SPORTS IN SOCIETY

SPORTS IN SOCIETY

Issues and Controversies

TENTH EDITION

Jay Coakley, Ph.D.
University of Colorado
Colorado Springs

Higher Education

Boston   Burr Ridge, IL   Dubuque, IA   New York   San Francisco   St. Louis
Bangkok   Bogotá   Caracas   Kuala Lumpur   Lisbon   London   Madrid   Mexico City
Milan   Montreal   New Delhi   Santiago   Seoul   Singapore   Sydney   Taipei   Toronto

 **Higher Education**

SPORTS IN SOCIETY: ISSUES AND CONTROVERSIES, TENTH EDITION

Published by McGraw-Hill, an imprint of The McGraw-Hill Companies, Inc., 1221 Avenue of the Americas, New York, NY 10020. Copyright © 2009 by The McGraw-Hill Companies, Inc. All rights reserved. No part of this publication may be reproduced or distributed in any form or by any means, or stored in a database or retrieval system, without the prior written consent of The McGraw-Hill Companies, Inc., including, but not limited to, in any network or other electronic storage or transmission, or broadcast for distance learning.

Some ancillaries, including electronic and print components, may not be available to customers outside the United States.

This book is printed on acid-free paper.

1 2 3 4 5 6 7 8 9 0 DOC/DOC 0 9 8

ISBN-13: 978-0-07-128528-5
MHID-10: 0-07-128528-8

To Maddie, Ally, and Cassidy
—each with her own way of doing sports

ABOUT THE AUTHOR

Jay Coakley and granddaughter,
Maddie, jogging along the Baltic Sea.

Jay Coakley is Professor Emeritus of Sociology at the University of Colorado in Colorado Springs. He received a Ph.D. in sociology at the University of Notre Dame and has since taught and done research on play, games, and sports, among other topics in sociology. Dr. Coakley has received many teaching, service, and professional awards, and is an internationally respected scholar, author, and journal editor. In 2004 the Citizenship Through Sport Alliance presented him with a national Citizenship Through Sport Award for his work to make sports and physical activities more inclusive. In 2007 the Institute for International Sport selected him as one of the 100 Most Influential Sports Educators, and the University of Chichester in West Sussex, England awarded him an Honorary Fellowship in recognition of his outstanding leadership in the sociology of sport. A former intercollegiate athlete, Coakley continues to use concepts, research, and theories in sociology to critically examine social phenomena and promote changes that will make social worlds more democratic and humane. He currently lives in Fort Collins, Colorado.

ABOUT THE COVER ARTIST

The cover image, *Double Dutch*, is a painting by Ernie Barnes, an internationally known artist and former professional football player. After his appointment as the Official Artist for the 1984 Los Angeles Olympic Games, Mr. Barnes's talent was recognized worldwide. Today he is hailed as the originator of Neo-Mannerist style and regarded as one of this country's foremost figurative painters.

The paintings of Ernie Barnes also became known to millions of people when they were used for the hit television show *"Good Times,"* and as the cover art on such popular albums as Marvin Gaye's *"I Want You,"* *"Donald Byrd and 125th Street, NYC,"* and B.B. King's *"Making Love Is Good for You."* His commissions include a painting that hangs permanently in the Carolina Panthers football stadium and a painting to commemorate the 50th Anniversary of the National Basketball Association that is displayed at the Naismith Memorial Basketball Hall of Fame.

The art of Ernie Barnes captures the spirit and determination of people as they express themselves through movement. For many people, his images of athletes capture the kinesthetic soul of sports. This is the fifth consecutive cover of *Sports in Society* that presents an Ernie Barnes image. Much of his current work, including his popular motivational poster series, can be viewed at www.erniebarnesart.com; his work is represented by The Company of Art, 8613 Sherwood, West Hollywood, CA 90069 (phone 800-858-2941). My thanks go to Ernie for sharing his images and ideas. *Double Dutch* was chosen for this cover to provoke thoughts about whose games are and aren't identified and funded as sports in society.

CONTENTS

6 Deviance in Sports: Is It Out of Control?   152

7 Violence in Sports: How Does It Affect Our Lives?   194

8 Gender and Sports: Does Equity Require Ideological Changes?   230

9 Race and Ethnicity: Are They Important in Sports?   274

10 Social Class: Do Money and Power Matter in Sports?   314

11 Sports and the Economy: What Are the Characteristics of Commercial Sports?   352

12 Sports and the Media: Could They Survive Without Each Other?   392

PREFACE

PURPOSE OF THIS TEXT

The tenth edition of *Sports in Society: Issues and Controversies* provides a detailed introduction to the sociology of sport. It uses sociological concepts, theories, and research to raise critical questions about sports and explore the dynamic relationship between sports, culture, and society. The chapters are organized around controversial and curiosity-arousing issues that have been systematically studied in the sociology of sport. Research on these issues is summarized so that readers can critically examine those issues.

All content is grounded in sociological research and theory and based on the assumption that a full understanding of sports must take into account the social and cultural contexts in which sports are created, played, given meaning, and integrated into people's lives.

FOR WHOM IS IT WRITTEN?

Sports in Society is written for everyone taking a first look at the relationships between sports, culture, and society. Readers don't need a background in sociology to understand and benefit from discussions in each chapter; nor do they need detailed knowledge of sport jargon and statistics. My goal is to help readers identify and explore critical issues related to sports in their personal experiences, families, schools, communities, and societies.

The emphasis on issues and controversies makes each chapter useful for people concerned with sport-related policies and programs. I've always tried to use my expertise to make sports more democratic, accessible, inclusive, and humane, and I hope to provide readers with the knowledge and desire to do the same.

CHANGES TO THIS TENTH EDITION

This edition has been heavily revised, and every section of the book, including all tables and figures, has been updated. New chapter opening quotes, photos, and examples have been added to maintain the timeliness of the content. This edition also is more carefully and clearly linked with the corresponding website (www.mhhe.com/coakley10e), and the Online Learning Center contains additional substantive materials related to each chapter topic.

Each chapter has been edited line-by-line to be more clear and concise. New research and theoretical developments are integrated into each section. There are about 600 *new* references included in this edition—nearly 1600 references in all—to assist those writing papers and doing research. Most new references identify materials published since the manuscript for the ninth edition left my hands.

The sociology of sport has expanded so much over the past decade that *Sports in Society* is now more of an introduction to the field than a comprehensive overview. To access materials from previous editions, including chapters on competition and coaching (fifth edition), and timely sections deleted from the sixth through ninth editions, visit the book's website (www.mhhe.com/coakley10e) and follow the links to Additional Readings for each chapter.

Revision Themes and New Materials

This edition puts a greater emphasis on the cultural, interactional, and structural dimensions of sports and sport experiences. Chapter 1 is revised to make readers aware of the differences between the sociology of sport and other sources of information about sports in society, such as blogs, media commentaries, and official sport organization sources. The concepts of culture, social interaction, and social structure, each of which is more prominently featured through the book, are explained in more detail. Sections on the body and sports, and sports as contested activities, are revised to make them more clear and relevant to readers.

The most significant change to this edition is a fully rewritten Chapter 2. The chapter from the ninth edition is now online and the new Chapter 2 focuses on the process of producing knowledge in the sociology of sport. Some instructors liked the former chapter on theories, but many others, along with the majority of students we've heard from, said that the chapter was confusing and left them feeling that knowledge in the field was not to be trusted because scholars disagreed on the validity and usefulness of various social theories. The new chapter is written to show readers that knowledge in the field is useful and organized around (1) a shared analytical focus on culture, social interaction, and social structure, and (2) a commitment to systematic and critical investigations of sports in society. The goal of the new chapter is to accurately represent the manner in which people in the field actually do the sociology of sport. Mike Messner's *Taking the Field* is used as a case study to give readers a first hand view of the important links between theory and research in the knowledge production process. New figures and diagrams provide concrete visualizations of major aspects of these links.

Chapter 3 is shortened and heavily edited so the content flows more clearly from ancient times to the nineteenth through twenty-first centuries. The revisions are designed to hold the readers' attention more closely and tie the chapter more directly with the other 15 chapters. The chapter on socialization (Chapter 4) is revised to reflect changes in Chapter 2, and there is a greater emphasis on socialization and health; the section on socialization as a community process is rewritten to be more clear and relevant to readers.

The extensive revisions in Chapter 5 surprise even me! My extensive reading, research, and thinking about youth sports informed a near-total rewrite of the chapter. There's a new section on variations in the organization of youth sports and how those variations influence the experiences of young people. This chapter includes new material on club sports and the myth that early sport specialization and year-round participation produce excellence. The recommendations also are rewritten to reflect more accurately the youth sport choices available to parents and children today.

Chapter 6 is rewritten to more clearly explain the theoretical approaches used when studying deviance in sports. The sections on deviant overconformity and the link between deviant over- and underconformity are rewritten for clarity's sake. There's new material on the deviance of people other than athletes and a new discussion of deviance and the development of commercial personas in sports. The chapter on violence (Chapter 7) is heavily edited with new material on mixed martial arts (cage fighting, ultimate fighting, etc.) and the involvement of women in more violent sports.

Chapter 8 has a new section on gender and fairness issues, and the material on "female athletes as invaders" is rewritten to account for changes. The gender classification section is thoroughly revised to help readers understand more clearly the ways that recent research has expanded our knowledge about sex and gender. The major changes in the chapter on race and ethnicity (Chapter 9) involve clarifications and examples of the influence of racial ideology in people's lives; completely rewritten sections on Latinos and Asian Pacific Americans; and a significant revision of material on the dynamics of racial and ethnic relations in sports and how progressive changes are and can be made.

Chapter 10, on social class and class relations, has new and more clearly written sections on class ideology, class relations and power in sports, and class relations in action. The material on economic and career opportunities in sports also is rewritten to reflect recent changes. The chapter on economics (Chapter 11) is updated with new information on salaries, and it's shortened to focus on sociological issues more exclusively. The media chapter (Chapter 12) is revised to reflect the rapid development and expansion of new media and shifts in the ideological themes that influence media coverage of sports. The sections on audience experiences, media and gambling, and sport journalism are rewritten with the latter section shortened.

The chapter on sports and politics (Chapter 13) is largely rewritten to reflect an abundance of new research worldwide. The section on government involvement in sports is revised to include new material on court cases, national identity, and social and economic development. The section on international relations and the Olympics is more concise and reflects new information about the Beijing Games and the upcoming Olympics in Vancouver and London. The section on politics in sports is shortened to allow for new material on nation-states, sports, and ideological hegemony; the global migration and recruitment of athletes in college and professional sports; and efforts to use sports to influence global labor issues, especially related to the manufacture of sports equipment, shoes, and apparel worldwide.

Chapter 14, on interscholastic and intercollegiate sports, is revised to focus more directly on sociological issues and acknowledge the diversity that characterizes school sports in the United States. New research informs revised material on current problems at the high school and college

levels. The chapter on sports and religions (Chapter 15) is shortened and includes new material on the concept of religion in sociology. The discussions of connections between sports and Islam, Buddhism, Hinduism, and Judaism are expanded, and there is a new "Reflect on Sport" box focusing on Muslim women who compete in sports wearing a hijab and veil. The chapter on the future of sports (Chapter 16) is extensively revised to reflect changes in Chapter 2, clarify connections between current trends and future realities, and more clearly outline vantage points for effective actions as an agent of change.

Suggested Readings and New Website Resources

Each chapter is followed by updated references to websites that are useful sources of information about the topics raised in the chapters. The Suggested Readings have been expanded for each chapter and included in the Online Learning Center (OLC); a link to the OLC ensures easy access to the annotated readings.

New Visual Materials

There are 135 photos, 24 figures, and 32 cartoons in this edition; 53 of the photos are new. These images are combined with new diagrams, figures, and tables to illustrate important substantive points, visually enhance the text, and make reading more interesting.

Online Learning Center

The website www.mhhe.com/coakley10e is an important feature associated with the tenth edition of *Sports in Society*. The site contains general information about this edition, along with links to supplemental materials associated with each chapter. Those materials include

- Annotated Suggested Readings
- A downloadable PowerPoint®presentation

- Updated URLs for website resources
- Discussion issues and questions
- Group projects
- Additional essays and readings that add depth and background to current chapter topics and enable instructors and students to read previous chapters on coaches and competition, including the full chapter on social theories as it appeared in the ninth edition
- True/false self-tests for each chapter
- Learning objectives for each chapter
- A cumulative 120-page bibliography that lists all references from this and the last five editions of *Sports in Society;* a companion 40-page bibliography on current research on intercollegiate sports
- Additional readings and current news articles
- A complete glossary of key terms

Sports in Society Blog

Read new articles, timely essays, and other relevant posts written by the author and other subject matter experts at http://sportsinsociety .blogspot.com. You are encouraged to contribute comments of your own about the book or any aspect of sports in society.

ANCILLARIES

Instructor's Manual and Test Bank

An instructor's manual and test bank is available to assist those using *Sports in Society* in college courses. It includes the following:

- *Chapter outlines.* These are full outlines that provide a section-by-section overview of each chapter. They are useful for test reviews and organizing lectures, and they may be reproduced and given to students as study guides.
- *Test questions (multiple choice).* These questions are designed to test students' awareness of the

central concepts and ideas in each chapter. For the instructor with large classes, these questions are useful for creating chapter and midterm tests, as well as final exams.
- *Discussion/essay questions.* These questions can be used for tests or to generate classroom discussions. They're designed to encourage students to synthesize and apply materials in one or more of the sections in each chapter. None of the questions asks the students to simply list points or give definitions.

Computerized Test Bank

A computerized version of the test bank for the instructor's manual is available in both IBM and Macintosh formats to qualified adopters. This software provides a unique combination of user-friendly aids and enables the instructor to select, edit, delete, or add questions and to construct and print tests and answer keys.

ACKNOWLEDGMENTS

This book draws on ideas from many sources. Thanks go to students, colleagues, and friends who have provided constructive criticisms over the years. Students regularly open my eyes to new ways of viewing and analyzing sports as social phenomena. Special thanks go to friends and colleagues who influence my thinking, provide valuable source materials, and willingly discuss ideas and information with me. Liz Pike and Chris Hallinan influenced my thinking as I worked with them on new versions of *Sports in Society* for the United Kingdom and Australia/ New Zealand; and Peter Donnelly, co-author of the first and second Canadian versions, has long influenced my thinking about sports in society. Laurel Davis-Delano deserves a special thanks for her insightful critique of the entire ninth edition and the new Chapter 2 on knowledge production for the tenth edition. Mike Messner's recent scholarly work inspired the revision of

Chapter 2, and Mike supported my use of his research as a case study in the chapter. Thanks also go to Becky Beal, Kevin Young, Liz Pike, and Jay Johnson for their professional photos used in these pages. Once again, I thank Ossur (www.ossur.com)—a company that designs and manufactures prosthetics and orthotics—for photos used in this and the previous edition.

Many thanks to Laura Stone, who did an excellent job of editing my words, and to Chris Johnson—a valued advocate who made sure that this edition is thoroughly revised with a focus on quality from an instructor and student perspective.

Special thanks to Nancy Coakley, who almost came to the point of sliding food under the office door as I worked continuously for eight months rewriting *Sports in Society*. Breaks were generally limited to hanging out with three granddaughters, watching them play games and sports, and listening to them and their friends talk about their experiences.

My appreciation also goes to the following reviewers, whose suggestions were crucial in planning and writing this edition:

Dean Anderson, Iowa State University
Jan Blade, Delaware State University
Philip Broyles, Shippensburg University
Jody Brylinsky, Western Michigan University
Doris Corbett, Howard University
Laurel Davis-Delano, Springfield College
Kellie Hagewen, University of Nebraska–Lincoln
Wardell Johnson, Eastern Kentucky University
Rick Jones, Marquette University
James LaPoint, University of Kansas
Michael Weissbuch, Xavier University

Finally, thanks to the students and colleagues who have e-mailed comments about previous editions. I take them seriously and appreciate their thoughtfulness—keep them coming.

Jay Coakley
Fort Collins, CO

SPORTS IN SOCIETY

(Christof Stache; AP/Wide World Photos)

THE SOCIOLOGY OF SPORT

What Is It and Why Study It?

THE DANGER, when fans view players as simply objects of entertainment, and when we don't need them to have opinions, is that they're simply drones out there for our pleasure. We objectify them.

—**Sally Jenkins, sports journalist,** *Washington Post* **(2005)**

Visit *Sports in Society*'s Online Learning Center (OLC) at www.mhhe.com/coakley10e for additional information and study material for this chapter, including the following:

• A complete chapter outline

• Learning objectives

• Practice quizzes

• Internet resources

• Related readings

• Essays

• Student projects

HOW DO YOU distinguish sports from entertainment, fakery from reality, when the two are so inseparable?

—**Selena Roberts, sports journalist,** *The New York Times* **(2007)**

SPORTS ARE . . . a multi-billion dollar business that saturates the mass media; young people's clothes are splattered with swooshes and team logos; school activities and year books point to sport's centrality in the social life of schools.

—**Mike Messner, Sociologist, University of Southern California (2006)**

NOW THAT THE sports business is a massive arm of the international entertainment industry . . . there's no way we can escape its economic, social and environmental footprints. . . . [T]he growing involvement of big business, of the media and of advertisers has helped reshape the rules of many games—and, in the process, fuelled new forms of exclusion.

—**John Elkington, environmentalist, president of Sustain Ability (2004)**

ABOUT THIS BOOK

Most of you reading this book have experienced sports personally, either as athletes or spectators. You're probably familiar with the physical and emotional experiences of playing sports and the rules and strategies of certain sports. You may even follow the lives of high-profile athletes at your school or on the national sports scene. Most of you have watched and read about sports and discussed them with family and friends.

This book assumes that you're interested in some facet of sports, but it is written to take you beyond scores, statistics, and sports personalities. The goal is to focus on the "deeper game" associated with sports, the game through which sports become part of the social and cultural worlds in which we live.

Fortunately, we can draw on our emotions and experiences as we consider this deeper game. Take high school sports in the United States as an example. When students play on a high school basketball team, we know that it can affect their status in the school and the treatment they receive from both teachers and students. We know it can also have implications for their prestige in the community, self-images and self-esteem, future relationships, opportunities in education and the job market, and their overall enjoyment of life.

Building on this knowledge enables us to move further into the deeper game associated with high school sports. For example, why do so many Americans place such importance on sports and accord such high status to elite athletes? Are there connections between high school sports and widespread beliefs about masculinity and femininity, achievement and competition, pleasure and pain, winning and fair play, and other important aspects of U.S. culture?

Underlying these questions is the assumption that sports are more than games, meets, and matches. They're important parts of social life that have meanings going far beyond scores and performance statistics. Sports are integral parts of the social and cultural contexts in which we live, and they provide stories and images that many of us use to evaluate our experiences and the world around us.

People who study sports in society are concerned with the deeper meanings and stories associated with sports. They do research to increase our understanding of (1) the cultures and societies in which sports exist, (2) the social worlds created around sports, and (3) the experiences of individuals and groups associated with sports.

ABOUT THIS CHAPTER

This chapter is organized to answer the following four questions:

1. What is sociology, and how is it used to study sports in society?
2. What are sports, and how can we identify them in ways that increase our understanding of their place and significance in society?
3. What is the sociology of sport, and how does it differ from other approaches to studying sports?
4. Why do sociologists study sports in society?

The answers to these questions will be our guides for understanding the material in the rest of the book.

USING SOCIOLOGY TO STUDY SPORTS

Sociology provides useful tools for investigating sports as social phenomena. This is because **sociology** *is the study of the social worlds that people create, organize, maintain, and change through their relationships with each other.*[1] The term

---

[1]Important concepts used in each chapter are identified in **boldface**. Unless they are accompanied by a footnote that contains a definition, the definition will be given in the text itself. This puts the definition in context rather than separating it in a glossary. Definitions are also provided in the index (p. xxx).

social world refers to *an identifiable sphere of everyday actions and relationships.* Social worlds are created by individuals, but they involve much more than individuals doing their own things for their own reasons. Our actions, relationships, and collective activities take the form of identifiable ways of life and social arrangements that we could not predict simply with information about each of us as individuals. These ways of life and social arrangements continue to exist as people collectively reproduce them through their interactions with each other. They change as people question, oppose, and replace them with alternative ways of life and social arrangements.

Social worlds can be as large and impersonal as an entire nation, such as the United States or Brazil, or as personal and intimate as your own family. But regardless of size, they encompass all aspects of social life: the values and beliefs that we use to make sense of our lives; our everyday actions and relationships; and the groups, organizations, communities, and societies that we form as we make choices, develop relationships, and participate in social life.

The goal of sociology is to describe and explain social worlds—how we create, re-create, and change them; how they are organized; and how they influence our lives and our relationships with each other. In the process of doing this, sociologists identify the social factors that enable us to see our lives and the lives of others "in context"—that is, in connection with complex and constantly changing social worlds. When we do this, we become aware of social circumstances that set limits and create possibilities in people's lives. This awareness is valuable because it helps us to anticipate and sometimes work around the constraints we face at the same time that we look for and take advantage of the possibilities. Ideally, it helps us gain more control over our lives as well as an understanding of other people and the conditions that influence their lives.

Key Sociology Concepts

When sociologists study sports and the social worlds associated with them, they focus on culture, social interaction, and social structure. **Culture** consists of *the shared ways of life and shared understandings that people develop as they live together.* **Social Interaction** consists of *people taking each other into account and, in the process, influencing each other's feelings, thoughts, and action.* **Social Structure** consists of *the established patterns of relationships and social arrangements that take shape as people live, work, and play with each other.*

These three concepts—culture, social interaction, and social structure—represent the central interconnected aspects of all social worlds. For example, a professional sport team is a social world formed by players, coaches, and team administrators. Over time every team creates and maintains a particular *culture* or way of life. Everyone involved with the team engages in *social interaction* as they take each other into account during their everyday activities on and off the playing field. Additionally, the recurring actions, relationships, and social arrangements that emerge as people interact with each other make up the *social structure* of the team. This combination of culture, social interaction, and social structure comprises the team as a social world.

Peer groups, cliques, and athletic teams are social worlds in which participants are known to one another. Communities, societies, concert crowds, and online chat rooms are social worlds in which participants are generally unknown to each other. This means that the boundaries of social worlds may be clear, fuzzy, or overlapping, but we generally know when we enter or leave a social world because each has identifying features related to culture, social interaction, and social structure.

We move back and forth between familiar social worlds without thinking. We make nearly automatic shifts in how we talk and act as we accommodate changing cultural, interactional, and structural features in each social world. However, when we enter or participate in a new or unfamiliar social world, we usually take the time to get a sense of what is happening. We watch what people are doing, how they interact with each other, and the recurring patterns that exist in their actions and relationships. If you've done this, you're ready to use sociology to study sports in society.

Sociological Knowledge Is Based on Research and Theory

Each time that I rewrite this book, my goal is to accurately represent research in the sociology of sport and discuss issues of interest to students. As I consider those issues, I seek information from research that is published in journal articles and books. I use newspaper articles and other media as sources for examples, but I depend on research findings when making substantive points and drawing conclusions. This means that my statements about sports and sport experiences are based, as much as possible, on studies that use surveys, questionnaires, interviews, observations, content analyses, and other accepted research methods in sociology.

The material in this book is different than material in blogs, talk radio, television news shows, game and event commentaries, and everyday conversations about sports. It is organized to help you critically examine sports as they exist in people's lives and the social contexts where people live, play, and work. I use research findings to describe and explain as accurately as possible the important connections between sports, society, and culture. I try to be fair when using research to make sense of the social aspects of sports and sport experiences. This is why there are over 1,400 books and articles listed as references for this book. Of course, I want to hold your attention as you read, but I don't exaggerate, purposely withhold, or present information out of context to impress you and boost my

"ratings." In the process, I hope that you will develop or extend your critical thinking abilities so that you can assess the merits of what people say about sports in society.

DEFINING SPORTS

Most of us know enough about the meaning of sports to talk about them with others. However, when we study sports, it helps to precisely define our topic. For example, is it a sport when young people choose teams and play a baseball game in the street or when thirty people of various ages spend an afternoon performing and learning tricks at a skateboard park? These activities are sociologically different from what occurs at major league baseball games and the X Games skateboard competitions. These differences become significant when parents ask if playing sports builds the character of their children, when community leaders ask if they should use tax money to fund sports, and when school principals ask if sports are valid educational activities.

When I say that I study sports, people ask if that includes jogging, double-dutch (jump rope—as pictured on the cover of this book), weight lifting, hunting, scuba diving, darts, auto racing, chess, poker, ultimate fighting, paintball, piano competitions, ballroom dancing, and so on. To respond is not easy, because there is no single definition that precisely identifies sports in all cultures at all times. Some people use a precise definition for practical reasons, whereas many others use a flexible approach and define sports in a way that fits the customs and traditions in particular societies at particular points in time.

A Precise Definition of *Sports*

Although definitions vary, many scholars identify **sports** as *well-established, officially governed competitive physical activities in which participants are motivated by internal and external rewards.*

This definition enables people to generally distinguish sports from other activities. For example, it is sociologically useful to distinguish a women's World Cup soccer match from what occurs when three girls kick a soccer ball around a backyard. Each of these activities involves different social dynamics, organization, and implications. The soccer played during the World Cup has official rules that standardize matches and make them comparable, regardless of who plays. Additionally, World Cup matches are controlled by FIFA (Fédération Internationale de Football Association), the official governing organization that develops and enforces rules for international soccer. The backyard soccer has no rules unless the three girls create them, and the girls answer to no governing organization. Both official soccer matches *and* informal games are important social phenomena, but sociologists know that it's important to distinguish between them because they have few sociological similarities (Mindegaard, 2007; Peterson, 2008).

In more general terms, a precise definition helps us distinguish sports from *play* and *dramatic spectacle*. The idea that people participate in sports for a combination of *internal and external rewards* means that sports involve the internal satisfaction associated with spontaneous play as well as the external satisfaction associated with displaying physical skills to gain public approval and other rewards. This is illustrated in Figure 1.1, where **play** is *an expressive activity done for its own sake*, and **dramatic spectacle** is *a performance meant to entertain an audience*. An example of play is four children spontaneously running around a kindergarten playground, yelling joyfully while throwing playground balls in random directions. These five-year-olds are motivated almost exclusively by the personal enjoyment and expression that is intrinsic to their actions. On the other hand, an example of dramatic spectacle is four professional wrestlers paid to entertain spectators by staging a skilled and cleverly choreographed tag-team match in which outcomes are prearranged to excite an audience.

Sports involve a balance between the elements of play and spectacle.
When sports emphasize elements of play, they are participant-oriented;
when they emphasize elements of spectacle, they are spectator-oriented.

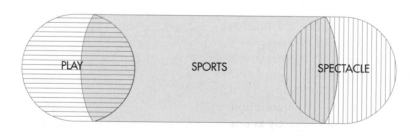

Focus:	Participants	-----	Spectators
Participants:	"Players"	-----	Characters (heroes & villains)
Rewards:	Intrinsic	-----	Extrinsic
Basis for action:	Authenticity	-----	Staged personas (cheats & spoilsports)
Action theme:	Spontaneous expression	-----	Choreographed drama
Structure:	Open/self-created	-----	Fixed by management
Dynamics:	Free flowing	-----	Anticipated and planned
Goal:	Personal enjoyment	-----	Entertain audience

FIGURE 1.1 *Sport* involves elements of *play* and *spectacle*. (Adapted from material in Stone, 1973)

> **OLC** **On the *OLC*:**
> See the OLC—Additional Readings for Chapter 1—for the author's article on the differences between play, games, and sports.

Sports differ from play and spectacle in that participation is motivated by intrinsic enjoyment *and* extrinsic rewards. Sports, therefore, contain elements of play *and* spectacle. This way of identifying sports is useful today when some spectator sports focus so much on entertaining an audience that events lose the element of play and become dominated by the element of dramatic spectacle.

Using a precise definition of sports has practical advantages, but it also has potentially serious problems. For example, when we focus attention only on official competitive events, we overlook the existence of physical activities among people who have neither the resources to formally organize their physical activities nor the desire to make them competitive. In the process, we unintentionally fail to understand the full range of social and cultural factors that influence how and when particular forms of physical activities are created and made an important part of people's lives.

Most people in the sociology of sport are aware of this possibility, so they use precise definitions of sport cautiously. At the same time, many scholars reject the idea that a single definition can be used to study sports in all cultures at all points in history. They prefer an alternative definitional approach based on the assumption that sports and the meanings given to them change over time and from one culture to another.

An Alternative Approach to Defining *Sports*

Those who reject the validity of a single definition identify sports by asking three questions:

1. What activities are defined as sports in a particular group or society?
2. Whose sports are most strongly supported and funded, especially with public facilities and money?
3. Who is advantaged and disadvantaged by the accepted definition of sports and the priorities used to allocate resources to sports?

Asking these questions opens the sociology of sport to a greater range of issues than is possible when using a static, precise definition. Seeking answers to these questions forces researchers to learn about the social, cultural, and historical contexts in which people create and organize physical activities and integrate them into their lives. We need this knowledge to accurately explain why sports exist and how they affect people's lives.

Those using this alternative approach assume that there are many ways to define sports, and that definitions vary over time and from one place to another. For example, people in England who played cricket and hunted foxes during the 1870s would be astonished that Americans define NFL football as a sport when the oversized players spend nearly 45 minutes of every 60-minute game walking to and from and standing in huddles, where they receive directions from a coach who does not play the game. Similarly, Americans today looking back at nineteenth-century British sports might say that they weren't "real" sports because the participants did not strive to set records or win championships. Looking ahead one hundred years, people might be playing virtual sports in challenging virtual environments and say that NFL football was not "real" sport because it lacked continuous action and damaged the health and well-being of participants.

An alternative definitional approach based on the three questions listed earlier takes into account that there are social, cultural, and historical differences in the ways that people define sports and include them in their lives. For instance, in cultures where cooperative relationships are highly valued and necessary for group survival, competing with others for rewards is likely to be seen as disruptive and even immoral (Kohn, 1986; Rosenau, 2003); therefore, their sports would be organized around the challenge of achieving a tie to end a game. At the same time, people in cultures where competition is highly valued would describe cooperative games with no winners and losers as pointless and boring; therefore, their sports would be organized around the challenge of outperforming or eliminating other participants. In the face of such differences, using a single definition of sports would clearly limit research and our understanding of sports and society.

Is this a sport? Rather than debating this question, most sociologists explain why certain ideas and beliefs about sports come to be widely accepted in a social world. According to many sport fans in the United States, "real" sports involve conquest, power, and physical domination of others—as in American football. In cultures where sports are defined in terms of the values and experiences of men, rhythmic gymnastics is not taken seriously as a sport, despite fitting most definitions. (*Source*: Efrem Lukatsky; AP/Wide World Photos)

Sports as Contested Activities

As scholars move away from a single definition of sports, they see sports as **contested activities**—that is, *activities for which there are no timeless and universal agreements about meaning, purpose, and organization.* This means that people disagree and sometimes struggle over *whose* ideas about sports will become generally accepted by others in a group or society. The most significant struggles are created by disagreements on one or more of three issues:

1. The meaning, purpose, and organization of sports
2. The people allowed to play sports, and the conditions under which they will play
3. The people and organizations that sponsor and provide the resources needed to play sports

Heated debates can occur when people disagree on these issues. History shows that some of these debates have caused bitter feelings and led to lawsuits, government intervention, and the passage of laws. For example, people in many states disagree about the meaning, purpose, and organization of cheerleading in U.S. high schools. Most school officials say that cheerleading is not a sport because its primary purpose is to support high school teams. But others argue that the cheerleaders at many schools are now organized as teams that compete in championships and bring recognition and rewards to their schools. This debate over the purpose of cheerleading will continue because the stakes are high: being designated an official high school sport brings funding and other support that affects the organization of cheerleading and the meaning it has in schools, communities, and American society.

Disagreements and struggles over the purpose, meaning, and organization of sports occur most often when they involve the funding priorities of government agencies (Eichberg, 2008). For example, if the primary purpose of sport is

to improve health and fitness for everyone, then funding should go to sports that are organized to provide widespread recreational participation that has net positive effects on physical well-being. On the other hand, if people see sports as "wars without weapons" with the purpose of pushing the limits of human capability, then funding should go to sports organized to produce high-performance athletes who can achieve competitive victories. This issue is regularly contested at the national and local levels of government, in universities and public school districts, and even in families, as parents decide how to use household resources.

The idea that sports are contested activities is most vividly demonstrated in disagreements over who is allowed to play sports and the conditions under which certain people can play. The cases that have involved extended struggles are listed in the box titled, "Who Plays and Who Doesn't."

The third issue making sports contested activities focuses on who should sponsor and provide the resources needed to play them. When people value the "common good" of a community and see sports contributing to the common good, it is likely that sport facilities and programs will be supported by public/government agencies and public/tax money. When people value individualism and see sports in terms of their contributions to individual development, it is likely that sport facilities and programs will be supported by individuals, families, and private-corporate sponsors. However, in both cases there will be struggles over the extent to which sponsors control sports and the extent to which sports are organized to be consistent with general community values.

Struggles related to these three issues show that using a single definition of sports may lead us to overlook the issue of why many people accept one definition of sports more than others in a particular social world. Many social factors, including who has power and resources,

Who Plays and Who Doesn't
Contesting a Place in Sports

Being cut from a youth sport team is a disappointing personal experience. But being in a category of people that is wholly excluded from all or some sports is more than disappointing—it is unfair and occasionally illegal. Most cases of categorical exclusion are related to gender and sexuality, skin color and ethnicity, ability and disability, age and weight, nationality and citizenship, and other "eligibility" criteria. Struggles occur in connection with questions such as these:

• Will females be allowed to play sports and, if they are, will they play the same sports at the same time and on the same teams that males play, and will the rewards for achievement be the same for females and males?

• Will sports be open to people regardless of social class and wealth? Will wealthy and poor people play and watch sports together or separately?

• Will people from different racial and ethnic backgrounds play together or in segregated settings? Will the meanings given to skin color or ethnicity influence participation patterns or opportunities to play sports?

• Will age influence eligibility to play sports, and should sports be age integrated or segregated?

Will people of different ages have the same access to participation opportunities?

• Will able-bodied people and people with disabilities have the same opportunities to play sports, and will they play together or separately? What meanings will be given to the accomplishments of athletes with disabilities compared to the accomplishments of able-bodied athletes?

• Will gay men and lesbians play alongside heterosexuals and, if they do, will they be treated fairly?

• Will athletes control the conditions under which they play sports and have the power to change those conditions to meet their needs and interests?

• Will athletes be rewarded for playing, what form will the rewards take, and how will they be determined?

Federal and local laws may mandate particular answers to these questions. However, traditions, local customs, and personal beliefs often support various forms of exclusion. The resulting struggles illustrate that sports can be hotly contested activities. *What do you think?*

influence the forms of sport that exist and the meanings given to them. Being aware of these factors enables us to *put sports into context* and understand them in the terms used by those who create, play, and support them. It also helps us see that the definition of sports in any particular context usually represents the ideas and interests of some people more than others. In the sociology of sport, this leads to questions and research on whose ideas and interests count the most when it comes to determining (1) the meaning, purpose, and organization of sports; (2) who plays under what conditions; and (3) who sponsors and controls sports. Material in

each of the following chapters summarizes the findings of much of this research.

WHAT IS THE SOCIOLOGY OF SPORT?

The sociology of sport is primarily a subdiscipline of sociology that studies sports as social phenomena. Most research and writing in the field focuses on "organized, competitive sports," although people increasingly study other forms of physical activities that are health and fitness oriented and informally organized. These include recreational, extreme, adventure, and virtual sports as well as fitness and exercise activities (Atkinson, 2007b; Eichberg, 2008; Honea, 2007; Martin and Miller, 1999; Mindegaard, 2007; Peterson, 2008; Rinehart, 2000; Rinehart and Syndor, 2003).

Research in the sociology of sport generally seeks to answer the following questions:

1. Why are some activities, and not others, selected and designated as sports in particular groups and societies?
2. Why are sports created and organized in different ways at different times and in different places?
3. How do people include sports and sport participation in their lives, and does participation affect individual development and social relationships?
4. How do sports and sport participation affect our ideas about bodies, human movement, masculinity and femininity, social class, race and ethnicity, work, fun, ability and disability, achievement and competition, pleasure and pain, deviance and conformity, and aggression and violence?
5. How do various sports compare with other physical activities in producing positive health and fitness outcomes?
6. How is the meaning, purpose, and organization of sports related to the culture, social structure, and resources of a society?
7. How are sports related to important spheres of social life such as family, education, politics, the economy, media, and religion?
8. How do people use their sport experiences and knowledge about sports as they interact with others and explain what occurs in their lives and the world around them?
9. How can people use sociological knowledge about sports to understand and participate more actively and effectively in society, especially as agents of progressive change?

Understanding the sociology of sport is easier if you learn to think of sports as **social constructions**—that is, as *parts of the social world that are created by people as they interact with one another under particular social, political, and economic conditions.* To stress this point, I generally use the term *sports* rather than *sport*. This emphasizes that the forms and meanings of sports vary from place to place and time to time. I want to avoid the inference that "sport" has an essential and timeless quality that exists separate from the contexts in which people create, play, and change sports in society.

The idea that sports are social constructions makes some people uncomfortable because they benefit from sports as they are currently defined, organized, and played. They don't want people to see sports as socially constructed activities that people can change if they wish to define, organize, and play them differently.

Differences Between Sociology and Psychology of Sport

For those new to sociology, a good way to understand the sociology of sport is to compare it to the psychology of sport. Psychologists study behavior in terms of attributes and processes that exist *inside* individuals. They focus on motivation, perception, cognition, self-esteem, self-confidence, attitudes, and personality. They also deal with interpersonal dynamics, including communication, leadership, and social influence, but they usually discuss these things in terms of how they affect attributes and processes that exist inside individuals. Therefore, they ask research questions such as, "How is the motivation of athletes related to their personality traits and self-perception of physical abilities?"

Sociologists, on the other hand, study actions and relationships in terms of the social contexts in which people live their lives. They focus on the reality *outside* and *around* individuals and deal with how people form relationships with one another and create social arrangements that enable them to control and give meaning

If sports are social constructions, it means that we create them and can change them. The sociology of sport helps people identify aspects of sports that could or should be changed; other people, including many associated with sports, resist the idea that sports are social constructions because they benefit from sports as they are currently defined and organized, and they don't want them changed.

to their lives. Sociologists ask questions about the ways that actions, relationships, and social life are related to characteristics that people define as socially relevant in their group or society. Therefore, sociological research focuses on the social meanings and dynamics associated with age, social class, gender, race, ethnicity, (dis)ability, sexuality, and nationality. It seeks to answer questions such as, "How do prevailing cultural beliefs about masculinity and femininity affect the organization of sport programs and the experiences of those who play sports?"

When psychologists apply their knowledge, they focus on the experiences and problems of particular individuals, whereas sociologists focus on group experiences and social issues that affect entire categories of people, such as Latinos, white men, lesbians, young people, high school students, and so on. For example, when studying

burnout among adolescent athletes, psychologists look at factors that exist *inside* the athletes themselves, such as the stress experienced by individual athletes and its impact on their motivation and performance (Cresswell and Eklund, 2006, 2007; Hodge, Lonsdale, and Ng, 2008; Smith, 1986). When applying their knowledge to prevent burnout, they help athletes manage stress through goal setting, personal skill development, and the use of relaxation and concentration techniques.

Sociologists, on the other hand, study burnout in connection with the social reality that surrounds adolescent athletes (Coakley, 1992; Ingham et al., 1999, 2002; Maslach and Leiter, 1997). They focus on the organization of sport programs and the relationships between athletes and other people, including family members, peers, and coaches. Because athletes are influenced by the social context in which they play sports, sociologists emphasize that reducing burnout requires changing the way youth sports are organized and altering athletes' relationships with parents and coaches so that the young people have more control over their lives and more opportunities to be involved in experiences and relationships outside sports.

Both approaches have value, although many people see a sociological approach as disruptive and difficult to apply. They feel that it's easier to change individual athletes and use stress management strategies than it is to change the relationships that influence athletes' lives and the social conditions in which athletes play their sports. Therefore, people who control sport programs often prefer psychological over sociological approaches. They don't want to change the organization and structure of their programs because it may jeopardize their status or power. Similarly, many parents and coaches prefer a psychological approach that focuses on stress management rather than a sociological approach that focuses on changing their relationships with athletes and the control they have over athletes' lives.

Using the Sociology of Sport

Sociology of sport knowledge is used in many ways. For example, it informs parents and coaches about the conditions under which youth sport participation is most likely to produce positive developmental effects. It explains why some sports have higher rates of violence than others and the ways to most effectively control sports violence. However, unless sociology of sport knowledge is combined with concerns for fairness and social justice, it can sometimes be used in negative ways. For example, it can show a football coach that one way to effectively control young men in U.S. culture is to threaten their masculinity and make them dependent on coaches for

> **The rituals of sport engage more people in a shared experience than any other institution or cultural activity today.**
> —Varda Burstyn, author, *The Rites of Men* (1999)

approval of their worth as human beings. And it also shows that this strategy increases the willingness of young men to play aggressively and put their bodies in jeopardy "for the good of the team"—an outcome that some coaches want to achieve.

This football coach example shows that the sociology of sport, like other scientific disciplines, is neither a pure nor objective enterprise. Like others who produce and distribute knowledge, those of us who study sports in society must consider why we ask certain research questions and how our research findings might affect people's lives. We can't escape the fact that social life is complex and characterized by inequalities, power differences, and conflicts of interests between different categories of people. Therefore, using knowledge in the sociology of sport is not a simple process that automatically brings about equal and positive benefits for everyone. In fact, it must also involve critical thinking about the potential consequences of what we know about sports in society. Hopefully, after reading this book you will be prepared and willing to do the following:

1. Think critically about sports so that you can identify and understand issues and controversies associated with sports in society.
2. Look beyond performance statistics and win–loss records to see sports as social constructions that can have both positive and negative effects on people's lives.
3. Learn things about sports that enable you to make informed choices about your sport participation and the place of sports in your community and society.
4. See sports as social constructions and be able to change them so they don't systematically disadvantage some categories of people as they privilege others.

Controversies Created by the Sociology of Sport

Research in the sociology of sport is usually controversial when it provides evidence that there should be changes in the organization of sports and the structure of social relations in society. Such evidence threatens some people, especially those who control sport organizations, benefit from the current organization of sports, or think that the current organization of sports is "right and natural." People in positions of power know that social and cultural changes can jeopardize their control over others and the privileges that come with it. Therefore, they prefer approaches to sports that blame problems on the weaknesses and failures of individuals. When individuals are identified as the problem, solutions emphasize the need to control individuals more effectively and teach them how to adjust to society as it is.

The potential for controversy created by a sociological analysis of sports is illustrated by reviewing research findings on sport participation among women around the world. Research shows that women, especially women in poor and working-class households, have lower rates of sport participation than do other categories of people (Donnelly and Harvey, 2007; Hargreaves, 1994, 2000; Tomlinson, 2007). Research also shows that there are many reasons for this, including the following:

1. Women are less likely than men to have the time, freedom, and money needed to play sports regularly.
2. Women have little or no control of the facilities where sports are played or the programs in those facilities.
3. Women have less access to transportation and less overall freedom to move around at will and without fear.
4. Women often are expected to take full-time responsibility for the social and emotional needs of family members—a job that seldom allows them time to play sports.

5. Most sport programs around the world are organized around the values, interests, and experiences of men.

These reasons all contribute to the fact that many women worldwide don't see sports as appropriate activities for them to take seriously.

> **OLC** **ON THE *OLC*:**
> See the OLC—Additional Readings for Chapter 1—for the author's article on the origins of the sociology of sport and the professional associations in the field.

It is easy to see the potential for controversy associated with these findings. They suggest that opportunities and resources to play sports should be increased for women, that women and men should share control of sports, and that new sports organized around the values, interests, and resources of women should be developed. They also suggest that there should be changes in ideas about masculinity and femininity, gender relations, family structures, the allocation of child-care responsibilities, the organization of work, and the distribution of resources in society.

People who benefit from sports and social life as they are currently organized are likely to oppose and reject the need for these changes. They might even argue that the sociology of sport is too critical and idealistic and that the "natural" order would be turned upside down if sociological knowledge were used to organize social worlds. However, good research always inspires critical approaches to the social conditions that affect our lives. This is why studying sports with a critical eye usually occurs when researchers have informed visions of what sports and society could and should be in the future. Without these visions, often born of idealism,

breaking BARRIERS

Cultural Barriers:
Aren't We Athletes?

Randy Snow won his first international track medal in 1984. He is a ten-time U.S. Open Wheelchair Tennis Champion, an International Tennis Federation Champion, U.S. Tennis Association Player of the Year, and winner of many athletic awards. Today he's a film producer and social activist who has received national citizenship awards. Asked about the Paralympics for elite athletes with physical disabilities, he says this:

> Paralympians are better athletes than our able-bodied counterparts. We work just as hard, do it for a lot less money, carry education to our venue as well as competition, and have overcome [physical challenges to do our sports]. Our stories display . . . true resiliency . . . therefore better matching us with the way life really exists (in Joukowsky and Rothstein, 2002a, p. 39).

Snow's comment plus the relative invisibility of sports for athletes with a disability raises a series of sociological questions:

1. Whose ideas and beliefs about sports come to be accepted as the *correct* ideas and beliefs in society?
2. Who is included and excluded from the processes through which ideas and beliefs are promoted and legitimized?
3. Who is advantaged and disadvantaged by decisions based on prevailing ideas and beliefs?
4. How can decision-making processes be revised so that decisions about sports are more representative of all people in society?

Most readers of this book don't have friends whose physical or intellectual impairments make them "disabled" nor have they ever met athletes from the Paralympic Games or the Special Olympics. This means that if I asked you to close your eyes and imagine five different sport scenes, few of you would picture a scene involving athletes with an amputated limb, in wheelchairs, blind, with cerebral palsy, or with intellectual disabilities.

This imagination exercise is *not* meant to evoke guilt. Our views of the world are based on personal experiences, and our experiences are influenced by the meanings given to age, gender, race, ethnicity, social class, sexuality, (dis)ability, and other characteristics that are defined as socially significant in our culture. Neither culture nor society forces us to think or do certain things, but the only way to mute cultural and social influence is to critically examine social worlds and understand that cultural meanings and social organization create constraints *and* opportunities in people's lives, including people with disabilities.

In each of the following chapters, a "Breaking Barriers" box presents the voices and experiences of people with disabilities. If you are *currently* able-bodied, each box alerts you to social and cultural barriers that constrain the lives of people with disabilities. If you have a disability, each box acknowledges the barriers that you, Randy Snow, and millions of others face in the pursuit of sport participation.

These barriers, according to many *currently* able-bodied people, are "just the way things are." Eliminating them is impossible or idealistic, they say, because they require changes in physical environments as well as the organization of relationships, schools, communities, and societies. However, this approach turns all of us into victims of culture and society. The alternative is to have informed and idealistic visions of what sports could and should be, making it possible to identify and eliminate barriers that prevent some people from playing sports.

Fung Ying Ki, a triple gold medal winner in the 2000 Sydney Paralympics, knew that it was possible to break barriers when she said, "I hope that, in the future, there will no longer be 'disabled athletes' in this world, only 'athletes'" (in Joukowsky and Rothstein, 2002a, p. 115). Working to achieve this future will make all of us more human and humane.

what would motivate and guide us as we participate in our communities, societies, and world? People who make a difference and change the world for the better have always been idealistic

and unafraid of promoting structural changes in societies. This is illustrated in the "Breaking Barriers" box above.

Are these athletes? Their times in the 100- and 200-meter sprints are better than all but a handful of sprinters worldwide. Why are some sports defined as more real or more important than others? Who determines this? These three sprinters run on Ossur's Cheetah Flex-Foot. Does this matter in terms of a definition of sport? (*Source*: David Biene; photo courtesy of Ossur)

Regardless of controversies, research and interest in the sociology of sport has increased significantly in recent years. This growth will continue as long as scholars in the field do research and produce knowledge that people find useful as they seek to understand social life and participate effectively as citizens in their communities and societies.

WHY STUDY SPORTS IN SOCIETY?

We study sports because they are socially significant activities for many people, they reinforce important ideas and beliefs in many societies, and they've been integrated into major spheres of social life such as the family, religion, education, the economy, politics, and the media.

Sports Are Socially Significant Activities for Many People

As we look around us, we see that the Olympic Games, soccer's World Cup, American football's Super Bowl, the Rugby World Cup, the Tour de France, the tennis championships at Wimbledon, and other sport megaevents attract global attention and media coverage. The biggest of these events are watched by billions of people in over two hundred countries. The media coverage of sport megaevents provides vivid images and stories that entertain, inspire, and provide for people the words and ideas they use to make sense of their experiences and the world around them. Even people with little or no interest in sports are forced to make them a part of their lives when family and friends insist on taking them to games and talking about sports.

> **OLC** ON THE *OLC*:
> See the OLC—Additional Readings for Chapter 1—for articles written or cowritten by the author on sports as social phenomena.

People worldwide increasingly talk about sports—at work, at home, in bars, on dates, at dinner tables, in school, with friends, and even with strangers at bus stops, in airports, and on the street. Relationships often revolve around sports, especially among men, and increasingly among women. People identify with teams and athletes so closely that the outcomes of games and matches influence their moods, identities, and sense of well-being. In a general sense, sports create opportunities for conversations that enable people to form and nurture relationships and even enhance their status as they describe and critique athletes, games, teams, coaching decisions, and the content of media commentaries. When people use sports this way, they often broaden social networks related to work, politics, education, and other spheres of their lives. This increases their **social capital,** that is, *the social resources that link them positively to social worlds* (Harvey, 2007).

When people play sports, their experiences are often remembered as special and important in their lives. The emotional intensity, group camaraderie, and sense of accomplishment that often occur in sports make sport participation more memorable than other activities.

For all these reasons, sports are logical topics for the attention of sociologists and others concerned with social life today.

Sports Reaffirm Important Ideas and Beliefs in Many Societies

We also study sports because many people use them to reaffirm ideas and beliefs that are important to them and widely accepted by others. In fact, a key research topic in the sociology of sport is the relationship between sports and cultural ideologies.

Ideologies *are webs of ideas and beliefs that people use to give meaning to the world and make sense of their experiences.* They are important aspects of culture because they embody the principles, perspectives, and viewpoints that underlie our feelings, thoughts, and actions. However, ideologies seldom come in neat packages, especially in highly diverse and rapidly changing societies. Various groups of people often develop their own ideas and beliefs for giving meaning to the world and making sense of their experiences, and they don't always agree with others. This can lead to struggles over whose ideologies provide the most accurate, useful, or moral ways of giving meaning to and explaining the world and the everyday events that affect people's lives.

As various people use and promote their ideologies in society, sports become socially relevant. As social constructions, sports can be organized to reinforce *or* challenge prevailing ideologies. People create and organize sports around their ideas and beliefs about bodies, relationships, abilities, character, gender, race, social class, and other attributes and characteristics that they define as important. Usually, the most popular forms of sports in a society reinforce and reproduce the ideologies favored by people with the most power and influence. This helps these ideologies become dominant because so many people in a society learn to use them as interpretive guides for making sense of the world and their experiences. When this occurs, sports help to produce forms of social organization that benefit powerful and wealthy people.

Gender Ideology   We can use gender ideology to illustrate the social significance of sports. **Gender ideology** consists of *a web of ideas and beliefs about masculinity, femininity, and male-female relationships in the organization of social worlds*. People use it to guide their definitions of what it means to be a man or a woman, their evaluations of people and relationships, and their sense of what is "natural" and "moral" when it comes to performing gender in their lives.

Dominant gender ideology in most societies emphasizes that men are naturally superior to women in activities that involve strength, physical skills, and emotional control. This belief has fostered in many cultures a form of "common sense" and a vocabulary that defines female inferiority in sports as "natural." Therefore, when a person throws a ball correctly, people learned to say that he or she "throws like a man." Throwing incorrectly means that a person "throws like a girl." The same has been true when running abilities and general sports abilities are evaluated. If sports are played correctly, they are played as a man would play them. If they are played incorrectly, they are played as a girl would play them.

The belief that playing sports, especially contact sports, would make boys into men has also been fostered by dominant gender ideology in many cultures. Consequently, when girls and women played these sports, many people described them as "unfeminine" or as "unnatural" or "immoral." Many people could not make sense of strong, competent women athletes, so they assumed that such women must be "male-like" or lesbians (Griffin, 1998; 2008). When this assumption was combined with related ideas and beliefs about nature and the body many people, including physicians and political and religious leaders, discouraged sport participation for girls and women and restricted their opportunities to play sports (Hargreaves, 1994; Lenskyj, 1986; Vertinsky, 1990, 1994).

This gender ideology was so widely accepted through most of the twentieth century that being female meant being a failure in sports (Lenskyj, 1986). Coaches of men's teams even used this idea to motivate players by "accusing" them of "playing like a bunch of girls" when they made mistakes or did not play aggressively enough. Most important, this ideology led people to exclude girls and women from sports and to give nearly all funding to programs for boys and men. Although many people have challenged and discredited this ideology in recent years, its legacy continues to privilege many boys and men and disadvantage many girls and women.

Fortunately, ideology can be and sometimes is changed. History shows that people regularly resist ideologies that they define as unfair, and sometimes organize social movements to change them. For example, many girls and women have used sports as sites or "social places" for challenging dominant ideas and beliefs about what is "natural and feminine." This has led others to question the validity of traditional ideology, form new ideas and beliefs about gender, and support structural changes in the gendered organization of sports and society as a whole.

Issues related to gender ideology are discussed in all of the following chapters, and especially Chapter 8. The box "The Body Is More Than Physical" deals with a related ideological issue in our lives: What do we consider "natural" when it comes to the body?

Racial Ideology   Sports often are sites for either reaffirming or challenging **racial ideology,** that is, the *web of ideas and beliefs that people use to give meaning to skin color and evaluate people and forms of social organization in terms of racial classifications.* Racial ideologies vary around the world, but they are powerful forces in many societies. They're used to place people into racial categories that are tied to assumptions about character traits and abilities, both intellectual and physical. These assumptions then serve as the foundation for important social practices and policies that affect people's lives.

The connections between sports and racial ideologies are complex. However, many people in the United States have long used widely shared ideas and beliefs about skin color to evaluate athletic potential and explain athletic success and failure. The beliefs that light-skinned people lack certain running and jumping abilities, whereas dark-skinned people excel in certain sports due to "natural" abilities, are expressions of what has been dominant racial ideology for at least a century in the U.S. This ideology has been challenged and discredited, but its legacy has shaped many aspects of existing social organization and cultural practices. This and related issues are discussed in Chapter 9.

Class Ideology   **Class ideology** consists of *a web of ideas and beliefs that people use to understand economic inequalities and make sense of their own positions and the positions of others in an economic hierarchy in society.* In the United States, for example, class ideology is organized around the beliefs that all people have opportunities to achieve economic success and that American society is a **meritocracy** *where deserving people become successful and where success is achieved by those who deserve it.* Sports provide many stories and slogans emphasizing that people can achieve anything through discipline and hard work, and that failure awaits the lazy and undisciplined. By extension, this ideology supports the assumption that wealth and power are earned by qualified and hardworking people of good character, whereas poverty and dead-end jobs signal a lack of character, qualifications, and a willingness to work.

This way of thinking legitimizes class inequality. It connects sports positively with capitalism and the belief that economic rewards identify deserving winners in a competitive world. This and related issues are discussed in Chapters 8 to 10.

Sports and Ideologies: Complex Connections When we think about sports and ideologies, it is important to know that ideology is complex and sometimes inconsistent and that sports come in many forms and have many meanings associated with them. Therefore, sports are connected with ideologies in various and sometimes contradictory ways. We saw this in the example showing that sports are sites for simultaneously reproducing *and* challenging dominant gender ideology in society.

Additionally, sports can have many different social meanings associated with them. For example, baseball is played by similar rules in Japan and the United States, but the meanings associated with baseball and with athletes' performances are different because of ideological differences between the two cultures. Team loyalty is highly prized in Japan, and emotional displays by players or coaches are frowned upon, whereas individualism is high prized in the United States, and emotional displays are seen as entertaining. Japanese baseball games can end in ties, but games in the United States must have winners and losers, even if it means playing extra innings.

The complex connections between sports and ideologies make it difficult to generalize about the role and consequences of sports in society. Sports have the *potential* to influence social worlds in many ways. This is another reason for studying them as contested activities and social constructions.

Sports Are Integrated into Major Spheres of Social Life

A reason for using sociology to study sports is that they are clearly connected to major spheres

> **[Sports] are why some people get out of bed. Sports define many of us. Some superstars command as much attention as heads of state and other leaders. Whether you weigh the good or bad of it—it's a fact.** —Bob Davis, vice president, American Program Bureau (1999)

of social life, including family, economy, media, politics, education, and religion. These connections are discussed through this book, but it is useful to highlight them here.

Sports and the Family   Family life in North America is often influenced by sports. Millions of children play organized sports and parents often administer programs, coach teams, attend games, and serve as chauffeur for child athletes. Family schedules are altered to accommodate practices and games, and watching sports can disrupt family life or bring family members together. In some cases, relationships between family members are nurtured and played out during sport activities or in conversations about sports. Family issues are discussed in Chapters 4 and 5.

Sports and the Economy   People in wealthy postindustrial societies spend billions of dollars each year on game tickets, sports equipment,

"This won't take long will it?"

Families and family schedules often are shaped by sport involvement, sometimes interfering with family relationships (left) and sometimes creating enjoyable time together (right).

The Body Is More than Physical
Sports Influence Meanings Given to the Body

Until recently, most people viewed the body as a fixed fact of nature; it was biological only. But many scholars and scientists now recognize that a full understanding of the body requires that we view it in social and cultural terms (Blake, 1996; Brownell, 1995; Butler, 2004; Cole, 2000a; Hargreaves and Vertinsky, 2006; Petersen, 2007; Shilling, 1993, 2007; Turner, 1997). For example, medical historians explain that the body and body parts have been identified and defined differently through history and from one culture to another. This is important because it affects medical practice, government policies, social theories, sport participation, and our everyday experiences (Fausto-Sterling, 2000; Laqueur, 1990; Lupton, 2000; Preves, 2005; Weil, 2006).

The meanings given to the body and body parts in any culture are the foundation for people's ideas and beliefs about sex, sex differences, sexuality, beauty, self-image, body image, fashion, hygiene, health, nutrition, eating, fitness, age and aging, racial classification systems, disease, drugs and drug testing, violence and power, and other factors that affect our lives. Cultural definitions of the body influence deep personal feelings such as desire, pleasure, pain, and other sensations that we use to assess personal well-being, relationships, and quality of life. For example, people in Europe and North America during the nineteenth century identified insensitivity to physical pain as a sign that a person had serious character defects, and they saw a muscular body as an indicator of a criminal disposition, immorality, and lower-class status (Hoberman, 1992).

Cultural definitions of the body have changed so that today we see a person's ability to ignore pain, especially in sports, as an indicator of strong moral character, and we see a muscular body as proof of self-control and discipline rather than immorality and criminal tendencies. But in either case, our identities and experiences are inherently embodied, and our bodies are identified in connection with social and cultural definitions of age, sex, sexuality, race, ethnicity, and disability, among other factors.

Definitions of the body are strongly related to sports in many societies. For example, our conception of the "ideal body," especially the ideal male body, is strongly influenced by the athletic body. In fact, the bodies of athletes are used widely as models of health and fitness, strength and power, control and discipline, and overall ability. In today's competitive sports, the body is measured, classified, conditioned, trained, regulated, and assessed in terms of its performance under various conditions. Instead of being experienced as a source of pleasure and joy, the body is more often viewed as a machine that achieves instrumental goals. As a machine, its parts must be developed, coordinated, maintained, and fixed when broken. Additionally, when the athletic body fails due to injuries, impairments, and age, it is reclassified in ways that dramatically alter identity, relationships, and status.

Socially constructing the body in this way emphasizes control and rationality. It leads people to accept and even seek forms of body assessment and regulation such as weigh-ins, measuring body-fat percentage, testing for aerobic and anaerobic capacity, observing physiological responses to stressors, doing blood analysis, dieting, using drugs and other substances, drug testing, and on and on.

The cultural conceptions of *body as machine* and *sport as performance* make it likely that athletes will use brain manipulations, hormonal regulation, body-part replacements, and genetic engineering as methods of disciplining, controlling, and managing their bodies. Measurable performance outcomes then become more important than subjective experiences of bodily pleasure and joy (Pronger, 2002). As a result, the ability to endure pain and stay in the game is an indicator of the "disciplined body;" and bodies that are starved to reduce body fat to unhealthy levels are viewed as "fit" and "in shape."

Continued

The steroid-enhanced body of Arnold Schwarzenegger made bodybuilding popular worldwide. A cutout of his pose as Mr. Olympia inspires the workouts of men who come to this gym in Ghazni, Afghanistan (in 2007). Although public displays of bodies are traditionally discouraged in Afghan culture, the notion that bodies can be sculpted to change men's lives is increasingly accepted. (*Source*: Musadeq Sadeq, AP Worldwide Photos)

Once we realize that human life is embodied and that bodies are socially constructed in the context of our culture, those who think critically ask the following questions:

1. What are the origins of prevailing ideas about natural, ideal, and deviant bodies in sports and in society?

2. What are the moral and social implications of the ways that the body is protected, probed, monitored, tested, trained, disciplined, evaluated, manipulated, and rehabilitated in sports?

3. How are bodies in sports marked and categorized by gender, skin color, ethnicity, (dis)ability, and age, and what are the social implications of such body marking and categorization?

4. How are athletic bodies represented in the media and popular culture, and how do those representations influence identities, relationships, and forms of social organization?

5. Who owns the body of an athlete, and what happens when it is sold as a billboard for advertising products and services?

These questions challenge taken-for-granted ideas about nature, beauty, health, and competitive sports. But learning about sports in society requires this form of critical inquiry to be done. *What do you think?*

participation fees, athletic club membership dues, and bets placed on teams and athletes. This affects local and regional economies. Throughout much of the world, sports and commerce have joined together so that corporate logos are now linked with sport teams and athletes, and they are displayed prominently in school gyms, arenas, stadiums, and other sports places.

Some athletes now make impressive sums of money from salaries, appearance fees, and endorsements. Corporations paid up to $3 million for thirty seconds of commercial time during the 2009 telecast of the Super Bowl and the International Olympic Committee takes in about $4 billion every four years from corporate sponsors. Sport stadiums, arenas, and teams are named after corporations, and corporate logos are so pervasive that many people associate certain sports, teams, and events with corporations and their products. Overall, sports are integrally tied to material and economic conditions in society. These issues are discussed in Chapters 10 and 11.

Sports and the Media   Television networks and cable stations pay billions of dollars for the rights to televise sports. NBC paid the International Olympic Committee (IOC) $2.3 billion for the rights to the 2004 and 2006 Summer Games and the 2006 Winter Games. Five media companies pay the NFL over $3.75 billion per year to televise their games. Commercial sports seldom prosper without media coverage and collecting rights fees from media companies.

The images and stories represented in media coverage of sports emphasize particular ideological themes, and they influence what people think and talk about every day. The media have converted sports into a major form of entertainment, athletes are now global celebrities, and corporations that sponsor media sports inscribe their logos in people's minds and use sports to promote lifestyles based on consumption. These issues are discussed in Chapter 12.

Sports and Politics   People in many societies link sports to national pride and identity. In the aftermath of the terrorist attacks of 9/11/01, many Americans used sport events as sites for reaffirming their collective sense of "we-ness." There were passionate expressions of unity and patriotism, combined with memorials to commemorate the victims of the attacks. This allowed spectators, even those watching on television, to reaffirm their sense of national identity.

Sports are widely used by nation-states wishing to gain global recognition or present a show of power and wealth to the rest of the world. China spent over $40 billion to host the 2008 Olympics in the hope of achieving these goals. Political leaders at various levels of government promote themselves by demonstrating personal interest in sports, and former athletes have used their name recognition and reputations from sports to be elected to political positions in the United States.

Additionally, sports themselves are political in that they involve decisions related to the control and sponsorship of events, eligibility and team selection, rules and rule changes, rule enforcement, and the allocation of rewards and punishments. Sport organizations exercise power over people's lives—a reason they often are described as governing bodies. These issues are discussed in Chapter 13.

Sports and Education   Sports are widely included in physical education, and interscholastic sport teams in some nations attract widespread attention. Some U.S. universities use intercollegiate teams as public relations and often make or lose millions of dollars in the process. U.S. schools often sponsor high-profile sport programs and teams, whereas schools in most other nations sponsor low-profile, club-based teams emphasizing participation and student control. These issues are discussed in Chapter 14.

Sports and Religion   There is an emerging relationship between sports and religion in certain

Table 1.1   Publication sources for sociology of sport research

JOURNALS DEVOTED PRIMARILY TO SOCIOLOGY OF SPORT ARTICLES

International Review for the Sociology of Sport (quarterly)
Journal of Sport and Social Issues (quarterly)
Sociology of Sport Journal (quarterly)
Sociology of Sport Online (sosol)

SOCIOLOGY JOURNALS THAT SOMETIMES INCLUDE ARTICLES ON OR RELATED TO SPORTS

American Journal of Sociology
American Sociological Review
British Journal of Sociology
Sociology of Education
Theory, Culture and Society

INTERDISCIPLINARY, SPORT SCIENCE, AND PHYSICAL EDUCATION JOURNALS THAT SOMETIMES INCLUDE ARTICLES ON OR RELATED TO SOCIOLOGY OF SPORT TOPICS

Adapted Physical Activity Quarterly
Avante
Canadian Journal of Applied Sport Sciences
Exercise and Sport Sciences Reviews
International Journal of Eastern Sports and Physical Education
Journal of Physical Education, Recreation, and Dance
Journal of Intercollegiate Sports
Journal of Issues in Intercollegiate Athletics
Journal of Sport Management
Journal of Sport Sciences
Journal for the Study of Sports and Athletics in Education
Physical Education Review
Quest
Recreational Sports Journal
Research Quarterly for Exercise and Sport
Sport, Education, and Society
Sport in Society (formerly *Culture, Sport, and Society*)
Sport Science Review
The Sport Journal (formerly *Journal of Sport Behavior*)
Women in Sport & Physical Activity Journal

JOURNALS IN RELATED FIELDS THAT SOMETIMES INCLUDE ARTICLES ON OR RELATED TO SOCIOLOGY OF SPORT TOPICS

Adolescence
Aethlon: The Journal of Sport Literature
Athletic Insight—The Online Journal of Sport Psychology
The British Journal of Sport History
Canadian Journal of the History of Sport
Coaching: An International Journal of Theory, Research and Practice
European Sport Management Quarterly
The European Sports History Review
International Journal of the History of Sport
International Journal of Religion and Sport
International Journal of Sport Communication
International Journal of Sport and Health Science
International Journal of Sports Psychology
International Review of Sport and Exercise Psychology
Journal of Coaching Education
Journal of Human Movement Studies
Journal of Leisure Research
Journal of the Philosophy of Sport
Journal of Popular Culture
Journal of Sport and Exercise Psychology
Journal of Sport History
Journal of Sport Media
Journal of Sports Economics
Leisure Sciences
Leisure Studies
Olympika: The International Journal of Olympic Studies
Soccer and Society
Society and Leisure
Sport, Ethics and Philosophy
Sport History Review
Sport Management Review
Sport in Society
The Sport Psychologist
Sporting Traditions
The Sports Historian
Youth & Society

societies. Local churches and church groups in the United States and Canada sponsor teams and leagues. Parishes and congregations revise Sunday worship schedules to accommodate members who won't miss an opening NFL kickoff. Athletes in the United States regularly express their religious beliefs, and nondenominational religious organizations use sports to attract and convert people to Christianity. Other U.S.-based religious organizations commonly use athletes as spokespersons, and some athletes now define their sport participation primarily in religious terms. These issues are discussed in Chapter 15.

Sports and Everyday Life   Data on youth sport participation, attendance at events, media coverage of sports, the number of people who consider themselves fans, the money spent on sports, and other information clearly indicate that the importance and visibility of sports has increased dramatically over the past few decades. This is reflected in the rapid expansion of research and scholarly discussions of sports in society. As I wrote this edition of *Sports in Society*, I included over 700 new references to books, journal articles, and relevent articles in the popular press that were not cited in the last edition. Keeping track of the literature is now a full time job. Table 1.1 on page 25 lists most of the journals that I used when seeking the latest research findings on topics discussed in this book.

summary

WHY STUDY THE SOCIOLOGY OF SPORT?

Sociology is the study of *the social worlds that people create, organize, maintain, and change through their relationships with each other*. Sociologists use concepts, research, and theories to describe and explain social worlds. In the process, they enable us to put the lives of individuals and groups into context. This makes us aware of the circumstances that set limits and create possibilities in people's lives. For most sociologists, the ultimate goal is to create the knowledge that enables people to understand, control, and change the conditions of their lives so that needs are met at both individual and group levels.

Sociologists use the concepts of culture, social interaction, and social structure as they systematically investigate social worlds. Sociological knowledge about sports and other social worlds is based on information collected in research. This makes it different from statements about sports that are based only on personal experience and opinions.

Defining sports presents a challenge. Some scholars define *sports* as *well-established, officially governed competitive physical activities in which participants are motivated by internal and external rewards*. However, using a single, static definition of sport is problematic if it leads us to ignore or devalue the lives of people who have neither the resources nor the desire to develop formally organized and competitive physical activities. For this reason, many people in the sociology of sport use an alternative definitional approach based on the assumption that popular conceptions of sports vary over time and from one social world to another. These scholars try to explain why certain activities, and not others, are identified as sports in a particular group or society, why some sports are more strongly supported and funded than others, and how various categories of people are affected by the prevailing definition of sports and related funding priorities.

This alternative approach emphasizes that sports are contested activities, meaning that people often disagree about their meaning, purpose, and organization. Furthermore, people often have different ideas about who should play sports and the conditions under which participation should occur. Debates over who plays and who doesn't often create heated exchanges and bitter feelings, because they are tied to notions of fairness, inclusion, and the allocation of resources in social worlds. Finally, sports are contested when people disagree over issues of sponsorship: the sports that will be sponsored, who will sponsor them, and how much control the sponsors will have over sports.

Learning to ask critical questions about sports in society is easier when people view sports as **social constructions**—that is, *parts of the social world that are created by people as they interact with one another under the social, political, and economic conditions that exist in their society.* This forces us to think about why sports take particular forms and who is advantaged and disadvantaged by prevailing ideas and the current organization of sports in a social world.

When sociologists study sports in society, they often discover problems created by the structure and organization of either sports or the social worlds in which they exist. When this happens, recommendations based on sociological research may threaten those with a vested interest in maintaining the status quo in sports. Although this leads some people to see the sociology of sport as controversial, most people in the field continue to do research and produce knowledge that they and others use to promote fairness and social justice.

People study sports in society because sports are socially significant activities for many people; they provide excitement, memorable experiences, and opportunities to initiate and extend social relationships. Sports also reaffirm important ideas and beliefs, especially those that comprise ideologies related to gender, race and ethnicity, and social class. Finally, people study sports in society because sports are deeply integrated in major spheres of social life such as family, economy, media, politics, education, and religion. Overall, sports have become such an integral part of everyday life that they cannot be ignored by anyone concerned with culture, social interaction, and social structure in societies today.

WEBSITE RESOURCES

Note: Websites often change. The following URLs were current when this book was printed. Please check our website (www.mhhe.com/coakley10e) for updates and additions.

www.alesde.ufpr.br/inicioen.html   Asociación Latinoamericana de Estudios Socioculturales del Deporte (ALESDE) is a recently formed Latin America sociology association dedicated to studying sports from social and cultural perspectives; this site will contain information about research as the association hosts conferences and sponsors a journal.

www.eass-sportsociology.eu/   The European Association for Sociology of Sport (eass) provides news, journal articles, policy information, and sponsors an annual conference focused generally on sports in European nations and the European Union.

www.issa.otago.ac.nz/   ISSA is the International Sociology of Sport Association; this organization is a subcommittee of ICSSPE, the International Council of Sport Science and Physical Education, and is affiliated with UNESCO, the United Nations Educational, Scientific and Cultural Organization.

www.mhhe.com/coakley10e   Click on chapter 1; also go to the Online Learning Center (OLC) at www.mhhe.com/coakley10e for an annotated list of readings and other materials related to this chapter. The OLC contains a chapter-by-chapter list of key concepts, a graded review test, and important sociology of sport information.

www.nasss.org/   The official site for the North American Society for the Sociology of Sport; the Resource Center contains a list of experts in the field, along with graduate programs specializing in the sociology of sport.

www.sociosite.net/topics/leisure.php#SPORT   This site, located in the Netherlands, provides excellent links to sites related to the sociology of sport.

(Jay Coakley)

PRODUCING KNOWLEDGE ABOUT SPORTS IN SOCIETY

What Is the Role of Research and Theory?

chapter

2

WE GET ALL JACKED UP about slobber-knocking tackles that serve as the NFL's rocking soundtrack. And maybe it's safer if we don't examine our delight in the pounding rhythms of the game too closely.

—Mark Kiszla, journalist, *Denver Post* (2007)

Visit *Sports in Society*'s Online Learning Center (OLC) at www.mhhe.com/coakley10e for additional information and study material for this chapter, including the following:

- A complete chapter outline
- Learning objectives
- Practice quizzes
- Internet resources
- Related readings
- Essays
- Student projects

... THE VERY PASSION we invest in sports can transform it from a kind of mindless escape into a site of resistance. It can become an arena where the ideas of our society are not only presented but also challenged.

—**Dave Zirin, Press Action Sportswriter of the Year (2005)**

Those of us who study sports in society want to understand four things:

1. The social and cultural contexts in which sports exist
2. The connections between those contexts and sports
3. The social worlds that people create as they participate in sports
4. The experiences of individuals and groups associated with those social worlds

We are motivated by combinations of curiosity, interest in sports, a desire to expand what we know about social worlds, and a desire to reduce social problems. Most of us also want to use what we know about sports in society to promote social justice, expose and challenge the exploitive use of power, and empower people so they can resist and transform oppressive social conditions.

As we study sports, we use research and theories to produce knowledge. **Social research** consists of *investigations in which we seek answers to questions about social worlds by systematically gathering and analyzing data.* Research provides data and systematic analyses that we use to expand what we know and to develop, revise, and refine theories about sports in society. **Social theories** are *logically interrelated explanations of the actions and relationships of human beings and the organization and dynamics of social worlds.* Theories also provide frameworks for asking research questions, interpreting information, and making sense of the meanings and stories associated with sports. Research and theories go hand in hand because sociologists use research to test the validity of theories, and they develop theories based on research findings.

The goal of doing sociology is to describe and explain social worlds logically and in ways that are consistent with evidence that is systematically collected and analyzed. When sociologists achieve this goal, their research and theories add to our knowledge about social worlds. This makes knowledge in the sociology of sport a more valid and reliable source of information than

what we read or hear in the media and online, where much of the content is based on opinions or perceived interests among media consumers. In practical terms, the knowledge produced in the sociology of sport helps us understand more fully the actions of individuals, the dynamics of social relationships, and the organization of social worlds. This, in turn, enables us to be more informed citizens as we participate in our schools, communities, and society.

OLC ON THE *OLC*:

See the OLC—Additional Readings for Chapter 2—for the author's explanation of the goals of social theory and why sociologists use more than one theoretical approach when they study social worlds.

The goal of this chapter is to answer these questions:

1. How is knowledge produced in the sociology of sport?
2. What are the primary data collection methods used in sociology of sport research?
3. Why is a critical approach often used when doing research and developing theories in the sociology of sport?

PRODUCING KNOWLEDGE IN THE SOCIOLOGY OF SPORT

Most of us regularly produce the practical knowledge that we use to navigate social worlds and manage our lives. We continually collect data and develop explanations of everyday experiences and events. For example, consider how you manage your life at home, school, work, and with friends. What strategies do you use to understand what occurs around you, and how do you make decisions about what to do in connection with the people and events in your life?

Most of us learn to navigate our social worlds and manage our lives by gathering information about people and things around us. We observe how others act and what occurs in various situations. And we use this information to develop experience-based explanations or "personal theories" about our experiences, people, events, and social worlds. These **personal theories** *are summaries of our ideas and explanations of social life and the contexts in which they occur.* We use them as guides when we make decisions and engage in actions through the day.

Think about life in your family as an example. You collect information and develop explanations to make sense of your family and your involvement in it. You may even develop explanations of how your family is related to the larger community and society in which you live. In the process, you develop "educated hunches" for why your family is more or less loving, strict, organized, wealthy, or supportive than other families. You also try to explain the impact of external factors on your family, such as the closing of your neighborhood high school that forced you to be bused 20 miles to another school, a nationwide economic recession during which your father lost his job, and the local decision to build a major highway that cut your neighborhood off from a previously accessible shopping area and recreation center.

The goal of our personal, experience-based data collection and theorizing is to make sense and gain some control of our lives and the social worlds in which we live. Personal theories are forms of practical knowledge that we use to anticipate events, the actions of others, and the consequences of our own actions in various situations. Without them, we would be passive objects in our social worlds—victims of culture and society. With theories, we become potentially active subjects—agents with the ability to participate intentionally and strategically in social worlds, reproducing or changing them as we take action alone and with others.

When Pierre Bourdieu, a famous French sociologist, discussed the practical knowledge that people develop through their personal experiences, he referred to it as "cultural capital" (Bourdieu, 1986). He explained that each of us can acquire and accumulate cultural capital as we expand our social and cultural experiences and make sense of them in ways that increase our understanding of ourselves, our relationships, and the ways that social worlds are organized. Although each of us has different opportunities and experiences, we can convert our personal theories into cultural capital. Like money, cultural capital has real value as we "cash it in" and use it to navigate, manage, and control our lives. But unlike money, cultural capital can be used over and over again without running up our bills.

As you consider these points, you may wonder how your personal research and theories differ from the research and theories in the sociology of sport. In what ways are they different? Can research and theories in the sociology of sport be used in combination with personal research and theories? Can they take their place? Are they more accurate and reliable to use? Are they useful to others who have theories of their own? These questions will be answered in the rest of the chapter and throughout this book.

Our personal research and theories are useful to us in our everyday lives, but they differ from research and theories in the sociology of sport. Personal research focuses on our immediate social worlds. We gather and analyze information, but we don't use carefully developed methods or follow systematic and rigorous guidelines as we do so (Lemert, 2002). Similarly, we develop personal theories for our own practical use. We don't systematically test them, compare them with related theories, and then make them public so that others may examine them and determine their overall validity across many social worlds beyond our own (Ritzer, 2003).

Research in the sociology of sport, unlike personal research, is designed to answer questions that go beyond the experiences and the social situations encountered by one person. Those doing the research collect data from people or in situations that are chosen because they can provide information to answer research questions. The researchers then analyze their data by using methods that have been developed and refined by other sociologists. If the analysis leads to clear conclusions, the researchers try to connect them with the conclusions and theories of other sociologists in the hope of expanding knowledge about the dynamics and organization of social life and social worlds. Finally, researchers are expected to publish their findings so that others can critically examine them to see if appropriate methods and procedures have been used and if the findings make sense when compared with other published studies.

People in the sociology of sport may study particular topics because they have a personal interest in them, but the process of doing research involves using methods that minimize the influence of personal values and experiences on the findings and conclusions. Basic research methods used in sociology of sport research are described later in the chapter (pages 44–48), but first we'll examine a case study that illustrates the ways that research is done and theory is used in the process of producing knowledge in the sociology of sport.

DOING RESEARCH AND USING THEORY IN THE SOCIOLOGY OF SPORT: A CASE STUDY

Mike Messner is a well-known and respected sociologist at the University of Southern California. One of his books, *Taking the Field: Women, Men, and Sports* (2002), was named best

The social worlds created around sports are so complex that it helps to have systematic research methods and logical theories to study and understand them. I attend youth sports events for personal reasons, but I use the knowledge produced by Mike Messner and others in the sociology of sport to help me make sense of what occurs at the events. (*Source*: Jay Coakley)

book of the year by his colleagues in the sociology of sport. In the first chapter of Messner's book, he described a situation that, in part, inspired him to do in-depth sociological research on the connections between sport and gender in the United States. The situation occurred as he accompanied his son to the opening ceremony of a youth soccer season. Here are his words:

> The Sea Monsters is a team of four- and five-year old boys. Later this day, they will play their first ever soccer game. A few of the boys already know each other from preschool, but most are still getting acquainted. They are wearing their new uniforms for the first time. Like other teams, they were assigned team colors—in this case, green and blue—and asked to choose their team name at their first team meeting. . . . A grandmother of one of the boys created the spiffy team banner, which was awarded a prize this morning. While they wait for the ceremony to begin, the boys inspect and then proudly pose for pictures in front of their new award-winning team banner. The parents stand a few feet away, some taking pictures, some just watching. . . .
>
> Queued up one group away from the Sea Monsters is a team of four- and five year-old girls in green and white uniforms. . . . They have chosen the name Barbie Girls and they too have a new team banner. But the girls are pretty much ignoring their banner, for they have created another, more powerful symbol around which to rally. In fact, they are the only team among the 156 marching today with a team float—a red Radio Flyer wagon base, on which sits a Sony boom box playing music, and a three-foot-plus tall Barbie doll on a rotating pedestal. Barbie is dressed in the team colors; indeed, she sports a custom-made green and white cheerleader-style outfit, with the Barbie Girls' names written on the skirt. Her normally all-blond hair has been streaked with Barbie Girl green and features a green bow with polka dots. Several of the girls on the team have supplemented their uniforms with green bows in their hair as well.
>
> The volume on the boom box nudges up, and four or five girls begin to sing a Barbie song. Barbie is now slowly rotating on her pedestal, and as the girls sing more gleefully and more loudly, some of them begin to hold hands and walk around the float, in synch with Barbie's rotation. Other same-aged girls from other teams are drawn to the celebration and, eventually, perhaps a dozen girls are singing the Barbie song. The girls are intensely focused on Barbie, on the music, and on their mutual pleasure.
>
> While the Sea Monsters mill around their banner, some of them begin to notice and then begin to watch and listen when the Barbie Girls rally around their float. At first, the boys are watching as individuals, seemingly unaware of each other's shared interest. Some of them stand with arms at their sides, slack-jawed, as though passively watching a television show. I notice slight smiles on a couple of their faces, as though they are drawn to the Barbie Girls' celebratory fun. Then, with side glances, some of the boys begin to notice each other's attention on the Barbie Girls. Their faces begin to show signs of distaste. One of them yells out, "NO BARBIE!" Suddenly, they all begin to move, jumping up and down, nudging, and bumping one another, and join in a group chant; "NO BARBIE! NO BARBIE! NO BARBIE!" They now appear to be every bit as gleeful as the girls as they laugh, yell, and chant against the Barbie Girls.
>
> The parents watch the whole scene with rapt attention. . . . "They are SO different!" exclaims one smiling mother approvingly. A male coach offers a more in-depth analysis: "When I was in college," he says, "I took these classes from professors who showed us research that showed that boys and girls are the same. I believed it, until I had my own kids and saw how different they are." "Yeah," another dad responds. "Just look at them! They are so different!"
>
> The girls meanwhile, show no evidence that they hear, see, or are even aware of the presence of the boys, who are now so loudly proclaiming their opposition to the Barbie Girls' songs and totem. The girls continue to sing, dance, laugh, and rally around the Barbie for few more minutes, before they are called to reassemble in their groups for the beginning of the parade.
>
> After the parade, the teams reassemble on the infield of the track, but now in a less organized manner. The Sea Monsters once again find

themselves in the general vicinity of the Barbie Girls and take up the "NO BARBIE!" chant. Perhaps put out by the lack of response to their chant, they begin to dash, in twos and threes, invading the girls' space and yelling menacingly. With this, the Barbie Girls have little choice but to recognize the presence of the boys; some look puzzled and shrink back, some engage the boys and chase them off. The chasing seems only to incite more excitement among the boys. Finally, parents intervene and defuse the situation, leading their children off to their cars, homes, and eventually to their soccer games. (from Messner, 2002, pp. 3–6)

As Messner observed these things, it caused him to think. As a father, he was concerned about the way his son would make sense of these experiences as a five-year-old boy in twenty-first-century America; and he considered what he would say to help his son define them in terms that would impact his development positively. But as a sociologist, Messner's thoughts went beyond his immediate experiences and his role as a father. He wondered why parents at the soccer ceremony accepted without question the idea that boys and girls are naturally different, even though many of the boys were initially interested in the playful actions of the girls and their use of the Barbie icon. Taking this thought a step further, he wondered if people who use "nature" to explain the actions of their children tend to overlook similarities between boys and girls and feel no need to discuss strategies to help their children understand that boys don't intimidate girls because it is part of their "nature."

Even though the boys' "playful actions" at the soccer ceremony did not physically hurt anyone, Messner wondered if certain sports are organized to reaffirm ideas about gender and nature so that many people believe that it is normal for boys and men to express aggression by intimidating others. This also made him think about the decision of the American Youth Soccer Organization (AYSO) officials to segregate soccer teams by sex, thereby eliminating opportunities for boys and girls to play together and discover that they often share interests and other characteristics. Without such opportunities, do boys and girls grow up thinking that males and females are naturally "opposites," even though they share many social, psychological, and physical attributes? And if this is so, what implications does it have for how we identify ourselves, form relationships, and organize our social worlds? As Messner asked these questions about sports and gender, he decided that he should do a full-scale research project to expand sociological knowledge about this topic.

At this point, Messner was at the beginning of a multistep process for producing knowledge in the sociology of sport and in science generally. These steps are listed in Figure 2.1, and we can use them as a guide as we discuss this case study.

Step 1: Observe social worlds and ask questions.

Producing knowledge always begins with observations of the world followed by questions about what is and is not observed. In this case, Messner observed a particular event and combined what he witnessed with his previous observations and knowledge of sports. As he organized his questions, it was clear that they were tied to his interests as a father, citizen, and sociologist. He had long-standing interests in the problems associated with definitions of masculinity in North America and issues of violence and gender equity in sports. These interests were grounded in his personal experiences in sports and his desire to make them, and social life generally, more fair and responsive to human needs (Messner and Sabo, 1994). With this as motivation, he launched his study of gender and sports.

Step 2: Identify issues, review past research, and use social theories and research methods to design the research project.

As Messner thought more deeply about his observations of sports, he formed questions around issues related to culture, social interaction, and

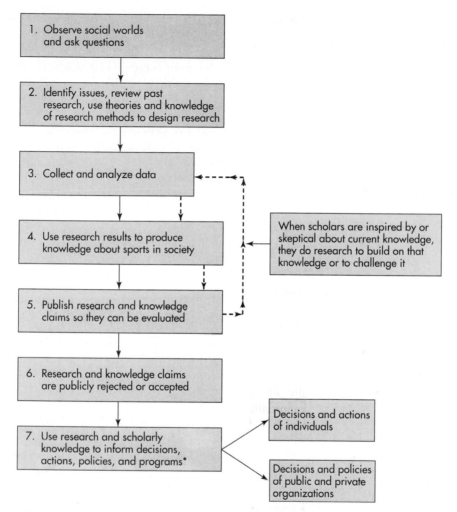

FIGURE 2.1 The seven-step process of producing knowledge in the sociology of sport
*As noted in Chapter 1, p. 15, when research and scholarly knowledge challenges those in power, it may be rejected or ignored.

social structure—the three concepts around which much sociological knowledge is organized. In connection with culture, he asked these questions:

- What words, meanings, and symbols do American children learn to use as they identify themselves and others?
- How do children learn and use cultural beliefs to separate all human beings into two distinct, nonoverlapping, and "opposite" sex categories,

even though males and females share many social, psychological, and physiological attributes and are not biological "opposites"?

In connection with social interaction, he asked:

- How do children perform gender in their everyday lives, and how do they learn to successfully present themselves to others as boys or girls?

- What happens in their relationships when they don't perform gender as others expect them to?

In connection with social structure, he asked:

- How are ideas and beliefs about gender integrated into the overall structure of the AYSO (American Youth Soccer Organization) and other sport organizations?
- How does the organization of sports at all levels create constraints and possibilities that influence the lives of boys and men in different ways than they influence the lives of girls and women?

To see if other researchers had already answered these questions or developed theories to guide his study, Messner reviewed many of the 326 sources he listed as references in his book. This "review of the literature," as it is called by researchers, indicated that there was a need to know more about the relationship between sports and the ways that people learn and incorporate ideas about gender into their identities, relationships, and the organization of social worlds.

As he designed his research project, Messner knew that social worlds are complex and must be viewed from different angles and vantage points to describe and explain them accurately. Therefore, he used a combination of cultural, interactionist, and structural theories as guides for conceptualizing his project. Each of these theories focuses on different aspects of social life. Table 2.1 summarizes the central features of these theories, showing that each one explains different aspects of social worlds, has a different focus of analysis, uses different concepts, and addresses different issues.

Messner used **cultural theories** because they *explain what we know about the ways that people think and express their values, ideas, and beliefs as they live together and create social worlds.* Research based on cultural theories focuses on the processes through which people create,

maintain, and change their collective ideas and beliefs about their lives and the social worlds in which they live. Cultural theories emphasize that people create symbols and give meaning to parts of their worlds that are important to them; in turn, those symbols and meanings influence their feelings, thoughts, and actions. Cultural theories utilize concepts such as values, norms, ideas, beliefs, ideology, symbols, and language because they are the reference points that people use to make sense of and give meaning to themselves, their experiences, and the world around them.

Cultural theories alerted Messner to the importance of symbols, such as names, colors, uniforms, banners, songs, and chants that were used to represent teams in the AYSO. Further, they suggested that it is important to examine the **narratives,** or *ways of representing and talking about objects, people, and experiences* that are used in connection with sports. Therefore, Messner directed his attention to the ways that particular ideas and beliefs about masculinity and femininity were included in these narratives.

OLC ON THE *OLC*:

See the OLC—Additional Readings for Chapter 2—for a summary of a study using interactionist theory to understand the meaning of pain in an athlete's life.

Messner also used **interactionist theories** because they *explain what we know about the origins, dynamics, and consequences of social interaction among people in particular social worlds.* These theories focus on processes of social learning and development and the social interaction and relationships through which people come to know and give meaning to themselves, others, and the things and events that occur in their social worlds. Interactionist theories use concepts such as social interaction, socialization, role models, significant others, self-concept, and identity to

Table 2.1   Central features of the three major types of theories used in the sociology of sport

Type of Theory	Help to Explain What is Known About	Major Focus of Analysis is the	Major Concepts Used in Analysis are	Research Includes Studies of*
Cultural Theories	Processes through which people create, maintain, and change their values, ideas, and beliefs as they play and watch sports	The ways people make sense of and give meaning to their experiences as sport participants and spectators	Values, norms, ideas, beliefs, ideology, symbols, and language associated with sports	- imagery and narratives in media coverage of men's and women's sports - the impact of racial ideology on the sport participation choices of individuals
Interactionist Theories	Social interaction and relationships in the social worlds created in connection with sports	Social learning and development; the interaction and relationships through which people learn about and give meaning to sports	Interaction, socialization, role model, significant others, self-concept, identity, and definition of the situation	- the process of normalizing pain and injury when playing sports - the process of developing and maintaining athletic identities
Structural Theories	The social organization and patterns of relationships that influence opportunities, decisions, and actions in sports	Impact of social organization on access to power, authority, status, resources, and economic opportunities in sports and society	Status, roles, groups, authority, power relations, social control, social inequality, social institutions, organizations, and societies	- gender equity in school sport programs; - who benefits when public money builds stadiums for professional sport teams

*See Messner (2002) Chapters 2, 3, and 4 for examples of these and other studies. Chapter 4, "Center of Attention: The Gender of Sports Media," summarizes studies guided by cultural theories. Chapter 2, "Playing Center: The Triad of Violence in Men's Sports," summarizes studies guided by interactionist theories. Chapter 3, "Center of the Diamond: The Institutional Core of Sport," summarizes studies guided by structural theories.

study social development during childhood, adolescence, and adulthood. This alerted Messner to the ways that youth sports are **sites,** or *identifiable social contexts,* where people learn what it means to be a man or woman, how to perform masculinity or femininity as they interact with others, and the ways that ideas and beliefs about gender are integrated into the organization of social worlds.

Finally, Messner used **structural theories** because they *explain what we know about forms*

of social organization that influence actions and relationships. These theories focus on the ways that relationships are organized and how they influence people's access to power, authority, material resources, economic opportunities, and other resources. Structural theories provide knowledge about recurring social patterns and arrangements that exist in important realms of everyday life, such as the family, religion, education, the economy, politics, and the media. They emphasize concepts such as status, roles, authority, power, social class, and social inequality to explain that the constraints and opportunities that exist in social worlds affect people differently, depending their social positions and relationships with others. Therefore, these theories alerted Messner to the ways that gender is used as a basis for organizing sports and identifying who has authority and power on AYSO teams, the AYSO administration, and in sports generally.

> ### OLC ON THE *OLC*:
>
> See the OLC—Additional Readings for Chapter 2—for the author's discussion of specific theories that have been used in the sociology of sport; these include structural-functionalism, conflict theory, symbolic interactionism, critical theory, feminist theory, and figurational theory.

Step 3: Collect and analyze data.

Using cultural theories as a guide, Messner collected information on the team names that players and coaches had selected for the 156 AYSO teams that season. Names, along with colors, uniforms, banners, and songs or chants, are symbols that people often use to represent sport teams in U.S. culture. **Symbols** are important to sociologists because they *are concrete representations of the values, beliefs, and moral principles around which people organize their ways of life.*

When Messner analyzed the 156 team names, he found that 15% percent of the girls' teams and 1% of the boys' teams chose sweet, cutesy names such as the Pink Flamingos, Blue Butterflies, Sunflowers, and Barbie Girls.[1] "Neutral" or paradoxical names such as Team Flubber, Galaxy, Blue and Green Lizards, and Blue Ice) were selected by 32 percent of the girls' teams and 13 percent of the boys' teams; and power

names such as Shooting Stars, Raptor Attack, Sea Monsters, Sharks, and Killer Whales were selected by 52 percent of the girls' teams and 82 percent of the boys' teams. Overall, boys were much more likely to avoid sweet, cutesy names and select power names. This is consistent with past research showing that people represent themselves and their groups with symbols and names that reaffirm their ideas about themselves. In this case, the boys and girls selected names that fit their gendered sense of who they

What does it mean when five-year-old girls choose Barbie as a representation of their team? On the one hand, Barbie represents traditional feminine values and ideals in U.S. culture. On the other hand, the girls connected Barbie to their sport participation. Is this a sign that traditional feminine values are changing or that the girls are creating a new form of femininity or that the girls value traditional femininity more than playing sports? The sociologists most likely to ask these questions are guided primarily by cultural theories.

---

[1]*Smurfs* was the only "sweet" name chosen by a boys' team.

were and how they wished to be perceived in the social world of AYSO youth soccer.

> **OLC ON THE *OLC*:**
> See the OLC—Additional Readings for Chapter 2—for the author's discussion of different forms of feminist theory and how they've been used in research on sports in society

When Messner used interactionist theory as a guide, he observed the actions of people at the AYSO event to see how they performed gender as they interacted with others. His observations of the children indicated that their performances clarified *and* blurred traditional gender distinctions. But the most noticeable gender performances occurred when the boys vocally objected to the girls' celebration of their Barbie icon and attempted to physically disrupt the celebration. At the same time, the girls were surprised by the boys' actions and either withdrew due to fear or stood their ground to challenge the boys. The parents reaffirmed the normalcy of these performances by attributing them to natural differences between boys and girls; they did not consider that the children's actions could be due to cultural norms, the interactional dynamics of the opening AYSO ceremony, or the overall social organization of the soccer league and most sports in U.S. society.

When Messner used structural theory as a guide, he collected data on the adult divisions of labor and power in the AYSO and each of the 156 teams. He found that there were gender-based limits for the actions and relationships of some children and adults, and gender-based possibilities for others. For example, the commissioner and assistant commissioner were men, as were twenty-one of thirty board members. Over 80 percent of the head and assistant coaches were men, whereas 86 percent of the team managers, or "team moms," as most people referred to them, were women. The coaches had formal

authority at the league and team levels, and the "team moms" performed support roles that were labor intensive, time consuming, and behind the scenes. Even when the soccer experiences of women surpassed those of men, they were less likely to volunteer as coaches. Men volunteered because they believed it was appropriate for them to play such a role, whereas the women felt less so,—and the men didn't believe they would make good "team moms."

As Messner collected and analyzed data on the organization of the AYSO, he also found that patterns of authority were *informally* structured by gender among the adults, whereas gender was *formally* and officially used to segregate boys and girls into separate leagues. According to AYSO leaders, the teams all age levels were segregated by sex to promote team unity. For the leaders, this made gender "appear to disappear" in the organization of the leagues and their decision making. By formally segregating the leagues and teams by sex, gender was erased from the day-to-day consciousness of coaches, officials, parents, players, and administrators, even though it was the primary organizing principle for the entire AYSO and the experiences of nearly 2,000 young people.

Messner pointed out that this type of social structure creates highly gendered experiences at the same time that people think that gender is irrelevant. For example, as the children played on sex-segregated teams, they had no opportunities to observe similarities in the sport skills, personalities, interests, and emotions of boys and girls or to learn to be teammates and friends with differently gendered peers. Coaches treated boys as they felt boys should be treated and girls as they felt girls should be treated without realizing that gender influenced the entire social context in which they coached. Gender was erased from their awareness at the same time that it organized and structured the experiences of everyone associated with the AYSO.

Collecting and analyzing data about the AYSO was a very small part of Messner's overall research project. He had already done similar studies of sports and gender in community, high school, college, and professional sports, and in media coverage of sports, in commentaries during sport events, in ads during sport events and in sport publications, and in the patterns of corporate sponsorships for sports. In other words, his systematic collection and analysis of data went far beyond the opening ceremony, the Sea Monsters and Barbie Girls, and the AYSO.

Step 4: Use research findings to produce knowledge about sports in society.

Messner's data and analysis enabled him to present detailed explanations of the many connections between gender and sports in the United States. He used the organized interpretive frameworks provided by cultural, interactionist, and structural theories to make sense of these connections and deepen our understanding of gender in social worlds. Figure 2.2 depicts Messner's overall explanation that **gender** is much more than a social category or trait that identifies a person; instead, it *is a social element woven into the fabric of social worlds as meaning, performance, and organization*. In the figure, a social world is represented as a flag with three sections. Gender is a long and strong thread that runs continuously through each section. As you view Figure 2.2, think of the "flag" as representing

the AYSO that Messner studied as part of his research project.

The gender thread in the culture section of the flag represents meaning—the meaning that people give to colors, names, objects, and various characteristics of human beings to mark them as masculine or feminine. Socially agreed-upon meaning is the foundation for constructing gender categories that are important to people in a social world. Gender categories are then used to identify objects and people in a way that allows inferences to be made about them. For example, pink isn't selected as a team color by boys or men because it has meaning associated with femininity. The five-year-old boys studied by Messner had learned *gender as meaning* to the extent that they did not name themselves the "Barbie Boys" or "Pink Monsters." This example may seem trivial, but gender as meaning is a key dimension of many social worlds, and it is learned, reaffirmed, and sometimes challenged and changed through sports in society.

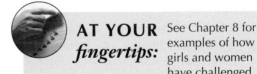

AT YOUR *fingertips:* See Chapter 8 for examples of how girls and women have challenged and blurred gender as meaning, see Chapter 8, pp. 262–265.

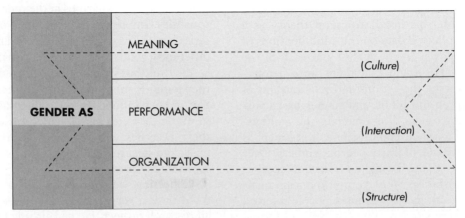

FIGURE 2.2 Gender as meaning, performance, and organization in social worlds.

The gender thread in the interaction section of the flag represents performance—the actions through which people "do" gender in their social relationships. These performances are constructed by people and then evaluated by others in terms of their beliefs about what it means to "act like a man" or "act like a women." In this sense, *gender is performance.* For example, a coach may refer to the boys on his team as "girls" when they don't perform as he expects them to perform *as men.* Similarly, a player on a girls' team who spits regularly on the field may be told by her coach to "act like a lady"— meaning that she is not performing gender as expected in U.S. culture.

The gender thread in the structure section of the flag represents organization—that is, the patterns of relationships in which positions, roles, and responsibilities are identified with gender. For example, men are more likely than women to be coaches in most sports because it is widely believed that successful coaches are aggressive, competitive, decisive, emotionally tough, knowledgeable about sports, and able to command respect and administer discipline—all of which are traits popularly associated with masculinity rather than femininity. This is why men coach nearly all men's teams and most women's teams, whereas women coach a minority of women teams and almost no men's teams. Similarly, the CEO of each major spectator sport in the United States is a man, and men own and manage over 99 percent of all teams in major spectator sports. The pattern of men in positions of control and women in support positions was clear in the AYSO, where the commissioner and assistant commissioners were men, as well as twenty-one of the thirty members of the board of directors, and 85 percent of the 156 head coaches. In this sense, gender is organization.

Part of Messner's contribution to what we know about gender and sport is showing us how gender constitutes a combination of meaning, performance, and organization in social worlds, especially those organized around sports. This is

important because it explains why it is so difficult to "ungender" sport; as long as we uncritically accept current meanings, performances, and organization, sport will remain gendered in ways that preclude equal treatment for men and women. However, once we see gender in these terms, it's possible to develop strategies to create equity in each of the realms represented in Figure 2.2.

Step 5: Publish research and knowledge claims so they can be evaluated.

After completing his project, Messner wrote a number of manuscripts reporting various aspects of his research findings that explained the social connections between gender and sports in the United States. At least three manuscripts were written as articles and submitted for possible publication in academic journals, and a long manuscript was written as a possible book and submitted to the University of Minnesota Press. The journal and book editors each asked respected scholars to critically review Messner's manuscripts and recommend whether they should be published as they were written, published after required revisions were made, or rejected for publication.

After receiving favorable reviews calling for minor revisions, each of Messner's manuscripts was accepted for publication. One of his articles was published in the journal, *Gender & Society* (Messner, 2000), and his book manuscript was published by the University of Minnesota Press (Messner, 2002).[2] In both cases, the editors and reviewers concluded that Messner's research produced worthwhile knowledge about sports and the ways that gender is woven into the fabric of social worlds.

Even though Messner was an established scholar and had tenure at the University of

---

[2]Other publications based on this research are Messner, Dunbar, and Hunt (2000); Messner, Duncan, and Cooky (2003); and Messner, Hunt, and Dunbar (1999); and Messner and Stevens (2002).

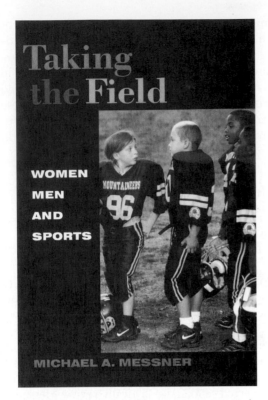

Reviewers determined that Messner's research was valid, that is, it measured what Messner claimed it measured and his conclusions were supported by the data. When research lacks validity in the eyes of reviewers, it is not published. Messner's book, pictured here, was also named the Outstanding Book of the Year by his colleagues in the North American Society for the Sociology of Sport. (*Taking the Field: Women, Men, and Sports* by Michael A. Messner, University of Minnesota Press, 2002)

Southern California, he, like most researchers, was expected to publish his work so that his knowledge claims[3] could be verified by a community of scholars who study gender, sports, and

related topics. This is because knowledge production in science is never a one-person job; it always depends on the critical review of a community of scholars. Messner understood this and published his research so that others could evaluate it. Although his manuscripts were published, most manuscripts submitted for publication are rejected because the reviewers find them to be lacking in quality or not contributing to knowledge production in a particular field.

Step 6: Research and knowledge claims are publicly rejected or accepted.

When research and knowledge claims are published, everyone can read them and determine if they should be accepted or rejected. If they are rejected, the research is not used by others; if they are accepted, other scholars may use them to guide their own research and to revise or extend existing theories.

Messner's claim that gender was more than a social category and should be viewed as a combination of meaning, performance, and organization was an important addition to sociological knowledge, and very useful for people who study gender and the connections between gender and sports. In his own research, Messner used this knowledge to theorize about sports as sites where ideas and beliefs about gender are created, maintained, and sometimes challenged and changed.

This knowledge is important because many people describe sports simply as a reflection of society—sites where aspects of culture and society are revealed to those who take a close look. But Messner's research findings challenged this view and provided evidence that sports are more than reflections of society; in fact, they are sites where ideas and beliefs about gender and other important aspects of our lives are created, reproduced, and changed. Therefore, sports constitute a significant social world to study, and the people associated with sports are most accurately viewed as agents involved in shaping social worlds rather than passive objects determined only by culture

---

[3]**Knowledge claims** *are statements that explain the "how and why" about a particular topic*—in this case, sports and gender in society. Knowledge claims occasionally take the form of a theory that the researcher has developed, but theory development is a long-term process that requires multiple studies by different researchers doing research in unrelated projects.

reflect on SPORTS   *Sports Are More Than Reflections of Society*

When people study the social aspects of sports, they often say that sports are reflections of society. This is true, but sports are much more than reflections. In fact, they are social constructions that actively influence what people do and how social worlds are organized. For example, many sports in the United States are organized in ways that perpetuate very limited ideas and beliefs about race, skin color, and race relations. This encourages people to accept these ideas and beliefs and avoid the following: (1) asking critical questions about race in social worlds; (2) considering the meaning of race and the racial categories that people use to classify themselves and others; (3) identifying the ways that ideas about race influence people's actions, their choices of what sports to play, and their expectations of how they might excel at certain sports; or (4) becoming aware of how race is woven into the organization of social worlds generally, and the ones organized around sports in particular.

At the same time, sports are also **sites,** that is, *identifiable social contexts*, where people can challenge and change ideas and beliefs about race and skin color—as Jackie Robinson did when he became the first African American to play in modern Major League Baseball in 1947, or when Tony Dungy became the first black head coach to win the Super Bowl in 2007.

This way of thinking about sports in society recognizes that people organize, perform, and give meaning

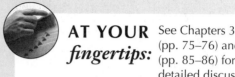

AT YOUR *fingertips:*   See Chapters 3 (pp. 75–76) and 9 (pp. 85–86) for detailed discussions of race and sports.

to sports in many different ways, and that sports are sites at which ideas, beliefs, and approaches to social relationships are created, maintained, and changed. Therefore, instead of merely reflecting society, sports comprise the "social stuff" from which society and culture are forever being created and reproduced. This makes them sociologically important.

When we understand the dynamic nature of social life, we realize that each of us is an agent that is involved in creating, maintaining, and changing the social and cultural worlds in which we live. Therefore, we are not destined to think about or do sports as they are portrayed in the narratives and images presented by media companies, Coca-Cola, Nike, General Motors, Budweiser, or other current sponsors of what we define as sports today. This opens our minds and makes it possible for us to think critically about sports and to work with others to make them what we decide they should and could be in our lives. *What do you think?*

. . . .

and society. This issue is discussed further in the box, "Sports are More Then Reflections of Society."

Messner's research made an important contribution to knowledge. His article in *Gender & Society*, "Barbie Girls vs. Sea Monsters: Children Constructing Gender," is frequently used by others as they develop ideas and do their own research on gender, sports, childhood, and other topics. His book, *Taking the Field*, received positive reviews and in 2004 was named the Outstanding Book of the Year by his colleagues in the North American Society for the Sociology

of Sport. *Taking the Field* remains on reading lists for many college courses worldwide, and researchers often use it as a guide when they study related topics.

Step 7: Use research and scholarly knowledge to inform decisions, actions, policies, and programs.

Hopefully, research-based knowledge does not just sit on the pages of journals and books. A primary goal of knowledge is to increase our understanding of the world so we can critically assess the organization and dynamics of people's lives and facilitate changes when and where changes will make social worlds more fair and just.

Earlier in this chapter (p. 31) it was noted that we often use "personal theories" to predict the consequences of what we or others might say or do. Even though our theories are usually incomplete, based on scanty information, and biased to fit our needs, we use them to anticipate the likely outcomes of what we say and do. In the case of sports, sociological knowledge and theories can complement, extend, and help us detect bias and validity problems in our personal theories. Therefore, we can use the research-based knowledge and theories in the sociology of sport to assess more fully and critically the consequences of what we and others say and do in connection with sports. This is helpful when we select a sport program for our child, create policies to increase healthy sport participation in our community, write a proposal to fund sport programs for employees at our workplace, or vote on a ballot issue that raises sales taxes to build a new stadium for the NFL team in our city.

> **OLC ON THE *OLC*:**
>
> See the OLC—Additional Readings for Chapter 2—for the author's description of how various theories can be used to inform practical decisions and deal with issues and controversies related to sports in social worlds.

Knowledge and theories in the sociology of sport enable us to use systematically collected data and view sports from multiple perspectives that go beyond our personal experiences and vantage points in social worlds. The sociology of sport does not claim to be the source of "ultimate truth," but it provides knowledge and theories based on systematic research carried out by people trained to study sports in society.

DATA COLLECTION IN SOCIOLOGY OF SPORT RESEARCH

Producing knowledge in the sociology of sport always involves the systematic collection and analysis of data. Data, in the form of facts, figures, and other information, are used to describe and document what occurs in sports and as a result of sports in society. They are used to describe trends, events, patterns, attitudes and beliefs, meanings, narratives, images, social characteristics, actions, relationships, and the organization of social worlds.

Depending on the topic studied and choices made by researchers, data are collected through quantitative approaches, qualitative approaches, or both. A **quantitative approach** *involves collecting information about people and social worlds, converting the information into numbers, and analyzing the numbers by using statistical procedures and tests.* Numbers often are presented in graphs and tables to represent statistical profiles and characteristics of people, events, and social worlds. Quantitative research is based on the assumption that social realities can be explained and understood by creating an overall view or a "big picture" of a social world (Lamb, 2007). Researchers use quantitative methods when they're interested in general patterns and relationships, such as the grade point averages of high school students who play particular sports compared to those who don't play on school teams (Carlson et al., 2005; Eitle, 2005; Guest and Schneider, 2003; Hunt, 2005; Spreitzer, 1995).

A **qualitative approach** *involves collecting information about people and social worlds, identifying patterns and unique features, and analyzing the information by using interpretive procedures and tests.* Information is presented in the form of detailed descriptions of the lived experiences of people, actual social events, and real social worlds. Qualitative research is based on the assumption that social worlds and the actions of individuals can be explained and understood when we know the meanings that underlie what people feel, say, and do (Denzin and Lincoln, 2000; Ellis and Bochner, 2000; Seale, 2004). Researchers use qualitative methods when they are interested in complex social realities and the meanings that people give to their sport experiences, such as how and why athletes make the decision to play while they are injured (Albert, 2004; Charlesworth and Young, 2004; Curry, 1992; Pike, 2004; Roderick, 2004; Thing, 2004).

Knowledge in the sociology of sport is based on both quantitative and qualitative research, and in each case, data are collected by (1) asking people written or verbal questions, (2) observing people and the social worlds of which they are a part,

and (3) investigating the content of documents or media. These methods are outlined in Figure 2.3.

Asking People Questions

Conducting a survey is a common method of collecting quantitative data. Surveys involve asking questions to obtain responses that enable researchers to do three things: (1) create statistical profiles of people, groups, communities, organizations, and societies; (2) identify recurring patterns and relationships that exist in social life; and (3) test hypotheses and answer questions about attitudes, opinions, and events (Schuman, 2002).

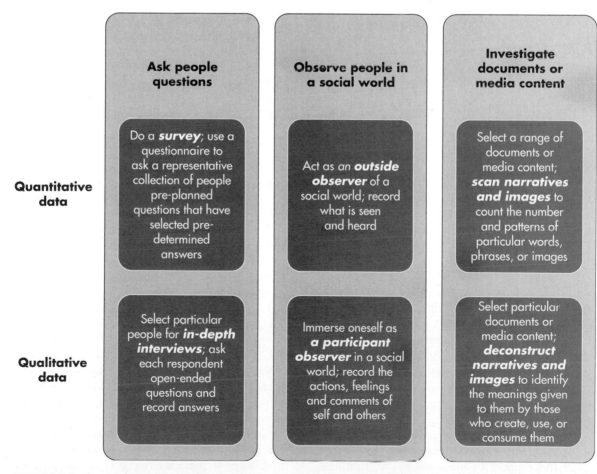

FIGURE 2.3 Three primary data collection methods used in the sociology of sport.

Surveys utilize either written questionnaires or interviews that are conducted face-to-face, over the telephone, or online. Questions are clearly worded so that respondents understand them, and they are designed to elicit very specific information.

Each of us has responded to survey questionnaires in which we are asked about our attitudes, opinions, preferences, backgrounds, or current circumstances. Additionally, we're usually asked to provide demographic data such as our age, gender, education, occupation, income, race and ethnicity, and place of residence. The goal of many surveys is to construct statistical profiles of the characteristics, attitudes, beliefs, and actions of respondents who represent or statistically match a larger collection of people. Researchers then compare and analyze those profiles to describe and even predict the patterns of how people will think and act in particular social situations.

In Messner's research project on gender and sports, he used data collected in a national survey of 800 boys and 400 girls, 10 to 17 years old, equally distributed across four ethnic backgrounds: White, African American, Latino, and Asian American. The data indicated that boys were five times more likely than girls to regularly watch sports on television. Thirty percent of boys across the four ethnic groups watched sports every day, whereas only 6 percent of girls did so.

In-depth interviews are used instead of surveys when researchers seek open-ended information about the details and underlying meanings of what people say and do. Conducting in-depth interviews is a time-consuming method of collecting data. Usually, interviews are done with people who have been carefully chosen because of their experiences, positions in an organization or community, or vantage point for viewing one or more social worlds. Interview topics or questions are presented so they will be understood by respondents. Interviewers attempt to develop trust and rapport to maximize the truthfulness of responses and listen carefully to what *is* and

is not said and either take notes or record the interview for later analysis.

Messner used data from in-depth interviews he conducted with thirty men who were former elite athletes (Messner, 1992). He learned that these men began playing sports with already-gendered identities, that is, with certain ideas about how to be a man in U.S. culture. As their athletic careers progressed, the men had experiences and formed attitudes consistent with dominant ideas about manhood. They believed that gender was grounded in nature and biological destiny, and this belief influenced the ways they performed masculinity in public, related to women, and evaluated their position and relative privilege in the overall organization of social worlds.

In summary, when data are collected by using surveys, researchers usually want to produce knowledge about general patterns and relationships in social wolds; when they use in-depth interviews, they want to produce knowledge about the details of everyday experiences and the meanings that people give to them.

Observing People and Social Worlds

Researchers in the sociology of sport often collect data by observing people in everyday life situations. They do this as (1) "outside observers," who are detached from the people and situations being studied, or (2) "participant observers," who are or become personally involved in the social worlds being studied. For example, Gary Alan Fine and Sherry Grasmuck each did classic studies of youth sport teams by collecting data as outside observers who attended practices and games and interviewed players and adults (Fine, 1987; Grasmuck, 2005); the late Janet Chafetz also studied youth sports as participant observer/"team helper" for her son's baseball team (Chafetz and Kotarba, 1991).

Collecting data through observational methods is time intensive. Relationships must be established so there is a requisite amount of trust and rapport developed with the people being studied. Actions, relationships, and social patterns and dynamics must be studied over time and from as many vantage points as possible so the data accurately depict the people and social worlds being studied. The goal of some sociologists who do observational research is to extend or challenge our knowledge of familiar groups and social worlds or introduce us to marginalized groups and unique social worlds about which we have little or no knowledge (Anderson, 2000, 2002, 2005; Atencio and Wright, 2008; Brittain, 2004; Curry, 1991, 1993, 1996, 1998; Huang and Brittain, 2006; Ravel and Rail, 2006, 2007).

Observational methods generally involve **fieldwork,** that is, *"on-site" data collection.* An **ethnography** *is fieldwork that involves observations and interviews;* in fact, ethnography literally means writing about people and how they live with each other (Adler and Adler, 2003; Hammersley, 2007). Ethnographies may take years to complete. They provide detailed descriptions and analyses of particular people and social worlds, such as sport teams, organizations, and communities.

Sociologist Reuben May (2008) did an ethnography in which he studied young men on a basketball team in a high school located in a poor, urban neighborhood. As the assistant coach of the team, he was a participant observer. May's observations and interviews occurred over seven years because he wanted to accurately represent the experiences and lives of the young men he coached—all African Americans. He organized his study to allow the young men to speak for themselves and describe their view of the world in which they lived. As he presented their stories, May put them into a social and cultural context so that he and his readers could make sense of them and extend our knowledge of sports in the lives of young African American men growing up in poor, urban neighborhoods today. In the process, he described the complexity and contradictions associated with sports in such a social world and identified the serious dilemmas faced by coaches as they try to help these players make the transition from high school to the rest of their lives.

Investigating the Content of Documents or Media

Research in the sociology of sport often involves collecting data from the narratives and images that represent ideas, people, objects, and events associated with sports. **Narratives** are *the stories that people tell about themselves and their social worlds.* They are an integral part of conversations, performances, and the media. They represent factual or fictional realities and they're usually combined with **images**—that is, *visual representations of ideas, people, and things.*

Now that most text, audio, and video can be digitized, researchers use complex software programs to analyze the narratives and images that are so pervasive in postindustrial, media-saturated societies (Cisneros-Puebla, 2007). Narratives and images include everything from tattoos and graffiti to billboards and computer pop-up ads; and they appear in print and electronic media and on the surfaces of public and privately owned spaces.

Sociology of sport scholars frequently investigate the content of sport documents and media because they contain narratives and images that people integrate into their lives and use as they make sense of and give meaning to themselves and the worlds around them. Numerous studies have been dedicated to identifying the patterns, themes, and meanings in narratives and images that people create, use, and consume in connection with sports and sport experiences. For example, researchers have analyzed data collected from sport team media brochures, newspaper articles, media commentaries during the Olympics and other sport events, the ads in sports magazines, the commercials aired during televised sport events, and sport books and films—many of which are discussed in chapter 12 on the media and sport.

In one of Messner's studies, he and his colleagues analyzed the content of network sports news from 1989 through 2004 (Table 2.2), and they also analyzed at regular intervals during 2004 the content of ESPN's one-hour evening *Sports Center* program and Fox's *Southern California Sports Report* (Table 2.3). The data indicated that stories about men's sports dominated television coverage between 1989 and 2004, despite dramatic increases in women's sport participation during that period. For example, during ESPN's prime time *Sports Center* program, there was only one highlight of women's sports for every 15 highlights of men's sports (Duncan and Messner, 2000, 2005). Messner and his colleagues concluded that this type of mainstream television news coverage perpetuates the notion that elite sports is a masculine activity in U.S. culture.

Messner and his colleagues also did a more in-depth analysis in which they *deconstructed* narratives and images to identify their underlying assumptions and the meanings they conveyed (Messner, Dunbar, and Hunt, 2000). This method of analyzing data enabled them to identify recurring themes that formed a master narrative about masculinity. These themes included the following: sports are a man's world, sports are wars and athletes are warriors, boys will be boys—and boys are basically violent, aggressive guys win and nice guys lose, women are sexy props, men sacrifice their bodies for their team, and the measure of a man is his "guts." Messner and his colleagues concluded that these themes formed a "Televised Sports Manhood Formula" that was consistently presented in sports programming.

These quantitative and qualitative methods of investigating the content of documents and media help us understand the complex connections between sports and other spheres of our lives. Scanning, analyzing, and deconstructing the narratives and images associated with sports are useful ways of identifying widely accepted ideas and beliefs about competition, authority structures, teamwork, dedication and practice, achievement, and success.

Table 2.2   Network sports news, by sex

	1989	1993	1999	2004
Men	92.0	93.8	88.2	91.4
Women	5.0	5.1	8.7	6.3
Neutral/Both	3.0	1.1	3.1	2.4

Source: Duncan and Messner, 2005; p. 9

Table 2.3   Percentage of 2004 sports highlights, by sex, on ESPN *sports center* and fox's *southern california sports report*

	ESPN	FOX
Men's Sports	97.0	96.3
Women's Sports	2.1	3.0
Both/Neutral	0.9	0.7

Source: Duncan and Messner, 2005; p. 10

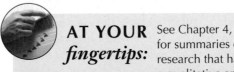 **AT YOUR** *fingertips:* See Chapter 4, for summaries of research that has used a qualitative approach and collected data by using interviews and participant observation.

USING A CRITICAL APPROACH TO PRODUCE KNOWLEDGE

A critical approach emphasizes that knowledge exists to empower people in a never-ending collective process of creating sustainable, just, and equitable ways of life (McDonald, 2002).

People using this approach want to produce and apply research-based knowledge to shrink the "the gap between what is and what could be" (Burawoy, 2004). They see social theories as guides for engaging in actions designed to improve people's lives.

> **OLC** **ON THE *OLC*:**
> See the OLC—Additional Readings for Chapter 2—for summaries of studies that used a critical approach when collecting and analyzing data about sports in society.

Those of us who use a critical approach in the sociology of sport want to produce knowledge and then use it to make sports more humane and inclusive activities that enhance individual and collective well-being. Therefore, we seek to identify problems, injustices, and exploitation in sports for the purpose of developing strategies to eliminate them. We promote, inform, and join public discussions and debates about important social issues in sports, and we feel a responsibility to study issues that concern everyone from athletes to spectators and sport administrators to those who are currently excluded from mainstream sports. This is why the *Breaking Barriers* essays are included in each chapter of this book. For example, the essay in this chapter, "Language Barriers," highlights the importance of using critically informed theories with clearly defined concepts to guide our thinking about sports for people with disabilities.

Like many people in the sociology of sport, Mike Messner used a critical approach in his research on gender and sports. While he performed the first six steps of the knowledge production process, he was aware of the seventh step—the ways that knowledge could be applied to real-world decisions, actions, policies, and programs so that sports could better serve the interests of more people. This led Messner to organize the last chapter of his book around the question, "Just do *what?*" The chapter presents thirty pages of recommendations for critically informed actions to make sports more fair, just, humane, equitable, and democratic. Referring to the Nike marketing slogan, "Just do it!," Messner emphasizes that without critically assessing what "it" is, we will reproduce sports as they are rather than actively changing and developing sports that involve fairness and equity along with excitement, physical challenges, and joy.

Sociology of sport research based on a critical approach usually involves asking one or more of the following questions when collecting and analyzing data:

- What values, ideas, and beliefs are associated with or promoted through sports, and who is advantaged or disadvantaged by them?
- What are the meanings currently given to sports and sport participation, and who is advantaged or disadvantaged by those meanings?
- How are sports, athletes, and other people associated with sports represented in media coverage, and how does that coverage influence people's lives?
- How are sports organized, and who is advantaged or disadvantaged by existing forms of organization in sports?
- Who has power in sports, to what ends is power used, and how are various categories of people affected by power relations associated with sports?
- Who accepts and who resists the prevailing social and cultural organization of mainstream sports, and what happens to those who resist?
- What strategies will effectively foster progressive changes in sports and the social worlds around them?

These questions show that a critical approach is organized around an awareness that people

breaking BARRIERS   Language Barriers

We're Not Handicapped—We Just Can't Hear

Len Gonzales is deaf. But more important, he's head football coach at the California School for the Deaf at Riverside (CSDR). When his team capped its 9–1 season by winning the 2004 championship of the San Joaquin High School League, a reporter asked Gonzales what other teams thought when they lost to CSDR. Gonzales explained that "teams hate to lose to us because they think we're a handicapped team. But we're not handicapped. We just can't hear" (in Reilly, 2004, p. 144).

Coach Gonzales is sensitive to the barriers created when people use the word *handicapped* to refer to physical and mental *impairments* and *disabilities.* Clear definitions of these words are necessary to understand and evaluate theories of disability.

An **impairment** *exists when a person has a physical, sensory, or intellectual condition that potentially limits full participation in social and/or physical environments.* Many people have impairments, such as those related to vision and hearing, which generally increase in number and severity as people age. This is part of normal, everyday life and many of us make personal adjustments to limit the impact of impairments on our lives. If we're lucky, we have access to technologies that make adjustments more effective. For example, I wear eyeglasses that "correct" my impaired vision. If I were a world-class archer I could be a member of the U.S. Archery Team, despite my impairment. I would face no barriers as long as I was allowed to wear eyeglasses; therefore, I would not have a disability.

An impairment becomes a **disability** only *when accommodations in social or physical contexts are not or cannot be made to allow the full participation of people with functional limitations.* This means that disabilities are created when relationships, spaces, and activities

Does this athlete have an impairment, a disability, or a handicap? His vision is impaired to the point that he needs a "guide runner." The Paralympic Games and sports for people with disabilities provide opportunities for athletes who are not eligible to participate in the Olympic Games and other sports because of legal restrictions or an absence of accommodations that would enable them to compete with temporarily able-bodied athletes. (*Source:* David Biene; photo courtesy of Ossur)

present barriers that limit the opportunities and experiences of people with particular impairments. For example, prior to the late-1990s, if my leg was amputated below the knee and I wore a prosthetic leg and foot, I would have been excluded from the U.S. Powerlifting Team because the International Powerlifting Federation rules stated that "Lifters without two real feet cannot compete in regular contests." This rule created a barrier that converted my amputation from an impairment into a disability. However, after the rule was changed, the barrier was eliminated so that my prosthetic leg and foot no longer classified me as disabled in powerlifting. My prosthesis was then similar to corrective eyeglasses or a contact lens. This means that disability often has less to do with impairment and ability than with barriers that limit participation (Brittain, 2004; Hargreaves, 2000; Higgins, 1992; Morris, 1996; Oliver, 1996). It also means that a person may be (dis)abled in one context but not in another (Friedman et al., 2004).

"Being handicapped" is something else again. People become **handicapped** *when others define them as inferior and "unable" due to perceived disabilities.* For example, when opposing players defined the football team from CSDR as handicapped, they hated losing to them because it meant that they lost to players that they defined as inferior and unable.

These definitions are based on theories that locate disabilities and handicaps in social and cultural arrangements rather than individuals. Thus, disabilities and handicaps are the result of the following:

- Environments organized to meet only the needs of temporarily able-bodied people

- Norms (rules) that disadvantage people with impairments
- Attitudes and beliefs that equate particular impairments and disabilities with inferiority and inability.

Definitions based on medical and psychological theories usually identify physical or intellectual disability as a characteristic of individuals and view it as a personal "abnormality." This is an important point, because if disability is an abnormal characteristic of an individual, treatment focuses on making the individual as "normal" as possible through personal coping strategies and assistive technologies. However, when disability is located in the barriers that restrict participation, the "treatment" is political action that eliminates social, cultural, legal, organizational, and environmental barriers.

Both medical/psychological and social/political approaches are needed, but people too often overlook the latter. Coping strategies and assistive technologies are clearly important for individuals with impairments, but eliminating barriers prevents impairments from becoming disabilities for entire categories of people in a social world (DePauw, 1997).

Leslie Little, a sailor with muscular dystrophy, helps us understand this point when she says, "Every day is a new adventure when I'm sailing . . . Plus, I'm not disabled when I'm on the water" (www.mdausa .org/publications/Quest/q82water.cfm). Therefore, a primary goal is to create barrier-free social and physical worlds like the world of sailing is for Leslie Little.

A critical approach to knowledge production in Northern Ireland focuses on the role of sport in eliminating sectarian (Protestant versus Catholic) violence. Administrators in the Irish Football Association have consulted with scholars in the sociology of sport as they develop strategies to make soccer more inclusive, just, and supportive of the well-being of athletes and spectators. (*Source*: Irish Football Association, Northern Ireland)

are positioned differently in social worlds, and they are affected differently by the prevailing meaning, purpose, and organization of sports. In other words, everyone does not benefit from sports in the same ways, and some people may be disadvantaged by the ways sports are organized and played in a particular social world. For example, an emphasis on high-performance sports in a society may exclude or discourage participation among many people who could benefit from the physical exercise provided by sports funded and organized for recreational purposes. In some cases, this would increase obesity rates in the society—a result that would be identified and studied by researchers using a critical approach.

Additionally, a critical approach heightens one's awareness that knowledge about social worlds can be applied in many ways. For example, Messner understood that knowledge about the relationship between masculinity and the cultures that exist in certain sports could be used to transform those cultures, thereby reducing male-on-male violence and the serious injuries that boys and men often see as normal in those sports. Therefore, in the last chapter of his book, he called for more activities that give boys and young men "the opportunity for healthy, respectful connection with others" (2002, p. 166). Similarly, he urged that we must reorganize certain sports so that boys and men do not have their "need for closeness, intimacy, and respect thwarted [and] converted into a narrow form of group-oriented bonding based on competitive one-upmanship, self-destructive behaviors, and sexually aggressive denigration of others" (2002, p. 166).

Because I use a critical approach to guide my thinking and research on sports in society, you will notice in the following chapters a concern with issues of fairness and equity in the discussions of issues and controversies. Underlying my critical discussions of sports issues is my desire to make available to more people the excitement, physical challenges, and joy that can be part of sport participation.

summary

WHAT IS THE ROLE OF RESEARCH AND THEORY?

Sociology of sport knowledge is produced through research and theories. Research provides data and systematic analyses to answer questions and validate or revise existing theories about sports in society. Theories provide logical explanations of people's actions and relationships and the organization and dynamics of social worlds. Additionally, theories guide research and the interpretation of research findings. This makes knowledge in the sociology of sport more valid and reliable than most of what we read, see, or hear in the media and discuss in our everyday conversations about sports.

Personal experience is a useful starting point for understanding the role of research and theory in knowledge production. This is because each of us gathers information about the people and things around us and uses it to develop experience-based explanations or "personal theories" about people, relationships, events, and social worlds.

We use personal theories to anticipate events, the actions of others, and the consequences of our actions in various situations. But these theories are limited because they focus on our individual circumstances and immediate social worlds. On the other hand, research and theories in the sociology of sport take us beyond the limitations of our own experiences and worlds. Social research follows systematic and rigorous guidelines for collecting and analyzing data, and social theories are systematically tested, compared with related theories, and presented for others to examine. The goal of social research and theory in the sociology of sport is to develop logical and verifiable explanations of the social worlds created in association with sports and the actions and relationships of people in those social worlds.

The case study of research done by Michael Messner illustrates that scholars in the sociology of sport use systematic and carefully planned methods as they do research and develop explanations of sports. The multistage process of producing knowledge consists of (1) observing social worlds and asking questions about sports; (2) identifying issues, reviewing past research, and using theories and specific research methods to design studies; (3) collecting and analyzing data; (4) using research findings to produce knowledge about sports in society; and (5) publishing research and knowledge claims. After publication, research and knowledge claims are subject to public scrutiny and evaluated as contributions to knowledge in the sociology of sport. Finally, research and scholarly knowledge is used to inform policies, programs, decisions, and actions related to sports.

Three types of theories guide most sociology of sport research. Cultural theories help us study and understand the meanings that people give to sports, sport experiences, and relationships formed in and through sports. Interactionist theories help us study and understand the origins, dynamics, and consequences of social relationships connected with sports. And structural theories help us study and understand the ways that various forms of social organization influence actions and relationships in sports and the social worlds associated with sports in society.

Many people in the sociology of sport use a critical approach as they do research and develop theory. This means that they are committed to producing knowledge that can be used to promote fairness and equity in sports and society, expose and challenge exploitation, and empower those who are disadvantaged by the current organization of sports in society. Overall, critical scholars are dedicated to the idea that sociological knowledge should be used to create and sustain social worlds in which basic human needs are satisfied and well-being is maintained fairly and equitably.

Research and theories in the sociology of sport help us understand that sports are more than mere reflections of society. Instead, sports are sites where meanings, relationships, and forms of social organization are created, maintained, and changed. Learning about the knowledge production process in the sociology of sport is part of the process of thinking critically about the issues and controversies discussed in the following chapters. When we use research and theories critically, we become aware of the deeper game associated with sports in society and this makes us more informed participants in our families, schools, communities, and societies.

WEBSITE RESOURCES

Note: Websites often change. The following URLs were current when this book was printed. Please check our website (www.mhhe.com/coakley10e) for updates and additions.

www.humankinetics.com/SSJ/journalAbout.cfm
The *Sociology of Sport Journal* (SSJ) is one of three primary journals in the sociology of sport and is the official journal of the North American Society for the Sociology of Sport (NASSS). This site provides access to the table of contents for every issue of this quarterly journal, 1984 to the present.

www.intute.ac.uk/socialsciences/cgi-bin/browse .pl?id=120997 Intute: Social Sciences provides Web resources for social science research; it is an excellent source for information on qualitative research methods. One site, for example, is Nationmaster: sports statistics by country (http://www.nationmaster.com/cat/spo-sports), which provides competition results enhanced by maps and charts.

http://irs.sagepub.com/ The *International Review for the Sociology of Sport* (IRSS) is one of three primary journals in the sociology of sport and is the official journal of the International Sociology of Sport Association (ISSA). This site provides access to the table of contents for every issue of this journal, 1966 to the present, and to abstracts of articles published between 1977 and the present.

http://jss.sagepub.com/ The *Journal of Sport and Social Issues* (JSSI) is one of three primary journals in the sociology of sport and is the journal of Sport in Society–A Northeastern University Center. This site provides access to abstracts of articles published between March 1977 and the most recent issue.

http://kerlins.net/bobbi/research/qualresearch/ bibliography/ This site provides an extensive bibliography on qualitative research methods. It is organized into more than 35 categories, so it is easy to use.

http://kerlins.net/bobbi/research/qualresearch/ bibliography/action.html This site provides descriptions of action research, a form of critical qualitative research used to change social worlds and produce knowledge. There are links to examples of social research in a critical tradition.

www.mhhe.com/coakley10e Go to "Additional Readings" for a full discussion of major theories used in sociology and the sociology of sport.

www.nova.edu/ssss/QR/web.html *The Qualitative Report* is a free, online journal dedicated to qualitative research; it presents many examples of qualitative research and has a feature called "Practicing Qualitative Research" in which there are practical, hands-on activities for students wishing to learn about and develop skills for doing qualitative research. Go to http://www.nova.edu/ssss/QR/QR3-4/jones.html

for the article, "Mixing Qualitative and Quantitative Methods in Sports Fan Research," by Ian Jones (*The Qualitative Report*, Volume 3, Number 4, December, 1997).

www.pollingreport.com/sports.htm This is an excellent source for quantitative data from polls and surveys in which questions were asked about sports; the polls are listed by date and present data in tables and graphs.

www.qualitative-research.net/fqs/fqs-eng.htm *Forum: Qualitative Research* is a free, online journal for qualitative research; its goal is to promote discussion and cooperation among qualitative researchers from different countries and social science disciplines. See Volume 4, No. 1, Art. 2, January 2003, for a special issue devoted to "Qualitative Research in Sport Sciences," and Volume 2, No. 1, February 2001, for an issue devoted to "Qualitative and Quantitative Research: Conjunctions and Divergences."

www.ringsurf.com/netring?action=info&ring= QualitativeResearch The Qualitative Research Web Ring is a source of information about all aspects of qualitative research.

www.sociologyprofessor.com/ An excellent site for those seeking information about theory and theorists in sociology.

www.sociosite.net/topics/sociologists.php When seeking information about a social theorist, this is a very useful site.

www.socqrl.niu.edu/FYI/theory.htm Created by the sociology department at Northern Illinois University, this site has links to helpful sites on social theory.

www.trinity.edu/~mkearl/index.html Site of *A Sociological Tour through Cyberspace*; links to many resources related to theory and other topics. The information is not sport related, but it is very helpful for those wishing to gain a better understanding of sociology as a discipline and theories used by sociologists.

(Jay Coakley)

STUDYING THE PAST

Does It Help Us Understand Sports Today?

OF THE THOUSANDS of evils . . . in Greece there is
no greater evil than the race of athletes. . . .

. . . Since they have not formed good habits, they
face problems with difficulty.

—**Euripides, Greek dramatist (fifth century BC)**

Visit *Sports in Society*'s Online Learning Center (OLC) at www.mhhe.com/coakley10e for additional information and study material for this chapter, including the following:

- A complete chapter outline
- Learning objectives
- Practice quizzes
- Internet resources
- Related readings
- Essays
- Student projects

THEY WHO LAID the intellectual foundations of the Western world were the most fanatical players and organizers of games that the world has ever known.

—C. L. R. James, sociologist and West Indian cricket player (1984)

To understand sports today, it helps to have a sense of what physical activities and games were like in past times. This chapter presents brief overviews of sport activities in different cultural and historical settings. My intent is *not* to provide an integrated overall history of sports. Such a history would look at the development and organization of physical games and sports across all continents from one cultural group to another over time. This is an ambitious and worthy project, but it is far beyond the scope of this chapter.

When studying sports in history it's important to know that people have defined "sports" in many ways over time and across cultures. For example, the formally organized, rule-governed, competitive physical contests that many people define as sports today were developed only during the last 200 years, mostly in Western Europe and North America. In fact, organized, rule-governed, competitive sports generally originated in England and were introduced to regions of the world that were colonized by the British or influenced by the British Empire. Even most of the historical information about sports in Asia, Africa, and Latin America comes from specific regions colonized by the British. Furthermore, it is usually presented from the perspectives of Europeans and North Americans, rather than the indigenous peoples in those regions.

This chapter draws on existing sport histories to focus on physical games and sportlike activities in (1) ancient Greece, (2) the Roman Empire, (3) parts of Europe during the Middle Ages, (4) parts of Europe during the Renaissance through the Enlightenment, and (5) the United States during the Industrial Revolution through recent times. These places and times are not meant to represent the experiences of most people around the world. However, they have been studied in enough detail that we can use them to understand the connections between physical games and sports and the everyday experiences of the people who create, play, and give them meaning in their lives.

UNDERSTANDING HISTORY WHEN STUDYING SPORTS IN SOCIETY

History is often viewed as a chronological sequence of events through which societies change from traditional to modern, primitive to civilized, underdeveloped to developed, and preindustrial to industrial to postindustrial. This approach enables people in postindustrial societies, such as England, the United States, and other wealthy nations, to conclude that they are the most civilized and developed people in world history. But this conclusion is misleading. For example, are postindustrial societies with lifestyles that deplete unrenewable natural resources, emit dangerous greenhouse gases into the atmosphere, and pollute life-sustaining water resources more advanced than traditional, premodern societies that sometimes had environmentally sustainable and relatively peaceful lifestyles? Similarly, are modern societies that have used weapons of mass destruction to kill all living things in large areas of the planet more civilized or developed than past societies that fought wars with handheld weapons? Answering "yes" to these questions requires assumptions about progress that can be challenged on scientific and moral terms.

This point about progress is useful to remember as we study the histories of sports. For example, when comparing American football or global soccer and rugby with traditional and local versions of games and physical contests, it is risky to conclude that today's sports are progressively better than games and sports in the past or in parts of the world that are not classified as postindustrial. Progressive changes do occur in history, but rather than fitting into a grand plan of progress, they are the result of actions taken by collections of people who possess the power and resources to make them happen. In other words, when we study sports through history we should not assume that changes represent progress along a one-way path of improvement and eventual perfection (Gruneau, 1988).

People in all cultures, both past and present, have incorporated physical activities into their ritual life. In prehistoric times, physical activities were tied to religious beliefs and the challenge of survival. People hunted for food and sometimes used their physical abilities to defend themselves, establish power over others, and appease their gods. Ritual games involved acting out events that had important meaning in their lives, but they were performed as religious worship, and their outcomes were determined by religious necessity as much as the physical abilities of the people involved (Guttmann, 1978).

The first physical games played by humans probably emerged from a combination of coping with physical challenges and performing religious rituals. Generally, the meaning, purpose, and organization of these games reaffirmed existing power structures and the belief systems that supported them. People may have used games to express their opposition to the status quo, but they would have been defined as troublemakers or worse by tribal leaders, kings, clergy, and other representatives of the existing social order.

The brief histories in this chapter represent a series of stories about people at different times and places struggling over and coming to terms with what they wanted their physical activities to be and how they wished to include them in their lives. These stories are organized around critical questions based on the cultural, interactional, and structural theories that sociologists use when they study social worlds. Therefore, the histories in the following sections call attention to the existence and consequences of power differences and social inequality in the social worlds being discussed. Inequalities related to wealth, political power, social status, gender, age, (dis)ability, race, and ethnicity influence how sports are organized and who plays and sponsors them in most times and places. Through the chapter we will pay special attention to these issues.

SIDELINES

"You weren't playing soccer last night—it won't be invented for another million years!"

In early human history, there were no sports as people in wealthy postindustrial societies define them today. Physical activities occasionally were included in community and religious rituals, but their purpose in ancient times probably was to appease the gods, rather than to entertain or build character.

CONTESTS AND GAMES IN ANCIENT GREECE: BEYOND THE MYTHS (1000 BC TO 100 BC)

The games played by early Greeks (circa 900 BC) were grounded in mythology and religious beliefs. They usually were held in conjunction with festivals that combined prayer, sacrifices, and religious services, along with music, dancing, and ritual feasts. Competitors were from wealthy and respected Greek families because they had money to hire coaches and the time to travel. Sport events were based on the interests of able-bodied young males. Warrior sports such as chariot racing, wrestling and boxing, javelin and discus throwing, foot racing, archery, and long jumping were especially popular. Violence, serious injuries, and even death were commonplace in comparison with today's sports (Elias, 1986; Kidd, 1984, 1996a; Mendelsohn, 2004). Greek women, children, and older people occasionally

reflect on SPORTS

Sports Today
What Makes Them Historically Unique?

The organized competitive sports so popular today are different from games and contests played in past times. Allen Guttmann's research shows that sports today have the following seven characteristics, which have never before appeared together in physical games and contests:

1. *Secularism.* There's no direct link to religious beliefs or rituals; the emphasis is on personal achievement and entertainment, not worship or the appeasement of gods.
2. *Equality.* Participation is open to everyone regardless of family or social background; all

contestants face the same competitive conditions.
3. *Specialization.* Participation is limited to a single event or position, and excellence depends on specific skills, rather than general physical abilities.
4. *Rationalization.* Rules regulate all conditions of participation, training methods are guided by "sport sciences," and competitors use rationally controlled strategies during events.
5. *Bureaucratization.* Governance is highly organized, and officials are trained to handle specific

Today's organized, competitive sports emphasize quantification. Performances are timed, measured, and recorded. The clock is crucial, and digital scoreboards now show times in hundredths of seconds. (*Source:* Thomas Kienzle, AP/Wide World Photo)

responsibilities related to athletes, teams, events, rule enforcement, and the certification of records.

6. *Quantification.* Precise timing and measurements are used to document performances and achievements.

7. *Records.* Achievements are compared over time to determine personal, national, and world records.

One or some of these characteristics had been present in games and contests during previous historical periods, but not until the nineteenth century did all seven appear together in what many scholars identify as *modern* sports (Dunning, 1999; Dunning and Sheard, 1979; Guttmann, 1978).

Today's sports are not superior to sports in past times and other places, but they are unique in terms of how they are organized and integrated into people's lives. When sociologists study sports in the context of culture and society, an awareness of these characteristics helps them identify what people value in their lives.

Table 3.1 summarizes Guttmann's comparison of contests, games, and sports in each of the places and time periods discussed in this chapter. The table shows that sports in postindustrial societies today differ from games and contests played in times past. The seven characteristics identified by Guttmann are useful to know when studying sports in society. But sports are social constructions, and they change in connection with social, economic, and political forces and as people seek and develop alternatives to current sports. The sports that people will play 50 years from now are likely to have characteristics that differ from these seven characteristics. *What do you think?*

Table 3.1 Comparison of the organizational characteristics of games, contests, and sport activities during selected periods in "Western" history*

Characteristic	Greek Contests and Games (1000 BC to 100 BC)	Roman Contests and Games (100 BC to AD 500)	Medieval Tournaments and Games (500 to 1300)	Renaissance, Reformation, and Enlightenment Games (1300 to 1800)	"Modern" Sports
Secularism	Yes and no**	Yes and no	Yes and no	Yes and no	Yes
Equality	Yes and no	Yes and no	No	Yes and no	Yes
Specialization	Yes	Yes	No	Yes and no	Yes
Rationalization	Yes	Yes	No	No	Yes
Bureaucratization	Yes and no	Yes	No	No	Yes
Quantification	No	Yes	No	Yes and no	Yes
Records	No	No	No	Yes and no	Yes

*Modified version of Table 2 in Guttmann (1978).

**This characteristic existed in some sports during this time, but not in others. For example, the games at Olympia in Greece spanned 1200 years, and the organization of certain events changed over time. Such variations also occurred during other time periods, as noted by the "Yes and no" descriptions in 11 places in the table.

played sports in these festivals, but they never played in the games held at Olympia.

The locations and dates of the Greek festivals were linked with religious beliefs. For example, Olympia was chosen as a festival site because it was associated with the achievements and activities of celebrated Greek gods and mythological characters. In fact, Olympia was dedicated as a shrine to the god Zeus about 1000 BC. Although permanent buildings and playing fields were not constructed until 550 BC, the games at Olympia were held every four years. Additional festivals involving athletic contests were held at other locations throughout Greece, but the Olympic Games became the most prestigious of these events.

Women were prohibited from participating as athletes or spectators at the Olympic Games. However, they held their own games at Olympia. These games, dedicated to the goddess Hera, the sister-wife of Zeus, grew out of Greek fertility rites. When women participated in sports, their purpose was to demonstrate strength, sexually attract men, and prepare to bear strong warrior sons (Perrottet, 2004). However, physical prowess was inconsistent with dominant definitions of femininity among the Greeks. Women were seen as inferior to men. They could neither vote nor be Greek citizens and did not participate in economic affairs. Wives were the property of their husbands and often were confined to the home.

The men's games at Olympia took on political significance as they grew in visibility and popularity. Winning became connected with the glory of city–states. In some cases, physically skilled slaves and young men from lower-status backgrounds were forced to become athletes; in other cases, wealthy patrons and government officials hired them to train for the Olympics and other games. Victorious slaves and hired athletes earned cash prizes and living expenses, and contrary to widely believed myths about amateur ideals among the Greeks, many male athletes saw themselves as professionals. During the second century BC, they even organized athletic guilds enabling them to bargain for rights, gain control over the conditions of their sport participation, and enjoy

material security when they retired from competition (Baker, 1988; Perrottet, 2004).

Most Greek athletes were so specialized in their physical skills that they made poor soldiers (Golden, 1998). They engaged in warrior sports, but they lacked the generalized skills of warriors. Furthermore, they concentrated so much on athletic training that they ignored intellectual development. This evoked criticism from Greek philosophers, who saw athletic contests as brutal and dehumanizing and the athletes as ignorant and nonproductive.

> **OLC ON THE *OLC*:**
> See the OLC—Additional Readings for Chapter 3—for links to articles about the Greek games at Olympia.

People today often romanticize Greek games and describe them as fostering a pure form of mind–body harmony. But research shows that athletes were regularly maimed and occasionally killed in their pursuit of victories and the rewards that came with them (Mendelsohn, 2004; Perrottet, 2004). Overall, fairness was not as important as honor, and athletic contests were connected with a cultural emphasis on warfare.

As shown in Table 3.1 on page 61, Greek contests and games were different from organized competitive sports of today (see the box "Sports Today," pp. 60–61). First, they were grounded in religion; second, they lacked complex administrative structures; and third, they did not involve measurements and record keeping from event to event. One similarity is that they often reproduced dominant patterns of social relations among people. The power and advantages that went with being wealthy, male, young, and able-bodied in Greece shaped the games and contests in ways that limited the participation of most people (Golden, 1998). Athletic excellence was defined in terms that favored the interests and abilities of young men. This meant that the abilities of others were substandard by definition—if you could not do it as a young, able-bodied Greek man did it, then you did not do it correctly.

ROMAN CONTESTS AND GAMES: SPECTACLES AND GLADIATORS (100 BC TO AD 500)

Roman leaders used physical contests and games to train soldiers and provide mass entertainment spectacles. They borrowed events from Greek contests and games, but they focused athletic training on preparing obedient soldiers. They were critical of the Greek emphasis on individualism and specialized physical skills that were useless in battle. Because Roman leaders emphasized military training and entertainment, the contests and games during the first century

AD increasingly took the form of circuses and gladiatorial combat. Chariot races were the most popular events during Roman spectacles.

Wealthy Romans recruited slaves as charioteers. Spectators bet heavily on the races, and when they became bored or unruly, the emperors gave them free food and raffled off prizes to prevent outbreaks of violence. This strategy pacified the crowds and allowed the emperors to use events to celebrate themselves and their power. Government officials controlled people throughout the Roman Empire by using similar strategies.

As the power and influence of the Roman Empire grew, spectacles consisting of contests and games became increasingly important as diversions for the masses. By AD 300, half the days on the Roman calendar were public holidays because slaves did most of the work. Many Romans held only part-time jobs, if they worked

The Flavian Amphitheater in Rome seated 45,000 to 55,000 spectators. Spectators could fill or exit the stadium in 15 minutes by using 76 numbered entrances. Now identified as the "Colosseum," it took eight years to build. When it opened in 80 AD, there were 100 days of games to display the power of the emperor and the wealth of the empire. Untold numbers of gladiators and animals were killed during the opening games. The Colosseum was the site of gladiatorial combat spectacles for over four centuries. (*Source:* Alexis Gonzalez, Aegis)

at all. This created a need for activities other than chariot races and boxing matches to attract and distract people. Bearbaiting, bullbaiting, and animal fights were added to capture spectator interest. Men and women were forced into the arena to engage in mortal combat with lions, tigers, and panthers. Condemned criminals were dressed in sheepskins to battle partially starved wild animals. Gladiators, armed with various weapons, were pitted against each other in gory fights to the death. These spectacles achieved two purposes for Roman rulers: They entertained an idle populace and disposed of socially "undesirable" people such as thieves, murderers, unruly slaves, and Christians (Baker, 1988).

Some Romans criticized these spectacles as tasteless activities, devoid of value. However, their criticisms were based not on concerns for human rights, but on their objections to events in which wealthy people and peasants mingled together. Other than some outspoken Christians, few people criticized the spectacles on moral or humanitarian grounds.

Women were seldom involved in Roman contests and games. They were allowed in the arenas to watch and cheer male athletes, but few had opportunities to develop athletic skills. Within Roman families, women were legally subservient to and rigidly controlled by men. As in ancient Greece, few women pursued interests outside the household.

The gladiatorial spectacles did not capture everyone's interest, but they attracted considerable attention in major cities. They continued until the Roman economy went into a depression and wealthy people moved from cities, taking their resources with them. As the Roman Empire deteriorated, there were not enough resources to support spectacles (Baker, 1988).

Although local folk games and other physical activities existed in the Roman Empire, we know little about them and what they meant in people's lives. The general population was interested in mild exercise and did not participate in the extreme competitions seen in gladiatorial

spectacles and used for military training. Common activities consisted of ball games played in connection with bathing in hot springs. Influenced by the Greeks, some Romans honored their gods by demonstrating skills in foot races, wrestling, and multiple forms of ball games. On occasions some women participated in ball games.

Roman contests and games differed from organized sports today. The achievements of athletes were seldom quantified, recorded, or used as a basis for evaluating future performances (review the box, "Sports Today," pp. 60–61).

TOURNAMENTS AND GAMES IN MEDIEVAL EUROPE: SEPARATING THE MASTERS FROM THE MASSES (500 TO 1300)

Sport activities in medieval Europe consisted of folk games played by peasants, tournaments staged for knights and nobles, archery contests, and activities in which animals were brutalized (Dunning, 1999). The folk games, often violent and dangerous and sometimes organized to maim or kill animals, emerged in connection with local peasant customs. The tournaments and archery contests were linked with military training and the desire for entertainment among the feudal aristocracy and those who served them.

Some local games of this period have interesting histories. As Roman soldiers and officials traveled around Europe during the fourth and fifth centuries, they built bathing facilities to use during their leisure time. To loosen up before their baths, they engaged in various forms of ball play. Local peasants during the early medieval period used the Roman activities as models and developed their own forms of ball games. They often integrated these games into local religious ceremonies and cultural events. For example, tossing a ball back and forth sometimes represented the conflict between good and evil, light and darkness, or life and death (Crowther, 2007).

As the influence of the Roman Catholic Church spread through Europe during the early years of the medieval period, these symbolic rituals were redefined in terms of Catholic beliefs. In these cases, sports and religion were closely connected with each other.

During most of the medieval period, the Roman Catholic Church accepted peasant ball games, even though they occasionally involved violence. Local priests encouraged games by opening church grounds on holidays and Sunday afternoons. As games became part of village life, people played them during festive community gatherings. These local ball games contained the roots for many contemporary games such as soccer, field hockey, football, rugby, bowling, curling, baseball, and cricket. However, the games in peasant villages had little structure and few rules. Local traditions guided play, and traditions varied widely from one community to the next.

The upper classes in medieval Europe paid little attention to and seldom interfered in the leisure of peasants. They saw peasant games and festivities as safety valves defusing mass social discontent. The sport activities of the upper classes were distinctively different from those of the peasants. Access to specialized equipment and facilities allowed them to develop early versions of billiards, shuffleboard, tennis, handball, and jai alai. Ownership of horses allowed them to develop forms of horse racing, while their stable hands developed a version of horseshoes. On horseback, the upper classes also participated in hunting and hawking. Owning property and possessing money and servants clearly influenced their sports.

Through the medieval period, the most popular sporting events among upper-class males were tournaments consisting of war games to keep knights and nobles ready for battle. Some tournaments resembled actual battlefield confrontations. Deaths and serious injuries occurred, victors carried off opponents'

> **Just as the dominant class writes history, so that same class writes the story of sport.** —James Riordan, social historian and former soccer player (1996)

possessions, and losers often were taken as prisoners and used as hostages to demand ransoms from opposing camps. Later versions of tournaments had lower stakes, but they also involved injuries and occasional deaths. Toward the end of the medieval period, colorful ceremonies and pageantry softened the warlike tournaments, as entertainment and chivalry took priority over military preparation and the use of deadly violence.

Women during this time seldom participated in physical games and sport activities. Gender restrictions were grounded in a male-centered family structure and Catholic teachings that women were inferior to men. A woman's duty was to be obedient and submissive; however, peasant women were involved in some of the games and physical activities that occurred during village festivals.

Among the aristocracy, gender relations were patterned so that men's and women's activities were clearly differentiated. Aristocratic women did little outside the walls of their dwellings, and their activities seldom involved rigorous physical exertion for fun. They sometimes engaged in "ladylike" games, but because women were subject to men's control and often viewed as sex objects and models of beauty, their involvement in active pursuits was limited. Feminine beauty during this time was defined in passive terms: The less active a woman, the more likely she was perceived as beautiful.

Even though some sports in Europe and North America today can trace their roots back to the medieval period, the contests and games of that time were not much like today's organized sports. They lacked specialization and organization, they never involved measuring or recording athletic achievements, and there was no commitment to equal and open competition among athletes from diverse backgrounds (review the box, "Sports Today," pages 60–61). Historian

Allen Guttmann has vividly described this last point:

> In medieval times, jousts and tournaments were limited to the nobility. Knights who sullied their honor by inferior marriages—to peasant girls, for instance—were disbarred. . . . Peasants reckless enough to emulate the sport of their masters were punished by death. (1978, p. 30)

Although some characteristics of medieval sport activities existed in the games and contests of the Renaissance, Reformation, and Enlightenment, these later periods involved important social transformations, which shaped the forms and meanings of physical activities and games.

AT YOUR *fingertips:* For more information on sports and religion, see chapter 15.

THE RENAISSANCE, REFORMATION, AND ENLIGHTENMENT: GAMES AS DIVERSIONS (1300 TO 1800)

The Renaissance

Wars throughout Europe during the fourteenth and fifteenth centuries encouraged kings, government officials, and church authorities to increase their military strength and prohibit popular peasant pastimes. Those in power wanted peasants to spend less time playing games and more time learning to defend the lands and lives of their masters. But, despite the pronouncements of bishops and kings, peasants did not readily give up their games. In fact, the games sometimes became rallying points for opposition to government and church authority.

At the same time that peasants were subjected to increased control, the "scholar–athlete" became the ideal "Renaissance man" among affluent people. Such a man was "socially adept, sensitive to aesthetic values, skilled in weaponry, strong of body, and learned in letters" (Baker, 1988, p. 59).

Throughout the Renaissance, women had relatively few opportunities to be involved in

tournaments and sport activities. Although peasant women sometimes played physical games, their lives were restricted by the demands of work in and out of the home. They often did hard physical labor, but they were not encouraged to engage in strenuous, public games and sports. Upper-class women sometimes participated in bowling, croquet, archery, and tennis, but involvement was limited because women were seen as "naturally" weak and passive. The ideal "Renaissance woman" was protected and put on a figurative pedestal, but she had little freedom because women were believed to be too fragile to leave the home and do things on their own. The code of chivalry, popular during this time, had less to do with protecting women than with reproducing **patriarchy,** that is, *a form of social organization in which rights are accorded only to or through men, with women being systematically controlled and oppressed.*

The Reformation

During the Protestant Reformation there were growing suspicions about the moral character of games and sports. Participation was discouraged, especially in regions where Calvinist or Puritan

"Why don't we settle this in a civilized way? We'll charge admission to watch!"

Dominant sport forms in many cultures are currently organized around a form of masculinity that emphasizes aggression, conquest, and dominance over others.

beliefs were popular. For example, between the early 1500s and the late 1600s, English Puritans tried to control leisure activities. Sports, they believed, undermined the work ethic. For them, sports were:

> . . . profane and licentious—they were occasions of worldly indulgence that tempted men from a godly life; being rooted in pagan and popish practices, they were rich in the sort of ceremony and ritual that poorly suited the Protestant conscience; they frequently involved a desecration of the Sabbath and an interference with the worship of the true believers; they disrupted the peaceable order of society, distracting men from their basic social duties—hard work, thrift, personal restraint, devotion to family, [and] a sober carriage. (Malcolmson, 1984, p. 67)

The primary targets of the Puritans were the pastimes and games of the peasants. Peasants didn't own property, so their festivities occurred in public settings and attracted large crowds. This made physical activities and games relatively easy to condemn and control. The Puritans did their best to eliminate collective festivities, especially those scheduled on Sunday afternoons. They objected to the drinking and partying that accompanied the games and disapproved of physical pleasure on the Sabbath.

The physical activities and games of the affluent were less subject to Puritan interference. Horse racing, hunting, tennis, and bowling took place on the private property of the wealthy, making them difficult for the Puritans to control. Similar to other times and places, power relations influenced who played sports as well as the conditions of participation. But despite Puritan influence and other barriers to participation, many peasants maintained certain games and sports.

During the early 1600s, King James I of England formally challenged Puritan influence by issuing *The King's Book of Sports*. Reissued in 1633 by Charles I, this book emphasized that Puritan ministers and officials should not discourage lawful recreational pursuits among English citizens. Charles I and his successors ushered in a new day for English sporting life. They revived traditional festivals and actively promoted and supported public games and sports. Consequently, cricket, horse racing, yachting, fencing, golf, and boxing became highly organized during the late 1600s and the 1700s, although participation patterns reflected and reproduced social class divisions in society.

In colonial America, Puritan influence was strong. Many colonists were not playful people because survival required full-time hard work. However, as colonial lifestyles became more routine, free time became available. Gradually, Puritan beliefs became less important than the desire to include recreation into everyday life. Towns abandoned or repealed Puritan "blue laws" that prohibited most leisure activities. In response, sports grew in popularity.

The games of indigenous people (that is, Native Americans) were not directly affected by Puritan beliefs during the colonial period. Along the eastern seaboard and in the Northeast, indigenous people continued to play the games that had been part of their cultures for centuries. This means that sports and sport participation have many histories across North America, even if they do not appear in history books. This reminds us that some voices, experiences, and perspectives are ignored or underrepresented in historical accounts of games, contests, and sports. The box "Lessons from History" emphasizes that most historical accounts do not represent the experiences and perspectives of Native Americans and others who lack the power to tell their stories and make them a part of dominant cultures.

> **Sports may be among the most powerful human expressions in all history.** —Gerald Early, Distinguished Professor, Washington University, St. Louis (1998)

The Enlightenment

During the Enlightenment period (1700 to 1800), many sport activities in Europe and North America began to resemble sport forms that we

Lessons from History
Who Tells Us About the Past?

History is much more than a chronological series of events. Historical research should take us inside the lives of people who have lived before us. It should give us a sense of how people lived and gave meaning to their experiences and the events of their times. Therefore, when we study sports, it is important to know whose voices and perspectives are used to construct historical accounts, and whose voices and perspectives are missing. This is the case when it comes to the physical activities, games, and sports of Native Peoples in North America.

Prior to the arrival of Columbus and other Europeans, the histories of Native Peoples were often kept in oral rather than written forms; they were local and personal histories. It was not until the late eighteenth century that accounts of the lives and cultures of Native Peoples were recorded in English. However, those accounts were written by Europeans with limited knowledge of the diverse languages, cultures, and complex social arrangements that made up the lives of nearly 500 unique cultural groups of Native Peoples in North America. This diversity was obscured by general accounts describing the lives and customs of "Indians," as if all native cultures were the same. These accounts provide limited information about the diverse games and sports played by Native Peoples. In many cases, accounts were written after the lives of Native People had been disrupted and influenced by European explorers and settlers. This history provides little information about the ways that traditional games and sports were played and integrated into the diverse cultures that existed in North America.

Europeans were seldom able to observe authentic expressions of traditional native cultures. When they did make observations, it was often under strained circumstances, and Native Peoples were unwilling to reveal their customs while being watched by outsiders who often viewed them as "oddities." The fact that the most important games in native cultures were connected with religious rites made it even less likely that Europeans

would be allowed to observe them in authentic, traditional forms or understand the meanings associated with them. By the time Native Peoples provided their own historical accounts in English, their cultures had changed in appreciable ways, and few people were willing to listen to their stories and publish them in forms that were considered "real history." In the meantime, experiences and meanings were lost forever.

Our limited knowledge about the histories of games and sports among Native Peoples demonstrates that social, political, and economic factors influence what is published as sport history. For example, if we want to understand an event, such as the establishment of the Iroquois National Lacrosse Team in 1983, we must also know the following:

- The histories and cultures of specific native societies and the six nations of the Iroquois Confederation
- The formal and informal political relationships between native societies and the U.S. government
- The experiences of Native Peoples in North America as they struggled to maintain their cultures while others tried to strip them of their language, religion, and customs

Knowing these things enables us to begin an investigation of the significance of the Iroquois National Lacrosse Team in terms of those who formed it, participated on it, and followed its matches. But without information based on the perspectives of those who lack power, our knowledge is diminished.

Social historian James Riordan (1996, p. vii) has said, "Just as the dominant class writes history, so that same class writes the story of sport." Therefore, when our knowledge of the past does not go beyond the experiences and perspectives of those with the power to tell their stories, it is incomplete. In the worst case, such histories reproduce stereotypes and justify discrimination against those who lack power. This is why some people call for more cultural diversity in courses taught in high schools and universities. *What do you think?*

are familiar with today. With some exceptions, they were no longer grounded in religious ritual and ceremony, they involved a degree of specialization and organization, achievements sometimes were measured, and records were kept more regularly. Furthermore, the idea that events should be open to all competitors, regardless of background, became increasingly popular. This commitment to equality and open participation was the ideological impetus for world-changing political revolutions in France and the United States.

Despite emerging similarities, sport activities during the Enlightenment differed from dominant sport forms today because they were defined strictly as diversions—as interesting and often challenging ways to pass free time. People *did not* see them as "character builders," nor as activities that could change individuals or social worlds. Therefore, there was no reason to organize sports for young people or create organizations to govern sports. Some people formed clubs, and they occasionally scheduled contests with others, but they did not form leagues or national and international associations. This, however, changed dramatically during the Industrial Revolution.

THE INDUSTRIAL REVOLUTION: THE EMERGENCE OF ORGANIZED COMPETITIVE SPORTS (1780 TO 1920)

The Industrial Revolution began in England around 1780 and became a part of life after 1800 in other European countries, the United States, and Canada. Organized competitive sports emerged during industrialization, but to understand how this occurred, sports must be analyzed as social constructions. People constructed and played sports as they coped with the realities of everyday life in rapidly changing families, communities, and societies. Depending on their position in society, they were either enabled or constrained by the powerful economic, political, and social factors that influenced everyone's life.

The development of factories, the mass production of consumer goods, the growth of cities, and increased dependence on technology were major characteristics of the Industrial Revolution. These factors changed the organization and control of work and the dynamics of community life. They also combined to increase the number and proportion of middle-class people in most industrializing societies.

The Early Years: Limited Time and Space for Sports

During the early years of the Industrial Revolution, few people had regular opportunities to play games and sports. Farm and factory workers had little free time. The workdays, even for many children, were long and tiring. Cities had few open spaces where people could play sports. Production took priority over play. Industrialists and politicians were not concerned with parks and public play spaces, mainly because they didn't want workers wasting time that could be used to expand the economy. Additionally, they feared that sports might provide workers with opportunities to organize themselves and challenge the status quo (Goodman, 1979; Mrozek, 1983).

Religious leaders in most industrializing countries endorsed restrictions on popular games and gatherings. Ministers preached about the moral value of work and the immorality of play and idleness. Many banned sports on Sundays and accused people of being sinful if they were not exclusively dedicated to work. They preached that work was a sign of goodness. Not everyone agreed, but working people had little leisure time. Survival depended on working long hours, regardless of what they thought about work, and they had little power to change the conditions of their lives.

In most countries, games and sports during this period existed *despite* the Industrial Revolution, *not* because of it. People in small towns and farm communities could maintain games and sport activities during their seasonal festivities, holidays, and public ceremonies. But people in

Early Americans had few play spaces. Playing in the streets was banned, but immigrant children were creative. Reformers who thought that introducing young boys to team sports would Americanize them and prepare them to be productive factory workers initiated the organized playground movement. When laws were passed to clear streets for commercial traffic, children like these would be chased home or arrested. (*Source:* McGraw-Hill)

cities had few opportunities to organize leisure activities, although the super wealthy lived highly publicized "lives of leisure" characterized by conspicuous and indulgent consumption (Veblen, 1899). Working-class people gradually gained opportunities to be spectators at new forms of commercialized sport events that were developed by wealthy entrepreneurs. These events differed from one nation to the next, but urban workers in most European and North American cities watched a combination of cricket, horse racing, boxing and wrestling, footraces, rowing and yachting races, cockfighting, bullbaiting, and circus acts, among other activities.

Rules that prohibited working-class people from forming crowds were suspended in the case of attending spectator sports that brought profits to influential people. When local events attracted

crowds that could not be controlled by authorities, they were defined as illegal. Some sport participation did occur among urban workers, but it was relatively rare during the early days of the Industrial Revolution. In the United States, for example, it usually was limited to activities such as bowling and billiards, played mostly by men. The constraints of work and the lack of money and facilities made it difficult for working-class people to engage in organized sports. Exceptions to this pattern were rare.

Similarly, African slaves, who made up 20 percent of the U.S. population during the early 1800s, had few opportunities to engage in any games or sports beyond those permitted by slaveholders. The dancing and other physical activities that occurred in slave quarters emphasized cooperation and community spirit—qualities required for survival (Wiggins, 1994). These activities took forms based on African traditions, and they were used to cope with the indignities of slavery. According to former slave and noted abolitionist Frederick Douglass, the games and holidays that the slaveholders permitted "were among the most effective means . . . of keeping down the spirit of insurrection among the slaves" (in Ashe, 1993, p. 10).

Between 1800 and 1850, progressives and reformers in Europe and North America became concerned about the physical health of workers. Some wanted to eliminate exploitation, whereas others simply wanted to keep workers strong and healthy so they would be more productive. Consequently, there were growing calls for funding open spaces and "healthy" leisure pursuits. Individuals were urged to become more fit by doing calisthenics, gymnastics, and outdoor exercises. In the United States, men were discouraged from hanging around pool halls, bowling alleys, and bars.

In the middle of the nineteenth century, exercises were often done by groups of men who worked together or had other community-based relationships with one another. The abolition of slavery in 1866 enabled 4.5 million former slaves to participate in communities and join these activities, but their participation was often subverted by forms of segregation maintained by whites. There was no emphasis on organized competition or keeping records of achievements during this time. The emergence of formally organized competitive sports would require more than increased free time and support for healthy activities. But this was the time during which the foundations for organized sports were established. The processes through which this occurred vary by nation. The material that follows focuses on the United States.

The Later Years: New Meanings, Purpose, and Organization for Sports

Since the late 1800s there has been a growing emphasis on organizing all spheres of social life in the United States. Clubs were formed to sponsor and control sport participation. Clubs were expensive, and most members were wealthy people in urban areas or students at exclusive eastern colleges. However, some sport competitions attracted spectators from all social classes.

The YMCA, founded in England in 1844 and the United States in 1851, was a clublike organization that had a less-exclusive membership. During the late 1800s it made popular the idea that physical conditioning through exercise and sports was compatible with Christian beliefs. This encouraged sport participation among hardworking middle-class people.

The games and sport activities of working-class people did not usually occur in clubs or organizations, and they seldom received publicity. An exception to this was baseball, a sport played by men from diverse backgrounds. Working-class men favored baseball, and it became increasingly popular. After the Civil War, baseball games were organized, sponsored, and publicized in many towns and cities. Leagues were established at various levels of competition, and men's professional baseball became increasingly popular. Professional women's teams existed, but they seldom received the sponsorship needed to grow in popularity. African American men developed teams and leagues around the country, although racism prevented them from playing in white-controlled leagues and stadiums.

As sport activities became more organized, they generally reinforced existing social and economic distinctions in Europe and North America. Upper-class clubs emphasized achievement and "gentlemanly" involvement—an orientation that ultimately led to definitions of amateurism. The definition of *amateur*, which first appeared in England, referred to those who played sport for the love of the game rather than material rewards. This definition became an effective tool for excluding working-class people from sports that were organized around the interests of upper-class people. The activities of the working classes, by contrast, involved local games and commercialized sports—a combination that ultimately led to professionalization. This dual development of amateurism and professionalization occurred in different ways in Europe and North America (Dunning, 1999).

New Ideas About Sports   Underlying the growing organization of sport activities between 1850 and 1920 was a new emphasis on the seriousness of sports. Instead of classifying sports simply as enjoyable diversions, people came to see them as tools for achieving goals such as economic productivity, national identity, political loyalty, and the development of positive character traits, especially among males. This new perspective was fueled by changes in every segment of industrial society.

During this period, and especially between 1880 and 1920, issues of power and wealth had a major impact on the ways that sports developed. For example, wealthy people in the United States often lived indulgent lives of leisure that included sports (Cavallo, 1981; Mrozek, 1983). Their participation in certain sports was meant to show others that they were so successful that they could "waste" time by playing economically nonproductive games (Veblen, 1899). Although the wealthy used sports to reinforce status distinctions between themselves and other social classes, their actions influenced the ways that sports were played and organized by others. This occurred because the status aspirations of many people led them to use the upper-class as their **reference group,** that is, a *group whose standards are used to evaluate self and others.*

This is how wealthy people influenced standards for facilities and equipment, the norms used by players and spectators, and the ways that people defined sports and integrated them into their lives. Over time, sports were widely seen as *consumer activities* to be played in *proper* attire, using the *proper* equipment in a *proper* facility, and preceded or followed by *proper* social occasions. Therefore, sports were supportive of the economy and often had worklike characteristics, even though most people saw them as escapes from work.

These ideas about the ways that sports "should be" played were important because they enabled wealthy people to reproduce their power and privilege without overtly coercing workers to think and do certain things during their leisure time. By promoting forms of sports that were both entertaining and supportive of capitalist expansion, they could maintain their power without being nasty and heavy-handed. Critical cultural theories explain that this is an example of how sports are political at the same time that most people see them as sources of excitement and enjoyment (Gramsci, 1971, 1988; Rigauer, 2000; Sage, 2000).

Middle- and working-class people, especially white males, had new opportunities to play sports during the period of 1880 to 1920. Labor unions, progressive government legislation, and economic expansion combined to improve working and living conditions. As the middle class expanded, more people had resources for leisure and sport participation. Progressive reforms at the turn of the twentieth century also led to the development of parks, recreation programs, and organized playground activities for urban residents, especially boys and young men.

New Ideas About Character Development   As opportunities for sport involvement increased during the early 1900s, they were shaped by factors beyond the interests of the participants themselves. Important new ideas about human behavior, individual development, and social life led to an emphasis on organized competitive sports as "character-building" activities.

Through the 1880s most people believed that human beings were not influenced by the physical and social environment in which they lived. They assumed that individual actions, personal development, and the organization of social life were determined by a combination of God's will, necessity, fate, and coincidence. But these ideas changed as Charles Darwin's ideas about evolution were increasingly accepted and as research by psychologists and sociologists documented that the social environment did influence people's actions as well as patterns of psychosocial growth and development.

This new way of thinking was a crucial catalyst for the growth of modern sports. It led people to see sports as potential educational experiences—experiences with important consequences for individuals, communities, and societies. This change was based on both behaviorist and evolutionary theories, which were popular at the time. For the first time in history, people saw sports as tools for changing behavior, shaping character, creating national loyalty, and training workers to use teamwork as a tool for being more productive. This, in turn, provided a new reason for organizing and promoting sport participation.

After the turn of the century, people began to think about the meaning and purpose of sports in new and serious terms. Sport participation was linked to many positive developmental outcomes. For example, some religious groups, later referred to as "muscular Christians" (see chapter 15), suggested a link between physical strength and the ability to do good works. Therefore, they promoted sport participation as an avenue for spiritual growth and a sign of moral righteousness. Others saw sports as tools for teaching immigrant children lessons that would turn them into contributing members of a corporate–bureaucratic–democratic society. They promoted organized playground programs that used team sports to suppress the traditional values of white ethnic groups (Italians, Irish, Germans, Jews, and others) and replace them with an Americanized view of the world. People interested in economic expansion saw organized sports as tools for generating profits by introducing untrained workers to tasks emphasizing teamwork, obedience to rules, planning, organization, and production. Sports, they thought, could create good workers who would tolerate stressful working conditions, obey supervisors, and meet production goals through teamwork on factory assembly lines.

In large part, organized sports became important because influential people believed that sport participation could be used to train loyal, efficient, and patriotic workers for the sake of capitalist expansion and the status of the United States as a world power. Sports were organized to emphasize competition and promote character development compatible with capitalist expansion and American military success. This was done through new "Americanized" sports such as football, baseball, and basketball. Soccer, very popular among many central and southern European immigrants during the early 1900s, was believed to undermine loyalty to the United States by perpetuating potentially dangerous identifiable links with "foreign" cultures. Therefore, soccer came to be viewed as dangerous and un-American. New immigrants who played soccer were perceived as unwilling to embrace an American identity. The legacy of these attitudes is a reason why soccer continues to struggle for full mainstream acceptance in the United States.

New Ideas About Masculinity and Femininity

The new belief that sports built character was applied primarily to males. The people who organized and sponsored new programs in the early twentieth century thought they could use sports, especially team sports, to tame what they perceived as the savage, undisciplined character of young men from Irish, Italian, and Greek immigrant families. Their intent was to create obedient citizens and productive workers. At the same time, people used sports to counteract what they believed to be the negative influence of female-dominated home lives on the development of boys in affluent families. Their goal was to turn these "overfeminized" boys into assertive, competitive, achievement-oriented men who would be leaders in business, politics, and the military. In this way, sports were heavily influenced by political and economic leaders who wanted to control the working class and prepare their sons to inherit positions of affluence and power (Burstyn, 1999; Goodman, 1979; Kidd, 1996a).

Although women's sport participation increased between 1880 and 1920, many sport programs ignored females. Organizers and sponsors did not believe that sport participation

Leisure activities among wealthy people in the early twentieth century included sports. However, physical activities and sports for girls and women often stressed balance and coordination, which were defined as "ladylike" qualities. Girls and women were often trained to be graceful and coordinated so that they might become "ladies." (*Source:* McGraw-Hill)

contributed to the positive development of girls and women. They sometimes included girls with boys in organized games at playgrounds, but they discouraged sex-integrated sports among children nearing the age of puberty. They believed that boys and girls who played sports together would become friends, lose their interest in being married and having children, and lose their motivation for maintaining a gender ideology based on the assumption of male superiority and female inferiority.

When boys were taught to play sports on playgrounds in the early 1900s, girls were told to sit in the shade and preserve their energy. Medical doctors during this time warned that playing sports would sap the energy that young women

needed to conceive and bear healthy children. Luther Gulick, who developed the recreational philosophy of the YMCA, wrote in 1906, "It is clear that athletics have never been either a test or a large factor in the survival of women; athletics do not test womanliness as they test manliness" (p. 158). Gulick also claimed to have scientific proof that strenuous activities were harmful to the minds and bodies of females. His ideas reaffirmed the prevailing gender ideology during the early twentieth century.

Organized activities for girls often consisted of domestic science classes to make them good wives, homemakers, and mothers. When playground organizers provided opportunities for girls to play games and sports, they designed activities that would cultivate "ladylike" traits, such as poise and body control. This is why so many girls participated in gymnastics, figure skating, and other "grace and beauty" sports (Burstyn, 1999; Hart, 1981). Another goal of the activities was to make young women healthy for bearing children. Competition was eliminated or controlled so that physical activities emphasized personal health, the dignity of beauty, and good form.

Limited opportunities and a lack of encouragement did not prevent women from participating in sports, but they restricted their involvement (Vertinsky, 1994). Some middle- and upper-class women engaged in popular physical exercises and recreational sport activities, but apart from limited intercollegiate games and private tournaments, they had few opportunities to engage in formal competitive events. The participation of girls and women from lower-income groups was restricted to informal street games, a few supervised exercise classes, and annual "field days" in public schools when girls had an opportunity to run short races and compete in other events that would not be too physically taxing.

Ideas about femininity changed between 1880 and 1920, but traditional gender ideology and many misconceptions about the physical and mental effects of strenuous activities on females prevented the "new woman" of the early twentieth century from enjoying the same participation opportunities and encouragement received by boys and men (Lenskyj, 1986). Medical beliefs supported this ideology by providing "scientific evidence" showing that women's bodies could not tolerate vigorous activities. These faulty beliefs and studies damaged the health of women during these years (Vertinsky, 1990).

New Ideas About Skin Color and Ethnicity   After the Civil War, some African Americans became involved in sports. Most participation occurred in segregated settings. This was especially true as whites established new forms of segregation and racism, designed to hold back the changes that threatened long-established social relationships organized around slavery and white supremacy. Whites in both northern and southern states became increasingly uncomfortable with the prospect of more open forms of race relations. This led them to draft "Jim Crow laws" that clearly divided people into categories of "white" and "black" and restricted the rights and opportunities of African Americans and all people who were not officially classified as "white."

Definitions of who counted as white changed over time as federal courts and the Supreme Court made decisions on the ancestral origins of Italians, Greeks, Armenians, and others. Definitions of who was black varied by state, but the general rule was that anyone with a black ancestor was not white, regardless of their appearance or skin tone. This has since come to be known as the "one-drop rule," meaning that only one drop of "black blood" made a person black (Davis, 2001).

Whites during this time (1890s to 1950s) increasingly believed that blacks were intellectually and physically inferior beings. During the early twentieth century, white scientists at Harvard and other prestigious universities published flawed studies "proving" white superiority and black inferiority.

As this racist ideology became more deeply embedded in the dominant culture of the United States, many whites came to view black athletes as a curiosity. When African Americans demonstrated skills in certain sports, whites quickly developed biological and genetic explanations for those skills. Therefore, many whites saw the achievements of blacks as "proof" that people with dark skin were less evolved than

---

OLC   ON THE *OLC*:
See the OLC—Additional Readings for Chapter 3—for the author's summary of information on medical myths about women in sports.

breaking **BARRIERS**

"Other" Barriers
They Found It Hard to Be Around Me

Danny was twenty-one years old, a popular and able-bodied rugby player. Then came the accident, the amputation of his right arm just below the shoulder, the therapy, and eventually, getting back with friends. But reconnecting with friends after suddenly acquiring a disability isn't easy. Danny describes his experience with these words: "A lot of them found it very difficult . . . to come to terms with it . . . And they found it hard to be around me, friends that I'd had for years" (in Brittain, 2004, p. 437).

Chris, an athlete with cerebral palsy and one of Danny's teammates on the British Paralympic Team, explains why his friends felt uncomfortable: "They have very little knowledge of people with a disability and [they think that] 'if I leave it alone and don't touch them and don't get involved, then it's not my problem'" (in Brittain, 2004, p. 437). Chris raises a recurring issue in the history of disability: What happens when people define physical or intellectual impairments as "differences" and use them to create "others" who are distinguished from "us normals" in social worlds?

Throughout history, people with disabilities have been described by words inferring revulsion, resentment, dread, shame, and a world of limitations. In Europe and North America, it took World War II and thousands of returning soldiers impaired by injuries before there were widespread concerns about the words used to describe people with disabilities. Gradually, people have learned that words like *retard*, *spaz* (spastic), *cripple, freak, deaf and dumb, handicapped, gimp, lame,* and *deformed* serve to undermine opportunities for people with disabilities. However, descriptions such as "she's a quad," "he's a CPer," "they're amputees," and "what a retard!" are still used to the point that people with disabilities are classified as "others," that is, not "normal people" like us.

When people with disabilities are defined as "others," coming face-to-face with disability causes many people to consider their own vulnerability, aging, and mortality. In the process, it highlights the faulty assumptions of normalcy around which many people have constructed identities and social worlds. This makes many "normal" people so uncomfortable that they often ignore, avoid, or patronize people with disabilities. This, of course, subverts the possibility of ever seeing the world through their eyes.

whites and had animal-like characteristics, making them successful in the sports that did not require intelligence. This racial ideology became deeply ingrained in U.S. culture, and its legacy continues to influence ideas about race and sport performance as well as the sport participation choices of young people in the twenty-first century. (This and related issues are covered in chapters 9 and 10.)

White ethnics during this time (1880–1920) also experienced discrimination limiting sport participation and forcing them to play their native games in ethnically segregated clubs. However, public schools became the settings in which many young men from Irish, Scandinavian, German, Jewish, Italian, Greek, Armenian, Spanish, Chinese, and other ethnic groups came

to learn, enjoy, and excel in "American sports" and abandon their passion for soccer.

New Ideas About Age and Disability Aging involves biological changes, but the connection between aging and sport participation depends largely on the social meanings given to those changes. Developmental theory in the early 1900s emphasized that all growth and character formation occurred during childhood and adolescence. Therefore, it was important for young people to play sports, but older people were already "grown-ups" and no longer needed the character-building experiences provided by sports.

Medical knowledge at the time also discouraged older people from engaging in sports. Strenuous activities were thought to put excessive demands

The uncomfortable dynamics associated with coming face-to-face with people classified as "others" causes many temporarily able-bodied people to avoid people with disabilities and manage how they deal with them. This occurs in various ways across cultures, but it often involves enlisting the services of experts to "handle" those who are "others." These experts may include doctors, mental health workers, psychiatrists, healers, shamans, witch doctors, priests, exorcists, and all professionals whose assumed competence gives them the right to examine, test, classify, and prescribe "normalizing treatments" for "others." Therefore, the history of disability is also the history of giving meaning to difference, creating "others," and using current knowledge to treat "otherness" and control "others" so they do not disrupt the illusion of normalcy in social worlds (Foucault, 1961/1967; Goffman, 1963).

As noted in *Breaking Barriers* in chapter 2, cultural traditions in the United States have long emphasized treatment-oriented approaches to fix impairments or help people adjust to living with disabilities. Only recently have these approaches been complemented by transformational approaches designed to create barrier-free social spaces. Disabilities are not stigmatized in these spaces, and the category of "other" becomes irrelevant. For example, the Special Olympics were created as barrier-free social spaces for people with intellectual disabilities, and the Paralympics serve the same purpose for people with physical disabilities ("para" here means *parallel with*, not *paraplegic*). Within these contexts, there are no "others" in terms of (dis)abilities.

Creating barrier-free social spaces is an idealistic project based on a critical approach to social worlds. Achieving success requires strategic actions that disrupt the "normal" order of social worlds so that people with disabilities are not systematically disadvantaged.

Jean Driscoll, eight-time winner of the Women's Wheelchair Boston Marathon, has experienced such transformed worlds. She says that when sports are transformed, "the focus turns from the person with a disability to the guy with a great shot or the gal with a fast 800-meter time." This, she says, "provides the perfect venue where 'actions speak louder than words'" (in Joukowsky and Rothstein, 2002a, p. 28).

on the heart and organs in aging bodies. This did not prevent some older people from playing certain sports, but it did prevent the establishment and funding of organized sport programs for older people. Furthermore, when older people were physically active, they participated by themselves or in age-segregated settings.

People with observable physical or mental impairments were denied opportunities to play sports and were often told that strenuous physical activities were bad for their well-being. During this time, widely accepted definitions of mental and physical disability gave rise to fears and prejudices that led many people to think it was dangerous to allow people with disabilities to become physically active or excited. Therefore, programs to build their bodies were discouraged.

This meant that people born with certain disabilities were isolated and destined to be physically inactive; obesity and problems caused by a lack of physical activity shortened their life expectancy. People with "acquired disabilities," usually those injured in war or accidents, were treated with physical therapy in the hope of some degree of rehabilitation. As explained in the "Breaking Barriers" box above, sports for most people with disabilities did not exist until after World War II.

SINCE 1920: STRUGGLES CONTINUE

By 1920 major connections between sports and American society had been firmly established. Sports were a growing part of people's everyday lives, and they were linked to major social institutions such as the family, religion, education, the economy, the government, and the media. Since 1920 the rate of change and the expansion of the visibility and importance of sports in people's lives have intensified. The past eight decades have been a time of many "firsts" in U.S. sports. They have also been a time for continuing struggles over the following:

1. The meaning, purpose, and organization of sports
2. Who plays sports under particular conditions
3. How and why sports are sponsored

As explained in chapter 1, sports are social constructions *and* contested activities. Therefore, we can outline social trends and patterns in recent history by focusing on issues and events related to these three realms of struggle. They are sensible reference points for discussing social history, and I use them to guide my choice of materials in the following chapters. They also provide a framework for understanding patterns and trends during the twentieth century. Table 3.2 highlights events related to major struggles and changes in sports, providing a feel for the social side of what has happened in recent sports history. Of course, the timing, dynamics, and outcomes of these struggles are also related to larger historical events and trends such as wars, economic recessions, suburbanization, the growth of universities, the civil rights and women's movements, the development and expansion of electronic media and other technologies, globalization, and the growing concentration of corporate power and influence around the world. Connections between the recent history of

sports and these trends and events are too complex to discuss in this chapter. But it is possible to outline major struggles from 1920 to the present.

Struggles over Meaning: Is Soccer Subversive?

Sports usually have multiple meanings in social worlds, and these meanings change over time. For example, national identity is a central realm of meaning connected with sports in the United States. Since 1920 certain sports and athletes have been associated with "Americanness." Through the 1960s, baseball was described as "America's pastime," and it was played by both men and women through the 1930s. But after World War II, it became primarily a men's game and has remained that way ever since; women turned to softball, which has never been described as "America's pastime," even though it was widely played through the early 1950s (Berlage, 1994). This is one of many examples illustrating that the meaning of sports changes as ideas about gender change.

In the 1960s, football emerged as the classic American sport. It emphasized strength, power, confrontation, and strategy—all of which were consistent with dominant values and cultural orientations during the Cold War between the United States and the Soviet Union. Men played football and defended turf from opponents, just as men in the military defended the United States from communist threats. College football became increasingly visible during the 1960s as baby boomers filled classrooms in record numbers; college administrators used football as a public relations tool and many students used it as a ritualized occasion for escaping coursework.

The sons of immigrants played baseball and football as they sought assimilation and acceptance in the United States. Sports such as rugby and soccer, born in England and nurtured in Europe, have never been associated with "Americanness" like baseball and football have. Soccer teams and leagues came and went during much of the twentieth century, but the meaning of

OLC **ON THE *OLC*:**
See the OLC—Additional Readings for Chapter 3—for the author's explanation of why 1920 is used as a turning point.

soccer was generally associated with ethnic communities, workers seeking to form labor unions, or European "wannabees." It wasn't until the 1970s that soccer began to gain popularity among boys and girls in white, middle-class families. But many Americans continue to see soccer as an international sport, and it has never been tied to national identity among more than a small proportion of the U.S. population. Soccer is no longer seen as subversive, but professional soccer struggles to attract fans and survive financially. The women's league suspended operations in 2003 after only three seasons, and after 12 seasons of operation the men's MLS experiences minimal success, selling only one-sixth as many game tickets as the NFL sells.[1] The current status of soccer was highlighted when Senator John Kerry, the Democrat Party presidential candidate in 2004, deliberately avoided talking about being a former varsity soccer player at Yale because it might turn off some voters. Instead, he presented himself as a windsurfer!

The meanings given to sports often vary from one region of a country to another. For example, stock car racing and the National Association for Stock Car Auto Racing (NASCAR) initially represented values, traditions, and histories common to the South, but they are now seen as a national sport. Rodeo traditionally had special meaning in midwestern and western rural areas, where livestock and horses were important to local economies and people's everyday lives. But today there are rodeo events held in New York City and other places where livestock are rarely seen (Haney and Pearson, 1999).

The meanings given to sports generally reaffirm the values and lifestyles of those who play

and watch them, and this has certainly been true since 1920. As cities have grown, so has basketball, often described as the city game (Axthelm, 1970). As African American men excelled at the highest levels of basketball, the game was defined by many people as a "black person's game." In the process, basketball was given special meaning in many black communities. At the same time, basketball was given other meanings by white boys growing up in Indiana, where "Hoosier Hysteria" occurs every fall during the boys' state high school basketball tournament. Basketball was given special meaning by girls who played on high school teams in Iowa, where girls' basketball was the major spectator event in the state through much of the twentieth century (McElwain, 2004). These examples remind us that understanding sports history depends on knowing what sports meant to those who played, watched, and sponsored them.

AT YOUR *fingertips:* For information on sports as contested activities and social constructions, see chapter 1, pages 10–11, 12.

Struggles over Purpose: Is Winning the Only Thing?

Meaning and purpose are closely aligned. On a general level, the central purpose of most sports between the 1920s and 1960s was to foster fitness and fair play. However, as occupational success and social mobility became increasingly important in a growing capitalist economy during the 1950s, there was a gradual turn toward an emphasis on competitive success and winning in sports. Competitive sports were seen to build the kind of individual character that many people felt was essential to American prosperity.

As sports teams and sports events were linked to schools, communities, and the nation, the primary purpose of sports continued to shift

---

[1]Women's Professional Soccer, the WPS, will be launched in the spring of 2009. The United Soccer Leagues (USL) of the United States, Canada, and Caribbean also provide a range of professional and amateur participation opportunities. The USL W-League consists of 41 teams for elite women players, and it allows NCAA college players to retain their eligibility (see USLsoccer.com).

During the twentieth century, sports clearly were linked to political and racial ideologies. At the 1936 Olympic Games in Berlin, Hitler and the Nazi Party used the games to promote their ideas about the superiority of the "Nordic race." This historic photo shows a German official giving the Nazi salute and Jesse Owens, the African American sprinter who won four gold medals during the games, giving the U.S. salute. Owens's success challenged Hitler's ideas about Nordic—that is, white—supremacy in sports. (*Source:* USOC Archives)

from fitness and fair play, as favored by educators, to the competitive success and victories that met the needs of commercial sponsors. By the 1960s, many people felt that "winning was the *only* thing" that mattered, although they often gave lip service to other purposes.

With the dramatic growth of media coverage during the 1970s, entertainment became an increasingly important purpose of sports. As this occurred, the styles and personas of athletes took on new meanings, and teams built public relations profiles around values and identities that resonated with current and potential spectators. This is when the Dallas Cowboys came to be known as "America's Team," and the Chicago Bears and Detroit Lions were known as "blue-collar" teams focused on the no-nonsense work ethic valued in traditional midwestern culture. Entertainment and winning came to be closely linked during this time; winning teams filled stadiums and generated revenue for sponsors and owners.

There is seldom complete agreement on the purpose of sports. For example, physical educators emphasize fitness and health, whereas people associated with the commercial media emphasize entertainment and revenue streams. This and other disagreements occur today as community residents debate whether recreation and mass participation are more important than competition and the development of elite athletes as the primary purpose of sports in their schools and youth programs.

Table 3.2   U.S. social history time line, 1920–1999

Since 1920 thousands of sports organizations have come and gone, hundreds of legal decisions have regulated and deregulated sports, and thousands of important struggles have occurred over (1) the meaning, purpose, and organization of sports, (2) who plays sports under what conditions, and (3) how and why sports are sponsored. This selective time line highlights events related to these struggles and the issues and controversies discussed in this book.

1920	Formation of the National Football League and a baseball league for black players.
1921	The National Collegiate Athletic Association (NCAA) sponsors the first national college sport championship (in track and field).
1922	The U.S. Supreme Court rules that professional sports are *not* a form of "commerce" and exempts them from antitrust laws; the first Women's Olympic Games are held (in response to the exclusion of women in many Olympic events).
1923	The eastern Colored League for black men is founded (dissolved in 1928).
1924	The first live radio coverage of the Olympics is broadcast (from Chamonix, France); the first Deaflympics (called The Silent Games) are held in Paris.
1926	Babe Ruth suffers from gonorrhea that is reported as "stomach cramps" in the media; the American Basketball League for men is formed (dissolved in 1931).
1927	Socialists and communists form the Labor Sports Union of America and sponsor soccer and other sports.
1929	Carnegie Foundation for the Advancement of Teaching publishes a report describing college athletics as too commercial and professionalized.
1932	The Summer Olympics are held in Los Angeles; Babe Didrikson sets two world records and wins two medals; the Labor Sports Union of America sponsors an alternative Olympics for working people.
1935	African American boxer Joe Louis defeats Italian champion Primo Carnera in a world heavyweight title bout before sixty thousand people in Yankee Stadium.
1936	The Olympic Games are held in Berlin; Jesse Owens wins four gold medals and challenges Hitler's ideas about race and white supremacy.
1939	Little League Baseball is founded; boxing becomes the first sport to receive regular TV coverage.
1943	All-American Girls' Professional Baseball League is founded (dissolved in 1954).
1946	NCAA members meet and draft a "sanity code" to restore honesty and integrity to intercollegiate athletics; the All-America Football Conference is formed (dissolved after 1949 season).
1947	Jackie Robinson signs with the Brooklyn Dodgers to become the first black since the nineteenth century to play Major League Baseball; the first Little League World Series tournament is held.
1948	The last baseball season is played by the Negro National League; the Stoke Mandeville Games for wheelchair athletes (mostly British war veterans) are held in England to coincide with the Olympic Games in London.
1949	The Ladies Professional Golf Association (LPGA) is established; the Basketball Association of America merges with the National Basketball League to form the National Basketball Association (NBA); Mexican American Richard "Poncho" Gonzalez wins the U.S. Open Tennis Championship.
1951	An American Council on Education study reports that college sports are too commercial and professionalized.
1952	The newly formed Soviet Union competes in the Olympic Games held in Helsinki, Finland; Sports Ambassadors, an evangelical Christian sport organization, is founded.
1953	The Little League World Series is televised for the first time.
1954	The first issue of *Sports Illustrated* is published; the Fellowship of Christian Athletes (FCA) is formed.
1957	Althea Gibson is the first black player to win a title at Wimbledon; ballplayers from Monterrey, Mexico, become the first non–U.S. team to win the Little League World Series (they win again in 1958).

(Continued)

Table 3.2   (*Continued*)

1960	Wilma Rudolph wins three gold medals at the Olympic Games in Rome, and Cassius Clay (Muhammad Ali) wins the gold medal in boxing; the American Football League (AFL) is formed; ABC is the first U.S. television company to pay $4 million for the rights to broadcast the Olympic Games in Rome; the first Paralympic Games for athletes with physical disabilities are held following the Summer Olympic Games in Rome; Charlie Sifford is the first black to play in a professional golf tournament; the NFL Dallas Cowboys are bought for $500,000; the Negro American League ceases operation.
1964	The Olympic Games in Tokyo are the first to be televised; Cassius Clay (Muhammad Ali) wins the world heavyweight boxing title; Billy Mills, an Oglala Sioux from the Pine Ridge reservation, wins the Olympic gold medal in the 10,000-meter competition; *Sports Illustrated* publishes its first "swimsuit edition."
1965	The Houston Astrodome, the first fully domed major stadium in the world, opens.
1966	The Major League Baseball Players' Association is formed; Athletes in Action is formed as an extension of the Campus Crusade for Christ; Texas Western College is first college team to start five black players in the NCAA tournament, beating a top-rated University of Kentucky team starting five white players.
1967	The first Super Bowl is played; the International Olympic Committee (IOC) defines and bans doping; the average annual salary of Major League Baseball players is $19,000; Muhammad Ali is stripped of his boxing title for "conscientiously objecting" to the Vietnam War and refusing induction into the army; Katherine Switzer registers as "K. Switzer," runs the all-male Boston Marathon, and men try to physically remove her from the course.
1968	Many black athletes boycott the Olympic Games in Mexico City in protest of racial discrimination; Tommy Smith and John Carlos support the boycott by raising gloved fists and standing barefooted on the victory podium at Olympics (see Chapter 16, p. 570); Mexican students protest against using public money for the Olympic Games, and police kill over thirty of them; Olympic drug testing begins; the first Special Olympics is held for athletes with intellectual disabilities; women athletes in the Olympics are forced to take a chromosome-based sex test to "prove" they are females; Arthur Ashe is the first African American man to win a U.S. Open Tennis title.
1969	The AFL and NFL merge to create one pro football league; Arthur Ashe and others form the Association of Tennis Professionals to represent players; Pancho Gonzalez defeats Puerto Rican American Charlie Pasarell in the longest match in Wimbledon history.
1970	The first *Monday Night Football* game is played and televised on ABC.
1971	An estimated 294,000 girls play varsity high school sports (1 of every 27 female students); the Association for Intercollegiate Athletics for Women (AIAW) is formed to govern intercollegiate sports for women; women are officially allowed to run the Boston Marathon for first time.
1972	Title IX, a law making gender discrimination illegal in schools that receive federal funds, is signed by President Richard Nixon; NCAA officials attempt to subvert Title IX; Palestinian terrorists capture eleven Israeli team members at the Olympic Village during the Summer Games in Munich—they kill two, and the nine others are killed during a failed rescue attempt; in response to requests from Native Americans, Stanford University drops "Indians" as its nickname.
1973	Billie Jean King defeats Bobby Riggs in a made-for-TV "Battle of the Sexes" tennis match; scholar–activist Harry Edwards publishes the first sociology of sport textbook; the NCAA establishes Divisions I, II, and III and defines all athletic scholarships in Divisions I and II as one-year renewable contracts; tests are developed to detect certain anabolic steroid use among athletes.
1974	World Team Tennis is founded; the World Football League is founded (bankrupt in 1975); the NCAA lobbies the U.S. Congress to exclude intercollegiate sports from Title IX law; Little League Baseball forms a softball programs for girls to legally justify excluding them from its baseball teams; an American Council on Education report concludes that college sports are too commercial and professionalized; Lee Elder is first black man to play the Masters golf tournament.

Table 3.2 (*Continued*)

1975	President Gerald Ford amends Title IX to clarify that the law *does* apply to interscholastic and intercollegiate sports because they are educational activities.
1976	The U.S. Supreme Court rules that Major League Baseball players are not permanently owned by teams; the ABA and NBA merge into one pro basketball league; twenty-nine nations, mostly from Africa and Asia, boycott the Olympic Games in Montreal to protest New Zealand's sporting ties with white supremacist South Africa; the NCAA passes Proposition 48 to expand academic requirements for athletes in Division I schools.
1977	Janet Guthrie is the first woman driver in the Indianapolis 500; the all-male IOC prohibits women from running the 3000-meter race (about 2 miles) to protect women from physical harm; six-time Mr. Olympia bodybuilder Arnold Schwarzenegger poses naked for numerous photos in *After Dark*, a gay magazine.
1978	U.S. Congress passes the Amateur Sports Act, establishing the U.S. Olympic Committee (USOC) as the central governing body of amateur sports; the North American Society for the Sociology of Sport (NASSS) is founded; three sociology of sport textbooks are published, including the first edition of *Sport in Society: Issues and Controversies.*
1979	The Office for Civil Rights of the U.S. Department of Education defines the legal meaning of Title IX and presents enforcement guidelines; ESPN, an all-sports cable television company, goes on air;
1980	U.S. men's hockey team defeats the heavily favored Soviet Union team at the height of the Cold War and then defeats Finland to win the gold medal at the Winter Olympic Games in Lake Placid, New York, in February; in July the United States and more than fifty other nations boycott the Summer Olympic Games in Moscow because the Soviet Union unilaterally (without United Nations approval) invaded Afghanistan in 1979.
1981	Major League Baseball players hold the first midseason strike (average annual salary for players is $185,000).
1982	NFL players strike for nine weeks (average annual salary for players is $90,000); the AIAW is dissolved as the NCAA takes over women's sports; the first Gay Games are held in San Francisco; testosterone is added to the IOC banned-substance list; the IOC allows amateur athletes to accept money from sponsors, which enables U.S. athletes to receive corporate money to compete with state-supported athletes from socialist nations.
1983	The U.S. Football League (USFL) plays its first game (dissolved in 1986).
1984	The Soviet Union and thirteen other nations don't trust U.S. security for their teams and they boycott the Olympic Games in Los Angeles; the Los Angeles Games are the first to make a profit for a host city, and this intensifies competition among cities bidding to host future games; the U.S. Supreme Court restricts Title IX by ruling that it applies *only* to the specific programs that directly receive federal money in a school; the Little League Baseball charter is rewritten to allow girls to play (after dozens of lawsuits brought by girls against Little League); the Texas State Legislature approves "no pass, no play" rules governing eligibility in Texas high school sports.
1985	For Super Bowl XIX, ABC sells the first million-dollar minute of advertising in television history.
1986	Lynette Woodward is the first woman to play on a men's pro-basketball team, The Harlem Globetrotters.
1988	U.S. Congress passes the Civil Rights Restoration Act and reaffirms that Title IX applies to entire schools, not just specific programs; Carl Lewis wins the gold medal in the 100-meter dash after the medal is stripped from Canadian sprinter Ben Johnson, who tests positive for steroids after setting a world record.
1990	The NCAA passes Proposition 42 to strengthen academic standards in Proposition 48; Olympic sports begin to abolish distinctions between amateur and professional athletes; Congress approves Student Right-to-Know Act, which requires public disclosure of graduation rates for varsity athletes and the general student body; Jean Driscoll sets a world record as she wins the first of seven consecutive wheelchair Boston Marathons.

(Continued)

Table 3.2   (*Continued*)

1991	The U.S. soccer team defeats Norway to win the first Women's World Cup; "Magic" Johnson announces that he tested positive for HIV, and his NBA career ends; the Women's Final Four of college basketball is televised live for the first time.
1992	At the Olympic Games in Barcelona, the USA basketball team ("The Dream Team") consisting of NBA players wins the gold medal; seven Native Americans file a lawsuit against the NFL team in Washington, D.C., for using the demeaning term "redskins" in their name; girls, for the first time, win all three divisions in the All-American Soap Box Derby.
1993	Sherry Davis is first woman to be a public address announcer at a Major League Baseball game; an obsessive fan of Steffi Graf jumps from the stands during a tennis tournament in Germany and stabs Monica Seles, ranked number one in the world at the time.
1994	The all-female Colorado Silver Bullets plays men's baseball teams; Major League Baseball season is canceled with seven weeks remaining as players start a 232-day strike opposing the owners' proposed team salary cap; Tonya Harding is banned for life from official figure skating events for conspiring to injure Nancy Kerrigan, her chief opponent at the Winter Olympics in Lillehammer, Norway.
1995	Julie Croteau is the first female assistant coach in men's collegiate division I baseball; 8,200 athletes participate in the fifth annual National Senior Games; 7,000 athletes from 143 countries compete at ninth Special Olympics World Summer Games; Native Americans protest use of their names and images as the Atlanta "Braves" and Cleveland "Indians" play in the World Series.
1996	Tiger Woods is the first golfer to win three consecutive U.S. amateur titles and is named PGA Tour Rookie of the Year; Karrie Webb is the first women to win more than a million dollars in one golf season; the Olympic Games are held in Atlanta, Georgia; boxer Christy Martin retains her women's boxing world title by defeating Deirdre Gogarty in a nationally televised bout.
1997	Jan Ullrich of Germany wins the Tour de France and admits in 2007 that he used performance-enhancing substances in 1997; Tiger Woods becomes first golfer with known African American ancestry to win the Masters golf tournament.
1998	Mark McGuire and Sammy Sosa hit 70 and 66 home runs, respectively, breaking a record set in 1961 (Roger Maris); McGuire admits taking androstenedione, a muscle builder that was legal in 1998; the NBA owners lock out players, cancelling over one-third of the season; the Winter Olympic Games are held in Nogano, Japan; the Fifth Gay Games are held in Amsterdam, The Netherlands.
1999	The U.S. Women's National Soccer Team wins the World Cup by defeating China before the largest crowd (90,185) ever to watch a women's sport event; Venus and Serena Williams are the first sisters since 1884 to meet in the finals of a major tennis tournament and Serena is the first black women to win the U.S. Open since it was done by Althea Gibson in 1958; the IOC investigates the Salt Lake City Olympic Organizing Committee for allegedly bribing IOC members while seeking to be named host city for the 2002 Winter Olympic Games.*

*Struggles and changes since 1999 are recent events rather than history, and they're covered in the following chapters.

Struggles over Organization: Can We Play without Managers, Coaches, and Referees?

Since 1920 there has been a clear trend toward organizing sports in formal and "official" ways. Mainstream sports are increasingly organized around standardized rules enforced by official governing bodies. Some people have resisted increased organization and rationalization, but resistance has not slowed or reversed this trend. Even many alternative and recreational sports have become increasingly organized as people try to make them safer, more accessible, or more commercially profitable.

Hundreds of sport organizations have come and gone over recent years, but the emphasis on organization has become increasingly prevalent.

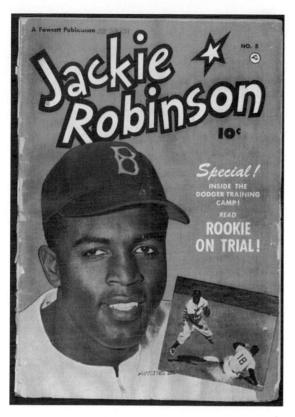

This is the cover of a Jackie Robinson comic book published in 1951. The headline, "Rookie on Trial," indicated that Robinson's performance in baseball was evaluated in connection with issues of racial desegregation in sports. Many others who have been "firsts" in their sport have felt the pressure that Robinson endured. (*Source:* American Memory Collection)

This is connected with classic and sometimes bitter struggles over who controls sports and the management strategies that should be used to maintain organizational consistency over time. In the process, governing bodies, coaches, and other officials have become key participants in an sports. In fact, many children today grow up thinking that sports cannot exist without coaches, referees, and sponsors, and this partially explains why sport management has become a popular major on many college campuses.

Struggles over Who Plays Sports: Does Everyone Play?

The most contentious struggles since the 1920s have revolved around participation in mainstream organized sports. Most sports were initially organized around various forms of exclusion and segregation based on race, ethnicity, gender, age, and (dis)ability. For example, men from relatively well-to-do white families have consistently had the greatest access to sport participation opportunities throughout their lives.

There have been constant struggles to expand participation opportunities for women, people from low-income neighborhoods, certain ethnic minorities, people with physical and intellectual disabilities, and people labeled as gay or lesbian. Each of these struggles has a complex history, but the general trend between 1920 and the early 1980s was to make participation more available. In some cases this was mandated when sports were funded by public money and played in public facilities.

Private clubs and organizations often maintained exclusionary membership criteria over the years, and many continue to do so today. Increased privatization since the 1980s has made it more financially difficult to initiate or maintain regular sport participation for marginalized populations, meaning that sports may be characterized by various forms of exclusion and segregation long into the future.

Struggles over the conditions of sport participation have also been widespread, and they've been complicated by the diversity of goals among those wishing to play. People in some marginalized social categories have fought to be fully integrated into mainstream organized sport programs, whereas others have fought to have separate opportunities that meet their specific needs and interests. For instance, not everyone wishes to play sports developed and organized around the interests and experiences of young, able-bodied, white, heterosexual males. Those who want alternatives to such sports often find it very difficult to rally support and funding for what they want.

Struggles over the conditions of sport partici-pation have also occurred as professional athletes have formed players' associations and bargained with team owners and leagues about the rights of players and the rules of their sports. College students have struggled to gain funding for club teams and gain access to the facilities they need to practice and play games. Many struggles since 1920 have occurred over issues of eligibility, the allocation of rewards to athletes, and the fund-ing of new or alternative sport participation opportunities. These continue today as people determine the conditions of sport participation in programs at all levels of competition.

Struggles over Sponsorships: Should Communities or Corporations Fund Sports?

Struggles over sponsorship issues are not listed among time line items in Table 3.2, but they have occurred regularly. For example, the Great Depression of the 1930s disrupted public and private sponsorships of many sports. However, as officials at all levels of government developed policies and programs to help people cope with the consequences of the depression, certain sport programs received public funding, espe-cially those for children and young people. After World War II, most American communities embraced the idea that tax money should be used to provide a range of sport participation oppor-tunities, especially for boys and young men.

As antitax sentiments became strong and cor-porate power grew rapidly during the 1980s, there was a significant shift in sponsorship patterns. After more than thirty years of consis-tent sponsorship by government agencies, sport programs began to lose public funding through the 80s. Some programs disappeared immedi-ately, others faded away, and others gained new funding from private and corporate sponsors. In recent years sport teams and organizations have increasingly sought corporate sponsors. In the process, corporations now influence the types of sports that enjoy popularity and who has oppor-tunities to play them.

ON THE *OLC*:
See the OLC—Additional Readings for Chapter 3—for the author's discussion of neo-liberal culture and sports.

As the twentieth century ended, many sports and sport programs were funded primarily to foster the interests of corporate sponsors. This created further struggles when sponsors were promoting the consumption of tobacco, alcohol, fast foods, products made in sweatshops, and ser-vices defined by some people as immoral, such as gambling, strip clubs, and escort services. These struggles have continued as people have cho-sen to play and watch sports that require large amounts of capital, but have not approved taxes to fund public sports and sport facilities. For example, community residents have approved taxes and bond issues to build $600-million sta-diums used by professional teams, whereas tax measures to use $600 million to build sixty state-of-the-art public recreation facilities around a city never make it to the ballot. Opposition to these trends has usually occurred on an individ-ual level as people use personal resources to seek alternatives to costly mainstream sports.

When we view sports from a global perspec-tive, it becomes clear that corporate sponsors support and promote the sports that attract people to consume their products and ser-vices. Sports that don't boost the bottom line of corporations are not sponsored, and those that do often receive the media coverage they need to grow and prosper. Although we don't yet under-stand all the dynamics and consequences of this form of sponsorship, it appears that they create greater similarities in the sports played by people across diverse cultures. As we assess this historical fact, we should not take it to mean that sports are evolving to fit a grand scheme for how physical activities *should* be organized or what they *should* mean in people's lives (Maguire, 1999). Instead, it likely means that large global corporations now have the power to define, organize, and present

The suburbanization that occurred after World War II through the 1960s was accompanied by the growth of youth sports for white boys and cheerleading for white girls. In this context, women who played sports during these years were often labeled as "dykes"; boys were often referred to as "sluggers." (*Source:* McGraw-Hill)

through the media particular sport forms for the entire world to see and to consider playing.

USING HISTORY TO THINK ABOUT THE FUTURE

As we study the past, we learn that struggles over the meaning, purpose, and organization of sports always occur in particular social, political, and economic contexts. Sports history does not just happen; it emerges in connection with the actions of people working with one another to construct sports to match their visions of what sports could and should be in their lives. The challenge, of course, has always been to develop the resources needed to realize particular visions.

Many people in recent history have ignored what others say is practical or realistic and pursued choices based on idealistic notions of what sports could be. On the one hand, some of these people have created a pervasive commercial sport culture that emphasizes entertainment and revenue production. On the other hand, there are people who have worked to bring about racial desegregation in sports, new opportunities for girls and women, new programs for people with disabilities, and the recognition and acceptance of gay and lesbian athletes. All these histories are worth knowing as we make decisions about what we want sports to be. Those decisions and the actions we take will create the sport histories of the future.

Historical and cultural variations in physical activities and games remind us that all cultural practices, even sports, serve a variety of social purposes. Because people create sport activities within the constraints of the social worlds in which they live, those with the most power generally have the greatest impact on how sports are defined, organized, and played. Sport activities do not totally reflect their desires, but they represent the interests of the powerful more than they represent the interests of others.

summary

CAN WE USE HISTORY TO UNDERSTAND SPORTS TODAY?

This selective overview of various sports histories shows us that physical activities and all forms of sports are integrally related to the social contexts in which they exist. Social and cultural changes, as well as shifts in who has power in a social world, influence the meaning, purpose, and organization of sports.

Games and contests in ancient Greece were grounded in mythology and religious beliefs. They revolved around the interests of able-bodied young men from wealthy segments of Greek city–states. As the outcomes of organized sports, such as the games at Olympia, took on political and social importance, male slaves and low-status workers were recruited, trained, and paid to be athletes. The existence of professional athletes, violence, and an emphasis on victory shows us a side of ancient Greek sports that contradicts popular beliefs and ideas promoted in connection with the modern Olympics. It also demonstrates that sports are seldom constructed to equally represent the interests and well-being of every category of people in a social world.

Roman contests and games emphasized mass entertainment. They were designed to celebrate and preserve the power of political leaders and pacify masses of unemployed and underemployed citizens in Roman cities and towns. Many athletes in Roman events were slaves or "troublemakers" coerced into battle with one another or wild animals. These spectacles faded with the demise of the Roman Empire. Critically assessing sports in Roman history makes us more aware of the interests that powerful people often have in sponsoring and promoting large spectator events.

Folk games and tournaments in medieval times clearly reflected and reproduced gender and social-class differences throughout Europe. Peasants played local versions of folk games in connection with seasonal events in village life. Knights and nobles engaged in tournaments and jousts, whereas other men in the upper class used their property and resources to develop and play various sports activities to occupy their leisure time. Studying the history of sports in medieval Europe shows us that gender and class relations had a major impact on sports and who played them.

Patterns from the medieval period continued through the Renaissance in Europe. However, the Protestant Reformation gave rise to negative attitudes toward any activities that interfered with work and religious worship. Peasants were affected most by these attitudes because they did not have the resources to resist the restrictive controls imposed by government officials who enforced Calvinist or Puritan rules. The games and sports of the wealthy generally occurred in the safe confines of their private grounds, so they could avoid most government restrictions.

The Enlightenment was associated with increased political rights and freedom to engage in diversionary games and physical activities. The men who combined highly developed sport skills with education and general cultural refinement during this period have subsequently been described as "Renaissance men," meaning that they embodied the ideal values of that time in European history.

Studying medieval Europe and the subsequent periods of Reformation and Enlightenment shows us how cultural ideology, power relations, and government policies influence who plays sports under particular conditions.

During the early days of the Industrial Revolution, the influence of the Puritans faded in Europe and North America, but the demands of work and the absence of spaces for play generally limited sport participation to wealthy people and certain rural residents.

This pattern began to change in the United States between the late 1800s and 1920. The combined influence of labor unions, progressive legislation, and economic expansion led to the creation of new ideas about sports, the consequences of sport participation, and who was best suited by nature to play sports. This meant that new sport programs and opportunities for involvement were strongly influenced by race, class, and gender ideologies and the needs of an economy dependent on mass production and consumption. It was in this context that people developed organized competitive sports. Studying this period shows us that the initial forms of today's sports were influenced by a complex interplay of social, political, and economic factors.

Sports histories since 1920 have revolved around continuing struggles over (1) the meaning, purpose, and organization of sports, (2) who participates in sports and the conditions of their participation, and (3) who sponsors sports and why. These struggles have occurred in connection with major historical events, trends, and changes. In most cases, powerful economic and political interests have prevailed in these struggles, but in some cases, people motivated by idealistic visions of what sports could and should be have prevailed. Every now and then, the visions of idealists have become realities.

Struggles over these three issues never end. Sports are never as everyone wants them to be. Being aware of this fact, along with past struggles, enables us to develop a deeper understanding of sports in our time and place.

WEBSITE RESOURCES

Note: Websites often change. The following URLs were current when this book was printed. Please check our website (www.mhhe.com/coakley10e) for updates and additions.

www.aagpbl.org/   Site of the All-American Girls Professional Baseball League; articles, photographs, interviews, and statistics on women's professional baseball from 1943 through 1954; this material inspired the feature film, *A League of Their Own.*

http://afroamhistory.about.com/od/athletes/Black _Athletes.htm   Links to biographies of African American athletes who have broken records, won medals, and excelled in sports.

http://archives.cbc.ca/IDC-1-41-1363-8434/sports/ paralympics/clip1   Information and video on "rehabilitation through sport"; explanation of the Stoke Mandeville Games and the origins of the Paralympics.

www.deaflympics.com/   Official site of the Deaflympics, established in 1924 as The Silent Games; this was the first international competitions for athletes with disabilities.

http://depthome.brooklyn.cuny.edu/classics/gladiatr/ index.htm   This site was developed by Roger Dunkle, an expert on Roman sports; excellent information and visuals related to the spectacles in which gladiators participated.

www.liu.edu/cwis/cwp/library/aaitsa.htm   An exhibit with histories of boxing, horse racing, cycling, track and field, baseball, basketball, and football, and the role the African American played in them; histories of key black athletes are provided.

www.melazerte.com/library/paralympics/chapter2 .htm   Excerpt from *Paralympics: Where Heroes Come*, by Dr. Robert Steadward and Cynthia Peterson (Edmonton, Alberta: One Shot Holdings Ltd., 1997); basic information on the origins of the Paralympics.

www.nassh.org   Site of the North American Society for Sport History; links to news, directory of scholars, publications, conferences, and other helpful sources.

www.salisbury.edu/seniorgames/NSGA%20History .htm   Site of the National Senior Games Association; formed in 1985, and it has had an interesting history since then.

www.sover.net/~spectrum/index.html   Site of the American Soccer History Archives; excellent information about the histories of both men's and women's soccer in the United States; links to articles and other sources.

www.studies.org/id70.html, www.studies.org/catalog/ i29.html, and www.studies.org/catalog/i22.html The Institute for Mediterranean Studies; site summarizes information and sells videotapes on the Olympic Games in ancient Greece and gladiator sports during the time of the Roman Empire.

www.zen20110.zen.co.uk/SportHistWeb/ SPORTS%20HISTORY/ISHPES/Conferences/ ishpes2.htm   Site for the International Society for the History of Physical Education and Sport; provides links to many other sites for sports history associations, journals, and scholarly resources.

(Jay Coakley)

SPORTS AND SOCIALIZATION

Who Plays and What Happens to Them?

Sport has influenced the path my life has taken . . .
Going into the field in Africa brought home
the reality that many children do not have the
opportunity to engage in sport or to play. I had
[mistakenly] believed that these benefits were
available to every child . . . Play is not a luxury; it
is an essential element to a child's development.

**—Silken Laumann, Right To Play Athlete
Ambassador and three-time Olympic Medalist
(2006a, 2006b)**

OLC Visit *Sports in Society*'s Online Learning Center (OLC) at www.mhhe.com/coakley10e for additional information and study material for this chapter, including the following:

- A complete chapter outline
- Learning objectives
- Practice quizzes
- Internet resources
- Related readings
- Essays
- Student projects

MANAGING PLAYER CONDUCT is the single biggest challenge American professional sports leagues face . . .

—**Robert Boland, Sports Management Department, New York University (2008)**

WHEN THEY DIDN'T HAVE any more baseball to play, it's like they got stuck. They didn't have the first idea of what to do with themselves [outside of sports].

—**Former major league baseball player about retired teammates (in Sokolove, 2004)**

IT WAS THROUGH SKATEBOARDING that I received my education in life. . . . I had so little confidence and self-esteem. I just felt lucky to have found something . . . that I was good at. . . . I'm not sure where I'd be without skateboarding.

—**Stacy Peralta, former skateboarder, producer of** *Dogtown and Z-boys* **(in Geffner, 2002)**

Whenever we discuss why people play sports, why they change or stop playing sports, and what happens to them because they play sports, in each case we deal with the process of learning and development that sociologists call socialization.

For nearly fifty years, people in the sociology of sport have done research to learn about three topics that are central to most discussions of sports and socialization:

1. The process of becoming involved and staying involved in sports
2. The process of changing or ending sport participation
3. The impact of being involved in sports

This chapter is organized around research on these topics. As you read, you'll see that we've learned much about socialization and sports, but our understanding remains incomplete. Some of what we've learned is so complex that the discussions carry over to Chapters 5 to 16.

The chapter closes with information about new types of research on socialization. This research is guided by cultural theories and a critical approach, and it focuses on socialization as a community and cultural process affecting many people at once.

WHAT IS SOCIALIZATION?

Socialization *is a process of learning and social development, which occurs as we interact with one another and become familiar with the social world in which we live.* It involves the formation of ideas about who we are and what is important in our lives. We are *not* simply passive learners in the socialization process. We actively participate in our own socialization as we form relationships and influence those who influence us. We actively interpret what we see and hear, and we accept, resist, and revise the messages that we receive about who we are and how we're connected with social worlds. Therefore, socialization is *not* a one-way process of social

influence through which we are molded and shaped. Instead, it is an interactive process through which we actively connect with others, synthesize information, and *make decisions* that influence our own lives and the social worlds in which we participate. These decisions, however, are often made in contexts out of our control; therefore, the decision-making options available to each of us vary depending on social circumstances. Additionally, some people are in better positions than others to control their options and the consequences of their decisions.

This definition of *socialization* is based on a *social interaction model* organized around a combination of cultural, interactionist, and structural theories. It leads researchers to assume that processes of social learning and development occur through social interaction, and that interaction is the basis for creating and maintaining the organization of our social worlds and the cultural framework that we use to give it meaning. For example, as children interact with their parents, family members, and peers, they learn to give meaning to the pain that comes with the bumps, bruises, and cuts caused by falling and crashing into things. However, if they play organized sports, their interaction with coaches, teammates, and even doctors often leads them to redefine pain and give new meanings to the bumps, bruises, and cuts that cause it. In fact, it may even lead them to define pain as a normal consequence of playing sports and to define sports injuries as symbols of their commitment to a team and their identity as an athlete. In this sense, socialization is a powerful and influential process.

The social interaction model is widely accepted today, but research done prior to the

ON THE *OLC*:
See the OLC—Additional Readings for Chapter 4—for Coakley's summary essay on socialization and sports.

1980s was often based on a *personal internalization model* of socialization. This model is based on structural theories that led researchers to assume that social learning occurs when people internalize the rules of society as they grow up in families, attend school, interact with peers, and receive images and messages through the media. Also assumed was that people learned to play the roles that kept a society operating efficiently. This theoretical approach inspired many studies of socialization, but its emphasis on socialization as a one-way learning process limited their accuracy and usefulness.

Most studies based on the personal internalization model produced inconsistent and contradictory findings about why people play sports, why they stop, and what happens to them as they play. However, some of the more recent studies using this model have been so carefully designed and use such good quantitative data from large, representative samples that they've provided detailed statistical analyses of the complex connections between sport participation and other aspects of people's lives (Curtis, McTeer, and White, 2003; Guest and Schneider, 2003; Loveless, 2002; Marsh and Kleitman, 2003; Miller et al., 1999; President's Council on Physical Fitness and Sports, 1997; Sabo et al., 1998, 2005; Spreitzer, 1995; Tracy and Erkut, 2002; Videon, 2002). The findings in these studies are useful because they identify general patterns in sport participation through the life course, the barriers that prevent or discourage some people from playing sports, and connections between sport participation and educational achievement, occupational success, sexual behavior and pregnancy rates, health and wellness, and general self-esteem. These patterns are discussed through this chapter.

Most current studies of sports and socialization are based on a social interaction model and use qualitative rather than quantitative research methods. Instead of using polls, surveys, or other quantitative methods that provide snapshots of people's lives, they use in-depth interviews and field observations to study smaller collections of people over time so they can provide continuous videos rather than single snapshots. Their goal is to obtain detailed descriptions of sport experiences as they occur in people's lives and then analyze the processes through which people make decisions about sport participation and give meaning to sport experiences. Finally, they seek to connect those decisions and meanings with the cultural and structural contexts in which sports and sport participation exist. This approach captures the complexity of the processes through which people become and stay involved in sports, change or end sport participation, and incorporate sports into their lives. The rest of this chapter uses both past and current research findings—the snapshots and the videos—to explain what we know about sports and socialization today.

"I know this is starting early, but I can't let him get too far behind the other kids if he's going to succeed in life."

Research guided by structural theories focused on who influences the sport participation patterns of children. Fathers and other family members are usually identified as *significant others* who influence when, how, and where children play sports.

BECOMING AND STAYING INVOLVED IN SPORTS

Carefully designed studies based on structural theories and a personal internalization model of socialization have found that sport participation is related to three factors: (1) a person's abilities, characteristics, and resources; (2) the influence of significant others, including parents, siblings, teachers, peers, and role models; and (3) the availability of opportunities to play sports in ways that are personally satisfying. These are the snapshot research findings that help us explain how and why people become involved and stay involved in sports. However, a more complete explanation is provided by detailed stories from people about their sport participation. When these stories are collected in research that is based on a social interaction model, they provide socialization videos rather than snapshots.

Studies using in-depth interviews, fieldwork, participant observation, and strategic conversations indicate that sport participation is connected to multiple and diverse processes that make up people's lives, and it occurs as people interact with others and make decisions based on available opportunities and the meanings they give to sports in connection with what they want to happen in their lives. These decisions and meanings are not permanent and often change as social conditions and relationships change. Furthermore, as people stay involved in sports, their reasons for participating usually change over time. When there are no reasons, they discontinue or change their sport participation—until things change again and there are new reasons to become re-involved.

Current knowledge about the processes through which people become and stay involved in sports has been produced through multiple studies across various populations of people in different situations. The most effective way to learn what we know about socialization is to review a few studies that highlight key aspects of these processes. The following summaries provide three sociological videos illustrating processes of becoming and staying involved in sports.

Example 1: The Process of Becoming an Elite Athlete

Chris Stevenson is a sport sociologist interested in how people become elite athletes. Using a social interaction model of socialization to guide his research, he interviewed and collected stories from elite athletes about how they were introduced to sports and became committed to sport participation. As he analyzed the stories, he noticed that they sounded much like descriptions of careers. In other words, they had identifiable beginnings, followed by a process of development, and ultimately an end. Stevenson felt that he could understand these careers in terms of the decisions that people made about sport participation and how those decisions were related to opportunities, developmental issues, and important relationships in their lives.

In one of his studies, Stevenson (1999) interviewed twenty-nine international athletes from England and Canada. At first, he was struck by the diversity of the stories the athletes told him, but as he analyzed them, he identified two processes experienced by nearly all the athletes.

First, there was a process of *introduction and involvement*, during which young people received support as they tried certain sports. His interviewees talked about being introduced to sports bit-by-bit over time as they interacted with important people in their lives. Gradually, they chose to specialize in a particular sport based on an evaluation of their potential for success and their sense of being personally connected with the people associated with the sport.

Second, there was a process of *developing a commitment* to sport participation. This process occurred as the athletes formed a web of personal relationships connected with their participation and established personal reputations and identities as athletes in their sports. Relationships and identities figured prominently in how they set priorities and made decisions about sport participation.

Staying involved depended on active and thoughtful efforts to develop their identities as athletes. This occurred as people who were important in their lives recognized and defined them as athletes. Over time, this social recognition supported deeper commitment to their sports and their lives as athletes.

Stevenson found that these processes did *not* occur automatically. The young people themselves helped them happen. Becoming and staying involved in sports was a complex process. The young people realized that they could not take for granted the social support they received for playing sports or the continued reaffirmation of their identities as athletes. They knew that the resources needed for participation could disappear and that changes in their lives could force them to alter the importance they gave to sport participation. Therefore, deciding to stay involved in sports was

a continuous process linked to relationships with those who supported and influenced them.

Stevenson's research shows that the socialization process is *interactive* and that each of us participates in our own socialization as we make decisions, become committed to particular identities, and express that commitment as we interact with those whose support we need. Additional research shows that the interactional contexts in which these decisions are made are influenced by structural and cultural factors. Structural factors include the availability of sport facilities, equipment, financial support, coaching, and competition opportunities (Houlihan and Green, 2007). Cultural factors include the importance given to particular sports in a social world and to the ways that one's age, gender, race, ethnicity, sexuality, and (dis)ability influence the meaning of being an athlete. For example, few boys in China play

Participation in sports is usually sponsored through important social relationships. This boy's participation in basketball is likely to be influenced by his father, an *agent of socialization* and a *significant other* in his life. However, continued participation also requires commitment to the sport, receiving material and emotional support, and establishing social relationships that support an identity related to basketball. (*Source:* McGraw-Hill)

competitive sports because the one-child policy enforced by the government leads parents to organize their sons' lives around school, home-work, and learning skills that will qualify him to be accepted into a university and then find a good job so he can support them when they become old. Consequently, boys spend seventy or more hours per week doing sedentary intel-lectual activities and have no time to be physi-cally active or play sports (Ying, 2007).

Example 2: The Process of Being Accepted as an Athlete

Peter Donnelly and Kevin Young are sociolo-gists who have studied sports as social worlds in which people form relationships and unique ways of life organized around shared interests. One of their studies focused on the process through which people became accepted members of the cultures organized around particular sports. Therefore, they've taken a closer look at some of the processes studied by Stevenson (Donnelly and Young, 1999).

Using data that Donnelly collected from expert rock climbers and Young collected from elite rugby players, they concluded that playing sports occurs in connection with complex pro-cesses of identity formation. They explained that becoming an athlete in a particular sport culture occurs through a four-phase process:

1. Acquiring knowledge about the sport
2. Interacting with people involved in the sport
3. Learning how participation occurs and what people in the sport expect from each other as athletes
4. Becoming recognized and fully accepted as an athlete in the sport culture

This finding shows that becoming involved in a sport depends on learning to "talk the talk and walk the walk" so that one is identified and accepted as an athlete *by other athletes*. This process of identification and acceptance is con-tinuous; it doesn't happen once and for all time.

When athletes can no longer talk the talk and walk the walk, interaction with other athletes declines, and support for their identity fades away. Membership in a sport culture is always temporary; it depends on what you do today, not what you did in the past.

To understand Donnelly and Young's find-ings, observe skateboarders, in-line skaters, snowboarders, beach volleyball players, basket-ball players, or members of any sport culture. Each culture has a unique vocabulary, its own way of referring to its members and what they do, unique ways of thinking about and doing their sports, and special understandings of what they expect from each other. New participants are tested and "pushed" by the "veterans" before being accepted as true skaters, riders, board-ers, volleyball players, or ballers. Vocabularies may change over time, but the process of being accepted as an athlete exists in all sport cultures.

Donnelly and Young help us understand that becoming and staying involved in a sport often depends on establishing social connections, being accepted in a sport culture, and receiving social support for the formation of an athlete identity. This finding helps to explain, for example, why there are so few girls and women in alternative sport cultures. Boys and men have defined rid-ing on a board, whether it is down a mountain, a wave, or a sidewalk curb as an activity that con-veys a valued form of masculinity (M. Donnelly, 2006; Rinehart, 2005). In the process, they create cultures that make it nearly impossible for girls and women to be accepted as authentic "board athletes." In other words, becoming and staying involved in sports is a complex, *interactive* social-ization and *identity formation* process.

Example 3: To Participate or Not to Participate

When I worked at the University of Chiches-ter in England, my colleague Anita White and I received a grant from a regional department of Sport England to study why most young people did not participate in a highly publicized, state-sponsored sport program. We designed a study in which we used in-depth interviews to explore how British adolescents in a working-class area east of London made decisions about what they did in their free time (Coakley and White, 1999).

> **OLC** **ON THE *OLC*:**
> See the OLC—Additional Readings for Chapter 4—for a link to the article on making decisions about sport participation by Coakley and White.

Data from our interviews indicated that the young people took a combination of factors into account as they made decisions about sport participation. These factors included the following:

1. Their ideas about the connection between sport participation and other interests and goals in their lives
2. Their desires to develop and display competence so they could gain recognition and respect from others
3. Social support for participation plus access to the resources needed for participation (time, transportation, equipment, and money)
4. Memories of past experiences with physical activities and sports
5. Sport-related images and meanings that were part of their social worlds

Overall, the young people decided to play sports when it helped them extend control over their lives, achieve development and career goals, and present themselves to others as competent. We also found that young women were less likely than young men to imagine that they could accomplish those things by playing sports. Therefore, the young women took sports less seriously and chose to participate less often.

The young people in our study made their decisions by determining if sport participation

would add something positive to their lives. They didn't passively respond to the world around them, and their decisions and sport participation patterns shifted over time, depending on access to opportunities, available resources, and changes in their identities. Therefore, socialization into sports was a *continuous, interactive process* grounded in the social and cultural contexts in which they lived.

Our study also found that people make decisions to participate in sports for different reasons at different points in their lives. This is consistent with theories stating that personal growth depends on accomplishing developmental tasks associated with various stages of childhood, adolescence, young adulthood, and adulthood. Therefore, the issues considered by seven-year-olds making decisions about sport participation differ from the issues considered by fourteen-year-olds, forty-year-olds, and sixty-year-olds (Porterfield, 1999; Stevenson, 2002). Furthermore, when seven-year-olds make decisions about sport participation today, they do so in different social and cultural contexts than the contexts in which seven-year-olds lived in 1970 or will live in 2020.

After analyzing our interview data, it was clear to Anita and me that sport participation decisions among these young people were clearly tied to their perceptions of the cultural importance of sports and the links between playing sports, gaining social acceptance, and achieving personal goals. Therefore, as we study why people become and stay involved in sports, we should take into account people's perceptions of how sport participation is related to their growth and development, how sports are integrated into their social worlds, and the extent to which participation is supported by widely accepted ideologies in their culture (Ingham et al., 1999).

I was recently reminded of these points when I read that some parents in Ethiopia now accept competitive running as a way for their daughters to achieve financial success. This change enabled many girls to take up running as a strategy to stay in school, avoid an arranged marriage (as a young teen), and seek a life that consists of more than washing laundry, preparing food, and obeying a husband who is likely to define her as a form of property (Wax, 2005). Running, for those girls lucky enough to be identified as talented, opens up developmental opportunities, gives them more control over their lives, and enables them to claim their bodies as their own. This is why thirteen-year-old Ethiopian girls are more likely to define running as an attractive activity than thirteen-year-old girls living in air-conditioned homes in a gated neighborhood in Beverly Hills, California—the context and consequences of their decisions are much different.

In summary, these three studies provide complementary videos about the process of becoming and staying involved in sports. They show that sport participation is grounded in decisions influenced by self-reflection, social support, social acceptance, and cultural factors. People don't make decisions about sport participation once and for all time; they make them day after day as they consider how sports are related to their lives. These decisions are made in particular social and cultural contexts and they are influenced by the meanings attached to gender, class, skin color, ethnicity, age, and physical (dis)abilities. None of us enters or plays sports in a vacuum.

CHANGING OR ENDING SPORT PARTICIPATION

Questions about becoming and staying involved in sports are usually accompanied by questions about changing or ending involvement. Much of the early research on this latter issue was guided by structural theories and an internalization model of socialization. Studies done between 1950 and 1980 were often designed to identify young people who dropped out of organized sport programs and then identify strategies to keep others from doing the same thing.

This topic was popular during these years because millions of baby boomer children

flooded playgrounds and primary schools, and parents thought that playing organized sports would build their character and teach them American values. At the same time, many coaches and others wanted to know how to develop elite sport skills among children and prepare them for higher levels of competition. There also were social critics and activists who did research to determine if rigidly organized, win-oriented programs turned children off to sport participation and exploited elite athletes in ways that left them unprepared for life after sport.

The carefully designed studies done during this time contributed the following to our knowledge of changing and ending sport participation:

- When people drop out of a particular sport, they don't drop out of all sports forever, nor do they cut all ties with sports.
- Many people play different and less-competitive sports as they become older, or they move into other sport roles such as coach, administrator, or sports businessperson.
- Dropping out of sports is usually connected with developmental changes and transitions in the rest of a person's life—changing schools, graduating, getting a job, getting married, having children, and so on.
- Dropping out of sports is not always the result of negative experiences, although injuries, exploitation, poor coaching, and abuse from coaches do influence some decisions to change or end participation.
- Problems may occur for those who end long careers in sports, especially those who have no identities apart from sports or lack social and material resources for making transitions into other careers and relationships.

Recent studies, especially those using qualitative research methods and a social interactionist model of socialization, have built on these findings and extended our understanding of the process of changing or ending sport participation. The following summaries of three studies are representative of this research.

Although people may drop out of sports at one point in the life course, they may return at a later point. This team of women, all over seventy years old, is playing an exhibition game against a group of younger women. The team is raising funds to travel to the national finals in the Senior Games. Most of these older women had not played competitive basketball for 30 to 50 years. (*Source:* Jay Coakley)

Example 1: Burnout Among Young Athletes

My work with coaches and my interest in identity issues led me to study young people who decided to quit sport at a time when they were experiencing great success, often as age-group champions in their sports (Coakley, 1992). People described these young people as "burned out," so I decided

OLC **ON THE OLC:**
See the OLC—Additional Readings for Chapter 4—for a link to the author's article on burnout among adolescents.

to interview former elite adolescent athletes who were identified as cases of burnout.

Data collected through in-depth interviews indicated that burnout during adolescence was grounded in the organization and authority structure of many high-performance sports for young people. It occurred when young athletes felt they no longer had control over their lives and could not explore, develop, and nurture identities apart from sports. This led to increased stress and decreased fun as they did their sports. Burnout occurred when stress became so high and fun declined so much that they no longer felt that continued participation was worth their effort.

The data also indicated that stress increased and fun decreased when sport programs were organized so that successful young athletes felt that they could not accomplish important developmental tasks during adolescence. My conclusion was that burnout could be prevented only if sport programs were reorganized so that young athletes had more control over their lives. Stress management strategies might delay burnout, but they would not change the underlying organizational and development barriers that caused burnout. Overall, my study led me to conclude that young people sometimes end sport participation during late adolescence when they feel that their career in sport prevents them from developing the autonomy and the multiple identities necessary to effectively claim adult status in U.S. culture.[1]

Example 2: Getting out of Sports and Getting on with Life

Konstantinos Koukouris (1994) is a physical educator from Greece who wanted to know why seriously committed athletes ended or reduced their sport participation. After analyzing questionnaire data from 157 former national athletes, Koukouris identified 34 who had ceased or reduced sport participation between the ages of eighteen and twenty-four. In-depth interviews with these people enabled him to identify patterns in the disengagement process.

His data indicated that ending or reducing sport participation was a voluntary decision among these athletes. But this decision was often part of a process during which they stopped playing and then started again more than once. In other words, they hadn't gone "cold turkey" as they withdrew from sport. Their decisions were usually associated with two practical factors: (1) the need to obtain a job and support themselves and (2) realistic judgments about their sport skills and the chances of

advancing to higher levels of competition. As they graduated from high school or college, the athletes faced the expectation that they should work and be responsible for their livelihoods. But jobs interfered with the time needed to train and play sports at an elite level. Furthermore, as they spent money to establish adult lifestyles, there was little left to pay for serious training. At the same time, their demanding training programs conflicted with their new adult lives.

When they ended serious training, many of these young adults sought other ways to be physically active or involved in sports. Some encountered problems, but most of them grew and developed in positive ways, much like their peers who had never played elite sports. Most of the former athletes perceived the end of their serious training and competition as an inevitable, necessary, and usually beneficial developmental change in their lives.

Example 3: Changing Personal Investments in Sport Careers

Garry Wheeler, from the University of Alberta, is concerned with the careers of athletes with disabilities and what happens when their playing careers end. Building on a previous study (Wheeler et al., 1996) of Paralympic athletes, Wheeler and his fellow researchers interviewed forty athletes from the United Kingdom, Canada, Israel, and the United States (Wheeler et al., 1999). The data indicated that athletes in each of these countries became deeply involved in sports and often achieved a high level of success in a relatively short time. Through sports they developed a sense of personal competence and established identities as elite athletes.

Ending active sport participation and making the transition into other spheres of life often presented challenges for these athletes. Retirement generally came suddenly and forced them to reinvest time and energy into other activities and relationships. As they reconnected with family members and friends, returned to school, and

---

[1]Burnout is studied more by psychologists than sociologists. Psychological research on burnout in sport is summarized in Cresswell and Eklund (2007); Goodger et al. (2007), and Gustafsson et al. (2007).

Many factors influence the decisions to drop out of sports or shift participation from one sport to another. Identity changes, access to resources, and life course issues are involved. As our circumstances change, so do our ideas about ourselves and about sports and sport participation. (*Source:* McGraw-Hill)

resumed occupational careers, some of the former athletes experienced emotional problems. However, most stayed connected with sports and sport organizations as coaches, administrators, or recreational athletes. Those few who hoped to regain their elite athlete status usually experienced difficulties during the retirement transition, whereas those who accepted the end of their competitive careers had fewer adjustment problems.

In summary, research shows that ending or changing sport participation often involves the same interactive and decision-making processes that occur as a person becomes and stays involved in sports. Just as people are not socialized into sports according to some formula, neither are they simply socialized out of sports according to a formula. Changes in participation are often the result of decisions associated with other life events, social relationships, and

cultural expectations related to development. This means that theories explaining why people play sports and change their participation over time must take into account identity issues and developmental processes that are part of the social and cultural contexts in which people make decisions about sports in their lives (Dacyshyn, 1999; Drahota and Eitzen, 1998; Swain, 1999). Furthermore, theories must take into account the personal, social, and material resources that former athletes possess as they make transitions to other relationships, activities, and careers. When problems occur during this transition, they are associated with the ways the athletes defined their sport identities and the resources they had to negotiate the transitional challenges they faced. Research suggests that if sport participation *expands* a person's identity, experiences, relationships, and resources, changes and retirement transitions are likely to be smooth and relatively problem free. Difficulties are most likely when a person has never had the desire or the chance to live outside the culture of elite sports and learn to negotiate their lives in nonsport social worlds (Messner, 1992; Murphy, Petipas, and Brewer, 1996).

> **OLC** **ON THE *OLC:***
> See the OLC—Additional Readings for Chapter 4—for a link to the author's article on retirement among elite athletes.

BEING INVOLVED IN SPORTS: WHAT HAPPENS?

Beliefs about the consequences of sport participation vary from culture to culture, but people in many cultures believe that playing sports builds character and improves health and well-being. These beliefs create encouragement for children to play sports, and they lead to support for funding sports programs in schools, building stadiums, promoting teams and leagues, and sponsoring international events such as the Olympic Games, the Paralympics, and world championships.

Do Sports Build Character?

For over a half century, researchers have examined the validity of the belief that "sport builds character." Many studies have compared the traits, attitudes, and behaviors of those who play organized sports with those who don't. These snapshot comparisons usually search for differences between members of U.S. high school varsity teams and students who don't play on varsity teams, but their findings have been inconsistent and confusing. This is because researchers have used inconsistent definitions and measures of *character* in their studies (Stoll and Beller, 1998). Furthermore, many of them have designed their studies around two faulty assumptions

(McCormack and Chalip, 1988). First, they've assumed that *all* athletes have the same or similar experiences in *all* organized competitive sports, and second, they've assumed that organized sports provide unique learning experiences that are not available in other activities. These faulty assumptions have caused researchers to overlook the following important things when they study sports and socialization:

1. Sport participation offers *diverse experiences*, both positive and negative, because sport programs and teams can be organized in vastly different ways. Therefore, we cannot make unqualified general statements about the consequences of sport participation. This point is explained in Reflect on Sports, pages 104–106.
2. People who choose or are selected to play sports often have different traits than those who do not choose or are not selected to play. Therefore, sports may not *build* character as much as they are organized to *select* people who already have certain character traits that are valued by coaches and compatible with highly organized, competitive activities.
3. The meanings given to sport experiences vary from one athlete to another, even when they play in the same programs and on the same teams. Therefore, the lessons that athletes learn and the ways they apply those lessons to their lives vary greatly.
4. As people change and grow older they often alter the meanings they give to their sport experiences and integrate them into their lives in new ways as they develop new ideas and values.
5. Socialization occurs through the social interaction that accompanies sport participation. Therefore, the meaning and importance of playing sports depend on a person's social relationships and the social and cultural contexts in which participation occurs.
6. The socialization that occurs in sports may also occur in other activities. Therefore,

people who do not play sports may have developmental experiences similar to the experiences of athletes.

Due to these oversights, studies that compare "athletes" with "nonathletes" have produced inconsistent and misleading "research results" about sports and socialization. After evaluating these studies, I've concluded that sport participation is most likely to have positive socialization consequences when it provides athletes with the following things:

- Opportunities to explore and develop identities apart from playing sports
- Knowledge-building experiences that go beyond the locker room and playing field
- New relationships, especially with people who are not connected with sports and do not base their interaction on a person's status or identity as an athlete
- Explicit examples of how lessons learned in sports may be applied to specific situations apart from sports
- Opportunities to develop and display competence in nonsport activities that are observed by other people who can serve as mentors and advocates outside sports

Alana Beard, a former all-American basketball player at Duke University, expressed some of these points when she said,

> I've developed a group of friends . . . and they know nothing about basketball. That's the best thing any athlete can do: get friends that don't know anything about your sport and accept you as just another friend and not because you're that basketball player. (Q and A, 2003, p. 28)

My review of past research also suggests that when playing sports *constricts* a person's opportunities, experiences, relationships, and general competence apart from sports, it is likely to have negative consequences for an athlete's overall development. Therefore, we cannot make a general statement that sports build *or* undermine character development. Neither positive nor negative character is automatically developed by playing sports. This is because sport experiences are diverse, and they are given meaning and incorporated into people's lives in various ways, depending on the social and cultural contexts in which they live (Hartmann, 2008; Kidd, 2007).

This conclusion does *not* mean that sports and sport participation are irrelevant in people's lives. We know that discourses, images, and experiences related to sports are vivid and powerful in many social worlds. Sports *do* affect our lives and the world around us. However, we cannot separate those affects from the meanings that we give to sports and how we integrate them into our lives. Therefore, if we want to know what happens in sports, we must study sport experiences in the contexts in which they occur. This type of research is exciting and provides insights into the complex connections between sports and socialization. Unfortunately, the uncritically accepted belief that "sports build character" prevents this research from being taken seriously and undermines research findings concluding that sports build character only under certain conditions. However, people in the sociology of sport continue to critically examine sports to identify the types of experiences most likely to create positive forms of socialization (Coakley, 2007; Donnelly, 2007; Hartmann, 2003b, 2008; Holt, 2007).

Do Sports Improve Health and Physical Well-Being?

An international organization called Sport for Development and Peace recently asked a team of scholars at the University of Toronto to answer this question (SDP/IWG, 2007). After a critical

---

OLC ON THE *OLC:*
See the OLC—Additional Readings for Chapter 4—for the author's discussion of why so many people believe that sports build character.

Power and Performance *versus* Pleasure and Participation
Different Sports, Different Experiences, Different Consequences

Sport experiences are diverse. It's a mistake to assume that all sports are organized around the same goals and orientations, played in the same spirit, or defined in the same way. For example, there are highly organized competitive sports, informal sports, adventure sports, recreational sports, extreme sports, alternative sports, cooperative sports, folk sports, contact sports, artistic sports, team sports, individual sports, and so on. However, at this point in history, the most dominant sport form in wealthy postindustrial nations is organized around a **power and performance model.**

Power and performance sports are highly organized and competitive; they emphasize the following factors:

- Using strength, speed, and power to push human limits and achieve competitive success
- Proving excellence through competitive success and attributing success to dedication, hard work, and sacrifice
- Being willing to risk physical well-being and play with pain
- Exclusive processes through which participants must meet elite performance standards if they wish to be included or continue playing
- A chain of command in which owners and administrators control coaches, and coaches control athletes
- Competing against opponents and defining them as enemies to be conquered

These points exaggerate the characteristics of power and performance sports to show that experiences in these sports are very different from experiences in other sport forms. Although many people use the power and performance model as a standard for defining "real" sports, it is not the only model around which sports are organized. For example, people in many societies often play other forms of sport, including various revisions of, alternatives to, and reactions against dominant sports.

The sport forms most unlike dominant sports today are organized around a **pleasure and participation model,** and they generally emphasize the following factors:

- Active participation that revolves around connections between people, the integration of mind and body, and sustaining the environment
- A spirit of personal expression, enjoyment, growth, good health, and mutual concern among all participants

Power and performance sports involve the use of strength, speed, and power to dominate opponents in the quest for competitive victories. (*Source:* Bob Jackson, *Colorado Springs Gazette*)

Pleasure and participation sports may involve competition, but the primary emphasis is on connections between people and on personal expression through participation. (*Source:* Susanne Tregarthen/Educational Photo Stock)

- Personal empowerment created by experiencing bodily wisdom and pleasure
- Inclusive processes through which participation is encouraged by accommodating (dis)ability differences
- Democratic decision-making structures in which relationships are characterized by cooperation and sharing power
- An emphasis on participating and competing *with* others who are defined as partners in creating and meeting physical challenges

Again, these points exaggerate the characteristics of pleasure and participation sports, but they show that experiences in these sports are very different from experiences in power and participation sports.

These two sport forms do *not* represent all the ways that sports might be organized, played, and defined.

There are sports that contain elements of both forms and reflect diverse ideas about what is important in physical activities. However, power and performance sports remain dominant today in the sense that they receive the most attention, support, and sponsorship. When people play or watch these sports, their socialization experiences are different from their experiences in pleasure and participation sports.

Power and performance sports are dominant today because they foster the interests of people and organizations with the resources to sponsor and stage sport events. History shows that wealthy and influential people in societies around the world have used different strategies to maintain their privileged positions. Some have used coercive strategies such as employing the police and military to maintain their control over resources and people, but most have used cultural strategies that foster the belief that they deserve their wealth and power and that society benefits from their resources.

In countries where wealth and power have been controlled by a monarchy, the privileged position of the royal family is based on the belief that it is their birthright to rule over others. Therefore, kings and queens maintain their privileged positions as long as their "subjects" believe that birthrights represent legitimate claims to wealth and power. This is why the church and state have usually been closely aligned in societies with monarchies—kings and queens use the clergy to promote the belief that their wealth and power are bestowed on them by a divine, supernatural source, such as a god.

In democratic countries, most people use *merit*, or "personal achievement," as a standard when judging whether the possession of wealth and power are legitimate. Therefore, it is only when most people believe that wealth and power are rightfully earned that those who possess them are seen in a positive way. When a democracy is characterized by widespread inequality, people with wealth and power promote the idea that

Power and Performance *versus* Pleasure and Participation (*Continued*)

they have earned their privileged positions through hard work and intelligence and that society as a whole benefits from their control and influence. In recent history, this idea has been promoted by emphasizing that *competition* is a natural part of social life and the only fair basis for determining who gets what in society. When there is widespread acceptance of this idea, people generally idealize and defer to wealthy and powerful people and believe that they deserve what they have.

Power and performance sports are widely promoted and sponsored by people with wealth and power because these sports are based on an ideology that celebrates competitive winners and defines competition as the only fair and natural way to distribute rewards. This ideology also explains and justifies economic inequalities as part of the natural order of things. The executives of major corporations realize this and collectively allocate billions of dollars annually to sponsor power and performance sports worldwide. They personally believe that rewards should go to winners, that winners deserve wealth and power, and that the ranking of people on the basis of wealth and power is fair and natural. By sponsoring power and performance sports and making them a major source

of enjoyment and excitement in people's lives, they promote these beliefs at the same time that they profit from selling vehicles, fast food, soft drinks, and beer advertised during sports events.

The sport forms that challenge this ideology may be popular among some people, but they don't receive many sponsorship dollars from wealthy and powerful people. For example, alternative sports such as skateboarding and disk sport (Frisbee) were often banned and associated with deviance until they were organized around a power and performance model. Free-flowing, expressive alternative sports that don't produce winners and losers receive little attention from powerful sponsors. But when ESPN used a power and performance model to restructure these sports in the X Games, corporate sponsors began to support them. Today, many of these sports have lost their alternative character. Celebrity athletes now hawk corporate products and lifestyles of consumption. At the same time, participation comes to be tied with brands and the quest for the latest piece of equipment, clothing, or energy drink endorsed by the athletes. This raises the question, "Who are the real winners and losers in power and performance sports?" *What do you think?*

review of English language studies worldwide, the scholars came to this conclusion:

> The physiological effects of participation in sport and physical activity are widely known, and one of the best established findings in the research literature. It is important to note that the effects are not a result of sport, . . . but of physical activity more generally. . . . Given clean air, adequate nutrition, and a variety of moderate levels of exercise, *there is a well-established direct positive relationship between physical health and physical activity*, including feelings of well being associated with increasing

physical fitness. In addition, research increasingly points to both the preventive and rehabilitative effects of physical activity with respect to some diseases. (SDP/IWG Secretariat, p. 4)

This is a carefully worded statement because the authors knew that it was important to distinguish between *exercise*, *physical activity*, and *sports* when talking about physical health and well-being. Similarly, a report by the U.S Surgeon General (USDHHS, 1996) included only two competitive sports in its recommended list of healthy physical activities. Apart from twenty minutes of playing basketball and forty-five minutes of playing volleyball, there were no other sports on the list because research indicated that the injury risks associated with nearly all competitive sports were so high that participation created more health costs than benefits (P. White, 2004; Young, 2004a).

The Sport–Health Connection   The relationship between sports, exercise, and health has been widely studied (Zakus, Njelesani, and Darnell, 2007). When sociologist Ivan Waddington (2000a, 2000b, 2007) reviewed research on this topic, he concluded that the healthiest of all physical activities were rhythmic, noncompetitive exercises in which individuals control and regulate their own body movements. The research also indicated that health benefits decline when there is a shift from self-controlled exercise to competitive sports. This is because the injury rates in competitive sports are high enough to increase health costs above what is considered "average" in most populations. This benefit–cost ratio becomes even less favorable when there is a shift from noncontact to contact sports and from mass sports to elite sports in which participants train intensely, play while injured, and perceive their bodies as tools for achieving competitive success.

Other scholars in the sociology of sport have made similar points. For example, Eric Dunning (1986) noted that many sports are mock battles during which aggressive and violent acts are common. Mike Messner (1992, 2002) explained that in heavy-contact sports, male athletes routinely turn their bodies into weapons and use them in ways that injure themselves and opponents. This orientation is so prevalent that Kevin Young (1993), classified men's heavy-contact professional sports as a "hazardous workplace" with injury rates that

> Athletic participation at the elite level is an egoistic, self-centered activity, as athletes must continue to hone their bodies. —George J. Bryjak, sociologist, University of San Diego, 2002

often are higher than rates at construction sites, oil-drilling rigs, and underground mines—the three most dangerous workplaces in North America. For example, of the approximately 1000 wrestlers age 45 and younger who worked on the professional wrestling circuit between 1997 and 2004, at least 65 died during those years (Swartz, 2004). Research also shows that athletes from youth sports through college suffer an alarming number of concussions, some of which cause permanent brain damage (Mihoces, 2007b; Nowinski, 2007; Roberts, 2007; Schwarz, 2007a, 2007b, 2007c; Tramontano, 2008).

A recent survey of worldwide research showed that "sport is the main cause of injury in adolescents" (Abernathy and Bleakley, 2007)—a finding that applies to girls and boys (Dick et al., 2007; Le Gall et al., 2008). For example, in 2005 to 2006, girls on U.S. high school soccer teams suffered an estimated 29,167 concussions (Gessel et al., 2007). Jennifer Waldron and Vikki Krane (2005) explained that female athletes often participate in contexts where there are group pressures to engage in risky and unhealthy actions as they seek to gain success and live up to the expectations of coaches and teammates. Overuse injuries also are a manifestation of these unhealthy actions (Jaffe, 2007; Le Gall et al., 2008; McMahon, 2007a, 2007b; Wen, 2007).

Although risks are highest in elite sports, they also exist in mass sports where injury rates are regularly higher than in other everyday activities. British researchers have found that the health benefits of playing sports outweighed costs among people aged forty-five years old and older, but the costs outweighed benefits for 15- to 44-year-olds. In financial terms, this meant that every young adult who regularly participated in exercise and sports "created" about $50 per year of costs more than if they had not participated regularly (Nichol et al., 1993). In other words, the "disease prevention benefits" were lower than the medical fees for treating exercise and sport-related injuries in younger adults.

These findings are limited in scope and need qualification, but they suggest that we must clarify what we mean when we say that "sports improve health and physical well-being." In practical terms, if you lack health insurance, it is best to stay fit by doing aerobics, walking, swimming, and jumping rope; and if you play football, rugby, hockey, or other competitive contact sports, you should have good health insurance because your medical bills are likely to be higher than average. Even if you play golf, softball, soccer and other sports that require sudden and forceful twisting motions or sprinting from a dead stop, it would be wise to be insured.

The Sport–Obesity Connection   Obesity is a highly publicized health issue today (Duncan, 2008). Nearly every discussion of this issue ends with the conclusion that eating right and exercising is the best way to avoid unhealthy weight gains. Furthermore, research consistently supports the value of exercise in controlling body weight.

Some people think that as sports become increasingly popular in a society, obesity rates decline, but data in the United States indicate otherwise: Obesity rates among young people and adults have more than doubled between 1985 and 2008—a period when competitive sports grew significantly in popularity. This does not mean that sports cause obesity, but it does mean that the popularity of sports in a society does not automatically inspire people to exercise in ways that reduce obesity.

Like the connection between sports and health, the connection between sports and weight is complex. Some competitive sports such as wrestling and gymnastics emphasize extreme forms of weight control; others emphasize weight gain for some or all participants. Many NFL players, for example, are encouraged to gain weight to the point that 56 percent of

the nearly 2200 players during the 2003 to 2004 season were classified as obese, and one-half of the obese players were severely so according to the body mass index (BMI) (Harp and Hecht, 2005). Although the BMI is not always a good measure for assessing the relationship between weight and health, the data in this study suggests that playing football is not a good way to control weight in healthy ways.

Expectations in football today often demand excessive eating and/or taking nutritional supplements to gain size. The consequences of these expectations are illustrated in Table 4.1. The table shows that between 1920 and 1985, no more than eight NFL players weighed over 300 pounds, but in 2006 there were 570 players over 300 pounds, and they claim to have gained weight by overeating. This takes a serious toll on overall health (Briggs, 2002; Longman, 2007b).

Research also shows that these patterns exist in college and high school football, which together have by far the most participants of all school-sponsored sports (Keller, 2007; Laurson and Eisenmann, 2007; Longman, 2007b). In fact, young men who play the line positions on high school football teams regularly have obesity rates that are twice as high as others their age. As one 332-pound 15-year-old high school lineman said, "They're going to notice me because of my size. . . .Most linemen in the NFL are 290 or 300" (Longman, 2007b).

Football is unique, but like other sports, it exists in a social world where expectations focus

Table 4.1   NFL players weighing over 300 pounds, by selected seasons

Year	Number of Players	Percent of All Players
1966:	3	0.2%
1976:	0	0.0%
1986:	18	0.7%
1996:	289	12.0%
2006:	570	19.9%

Source: Frias and Hartnett (2006).

on competitive success rather than healthy actions and overall fitness. If playing sports is to have a positive impact on the long-term physical well-being of people, regardless of age, it should be accompanied by information about good health and fitness combined with effective encouragement to use this information in connection with sport participation.

How Do Sports Affect Our Lives?

Sports and sport participation affect the lives of many people around the world. We're learning more about this impact through three types of studies based on a combination of cultural, interactionist, and structural theories:

1. Studies of sport experiences as presented through the voices of sport participants
2. Studies of the social worlds that are created and maintained in connection with particular sports
3. Studies of sports as sites, or "social locations," where dominant ideas and ideologies are expressed and sometimes challenged and changed

Most of these studies are grounded in a critical approach. Taken together, they help us rethink socialization issues and expand our understanding of how social learning occurs in social worlds. Today we view sports as *sites* for socialization experiences, rather than *causes* of specific socialization outcomes. This is an important distinction that highlights two things. First, sports are social locations rich in their potential for providing memorable and meaningful personal, social, and cultural experiences. Second, sports *by themselves* do not cause particular changes in the character traits, attitudes, and actions of athletes or spectators. Therefore, when positive or negative socialization outcomes occur in connection with sports, we don't simply say that sports caused them. Instead, we view sports as sites where people have potentially influential experiences and then we look for and try to

understand the relationships and social processes through which particular forms of socialization occur (SDP IWG Secretariat. 2007).

The following summaries of selected studies illustrate how this approach to socialization enables us to understand more fully the social dimensions of sports and the connections between sports and the larger social and cultural contexts in which they are produced, reproduced, and changed.

Real-Life Experiences: Sport Stories from Athletes

The following examples provide three socialization "videos." They present the perspectives of the participants themselves, and they help us understand how people give meaning to sport experiences and integrate them into their lives.

Example 1: The Moral Lessons of Little League Sociologist Gary Alan Fine (1987) spent three years studying boys in Little League baseball. He focused on the moral socialization that occurred as the boys interacted with each other, coaches, and parents. He found that the moral messages that coaches and parents presented to the boys were based on adult views of the world. But the boys heard and interpreted these messages in terms of their perspectives as eleven-year-old boys concerned with peer acceptance and learning what it means to be a man in U.S. culture. Socialization was an interactive process in which the boys played key roles in what and how they learned. What happened to the boys as they played baseball resulted from a combination of adult influence, the developmental issues associated with preadolescence, and the social reality of being eleven-year-old boys in U.S. culture during the late 1980s.

Among other things, the boys learned to define *masculinity* in terms of toughness and aggression and to express disdain for all females and those boys labeled as weak or unwilling to take risks on or off the playing field. They learned other things as well, but their emerging

Sports in many cultures are no longer seen as exclusively masculine activities. However, traditional gender definitions and associated clothing may still keep some girls out of the action. (*Source:* Jay Coakley)

ideas about manhood influenced how they saw themselves and their relationships with others. Playing baseball did not *cause* the boys to define *masculinity* in a particular way, but was an important site where they were introduced to ideas and beliefs about what it means to be a man and how to act manly.

The relevance of these socialization experiences was important for the boys because the ideological notion that men are tough and aggressive was clearly endorsed by coaches, parents, and peers. It was promoted in team strategies, player evaluations, and peer acceptance, and it was reinforced by cultural messages that the boys received in the media and other spheres of their lives. Therefore, playing baseball was a heavily gendered experience for the boys. It was linked

with the development of their identities as males and athletes. Similar findings have been widely reported in studies across a range of youth sports and in various cultures over the past two decades (Bhana, 2008; Craig and Liberti, 2007; Hills, 2007; Ingham and Dewar, 1999; Messner, 2002).

Example 2: Lessons in the Locker Room   Sociologist Nancy Theberge (1999, 2000b) spent two years studying an elite women's ice hockey team in Canada. As she observed and interviewed team members, she noted that their experiences and orientations were influenced by the fact that men controlled the team, the league, and the sport itself. Within this structure, the women developed a professional approach to participation. They focused on hockey and were serious about playing well and winning games. In the process, they developed close connections with each other. The team became a community with its own dynamics and internal organization. Within this constructed community, the athletes learned things about hockey, their teammates, and themselves. The meanings that the players gave to their hockey experiences and the ways they integrated them into their lives emerged as they interacted with each other both on and off the ice.

The locker room was a key place for interacting with teammates and giving meaning to their sport experiences. Its emotional climate, especially *after* a practice or game, encouraged talk about their lives outside hockey. This talk gave shape and meaning to what they did on the ice. It also served as a means for expressing feelings and thoughts about men, sexuality, male partners or female partners, and families. The women talked and joked about men but didn't degrade or reduce them to body parts in their comments. They made references to sex and sexuality in their conversations, but the substance of these references was neither hostile nor based on stereotypes. This was very different from what has reportedly occurred in some men's locker rooms, where women have been routinely derogated and objectified, and homosexuality has been scorned if it is discussed at all (Clayton and Humberstone, 2006; Curry, 1993).

Theberge's study shows us that playing sports is both a physical and a social experience. Hockey was a site for memorable experiences, but it was only *through social relationships* that those experiences were given meaning and incorporated into the women's lives. Theberge also gathered data on relationships between the athletes and others, including coaches, managers, trainers, friends, family members, sport reporters, and even fans. She realized that if she wanted to know what happens in sports, she had to understand the relationships and interaction through

> [As a player, it was] what do I eat? What's going to be good for my tennis? When do I practice? It was me, me, me, and that gets very old and very empty.
>
> —Chris Evert, former professional tennis player, 2003

which socialization occurs among athletes.

Example 3: Stories of Gay Male Athletes The meanings given to sport experiences vary from one person to another because social relationships are influenced by social definitions given to age, gender, socioeconomic status, ethnicity, skin color, (dis)abilities, and sexuality. This point was highlighted in Dan Woog's interviews with gay male athletes in the United States. Woog, a journalist, used data collected in his interviews to present twenty-eight stories about athletes, coaches, referees, administrators, and others in sports (Woog, 1998).

The stories indicated that gay men were especially cautious about coming out in sports. Successfully combining gay and athlete identities was a challenging process for nearly all the men. Woog observed that the social contexts and relationships associated with individual sports, such as running and swimming, generally were more gay friendly than most team sports, depending on the ways that athletes and coaches defined the link between heterosexuality and masculinity.

Being "out" was liberating for most of the men, but it was also dangerous for some of them. They cared deeply about sports, and many feared that being out might lead others to exclude them from teams and deny them the chance to play. Positive experiences among openly gay athletes were most likely when organizations supported them both on and off the field (such as in their schools), when family and friends provided overt support, and when someone in their sport, such as a teammate or coach, served as their advocate and showed others that sexuality should not undermine acceptance and friendship.

Despite similarities between the experiences of gay and straight men in sports, the meanings given to those experiences and how they are integrated into people's lives differ because of the different ways that *heterosexuality* and *homosexuality* are defined. Those definitions influence people's lives *and* the meaning and impact of sport experiences. As they change, so do the dynamics of socialization among people, gay and straight, who play sports (see Anderson, 2000, 2002, 2005).

OLC ON THE *OLC:*
See the OLC—Additional Readings for Chapter 4—for summaries of additional research about what happens to young people who play sports.

Social Worlds: Living in Sports

Some sociologists have studied socialization processes in connection with the social worlds in which they occur. **Social world** is a term used in interactionist theory to refer to *a way of life and an associated mind-set that revolve around a particular activity and encompass all the people and relationships connected with it.* Qualitative research methods are most often used to study social worlds. Researchers use participant observation and interviews to view sport participation in the overall context in which it occurs. Studies are based on the assumption that we can't understand who athletes are, what they do, and how sports influence their lives unless we also understand the social worlds in which they give meaning to sport experiences and integrate them into their lives. This is especially true when the lives of athletes revolve completely around a particular sport—that is, when the social world of their sport is their entire world.

Studies of the social worlds created around specific sports provide useful information about socialization processes and experiences. The following summaries of four ethnographic studies are representative of this type of research.

Example 1: Learning to Be a Hero Sociologists Patti and Peter Adler spent nearly ten years studying the social world of a high-profile college

basketball team. Much of their data, presented in the book *Backboards and Blackboards* (1991), focuses on how the self-conceptions of young men changed as they lived in the social world of big-time intercollegiate basketball. The Adlers found that the young men, about 70 percent of whom were African Americans, usually became deeply engulfed in their roles as athletes. This influenced how they viewed themselves and allocated their time between basketball, social life, and academics. This "role engulfment" intensified as the young men became increasingly committed to identities formed around their relationships with teammates, coaches, and others associated with basketball. Everyone they met supported and reinforced their identities as athletes. As a result, the social world of intercollegiate basketball became the context in which the young men identified themselves, set goals, and viewed the rest of the world.

The Adlers noted that the young men learned to set goals, focus their attention on specific tasks, and make sacrifices to succeed in basketball. However, there was no apparent evidence that the athletes applied these lessons to other aspects of their lives. The social world of basketball separated them so much from the rest of life that the lessons they learned in that world stayed there.

The Adlers' study raises an important point about socialization: When the social world in which athletes play their sport is so separate from other spheres of life and role engulfment confines athletes to that world, it is difficult to take the learning that occurs through sport participation and transfer it to nonsport worlds. There's a need for further studies on role engulfment and how it influences the socialization experiences of athletes from different backgrounds, in different sports, and over the course of an athlete's time in college (Miller and Kerr, 2003).

Example 2: Realizing That Image Isn't Everything Anthropologist Alan Klein studied the social world of competitive bodybuilding for seven years. In his book, *Little Big Men* (1993), he explains that much of the lives of the bodybuilders revolved around issues of gender and sexuality.

The bodybuilders, both male and female, learned to project public images of power and strength, although privately they experienced serious doubts about their identities and self-worth. The social world of bodybuilding seemed to foster a desperate need for attention and approval from others, especially other bodybuilders. Ideas about masculinity within the social world were so narrow and one dimensional that the male bodybuilders developed homophobic attitudes and went to great lengths to assert their heterosexuality in public. Also, the emphasis on body size and hardness created such insecurities that the men learned to present and even define themselves in terms of exaggerated caricatures of masculinity—like comic-book depictions of manly men.

Overall, bodybuilding was a site for powerful socialization experiences. But instead of enhancing self-esteem and confidence among the men, these experiences fostered a sense that one would never fully measure up to the ideals that were so prevalent in the social world of the gym. It was in this context that men made decisions about using muscle-building substances and engaging in risky actions to make the money needed to pay for training and supplements. Without understanding the social world of the gym, it is difficult to make sense of the lives of the bodybuilders.

> I don't know what life is like, I don't know how regular people live. I just can never understand it. My first job was the NBA. —Tracy McGrady, NBA player, 2005

Example 3: Living in the Shadow of a Man's World

Sociologist Todd Crosset (1995) spent fourteen months studying the social world of women's professional golf. He found that being on the LPGA tour created and in fact required a mind-set focused on using physical competence as a basis for evaluating self and the other golfers. He described this mind-set as "an ethic of prowess" and explained that it existed partly because the women wanted to neutralize the potentially negative effects that dominant ideas about gender could have if those ideas entered the social world of women's professional golf.

One of the golfers interviewed by Crosset said that much of what she did in her life was a response to the notion that "*athlete* is almost a masculine noun" in U.S. culture. Another explained, "We are different than the typical married lady with a house full of kids in what we think and do." Overall, the data collected in Crosset's interviews led him to conclude that the social world of the LPGA was created, in part, as a defensive response to gender relations in U.S. culture. Even as women professional athletes have become increasingly visible and accepted, discussions continue on their sexuality and whether they can maintain "normal" lives as full-time pro athletes. These issues are not as widely discussed as they were in the past, but the women of the LPGA continue to deal with realities that are seldom faced by male golfers on the PGA tour.

Example 4: Surviving in a Ghetto

Sociologist Loïc Wacquant (1992, 2004) spent three years studying the social world of boxers in a gym located in a black neighborhood in Chicago. His observations, interviews, and experiences as a boxer helped him uncover the ideas and meanings that constitute the life and craft of boxing. He explains that the social world of the boxing gym is very complex: It is created in connection with the social forces in an ethnically segregated ghetto and its masculine street culture, but it also shelters black men from the full destructive impact of those forces.

To learn the "social art" of boxing, the men at the gym engaged in an intense regimen of body regulation focused on the physical, visual, and mental requirements of boxing. They had to "eat, drink, sleep and live boxing," and in the process, they developed what Wacquant described as a *socialized lived body*, which was at the very core of their identities and actions.

The social world of the boxing gym was a workplace, a refuge, and a place where dreams were pursued by men dedicated to disciplining their bodies and souls (Wacquant, 2004). Immersing themselves in this world separated the men from their peers on the streets and kept them alive by helping them navigate their lives in dangerous neighborhoods devoid of hope or opportunity. For these men, boxing was a powerful socialization experience, but it can be understood only in connection with social and material conditions that constituted the social world of their everyday lives. In fact, the gym studied by Wacquant would never exist in an upper-middle-class white neighborhood; it would make no sense there.

In summary, these four studies of social worlds created around sports help us understand more fully the contexts in which athletes and others connected with sports form identities, make decisions, and give meaning to their experiences. Research that takes us into those worlds helps us make sense of actions that sometimes appear strange or even irrational from an outsider's perspective. This doesn't mean that we approve of everything that occurs in those worlds, but insightful research provides the information needed to make sports more humane and healthy activities.

Ideology: Sports as Sites for Presenting Ideas and Beliefs

Socialization research has focused mostly on what occurs in the lives of individuals and within bounded social worlds. However, researchers now combine cultural theories with a poststructuralist methodological approach to do studies of *socialization as a community and cultural process.*[2] These studies go beyond looking at the experiences and characteristics of athletes and the organization of social worlds. Instead, they focus on sports as sites at which people collectively create and learn "stories," which they use to give meaning to and make sense of the world and their lives. These stories are sociologically relevant because so many people use them as vehicles for presenting ideas and beliefs about everything from morality and work to capitalism and lifestyles of consumption. The stories that constitute sports have their own vocabularies and images. The meanings in these stories shift, depending on who tells and hears them, and they often identify important cultural issues in everyday life. Researchers in the sociology of sport conduct studies to identify these stories, explain how they fit into the culture, and show how people use them in connection with what they think and do.

Researchers using cultural theories and a poststructuralist approach are primarily concerned with whose stories about sports become dominant in the culture and whose stories are ignored. The dominant or most widely told stories are culturally important because they are based on ideological assumptions of what is natural, normal, and legitimate in social worlds; therefore, they promote ideas and beliefs that often privilege some people more than others. For example, the stories that constitute sports often revolve around heroic figures—warriors who are big, strong, aggressive, record-setting competitors. As researchers have deconstructed or taken these stories apart to examine the assumptions on which they are based, they've found that many of them celebrate values, ideas, and beliefs that serve the interests

---

[2]Poststructuralism is a theoretical and methodological perspective based on the assumption that culture today revolves primarily around language and rapidly changing media images and representations.

  This perspective was developed because structuralist theory, focusing almost exclusively on the organization of social systems and economic relationships, was considered to be out of date and unable to adequately explain current realities in social worlds.

  The scholars who do poststructuralist research focus primarily on language and media representations because they assume that social life in today's postmodern cultures is much more fluid than it was in the past. This fluidity exists because social worlds are constantly negotiated, constructed, challenged, and changed through discourses that represent people, ideas, and things. This results in social worlds full of diversity and internal inconsistencies that cannot be explained through a structural analysis that focuses

OLC ON THE *OLC:*
On the OLC—Visit the Online Learning Center and download Additional Readings for Chapter 4 for the author's discussion of the concept of competition and the importance of competition as a value in U.S. culture.

and the conditions under which sports and sport stories become a part of people's lives. This research is important in the knowledge-building process because it deals with the ways that sports influence culture and society as a whole, and thereby affects people's lives even when they don't participate in or care about sports.

of unregulated capitalist expansion and traditional notions of masculinity based on the ability to dominate others through the use of physical strength, power, and speed (Burstyn, 1999).

Researchers using a poststructuralist approach also study untold stories representing voices that are silenced or "erased" from the widely circulated and accepted stories in the dominant culture. For example, they've done studies of sports media coverage to learn what *is* and what *is not* contained in the **discourses**—that is, *the combination of commentaries, images, and other representations of people, events, and things*—that "create" sports and give them meaning. These studies are important because they give us a fuller understanding of the ways that sports are connected with patterns of advantage and disadvantage in societies.

Research based on cultural theories and a poststructuralist approach is difficult to do because it requires a deep knowledge of history

> Sport serves as one's means of socializing the population and of installing their respect and conformity to those in power. Sports attractiveness in this process is that it provides the opportunity for large masses of the population to be part of the action through ritual and ceremonies. —Bob Chappell, Sport Scientist, Honorary Fellow, Brunel University (2007, p. 172)

The Politics of Socialization as a Community and Cultural Process Critical research on socialization as a community and cultural process is partly inspired by the ideas of the Italian political theorist Antonio Gramsci. When the fascist government in Italy imprisoned Gramsci for speaking out against their oppressive policies, he used his time in prison (1928–1935) to think about why people in Italy and elsewhere had not revolted against exploitive forms of capitalism in Western societies. Gramsci concluded that revolutions had not occurred because popular notions of common sense and widely accepted ideas about organizing society were actually supportive of the powerful people who exploited and oppressed the general population. After carefully studying historical evidence from around the world, he explained that leaders often maintained power by convincing the people that they governed of three things: (1) that life was as good as it could be under present conditions, (2) that any positive things that people experienced were due to the goodwill and power of current leaders, and (3) that changing the current structure of their society would threaten everything that people valued.

Although Gramsci never talked about sports, he used historical data to conclude that current leaders could most effectively maintain their positions by providing people with exciting and pleasurable experiences that promoted particular

---

on relatively stable sets of relationships and social processes.

Studies done by poststructuralists often deal with the ways that images, identities, symbols, and meanings are constructed through media representations that collectively constitute the contexts of our lives. Poststructuralist scholars use a critical approach and sometimes do research that intentionally disrupts dominant cultural meanings and representations that are the foundation for oppressing some people and privileging others.

ideas and beliefs in support of their power. In other words, powerful people could preserve their power by sponsoring forms of popular entertainment that perpetuated ideological perspectives supportive of current economic and political structures. If this was done successfully, there would be little support for radical or structural changes because people would want to undermine the primary sources of excitement and pleasure in their lives (Chappell, 2007).

Gramsci's analysis explains why large corporations spend billions of dollars every year to sponsor power and performance sports and present their commercial messages in connection with these sports. For example, Coca-Cola, General Motors, and McDonald's have each spent well over a billion dollars sponsoring and presenting advertising messages during the 1996, 2000, 2004, and 2008 Olympic Games. These expenditures were made to promote sales, but more important, they were made to use the Olympics as a site for delivering cultural messages that encouraged people to see these transnational corporations as benevolent sources of excitement and pleasure. If these messages were widely accepted, people would be less likely to criticize these corporations or support legislation that would curb their power and influence. Therefore, the corporate executives who made the decisions to sponsor the Olympics wanted people watching the events to agree that competition was the fair and natural way to allocate rewards. They realized that this belief and the free market ideology that is organized around it were the foundation of their personal status and wealth as well as the success of the corporation for which they worked. For them, Olympic sports provide a model of life that fits their interests.

The people who run Coca-Cola and General Motors want to sell Coke and cars, but they don't spend billions of sponsorship dollars only to boost next year's sales figures. Their more important goal is to effectively promote lifestyles organized around consumption and the use of corporate brands and logos as status and identity symbols. They want to convince people that corporations are the source of their excitement and pleasure, and the sponsors of the athletes, teams, and sports they love so dearly. Coke and General Motors executives want people to associate their good and memorable times with corporations and their products and to use consumption as the primary measure of progress and prosperity. To the extent that people in society accept this ideology, the power of corporations is nearly guaranteed. This is why the marketing departments of major corporations often use power and performance sports as "outposts" to promote their interests.

TV viewers of the Super Bowl may not realize it, but the biggest stakes associated with that event have nothing to do with the score and everything to do with how viewers integrate into their lives the cultural messages that are deeply embedded in the narratives and images presented in everything from the pregame show through the game, commercials, and postgame show.

Many sociologists refer to this process of forming consent around a particular ideology as the process of establishing hegemony (heh-g̃em-ō-nee). In political science and sociology, **hegemony** is a *process of maintaining leadership and control by gaining the consent and approval of other groups, including those who are being led or controlled.* For example, American hegemony in the world exists when people worldwide accept U.S. power and influence as legitimate. Hegemony is never permanent, but it can be maintained in a social world as long as most people in it feel that their lives are as good as can be expected and that there is no compelling reason to change their current organization. Similarly, corporate hegemony is maintained as long as most people accept a view of the world that discourages them from objecting to corporate policies, profits, and executive pay packages. Like Gramsci, corporate executives know that preserving corporate power depends on establishing "ideological outposts" in people's heads. Sports, because they are exciting and pleasurable activities for so many people, are important sites for constructing these mental outposts. Once established, the outposts serve as terminals for delivering corporate messages directly into the popular psyche. To paraphrase Gramsci's conclusion about hegemony, "it is difficult to fight an enemy that has outposts in your head."

Research on Socialization as a Community and Cultural Process   It is difficult to understand socialization as a community and cultural process unless we see it in action. The following examples of research highlight this approach to sports and socialization.

When anthropologist Doug Foley (1999b) did an ethnographic study of a small town in southern Texas, he focused part of his attention on the connection between sports and community socialization processes. High school football games were the most visible and popular events in the town, and the local team was important in the lives of many townspeople. As Foley observed social dynamics in the town and interviewed people about local events, he discovered that the stories created around high school football reaffirmed established ways of thinking and doing things in the town. As a result, sports served as a site for maintaining forms of social inequality that made life good for a few and difficult for many residents. For example, even though a young Mexicana could become a cheerleader and a young Mexicano from a poor family could be a star on the football team, this did nothing to improve the political and economic status of women, citizens with Mexican heritage, and low-income people in the town.

The experiences and meanings associated with football reproduced ideologies that supported and justified inequalities of gender, ethnicity, and social class. Even though particular individuals benefited from sport participation, the vocabularies and images associated with sports perpetuated actions and forms of social organization that

> **In his own way, [Michael] Jordan did spread an ideology. It was that sports are not just games but tools for advertisers. It was that basketball isn't a playground thing, but a corporate thing.** —Jay Weiner, *BusinessWeek* (1999)

maintained existing patterns of power and privilege. Foley summarized the findings of his ethnography in this way:

> Local sports, especially football, socialize every new generation of youth into the local status hierarchy, both inside and outside the school. Each new generation of males learns to be individualistic, aggressive, and competitive within a group structure. . . . (1999b, p. 138)

Other studies have used a poststructuralist approach and focused on the ways that popular images connected with sports become influential cultural symbols as they are represented in the media and everyday conversations. For example, cultural studies scholar David Andrews and his colleagues have studied Michael Jordan as an iconic figure that influenced the attitudes and experiences of people worldwide, especially a generation of young people in the United States (Andrews, 1996a, 1996b; 2001; Andrews and Jackson, 2001; and

When corporations invest money to have their names, logos, and products associated with sports, they are looking for more than sales. In the long run, their executives hope that people will believe that their enjoyment of sports depends on corporations. This will make them more likely to support and less likely to interfere with corporate interests. (*Source:* Jay Coakley)

breaking BARRIERS

Socialization Barriers:
Living in the Empire of the Normal

The images of productive, healthy, beautiful, and ideal bodies in U.S. culture are always images of *able bodies*. Images of impaired bodies are seldom seen, except in notices for fund-raising events to "help the disabled." Images representing bodies with disabilities as valued, beautiful, healthy, fit, or athletic are practically nonexistent (Seeley and Rail, 2004). This is because the United States and most postindustrial societies are part of the "Empire of the Normal," where bodies with disabilities are marginalized and managed by medical experts (Couser, 2000; MacLeod, 2008).

When bodies with disabilities are encountered in the Empire of the Normal, people want to know, "*What happened to you?*" They demand a story that explains why a body is different than normal—that is, why it is abnormal. As people with disabilities tell their stories day after day, their identities come to be organized around their "difference," rather than their similarity with other people (Thomson, 2000, p. 334).

This information is important for those of us who want to understand sports and socialization in more detail. When people with disabilities decide to play sports in the Empire of the Normal, they're often referred to programs by medical personnel, such as physical therapists, nurses, doctors, and hospital staff (Schilling, 1997). In fact, the Paralympic sports were originally developed in a British medical center for war

When people see a body with a disability, they often want to hear the story that accounts for its difference from "normal" bodies. Over time, this may lead to the development of an identity organized around a person's account of "why my body is different from your body." (*Source:* David Biene; photo courtesy of Ossur)

McDonald and Andrews, 2001). These researchers meticulously deconstructed the cultural stories that were created around Jordan, mostly between 1982 and 1995. This involved analyzing commercials, commentaries, and various forms of media coverage. One of their findings was that the "Jordan persona" was severed from African American experiences and culture so that white America, seeking evidence that it was color-blind and open to all, could comfortably identify with it and approve of their children hanging Jordan posters on bedroom walls in their all-white neighborhoods. Race and skin color were

strategically erased from Jordan's public persona thereby allowing it to become a sign that could be attached to any corporate brand, including Nike, Wilson, Hanes underwear, Jordan brand apparel, Bijan (the Michael Jordan fragrance), Coca-Cola, Gatorade, McDonald's, Wheaties, Ball Park Franks, Quaker Oats, Sara Lee, CBS SportsLine, MJ's sports videos, MCI telephone long-distance service, General Motors, Chevrolet, Rayovac, and others (Denzin, 2001; McDonald and Andrews, 2001).

In the United States, Jordan's persona was shaped in connection with capitalism and veterans with spinal cord injuries. Ludwig Guttmann, the neurosurgeon founded the center, felt that playing sports was effective therapy for many of his patients. When he scheduled public games for people with disabilities at the same time as the 1948 Olympics in London, he was described as a radical because he disrupted the Empire of the Normal and forced people to confront bodies with disabilities. The longstanding rule in the Empire had always been "Out of sight, out of mind" when it came to those bodies.

When people with disabilities become involved in sports, their decisions to stay involved are related to their sense of how other people define their bodies and treat them as athletes. Also important is access to participation opportunities, resources for transportation and adapted equipment, knowledgeable coaches, and programs that inspire achievement and success.

Changing or ending sport participation occurs in connection with many of the same factors that lead able-bodied athletes to disengage from sports. Injuries, a sense of reaching one's goals or hitting one's limits, responsibilities related to work and family, a lack of resources, and new opportunities to coach or work in sports influence decisions to alter or end sport participation.

What happens to athletes with disabilities when they play sports? Research on this question is scarce,

but it's reasonable to hypothesize that, like able-bodied athletes, socialization experiences among athletes with disabilities depend on their relationships, the general social and cultural context in which participation occurs, and the meanings given to participation. When power and performance sports are defined as the only "real" sports in a social world, people with disabilities seldom play with or alongside able-bodied athletes. Instead, they are forced to play in segregated or "special" programs and the meanings they give to their sport participation are then developed in those contexts.

Today some athletes with disabilities see sports as sites for effectively challenging dominant body images in the Empire of the Normal. They want to break through and break down the walls of the empire; they want to challenge the notion that disabled bodies need to be cured, fixed, regulated, and separated from other bodies (Thomson, 2002, p. 8).

Pam Fernandez, an eight-time U.S. National Champion in Road and Track cycling, speaks from experience when she says, "If we could somehow bring the respect, dignity, and camaraderie of the Paralympic Village to the rest of the world, we could teach a lifetime of lessons in a single day" (in Joukowsky and Rothstein, 2002b, p. 93). This is the form of socialization needed to bring down the Empire of the Normal.

· ·

traditional family values, and he was represented as both a brand sign and a family man (Andrews, 2001; Andrews and Jackson, 2001). As the media transmitted the Jordan persona around the world, it was often associated with American capitalist expansion and the power of transnational corporations such as Nike. However, among Black Britons striving to transcend the legacy of being colonized by white people from England, the Jordan persona represented black empowerment and resistance to white supremacy. Among whites in New Zealand, it represented the NBA, American popular culture, and African American

prowess in sports. In Poland, the Jordan persona represented the American Dream, freedom, independence, the self-made man, opportunity, wealth, and other American values that stood in opposition to the communism that Poles had recently rejected in their lives.

The research by Andrews and his colleagues shows that sports and celebrity athletes are given multiple and sometimes contradictory meanings by different people in different cultural contexts. Therefore, the significance of sports in the socialization that occurs at the community and cultural level can be understood only

"I think these guys give different meanings to their boxing experiences."

The meanings given to sports vary from one person to another. However, many power and performance sports are organized to encourage orientations that emphasize domination over others. Those who do not hold this orientation may not fit very well in these sports.

in connection with local history, ideologies, and power relations. In other words, the influence of sports on people's lives cannot be captured in a single statement about building character, bringing people together, creating responsible citizens, promoting conformity, or fostering warfare. The connection between sports and socialization is much more complex than that and can be explained only by studying sports in the contexts in which people give them meaning and make them a part of their lives. This final point of the chapter is illustrated further in the "Breaking Barriers" box on pages 118–119.

summary

WHO PLAYS AND WHAT HAPPENS?

Socialization is a complex, interactive process through which people learn about themselves and the social worlds in which they participate. This process occurs in connection with sports and other activities in people's lives. Research indicates that playing sports is a social experience as well as a physical one.

Becoming involved and staying involved in sports occur in connection with general socialization processes in people's lives. Decisions to play sports are influenced by the availability of opportunities, the existence of social support, processes of identity formation, and the cultural context in which decisions are made.

Research indicates that sport participation decisions are related to processes of individual development, the organization of social life, and cultural ideology. People do not make decisions about sport participation once and for all time. They make them day after day, as they set and revise priorities in their lives. Research on sport-related decisions explains the social dynamics of early experiences in sports and identifies the agents of socialization and significant others who influence those decisions. Reasons for staying in sports change over time as people's lives change, and it is important to study the contexts in which these changes occur.

Changing or ending active sport participation also occurs in connection with general socialization processes. These processes are interactive and influenced by personal, social, and cultural factors. Changes in sport participation are usually tied to a combination of identity, developmental, and life course issues. Ending sport participation often involves a transition process, during which a person disengages from sport, redefines personal identity, reconnects with friends and family members, and uses available resources to become involved in other activities and careers. Just as people are not socialized into sports, they are not simply socialized out of sports. Research shows that changing or ending a career as a competitive athlete occurs over time and is often tied to events and life course issues apart from sports. These connections are best studied by using research methods that enable us to identify and analyze long-term transition processes.

Socialization that occurs as people participate in sports has been widely studied, especially by people wanting to know if and how sports build character. Much of this research has produced inconsistent findings because it has been based on oversimplified ideas about sports, sport experiences, and socialization. Reviews of this research indicate that the most informative studies of sports and socialization take into account variations in the ways that sports are organized, played, and integrated into people's lives. This is important because different sports involve different experiences and produce different socialization patterns. For example, the experience and meaning of playing power and performance sports is different from the experience and meaning of playing pleasure and participation sports. The continued visibility and popularity of power and performance sports are related to issues of wealth and power in society because they promote an ideology that supports the interests of existing leaders and wealthy people.

We know that sports have an impact on people's lives. The most informative research on what happens in sports deals with (1) the everyday experiences of people who play sports, (2) the social worlds created around sports, and (3) community and cultural processes through which ideologies are created, reproduced, and changed. As we listen to the voices of those who participate in sports, study their lives in sports, and identify the ideological messages associated with sports, we learn that there is a complex relationship between sports and socialization.

Most scholars who study sports in society now see sports as sites for socialization experiences, rather than causes of specific socialization outcomes. This distinction recognizes that powerful and memorable experiences can occur in connection with sports, but the impact of those experiences depends on the relationships through which they are given meaning and the social and cultural factors that influence the relationships. Therefore, the most useful research in the sociology of sport focuses on the importance of social relationships and the contexts in which

sport experiences are given meaning by a wide and diverse range of people who play or watch sports in one form or another.

WEBSITE RESOURCES

Note: Websites often change. The following URLs were current when this book was printed. Please check our website (www.mhhe.com/coakley10e) for updates and additions.

www.charactercounts.org/sports/sports.htm A loosely organized coalition of individuals and organizations committed to the idea that sports should build positive character; the goal of the coalition is to change the ways that individuals play, coach, and watch sports.

http://iwg.sportanddev.org/data/htmleditor/file/ Lit.%20Reviews/literature%20review%20SDP .pdf A literature review and summary of research on *"The use of sport to foster child and youth development and education"* prepared by Peter Donnelly and his colleagues (2007) at the University of Toronto; this is one of five helpful literature reviews on sociology of sport topics.

www.mhhe.com/coakley10e Click on chapter 4; see information on the concept of competition, the relationship between competition and culture, the persistent belief that sports build character, and what current socialization research does not tell us.

www.responsiblesports.com/ Responsible Sports is an organization that supports volunteer youth sport coaches and parents who help children succeed both on and off the field; experts provide advice about keeping young athletes positive and translating field lessons to life lessons.

www.righttoplay.com/site/PageServer *Right to Play* uses strategically designed sports and games to improve health, build life skills, and foster peace for children and communities affected by war, poverty, disease; this is "youth sports" where children's rights and survival are the stakes.

www.sportsmanship.org A loosely organized coalition of organizations with the goal of fostering changes so that sports will build positive character traits; the focus is on changing individuals, rather than organizations.

(Jay Coakley)

SPORTS AND CHILDREN

Are Organized Programs Worth the Effort?

> . . . INNOVATION AND PASSION bloom when children are given the time and space to create games on their own. [These games] are an inspired place in which improvisation rules, rewards are intrinsic, playing personalities are developed—and a child learns to see things that don't reveal themselves as readily in formal games.
>
> **—Tom Farrey, ESPN journalist (2008)**

(OLC) Visit *Sports in Society*'s Online Learning Center (OLC) at www.mhhe.com/coakley10e for additional information and study material for this chapter, including the following:

- A complete chapter outline
- Learning objectives
- Practice quizzes
- Internet resources
- Related readings
- Essays
- Student projects

WE NEED TO GIVE community stakeholders in low-income neighborhoods the resources they need to expand and improve their sports and physical activity programs so that we can get kids off the sidelines and into the game.

—**Timothy Johnson, Executive Director, Team-Up for Youth, Oakland, CA (2007)**

CHILDREN'S PLAY IS so focused on lessons and leagues [that] kids aren't getting a chance to practice policing themselves. When they have that opportunity, . . . the results are clear: Self-regulation improves.

—**Alix Spiegel, PBS, Morning Edition (2008)**

WE HAVE A TENDENCY to overcoach kids . . . When I coach my kids' teams, people look at me like I'm crazy, because they know I'm involved in pro soccer and yet I'm not trying to impose structure on them. I don't insist on positional play. I want them to work it out.

—**Ivan Gazidis, deputy commissioner, Major League Soccer (in Farrey, 2008)**

According to Census Bureau estimates, there were about 51 million six- to eighteen-year-olds living in the United States in 2008. Estimates of youth sport participation range from 15 million to 46 million six- to eighteen-year-olds, depending on who does the counting and what counts as sports (Farrey, 2008; Fullinwider, 2006). As best as I can tell, during a given year, about 15 to 20 million U.S. children and youth participate in organized sports, excluding high school teams.[1]

When, how, and to what end children play sports are issues that concern parents, community leaders, and child advocates in national and international organizations. When sociologists study youth sports, they focus on the experiences of participants and how those experiences vary depending on the social and cultural contexts in which they occur. Research done by sociologists and other professionals has influenced how people think about and organize youth sports, and it continues to provide valuable information that parents, coaches, and program administrators can use when organizing and evaluating youth programs.

This chapter summarizes part of that research as we discuss five topics that are central to understanding youth sports today. These are

1. The origin and development of organized youth sports
2. Major trends in youth sports
3. Variations in the organization of youth sports and in the sport experiences of young people
4. Youth sports and issues related to access, psycho-social development, and family dynamics
5. Recommendations for improving youth sports

An underlying question that guides our discussion of these topics is this: Are organized youth sports worth the massive amount of time, money, and effort that people put into them? I first asked this question when my son and daughter played sports as children, and I continue to ask it as I talk with parents and work with coaches and policy makers who make extensive commitments to organizing sports for young people.

ORIGIN AND DEVELOPMENT OF ORGANIZED YOUTH SPORTS

During the latter half of the nineteenth century, people in Europe and North America began to realize that child development was influenced by the social environment. This created a movement to organize children's social worlds with the goal of building their character and turning them into hard-working, productive adults in rapidly expanding capitalist economies (Chudacoff, 2007). It wasn't long before organized sports for young boys were organized and sponsored by schools, communities, and church groups. The organizers hoped that sports, especially team sports, would teach boys from working-class families to obey rules and work together productively. They also hoped that sports would toughen middle- and upper-class boys and turn them into competitive men, despite the "feminized" values they learned from their stay-at-home mothers. At the same time, girls were provided activities that taught them to be good wives, mothers, and homemakers. The prevailing belief was that girls should learn domestic skills rather than sport skills when they went to schools and playgrounds. There were exceptions to these patterns, but after World War II, youth programs were organized this way in Western Europe and North America.

---

[1]High school teams are not discussed here because they are covered in Chapter 14. The data on youth sport participation are confusing because some figures double and triple count children who play two or more sports; some figures include informal physical activities, such as riding a skateboard once during a year or wading in the water at a beach, as participating in a sport; and other figures are based only on official counts from national youth sport organizations, such as Little League, Inc., US Youth Soccer, the American Youth Soccer Organization, and others. For example, the Sporting Goods Manufacturer's Association counts being in the water for a few minutes at a local pool as "participation in swimming," because it involves buying and wearing a bathing suit, which is what concerns members of this organization.

The Postwar Baby Boom and the Growth of Youth Sports

The baby-boom generation was born between 1946 and 1964. Young married couples during these years were optimistic about the future and eager to become parents. As the first wave of baby boomers moved through childhood during the 1950s and 1960s, organized youth sports grew dramatically, especially in the United States. Programs were sponsored by public, private, and commercial organizations. Parents also entered the scene, eager to have their sons' characters built through organized competitive sports. Fathers became coaches, managers, and league administrators. Mothers did laundry and became chauffeurs and short-order cooks so their sons were on time for practices and games.

Most programs were for boys eight to fourteen years old, and they were organized with the belief that playing sports would prepare them to participate productively in a competitive economy. Until the 1970s, girls were largely ignored by these organizers and sat in the bleachers during their brothers' games and, in the United States, given the hope of becoming high school cheerleaders. Then came the women's movement, the fitness movement, and government legislation prohibiting sex discrimination. These changes stimulated and mandated sport programs for girls (see Chapter 8). Beginning in the mid-1970s these programs grew rapidly, and by the 1990s, girls had nearly as many opportunities as boys.

Participation in organized youth sports is now a valued part of growing up in most wealthy nations. Parents and communities use their resources to sponsor, organize, and administer a variety of youth sports. However, some parents today question the benefits of programs in which winning is more important than overall child development; others seek out win-oriented programs, hoping their children will become the winners. A few parents encourage their children

For a century now, youth sport has been more proving ground than playground—an enterprise laced with purpose and emotion, even the hopes of a nation. —Tom Farrey, ESPN (in *Game On*, 2008, p. 99)

to engage in unstructured, noncompetitive physical activities—an alternative that many children prefer over organized, adult-controlled sports (Honea, 2007; Midol and Broyer, 1995; Rinehart, 2000; Rinehart and Grenfell, 2002; Rinehart and Syndor, 2003).

Social Change and the Growth of Organized Youth Sports

Since the 1950s, an increasing amount of children's after-school time and physical activity has occurred in adult-controlled organized programs. This growth is partly related to changing ideas about family life and childhood in **neoliberal societies,** that is, *societies in which individualism and material success are highly valued and there is a decline in publicly funded programs and services.* The following five changes are especially relevant to the growth of organized youth sports.

First, the number of families with both parents working outside the home has increased dramatically. This has created a demand for organized and adult supervised after-school and summer programs. Organized sports have grown because many parents believe they offer their children opportunities to have fun, learn adult values, become physically fit, and acquire positive status among their peers (Dukes and Coakley, 2002).

Second, since the early 1980s, there's been a major cultural shift in what it means to be a "good parent." Good parents today are those who can account for the whereabouts and actions of their children twenty-four/seven. This expectation is a new component of parenting ideology, and in recent years it has led many parents to seek organized, adult-supervised programs for their children. Organized sports are favored by parents because they provide adult leadership for children, predictable schedules, and measurable indicators of a child's accomplishments. When a child succeeds, parents can claim that they

To meet cultural expectations for the "good parent," mothers and fathers often are attracted to youth sport programs that use symbols of progressive achievement and skill development. Karate, with achievement levels signified by belt colors, is appealing to some because the visible and quantifiable achievements of their children can be used as proof of their parental moral worth. (*Source:* Jay Coakley)

are meeting cultural expectations. In fact, many mothers and fathers feel that their moral worth as parents is associated with the visible achievements of their children—a factor that further intensifies parental commitment to youth sports (Coakley, 2006; Dukes and Coakley, 2002).

Third, there's been a growing belief that informal, child-controlled activities inevitably lead to trouble—much like what occurs in the novel *Lord of the Flies*. This belief often leads adults to view children as threats to social order (Sternheimer, 2006) and to see organized sports as ideal activities that keep children occupied, out of trouble, and under the control of adults.

Fourth, many parents, responding to the fear-producing stories highlighted in media news, now see the world outside the home as dangerous for their children. They regard organized sports as safe alternatives to informal activities that occur outside the home's locked doors and fenced backyards. Even when sports have high injury rates and coaches use methods that border on abuse, parents still feel that organized programs are needed to protect their children (Gorman, 2005; Nack and Munson, 2000; Nack and Yaeger, 1999; Pennington, 2005).

Fifth, the visibility of high-performance and professional sports has increased people's awareness of organized competitive sports as a valued part of culture. As children watch sports on television, listen to parents and friends talk about sports, and hear about the wealth and fame of popular athletes, they often see organized youth sports, especially those modeled after professional sports, as attractive activities. And when children say they want to be gymnasts or basketball players, parents often look for the best-organized programs in those sports (Opdyke, 2007). Therefore, organized youth sports have become popular because children see them as enjoyable and culturally valued activities that will gain them acceptance from peers and parents alike.

Together, these five social changes have boosted the popularity of organized youth sports in recent decades. Knowing about them helps to explain why parents invest so many family resources into the organized sports participation of their children. The amount of money that parents spend on participation fees, equipment, travel, personal coaches, high-performance training sessions, and other items defined as necessary in many programs has skyrocketed in recent years (Bick, 2007; Giordana and Graham, 2004; King, 2002; MacArthur, 2008; Moore, 2002; Poppen, 2004; Sokolove, 2004a; Weir, 2006; Wolff, 2003). For example, when my students and I recently interviewed the parents of elite youth hockey players who traveled to Colorado for a major tournament, we discovered that the families had spent $5,000 to $20,000 per year to support their sons' hockey participation. As they added up their expenses, many of them shook their heads and said, "I can't believe we're spending this much, but we are." And then they quickly explained that it was worth it because their son would benefit from the experience, and the whole family enjoyed traveling together. Other parents have gone even further—remortgaging houses and spending hundreds of thousands of dollars to nurture the sport dreams of a child (Weir, 2006).

One of the troubling issues raised by these changes is that mothers and fathers in working-class and lower-income households are increasingly defined as irresponsible and "bad" parents because they lack the resources to put their children in adult-supervised after-school sport programs as wealthier parents do. Parents without resources may also be perceived as uninterested in nurturing the dreams of their children. In this way, organized sports for children become linked to political issues and debates about family values

and the moral worth of parents in lower-income households.

MAJOR TRENDS IN YOUTH SPORTS TODAY

In addition to their growing popularity, youth sports are changing in five socially significant ways.

First, organized programs are becoming increasingly privatized. This means that more youth sports today are sponsored by private and commercial organizations, and fewer are sponsored by public, tax-supported organizations.

Second, organized programs increasingly emphasize the "performance ethic." This means that participants in youth sports, even in recreational programs, are encouraged to evaluate their experiences in terms of the progress they make in developing technical skills and moving to higher levels of competition.

Third, there's an increase in private, elite sport-training facilities that are dedicated to producing highly skilled and specialized athletes who can compete at the highest levels of youth sports. This means that parents often spend significant amounts of money to "train" their children in particular sports.

Fourth, parents are increasingly involved in and concerned about the participation and success of their children in organized youth sports. This means that youth sports are now serious activities for both adults and children, and adults are more likely to act in extreme ways as they advocate the interests of their children.

Fifth, participation in alternative and action sports has increased. This means that many young people prefer unstructured, participant-controlled sports such as skateboarding, in-line skating, snowboarding, BMX biking, Frisbee, jumping rope, and other physical activities that have local or regional relevance in their lives.

These five trends have an impact on who plays and what happens in organized youth sports. This is discussed in the following sections and in the

reflect on
SPORTS

Sponsorship Matters:
Variations in the Purpose of Organized Youth Sports

The purpose of organized youth sports often varies with the goals of those who pay for them. Forms of sponsorship differ from one program to another, but they generally fall into one of the following four categories:

1. *Public, tax-supported community recreation organizations.* This includes local parks and recreation departments and community centers, which traditionally offer free or low-cost sport programs for children. The programs are usually inclusive and emphasize overall participation, health, general skill development, and enjoyment.

2. *Public-interest, nonprofit community organizations.* These include the YMCA, the Boys and Girls Club, the Police Athletic League (PAL), and other community-based clubs, which traditionally have provided a limited range of free or low-fee sport programs for children. The goals of these programs are diverse, including everything from providing a "wholesome, Christian atmosphere" for playing sports to providing "at-risk children" with opportunities to play sports and engage in other activities designed to keep them off the streets.

3. *Private-interest, nonprofit sport organizations.* These include organizations such as the nationwide Little League, Inc., Rush Soccer (rushsoccer .com), and local organizations operating independently or through connections with larger sport organizations, such as national federations. These organizations usually offer more exclusive opportunities to selective groups of children, generally those with special skills from families who can afford relatively costly participation fees.

4. *Private commercial clubs.* These include gymnastics, tennis, skating, soccer, and many other sport clubs and training programs. Many of these organizations have costly membership and participation fees, and some emphasize intense training, progressive and specialized skill development, and elite competition.

Because these sponsors have different missions, the sports programs they fund are likely to offer different types of experiences for children and families (King, 2002). This makes it difficult to generalize about what happens in organized programs and how participation affects child development and family dynamics.

When public funds disappear due to tax cuts, one of the first things to be eliminated is youth sport programs—the type in category 1 (above). This has many effects. It limits opportunities for children from low-income families and funnels them into the one or two sports that may survive the cuts. Additionally, it creates a demand for youth sports in the remaining three sponsorship categories. Sponsors in categories 3 and 4 often thrive if they serve people with the money to pay for their programs.

Overall, this means that the opportunities and experiences available to young people are influenced by local, state, and national politics, especially those related to taxation and public spending. At present, opportunities and experiences are strongly influenced by voters and political representatives who say that tax money should not be used to fund sports for children. *What do you think?*

---

box "Sponsorship Matters: Variations in the Purpose of Organized Youth Sports."

The Privatization of Organized Programs

Privatization is a prevalent and alarming trend in youth sports today. Although organized sports are widely popular in the United States, there has been a decline in publicly funded programs with free and open participation policies. As local governments have faced budget crises because of federal and state tax cuts beginning in the 1980s, various social services, including youth sports, have been downsized or eliminated. Some publicly funded programs have tried to survive by imposing participation fees, but most have dropped programs. In response, middle- and upper-middle-class parents have organized sport clubs and leagues for their children. These organizations depend on fund-raising, membership dues, and corporate sponsorships. They offer opportunities to children from well-to-do families and neighborhoods, but they're too expensive and inconveniently located for children from low-income families and neighborhoods.

Private, for-profit sport programs also have become major providers of youth sports as public programs have been eliminated. These commercial programs are usually selective and exclusive, and they provide few opportunities for children from low-income households. The technical instruction in these programs often is good, and they provide closely regulated skills training for children from wealthier families. Through commercial programs, some parents hire private coaches for their children at rates of $35 to $150 per hour (Bick, 2007; Ellin, 2008; Farrey, 2008; Giordano and Graham, 2004; King, 2002; Poppen, 2004; Sokolove, 2004c; Wolff, 2003).

There are two negative consequences of privatizing youth sports. *First*, privatized programs reproduce the economic and ethnic inequalities that exist in the larger society. Unlike public programs, they depend on the resources of participants, rather than entire communities. Low-income and single-parent families often lack money to pay for dues, travel, equipment, and other fees. To the extent that ethnic minorities have lower household incomes and overall family wealth and more single-parent households than members of the dominant group, this creates and accentuates ethnic segregation and social-class divisions in communities (Farrey, 2008; Kooistra, 2005).

Second, as public parks and recreation departments cease to offer programs, they often become brokers of public parks and rent them to private sport programs. The rental fees are usually very reasonable, which means that the

> **Philadelphia Area Girls Soccer—the biggest local girls' league, which has been around in one form or another since the '80s—runs soccer leagues from as far away as Baltimore and Harrisburg, and from all over Philadelphia, a city that's 43 percent African-American. The league has 9,200 girls, 85 clubs and 556 teams. But only one of those teams is predominantly African-American.** —Steven Wells, journalist (2008)

private programs benefit from tax-supported facilities without being held accountable for running their programs to benefit the entire community. For example, such private programs may not be committed to gender equity or other policies of inclusion that are a key part of public programs. This occurred in Los Angeles during the late 1990s, when 83 percent of the participants in private programs were boys and only 17 percent were girls. This meant that local taxpayers were subsidizing the perpetuation of gender inequities in their own city—a violation of all local laws—until changes were made.

When privatization occurs, market forces become primary factors shaping who plays youth sports under what conditions. People with resources don't see this as a problem because they have the money to pay for their children's participation and choose the programs they want. But people with few resources face a double bind: They can't pay for their children's participation, and they often are accused of not caring for, controlling, or taking an interest in their children. There are obvious problems associated with privatization, and they disproportionately affect poor people with little political power; therefore, these problems receive little attention from the media or most current politicians.

Emphasis on the Performance Ethic

The **performance ethic** *is a set of ideas and beliefs emphasizing that the quality of the sport experience can be measured in terms of improved skills, especially in relation to the skills of others.* It has become increasingly prevalent in youth sport programs, where *fun* is now defined in terms of becoming a better athlete, becoming more competitive, and being promoted into more highly skilled training and competition categories. Often the categories have names that identify skill levels, so there may be gold, silver, and bronze groups to indicate a child's relative status in programs. "Travel teams" are now an important category in many sports because they separate certain young people from others on the basis of skills. Many parents like this because it enables them to judge their child's progress and prove to themselves and to others that they are "good parents."

Private and commercial programs emphasize the performance ethic to a greater degree than do public programs. Their directors and coaches tout them as "centers of athletic excellence" to attract parents willing and able to pay high fees for membership, participation, and instruction.

In some cases, the profiles and achievements of successful athletes and coaches who have trained or worked in the program are highlighted to justify costly memberships and dues.

Parents of physically skilled children sometimes define membership fees, equipment, travel, and training expenses, which can be shockingly high, as *investments* in their children's future. They may even use performance-oriented programs to develop social networks that can provide information about college sports, scholarships, coaches, and sport organizations. Overall, they want their children's sport participation to have developmental, educational, and eventual occupational payoffs.

As publicly funded youth sports are downsized or eliminated, private clubs provide participation opportunities. Membership fees in many club programs are too costly for most families. Additionally, children may not enjoy the emphasis on the performance ethic that is common in these programs. (*Source*: Travis Spradling, *Colorado Springs Gazette*)

Of course, the application of the performance ethic is not limited to organized sports; it influences a range of organized children's activities, and it is changing childhood from a time of exploration and freedom to a time of preparation and controlled learning (Chudacoff, 2007; Elkind, 2007; Laumann, 2006b; MacArthur, 2008; Rosenfeld and Wise, 2001). Children's sports reflect this larger trend (Sokolove, 2004a; Wolff, 2003).

New, Elite, Specialized Sport-Training Programs

The emphasis on performance is also tied to a third trend in youth sports—the development of elite, specialized training programs and leagues (Bick, 2007; King, 2002; Sokolove, 2004c; St. Louis, 2007; Wolff, 2003). Many private and commercial programs encourage early specialization in a single sport because these programs have year-round operating expenses that are paid from membership fees through the year. If young people played multiple sports and did not pay dues through the entire year, these programs could not to meet their expenses or produce profits for owners. Therefore, owners and staff develop clever rationales to convince parents and athletes that year-round participation in a single sport is necessary to stay on track for future success. As parents accept these rationales, "high-performance" teams, training schools, clubs, and programs grow in number and size (see imgacademies.com; velocitysp.com; catzsports.com; Coakley, forthcoming).

Commercial clubs for gymnastics, figure skating, ice hockey, soccer, tennis, volleyball, lacrosse, and other sports now declare an explicit emphasis on making children into headline-grabbing, revenue-producing sport machines. Children in these programs even become marketing tools for program managers and symbols of the moral worth of parents, who pay the bills and brag to friends about their children's accomplishments and how much they have done to make their children successful (Dukes and Coakley, 2002; Grenfell and Rinehart, 2003; Mahany, 1999; Rinehart and Grenfell, 1999). For example, eleven-year-old standout athletes may be used by clubs as marketing hooks to recruit dues-paying members. When this occurs, the adults who work at the club and depend on dues to pay their salaries become financially dependent on the eleven-year-olds that they train to succeed (and attract attention) in high-profile competitive events.

Children in high-performance training programs work at their sports for long hours week after week and year after year (King, 2002; Wolff, 2003). They compete regularly, their images and accomplishments may be used to market commercial training programs, they sometimes appear on commercial television and attract paying spectators to events at which they perform, and a few even have product endorsement contracts. All this occurs without government regulation, which might protect the interests, bodies, health, and overall development of child athletes. When the livelihoods of coaches and other adults depend on the performances of child athletes, some child advocates wonder whether elite training becomes a form of child labor (Donnelly, 1997, 2000; Donnelly and Petherick, 2004).

Existing child labor laws in many postindustrial societies prevent adults from using children as sources of financial gain in other occupations, but there are no enforceable standards regulating what child athletes do or what happens to them. Governments in a few countries mandate certain forms of coaching education, but coaches in the United States need no such training to work with children. They can use fear, intimidation, and coercion to turn a few children into medal-winning athletes and damage other "less-talented" children in the process without being held accountable to anything but market forces. Parents can live off their children's earnings, and commercial events can be scheduled around their talents. The results of this situation are sometimes frightening, but many parents and young athletes continue to believe that unless coaches are coercive, controlling, and abusive, they cannot effectively motivate and train successful elite athletes (Coakley, 1994; Coakley and Donnelly, 2004; MacArthur, 2008; Ryan, 1995).

Emile Therion, the former president of the Canada Safety Council, says that subjecting children to the demands and pressures of highly competitive sports "makes no sense whatsoever" and "flies in the face of public health and injury prevention, and . . . borders on child abuse" (CBC Sports, 2007). This statement creates defensiveness among the people who administer and coach in these programs, but it suggests that there is a need to have more public discussions about where the line should be drawn to separate abuse from the motivational and training strategies used by some coaches (American Academy of Pediatrics, 2000; Gorman, 2005; Pennington, 2005; Sokolove, 2004a). The argument generally used to avoid this discussion is that the children themselves want to specialize, be pushed, and excel in sports. But these children have not reached the age when they can give legally "informed consent." In addition, we don't allow ten-year-olds to work 40 hours a week as actors just because they like it and their parents approve; we have rules that regulate what child workers can do, even when the children are having fun as they work.

Increased Involvement and Concerns Among Parents

Youth sports have become serious business in many families. The expectation that good parents control the actions and nurture the dreams of their children 24/7 has made parenthood today more demanding than ever before. Many parents now feel compelled to find the best-organized youth sport programs for their children and ensure that their children's interests are being met in those programs.

Even though multiple factors influence child development, many people attribute the success or failure of children entirely to their parents.

> **ON THE *OLC*:**
> See the OLC—Additional Readings for Chapter 5—for Coakley's article on fathers and youth sports

When children are successful in sports, their parents are perceived to be parenting the correct way. For example, when Tiger Woods began winning tournaments, everyone attributed his success to Earl Woods, his father. The same thing occurred with Richard Williams, the father of Venus and Serena Williams. When a child succeeds, parents are congratulated, and people want to know what they did to "create" a prodigy; when a child fails, the moral worth of parents is questioned, and people want to know what parents did wrong.[2]

Under these conditions, a child's success in sports is especially important for parents. Youth sports are highly visible activities and become sites where mothers and fathers can prove their moral worth as parents. This greatly increases the stakes associated with youth sports and causes parents to take youth sports and the success of their child athletes very seriously. The stakes associated with youth sports are increased even further when parents expect their children to receive college scholarships, professional contracts as athletes, or social acceptance and popularity in school and among peers. When parents think in these terms, the success of their children in youth sports is linked to anticipated social and financial payoffs.

---

[2]When Tiger Woods won the famed Master's golf championship as a 21-year-old, people wanted to know how his father did it. In response, Earl Woods teamed with a golf writer to publish his book of advice, *Training a Tiger: A Father's Guide to Raising a Winner*. In the first chapter he explains that "It all starts with a parent's desire to make the child's life better . . ." The book hit the *New York Times* top 10 best-seller list, and Earl Woods joked that he was making more money on the book than Tiger made winning tournaments. Similarly, so many people wanted to know how Richard Williams "created" his tennis superstar daughters, that he authorized a film, *Raising Tennis Aces: The Williams Story*, in which he discussed his developmental strategies.

As the moral, financial, and social stakes associated with youth sport participation have increased, youth sports have become sites for extreme actions among some adults (Engh, 1999; Farrey, 2008; Nack and Munson, 2000). Parents may be assertive and disruptive as they advocate the interests of their children with coaches and sport program administrators. Some parents are obnoxious and offensive as they scream criticisms of coaches, referees, players, and their own children. A few have even attacked other people over sport-related disagreements.

As the actions of parents have become more extreme, some sport programs now sponsor parent education seminars combined with new rules and enforcement procedures to control parents at practices and games. These strategies are useful, but their success depends on administering them with an understanding of the cultural expectations that exist for this generation of parents. As long as parental moral worth is linked to the achievements of their children, and parents feel morally obliged to nurture the sport dreams of their children, parents will be deeply involved in and concerned about youth sports. Furthermore, when parents make major financial sacrifices and invest vast amounts of time in their children's sports without receiving the community support that families through history have always needed to thrive, their actions will be difficult to control. When cultural ideology emphasizes that parents are solely responsible for their children, mothers and fathers will assertively advocate the interests of their children. If they don't, who will? Under these cultural circumstances, many parents conclude that it is their moral obligation to get in the face of anyone standing in the way of their child's success in sports.

Increased Interest in Alternative and Action Sports

As youth sports have become increasingly structured and controlled by adults, some young people have sought alternatives allowing them to engage more freely in physical activities on their own terms. Because organized youth sports are the most visible and widely accepted settings for children's sport participation, these unstructured and participant-controlled activities are referred to as alternative sports—alternatives, that is, to organized sports.

Alternative sports, or "action sports," as many now refer to them, encompass a wide array of physical activities. Their popularity is based in part on children's reactions against the highly structured character of adult-controlled, organized sports. For example when legendary skateboarder Tony Hawk was asked why he chose to skateboard rather than do other sports, he said, "I liked having my own pace and my own rules . . . and making up my own challenges" (in Finger, 2004, p. 84). Similarly, when Sonja Catalano, the president of the California Amateur Skateboard League, was asked why skateboarding became popular, she explained, "We didn't . . . have any parents. That's what drew a lot of kids . . . It was their thing" (Higgins, 2007).

When I observe children in action sports, I'm regularly amazed by the physical skills that they develop without adult coaches and scheduled practices and contests. Although I'm concerned about injury rates and the sexism that often is a part of these sports, I'm impressed by the discipline and dedication of young action sport participants who seek challenges apart from adult-controlled sport settings (Beal and Weidman, 2003). The norms in these participant-controlled activities vary from one location to another, but most young people use them as guides as they share the spaces used in their sports (Rinehart and Grenfell, 2002).

Mark Shaw, winner of the first International Mountain Board Championships in 2000, explained that action sports often are attractive to young people because the older and more skilled participants teach tricks and give helpful advice to those with less experience. He explained, "I look forward to helping young skaters . . . at the park each weekend almost as much as I look forward to skating and my own progression on the board" (2002, p. 3). Many young people find this

Many young people seek alternatives to adult-controlled youth sports. Skateboarding and BMX biking are popular alternative sports that young people use to express themselves as they learn skills on their own terms. The experience of creating your own sports and playing them on your terms is very different from the experience of playing organized youth sports under the supervision of parents, coaches, referees, and league administrators. (*Source:* Jay Coakley)

orientation and the sense of community it creates to be more welcoming than what occurs in organized youth sports.

Participation in alternative and action sports has become so widespread that media companies and corporations wishing to turn young people into consumers have sponsored competitive forms of these sports and hype them as "extreme" and high-risk activities. These sponsored events, such as the X Games, Gravity Games, and the Dew Action Sports Tour provide exposure and support for athletes, but they alter the activities by making them more structured and controlled. At this point, we need research on the ways that this occurs and its implications for the participation experiences of young people. Adult intervention in these activities remains relatively limited, but in the future we will see skateboard and BMX coaches and organized programs. If

this occurs, children will seek other opportunities to play sports on their own terms.

DIFFERENT EXPERIENCES: VARIATIONS IN THE ORGANIZATION OF YOUTH SPORTS

Between 1970 and 1990, much of my research compared the experiences of young people in formally organized, adult-controlled sports with their experiences in player-controlled informal sports, such as pickup games. The data that my students and I collected over three years showed that experiences in these two contexts varied greatly. Informal sports were primarily action centered, whereas organized sports were primarily rule centered (Coakley, 1983b, 1992; White and Coakley, 1986). When children and young people created their own games, they emphasized action, exciting challenges, and opportunities for personal expression and maintaining friendships. In contrast, organized, adult-controlled sports emphasized learning rules, positions, skills, and the competitive strategies developed by coaches.

The different experiences in these two types of youth sports have important implications for what children learn, the meanings they give to their experiences, and the ways they integrate sports into their lives (Baker and Coté, 2006). Despite this, research on this issue has been scarce after 1980s. This is due to three factors. First, there has been a rapid and continuous decline in the informal games played by children. Second, parents have increasingly objected to anyone studying their children's lives. And third, the "Human Subjects" and Research Ethics Review Committees at most universities have regularly demanded that researchers obtain written approval from all parents whose children might be interviewed or observed in a study—even when the study involves hundreds of children on dozens of teams, or children who spontaneously create pickup games played in parks, school grounds, streets, vacant lots, driveways, and yards (Campbell, 2008).

> **OLC ON THE *OLC*:**
> See the OLC—Additional Readings for Chapter 5—for a summary of Coakley's research on informal games and organized sports.

For these reasons, most recent studies focus on organized youth sports but seldom involve in-depth or spontaneous conversations with children playing informal games. There's no recent research that compares the experiences of young people in organized, adult-controlled sports with their experiences in other types of sports and physical activities. However, we can use research from a variety of disciplines to identify the full range of experiences available to young people and to think critically about the merits of organized programs. This will help us determine whether the organized sports that exist today are worth all the time, money, and effort that adults put into them.

Informal, Player-Controlled Sports: A Case of the Generation Gap

The structure and culture of childhood have changed dramatically over the past two generations.[3] When I was growing up in the 1950s and 1960s, I spent at least fifteen hours playing in "pickup games" and informal, player-controlled sports for every one hour I spent playing games or practicing in an organized sport. Few of my sport experiences were ever seen or evaluated by parents, coaches, or referees. They were *my* experiences, and it was up to me to give them meaning because neither parents nor coaches were there to provide their interpretations, praise, or criticisms. I decided if I had fun, played well, succeeded, or failed. My judgments were influenced by peers with whom I played and by my general experiences, but there were no "outside spectators" shaping my perspectives. Further, there were no official statistics, scores, records, game films, or coaches' ratings to influence how I defined, evaluated, and then integrated these experiences into my life.

I played on high school teams in five different sports (over four years) and played other sports during summers. Only in college did I specialize because I had a full, four-year basketball

---

[3]The recent history of children's lives, including the over-scheduling of highly structured activities and the alarming decline of informal play and games involving physical activity has been documented and discussed by many experts on childhood and childhood development, as well as journalists and scholars studying popular culture (Coakley, 2008b; Chudacoff, 2007; Coté, Baker, and Abernathy, 2008; Coté and Fraser-Thomas, 2007; Coté, and Hay, 2002; Elkind, 2007, 2008; Farrey, 2008; Ginsburg, 2006; Joiner, 2007; Mintz, 2006; Schultz, 1999; Sternheimer. 2006; Williams and Feldman).

scholarship, and there was a team rule prohibiting involvement in sports that might cause injuries or distract attention from basketball training. However, I golfed, swam, and played in softball, handball, and basketball leagues during summers. Although I played over 130 basketball and baseball games as a college athlete, my parents saw none of them, nor did I expect them to do so.

Two generations later, Maddie, my eleven-year-old granddaughter has played for two years on a club travel team organized by a local nonprofit soccer organization. Her team is one of five travel teams for girls her age in our city of 180,000 people. Every travel team plays two seasons, one in fall and another in spring. About half the games are out of town, and each involves two to seven hours of round-trip driving. Maddie's team also plays in an indoor league between seasons and in three to four major tournaments that require significant travel during the year. Additionally, it is highly recommended that all travel team members play in one or more summer soccer camps.

When I was ten years old, and when Maddie's mom was ten years old, we were never asked to be so committed to a single sport. My parents could not and would not have supported such intense, specialized sport participation, and I would not have allowed Maddie's mother to specialize this way when she was ten years old. Maddie, a coordinated and strong girl, has cut back on basketball and dropped out of karate, two sports that she enjoys. Her involvement in swimming, ice skating, and in-line skating has, for the most part, been "postponed" for the sake of soccer.

Although Maddie has played organized soccer since she was four years old, she's played in very few informal sports and pickup games. She lacks time to do so, and her parents, like most parents today, don't feel comfortable allowing her to roam around the neighborhood to find other players and create informal games in places that cannot be predicted ahead of time. Even if she did have permission to roam the neighborhood, she would not find peers with whom she could create informal games. This is because parents today fear that their unsupervised children could be exploited by strangers or create trouble of their own doing.[4] Therefore, for every one hour that Maddie has played informal games, she has spent at least twenty hours practicing or playing games on organized teams under the watchful eyes of coaches, referees, and parents. Only once in seven years of playing organized sports has Maddie played an official game without multiple family members in attendance.

Maddie and I typify our respective generations when it comes to sports. My experiences were enjoyable, and I think I benefited from them; Maddie, at eleven years old, says the same thing, even though her experiences have been very different than mine. This raises the sociological question of whether we can make sense of the differences between them. Fortunately, there is research to help us think critically about the changes over the past two generations and the implications that they have for young people and the place of sports in their lives.

Developmental Issues and the Organization of Children's Sports

Informal games exist when young people come together and agree to organize themselves for the sake of having fun. My research indicates that informal games involve *fun* to the extent that they provide action, exciting challenges, and opportunities for personal expression and the maintenance of friendships (Coakley, 1983b). On an individual level, *fun* requires personal involvement in the action of a game and facing game-based challenges that test and extend personal skills. When the players are mixed ages, a seven-year-old playing with older children may have fun without a high level of personal involvement in the action, whereas the older and more skilled players require continuous personal involvement to have fun and they often alter rules to create exciting challenges.

---

[4]Remnants of informal street games can be found in some cities, although many now have laws preventing young people from using streets, alleyways, and vacant lots for game playing (steetplay.com; Whoriskey, 2002).

Maddie and most girls on the travel teams for eleven-year-olds have played organized soccer for at least six years. There's been little time for informal games. Instead, they've learned about soccer under the watchful eyes of adults who organize their teams, practices, schedules, games, tournaments, and camps and tell them what they should practice during their "free time." Under these conditions, how do girls and boys learn to make informed choices about their future sport participation? (*Source:* Jay Coakley)

Nearly all informal games are organized to maximize action. When there's plenty of space to play and few available players, the game rules are interpreted and adjusted to keep everyone involved, so that players don't quit and destroy the game. When space is limited and many young people want to play, game rules are enforced more strictly, and those who aren't selected to play are relegated to the sidelines; furthermore, the team winning a game may claim the right to play against a challenger that replaces the losing team. But in all cases, the emphasis is on action and exciting challenges. Action keeps alive a "spirit of play," and challenges require players to focus on testing their skills.

Research shows that informal games help children learn to cooperate and express themselves physically through a wider range of movements than they would try if coaches were evaluating them (Ginsburg, 2007; Henricks, 2006). For example, when Tom Farrey, a longtime writer and television correspondent with ESPN, investigated why France produces great soccer talent, he was told by André Mérelle, the director of youth soccer development in France, that they emphasize the importance of unstructured play and informal games for French children. Mérelle told Farrey this:

> Everyone wants to win games. That's good. But *how* do you win? If you're too focused on winning games, you don't learn to play well. You get too nervous, because you're always afraid to make errors. (in Farrey, 2008, p. 75)

As Farrey talked with Zinedine Zidane, three-time World Player of the Year, Thierry Henry, rated a top player in the world, and other soccer standouts in France, he concluded that the French developmental approach succeeds because it emphasizes informal play—no uniforms, positions, lined fields, game clocks, league standings, or adults yelling instructions from the sidelines. Without the constraining structures and adult expectations that characterize organized youth sports, young people learn to improvise, feel the joy of intrinsic satisfaction, and develop a playing style and personality that make them unique. This allows them to claim ownership of soccer, rather than feeling that soccer owns them. Further, as French coaches explained, informal games are the places where children develop a personal "feel" for the game and a vision for what occurs and is possible on the field of play—things that are not learned as readily in organized, adult-controlled games in which the structure and rhythm of play are dictated by rules, coaches, and referees.

Consensus among sport development experts worldwide is that children under eight years old should not play highly organized sports or on (soccer) teams with more than five players (Farrey, 2008). From eight to fourteen years old, games can be increasingly organized, but positional play should not be emphasized. There should be no travel teams and no more than one game per week or thirty to thirty-five games per year. Most important, say the experts, is that all coaches must complete a coaching education course and be regularly recertified through continuing coach education. When coaches learn about child development, they can facilitate participation opportunities through which young people are likely to develop a passion for the sport and the awareness that the sport enables them to be creative and expressive.

Developmental research supports the approach used in French soccer (Bloom, 1985; Coté and Fraser-Thomas, 2007). When Benjamin Bloom, a noted educational psychologist from the University of Chicago, studied 120 individuals who were recognized world-class talents in classical piano, sculpting, mathematics, Olympic swimming, professional tennis, and

neurological research, he concluded that talent development occurred over a long period of time under special conditions. In all cases, the talent development process began with exploration, play, and expressive fun. It did not begin with structured activities organized by other people, early specialization, or childhood commitments to long-term goals. Nor did it begin with pep talks about hard work, sacrifice, dedication, and the need to constantly practice. It began with opportunities to freely and playfully explore an activity and discover that it required creativity and effort. Talent development ultimately depended on whether the young people emotionally bonded with the activity, claimed it as their own, and identified what they wanted to learn so they could master a set of skills. When this occurred, the young people came to be driven by the feelings of exhilaration that occurred as they met and mastered new challenges. Bloom found that this process took at least ten years to occur, but when it did, the young people, usually in their midteens, were ready to specialize and make the commitments required to excel. At this point, fun merged with the hard work of mastering skills, and this merger fueled the passion and drive that enabled them to achieve excellence.

Bloom's findings have been widely supported by other scholars who study the development of excellence in sports (Coté and Fraser-Thomas, 2007). For example, reports on the experiences of U.S. Olympians indicate that they attribute their success to being introduced to sports through unstructured play and informal games and having opportunities to play multiple sports through junior high school (Gibbons et al., 2003).

We know that the existence of informal games and sports require and foster creativity, interpersonal skills, and problem-solving abilities among the players (Coté and Fraser-Thomas, 2007; Elkind, 2007, 2008). Creating games requires knowledge of game models, but maintaining them in the face of multiple unanticipated challenges requires keen conflict resolution skills and an ability to develop on-the-spot solutions to problems. Players must understand the basic requirements of an organized activity so they can create games to fit here-and-now circumstances; additionally, they must form teams, cooperate with peers, develop rules, and take responsibility for following and enforcing the rules (Adler and Adler, 1998). These are important lessons, and we need research to explain when and how children learn them in different types of sport experiences and whether the learning that occurs in sports is used by children in their relationships and activities apart from sports.

"Uniformed Childhood": Are Today's Organized Sports Worth the Effort?

A recent project sponsored by the Citizenship Through Sport Alliance (CTSA) brought together a panel of experts to assess the current state of organized youth sports in the United States. Using their collective knowledge, the panelists created a Youth Sports National Report Card.[5] They also issued grades for twenty-five important elements of existing organized sport programs. The elements were divided into sets of five, with each set related to a major topic. The topics and the overall grade for each are

1. Child-Centered Philosophy: D
2. Coaching: C
3. Health and Safety: C+
4. Officiating: B−
5. Parental Behavior/Involvement: D

The panel consisted of a diverse collection of men and women, including researchers, youth sports organization leaders, authors, attorneys, youth coaches, and parents. The goal was to identify where youth sports were succeeding or failing and to alert people to the need for improving the sports experiences of children. Each panelist supported youth sports and recognized that, when done correctly, they improve the physical fitness of participants and provide positive learning experiences. They also recognized that the adults who organize, coach, and maintain these programs are sincerely interested in the well-being of young people.

> **OLC** **ON THE *OLC*:**
> See the OLC—Additional Readings for Chapter 5—for copies of the Youth Sports Report Cards developed in the project sponsored by the Citizenship Through Sports Alliance.

In addition to issuing grades, the panel also identified specific problem areas that needed attention. The problem statements noted that, in general, youth sports have

- Lost their child-centered focus, meaning that there is too little emphasis on the child's experience and too much emphasis on winning
- Been distorted by overinvested sports parents, who have unrealistic expectations and often undermine for their own child and others the benefits of playing sports
- Failed to adequately evaluate and train the people who coach young people
- Overemphasized early sports specialization that often leads to burnout, overuse injuries, and a hypercompetitive culture and organized atmosphere focused on travel teams
- Ignored the interests and developmental abilities of children who view sports as a source of fun, friends, physical action, and skill development (http://www.sportsmanship.org/News/1105%20Report%20Card-Fgrade.pdf)

---

[5]Grading key for each topic: A= Outstanding; B = Good; C = Fair; D = Poor; F = Failing. Information about CTSA and multiple versions of the Youth Sports National Report Card are available at www.sportsmanship.org/. Copies of the report cards and factors to be considered when giving grades can be downloaded and used to assess programs in your community and to determine where changes should be made to improve them.

breaking BARRIERS

Mainstreaming Barriers
Will They Let Me Play with My Brace?

Ally was born with physical impairments—no fine motor movement in her left hand, a left leg that had to be stabilized by a brace, and a loss of 40 percent of her left-side peripheral vision. She didn't see her impairments as disabilities because she learned that every person's body was unique and capable of many things. Like other children, she developed physical skills and learned about her strengths and weaknesses. After playing soccer informally with her parents and sisters and watching her older sister play on a local team, she said she wanted play on an organized team. Then she asked, "Will they let me play with my brace?"

Ally's brace had never been an issue in her family. But as she watched sports on television, attended high school and college volleyball and basketball games, and watched her mom and sister play soccer and softball, she'd never seen athletes with leg braces. As a six-year-old, she had seen enough to wonder if there was space for her in sports.

The youth soccer programs where Ally lived were covered by the Americans with Disability Act (ADA), signed into law in 1990. When applied to youth sports, this law states that neither public nor private programs open to everyone are allowed to exclude children with disabilities unless their participation creates direct threats to the health and safety of able-bodied participants. These threats must be real, based on objective information, and unavoidable, even *after* reasonable efforts have been made to eliminate them. In Ally's case, it was easy to follow the law: She wore one shin pad on the front of her leg and another on the back, and her participation did not require the league to make accommodations causing "undue burden" or "fundamental alteration of the program" (Block, 1995).

According to the ADA, if playing in a program required tryouts for everyone, Ally could not be cut because she had a disability, but she could be cut if she did not meet the same skills standards used to cut others. Her coaches could not say that all players must run without a limp to make the team, but they could say that running was a prerequisite for team eligibility.

Ally had a great time playing her first year, despite surgery to lengthen her Achilles tendon and playing part of the season wearing a walking boot over her cast. But during her seven-year-old season, the coaches and parents put more emphasis on the performance

After Ally dropped out of youth soccer, she played youth basketball for a year and continued learning karate in a dojo committed to teaching all children. Among her most enjoyable sports experiences are those sponsored by the U.S. Paralympic Academy. After learning how to wheel this borrowed chair with one hand while handling a basketball, she wanted to practice and play wheelchair basketball. But there were no organized programs in her community. (*Source:* Jay Coakley)

OLC ON THE *OLC*:

See the OLC—Additional Readings for Chapter 5—for the Americans with Disability Act regulations

ethic. When Ally's lack of peripheral vision caused her to collide with others and sustain a few minor injuries, she became discouraged. Her coach helped everyone on the team understand the implications of Ally's vision impairment, but it was difficult to do this with members of opposing teams. As the season progressed, some parents of Ally's teammates expressed concern that accommodating Ally was jeopardizing the team's success.

When it came time to sign up for the next season, Ally said that she didn't want to play. Her main complaint was not that she felt inferior in terms of skills or that she had frequent collisions, but that opposing players never asked her if she was okay after collisions left her lying on the field. Her parents explained that children playing soccer were not expected to say they're sorry when they knock opponents down, but Ally was not willing to accept this, especially after she'd been taught to always say she was sorry if she knocked someone down. Two years later, when she began to understand this qualification, she resisted playing because she felt her skills were not as good as those of her peers. Additionally, she'd seen her sister's competitive travel team play and knew that "the performance ethic" pervaded the culture of youth soccer. Her parents knew that even the "recreational" teams in town emphasized the performance ethic to a degree that would make it difficult to accommodate a player with special needs and with skills that would not win games.

Ally's story is not unique. Children with disabilities generally have only two options if they wish to play sports: Find an organized adapted program, or play informal games in which peers are willing and able to develop adaptations. Unfortunately, very few communities have adapted youth sport programs, and informal games are scarce and seldom involve children who know how to quickly or easily include a child with disabilities. As a result, most children with disabilities are excluded from youth sports. Without advocates, they remain on the sidelines.

This outcome was noted by a ten-year-old boy with cerebral palsy when he said that other kids "like me but . . . if I'm trying to get in a game without a friend, it's kind of hard" (in Taub and Greer, 2000, p. 406). Other children with disabilities describe their experiences with these statements: (a) "[Kids] try and shove me off the court, [and] tell me not to play," (b) "they just don't want me on their team," and (c) "there's a couple of people that won't let me play" (in Taub and Greer, 2000, p. 406). When these things occur, children with disabilities miss opportunities to make friends and participate in activities that have "normalizing" effects in a culture where sports often are contexts for social acceptance and self-validation.

Although the achievement of inclusion requires sensitivity, experience, and effort, it is worth it when children—in this case, children with cerebral palsy—say things like this:

> [Playing games] makes me feel good 'cause I get to be with everybody, . . . and talk about how our day was in school while we play.
>
> Playing basketball is something that I can do with my friends that I never thought I could do [with them], but I can, I can! (in Taub and Greer, 2000, pp. 406 and 408)

Eliminating barriers to mainstreaming is a challenge, but when we are creative and open to expanding our experiences, it's not impossible.

The panel also created a Youth Sports Community Report Card for Parents (in English and Spanish) to enable mothers and fathers to evaluate programs serving young people ages six to fourteen in their communities (www.sportsmanship.org/ News/1105%20RCARD_COM_P.pdf). A third report card was designed for youth sports leaders to evaluate their programs and identify needed improvements for teams and leagues (www.sports manship.org/News/1105%20COM%20RCARD .pdf). These tools were intended to facilitate discussions about the organization of youth sports and how it might be improved to benefit all young people.

As a panel member participating in the "report card project," I also was concerned with three issues central to a sociological assessment of organized youth sports: access, development, and family dynamics.

Access issues   There are many good things about youth sports in the United States, but those good things are experienced by fewer and fewer young people (SGMA, 2006). For example, over the past forty years, most organized programs have become less accessible to children who are genetically average, living in low-income or one-parent households, and late physical bloomers; most important, they've ignored those who need exercise the most—children who are (dis)abled or clinically obese (Farrey, 2008). A seldom-discussed aspect of access is highlighted in the "Breaking Barriers" box on pages 140–141.

Access to youth sports in middle- and working-class areas has been severely cut in many large cities. For example, when Baltimore used $200 million of tax money to fund a baseball stadium in 1993, money for other programs was cut, which caused nearly 150 neighborhood recreation centers to close over the rest of the decade; park and recreation staff, numbering 1400 in 1990 declined to 365 nine years later. Carmelo Anthony, currently an NBA player with the Denver Nuggets, was nine years old when these centers began to close. He now explains that he was able to play organized basketball only because "drug dealers funded our programs. I was like 10 when they started buying my uniforms and it went on until I was 13 or 14" (Farrey, 2008, p. 237).

The Baltimore experience has been duplicated in dozens of U.S. cities as they've collectively spent over $20 billion since 1990 to subsidize professional sport franchises and their wealthy owners. Baltimore's "investment" in Camden Yards, where the Orioles play major league baseball, boosted the value of the team, increased profits to $25 million the next year, and allowed the team owner to sell the franchise for a $100 million more than he paid for it five years earlier. As this and similar deals have occurred in city after city, youth sports and other programs for young people have been cut. At the same time, private and club sport programs have been created to serve the needs of families that could afford them. These programs have generally been organized around a "competitive travel team model" that was and remains attractive to parents who see the sport accomplishments of their children as proof of their parental moral worth. As a result, there aren't enough votes to pass legislation that calls for taxes to fund local public programs and neighborhood teams that are free or low cost and open to everyone.

These political and economic dynamics help explain why overall sport participation among children has declined since the 1990s, even though particular "suburban" sports such as soccer, lacrosse, and volleyball have shown increases (SGMA, 2006). Organized youth sports built around a democratic model have been replaced by a top-down elitist approach. Even when professional sport teams and their multimillionaire players donate money to youth sports, they don't even begin to provide opportunities for those who need physical activities the most. For example, when the Denver Nuggets, playing in a nearly rent-free, heavily subsidized arena, paid Carmelo Anthony $80 million for five years, Anthony pledged $300,000 annually for five years to reopen

This Brooklyn team is a rarity at a time when few young people outside wealthy areas in large cities have access to organized youth sports. Too often, public money in cities is used to build stadiums and arenas that are used nearly rent free by professional men's teams owned by very wealthy white men. Filled with expensive luxury suites and club seats, these facilities generate impressive profits going to owners and highly paid athletes. The "economic logic" is that money generated by the facilities will trickle down to fund children's programs. But young people seldom see any resources trickling in their direction. (*Source:* Bebeto Matthews, AP/Wide World Photos)

an abandoned Boys and Girls Club in Baltimore. The club serves about 250 young people daily, but there are 160,000 young people in Baltimore who need such programs. Anthony was generous, but his money funds only a few sports for only one-tenth of one percent of the young people who need sport programs in Baltimore.

According to Bobby Dodd, president of the Amateur Athletic Union, which

Whole industries have grown up around the concept that sports for children age 10 and even younger aren't for fun or fitness, but a means to a lucrative career or at least a college scholarship. —Editors, *Rocky Mountain News* (2005)

sponsors youth sports and national championships for children as young as six years old, "Youth sports is a business. Across America, it's a business" (in Farrey, 2008, p. 141). This statement is an exaggeration, but it highlights the root of many youth sports access barriers. When we look beyond the impressively organized programs in many communities, the beautiful and well-maintained fields and facilities, and the thousands of coaches committed to producing excellent players and teams, youth sports are increasingly exclusive. For example, John Thomas, a director of coaching for United States Youth Soccer, said in 2007 that in all his travels across the United States over the last decade, he'd "never come across a mostly African-American girls' traveling team" (in Wells, 2008). The dynamics underlying this type of exclusion was analyzed by sociologist Paul Kooistra, who concluded that

> Competitive youth soccer in the United States is really the middle-class equivalent of dressage or polo. It provides a way middle-class parents can separate themselves and their children from lower social classes and minorities. (in Wells, 2008)

Middle-class parents will disagree with Kooistra's statement about *why* many youth sports do not include poor, working-class, and ethnic minority children, but Kooistra accurately identifies exclusion as a problem. Unless this problem is directly confronted nationwide, fitness among young people may remain at a level that signals expanded health costs in the future.

Development issues   Research shows that playing youth sports can enhance social and physical development, but it doesn't do this automatically, nor is it likely when programs are not organized to match the overall maturational level of the children who play in them.

It's *never* too early for a child to engage in expressive physical activities in safe environments. In fact, the more activity, the better; and the more socially and physically diverse the activities, the better (American Academy of Pediatrics, 2000). But to put four- and five-year-olds in organized competitive sports is much like creating a system of arranged marriages for twelve-year-olds who are clearly too young for intimate relationships and long-term commitments. Additionally, when children begin playing organized sports early and specialize in one or two sports year-round, they're more likely than other children to suffer overuse injuries and burnout (Coakley, forthcoming; Coté and Fraser-Thomas, 2007; Farrey, 2008).

> ### ON THE *OLC*:
> See the OLC—Additional Readings for Chapter 5—for Coakley's article on the pros and cons of early childhood specialization in sports and other materials on this topic

Contributing to burnout and dropout is the fact that most children under eight years old don't yet have the cognitive and social abilities they need to fully or meaningfully comprehend competitive relationships (Coté and Fraser-Thomas, 2007; Selman, 1971, 1976). A prerequisite for understanding competition is the ability to form and nurture cooperative relationships, which are the foundation of orderly competitive sports. When children play organized, competitive sports before they've played informal games, they often don't know their role in creating fair and ethical competition in organized games. Children who don't understand the dynamics of cooperation are difficult to coach on organized teams, and the results often lead to unhappy experiences for coaches, players, and parents (Coakley, forthcoming).

Coaches unwittingly contribute to burnout and dropout when they try to teach complex team strategies to children under twelve years old (Coté and Fraser-Thomas, 2007). For example, to understand one's position in any team (ball) sport requires a player to do three things simultaneously: (1) mentally visualize the ever-changing locations of all teammates and opponents over the entire field, (2) assess the spacial relationships between all players relative to the ball, and (3) synthesize this information to determine *where* one's position should be. Because most children younger than twelve years old don't have the cognitive ability and social experience to think in these terms, coaches must condition them to do so if they are to stay "in position." But doing the repetitive drills and plays over and over again to condition players to be in position makes practices so boring that children often lose interest in the sport; at their age they cannot appreciate the need for such an approach. To make things worse, when they play games, the coaches and their parents are constantly yelling at them to "spread out" and "get in position." This is so distracting that many children don't fully enjoy the experience of participation.

When adults ignore developmental issues, they tend to create organized sports that favor children who mature early. These children are bigger, faster, and stronger than their peers, and they're the ones who win games and championships. But they're not often the ones most likely to be the best players a few years later when others have matured physically and have the attributes to excel in particular sports. Unfortunately, many youth sports today are organized so there is a "pipeline" through which children move from one competitive level to the next. If children aren't in the pipeline by the age of nine or ten, they're unlikely to be selected for elite teams after that age. This means that many young people who could be excellent players at eighteen years old were cut out of the pipeline seven to ten years earlier and could never find their way back into it because they didn't have enough experience or name recognition among the insider club team coaches. This, in turn, undermines overall skill development in U.S. sports (Farrey, 2008).

AT YOUR *fingertips*   Table 13.1 (p. 457) presents comparative data on the success of U.S. athletes and teams in Olympic competition.

Youth sports programs in the United States are diverse, and some offer children opportunities for pleasure, healthy exercise, friendships, and learning about achievement and teamwork in structured activities (Coté and Fraser-Thomas, 2007; Fullinwider, 2006). However, many programs are organized so that they wear out and burn out early bloomers, cut out or keep out late bloomers, and exclude young people

Organized youth sports are a luxury item in most of the world. The parents of this ten-year-old Kenyan boy don't have the resources to nurture his sport dreams. But using his bare feet and a ball of rags bound with twine, he's managed to develop impressive soccer skills. The meaning he gives to kicking this ball likely differs from the meanings that privileged ten-year-old American boys give to kicking dozens of "official soccer balls" purchased by parents and clubs. (*Source:* Kevin Young).

uninterested in making premature long-term commitments to a particular sport.

Family dynamics issues   Organized youth sports are luxury items unavailable to most children around the world. They require time, money, and organizational resources that are scarce outside middle-class families in relatively wealthy societies. This means that playing organized sports is usually a family affair, especially when neighborhood-based, public programs don't exist and parents are the total support system for a child's participation.

Research on family dynamics and youth sports is scarce, but we know that youth sports can bring family members together in supportive ways and that it also can create tensions and problems in family relationships. Jeff Opdyke (2007), a reporter who covers family and money issues for the *Wall Street Journal*, recently noted that youth sports in the United States have been transformed from a child's recreation into a professionalized activity that dominates family life, "often splitting the family apart" and always taxing the family budget. When I read this I expected Opdyke to advise parents on reorganizing youth sports to avoid family turmoil, but he thought of his own son and came to a very different conclusion. He said,

. . . the bigger reality is this: Despite any inconveniences, we, as parents, owe him a chance to pursue his passion. If he never makes it past this level, it should be because he called it quits on his own or his skills could take him no further. It should not be because our schedules were too hectic to accommodate his dreams. (Opdyke, 2007)

This belief that parents are morally obliged to nurture the dreams of their children, regardless of cost and sacrifice, is now a widely accepted part of neoliberal American culture. Although children in the 1970s and 1980s often stayed in sports to please and gain attention from their parents—especially their fathers, who were often emotionally distant from them (Messner, 1992, 2002)—it is the parents who feel pressure today (Coakley, 2006). As a result, they change family schedules, give up weekends to attend games, organize vacations around out-of-town tournaments, chauffeur children to practices at all hours of the early morning and late afternoon, abandon family dinners, and perform uncounted

When children have schedules that are full of organized youth sports, they have little time to be with their parents. The irony is that many parents spend more time making it possible for their children to play sports than they spend with their children.

hours of volunteer labor to create leagues and teams that are the envy of parents everywhere.

Research shows that organized youth sports could not exist without the volunteer labor of parents, especially mothers (Chafetz and Kotarba, 1999; Thompson, 1999a, 1999b). Mothers drive children to practices and games, fix meals at convenient times, launder dirty training clothes and uniforms, and make sure that equipment is ready. They raise funds for teams and leagues; purchase, prepare, and serve food during road trips and postgame get-togethers; form and serve on committees that supervise off-the-field social activities; and make phone calls and develop websites to communicate information to other team parents. Mothers also manage the activities of brothers and sisters who are not playing games and provide emotional support for their child-athletes when they play poorly or receive self-deflating criticism from coaches and coachlike fathers. Fathers also provide valuable labor, but it's mostly devoted to on-the-field and administrative matters such as coaching, league administration, facility management, and field maintenance.

These patterns of parental labor reproduce a gendered division of labor in families, communities, and the minds of children, who are keen observers of how their parents perform their roles (Chafetz and Kotarba, 1999). More research is needed on this and other aspects of family life and youth sports. We know little about fatherhood and sports and the ways that fathers use sports as a site for parenting their children, at least the ones who play sports (Coakley, 2006). As one mother explains, "My husband was a big athlete . . . [and the] best way he knows . . . to be a good father is through sports" (Joiner, 2007).

> **ⓞ ON THE *OLC*:**
> See the OLC—Additional Readings for Chapter 5—for Coakley's article, "The Good Father: Parental Expectations and Youth Sports."

RECOMMENDATIONS FOR IMPROVING YOUTH SPORTS

Recommendations usually focus exclusively on organized youth sports. However, informal and alternative sports also have problems that need to be addressed. Many children opt for these sports because they provide action, exciting challenges, and opportunities for personal expression and maintaining friendships. But they often involve physical risks and various forms of exclusion. This suggests that adults should foster participation opportunities for children interested in joining informal games and participating in action sports. For example, instead of passing laws to prohibit skateboarding or in-line skating, adults can work with young people to design and provide safe settings for them to create their own activities and norms that are inclusive (Donnelly and Coakley, 2003).

The challenge for adults is to be supportive and provide guidance without controlling young people who need their own spaces to create physical activities. Adult guidance can make those spaces safer and more inclusive—for boys and girls as well as children with disabilities and from various ethnic and social class backgrounds. The gender exclusion that exists in certain alternative sports is especially problematic and begs for creative solutions that make the cultures of those sports more inclusive (Beal and Weidman, 2003; Laurendeau and Sharara, 2008).

As the tradition of informal games has nearly disappeared among young people today (see footnote 3), there is a need to consider ways to revive it and also to develop what might be called **hybrid sports** that *combine features of player-controlled informal games and adult-controlled organized sports.* Hybrid games have not been studied, but they come in at least two forms. *First,* there are informal games in which adults provide subtle guidance to children, who create and control most of what occurs as they play games in safe settings that are familiar and accessible to them. *Second,* there are organized sport teams on which parents and coaches encourage un- or semistructured play during practices and also include children in decision-making, rule enforcement, and conflict resolution processes. As more adults learn that positive child development requires involvement in unstructured play and informal games, there will be attempts to facilitate them.

Improving Organized Sports

When considering improvements for organized youth sports, programs and teams should be evaluated in terms of whether they are child centered and organized to match the developmental age of children, rather than the adults who organize them. This makes children a valuable source of information about needed improvements. If children define fun in terms of action, exciting challenges, personal expression, and reaffirming friendships (see p. 136), it makes sense to organize youth sports so that these aspects of experience are emphasized.

Action can be increased by altering or eliminating certain rules, changing the structure of games, and using smaller teams and playing areas. But many adults resist these changes because they want games to resemble what occurs in elite, adult sports. They say that children must play "the real thing" to learn the sport properly, and they forget that children are more interested in fun than mimicking adults and following rules that were never intended to maximize a child's fun. Therefore, adults need to control their emphasis on rules, order, standardized conditions, predictability, and performance statistics, and they should abandon tactics that slow and stop action; after all, high-scoring games are fun, even if many adults see them as undisciplined free-for-alls.

Exciting challenges are destroyed by blowouts. This is why children often include handicaps, "do-overs," and other adjustments that preserve the excitement of competition. Motivation depends on perceived chances for success, and close games keep children motivated by making the game exciting. When the adults who control youth sports resist changes that affect

game scores and outcomes, some people call for "mercy rules" that stop games or run game clocks continuously to shorten games with lopsided scores. But this subverts action and excitement for young people, who would alter games to keep them challenging rather than simply cutting them short. Therefore, adults should promote exciting and challenging action in youth sports rather than giving priority to winning games, developing a killer instinct in players, and qualifying for postseason tournaments.

Personal expression is maximized when games are organized to allow for creative and expressive action. Rigid systems of control and specialization by position restrict the range of players' experiences and opportunities to express themselves. Reducing team size increases opportunities for personal involvement and expression. For example, ice hockey games for children under twelve years old could be played across the width of the rink, thereby allowing three times as many teams to compete at the same time. Basketball could be reorganized so that first-string, three-player teams play a half-court game at one basket, while second- and third-string teams play at other baskets; a combined score would determine the overall winner. But these strategies require adults to revise their approach to youth sports so that the identification of mistakes is less important than encouraging children to express themselves and try new things.

Reaffirming friendships is central in the lives of children. Organized sports provide contexts for making friends, but friendships are difficult to nurture when children see each other only at adult-controlled practices and games. Additionally, making friends with opponents is seldom considered a high priority in organized sports. Therefore, youth teams should be neighborhood and school based whenever possible. Pregame warmups should mix players from both teams, and players should introduce themselves to the person they line up with as each quarter or half begins. Unless children learn that games cannot exist without cooperation between opponents, they will have no

When coaches and parents constantly shout directions during games, it's unlikely that children will feel comfortable engaging in personally expressive actions. This makes it nearly impossible for children to emotionally bond with and begin claiming ownership of a sport. Instead, many of them view organized sports as an adult thing that they'll eventually outgrow—much like braces on their teeth (Farrey, 2008). (*Source:* Jay Coakley)

understanding of fair play, why rules exist, why rule enforcement is necessary, and why players should follow game rules. Without this understanding, children don't have what it takes to maintain fair play at the same time that they strive for competitive success. When this occurs, youth sports are *not* worth our time and effort.

Obstacles to Change

A serious obstacle to change is that many people who currently control youth sport programs are mostly concerned about making them bigger, increasing the emphasis on the performance ethic, going to state and national tournaments, and developing more structures to control children, parents, referees, and coaches.

Coaching education can be an effective tool for improving youth sports when they lead coaches to put the needs of young people ahead of winning and producing age group champions. However, current programs don't teach coaches to critically assess and change the structure of youth sports programs. Their major focus is to keep coaches organized as they teach techniques and tactics safely. Additionally, unless coaching education instructors are prepared to keep coaches focused on the overall development of young people, there's a tendency in some courses to help coaches become "sports efficiency experts," rather than teachers who enable young people to make responsible and informed decisions about physical activity and sports in their lives. Unfortunately, turning child athletes into decision makers who control their sport lives and the contexts in which they play sports is not a goal of current coaching education programs.

summary

ARE ORGANIZED PROGRAMS WORTH THE EFFORT?

Although physical activities exist in all cultures, organized youth sports are a luxury. They require resources and discretionary time among children and adults. They exist only when children are not required to work and when adults believe that experiences during childhood influence individual growth and development. Youth sports have a unique history in every society where they exist, but they characteristically emphasize experiences and values that are central to the dominant culture.

The growth of organized sports in North America and much of Europe is associated with changes in the family that occurred during the latter half of the twentieth century. Many parents now see organized sports as vehicles to control children and ensure that boys and girls have access to important developmental experiences.

Major trends in youth sports today include the privatization of organized programs, an emphasis on the performance ethic, the development of high-performance training programs, and increased involvement among parents. In response to these trends, some young people have turned to informal, alternative, and action sports that they can control on their terms.

Children's sport experiences in the United States have changed dramatically over the past two generations. Informal, player-controlled sports were prevalent in the past, whereas organized adult-controlled sports are prevalent today. The decline of loosely structured, informal play and games has influenced the extent to which physical activities are the source of expressive fun among children. This is important in light of research showing that the talent development process in children usually begins with opportunities to freely and playfully explore an activity and discover that it enables them to be creative and expressive. Unless young people have opportunities to emotionally bond with particular physical activities, claim them as their own, and identify what they want to learn, excellence is rarely achieved.

The overall benefits of organized youth sports today are limited primarily because they've lost a child-centered focus, neglected the evaluation and training of coaches, and reflect too much the orientations of overzealous parents who have unrealistic expectations. Many programs are costly and designed to favor children who are bigger, faster, and stronger than their peers. This creates access issues that affect children from lower-income families and those whose abilities are average or below. The emphasis on early specialization in a single sport and year-round participation tends to wear out early bloomers, deny access to late bloomers, and exclude those who aren't inclined or selected to be on elite teams. Interactionist research shows that, prior to eight years old, children lack the abilities required for fully meaningful participation in organized competitive sports, especially team sports in which complex strategies are used. These abilities are not fully developed until twelve years of age in most children.

Because youth sport participation requires extensive resources, they depend on parental support, and they influence family dynamics. Influence may be positive or negative, but the scarcity of research on families and youth sports makes it difficult to identify the conditions under which positive or negative outcomes are most likely.

Recommendations for improving youth sports emphasize that there should be action, exciting challenges, and opportunities for personal expression and the maintenance of friendships. This requires more open and flexible structures and less overt control by adults. The goal of such changes is to provide young people with opportunities to learn that cooperation and an understanding of rules and rule enforcement is the foundation of competitive sports played fairly and ethically.

A major obstacle to change is that there are vested interests in maintaining and expanding programs as they are currently organized. Coaching education programs could facilitate critical thinking among those who work most directly with children in these programs, but they tend to emphasize organization and control rather than critically assessing and changing youth sports.

Overall, organized sports for children *are* worth the effort—*if* adults put the needs and interests of children ahead of the organizational needs of sport programs and their own needs to gain status through their association with successful and highly skilled child athletes.

WEBSITE RESOURCES

Note: Websites often change. The following URLs were current when this book was printed. Please check our website (www.mhhe.com/coakley10e) for updates and additions.

http://deepfun.com/junkyard-sports.html This site, maintained by Bernie De Koven, contains practical descriptions of how play and games can occur in any environment by using creativity rather than special equipment.

http://ed-web3.educ.msu.edu/ysi/ The Institute for the Study of Youth Sports at Michigan State University; the Institute's mission is to do scientific research and provide leadership and assistance that transforms youth sports so that the beneficial effects of participation are maximized and the detrimental effects are minimized. This is a very helpful site with useful links to other sites.

http://findarticles.com/p/articles/mi_qa3841/is_200404/ai_n9389930/print Online article: Sport Specialization in Youth: A Literature Review by Mark Hecimovich (2004).

www.keap.net Keep 'em All Playing, a parent organization in Edina, MN, wants to initiate a movement to restore youth sports as public, community-supported activities, because private and commercial programs distort the purpose and importance of youth sports. KEAP identifies the selection policies of competitive sport organizations as "a form of discrimination" that should make them ineligible to use public fields and facilities.

www.mhhe.com/coakley10e Click on chapter 5 to find information on studying gender in children's sports, an observation guide for studying a youth sport event; in-depth discussion of when children are ready to play sports; materials on parent–child relationships and youth sports; and discussion of social factors influencing youth sports.

www.momsteam.com Information at this parents' site is designed to create a safer, saner, less-stressful, and more-inclusive youth sports experience; it is by and for mothers of children in organized youth sport programs, but is useful for fathers as well.

www.nays.org The National Alliance for Youth Sports, a nonprofit organization with the goal of making sports safe and positive for children; useful links to other youth sport sites.

www.positivecoach.org/ The Positive Coaching Alliance (PCA) has partnered with over 1,100 youth sports organizations, leagues, schools, and cities in the United States to change the culture of youth sports.

www.righttoplay.com Right To Play (Toronto, Canada) is an international humanitarian organization that uses sport and play to promote health and development among children in high-poverty regions of the world; it focuses on community development and provides an evaluation system to assess programs and teams, identify and anticipate problems, and provide corrective action.

www.sportinsociety.org/uys.html The site of the Urban Youth Sports Program of the Center for the Study of Sport in Society; focuses on issues in Boston, but it provides a useful conceptual model for what might be done in other cities to overcome barriers that limit youth sport participation and to increase opportunities for healthy development.

www.sportsparenting.org/csp The Center for Sports Parenting offers guidance to parents and other adults involved in youth sports.

www.youth-sports.com A general site for information, advice, and instructional products for parents, coaches, and children involved in youth sports; links to useful articles on many topics.

(Mark Reis, *Colorado Springs Gazette*)

DEVIANCE IN SPORTS

Is It Out of Control?

WHERE DO ACCEPTABLE practices end and cheating begin? Why is it okay for a cyclist to sleep in an oxygen tent but not okay to inject EPO?

—**Paula Parrish, journalist, 2002**

(OLC) Visit *Sports in Society*'s Online Learning Center (OLC) at www.mhhe.com/coakley10e for additional information and study material for this chapter, including the following:

- A complete chapter outline
- Learning objectives
- Practice quizzes
- Internet resources
- Related readings
- Essays
- Student projects

IF I HADN'T HAD the injections [of painkillers], I don't think I would have been able to skate.
—**Johnny Weir, two-time U.S. figure skating champion, 2005**

IT'S NO SECRET what's going on in baseball. At least half the guys are using steroids. They talk about it. They joke about it. . . . At first I felt like a cheater. But I looked around, and everybody was doing it.
—**Ken Caminiti, Major League Baseball player, 2002**

BEING TOO MORALISTIC about our games is like going to the circus and being indignant about how the clowns act.
—**Dan Le Batard, ESPN journalist, 2005**

Deviance among athletes, coaches, agents, and others connected with sports attract widespread attention. Media stories about on-the-field rule violations and off-the-field criminal actions have become so common that many people think that deviance in sports is out of control. News about drug and substance use among athletes promotes this perception. For those who cling to the myth that sports build character, these stories lead them to conclude that the moral fabric of society itself is eroding. They say that money, greed, and undisciplined athletes have destroyed the "natural" purity of sport and the existence of ethics and fair play.

Because many people think this way, the purpose of this chapter is to examine deviance in sports. We focus on four questions as we deal with this issue:

1. What problems do we face when studying deviance in sports?
2. What is deviance, and how does sociological knowledge about it help us understand sports as a social phenomena?
3. Are rates of deviance among athletes (on- and off-the-field), coaches, and others connected with sports out of control?
4. Can sociology help us explain the use of performance-enhancing substances in sports and determine if and how it should be controlled?

These questions direct our attention to important issues in the study of sports in society.

PROBLEMS FACED WHEN STUDYING DEVIANCE IN SPORTS

Studying deviance in sports presents problems for four reasons. First, *the types and causes of deviance in sports are so diverse that no single theory can explain them all* (Atkinson and Young, 2008). For example, think of the types of deviance that occur just among male college athletes: talking back to a coach at practice, violating rules or committing fouls on the playing field during a match or game, taking megadoses of performance enhancing substances in the locker room, hazing rookie team members by demeaning them and forcing them to do illegal things, binge drinking, fighting in bars, harassing women, engaging in group sex, sexual assault, turning in coursework prepared by others, betting on college sports, overtraining and jeopardizing health, playing with painful injuries and using painkillers to stay on the field, destroying hotel property during a road trip after an embarrassing loss or a difficult win, and going home over a holiday to meet agents who have given money to their parents and bought a car for them to use when they return to campus. This diverse list includes only a sample of cases reported for one group of athletes at one level of competition over the past decade. The list would be more diverse if we included all athletes and if we were to also list examples of deviance that occur among coaches, administrators, team owners, and spectators. Therefore, it is important to study deviance in the contexts in which it occurs and not expect that a single theory will explain all or even a significant part of it.

Second, *actions accepted in sports may be deviant in other spheres of society, and actions accepted in society may be deviant in sports.* Athletes are allowed and even encouraged to do things that are outlawed or defined as criminal in other settings. For example, some things that athletes do in contact sports would be classified as felony assault if they occurred on the streets; boxers would be criminals outside the ring. Ice hockey players would be arrested for actions they define as normal during their games. Racecar drivers would be ticketed for speeding and careless driving. Speed skiers and motocross racers would be defined as criminally negligent outside their sports. However, even when serious injuries or deaths occur in sports, criminal charges are seldom filed, and civil lawsuits asking for financial compensation are rare and generally unsuccessful when they go to court (Atkinson, and Young, 2008; Young 2002a; 2004b).

Coaches treat players in ways that most of us would define as deviant if teachers treated students or employers treated employees similarly. Team owners in North American professional sports clearly violate the antitrust laws that apply to other business owners. Fans act in ways that would quickly alienate friends and family members in other settings or lead people to define them as mentally deranged.

On the other hand, if athletes take the same drugs or nutritional supplements used by millions of normal citizens, they may be banned from their sports and defined as deviant, even by the people using those drugs and supplements to enhance their performance in their non-sport jobs. Athletes who miss practices or games due to sickness or injury often are defined as deviant by coaches and teammates, even though taking "sick days" is accepted as normal outside sport. Certain college

athletes violate rules if they hold jobs during the school year, and coaches may punish players who fail to attend class, whereas other students work and cut classes without violating rules or being sanctioned. Youth league players may be benched for a game if they miss practice to attend a family picnic, despite the value given to the family outside sports. The fact that norms seem to be applied and enforced differently in sports makes it difficult to use studies of deviance in other contexts to understand what occurs in sports.

Third, *deviance in sports often involves an uncritical acceptance of norms, rather than a rejection of norms.* Athletes often go overboard in their dedication to sport and their willingness to pay the price, play with pain, and live their dreams. Their attitudes and actions are *supranormal* in the sense that they overconform to norms widely accepted in society as a whole. Instead of setting limits on what they

Understanding deviance in sports is a challenge because athletes often do things that are not accepted in other settings. Many of the actions of boxers, football and hockey players, racecar drivers, and wrestlers would be criminal acts off the field. (*Source: Colorado Springs Gazette*)

are willing do as athletes, they evaluate themselves and their peers in terms of their dedication to the game and their unqualified willingness to go over-the-top and exceed normative limits, even if they jeopardize health and well-being in the process.

This "over-the-top deviance" is often danger-ous, but athletes learn to accept it as part of the game they love to play and as the basis for being accepted into the culture of high-performance sports. When normative overconformity takes the form of extreme dedication, commitment, and self-sacrifice, it brings praise rather than punishment from coaches and fans. It's even used to reaffirm cultural values related to hard work, competition, achievement, and manliness. In the process, people overlook its negative con-sequences for health, relationships with family and friends, and overall well-being.

This practice of overconformity to norms makes it difficult to understand much of the deviance in sports because it doesn't fit the belief that deviance always involves *subnormal* or *under-conforming* attitudes and actions based on a rejec-tion of norms. However, both *supranormal* as well as *subnormal* attitudes and actions are *abnor-mal*, that is, deviant (Heckert and Heckert, 2002, 2007; West, 2003). When people don't distin-guish between these different forms of deviance, they often define athletes as role models, even though much of what athletes do is dangerous to health and well-being and beyond the limits of acceptance in other spheres of life.

Fourth, *training and performance in sports are based on such new forms of science and technology that people have not yet developed norms to guide and eval-uate the actions of athletes and others in sports.* Sci-ence and medicine once used only to treat people who were sick are now used regularly in sports (Pennington, 2007). The everyday challenge of training and competition in sports often pushes bodies to such extremes that continued participa-tion requires the use of new medical treatments and technologies just to stay on the field (Farrey, 2006a; 2007).

Using nutritional supplements is now a stan-dard practice in nearly all sports. As one high school athlete explained, supplements "are as much a fixture in sports participation as mouth guards and athletic tape" (in Mooney, 2003, p. 18). Ingesting substances thought to enhance performance is a taken-for-granted part of being an athlete today. In 2005 the athletic departments at the University of Texas and Texas A&M spent over $200,000 on supplements for their football players. Athletes in high-performance sports buy supplements online and at local stores, not because they want to take shortcuts, but because they want to be all they can be in sports; they don't think critically, they "just do it" (Leitch, 2008).

A survey of the ads for performance-enhancing substances in any *Flex, Muscle and Fitness, Planet Muscle,* or *Muscle and Body* magazine leads to the conclusion that "strength and high performance (and a "hot body") are just a swallow away." Online promotions push protein drinks, amino acids, testosterone boosters, human growth hor-mone boosters, insulin growth factor, vitamins, and hundreds of other supplements that will help athletes get the most from their workouts, recover more quickly from injuries, and build a body that can adjust to overtraining and become stronger in the process. If you don't like to swallow, there are rub on creams and patches that do the job. Using the Internet to obtain various substances has occurred since the early 1990s (even though U.S. federal investigators did not discover this until 2005—see Denham, 2007b). In the meantime, it's become much more difficult to determine just what actions are deviant and what actions are accepted parts of athletic training; in fact, "normal training" is now an oxymoron because all training involves excess and ignoring limits and boundar-ies accepted as normal in society as a whole.

DEFINING AND STUDYING DEVIANCE IN SPORTS

When a softball player punches an umpire after a disputed call, it's a deviant act because it vio-lates a norm. Similarly, when a college football coach provides funds to hire prostitutes for high school recruits or when an Olympic judge alters scores to ensure a victory for a particular figure skater, we know that deviance has occurred. In each case, norms are violated.

A **norm** is *a shared expectation that people use to identify what is acceptable and unacceptable in a social world.* Norms exist in all social worlds and serve as the moral standards that people use to identify deviance. **Deviance** *occurs when a person's ideas, traits, or actions are perceived by others to fall outside their normal range of acceptance in a society.*

Studying deviance is often tricky because norms take different forms, vary in importance, change over time, and differ from one social world to another. **Formal norms** *are official expectations that take the form of written rules or laws*, whereas **informal norms** are *customs or unwritten, shared understandings of how a person is expected to think, appear, and act in a social world.*

When basketball players dribble the ball out of bounds or shove a referee in anger over a foul call, they violate formal norms that are written in the official rule book. These norms are enforced by "officials" given the authority to sanction or punish violators. When two college basketball players don't face the U.S. flag during the national anthem or don't participate in a pregame team ritual, they violate unwritten, informal norms. In response, fans may deride or "boo" players that don't conform to flag-related customs, and teammates may refuse to talk with players that don't meet their expectations for togetherness. This means that there are two forms of deviance: **formal deviance,** which involves *violations of official rules and laws that are punished by official sanctions administered by people in positions of authority*, and **informal deviance,** which involves *violations of unwritten customs and shared understandings that are punished by unofficial sanctions administered by observers or peers.*

These definitions of norms and deviance appear to be straightforward, but there are different ways to interpret norms and identify deviance when studying sports in society.

Two Approaches to Studying Deviance

When norms are viewed as representing absolute, unchanging truths about right and wrong and good and evil, deviance is identified differently than when norms are viewed as social constructions that people create as they interact with each other and organize their social worlds to meet individual and collective needs.

The truth-based, or **absolutist approach** to deviance *assumes that social norms are based on essential principles that constitute an unchanging foundation for identifying good and evil and distinguishing right from wrong.* According to this approach, all norms represent particular *ideals*, and whenever an idea, trait, or action departs from an ideal, it is deviant; the greater the departure from the ideal, the more

"It's time to lock up these athletes; they're a bunch of thugs."

When people use an absolutist approach, they see any departure from their ideals as deviance. The cause of deviance, according to this approach, rests in the weak or distorted character of individuals who can be controlled only by making more rules and enforcing them more strictly. But this approach does little to explain and deal with most deviance in sports today.

serious the deviance. This approach is illustrated in Figure 6.1, where the solid, vertical line signifies a particular ideal, and the dotted, horizontal line represents departures from the ideal in the form of increasing degrees of deviance. The most extreme deviance occurs when there is a major departure from the ideal; sometimes, people refer to this type of deviance as perversity or evil. For example, if obedience to the coach is a team norm, any form of disobedience is deviant. The greater and more frequent the disobedience, the more serious the deviance; chronic or consistent deviance would eventually be seen by absolutists as evil and a sign of perverted character.

The absolutist approach has not contributed to a sociological understanding of deviance in sports, but it is often used by fans, media people, and the general public as they discuss rule violations and crimes by athletes and coaches. It's important for sociologists to understand this approach because it helps them explain the way many people respond to deviance and why there are so many disagreements when people discuss deviance in sports. For example, if you and I use an absolutist approach but hold different ideals, it becomes difficult for us to jointly study deviance. Let's say that my ideal is fair play, and your ideal is achieving excellence as demonstrated through winning, According to my ideal, all violations of game rules would be deviant, whereas you would say that a player was deviant if your team lost because she refused to commit a strategic foul in the closing minutes of a game. If we don't share the same ideals, we identify *deviance* in differently.

Another problem with an absolutist approach is that it leads many people to think that controlling deviance always requires more rule enforcement and increasingly severe penalties for deviations from the ideal. This leads people to develop more rules, make them stricter, and create more efficient methods of detection and punishment. But this approach undermines creativity and change, creates resistance to rules, and makes people defensive about their own attitudes and actions. When strict conformity to a specific ideal is the only way to avoid deviance, people always wonder if they are doing something wrong.

Despite these problems, many people use an absolutist approach when they discuss deviance in sports. When the actions of athletes don't match their ideals, they define the athletes as deviant. They argue that the only way to control deviance is to "get tough," make punishments more severe, and eliminate the "bad apples" that lack moral character and will always be moral failures. In other words, those who use an absolutist approach see deviance as located in the person who engages in it and concludes that the only way to control deviance is to police and punish individual rule violators.

Most sociologists reject an absolutist approach and use an interaction-based, constructionist approach to identify and deal with deviance. A **constructionist approach** assumes that **deviance** occurs when *ideas, traits, and actions fall outside the socially determined boundaries that people in a social world generally use to determine what*

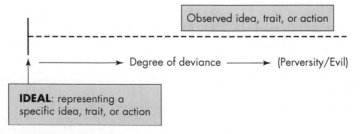

FIGURE 6.1 An *absolutist approach* to deviance: Using ideals to judge ideas, traits, and actions.

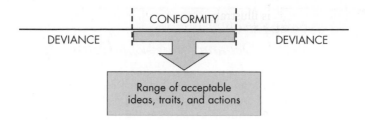

FIGURE 6.2 A *constructionist approach* to deviance: negotiating normative limits to permit a range of acceptable ideas, traits, or actions.

is acceptable and unacceptable in a society or social world. This approach is based on a combination of cultural, interactionist, and structural theories in sociology, and it emphasizes the following four points:

1. Norms are socially constructed as people interact with each other and use their values to determine a range of acceptable ideas, traits, and actions. This point is illustrated in Figure 6.2, where the vertical hash marks crossing the horizontal line represent the boundaries that separate what is accepted from what is deviant. This means that conformity does not usually require everyone to think, look, and act exactly alike to avoid deviance—there is a range of acceptance associated with nearly all norms.

2. Deviance is socially constructed as people negotiate the boundaries of their acceptance. The ideas, traits, and actions that fall outside the range of unacceptance are defined as deviant. However, boundary negotiation occurs continuously, and the vertical hash lines that represent normative boundaries move one way or the other over time as norms change. An example of this negotiation process is highlighted in Breaking Barriers (pp. 160–161).

3. The process of negotiating normative boundaries and the range of social acceptance is influenced by the power dynamics that exist in a society or social world. People who possess power and authority generally

have the most influence in determining normative limits, because they administer formal sanctions, including both punishments and rewards.

4. Most ideas, traits, and actions in a social world fall into a normally accepted range. This is illustrated in Figure 6.3 (on page 162), where those that fall outside this "bell-shaped" normal range involve deviant underconformity in the shaded area on the left side of the range *or* deviant overconformity in the shaded area on the right side.

As represented in Figure 6.3, a constructionist approach is useful when studying deviance in sports, especially when deviance involves the use of certain performance-enhancing substances and other extreme actions that most people in society define as outside the normal range of acceptance. **Deviant underconformity** *consists of subnormal ideas, traits, and actions that indicate a rejection of norms or ignorance about their existence,* such as bar fighting, sexual assault, or referring to a person with mental retardation as a "retard." **Anarchy** is *the social condition that exists when widespread underconformity creates general lawlessness.*

Deviant overconformity *consists of supranormal ideas, traits, and actions that indicate an uncritical acceptance of norms and a failure to recognize any limits to following norms,* such as playing despite broken bones and torn ligaments or using painkilling drugs to stay in the game. **Fascism** *is the social condition that exists when widespread overconformity*

Acceptance Barriers
What Is Deviance and Who Defines It?

Oscar Pistorius is a record-setting sprinter from South Africa. Sometimes identified as "Blade Runner" and "the fastest man on no legs," he was born without a fibula bone in both legs. The fibula is the long, slender bone that goes from the knee to the ankle alongside the tibia, or shin bone. Oscar's parents determined that a below-the-knee prosthetic leg and foot would enable him to live more normally. So in late 1987 they arranged a surgery in which doctors amputated the legs of their 11-month-old son below the knee.

As an active, athletic boy, Oscar dreamed of playing elite rugby. Never experiencing a body without prosthetic legs, he did everything his friends did and didn't consider himself handicapped. Through middle and high school he wrestled and played cricket, rugby, water polo, and tennis. After he shattered his knee playing rugby in late 2003 his doctor told him to use running as physical therapy. In January 2004, at the age of 17, he began to train as a sprinter. Two months later he competed in his first 100-meter race, winning a gold medal and setting a world record time of 11.51 seconds.

Through the summer of 2004 he continued to compete and set records. In September of that year he competed in the Paralympic Games in Athens, Greece, where he won a silver medal in the 100 meters and a gold medal in the 200 meters, setting world records four times during his heats.

Between 2005 and mid 2008, Pistorius competed in many Open/Able-bodied meets as well as T43 and T44 races—the categories used for runners with both legs amputated below the knee and with one leg amputated below the knee, respectively. Breaking his own records over 25 times, he holds all world records in the T43 and T44 100-, 200-, and 400-meter sprints, and he has steadily improved his placement against elite international able-bodied sprinters in the 200- and 400-meter races. His best time in the 100 meters was 10.91 seconds, and his best time in the 400 meters was 46.34 seconds, just 2.34 seconds slower than the 2004 Olympic men's gold medal time of 44.00 seconds.

Team OSSUR, the company that makes the carbon-fiber Flex-Foot Cheetah prosthesis (see photo), sponsors Pistorius and other record-setting Paralympic sprinters. The Flex-Foot replicates the hind leg of a cat with a small profile foot that extends and reaches out to contact the ground, while the large thigh muscles pull the body forward. These prosthetic legs return about 95 percent of the energy put into them by the runners' upper legs, whereas a human lower leg returns about 200 percent of the energy put into them. OSSUR researchers hope to eventually duplicate the running power of a human leg, but they say that reaching their goal will take some time.

In 2007 Pistorius adopted a new training regimen similar to the one used by elite, able-bodied sprinters. He felt that his hard work would improve his performance, especially in the 400-meter sprint. However, his hopes of qualifying for and competing in the 2008 Olympics in Beijing were dashed when the International Association of Athletics Federation (IAAF), the global governing body for track and field, banned him. Research commissioned by the IAAF concluded that his prosthetic legs gave him an advantage over able-bodied runners (IPC, 2008; Tucker and Dugus, 2008, 2007a, b, c, d; Wikipedia, 2008) and the members of the IAAF board defined Pistorius as deviant—his body, they said, was abnormal (supranormal according to the terms used in this chapter). Pistorius appealed the IAAF decision and asked the International Court of Arbitration for Sport to consider research that went beyond laboratory tests that focused only on the carbon fiber leg *apart from* the human leg. He felt there should be field tests on a running track while he ran under race conditions. He knew from experience that the blade-like legs slowed him down at the start of a race, provided poor traction on a wet track, produced rotational forces that were difficult to control, and gave him none of the maneuverability and control that are supplied by the human lower leg, ankle, and foot (Longman, 2007; McHugh, 2007; Ossur, 2008).

Independent researchers conducted further studies, and after the international court reviewed the new research findings, they overturned the IAAF ban in May, 2008 and ruled that Pistorius was eligible to qualify for the Olympics and participate in other international events (Director, 2008; Robinson and Schwarz, 2008). Pistorius was elated, and said, "It's not just about me; it's about the extra opportunity for amputee athletes."

This case raises provocative issues about what counts as deviance in sports and who draws the line to distinguish what is acceptable and what is not. The merger of sports and technology has led to heated debates over these issues. Pistorius knew that it was risky to challenge

In 2008 Oscar Pistorius (No. 1853) was banned from racing in the Olympics. International (IAAF) track and field officials concluded that his carbon fiber legs gave him an unfair advantage over able-bodied runners. The IAAF decision was overturned by the International Court of Arbitration for Sport. This opened the door for Pistorius to compete in the 2008 Olympic Games in Beijing, but he failed to qualify. (*Source:* David Biene; Photo courtesy of Ossur, www.ossur.com)

the "Empire of the Normal" as it existed in the IAAF. But he also knew that definitions of *deviant* and *normal* are social constructions, and that baseball players have "assistive" laser eye surgery to improve their vision; that football, baseball, and tennis players have "assistive" elbow and knee reconstructions that use super strong ligaments taken from other parts of their bodies; that endurance athletes sleep in "assistive" hyperbaric chambers to enhance the oxygen-carrying capacity of their red blood cells (to increase their endurance); and that swimmers wear NASA-designed, ultra-light, seamless, water-resistant full body "assistive" swim suits that improve their times. He thought that if these things were not considered to be illegal forms of "techno-doping," his legs should not be considered deviant.

Pistorius did not qualify for the 2008 Olympics in Beijing—missing by seven tenths of a second in the 400-meters (46.25 vs 45.55), but he will train to run in the 2012 Games in London. Even if he doesn't qualify in 2012, his case has shown us that the line between normal and deviant shifts and changes depending on who draws it and what criteria they use. It also forces us to reconsider our ideas about what constitutes an "assistive" device, about what athletes look like, and about why we separate people into distinct able-bodied and disabled categories when real bodies are so much more complicated than that.

As new technologies enable people with various impairments to compete at elite levels, officials who determine eligibility must think more clearly and critically about their definitions of normal and deviant and their conception of human perfection. But can this occur if none of the decision-makers have experiences or bodies like those of Oscar Pistorius? *What do you think?*

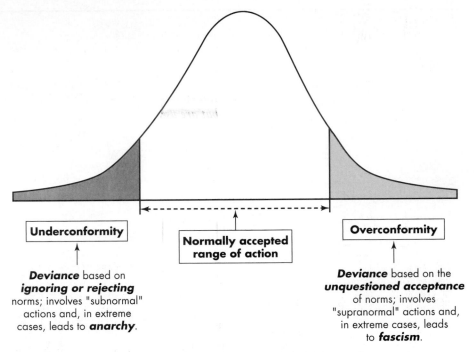

Underconformity	Normally accepted range of action	Overconformity
Deviance based on **ignoring or rejecting** norms; involves "subnormal" actions and, in extreme cases, leads to **anarchy**.		**Deviance** based on the **unquestioned acceptance** of norms; involves "supranormal" actions and, in extreme cases, leads to **fascism**.

FIGURE 6.3 Two types of deviance in sports. Most actions in sports fall within a normally accepted range in society as a whole. Deviance occurs when ideas, traits, or actions go beyond normative limits on either side of this range.

creates unlimited obedience to norms or the commands of leaders.

Both types of deviance involve abnormal ideas, traits, or actions, and both can be dangerous, just as both anarchy and fascism are dangerous.

Deviant Overconformity in Sports

Research shows that deviant overconformity is a significant problem in sports. When sociologists Keith Ewald and Robert Jiobu (1985) studied men who were seriously involved in bodybuilding or competitive distance running, they found that some of the men engaged in unquestioned overconformity to norms related to training and competition. The men trained so intensely and so often that their family relationships, job performance, and/or physical health deteriorated, yet they never questioned their actions or the norms of their sport cultures. This study was published

over twenty years ago, but athletes today are just as likely, if not more likely, to ignore normative limits and do anything it takes to train and participate in sports. Former NFL player Matt Millen explains in this way:

> You have to be selfish, getting ready for a game that only a handful of people understand. It's tough on the people around you. . . . It's the most unspoken but powerful part of the game, that deep-seated desire to be better at all costs, even if it means alienating your family or friends. [Athletes] will do anything to [stay in the game], even if it means sacrificing their own physical or mental well being." (in Freeman, 1998, p. 1)

Another player reaffirms Millen with these words:

> . . . I had a pretty high pain threshold. I was willing to do anything to be successful, anything. When I got hurt, I just made sure to get myself

back into a game as soon as possible. It was do-what-you-have-to-do, and I did it all. (in Leahy, 2008, p. W08)

Research has identified many forms of deviant overconformity, including self-injurious over-training, extreme weight control strategies, taking untested or dangerous performance enhancing substances, and playing while injured.[1] When studying deviance in sports, it's important to distinguish between those actions based on indifference to or rejection of norms and those actions based on a blind acceptance of norms and a willingness to surpass normal limits to follow them. Such a distinction is identified only by examining the organization and dynamics of sports cultures and the meanings that athletes give to their sport participation. For example, within the culture of high-performance sports, athletes are expected to live by a code that stresses dedication, sacrifice, and a willingness to put one's body on the line for the sake of their sport and their teammates. Following this code to an extreme degree is seen as a mark of a true athlete who is accepted and respected by peers as one of them (Donnelly, 1996b; Howe, 2004; Ingham et al., 1999, 2002; Johns, 1997; Leahy, 2008; Waldron and Krane, 2005). This creates a set of conditions in which athletes are likely to *overconform* to norms

embodied in the code or ethic of contemporary power and performance sports.

The Sport Ethic and Deviance in Sports

An **ethic** is *an interrelated set of norms or standards that are used to guide and evaluate ideas, traits, and actions in a social world.* Research suggests that elite athletes and coaches use a **sport ethic** to guide and evaluate attitudes and actions in the social world of power and performance sports (Hughes and Coakley, 1991). This ethic is formed around four general norms (see Figure 6.4):

1. *Athletes are dedicated to "the game" above all other things.* This norm stresses that athletes must love "the game" and prove it by giving it top priority in their lives. They must have the proper attitude and demonstrate their unwavering commitment to the game by meeting the expectations of fellow athletes, making sacrifices to stay in their sport, and facing the demands of competition without backing down. Coaches' pep talks and locker-room slogans proclaim the importance of

---

[1]Many studies identify deviant overconformity, although they may not all use the concept as described in this chapter. These studies (along with detailed media reports) include Beals, 2000; Beals and Hill, 2006; Busch, 2007; Cotton, 2005; Curry, 1993; Curry and Strauss, 1994; Davis, 1999; Donnelly, 1993; Franseen and McCann, 1996; Grant, 2002a, 2002b; Haney and Pearson, 1999; Hawes, 2001; Howe, 2004; Ingham et al., 2002; Johns, 1992, 1996, 1997, 2004; Johns and Johns, 2000; Keown, 2004; P. King, 2004; Leahy, 2008; Liston et al., 2006; Lyons, 2002; Nixon, 1993a, 1993b, 1994a, 1994b, 1996a, 1996b; Peretti-Watel et al., 2004a, 2004b; Pike, 2004, 2005; Pike and Maguire, 2003; Schefter, 2003; Schwarz, 2007a, 2007b, 2007c, 2007d; Sundgot-Borgen, 2001; Thompson and Sherman, 1999; Waldron and Krane, 2005; White and Young, 1997; Wilmore, 1996 (a review of thirty-five studies related to eating disorders); Wood, 2004; Young and Charlesworth, 2005; Young and White, 1995; Young, 2004; Young et al., 1994.

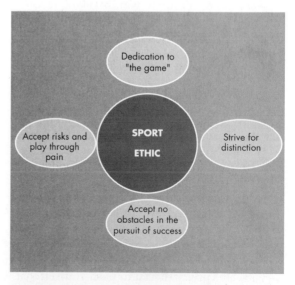

FIGURE 6.4 The four primary norms of the Sport Ethic

this norm. It was explained in these terms by a college football player who continued to play after each of ten knee operations over a period of six years: "I've told a hundred people that if I got a chance to play in the NFL, I'd play for free. It's never been about money. It's never been about anything but playing the game" (in Wieberg, 1994, p. 8C). When NBA player Alonzo Mourning faced a life-threatening kidney disease and played while waiting for a transplant, all-star player Jason Kidd said, "For him to come out and almost kill himself to just play the game that he loves, it just shows the kind of person 'Zo is" (in Canavan, 2003, p. D3). Athletes often make statements like these, and retired athletes regularly say that they miss the game and want to give back to it, even when playing it left them with permanent disabilities.

2. *Athletes strive for distinction.* The Olympic motto *Citius, Altius, Fortius* (swifter, higher, stronger) captures the meaning of this norm. Athletes are expected to relentlessly seek to improve and achieve perfection. Winning symbolizes improvement and establishes distinction; losing is tolerated only because it increases the desire to win. Breaking records is the ultimate mark of distinction because it reaffirms that athletes are a special group dedicated to pushing limits, exceeding others, and being the best they can be, no matter what it takes. This norm is highlighted by a former U.S. gymnast who explained that "the harder you train, the more pounding the body takes. . . . We're clearly pushing the envelope. All it takes is one or two gutsy guys to exceed the difficulty level, then everyone tries it" (in Becker, 1999, p. 4E). Justin Wadsworth, the top U.S. Nordic skier in the 30-kilometer race, pushed his body so hard during the 2002 Olympics in Salt Lake City that he suffered internal bleeding due to his exertion. From his hospital bed he said, "It's pretty special to push yourself that hard," and his coaches and fellow athletes agreed with him (Berger, 2002).

3. *Athletes accept risks and play through pain.* According to this norm, athletes are expected to endure pressure, pain, and fear without backing down from competitive challenges. When athletes talk about this, they simply say that "this is part of the game." But in sociological terms, it shows that athletes are participants—along with coaches, trainers, owners, and others—in a **culture of risk** *where a player's willingness to compete in pain while subjecting one's body to danger on the field is the mark of a true athlete* (Leahy, 2008; Liston et al., 2006; Murphy and Waddington, 2007). The language used in sports emphasizes the importance of this norm. Longtime NFL quarterback Troy Aikman explains that "you earn respect in the locker room [by] going out and putting your body through things that most people wouldn't attempt. . . .[T]he most important thing . . . in my career was to have the respect of the guys in the locker room. To go out and play through injury and . . . significant pain is part of that process" (Klis, 2008, 7D). Similarly, NBA player Allen Iverson says that playing with injuries "is what I do. . . . My team-mates need me . . . And I need to be with my team-mates" (*Denver Post*, 2000, p. 4D). U.S. javelin thrower Breaux Greer predicted success at the 2008 Olympic games because "I can take more pain than anyone" (Grant, 2008, p. 70). He plays through pain but he takes Vicodin to sleep and plenty of caffeine to start the day—and his philosophy, "LIFE WITHOUT LIMITS," is written on his coffee cup. Coaches seek players like these—willing to take risks and play through pain—and use them as examples of what they expect from everyone on the team.

4. *Athletes accept no obstacles in the pursuit of success in sports.* This norm stresses "the dream" and the obligation to pursue it at all costs. Athletes don't accept obstacles without trying to overcome them and beat the odds; dreams, they say, are achievable unless one quits. Champion boxer Lucia Rijker (who

starred in the film *Million Dollar Baby*) stated this norm succinctly as she trained for a bout: "I use obstacles as wood on a fire" (in Blades, 2005, p. 96). And after Buddy Lazier won the Indianapolis 500 while driving the race with a broken back, his father said, "He absolutely never said quit. He was not going to be robbed of this opportunity" (in Ballard, 1996, A1).

The sport ethic is linked to deviance because overconformity to its norms is expected in many sports, even though it is defined as deviant apart from sport and may lead to injuries that irreparably damage the health and well-being of athletes. Overconformity is also important when athletes claim and reaffirm identity in the context of a sport. Only when players show they're willing to put themselves on the line for the sake of their sport will other players recognize and respect them as athletes—as members of a special class of people living at a level of intensity, dedication, and risk that outsiders cannot understand.

> **OLC ON THE *OLC*:**
> See the OLC—Additional Readings for Chapter 6—for the author's analysis of deviant overconformity in Nike ads from the 1990s.

When athletes don't critically assess the norms of the sport ethic and make a decision to set limits on their conformity, they reproduce a culture in which deviance is common and dangerous. This is relatively easy to do because people with power in sports pay little attention to overconformity or efforts to control it; instead, they focus on controlling deviant underconformity, such as failing to obey a coach.

The danger of overconformity to the sport ethic was explained by Alberto Salazar, a former marathoner and coach for Mary Decker Slaney, a legendary middle-distance runner during the 1970s and 1980s. After multiple injuries and nineteen sport-related surgeries, Slaney attempted a comeback while she lived in constant pain; she trained excessively, hoping to make the U.S. Olympic team in 1996 and again as a 42-year-old in 2000. Salazar understood Slaney's overconformity to the norms of the sport ethic, but he also recognized its dangers with this comment:

> The greatest athletes want it so much, they run themselves to death. You've got to have an obsession, but if unchecked, it's destructive. That's what it is with [Slaney]. She'll kill herself unless you pull the reins back. (in Longman, 1996, p. B11)

Research documents these dangers in the case of athletes who experience successive concussions as they "suck it up" and return to play. These players are much more likely to suffer cognitive impairment, chronic memory loss, clinical depression, early-onset dementia, and osteoarthritis (Callahan et al., 2002; Guskiewicz et al., 2003, 2005, 2007); and they're more likely to suffer catastrophic head injuries and even death than players who have not had a history of concussions (Mueller and Cantu, 2008; Schwarz, 2007a, 2007b, 2007c, 2007d). These findings, along with findings from other studies on deviance and sports, indicate that deviant overconformity is more dangerous than deviant underconformity and is a central problem in sports today. Without critically assessing the culture of high performance sport, this form of deviance will persist.

Deviant underconformity, based on rejecting norms or refusing to take them seriously, also is a problem in sports, but when athletes underconform, they are punished immediately. Underconformers usually are selected out of high-performance sport cultures, whereas overconformers are praised. Media stories glorify overconforming athletes as role models—as warriors who play with broken bones and torn ligaments, endure surgery after surgery, and willingly submit to injections of painkilling drugs to stay in the game. Spectators express awe when they hear these stories, even though they realize that athletes have surpassed the normative limits that are normally used in the society as a whole. But people allow deviant overconformity in sports because they can use it to reaffirm values such as dedication, hard work, and achievement; at the same time, they condemn deviant underconformity because it threatens their values. Therefore, most athletes avoid asking critical questions, even though their overconformity to the norms of the sport ethic creates problems, causes pain, disrupts family life, jeopardizes health and safety, and shortens their life expectancy (Callahan et al., 2002; Guskiewicz et al., 2003, 2005, 2007; Leahy, 2008; Safai, 2003; Schwarz, 2007a, 2007b, 2007c, 2007d; Tracey and Elcombe, 2004; White, 2004).

Even when athletes suffer life-changing injuries due to their overconformity, they still express pride in their deviance. For example, a former NFL player who says that his current life is like being locked in a torture chamber due to his chronic pain and disabling injuries, looks back at the way he played while injured and says, "I guess I'm proud about being a champion, giving everything I had. Even if it ruined me" (in Leahy, 2008, p. W08). This illustrates how powerful the sport ethic can be when athletes internalize it and use their own overconformity as a basis for evaluating themselves and sustaining their identity. Coaches foster this form of internalization. The head football coach at the University of Colorado says to succeed in a culture organized around the sport ethic, you've "got to be a little abnormal"—although what he really means is that you've got to be supranormal (A. Murphy, 2006, p. 65).

Why Do Athletes Engage in Deviant Overconformity?

Many, but not all, athletes overconform to the norms of the sport ethic. Overconformity is generally due to these three factors:

1. Playing sports is so exciting and exhilarating that athletes will do almost anything to stay involved.
2. Being selected to play high-performance sports often depends on a perceived willingness to overconform to the norms of the sport ethic; coaches praise overconformers and use them as models on their teams.
3. Exceeding normative boundaries infuses drama and excitement into people's lives because it increases the stakes associated with participation and bonds athletes together through a "bunker mentality" in which putting one's body on the line is mutually expected and respected.

When overconformity is accepted as "the standard," athletes themselves don't see it as deviant. In fact, it is necessary in the process of having their identities as athletes acknowledged and reaffirmed. When athletes stop overconforming, other athletes marginalize and eventually exclude them, forcing them to withdraw from their special in-group. Most athletes fear and seek to avoid this exclusion because it exiles them to the everyday world, where people live boring lives and never push limits as athletes do. As a result, they often conclude that overconformity, even when it is dangerous and disruptive, is a small price to pay to live such an exciting life and gain respect from other athletes.

The frequency and degree of overconformity to the sport ethic varies among athletes. Those most likely to overconform are:

1. Players with low self-esteem and a deep need to be accepted as athletes by their peers in sport
2. Players who see achievement in sports as their only way to get ahead and be treated with respect in the world at large
3. Male players who link their identities as athletes and as men so that being an athlete and being a man become one and the same in their minds

Therefore, athletes who perceive that their identities or future chances for recognition and success depend exclusively on sport participation are most likely to engage in deviant overconformity. An athlete's vulnerability to group demands, combined with the desire to gain or reaffirm group membership, is a critical factor underlying this form of deviance (Waldron and Krane, 2005). Many coaches realize this and create team environments that keep athletes in a perpetual state of adolescence—a developmental stage characterized by identity insecurities and a strong dependence on peer acceptance. This encourages a never-ending quest to confirm identity and eliminate self-doubt by going overboard to make the coach happy and earn respect in the locker room. This dependency-based overconformity to the sport ethic increases the likelihood that athletes will engage in dangerous forms of deviance. If coaches wanted to control all forms of deviance on their teams, they would help athletes set limits on conformity to the norms of the sport ethic. This is done by encouraging athletes to critically assess why they do what they do in sports, and how they want their sport participation to be integrated with the rest of their lives; but few coaches ever do this.

Deviant Overconformity and Group Dynamics

Being an athlete is a social experience as well as a physical one. At elite levels of competition, athletes form special bonds with each other, due in part to their collective overconformity to the norms of the sport ethic. When team members collectively dedicate themselves to a goal and willingly make sacrifices and endure pain in the face of significant challenges, they often create a social world in which overconformity to their norms and ideals becomes "normalized," even as it remains deviant in society as a whole (Albert, 2004; Curry, 1993; Pike, 2004, 2005; Theberge, 2008; Young, 2004a). As they push the envelope together, the bonds between athletes become extraordinarily powerful. Their overconformity sets them apart culturally and physically, from the rest of the community, and this allows them to

> You do whatever it takes to play . . . You get hurt, you find a way. . . . You just suck it up and push through, and if you can't, you're out. There's a saying around locker rooms: "No one has ever made the club from the tub." —Dave Pear, former NFL player, disabled (in Leahy, 2008, p. W08)

assume that "outsiders" cannot understand who they are and what they do. Athletes may appreciate fan approval, but they don't look to fans for reaffirmation of their identity as athletes because fans are ignorant of what it takes to pay the price day after day, face risk and pain, subordinate one's body and being to the needs of the team, and do anything required to be among a select few who can perform as no others in the world can perform. Only other athletes understand this, and this makes everyone else peripheral to an athlete's life in sports, even spouses and family members.

The separation between athletes and the rest of the community makes the group dynamics associated with participation in high-performance sports very powerful. Other selective and exclusive groups, usually groups of men, experience similar dynamics. Examples are found in the military, especially among Special Forces units. Former soldiers sometimes talk about these dynamics and the powerful social bonds formed while they faced danger and death with their "teams." In his book about astronauts and test pilots (*The Right Stuff*, 1979), noted author Tom Wolfe explained that trusting your life to fellow pilots when a small mistake or misjudgment means automatic death creates special bonds and strong feelings that you and your peers are uniquely separate from "normal people." These bonds and the desire to remain connected with the select men that have unique and exhilarating experiences can be so strong that the pilots and astronauts support increasingly extreme and deviant forms of overconformity among themselves. As a result, what happens on the team stays in the team, even when it should be reported to authorities, and even when many team members know it isn't right.

As high-performance athletes strive to maintain their identities and membership in their elite in-group, they often develop the sense that they are unique and extraordinary people. They often hear this day after day from coaches to fans and people on the street. They read it in newspapers and magazines, and they see it on TV and the Internet. And when this sense of being unique and extraordinary becomes extreme, as it often does among celebrated high-profile athletes, it can take the form of **hubris**—that is, *pride-driven arrogance and an inflated sense of self-importance that leads one to feel separate from and superior to others*. Hubris is so common in some sports that it is a key feature of the public personas of many athletes. Some athletes even market it and use it to attract attention and make people remember them.

The dynamics leading to hubris among athletes are clear. First, athletes bond together in ways that encourage and normalize deviant overconformity. Second, collective overconformity creates a sense of specialness and separates athletes from the rest of the community at the same time that it inspires awe and admiration from fans. Third, the unique experiences associated with team membership leads athletes to feel a sense of entitlement. Fourth, athletes see people outside their sport culture as incapable of understanding them and their lives, and therefore undeserving of their concern or, in some cases, their respect.

Rather than being driven by the desire to win or make money, deviant overconformity and hubris are tied to a powerful desire to play the game, gain the respect of peers in the locker room, maintain an identity as an athlete, and remain an accepted member in an elite athletic in-group. This is not to say that winning and money are irrelevant to elite athletes; they *are* important, but they *don't* fully explain deviant overconformity. Therefore, overconformity occurs on teams and among athletes who will never win championships, play in televised games, achieve public fame, or receive college scholarships or professional contracts (Liston, 2007). The roots of deviant overconformity are grounded in the culture

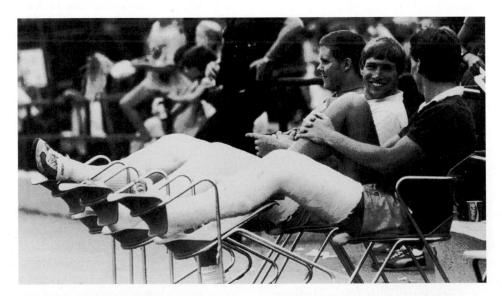

Overconformity to the norms of the sport ethic often jeopardizes the health and well-being of athletes. These injured football players put their bodies on the line for their team. Fans, coaches, and teammates praise their unquestioned and unlimited dedication and commitment—and they also expect them back on the field when the casts come off. (*Source:* Bobette Brecker, University of Colorado Media Relations)

and social organization of sports; they're intertwined with processes of identity development and group dynamics and nurtured by coaches and administrators who benefit when athletes uncritically accept the norms of the sport ethic. Fines and jail sentences can't control this form of deviance; the social processes that operate in the social world of many sports guarantee that overconformity will continue season after season. The source of deviant overconformity is the culture and organization of high performance sports, not the moral character of those who play them.

Deviant Overconformity and Deviant Underconformity: Is There a Connection?

The relationship between deviant overconformity and rates of deviant underconformity has not been studied in the sociology of sport at this point. Figure 6.5 presents a set of hypotheses about this relationship. These hypotheses are based on the following questions:

- If the social bonds created in sports are powerful enough to normalize deviant overconformity that jeopardizes health and well-being among athletes, are they powerful enough to foster other forms of deviance in and by groups of athletes?
- When the dynamics of high-performance sports separate athletes from the rest of the community, does this lead athletes to view nonathletes as outsiders undeserving to the point that athletes might demean, harass, or assault those they perceive as least deserving?
- If athletes develop hubris, might they feel entitled to the point of assuming that community laws don't apply to them?
- If fans and others in the general community view with awe and fascination athletes who engage in entertaining forms of deviant overconformity, are they less likely to enforce laws and other community standards when athletes violate them?

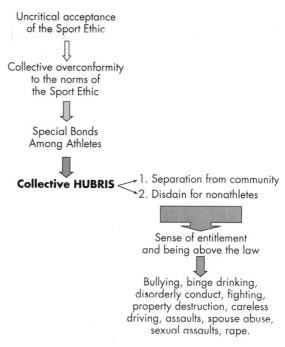

FIGURE 6.5 Hypothesized relationship between deviant overconformity and deviant underconformity.

Research is needed to answer these questions and develop these hypotheses more clearly. My sense is that long-term overconformity to the sport ethic creates social conditions and group dynamics that encourage certain forms of deviant underconformity such as binge drinking, academic cheating, group theft and property destruction, drunken and careless driving, sexual harassment, physical assault, spousal abuse, and sexual assault. Statements by athletes indicate that this connection may exist. For example, when an NFL football player was asked about off-field sexual relationships, he proudly said, "Hey, I have no problem sharing women with my teammates. These guys go to battle with me" (in Nelson, 1994, p. 144). Similarly, it's common for male high school and college athletes to maintain group silence after witnessing teammates gang rape a woman (Curry, 1991, 1996, 1998; Lefkowitz, 1997). At a less-extreme level, groups of athletes from certain school teams have taunted and harassed other students, whom they defined as "unworthy" of respect because of how they looked or dressed (ESPN, 1999)—a practice that can irritate, frustrate, and anger other students.

As outlined in Figure 6.5, when athletes in a sport or on a team accept without question or qualification the norms of the sport ethic, there is no moral basis for setting limits on their conformity to them; in fact, overconformity comes to be connected with a sense of moral righteousness. When athletes collectively overconform to these norms by being extremely dedicated to the game, striving for distinction, risking injury and playing in pain, and following sport dreams no matter the cost, they develop special social bonds with each other. These bonds then serve as the foundation for developing hubris, or pride-driven arrogance. Hubris supports social dynamics that separate athletes from the general community and lead them to look with disdain on outsiders who cannot understand or appreciate their commitment and sacrifice. This creates among athletes a sense of entitlement to the point that they feel free to ignore the laws governing the general community.

> **OLC** **ON THE *OLC*:**
> See the OLC—Additional Readings for Chapter 6—for a discussion of hazing on sport teams and how it is related to the model in Figure 6.5.

The adulation accorded to athletes who entertain others as they push limits and overconform to the norms of the sport ethic has, in some cases, interfered with the enforcement of laws and community standards off the field. Kathy Redmond, founder of the National Coalition Against Violent Athletes, has noted that people in society don't "want to admit that this athlete whom we live vicariously through . . . is capable of deviant behavior" (Cronin, 1998, p. C3). For example, boosters and fans who express "get-tough-on-crime" attitudes have threatened women who are alleged assault and rape victims of athletes (Benedict, 1997; Lipsyte, 1998). This occurred in 2004 to the woman who alleged she was raped by NBA player Kobe Bryant; it occurred between 2001 and the present (2008) to a woman who said that she was raped multiple times by University of Colorado football players and recruits; and it occurred in 2008 to the four women students at the University of Washington, each of whom was allegedly raped by members of the football team (Armstrong and Perry, 2008a, 2008b, 2008c). Community perception of athletes (and women) make these cases difficult to prosecute; law enforcement officers have sought autographs from and have posed for photos with athletes charged with these crimes, and judges who have season tickets to the athletes' games may rule on these cases without declaring a conflict of interest (Armstrong and Perry, 2008a, 2008b, 2008c; Wilson, 2008a). In the end, many people marginalize or condemn the alleged victim rather than the athlete.

Controlling Deviant Overconformity in Sports

Deviant overconformity presents special social control problems in sports. Coaches, managers, owners, and sponsors—people who exercise control and enforce norms—often benefit when athletes overconform to the norms of the sport ethic. In their eyes, athletes who willingly put their bodies on the line for the team are a blessing, not a curse. In the eyes of the athletes, their overconformity is proof of their dedication and commitment; and in the eyes of fans and media people it is seen as exciting, a way to win games, and a wonderful boost to media ratings. Therefore, deviant overconformity goes unpunished, even though it often consists of dangerous actions that everyone sees as falling outside normative boundaries.

The issue of social control is further complicated by the tendency to promote overconformers into positions of power and influence in sports. As players they've proved that they are willing to do anything it takes to win, so they're seen as ideal coaches and managers. This creates a situation in which deviance and related ethical infractions among athletes are rooted in the organization of sports, athletes' relationships with each other, and willful neglect on the part of coaches and administrators.

To control deviant overconformity, athletes must learn how and when to set limits as they play sports. But this learning conflicts with the ethos of overconformity that is central in many elite sport cultures. Deviant underconformity is much easier to control because it is quickly identified by authority figures, and everyone understands that it will be punished. For example, when a fourteen-year-old gymnast is late for practice, her coach immediately sanctions her for violating team norms. But when the same gymnast loses weight and becomes dangerously thin as she strives for distinction and pursues her sport dream, many coaches, parents, and judges don't see deviance as much as they see a dedicated athlete willing to suck it up and pay the price—that is, until stress fractures or anorexia interfere with competition and put the athlete in the hospital.

Another barrier to controlling deviant overconformity is that people associated with sports resist asking critical questions about the goals, purpose, and organization of sports. Without asking critical questions, dangerous forms of deviance persist, including the use of performance-enhancing substances. But many coaches encourage deviant overconformity by telling athletes that the team is their family and that family members put their bodies on the line for each other when they go to battle. Similarly, they often claim that "outsiders are out to get us, so we must stick together because nobody else

truly understands us and our love of the game and for each other." This, in turn, promotes hubris and further separates athletes from the general community and its laws.

Fans also want athletes to exceed normative limits and put their bodies on the line. They see this as exciting and entertaining because it heightens the stakes associated with competition. Fans don't realize that if they accept deviant overconformity, deviant underconformity often follows in its wake. This, in turn, threatens the veracity of the fans' belief that sport builds character. But in an effort to maintain the myth and preserve the excitement, fans, including many people in the sports media, condemn a few players that are easy targets to them and say that deviance is the result of weak moral character among a few bad apples.

Another strategy to control deviant overconformity is to directly assist athletes to connect more meaningfully with people in the general community. Under certain circumstances this helps athletes identify with the community and its norms and it decreases their sense of hubris. But this occurs only when people in the general community can integrate athletes into their social worlds without treating them only as celebrities.

> **I feel like I've been coached that way my whole life—to play dirty and to play mean.** —Jeremy Shockey, NFL player (in Lieber, 2003, p. 1C)

RESEARCH ON DEVIANCE AMONG ATHLETES

Media stories about deviance among athletes are reported daily. But do athletes have higher rates of deviance than others? Few studies have tried to answer this question, and no studies make distinctions between deviant overconformity and underconformity because the former is rarely identified and counted as deviance by sociologists or criminologists (Goode, 1991; West, 2003).

At present, I would argue that deviant overconformity is out of control, especially if the use of performance-enhancing substances is considered

Today's media coverage and video technology enables us to see rule violations in slow motion, stop action, and replays. Contrary to popular opinions, research indicates that many forms of deviance were more prevalent before video technology could provide close-ups like this. (*Source:* Jasper Juinen, AP/Wide World Photos)

to be this form of deviance—an issue discussed later in the chapter. Most people focus attention on deviant underconformity and highlight lists of arrest records and criminal charges filed against athletes. They claim that this form of deviance is out of control in sports, but they can't say if rates are higher today than in the past, or if they are higher than rates among comparable people who are not athletes.

Most media reports focus on the deviance of athletes rather than coaches, administrators, and team owners. They blame deviance on the character weaknesses of athletes and the greed of others associated with sports. These reports ignore the possibility that deviance is grounded in the culture and organization of sports and the social dynamics that exist in the social worlds that are created around sports.

Deviance on the Field and Around Sports

This deviance includes cheating, gambling (by players), shaving points, throwing games or matches, engaging in unfair conduct, fighting, taking illegal performance-enhancing drugs, and

other actions that violate rules of the game. Some people claim that this deviance has become serious today because financial stakes have become so great in sports. But historical research indicates that cheating, dirty play, fighting, and the use of violence are less common today than in the days before television coverage and mega-salaries (Dunning, 1999; Guttmann, 2004; Maguire, 1988; Scheinin, 1994). It also shows that sports today are more rule-governed than in the past and that on-the-field deviance today is more likely to be punished and publicly criticized. Therefore, saying that these particular forms of deviance are out of control.

Comparing rates of on-the-field deviance among athletes from one time period to another is difficult because rules and enforcement standards change over time. Research shows that athletes in most sports interpret rules very loosely during games, and they create informal norms, which stretch or bend official rules (Shields and Bredemeier, 1995). But this is not new. Athletes in organized sports have traditionally "played to the level" permitted by umpires and referees—that is, they adjust their actions according to the way that referees enforce rules during a game. However, this does not mean that players ignore rules or that deviance is out of hand. Nor does it mean that we ought to ignore deviance when it occurs on the field.

The perception that deviance has increased on and around the field is partly due to the constant addition of new rules in sports. Rulebooks in sport organizations today have hundreds of rules that didn't exist a generation ago. The National Collegiate Athletic Association (NCAA) and other sport-governing organizations today have hundreds of rules and regulations that didn't exist in the past, and every year more rules are added. International sport organizations now provide catalogs listing banned substances. Overall, there are more ways to be deviant in sports today than at any time in history. Furthermore, the forms of surveillance used today and the increased emphasis on rule enforcement means that more rule violators are caught than ever before.

Finally, evidence shows that athletes in power and performance sports expect and engage in certain forms of on-the-field deviance, such as "good fouls" and "cheating when you can get away with it" (Anonymous, 1999; Atkinson and Young, 2008; Bowden, 2008; Kihl, 2007; Pilz, 1996; Shields et al., 1995). This is most prevalent at higher levels of competition, it increases with the number of years that people play sports, and it is more common among men than women. These patterns are consistent with other research suggesting that participation in power and performance sports does not generally promote moral development or moral decision making (Stoll and Beller, 1998, 2000). However, there are no historical studies showing that deviant underconformity on and around the field is more common now than in the past, and this form of deviance doesn't seem to be out of control. However, deviant underconformity does exist in sports, and efforts should be made to control it without violating individual rights or principles of due process. A form of deviance that is more prevalent today is deviant overconformity in the form of using banned and illegal performance-enhancing substances. This is clearly a serious problem that has been out of control for some time, and it will be discussed later in the chapter (pp. 179–191)

Deviance off the Field and away from Sports

Off-the-field deviance among athletes attracts widespread media attention. When athletes are arrested or linked to criminal activity, they make headlines and become lead stories on the evening news (Starr and Samuels, 2000). However, research doesn't tell us if the rates of off-the-field deviance have gone up or down over time or if general rates are higher among athletes than their peers in the general population. The studies that deal with this have focused primarily on three topics: (1) delinquency and sport participation among high school students, (2) academic cheating and excessive alcohol use among high school and college athletes, and (3) particular felony rates among athletes.

Delinquency Rates   Research on high school students shows that delinquency rates among athletes often are lower than rates for other students from similar backgrounds. With a few exceptions, this finding applies for athletes in various sports, athletes in different societies, and both boys and girls from various racial and social-class backgrounds (Hartmann and Massoglia, 2008; McHale et al., 2005; Miller et al., 2002).

The problem with most of these studies is that they don't take into account three important factors: (1) students who have histories of deviance are less likely than other students to try out and be selected for sport teams, (2) athletes may receive preferential treatment enabling them to avoid being labeled delinquent, and (3) deviance among high school athletes may be obscured by a "facade of conformity"—that is, athletes who conform to norms in public, but violate them in private where

Is Sport Participation a Cure for Deviance?

We often hear that sports keep kids off the streets and out of trouble and build character in the process. And then we hear about athletes who are living proof that years of playing sports don't make people into models of character. How do we make sense of this conflicting information?

Fortunately, research can help. A classic study by sociologist Michael Trulson (1986) suggests that *only certain types of sports and sport participation* can lower delinquency rates among young people. Trulson worked with thirty-four young men, ages thirteen to seventeen, who were classified as delinquents. He tested them for aggression and personality adjustment and divided them into three groups matched on important background characteristics. For six months, each group met three times a week for training sessions with the same instructor. Group 1 received traditional Tae Kwon Do training, taught with a philosophy emphasizing nonviolence, respect for self and others, physical fitness, self-control, patience, perseverance, responsibility, and honor. Group 2 received a form of martial arts training that emphasized free-sparring and self-defence techniques—and the coach provided no philosophy during the training. Group 3 received no martial arts training, but engaged in regular sessions during which they jogged and played basketball and football under the instructor's coaching and supervision.

Trulson's findings indicated clear changes in Group 1. After six months, the young men in this group had fewer delinquent tendencies, less anxiety and aggression, improved self-esteem and social skills, and more awareness of commonly held values. Those in Group 2 had increased delinquent tendencies and were more aggressive and less adjusted than when the study began. Those in Group 3 showed no change in delinquent tendencies or on most personality measures, but their scores on self-esteem and social skills improved over the six months.

THE MORAL OF THE STORY

Sport participation is most likely to keep young people out of trouble when it emphasizes (1) a philosophy of nonviolence, (2) respect for self and others, (3) the importance of fitness and self-control, (4) confidence in physical skills, and (5) a sense of responsibility. When these five things are absent, sport participation does little apart from keeping young people under adult control for the time that they play.

Simply taking young people off the streets is just the beginning. If they play sports that emphasize confrontation, dominating others, using their bodies as weapons, and defining masculinity or success in terms of conquest, we *cannot* expect rates of deviance to decrease. Personal change is a complex process, and it doesn't occur through sports unless participation is accompanied by strategic efforts to teach young people how to make positive moral, economic, and social choices outside of sports. This doesn't mean that all

detection is rare (Miracle and Rees, 1994). This means that many studies may not have valid measures of delinquent actions by athletes and, as a result, underestimate their delinquency rates.

A recent study using longitudinal data (1994–2001) collected from a national sample of students in grades 7 to 12 found that football players and wrestlers were more likely to be involved in serious fights than young men in other sports or not involved in school sports (Kreager, 2007). This raises issues that are discussed in the chapter on "Violence in Sports," but the point in

this chapter is that some studies on sport participation and delinquency may overlook patterns of norm violations among certain athletes or analyze data out of context so they can't explain why certain patterns exist.

Even when sport programs are designed as "interventions" for "at-risk youth," success is difficult to achieve. In a review of this issue, Doug Hartmann (2003b) noted that we lack a clear theory to explain how and why we might expect sport-based intervention programs to be effective in reducing delinquency or producing other positive sports should be designed as treatment programs, but it does mean that playing sports can't be expected to keep young people out of trouble unless it facilitates connections with adults who support them, advocate their interests, and provide them with opportunities to make positive choices in their lives (Coakley, 2002).

A WORD OF CAUTION

A study by sociologist Eldon Snyder (1994) suggests that when athletes form special bonds with each other, become arrogant about their unity and uniqueness, and become subjectively separated from the general community, sport participation can be positively associated with deviance. Snyder did a qualitative analysis of a case in which nine college athletes at a major university were arrested after committing dozens of burglaries over two years. Seven of the athletes were on the men's swim team, one was on the track team, and one was a former member of the women's swim team (and dating one of the men); they all came from middle-class families. Snyder examined records, testimony, and court documents in the case, including statements by athletes, parents, lawyers, and others. He did *not* conclude that sport participation had *caused* these young people to be deviant. Instead, he concluded that playing sports had created the social bonds and dynamics out of which the deviance of this group emerged. Snyder could not explain the

criminal acts of these young people, but he noted that sport participation certainly did not deter deviance in their case. This conclusion is consistent with Peter Donnelly's (1993) research showing that certain forms of binge deviance sometimes occur among elite athletes, especially after major competitions, at the end of their seasons, and immediately following retirement.

A FINAL NOTE

These studies show that neither virtue nor deviance is *caused* by playing sports. But sports offer young people the possibility of powerful and exciting physical and social experiences that can be organized so that participants receive thoughtful guidance from adults who can help them develop self-respect and become connected to the general community. When this occurs, good outcomes are likely. However, when playing sports separates athletes from the general community and fosters overconformity to the norms of the sport ethic, good outcomes are unlikely. The social bonds formed among athletes can take them in many directions, including deviant ones. Sport programs are effective only when they enable people to live satisfying lives in the world beyond sports; simply taking young people off the streets for a few hours a week so that they can bounce basketballs or kick soccer balls does little more than provide temporary distraction. *What do you think?*

effects. Most of these programs have little effect because they do nothing to change the unemployment, poverty, racism, poor schools, and other delinquency-related factors that exist in most neighborhoods where sports for at-risk youth are offered (Coakley, 2002; Hartmann, 2003b; Hartmann and Depro, 2006; Hartmann and Massoglia, 2007; Hartmann and Wheelock, 2002).

We know from chapter 4 (pp. 102–107) that we cannot make generalizations about athletes because sport experiences vary from program to program and because sport participation

constitutes only one part of a person's experiences. Therefore, when someone says that "playing sports kept me out of trouble," we should investigate what that statement means in that person's life and then identify aspects of sports experiences that enable young people see positive alternatives and make good choices in their lives. Until this research is done, our conclusion is that sport participation creates neither "saints nor sinners," although both may play sports. This issue is discussed further in the box, "Is Sport Participation a Cure for Deviance?"

Academic Cheating   Despite highly publicized cases of college athletes having their coursework completed by "academic tutors," the charge that college athletes generally engage in academic cheating more often than other students, has never been studied systematically. If we compared athletes with other students, we might find comparable rates but different methods of cheating. A varsity athlete may be more likely to hand in a paper written by an "academic tutor," whereas other students would obtain papers from files maintained at a fraternity house, from an online site, or from a professional writer hired by a parent (Kristal, 2005). However, when a regular student is caught turning in a bogus paper, the case will not make national news, the student will not be rebuked by people around the nation, the reputation of the university will not be questioned in the national media, and no faculty members will be fired for not policing students effectively—as might occur if the cheater were an athlete.

Do athletes cheat more often because the stakes associated with making particular grades are higher for them than for other students, or do athletes cheat less because they are watched more closely and have more to lose if they are caught? We don't know the answer to this question, and we need studies comparing athletes with other students generally, with other students who would lose their scholarships or job opportunities if they did not maintain minimum grade point averages, and with other students who are members of tightly knit groups organized around nonacademic activities and identities. Only then will we be able to make definitive statements about academic cheating and sport participation.

Alcohol Use and Binge Drinking   Underage and excessive alcohol consumption in high school and college is not limited to athletes. However, data collected through the 1990s indicated that male and female intercollegiate athletes engaged in more alcohol use, abuse, and binge drinking than other male and female students (Bacon and Russell, 2004; Eccles and Barber, 1999;

Naughton, 1996; Wechsler et al., 1997; Wechsler and Wuethrich, 2002). But a study of U.S. high school students suggests that rates of alcohol use may be lower among under eighteen-year-old teens who play on sport teams than other teens (SAMHSA, 2002). This may mean that norms related to alcohol use are different among junior and senior high school athletes than among college athletes or that young people under eighteen years old who play sports are more closely monitored and controlled by their parents and other adults than is the case for other young people or college athletes.

Research on this topic is important because alcohol use and abuse is related to other forms of deviance. For example, we don't know if deviant overconformity and the associated group dynamics that exists among college athletes contributes to alcohol use and binge drinking. Slamming drinks and getting drunk with teammates may not be very different, in sociological terms, from playing with an injury to gain approval in a sport culture. When teammates who take risks together and depend on each other say, "Let's do some tequila tonight," do players uncritically overconform by downing multiple shots? Research is needed to see if, why, when, and how often this occurs.

Felony Rates   Widely publicized cases of assault, hard-drug use, and driving under the influence (DUI) in which male athletes are the offenders have made it important to study these forms of deviance. At this point, research is scarce, and existing studies report mixed findings (see Crosset, 1999, for a review and critique of research on sexual assault, in particular).

Another problem with studies of felony rates is that data on arrest rates for athletes are seldom compared with arrest rates in the general population or in populations comparable to the athletes in age, race/ethnicity, and socioeconomic background. For example, after a study by Jeff Benedict and Don Yaeger (1998) reported that 21.4 percent of a sample of NFL players had been arrested at least once for something more serious than minor crimes since the year they started college, most people were horrified. However, a follow-up study by Benedict and crime statistics expert Alfred Blumstein (Blumstein & Benedict, 1999) showed that 23 percent of the males living in cities of 250,000 or more people are arrested for a serious crime at some point in their lives, usually during young adulthood; in particular, the arrest rate is 14 percent for whites and 51 percent for blacks. When the domestic violence and nondomestic assault rates among NFL players were compared with rates for young adult males from similar racial backgrounds, Blumstein and Benedict found that the arrest rate for NFL players was less than half the arrest rate for males in the general population. This pattern was nearly the same when the rate for white NFL players was compared with the rate for young, white men generally, and when the rate for black NFL players was compared with the rate for young black men generally.

When Blumstein and Benedict compared arrest rates for property crimes, NFL players had distinctively lower rates than the rest of the population, a finding the researchers explained partly in terms of the salaries of NFL players. However, their overall conclusion was that NFL players do not have crime rates that are as high as the rates for young men in the general population. Of course, this doesn't mean that crimes perpetrated by athletes are not a problem or that professional sport leagues and universities should ignore them. In fact, part of the problem associated with crimes by people in sports is that leagues and universities have neglected their responsibility in holding coaches, athletes, and administrators accountable for criminal actions (Armstrong and Perry, 2008a, 2008b, 2008c; Thiel, 2008).

Lawyer Jeff Benedict also collected data on NBA players during the 2001 to 2002 season and found that 40 percent of them had a police record involving a serious crime—a lower rate than young black men in the general population. After doing over four hundred interviews, reviewing police records, and searching court

documents, Benedict focused on the issue of sexual assault and concluded that the social world of NBA basketball is organized so that it is "nearly impossible for a rape victim to file a criminal complaint against an NBA player without being labeled a groupie or a gold digger." He suggested that "it takes a victim nothing less than Snow White to obtain a conviction in a sexual assault case against a celebrity athlete and emerge with a reputation still intact" (Benedict, 2004, p. 29). This issue—the incidence of assault and sexual assault among male athletes—is especially important, and it is discussed fully in chapter 7, "Violence in Sports" (pp. 213–216)

Using Deviance to Create Commercial Personas in Sports

Do people in sports engage in deviance for commercial purposes? For instance, coaches and players might stage actions that deliberately violate norms for the purpose of entertaining spectators. Two British sociologists, Tony Blackshaw and Tim Crabbe (2004), refer to this as **consumptive deviance** *that involves actions and appearances that can be imagined as "real" deviance without producing any real negative consequences for anyone involved.* Professional wrestling uses this form of deviance as part of its staged-performance that exists only for the melodramatic moment in which it occurs.

It certainly appears that some athletes create public personas as "bad boys" and then use them to attract endorsements from companies that sell products to young people who see themselves as living outside normative boundaries. These personas often are organized around a particular physical appearance along with a presentation of self that is anticonformist. NBA player Dennis Rodman (Chicago Bulls) did this in the 1990s with his increasingly tattooed and pierced body. Allen Iverson did it with his now signature cornrows along with tattoos and a defiant self-presentation when he first entered the NBA (Philadelphia 76ers). And both these players successfully marketed and sold their deviant personas in connection with product endorsements; they also were able to generate a "buzz" that attracted attention to them, their teams, and the NBA, even though NBA officials formally disapproved of their actions and appearance.

The use of consumptive deviance to construct marketable personas occurs in many sports, although it is most effective in basketball, where a player's full physical appearance is readily observable. Athletes today want to establish themselves as "brands," and one of the ways to do this is to create an appearance and persona that is defined as deviant and attracts attention because it is so—without hurting anyone in the process.

Why Focus on Deviance Only Among Athletes?

This chapter focuses on deviance among athletes. This is an important issue, but clearly, athletes are not the only ones in sports who violate norms. The following list identifies other examples of sport-related deviance:

- Coaches who hit players, treat them inhumanely, use male players' insecurities about masculinity to motivate them, sexually harass women in and out of sports, subvert efforts to follow Title IX law that mandates equal participation opportunities for girls and women in sports, and violate NCAA or other organizational rules
- Coaches or team management that engage in unlawful forms of spying on opposing players or teams or altering the physical conditions of an event to gain unfair competitive advantage (Bowden, 2008)
- High school and college program administrators who operate sport programs that do not honor promises to athletes, fail to provide athletes with proper health and accident insurance, or ignore violations of rules set by the school of official governing bodies, such as the NCAA or state high school activities associations (Zimbalist, 1999)

When a black NBA player loses his temper, throws a ball in anger, and appears ready to fight, many people "see" deviance. When a white coach does similar things—throws towels, chairs, and rolled-up programs, and appears ready to fight—many people "see" him—Bobby Knight, for example—as a legend, as an authority figure who effectively controls subordinate players (with tactics that would be defined as criminal if a teacher used them in the classroom). Are race and roles (authority) related to what is classified as deviance in sports? This question must be answered to understand sports in society. (*Source:* Jake Schoellkopf; AP/Wide World Photos)

- Sport team owners who violate antitrust laws, collude with each other to depress player salaries, and deliberately mislead city officials and voters to obtain public money to build stadiums and arenas
- Sport administrators (including those on the International Olympic Committee and related organizations) who take bribes and gifts in return for favors and who violate public trust and organizational principles by making decisions clearly based on their personal interests (see Jennings, 1996a,

1996b, 2006; Jennings and Sambrook, 2000)

- Judges and other officials in events who take bribes or make agreements with others (such as gamblers) to alter the outcomes of events
- Media promoters and commentators who deliberately distort and misrepresent sport events so that they can generate high television ratings or newspaper/magazine sales
- Agents who mislead athletes, misrepresent themselves, or violate rules as they solicit college student-athletes and represent professional athletes
- Parents/spectators who berate, taunt, and fight with each other, referees, and players as they watch their children in youth sports
- Spectators who verbally demean and attack athletes and coaches with hateful personal comments, throw objects at athletes, fight with each other, destroy property as they lament a loss or celebrate a win, place illegal bets on sports, and sell forged autographs of athletes

Some of these and other examples of deviance are discussed in chapters 5, 7, 8, and 11 to 14. At this point it should be noted that controlling deviance among those who have power in sports is difficult because they are the ones who make and enforce the rules, or know how to circumvent and "stretch" them without being identified as formally deviant or legally criminal. This shows that power relations influence what and who is defined as deviant in sports. People with power have more influence than others when it comes to negotiating the limits of normative conformity and the range of ideas, traits, and actions that are acceptable.

Research on the deviance of sport team owners, administrators, managers, coaches, and referees is scarce because sociologists have little access to data for their studies. This is why some of the most revealing work in this area is done by investigative journalists who have resources and contacts that enable them to collect data (Assael,

> **We've taught illegal tactics to survive** —Billy Tubbs, basketball coach, Texas Christian University (in Wolff, 2000, p. 47)

2007b, 2007c; Bissinger, 1990; Brennan, 1996; Farrey, 2008; Jennings, 1996a, 1996b, 2006, Jennings and Sambrook, 2000; Ryan, 1995; Zirin, 2005b, 2007).

PERFORMANCE-ENHANCING SUBSTANCES: DEVIANT OVERCONFORMITY IN SPORTS

The use of performance-enhancing substances in sports is commonplace (Lippi et al., 2008). A widely quoted expert on drug use in sports recently said, "You've got to be a moron to not connect the dots. Doping is everywhere. There are only a few good apples in the barrel, and they're not winning any medals" (in Patrick, 2006, p. 10C).

Media stories about athletes using performance-enhancing substances are no longer shocking. However, most people don't know that drug and substance use in sports has a long history. For centuries athletes have taken a wide variety of everyday and exotic substances to aid their performances, and this has occurred at all levels of competition. In fact, research suggests that athletes in past centuries would have taken the same substances that athletes take today if the substances had been available (Dimeo, 2007; Hoberman, 1992, 2004; Todd, 1987). This makes it difficult to say that money, television, and the erosion of traditional values are the causes of this form of deviance. The use of performance-enhancing substances *predates* commercial sports and television, and it occurred regularly when so-called traditional values were widely accepted. Therefore, we must look beyond these factors to

> **OLC** **ON THE** *OLC*:
> See the OLC—Additional Readings for Chapter 6—for a summary of this history and examples of how substances have been used by athletes in the past.

explain why athletes use performance-enhancing substances.

Research also suggests that substance use is not caused by defective socialization or a lack of moral character among athletes; in fact, it often occurs among the most dedicated, committed, and hard-working athletes in sports. At this point, it appears that most substance use and abuse is tied to an athlete's uncritical acceptance of the norms of the sport ethic. Therefore, it is grounded in overconformity—the same type of overconformity that occurs when distance runners continue training with serious stress fractures; when female gymnasts control weight by cutting their food consumption to dangerous levels; and when NFL players take injections of painkilling drugs so they can put their already injured bodies on the line week after painful week.

Sports provide powerful and memorable experiences, and many athletes are willing to "set no limits" in their quest to maintain participation and their identities as members of a select group sharing lives characterized by intensity, challenge, and excitement. Athletes seek victories because winning enables them to continue playing, but their desire to win is secondary to their desire to play and to retain respect from other athletes. These dynamics encourage overconformity to the norms of the sport ethic, and they affect athletes at various levels of sports—from local gyms, where high school players work out, to the locker rooms of professional sport teams; they affect both women and men across many sports, from the 100-meter sprint to the marathon and from lacrosse to football.

The point here is that athletes use substances like HGH (Human Growth Hormone) for reasons that differ greatly from the reasons that an alienated 25-year-old shoots meth to get high and zone out. The alienated 25-year-old rejects society's norms, whereas most athletes using performance-enhancing substances accept society's norms and uncritically overconform to them. Therefore, we need different explanations to understand the athletes and control their actions. The explanations and methods of control used to deal with people who reject norms and use heroin, cocaine, and methamphetamines are not relevant when trying to limit the use and abuse of performance-enhancing substances in sports.

Defining and Banning Performance-Enhancing Substances

Defining *performance-enhancing substances* is difficult. Substances can include anything from aspirin to heroin; they may be legal or illegal, harmless or dangerous, natural or synthetic, socially acceptable or unacceptable, commonly used or exotic. Furthermore, they may produce real physical changes, psychological changes, or both. This means that sport organizations face challenges whenever they develop antidoping programs and must define what they mean by doping.

Most antidoping policies are justified by saying that drugs are *foreign* to the body, *unnatural*, *abnormal*, *artificial*, *unfair*, and *dangerous* to use. This sounds like a reasonable approach, but there is little agreement about the definitions of these terms. For example, what is a substance *foreign* to the body, and why are the *foreign* substances of aspirin and ibuprofen not banned, whereas the hormone testosterone and naturally grown marijuana are banned? What is an *abnormal* quantity when megadoses of vitamins are okay, but small doses of decongestants are banned? What is *abnormal* and *dangerous* when athletes are legally rehydrated by intravenous needles inserted into their veins, but are stripped of medals for swallowing a prescribed medication for chronic asthma?

With an explosion of scientific discoveries that are now being applied to sports, anyone would struggle to define these terms in light of the following questions:

- Why are needles permitted to drain fluid from the knees of NFL players and inject their bodies with cortisone and painkillers, but the same needles are considered *dangerous* and *artificial* when used to inject into a cyclist or distance runner their own *natural* red blood cells that have been carefully stored for them (blood boosting)?

- Why is the electronic stimulation of muscles not banned, even though it is *unnatural* and *artificial?*
- Why is a knee replacement considered *natural*, whereas a prosthetic foot is considered *unnatural?*
- Why are biofeedback and other psychological technologies defined as *natural* and *fair*, whereas taking certain naturally grown herbs is classified as *unnatural* and *unfair?*
- Are vitamins, amino acids, caffeine, Gatorade, protein drinks, creatine, eyeglasses, and sunglasses *natural* or *artificial*, and why are none of these banned?
- Why is it considered *fair* to wear contact lens that enhance visual acuity and block selected wavelengths of light so that athletes can see more clearly a fast-moving ball in baseball, tennis, lacrosse, or soccer?
- Is it *normal* when athletes deprive themselves of food so they can make weight or meet the demands of a coach who measures body fat every week?
- Why aren't athletes stripped of medals when they engage in abnormal strategies such as purging or wearing rubber suits to lose weight?
- What is *natural, normal,* or *fair* about any of the social, psychological, biomechanical, environmental, and technological methods of manipulating and changing athletes' bodies and minds in today's high-performance sports?
- Is it natural and fair when college football players are hydrated with IVs so they can play when the weather is so hot that heat strokes become likely?
- And what is *normal* about twelve-year-old gymnasts taking multiple anti-inflammatory pills every day so that they can train through pain? Are they different from hockey players who pop multiple Sudafed pills (containing pseudoephedrine) to get "up" for a game, or from baseball players who have long used nicotine (in chewing tobacco) and various amphetamines to stay alert during 4-hour long baseball games (Schmidt, 2008; Sokolove, 2006)?

There are unending questions about what is *foreign* to the body, *unnatural, abnormal, artificial, unfair,* and *dangerous.* This creates endless debates about the definition of *doping* and its technical and legal meaning (Bell, 2008; Shapin, 2005). This is why the International Olympic Committee (IOC) has revised its definition at least three times since 1999 and why the policies of sport organizations are so diverse. As WADA, USADA, the IOC, and decision makers in professional, college, and high school sports all debate drug and testing policies in their respective organizations, there are uncounted physicians, pharmacists, chemists, inventors, and athletes who continue to develop new and different aids to performance—chemical, *natural,* genetic, and otherwise. For example, Anthony Almada and former partner Bill Phillips, founders of EAS (Experimental and Applied Sciences), a major supplement producer and distributor, made hundreds of millions of dollars by knowing the loopholes in every sport's drug policy and creating substances that fit through the holes. This game of scientific hide and seek continues today despite new definitions and policies. It will become more heated and controversial as scientists manipulate the brain and nervous system and use genetic therapies and engineering to improve athletic performance (Loland, 2003; Pennington, 2007; Reynolds, 2007a, 2007b; Schneider and Hong, 2007; Sokolove, 2004b; Tamburrini, 2003; Wilson, 2008b). With new performance-enhancing technologies, we are approaching a time when defining, identifying, and dealing with doping and drugs will be only one of many strategies for manipulating athletes' bodies and improving performance (Assael,

2007c; Berry, 2008; Bjerklie and Park, 2004; Blue, 2008; Schneider and Friedmann, 2006).

Further complicating antidoping policies is confusion about the effects of various substances on athletic performance. Research ethics prevent studies that measure the impact of megadoses and multiple combinations of substances that are "stacked and cycled" by athletes (Bell, 2008; Interlandi, 2008); nor do the people used in drug studies work out with the same intensity, regularity, or resistance that characterize the workouts of dedicated elite athletes. Therefore, athletes learn things in gyms and locker rooms faster than scientists learn them in the lab, although the validity of locker-room knowledge is often questionable. Furthermore, by the time researchers discover valid information about a substance, athletes have moved on to others, which are unknown to researchers or insufficiently tested. This is why most athletes ignore "official statements" about the consequences and dangers of doping—the statements are well behind the "inventors" who supply new substances and the athletes who have experimented with them.

As the wealth of athletes and the market for substances have grown, so have the labs that are dedicated to "beating the system" with "designer drugs," undetectable substances, and masking agents that hide certain molecules in the testing process. For example, IGF-1 (insulin-like growth factor-1) is a muscle builder that is undetectable with current tests. The same is true for dozens of other "designer substances" rumored to be available for the right price (Assael, 2003, 2005, 2007c; Blue, 2008; Sokolove, 2004b).

The Internet has made information about and access to hundreds of substances immediately available to athletes worldwide (see Website Resources at the end of the chapter). Muscle, fitness, and bodybuilding magazines provide dozens of references to these sites. Despite antidoping policies in sports, most athletes know that those who control sport organizations are not eager to report positive tests because it

jeopardizes the billions of dollars that corporate sponsors and TV networks pay for events that are promoted as "clean and wholesome" (Assael, 2007a; *ESPN The Magazine*, 2005; Jennings and Sambrook, 2000).

The lack of effective antidrug enforcement in Major League Baseball (MLB) led the U.S. Congress to become involved in 2004 when it was discovered that anabolic steroid and amphetamine use was widespread among players. After identifying steroid use by athletes and young people as a national public-health crisis, Congress passed the *Anabolic Steroid Control Act of 2004*. As a result, both anabolic steroids and prohormones (used to stimulate the "natural" production of testosterone) were added to the list of controlled substances so that possession, as of 2005, became a federal crime. This law and the threat of additional legislation led MLB to initiate a drug-testing program with clear-cut penalties for first, second, and third violations.

Effective testing and control was not achieved after federal laws were changed (Assael, 2007a; Keating, 2005). Testing was increasingly expensive as it was expanded to detect more substances, and it did not guarantee detection of all performance-enhancing substances. To test effectively, it would cost billions of dollars because all athletes at all levels would have to be tested randomly at least four times a year. This is not feasible, and existing tests fail to detect a number of key substances.

Seeing the failure of antidoping policies, the U.S. Congress intervened again in 2006 through 2008 with a series of committee investigations and grand jury hearings. But these efforts were ineffective because people in the Congress knew little about the extent or variety of substance use, athletes resisted their questions or lied with their responses, and leaders of sport organizations, including the players' associations in professional sports, responded slowly in the face of incomplete and contradictory evidence.

This has led some people to ask why performance-enhancing substances should be banned in sports when they are widely accepted in the United States (Bell, 2008; Kayser, Mauron, and Miah, 2005; Tierney, 2008). The use of tranquilizers, pain controllers, mood controllers, chemical stimulants, antidepressants, decongestants, steroid inhalers, diet suppressants, fat burners, vitamins, creatine, insulin, caffeine, nicotine, muscle builders, prohormones, and hormones, among dozens of other subbstances is pervasive. Drug companies market these products as necessary for social and career success, sexual performance, health maintenance, strength building, and counteracting the negative effects of aging. For example, many men use, legally or illegally, thyroid hormone, testosterone, amino acids, anabolic steroids, human growth hormone (HGH), HGH stimulants, androstenedione, DHEA, and creatine.[2] These products generate billions of dollars of annual sales worldwide, and as of 2007, an estimated two million men in the United States had used or were using patches, gels, injections, and pills to stimulate the production of testosterone, and at least 30,000 Americans had used HGH (Interlandi, 2008).

The list of widely used substances changes and grows longer as new discoveries are made and new supplements are produced and sold. When people learn that millions of 40-plus-year-old men take testosterone and HGH to stay productive in their jobs, they often ask, "Why is it wrong for a 35-year-old athlete, dedicated to a sport and concerned with keeping the only job he's ever known, to use the same substances?"

These issues lead to an important question: Why control athletes in ways that other people

are not controlled? Do colleges ban caffeine and other drugs that students use to study all night and be mentally primed to take final exams? Do teachers make students sign an oath to avoid drugs that might help them improve their grade in a course? Do employers tell executives not to use hormone therapies that will keep them fit for work? Do wives tell their husbands not to take Viagra, Cialis, Levitra, or other substances that improve sexual performance? Does a person condemn a surgeon for taking 200 mg of Provigil (modafinil) to stay alert and focused during a successful emergency operation that saved her son's life after a serious skiing accident? Did the people of California elect Arnold Schwarzenegger as their governor even though he used steroids for twelve years to gain and retain the Mr. Olympia title and become a bulked-up film star (Assael, 2007c)? Why should athletes be tested and denied access to substances, when others competing or working for valued rewards and

"Hey smart guy, did you mix the growth hormones with the 'miracle seaweed extract' I bought online?"

The negative side effects of various combinations of substances are difficult to identify. Controlled studies of banned substances cannot be done effectively because it isn't ethical to experiment with the same dosages that athletes use. This means that the side effects of many substances are unknown.

---

[2]Dehydroepiandrosterone (DHEA) is a manufactured hormone widely available over the counter. Natural DHEA is produced by adrenal glands, and it stimulates the production of testosterone. Athletes may use it to maintain lean body mass, and most sports don't ban it currently. Creatine is widely used by athletes as a training aid. It is a compound produced by the liver, kidneys, and pancreas; it facilitates the renewal of anaerobic energy reserves, delays the onset of fatigue during intense exercise, and cuts recovery time between workouts.

serving in powerful positions are allowed and even encouraged to take them? As these questions are asked, it remains difficult to define drugs, doping, and substance abuse in sports.

Why Is the Challenge of Substance Control So Great in Sports Today?

Many factors influence athletes to seek substances that help them pursue their dreams and stay involved in the sports they love and the jobs for which they are paid. These factors include the following:

1. *The visibility and resources associated with sports today have fueled massive research and development efforts, and this has dramatically increased the number and availability of performance-enhancing substances.* Entrepreneurs and corporations have developed performance-enhancing substances as forms of "alternative medicine" that make them substantial profits. Aging baby boomers (the massive population cohort born between 1946 and 1964) see these substances as health aids and tools for preserving youth. This market of 70 million Americans is an incentive for the supplement industry to produce and distribute an ever-expanding array of substances.

2. *People in postindustrial societies are deeply fascinated with technology and want to use it to extend human limits.* Advertising messages that promote hyperconsumption as a lifestyle encourages this fascination. Athletes, because they live in these societies and seek to excel in their sports, hear those messages loud and clear. Like many of us, they use consumption as a tool to pursue their dreams. Consuming substances is simply another manifestation of their overconformity to the norms of the sport ethic, and they see it as part of their dedication and willingness to pay the price to stay in the game.

3. *The rationalization of the body has influenced how people conceptualize the relationship between the body and mind.* People in postindustrial societies see the body as a malleable tool serving the interests of the mind. Separating the body from the mind is common in cultures with Judeo-Christian religious beliefs, and it leads people to objectify their own bodies, view them as machines, and use them as tools for doing what the mind commands. Using substances to improve the body and what it can do fits with this orientation and is consistent with the way that athletes use their minds to ignore or redefine physical pain and injury (Grant, 2002a, 2002b).

4. *There is a growing emphasis on self-medication.* People in wealthy postindustrial societies increasingly seek alternatives to mainstream medicine. They obtain medical information online and from friends, and they're willing to try substances they purchase online and over the counter without a doctor's advice or approval. In the United States, the Dietary Supplement Health and Education Act of 1994 deregulated "nutritional" and performance-enhancing substances and allowed them to be produced, distributed, and consumed without testing and approval by the U.S. Food and Drug Administration (FDA).[3] This was great for business, but it flooded the market with untested products that people bought out-of-pocket because health insurance companies don't pay for untested therapies.

5. *Gender relations are changing in contemporary society.* As traditional ideas about masculinity and femininity have changed, some men seek to develop a physique that reaffirms an ideology of male strength and power. At the same time, changes have led many women to revise their notions of femininity and do whatever it takes to achieve strength, power, and physical ability and lose weight at the

---

[3]The politics behind this legislation and the growth of the nutritional supplement business is discussed in many sources that deal with doping and sports (Assael, 2007c; Bell, 2008; Denham, 2006b, 2007a).

same time. Therefore, men and women define performance-enhancing and body-shaping substances as valuable aids in their quests to preserve or challenge prevailing gender ideology.

6. *The organization of power and performance sports encourages overconformity to the norms of the sport ethic.* Continued participation in these sports depends on competitive success, and this fuels the search for training strategies that can provide athletes with "the edge" that enables them to succeed. New technologies, including performance-enhancing substances, can provide such an edge.

7. *Coaches, sponsors, administrators, and fans clearly encourage deviant overconformity.* When athletes make sacrifices and put their bodies on the line for the sake of the team, the school, the community, or the nation, they're defined as heroes. The duty of heroes is to do what it takes to get the job done. For example, a former NFL player who had twenty-nine surgeries during his career, including twenty on his knees, explained that he took anything he could to play the game he loved: "You name it, I've taken it—in excess. Too much at times. But that's the way you get through" (in Schefter, 2003, 6J).

8. *The performance of athletes is closely monitored within the social structure of elite sports.* Elite sports are organized to emphasize (a) control, especially an athlete's control over her body; (b) conformity, especially to the demands of a coach; and (c) shame, especially when an athlete lets down teammates, parents, schools, communities, clubs, and corporate sponsors. This creates a powerful incentive to do whatever it takes to succeed on the field.

When these eight factors are combined, it's easy to see that access to substances and the willingness to use them are high. These conditions exist today, and this makes it more difficult than ever to control substance use.

Drug Testing as a Deterrent

Drug testing is controversial. There are powerful arguments for and against it. The arguments in favor of testing are these:

1. *Drug testing is needed to protect athletes' health and reduce the pressures to take substances to keep up with competitors.* In elite cycling, the blood-boosting drug EPO was implicated in the deaths of about twenty riders from Europe between 1988 and 2000 (Zorpette, 2000), and seven of the eight elite cyclists who died over a thirteen-month period in 2003 and early 2004 were victims of heart attacks, often caused by circulatory problems (Henderson, 2004). EPO causes a person's blood to thicken and clot, and it can be fatal when taken in high doses. In professional wrestling, steroids are suspected in at least 65 deaths among wrestler-performers under the age of forty-five between 1997 and 2007 (Sandomir, 2007; Swartz, 2004, 2007). Furthermore, the use of steroids and other substances may partially account for the rising injury toll in certain sports in which severe muscle and tendon tears and bone fractures are common (Keating, 2004b; Verducci, 2002). Other serious health risks are associated with various substances, including ephedrine; steroid precursors, such as androstenedione; diuretics; Epogen; and beta-blockers (Meyer, 2002).

> IIow different is steroid use from cosmetic surgery for the male TV newsies reporting these stories, from Botox for actresses, beta-blockers for public speakers[?]
> —Robert Lipsyte, journalist, 2005

2. *Drug testing is needed to achieve a level playing field where competitive outcomes reflect skills and training rather than access to substances.* Many athletes and spectators believe that some of the most visible and talented athletes today owe part of their success to drugs. This damages the integrity of sports and jeopardizes

sponsorships, television rights fees, and the willingness of spectators to buy tickets and pay cable fees so that they can see games.

3. *Requiring people to submit to drug tests is legally justified because athletes influence young people.* Furthermore, the U.S. Supreme Court ruled in 2002 that schools may conduct drug tests on all students involved in sports and other extracurricular activities because drug use by young people is a serious national problem, and schools have "custodial responsibilities" for their students (Lewin, 2002). When the U.S. Congress discussed the Professional Sports Responsibility Act of 2005, its goal was to mandate uniform testing and sanctions partly because it would protect children who use athletes as role models.

4. *Drug testing is part of normal law enforcement because drug use is illegal and must be controlled, just as other criminal acts are controlled.* This means that punishments must be clearly explained, fairly administered, and severe enough to deter future substance use.

5. *Drug tests must be expanded to preserve the current meaning of sports and athletic achievements.* According to a member of the World Anti-Doping Agency (WADA), if doping and other technologies cannot be controlled, it will mark "the end of sport as we know it" (Swift and Yaeger, 2001, p. 91). Unless drug testing succeeds, there will be no precedent for controlling future technologies, such as genetic manipulation, that will turn sports into circus-like spectacles in which genetic engineers compete against each other to produce the most superhuman bodies (Gibbs, 2008). These technologies already exist, and many athletes are eager to try them (Barry, 2008; Miah, 2004; Reynolds, 2007a, 2007b; Wilson, 2008b). For example, there are reports of top professional soccer players storing stem cells from the umbilical cords of their newborn children so the cells can be used in future treatments to restore the players' bodies after serious injuries (Cannella,

2006). Testing is the only hope of preventing such things.

> **OLC ON THE *OLC*:**
> See the OLC—Additional Readings for Chapter 6—for additional materials on drug testing in sports.

The arguments against testing emphasize the following points:

1. *Testing is ineffective because athletes are one step ahead of rule makers and testers.* By the time substances are banned and tests are developed to detect them, athletes are taking new substances that tests cannot detect or are not calibrated to detect (Assael, 2005, 2007b, 2007c; Bell, 2008; Sokolove, 2004b; Zorpette, 2000). Don Catlin, head of the UCLA lab that does all the tests for WADA, says, "You may think testing is wonderful and great, but . . . [athletes] have little trouble beating the test and there are many doctors telling them how to do it" (in Patrick, 2005). The NFL policy, reputedly the toughest in pro sports, was described by the founder of a supplement company as having "numerous loopholes." He noted that "athletes are out there looking for anything to give them an edge. And there are always people out there to fill that need" (in Saunders, 2005). When the U.S. Drug Enforcement Agency (DEA) in 2007 identified thirty-seven Chinese factories shipping large amounts of HGH to doctors and pharmacists in the United States, it was clear that developing and selling performance-enhancing substances had become a global industry that is unregulated in many countries (Assael, 2007b, 2007c). To complicate matters, new performance-enhancing substances made from herbs and plants unknown in Western medicine may already exist (Schneider and Hong, 2007).

This creates an impossible challenge for sport organizations that want to ban them, because English words for these substances don't even exist at this time.

2. *Requiring people to submit to drug tests without cause violates rights to privacy and sets precedents for invasive testing that produces medical information that could be used against a person's interest outside of sports.* If protocols for future tests require blood samples, muscle biopsies, genetic testing, and DNA analysis, test results could lead some people to be stigmatized as "impure," "contaminated," or abnormal for medical or biological reasons (Kayser and Smith, 2008; Malloy and Zakus, 2002). This is an unreasonable price to make a person pay to play a sport.

3. *Drug tests are expensive and drain resources that could be used to fund health education programs for athletes.* The test administered to athletes in Olympic sports by the United States Anti-Doping Agency (USADA) and WADA costs well over $300 per athlete per administration. Testing 100,000 potential Olympic athletes around the world four times a year would cost about $120 million. Furthermore, athletes taking substances are unlikely to be deterred by a test administered only four times a year, especially if it is calibrated to detect only a limited number of substances. High schools face similar cost issues. In a school district with 10,000 high school students, in which 4000 students play sports, a basic test for illegal street drugs

"Don't worry, most of these are legal and the others won't show up on the drug tests!"

Some athletes take multiple "nutritional supplements." The industries that produce them are unregulated and often claim that certain products are performance enhancing.

costs $15 to $20 per student, or $60,000 for the district. A test for a limited range of popular performance-enhancing substances given once per year would cost the district at least $250,000; but it would have little effect because athletes could take substances during the off-season while they train and then stop prior to the season when they would be tested. This teaches athletes nothing about health or how to set health priorities as they play sports.

4. *Drug tests often cannot detect substances that are designed to match substances naturally produced by the body.* EPO (erythropoietin), HGH (human growth hormone), IGF-1 (insulin-like growth factor-1), and testosterone are powerful performance enhancers produced by the body, and normal levels of these substances vary from person to person.[4] This makes it difficult to determine an amount of each substance that would be considered illegal for all bodies (Berry, 2008). And, once legal levels are determined, athletes who test positive frequently use lawsuits to challenge the limits in individual cases (Walsh, 2007).

5. *Drug tests provide an incentive for developing forms of genetic engineering that alters physical characteristics related to performance.* When genetic engineering occurs, it will make steroids and other drugs obsolete. Gene therapies are seen as crucial treatments to deal with the negative effects of aging and to cure

or reduce the symptoms of certain diseases. These therapies will make "gene doping" possible for athletes—therapies to enhance muscle size, strength, and resiliency (Assael, 2005; Barry, 2008; Longman, 2001; Parrish, 2002; Reynolds, 2007a, 2007b; Sokolove, 2004b; Sweeney, 2004; Swift and Yaeger, 2001; Zorpette, 2000). Gene doping and other forms of genetic manipulation will be difficult if not impossible to detect, and tests will cost at least $1000 per athlete (Sweeney, 2004). Chuck Yesalis, a professor at Penn State who has studied drugs in sports for many years, argues that all forms of testing will be irrelevant when athletes use genetic engineering (Patrick, 2002, p. 6C).

In the face of arguments for and against drug testing, many athletes have mixed feelings about testing policies and programs. They realize that political and economic interests can cloud the validity and reliability of testing programs. They also know that drug testing is a complicated scientific and bureaucratic process and that mistakes can occur at many points. This has already provoked legal challenges to test results. These challenges are complicated because they often cross national borders where judicial processes and definitions of individual rights and due process are inconsistent. In the meantime, athletes know that fellow athletes continue to overconform to the sport ethic and seek creative ways to push their bodies to new limits in the pursuit of dreams.

When drug testing is done by the same organizations that promote and profit from sports, athletes have good reason to have mixed feelings. Promoting, profiting, and policing just don't go together. To avoid conflicts of interest, international athletes in Olympic sports are now tested by "independent" agencies. WADA conducts random, unannounced tests around the world. The USADA conducts similar tests on U.S. athletes wherever they are training around the world. These two agencies work together. However, part of the funding for the USADA

---

[4]EPO (erythropoietin) is a protein hormone that is produced by cells in the kidneys. It promotes the production of red blood cells, the cells that carry oxygen. Therefore, it can be useful to endurance athletes looking to increase the oxygen-carrying capacity of their blood. HGH (human growth hormone) is a hormone produced naturally by the pituitary gland, and it stimulates physical growth in children. However, it can be used to increase muscle mass and overall strength in adults, and some adults take it in the belief that it slows the aging process. IGF-1 (insulin-like growth factor-1) is a protein that helps muscles grow and repair themselves when they are damaged. It can be used to reduce muscle-recovery time after strenuous workouts.

comes from the U.S. Olympic Committee, and this causes some people to wonder about how independent the agency is, despite its claim to be so. Both USADA and WADA claim to have an educational emphasis, but many experts see their approach to doping control as repressive and punitive (Kayser and Smith, 2008; Soek, 2006). Additionally, their educational programs won't be effective until they understand deviant overconformity among athletes and the need to help athletes set limits as they make decisions and follow their dreams in the context of current sport cultures. But it's unlikely that these organizations would use such an approach.

Controlling Substance Use in Sports: Where to Start

Today's athletes, like their counterparts in the past, seek continued participation and excellence in sports. When they overconform to norms promoting sacrifice and risk in the pursuit of distinction and dreams, they're also likely to seek training methods and technologies that are performance enhancing, even if they are considered deviant by people outside of sports. A physician who works with athletes explains that in his experience, "athletes don't use drugs to escape reality—they use them to enforce the reality that surrounds them" (DiPasquale, 1992, p. 2). This forces everyone who consumes sport for entertainment to ask if it is reasonable to praise athletes as warrior-heroes when doctors give them injections of cortisone and painkilling drugs to stay on the field, and then condemn them as cheaters when they take steroids, HGH, and other substances to heal injuries more quickly, rebuild muscles damaged by overtraining, or relax and recover after exhausting and tightly scheduled competitions (Farrey, 2007; Olney, 2006). Similarly, is it reasonable to condemn athletes for failing to be positive role models for children, when we expect them to do anything to stay on the field and play sports that involve brutal body contact and grueling physical challenges?

A central point in this chapter is that athletes use performance-enhancing substances not because they lack character or are victims of evil or exploitive coaches, but because they uncritically accept and overconform to the norms of the sport ethic in an effort to remain in sports and be accepted as athletes. This is why tougher rules and increased testing have not been effective. Moral panics over drug use and oversimplified solutions will not stop athletes from using substances that they see as necessary to maintain their identities and continue experiencing the joy and excitement of playing elite sports.

The use of performance-enhancing substances and future forms of genetic manipulation cannot be effectively controlled in elite sport cultures as they are now organized. Effective control requires both cultural and structural changes in sports so that athletes, coaches, and others critically assess the sport ethic and control deviant overconformity, or redefine the sport ethic to include new norms (Shogan and Ford, 2000). Here are suggestions on where to begin these processes:

- *Critically examine the deep hypocrisy involved in elite power and performance sports.* It isn't possible to effectively control the use of performance-enhancing substances when federations and teams encourage general overconformity to the norms of the sport ethic. Therefore, there's a need for critical discussions of limits on the use of currently accepted performance-enhancing strategies, such as injecting painkilling drugs and massive doses of vitamin B_{12}, hydration therapies, playing with pins in broken bones and with high-tech "casts" to hold broken bones in place during competition, and using special harnesses to restrict the movement of injured joints. These practices are common, and they foster a sport culture in which the use of performance-enhancing substances is defined as logical and courageous.
- *Establish rules clearly indicating that certain risks to health are undesirable and unnecessary in sports.* When sixteen-year-old girls who

compete with training-induced stress fractures in elite gymnastics are turned into national heroes and poster children for corporate sponsors, we promote deviant overconformity in sports. This sets up athletes for permanent injuries and disabilities. This is clearly a problem, and sport organizations should not allow it to occur.

- *Establish a "harm reduction" approach in which athletes are not allowed to play until certified as "well" (not simply "able to compete") by two independent physicians or medical personnel.* This approach differs from current practices in which trainers and medical personnel do what they can to get injured athletes back on the field as quickly as possible (*ESPN The Magazine*, 2005; Lippi et al., 2008; Safai, 2003; Waddington, 2007). Trainers and physicians should be health advocates paid by someone other than team management. As one former NFL player explains, "I see guys playing in games that I don't think a personal advocate would allow them to do. The doctor who is supposed to be looking out for you is also the same guy who may put you into a game that the team has to win. You're mixing business with medicine" (in Schwarz, 2007b). The focus of a player health advocate would be protecting the long-term well-being of athletes. Therefore, instead of testing for drugs, athletes should be tested to certify that they are healthy enough to participate. If drugs damage their health or make it dangerous for them to play, they would not be certified. Only when their health improves and meets established guidelines would they be allowed back on the field. This would be a major step in creating a new sport culture.
- *Establish injury and health education programs for athletes.* This is a first step in establishing a sport culture in which *courage* is defined as recognizing limits to conformity and accepting the discipline necessary to accurately and responsibly acknowledge the consequences of deviant overconformity and sports injuries.

Learning to be in tune with one's body rather than to deny pain and injury is important in controlling the use of potentially dangerous performance-enhancing substances.

- *Establish codes of ethics for sport scientists.* Too many sport scientists assist athletes as they overconform to the norms of the sport ethic, rather than helping them raise critical questions about the dangers that deviant overconformity presents to their health and development. This makes those sport scientists part of the problem, rather than part of the solution. For example, sport psychology should be used to help athletes understand the consequences of their choices to play sports and help them critically assess *why* they're doing what they're doing and *what* it means in their lives. Using science to encourage or enable athletes to give body and soul to their sports without asking these critical questions is to leave the door open for deviant overconformity, including the use of performance-enhancing substances.
- *Make drug and substance education a key part of health education programs.* Parents, coaches, league administrators, managers, and trainers should participate with athletes in educational programs in which they consider and discuss the norms of the sport ethic and how to prevent deviant overconformity. Unless all these people understand their roles in reproducing a culture supportive of substance use and abuse, the problems will continue.

We now face a future without clearly defined ideas about the meaning of achievement in sports (Gibbs, 2008). There are new financial incentives to succeed in sports, athlete identities have become central in the lives of many sport participants, and performance-enhancing technologies have become increasingly effective and available. Therefore, we need *new* approaches and guidelines. Old approaches and guidelines combined with coercive methods of control have not been effective. Trying to make sports into what we believe they were in the past is futile. We face new issues and challenges, and it will take new approaches to deal with them effectively (Kix, 2007; Smith, 2005a).

Widespread participation is needed if sport cultures are to be successfully transformed. At present, both nation states and corporate sponsors have appropriated the culture of power and performance sports and used it to deliver messages that foster forms of deviant overconformity for the sake of national and corporate interests. There is no conspiracy underlying this, but it creates a challenge that can be met only through our collective awareness of what needs to be done, followed by collective efforts to do it. Even then changes will be incremental rather than revolutionary, but changes are possible if we work to create them in our sports, schools, and communities.

summary

IS DEVIANCE IN SPORTS OUT OF CONTROL?

The study of deviance in sports presents challenges due to four factors: (1) The diverse forms and causes of deviance in sports cannot be explained by a single theory; (2) the ideas, traits, and actions accepted in sports may be deviant in the rest of society at the same time that things accepted in society may be deviant in sports; (3) deviance in sports often involves accepting norms uncritically and without limits, rather than rejecting them; and (4) training in sports now uses so many new forms of science and technology that we lack norms to guide and evaluate the actions of athletes and others in sports.

People who assume that social reality contains absolute truths about right and wrong and good and evil often use an absolutist approach to deviance. They believe that unchanging moral truths are the foundation for all norms. Therefore, every norm represents an ideal, and every action, trait, or idea that departs from that ideal is deviant, immoral, perverse, or evil. When this approach is used, deviance becomes increasingly serious as the departure from the ideal increases. For example, if using drugs violates an absolute principle of fairness in sports, any use of drugs at any time or place would be deviant, and if the drug use continued over time, it would eventually be defined as immoral or evil.

Sociologists generally use a constructionist approach to study and explain deviance in sports. This approach, based on a combination of cultural, interactionist, and structural theories, emphasizes that norms and deviance are socially constructed through social interaction as it occurs in a particular social and cultural context. This approach highlights a distinction between deviant underconformity and overconformity. This is important because the most serious forms of deviance in sports occur when athletes, coaches, and others overconform to the norms of the sport ethic—a cluster of norms that emphasizes dedication to the game above all else, striving for distinction, taking risks and playing through pain and injury, and overcoming all obstacles in the pursuit of sport dreams. When limits are not set in the process of conforming to these norms, deviant overconformity becomes a problem.

Research supports this approach. Most on-the-field and sport-related actions fall within an accepted range; when they fall outside this range, they often involve overconformity to the norms of the sport ethic. Rates of off-the-field deviance among athletes are a problem, although they are generally comparable with rates among peers in the general population; when rates are high, as they are with binge drinking and sexual assault, they may be connected with the dynamics and consequences of overconformity to the sport ethic.

The use and abuse of performance-enhancing substances is a widespread form of deviance among athletes, despite new rules, testing programs, current educational programs, and strong punishments for violators. Historical evidence suggests that recent increases in rates of use are due primarily to increases in the supply and range of available substances, rather than changes in the values and moral characters of athletes. Most athletes throughout history have sought ways to improve their skills, maintain their athlete identity, and continue playing their sports, but today their search is likely to involve the use of widely available performance-enhancing substances.

Despite new enforcement efforts by sport organizations, athletes using performance-enhancing substances have generally stayed one jump ahead of the rule makers and testers. When one drug is banned, athletes use another, even if its more dangerous. If a new test is developed, athletes switch to an undetectable drug or use masking agents to confuse testers. The use of HGH, blood doping, testosterone, and many new substances still escape detection, and testing programs often are problematic because they are expensive, violate privacy rights or cultural norms in many societies, and produce inconsistent results. However, many people are strongly committed to testing, and new testing procedures are constantly being developed. The prospect of "gene-doping," or performance-enhancing genetic manipulation, will present significant challenges for testing in the future. In the meantime, testers are struggling to stay ahead of athletes who continue to overconform to the norms of the sport ethic.

Controlling deviant overconformity requires a critical assessment and transformation of the norms and social organization of sports. The goal is to strike a balance between accepting and questioning norms and setting limits on conformity so that athletes who engage in risky and self-destructive forms of deviant overconformity are not defined and presented as heroes. The use of new performance enhancing technologies can be controlled only through new strategies that recognize the reality and dynamics of deviant overconformity.

An effective transformation of sports also requires that all participants be involved in a continual process of critical reflection about the goals, purpose, and organization of sports. Controlling deviance requires an assessment of the values and norms in sports, as well as restructuring the organizations that control and sponsor sports. Critical assessment should involve everyone, from athletes to fans. It is idealistic, but it is worth trying.

 ## WEBSITE RESOURCES

Note: Websites often change. The following URLs were current when this book was printed. Please check our website (www.mhhe.com/coakley10e) for updates and additions.

www.alfred.edu/news/html/hazing_study.html A report of the National Survey of Initiation Rites and Athletics for NCAA Sports; excellent source of hazing data from U.S. colleges, universities, and high schools.

http://bodybuilding.com/store/hardcore.htm Lists producers of "nutritional supplements," chemical compounds, and what many consider to be performance-enhancing drugs; provides online shopping for bodybuilders, athletes, and anyone else looking for substances believed to build muscles and increase training effects.

http://bodybuilding.com/store/hgh.html Information on HGH and other substances for which there are no tests in most sports.

www.champion-nutrition.com/champion/ Lists hundreds of "products" available for people wanting to build strength and mass, boost endurance, and recover more rapidly from hard workouts.

www.espn.go.com/special/s/drugsandsports This site provides basic information on a variety of drugs used by athletes; ESPN regularly includes on its site information about deviance in sports as it hits the news.

www.mhhe.com/coakley10e Click on chapter 6 for information on the history of performance-enhancing drug use and drug testing in high-performance sports and for information on recent cases of athletes testing positive for certain drugs.

http://multimedia.olympic.org/pdf/en_report_817. pdf The IOC Anti-Doping Rules Applicable to the 2004 Athens Olympic Games, 4 June 2004, 25 pages.

www.ncava.org National Coalition Against Violent Athletes; materials on athletes and violent behavior, support for victims, advocacy, referrals, prevention programs, and research.

www.sports.findlaw.com Presents sport law news on current and past cases sport by sport; has a list of the "Tarnished 20," which identifies universities where people associated with sport programs have violated rules.

www.sportslaw.org The Sports Lawyers Association often refers to deviance in sports in terms of the legal issues raised; this site lists articles and recent cases.

www.t-nation.com/ Testosterone Nation, a site widely used by people who take bodybuilding compounds and drugs, seek information on what drugs to use, how to obtain them, and what others say about them.

www.usantidoping.org U.S. Anti-Doping Agency, the official performance-enhancing drug education and substance-testing agency in the United States; online materials illustrate how the agency presents regulatory and educational materials to athletes and others.

www.wada-ama.org World Anti-Doping Agency, the official worldwide drug- and substance-testing agency; online materials illustrate how the agency presents regulatory and educational materials.

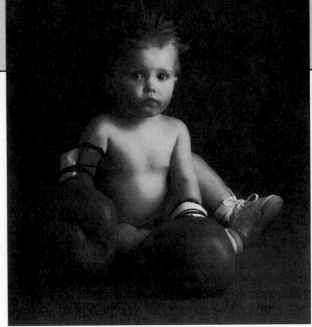

(McGraw-Hill)

VIOLENCE IN SPORTS

How Does It Affect Our Lives?

IT'S THE MOST PERFECT feeling in the world to
know you've hit a guy just right, that you've
maximized the physical pain he can feel. . . . You
feel the life just go out of him. You've taken all
this man's energy and just dominated him.

—Michael Strahan, NFL player, 2007
(in Layden, 2007)

(OLC) Visit *Sports in Society*'s Online Learning
Center (OLC) at www.mhhe.com/coakley10e
for additional information and study material
for this chapter, including the following:

- A complete chapter outline
- Learning objectives
- Practice quizzes
- Internet resources
- Related readings
- Essays
- Student projects

I DRILLED HIM as good as I can drill him, right in
the rib cage. You could hear the air go out of him,
and it was beautiful.

　　　—Goose Gossage, Hall of Fame major league
　　　　pitcher, 2008 (in Etkin, 2008).

YOU CAN'T TAKE the violence out of the game,
and that's okay, because it wouldn't be football
without the violence, I guess. But if you can't take
the violence out, you gotta at least help the people
who get hurt.

　　　—Dave Pear, former NFL player (disabled), 2008

I DON'T WANT TO SOUND LIKE I'm bragging,
because I'm not, but back [in the 1960s, when I
played basketball] the violence was much more
intense.

　　　—Satch Sanders, former NBA player, 1999

Discussions of violence in sports, like discussions of deviance, are often connected with people's ideas about the moral condition of society as a whole. When athletes engage in quasi-criminal violence on the field or criminal violence off the field, many people see it as evidence that the moral foundation of society is eroding. They fear that young people who look up to athletes as role models are learning a warped sense of morality.

Statements about violence in sports are often confusing. Some people say that violence is an inherent part of many games, whereas others say that it destroys the dynamics of games. Some people say that violence in sports reflects natural tendencies among males in society, whereas others say that men use violence in sports to promote the idea that physical size and strength is a legitimate basis for maintaining power over others. Some say that violence in sports is worse today than ever before, whereas others say it is less common and less brutal than in the past.

Contradictory statements and conclusions about violence in sports occur for four reasons. *First*, many people fail to define important terms in their discussions. They use words such as *physical, assertive, tough, rough, competitive, intense, intimidating, risky, aggressive, destructive,* and *violent* interchangeably. *Second*, they may not distinguish players from spectators, even though the dynamics of violence differ in these two groups. *Third*, they categorize all sports together, despite differences in meaning, purpose, organization, and amount of physical contact involved. *Fourth*, they may not distinguish the immediate, short-term effects of experiencing or watching violence in sports from more permanent, long-term effects.

The goal of this chapter is to enable you to include information based on research and theories in your discussions of violence in sports. Chapter content focuses on five topics:

1. A practical definition of *violence* and related terms
2. A brief historical overview of violence in sports
3. On-the-field violence among players in various sports
4. Off-the-field violence among players and the impact of sports violence on their lives apart from sports
5. Violence among spectators who watch media coverage of sports and attend events in person

In connection with the last three topics, I will use research findings to identify strategies for controlling violence on and off the field.

WHAT IS VIOLENCE?

Violence *is the use of excessive physical force, which causes or has obvious potential to cause harm or destruction.* We often think of violence as actions that are illegal or unsanctioned, but there are situations in which the use of violence is encouraged or approved in most groups or societies. For instance, when violence involves deviant underconformity to social norms, it is often classified as illegal and sanctioned severely. However, when violence occurs in connection with enforcing norms, protecting people and property, or overconforming to widely accepted norms, it may be approved and even lauded as necessary to preserve order, reaffirm important social values, or entertain spectators. Therefore, violence may be tolerated, or even glorified, when soldiers, police, and athletes are perceived to be protecting people, reproducing accepted ideologies, or pursuing victories in the name of others.

When violence occurs in connection with the widespread rejection of norms in a social world, it may be described as anarchy or lawless mayhem. When it occurs in connection with extreme methods of social control or extreme overconformity to norms, it often is associated with a sense of moral righteousness, even when people are maimed or killed and property is destroyed. Under certain political conditions, this latter expression of violence is tied to fascism and dictatorial leaders.

In the case of sports, punching a referee who penalizes you or a coach who reprimands you is violence based on a rejection of norms. These actions are defined as illegal and punished severely by teams and sport organizations, even if the referee or coach is not seriously injured. However, it is different when a football player delivers a punishing tackle, breaking the ribs or blowing out the knee of an opposing running back after his coach told him to be aggressive and put his body on the line for the team. Such violence involves overconformity to norms and is seen as entertaining, highlighted on video replays, and used by teammates and many other players as a mark of one's status in football culture. The player might even feel righteous in being violent, despite the harmful consequences, and would not hesitate to be violent again. His violence is not punished because it helps achieve a valued goal for the team and the people it represents. Furthermore, his ability to do violence and endure it when perpetrated by others is used to affirm his identity as an athlete and a football player.

The term **aggression** is used in this chapter to refer to *verbal or physical actions grounded in an intent to dominate, control, or do harm to another person.* Aggression is often involved in violence, but violence may occur inadvertently or carelessly without aggressive intent. This definition allows us to distinguish aggressive actions from other actions that we might describe as assertive, competitive, or achievement oriented. For example, a very competitive person may use violence during a game without the intent to dominate, control, or harm others. However, there is often a difference between being aggressive and simply being assertive or trying hard to win or achieve other goals. The term **intimidation** is used to refer to *words, gestures, and actions that threaten violence or aggression.* Like aggression, intimidation is used to dominate or control another person. These definitions focus our discussion, but they will not eliminate all conceptual problems.

VIOLENCE IN SPORTS THROUGH HISTORY

Violence is not new to physical activities and sports (Dunning, 1999; Guttmann, 1998; 2004). As noted in Chapter 3, so-called blood sports were popular among the ancient Greeks and throughout the Roman Empire. Deaths occurred regularly in connection with ritual games among the Mayas and Aztecs. Tournaments in medieval and early modern Europe were designed as training for war and often had warlike consequences. Folk games were only loosely governed by rules, and they produced injuries and deaths at rates that would shock and disgust people today. Bearbaiting, cockfighting, dog fighting, and other "sporting" activities during those periods involved treatment of animals that most people today would define as brutal and violent.

Research indicates that, as part of an overall civilizing process in Europe and North America, modern sports were developed as more rule-governed activities than the physical games in previous eras. As sports became formally organized, official rules prohibited certain forms of violence that had been common in many folk games. Bloodshed decreased, and there was a greater emphasis on self-control to restrict physical contact and the expression of aggressive impulses in the emotional heat of competition (Dunning, 1999).

Social historians also point out that rates of violence in sports do not automatically decrease over time. In fact, as actions and emotional expression have become more regulated and controlled in modern societies, players and spectators view the "controlled" violence in sports as exciting. Furthermore, the processes of commercialization, professionalization, and globalization have given rise to new forms of instrumental and "dramatic" violence in many sports. This means that goal-oriented and entertainment-oriented violence have increased, at least temporarily, in many Western societies. Sociologist Eric Dunning (1999) notes that violence remains a crucial social issue in modern sports because their goal is to create tension rather than relieve or discharge it. Additionally, violent and aggressive sports serve, in patriarchal societies, to reproduce an ideology that naturalizes the power of men over women. Overall, historical research shows that sports are given different meanings by time and place and that we can understand violence in sports only

SIDELINES

"Now that we've invented violence, we need a sport so we can use it without being labeled as uncivilized."

Violence in sports is not new, but this does not mean that it is a natural or inevitable part of sport participation among men or women.

when we analyze it in relation to the historical, social, and cultural contexts in which it occurs.

VIOLENCE ON THE FIELD

Violence in sports comes in many forms, and it is grounded in social and cultural factors related to the sport ethic, commercialization, gender ideology and ideas about masculinity, the dynamics of social class and race, and the strategies used in sports. Violence also has significant consequences for athletes and presents challenges for those who wish to control it. As we discuss these topics, it is useful to consider the different types of violence that occur in sports.

> There are a lot of unwritten rules in the game of baseball that you tacitly accept when you put on the uniform. When one of those is broken, there is yet another unwritten rule of retaliation. —Doug Glanville, former minor league baseball player, 2008

Types of Violence

The most frequently used typology of on-the-field violence among players was developed by the late Mike Smith, a respected Canadian sociologist

(1983; see Young, 2000, 2002a; 2007a). Smith identified four categories of violence in sports:

1. *Brutal body contact.* This includes physical practices common in certain sports and accepted by athletes as part of sport participation. Examples are collisions, hits, tackles, blocks, body checks, and other forms of forceful physical contact that can produce injuries. Most people in society define this forceful physical contact as extreme, although they don't classify it as illegal or criminal, nor do they see a need to punish it. Coaches often encourage this form of violence. As one coach said after a big playoff victory in high school football, "We preached to the kids all week that we had to get back to what we do best—playing smash-mouth football" (in Trivett, 1999, p. 30C).

2. *Borderline violence.* This includes practices that violate the rules of the game but are accepted by most players and coaches as consistent with the norms of the sport ethic and as useful competitive strategies. Examples are the "brush back" pitch in baseball, the forcefully placed elbow or knee in soccer and basketball, the strategic bump used by distance runners to put another runner off stride, the fistfight in ice hockey, and the forearm to the ribs of a quarterback in football. Although these actions are expected, they may provoke retaliation by other players. Official sanctions and fines are not usually severe for borderline violence. However, public pressure to increase the severity of sanctions has grown in recent years, and the severity of punishments has increased in some sports.

3. *Quasi-criminal violence.* This includes practices that violate the formal rules of the game, public laws, and even informal norms among

players. Examples are cheap shots, late hits, sucker punches, and flagrant fouls that endanger players' bodies and reject the norm calling for dedication to the game above all else. Fines and suspensions are usually imposed on players who engage in such violence. Most athletes condemn quasi-criminal violence and see it as a rejection of the informal norms of the game and what it means to be an athlete.

4. *Criminal violence.* This includes practices that are clearly outside the law to the point that athletes condemn them without question and law enforcement officials may prosecute them as crimes. Examples are assaults that occur after a game and assaults during a game that appear to be premeditated and severe enough to kill or seriously maim a player. Such violence is relatively rare, although there is growing support that criminal charges ought to be filed when it occurs. This support grew recently after a hockey player intentionally smashed an opponent's head with his stick. The act was such a blatant and dangerous assault that a fellow player known for his on-ice violence said, "He's lost the respect of every player in the league."

Sociologist Kevin Young (2002a, 2004b, 2007a) has noted that this is a useful general typology but that the lines separating the four types of violence shift over time as norms change in sports and societies. Furthermore, the typology fails to address the origins of violence and the relationship of violent acts to the sport ethic, gender ideology, and the commercialization of sports. Despite these weaknesses, this typology enables us to make distinctions between various types of violence discussed in this chapter.

Violence as Overconformity to the Norms of the Sport Ethic

In Pat Conroy's novel *The Prince of Tides* (1986), there is a classic scene in which the coach addresses his team and describes the ideal football player. He uses words that many athletes in heavy-contact sports have heard during their careers:

> Now a real hitter is a head-hunter who puts his head in the chest of his opponents and ain't happy if his opponent is still breathing after the play. A real hitter doesn't know what fear is except when he sees it in the eyes of a ball carrier he's about to split in half. A real hitter loves pain, loves the screaming and the sweating and the brawling and the hatred of life down in the trenches. He likes to be at the spot where the blood flows and the teeth get kicked out. That's what this sport's about, men. It's war, pure and simple. (p. 384)

Many coaches don't use such vivid vocabulary because they know it can inspire dangerous forms of violence. However, some coaches and team administrators seek athletes who think this way. For example, during a recent NFL draft, a reporter observed that the coach of the team in his city was seeking "cold-blooded defenders who smile when quarterbacks bleed" (Kiszla, 2001, p. 3D).

When athletes think this way, violence occurs regularly enough to attract attention. Journalists describe it, sociologists and psychologists try to explain it, and athletes brag or complain about it. When an athlete dies or is paralyzed by on-the-field violence, the media present stories stating that violence is rampant in sports and in society, and then they run multiple replays or photos of violent acts, knowing that this will increase their ratings or sales.

Although players may be concerned about brutal body contact and borderline violence in their sports, they generally accept them. Even when players don't like them, they may use them to enhance their status on teams and their popularity among spectators. Athletes whose violence involves overconformity to the sport ethic become legends on and off the field. Athletes who engage in quasi- and criminal violence often are marginalized in sports and may face criminal charges, although prosecuting such charges has

Violence is often connected with overconformity to the norms of the sport ethic. This high school rugby jacket presents violence as part of team culture. By associating violence with excellence, players learn what is expected on the field, even if they do not feel comfortable with brutal body contact and borderline violence. (*Source:* Jay Coakley)

been difficult and convictions are rare (Young, 2000, 2002a, 2004b, 2007a).

Violence as deviant overconformity is also related to insecurities among athletes in high-performance sports. Athletes learn that "you're only as good as your last game," and they know that their identities as athletes and status as team members are constantly tested. Therefore, they often take extreme measures to prove themselves, even if it involves violence. Violence reinforces feelings of self-worth by inviting affirmation from other athletes. This is why athletes who don't play in pain are defined as failures, whereas those who do are defined as courageous.

Willingly facing violence and playing in pain honors the importance of the game and expresses dedication to teammates and the culture of high-performance sport.

It is important to understand that violent expressions of deviant overconformity are not limited to men, even though they are more common among male athletes than female athletes. Women also overconform to the norms of the sport ethic, and when they play contact sports, they face the challenge of drawing the line between physicality and violence. For example, when sociologist Nancy Theberge (1999) spent a full season studying the sport experiences of women on an elite ice hockey team in Canada, she discovered that the women loved the physicality of hockey, even though body checking was not allowed. As one woman said,

> I like a physical game. You get more fired up. I think when you get hit . . . like when you're fighting for a puck in the corner, when you're both fighting so you're both working hard and maybe the elbows are flying, that just makes you put more effort into it. (in Theberge, 1999, p. 147)

The experience of dealing with the physicality of contact sports and facing its consequences creates drama, excitement, strong emotions, and special interpersonal bonds among female athletes just as it does among men. Despite the risk and reality of pain and injuries, many women in contact sports find that the physical intensity and body contact in their sports make them feel alive and aware. Although many women are committed to controlling brutal body contact and more severe forms of violence, the love of their sport and the excitement of physicality can lead to violence grounded in overconformity to the norms of the sport ethic.

Commercialization and Violence in Sports

Some athletes in power and performance sports are paid well because of their ability to do violence on the field. However, it would be inaccurate to identify money as the sole cause of violence in sports. Violent athletes in the past were paid very little, and athletes in high schools, colleges, and sport clubs today are paid nothing, yet many of them do violence despite the pain and injuries associated with it.

Commercialization has expanded opportunities to play certain contact sports in some societies, and media coverage makes these sports and the violence they contain more visible than ever before. Some sociologists note that the media tend to make events appear more violent than they actually are (see Weed, 2001; Poulton, 2005)—a point covered in the discussion of media influence in Chapter 12. Children watch this coverage and may imitate violent athletes when they play informal games and organized youth sports, but this does not justify the conclusion that commercialization is the cause of violence in sports.

Football players and athletes in other heavy contact sports engaged in violence on the field long before television coverage and the promise of big salaries. Players at all levels of organized football killed and maimed each other at rates that were far higher than the death and injury rates in football today. There are more injuries in football today because there are more people playing football. Violence in certain sports is a serious problem that must be addressed, but to think that it is caused mainly by commercialization and money would be a mistake.

This is an important point because many people who criticize sports blame violence and other problems on money and greed. They claim that if athletes were true amateurs and played for love of the game instead of money, there would be less violence. However, this conclusion contradicts research findings, and it distracts attention from the deep cultural and ideological roots of violence in particular sports and societies. We could take money away from athletes tomorrow, but violence would be reduced only if there were changes in the culture in which athletes, especially male athletes, learn to value and do violence in sports.

Many people resist the notion that cultural changes are needed to control violence because it places the responsibility for change on all of us. It is easy blame violence on wealthy and greedy team owners, athletes without moral character, and TV executives seeking higher viewer ratings, but it is more difficult to critically examine our culture and the normative and social organization of the sports that many people watch and enjoy. Similarly, it is difficult for people to critically examine the definitions of *masculinity* and the structure of gender relations that they have long accepted as part of the "natural" order of things, but such critiques are needed if we wish to understand and control violence in sports.

The point emphasized in this section is that commercialization is not the *primary* cause of violence in sports. But money is not irrelevant. Consider the following statements made by a boxer and two football players:

> I'm challenging Laila Ali. . . . Kicking [her] butt will be a walk in the park. . . . And if she wants a rematch, I'll dust her off again. (Jacqui Frazier-Lyde in Farhood, 2000, online)

> I want to hurt him. . . . I love to see people bleed. I do my talking [in the NFL] by hitting my man, throwing him on the ground, jumping on him. (Orlando Brown in Montville, 1999, p. 100)

> The first thing on our mind is to be violent and disruptive and rip someone's head off. (Marcus Stroud in Fleming, 2005, p. 66)

These are three among dozens of similar statements from popular sports publications. They express the language and rhetoric that has come to be used in certain commercial sports. The most extreme examples of this rhetoric can be found in professional wrestling and mixed martial arts (Ultimate Fighting Championship and Cage Fighting Championship). Therefore, when images of intimidation are used by Jacqui Frazier-Lyde (daughter of former heavyweight boxing champion Joe Frazier) as she challenges Laila Ali (daughter of Muhammad Ali) to a prize fight with a big payoff and when NFL players tell reporters that they want to hurt one another and rip someone's head off, their violent rhetoric tells us less about the way they *play sports* than it does about how they want us to *think* they play sports.

Professional athletes are entertainers, and they use a promotional and heroic rhetoric that presents images of revenge, retaliation, hate, hostility, intimidation, aggression, violence, domination, and destruction. These melodramatic images attract attention and serve commercial purposes. The NFL, the NHL, and even the NBA use these images to hype their games. They sell videos that present image after image of glorified violence in slow-motion close-ups accompanied by sounds of bodies colliding, bones and tendons snapping on impact, and players gasping in agony and pain. In true promotional fashion, the same media companies that sell or promote these videos also publish articles that condemn violence and violent players. Their marketing people know that violence *and* moral outrage about violence attract audiences and generate profits (Layden, 2007). ESPN has done this with its popular and controversial segment called "Jacked Up," during which they televise the five most violent hits of the week in the NFL.

Does this commercially inspired rhetoric represent real on-the-field orientations among athletes, or is it part of a strategy to make money by creating personas and attracting attention? Research is needed to answer this question, but my sense is that most athletes don't relish hurting opponents and seeing them bleed. At the same time, some athletes have become experts at using violent rhetoric to enhance the entertainment value of what they do and boost attendance at the events in which they participate. When the boxer Mike Tyson, renowned for his own violence in the ring, refereed the Cage Fighting world championships in Manchester, England, in 2006, he is said to have stated that he would not stop a fight until there was an eyeball rolling across the canvas. According to Tyson, Cage Fighting (also known as mixed martial arts, ultimate fighting, and No Holds Barred):

Is basically bone against bone, so there's probably going to be some blood and broken bones. It's a bit gory, not for the weak to watch. (in *The Observer*, March 19, 2006, p. 22)

Such rhetoric is part of the spectacle dimension of sports, similar to dramatic storylines delivered by paid announcers, sexy performances by cheerleaders and halftime dancers, and use of toy tomahawks for the symbolic "chopping" of opponents. However, it raises this question: How far can the spectacle be emphasized before people conclude that a particular sport has lost its authenticity as a game and has become choreographic violence devoid of play? Professional wrestling (WWE) crossed this line long ago, and the Ultimate Fighting Championship (UFC) seems to be crossing it now. Many people will watch violence in the context of an authentic game, but few will pay to watch violence week after week when it is not part of a goal-oriented structure that gives it meaning beyond the blood and gore.

Violence and Masculinity

Violence in sports is not limited to men. However, research based on critical feminist theory indicates that *if we want to understand violence in sports, we must understand gender ideology and issues of masculinity in culture.* Sociologist Mike Messner explains:

Young males come to sport with identities that lead them to define their athletic experience differently than females do. Despite the fact that few males truly enjoy hitting and being hit, and that one has to be socialized into participating in much of the violence commonplace in sport, males often view aggression, within the rule-bound structure of sport, as legitimate and "natural." (1992, p. 67)

Messner notes that many male athletes learn to define injurious acts as a necessary part of the game, rather than as violence, as long as those acts occur within the rules of the game and within the informal norms players use to evaluate each other.

Both men and women are capable of violence on and off the playing field. However, women may not connect violent actions to their identities in the same way that some men do. Prevailing definitions of *masculinity* lead many people to feel that violence is more "natural" for men than for women, and it may lead men to feel more comfortable with violence in their sports. (*Source:* Daniel Maurer, AP/World Wide Photos)

In many societies, participation in power and performance sports has become an important way to prove masculinity. Boys discover that if they play these sports and others see them as being able to do violence, they can avoid social labels such as *pussy*, *girl*, *fag*, *wimp*, and *sissy* (Ingham and Dewar, 1999). In a review of the research on this issue, Phil White and Kevin Young (1997) note that if a boy or young man avoids these sports, he risks estrangement from his male peers.

Boys and men who play power and performance sports learn quickly that they are evaluated in terms of their ability to do violence in combination with physical skills (Lance, 2005). This learning begins in youth sports, and by the time young men have become immersed in the social world of most power and performance

sports, they accept brutal body contact and borderline violence as part the game as it is played by "real" men. For example, when Ozzie Guillen, manager of the Chicago White Sox, was asked to comment about some of his players who complained about a vicious collision between a teammate and the catcher on the opposing team, he said, "If we don't like it, [we should] go and play softball or go play tennis. I don't want them to be a bunch of ladies playing this game" (*Denver Post*, 2004). When gender is viewed in these terms, the ability to do violence becomes "one of the cornerstones of masculinity" (White and Young, 1997, p. 9).

A tragic example of the connection between masculinity and violence in sports occurred at a Massachusetts hockey rink a few years ago. As a few boys practiced hockey skills during an

breaking BARRIERS

Ideological Barriers
The Hit Isn't Real Unless It Bends Steel

Murderball is unique. It's four-on-four competition with players in wheelchairs customized to function like mini-chariots, with angled wheels, bucket seats, safety harnesses, and protective metal bars that shield legs and feet during crashes. Using a volleyball on a basketball court, the teams engage in a contest that resembles a mix of rugby, team handball, and football that was organized by an X Games promoter.

In the Paralympics, murderball is officially called wheelchair rugby. Many people call it quad rugby because participants have quadriplegia or limited use of three or four limbs. Each of the twelve members of a team is rated in terms of upper-body muscle function, from 0.5 (most impaired) to 3.5 (least impaired). During games the four players on the court from each team may not exceed a cumulative rating of 8.0 points. Participation is open to men and women, but most teams are all-male. During the four eight-minute quarters, points are scored when a player possessing the ball crosses the opponents' end line.

Wheelchair rugby was invented in Canada in 1981 and first played in the Paralympics in 1996. It

Wheelchair rugby, a.k.a. *quad rugby* and *murderball*, is played in the Paralympics. Pictured are the Portland Pounders, one of many teams in North America. Some quad rugby players use a highly masculinized vocabulary to describe the intimidation and violence that occur in their games. Wheelchair rugby challenges stereotypes about people with a disability, but it also reaffirms a gender ideology in which manhood is defined in terms of the ability to do violence. When sports embody contradictory ideological themes, making clear sense of them is difficult. (*Source:* Jason E. Kaplan Photography, Portland, Oregon)

informal skating session, a father became angry because his son failed to defend himself when other boys pushed him around. The father entered the rink and told his son to "be a man" on the ice. The boy turned away and walked to the locker room, but his father continued to harass him. Another father passed by and told his fellow dad to ease up because it was a minor incident. This further irritated the angry father, and he punched the man who gave him the unwanted advice. He exited the rink and then came back, found the man whom he had punched, and beat him to death in the lobby of the rink, in front of a few children, mothers, and a rink employee.

This case was covered in the media as an extreme example of parental "rink rage," but it was never discussed as an expression of ideas about masculinity in American society. The father, who was later convicted of voluntary manslaughter, first became enraged when his son failed to meet immediately became popular among men with multiple limb impairments, especially those who favored power and performance sports involving heavy physical contact. Paul Davies, a former player and now manager of the British national team, describes wheelchair rugby as "a real in your face sport [resembling] chess with violence" (BBC Sport Academy, 2005).

Many wheelchair rugby players have impairments caused by accidents in risky activities, including sports. They like wheelchair rugby because it differs from other sports in the Paralympics. When players and other insiders refer to the sport as *murderball*, it implies a closer connection to able-bodied heavy-contact sports than there is for other Paralympic sports.

Some athletes say that murderball allows them to express their aggression and gain a sense of control over their bodies. But as one member of the U.S. team said, "Of course, you're gonna have healthy aggression and unhealthy aggression." And then one of his teammates added, "But when you can use your body and your chair just to go knock the shit out of somebody, it helps" (in Anderson, 2005; from the documentary film, *Murderball*).

Although other Paralympic sports are organized so that violence is inconsistent with the strategy and rhythm of participation, some athletes with disabilities want to play a violent sport and reaffirm their identities as athletes and men by doing violence. For example, when the U.S. team faced Canada in the gold medal game of the 2002 Wheelchair Rugby World Championships, the coach reminded the players that, "It's not buddy-buddy time anymore,

guys." And when a member of the U.S. team was asked about their goal for the 2004 Paralympics in Athens, he quickly replied, "We're not going for a hug, we're going for a f___ing Gold Medal" (in *Murderball*, 2004).

"Hugs" are associated with the Special Olympics, which are organized to emphasize play and personal accomplishment among athletes with intellectual disabilities. There is little emphasis on competitive success in the Special Olympics and none on dominating opponents. Volunteer coaches frequently hug athletes who complete an event, regardless of the outcome.

Many Paralympians, influenced by the ideology of ableism, want to distance themselves from the Special Olympics because it doesn't match dominant sport forms in society and it perpetuates the idea that people with disabilities cannot play "real" sports—that is, the sports played by able-bodied male athletes.

Ableism is a *web of ideas and beliefs that people use to classify bodies perceived as unimpaired as normal and superior and bodies perceived as (dis)abled as subnormal and inferior.* This ideology is widespread in society and many people, including some with disabilities, use it to evaluate themselves and others. Similarly, some murderball athletes use traditional gender ideology to connect power, status, and male identity with the ability to do violence. As expressed through words on a player's T-shirt: "The hit isn't real unless it bends steel" (Grossfeld, 2005). This is not surprising because none of us lives outside the influence of ideology, even when we move around in wheelchairs.

his definition of how a man should behave on the ice, and then he killed another man who told him that the issue was minor. This case highlights the problems associated with a gender ideology that leads people to think that masculinity is proved by doing violence in sports.

When women do violence in sports, it may be seen as a sign of commitment or skill, but it is not seen as proof of femininity. Dominant gender ideology in many cultures links manhood with

the ability to do violence, but there is no similar link between womanhood and violence. Therefore, female athletes who engage in violence do not receive the same support and rewards that men receive—unless they wrestle in the WWE, do mixed martial arts in Fatal Femme Fighting, or skate on a roller derby team where the sport personas of female athletes are constructed, in part, to shock or titillate spectators (Berra, 2005; Blumenthal, 2004). The emergence of women's boxing provides a context in which female athletes are rewarded for doing violence, but most female boxers do not feel that doing violence in the ring makes them more of a woman than the boxers they defeat.

Overall, none of us lives outside the influence of ideology. This point is highlighted in connection with a rapidly growing sport that participants call murderball. Officially known as wheelchair rugby, murderball is the focus of Breaking Barriers on pages 204–205.

> **OLC ON THE *OLC*:**
> See the OLC—Additional Readings for Chapter 7—for the author's review of the documentary film, *Murderball.*

The Institutionalization of Violence in Sports

Certain forms of violence are built into the culture and structure of particular sports (Guilbert, 2004). Athletes in these sports learn to use violence as a strategy, even though it may cause them pain and injury. Controlling institutionalized violence is difficult because it requires changing the culture and structure of particular sports—something that most people in governing bodies are hesitant to do. These topics are discussed in the following sections.

Learning to Use Violence as a Strategy: Non-contact Sports   In some non-contact sports, participants may try to intimidate opponents, but violence is rare. For example, tennis players have been fined for slamming a ball to the ground in protest or talking to an official or opponent in a menacing manner, but they're seldom, if ever, rewarded for violent actions. Therefore, it is doubtful that playing or watching non-contact sports teaches people to use violence as a strategy on the field.

Athletes in non-contact sports may use violent images as they describe competition, but they

don't have actual opportunities to convert their words into deeds. For example, a sprint cyclist on the U.S. cycling team used violent imagery to describe his approach to competition on the track:

> I am really aggressive out there. I pretty much hate the guy I'm racing. It wouldn't matter if it were my brother. . . . I want to destroy the guy. End it quick. Boom. One knockout punch. (in Becker, 1996, p. 4E)

Of course, cycling does not allow him to physically destroy or punch a competitor, but the language he used had violence built into it.

Men who play non-contact sports use violent images in their descriptions of competition much more often than women use them. The use of a "language of violence" is clearly linked to masculinity in most cultures. Women may use it on occasion, but men use it more frequently. Part of the reason for this difference is that many women realize that a language of violence reaffirms a gender ideology that privileges men, works against women's interests, and subverts the health and well-being of everyone in society.

Learning to Use Violence as a Strategy: Men's Contact Sports   Athletes in heavy contact and collision sports learn to use intimidation, aggression, and violence as strategies to achieve competitive success on the field. Success in these sports depends on the use of brutal body contact and borderline violence. Research shows that male athletes in these sports readily accept certain forms of violence, even when they involve rule violations, and this acceptance increases with the frequently and force of collisions in a sport (Pilz, 1996; Shields and Bredemeier, 1995; Weinstein, Smith, and Wiesenthal, 1995; White and Young, 1997). These athletes routinely disapprove of quasi-criminal and criminal violence, but they accept brutal body contact and borderline violence as long as it occurs within the rules of the game. They may not intend to hurt, but this does not prevent them from doing things that clearly put their bodies and the bodies of opponents in harm's way.

In boxing, football, ice hockey, rugby, and other heavy-contact and collision sports, athletes also use intimidation and violence to promote their careers, increase drama for spectators, and enhance publicity for their sports and sponsors. They realize that doing violence is expected, even if it causes harm to themselves and others. This was illustrated in 2004 when Brian Burke, the general manager of the NHL Vancouver Canucks, promised that his team would go after an opposing player who had injured one of their players in a previous game. Burke stated, "There's definitely a bounty on his head . . . It's going to be fun when we get him" (in Sadowski, 2005, p. 7C). In the game that followed this comment, a Canucks player wrapped his left arm around the target player's neck, punched his head repeatedly, and slammed him to the ice. This "fun" resulted in a broken neck, a closed head injury, and deep cuts on the face of the victim. The Canucks were fined $250,000, and the attacking player was suspended, causing him to lose $502,000 of his $6.8 million salary. The victim sustained serious physical and neurological damage and has not played hockey since being attacked. The attacker was charged with criminal assault and, after pleading guilty, was sentenced to twelve months of probation and eighty hours of community service; additionally, he was prohibited from ever playing against the person he attacked, but he currently plays in the National Hockey League (NHL) and earns a multimillion-dollar salary.

Violence is also incorporated into game strategies when coaches use players as designated agents of intimidation and violence for their teams. These players are called "enforcers," "goons," and "hit men," and they are expected to protect teammates and strategically assist their teams by intimidating, provoking, fighting

> With the smart coach, fighting is a tool. . . . Fighting can be used to inspire your team, send a message, change momentum. —Barry Melrose, ESPN hockey announcer, 2002

with, or injuring opponents. Their violent acts are an accepted part of certain sports, including hockey and basketball. For example, former Los Angeles Lakers player Rick Fox regularly played the role of enforcer on the basketball court. To do it right, he says, "You have to look within and find the evil that's inside of you. It's not the kind of talk you want your kids to hear, but we're grown men" (in AP, 2000).

Players who act as enforcers are paid primarily for their ability and willingness to do violence. However, every time they maim or come close to killing someone on the ice, court, or playing field, people raise questions about institutionalized violence in sports. Football, basketball, and baseball have taken actions to control certain forms of institutionalized violence, but hockey has been slow to do so. Once violence is built into the culture, structures, and strategies of a sport, controlling or eliminating it is difficult.

Learning to Use Violence as a Strategy: Women's Contact Sports   Information on violence among girls and women in contact sports remains scarce even though more women are participating in them (Lawler, 2002; Young 2007a). Participation creates the possibility for cases of violence among female athletes, but few studies explore if and why it occurs.

Women's programs have undergone many changes over the past thirty years. They have become more competitive with a greater emphasis on power and performance and higher stakes associated with success. Today, as women become increasingly immersed in the social world of elite power and performance sports, they become more tolerant of rule violations and aggressive actions on the playing field, but this pattern is less clear among women than men (Nixon, 1996a, 1996b; Shields and Bredemeier, 1995; Shields et al., 1995; Tucker and Parks, 2001; Young, 2007a).

In the words of one researcher, "We know of no biological reasons that would prevent women from using intimidation and violence or being as physically aggressive as men" (Dunn, 1994). However, most girls and women become involved in and learn to play sports in ways that differ from the experiences of most boys and men. As women compete at higher levels, they often become similar to men in the way they embrace the sport ethic and use it to frame their identities as athletes. Like men, they are willing to dedicate themselves to the game, take risks, make sacrifices, pay the price, continue playing despite pain and injury, and overcome barriers. However, it is rare for them to link toughness, physicality, and aggression to their gender identities. In other words, women do not tie their ability to do violence to their definitions of what it means to be a woman in society. Similarly, coaches don't try to motivate female athletes by urging them to "go out and prove who the better woman is" on the field. Therefore, at this time, women's contact sports are less violent than men's contact sports.

With this said, many research questions have not yet been answered: Do elite female athletes develop the same form of hubris (pride-based arrogance) that many elite male athletes develop? If so, how is it linked to their identities, and how do they express it in sports? Do female athletes use a rhetoric of violence when they talk about sports? Some studies suggest that they don't (Nelson, 1994, 1998; Theberge, 1999; Young and White, 1995), but more information is needed. A good place to start might be with the women now playing heavy-contact sports such as football, ice hockey, rugby, and boxing or participating in dramatic spectacles such as ultimate fighting and professional wrestling.

SIDELINES

"When are you gonna learn when it's necessary to use unnecessary roughness?"

Physical intimidation and violence are used as strategies in men's contact sports. They have been effective in winning games and building the reputations of players and teams.

> Becky Zerlentes took a shot to the head above her left eye, then staggered forward and fell to the canvas. . . . [She] never regained consciousness and died, becoming the first female boxer to die in a sanctioned event. — *CBS News*, 5 April 2005

Pain and Injury as the Price of Violence

Many people think about sports in a paradoxical way: They accept violence in sports, but the injuries caused by that violence make them uneasy. They seem to want violence without consequences— like the fictionalized violence they see in the media and video games in which characters engage in brutality without being seriously or permanently injured. However, sports violence is real, and it causes real pain, injury, disability, and even death (Dater, 2005; Farber, 2004; Leahy, 2008; Rice, 2005; Smith, 2005b; Young, 2004a).

Ron Rice, an NFL player whose career ended when he tackled an opponent, discusses the real consequences of violence. The brutal body contact of the tackle left him temporarily paralyzed and permanently disabled. He remembers that "before I hit the ground, I knew my career was over. . . . My body froze. I was like a tree that had been cut down, teetering, then crashing, unable to break my fall." Reminiscing about his life as a football player, Rice says that he was "programmed from a very young age to live and think a certain way," to be a warrior who keeps going no matter what (Rice, 2005). He did just that, and today he lives with chronic pain in his neck, wrists, hands, ankles, knees, and back—the toll of doing violence to others and enduring it in return. Rice says, "I'm 32 now, . . . These injuries are a part of my life. And I got off easy compared to a lot of these guys" (Rice 2005, p. 83).

Research on pain and injury among athletes helps us understand that violence in sports has real consequences. As noted in chapter 6, studies indicate that professional sports involving brutal body contact and borderline violence are among the most dangerous workplaces in the occupational world (Leahy, 2008; Nixon, 2000; Waddington, 2000a, 2000b; White, 2004; White and Young, 1997; Young, 1993, 2000, 2004a). The same could be said about high-profile power and performance intercollegiate sports in which 80 percent of male and female athletes sustain at least one serious injury while playing their sports and nearly 70 percent are disabled for two or more weeks (Nixon, 2000). Rates of disabling injuries vary by sport, but they are high enough in many sports to constitute a serious health issue (Gessel et al., 2007; Mueller and Cantu, 2008; see Chapter 4, pp. 103–108). The "normal" brutal body contact and borderline violence in contact and collision sports regularly cause arthritis, concussions, bone fractures, torn ligaments, and other injuries. In other words, the violence inherent in power and performance sports takes a definite toll on the health of athletes (Leahy, 2008; Theberge, 2008c; Young, 2004a).

Research shows a close connection between dominant ideas about masculinity and the high rate of injuries in many sports. Ironically, some power and performance sports are organized so that players feel that their manhood is up for grabs. Men who define *masculinity* in terms of physically dominating others often use violence in sports as an expression of this code of manhood. Until they critically examine issues related to gender and the organization of their sports, they will mistakenly define violence as a source of rewards rather than a source of chronic pain and disabilities that constrain and threaten their lives.

Controlling On-the-Field Violence

The roots of violence on the playing field are deep. They're grounded in overconformity to the sport ethic, processes of commercialization, and definitions of masculinity. Therefore, many of the men who control and play power and performance sports resist efforts to reduce violence. They understand that their identities in the context of these sports depend on approving and doing violence and that competitive success often requires the strategic use of violence.

Brutal body contact is the most difficult type of violence to control. It is grounded in the culture of power and performance sports and its incorporation of dominant gender ideology. Unfortunately, about 90 percent of the serious injuries in these sports occur *within the rules* of the games and contests. This means that many men inevitably pay the price for their destructive definitions of *sports* and *masculinity*.

Efforts to control brutal body contact require changes in gender ideology and the cultures of certain sports. These changes won't occur without persistent and thoughtful strategies to document the dangers of the actions and the language that men and women use to reproduce violent sport cultures and the gender ideology that supports them. People should demand and keep accurate records and publish information on injuries on a team-by-team, league-by-league, and sport-by-sport basis. Parents should be informed of these rates before they enlist their children in the service of reproducing patriarchy and a gender ideology that jeopardizes health and development. People should also calculate the cost of injuries due to brutal body contact and other types of violence in terms of medical expenses, lost work time and wages, days missed in college classes, disability payments, family problems, and even loss in life expectancy. Looking at these statistics will help us understand the connections between sport participation and health.

It is less difficult to control borderline, quasi-criminal, and criminal violence in sports, although many people continue to resist taking necessary actions. Enforcers, instead of being hired explicitly to do violence, should be suspended without pay for violent acts; additionally, teams should be prohibited from replacing them during the suspension period and coaches and team owners should be fined for the violent actions of their players. Unless these or similar actions are taken, owners will simply replace one headhunting enforcer with another. As long as owners and league officials escape sanctions, they have little incentive to control violent players who boost their profits. Suspensions prevent players from doing what they love to do, and if they cannot be replaced on rosters, the suspensions encourage coaches and team owners to use their power to discourage violence on the field.

VIOLENCE OFF THE FIELD

When athletes in contact sports are arrested for violent crimes, many people assume that their violence off the field is related to the violent strategies they've learned on the field. For example, *New York Times* columnist Robert Lipsyte says,

> Felony arrests among pro and college [male] athletes may or may not be rising, but better reporting makes it clear that many of them cannot turn off their aggressive behavior at the buzzer. (1999, p. 11)

Ultimate Fighting, AKA Mixed Martial Arts, Cage Fighting, Tough Man Contests, and Fatal Femmes Fighting (www.fatalfemmesfighting.com/), involves one-on-one violence. It is among the fastest growing spectator events in the world. The only way to control violence in these events is to ban the events. So far, bans have been successfully resisted by event organizers and competitors. (*Source:* Jon Super, AP/ Wide World Photos)

Jessie Armstead, a linebacker in the NFL, says making the transition from a violent playing field to life off the field is not easy for many players:

> When you think about it, it is a strange thing that we do. During a game we want to kill each other. Then we're told to shake hands and drive home safely. Then a week later we try to kill each other again. (in Freeman, 1998, p. 1)

John Niland, a former NFL player, supports this:

> Any athlete who thinks he can be as violent as you can be playing football, and leave it all on the field, is kidding himself. (Falk, 1995, p. 12)

These statements as well as statements in a study of professional hockey players (Pappas, McKenry, and Catlett, 2004) suggest that the violence used strategically on the field carries over into athletes' lives off the field. However, research on the carryover issue is difficult to do, and good studies are rare. When people refer to statistical correlations that show a relationship between playing certain sports and high rates of off-the-field violence, it does not prove that playing violent sports causes people to be violent outside of sports. Two other issues must be considered before causality can be established.

First, the people who play violent sports may have used violence to establish status or cope with problems prior to their sport participation. In other words, violent sports attract people who already feel comfortable about doing violence.

Second, off-the-field violence among athletes may be due to unique situational factors encountered more often by athletes than by other people. For example, athletes known for their toughness on the field may be encouraged, dared, or taunted by others to be tough on the streets. In some cases, they are challenged to fight because of their reputations in sports. This is most likely to occur when athletes who grew up in high-crime neighborhoods return home and are identified as "marks" by locals who push drugs or run scams to make money. If athletes hang out in those neighborhoods, they're likely to attract locals who define them as "sellouts" to big money and corporate sponsors. Some of these locals would like nothing better than to enhance their own credibility on the streets by successfully confronting an athlete known for his toughness. If trouble occurs and athletes are arrested for fighting in these circumstances, it is misleading to say that their actions were caused by what they learned in sports.

Control versus Carryover

Does playing sports teach people to control violent responses in the face of adversity, stress, defeat, hardship, and pain? Or does it create identities, personal orientations, and social dynamics that make off-the-field violence more likely?

Trulson's research that was summarized in Chapter 6 (p. 174) showed that aggressive tendencies among male juvenile delinquents decreased after they received training in the philosophy and techniques of tae kwon do (Trulson, 1986). The philosophy emphasized respect for self and others, confidence, physical fitness, self-control, honor, patience, and responsibility. Similar young men who received martial arts training *without* the philosophy actually measured higher on aggressive tendencies after a training period, and young men who participated in running, basketball, and football with standard adult supervision didn't change at all in terms of their aggressive tendencies.

French sociologist Loïc Wacquant studied these issues for three years as he trained and gained the trust of the men who worked out at a traditional, highly structured, and reputable boxing gym in a Chicago neighborhood. During that time, he observed, interviewed, and documented the experiences and lives of more than fifty professional boxers. He not only learned the craft of boxing but also became immersed in the social world in which the boxers trained. He found that the social world encompassed by this gym was one in which the boxers learned to value their craft and dedicate themselves to the idea of being a professional boxer; they also learned to respect fellow boxers and accept the rules of sportsmanship that governed boxing as a profession. In a low-income neighborhood where poverty and hopelessness promoted intimidation and violence, these boxers accepted norms that disapproved of fighting outside the ring, they avoided street fights, and they internalized the controls necessary to follow a highly disciplined daily training schedule.

When Wacquant (1995a) asked the boxers about a boxing-violence connection, their responses challenged popular beliefs. Two boxers answered with these statements:

> Boxin' doesn't jus' teach you violence. I think, boxin' teaches you discipline an' self-respect an' it's also teachin' you how to defen' yourself. . . . Anybody who feels that it teaches you violence is a person tha's really a, a *real incompetent mind* I think. (Twenty-four-year-old night security guard who trained at the gym for eight years, pp. 494–95)

> Man, the sports commentators an' the writers and stuff, they don't know nuthin' abou' the boxin' game. *They ignorant.* I be embarrassed to let somebody hear me say [chuckles in disbelief], "Boxing teach you violence." . . . Tha's showin' *their* ignorance. For one thin', they lookin' at it from a spectator point of view . . . on the *outsi' lookin' in,* but [the boxer's] *insi' lookin out.* (Twenty-eight-year-old part-time janitor, seven years in the ring, p. 489)

These statements are not meant to support professional boxing. However, when they are combined with research findings in the studies by Trulson and Wacquant, it is reasonable to conclude that participation in sports, even martial arts and boxing, can teach people to control aggression and violence. Of course, this outcome depends greatly on the conditions under which sport participation occurs. *If* the social world formed around a sport promotes a mind-set and norms emphasizing non-violence, self control, respect for self and others, physical fitness, patience, responsibility, and humility (the opposite of hubris), then athletes *may* learn to control violent behavior off the field. Those most likely to benefit seem to be young men who lack structured challenges and firm guidance as they navigate their way through lives in which there are many incentives to engage in violence.

Unfortunately, many sports are not organized around these norms. Instead, most sport cultures emphasize hostility, physical domination, and a willingness to use one's body as a

Some sports, even at the youth level, use symbols and language that encourage orientations supportive of violence. Coaches award skull-and-crossbones decals, as shown on this player's helmet, to 11-year-olds who make "big hits" and intimidate the opposition. (*Source:* Jay Coakley)

weapon. They're also organized to produce hubris, isolate athletes from the community and encourage them to view outsiders as unworthy of their respect. For example, recent research on thirteen- to seventeen-year olds in U.S. schools shows that sport participation, especially for young men in contact sports, is associated with fighting and delinquency off the field (Kreager, 2007; Roche, 1999; Portes, 1998; Wright and Fitzpatrick, 2006). Sociologist Derek Kreager analyzed data from a national sample of 6,397 seventh- to twelfth-graders and found that football players and wrestlers were over 40 percent more likely to be involved in fights than male peers who didn't play high school sports. Playing basketball and baseball were unrelated to fighting, and male tennis players had a 35 percent *lower* risk of fighting than male peers who didn't play sports. The likelihood of fighting also increased with the proportion of football players in a young man's friendship network.

In another national study, Wright and Fitzpatrick (2006) found that certain high school sports were associated with status dynamics that created or intensified ingroup versus outgroup differences among young people. Other research suggests that these status differences frequently take the form of a social hierarchy that is sustained, in part, through harrassment, bullying, and fighting; in many cases, athletes from certain sports were the perpetrators of these actions (ESPN, 1999).

More research is needed to understand the social worlds of athletes in particular sports, the meanings that athletes attach to their actions, and the place of violence in sport cultures. Similarly, we need to know more about issues of identity, group dynamics among athletes, ideological issues, and social factors associated with violence. Sport participation does not automatically teach people to control violence, nor does the violence used in certain sports inevitably carry over to other relationships and settings. Instead of seeking examples of carryover or control, perhaps we should look for cultural connections between sports and ideologies associated with high rates of violence. This topic is discussed in the box titled "Violence on the Field" on the next page.

Assaults and Sexual Assaults by Male Athletes

Highly publicized cases in which male athletes are accused or convicted of assault, sexual assault, rape, gang rape, and even murder create the impression that violence in certain sports influences off-the-field actions and relationships, especially relationships with women. Athletes are public figures and celebrities, so when they

are accused and arrested, we hear and read about it time and time again. This repetition also creates the impression that male athletes are violent and misogynist.

Violent crimes by male athletes are a serious problem. On this, there is no question (Armstrong and Perry, 2008a, 2008b, 2008c; Benedict, 1997, 1998, 2004; Lefkowitz, 1997; Robinson, 1998). Furthermore, the victims of these crimes are often subject to various forms of character assassination and harassment to a degree that may exceed that of victims of similar crimes committed by men who are not celebrity athletes (Hnida, 2006). Therefore, there is a clear need for sport teams and organizations to directly and assertively address this issue. But there's also a need to understand the role of sport participation in violent off-the-field actions and crimes. Without this understanding, the efforts of teams and organizations are likely to be ineffective.

As noted previously, some research indicates that high school athletes in certain sports are involved in fighting more frequently than their peers, but we lack studies that compare specific rates of off-the-field violence for athletes of different ages with the rates for similar peers who don't play elite sports.

Research on the conversations and biographies of athletes suggests that the social worlds created around men's power and performance sports subvert respect for women and promote the image of women as "game" to be pursued and conquered (Curry, 1991, 1996, 1998; Lefkowitz, 1997; Messner and Stevens, 2002; Nack and Munson, 1995; Reid, 1997). However, as noted in Chapter 6, data on the arrest records of NFL players raise questions about the extent to which this is a problem related to sports or whether it is primarily a part of a larger problem in U.S. culture generally (Blumstein and Benedict, 1999).

In the late-1990s, sport sociologist Todd Crosset (1999) reviewed all the published research on sexual assaults by male athletes to determine if there was cause to say that they are disproportionately involved in violence

reflect on SPORTS

Violence on the Field
Does It Distort Our Ideas About Gender?

"Men are naturally superior to women." This is a contentious statement today. However, many people still believe it, mostly because the current hierarchical structure of gender relations depends on its acceptance.

The ideology of male superiority is clearly reaffirmed through sports such as ultimate fighting, boxing, football, wrestling, ice hockey, rugby, and other heavy-contact sports that are valued and viewed worldwide (Burstyn, 1999; Connell, 1995; Messner, 2007a). The violence in those sports supports the belief that hierarchical distinctions between men and women are grounded in nature and cannot be altered.

Power and performance sports emphasize sex *difference* in terms of physical strength, *control* through domination, and *status* as an outcome of victories over others. This "naturalizes" hierarchical differences and reaffirms the belief that power is the basis for success and a person's status or rank compared to others. These ideas and beliefs are perpetuated through the stories that people tell about power and performance sports and how victories and championships are won only by using strength and strategic violence to dominate others (Burstyn, 1999).

The gender ideology formed around these ideas and beliefs has been central in U.S. culture. The stakes associated with preserving this ideology are so high that male boxers are paid millions of dollars for three to thirty-six minutes of brutalizing one another in the ring. Heavyweight boxers are among the highest-paid athletes in the world because they promote the idea that man versus man violent confrontations are "nature in action," even though the combatants often lose millions of brain cells as they "prove" male superiority.

The irony in this approach is that, if a gender hierarchy were truly fixed in nature, there would be no need for sports to reaffirm "natural" differences between men and women. Gender would simply exist without spending so much time and effort teaching girls and boys how they should perform gender.

Power and performance sports are used as valuable aids in this teaching and learning process, and the men who play them sometimes serve as the teachers. For example, when rules were passed to partially limit fighting in ice hockey, Tie Domi, an American player with a reputation for being violent, complained, "If you take out fighting, what comes next? Do we eliminate checking? Pretty soon, we will all be out there in dresses and skirts" (Domi, 1992, p. C3). Domi's point was that, unless men can do violence in hockey, there will be nothing that makes them different from women, and the preception in certain sports is that there is nothing worse for a man than being like women—except, perhaps, being gay.

When women participate in violent sports they potentially disrupt the "logic" used to reaffirm traditional gender ideology. This causes some people to argue that women should not participate in these sports, and to treat women athletes in these sports as jokes, oddities, or freaks of nature; these people may watch as women box, cage fight, or wrestle, but they don't take them seriously as athletes or they sexualize them to reaffirm the "logic of sex differences" on which traditional gender ideology is based (see www .fatalfemmesfighting.com/).

The participation of women in violent sports often creates a dilemma for people who advocate progressive changes in traditional gender ideology. Although participation contradicts the ideological belief that women are frail and vulnerable, it also reaffirms the beliefs that have traditionally disadvantaged women through history. For this reason, some women advocate equal opportunities in sports at the same time that they seek alternatives to violent sports. Their goal is to promote sports in which women can be strong and assertive without being violent.

These issues and controversies illustrate that sports have an impact on our lives regardless of our own involvement in them as athletes or spectators. *What do you think?*

against women. His review indicated that male intercollegiate athletes, in particular, seem to be involved in more sexual assaults than other male students, but the differences were not statistically significant in the studies of this issue, and background differences between athletes and other students made the data in these studies difficult to interpret.

In his conclusion, Crosset explained that the evidence did not warrant a conclusion that playing power and performance sports causes men to engage in violence against women. He also noted that some efforts to seek such a causal link may lead researchers to overlook important cultural and ideological issues and distract attention from three important points:

1. Violence against women occurs regularly and is a serious problem in the United States and many other societies.
2. Some male athletes have perpetrated sexual assault and rape, but nearly all violence directed against women is perpetrated by heterosexual men who are *not* currently playing competitive sports.
3. The problem of violence against women in the United States must be understood within the context of U.S. culture and the forms of gender relations that exist in all spheres of society, including sports, if efforts to lower the rates of sexual assault and rape are to succeed.

Building on Crosset's analysis and combining it with other research on patterns of violence in all-male groups, violence against women by male athletes is associated with the extent to which the culture of men's sports

- supports the belief that violence is an effective strategy for establishing one's manhood, achieving status as an athlete, and controlling women
- fosters social bonds and a related sense of hubris that separates athletes from the rest of the community

- creates a sense of privilege based on the belief that people outside the fraternity of elite athletes do not deserve respect and that elite athletes live outside the norms of the general community
- supports the belief that women, apart from mothers and sisters, are celebrity-obsessed "groupies" who can be exploited for sexual pleasure without consequences
- is viewed with such awe and idealism that people and institutions in the general community fail to hold elite athletes accountable for violations of community norms and rules

Research on these factors will help us understand violence against women *in the full social and cultural contexts in which it occurs.*

As noted in Chapter 6, the social dynamics in certain all-male sport groups encourage athletes to demean and humiliate those who don't match their unique, elite status. This suggests that off-the-field violence is not simply the result of carryover from on-the-field violence. Instead, it is action grounded in complex social processes related to the social worlds in which athletes live, define their identities, and deal with social relationships. As athletes are increasingly separated from the rest of the community, it becomes more important to understand these processes if we wish to explain and reduce assault rates among athletes.

When discussing this issue, it's important to remember that even if studies indicated that male athletes had higher sexual assault rates than other categories of people, this would not change the fact that males who don't play elite sports perpetrate nearly all violence, including violence against women. Jackson Katz, a violence prevention expert, explains that it would be useful to explain why some male athletes assault women, but this is only part of what we need to know when trying to answer the main question of why "stockbrokers, teachers, priests, auto mechanics, and Ivy League students" also assault women

(Katz, 2003). Although people from all racial and ethnic groups, social classes, and occupational categories perpetrate violence, it is clear that men commit nearly all rapes.

Finally, the focus on athletes should not distract attention from other sport-related assault issues. For example, sexual assaults, including statutory rape, by coaches have a greater impact in sports and on people's lives than sexual assaults by athletes (Brackenridge, 2001; Brackenridge and Fasting, 2003; Fasting, Brackenridge, and Sundgot-Borgen, 2004). Research done by journalists at the *Seattle Times* (2003) found that 159 coaches in the state of Washington (where only 2 percent of the U.S. population lives) were fired or reprimanded for sexual offenses between 1993 and 2003. Offenses ranged from harassment to rape, nearly all involved heterosexual male coaches victimizing girls, and about 60 percent of these coaches continued to coach or teach after the misconduct was known. Even though 159 coaches were fired or reprimanded, most reports of misconduct were neither investigated by school authorities nor reported to the police. Even when misconduct was admitted, the incidents were kept secret if the coaches agreed to leave their jobs. Sexual offenses in private sport clubs were especially problematic because clubs seldom regulate coaches' conduct, and most parents trust coaches even when evidence arouses suspicions of misconduct (Willmsen and O'Hagan, 2003).

Crimes of assault and sexual assault go far beyond the realm of sport, but when they are committed by celebrity athletes or coaches, they may be reported less often than in other cases, victims may be intimidated by fans and representatives of teams and sport organizations, prosecutors may not file charges, "settlements" may be reached to avoid criminal prosecution, and verdicts may be debated after trials have been held. Even if future research indicates that neither athletes nor coaches have assault rates higher than others, there is a need to address the unique issues associated with sport cultures and the experiences of the victims in these cases.

VIOLENCE AMONG SPECTATORS

Do sports incite violence among spectators? This is an important question because sports capture widespread public attention around the world and spectators number in the billions. To answer this question, we must distinguish between watching sports on television and attending events in person. Further, we must study spectators in context if we wish to understand the emotional dynamics of identifying with teams and athletes, the meanings that spectators give to particular sporting events, and the varying circumstances under which people watch sports.

Violence Among Television Viewers

Most people watch sports on television in their homes. They may express emotions and become angry at certain points, but we don't know much about when and why people express anger through violence directed at friends and family members at home. Nor do we know much about violence among people who watch televised sports in public settings such as bars, pubs, and around large video screens in public areas.

"Hey, watch it, pal! You stepped on my foot."

The language used by some spectators often refers to violence, but it is not known if such language actually incites violent actions.

Thousands of diverse fans gathered around public video screens when the 2007 Rugby World Cup was hosted in Paris. These fans, mostly French, with large groups from England, Ireland, Australia, and New Zealand, were expressive, but violence was not observed by the author, who took this photo and talked with people in the crowd. (*Source: Jay Coakley*)

Most people who watch media sports outside the home restrict their emotional expressions to verbal comments. When they express anger, they nearly always direct it at the players, coaches, referees, or media commentators rather than fellow viewers. Even when emotional outbursts are defined as too loud or inappropriate, fellow viewers usually try control the offender informally and peacefully. When fans from opposing teams watch an event at the same location, there often are sources of mutual identification that defuse differences and discourage physical violence, although verbal comments may become heated.

Since the mid-1990s, the cases of celebratory violence after a favored team wins a big game or championship have increased among men watching sports in bars or other public places. Predicting such violence is difficult, but a combination of heavy alcohol consumption and the presence of peers who encourage extreme actions increase its likelihood.

The belief that watching sports is associated with violence has led some people to wonder if watching sports—the Super Bowl, for example—is associated with temporary spikes in the rates of domestic violence in a community or the nation as a whole. During the 1990s, a journalist misleadingly reported that women's shelters were filled on Super Bowl Sunday because of increased domestic violence on that day. Subsequent examination of his sources and reliable research on this topic proved that he was wrong (Cohen 1994; Sachs and Chu, 2000), but the belief persists. Of course, the anger caused by a televised sport event *could* be a factor in particular cases of domestic violence, but the roots of such violence run deep, and to blame it on watching sports overlooks more important factors. Furthermore, we don't know enough about the ways that spectators integrate televised sport content into their lives to say that watching sports does anything except provide focused social occasions (Coakley, 1988–1989; Crawford, 2004).

Violence at Sport Events

Spectators attending non-contact sport events seldom engage in violence. They may be emotionally expressive, but violence directed at fellow fans, players, coaches, referees, ushers, or police is rare. The attack and wounding of number-one ranked tennis player Monica Seles in 1993 stands out as one of the only violent incidents at a non-contact sport event, and that incident had more to do with celebrity stalking than with the dynamics of a sport event. Of course, there are occasions when fans use hostile words or engage in minor skirmishes when someone spills a drink on another person, but such cases of violence are usually controlled effectively by the fans themselves. The exception is when there are pre-existing hostilities between particular fans looking to confront each other.

Spectators attending contact sports tend to be vocal and emotional, but most of them don't engage in violent acts. However, crowd violence occurs with enough regularity and seriousness in certain sports to be defined as a problem for law enforcement and a social issue for which it would be helpful to have an explanation (Briggs, 2004; Lewis, 2007; Upton, 2005; Young, 2002b; 2007b).

Historical Background   Media reports of violent actions at sport events around the world, especially soccer matches in Europe and college football games in the United States, have increased our awareness of crowd violence. However, crowd violence is not new. Data documenting the actions of sport spectators through the ages are scarce, but research suggests that spectator

violence occurred in the past and much of it would make crowd violence today seem rare and tame by comparison (Dunning, 1999; Guttmann, 1986, 1998; Scheinin, 1994; Young, 2000).

Roman events during the first five centuries of the first Christian millennium contained especially brutal examples of crowd violence (Guttmann, 1986, 1998; 2004). Spectators during the medieval period were not much better, although levels of violence decreased in the late medieval period. With the emergence of modern sports, violence among sport spectators decreased further, but it remained common by today's standards. For example, a baseball game in 1900 was described by a journalist in this way:

> Thousands of gun slinging Chicago Cubs fans turned a Fourth of July doubleheader into a shootout at the OK Corral, endangering the lives of players and fellow spectators. Bullets sang, darted, and whizzed over players' heads as the rambunctious fans fired round after round whenever the Cubs scored against the gun-shy Philadelphia Phillies. The visiting team was so intimidated it lost both games . . . at Chicago's West Side Grounds. (Nash and Zullo, 1989, p. 133)

This newspaper account also reports that when the Cubs scored six runs in the sixth inning of the first game, guns were fired around the stadium to the point that gun smoke made it difficult to see the field. When the Cubs tied the score in the ninth inning, fans again fired guns, and hundreds of them shot holes in the roof of the grandstand, causing splinters to fly onto their heads. As the game remained tied during three extra innings, fans pounded the seats with the butts of their guns and fired in unison every time the Phillies' pitcher began his windup to throw a pitch. It rattled him so much that the Cubs scored on a wild pitch. After the score, a vocal and heavily armed Cubs fan stood up and shouted, "Load! Load at will! Fire!" Fans around the stadium emptied the rest of their ammunition in a final explosive volley.

Between 1900 and the early 1940s, crowd violence was common: Bottles and other objects were thrown at players and umpires, and World Series games were disrupted by fans angered by umpires' calls or the actions of opposing players (Scheinin, 1994). Players feared being injured by spectators as much as they feared the "bean balls" thrown regularly at their heads by opposing pitchers. During the 1950s and 1960s, high school basketball and football games in some U.S. cities were sites for local youth gang wars. Gang members and a few students used chains, switchblade knives, brass knuckles, and tire irons to attack each other. During the late 1960s and early 1970s, some high school games in Chicago were closed to the public and played early on Saturday mornings because the regularly scheduled games had become occasions for crowd violence, much of it related to racial and ethnic tensions in the city.

These examples are not meant to minimize the existence or seriousness of crowd violence today. They are mentioned here to counter the argument that violence is a bigger problem today than in the past, that coercive tactics should be used to control unruly fans, and that there is a general decline of civility among fans and in society as a whole (Jayson, 2004; Saporito, 2004; Wulf, 2004). Some spectators do act in obnoxious and violent ways today. They present law enforcement challenges and interfere with the enjoyment of other fans, but there is no systematic evidence that they are unprecedented threats to the social order or signs of the decline of civilization as we know it.

Celebratory Violence   Oddly enough, some of the most dangerous and destructive crowd violence occurs during the celebrations that follow victories in important games (Lewis, 2007). Until recently, when middle-class, white college students tore down expensive goalposts after football victories or ransacked seats and threw seat pads and other objects onto the field, it was treated as displays of youthful exuberance and loyalty to the university. However, in the wake of injuries and mounting property damage

associated with these incidents, local and university authorities have banned or limited alcohol sales in stadiums and arenas, and they now use police and security officials to prevent fans from rushing onto the playing field when games end. Cases of celebratory violence still occur, but new methods of social control have been reasonably successful in preventing them from happening *inside* the stadium.

Controlling celebratory violence is especially difficult when crowds gather in multiple locations throughout a city. Local police are usually prepared to anticipate celebratory crowds around the stadium, but effective control depends on specialized training, advance planning, and officers who can intervene without creating backlash in the crowd. Breakdowns are relatively common in the face of massive crowds and uncertainty about what might happen. For instance, when thousands of Boston Red Sox fans gathered to celebrate winning the World Series in October 2004, a Boston police officer carelessly shot a projectile filled with pepper spray at a crowd and hit a young woman in the eye. She died of head injuries caused by the impact. In most cases, however, deaths occur when crowds move suddenly and trample people or when people are pushed in the way of vehicles with panicked drivers trying to escape the danger.

Sociologists have studied crowds and crowd dynamics, but scholars in the sociology of sport usually lack the resources to study sport-related celebratory violence. However, if celebratory violence continues to occur, resources will be allocated for law enforcement research. Furthermore, professional sport teams will develop strategies to defuse violence through announcements by highly visible players and respected coaches, bar owners will be asked to control drinking and contain the movement of their customers, and universities will attempt to control the binge drinking that accompanies most celebratory violence. Fans will be encouraged to BIRG, that is, "bask in the reflected glory" of the moment, but the goal will be to facilitate the formation of norms that discourage violence in connection with BIRGing.

We need research on so-called celebratory riots. Research on other forms of collective action suggests that celebratory riots may not be as spontaneous and unplanned as many people think.

Research and Theories About Crowd Violence

Researchers in the United States often study violence, but seldom have they studied violence at sport events. The research that does exist has focused primarily on issues of race relations, and little attention has been given to other issues.

European scholars, especially in Great Britain, have done most of the research on crowd violence, and their studies have focused almost exclusively on soccer and "soccer hooliganism." Social psychological research has emphasized that displays of intimidation and aggression at soccer matches involve ritual violence, consisting of fantasy-driven status posturing by young males who want to be defined as tough and manly (Marsh, 1982; Marsh and Campbell, 1982). These studies describe classic examples of ritualistic aggression, but they understate the serious and occasionally deadly violence perpetrated by soccer fans, especially during pre- and post-game activities.

Research inspired by structural theories, especially forms of Marxism, emphasize that violence at soccer matches is an expression of alienation among disenfranchised working-class men (Taylor, 1982a, 1982b, 1987). In addition to losing control over the conditions of their work lives, these men also feel marginalized by the recently commercialized clubs that sponsor elite soccer in England. This research connects certain forms of violence with class conflict in society, but it doesn't explain why violence at soccer matches has not increased proportionately in connection with the declining power of the working class in England.

Research inspired by interactionist and cultural theories has emphasized a variety of factors, including the importance of understanding the history and dynamics of the working-class and youth subcultures in British society and how those subcultures have been influenced by the professionalization and commercialization of society as a whole and soccer in particular (Clark, 1978; Critcher, 1979). However, the data presented in this research are not very strong, and more work is needed to develop critical analyses of crowd violence across various situations.

Much of the recent research on soccer violence has been based on figurational theory, an explanatory framework based on a synthesis of knowledge from biology, psychology, sociology, and history. This work, summarized by Dunning (1999), Dunning, Murphy, and Williams (1988), Dunning et al. (2002), and Young (2000, 2007a, 2007b), emphasizes that violence and hooliganism (rowdy and destructive actions) is grounded in long-term historical changes that have affected working-class men, their relationships with each other and their families, and their ideas about community, violence, and masculinity. Taken together, these changes have created a *social figuration*, or a set of historically concentrated social processes, in which soccer represents the collective turf and identity of people in local communities, espcially young British men. Soccer then becomes a site for these men to defend and/or assert community and identity through violence directed at the new status quo. This research provides valuable historical data and thoughtful analyses of the complex social processes in which particular forms of sport violence are located. In fact, is has been used as a guide by officials formulating recent policies of social control related to soccer crowds in England and around Europe (Spaaji, 2008).

As the police have become more sophisticated in anticipating violence associated with soccer crowds, young men, some of whom may not be avid soccer fans, take it as a challenge to outsmart them and create discord and violent confrontations with rival groups. Research indicates that current forms of hooliganism involve semi-organized confrontations that are strategically staged to cause havoc and avoid arrest. The police in this situation play the role of umpire between groups and attempt to confine confrontations to spaces where they are prepared to deal with them and make arrests before serious injuries and property damage occur (Armstrong, 1998; 2007; Brown, 1998; Dunning et al., 2002; Giulianotti and Armstrong, 2002).

Cell phones, handheld GPS devices, and other communications technology are used by the young men to formulate on-the-spot strategies and escape detection and arrest. The police use similar technologies along with surveillance cameras to contain violence. The dynamics associated with this form of violence are not related to sports to the same degree as the so-called hooliganism of the past. Today, soccer matches and tournaments are not the primary focus of those involved in the violence; instead, the perpetrators simply use soccer matches as occasions for seeking excitement through violence.

General Factors Related to Violence at Sport Events

Crowd violence at sport events is a complex social phenomenon. Research shows that it is related to three general factors:

1. The action in the sport event itself
2. The crowd dynamics and the situation in which the spectators watch the event
3. The historical, social, economic, and political contexts in which the event is planned and played

Violence and Action in the Event If spectators perceive players' actions on the field as violent, they are more likely to engage in violent acts during and after games (Smith, 1983). This point is important because spectators' perceptions often are influenced by the way in which events are promoted. If an event is hyped in terms of violent images, spectators are more likely to perceive violence during the event itself and then to be violent themselves. This leads some people to argue that promoters and the media have a responsibility to advertise events in terms of the action and drama expected, not the prospect of blood and violence.

Research by Daniel Wann and his colleagues (1999; 2001a, b; 2002; 2003; 2004) has shown that the perceptions and actions of spectators depend on the extent to which they identify with teams and athletes. Highly identified fans are more likely than others to link their team's performance to their own emotions and identities. Although, by itself, this does not cause violence, it predisposes fans to take action if and when they have opportunities to do something that they think might help their team. This is important because team personnel and venue management encourage fans to believe that they can motivate home team players and distract visiting team players. Although most fans restrict their "participation" to cheering, stomping, and waving objects, some systematically harass and taunt opposing players.

Taunts from fans are not new, but they've become especially personal and offensive in recent years. Players are expected to ignore taunts, but on occasion some have gone into the stands to attack an obnoxious fan. This has occurred more often in Latin America and Europe than North America, but it appears to be increasing in the United States and Canada. In 2005 there was a highly publicized case when three NBA players on the Indiana Pacers fought with fans during a game with the Detroit Pistons after a fan hit a player with a cup of liquid and ice thrown from the stands. The cup was thrown following an incident of brutal body contact on the court. For a few moments, many people feared a major riot, but players, coaches, security officers, and fans intervened to prevent an escalation of violence. As a result, the three visiting players involved in the fight were suspended for a total of 128 games and forfeited about $11 million dollars of salary between them. Two of these players were charged with assault and battery, two players from the Pistons also were suspended for multiple games, the owner of the Indiana Pacers paid the NBA a fine of nearly $3 million, and two fans were charged with minor crimes and one had his Pistons season tickets revoked.

This incident created discussions throughout the United States. In sociological terms, it highlighted the need to manage more carefully the relationship between players and fans. However, this is a challenge under current circumstances. Fans pay high prices for tickets, they're encouraged by management and media personnel to be emotionally expressive, they expect players to give them their money's worth, and they often detest what they perceive as arrogance displayed by highly paid players. To complicate matters, over 90 percent of fans are white, and a large percentage of the players are black (75 percent in the NBA). This can frame the expectations and perceptions of fans and the attitudes of players in volatile racial terms—as if did in Detroit.

From the players' perspective, the possibility of fan violence creates a strong sense of vulnerability. They realize that they're standing amidst thousands of fans who could kill or main them in minutes if a mass brawl occurred. For example, a Pacers player who was suspended for thirty games and lost $1.7 million in salary for coming to the aid of his teammate in 2005 said this:

> I regret the incident . . . But I never regret helping my teammate. We shine together; we go down together. If my teammate feels threatened, I'm going to be there for him. . . . I protect my brother, my family. . . . Players understand [what I mean]. If you were a player, you would too. (in Le Batard, 2005b, p. 14)

This statement emphasizes the strong bonds between athletes and how those bonds lead athletes to protect each other when there are player-fan confrontations.

Also important in the sport event are the calls made by officials. When fans believe that a crucial goal or a victory has been "stolen" by an unfair or clearly incompetent decision made by a referee or an umpire, the likelihood of violence during and after the event increases (Murphy, Williams, and Dunning, 1990). This is why it is important to have competent officials at crucial games and matches and why it is important for them to control game events so that actions perceived as violent are held to a minimum.

The knowledge that fan aggression may be precipitated by a crucial call late in a close, important contest puts heavy responsibility on the officials' shoulders. For example, the brawl at the Detroit–Indiana NBA game occurred after a flagrant foul by a Detroit player. The officials had allowed players to continue the rough play that had characterized the game, even though there was less than a minute to play and the Pacers were winning by 15 points. Would the brawl have occurred if the officials had controlled the game differently in the final quarter? We don't know, but officials are important when it comes to managing games in ways that make crowd violence less likely.

Violence, Crowd Dynamics, and Situational Factors   The characteristics of a crowd and the immediate situation associated with a sport event also influence patterns of action among spectators. Spectator violence is likely to vary with one or more of the following factors:

- Crowd size and the standing or seating patterns of spectators
- Composition of the crowd in terms of age, sex, social class, and racial/ethnic mix
- Importance and meaning of the event for spectators
- History of the relationship between the teams and among spectators
- Crowd-control strategies used at the event (police, attack dogs, surveillance cameras, or other security measures)
- Alcohol consumption by the spectators
- Location of the event (neutral site or home site of one of the opponents)
- Spectators' reasons for attending the event and what they want to happen at the event
- Importance of the team as a source of identity for spectators (class identity, ethnic or national identity, regional or local identity, club or gang identity)

Instead of discussing each factor in detail, contrasting pairs of game situations will be used to illustrate how the factors might influence spectator violence.

The *location of an event* is important because it influences who attends and how they travel. If the stadium is generally accessed by car, if

spectators for the visiting team are limited due to travel distance and expense, and if tickets are costly, it is likely that the local people attending the game have a vested interest in maintaining order and avoiding violence. On the other hand, if large groups of people travel to the game in buses or trains and if tickets are relatively cheap and many of the spectators are young people more interested in creating a memorable experience than simply seeing a game, confrontations between people looking for exciting action increase, as does the possibility of violence. If groups of fans looking for excitement have consumed large amounts of alcohol, the possibility of violence increases greatly.

If spectators are respected and treated as valued guests rather than bodies to be controlled, and if stadium norms emphasize service as opposed to social control, people are less likely to engage in defensive and confrontational actions that could lead to violence. If the stadium or arena is crowded and if the crowd itself is composed mostly of young men rather than men and women of all ages, there is a greater chance for confrontations and violence, especially if the event is seen as a special rivalry whose outcome has status implications for the schools, communities, or nations represented by the teams.

Spectator violence, when it does occur, takes many forms. There have been celebratory riots among the fans of the winning team, fights between fans of opposing teams, random property destruction carried out by fans of the losing team as they leave town, panics incited by a perceived threat unrelated to the contest itself, and planned confrontations between groups using the event as a convenient place to face off with each other as they seek to enhance their status and reputation or reaffirm their ethnic, political, class, national, local, or gang identities. Each of these has different dynamics and requires specific methods of control.

Whenever thousands of people gather together for an occasion intended to generate collective emotions and excitement, it's not surprising that crowd dynamics and circumstances influence the actions of individuals and groups. This is especially true at sport events where collective action is easily fueled by what social psychologists call **emotional contagion,** *a condition in which social norms are formed rapidly and are followed in a nearly spontaneous manner by large numbers of people.* Although this does not always lead to violence, it increases the possibility of potentially violent confrontations between groups of fans and between fans and agents of social control, such as the police.

Violence and the Overall Context in Which Events Occur   Sport events do not occur in social vacuums. When spectators attend events, they take with them the histories, issues, controversies, and ideologies of the communities and cultures in which they live. They may be racists who want to harass those they identify as targets for discrimination. They may come from ethnic neighborhoods and want to express and reaffirm their ethnicity or from particular nations and want to express their national identity. They may resent negative circumstances in their lives and want to express their bitterness. They may be members of groups or gangs in which status is gained partly through fighting. They may be powerless and alienated and looking for ways to be noticed and defined as socially important. They may be young men who believe that manhood is achieved through violence and domination over others. Or they may be living lives so devoid of significance and excitement that they want to create a memorable occasion they can discuss boastfully with friends for years to come. In other words, when thousands of spectators attend a sport event, their actions are grounded in multiple factors far beyond the event and the stadium.

When tensions and conflicts are intense and widespread in a community or society, sport events may become sites for confrontations. For example, some of the worst spectator violence in the United States has been grounded in racial

tensions aggravated by highly publicized rivalries between high schools whose students come from different racial or ethnic backgrounds (Guttmann, 1986). In cities where housing segregation has created heavily segregated schools, racial and ethnic conflicts have contributed to confrontations before, during, and after games. Gangs, some of whose members have weapons, may stake out territories around a sport stadium so that a game becomes an occasion for displays of gang power. Similarly, when the "ultras," organized groups of fans prevalent in Italy during the 1990s, attended soccer games, they often used violence to express their loyalty to peers and the teams they followed (Roversi, 1994). The ultras have developed in recent years into commercial enterprises run by business people. However, the violence continues and recent events for which they have been credited include hospitalizing four British fans attending a game in Italy in 2000, and stabbing to death a policeman in 2007.

Finally, it must be noted that nearly all crowd violence involves men. This suggests that future research on this topic must consider the role of masculinity in crowd dynamics and the actions of particular segments of crowds (Hughson, 2000). Female fans generally don't tip and set cars on fire or throw chairs through windows when they celebrate a victory. They may become involved in fights, but this is relatively rare. Crowd violence may be as much a gender issue as it is a racial or social class issue, and controlling it may involve changing notions of masculinity as much as hiring additional police to patrol the sidelines at every event.

Controlling Crowd Violence

Effective efforts to control spectator violence are based on an awareness of each of the three factors previously discussed. *First,* the fact that perceived violence on the field is associated with crowd violence indicates a need to control violence among players during events. If fans don't

Fearing mass violence, this officer aims pepper spray at fans, mostly males, who occupied the field after a major college football game. A more effective strategy is to contain them and then disperse them in small groups in different directions. Using pepper spray may incite or escalate violence in such situations. (*Source:* Mark Hall, AP/Wide World Photos)

define the actions of players as violent, the likelihood of crowd violence decreases. Furthermore, if events are not promoted as violent confrontations between hostile opponents, fans are less likely to perceive violence on the field.

Perceived hostility and violence can be defused if players and coaches make public announcements emphasizing the skills of the athletes involved in the event and their respect for opponents. High-profile or celebrity fans for each team could make similar announcements.

The use of competent and professionally trained officials is also important. When officials maintain control of a game and make calls the spectators define as fair, they decrease the likelihood of spectator violence grounded in anger and perceived injustice. Referees also could meet with both teams before the event and explain the need to leave hostilities in the locker rooms. Team officials could organize pre-game unity rituals involving an exchange of team symbols and displays of respect between opponents. These rituals could be covered by the media so that fans could see that athletes do not view their opponents as enemies. But these strategies conflict with commercial media interests in hyping games as wars without weapons; therefore, we're faced with a choice: protect the safety of fans and players versus preserve media profits and gate receipts for team owners.

Second, an awareness of crowd dynamics and the conditions that precipitate violence is critical. Preventive measures are important. The needs and rights of spectators must be known

Terrorism
Planned Political Violence at Sport Events

The visibility of sport events and the concentration of many people in one place make sport venues a possible target of terrorist attacks. After deadly terrorist attacks in New York, Washington, DC, London, Madrid, and other cities worldwide, most people today have a heightened awareness of terrorism and its possible impact on their lives (GAO, 2006).

An integral part of planning major sport events today is establishing effective security measures at arenas and stadiums. Spectators often are searched as they enter venues, and rules regulate what they may bring with them. However, most security measures are discreetly enacted and take place behind the scenes in the form of bomb searches, electronic surveillance, and undercover tactics.

As sport teams and venues deal with security issues, their costs increase. In fact, it is estimated that world organizers of sport events spend around $2 billion per year on security. During the 2004 Summer Olympic Games in Athens, over $2 billion was spent on security. Similar expenses for the 2008 Olympic Games were difficult to estimate because security forces were deployed across the entire nation, with 100,000 trained antiterrorists and 300,000 public surveillance cameras used in Beijing alone. The day after London was awarded the summer Olympic Games for 2012, it was the target of a terrorist attack, and it is estimated that the cost of security for the London Games will be at least $2 billion.

Although people in the United States have only recently become sensitive to the threat of political terrorism, others around the world have lived for many years with the threat and reality of terrorist acts. Furthermore, terrorism is not new to international sports. For instance, during the early morning hours of September 5, 1972, members of a Palestinian terrorist group called Black September entered the Olympic Village in Munich, Germany. Dressed in athletic warm-up suits and carrying sport bags containing grenades and automatic weapons, they entered a bedroom that housed Israeli athletes participating in the Summer Olympic Games. They shot and killed a wrestling coach and a weightlifter and captured nine other Israeli athletes, one of whom was from the United States.

After a twenty-one-hour standoff and a poorly planned rescue attempt, seventeen people were dead—ten Israeli athletes and one coach, one West German police officer, and five terrorists. The remaining terrorists were sought out and killed by Israeli commandos. The Olympics were suspended for a day, but events resumed and the closing ceremonies occurred as planned. About $2 million had been spent on security during the Olympics in Munich; thirty-two years later Athens spent over 1000 times that amount.

Although the terrorism in Munich is remembered by many people who currently plan the Olympic Games, it is seldom mentioned in the media coverage of the Olympics. The reasons for this are complex, but it is clear that many people don't want their favorite sport events disrupted or defined in connection with the nasty realities of everyday life, even though sports cannot be separated from the world in which they exist.

Because terrorism occurs regularly, it is useful to remember that sports cannot be separated from policies, events, and material conditions of life that create deeply felt resentment and hatred among people around the world. This means that everyone has an interest in learning more about the world and how peace might be achieved. This takes time and commitment on our part, and it won't be easy to change the conditions that precipitate terrorism. In the meantime, none of us can escape the threat of terrorism at the high-profile sport events we attend. *What do you think?*

and respected. Crowd-control officials must be well trained so that they know how to intervene in potentially disruptive situations without escalating violence. Alcohol consumption should be regulated realistically, as has been done in many venues worldwide. Venues and the spaces around them should be safe and organized, to enable spectators to move around while limiting contact between hostile fans of opposing teams. Exits should be accessible and clearly marked, and spectators should not be herded like animals before or after games. Encouraging attendance by families is important in lowering the incidence of violence.

Third, an awareness of the historical, social, economic, and political issues that often underlie crowd violence is also important. Restrictive law-and-order responses to crowd violence may be temporarily effective, but they will not eliminate the underlying tensions and conflicts that often fuel violence. Policies dealing with oppressive forms of inequality, economic problems, unemployment, lack of political representation, racism, and distorted definitions of masculinity are needed. These factors often lead to tensions, conflicts, and violence. As noted in the box on terrorism (page 226), dealing with the threat of political terrorism at sport events also requires an awareness of these factors on a global level. For example, current and past wars often create tensions that will precipitate sport-related violence under particular conditions.

In addition to strategies in each of these three categories, social control can be maintained by establishing visible and meaningful connections between teams and the communities in which they're located. This can defuse potentially dangerous feelings among groups of spectators and community residents. However, this does not mean that teams merely need better public relations. There must be *actual* connections between the teams (players) and the communities in which they exist. Effective forms of community service are helpful, and team owners must be visible supporters of community events and programs.

Teams must develop programs to assist in the development of local neighborhoods, especially those around their home stadium or arena. The goal of these strategies is to create antiviolence norms among spectators and community residents. Shaping norms can be difficult, but it's a more effective strategy than using metal detectors, moving games to remote locations, hiring hundreds of security personnel, patrolling the stands, using surveillance cameras, scheduling games at times when crowds will be sparse, and recruiting police and soldiers to brandish automatic weapons. Of course, some of these tactics can be effective, but they destroy part of the enjoyment of spectator sports. Therefore, they should be last resorts or temporary measures used only during the time it takes to develop new spectator norms.

OLC ON THE *OLC*:
See the OLC—Additional Readings for Chapter 7—for an essay on violence in animal sports, including dog racing and dog fighting.

summary

DOES VIOLENCE IN SPORTS AFFECT OUR LIVES?

Violence is not new to sports. Athletes throughout history have engaged in actions and used strategies that cause or have the potential to cause injuries to themselves and others. Furthermore, spectators throughout history have regularly engaged in violent actions before, during, and after sport events. However, as people define violence in sports as controllable rather than as a fact of life, there's a tendency to view it as a problem in need of a solution.

Violence in sports ranges from brutal body contact and borderline violence to quasi-criminal and criminal acts. It is linked with overconformity to the sport ethic, commercialization, and cultural definitions of masculinity. It has become institutionalized in most contact sports as a strategy for competitive success, even though it causes injuries and permanent physical impairments to athletes. The use of enforcers is one example of institutionalized violence in sports.

Controlling on-the-field violence is difficult, especially in men's contact sports, because it is often tied to players' identities as athletes and men. Male athletes in contact sports learn to use violence and intimidation as strategic tools, but we don't know if the strategies learned in sports influence the expression of violence in relationships and situations that occur off-the-field.

Among males, learning to use violence as a tool within a sport is frequently tied to the reaffirmation of a form of masculinity that emphasizes a willingness to risk personal safety and intimidate others. If the boys and men who participate in certain sports learn to perceive this orientation as natural or appropriate, and receive support for this perception from sources inside sports and the general community, then their participation in sports may contribute to off-the-field violence, including assault, sexual assault, and rape. However, such learning is not automatic, and men may, under certain circumstances, even learn to control anger and their expressions of violence by playing certain sports.

The most important impact of violence in sports may be its reaffirmation of a gender ideology that assumes the "natural superiority of men." This ideology is based on the belief that an ability to do violence is an essential feature of manhood.

Female athletes in contact sports also engage in aggressive and violent acts, but little is known about the connections between these acts and the gender identities of girls and women at different levels of competition. Many women prefer an emphasis on supportive connections between teammates and opponents as compared with the power and performance aspects of sports. Therefore, aggression and violence do not occur in women's sports as often or through the same identity dynamics as they occur in men's sports.

Violence occurs among spectators who view sport events through the media as well as those attending live events. Research is needed to explain the conditions under which violence occurs in crowds watching or listening to media representations of events. Studies of violence at the sites of events indicates that crowd violence is influenced by perceived violence on the field of play, crowd dynamics, the situation at the event itself, the overall historical and cultural contexts in which spectators give meaning to the event, and their relationships with others in attendance. Isolated cases of violence, including celebratory violence, are best controlled by improved crowd management, but chronic violence among spectators usually signals that changes are required in the culture and organization of sports and/or the social, economic, and political structures of a community or society.

Terrorism in the form of planned, politically motivated violence at sport events is rare, but the threat of terrorism alters security policies and procedures at sport venues. The terrorist attack at the 1972 Olympic Games reminds us that global issues influence our lives, even when we attend our favorite sport events. Just as violence in sports affects our lives, the social conditions in which we live affect violence in sports.

WEBSITE RESOURCES

Note: Websites often change. The following URLs were current when this book was printed. Please check our website (www.mhhe.com/coakley10e) for updates and additions. Click on chapter 7 for information and critique of instinct theory and frustration-aggression theory as applied to violence in sports; discussion of cultural patterning theory and violence associated with sports.

www.answers.com/topic/violence-in-sports
    Encyclopedia-like information about violence in sports; good links to sites on specific topics.

www.coe.int/t/dg4/sport/violence/Default_en.asp Council of Europe site presents documents stating the council's official position on spectator violence, mostly in connection with football matches.

www.ericdigests.org/pre-9214/sports.htm Explores various aspects of violence in sports, especially youth sports.

www.ncava.org Site of the National Coalition Against Violent Athletes presents information to educate the public and to support and assist victims of violence by athletes.

www.sportinsociety.org/vpd/mvp.php Mentors in Violence Prevention (MVP) is a gender violence prevention and education program based at Northeastern University's Center for the Study of Sport in Society; it enlists high school, collegiate, and professional athletes in the effort to prevent all forms of men's violence against women.

www.un.org/Depts/dhl/resguide/r58.htm Links to two UN resolutions: "Building a Peaceful and Better World Through Sport and the Olympic Ideal" (A/RES/58/6) and "Sport as a Means to Promote Education, Health, Development and Peace" (A/RES/58/5).

www.un.org/sport2005/ The site for the UN International Year for Sport and Physical and links to sites on sexual harassment in sports; click on "Resources" to see UN resolutions related to sports and peace.

http://youthsports.rutgers.edu/resources/general -interest/parental-violence-in-youth-sports -facts-myths-and-videotape Article on "Parental Violence in Youth Sports: Facts, Myths, and Videotape," by Gregg S. Heinzmann, Director, Youth Sports Research Council at Rutgers University.

(Marc Piscotty, *Rocky Mountain News*)

GENDER AND SPORTS

Does Equity Require Ideological Changes?

ALL MY LIFE, I believed that I couldn't show weakness. I couldn't pull myself out if I was hurt, I couldn't let people say, "She's just a girl." . . . I had to be tougher [than men], because only then did you get respect.

> —**Lauren Arase, goalie for NCAA soccer champions**

OLC Visit *Sports in Society*'s Online Learning
Center (OLC) at www.mhhe.com/coakley10e
for additional information and study material
for this chapter, including the following:

- A complete chapter outline
- Learning objectives
- Practice quizzes
- Internet resources
- Related readings
- Essays
- Student projects

I FEEL NOW that I am more fit physically, I am
more at peace and I have more confidence. I have
gained these traits through the sport and they
are important for me as I am a doctor and my
occupation requires physical effort.

> —**Dr. Sara, physician, Saudi Arabia (in El Qarany,
> 2006)**

IT NEVER FELT RIGHT to take my clothes off. It
never felt like me. It sucks. When you're a woman
in sports, people want you to show some skin.

> —**Gretchen Bleiler, Snowboarder, three-time X
> Games gold medalist, Olympic silver medalist
> (in Roenigk, 2008)**

IT'S IMPORTANT TO HEAR from women
who overcome stereotypes, ignorance and
inequality . . . to be an athlete, [to be] strong and
not feel sorry for kicking someone's butt.

> —**Serena Williams, Nike ad (in Howard, 2007)**

Gender and gender relations are central topics in the sociology of sport. Its important to explain why most sports around the world have been defined as men's activities, why half the world's population generally was excluded or discouraged from participating in many sports through history, and why there have been dramatic increases in women's participation since the mid-1970s. To explain these things we must understand the relationship between sports and widespread beliefs about masculinity, femininity, homosexuality, and heterosexuality.

Discussions and research on gender relations and sports usually focus on two interrelated issues. One is fairness and equity, and the other is ideology and power. *Fairness and equity issues* revolve around topics such as the following:

- Sport participation patterns among girls and women in comparison with boys and men.
- Gender inequities in participation opportunities, support for athletes, and jobs in coaching and administration.
- Strategies for achieving equal opportunities for girls and women.

Ideology and power issues revolve around topics such as these:

- The production and reproduction of gender ideology in and through sports.
- The influence of gender ideology on people's lives and on the achievement of gender equity in sports.
- Cultural and structural changes that are required to achieve full gender equity in sports.

The goal of this chapter is to discuss these two sets of issues and show that, even though many people deal with them separately, they go hand in hand. We cannot ignore either one if we define sports as important in the lives of human beings.

PARTICIPATION AND EQUITY ISSUES

The single most dramatic change in sports over the past two generations has been increased participation among girls and women. This phenomenon has occurred mostly in wealthy postindustrial nations, but there also have been increases in many developing nations. Despite resistance against change, more girls and women now participate in sports than ever before.

Reasons for Increased Participation

Since the mid-1960s, five interrelated factors account for the dramatic increases in sport participation among girls and women:

1. New opportunities
2. Government legislation mandating equal rights
3. The global women's rights movement
4. The health and fitness movement
5. Increased media coverage of women in sports

New Opportunities   New participation opportunities account for most of the increased sports participation among girls and women since the mid-1970s. Prior to that time, many girls and women did not play sports for one simple reason: teams and programs did not exist. Young women today may not know it, but the participation opportunities they enjoy were not available to many of their mothers or any of their grandmothers. Teams and programs developed since the mid-1970s have inspired and supported interests ignored in the past. Girls and women today do not receive an equal share of sport resources in most organizations and communities, but their increased participation clearly has been fueled by new opportunities. In part, these opportunities are the result of organized political action and government legislation.

Government Legislation Mandating Equal Rights   Many girls and women would not be playing sports today if it weren't for local and national legislation mandating equal rights. Policies and rules requiring gender equity are primarily the result of persistent political actions advocating equal rights for girls and women. Activist individuals and groups often have consisted of feminists committed to gender equity. For example, the U.S. Congress passed Title IX of the Educational Amendments in 1972 only after years of lobbying by concerned citizens. Title IX law declared that *no person in the United States shall, on the basis of sex, be excluded from participation in, be denied the benefits of, or be subjected to discrimination under any educational program or activity receiving federal financial assistance.* This law made sense to most people when it was applied to education in the classroom, but when it was applied to sports, many people resisted it.

The men who controlled athletic programs in high schools and colleges thought that sharing half of all sport resources with women was an outrageous and subversive idea, and they delayed the enforcement of Title IX for nearly seven years after it became law. Many men and some women claimed that equity was unfair because men would have to share the resources that they assumed belonged only to them. The story of support and resistance related to this law is told in the box "Title IX" (see page 234).

Many nations now have laws and policies that support equal rights for girls and women in sports. In 1994 women around the world formed the International Working Group on Women and Sport (the IWG; see www.iwg-gti.org) to promote the enforcement of these laws and policies. With the assistance of local and national women's organizations, the IWG has successfully pressured resistant governments and sport organizations to pass equal rights legislation of their own. This has been a challenge, however, because the men who control power in these governments and organizations believed that if girls and women played sports it would threaten the positions of privilege enjoyed by many men and violate important moral principles grounded in nature and/or their religious beliefs.

Although activist women and men dedicated to gender equity have produced many important changes, at least half of the 3.3 billion girls and women in the world today lack regular access to sport participation opportunities.

The Global Women's Rights Movement The global women's movement over the past half century has emphasized that girls and women are enhanced as human beings when they develop their intellectual *and* physical abilities. This idea has inspired a wide range of sport participation, even among girls and women who, in the past, never would have thought of playing sports (Fasting, 1996).

The women's movement also has brought about changes in the occupational and family roles of women. These changes have enabled many women to acquire the time and resources they need to play sports. As women's rights have expanded and as male control over the lives and bodies of women has weakened, more women have chosen to play sports. Additional changes are needed, especially in poor nations and among low-income women in wealthy nations, but the sport participation opportunities available to women today are far less restricted than they were a generation ago.

The global women's movement has fueled the formation and growth of many political action organizations worldwide. The IWG emerged from a 1994 conference that brought women delegates from eighty countries to Brighton, England, to discuss "women, sport, and the challenge of change." After three days of discussion and debate, the delegates unanimously passed a set of global gender equity principles now known as the "Brighton Declaration." This document, updated and reaffirmed at world conferences on women in sport in Windhoek, Namibia (1998), Montreal, Canada (2002), and Kumamoto, Japan (2006), continues to be used to pressure governments and sport organizations to create new opportunities for girls and women in sports.

Lobbying efforts by representatives from these and other organizations led to the inclusion of statements related to sports and physical education in the official Platform for Action of the United Nations Fourth World Conference on Women, held in Beijing, China, in 1995. These statements called for new efforts to provide sport and physical education opportunities to promote

reflect on **SPORTS**

Title IX
Can a Law Create Gender Equity?

Title IX is a U.S. law prohibiting gender discrimination in schools that receive federal funds through grants, scholarships, or other support for students. Passed in 1972, the law states that federal funds can be withdrawn from a school engaging in intentional gender discrimination in the provision of curriculum, counseling, academic support, or general educational opportunities; *this includes interscholastic or school-sponsored sports.*

Young women today benefit from the passage of Title IX without knowing much or anything about it. This essay provides the background, history, and current status of a law that has changed the face of sports in the United States and influenced women's sports worldwide. Because it has been so effective in bringing about change, Title IX has supporters *and* opponents, and it continues to create heated debates about the organization and culture of sports today.

BEFORE TITLE IX: PLAY DAYS AND CHEERLEADERS

Prior to 1972, sports were almost exclusively a "guy thing" in American schools. In 1971 there were 3.7 million boys and 295,000 girls playing high school sports. For every 12.5 boys on teams, there was only 1 girl on a team. Similarly, out of every dollar spent on high school teams, boys received 99 cents and girls received the remaining penny for their teams.

At the college level, 180,000 men and 32,000 women played on intercollegiate teams in 1971; 1 of every 10 male college students played intercollegiate sports, but only 1 of every 100 female students played on a college team. Women's intercollegiate programs received only 1 percent of the athletic budget, even though student fees paid by female students and taxes paid by female workers were used to fund intercollegiate athletic programs.

For most of the twentieth century few schools sponsored competitive teams for girls and young women. Instead, they usually sponsored semi-annual "field days" during which girls could compete in running races and other field events. Until the 1960s there were widely believed myths that vigorous sports would harm the female body and make it difficult for a woman to conceive, carry, and give birth to children. (*Source:* McGraw-Hill)

In the pre–Title IX era, most elementary and high school girls played sports only on annual "play days" when track and field events were scheduled for them. Girls were cheerleaders for the boys' teams, they joined pep clubs and attended games, but very few had opportunities to play on teams like the ones provided for boys. The situation was much the same at the college level. In fact, if you know women older than fifty-five (in 2010), ask them to tell you about those days.

> **OLC ON THE *OLC:***
> See the OLC—Additional Readings for Chapter 8—for a brief history and discussion of cheerleaders in U.S. sports.

TITLE IX: A HISTORY OF RESISTANCE AND PROGRESS

In 1972 Congress decided to update the 1964 Civil Rights Act, which prohibited discrimination based on "race, color, religion, or national origin" in public education, public facilities, publicly funded programs, and private companies engaged in interstate commerce. Most congressmen, many of whom had daughters, wanted to extend the law to prohibit gender discrimination in public education, so they passed the Education Amendments to the Civil Rights Act, and President Nixon signed the legislation.

Title IX was a section of the Amendments that applied to educational opportunities in schools. Its purpose was to eliminate gender-based barriers to all programs defined as "educational." When Title IX was passed, it wasn't controversial. The women's movement and the civil rights movement were in full swing, and most people wanted their daughters to have the same educational opportunities as their sons. But, when people realized that Title IX could be applied to sport programs, sparks began to fly.

Gender equity sounded good in theory, but when the men who controlled and played high school and college sports realized that they now had to share their resources with girls and women, many of them objected and claimed that Title IX was unfair to them. "What

was *equity?*" the men wanted to know. Did the law mean that boys and men had to give girls and women more than one percent of the total athletic budget? How much more would they have to share? Certainly, "equity" did not mean a 50-50 split—or *did* it? Sharing more than one percent of sport resources, they said, wouldn't be fair to boys and men because they had come to believe that those resources were "rightfully" and "naturally" theirs. Did "equity" mean that schools should have as many girls' and women's teams as boys' and men's teams, and that the number of female players should equal the number of male players?

The men who controlled sports, and had organized them around their values and experiences, saw the pursuit of equity as a radical, subversive, and destructive concept. They wanted the term clarified, so the Office of Civil Rights (OCR) in the U.S. Department of Education developed a conceptual clarification of the meaning of Title IX. In the meantime, men at the NCAA and at other sport organizations worked to undermine the law because treating women as equals would mean that they would lose some of their control over sport resources and athletic policies. Dividing budgets, teams, and scholarships by two was, in their minds, out of the question. So they resisted Title IX and pushed to have it repealed.

After receiving nearly 10,000 comments, questions, and complaints about Title IX, the OCR published additional legal clarifications in 1975. OCR officials told high schools that they had one year to comply with the regulations, and universities had three years to comply. But resistance to the law continued to grow as male athletes, coaches, and athletic directors complained that equity could not be measured in legal terms. In response, the OCR in 1979 established three legal tests to assess compliance with Title IX law. According to the OCR enforcement guidelines, a school legally complied with Title IX if it met *any one* of the following three tests:

1. *Proportionality test.* Equity exists when a school has nearly the same proportion of women playing sports as the proportion of women enrolled as full-time (undergraduate) students. For example, if 51 percent of students in the school are women,

Title IX (*Continued*)
Can a Law Create Gender Equity?

women should make up between 46 percent and 56 percent of all athletes—a 5-percentage-point variation in either direction was within legal limits.

2. *History of progress test.* Equity exists when a school has a clear history and continuing practice of expanding its sport programs for female athletes.

3. *Accommodation of interest test.* Equity exists when a school demonstrates that its sports program fully accommodates the interests of female students and potential students (that is, younger girls in the region from which the university recruits students).

This three-part test did not eliminate resistance to Title IX, but it gave people a legal basis for filing lawsuits against schools that did not provide equitable opportunities to play sports. This infuriated Title IX opponents, so they complained to President Ronald Reagan, lobbied men in Congress, and filed suits to overturn the law. When one of those lawsuits reached the U.S. Supreme Court in 1984, the court ruled in a split decision that Title IX applied *only* to programs that *directly* received money from the federal government and, because *varsity sports did not directly receive federal funds*, the law *did not* apply to them. This made the law irrelevant, and the OCR was forced to drop its investigations of nearly 800 complaints against schools charged with violating Title IX.

Title IX was not enforced after 1984, and this led the U.S. Congress to pass the Civil Rights Restoration Act in 1987. This act declared that Congress had originally intended Title IX to be applied to sport programs because school sports were educational. President Reagan disagreed and promptly vetoed the Civil Rights Restoration Act, and Congress overrode Reagan's veto in 1988. But men still did not understand what equity meant in sports, so in 1990 the OCR provided an even more detailed guide that explained *equity* in connection

> **Parity in funding must be more than a goal. It must be a reality. That means more money for operating women's sports programs. . . . Justice often comes with a price tag.** —Donna Shalala, former U.S. Secretary of Health and Human Services, 2002

with all aspects of athletic programs, such as scholarships, facilities, scheduling, coaching, and other forms of support for athletes, teams, and athletic programs.

In a case filed by a woman against a university the Supreme Court ruled in 1992 that a person could be awarded monetary damages if she (or he) proved that a school intentionally violated Title IX. This ruling marked a major turning point for women's sports because it meant that schools could be forced to pay damages if they lost a Title IX case. Prior to 1992, a school that violated Title IX could only be required to eliminate gender inequities in the future, without being held financially liable for past discrimination. This stipulation limited the effectiveness of Title IX because no school had ever lost any federal funding for violating the law; the OCR had always been more interested in fixing inequities than punishing schools. As of 2008, this record has not changed: *No school has ever lost a penny of federal money, even though the majority of schools have violated the law for more than thirty-five years!*

After 1992 Title IX was easier to enforce, and the law gained credibility among many Americans in 1994 when Congress passed the Equity in Athletics Disclosure Act. This act required every university with students receiving financial aid from the federal government to provide an annual report containing specific data on athletic participation, staffing, and budgets for all men's and women's sports. The purpose of this report was to enable prospective students and their parents to see the "equity record" for the schools they might attend. These data (available online at http://ope.ed.gov/athletics/) have opened universities' equity/inequity records to public scrutiny.

Since 1994 there has been slow progress toward gender equity in high schools and universities. Resistance to Title IX remains strong among people with vested interests in certain men's sports. For example, Brown University objected on legal grounds to the three-part test, but the legality of the test was upheld in a 1996 court decision. After the Brown case, the OCR clarified for the third time the meaning of the three-part test. In 1997 it clarified the ways that sexual harassment violated Title IX, and in 1998 it clarified the meaning of equity in relation to athletic scholarships.

Resistance to Title IX hit another peak in 2001 after the election of George W. Bush. Some Bush supporters thought he would support a critical review of Title IX. They joined with others, including representatives of men's teams that had been cut from intercollegiate sport programs since 1981. They argued that Title IX created a system of illegal "preferences" for girls and women and unfairly discriminated against men's sports in the process. Men had suffered, they argued, because athletic departments cut men's teams to meet the proportionality test of Title IX.

In response to this argument, President Bush appointed his Secretary of Education to chair a 15-member Commission on Athletic Opportunity (CAO). The CAO was charged with determining whether Title IX was adversely affecting men and in need of modification. Commission members had heated discussions during their meetings, and the CAO report was controversial when it was released in 2003.

Advocates of girls' and women's sports criticized the report because the commission's recommendations were confusing and contradictory. Opponents of Title IX were hopeful that the recommendations would protect all men's teams. As people debated the lengthy list of recommendations, Ted Leland, athletic director at Stanford University and co-chair of the commission, said, "Let us remember, the commission is not the last word on Title IX. Rather, [it] is the first step in what will be a long process." What Leland forgot to say was that the process of achieving gender equity was already thirty years old in 2003, and that hundreds of steps, backward and forward, had already been taken.

After the report was released, a U.S. district court judge ruled against the National Wrestling Coaches Association and their claim that Title IX created a gender-based quota system that forced schools to cut men's teams. The ruling explained that Title IX provided flexible guidelines for achieving equity, and it could not be blamed when administrators chose to cut men's teams. Schools, the judge explained, cut teams for many reasons, including budget constraints, liability costs, lack of specialized training spaces, and other factors unrelated to gender equity. In the wake of this decision and in the face of the upcoming 2004 presidential election, the Bush administration decided not to make changes in Title IX. However, the resistance and controversies continued.

In 2005 the Supreme Court heard a crucial Title IX case and ruled in a 5–4 split decision that a coach who was fired after reporting Title IX violations at his school has the right to sue the school and try to prove that he was fired for making a sex discrimination complaint (www.pbs.org/newshour/bb/law/jan-june05/scotus_3-29.html). This decision is important because it protects "whistle-blowers" who identify inequities. However, a week before this decision, the U.S. Department of Education released a letter stating that with approval from the Bush administration it was changing its interpretation of the third equity test—the "accommodation of interest test." The new interpretation indicated that all schools are presumed to comply with this test if they conduct a web-based survey and do not find a pattern of unmet interests among current female students or if the sport that women wanted to play was not sponsored by nearby schools, thereby making it difficult to schedule competitions.

This move by the Bush administration angered Title IX advocates because it ignored the CAO report and required women students to prove the existence of unmet interest to achieve equity. This, they argued, was a flawed methodology because (1) students don't take online surveys seriously; (2) women often don't express their interests in sports in the same ways that men express their interests; (3) women interested in a sport would not enroll in a school that did not offer the sport; (4) college teams recruit athletes for specific sports rather than waiting for them to show up and prove their interest; (5) men's teams don't require

reflect on SPORTS

Title IX *(Continued)*
Can a Law Create Gender Equity?

"interest surveys;" and (6) higher education is supposed to provide contexts in which students *develop* new interests and skills in addition to cultivating existing interests and skills.

Most university administrators recognized that the interpretation made by the Bush administration was deeply flawed and would not stand up in court, so they have not sought equity compliance by using online interest surveys.

THE SOCIOLOGY OF TITLE IX

As you read these words, the story of Title IX continues. It tells us that the law can be a powerful tool for making changes in society. Between 1971 and 2008, for example, the number of girls playing varsity high school sports increased from 295,000 to about 3.06 million—more than a 1000-percent increase! Instead of 1 of every 27 high school girls playing on teams, now 1 in 3 play. At the college level, the number of women playing on sport teams at all four-year colleges and universities has increased from 32,000 to over 180,000—nearly a 600-percent increase! Today, about 5 percent of all female college students play intercollegiate sports. At the same time, more than 4.3 million boys play high school sports and 265,000 men play in college (see Chapter 14 for data on participation over time). Another important outcome of Title IX is that many boys and men have learned to see and respect women as athletes—something that seldom occurred prior to 1972.

Title IX has benefited millions of girls and women, but it remains controversial. When James Madison University officials announced in 2006 that they would cut seven men's and three women's teams to comply with Title IX, students went to nearby Washington, DC, to demand reforms in the law. But a consultant who worked with JMU officials said the cuts were part of a business decision that involved building a more visible football team with 90 members, 11 coaches, and 85 scholarships. (*Source:* Ron Edmunds, AP/Wide World Photos)

The story of Title IX also demonstrates that laws don't exist in a social and cultural vacuum. Their effectiveness depends on the extent to which people think they are legitimate and necessary. When laws

the education, health, and human rights of girls and women in countries around the world; these will be reviewed and new strategies developed for the United Nations Fifth World Conference on Women in Sophia, Bulgaria in 2010. Overall, this initiative based in the women's movement has become an established global movement to promote and guarantee sport participation opportunities for girls and women.

The Health and Fitness Movement Since the mid-1970s, research has made people more aware

of the health benefits of physical activity (Bailey, Wellard, and Dismore, 2004; Oglesby, 2006; 2007; Sabo et al., 2004; U.S. Surgeon General, 1999a, 1999b; World Health Organization, 2007). This awareness has encouraged women to seek opportunities to exercise and play sports. Although much of the publicity associated with this movement has been influenced by traditional ideas about femininity and tied to the prevailing feminine ideal that emphasizes being thin and heterosexually attractive, there also has been an emphasis on the *development of physical strength and competence*. Muscles threaten vested interests, ideology, or deeply held principles, people often will resist them, especially if they have the power to do so. This means that the histories of certain laws involve extended struggles over what different groups of people think is important and how they want to organize their lives. Developing consensus about laws that threaten the status quo is seldom easy.

The fact that laws, like sports, are social constructions means that they can be changed. When Title IX was passed in 1972, the time was right to make the case for gender equity in education. Many people were ready and eager to embrace it. But enforcement was bound to evoke resistance among those whose power and privilege was threatened. Sport programs have generally reaffirmed and reproduced male power and privilege, so it is not surprising that many men have strongly resisted Title IX and its definitions of gender equity.

Some people argue that inequities today exist only because girls and women are not as interested in sports as boys and men are. Others argue that more changes are needed and that differences in interest result from other inequities related to socialization, encouragement, and a general cultural devaluation of women's sports relative to men's sports. Young women, they say, are discouraged when they are told that they play

like men if they excel in sports or if their programs are second-class. Some people question the use of the proportionality test in universities because the ratio of female to male students has gone from 40:60 to nearly 60:40 over the last forty years, and this means that women should receive more than half of all resources and opportunities in sports. Some people say that if high school cheerleading was officially classified as a sport, most high schools could achieve equity. Others argue that cheerleading reaffirms traditional definitions of femininity and discourages the very cultural changes needed to build increased interest in sports among girls and women.

These and other issues will continue to influence discussions and policies about gender equity (Blumenthal, 2005; Suggs, 2005). There is much less inequity today than in 1972, but sports continue to be organized primarily around the values and experiences of men rather than women. Therefore, struggles over equity and Title IX are likely to continue for some time (Cheslock, 2007). *What do you think?*

Note: Materials in this section are based on many sources; most are summarized in Carpenter and Acosta (2005), Hogshead-Makar and Zimbalist (2007), McDonagh and Pappana (2008), and Suggs (2005).

- -

have become increasingly accepted as desirable attributes for women of all ages (Kruger, Carlson, and Kohl, 2006; Ross and Shinew, 2008). Traditional standards for body image remain, as illustrated by clothing fashions and marketing strategies associated with women's fitness, but many women today reject or temporarily ignore those standards and focus on physical competence and the good feelings that go with it rather than aspiring to look like airbrushed and/or anorexic models in fashion magazines (Krane et al., 2004).

Companies that produce sporting goods and apparel also have recognized that women can be serious athletes. They continue to promote unreal body images, but they also pay more attention to function and performance in their designs and marketing approaches. For example, they produce ads that appeal to women who see sport participation and achievements as symbols of independence and power. In the process, they encourage and promote sport participation among girls and women at the same time that they present frail, underweight models in other ads (Wearden and Creedon, 2002).

Increased Media Coverage of Women in Sports   Even though women's sports are not covered as often or in the same detail as men's sports, girls and women now can see and read about the achievements of female athletes in a wider range of sports than ever before. This exposure encourages girls and women by publicly legitimizing their participation and providing alternatives to media content that portrays women in powerless and/or sexually objectified terms (Buysse and Embser-Herbert, 2004; Heywood and Dworkin, 2003; Kane, 2002; Kane and Buysse, 2005; Kilbourne, 2007). For example, when girls watch women who are physically strong and competent athletes, it becomes easier for them to envision themselves as athletes and to view sports as human activities, not male-only activities.

AT YOUR *fingertips*   For more information on the media coverage of women in sports, see pages 419–425.

The media people who make decisions about sports programming and coverage of women's sports are beginning to realize that women make up half the world's population and therefore half the world's consumers. As they use sports to attract an audience of women that they can sell to sponsors, these people can provide both narratives and images that regularly challenge traditional ideas and beliefs about the characteristics and potential of girls and women on and off the field (Lafferty and McKay, 2004; Thomsen, Bower, and Barnes, 2004).

Reasons to Be Cautious When Predicting Future Participation Increases

Increases in the sport participation rates of girls and women have not come easily. Progress has been remarkable, but gender equity is far from

being achieved in U.S. sports and sports worldwide. Furthermore, past progress does not guarantee continued progress in the future. In fact, there are seven reasons to be cautious about the pace and extent of future increases in sport participation:

1. Budget cuts and privatization of sport programs
2. Resistance to government regulations
3. Backlash among people who resent changes that threaten dominant gender ideology
4. Underrepresentation of women in decision-making positions in sports
5. A cultural emphasis on "cosmetic fitness" for women
6. Trivialization of women's sports
7. Homophobia and the threat of being labeled "lesbian"

Budget Cuts and the Privatization of Sport Programs   Gender equity is often subverted by budget cuts. Compared with programs for boys and men, programs for girls and women tend to be more vulnerable to cuts because they are less well established and they have less revenue-generating potential and less administrative, corporate, and community support. As one woman observed, "It seems like the only time women's programs are treated equally is when cuts must be made."

Because sport programs for girls and women often are relatively new, they have developmental and promotional costs that long-standing and well-established programs for boys and men don't have. Therefore, "equal" budget cuts cause women's programs to fail at a faster pace than men's programs because they haven't developed institutional support or market presence. Many programs for boys and men are less vulnerable because they've had more than a century to develop legitimacy, value, support, and fans. When they face financial crises, they can attract sponsors, whereas many girls' and women's programs face greater struggles to do so.

As public, tax-supported sport programs are cut, opportunities to play sports become privatized. Privatization has a negative impact on girls and women, especially in low-income households. Public sport programs are accountable to voters and regulated by government rules mandating equal rights and opportunities. But private programs are accountable only to the needs of dues-paying members, which means that they respond to market forces rather than to a commitment to equal rights and opportunities.

When free and affordable public programs are cut, people must buy access to sport participation from commercial providers. This is easy for females from well-to-do backgrounds: They just buy what they want, and commercial providers want their business. "Free-enterprise sports" are great for people with money. But they are neither "free" nor are they "enterprising" when it comes to providing opportunities for women with few financial resources. Commercial programs serve only those who can buy what's for sale. When money talks, poor people are seldom heard, and poor girls and women are silenced. Therefore, future participation increases may be distributed unevenly among girls and women, and those who lack resources may suffer participation setbacks in the future (Braddock et al., 2005; Sabo et al. 2004). Research also shows that when the quality of sport programs is poor, as often occurs when there is a lack of public funding, girls lose interest and don't take sport participation seriously (Cooky, 2004).

When sport programs have been cut in U.S. public schools, booster organizations are more likely to step up and provide funds and facilities for boys' sports, such as football, than to offer funding for girls' sports (Wieberg, 2004). Boosters aren't required to follow Title IX law because they're private organizations and receive no support from the federal government. For example, when the city of Los Angeles cut many public sport programs and let private sport programs use public parks, the private programs offered four times as many participation opportunities for boys as for girls. The organizations claimed that boys wanted to play sports and girls did not. Title IX does not apply to state,

county, and city sport programs because they are not connected with public education. The officials in Los Angeles struggled for over five years to resolve these gender inequities, but no resolution came until the California State Legislature passed a law requiring that all city and county sport programs be gender balanced. This occurred in 2005, and today California continues to be the only state with such a law.

Resistance to Government Legislation   Those who benefit from the status quo often resist government legislation that mandates change. For example, some people argue that Title IX represents unwarranted government interference in their lives. They also say that girls and women would already have opportunities to participate if they were genuinely interested in sports, and that laws mandating gender equity interfere with the natural order of sports in society (Gavora, 2002; Knudson, 2005). These people seemingly want to turn back the clock, and they have impeded the implementation and enforcement of Title IX over the years. Resistance to government legislation has a long history in the United States, and it is not likely to go away any time soon.

Backlash Among People Threatened by Changes in Dominant Gender Ideology   When women play certain sports, they become strong. Strong women challenge the prevailing gender ideology that influences the norms, legal definitions, and opportunity structures that frame people's lives, relationships, and identities.. Those who are privileged by this gender ideology describe strong women as abnormal and they put down certain women's sports that involve strength and brutal body contact. These people want things to be as they were in the past, when men played and women watched, cheered, and played sports like "proper ladies."

A variation of this type of backlash began in 2002 after Martha Burk, a psychologist and director of the National Council of Women's Organizations, which represents 6 million members and 160 organizations, wrote to Hootie Johnson, then-chairman of the Augusta National Golf Club, Incorporated. Burk asked Johnson to open the prestigious, all-male Augusta Club to women members. The club is a for-profit organization that produces the financially profitable annual Masters Golf Tournament, which receives global media coverage. Its members, most of whom are powerful white businessmen, receive public attention and have their status boosted by this event, and women executives feel that this type of gender exclusion further privileges their male peers and disadvantages them. In response to Burk's request, here is what Johnson said:

> We will not be bullied, threatened or intimidated. We do not intend to become a trophy in their display case. . . . There may well come a day when women will be invited to join our membership, but that timetable will be ours, and not at the point of a bayonet. (in Brennan, 2002, p. 3C)

Johnson clearly objected to changes threatening a gender ideology that supported his power and privilege and that of other wealthy (white) men. He said that all membership matters are voted on by existing members who have maintained the organization's male-only membership policy.[1] Giving in to a request by women was ideologically intolerable for him, and he and his peers succeeded in demonizing Burke by calling

her a "radical feminist." Augusta National continues its policy of gender exclusion, and the media have dropped the story.

Of course, private clubs have the right to maintain policies of gender (and racial) exclusion, but the responses of Johnson and his successor (Billy Payne) are indicative of equity backlash by powerful men who run a lucrative sport business (Associated Press, 2007). As Burk has said, "It's golf, it's sports, it's power, it's men, it's money—and all those things together make for a volatile mix" (The Daily Show, 2003). To the extent that other men in positions of power in sport organizations think like Johnson, progress toward gender equity is slowed.

Underrepresentation of Women in Decision-Making Positions in Sports   Despite increased sport participation among girls and women, women have suffered setbacks in the ranks of coaching and sport administration in women's programs. For example, in the years immediately following the passage of Title IX in the United States, there was a decline in the number and proportion of female head coaches and administrators (Acosta and Carpenter, 2004; Carpenter and Acosta, 2005; Parkhouse and Williams, 1986). As women's sports became more important in high schools and colleges, men replaced female coaches and administrators.

Many men do a good job of coaching and administering women's sports, but unless girls and young women see women in decision-making positions in their programs, they're unlikely to envision themselves as full participants in sports and sport organizations. When women are not visible leaders in sport programs, it appears that women's abilities and contributions in sports are less valued than men's. This conclusion limits further progress toward gender equity (Hogshead-Makar and Zimbalist, 2007; Ligutom-Kimura, 1995).

Continued Emphasis on "Cosmetic Fitness"
Competing images of female bodies exist in

---

[1]Augusta National is built on a former plantation close to the Georgia-South Carolina border. When the governing bodies for professional golf ruled in 1990 that their official tournament events would no longer be held at clubs that formally excluded women and racial minorities, the major television networks threatened to withdraw coverage from the Masters. Fearing lost revenue from the sale of its media rights, Augusta National voted in a black member. But unlike other major tournaments, the Masters event is a private business that isn't governed by the PGA Tour, and it continues to be profitable because the networks and sponsors support the tournament despite its policy of excluding women. This upsets many women who work for CBS (the only network to ever cover the event) and the sponsors, but these women have learned that to challenge this bastion of male privilege can be very dangerous to their careers.

many cultures today (J. S. Maguire, 2008; Ross and Shinew, 2008). Girls and women receive confusing cultural messages that they should be "firm but shapely, fit but sexy, strong but thin" (Markula, 1995). Although they see images of powerful female athletes, they cannot escape images of fashion models whose bodies are shaped by food deprivation and multiple cosmetic surgeries. Girls and women also hear that physical power and competence are important, but they see disproportionate rewards going to women who look young, vulnerable, and nonathletic. They are advised to "get strong but lose weight" and they learn that muscles are good but too many muscles are unfeminine. They're told that athletic women are attractive, but they see men attracted to professional cheerleaders and celebrity models with breast implants and airbrushed publicity photos. They also see attractive athletes, such as Russian tennis player Maria Sharapova, "packaged and sold as the . . . giggly gal who just wants to have fun: Hillary Duff with a forehand"—even though she's not that way (Glock, 2005). Therefore, they may conclude that even if you're a good athlete, hot looks bring real fame and celebrity. And they know that Anna Kournikova turned her looks, not her success in tennis, into fame, and they see that her fame has lasted far longer than her tennis skills would have lasted.

Cultural messages that promote athletic performance are clearly outnumbered and out-hyped by cultural messages promoting appearance and beauty (Hargreaves, 1994; Heywood and Dworkin, 2003; Kane, 2002; J. S. Maguire, 2008). Effective commercial messages for everything from makeup to clothing are based on the well-established marketing assumption that insecurities about appearance promote consumption, whereas positive body image does not. Therefore, even many ads that show women doing sports are carefully staged to make women consumers feel insecure rather than confident about their bodies. This marketing approach is so powerful that some women avoid sports

"What used to be a parade of womanly stars [in tennis]—from Chris Evert to Monica Seles, from Jennifer Capriati to Serena Williams—has turned into a runway of lollipops in Lycra. Thin has now been confused for fit among some female pros" (Roberts, 2006). Former tennis star Anna Kournikova, no longer competitive on the pro tour, now does exhibition matches for crowds that are impressed by cosmetic fitness. (*Source:* AP Photo/ Terry Renna, AP/Wide World Photos)

until they are thin enough to look "right" and wear the "right" clothes; other girls and women combine participation with pathogenic weight-control strategies to become dangerously thin (Beals, 2000; Hawes, 2001; Johns, 1997; Madison and Ruma, 2003; Wilmore, 1996).

Overall, the tensions between cosmetic fitness and being strong and physically skilled create for many girls and women the challenge of negotiating the mixed meanings they and others give to their bodies (Dworkin, 2001; Garrett, 2004;

Narrative Barriers
I Was Too Ashamed of My Body

Anna was born with underdeveloped arms and feet. Despite encouragement and support from a close friend, she resisted going to the gym and becoming involved in sports. She explains that

> I really wanted to go—inside, I was dying to be physical, to have a go at "pumping iron." . . . But at the time I just couldn't say yes. . . . I was too ashamed of my body. . . . It was the same thing with swimming. I just couldn't bear the thought of people looking at me. I felt *really* vulnerable. (in Hargreaves, 2000, p. 187)

Anna's fear that her body would be seen and judged is not unique. Negotiating the meanings that we give to our bodies is a complex and challenging process. But in contemporary cultures it is more challenging for women than men, and more challenging for people with disabilities than their able-bodied peers.

When femininity is tied to physical attractiveness and sexual desirability, the women who accept dominant gender ideology often make choices that interfere with sport participation. For example, a young woman with an amputated leg may choose a prosthesis that is more natural looking, rather than one suited to sport participation. As one woman explained, "It's one thing to see a man with a Terminator leg. . . . It may inspire people to say, 'Cool.' But body image for women in this country is model thin and long sexy legs" (in Marriott, 2005). For example, Nick, a twenty-year old college student who lost his legs after contracting a rare bacterial disease when he was fourteen, says, "I love my Terminator legs," and he doesn't think twice about plugging them into the nearest electrical outlet when they run short on their charge.

Although Nick loves his "Terminator legs," negotiating the meaning given to one's body is more challenging for men with disabilities than for most able-bodied men—especially when they accept a gender ideology that ties masculinity to power and the ability to outperform or dominate others. This was the

case for Mark, who had trouble starting his car after filling it with gas and putting his wheelchair in the back. A man who had just driven up behind him laid on his horn and shouted obscenities. Mark said that prior to the accident that paralyzed his legs he "would have got out of the car and . . . laid him out, but now I'm useless . . . This is why I say my manhood has been shattered" (in Sparkes and Smith, 2002, p. 269).

Although Mark did not use the same words that Anna used, he also felt vulnerable. When men with disabilities feel vulnerable, some may do what Anna did and avoid sport participation, whereas others may view sport as a site for asserting or reaffirming masculinity.

Sociologists Brett Smith and Andrew Sparkes (2002) point out that people create identities, including feminine and masculine identities, through narratives—that is, stories they tell others about themselves. Their research indicates that playing power and performance sports provides men with a masculinizing narrative—a story in which manhood is constructed through physical accomplishments and dominance over other men. These narratives are the foundation of hegemonic masculinity in many societies. But the identity-creating narratives available to women with disabilities are unlikely to involve sport participation, because sports don't contain femininity stories.

Overall, men and women with disabilities would benefit if they had access to narratives that construct gender in less constraining terms (Thomas, 1999). When there are multiple ways to be a woman or a man, people with visible disabilities have more options for negotiating the meanings that they and others give to their bodies. Maybe this would enable Anna to become more physical and have a go at pumping iron. And maybe it would enable Mark to accept help or play sports that don't involve physical domination over others and still feel like a man.

Heywood and Dworkin, 2003; Krane et al, 2004; Shakib, 2003; Wedgewood, 2004; Young, 1998). This challenge is doubly daunting for female athletes with disabilities, as explained in "Breaking Barriers," page 244.

When the goal of playing sports is cosmetic fitness, women define their participation as a means of meeting expectations based on dominant gender ideology, burning calories so they can eat without guilt, or punishing themselves when they've eaten too much (Krane et al., 2001). Additionally, young women seeking cosmetic fitness sometimes drop out of sports if they gain weight while they train, and others drop out after achieving weight-loss goals. Overall, it appears that cultural messages about cosmetic fitness interfere with further increases in sport participation among girls and women.

Trivialization of Women's Sports "Women play sports, but they are not as good as men and people want to see the best." Statements like this assume that "real" sports involve "manly" things, such as intimidation, violence, and physical domination over others, and that women's sports are second-rate. This orientation is widespread enough that it interferes with achieving gender equity in sports (Laurendeau, 2004; 2008; Vincent, 2004).

Power and performance sports are historically grounded in the values and experiences of men, and they use evaluative standards that disadvantage women. Women play football, but they don't hit as hard as NFL players. They play basketball, but they don't dunk as dramatically as NBA players. They play hockey, but they don't check or fight as in the NHL. They do sports, but they don't do them as men can do them. Therefore, they don't do them well enough to receive equal support. A high school senior who played on his schools' basketball team expressed this "gender logic" in these words: "Watching the girls' basketball team is like watching elementary school kids trying to play. It's not exciting. I mean you watch them because it's your kids out

there playing. But it's not exciting" (Shakib and Dunbar, 2002, p. 363).

An extension of this "logic" was used in 2004 by the president of FIFA, the world-governing body for soccer, when he told international women players that more spectators would watch them if they would wear tighter shorts (Christenson and Kelso, 2004). He assumed that the women's game was trivial, compared with the men's game, and using sex appeal would make it more fan-friendly—a strategy that appears to have helped women in beach volleyball.

When enough people trivialize women's sports by dismissing competent female athletes or defining them primarily as sex objects, it is difficult to consistently generate gate receipts and commercial sponsorships to sustain elite and professional programs. This is why the Women's United Soccer Association (WUSA) and other professional women's sports have not been successful. Even though it's no longer considered appropriate to say that a person "throws like a girl" when he or she doesn't throw well, many people continue to think that playing like women is second-rate by definition. This form of trivializing women's sports and female athletes subverts gender equity at all levels of sport.

Homophobia and the Threat of Being Labeled "Lesbian" **Homophobia** is *a generalized fear or intolerance of lesbians, gay men, bisexual, transsexual, and intersexed people—that is, anyone who isn't clearly classifiable as a heterosexual male or female* (Griffin, 1998). It is based on the notion that homosexuality is deviant or immoral, and it supports prejudice, discrimination, harassment, and violence directed toward those identified or believed to be non-heterosexual. Homophobia is a powerful cultural factor that has discouraged many girls and women, including those who are heterosexual, from playing certain sports or making sports an important part of their lives.

Homophobia causes some parents to steer daughters away from teams, programs, and sports that they believe attract lesbians or have lesbian coaches. Homophobia and public expressions of homophobic discourse influence and often limit the sport participation choices available to women (Dworkin, 2003; Howe, 2003; Veri, 1999). When women fear the label of *lesbian* or fear being associated with lesbians, they may avoid certain sports, limit their commitment to sports, de-emphasize their athletic identities, or emphasize a "presentation of self" that appears to be heterosexual. Closeted lesbian athletes may fear the loss of secrecy so much that they limit their relationships with teammates and become lonely and isolated in the process (Bredemeier et al., 1999; Griffin, 1998; Lenskyj, 2003; Swoopes, 2005).

Heterosexual men may use homophobic discourse to tease female athletes and control all women who are intimidated by it. This occurs in some high schools and colleges, and it can cause women to become so defensive that they give sport participation a lower priority in their lives. Effectively challenging homophobic discourse and forcing others to confront their homophobia is a daunting task. Some people, gay and straight, are good at this, but most people lack the experience to do it effectively or with confidence.

In the meantime, many female athletes go out of their way to emphasize traditional feminine attributes and even say in interviews that being an athlete is not nearly as important as eventually getting married, settling down, having children, and becoming a nurturing homemaker. Like athletes, people who market women's sports often avoid acknowledging lesbians for fear that it will decrease attendance among potential spectators who are homophobic. Players know this and often say that if a woman wants to make a team, she had better grow her hair long and talk about wanting to be married and have children. As one international player said, it is well known that team officials "don't want a bunch of dykes representing our country [in the Olympics]" (Hall, 2002, p. 200).

Homophobia affects all women: it creates fears, pressures women to conform to traditional gender roles, and silences and makes invisible the lesbians who manage, coach, and play sports (Griffin, 1998; Hall, 2002; Lenskyj, 1999; Nelson, 1998).

Gender and Fairness Issues in Sports

Sport participation among girls and women will not continue to increase automatically (Cooky and McDonald, 2005). Without efforts to maintain progress toward achieving gender equity, there's a tendency in most cultures to give priority to men's sports and male athletes. This is because sport worlds usually are[2]

1. *male-dominated*, so that power and qualifications are associated with manhood and men—that is, being qualified in a sport world means possessing characteristics associated with masculinity;
2. *male-identified*, so that a typical sport world is a "man's world"—that is, people assume it involves men and is about men, unless it is identified as "women's sports"—such as "the Women's World Cup" or "the Women's Final Four";
3. *male-centered*, so that men and men's lives are the expected focus of attention when people talk about sport stories, legends, records, events, halls of fame, and media programming.

These are useful concepts to understand when studying sports in society. For example, in *male-dominated social worlds*, women are considered to be qualified when they perform like men. Therefore, female athletes are assumed to be good when "they play like men," and a female coach, official, or administrator is considered qualified when she does her job "like a man (would do it)." And if a woman were named head coach of a major college men's football or basketball team, most people would closely examine her credentials and then wonder if she would be able to handle the job as a man would handle it.

---

[2]This framework was developed by Allan Johnson in his chapter on "How systems of privilege work" in *Privilege, Power, and Difference* (McGraw-Hill, 2006).

In *male-identified social worlds*, women in positions of power or authority arouse suspicion about how they obtained their power and what they might do with it. However, if they attempt to reduce those suspicions by "fitting in" with men, some people will define them as abnormal or untrustworthy, and, therefore, undeserving of their position. This makes it relatively easy to discredit women leaders in sports—people can say that they obtained their positions by gaining the favor of men, abandoning women, or being a manipulative "stealth feminist" or a lesbian who doesn't like men and has an agenda that will undermine the men in sports.

In *male-centered social worlds* people assume that men are the center of attention. For example, when U.S. students go to a movie that focuses on women they may describe it as a "chick flick"; and when a film is about gays or lesbians, they may describe it as a "gay" or "lesbian" film. But when a film is about men and men's heterosexual lives, they don't describe as a "dick flick" or "hetero man movie." It's similar in sports. Therefore, the World Series, the Super Bowl, the Little League World Series, the World Cup, and the Masters (Golf Tournament), are not described as "men's events," nor are pro football stadiums referred to as "men's sport centers," even though they're all about men and men's culture. In male-centered sports, it assumed that men are the center of attention without needing to say it.

The following sections on sport participation, support for athletes, and jobs for women in sports illustrate what it means when we say that sports are organized to be male dominated, male identified, and male centered.

Participation Opportunities: Organized and Mainstream Sports   Prior to the early 1970s, most people did not question the male-dominated/identified/centered organization of sports. They believed that females were naturally frail and unsuited for most sport participation. When girls and women were encouraged to be physically active, they were steered into figure skating, ice dancing, gymnastics, swimming, tennis, golf, and other sports that were assumed to not require strength, power, and speed—traits associated with masculinity. Some girls and women ignored these assumptions and played sports involving strength, power, and speed—and they lived with the consequences, which often involved some form of social rejection. But overall, there were limited opportunities for girls and women to play sports.

Over the past fifty years, female athletes have demonstrated clearly that notions of female frailty are grounded in ideology rather than nature. They've expanded ideas about what girls and women can and should be encouraged to do in sports. Today, most people in the United States and many other nations agree that women should have opportunities to play sports. But there continue to be disagreements about girls and women playing certain contact sports, playing certain sports with men, and having access to the same resources that men have.

These disagreements have perpetuated inequities in participation opportunities in many international sports (White and Kay, 2006; Young and White, 2007). Although important changes have occurred since the early 1980s, female athletes remain underrepresented in international competitions. The data in figure 8.1 and table 8.1 illustrate that women in the modern Summer Olympic Games have always had fewer events than men have had, with fewer women participating than men. The International Olympic Committee (IOC), which from 1894 to 1981 had no women members, did not approve a women's 1500-meter run until the 1972 Games in Munich. It was not until the 1984 Games in Los Angeles that women were "allowed" to run the marathon; women waited until 1988 to

> It's unfortunate that [some golf clubs have policies that exclude women and minorities], but it's just the way it is.
> — Tiger Woods, professional golfer (in Dodd, 2002, p. 1C)

run the Olympic 10,000-meter race, until 1996 to run the 5000-meter race, and until 2004 to wrestle. But despite these changes, sports remain characterized by deep gender inequalities.

The factors that stall equity in participation are both ideological and structural. This means that they are based on (1) *webs of ideas and beliefs* about what is and isn't appropriate for girls and women to do (*gender ideology*) and (2) the organization of *opportunities* and the distribution of *resources* to take advantage of opportunities (*social structure*). In some cases, ideological barriers are grounded in traditional religious beliefs, making them very difficult to change. For example, strict Islamic beliefs in certain nations forbid women from publicly exposing any skin to the sight of men (Kay, 2006). Similarly, women in traditionally Catholic nations face restrictions grounded in beliefs about their reproductive and childrearing roles. The influence of fundamentalist Christian beliefs varies greatly, but it has led to excluding women from

sport roles in the United States and worldwide (Rock, 2008).

Structural barriers are influenced by ideological barriers, but they're directly grounded in socioeconomic factors. When women are positioned in roles and situations that preclude or diminish their access to resources, this limits sport participation and makes it impossible for them to train as elite competitors (Donnelly and Harvey, 2007).

For both ideological and structural reasons, women have relatively few opportunities to play professional sports. Until recently, few people would pay to watch women play anything but "ladylike" sports in which they competed alone (figure skating, golf) or competed with nets or dividers separating opponents and preventing physical contact (tennis, volleyball). Although more people today are willing to pay to watch women play various sports, the most popular spectator sports continue to be tennis, figure skating, gymnastics, and golf—all of

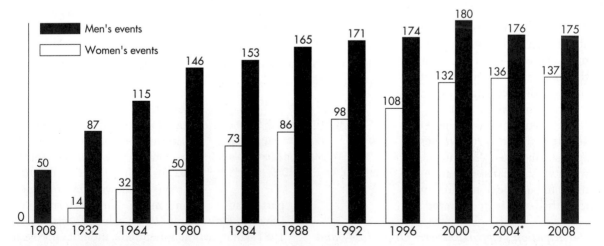

*Ten events in 2008 were mixed, or open to both men and women. These ten are added to the totals for both men and women. This way of handling mixed events is used for each of the other years in this graph.

FIGURE 8.1 Number of Summer Olympic events open to women and to men, 1908–2008.

Table 8.1 Male and female athletes in the modern Summer Olympic Games, 1896–2008

Year	Place	Countries Represented	Male Athletes	Female Athletes	Percent Female
1896	Athens	14	241	0	0.0
1900	Paris	24	975	22	2.2
1904	St. Louis	12	645	6	0.9
1908	London	22	1971	7	1.8
1912	Stockholm	28	2359	48	2.0
1916		Olympics scheduled for Berlin canceled because of World War I.			
1920	Antwerp	29	2561	65	2.5
1924	Paris	44	2954	135	4.4
1928	Amsterdam	46	2606	277	9.6
1932	Los Angeles	37	1206	126	9.5
1936	Berlin	49	3632	331	8.4
1940		Olympics scheduled for Tokyo canceled because of World War II.			
1944		Olympics canceled because of World War II.			
1948	London	59	3714	90	9.5
1952	Helsinki	69	4436	519	10.5
1956	Melbourne	72	2938	376	11.3
1960	Rome	83	4727	611	11.4
1964	Tokyo	93	4473	678	13.2
1968	Mexico City	112	4735	781	14.2
1972	Munich	122	6075	1059	14.8
1976	Montreal	92	4824	1260	20.7
1980	Moscow	81	4064	1115	21.5
1984	Los Angeles	140	5263	1566	22.9
1988	Seoul	159	6197	2194	26.1
1992	Barcelona	169	6652	2704	28.9
1996	Atlanta	197	6806	6806	34.0*
2000	Sydney	199	6582	4069	38.2
2004	Athens	201	6262	4306	40.7
2008	Beijing	204§	6450	4746	42.4

Source: www.olympic.org/uk/games/index_uk.asp.

*Twenty-six countries sent only male athletes to the 1996 Summer Games.

§This includes 192 of the 195 countries in the world plus 12 territories or other areas that the IOC allows to have a National Olympic Committee and send athletes to the games.

Note: These data show 112 years of gradual progress toward gender equity. At this rate, the 2016 or 2020 Summer Games may have equal numbers of men and women. The number of athletes participating in 1976, 1980, and 1984 was lower than expected, due to boycotts. The numbers for 2008 are estimates that were made as the games occurred.

which are consistent with traditional notions of femininity.

Additionally, women in elite sports are often referred to as "ladies," and events are promoted with an emphasis on heterosexual habits, lifestyles, and "looks," and an acknowledgment of children, husbands, or the hope to have them someday. This approach, grounded in subtle homophobia, continues to shape the public image of all women's sports. The goal of people who use it is to make invisible the lesbians who participate in many college, professional, and international events. But in the long run, this approach, along with other ideological and structural factors, will restrict the growth of women's professional sports and the inspiration they provide for girls and women. Growth will not expand significantly until more people embrace multiple and diverse notions of womanhood.

> **OLC** ON THE *OLC:*
> See the OLC—Additional Readings for Chapter 8—for an essay on women's professional basketball in the United States

Participation Opportunities: Informal and Alternative Sports   Informal games often have gender dynamics that present girls and women with special challenges for gaining access to participation and claiming identities as athletes. Similar challenges exist in alternative or action sports, both informal and formal. This is because boys and men generally control who plays and who is defined as a "fellow" athlete.

Regardless of where informal sport participation occurs, the contexts are nearly always male dominated/identified/centered. This discourages the participation of girls and women. In fact, they must be exceptionally good athletes and have clever inclusion strategies to be given a chance to play and be accepted as an athlete by male peers. Inclusion strategies vary (Laurendeau and Sharara, 2005), but the most reliable is to be "sponsored" by an influential male who vouches for a female's "right" to demonstrate what she can do as an athlete. Laws such as Title IX don't apply to these settings, and changes usually come slowly.

The methods and dynamics of excluding or restricting the participation of girls and women in informal sports have received little attention in the sociology of sport. However, we do know that females face unique participation and identity challenges in informal and alternative sports and that there are equity and fairness issues related to who plays under what conditions (Laurendeau and Sharara, 2005; Wheaton and Beal, 2003). Therefore, many girls and women feel unwelcome. At the same time, many boys and men assume that they have priority when using facilities or resources. It's a "Catch-22" situation for girls and women: Sports are organized so that women have fewer opportunities than men to develop interests and skills, and then women are denied opportunities because they have fewer interests and skills!

Research on alternative sports shows that they are clearly organized around the values and experiences of boys and young men (Anderson, 1999; Honea, 2007; Laurendeau, 2008; Laurendeau and Sharara, 2005; Rinehart and Syndor, 2003). Observations at nearly any noncommercial skateboard park reaffirms this point. Girls and young women are usually spectators—"skate Bettys" ("groupies" with boards), or they're cautious participants who must work harder than their male peers to be taken seriously as athletes (Beal and Weidman, 2003). Additionally, a disproportionate number of girls are inline skaters, which puts them lower in the skateboard park status hierarchy. The few girls who do claim space for themselves in bowls or ramp areas have earned the "right" to participate, but they have done so on terms set by the boys.

Alternative sports have emerged in connection with the lifestyles of boys and young men who value, among other things, facing one's fears, taking risks, and pushing normative limits. The boys and young men in these sports say that inclusion is based on skill, guts, and aggressiveness, not gender. In fact, it is common in action sports for participants to say that you can't be great unless you have big *cahones* and that success requires that an athlete go "balls to the wall" (Meadows, 2006; Roenigk, 2006). Therefore, girls identified as athletes in "extreme" versions of action sports are those who have "balls" and demonstrate "Kodak Courage"—that is, enough skill and guts to attempt and occasionally accomplish creative and dangerous tricks that others want to see (Kay and Laberge, 2003).

The consequences of the male-dominated/identified/centered culture and organization of alternative sports are seen in media-created, corporate-sponsored versions such as the X Games, Extremity Games, Gravity Games, Velocity Games, and Dew Action Sports Tour. For example, there were fifty-six female athletes in the 1995 X Games, twenty-six in 2003, and only four of the fifty-four *invited* participants in 2005 were women. The 2007 Extremity Games had 14 events for men and 3 for women. Recent Dew Action Sports Tour events had no women on the invited list of participants. Patterns vary from one alternative sport to another, but including women does not appear to be a high-priority goal (M. Donnelly, 2006).

Support for Athletes Female athletes in most North American high schools and colleges seldom receive the same support enjoyed by the boys and men. This also occurs in sport-sponsoring organizations worldwide. Historically, serious inequities have existed in the following areas:

- Access to facilities
- Quality of facilities (playing surfaces, locker rooms, showers, and so on)
- Availability of scholarships*
- Program operating expenses
- Provision and maintenance of equipment and supplies
- Recruiting budgets*
- Scheduling of games and practice times
- Travel and per diem expenses
- Opportunity to receive academic tutoring*
- Numbers of coaches assigned to teams

These apply primarily to U.S. colleges and universities.

Girls and women are eager participants in action sports such as climbing. However, boys and men control who plays and who is defined as an athlete in these sports, and girls and women are seldom taken seriously unless they perform like boys and men. This girl outclimbs boys her age, but she is marginalized by the vocabulary that boys use when they climb together (Laurendeau, 2008). (*Source:* Jay Coakley)

- Salaries for administrators, coaches, trainers, and other staff
- Provision of medical and training services and facilities
- Publicity for individuals, teams, and events

Inequities in some of these areas remain a problem in many schools, but they are an even greater problem in community programs where they often go undetected unless someone digs through data from many sources.

Most people today realize that a lack of support for female athletes subverts sport participation among girls and women (Cooky, 2004). For well over a century, men built their programs, shaped them to fit their interests and values, generated interest in participation, sold them to sponsors, and marketed them to spectators. During this time, public funds and facilities, student fees, and private sponsorships created and maintained programs for boys and men. Girls and women today want only the same treatment that boys and men have enjoyed—no handouts; just the same investment that was made in developing sports for boys and men (Lamb, 2000). For those who believe in fairness, its difficult to argue with this point.

Jobs for Women in Coaching and Administration

Most sport programs are controlled by men. Although women's programs have increased in number and importance around the globe, women often have lost power over them. Data at all levels of competition show that women don't have equal opportunities when it comes to jobs in coaching and administration. Women are especially underrepresented at the highest levels of power in sports. A thirty-six-year study by Vivian Acosta and Linda Carpenter (Carpenter and Acosta, 2005, 2008) documents gender trends for U.S. college coaching and administration in NCAA institutions:

- When Title IX became law in 1972, women coached 90 percent of women's teams in the

NCAA; by 1978, the proportion dropped to 58 percent; in 2008, it was down to 43 percent.
- Between 1998 and 2008, there were 2,755 new NCAA teams for women; of the head coaches hired for those teams, 1,868 (68 percent) were men and 887 (32 percent) were women.
- In 1998, 188 (19 percent) of all NCAA institutions had a woman as an athletic director; this number grew slightly to 224 (21 percent) in 2008 (men held this position in 807 institutions in 1998 and in 809 in 2008).
- The athletic departments that had female athletic directors in 2008 also had higher proportions of women coaches.
- The proportion of female coaches and administrators declines as levels of competition and job salary increase.
- Women held only 11 percent of the full-time sports information director positions in universities in 2008, and 27 percent of athletic trainer positions.
- Women accounted for less than 2 percent of men's team coaches, and most of those coaches worked with gender-combined teams in swimming, cross-country, or tennis.

Table 8.2 presents longitudinal data on the proportion of women's teams with female head coaches for the ten most popular women's intercollegiate sports from 1977 to 2008. Only soccer had a higher proportion of women coaches in 2008 than in 1977, and the gain was small. Eight of the other nine sports showed at least a 15-percentage point decline in female head coaches between 1977 and 2008. What would men say if nearly 80 percent of the administrators and head coaches of all athletic departments and intercollegiate teams were women? They would be outraged; they would file lawsuits and demand affirmative action programs—and they would be justified in doing so.

The coaching and administration situation is much the same worldwide. Over 80 percent of all

Table 8.2 Percentage of women's teams with female head coaches for the ten most popular women's intercollegiate sports in all NCAA divisions, 1977–2008

Sport	1977	1987	1997	2002	2004	2008	Percentage Point Change, 1977–2008
Basketball	79.4	59.9	65.2	62.8	60.7	59.1	−20.3
Volleyball	86.6	70.2	67.8	57.3	59.5	55.0	−31.6
Cross-country	35.2	18.7	20.7	21.3	22.0	19.2	−16.0
Soccer	29.4	24.1	33.1	30.7	30.1	33.1	+3.7
Softball	83.5	67.5	65.2	65.1	64.8	64.7	−18.8
Tennis	72.9	54.9	40.9	34.5	34.6	29.8	−43.1
Track	52.3	20.8	16.4	19.0	19.7	18.0	−34.3
Golf	54.6	37.5	45.2	39.2	41.7	38.8	−15.8
Swimming/diving	53.6	31.2	33.7	23.0	25.6	24.3	−29.3
Lacrosse	90.7	95.1	85.2	85.9	86.2	84.6	−6.1

Modified from Carpenter and Acosta (2008). In 2008, 43 percent of the coaches of women's teams were women. This is the lowest representation of women as coaches of women's teams in the history of college sports. In 1972, women coached 90 percent of all women's teams, but there were far fewer teams.

national team coaches worldwide are men. The IOC, the most powerful administrative body in global sports, had *no* women members for 85 years (1896 to 1981). IOC membership in 2008 consisted of 94 men and 16 women, and its 15-member executive committee had only 1 woman. Most of the 205 National Olympic Committees have executive staffs that are less than 20 percent female, and only 2 of 35 International Sports Federations have women as presidents (Canadian Press, 2008; White and Henry, 2004).

Reasons for the underrepresentation of women in coaching and administrative positions in women's sports include the following:

- Men use well-established connections with other men in sport organizations to help them during the job search and hiring process.
- Compared with men, most female applicants for coaching and administrative jobs do not have the strategic professional connections and networks to compete with male candidates.
- Job search committees often use ideologically based evaluative criteria, making it likely

that female applicants for coaching and administrative jobs will be seen as less qualified than men.

- Support systems and professional development opportunities are scarce for women who want to be coaches or administrators and for women already in coaching and administrative jobs.
- Many women know that it is difficult to work in athletic departments and sport organizations that are male-dominated/identified/centered.
- Sport organizations are seldom organized in family-friendly ways.
- Sexual harassment is more often experienced by women than by men, and female coaches and administrators often feel that they are judged by more demanding standards than those by which men are judged.

These factors affect aspirations and opportunities. They influence who applies for jobs, how applicants fare during the hiring process, how coaches and administrators are evaluated, who enjoys their job, and who is promoted into higher-paying jobs with more responsibility and power (Bruening and Dixon, 2008).

SIDELINES

©1982 M.T.F.-T.W.S.-Lakewood, CO

Women traditionally have been expected to play support roles for men in sports as well as in society at large. This situation is changing, but these role expectations are still present in the gendered social structures of many organizations and societies.

People on job search committees seek, interview, evaluate, and hire candidates who they think will be successful in sport programs that are male-dominated/identified/centered. After looking at objective qualifications, such as years of experience and win–loss records, search committee members subjectively assess such things as a candidate's abilities to recruit and motivate players, raise money, command respect in the community (among boosters, fans, sport reporters), build toughness and character among players, maintain team discipline, and "fit" into the athletic department or sport organization.

None of these assessments occurs in a vacuum, and some are influenced by gender ideology in addition to the facts. Although people on search committees do not agree on all things, many think in terms that favor men over women (Gregory, 2009; Hovden, 2000). This is because coaching and other forms of leadership often are seen as consistent with traditional ideas about masculinity: If you "coach like a girl," you are, by definition, doing it wrong; if you "coach like a man," you are doing it right. In a male-dominated and male-identified organizational culture, this is taken for granted.

Under these conditions, women are hired only when they present compelling evidence that they can do things as men have done them in the past. In sport programs and athletic departments where men have routinely been hired and women have been ignored, there may be pressure to recruit and hire women so that charges of discrimination can be deflected. When a woman is hired in such circumstances, the selection committee may say that "*We had to hire a woman.*" But a more accurate statement would be "*We've favored men for so long that people were going to rightfully accuse us of gender discrimination if we didn't hire a woman or two.*"

When women are hired, they are less likely than men to feel welcome and fully included in sport organizations. Therefore, they often have lower levels of job satisfaction and higher rates of job turnover. This causes some people to conclude that women simply don't have what it takes to survive in sports. But this conclusion ignores the fact that job expectations in sports have been developed over the years by men who've had wives to raise their children, provide them and their teams with emotional support, host social events for teams and boosters, coordinate their social schedules, handle household finances and maintenance, make sure they're not distracted by family and household issues, and faithfully attend games season after season. If female coaches and administrators had an opportunity to build programs and coach teams under similar conditions, job satisfaction would be high and turnover would be low (Bruening et al., 2007).

Finally, some sport organizations have records of being negligent in controlling sexual harassment and responding to complaints from women who wish to be taken seriously in the structure and culture of sport organizations and programs. This means that people in the programs must critically assess the impact of male-dominated/identified/centered forms of social organization on both males and females. Unless this assessment takes place and changes are made, gender equity will never exist in the ranks of coaching and administration (Claringbould and Knoppers, 2008; Cunningham, 2008; Cunningham and Sagas, 2008; Fink, 2008; Gregory, 2009; Hoeber, 2007; Knoppers and Anthonissen, 2008).

AT YOUR *fingertips* For more information on jobs and mobility in sports, see pages 345–349.

Strategies to Achieve Equity

Most men support the idea of gender equity, but few are willing to give up their power and change the culture of sport organizations to achieve it (Gregory, 2009). This reluctance has forced proponents of gender equity to turn to governments for assistance or to file lawsuits. Governments have been helpful, but they're slow to respond. Legal actions have been effective, but they require money and long-term commitments. Therefore, in the hope of fostering progressive changes, people have formed grassroots organizations to support and publicize sport programs for girls and women and the achievements of female athletes. Along with these efforts, individuals and groups have used the following strategies to effectively promote gender equity:

- Confront discriminatory practices in the athletic department and become an advocate for female athletes, coaches, and administrators.
- Insist on fair and open employment practices in the entire organization, including the athletic department.
- Record equity data and have an independent group issue a public "gender equity report card" every three to four years for your athletic department or sport program.
- Learn and educate others about the history of discrimination in sports and how to recognize the subtle forms of discrimination that operate in sport worlds that are male dominated, male-identified, and male-centered.

- Object to practices and policies that decrease opportunities for women in sports, and inform the media of them.
- When possible, package and promote women's sports as revenue producers, so there will be financial incentives to increase participation opportunities for women.
- Recruit female athletes into coaching by establishing internships and training programs.
- Use women's hiring networks when seeking coaches and administrators in sport programs.
- Create a supportive work climate for women and establish policies to eliminate sexual harassment in a sport program and athletic department.

These suggestions emphasize a combination of public relations, political lobbying, pressure, education, and advocacy. They're based on the assumption that increased participation and opportunities for women come only through struggle and that favorable outcomes depend on persistence and organization.

Girls and Women as Agents of Change   Some people assume that women are empowered when they play sports and that they then become active agents of gender equity in sports and society. But this claim is only partially supported by research (Eitle and Eitle, 2002; Stoelting, 2004).

Sport participation enables girls and women to connect with the power of their bodies and reject notions that females are naturally weak, dependent, and powerless. Because identity and a personal sense of power are partly grounded in one's body and body image, sport participation can help women overcome the feeling that their bodies are objects to be viewed, evaluated, and consumed. Furthermore, the physical skills and strength often gained through sport participation can help girls and women feel less vulnerable, more competent and independent, and more in control of their physical safety and psychological well-being (see Blinde, Taub, and Han, 1994; Chastain, 2004; Ference and Muth, 2004; Fredrickson and Harrison, 2005; Pelak, 2002, 2005; Ross and Shinew, 2008; Roth and Basow, 2004; Theberge, 2000a; Wedgewood, 2004).

Empowerment does not occur automatically when a girl or woman plays sports, nor is a sense of empowerment always associated with a desire or an ability to actively promote fairness and equity issues in sports or other spheres of life. Feeling competent as athletes does not guarantee that women will critically assess gender ideology and gender relations or work for fairness and equity in sports or society. For example, some female athletes express negative attitudes toward feminism and distance themselves from social activism related to women's issues. In other words, those who play elite-level sports often avoid becoming "boat rockers" who are critical of the gender order (McClung and Blinde, 1998; Young and White, 1995). There are four reasons for this lack of activism:

1. Many female athletes feel that they have much to lose if they're associated with civil and human rights issues for women because others might identify them as ungrateful or marginalize them by tagging them with labels such as *radical, feminist*, or *lesbian*.
2. The corporation-driven "celebrity feminism" promoted through media sports today focuses on individualism and consumption rather than everyday struggles faced by ordinary girls and women who want to play sports but also need to find child care, health care, and a decent job in order to do so (Cole, 2000b; Cooky and McDonald, 2005).
3. The "empowerment discourses" associated with fitness and sports often emphasize *individual* self-empowerment through physical changes that enhance self-image and self-esteem (Cooky, 2006; Cooky and McDonald, 2005; MacNeill, 1999; J. S. Maguire, 2006, 2008); they do not emphasize social or cultural changes at an institutional level.

4. Female athletes, even those with high media profiles and powerful bodies, have little control over their own sport participation and little political voice in sports or society as a whole (Lowe, 1998).

Similarly, women hired and promoted into leadership positions in major sport organizations are expected to promote power and performance sports in society. The men who control many sport organizations are not usually eager to hire women who put *women's issues* on the same level as *sport issues*. Of course, not all female leaders become uncritical cheerleaders for power and performance sports, but it takes effort and courage to critically analyze sports and use one's power to change them. Without this effort and courage, gender inequities will persist.

Boys and Men as Agents of Change Gender equity is not just a woman's issue. It also involves creating options for boys and men to play sports that are not based exclusively on a power and performance model. Sports that emphasize aggression and domination often encourage orientations and actions that lead to chronic injuries, an inability to relate to women, fears of intimacy with other men, homophobia, and a compulsive concern with comparing oneself with other men in terms of what might be called "life success scores" (Burstyn, 1999; Messner, 2002, 2007a, 2007b).

Sports privilege men over women, but they also privilege some men over others. When men realize that certain sports perpetuate attitudes and orientations that often undermine their relationships with one another and with women, they are more inclined to view sports critically. Bruce Kidd, a former Olympic runner and now a physical educator and social scientist, used his experiences to offer the following observations:

> Through sports, men learn to cooperate with, care for, and love other men, in [many] ways, but they rarely learn to be intimate with each other or emotionally honest. On the contrary, the only way many of us express fondness for other men is by teasing or mock fighting. (1987, p. 259)

Developing physical skills often improves health and provides girls and women with a sense of empowerment. This is true for Reshma, a seven-year-old in Dhaka, Bangladesh. However, if the culture and social structure in Bangladesh are organized to systematically prevent females from gaining power in her community and society, Reshma's joy and sense of empowerment from winning this race will be temporary and difficult to convert into the power to make needed institutional changes as an adult. (*Source:* Photo courtesy of The Hunger Project; www.thp.org/)

Men who want to move beyond an expression of fondness based on teasing and mock fighting have good reason to join with those women concerned with critically assessing dominant sport forms in their society (Anderson, 2005; Pronger, 1999).

Facing Football: A Challenge for Equity Strategies In the box "Title IX" on pages 234–239, we did not explore the primary obstacle to achieving gender equity in

> The reason I need sports in my life is that it's the only aspect of my existence that I understand completely. . . . And this is true for a lot of men. . . . It is the only subject that allows us to see—or at least feel—the truth. —Chuck Klosterman, journalist, 2003.

high school and college sport programs: the place of high-profile football teams in the culture and structure of high school and university athletic departments.

High schools and colleges often fail to meet equity goals because of the size and cost of football teams. When teams have 80 to 120 team members, award eighty-five scholarships, employ multiple coaches, and have high operational costs, there is little chance for a women's sport program to match the men's program in terms of budget and number of athletes. Despite this, university officials resist cutting the size and budgets of football teams—even though all but about seventy big-time football programs report considerable financial losses every year. This management decision puts many athletic directors in a position where they must cut expenses by cutting non-revenue-producing men's teams such as wrestling, gymnastics, and diving. The men on these teams then feel victimized by Title IX rather than by management strategies that give priority to football. But these men find it easier to blame women and Title IX than to challenge football because the culture and structure of the entire athletic department often revolves around football. Defining the loss of men's teams as a men-versus-women conflict makes more sense to many men than challenging the sport (football) that reproduces the gender ideology that many of them have used to form their identities and achieve social status since they were boys.

When football is the "cultural and structural centerpiece" in schools and communities, gender equity is chronically out of reach. Ironically, some of the best-funded intercollegiate women's sport programs exist in the sixty to seventy universities where big-time Division 1 football teams enjoy big payouts from bowl games and make their athletic department resource-rich. However, all other universities—over 400 of them—have football teams that don't play in lucrative bowl games; these teams incur major financial losses and depend on support from boosters whose identities are deeply grounded in football and the ideologies it reproduces. These ideologies aren't compatible with achieving gender equity, and it is important to understand their impact on the distribution of power and resources in sports.

IDEOLOGY AND POWER ISSUES

Ideologies often are so deeply rooted in our social worlds that we seldom think about or question them. We simply take them for granted and use them as forms of "cultural logic" to make sense

of the world. This is especially the case with gender ideology.

Gender is a central organizing principle of social life, and gender ideology influences our identities and relationships as well as how we organize social worlds. It influences what we wear, how we walk, how we present ourselves to others, and how we think about and plan for our future. The tendency to ignore gender ideology in sports limits the effectiveness of strategies to achieve equity. In fact, without transforming the gender ideology that has been used to organize, play, and make sense of sports, gender equity will never be achieved.

Gender Ideology in Society

Gender ideology varies from culture to culture. In societies where men control a disproportionate share of power and resources, gender ideology is based on a *simple binary classification model.* According to this model, all people are classified into one of two **sex categories:** *male or female* (see figure 8.2). These categories are defined in biological terms, and they are viewed in terms of difference and opposition; in fact, they're usually identified as "opposite sexes." All people in the male category are believed to be naturally different from all people in the female category, and they are held to different normative expectations when it comes to feelings, thoughts, and actions. These expectations shape the ways that people define and identify **gender**—that is, *what is considered masculine and what is considered feminine in a group or society.*

The two-category gender classification model is so central to the way people see the world that they resist thinking about gender critically and are likely to feel uncomfortable when people don't fit neatly into one sex category or the other.

It takes dedication and hard work to maintain ideas about gender when they are based on a two-category sex classification model (Butler, 2004; Fenstermaker and West, 2002). This is because such a model is inconsistent with biological evidence showing that anatomy,

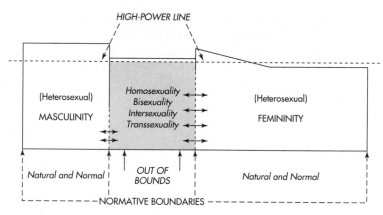

Note: This diagram refers to dominant ideas and beliefs about gender categories; it does *not* refer to people or their actions. Therefore, heterosexual masculinity and heterosexual femininity are depicted as separate, nonoverlapping categories; in other words, most people believe that humans fall into one or the other category. Each category has normative boundaries that identify the limits of widely accepted beliefs about what is "natural and normal" for males or females. The heterosexual "FEMININITY" category is wider than the heterosexual "MASCULINITY" category because girls and women have more latitude in what they can do without being defined as deviant, or *out of normative bounds* in terms of gender. The ways of thinking, feeling, and acting that are perceived to be outside the "natural and normal" categories of heterosexual masculinity or femininity are listed in the gray area of the diagram. This placement reflects that fact that those who use the two-category classification model see them as gender nonconforming. People in this gray area include gay men, lesbians, bisexuals, the intersexed, and transsexuals (GLBITs).

The short double arrows (◄——►)indicate two things: (1) feelings, thoughts and actions that cross over normative boundaries, and (2) efforts to push normative boundaries to make space for alternative expressions of masculinity and femininity, to create new sexual categories, or to transcend sexual categories by blurring or erasing the boundaries.

The "high-power line" at the top of the diagram indicates that heterosexual men are more likely to occupy high-power and influential positions, such as heads of state, members of the Senate and Congress, CEOs, and top-level leaders and decision makers in religious organizations, education, media, and sports. The high-power line represents the "glass ceiling" for women and GLBITs, although some have cracked through it in certain spheres of social life.

FIGURE 8.2 A two-category classification model: Identifying sex and defining gender in U.S. culture.

hormones, chromosomes, and secondary sex characteristics vary in complex ways that cannot be divided into two distinct, nonoverlapping sex categories. Noted biologist Anne Fausto-Sterling explains that sex in bodily terms is simply too complex for only two categories. She notes that "There is no either/or; rather, there are shades of difference" (2000, p. 3). In other words, real bodies have physiological and

biological traits that vary along various continua rather than falling neatly into two separate, different, and opposite categories.

Classifying all bodies into two categories is reflects social and cultural ideas rather than biological facts (Cheshire and Valentine, 2007; Crawley, Foley, and Shehan, 2007). But this doesn't mean it is unimportant or without life-altering consequences. In fact, when people are born with physical traits that don't fit neatly into one sex category or the other, the gender ideology used by physicians and parents has led them to surgically "fix" genitals and reproductive organs so the infant will appear to fit into a single category (Fausto-Sterling, 2000; Preves, 2005; Quart, 2008). This approach is changing now that more people realize that bodies are more complex than a two-category model leads us to believe, and that sex as well as gender is a social construction (Laqueur, 1990; Preves, 2005).

Hormones vary from one body to the next, and nearly all bodies have some amount of both testosterone and estrogen. However, testosterone is identified as a "male hormone" and estrogen as a "female hormone." This way of thinking about and referring to hormones is misleading, but it enables people to maintain their two-category classification model without asking critical questions about it (Garbarino, 2006; Preves, 2005; Rivers, 2007). Even chromosomal patterns do not fit neatly into two distinct categories, nor do secondary sex characteristics, which vary greatly from one body to the next, even those classified into a single sex or gender category (Boylan, 2008; Genel, 2000; Warren, 2003). But people in certain cultures do their best to cover those variations with sex-appropriate clothes and body management strategies that are consistent with prevailing definitions of masculinity and femininity. Most people spend considerable time, energy, and money to ensure that their physical characteristics and appearance fit general expectations based on the two-category sex classification model. Those who ignore, cannot conform with, or choose not to conform with these expectations risk being marginalized or treated as if they are "out of gender bounds" in the gender order (Fenstermaker and West, 2002). For example, a woman who doesn't remove natural hair growth above her upper lip or on other parts of her body risks ridicule, as does a slender man with "fine" features who doesn't avoid effeminate gestures and clothing (Crawley, Foley, and Shehan, 2007).

The overall point of this section is that physical variation is real, but to categorize all humans into two distinct, nonoverlapping, "opposite" categories requires that we ignore many aspects of this variation and assume that socially constructed definitions of what males and females are "supposed to be" in physical terms are biologically valid (Butler, 2004). When this assumption is made in sports, gender equity becomes difficult, if not impossible, to achieve.

Being "Out of Bounds": A Challenge for GLBITs   A major problem created by a two-category classification model is it causes people to have relatively fixed ideas and beliefs about the ways that males and females are supposed to think, feel, and act. Further, it leads to the assumption that heterosexuality is natural and normal and that those who express feelings, thoughts, and actions that cannot be classified into the categories of heterosexual masculinity or heterosexual femininity are innatural and abnormal and therefore "out of bounds" when it comes to gender (review figure 8.2).

When gender ideology is based on this model, gay men, lesbians, bisexuals, intersexuals, and transsexuals are gender-nonconforming people who are socially positioned outside or between the accepted two categories. In other words, a two-category model provides no legitimate social space or recognition for gender nonconformists. This, in turn, fosters homophobic responses to anyone who isn't clearly classifiable as a heterosexual male or female (Vitello, 2006). This is not surprising because many people fear things that don't make sense in terms of their view of the world—and the only two sex and gender categories that make sense to many people are heterosexual male and heterosexual female.

Power in Society: Gender Ideology in Action   Another important aspect of a two-category model is that the categories are seldom defined as being equal in social, cultural, or physical terms. For example, as represented in figure 8.2, males have access to higher levels of privilege, power, and influence than females have, and men occupy the highest levels of power and influence in greater numbers than women do. This structure benefits men relative to women, and it also means that men have a greater stake in preserving the two-category approach to sex and gender and making sure that other men do not push or cross the gender boundary that separates "real heterosexual men" from all women and from men who are "out of gender bounds" in their view.

To the extent that boys and men learn this approach, they maintain more tightly defined and restrictive normative boundaries associated with masculinity than most women maintain in connection with femininity or that GLBITs maintain in connection with most normative boundaries based on a two-category model of sex and gender. After all, if boys and men want to retain their greater access to positions of power and influence, they must do two things: (1) promote the belief that power and influence are legitimately linked with characteristics that are defined as masculine, and (2) maintain the boundaries of masculinity so that boys and men learn, value,

and accept those characteristics as a basis for their feelings, thoughts, and actions. This is why men strictly police their gender boundaries and punish or reject those who push or move outside them. Women, on the other hand, have less to lose and more to gain in terms of power and influence if they push or blur boundaries. Therefore girls and women have more latitude or permission to exhibit a wider range of feelings, thoughts, and actions than boys and men have, although they too must be sensitive to gender boundaries if they wish to avoid sanctions (Orenstein, 2008).

This is why boys are teased for being "sissies," whereas girls are usually praised for being "tomboys." It's also why figure skating or synchronized swimming aren't as attractive to boys and men as ice hockey and water polo are to girls and women (Laberge and Albert, 1999).

OLC **ON THE *OLC:***

See the OLC—Additional Readings for Chapter 8—for an example of men policing gender boundaries more carefully than women police them.

Gender ideology is changing. However, when men or women become seriously involved in sports that challenge the two-category sex and gender classification model, some people may tease or discourage them.

Challenging Gender Ideology: Blurring the Old Boundaries   Not everyone accepts the boundaries or conforms to the norms based on a two-category gender classification model. The double arrows that intersect normative boundaries in figure 8.2 represent efforts by men and women to push, bend, blur, and erase normative boundaries, or escape their constraints. Of course, women do more pushing and bending than men do, but there always are potential costs associated with challenging gender boundaries (except on Halloween!). However, as boundary pushers and gender benders raise critical issues they may encourage some people to critically assess definitions of *masculinity* and *femininity*. Under certain conditions, this can alter normative boundaries so that men and/or women face fewer gender constraints on their feelings, thoughts, and actions. But changes usually come slowly because so many people use the two-category model as a guide for perceiving and making sense of themselves, their relationships, and the world around them.

Gender Ideology in Sports

Ideas and beliefs about gender are a crucial part of the foundation on which sports are organized, promoted, and played. Sports are sites for reaffirming beliefs about male–female *difference* and valorizing masculine characteristics (Messner, 2007b). Consequently, women's sports may not be seen as "real" or as good as men's sports; similarly, female athletes may be seen as deviant when they push, blur, or bend the boundaries of heterosexual femininity. But sports also are sites for challenging and revising gender ideology—a fact that makes it interesting to study gender when analyzing sports in society.

Celebrating Masculinity   Because gender is not fixed in nature, gender ideology is preserved only if people police gender boundaries and maintain them through myths, rituals, and everyday cultural practices. In other words, people must *perform* gender in conformity with the two-category model to keep the model viable.

Gender ideology is most effectively maintained when gender categories become embodied aspects of people's lives—a foundation for people as they experience the world with and through their bodies (Fenstermaker and West, 2002). This is why sports are so socially relevant: they offer forms of movement that reproduce or challenge a very important organizing principle on which much of the status quo rests (Messner, 2002).

Sports are generally sites for preserving gender ideology. The meaning of gender and its application in people's lives are symbolized and powerfully presented in the bodily performances that occur in sports. For example, many people use men's achievements in power and performance sports as evidence of men's aggressive nature, their superiority over women, and their rights to claim social and physical space as their turf. Sociologist Doug Hartmann explains:

> [Sport] makes male advantages and masculine values appear so normal and "natural" that they can hardly be questioned. Therein may lie the key to the puzzle connecting men and the seemingly innocent world of sports: they fit together so tightly, so seamlessly that they achieve their effects—learning to be a man, male bonding, male authority, and the like—without seeming to be doing anything more than tossing a ball or watching a Sunday afternoon game. (2003b, p. 20)

This explanation helps us understand why Bruce Kidd (1987) describes sports stadiums and domed arenas as "men's cultural centers." These facilities, often built with public funds, host events that present a manhood based on aggression, physical power, and the ability to intimidate and dominate others. Therefore, the sports that are played in them generally reproduce a particular gender ideology that privileges men and favors a particular form of manhood (Barnes, 2006).

Female Athletes as Invaders   When girls and women play certain sports, they may be seen as invaders of male turf. Traditionally, "women's sports" have been those that emphasize grace, beauty, and coordination (Hart, 1981). In fact, during much of the twentieth century, women

Traditional gender ideology is reproduced in many men's sports. Some of those sports provide a vocabulary and a set of symbols and stories that erase diverse and contradictory masculinities and present a homogenized manhood in which the heroic warrior is the model of a real man (Burystn, 1999). For boys this can inspire fantasies in which playing the role of warrior and superhero is the substance of being a man. (*Source:* Jay Coakley)

were told by medical experts that playing strenuous sports would damage their uteruses and breasts and endanger their abilities to give birth and nurture children. Today's college students laugh at these myths because they know about research that refutes them. However, people who lack access to this research may use gendered myths to guide their personal decisions and public policies related to sports and sport

OLC ON THE *OLC*:

See the OLC—Additional Readings for Chapter 8—for the author's essay on myths about the consequences of vigorous exercise on the bodies of women and their relationships with men.

participation. This is especially true in cultures where literacy rates are low and men control the production and distribution of knowledge.

When female athletes push, blur, and bend the boundaries of gender, they inspire some people and threaten others, and they're described as both ideal role models and invaders. For example, when golf superstar Annika Sorenstam became the first woman to compete on the traditionally male-only PGA Tour, she was described favorably by some people, whereas others objected and sided with a male pro golfer who saw Sorenstam as an invader and declared, "I'll do what men do, and she should do what women do"—which is to play with women only (*Newsweek*, 2004, p. 122). Sorenstam ignored his comment and beat him by three strokes in the tournament, showing that his assumptions about sex and gender were inconsistent with the facts. Similarly, when golfer Michelle Wie played in her first men's tournament in 2005, an analyst for the Golf Channel wondered if her presence would turn the PGA into "a freak show" (Kensler, 2005).

These cases involve golf, a sport not known as a "men's sport." The tendency to perceive girls and women as invaders increases when they become involved in baseball, wrestling, boxing, football, and other sports that some men use as sites for establishing and expressing their masculinity. Former Stanford basketball player, Mariah Burton Nelson discussed this issue in 1994 when she wrote a controversial book titled, *The Stronger Women Get, The More Men Love Football*. Her point was that women who are strong athletes threaten everyone who uses the two-category model of gender, and this forces them to use football (and other heavy contact and conquest sports) as "proof" that men and women are clearly different and that men are superior to women. Interestingly, every year since 1994 has shown women athletes to be stronger and stronger, and all indicators of football's popularity in the United States have increased in each of those years. The irony: women's invasion of sports has increased the popularity of football! But this irony can be explained in connection with the dynamics associated with gender ideology.

Of course, many girls and women who play previously identified "men's sports" don't want to be seen as invaders. After all, invaders are usually resisted, attacked, and harmed, as when

Katie Hnida became a kicker on the University of Colorado football team in 1999. She was mocked and ridiculed by teammates who also sexually taunted her and exposed their genitals to her with threatening comments. After being physically mistreated on the field, raped by a teammate presenting himself as a "sensitive friend," and discredited by the coach and athletic director, she became fearful and depressed and dropped out of school. After two years of therapy, she enrolled at the University of New Mexico, made the football team and became the first woman in big-time college football to score points in a game (Hnida, 2006; Reilly, 2004a).

To avoid being labeled as invaders, some girls and women try to be more feminine by referring to themselves as "ladies" and wearing heterosexualized "femininity insignias" such as hair ribbons, ponytails, makeup, dresses, hose, heels, and engagement or wedding rings. When interviewed, they may say how they like to party at clubs (where other heterosexuals party) and talk about boyfriends or husbands and their desire to eventually settle down and have children—like "normal" women.

The dynamics of this process, referred to as the "female apologetic," are especially apparent among female bodybuilders who often are required to wear femininity insignias to offset the fact that their bodies clearly blur, bend, and even erase gender boundaries when it comes to accepted ideas about muscles. Expressions of the female apologetic vary by the age of the athletes, but many girls and women feel a need to combine the "girly girl" and "sporty girl" personas in some way (Cooky, 2004).

OLC ON THE *OLC*:

See the OLC—Additional Readings for Chapter 8—for the author's summary of data on the annual increases in the popularity of football every year since 1994, and evidence of women athletes who have blurred and bent gender boundaries related to strength during those years.

OLC ON THE *OLC*:

See the OLC—Additional Readings for Chapter 8—for the author's essay on women's bodybuilding and its connection with femininity

The most direct and insulting indication that strong women were seen as (alien) invaders in sports were the "fem tests" they were required to take from the mid-1960s through the late-1990s. These tests, approved by the IOC and most other male-dominated/identified/centered sport organizations, made women athletes prove they were women (see www.pponline.co.uk/encyc/0082.htm; AMA, 1996). The assumption underlying the test was that if a girl or woman was really good in sports, she might not be a real girl or woman! This test was an improvement over stripping naked for a panel of doctors as they had been forced to do previously, but clearly humiliating (Genel, 2000).

Many female athletes objected to these tests, and many rule-making organizations in sports eliminated them in the mid-1990s. However, all 3500 female athletes at the 1996 Olympic Games in Atlanta were required to take the test or show their "fem card" from a previous test to certify they were "real" women. The IOC continued testing through 1999 but dropped it before the 2000 Sydney Games in response to protests and research that challenged the test's validity. The organizers of the 2008 Olympic Games in Beijing set up a "gender test lab" where they drew blood samples from female athletes whose appearance was "suspect" (Boylan, 2008; Thomas, 2008b). But this received very little attention from the press, even though only one athlete in Olympic history has ever been identified as a gender fraud (Boylan, 2008; Thomas, 2008).

Traditional gender ideology and associated expressions of homophobia continue to exist, but their consequences are not perceived by all girls and women in sports. Furthermore, the recent achievements of female athletes have challenged certain ideas and beliefs about gender and encouraged some people to think in new ways about masculinity, femininity, and gender

> Gender is much more than a biochemical construct. It's bizarre to think you can determine whether someone is male or female based on [lab] tests. — Andrew Pipe, former president of the Canadian Academy of Sports Medicine and chair of the Canadian Center for Ethics in Sport (in Lehrman, 1997).

relations (Caudwell, 2006; Theberge, 2000a). When this type of reassessment occurs, women's sports are important sites for pushing the normative boundaries of *femininity*.

Gender Ideology: Challenges Faced by GLBITs in Sports

When a two-category classification model is used to identify sex and define *gender*, the identities and actions of gay men, lesbians, bisexuals, intersexuals, and transsexuals (GLBITs) are outside normative boundaries (refer to figure 8.2, page 259). Therefore, GLBITs are sometimes feared, marginalized, or seen as abnormal, immoral, or both. They may be harassed and, in extreme cases, physically attacked (Smith, 2005b; Wertheim, 2005).

Discussions about the identities and lives of GLBITs sometimes evoke strong emotions, defensive reactions, and moral judgments. Exceptions to this exist when people don't accept the two-category model and define *gender* in terms that reflect the realities of people's identities and lives.

The same is true in sports. GLBITs play sports, but any acknowledgment of their sexual identities is carefully avoided. This indicates that many people have mixed or confused feelings about sexual identities that don't correspond directly with heterosexual masculinity or femininity. For example, a 2005 survey of a nationally representative sample of Americans indicated that 78 percent of adults agreed that "It is OK for gay athletes to participate in sports, even if they are open about their sexuality" (NBC/USA Network, 2005). But about one in four said that openly gay athletes would hurt their teams and sport and would turn them off as fans. Forty-four percent agreed that homosexual behavior was a sin, half said that media coverage of gay athletes would cause negative reactions, over 60 percent agreed that "America is not ready to accept gay athletes," and nearly 70 percent said that being openly gay would hurt an athlete's career. Additionally, about 40 percent of youth sport coaches and 20 percent of college and professional coaches thought it was inappropriate for homosexuals to work in sports!

These data obscure the fact that acceptance of gay men and lesbians has increased in society *and* in sports (Anderson, 2000, 2002, 2005). Today, there are teams and sport programs in which they are accepted and supported by heterosexual athletes and coaches, and there are more teams and programs exclusively for those with sexualities that are not clearly heterosexual (Elling, de Knop, and Knoppers, 2003). But significant challenges remain for lesbian and gay athletes; even when acceptance occurs, it often is on terms set by heterosexual others (Anderson, 2002). Therefore, many gay and lesbian athletes remain closeted, pass as heterosexual, or selectively reveal their identity to trusted others and in situations where their sexuality is accepted (Griffin, 1998). Because of varying levels of acceptance, identity management strategies often differ between athletes in women's and men's sports.

The challenges faced by intersexuals and transgendered persons have been studied only recently, and data are scarce.[3] Ann Travers (2006) has studied lesbian softball leagues throughout North America and investigated the tensions around policies that allowed or excluded the participation of transgendered persons. She found that because many lesbians view sex in terms of two categories, they were uncertain about allowing someone to play who didn't clearly fit in either one. Travers also explains that some leagues and tournaments use a policy based on

standards developed and approved by the IOC in 2003. This policy indicates that adults are eligible to play in their chosen gender category if they meet one of two conditions:

1. Present a letter from a certified medical practitioner who states that the person has been actively involved in sex-reassignment hormone treatment for a minimum of two full years, or
2. Provide proof that one has lived as the self-identified gender for a minimum of two years

Although this decision assumes a two-category model of sex and gender, it recognizes that both sex and gender are changeable. This is a significant new standard that now applies worldwide in international sports (Cavanagh and Sykes, 2006).

Not yet studied in the sociology of sport are the intersexed—that is, people born with some combination of male and female anatomical, physiological, or chromosomal characteristics (Preves, 2005). Many parents and physicians today do not alter the physical traits of intersexed infants, preferring to allow the person to choose what should be done when the age of informed consent is reached. I've not heard of anyone questioning the participation of an intersexed child in a youth sport league, but if it occurs, it will force people to deal with the real diversity of nature rather than using two socially constructed sex categories to classify all human beings. In the absence of sex reassignment treatment, how is an intersexed person to be included in sports?

Lesbians in Sports Acceptance of gender-nonconforming athletes is greater in women's than men's sports. When the first high-profile female athletes came out as lesbians in the 1980s, they were the focus of praise, hostility, and endless media discussions and debates. As other elite female athletes come out today, they face short-term media attention, some negative

---

[3]See the OLC for definitions and explanations of these terms. See also Pat Grifffin's discussion of issues faced by gender nonconforming people at http://www.womenssports-foundation.org/cgi-bin/iowa/issues/itat/news/?record=1076. The IOC policy can be seen at http://www.olympic .org/uk/includes/common/article_print_uk.asp?id=841

reactions from fans and other athletes, and the personal challenges that most women face when they come out with friends and family (Barnes, 2006). But they're also likely to find people who will support them, even if some corporations are hesitant to sign them to endorsement contracts (Swoopes, 2005).

> **OLC ON THE *OLC*:**
> See the OLC—Additional Readings for Chapter 8—for an essay on the feelings of a girl who didn't "fit" within the two-category model of gender.

Pat Griffin's groundbreaking book *Strong Women, Deep Closets: Lesbians and Homophobia in Sports* (1998) provides clear evidence that "sports and lesbians have always gone together" (p. ix). She notes that this evidence has been ignored in the popular consciousness, largely because of cultural myths about lesbians. Although most myths have been challenged and discredited, some people continue to believe them. For example, some think that lesbians are predatory and want to "convert" others to their "way of life," which is imagined to be depressing and immoral. When lesbian athletes perceive that people think this way, they often turn inward and experience isolation and loneliness. When heterosexual athletes believe these myths or even wonder about their veracity, they fear and/or avoid lesbian athletes and coaches; when coaches and administrators believe them, they're less likely to hire and promote lesbians in coaching and sport management.

Some women's sports and teams are characterized by a "don't ask, don't tell" atmosphere in which lesbians hide their identity to play the sports they love without being marginalized or harassed. However, this strategy has costs, and it

Being a gay icon is a great honor for me. I'm quite sure of my feminine side. —David Beckham (in Wahl, 2003)

doesn't encourage changes that might defuse or erase homophobia in women's sports. Overall, a "don't ask, don't tell" approach affects both heterosexual women and lesbians, all of whom restrain their actions to avoid suspicions or being labeled as lesbians.

Griffin encourages people to be open and truthful about sexual identity, but she explains that lesbians must be prepared to handle everything from hostility to cautious acceptance when they come out. She points out that handling challenges is easier (a) when friends, teammates, and coaches provide support; (b) when there are local organizations that challenge homophobia and advocate tolerance; and (c) when there is institutionalized legal protection and support for gays and lesbians in organizations, communities, and society.

Gay Men in Sports Changes related to attitudes about homosexuality have not been as significant in men's sports as in women's sports. The culture of many men's sports continues to support a vocabulary of exclusion, marginalization, and homophobia. However, this does not always predict the regularly supportive responses of many heterosexual athletes when a teammate comes out (Anderson, 2005; Bull, 2004). Men's sports have always been key sites for celebrating and reproducing dominant ideas about heterosexual masculinity. Playing certain sports has been a rite of passage for boys to become men, and male athletes in contact and power sports are held up as models of heterosexual manhood in society. Therefore, there is much at stake in maintaining the silence about gay men in sports and discouraging gay male athletes from revealing their identities. This is necessary to maintain the integrity of existing normative gender boundaries and the privilege that is available to some men as long as the two-category model is widely accepted and used (Pronger, 1999, 2002). Policing gender boundaries in and through men's sports preserves the glorified status of male athletes and men's access to power and influence in society as a whole.

Because of these dynamics, the message to boys and men in sports is loud and clear: "Don't be a fag," and "don't play like a girl." The message to gay males of all ages is also clear: "Don't challenge the two-category gender classification model because it works for us men and has given some of us power and privilege in sports and society." When combined, these messages create commitment to the cult of masculinity and a fear of homosexuality in men's sports (Anderson, 2005; Tuaolo, 2002).

These messages also create a context in which boys and men resist or feel ashamed of their feelings of affection toward other men. In the process, they may mimic violent caricatures of masculinity to avoid being labeled "fags" (Messner, 1996). Consequently, connections between male athletes are expressed through bell-ringing head-butts, belly bashers, arm punches, forearm crosses, fist bumping, and other ritualistic actions that disguise intimacy (Barnes, 2006).

The power of gender ideology among male athletes is illustrated with a simple example: The first man to come out as gay in a major men's team sport will be guaranteed a spot in sport history. He will be seen as a hero by closeted and openly gay men of all ages. He will be on every talk show on television and radio. His website will receive millions of hits. Corporations that market to the gay demographic will offer endorsement deals. He will be an overnight celebrity and eventually defined as a hero in the company of Jackie Robinson, Muhammad Ali, and others who stood up for a principle that would later be taken for granted in the culture as a whole.

So why hasn't an active, high-profile athlete come out of the closet? Research by sociologist Eric Anderson (2005), who in 1993 was the first openly gay male high school coach in the United States, indicates that all male athletes, including gays, have learned to see themselves in strict ideological terms and conform to the norms of hegemonic masculinity in cultlike ways, even

when they would benefit by leaving the cult. This explanation highlights the point that problems for gay athletes are ultimately grounded in a sport culture organized around a two-category gender classification model. Therefore, solutions rest in finding strategies to change gender ideology and the ways that we do sports.

Strategies for Changing Ideology and Culture

Gender equity ultimately depends on transforming gender ideology and changing the ways we do sports in society. These are complex and challenging tasks.

Alternative Definitions of Masculinity   Dominant gender ideology naturalizes the idea that masculinity is associated with aggression and a desire to physically dominate others. Men with the power and willingness to do whatever it takes to dominate others are defined as heroes in sports, business, and politics. Men who are seen as nurturing and supportive of others are defined as effeminate and unmanly.

As boys and men apply this ideology to their lives, they learn to view manhood in terms of things that jeopardize the safety and well-being of themselves and others. They may ride the tops of elevators, drive cars at breakneck speeds, play various forms of "chicken," drink each other under the table, get into fights, use violence in sports as indicators of manhood, use dangerous substances to build muscles, avoid interacting with women as equals, keep sexual scores in heterosexual relationships, and physically control girlfriends and wives. Some men even learn that size and toughness allow them to violate norms and control others through fear and physical coercion.

Despite the dangers and socio-emotional isolation caused by this ideology, male athletes are seldom criticized for using it to guide their words and actions in sports. Coaches want athletes who can hurt others without hesitation or remorse and define it "as part of the game." But in the larger social and cultural context, does this ideology destroy men's ability to empathize with others and feel their pain, even the pain of opponents? Does it discourage the development of intimate and supportive relationships with other men or with women? Does it lead to high rates of assault and sexual assault in society?

The frightening record of men's violence suggests that it would be useful to answer these questions and create new cultural space for alternative definitions of masculinity. The dual notion that "boys will be boys" and that men's lives are shaped by testosterone continues to be closely associated with seriously dangerous actions worldwide. Joe Ehrmann, a former NFL player and currently a successful high school coach, challenged these

ideas on his football team by defining masculinity in terms of forming relationships and in connection with "the capacity to love and be loved" (in Marx, 2004, p. 4). Ehrmann wants to create with his players a new form of masculinity organized around empathy, inclusion, and integrity. This, he says, would enable his players to become effective agents of progressive change as adults.

Alternative Definitions of Femininity The experiences of many female athletes also suggest a need for alternative definitions of *femininity*. Additionally, research suggests that parents and other adults tend to monitor the bodies and actions of girls more closely than they do for boys, even during infancy (Fredrickson and

Hundreds of roller derby teams have been formed as women seek new sport experiences. The athletes on these teams embrace a wide array of ideas and beliefs about femininity, and many of them are gender nonconformers who reject a two-category model of gender. Derby teams and derby bouts are sites where alternative definitions of femininity presented to spectators. (*Source:* Daniel K Photography; www.danielkphoto.com)

Harrison, 2005; Young, 1990). This pattern of protectiveness often limits the range of physical skill development and sport participation among many girls. Alternative definitions of femininity are needed to reduce this monitoring of girls, thereby encouraging them to explore and connect with the power of their bodies across many activities, including competitive sports.

OLC   ON THE *OLC*:
See the OLC—Additional Readings for Chapter 8—for an essay on the "conditional permissions" that girls sometimes receive when it comes to playing informal games and pick-up sports

---

Sports today constitute ideal contexts in which large and strong girls and women who don't possess traditionally feminine characteristics can challenge gender ideologies. In the process, they serve as models for new femininities that recognize and support women whose physicality and view of themselves are not supported by traditional notions of femininity (Migliaccio and Berg, 2008).

Changing the Way We Do Sports   Gender equity involves more than creating new ways to define and portray masculinity and femininity. It also requires changes in the ways that sports are defined, organized, and played. New and creative sport programs, new vocabularies to describe sports, new images that people can associate with sports, and new ways to evaluate success and enjoyment in sports are the foundation of such changes (Burstyn, 1999; Hargreaves, 2000). When women and men who participate in sports as athletes, coaches, and administrators can critically assess sports and sport organizations from the inside, changes are more likely to occur (see Chapter 16).

One strategy for achieving gender equity is to develop new programs that change how we do sports. Possibilities include the following:

1. Programs that promote lifetime sport participation and emphasize combinations of competition and partnership, individual expression and teamwork, and health and skill development
2. Programs that embody an ethic of care and promote personal connections between teammates and opponents (Duquin, 2000)
3. Programs that provide coaching and administrative opportunities for gender-nonconforming people, thereby adding new voices in decision-making processes, expanding ideas about the organization and purpose of sports, and opening sports to a wider range of participants
4. Programs that bring together boys and girls, men and women, and heterosexuals and GLBITs in shared sport experiences that promote new ideas about gender and sports in society

New programs are useful, but strategies to effect change must also take into account the political challenges that are associated with creating new ways to do sports. These include the following:

1. When women's sport programs are structured differently from men's programs, it is difficult to determine whether there are equal opportunities for girls and women.
2. New and different sport programs for girls and women run the risk of being perceived as "second-class," thereby perpetuating notions of female inferiority.
3. New sport programs are difficult to promote, and it is easier to apply pressure for equal resources in schools and other organizations when asking for comparable programs rather than new and different ones.
4. Sports that do not reproduce dominant gender ideology often are devalued, defined

as "not real," and are (under)funded accordingly.

In the long run, achieving gender equity requires a dual approach: creating new and different sports as well as expanding opportunities and gaining power in established sports. Changes will occur if people currently in positions of power and influence envision and create alternatives for the future, *and* if those who envision new forms of sport gain access to power and resources so they can develop new and different programs.

All of us participate in ideological and cultural change when we critically assess how we talk about and do sports. This occurs when we avoid using labels such as *sissy*, *tomboy*, *fag*, and *wimp* in conversations, object to coaches who motivate young men by telling them to go out and prove their masculinity on the playing field, speak out against language that bashes GLBITs and demeans women, and avoid using military metaphors that further masculinize sports (for example, "throwing long bombs," "he/she is a warrior," "putting in the big guns," and "punishing opponents").

Overall, gender equity depends on doing sports inclusively. There is no need to make all sports match the ones played by men who are fascinated by domination and conquest. Full equity means that all people have a wide range of choices when it comes to organizing, playing, and giving meaning to sports.

summary

DOES EQUITY REQUIRE IDEOLOGICAL CHANGES?

Sport participation among girls and women has increased dramatically since the late 1970s. This change is the result of new opportunities, equal rights legislation, the women's movement, the health and fitness movement, and increased publicity given to female athletes.

Despite recent increases in participation, gender equity is far from being achieved, and future increases in participation rates will not be automatic. The reasons to be cautious when anticipating more changes in the future include budget cuts and privatization of sports, resistance to government policies and legislation, backlash in response to changes favoring strong women, a relative lack of female coaches and administrators, a cultural emphasis on cosmetic fitness among women, the trivialization of women's sports, and the existence of homophobia.

More women than ever are playing sports and working in sport organizations, but gender inequities continue to exist in participation opportunities, support for athletes, jobs for women in coaching and administration, and informal and alternative sports. These inequities persist because sports have traditionally been organized to be male dominated, male identified, and male centered.

Even when sport participation creates feelings of personal empowerment among women, the achievement of full gender equity is impossible without a critical analysis of the gender ideology used in sports and society. Critical analysis is important because it gives direction to efforts to achieve equity and it shows that there are reasons for men to join women in trying to achieve equity.

The major point of this chapter is that gender equity in sports is integrally tied to ideology and power issues. Full equity will not be achieved without changes in how people think about masculinity and femininity and in the ways that sports are organized and played.

Dominant sport forms in society are currently based on a two-category gender classification model, which leads to the conclusion that girls and women are by definition inferior to boys and men. Gender ideology based on this classification model is organized around ideas and beliefs about male–female differences and the "natural" superiority of men over women. These ideas and beliefs also marginalize gay men, lesbians, bisexuals, the intersexed, and transsexuals and erase their existence in sports. Therefore, sports celebrate a form of masculinity that marginalizes women and many men. As this form of masculinity is celebrated through sports, sexism and homophobia come to be integrated into the structure of sports and sport organizations.

When gender ideology and sports are organized around the values and experiences of heterosexual men, real and lasting gender equity depends on changing dominant definitions of masculinity and femininity and the way we do sports. Useful strategies include developing new sports and sport organizations and changing existing sports from the inside and through outside actions and pressure. Changes also depend on using new ways to talk about sports. Until gender ideology and sports change, full gender equity will not be achieved.

WEBSITE RESOURCES

Note: Websites often change. The following URLs were current when this book was printed. Please check our website (www.mhhe.com/coakley10e) for updates and additions.

www.mhhe.com/coakley10e Click on chapter 8 for a discussion of cheerleaders, myths about the impact of strenuous exercise on women, and other gender issues.

www.aahperd.org/nagws/ The National Association for Girls and Women in Sport actively advances gender equity in U.S. schools; the site provides information on Title IX.

www.feminist.org/sports/ The Feminist Majority Foundation provides links to many sites and resources on gender equity in sports at all levels of participation.

www.gssf.co.nr/ This is the site of the Gender Sport and Society Forum, an online project dedicated to scholars and students with an interest in all social issues related to gender and sport; the site is maintained by Emma Rich of Loughborough University in England and includes an excellent bibliography and many other helpful resources.

www.iwg-gti.org The site of the International Working Group on Women and Sport contains information on programs, policy issues, and problems faced by girls and women in more than 100 nations.

http://raw.rutgers.edu/womenandsports/Websites/ A valuable gateway site for links to sites on women in sports.

www.savetitleix.com/ This site provides up-to-date information about challenges to Title IX and what is being done to resist them.

www.statusofwomen.ca.gov/doc.asp?id=640 Provides information on Title IX athletics compliance at California's public high schools, community colleges, and universities; written by Margaret Beam, Bonnie Faddis, and Patricia Ruzicka. Portland, RMC Corporation for the California Postsecondary Education Commission, March 22, 2004, 55 pages.

www.titleix.info/index.jsp The site of *I Exercise My Rights*, a public service, informational campaign that helps people understand the spirit and the legal letter of Title IX; includes links to descriptions of legal cases and other resources related to girls and women in sports.

http://webpages.charter.net/womeninsport/ This site contains R. Vivian Acosta and Linda Jean Carpenter's latest report on gender equity in U.S. universities; summary data is found on pages 252–253 in this chapter.

www.womenssportsfoundation.org/ The site of the Women's Sports Foundation, the most recognized sport organization for women in the United States; contains excellent links to many sites.

http://cehd.umn.edu/tuckercenter/ The Tucker Center for Research on Girls and Women in Sport lists references to research on gender and sports, including studies that focus specifically on homophobia and sport.

http://outsports.com/ Based in Los Angeles, Outsports.com provides a full range of information for the gay sports community, including links to current news and other stories about gays and lesbians in sports. If a professional athlete in one of the major men's team sports ever came out, it would be covered on this site.

www.womenssportsfoundation.org/Issues-And-Research/Homophobia.aspx It Takes A Team! Educational Campaign for Lesbian, Gay, Bisexual and Transgender Issues in Sport; an educational project with resources focused on eliminating homophobia as a barrier to all women and men participating in sport.

www.xtremecentral.com/WASN/WASNintro.htm The site of the Women's Aggressive Skating Network; designed to showcase "Outrageous Women Doing Incredible Things," and linked to http://www.bladegirlz.com/—a site for young women in extreme sports.

(Jay Coakley)

RACE AND ETHNICITY

Are They Important in Sports?

ATHLETES ARE LIMITING themselves by what they see
in the mirror. We become slaves to our stereotypes.
Athletes of all races commit the same error.

—**Mark Kiszla, sports columnist,** *Denver Post,*
2005

OLC Visit *Sports in Society*'s Online Learning Center (OLC) at www.mhhe.com/coakley10e for additional information and study material for this chapter, including the following:

- A complete chapter outline
- Learning objectives
- Practice quizzes
- Internet resources
- Related readings
- Essays
- Student projects

A GROUP OF SIXTH GRADERS tied me to a tree, spray-painted the word "nigger" on me, and threw rocks at me. That was my first day of school [as a 5-year-old]. And the teacher really didn't do much of anything.

—**Tiger Woods, pro golfer (in Barkley, 2006)**

JUST AS JEWS, ASIANS AND ITALIANS have used sports to break down racial barriers, Mexican Americans have challenged stereotypes through their performances on the field.

—**Jeff Stoughton journalist,2005**

I'M PROUD THAT I'M FULLY KOREAN, and that I'm fully American. I want to represent hope, the belief that it can happen.

——**Michelle Wie, pro golfer (in Adelson, 2006)**

Sports involve complex racial and ethnic issues, and their relevance has increased as global migration and political changes bring together people from many racial and ethnic backgrounds. The challenges created by racial and ethnic diversity are among the most important ones that we face as we live, work, and play together in the twenty-first century (Edwards, 2000).

Ideas and beliefs about race and ethnicity traditionally influence self-perceptions, social relationships, and the organization of social life. Sports reflect this influence and are sites where people challenge or reproduce racial ideologies and existing patterns of racial and ethnic relations in society. As people make sense of sports and give meaning to their experiences and observations, they often take into account their beliefs about skin color and ethnicity. The once-popular statement, "White men can't jump," is an example of this.

Not surprisingly, the social meanings and the experiences associated with skin color and ethnic background influence access to sport participation, decisions about playing sports, the ways that people integrate sports into their lives, and the organization and sponsorship of sports. People in some racial and ethnic groups use sport participation to express their cultural identity and evaluate their potential as athletes. In some cases, people are identified and evaluated as athletes, coaches, or media commentators based on the meanings given to their skin color or ethnic background. Sports also are cultural sites where people formulate or change ideas and beliefs about skin color and ethnic heritage.

This means that sports are more than mere reflections of racial and ethnic relations in society: they're sites where racial and ethnic relations occur and change. Therefore, the depth of our understanding of sports in society depends on what we know about race and ethnicity in various social worlds.

This chapter focuses on the following topics:

1. Definitions of *race* and *ethnicity*, as well as the origins of ideas about race in cultures today
2. Racial classification systems and the influence of racial ideology in sports

3. Sport participation patterns among racial and ethnic minorities in the United States
4. The dynamics of racial and ethnic relations in sports

DEFINING *RACE* AND *ETHNICITY*

Discussions about race and ethnicity are confusing when people fail to define their terms. In this chapter, **race** refers to *a population of people who are believed to be naturally or biologically distinct from other populations*. Race exists only when people use a classification system that divides all human beings into distinct categories, which are believed to share genetically-based physical traits passed from one generation to the next. Racial categories are developed around the meanings that people give to real or assumed physical traits that they use to characterize a racial population.

Ethnicity is different from race in that it refers to *a cultural heritage that people use to identify a particular population*. Ethnicity is *not* based on biology or genetically determined traits; instead, it is based on cultural traditions and history. This means that an **ethnic population** is *a category of people regarded as socially distinct because they share a way of life, a collective history, and a sense of themselves as a people*.

Confusion sometimes occurs when people use the term *minority* as they talk about racial or ethnic populations. In sociological terms, a **minority** is *a socially identified population that suffers disadvantages due to systematic discrimination and has a strong sense of social togetherness based on shared experiences of past and current discrimination*. Therefore, *not all* minorities are racial or ethnic populations, and *not all* racial or ethnic populations are minorities. For example, whites in the United States often are identified as a race, but they would not be a minority unless another racial or ethnic population had the power to subject them to systematic discrimination that would collectively disadvantage whites as a population category in American society. Similarly, Polish people in Chicago are considered an ethnic population, but not a minority. Mexican Americans, on the other hand, are an ethnic population that is a minority because of past and current discrimination experienced by people with a Mexican heritage.

African Americans often are referred to as a race because of the meanings that people have given to skin color in the United States; additionally, they are referred to as an ethnic group because of their shared cultural heritage. This has led many people to use *race* and *ethnicity* interchangeably without acknowledging that one is based on a *classification of physical traits* and the other on *the existence of a shared culture*. Sociologists attempt to avoid this conceptual confusion by using the term "race" only to refer to the social meanings that people have given to physical traits. These meanings, they say, have been so influential in society that shared ways of life have developed around them. Therefore, many sociologists today focus on ethnicity rather than race, except when they study the social consequences of widespread ideas and beliefs about skin color.

This information about race confuses many people who have been socialized to take for granted that race is a biological reality. To be told that race is based on social meanings rather than biological facts is difficult to accept until they learn about the origins of the concept of race and the development and the use of racial ideologies in various societies.

CREATING RACE AND RACIAL IDEOLOGIES

Physical and cultural diversity is a fact of life, and people throughout history have categorized one another, often using physical appearance and cultural characteristics to do so. However, the idea that there are distinct, identifiable races is a recent invention. Europeans developed it during the seventeenth century as they explored the world and encountered people who looked and lived unlike anything they'd ever known. As they colonized regions on nearly every continent, Europeans developed classification systems to distinguish the populations that they encountered. They used the term *race* very loosely to refer to people with particular religious beliefs (Hindus), language or ethnic traditions (the Basque people in Spain), histories (indigenous peoples such as New World "Indians" and "Aborigines"), national origins (Chinese), and social status (chronically poor people, such as Gypsies in Europe or the Untouchables in India).

> ## ON THE *OLC:*
> See the OLC—Additional Readings for Chapter 9—for a summary of current knowledge about race and quotes from scientists who have produced this knowledge.

More specific ideas about race emerged in connection with religious beliefs, scientific theories, and a combination of political and economic goals (Fredrickson, 2003; Omi and Winant, 1994, Winant, 2001, 2004, 2006). And over time, people in many societies have come to use the term *race* to identify populations that they believe are naturally or biologically distinct from other populations. This shift from a descriptive to a biology-based notion of race occurred as light-skinned people from northern Europe sought justification for colonizing and exercising power over people of color around the world. Intellectuals and scientists in the seventeenth though twentieth centuries facilitated this shift by developing appearance-based racial classification frameworks that enabled them to "discover" dozens of races, subraces, collateral races, and collateral subraces—terms that many scientists used as they analyzed the physical variations of people in colonized territories and other regions of the world.

Faulty "scientific" analyses combined with the observations and anecdotal stories told by explorers led to the development of racial ideologies. As noted in Chapter 1, **racial ideology** consists of *a web of ideas and beliefs that people use to give meaning to skin color and evaluate people in terms of racial* *classifications.* The racial classification models developed in Europe were based on the assumption that the appearance and actions of white Europeans were normal and that all deviations from European standards were strange, exotic, primitive, or immoral (Carrington, 2007; Carrington and McDonald, 2001). In this way, the "whiteness" of northern Europeans became a standard against which the appearance and actions of *others* ("*those people*") were measured and evaluated. In other words, the regions that were white-dominated also became white-identified and white-centered in a social and cultural sense.

From the eighteenth through much of the twentieth century, many whites used these racial ideologies to conclude that people of color around the world were primitive beings driven by brawn rather than brains, instincts rather than moral codes, and impulse rather than rationality. This way of thinking allowed whites to give themselves "moral permission" to colonize and subsequently exploit, subjugate, enslave, and even murder dark-skinned peoples without guilt or the sense that they had sinned in religious terms (Carrington, 2007; Carrington and McDonald, 2001; Fredrickson, 2003; Hoberman, 1992; PBS, 2006; Smedley, 1997, 1999; Winant, 2001, 2004, 2006). Some whites also used racial ideology to define people of color as pagans in need of spiritual salvation. These whites worked to "civilize" and save the souls of dark-skinned people to the point that white historians identified people of color as "the white man's burden." Over time, these racial ideologies became widely accepted, and whites used them to connect skin color with other traits including intelligence, character, and physical characteristics and skills; and in the United States, they were used to strip humanity from "black, red, and yellow" people.

Racial Ideology in the United States

Racial ideology in the United States is unique. It emerged during the seventeenth and eighteenth centuries as proslavery colonists developed justifications for enslaving Africans and treating them inhumanely. By the early nineteenth century, many whites believed that race was a mark of a person's humanity and moral worth. Africans and Indians, they concluded, were subhuman and incapable of being civilized. By nature, these "colored peoples" were socially, intellectually, and morally inferior to light-skinned Europeans—a fact that was accepted without question by most whites (Morgan, 1993; PBS, 2006; Smedley, 1997). This ideology became popular for three reasons.

First, as the need for political expansion became important to the newly formed United States, the (white) citizens and government officials who promoted westward territorial expansion used racial ideology to justify killing, capturing, and confining "Indians" to reservations.

Second, after the abolition of slavery, white Southerners used the "accepted fact" of black inferiority to justify hundreds of new laws that restricted the lives of "Negroes" and enforced racial segregation in all public settings; these were called Jim Crow laws (DuBois, 1935).

Third, scientists at prestigious universities, including Harvard, did research on race and published influential books and articles claiming to "prove" the existence of race, the "natural superiority" of whites, and the "natural inferiority" of blacks.

The acceptance of this ideology was so pervasive that the U.S. government established policies to remove Native Americans from valued lands, and in 1896 the U.S. Supreme Court ruled to legalize the segregation of people defined as "Negroes." The opinion of the court was that "if one race be inferior to the other socially, the Constitution of the United States cannot put them on the same plane" (U.S. Supreme Court, *Plessy* v. *Ferguson*, 1896). This ruling, even more than slavery, has influenced race relations from 1896 until today because it legitimized hundreds of laws, political policies, and patterns of racial segregation that connected whiteness with privilege, full citizenship, voting rights, and social-intellectual-moral superiority over people of color in the United States (Nobles, 2000).

As patterns of immigration changed between 1840 and 1920, people came to the United States from Ireland, southern Europe (Italy, Greece, Sicily), China, Japan, and Israel. At the same time, dominant racial ideology was used to link whiteness with one's identity as an American. Therefore, the question of who counted as white was often hotly debated as immigrant populations tried to claim American identities. For example, through the late 1800s and early 1900s, Irish, Jewish, Italian, Japanese, Chinese, and all Eastern European and Western Asian populations were considered to be nonwhite and, therefore, unqualified for U.S. citizenship. As some members of these ethnic populations objected to being classified as "colored" and denied citizenship, they took legal cases all the way to the Supreme Court to prove that they had ancestral links to "real" white people. It took some of these people many years to establish or prove their whiteness because whites with Western and Northern European backgrounds carefully maintained racial ideology to preserve their privilege in U.S. culture and society. The traditional belief that whiteness is a pure and innately special racial category has, through the twentieth century, created a deep cultural acceptance of racial segregation and inequality and strong political resistance to policies that are designed to address the racial and ethnic inequities that remain part of American society (Shapiro, 2004).

The Problem with Race and Racial Ideology

Research since the 1950s has produced overwhelming evidence that the concept of *race* is not biologically valid (Graves, 2002, 2004; Omi and Winant, 1994; PBS, 2006). This point has received powerful support from the Human Genome Project, which demonstrates that external traits such as skin color, hair texture, and eye shape are not genetically linked with patterns of internal differences among human beings. We now know that there is more biological diversity within any so-called racial population than there is between any two racial populations, no matter

how different they may seem on the surface (AAA, 1998; PBS, 2006; Williams, 2005).

Noted anthropologist Audrey Smedley (2003) explains that the idea of race has had a powerful impact on history and society, but it has little to do with real biological diversity among human beings. This is because the concept of *race* identifies categories and classifications that people use to explain the existence of social differences and inequalities in social worlds. In this sense, race is a biological myth based on socially created ideas about variations in human potential and abilities that are assumed to be biological.

This conclusion is surprising to most people in the United States because they've learned to "see" race as a fact of life and use it to sort people into what they believe to be biology-based categories. They've also used ideas and beliefs about race to make sense of the world and the experiences of various people. Racial ideology is so deeply rooted in U.S. culture that many people see race as an unchangeable fact of nature that cannot be ignored when it comes to understanding human beings, forming social relationships, and organizing social worlds.

To put biological notions of race aside requires a major shift in thinking for many people. This is difficult to do because it complicates the world and changes our sense of how it is organized and how it operates. But when we move beyond traditional racial ideology in the United States, we see that definitions of race and approaches to racial classification vary widely across cultures and over time. Thus, a person classified as black in the United States is not considered to be "black" in Brazil, Haiti, Egypt, or South Africa, where approaches to racial classification have been created under different social, cultural, and historical circumstances. For example, golfer Tiger Woods is classified as black in the U.S., Asian in Japan, and Thai in Thailand where his mother was born. Additionally, definitions of race have varied from one U.S. state to another through much of the twentieth century. This created confusion because people could be legally classified as black in one state but white in another; and to add to the confusion, definitions within states changed over time as social norms changed (Davis, 2001). These cultural and historical variations indicate that race is a social construction instead of a biological fact.

Another problem with *race* is that racial classification models force people to make clear racial distinctions on the basis of *continuous traits* such as skin color and other physical traits possessed to some degree by all human beings. Height is an example of a continuous physical trait: All humans have some height, although height measurements vary along a continuum from the shortest person in the world to the tallest. If we wanted to classify all human beings into particular height categories, we would have to decide where and how many lines we should draw along the height continuum. This could be done only if the people in charge of drawing the lines could develop shared agreements about the meanings associated with various heights. But the agreements made in one part of the world would likely vary from the agreements made in other parts of the world, depending on social and cultural factors that influenced the relevance of height. Therefore, in some societies a 5-foot, 10-inch-tall man would be classified as tall, whereas other societies might define "tall" as 6 feet, 5 inches or more. To make classification matters more complicated, people sometimes change their ideas about what they consider to be short or tall, as Americans have done through the twentieth century. Additionally, evidence clearly shows that the average height of people in different societies changes over time as diets, lifestyles, and height preferences change, even though height is a physical, genetically based trait (Bilger, 2004). This is why the Japanese now have an average height nearly the same as Americans, and northern Europeans have surpassed Americans in average height (Komlos and Lauderdale, 2007).

Like height, skin color also is a continuous physical trait. As illustrated in Figure 9.1, it varies from *snow white* at one end of the spectrum to *midnight black* on the other, with an infinite array of shades in between. When skin color is used to identify racial categories, the lines drawn to identify different races are based on the meanings given to skin color by the people who are doing the classifying. Therefore, the identification of races is based on social agreements about where and how many racial dividing lines to draw; it is not based on objectively identifiable biological division points. For example, racial classification in the United States was traditionally based on the "one-drop rule." This meant that any person with a black ancestor was classified as "Negro"

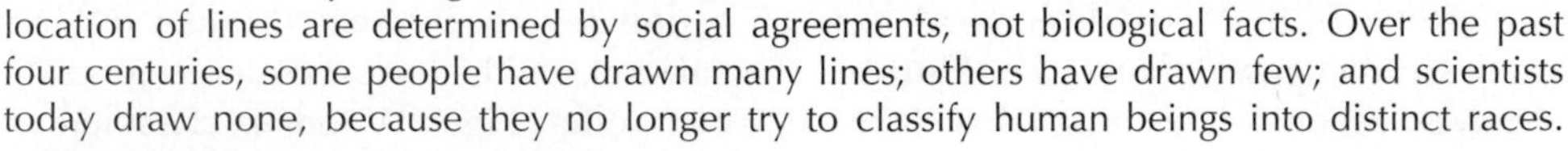

Snow white   Midnight black

Skin color continuum

Skin color is a continuous trait that varies from snow white to midnight black with a infinite number of skin tones in between. As with any continuous trait,* we can draw as many "racial category lines" as we choose and locate them anywhere on the continuum. We could draw 2 or more lines, depending on our ideas about "race." Our decisions about the number and location of lines are determined by social agreements, not biological facts. Over the past four centuries, some people have drawn many lines; others have drawn few; and scientists today draw none, because they no longer try to classify human beings into distinct races.

*Continuous traits are such things as height, weight, nose width or length, leg length or leg length to body height ratio, number of fast or slow twitch muscle fibers, brain size or weight—any trait that varies continuously from low to high or from a few to many.

FIGURE 9.1 Racial Ideology: Drawing Lines and Creating Categories.

(black) and could not be considered white in legal terms even if he or she appeared to be white, although some people with black ancestors "passed" as white. This approach to racial classification was based on decisions that white people made in an effort to perpetuate slavery, maintain the "purity" of the "white race," discourage white women from forming sexual relationships and having children with black men, deny interracial children legal access to the property of their white parent, and guarantee that white men would retain power and property in society (Davis, 2001). The uniquely American one-drop rule was based on a social agreement among white men, not on some deep biological significance of "black blood" or "white blood."

The problem with using the one-drop rule to define race is that "mixed-race" people are erased in history and sports. Additionally, it creates social and identity confusion. For example, when golfer Tiger Woods was identified as "black," he declared that he was "Cablinasian"—a term he invented to represent that he is one fourth Thai, one-fourth Chinese, one-fourth African American, one-eighth Native American, and one-eighth white European (Ca-bl-in-asian = *Ca*ucasian + *Bl*ack + *In*dian + *Asian*). However, when people use the one-drop rule, they ignore diverse ancestry and identify people as black if they are not "pure" white. This is why mixed-race persons in sports are described as black, even though a parent or multiple grandparents are white, Asian, and Latino (Middleton, 2008).

To say that race is a social construction does not deny the existence of physical variations between human populations. These variations are real and some are meaningful, such as those having medical implications, but they don't correspond with the skin-color–based racial classification model widely used in the United States. Additionally, scientists now know that physiological traits, including particular genetic patterns, are influenced by the experiences of particular individuals and the long-term experiences of particular populations. Therefore, a population

that has lived for centuries in a certain mountainous region in Africa may have more or less of a specific trait than a population that has lived for centuries in Norway, but this does not justify classifying these populations as different races on the basis of skin color.

Even though race is not a valid biological concept, its social significance has profoundly influenced the lives of millions of people for three centuries. As people have developed webs of ideas and beliefs around skin color, the resulting racial ideologies have become deeply embedded in many cultures. These ideologies change over time, but they continue to exert a powerful influence on people's lives (Fields, 1982).

The primary problem with *race* and racial ideologies is that they have been used for three centuries to justify the oppression and exploitation of one population by another (Carrington, 2007; Fredrickson, 2003; Klein, 2008; Smedley, 1997, 1999; Winant, 2001, 2006). Therefore, they've fueled and supported **racism,** defined as *attitudes, actions, and policies based on the belief that people in one racial category are inherently superior to people in one or more other categories.* In extreme cases, racial ideology has supported beliefs that people in certain populations are (1) childlike beings in need of external control, (2) subhuman beings that can be exploited without guilt, (3) forms of property that can be bought and sold, or (4) evil beings that should be exterminated through **genocide,** or *the systematic destruction of an identifiable population.*

Another problem with race and racial ideologies is that they foster the use of **racial stereotypes,** or *generalizations used to define and judge all individuals who are classified in a particular racial category.* Because stereotypes provide ready-made evaluative frameworks for making quick judgments and conclusions about others, they're widely used by people who don't have the opportunity or aren't willing to learn about and interact with those who have experiences that are influenced by popular beliefs about skin color. Knowledge, when used critically, undermines

Tiger Woods is only one-fourth African American, yet he is often identified as black because of the way race has been defined by most people in the United States. Annika Sorenstam, a highly talented Swedish golfer, is defined as white, even though her physical characteristics are quite different from those of Italians, Greeks, and others commonly described as whites according to the racial classification system currently used by many people in the United States. (*Source:* Mark J. Terrill, AP/Wide World Photos)

racial stereotypes and gradually subverts the ideologies that support them and the racism that often accompanies them.

Race, Racial Ideology, and Sports

None of us is born with a racial ideology. We acquire it over time as we interact with others and learn to give meanings to physical characteristics such as skin color, eye shape, the color and texture of hair, or even specific bodily movements. These meanings become the basis for classifying people into racial categories and associating categories with particular psychological and emotional characteristics, intellectual and physical abilities, and even patterns of action and lifestyles.

This process of creating and using racial meanings is built into the cultural fabric of many societies, including the United States. It occurs as we interact with family members, friends, neighbors, peers, teachers, and people we meet in our everyday lives. And it is reproduced in connection with general cultural perspectives as well as images and stories in children's books, textbooks, popular films, television programs, video games, song lyrics, and other media content. We incorporate these perspectives, images, and stories into our lives to the extent that we perceive them to be compatible with our experiences. In this sense, race is much like gender: it consists of meaning, performance, and organization (see chapter 2, pp. 40–41).

The influence of race and racial ideologies in sports has been and continues to be significant in the United States (Brown et al., 2005; Buffington, 2005; King, 2007; Woodward, 2004). For example, through the nineteenth and much of the twentieth century when African Americans engaged in clearly courageous acts, many whites used racial ideology to conclude that such acts among blacks were based on ignorance and desperation rather than *real* character. Some white people went so far as to say that blacks, including black athletes, did not feel pain in the same way that whites did and this permitted black people to engage in superhuman physical feats and endure physical beatings, as in the case of boxers (Mead, 1985). Many whites concluded that the success of black athletes was meaningless because blacks were driven by simple animal instincts instead of the heroic and moral character that accounted for the achievements of white athletes. For example, when legendary boxer Joe Louis defeated a "white" Italian for the heavyweight championship of the world in 1935, the wire service story that went around the world began with these words:

> Something sly and sinister and perhaps not quite human came out of the African jungle last night to strike down [its opponent] . . . (in Mead, 1985, p. 91)

Few people today would use such blatantly racist language, but traditional ideas about race continue to exist.[1] Therefore, when eight blacks line up in the Olympic finals of the 100-meter dash or play in an NBA All-Star game, many people talk about "natural speed and jumping abilities," and some scientists want to study dark-skinned bodies to discover the internal physical traits that will explain why they outperform whites.

OLC ON THE *OLC*:

See the OLC—Additional Readings for Chapter 9—for further discussion of the media coverage of Joe Louis and Michael Phelps.

---

[1]Mainstream media do not contain words like this, but there are online sources in which words such as these are used regularly today (King, 2007).

On the other hand, when white athletes do extraordinary physical things, dominant racial ideology leads people to conclude that it is either expected or a result of fortitude, intelligence, moral character, strategic preparation, coachability, and good organization. Therefore, few people want to study white-skinned bodies when all the finalists in multiple Olympic Nordic (cross-country skiing) events are "white." When white skiers from Austria and Switzerland—countries half the size of Colorado, with one-twentieth the population the United States—win World Cup championships year after year, people don't say that they succeed because their white skin is a sign of genetic advantages. Everyone already knows why the Austrians and Swiss are such good skiers: They live in the Alps, they learn to ski before they go to preschool, they grow up in a culture in which skiing is highly valued, they have many opportunities to ski, all their friends ski and talk about skiing, they see fellow Austrian and Swiss skiers winning races and making money in highly publicized (in Europe) World Cup competitions, and their cultural heroes are skiers. But this is a cultural explanation, not a biological one.

When athletes are white, racial ideology focuses attention on *social* and *cultural* factors rather than biological and genetic factors. This is why scientists don't do studies to identify hockey genes among white Canadians, weightlifting genes among white Bulgarians, or swimming genes among white Americans. Dominant racial ideology prevents people from seeing "whiteness" as an issue in these cases because it is the taken-for-granted standard against which everything else is viewed. When dominant racial ideology serves as the cultural foundation of a white-dominated, white-identified, and white-centered society, the success of white athletes is seen as "normal"—the way it always has been. At the same time, the success of black athletes is seen as an invasion or a takeover—a "problem" in need of an explanation focused on dark-skinned bodies.

"Jumping Genes" in Black Bodies
Why Do People Look for Them, and What Will It Mean If They Find Them?

When people seek genetic explanations for the achievements of black athletes, sociologists raise questions about the validity and purpose of the research. Let's use the search for "jumping genes" to explore whether these questions are justified. Our questions about research on this issue are based on two factors: (1) many current ideas about the operation and effects of genes are oversimplified and misleading, and (2) jumping is much more than a simple physical activity.

OVERSIMPLIFIED AND MISLEADING IDEAS ABOUT GENES

Most people have great hopes for genetic research. They see genes as the building blocks of life that will enable us to explain and control everything from food supplies to human feelings, thoughts, and actions. These hopes have inspired studies seeking genes for violence and intelligence as well as genes that enable people to sprint fast, run record-setting marathons, and jump high. Genes, in the minds of many people, constitute the "magic bullet" that will enable us to understand the world and everyone in it.

According to Robert Sapolsky (2000), a professor of biology and neurology at Stanford University, this notion of the "primacy of the gene" fosters deterministic and reductionist views of human actions and social problems. The actions of human beings, he explains, cannot be reduced to particular genetic factors. Even though genes are important, they do not work independently of the environment. Research shows that genes are activated and suppressed by many environmental factors; furthermore, even the *effects* of genes inside the human body are influenced by numerous environmental factors, including the body itself.

Genes are neither autonomous nor the sole causes of important, real-life outcomes associated with our bodies and what they do. The influence of genes is regulated by chemicals that exist in cells as well as chemicals, such as hormones, that come from other parts of the body. These chemicals and hormones are influenced, in turn, by a wide range of external environmental factors. For example, when a mother rat licks and grooms her infant, her actions initiate biochemical processes that activate genes regulating the

physical growth of the infant rat. Therefore, geneticists have concluded that the operation and effects of genes cannot be separated from the environment that switches them on and off and influences their effects in the body (Davids et al., 2007).

The point is this: genes do not exist and operate in environmental vacuums. This is true for genes related to diseases and genes related to jumping. Furthermore, we know that physical actions such as jumping, running, and shooting a basketball all involve one or more clusters of multiple genes. To explain overall success in a sport such as basketball or soccer requires an investigation of "at least 124 genes and thousands, perhaps millions, of combinations of those genes," and this would provide only part of an explanation (Farrey, 2005). The rest would involve research on why people choose to do certain sports, why they're motivated to practice and excel, how they're recognized and identified by coaches and sponsors, and how they're able to perform under particular conditions.

This means that discovering "jumping genes" would be exciting, but it would *not* explain why one person jumps higher than another, *nor* would it explain why people from one population jump, on average, higher than people from other populations. Furthermore, no evidence shows that particular genes related to jumping or other complex sport performances vary systematically with skin color or any socially constructed ideas about race and racial classifications (PBS, 2006, episode 1).

JUMPING IS MORE THAN A PHYSICAL ACTIVITY

Jumping is much more than a mechanical, springlike action initiated by a few leg muscles. It is a total body movement involving neck, shoulders, arms, wrists, hands, torso, waist, hips, thighs, knees, calves, ankles, feet, and toes. Jumping also involves a timed coordination of the upper and lower body, a particular type of flexibility, a "kinesthetic feel," and a total body rhythm. It is an act of grace as much as power, a rhythmic act as much as a sudden muscular burst, an individual expression as much as an exertion, and it is tied to a sense of the body in harmony with space as much as overcoming resistance through physical force.

Athletes in different sports jump in different ways. Gymnasts, volleyball players, figure skaters, skateboarders, mogul skiers, BMX bikers, wakeboarders, basketball players, ski jumpers, high jumpers, long jumpers, triple-jumpers, and steeple-chase runners all jump, but their techniques and styles vary greatly from sport to sport and person to person. The act of jumping among people whose skin color and ethnic heritage have been given important social meanings is especially complex because race and ethnicity are types of performances in their own ways. In other words, performing race and ethnicity often involves physical expressions and body movements that are grounded in the cultural–kinesthetic histories of particular populations and to stereotypes about them.

Noted scholar Gerald Early (1998) explains that playing sports is an *ethnic performance* because the relevance and meaning of bodily movements vary from one cultural context to another. For example, jumping is irrelevant to the performances of world leaders, CEOs of major corporations, sport team owners, coaches, doctors, and college professors. The power, influence, and resources that these people possess do *not* depend on their jumping abilities. The statement that "white men can't jump" isn't defined as a racial slur by most whites, because jumping deficiencies have not stopped them from dominating the seats of power in the U.S. (Myers, 2000). Outside of a few sports, jumping ability has nothing to do with success, power, or wealth. As Public Enemy rapped in the 1998 film, *He Got Game*, "White men in suits don't *have* to jump."

To study the physical aspects of jumping, sprinting, and distance running is important because it helps us understand human biology more fully. But this research will not explain why people in some social and cultural populations jump well in certain sports and not others, or not at all. Such explanations must take into account the historical, cultural, and social circumstances that make jumping and running important in some people's lives and why some people work so hard to develop their jumping and running abilities. There certainly are genes related to jumping, but

"Of course, white folks are good at this. After 500 years of colonizing the world by sea, they've been bred to have exceptional sailing genes!"

This statement is laughable when made about whites. However, similar statements about blacks have been used by scientists as a basis for hundreds upon hundreds of studies over the last century. As a result, racial ideology has influenced the process of knowledge production as well as everyday explanations of social worlds and the actions of individuals.

its wrong to assume that they operate independent of environmental factors, that they are connected with skin color, or that they correspond with the racial categories that people have constructed for social and political purposes. Knowledge about genes is important, but it will never explain the complex physical and cultural performance of slam dunks choreographed by NBA players with varying skin color from 31 nations (in 2008). Nor will it explain the amazing vertical leaps and amazing hang time of the European, Brazilian, Chinese, and Japanese volleyball players who have won so many international events. Nor will it tell us why whites have always won America's Cup yacht races and nearly every "big air" event in action sports. *What do you think?*

This way of thinking about skin color was clearly illustrated in 1997 when the white editors of *Sports Illustrated* decided that a feature-length cover story should be titled "What Happened to the White Athlete?" (Price, 1997). The story was based on their belief that blacks had taken over sports and that white athletes were fast disappearing. However, the story focused only on the most visible revenue-producing sports and ignored the fact that white athletes made up all or nearly all participants in dozens of other sports at all levels of competition. The editors at *Sports Illustrated* are not unique in the American sports media, where racial ideology regularly influences the selection of stories and the ways they are told. This partly explains why race-related ideas and beliefs tend to be self-perpetuating, even when they portray reality in distorted and inaccurate terms.

Like all of us, if scientists and editors do not ask critical questions about racial ideology, it will influence their explanations of human performance in sports. These explanations are based on three things: (1) the facts people choose to examine, (2) the ways that people classify and organize those facts, and (3) the theories people use to analyze and interpret the facts that they have classified and organized. Therefore, if people are not critically self-reflective as they observe, analyze, and explain the actions of human beings, racial ideology will influence the process of producing knowledge (St. Louis, 2003). This is highlighted in the box "'Jumping Genes' in Black Bodies" on pages 284–285.

Racial Ideology and a Sense of Athletic Destiny Among African American Men Does racial ideology influence the ways that African Americans interpret their own physical abilities and potential as athletes? This is a controversial question. Research combined with statements by athletes and coaches suggests that many young blacks, especially men, grow up believing that the black body is superior when it comes to physical abilities in certain sports (Harrison

and Lawrence, 2004; Harrison, Azzarito, and Burden, 2004; Lawrence, 2005; Liddle, 2003; May, 2008; Stone et al., 1997, 1999). This belief inspires some young people to believe it is their biological and cultural destiny to play certain sports and play them better than others. This inspiration is intensified when young blacks feel that their chances of gaining respect and material success are dismal in any realm other than a few sports.

Figure 9.2 outlines a hypothesized sociological explanation of the athletic achievements of African American male athletes. The top section of the figure shows that racial stereotypes about the innate physical abilities of blacks have been a part of U.S. history and culture. When these stereotypes are combined with restricted opportunities in mainstream occupations and heavily sponsored opportunities to develop skills in certain sports, many young blacks are motivated to play those sports. Over time they come to believe that it is their destiny to excel in those sports, especially relative to whites (see the middle section of Figure 9.2). When this sense of destiny is widespread and strong, it creates a context in which the achievements of blacks are driven to record-setting levels (see the bottom section of Figure 9.2).

Does this sociological approach explain the notable achievements of African American men in basketball, football, track, and boxing? Former NBA player Charles Barkley, an outspoken observer of sports in U.S. culture, claims that it does. He notes that social, cultural, and historical factors have all combined so that "every black kid in the country thinks the only way he can be successful is through athletics" (in McCallum, 2002, p. 34; see also Barkley, 2006).

Apart from Barkley's anecdotal analysis, historical evidence indicates that a perceived collective sense of biological cultural destiny can dramatically influence an entire population. For example, three centuries ago, white men from the small island nation of England felt that it was their biological and cultural destiny to colonize

When these three social and cultural conditions are added together:

A long history of racial ideology that has emphasized
"black male physicality" and innate, race-based physical abilities among blacks
+
A long history of racial segregation and discrimination, which has limited
the opportunities for black men to achieve success and respect in society
+
The existence of widespread opportunities and encouragement
to develop physical skills and excel in a few sports

There are two intermediate consequences:

Many blacks, especially young men, come to believe
that it is their biological and cultural destiny to become great athletes.
+
Young black men are motivated to use every opportunity
to develop the skills they need to fulfill their destiny as athletes.

The resulting hypothesis is this:

This sense of biological and cultural destiny, combined with
motivation and opportunities to develop certain sport skills,
leads some black males, especially those with certain physical
characteristics, to be outstanding athletes in certain sports.

FIGURE 9.2 A sociological hypothesis to explain the achievements of black male athletes.

and rule other parts of the world. This belief was so powerful that it led them to conquer over one-half the world as they formed the British Empire! This dwarfs the achievements of blacks in certain sports today. Further, it is clear that British colonization was driven by a combination of historical, cultural, and social factors; it was not due to British genes. Overall, when social worlds are organized to foster a sense of destiny among particular people, it shouldn't be surprising when those people achieve notable things in pursuit of what they believe they can accomplish.

The Challenge of Escaping Racial Ideology in Sports The most effective way to defuse racial ideology is for people to understand each other's history and heritage and to depend on each other to achieve their goals. However,

Many African American men grow up taking sports, especially basketball and football, very seriously. By age eleven this boy has learned not to smile when presenting himself as an athlete. His father reminded him to look serious and tough for this photo because it represented an identity that should be taken seriously. (*Source:* Jay Coakley)

when ethnic segregation exists, as it does in U.S. schools, for example, there is a tendency for black males to be "tagged" in a way that subverts their success in claiming identities that don't fit expectations based on racial ideology. Educator Amanda Godley (1999) found this to be true when she studied student interactions in a California high school. When young black men were in the honors program and played on a school team, other students and teachers identified them as *athletes* rather than *honor*

students. At the same time, Asian and white students (male or female) in the honors program and on school teams were clearly identified as honor students rather than as athletes. There was no specific pattern in the way that young black women were identified. In other words, racial ideology had a uniquely powerful impact on identity dynamics for black males—a finding that is consistent with other research.

Educator C. Keith Harrison found similar identity dynamics on major university campuses. As two black male college athletes in one of his studies noted, "Everyone around perceives us being there only for our physical talents," and "Everything is white [on campus], only sports [are] for blacks" (1998, p. 72). This is not a new phenomenon (Adler and Adler, 1991), but its consequences are frustrating for black men who want to expand their social identities beyond sports, or who don't play sports and don't want to be identified with them.

More research is needed on this issue, but it appears to be difficult for some black men to escape the influence of racial ideology that encourages people to "see" them in athletic terms, especially in situations where whites constitute a clear numerical majority (T. Brown et al., 2003). When these identity dynamics occur, relationships in schools may be organized so that black male students are academically marginalized. We need to know more about the conditions under which this marginalization occurs and how it affects everyone involved. At this point, many people say that it occurs because black students, especially young men, avoid and devalue an academic identity, but this factor is less important than the perceptions of others and their willingness to acknowledge certain identities and skills and ignore others.

These identity dynamics can undermine the positive consequences of sports in the lives of many blacks, because it frames their achievements in sports in racial terms. This point was made in more specific sociological terms by prize-winning author John Edgar Wideman—the father of Jamila Wideman, who played basketball at Stanford and in the WNBA. As Wideman analyzed race and basketball in the United States, he explained that basketball "functions to embody racist fantasies, to prove and perpetuate 'essential' differences between blacks and whites, to justify the idea of white supremacy and rationalize an unfair balance of power . . . between blacks and whites." (in Lipsyte, 2001, p. S13). His purpose was not to discourage young blacks from playing basketball or any other sport but to emphasize that current racial ideology shapes popular perceptions of sports in ways that perpetuate the racial status quo and make it difficult to use sports to create a fair and just society.

Racial Ideology and Sport Choices Among Whites A few years ago, I invited five children to be on a youth sports panel in my sociology of sport course. All were white ten- to twelve-year-olds who were heavily involved in sports. During the discussion, a sixth-grade boy known in his nearly all-white elementary school for his sprinting and basketball skills was asked if he would play those sports in junior high school. Surprisingly, he said no. When asked to explain, he said, "I won't have a chance because the black kids will beat me out." He added that this did not upset him because he would play soccer and run cross country instead. He also said that he'd never played sports with black peers in elementary school, but he had watched TV and had seen blacks play basketball and win Olympic medals in the sprinting events.

About the same time that this sixth-grader was using racial ideology to make sport participation decisions, an 18-year-old white male who was named the state's best football *and* basketball player was asked by a sportswriter which sport he would play in college. The young man said, "I guess, right now, I'd take football because it's more unique to be a 6-6 quarterback . . . than a 6-6 *white* forward." This decision clearly took into account his whiteness *and* dominant racial ideology in relation to sports.

Both of these young people had watched sports on television and listened to people discuss the abilities of athletes. In the process, they developed ideas about race, physical abilities, and their chances for success in various sports. Their whiteness, a taken-for-granted characteristic in the rest of their lives, strongly influenced their decisions about playing sports. Ironically, they limited their options because of their skin color—although they had so many options that this didn't bother either of them.

The racial factors that influenced these two students may also explain why the official times of white runners in certain sprints and long-distance road races have actually become slower since the 1950s and 1960s. Whites' genes have not changed, but their choices and motivation appear to have changed as American schools were desegregated and certain sports came to be identified as "black sports" and "white sports" (Bloom, 1998; George, 1994; Merron, 1999; Weir, 2000). For example, when Tim Layden, a *Sports Illustrated* journalist, returned to the high school that inspired the 2000 film *Remember the Titans*, he noted that the football team at the school was no longer racially integrated as it had been in 1971, the year depicted in the film. One of the players on the 2002 team told Layden that "most white kids around here wouldn't even think of coming out for football. They think it's a black sport" (Layden, 2001, p. 79).

Research suggests that choices and achievements in sports are influenced by racial ideology and the stereotypes it supports, but this is a tricky issue to study (Harrison and Lawrence, 2004; Harrison, Lee, and Belcher, 1999; Stone et al., 1997, 1999). The influence of ideology is subtle and difficult to measure. Therefore, researchers must use creative methods to examine how racial ideology affects people's lives and the organization of the social worlds in which choices are made.

Racial ideology operates in diverse ways. In some cases, it influences whites to avoid the sports in which blacks have a record of excellence. This way of thinking did not influence the white teen on this team, nor does it influence whites in Europe and Australia where racial ideology does not discourage them from playing basketball and learning to run and jump as NBA players do. (*Source:* Courtesy of Preston Miller)

Racial Ideology, Gender, and Social Class

Racial and gender ideologies are interconnected in U.S. sports (Ferber, 2007). Research shows that the implications of racial ideology for black men are different from those for black women (Bruening, 2005; Bruening et al., 2005; Corbett and Johnson, 2000; Daniels, 2000; Majors, 1998; Smith, 2000; A. Solomon, 2000; Winlock, 2000). This is partly because the bodies of black men in U.S. culture have been viewed and socially defined differently from the bodies of black women.

Over the past three centuries, but especially during the last century, many whites in the United States grew up fearing the power of black male bodies, feeling anxious about their sexual capacities and being fascinated by their movements. Ironically, this consequence of racial ideology enabled a few black men to use their bodies as entertainment commodities, first on stage in music and vaudeville theater and later on athletic fields. Black female bodies, on the other hand, were seen in sexualized terms or in terms of the nurturing nanny—neither of which made them valuable entertainment commodities in sports (Corbett and Johnson, 2000; Winlock, 2000).

Being feared by whites who wanted to prevent black men from having any contact with white women led to forms of discrimination that systematically denied them opportunities to be successful breadwinners and providers for their wives and families. To cope with being feared and marginalized, some African American men developed a presentation of self that they could use to maintain social distance from others and establish a sense of personal significance that would gain them respect. Educator Richard Majors has described this presentation of self as **"cool pose,"** *which involves "unique, expressive, and conspicuous styles of demeanor, speech, gesture, clothing, hairstyle, walk, stance, and handshake"* (Majors, 1998, p. 17). Cool pose is partly an *interpersonal* strategy used to gain respect after being denied personal significance and success in jobs, politics, and education. But it also is a defensive-protective strategy that oppressed people use to appear tough, detached, and in control so that others will keep their distance and not hurt them.

According to Majors, cool pose says different things to different people. To the white man, it says, "You can try to hurt me again and again, but you'll never break me (and if I'm hurting or weak, I'll never let you know)." It also says, "See me, touch me, hear me, but, white man, you can't copy me" (Majors, 1986, pp. 184–85). To everyone, cool pose says, "Don't mess with me; I know how to handle myself, so you'd better keep your distance from me if you don't want trouble." In racial and gender terms, cool pose is a form of masculinity that is performed by black males who face emasculating status threats in everyday life; this performance is designed to cover the frustration and self-doubt caused by the experience of being marginalized in schools, the mainstream economy, and society in general.

Majors suggests that cool pose shapes the public personas of many black men and it is especially evident in sports. This point raises interesting sociological questions. Is cool pose the basis of the personal style that has become such a big part of basketball? Is it the basis for certain forms of "trash talking" on the playing field? Is it used strategically to intimidate white opponents? Does it boost the commercial value of sports among whites who will buy tickets and watch events so they can see creative dunks and other moves inscribed with the "cool pose" personas of black men? Is cool pose limited to black men, or are forms of cool pose used by other people who are oppressed and seek to project an appearance of personal power that keeps those who might hurt them at a distance? These questions have not been answered, but they remind us of the subtle consequences of racial and gender ideology in our everyday lives (see Wilson, 1999).

Racial and gender ideology create slightly different challenges for black female athletes. For example, Donna Daniels, an African American studies scholar, suggests that the norms for physical appearance among females in predominantly white cultures have been racialized so that black female athletes exist in a realm outside the normal range of acceptance. To gain acceptance, they must carefully "monitor and strategize about how they are seen and understood by people who are not accustomed to their physical presence or intellect, whether on the court, field, or peddling a product" (2000, p. 26). If they're not careful, there's a danger that people will interpret their confidence and intelligence as arrogance and cockiness or as an indication that they are "too black."[2] Therefore, some black women learn to present themselves to others in a way that tones down their toughness and makes them appear amicable and nonthreatening—much like Oprah

---

[2]Many people in 2008, including media people, interpreted Michelle Obama (wife of then–Senator Barack Obama) in these terms, identifying her as "too black" and a "typical angry black woman." Her confidence and intelligence were viewed by many as arrogance and cockiness.

Winfrey—lest they face chronic marginalization in the cultural mainstream.

This point was poignantly illustrated when radio and talk show host Don Imus saw the strength and toughness of the black women on the Rutgers University basketball team and could find no other words to describe them except "some rough girls from Rutgers . . . some nappy-headed ho's." As for Rutgers' opponents, Imus said, "The girls from Tennessee—they all looked cute." Then the show's executive producer said that the game pitted "the jigaboos versus the wannabes." To Imus and his producer, both of whom were fired for their on-air conversation, the appearance of the women from the Rutgers team was "too black," and outside of their "normal range of acceptance." This was reminiscent of ways that the media in the 1990s pathologized the bodies of Venus and Serena Williams as exotic yet repulsive, animalistic yet supremely athletic, unfeminine yet erotic (McKay and Johnson, 2008; Spencer, 2004).

This type of response among potential fans was anticipated by the marketing people at the WNBA. When they first promoted the league, they presented ad after ad highlighting black players who had modeling contracts or newborn babies (Banet-Weiser, 1999; A. Solomon, 2000). When lip gloss and cute infants were not used, the ads depicted nicely groomed black players in nurturing and supportive roles, especially with children.

At the same time, the NBA was using the sounds and images of urban hip-hop to recruit young males as fans. They knew that over 70 percent of the young people who consume elements of hip-hop culture are whites and that hip-hop could be used to market the NBA across ethnic groups. This approach was abandoned after a couple of years because NBA executives and owners thought it was alienating existing season-ticket holders, most of whom were (and remain) relatively wealthy white men who see hip-hop as too urban, too street, too tattooed, too cornrowed—"too black" to fit into their

"normal range of acceptance" (Hughes, 2004; Long and McNamee, 2004; Platt, 2002; Simons, 2003; Zirin, 2004b). NBA commissioner David Stern even established a "dress code" in 2005 as he tried to successfully walk the line drawn by the combination of racial and gender ideology in the early twenty-first century.

> **OLC** **ON THE *OLC*:**
> See the OLC—Additional Readings for Chapter 9—for short essays on "racial ideology in action" in sports.

As social conditions change, so do ideas and beliefs about race and the bodies of athletes. For example, boxers today are more apt to be Latino and Eastern European than black. Large numbers of upper-middle-class whites now play the Native American game of lacrosse, and Africans are widely recruited by previously all-white men's soccer clubs in Europe. At the same time, white Americans are being replaced by young women from Russia at the top levels of professional tennis, one-third of the players on Major League Baseball (MLB) teams are now from Latin America and Asia, and over 25 percent of all NBA players were born outside the United States. To explain these things, we must understand social and cultural changes as well as shifts in racial, ethnic, gender, and political ideologies. Information on genes may not help much, if at all, when developing our theories.

SPORT PARTICIPATION AMONG ETHNIC MINORITIES IN THE UNITED STATES

Sports in the United States have long histories of racial and ethnic exclusion (Bretón, 2000; Brooks and Althouse, 2000; Corbett and Johnson, 2000; Harrison, 1998; Hartmann, 2003a, 2004; C. R. King, 2004a; Miller and Wiggins, 2003; Niiya, 2000; Wiggins, 2003). Men and women in all ethnic minorities traditionally have been under-represented at all levels of competition and management in most competitive sports, even in high schools and community programs. Prior to the 1950s, the organizations that sponsored sport teams and events seldom opened their doors fully to African Americans, Latinos, Native Americans, and Asian Americans. When members of minority groups played sports, they usually played among themselves in games and events segregated by choice or by necessity (Giles, 2004; Miller and Wiggins, 2003; Niiya, 2000; Powers-Beck, 2004; Ruck, 1987).

Sport Participation Among African Americans

Prior to the 1950s, most whites in the United States consistently avoided playing with and against blacks. Blacks were systematically excluded from participation in white-controlled sport programs and organizations because whites believed that blacks didn't have the character or fortitude to compete with them. Since the 1950s, the sport participation of blacks has been concentrated in only a few sports. Even today, 41 million black Americans are underrepresented in or absent from most sports at most levels of competition (in 2009). This fact is often overlooked because a few of the most popular spectator sports involve high proportions of black athletes. People see this and don't realize that African Americans are absent or nearly absent in thirty-nine of forty-four men's and women's sports played in college, most of the dozens of sports played at the international amateur level, and all but five of the dozens of professional sports in the United States. There is a similar pattern in Canada and in European countries with strong sporting traditions.

The exceptions to this pattern of exclusion stand out because they *are* exceptions. The underrepresentation of blacks in most sports is much greater than the underrepresentation of whites in basketball, football, and track and field.

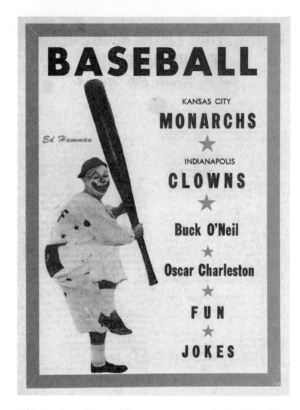

African American athletes were not taken seriously by most white people through much of the twentieth century. To earn a living playing sports, they often had to present themselves in ways that fit the racial stereotypes held by whites. The Indianapolis Clowns baseball team and the Harlem Globetrotters basketball team joked around and behaved in childlike ways so that whites would pay to watch them. Racism provided limited cultural space for blacks to be entertainers for the enjoyment of whites, and blacks faced near-total exclusion in other spheres of social life, including mainstream sports. (*Source:* American Memory Collection)

Additionally, there are proportionately many more whites who play basketball and football in high school and college than there are blacks who play tennis or golf at those levels. Finding black drivers at an Indy-car or NASCAR race is difficult or impossible; drivers, support personnel, and nearly 100 percent of the spectators are white, but the races are never described as white events (King, 2007c; Kusz, 2007). In a *white-centered* cultural setting where the lives of whites are the expected focus of attention, whites don't think about the whiteness of these sports. And in *white-dominated, white-identified* settings where the characteristics of whites are used as the standards for judging qualifications, most whites never think that they might have an advantage when it comes to fitting in or being hired and promoted; at the same time, blacks and other ethnic minorities must be careful not to be too black or too ethnic if they wish to succeed.

Throughout U.S. sports history, the participation of black females has been severely limited and has received little attention, apart from that given to occasional Olympic medal winners in track events. Although black women face a "double-dose" of consequences fostered by gender and racial ideologies, there have been few studies of their experiences in sports. The studies that have been done suggest that black women are keenly aware of the need to "tone down" their toughness and confidence lest they turn off people who think like Don Imus, even though they don't say what he said (Bruening, 2005; Bruening et al., 2005; Corbett and Johnson, 2000; Green, 2000; Smith, 2000). In the case of black girls, a recent study by ethnomusicologist Kyra Gaunt (2006) shows that games in urban girl culture traditionally combine songs, chants, handclapping, footstomping, and rhythmic movement—a combination that doesn't fit with widely used definitions of sport (Cole, 2006). Many of these games, including traditional double-dutch, involve complex physical challenges combined with a body-conscious physicality and embodied musicality traceable to African origins. This combination of music and complex physical challenges in the games of black girls has yet to be studied in the sociology of sport—a fact that influenced my choice of the double dutch image that is on the cover of this book.

Overall, rates of sport participation in middle- and upper-middle-income white communities in the United States are much higher than those in most predominantly black communities, especially those where resources are scarce. Racial ideology causes many people to overlook this fact. They see only the black men who make high salaries in high-profile sports and assume that blacks have "taken over" sports, that discrimination is gone, and that the nation is now color blind. Overall, this is how dominant racial ideology erases people and problems that cause discomfort among the racially privileged.

Sport Participation Among Native Americans

There are 4.5 million Native Americans/Alaskans in the United States (including those who identify as Native American plus one other "race"), and about 820,000 of these people live on reservations. Although the U.S. census counts Native Americans as a single demographic category, they comprise dozens of diverse cultural populations. The differences between many of these populations are socially significant. However, most non-Native Americans tend to erase these differences by referring generally to "Indians" and envisioning stereotypical habits and dress—long hair, feathers, buckskin, moccasins, bows and arrows, horseback riding, war-whooping, tomahawk-chopping, and half-naked, even in cold northern states.

Native American sport participation patterns are diverse. They vary with cultural traditions, socioeconomic status, and whether people live on or off reservations. For example, participation patterns are heavily affected by a poverty rate of nearly 30 percent generally and up to 50 percent on reservations—more than twice the poverty rate in the United States as a whole (about 12.3 percent in 2007).

Many sports in traditional Native American cultures combine physical activities with ritual and ceremony (Keith, 1999; King, 2004a; Nabokov, 1981; Oxendine, 1988; Powers-Beck, 2004). Although individual Native American athletes

reflect on
SPORTS

Identity Theft?
Using Native American Names and Images in Sports

Using stereotypes to characterize Native Americans is so common that most people don't realize they do it. When people take Native American images and names, claim ownership of them, and then use them for team names, mascots, and logos, sports perpetuate an ideology that trivializes and distorts the diverse histories and traditions of native cultures. No other ethnic population is subject to this form of cultural identity theft. As sportswriter Jon Saraceno exclaims, "Can you imagine the reaction if any school dressed a mascot in an Afro wig and a dashiki? Or encouraged fans to show up in blackface?" (2005, p. 10C).

To understand this issue, consider this story told by the group, Concerned American Indian Parents:

> An American Indian student attended his school's pep rally in preparation for a football game against a rival school. The rival school's mascot was an American Indian. The pep rally included the burning of an Indian in effigy along with posters and banners labeled "Scalp the Indians," "Kill the Indians," and "Let's burn the Indians at the stake." The student, hurt and embarrassed, tore the banners down. His fellow students couldn't understand his hurt and pain.

This incident occurred in a public school in 1988, twenty years after the National Congress of American Indians initiated a campaign to eliminate stereotypes of "Indians" in U.S. culture. In 1970 about 3000 schools were using Native American images, names, logos, and mascots for their sport teams. Many of these changed their names and mascots when they realized that it wasn't right to use the identities of other human beings to represent and promote themselves. However, hundreds of schools and a few professional teams still engage in this form of identity theft as they call themselves "Indians," "Savages," "Warriors," "Chiefs," "Braves," "Redskins," "Red Raiders," and "Redmen" and have mascots who cross-dress as Indians by donning war bonnets and paint, brandishing spears and tomahawks, pounding tom-toms, intoning rhythmic chants, and mimicking religious and cultural dances (King, 2004b; King and Springwood, 2001a, 2001b). Some schools continue to display "*their* Indian" on gym walls and floors, scoreboards, and products they sell for a profit. They say that they're engaging in a "harmless" tradition that "honors" the

When teams use Native American names and mascots, they enable fans to express their ignorance and/or racist ideas. Despite the stated "honorable intentions" of team sponsors, they cannot control the insensitive displays, chants, and actions of fans. This occurs in Cleveland where the "Indians" and "Chief Wahoo" inspire these young fans. Similar forms of identity derogation and theft occur in many towns and cities. (*Source:* Tony Dejak, AP/Wide World Photos)

"Indians" from whom they've taken images and identities. But is it possible to honor someone you don't know and won't listen to?

What if the San Diego Padres' mascot were a fearsome black-robed missionary who walked the sidelines swinging an 8-foot-long rosary and carrying a 9-foot-long faux-crucifix? And what if he led fans in a hip-hop version of the sacred Gregorian chant as spectators waved plastic crucifixes and rapped the lyrics of their chant? People would be outraged because they know the history and meaning of Christian beliefs, objects, and rituals. If more Americans knew the histories, cultural traditions, and religions of the 500 Native American tribes and nations in the United States today, would they be as likely to use Native American team names and allow naïve students to dress in costumes made of items defined as sacred in the animistic religious traditions of many Native Americans? Would they allow fans to mimic sacred chants and perform war-whooping, tomahawk-chopping cheers based on racist images from old "cowboy and Indian" movies?

At most schools that use Native American mascots and names, support runs very deep among school and team supporters (Davis-Delano, 2007; Williams, 2007). However, an increasing number of public school officials and state legislators now realize that it's cruel and inconsiderate to misrepresent people whose ancestors were massacred, ordered off their lands at gunpoint, and confined to reservations by U.S. government agents. They also realize that romanticizing a distorted version of the past by taking the names and images of people who currently experience discrimination, poverty, and the negative effects of stereotypes is clearly an act of careless white privilege and hypocrisy. Therefore, some states and school districts now have policies banning such practices.

OLC **ON THE *OLC*:**
> See the OLC—Additional Readings for Chapter 9—for current information on mascot issues.

In 2003 the National Collegiate Athletic Association (NCAA) recommended that all universities using American Indian names, mascots, or logos review their practices and determine if they undermined the NCAA's commitment to cultural diversity. In 2005 the NCAA banned the display of Native American names, logos, and mascots on uniforms and other clothing and at NCAA playoff games and championships. But NCAA officials made an exception for Florida State University (FSU), whose officials claimed they had tribal permission to use the Seminole name and logo image in an honorable way (Staurowsky, 2007). "Honorable" for FSU means having a white European American student paint his face, put on a headband and a colorful shirt, carry a feather-covered spear, and ride into the football stadium on a horse named Seminole. And at the FSU web store (www.nolesstore.com), fans can honor *their* "nole," as they call "their Indian," by buying products adorned with the painted and feathered "Seminole face." These products include floor mats, welcome mats, stadium seats, paper plates, and other things that fans use to sit, stand, and wipe their feet on. This is a strange way to show honor, but it makes money for the university and keeps the wealthy boosters happy, even if it mocks the courses in their history department and makes the FSU diversity policy a symbol of hypocrisy.

The insensitivity of people at FSU is not an isolated or rare case (Davis-Delano, 2007; Williams, 2007). For example, in 2005 the California State Legislature passed a bill banning the use of "Redskins" as a public school nickname, because many Native Americans consider it the equivalent of *nigger, spic, kike, chink, slope,* and *camel jockey*. However, Governor Schwarzenegger vetoed the bill, saying it was a trivial matter. In 1999 a panel in the U.S. Patent and Trademark Office ruled that "Redskins," "Redskinettes," and the logo of a feathered "Redskin" man as used by Washington, DC's NFL team "disparaged" Native Americans. The panel canceled six exclusive trademarks, ending the NFL's exclusive ownership of the "Redskins" name and logo. But in 2003 a federal district court judge overturned the panel's ruling because Native Americans had not objected back in 1967 when the trademarks were registered. Although this decision is under appeal (in 2009; see Elman, 2006), the NFL still controls its "Redskins"—located in the capital city of the government that broke all but one of over 400 treaties with Native Americans. This case symbolizes the history of oppression endured by Native Americans.

Some people say that this issue is an example of petty political correctness. But what would they say if their name and reputation was taken by an organization and represented in ways that met the organization's goals? Would they say that this is a form of identity theft?

What do you think?

have done well and set records over the past century, public recognition has often been limited to those few standouts on the football and baseball teams from reservation schools. For example, when Jim Thorpe and his teammates at the Carlisle School, a segregated government training school, defeated outstanding college teams in 1911 and 1912, they attracted considerable attention (Bloom, 2000; Oxendine, 1988). But apart from a few teams and individual athletes in segregated government schools, Native American sport participation has been limited by poverty, poor health, lack of equipment and facilities, and a lack of understanding by those who control sports (Draper, 2005).

Native Americans who can play intercollegiate sports often fear being cut off from their cultural roots and identities. For example, Billy Mills, gold medalist in the 10,000-meter race at the 1964 Olympics, explains that being immersed in a sport program that does not acknowledge or support your culture is "like walking death." He speaks for many traditional Native Americans when he says that "if you go too far into [white] society, there's a fear of losing your Indianness. There's a spiritual factor that comes into play. To become part of white society you give up half your soul" (in Simpson, 1996, p. 294).

Native Americans who grow up learning their culture often feel disconcerting tension between the dominant American culture and their way of life. They say that when you leave your customs, religious ceremonies, families, and community behind, you must be prepared to live without the things that have made you who you are (Bloom, 2000; Clancy, 1999; Draper, 2005). This is a challenge that most people in any culture would find daunting or avoid altogether.

Cultural tensions felt by Native Americans are heightened when they attend schools or watch games between teams named Indians, Redskins, Redmen, and Savages and with mascots that mimic stereotypes of "Indians." Watching or playing sports under such conditions involves losing control of one's identity. It is depressing to see a distorted or historically inappropriate caricature of a Native American on the gym wall of a school where students have no knowledge of local or regional native cultures. It means that one must (1) swallow cultural pride, (2) repress anger against insensitive, historically ignorant non-Native Americans, and (3) suspend hope of being understood in terms of your identity and cultural heritage.

Native American athletes also face challenges when their orientations don't fit with the culture of the power and performance sports sponsored by most schools. Through the years, some white coaches who have worked in reservation schools have tried to strip students of cultural traditions that emphasize cooperation and replace them with Euro-American orientations that favor competition. Some coaches, frustrated by lack of competitive aggression among some populations of Native Americans, have tried to instill a "killer instinct" in their athletes.

When Native Americans don't give up their cultural souls voluntarily, some white coaches ask for them in the name of winning and cultural assimilation. Other coaches simply avoid recruiting Native American athletes because they don't want someone who might not fit in with teammates and campus culture. This is a problem that affects many Native American high school students who play basketball, a popular sport on reservations and one in which young Native Americans often excel (Draper, 2005).

Fortunately, Native American sport experiences do not always involve dramatic cultural compromises. Some Native Americans play sports in contexts in which their identities are respected and supported by others (Bloom, 2000; Clancy, 1999; King, 2004a; King and Springwood, 2001a, 2001b; Paraschak, 1995, 1999; Schroeder, 1995). In these cases, sports provide opportunities for students to learn about the cultural backgrounds of others. In other cases, Native Americans adopt Euro-American ways and play sports without expressing any evidence of their cultural heritage; that is, they "go along with" the dominant culture, even if they don't agree with or accept all of it. And there are cases in which Native Americans redefine sport participation to fit their cultural beliefs—a strategy used by many ethnic minorities who play sports developed by and for people in the dominant culture (Brenner and Reuveni, 2006; Maguire, 1999).

Sport Participation Among Latinos and Latinas

Latinos in the United States include people from diverse cultures.[3] They may share language, colonial history, or Catholicism, but their cultures, histories, and migration patterns vary greatly. Mexican Americans constitute the largest Latino/a group (67 percent), followed by Puerto Ricans (9 percent), Cubans (4 percent), Central and South Americans (14 percent), and other Hispanic people (6 percent). Overall, the Latino population numbers more than 45 million people in 2009, making it the largest ethnic population in the United States.

When dealing with sports in the United States, it's useful to distinguish between three categories of Latinos: (1) native born and naturalized citizens, (2) Latin Americans working as athletes in the U.S., and (3) workers and their family members who are in the U.S. without legal approval. The role of sports varies greatly in the everyday lives of people in each of these three categories.

Native-Born and Naturalized Citizens with Latino Heritage Because much of the southwestern United States (California, Texas, Nevada, Utah, most of Arizona, and parts of New Mexico, Colorado, and Wyoming) was part of Mexico prior to the mid-nineteenth century, the ancestors of Latinos were living in this region long before 1620 when European pilgrims docked the *Mayflower* in Plymouth Harbor. Therefore, Latino people have played major roles in establishing communities, schools, businesses, churches, hospitals, and sport programs in the Southwest, which is home to 25 percent of the total U.S. population. Unsurprisingly, they've also played and been successful in the same sports as others in the Southwest (Mendoza, 2007).

The exceptions to this pattern involve people who emigrated from Mexico and other parts of Latin America during the twentieth century to work in low-status jobs in U.S. industry and agriculture. Many people in this category are naturalized citizens or their children who were born in the United States. They frequently maintained family connections in Mexico and have generally experienced systematic, long-term ethnic discrimination. Work patterns, poverty, segregation, general discrimination, and cultural traditions have influenced their sport involvement. Scarce time, resources, and little access to facilities and teams have restricted participation. Anglo stereotypes often portrayed Mexicans and Mexican Americans as lazy and intellectually and physically inferior to whites (Iber and Regalado, 2007).

When anthropologist Doug Foley (1990a, 1990b, 1999b) studied "Mexicano-Anglo relations" associated with high school football in a small Texas town, he found that working-class Mexican males (*vatos*) rejected sport participation but used Friday night football games as occasions for publicly displaying their "style" (cool pose?) and establishing social reputations in the community. Foley also described how the Mexicans protested a high school homecoming ceremony that marginalized Mexicans and gave center stage to Anglos. Additionally, the Mexican man who was the head football coach resigned in frustration when faced with the bigotry and contradictory expectations of powerful Anglo boosters and school board members.

---

[3]*Latino* is the term used by people from Latin America to identify themselves as a single population with shared political interests and concerns. It was created as an alternative to *Hispanic*, a term used by the U.S. Census Bureau to refer to people of any race who have "Spanish/Hispanic/Latino origin." I use *Latino* because it is more socially and politically meaningful than *Hispanic*, which is mostly a demographic term.

Foley concluded that despite being a site for resistance against prevailing Anglo ways of doing things in the town, high school football ultimately perpetuated the power and privilege of the local Anglos. As long as Mexicanos saw and did things the Anglo way, they were accepted. But when they raised ethnic issues they were ignored, opposed, or marginalized.

There's a need to update Foley's work and to do research in urban areas as well as smaller towns. We know little about sports in the lives of young people who are first-, second-, and third-generation Latinos in the United States. There are anecdotal accounts of young people who overcome barriers to play on school teams or at the professional level, but in-depth, community-based research is lacking.

Similarly, there's been little research on Puerto Ricans in northeastern states, especially New York, and Cubans in southeastern states, especially Florida. Among those who are second- or third-generation residents of the United States, sport participation patterns match the patterns of those with similar family incomes and levels of education. For example, the relatively poor Puerto Ricans in New York City and other urban areas on the eastern seaboard have sport participation patterns matching other populations with scarce resources. Boxing, baseball, and soccer are among the most popular sports. The relatively wealthy Cubans who came to the U.S. when Castro and his communist party came to power in 1959 have sport participation patterns that match their socioeconomic counterparts. More recent Cuban immigrants have patterns closer to those of recent immigrants from Mexico—boxing, soccer, and baseball among the men and softball and some basketball among the women.

Research on Latinas in the United States indicates that diverse ethnic traditions and gender norms influence their sport participation (Acosta, 1999; Jamieson, 1998, 2005, 2007; Sylvester, 2005a, 2005b, 2005c). First-generation Latinas often lack parental support

Lisa Fernandez, probably the best player in softball history, led the U.S. team to three gold medals (Atlanta, Sydney, and Athens). Her father was born in Cuba and played baseball there; her mother was born in Puerto Rico and played stickball after moving to New York. Fernandez continues to be an inspiration for many Latinas who play sports. (*Source:* Elaine Thompson, AP/Wide World Photos)

to play sports. Parents control their daughters more strictly than they control their sons, and daughters are expected to do household tasks such as caring for siblings, assisting with meal preparation, and cleaning house—all of which interfere with playing sports in households where meeting expenses is a struggle and transportation to practices and games is unavailable or costly.

Second- and third-generation Latinas face fewer parental constraints, and many parents are willing to use family resources to fund their daughters' sport participation. However, talented high school players often remain hesitant to play intercollegiate sports if it means going to a college far from home where there is little support for their Latina identities and traditions. Katherine Jamieson's (1998, 2005, 2007) research describes the unique identity management experiences of Latina intercollegiate athletes who must bridge a cultural divide as they live, study, and play with others who know little about merging cultural identities and managing relationships in two cultural spheres.

Young Latinas today are more likely than their peers in past generations to see athletes who look like them. There's some media coverage showing Latinas in golf, softball, and soccer, but most inspiration comes from older sisters and neighbor girls who play sports. Research on the experiences of Latinas is important because it helps us understand the dynamics faced by young women caught up in the experience of immigration and making their way in a new society. At this point, we know next to nothing about the experiences of younger Latinas as they combine family life with school, sports, and jobs, and about adult Latinas who play sports in local leagues. Women playing in local leagues often use their participation to maintain regular contact with relatives and friends in the U.S. and Mexico, which makes soccer and softball especially important in their lives.

Latin Americans Working as Athletes in U.S. Sports

For well over a century boys and young men from poor families in Cuba, Puerto Rico, the Dominican Republic, Mexico, and Venezuela have dreamed about playing professional baseball in their home countries or the United States (Burgos, 2007; Regalado, 2008).

Between 1880 and the late 1930s players from Latin America—often from Cuba—played on white U.S. professional teams and Negro League teams. Although they faced strong discrimination on white teams, they learned that they could negotiate team membership by using their Spanish names to claim they were not "black." Whites often accepted this in the interest of including highly skilled players on their teams, even when the Latino players were dark-skinned. Therefore, Latino players quietly passed through "the color line" and disrupted the "one-drop" racial classification model that was used in Major League Baseball. Additionally, many white, black, and Latino players had played in integrated Latin American leagues in the decades prior to the desegregation of MLB (Burgos, 2007).

These factors, according to historian Adrian Burgos (2007), helped erode resistance to desegregation and made it easier for Branch Rickey to convince his co-owners of the Brooklyn Dodgers to make Jackie Robinson a team member in 1947. This means that breaking the color line in baseball was a multi-ethnic process rather than a single event in black-white relations. Latino players had long been involved in weakening the color line and demonstrating that the definition of race used in the United States was arbitrary and inconsistent. In fact, during the early twentieth century, some African Americans were known to learn Spanish and take Spanish names so they could pass as Cubans or Dominicans and play on U.S. teams.

Latinos constitute nearly 25 percent of the players in MLB today and about 40 percent of all minor league players; 85 percent of players born outside the U.S. come from Latin America. This is part of a century-long process through which players learned skills in community and professional leagues in Latin America, and more recently, in baseball training academies, mostly in the Dominican Republic (Klein, 2006). Baseball has long been seen as the ticket to take a young man out of poverty, enabling him to support his extended family and make contributions to his local community.

When scouts for MLB teams realized that there was so much baseball talent in the Dominican Republic they began to build training academies to gain access to the young players and then assess, develop, and control them. This began in the 1970s and continues today, although Dominicans with ties to their communities have now developed their own academies so they can "broker" players to academies sponsored by Major League teams (Klein, 2006). In this way, the Dominicans have regained control over their own talent so that Major League teams don't just take the best players and destroy the local leagues and teams. The success of the academies is seen through the 95-100 Dominicans who currently play on MLB teams; in fact, over the years, 70 MLB players have come from San Pedro de Macorís, a city of 200,000 people, and in 1990 it was the birthplace of five of the 26 starting shortstops in the major leagues (Dannheisser, 2008).

Once Latino players sign contracts with MLB teams, they face significant cultural adjustments and language problems; they also face the strain of living in a society where few people understand their cultural backgrounds (Bretón and Villegas, 1999; Burgos, 2007; Klein, 1991, 2006). This is partly why 90 to 95 percent of Latino players who sign contracts never make it beyond the minor leagues. Even those lucky enough to make minor league teams often are cut after a year or two, and rather than return home as "failures," they often find ways to remain in the United States as undocumented workers at low-wage jobs. Writer Marcos Bretón notes that "these castoffs represent the . . . rule rather than the exception in the high-stakes recruitment of ball players from Latin America and the Caribbean" (2000, p. 15), but their stories remain untold in U.S. and Canadian media.

Since the 1970s, the proportion of Latin American players has increased in U.S. professional leagues because they constituted a pool of cheap baseball labor. Established Latino stars are well paid, but young players have signed for a fraction of the money paid to new players born and trained in the United States. For example, a vice president of a MLB team said recently that it costs less to sign five Latin American players than one player from the United States. This "boatload approach" to signing these players has begun to change now that Latino "agents" are advocating the interests of many new players and as MLB teams have fewer visas they can give to non-citizen players because of new immigration and homeland security policies (Klein, 2006).

One of the major problems now faced by Latino players is that they are more likely to test positive for drugs than players raised in the United States. Since 2005 when MLB initiated its new drug-testing policy, most of the Latinos who have tested positive have spoken little English, have not known all the substances on the list, and have come from countries where medical care is scarce and taking vitamins, supplements, and over-the-counter drugs is common (Gordon, 2007; Jenkins, 2005; LeBatard, 2005). Many drugs are less regulated in Latin America than in the United States, and some, including anabolic steroids, are available over the counter. The cheapest and most accessible steroids are those used by ranchers and farmers to increase the growth of their animals. Therefore, when young baseball players are desperate to escape poverty and hunger and hope to support their families, they may take these drugs despite the risks to their health.

On the positive side of things, Latino players today enjoy the benefits of a visible and growing Latino culture in the United States, a growing Spanish-language media, a shared identity with many other players, and increased salaries that give them financial leverage that players in previous eras never had. Stereotypes continue to exist, but they are not as widely held as in the past, and when they are used in public, they are more likely to be challenged.

Undocumented Workers and Their Family Members We know little about sports in the lives of undocumented Latino workers and their families, who number in the millions. Sport involvement patterns are likely to vary with their income, education, and the number of years they've been in the United States. In some cases, sports may be used as a means of assimilating into and expressing familiarity with U.S. culture and developing relationships with non-Latinos. In other cases, workers and their families may use weekend soccer, baseball, and softball games to come together and exchange information about jobs, friends and family in Mexico, transferring money home, obtaining medical care and housing, and other things crucial to survival and maintaining support that can be helpful when a crisis strikes—a regular occurrence for many of these workers and their families.

A Need for Research   Knowledge about the sport experiences of Latinos and Latinas is important because they are the fastest-growing ethnic population in the United States. Physical educators, coaches, and sport administrators need research that helps them to provide services and opportunities that meet the needs of Latinos. For example, the economic success of professional soccer in much of the United States depends on being sensitive to the interests and orientations of Latino athletes and spectators. Latinos are eager to have their cultural heritage recognized and incorporated into sports and sport experiences in the United States and into the awareness of their fellow citizens (Otto, 2003). In the public sector, there's a growing need for inclusive programs that provide participants from diverse backgrounds with opportunities to learn about the heritage and personal orientations and circumstances of their Latino peers.

Existing research indicates that sports are related to ethnicity in three ways: (1) they can be used to break down social and cultural barriers, discredit stereotypes, and facilitate assimilation; (2) they can be used by ethnic groups to preserve and extend in-group relationships that support ethnic identities and make it possible to effectively bridge the gap between their native culture and dominant U.S. culture; and (3) they

can be used to maintain segregated lifestyles that prevent people from having experiences and gaining knowledge that often leads to intergroup understanding, tolerance, and cooperation.

Sport Participation Among Asian Pacific Americans[4]

There are about 15 million Asian Pacific Americans (APAs) in the United States. The legacy of wars and the global migration of labor has brought people from many Asian Pacific cultures to the United States. Most live on the West Coast and in cities where particular jobs have been plentiful. However, the heritage and histories of APAs are very diverse, representing at least 18 nations and dozens of cultures. This diversity is often ignored in media coverage and research that focuses on "Asians."

Although people with Chinese and Japanese ancestry have long played sports in their own communities (Niiya, 2000), the recent success and popularity of APA athletes has raised important issues about ethnic dynamics in sports. For example, the popularity of Yao Ming (Chinese) in the NBA, Japanese and Korean baseball players, Tiaina "Junior" Seau in the NFL, golfers Tiger Woods (Chinese and Thai) and Se Ri Pak (Korean), speed skater Apolo Anton Ohno, and figure skaters Kristi Yamaguchi (Japanese) and Michelle Kwan (Chinese) highlights the extent to which many Asians and Asian Americans have embraced sports played in the United States. The popular all-star baseball player Ichiro Suzuki has attracted so many Japanese spectators to Safeco

---

[4]At this point in time, the literature related to North America focuses primarily on Asians whose ancestry is from Pacific Rim nations and cultures. This excludes people from countries in South Asia, including India, and in Western Asia, including Persian Gulf countries and cultures (or "The Middle East" from a British geographical standpoint). The literature in Europe, especially research done in Britain, focuses more on ethnic populations from South and Western Asia (Fleming, 2007; Fleming and Tomlinson, 2007; Long, Carrington, and Spracklin, 2007).

When Yao Ming entered the NBA, he disrupted widespread stereotypes about the physical characteristics of Chinese people. As a result, many people realized that it is not possible to use a single generalization to describe 1.4 billion Chinese people from dozens of ethnic populations that have little in common physically or culturally. (*Source:* EyePress, AP/Wide World Photos)

Field in Seattle that signs in the stadium are now posted in both Japanese and English—although we don't have good information on the impact of Suzuki and other APA players on ethnic relations in the stadiums and communities where they play and live.

Historical research shows that certain sports have provided APAs with opportunities to challenge and discredit stereotypes about their lack of height and strength, their introverted "nature," and their singular dedication to intellectual development (Lapchick, 2007; Liang, 2007; Regalado, 2006). Yun-Oh Whang, a native Korean and a professor of sports marketing, acknowledged this point when he said:

> Asian Americans put huge value on education. [Therefore, it] is common that coaches and teachers at schools presume that an Asian American

kid belongs in the science lab, not on the football field. This is why it is so important that Asian American athletes have to rise to the top and show the general public that Asian Americans can also achieve excellence in sports. (in Lapchick, 2007).

Additionally, playing sports has been a way for some APAs to gain greater acceptance in schools and local communities.

The experiences and sport participation patterns of APAs often vary depending on their immigration histories. Chinese Americans and Japanese Americans whose families have lived in the United States for four or more generations have different experiences from those of first- and second-generation Americans from Vietnam, Thailand, Cambodia, Laos, the Philippines, Malaysia, and Indonesia. Researchers must be sensitive to these differences and the ways that they influence sport participation patterns and experiences. Gender and social class variations among APAs also are important areas for study (Wong, 1999).

Anthropologist Mark Grey (1999) dealt with some of these issues in a study of high school sports and social relations between recent refugees from Southeast Asia and the established residents of Garden City, Kansas. Grey reports that the Asian students often had a difficult time fitting into sports organized around the values and experiences of European Americans. When these students didn't try out for football, basketball, baseball, and softball, they were seen by many long-time residents as unwilling to become "true Americans." This created tensions that contributed to the social marginalization of Asian students and families.

> ## OLC ON THE *OLC:*
>
> See the OLC—Additional Readings for Chapter 9—for a list of references on the men from Samoa who play in college and professional football, including a 2007 series of articles in *ESPN—The Magazine.*

A relatively exceptional pattern exists in the case of young men from the Samoan Islands (American Samoa and Western Samoa, including Tonga) who come to the United States to play football (Feldman, 2007; Garber, 2007a, 2007b; T. Miller, 2007). With a population the size of Anchorage, Alaska (260,000 people), these islands were the birthplace of twenty-eight NFL players in 2007, plus many college football players. Universities also recruit many players from neighboring Tonga Island, which has a population the size of Peoria, Illinois (115,000). The sport traditions on all of these islands tend to involve rugby and cricket more than American sports, but young men from low-income families have defined football as their ticket to upward mobility, much as the young men from

the Dominican Republic see baseball. At this point, research is needed on the conditions under which this and other patterns occur.

The participation of APA athletes in elite sports has elicited prejudiced statements from some athletes. Shaquille O'Neil responded in 2003 to a journalist's question about playing against Yao Ming by saying, "Tell Yao Ming, 'ching-chong-yang-wah-ah-so." Pro golfer Jan Stevenson, a native of Australia currently residing in Florida, said in 2003 that Asian women golfers "are killing our tour." She explained that the Korean and Japanese pros didn't promote women's golf because they lacked emotional expressiveness, refused to speak English—even when they could do so, and rarely spoke to fans and reporters (Adelson, 2003; Blauvelt, 2003). Public comments such as these are rare, but they point to the challenges faced when people from different cultural and ethnic backgrounds participate in sports that are organized around only the cultural orientations and traditions of Europeans and North Americans.

AT YOUR *fingertips* For more information on globalization and the migration of athletes worldwide, see Chapter 13, pp. 461–463.

Currently, we need to know more about the ways in which images of Asian and Asian American athletes are taken up and represented in the U.S. media and in the minds of Americans. Research is also needed on the dramatic rise in popularity of various martial arts in the United States. Karate, judo, tae kwon do, and other sports with Asian origins have become especially popular among children, but we don't know if participation in these martial arts has increased children's knowledge and awareness of Asian cultures, influenced ethnic relations in elementary schools, or discredited anti-Asian stereotypes among children and others who participate in these sports. It may be that these sport forms become so Americanized that their Asian roots are lost or ignored by participants—but we don't know.

THE DYNAMICS OF RACIAL AND ETHNIC RELATIONS IN SPORTS

Racial and ethnic relations in the United States are better today than in the past, but many changes are needed before sports are a model of inclusion and fairness. The challenges today are different from the ones faced twenty years ago, and experience shows that when current challenges are met, a new social situation is created in which new challenges emerge. For example, once racial and ethnic segregation is eliminated and people come together, they must learn to live, work, and play with each other despite diverse experiences and cultural perspectives. Meeting this challenge requires a commitment to equal treatment, *plus* learning about the perspectives of others, understanding how they define and give meaning to the world around them, and then determining how to form and maintain relationships while respecting differences, making compromises, and supporting one another in the pursuit of goals that may not always be shared. None of this is easy, and challenges are never met once and for all time.

Many people think in fairy-tale terms when it comes to racial and ethnic relations. They believe that opening a door so that others may enter a social world is all that's needed to achieve racial and ethnic harmony. However, this is merely a first step in a never-ending process of nurturing relationships, producing an inclusive society, and sharing power with others. Racial and ethnic diversity brings potential vitality and creativity to a team, organization, or society, but this potential does not automatically become reality. It requires constant awareness, commitment, and work to achieve and maintain

it (Cunningham, 2007a, 2007b; Fink and Cunningham, 2005).

The following sections deal with three major challenges related to racial and ethnic relations in sports today: (1) eliminating racial and ethnic exclusion in sport participation, (2) dealing with and managing racial and ethnic diversity by creating an inclusive culture on sport teams and in sport organizations, and (3) integrating positions of power in sport organizations.

> **OLC ON THE *OLC:***
> See the OLC—Additional Readings for Chapter 9—for references to research on racial and ethnic diversity and diversity management in sport organizations.

Eliminating Racial and Ethnic Exclusion in Sports

Why are some sports characterized by disproportionately high rates of participation by racial and ethnic minorities, whereas others have little or no racial or ethnic diversity? When sociologist Harry Edwards (1973) answered this question in the early 1970s, he said that certain sports had built-in characteristics that made them easier to desegregate. These remain timely and include the following:

1. The people who control teams in commercial sports can maximize their profits when they employ the best players regardless of skin color or ethnicity.
2. Athlete performance can be measured in concrete, objective terms that are not usually influenced by racial ideology.
3. All players on a sport team benefit when a teammate performs well, regardless of the teammate's skin color or ethnicity.
4. When ethnic minority athletes excel on the playing field they are not automatically promoted into leadership positions where they would have control over white players.

5. Friendships and off-the-field social relationships between teammates are not required for team success.
6. All athletes with scholarships or pro contracts are controlled by coaches, managers, administrators, and owners who are almost always white.

These six characteristics limit the threats that cause whites in nonsport situations and organizations to fear and resist racial and ethnic desegregation. Therefore, when the people who controlled professional teams and revenue-producing college teams realized that they could benefit financially from recruiting ethnic minority players without giving up power and control and without disrupting the existing structure and relationships in their sports, they began to do so.

Desegregation occurs more slowly in sports that lack the characteristics listed above. Golf, tennis, swimming, and other sports played in private clubs where social interaction is personal and often involves male-female relationships have been slow to welcome racial and ethnic diversity. As social contacts become increasingly close, people are more likely to enforce various forms of exclusion. This is why informal practices of racial and ethnic exclusion still exist in many private sports clubs and why it remains difficult to name more than a few African Americans, Latinos, and Asian Pacific Americans playing in the major professional golf and tennis tours or in club-based sports such as lacrosse. Private golf and tennis clubs in the United States have many more black, Latino, and Asian people working in low-wage service jobs than playing on courses and courts and watching their children take lessons.

The most significant forms of racial and ethnic exclusion today occur at the community level where they are hidden behind the fees and other resources required for sport participation. People can claim to have ethnically open sport programs when in reality their location, fees, and the lack of public transportation preclude ethnically inclusive participation. This point also applies to people with disabilities, as noted in Breaking Barriers on page 307.

As public programs are dropped and sports are offered primarily by commercial providers, patterns of exclusion reflect race and ethnicity to the extent that race and ethnicity influence education and income. This type of exclusion occurs in the United States and is difficult to eliminate because market forces do the dirty work of segregation without race or ethnicity even being mentioned. Developing strategies to undermine these dynamics and make sports more inclusive is one the most difficult challenges we now face.

Dealing With and Managing Racial and Ethnic Diversity in Sports

As sports become more global, as teams recruit players worldwide, and as global migration demands more inclusive sports, there will be many new racial and ethnic challenges. It's naïve to think that sports can avoid issues that exist in the rest of the world today, or that inclusion doesn't require a continuous effort for as long as sport organizations exist. A brief look at racial dynamics and issues in U.S. Major League Baseball illustrates this point.

History shows that, after Branch Rickey signed Jackie Robinson to a contract with the Brooklyn Dodgers in 1946, many new challenges confronted Rickey, Robinson, the Dodgers organization, players throughout the league, other baseball teams in the National League, and spectators attending baseball games. Rickey had to convince his partners in the Dodgers organization and other team owners that it was in their interest to abandon their practice of segregation. Robinson had to endure unspeakable racism from opponents, spectators, and others. To control his anger and depression, he needed support from Rickey, his coach, and his teammates.

As thousands of African American fans wanted to see Robinson, the Dodgers and other teams had to change their policies of racial exclusion and segregation in their stadiums. Teammates on the Dodgers were forced to decide if and how they would support Robinson on and off the

Point-of-Entry Barriers
We Are Out There

Toni Davis was training for the 2004 Paralympics in Athens. As a swimmer, she'd heard about Martiza Correia, a new member of the U.S. Olympic team. Correia had broken U.S. swimming records held by the highly touted Amy Van Dyken and Jenny Thompson in the 50- and 100-meter freestyle. When Davis looked online for information about the new record-setting swimmer, she discovered that Correia was an African American like her. Davis was heartened and declared proudly, "*We are out there.*"

When Davis referred to "we," she meant *black swimmers*. As a former intercollegiate athlete, she knew that a black person on a swim team caused many people to do a double take. She also knew that when people saw her—a black swimmer with only one arm—they often did a triple take.

Davis says that she gets more looks for having one arm than for being black, but she knows that race influences choices and opportunities in sports. "What we need to do for minority kids," Davis explains, "is to have low-cost programs that enable them to be in the water and receive the instruction they need to develop their abilities" (Schaller, 2005).

Davis knows that sport participation always has a point of entry—a time and place at which a person is hooked up with an opportunity. In the case of people with a disability, the point of entry is often made available through rehabilitation, occupational therapy, and medical care programs, or through a local network of friends and family.

Taking advantage of an entry opportunity is never automatic. People from an ethnic minority are most likely to enter a program when they see others who will understand them and with whom they can identify. If everyone in a program, including administrators and coaches, is white, they'll think twice before taking a first step toward participation. "Fitting in" is always an issue when initiating or continuing participation.

Point-of-entry opportunities have complex dynamics related to race, ethnicity, health care, medical insurance, trusting medical providers, transportation, and the "look and feel" of a sport program. If ethnic inclusiveness is not apparent, people of color may back off to avoid being labeled as "different." Playing sports is fun, but it becomes tedious when people constantly do triple takes when they see you.

Eliminating point-of-entry barriers related to race and ethnicity is a major challenge in sports for people with disabilities. As in most sport organizations, there's a need to recruit coaches and administrators from underrepresented ethnic populations. Inclusiveness must be apparent so that prospective participants can see people who look like them. Additionally, there's a need to create new entry points that are part of the structure of everyday life in neighborhoods and communities where ethnic minorities live and work. Churches, schools, hospitals, medical clinics, and veterans' organizations are sites at which institutionalized entry points can be created. Once they exist, more people from ethnic minority backgrounds will join Toni Davis in declaring proudly, "We are out there."

- -

field. The team's coach had to manage interracial dynamics he knew nothing about: Who would be Robinson's roommate on road trips, where would the team stay and eat in cities where hotels and restaurants excluded blacks, and what would he say to players who made racist comments that could destroy team morale? These questions had never been asked in the past because Major League Baseball had been played by whites only.

White baseball fans who had never met a black person now faced the prospect of sitting next to one if they wanted to attend a game. Blacks, uncomfortable with whites, faced a similar challenge. Stadium managers faced the challenge of serving food to people with different tastes and traditions; white, working-class service workers had to serve black customers—a totally new experience for them. Journalists

Eliminating racial barriers to sport participation is as important today as it was when Jackie Robinson joined the Brooklyn Dodgers in 1947. After the desegregation of Major League Baseball, there were new challenges associated with managing intergroup relations on teams and integrating positions of power in sport organizations. (*Source:* American Memory Collection)

and radio announcers had to decide how they would represent Robinson's experiences in their coverage—would they talk about racism on the field and in the clubhouse and about the way Robinson handled it, or would they ignore race, even though it was relevant to the game?

These are only some of the new challenges created when MLB was desegregated. And as these challenges were met, new ones emerged. As other black players were signed to teams, players began to racially segregate themselves in locker rooms. Black players could not buy homes in segregated white areas of the cities where they played, and when they challenged records set by whites, they received death threats. Stadium security became an issue, some teams became racially divided, and black players often felt marginalized because all coaches, managers, trainers, and owners were white.

Even the positions played by blacks and whites fit patterns shaped by racial ideology.

Blacks, expected to be fast and physically gifted, played outfield in baseball and defensive back in football—positions believed to call for speed and quick reactions—whereas whites, expected to be smart, played the positions believed to require intelligence and decision-making skills, such as pitcher in baseball and quarterback in football. These position placements, or "stacking" patterns, prevented most blacks from playing the positions at which they would be identified as good candidates for coaching jobs after they retired. This is related to a challenge that has become chronic in baseball and most other sports: the lack of black CEOs, general managers, and head coaches.

This example illustrates that challenges related to race and ethnicity are an ever-present part of our lives; they will exist as long as skin color and ethnicity influence people's lives and are viewed as socially important. This is not new, nor is it unique to sports. Managers and coaches must now be ready and able to work effectively

OLC ON THE *OLC*:

See the OLC—Additional Readings for Chapter 9—for a detailed and illustrated discussion of "stacking," an essay on the profit motive as an incentive for desegregation in sports, and references on management issues related to racial and ethnic diversity in sport organizations.

with players from multiple cultural and national backgrounds, meld them into a team, defuse and debunk players' racial and ethnic stereotypes, and facilitate respect for customs and lifestyles they've not seen before. Even determining the food to be served in pre-game meals now requires creative management strategies.

Athletes and coaches must learn new ways to communicate effectively on ethnically diverse teams, and marketing people must learn ways to promote racially and ethnically diverse teams to predominantly white, Euro-American fans. Ethnic issues enter into sponsorship considerations and products sold at games, and ethnic awareness is now an important qualification for those who handle advertising and sponsorship deals. For example, the success of professional soccer in the United States depends partly on attracting ethnic spectators to games and television broadcasts. Spanish-speaking announcers are crucial, and deals must be made with radio and television stations that broadcast in Spanish.

Teams in the NFL and NBA now face situations in which 70 to 85 percent of their players are black, whereas 90 to 95 percent of their season ticket holders are white. Many people are aware of this issue, but it's rarely discussed because Americans have a "civic etiquette" that keeps these issues "off the table" in public settings (Eliasoph, 1999). But if the challenges related to race and ethnicity in sports are to be met, changes in this etiquette are needed so that open and honest discussions can occur.

Integrating Positions of Power in Sport Organizations

Despite progressive changes in many sports, positions of power and control are held primarily by white, non-Latino men. There are exceptions to this pattern, but they do not eliminate pervasive and persistent racial and ethnic inequalities related to power and control in sports.

Data on who holds positions of power change every year, and it is difficult to obtain consistent information from sport teams and organizations. Fortunately, Richard Lapchick, director of The Institute for Diversity and Ethics in Sport (TIDES) at the University of Central Florida, often publishes *Racial and Gender Report Cards* for the NCAA and many professional sports (http://www.ncasports.org/press_releases.htm). They contain data on the racial and ethnic composition of players in major professional team sports and an analysis of the number and types of jobs held by women and people of color in major professional and university sports organizations. The report cards cover everyone from owners and athletic directors to office staff, athletic trainers, and radio and television announcers.

The data in Table 9.1 were drawn from six recent report cards on professional leagues and teams. The percentages in the table describe the racial and ethnic composition of players, assistant coaches, head coaches, vice presidents, chief operating officers and general managers, team chairmen and presidents, and team owners. The data show that whites are overrepresented in every power position in the major professional sports played in the United States. Blacks are overrepresented among players in a few sports, but they generally play under the control and management of whites (Hughes, 2004).

Patterns are similar in most other sport organizations at nearly all levels of competition. Black, Latino, and Asian players at all levels are aware that whites have a disproportionate share of power and control in sports. When they see good minority candidates passed over as white candidates are selected for important jobs

Table 9.1 Who plays, coaches, and has the power: Race and ethnicity in major professional sports in North America.

League	Players (%)	Assistant Coaches (%)	Head Coaches (%)	VPs (%)	General Manager* (%)	CEO/ President (%)	Major Owners (%)
NBA: Whites	21	59	60	85	73	87	98
(2007) Blacks	75	40	40	11	27	13	2
Latinos	3	1	0	3	0	0	0
Asians	<1	0	0	1	0	0	0
Others†	1	0	0	0	0	0	0
NFL: Whites	31	62	78	92	87	100	100
(2006) Blacks	67	35	22	8	13	0	0
Latinos	<1	2	0	1	0	0	0
Asians	2	1	0	0	0	0	0
Others	1	0	0	0	0	0	0
MLB: Whites	60	96	80	90	93	100	97
(2007) Blacks	8	13	7	4	3	0	0
Latinos	29	17	13	4	3	0	3
Asians	3	1	0	2	0	0	0
Others	0	0	0	0	0	0	0
NHL:‡ Whites	98	100	100	96	100	100	94
(2003) Blacks	1	0	0	3	0	0	0
Latinos	1	0	0	0	0	0	0
Asians	1	0	0	1	0	0	6
Others	1	0	0	0	0	0	0
MLS: Whites	64	76	91	100	100	70	NA§
(2006) Blacks	17	3	0	0	0	0	NA
Latinos	15	18	9	0	0	20	NA
Asians	3	0	0	0	0	10	NA
Others	3	3	0	0	0	0	NA
WNBA: Whites	36	59	86	90	82	89	95
(2007) Blacks	63	41	14	10	18	11	5
Latinos	0	0	0	0	0	0	0
Asians	0	0	0	0	0	0	0
Others	0	1	0	0	0	0	0

Source: Lapchick (2008c).

*These men are responsible for the day-to-day operation of teams (no women were in this position).

†"Others" consist of Native Americans and people who are unidentifiable by race or ethnicity.

‡Data are for 2002–2003 because the 2004–2005 season was canceled.

§NA means "Not Applicable" because the MLS is a monopoly with investor/franchise holders rather than owners.

in sport organizations, they question the attitudes and orientations of owners and other decision makers in sports. They know that there is a difference between desegregating sports to make more money and being inclusive to the point of sharing power in sport organizations. The data suggest that full inclusion in the form of sharing power is a long way from being achieved.

Overall, people do not give up racial and ethnic beliefs easily, especially when they come in

> **OLC ON THE *OLC*:**
> See the OLC—Additional Readings for Chapter 9—for the author's essay on sports as sites for transforming the racial attitudes of individuals.

the form of well-established ideologies rooted deeply in their cultures. Those who benefit from dominant racial ideology generally resist changes in the relationships and social structures that reproduce it. This is why certain racial and ethnic inequities have remained a part of sports.

Sports may bring people together, but they do not automatically lead them to adopt tolerant attitudes or change long-standing policies of exclusion. For example, white team owners, general managers, and athletic directors in the United States worked with black athletes for many years before they ever hired black coaches or administrators. It often requires social and legal pressures to force people in positions of power to act more affirmatively in their hiring practices. In the meantime, blacks and other ethnic minorities remain underrepresented in coaching and administration.

Although there is resistance to certain types of changes in sports, many sport organizations are more progressive than other organizations when it comes to improving racial and ethnic relations. However, good things do not happen automatically or as often as many think, nor do changes in people's attitudes automatically translate into changes in the overall organization of sports. Challenging the negative beliefs and attitudes of individuals is one thing; changing the relationships and social structures that have been built on those beliefs and attitudes is another. Both changes are needed, but neither will occur automatically just because sports bring people together in the same locker rooms and stadiums.

The reports cards published by Lapchick and TIDES and similar studies on hiring practices done by Black Coaches and Administrators (http://bcasports.cstv.com/) have kept a bright light shining on the racial and ethnic composition of major sport organizations in the United States. This light creates heat that makes decision-makers uncomfortable if they are not making progress toward full racial and ethnic inclusion. Public scrutiny is an effective strategy because progress comes only when those in power work to bring about change. It has never been easy for people to deal with racial and ethnic issues, but if it is done in sports, it attracts public attention that can inspire changes in other spheres of life.

The racial and ethnic diversity training sessions used over the past two decades have produced some changes, but promoting positive changes in ethnic relations today requires leaders who are trained specifically to create more inclusive cultures and power structures in sport organizations. This means that training must go beyond athletes and include everyone from team owners and athletic directors to mid-level management, coaches, and people in marketing, media, and public information. When training programs are directed primarily toward employees, the employees won't take them seriously if they don't see their superiors making a personal commitment to them.

Even people who are sensitive to ethnic diversity issues require regular opportunities to renew and extend their knowledge of the experiences and perspectives of others who have different vantage points in social worlds. This means that effective training requires information and approaches organized around the perspectives of underrepresented ethnic populations. This is crucial because progressive change takes into account the interests of those least likely to be heard or to hold positions of power.

summary

ARE RACE AND ETHNICITY IMPORTANT IN SPORTS?

Racial and ethnic issues exist in sports, just as they exist in other spheres of social life. As people watch, play, and talk about sports, they often take into account ideas about skin color

The Irish Football Association (IFA) uses soccer as a site for eradicating the Protestant-versus-Catholic sectarianism that has caused decades of violence and terrorism in Northern Ireland. IFA officials also work with other European soccer leagues to eliminate racist displays and chants that some fans direct at African players on European and African teams. Bigotry in any form, whether expressing sectarianism or racism, is not welcome at football matches in Northern Ireland. (*Source:* Mike Collins, Irish Football Association, Northern Ireland)

and ethnicity. The meanings given to skin color and ethnic background influence access to sport participation and the decisions that people make about sports in their lives.

Race refers to a category of people identified through a classification system based on meanings given to physical traits among humans; *ethnicity* refers to collections of people identified in terms of their shared cultural heritage. Racial and ethnic *minorities* are populations that have endured systematic forms of discrimination in a society. The idea of race has a complex history, and it serves as the foundation for racial ideology, which people use to identify and make sense of "racial" characteristics and differences. Racial ideology, like other social constructions, changes over time as ideas and relationships change. However, over the past century in the United States, dominant racial ideology has supported the notion that there are important biological and cognitive differences between people classified as "black" as opposed to "white," and that these differences explain the success of blacks in certain sports and sport positions.

Racial ideology influences the ways that many people connect skin color with athletic performance. At the same time, it influences sport participation decisions and achievement patterns in sports. Race, gender, and class relations in American society combine to create a context in which black males emphasize a personal presentation of self that is described as "cool pose"—a stylized persona that adds to the commodity value of the black male body in sports and enables some black athletes to use widely accepted ideas about race to intimidate white opponents in sports.

Sport participation patterns among African Americans, Native Americans, Latinos, and Asian Pacific Americans each have unique histories. Combinations of cultural, social, and political factors have influenced those histories. However, sport participation in ethnic minority populations usually occurs under terms set by the dominant ethnic population in a community or society. Minority populations are seldom able to use sports to challenge the power and privilege of the dominant group, even though particular individuals may experience great personal success in sports.

The fact that some sports have histories of racially and ethnically mixed participation does not mean that problems have been eliminated. Harmonious racial and ethnic relations never occur automatically, and ethnic harmony is not established once and for all time. As current problems are solved, new relationships and new challenges are created. This means that racial and ethnic issues require regular attention if challenges are to be anticipated accurately and dealt with successfully. Success also depends on whether members of the dominant ethnic population see value in racial and ethnic diversity and commit themselves to dealing with diversity issues alongside those who have different ethnic backgrounds.

Sports continue to be sites for racial and ethnic problems. But despite problems, sports also can be sites for challenging racial ideology and transforming ethnic relations. This happens only when people in sports plan strategies to encourage critical awareness of ethnic prejudices, racist ideas, and forms of discrimination built into the cultures and structures of sport organizations. This awareness is required to increase ethnic inclusion, deal with and manage ethnic diversity, and integrate ethnic minorities into the power structures of sport organizations. Without this awareness, ethnic relations often become volatile and lead to overt forms of hostility.

WEBSITE RESOURCES

Note: Websites often change. The following URLs were current when this book was printed. Please check our website (www.mhhe.com/coakley10e) for updates and additions.

www.mhhe.com/coakley10e Click on Chapter 9 for discussion guides for *Hoop Dreams* and *In Whose Honor*, brief readings on the history of racial desegregation in U.S. sports, and stacking in the NFL and Major League Baseball.

www.asian-nation.org/sports.shtml Articles and links to articles on Asians in sports.

www.asianathlete.com/WebLinksPage.aspx Links to sites on Asians in sports.

www.bus.ucf.edu/sport/cgi-bin/site/sitew .cgi?page=/ides/media.htx The DeVos Sport Business Management site has links to recent news releases from The Institute for Diversity and Ethics in Sport; data on graduation rates for university teams in postseason tournament and bowl games, and the *Racial and Gender Report Card*—a research document that analyzes hiring practices in major sports organizations in the United States.

http://home.earthlink.net/~prometheus_6/ RaceReadings.htm Short essays and interviews on race with scholars from many academic disciplines; excellent source for those wanting to understand race as a concept and as lived experience.

www.nativeculturelinks.com/mascots.html Links to websites and articles on Native American names and mascots used by sports teams.

www.pacificcitizen.org/sports.htm The sports section of a widely read newspaper for Asian Americans; provides current stories plus an easy-to-use archive.

www.pbs.org/race/000_General/000_00-Home.htm Site for the three-part series, *Race—The Power of An Illusion*, first shown in 2004; information for students and instructors; links to summaries of each part of the series, and links for those wishing to explore the topic of race in more detail.

http://racerelations.about.com/od/racesports/Race_ Sports.htm Site with links to articles on diversity and other sources that cover race and ethnicity-related issues in sports.

www.shipbrook.com/jeff/ChiefWahoo/ A video parody focused on Chief Wahoo, the mascot and logo of the MLB team in Cleveland; highlights points made in this chapter.

www.sportinsociety.org/vpd/ptw.php Project TEAMWORK is a diversity awareness and conflict-resolution program that teaches high school students to combat discrimination.

www.umich.edu/~ac213/student_projects05/ls/ Focuses on Latinos in sports in the United States; provides information sport-by-sport and on the barriers that Latinos faced in breaking into the four major men's sports in the United States.

(John Sutherland)

SOCIAL CLASS

Do Money and Power Matter in Sports?

BENEATH THE THIN LAYER of sport entertainment
that makes its way onto television are the bulk of
college athletes: Well-off and white.

—Tom Farrey, ESPN journalist (2008)

Visit *Sports in Society*'s Online
Learning Center (OLC) at www.mhhe.com/
coakley10e for additional information and
study material for this chapter, including the
following:

- A complete chapter outline
- Learning objectives
- Practice quizzes
- Internet resources
- Related readings
- Essays
- Student projects

THE SUPER BOWL as a live event is primarily a
perk for the nation's elite, and an opportunity
for companies to sell their products to a coveted
demographic of influencers and decision-makers.

—Katie Thomas, *New York Times* **sports reporter
(2008)**

IT CAN BE A STRAIN on families . . . We spent
hundreds of thousands of dollars on Heather.
Tournaments, hotel accommodations, private
lessons, food, travel, sitters for siblings or pets—all
those things cost money.

—Jan Peck, mother of an Olympian on the U.S.
soccer team (in Ellin, 2008)

GROWING UP IN the Robert Taylor Homes [in
Chicago], you have three choices. You can be a
gang banger, a rapper or a basketball player.

—Jay Straight, college student and basketball
player (in Berger, 2004)

315

People like to think that sports transcend issues of money, power, and economic inequalities. They see sports as open to everyone, watch them on "free" television, and define success on the playing field in terms of individual ability and hard work. However, all organized sports depend on material resources, and those resources must come from somewhere. Therefore, playing, watching, and excelling in sports depend on resources supplied by individuals, families, governments, or corporations.

More than ever before, it takes money to play sports and develop sport skills. Tickets are expensive, and spectators often are divided by social class in the stadium: The wealthy and well connected sit in luxury suites and club seats, whereas fans who are less well off sit in other sections, depending on their ability to pay for premium tickets or buy season tickets. Today it takes money to watch sports on television as satellite and cable connections come with ever-increasing monthly subscriber fees and pay-per-view costs skyrocket. This means that sports and sport participation are closely connected with the distribution of economic resources in society.

Many people believe that sports are a new path to economic success for people from all social classes. Rags-to-riches stories are common when people talk about athletes. However, these beliefs and stories distract attention from the ways in which sports reflect and perpetuate existing economic inequalities.

This chapter deals with matters of money and wealth, as well as larger sociological issues related to social class and socioeconomic mobility. Our discussion focuses on the following questions:

1. What is meant by *social class* and *class relations?*
2. How do social class and class relations influence sports and sport participation?

> [Sport] serves to reproduce social and economic distinctions and preserve the power and influence of those who control resources in society. — Alan Tomlinson, sociologist, University of Brighton, England, 2007

3. Are sports open and democratic in the provision of economic and career opportunities?
4. Does playing sports contribute to occupational success and social mobility among former athletes?

SOCIAL CLASS AND CLASS RELATIONS

Understanding social class and the related concepts of social stratification, socioeconomic status, and life chances is important when studying social worlds. Economic resources are related to power in society, and economic inequalities influence many aspects of people's lives.

Social class refers to *categories of people who share an economic position in society based on their income, wealth (savings and assets), education, occupation, and social connections.* People in a particular social class also share similar **life chances**—that is, *similar odds for achieving economic success and power in society.* Social classes exist in all industrial societies because life chances are not equally distributed across all populations.

Social stratification refers to *structured forms of economic inequalities that are part of the organization of everyday social life.* In other words, in comparison with people from upper social classes, people from lower social classes have fewer opportunities to achieve economic success and power. Children born into wealthy, powerful, and well-connected families are in better positions to become wealthy, powerful, and well-connected adults than are children born into poor families that lack influence and social networks connecting them with educational and career opportunities.

Most of us are aware of economic inequalities in society. We see them all around us and in television programs like MTV's *Cribs* (the contemporary young people's version of a previous program, *Lifestyles of the Rich and Famous*). We know they exist and influence people's lives, but there are few public discussions about the impact of social class on our views of ourselves and others, our social relationships, and our everyday lives (Perrucci and Wysong, 2003). In other words, we don't discuss **class relations**—the *ways that social class is incorporated into our everyday lives*. We often hear about the importance of equal opportunities in society, but there are few discussions about the ways that people in upper socioeconomic classes use their income, wealth, and power to maintain their privileged positions in society and pass that privilege from one generation to the next. Instead, we hear "rags to riches" stories about individuals who overcame poverty or a lower-class background to become wealthy, stories about "millionaires next door," and stories CEOs who are "regular guys" with average incomes of $11 million a year. Ignored in the media and popular discourse are the oppressive effects of poverty and the limited opportunities available to those who lack economic resources, access to good education, and well-placed social connections. Those stories are too depressing to put in the news, claim executives for the commercial media— people don't like to hear about them, and they lower the audience ratings. However, social-class differences are real; they have real consequences for life chances, they affect nearly every facet of people's lives, and all of this is clearly documented by valid and reliable data (Collins and Yeskel, 2005; Lardner and Smith, 2005; Perrucci and Wysong, 2003; Rose, 2007; Sernau, 2005).

People in the United States often shy away from critical discussions of social class and class relations because they're uneasy about acknowledging that equality of opportunity is largely a myth in their society (hooks, 2000; Sage, 1998). This is especially true in regard to sports and sport participation—a sphere of life in which most people believe that money and class-based privilege don't matter.

The discussion of social class and class relations in this chapter is grounded in a critical approach that identifies who benefits and who is disadvantaged by the ways that sports are organized and played. The focus is on economic inequality, the processes through which inequality is reproduced, how it benefits wealthy and powerful people, and how it affects sports and the lives of people associated with sports.

SPORTS AND ECONOMIC INEQUALITY

Money and economic power exert significant influence on the goals, purpose, and organization of sports in society (Bairner, 2007; Gruneau, 1999; Sugden and Tomlinson, 2000; Tomlinson, 2007). Many people believe that sports and sport participation are open to all people and that inequalities related to money, position, and influence have no effect on the organized games we play and watch. However, formally organized sports could not be developed, scheduled, or maintained without economic resources. Those who control money and economic power use them to organize and sponsor sports. As they do so, they give preference to sport forms that reflect and maintain their values and interests.

The wealthy aristocrats who developed the modern Olympic Games even used their power to establish a definition of *amateur* that favored athletes from wealthy backgrounds. This definition, which excluded athletes who used their sport skills to earn a living, has been revised over the years so that participants can include those who are not independently wealthy. However, money and economic power now operate in different ways as elite-level training has become privatised and costly in many countries.

Elite and powerful people have considerable influence over what "counts as sport" and how sports are organized and played in mainstream social worlds. Even when grassroots games and physical activities become formally organized as sports, they don't become popular unless they can be used to reaffirm the interests and ideologies of sponsors with resources. For example,

ESPN organized and televised the X Games to fit the needs of corporate sponsors that buy advertising time to promote their products to young males. Even informal games require facilities, equipment, and safe play spaces—all of which are more plentiful in upper- and upper-middle-income neighborhoods. Low-income neighborhoods generally lack what is needed to initiate and sustain informal activities; families don't have large lawns at their homes, they don't live on safe cul-de-sacs without traffic, and well-maintained neighborhood parks are in short supply. This is why social class and class relations must be taken into account when we study sports in society and try to explain the patterns of sport participation we see around us.

The Dynamics of Class Relations

To understand the dynamics of class relations, think about the way that age relations operate in sports. For example, even though young people are capable of creating and playing games on their own, adults intervene and create organized youth sport programs. These programs emphasize the things that adults think are best for their children. As noted in Chapter 5, adults have the resources to develop, schedule, and maintain organized sports that reflect their ideas of what children should be doing and learning. Children often enjoy these adult-controlled sports, but their participation occurs in a framework that is determined by adults and organized to legitimize and reproduce adult control over the lives of children.

Age relations are especially apparent in youth sports when participants don't meet adult expectations or when they violate the rules developed by adults. The adults use their power to define deviance, identify when it occurs, and demand that children comply with rules and expectations. Overall, the adults use their superior resources to convince young people that "the adults' way" is "the right way" to play sports. When young people comply with adults' rules and meet the adults' expectations, they're

rewarded and told that they have "character." This is why many adults are fond of college and professional coaches who are autocratic and controlling. These coaches reaffirm the ideas that it is normal and necessary for adults to control young people and that young people must learn to accept that control. In this way, sports reproduce a hierarchical form of age relations, with adult power and privilege defined as normal and necessary aspects of social worlds.

Class relations work in similar ways. People with resources sponsor sports that support their ideas about "good character," individual responsibility, competition, achievement, and proper social organization. In fact, whenever people obtain power in a social world, they define "character" in a way that promotes their interests. For example, when wealthy and powerful people play sports in exclusive clubs, such as Augusta National (golf club) in Georgia, they use a class ideology that legitimizes their right to do so and establishes their membership in such a club as a privilege they deserve for being the winners in society. Similarly, they sponsor sports that can be presented in ways that reaffirm the existing class structure in society and the ideology that supports it. This is partly why popular spectator sports worldwide emphasize competition, individualism, highly specialized skills, the use of technology, and dominance over opponents. When these values and cultural practices are widely accepted, average people are more likely to believe that the status and privilege of the wealthy and powerful are legitimate and deserved. Sports that emphasize partnership, sharing, open participation, nurturance, and mutual support are seldom sponsored because people with power don't want to promote values that reaffirm equality and horizontal forms of social organization in society.

Class Ideology in the United States

Sociologists define **class ideology** as a *web of ideas and beliefs that people use to understand economic inequalities, identify their class position, and*

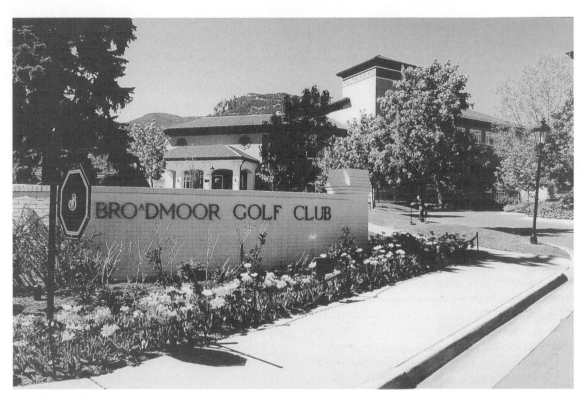

BROADMOOR GOLF,
TENNIS CLUB & SPA
Members and Guests Only

The belief that wealth and power are achieved through competitive success implies that being wealthy and powerful is proof of one's abilities, qualifications, and overall moral worth. Exclusive sports clubs reaffirm this belief and reinforce the idea that class privileges enjoyed by powerful and wealthy people are deserved; and the clubs are sites for establishing relationships that are used to perpetuate status. (*Source:* Jay Coakley)

evaluate the impact of economic inequalities on the organization of social worlds. Dominant class ideology in the United States has long been organized around two themes: the American Dream and a belief that the United States is a meritocracy.

The American Dream is *a hopeful vision of boundless opportunities for individuals to succeed economically and live a happy life based on consumption.* It focuses attention on individual aspirations and often blurs an awareness of social class differences in material living conditions and differential life chances among categories of people. The uniquely American belief that "you can be anything you want to be" never acknowledges that a person's class position influences life chances or

that life chances influence patterns of social and economic mobility in all social classes. Therefore, Americans often dream about what they hope to be in the future rather than critically examining their current economic circumstances and the ways that class relations affect their lives. The belief that "you can be anything" also discredits poor and low-income people by associating poverty with individual failure, laziness, and weakness of character.

The American Dream is usually connected with a belief that the United States is a **meritocracy**—*a society in which rewards go to people who deserve them due to their abilities and qualifications.* Believing that the United States is a meritocracy helps people explain and justify economic inequalities. It supports the assumption that success is rightfully earned and failure is caused by poor choices and a lack of ambition.

Sustaining widespread beliefs that the United States is a meritocracy requires that people also believe that individual ability, qualifications, and character are objectively proven through competitive success, that humans are naturally competitive, and that competition is the only fair way to allocate rewards in a society. This is why people with money and power like to use sports as a metaphor for life—it identifies winners like them as deserving individuals who have outperformed others in a natural process of individual competition and achievement. This also is why CEOs hire successful coaches as keynote speakers at annual corporate meetings—they know that coaches will reaffirm the idea that the business world, like sports, is organized so that only the best, brightest, and hardest workers make it to the top, and that those at the top deserve what they receive.

Figure 10.1 shows that class ideology in the United States is a web of ideas and beliefs related to the American Dream, meritocracy, and competition; it illustrates that inequality is a result of people receiving what they deserve; it emphasizes that opportunities exist and that success is achieved

only when people develop abilities and work hard; and it justifies inequality as a natural result of competition in a society where merit counts.

One of the outcomes of such an ideology is that competitive success comes to be linked with moral worth. People assume that "you get what you deserve, and you deserve what you get." This belief, of course, works to the advantage of people with wealth, because it implies that they deserve what they have and that inequality is a fair and natural outcome of competitive processes. A related belief is that as long as competition is free and unregulated, only the best will succeed and only the lazy and unqualified will fail.

Promoting this ideology is difficult when it conflicts with the real experiences of many Americans who work hard and haven't achieved success in the form of the American Dream or have seen their success disappear due to factors beyond their control. Therefore, people in the upper classes are most likely to retain their position and status *if* they can create widespread agreement that competition is a natural and fair way to allocate rewards and that the winners in competitive processes deserve the rewards they receive. This, of course, is how sports come to be connected with class relations in society. Sports offer "proof" that inequalities are based on merit, that competition identifies winners, and that losers should work harder or change themselves if they want to be winners, or simply get up and try again. Most important, sports provides a metaphor for society that portrays social class as a characteristic of individuals rather than an economic structure that influences life chances and the distribution of resources in society.

Alan Tomlinson, a British sociologist who has studied power and social class for decades, has noted that sport, as it is sponsored and played today, "ultimately serves to reproduce social and economic distinctions and preserve the power and influence of those who control resources in society." As a result, he says, sports today "cannot be fully understood unless this key influence and core dynamic is fully recognized" (2007, p. 4695).

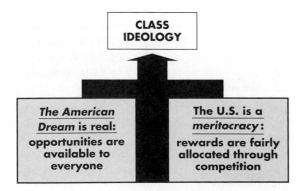

FIGURE 10.1 Major beliefs that inform and support class ideology in the United States.

Class Relations and Who Has Power in Sports

Decisions that affect the meaning, purpose, and organization of sports are made at many levels—from neighborhood youth sport programs to the International Olympic Committee. Although scholars who study sports in society identify people who exercise power in various settings, they usually don't rank those with power in and over sports. But *The Sporting News*, a national weekly newspaper in the United States, regularly publishes a rank-ordered list of "the most powerful people in [U.S.] sports." Their most recent rankings and rankings from 2004 are listed in Table 10.1, which includes twenty-eight men and no women. Twenty-six of the men are white, non-Latinos; one is African American; and one is Latino. Ten men represent media companies, nine represent sport organizations, six represent corporate sponsors, and three are involved in the Congressional investigation of steroids in sports. There are no coaches or current athletes on the list.

> ⓄⓁⒸ **ON THE *OLC*:**
> See the OLC—Additional Readings for Chapter 10—for past lists of the 25 most powerful people in sports.

If we combine the information is this table with the information in Table 9.1 (page 310) in the last chapter, it is clear that white men hold nearly 100 percent of the major power positions in elite sports today. These men have much in common with other economic elites in the United States. Collectively, they benefit from a class ideology that legitimizes the existing status and power hierarchy in American society and supports the idea that the current level of economic inequality, even though it is greater than it has been for nearly a century, is good for the country. This is why they are sincerely committed to a form of sport—elite men's sports—in which competition, conquest, individualism, authority, and consumption are highlighted in everything from media coverage and stadium design to team logos and ads for upcoming games and contests.

The rest of the Power 100 rankings are little different than the top 25, although they include three women (#65, #93, and #99), five African Americans, three Latinos, and three Asian Pacific Americans (including Tiger Woods). Although the power wielded by these and other powerful people in sports does not ignore the interests of common folk in the United States and worldwide, it clearly focuses on the expansion and profitability of the organizations represented by the power holders. Therefore, sports are sponsored and presented to highlight the meanings and orientations valued by economic elites at the same time that they provide exciting and enjoyable experiences to people like you and me.

This relationship between sports and social class explains why many of us in the sociology of sport use a combination of structural and cultural theories to help us understand sports in society. For example, Antonio Gramsci, an Italian political theorist, developed a theory stating that members of the "ruling class" in contemporary societies maintain their power to the extent that they can develop creative ways to convince most people that their society is organized as fairly and efficiently as possible under current national and global conditions. One of the strategies for doing this is to become the primary providers of popular pleasure and entertainment—the things that give people joy and excitement—and use this forum to promote particular ideas and beliefs about what should be important in people's lives. In other words, sports and other forms of exciting entertainment become cultural vehicles for establishing "ideological outposts" in the minds of people who are ruled. These outposts can then be used to relay other messages into the popular consciousness—messages from sponsors and media commentators who reaffirm a class ideology legitimizing current forms of class inequality in the United States and

Table 10.1   The 2006 Top 25 in *The Sporting News*' "Power 100" and previous ranking in 2004

Rank in 2006	Name	Position	Organization	Rank in 2004
1	David Stern	Commissioner	NBA	4
2	George Bodenheimer	President Co-chair	ESPN & ABC Sports Disney Media Networks	5
3	Paul Tagliabue	Commissioner	NFL	1
4	Bud Selig	Commissioner	Major League Baseball	3
5	Brian France	Chairman/CEO	NASCAR	2
6	Gary Bettman	Commissioner	NHL	*
7	Dick Ebersol	Chairman	NBC Sports	9
8	Sean McManus	President	CBS News and CBS Sports	*
9	David Hill	Chairman/CEO	FOX Sports Television Group	8
10	Brian Roberts	Chairman and CEO	Comcast	*
11	Ted Forstmann (NR)	Chairman	IMG	6
12	Gene Upshaw	Executive director	NFLPA	
13	August Busch IV Tony Ponturo	President V.P., global media/ marketing	Anheuser-Busch	7
14	Phil Knight	Chairman	Nike	10
15	John Skipper	Executive V.P. of content	ESPN	*
16	Adam Silver	President and COO	NBA Entertainment	*
17	Bill Daly	Executive V.P. and chief legal officer	NHL	*
18	Roger Goodell	Executive V.P. and COO	NFL	12
19	William Perez	President and CEO	Nike, Inc.	*
20	Ed Goren	President and executive producer	FOX Sports	22
21	Steve Bornstein	President and CEO	NFL Network	25
22	David Levy	President President	Turner Sports/ Turner Entertainment ad sales and marketing	*
23	Erich Stamminger	CEO & directs global marketing	Adidas	*
24	Sens. John McCain & Jim Bunning Tom Davis	U.S. Rep. Congressional steroids enforcers		*
25	Jeff Shell	President	Comcast Programming	*

*These people were unranked in 2004, that is, they were not listed in the Top 25.

worldwide. This critical theoretical approach helps us see the dynamics of class relations and the process of hegemony at work in sports and other spheres of our lives.

SOCIAL CLASS AND SPORT PARTICIPATION PATTERNS

In all societies, social class and class relations influence who plays, who watches, who consumes information about sports, and what information about sports is available in mainstream media.[1] Patterns of sport participation, whether they include playing, watching, or consuming media coverage of sports, are closely associated with money, power, and privilege. At a basic level, organized sports are a luxury item in the economies of many nations, and they are most prevalent in wealthy nations where people have discretionary money and time.

AT YOUR *fingertips* For more information on the relationship between wealth and sports, see Chapter 11, p. 356 and pp. 372–379.

Active sport participation, attendance at events, and consuming media sports are positively correlated with a person's income, education, and occupational status (Booth and Loy, 1999; CBC, 2005; Donnelly and Harvey, 1999; Farrey, 2008; Scheerder et al., 2002; T. Wilson, 2002). For example, Olympic athletes tend to come from more privileged populations in society (Collins and Buller, 2003; Kidd, 1995). This was documented in a 1996 analysis of U.S. Olympic teams across all sports (*Atlanta Journal/Constitution*, 1996, p. H7), and it remains true today.

Training at the elite level requires considerable resources. Some costs may be covered by sponsors for those lucky enough to have them, but others must be covered by personal funds (Ellin, 2008). For example, when the record-setting swimmer 41-year old Dara Torres trained for the 2008 Olympics, she spent about $100,000 per year for her support staff, including a pool coach, a strength and conditioning coach who also is her dietician, two full-time people who stretch her muscles, a physical therapist, a masseuse, and a nanny to care for her daughter (Crouse, 2007).

Even the health and fitness movement, often described as a grassroots phenomenon in North America, involves mostly people who have higher-than-average incomes and education and work in professional or managerial occupations. For the most part, people in low-income jobs don't run, bicycle, or swim as often as their high-income counterparts. Nor do they play as many organized sports on their lunch hour, after work, on weekends, or during vacations. This pattern holds true throughout the life course, for younger and older people, men and women, racial and ethnic populations, and people with disabilities: Social class is related strongly to participation among all categories of people.

Over time, economic inequality in society leads to the formation of class-based lifestyles that involve particular forms of sports (Bourdieu, 1986a, 1986b; Dukes and Coakley, 2002; Laberge and Sankoff, 1988). For the most part, sport participation in various lifestyles reflects patterns of sponsorship and access to participation opportunities. For example, the lifestyles of wealthy people routinely include golf, tennis, skiing, swimming, sailing, and other sports that are self-funded and played at exclusive clubs and resorts. These sports often involve expensive facilities, equipment, and/or clothing, and generally require that people have jobs and/or lives in which they have the control, freedom, and time needed to participate; some people also combine sport participation with their jobs by using facilities that their business associates also use. This has interesting implications in the United States, where companies pay the club memberships of their top executives and then classify most club expenses as "business deductions" on the corporation's tax

---

[1] This was especially apparent in the media coverage of the 2008 Olympic Games in Beijing, China (Zirin, 2008a).

returns. Taking these deductions reduces the company's taxes and reduces the tax revenues that fund public sport programs for people who cannot afford golf, tennis, or elite health club memberships.

The lifestyles of middle-income and working-class people, on the other hand, tend to include sports that by tradition are free and open to the public, sponsored by public funds, or available through public schools. When these sports involve the use of expensive equipment or clothing, participation occurs in connection with various forms of financial sacrifice. For instance, buying a motocross bike so his child can ride and race means that a father must work overtime, cancel the family vacation, and organize family leisure around motocross races.

The lifestyles of low-income people and those living under the poverty line seldom involve regular forms of sport participation, unless a shoe company identifies a young potential star and sponsors his or her participation. When people struggle to stretch the family budget, they seldom can maintain a lifestyle that includes regular sport participation. Spending money to play or watch sports is a luxury that most low-income people can't afford.

Homemaking, Child Rearing, and Earning a Living: Class and Gender Relations in Women's Lives

The impact of social class often varies by age, gender, race and ethnicity, and geographic location. For example, married woman with children are less likely than their male counterparts to have the time and resources to play sports (Raisborough, 2006; Thompson, 1999a, 1999b). To join a soccer team that schedules practices late in the afternoon and plays games in the

> **It cost hundreds of thousands of dollars over the years [to pay for his training and competitions]. But I knew I was going to do whatever I had to make sure he followed his dream.** —David Ali, father of a 19-year-old boxer on the 2008 U.S. Olympic team (in Ellin, 2008)

> **My only brother was not required to help out around the house, but was encouraged to go out and play football with his friends.** — Dr. Beatriz Vélez (2003)

evening or on weekends is all but impossible when you're the family cook, chauffeur, housekeeper, and homework supervisor.

On the other hand, married men with children are less likely to feel such constraints. When they play softball or soccer after work, their wives may delay family dinners or keep dinner warm until they arrive home. When they schedule a golf game on a Saturday morning, their wives make breakfast for the children and then chauffeur one or more children to their youth sport games.

Women in middle- and lower-income families are most constrained by homemaking and child rearing responsibilities. Unable to pay for child care, domestic help, and sport participation fees, these women have few opportunities to play sports. They also lack time, transportation to and from sport facilities, access to gyms and playing fields in their neighborhoods, and the sense of physical safety that enables them to feel secure enough to leave home and travel to places where they can play sports. When playing a sport requires multiple participants, the lack of resources among some women affects others, because it reduces their prospects for assembling the requisite number of players. This is also true for men, but women from middle- and lower-income families are more likely than their male counterparts to lack the network of relationships out of which sport interests and participation emerge and are supported.

Women from upper-income families, on the other hand, usually face few constraints on sport participation. They can afford child care, domestic help, carry-out dinners, and sport fees. They participate by themselves and with friends and family members. Their social networks include

The sports played by young people in low-income families often occur in public areas such as this public school playground. Young people in upper- and upper-middle-class families have resources to purchase access to privately owned sport facilities and spaces. This results in different sport experiences and different sport participation patterns from one social class to another. (*Source:* Tini Campbell)

other women who also have resources to play sports. Women who grow up in these families play sports during their childhoods and attend schools with good sport programs. They seldom experience the same constraints as their lower-income counterparts, even though their opportunities may not equal those of their upper-income male peers.

The sport participation of girls and young women also is limited when they're expected to shoulder responsibilities at home. For example, in low-income families, especially single-parent and immigrant families, teenage daughters often are expected to care for younger siblings after school until early evening when their parents return from work. According to one girls' team coach in a New York City high school, "It's not at all unusual that on a given day there may be two or three girls who aren't [at practice] because of responsibilities at home" (Dobie, 1987). The

reflect on SPORTS

Public Money and Private Profits
When Do Sports Perpetuate Social Inequality?

The dynamics of class relations sometimes have ironic twists. This is certainly true when public money is used to build stadiums and arenas that are then used by wealthy individuals who own professional sport teams that often bring them large profits. Since 1990, over $22 billion of public money in the United States has been spent to build these facilities that add to the wealth of powerful individuals and corporations and then subsidize their real estate developments in the area immediately around the facilities (Brown et al., 2004; Cagan and deMause, 1998; Curry et al., 2004; Delaney and Eckstein, 2003; Friedman et al., 2004; Sandomir, 2008a, 2008b).

Furthermore, wealthy investors often purchase the tax-free municipal bonds that cities sell to obtain the cash to build these facilities. This means that while city and/or state taxes are collected from the general population to pay off the bonds, wealthy investors receive tax-free returns, and team owners use the facilities built by taxpayers to make large amounts of money for themselves. When sales taxes are used to pay off bonds, people in low- and middle-income households pay a higher percentage of their annual incomes to build the stadiums than people in higher-income households. This amounts to a case of the poor subsidizing the rich with government approval.

According to a U.S. senator who reviewed research conducted by the non-partisan Congressional Research Service, the use of tax-exempt bonds to finance stadiums "amounts to little more than a public housing program for millionaire team owners and their millionaire employees [athletes]" (Welch, 1996, p. A1). The senator also asked, "Do [Americans] have enough money to finance stadiums for [wealthy team] owners . . . at the same time we are cutting Head Start Programs [for low-income children]?" (in Brady and Howlett, 1996, p. 13C). Nearly ten years later, Republican Senator John McCain stated that "owners have too much political power in major cities. I mean, how else could they get the people to build stadiums for 'em?" (in Keating, 2004a).

Ironically, the average residents whose taxes build stadiums and arenas usually can't afford to buy tickets to sports events in these venues. One reason for high ticket prices is that corporate accounts are used to buy so many tickets to games that the team owners raise ticket prices to match the demand. Higher prices seldom discourage corporate decision makers because they claim a portion of the ticket costs as a business deduction, thereby reducing their taxes so they receive an indirect reduction in ticket costs of about 35 percent. As a result, tax revenues decline and the government has less money to fund sport programs for average taxpayers, and most of those taxpayers can't afford the expensive tickets. This means that

"I thought they said 'Sport brings everyone together' when they used our tax money to build this place!"

As they sit in the distant bleachers and spot wealthy people in luxury boxes and club seats, these fans discover that the dynamics of social class operate in sports. To say that "sports transcend social class" is to ignore the dynamics that often segregate people by class and favor the wealthy and powerful.

stadiums today seldom are places where social classes mix as they cheer for the same team. In fact, when corporate credit cards are used to purchase blocks of season tickets, as they are in most venues, the only mixing of social classes is between "the haves" and "the have-mores" (Thomas, 2008). Meanwhile, team owners misleadingly blame players' salaries for escalating ticket prices.

The dynamics of class relations do not stop here. After contributing public money to build stadiums and arenas, local and state governments often give discounted property tax rates to team owners and their real estate partners who develop areas around the new venues. Property taxes are the main source of revenues for public schools, so urban public schools often have less money as owners increase their wealth. Meanwhile, professional teams sponsor a few charity programs for "inner-city kids" and occasionally send players to speak at urban schools—all of which garner press coverage that describes team owners and millionaire athletes as great public servants! As school systems fail due to poor funding and teachers complain about this scam, local editorials and letters to the editor accuse educators of wasting public money and demand that they become more frugal.

This method of transferring public money to wealthy individuals has occurred during a time when social services for the unemployed, the working poor, and children are being cut. When Carl Pohlad, the owner of the Minnesota Twins baseball team, was asked about this, he said, "Sports is a way of life, like eating. People say, 'You should pay to feed the homeless.' But the world doesn't work that way" (Cagan and deMause, 1998: 162). A similar argument convinced public officials in Washington, DC, to spend $611 million of taxpayer money to build a baseball stadium that opened in 2008. Journalist Dave Zirin (2008a) notes that this decision was made "in a city that has become a ground zero of economic segregation and gentrification. . . . a city set to close down a staggering twenty-four public schools."

WHAT ABOUT JOBS CREATED BY SPORTS?

Jobs are created whenever $300 to $900 million is spent in a city. But those jobs also would be created if the arenas and stadiums were privately financed. Furthermore, when cities spend public money to build stadiums for professional teams, they create far fewer jobs than could be created by other forms of economic development. The congressional study cited previously found that *each new job* created in connection with the state-financed $222-million football stadium that opened in Baltimore in 1998 cost about $127,000. Meanwhile, the cost of creating one job through the Maryland economic development fund was about $6,250 (in 1998 dollars). This means that for each job created by the new stadium, about 21 jobs could have been created if public money had been invested in other development projects. This is true because sport facilities employ few people, they sit empty most of the time, and the jobs they generate are mostly low-paying and seasonal.

WHO ELSE BENEFITS?

Sport team owners are not the only wealthy and powerful people who benefit when stadiums and arenas are built with public money. New publicly financed sport facilities increase property values in urban areas in which major investors and developers can initiate profitable projects. Others also may benefit as money trickles down to the rest of the community, but the average taxpayers who fund the facilities will never see the benefits enjoyed by the wealthy few. Additionally, these developments often require the displacement of housing for people living near or below the poverty line, and this housing is seldom replaced (Delaney and Eckstein, 2003; Zirin, 2008a).

Publicly financed sport venues may provide the illusion of unity in a city, but they are mostly vehicles for transferring public money to wealthy individuals and corporations. Behind the illusion often exists disunity and class inequality.

What do you think?

coach also explained that child care duties kept many girls from going out for teams. His solution was to coordinate a cooperative child-care program at practices and games, so that girls from low-income families could meet family expectations *and* play sports. However, when coaches cannot be so accommodating, girls drop out of sports because they have responsibilities at home (Sylwester, 2005b).

Boys and girls from higher-income families seldom have household responsibilities that force them to drop out of sports. Instead, their parents drive them to practices, lessons, and games; make sure they have all the equipment they need; and make sure they have cars when they are sixteen years old, so they can drive themselves to practices and games.

The implications of social class dynamics become very serious when health and obesity issues are considered. Limited opportunities to exercise safely and play sports are among the factors contributing to high rates of obesity, diabetes, and heart disease, especially among girls and women from low-income households (NHANES, 2002). The availability of facilities, safe spaces, transportation, and sports programs all vary by social class, and girls and women in low-income households experience the effects of social class in different and more profound ways when it comes to involvement in physical activities and sports.

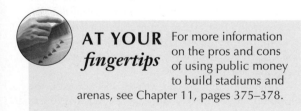

AT YOUR *fingertips*   For more information on the pros and cons of using public money to build stadiums and arenas, see Chapter 11, pages 375–378.

Being Respected and Becoming a Man: Class and Gender Relations in Men's Lives

Many boys and young men use sports to establish a masculine identity, but the dynamics of this process vary by social class. For example, in a qualitative analysis of essays written about sports by fifteen- and sixteen-year-old French Canadian boys in the Montreal area, Suzanne Laberge and Mathieu Albert (1999) discovered that upper-class boys connected their sports participation with masculinity because playing sports, they said, taught them leadership skills, and being a leader was central to their definition of masculinity. Middle-class boys said that playing sports provided them with opportunities to be with peers and gain acceptance in male groups, which fit their ideas of what they needed to do to establish identities as young men. According to working-class boys, playing sports enabled them to display toughness and develop the rugged personas that matched their ideas of manhood. In this sense, social class influenced the ways that sports and sport experiences were integrated into young men's lives.

Sociologist Mike Messner (1992, 2007a) has noted that boys in U.S. culture are more likely to make commitments to athletic careers at a young age when they perceive limited options for other careers and when their family situation is financially insecure. This means that the personal stakes associated with playing sports are different and often greater for boys from low-income households than they are for boys from higher-income households. Similarly, male athletes from poor and working-class households often use sport participation to obtain "respect" in a society where they often lack other means to do so. A former athlete who grew up in a poverty-level family and later became a junior high school coach explained the issue in this way:

> For . . . the poorer kids, [sports are] their major measuring stick. . . . They constantly remind each other what they can't do in the sports arena. It's definitely peer-acceptable if they are good at sports—although they maybe can't read, you know—if they are good at sports, they're one of the boys. Now I know the middle- and upper-class boys, they do sports and they do their books. . . . but as a whole, [they put] less effort into [sports]. (Messner, 1992, pp. 57–58)

This coach also noted that social class factors create social conditions under which young men from low-income households often have more at stake when it comes to playing sports. This usually creates pressure for them because they often lack the material resources required to train, develop skills, and be noticed by people who can serve as their advocates. Unless public school athletic programs and coaches can provide these things, these young people—boys and girls alike—have fewer opportunities for moving up to higher levels of competition than their upper-income peers have. The last remaining exceptions to this social class discrepancy are in football, basketball, and track, which are usually funded in public schools, often have qualified coaches, and provide opportunities to be seen by potential advocates.

ON THE *OLC:*

See the OLC—Additional Readings for Chapter 10—for an essay on the correlation between the per capita production of professional footbal players and poverty rates state-by-state.

Young people from upper-income households often have so many opportunities that they seldom see sports as high-stakes, career-related activities in their lives. For a young person with a car, nice clothes, money for college tuition, and good career contacts for the future, playing sports can be fun, but it's not perceived as necessary for economic survival, gaining respect, or establishing an identity (Messner, 1992; 2007a). Therefore, young men from middle- and upper-income backgrounds often disengage gradually from childhood dreams of becoming professional athletes and develop new visions for their futures. For them, playing sports does not hold the same life significance as it does for their peers from working-class and low-income households.

Fighting to Survive: Class, Gender, and Ethnic Relations Among Boxers

Chris Dundee, a famous boxing promoter, once said, "Any man with a good trade isn't about to get himself knocked on his butt to make a dollar" (in Messner, 1992, p. 82). What he meant was that middle- and upper-class boys and men have no reason to play a sport that destroys brain cells, that boxers always come from the lowest and most economically desperate income groups in society, and that boxing gyms are located in neighborhoods where desperation is most intense and life-piercing (Wacquant, 2004).

The dynamics of becoming and staying involved in boxing have been studied and described by French sociologist Loïc Wacquant (1992, 1995a, 1995b, 2004). As noted in Chapter 7, Wacquant spent over three years training and hanging out at a boxing gym in a black ghetto area in Chicago. During that time, he documented the life experiences of fifty professional boxers, most of whom were African Americans. His analysis shows that deciding to dedicate oneself to boxing is related to a combination of class, race, and gender relations in the United States. Statements by the boxers themselves illustrate the influence of this combination of factors:

> Right [in the area where I lived] it was definitely rough, it was dog-eat-dog. I had to be a mean dog . . . young guys wan'ed to take yer money and beat ya up an' you jus' had to fight or move out the neighbo'hood. I couldn't move, so I had to start fightin'. (in Wacquant, 1992, p. 229)

> I used to fight a lot when I was younger *anyway* so my father figure like, you know, [said] "If you gonna fight, well why don't you take it to a gym where you gonna learn, you know, a little more basics to it, maybe make some money, go further and do somethin' . . . insteada jus' bein' on the streets you know, and fightin' for nothing." (in Wacquant, 1992, p. 229)

The alternative to boxing for these young men often was the violence of the streets. When Wacquant asked one boxer where he'd be today if he hadn't started boxing, he said,

If it wasn't for boxin,' I don't know where I'd be . . . Prob'ly in prison or dead somewhere, you never know. I grew up in a tough neighbo'hood, so it's good for me, at least, to think 'bout what I do before I do it. To keep me outa the street, you know. The gym is a good place for me to be every day. Because when you're in d'gym, you know where you are, you don' have to worry about getting' into trouble or getting shot at. (in Wacquant, 2004, p. 239)

Wacquant explains that most boxers know they would not be boxing if they had been born in households where resources and other career opportunities existed. "Don't nobody be out there fightin' with an MBA," observed a trainer-coach at the gym (in Wacquant, 1995a, p. 521). Wacquant notes that these men see boxing as a "coerced affection, a captive love, one ultimately born of racial and class necessity" (1995a, p. 521). When he asked one boxer what he would change in his life, the answer represented the feelings of many men at the gym:

I wish I was born taller, I wish I was born in a rich family, I . . . wish I was smart, an' I had the brains to go to school an' really become somebody real important. For me I mean I can't stand the sport, I hate the sport, [but] it's carved inside of me so I can't let it go. (in Wacquant, 1995a, p. 521)

The boxers were attached to their craft, but over 80 percent didn't want their children to be boxers. One said,

No, no fighter wants their son [to box], I mean . . . *that's the reason why you fight, so he won't be able to fight.* . . . It's too hard, jus' too damn hard. . . . If he could *hit the books* an' study an' you know, with me havin' a little background in school an' stuff, I could help him. My parents, I never had nobody helpin' me. (in Wacquant, 1995a, p. 523)

These mixed feelings about boxing were pervasive; the men were simultaneously committed to and repulsed by their trade, and their participation was clearly connected with the dynamics of social class in their lives. Boxing and the gym provided for them refuge from the violence,

hopelessness, and indignity of the racism and poverty that had framed their lives since birth. They excelled at the sport because being a young, poor, black man in America "is no bed of roses" (Wacquant, 2004, p. 238).

Class Relations in Action: Changing Patterns in Sport Participation Opportunities

Publicly funded youth sport programs have been reduced or eliminated in many U.S. communities, and varsity teams in low-income school districts are being eliminated. When this occurs, fewer young people from low-income neighborhoods have opportunities to play sports, especially those requiring large fields and safe, functional facilities. This is why basketball remains a primary focus among low-income boys and girls; public schools usually can offer basketball teams and coaches if they have a usable gym that has not been converted into a permanent lunchroom or classroom.

 **AT YOUR** *fingertips* For more information on reductions in public funding for sport programs, see Chapter 5, pp. 128–129.

School sport programs in middle- and upper-income areas also may be threatened by financial problems, but they're maintained by "participation fees" paid by athletes' parents. These fees, as high as $250 per sport, guarantee that teams across many sports are available for young people lucky enough to be born into well-to-do households. Additionally, when school teams don't meet the expectations of well-to-do parents, they either vote to raise more public funds or use private funds to build new fields and facilities, hire coaches, and run high-profile tournaments that

Boxing has long been a sport for men from low-income groups. As a long-time boxing coach says, "If you want to know who's at d' bottom of society, all you gotta to do is look at who's boxin" (in Wacquant, 2004, p. 42). (*Source:* McGraw-Hill)

often attract college coaches who recruit athletes with scholarships. Therefore, when tax revolts and political decisions cause public programs to disappear, well-to-do people simply buy private sports participation opportunities for their children (Coakley, 2002). This highlights the influence of social class in sports. In fact, when it comes to sport participation today, the socio-economic status of an athlete's family has never been more important, because participation now depends on family resources. This affects everyone, but for people with disabilities it has special implications, as explained in "Breaking Barriers," page 332.

breaking **BARRIERS**

Resource Barriers
I'm Trying to Make Do

We occasionally hear heartening stories about people using assistive devices made of Kevlar, carbon fibrer, and other high-tech materials. These materials are now used to make light, maneuverable, and fast racing chairs, revolutionary running prostheses, and racing mono-skis that can negotiate steep Alpine slopes.

This technology is seductive for those who see it for the first time—so seductive that they focus on the device and overlook the person using it (Belson, 2002). However, as most athletes know, technologies are only as good as the people who use them. And most people with disabilities know that adaptive technologies for sports are prohibitively expensive.

Diane Cabrera discovered this when cancer took her leg in 2001. Her new prosthesis enabled her to walk, but it cost $11,000, and her HMO covered only $4000 per year. She spread payments over two years and struggled to find $2200 for co-pays related to diagnostics, fitting, tuning, and maintaining the device. When she needed a new leg socket in 2005, because her original prosthesis no longer fit correctly, she put it off due to cost. When asked about this, Diane said with resignation, "I'm trying to make do right now."

"Make do right now." That's what many people do today when they need assistive devices like prostheses and more mobile chairs. Unless you're wealthy, have insurance that covers more than $1500 a year for prosthetic limbs, or find a charity with deep pockets, you must learn to "make do." Most below-the-knee prosthetics cost $7000 to $12,000, and an arm or an above-the-knee prosthetic leg costs $12,000 to $30,000. Prosthetic limbs and adaptive devices for sports cost the most and usually require replacement every year or two. The price of a racing wheelchair is at least $4000, and Kevlar wheels push that cost up to $6000 and more.

The cost of equipment is a major barrier to sport participation among most people with disabilities, especially considering the following statistics (McKay, 2005; U.S. Department of Labor, 2005):

- Unemployment rates among people with disabilities are three times higher than among able-bodied people, and people with "serious or significant" disabilities have the highest rate of any category of Americans—about 70 percent for working-age people.
- Only thirty-five percent of people with disabilities report that they work full or part time, compared with 78 percent of currently able-bodied people.
- People with disabilities are three times more likely than able-bodied people to live in households making less than $15,000 per year, which is below or just above the poverty line, depending on household size.
- Compared to able-bodied people, those with disabilities have less access to transportation and are more likely to go without needed medical care.

Federal government assistance for people with disabilities has been cut recently—even for Iraq veterans. States have not picked up the slack; charity support is spotty, uneven, and declining; and community programs are scarce, even for people with dependable transportation. A few elite athletes with disabilities are sponsored by companies that sell prostheses and other adaptive technologies, but class-based barriers for others are formidable. This forces many people with disabilities to join Diane Cabrera and "make do right now."

When we compare the availability and quality of school and club sport programs by social class, we notice the existence of *savage inequalities*, as documented continuously over the past three decades by educator Jonathan Kozol (1991, 2002, 2005). These inequalities signal the dismal life chances of young people facing barriers rooted in poverty. With funds being cut and coaches laid off, schools in poor neighborhoods struggle to maintain sport programs while looking for new funding from corporations. But corporations usually sponsor only the sports that promote their brand and products. For example, a shoe company will support basketball because it fits with its marketing and advertising programs. Corporate funders support individuals, teams, and sports that generate product visibility through media coverage and high-profile state and national tournaments. This keeps certain sports alive, but only on terms that continue to meet corporate interests. This highlights clearly the link between sports and class relations.

Class Relations in Action: The Cost of Attending Sport Events

It remains possible to attend some sports events for free. High school and many college games and meets in the United States are affordable for many people, and in some communities the

Children in middle-class suburban areas often have safe streets on which to play. The boys in this cul-de-sac have multiple portable basketball goals, and they occasionally play full-court games in the street. They also play other sports and enjoy water-skiing behind boats owned by neighbors. Sports are important to them, but mainly as a source of sociability. (*Source:* Jay Coakley)

tickets for minor league sports are reasonably priced. But tickets to most major intercollegiate and professional games are beyond the means of most people, even those whose taxes were used to build the venues in which the games are played. The cost of attending these events has increased much more rapidly than the rate of inflation over the past fifteen years.

Table 10.2 shows that the inflation rate between 1991 and 2008 was 52 percent, whereas average ticket prices increased 194 percent, 166 percent, 190 percent, and 143 percent for MLB, the NFL, the NBA, and the NHL respectively, during the same period. Therefore, ticket prices have increased three to four times the rate of inflation—partly due to increased costs at new stadiums and arenas, but mostly due to team owners wanting to attract people with money to spend on food, drinks, apparel, and everything else they sell. This is why new facilities resemble giant circular shopping malls built around a central entertainment stage. They house expensive luxury suites and separate club seating, where high-income spectators have special services available—wait staff, hot food menus, private restrooms, televisions, refrigerators, lounge chairs, temperature controls, private entrances with no waiting lines or turnstiles, and special parking areas—so that attending a game is no different from going to an exclusive private club.

As tickets become more expensive and spectators are increasingly segregated according to their ability to pay, social class and class relations become more evident in the stands. Spectators may cheer at the same times and experience similar emotions, but this is the extent to which social-class differences are transcended at the events, and the reality of social class returns as soon as people leave the stadium.

Efforts by some fans wanting to reduce ticket prices seldom develop traction because people in luxury boxes, club seats, and other premium seats don't want to be identified with spectators who can't afford high-priced tickets and concessions. Expensive tickets are status symbols for wealthy spectators; they *want* class distinctions to be part of the sport experience, and they are willing to pay—or have their corporation pay—high prices so they can conspicuously display their status and

Table 10.2   Escalating ticket prices versus inflation in the United States, 1991–2008

	AVERAGE TICKET PRICE					Thirteen-Year Increase (%)
	1991 ($)	1996 ($)	2001 ($)	2004 ($)	2008 ($)	
Major League Baseball	8.64	11.20	19.00	19.82	25.40	194
National Football League	25.21	35.74	53.64	54.75	67.11	166
National Basketball Association	22.52	31.80	51.02	60.72*	65.41*	190
National Hockey League	24.00†	38.34	47.70	50.55*	58.23*	143†

Inflation rate from 1991 to 2008 = 52%§

Source: Adapted from data in Team Marketing Report, www.teammarketing.com.

*The Team Marketing Report did not include for 2004 and 2008 the average *premium* ticket price for NBA and NHL games in its basic average ticket price. Therefore, I assumed that 15 percent of NBA and NHL tickets were sold at the average premium price and calculated the approximate average for the entire venue.

†This is an estimate because no NHL data were available prior to 1994.

§Represents the official rate of inflation as determined by the U.S. government (http://www.westegg.com/inflation/)

have an experience with other wealthy people, except for the waitstaff who serve them.

Attendance and seating at many events, from the opening ceremonies at the Olympics to the NFL Super Bowl, are now tied to conspicuous displays of wealth, status, influence, and corporate power. After observing the 2008 Super Bowl and the events leading up to the game, journalist Dave Zirin (2008b) concluded that "Before it is anything else, before it's even a football game, the Super Bowl is ... a two-week entertainment festival for the rich and shameless." Those attending the game in 2008 had an average household income of $222,318—nearly five times greater than the median U.S. household (Thomas, 2008). This is an important point, because efforts to make games affordable to the people whose taxes build the facilities will fail as long as corporations use them as party sites for executive and customers.

> Who has the motive to invest in the . . . longlasting success of African [soccer] football? African governments . . . have more important things to worry about. When they have some spare cash, they are not usually thanked by their impoverished peoples for sinking it into fancy new stadiums. —David Runciman, Political Scientist, Cambridge University (2006)

GLOBAL INEQUALITIES AND SPORTS

When we discuss social class and sports, it's essential to think beyond our own society. Inequalities exist at all levels of social organization—in families, groups, organizations, communities, societies, and the world. Global inequalities related to per capita income, living standards, and access to developmental resources cause many of the most serious problems that we face today. Research shows that the gap between the richest and poorest people worldwide is growing wider. For example, people in the United States, *on average*, spend about $65 per day to live as they do—and this includes everyone, even newborns. In the thirty-nine nations classified as

"less developed countries" (LDCs), people spend about 60 cents a day to live as they do. In terms of consumption, an average person in the United States spends per day about 100 times more than nearly half the individuals in the world spend per day. But these figures actually *understate* standard-of-living differences between Americans and people in LDCs because the U.S. gross domestic product (GDP), which is money generated by the economy, is over 125 times higher than the GDPs in an average LDC.

Another way to view social class in global terms is to determine how many of the 6.7 billion people in the world (as of mid-2008) live on less than $2 a day, an amount that international organizations agree is clearly below basic subsistence levels in any country, regardless of cost of living. As of 2008, about 2.6 billion people lived on less than $2 per day, and one billion of them lived on less than $1 a day. As a point of comparison, the *median* income for U.S families in 2006 was about $59,000 per year (www.infoplease.com/ipa/A0104688.html).

The meanings given to this global gap between the wealthy and poor differ depending on the ideologies that people use to guide their understanding of world affairs. But apart from ideological interpretations, it is clear that about 40 percent of all people in the world have few resources to use on anything beyond basic survival. They may play games, but they seldom have the resources needed to organize and play sports as we know them. For these people, the sports played in the United States and other post-industrial nations are clearly out of reach. They can't understand how or why Tiger Woods made $115 million in 2008, an amount more than 250,000 people like them spend during an entire year (Freedman, 2008a). Similarly, the workers who make

Since 2003 the annual Homeless World Cup has been held in different cities where national teams comprising homeless people, mostly men, compete during a three-day tournament. This event was initiated by two editors of newspapers that serve homeless people. Their readers sometimes played informal soccer games, so they recruited sponsors and have organized the event each year. In 2007, teams from 48 countries were funded to play in Copenhagen, Denmark. In additional to being a sport event, the tournament is a site for initiating and sustaining political strategies advocating the rights of homeless people worldwide. (*Source:* Jay Coakley)

less than $1 an hour producing the balls, shoes, and other equipment and clothing used by most Americans who play sports, would question the fairness of such inequality (Weiner, 2004).

When a dirt soccer pitch or basketball court exists in communities where people struggle to survive, it often attracts young people who may have seen televised soccer or basketball games. This has not escaped the attention of people who identify potential elite athletes for U.S. colleges or professional soccer and basketball teams in wealthy nations. According to a *Sports Illustrated* article (Wahl, 2004), the scouts that visit these areas are "on safari for 7-footers." When they find a good prospect, they know that he has no agent to represent him and will sign a contract for a low sum of money in "Western" terms, and be thankful to do so. Only a few of these prospects have made it to the NBA or other top professional leagues, and many of those who do make it, use much of their money to buy food and medical care for people in their home village. This is one of many ways that class relations operate on a global scale.

ECONOMIC AND CAREER OPPORTUNITIES IN SPORTS

Many people in the U.S. see sports as a sphere in which people from low-income and poor backgrounds can experience upward social mobility.

Social mobility is a term used by sociologists to refer to *changes in wealth, education, and occupation over a person's lifetime or from one generation to the next in families.* Social mobility can occur in downward or upward directions. On a general level, career and mobility opportunities exist in sports and sport organizations. However, as we consider the impact of sports on mobility in the United States, it is useful to know the following things about sport-related opportunities:

1. The number of paid career opportunities in sports is limited, and the playing careers of professional athletes are short-term.
2. Opportunities for women are growing but remain limited on and off the field relative to men.
3. Opportunities for blacks and other ethnic minorities are growing but remain limited on and off the field relative to whites with European heritage.

These points are discussed in the following sections.

Career Opportunities Are Limited

Young athletes often have visions of playing professional sports, and their parents may have similar visions. But the chances of turning these visions into realities are remote. The odds or chances for a person to become a college or professional athlete are difficult to calculate, and many different methods have been used. For example, we could calculate odds for all high school or college athletes in a particular sport, or for high school or college athletes from particular racial or ethnic groups, or for any male or female in a particular age group of the total population of the United States. Additionally, the calculations could be based on the number of players in the top league in a sport, such as the NHL in hockey, or they could be based on the number of professional hockey players in Europe and on minor league teams in North America. The fact that about 75 percent of the players in the NHL come from outside the United States

means that it is meaningless to calculate the odds of a U.S. high school hockey player making it to the NHL without taking this into account.

The point here is that all calculations must be qualified, and many estimates reported in the media are inaccurate. The data in Table 10.3 represent calculations made by NCAA researchers in 2004. The footnotes for the table explain the limitations of these calculations and suggest that most of the odds listed in the table are overestimates of the chances of moving from one level of competition to the next in these sports. At any rate, the NCAA calculations indicate that playing at the professional level is a long shot. In fact, if there was a race horse that had similar odds of winning a race, nobody would even think of betting on it.

Additionally, professional sport opportunities are short-term, averaging three to seven years in team sports and three to twelve years in individual sports. This means that, after playing careers end, there are about *forty additional years* in a person's work life. Unfortunately, many people, including athletes, coaches, and parents, ignore this aspect of reality.

Media coverage focuses on the best athletes in the most popular sports, and they have longer and more lucrative playing careers than others. Little coverage is given to the more typical cases—that is, those who play for one or two seasons before being cut or forced to quit for other reasons, especially injuries. We hear about the long football careers of popular quarterbacks, but little about the many players whose one-year contracts are not renewed after their first season. The average age of players on the *oldest* NFL team in 2008 was less than 28 years old. This means that few players older than thirty are still in the league. Much more typical than 30-year-old players contemplating another season are 22-year-olds facing the end of their professional sport careers.

Finally, many professional athletes at the minor league level make less than workers in non-sport occupations. For example, over 100 of the 335 players in Major League Soccer in 2008

Table 10.3   Estimated probability of competing in athletics beyond the high school interscholastic level*

Athletes	Men's Basketball	Women's Basketball	Football	Baseball	Men's Ice Hockey	Men's Soccer
HS athlete	549,500	456,900	983,600	455,300	29,900	321,400
HS senior athlete	157,000	130,500	281,000	130,100	8,500	91,800
NCAA athlete	15,700	14,400	56,500	25,700	3,700	18,200
NCAA 1st year roster slots	4,500	4,100	16,200	7,300	1,100	5,200
NCAA senior athlete	3,500	3,200	12,600	5,700	800	4,100
NCAA athlete drafted	44	32	250	600	33	76
Percent HS to NCAA	2.9	3.1	5.8	5.6	12.9	5.7
Percent NCAA to pro	1.3	1.0	2.0	10.5	4.1	1.9
Percent HS to pro	0.03[†]	0.02	0.09	0.5	0.4	0.08

Source: NCAA, 2004, online, www.ncaa.org/research/prob_of_competing/probability_of_competing2.html#m_ice_hockey.

*These numbers, based on estimated data, are rough approximations of reality. The numbers for NCAA players do not include players at non-NCAA schools, players from outside the United States recruited by NCAA schools, players in North American professional leagues who haven't attended high school or college in the United States, or U.S. high school and college players that play professional sports in other countries. Therefore, the odds of a U.S. high school or college athlete making it to the next levels of competition in these sports are lower than these numbers suggest; in ice hockey, for example, they are very much lower.
†How to read the last line: For men's basketball, 3 of every 10,000 high school players will be drafted by the NBA, or 1 of every 3,333. But this does not mean these selected players will make teams. In women's basketball, 2 in 10,000 high school players, or 1 of every 5000 will be drafted; in football it is 9 of every 10,000 high school football players, or 1 of every 1100.

made $17,700 or less (www.mlsplayers.org/ salary_info.html). Another 64 players made less than $50,000, and two-thirds of all MLS players did not make $100,000 in 2008. Elementary school teachers have higher salaries than many of these players, and they also have greater financial security and stability, along with a pension plan.

Opportunities for Women Are Growing but Remain Limited

Career opportunities for female athletes are limited relative to opportunities for men. Tennis and golf provide opportunities, but the professional tours for these sports draw athletes worldwide. For women in the United States, this means that the competition to make a living in these sports is great. More than 1,100 players competed in Women's Tennis Association (WTA) tournaments in 2008, but only 98 were from the United States, and many of those were naturalized citizens who came to the U.S. as top-level players. Only nine of the 100 top-ranked players in May 2008 were American, and those who are ranked below the top 100 seldom make enough prize money to cover their expenses on the tour.

In the Ladies Professional Golf Association (LPGA), there were about 500 players in 2008, and only eight of the top 30 money winners in 2007 were from the United States. Fewer than 40 of the approximately 80 million adult women in the United States make enough prize money to cover their expenses as professional golfers.

There are opportunities in professional basketball, volleyball, figure skating, bowling, skiing, bicycling, track and field, and rodeo, but the number of professional female athletes in these sports remains low, and only a few women make large amounts of money. For example, when *Sports Illustrated* in 2007 listed the top 50 money-making athletes born in the

United States and the top 20 from the rest of the world, only two women made the lists—golfer Michelle Wie from the United States and tennis player Maria Sharapova from Russia (Freedman, 2007a, 2007b). But their combined prize money (no endorsements) for the year amounted to less than five percent of what boxer Oscar De La Hoya earned for one championship fight lasting 36 minutes! This startling difference says much about the influence of gender ideology on the rewards people receive in sports.

Professional leagues for women now exist in basketball and beach volleyball, but they have provided career opportunities for fewer than 400 athletes at any given point in recent years. The Women's United Soccer Association (WUSA) employed about 170 players for the two years it operated, and about 40 of those players were from outside the United States. The combined salaries for *all* WUSA players during the 2002 season was $6.76 million, which was less than the annual salary of most individual star players on European men's teams.

In the WNBA, the pay is a fraction of what men in the NBA make—an average of $46,060 during the 2008 season. First-year players in 2008 made between $34,500 and $44,064, fourth-year players made between $42,229 and $56,182, and no player could make more than $95,000. This means that the highest-paid WNBA player in 2008 made in a year what Shaquille O'Neill made for every twelve minutes he played during the regular season. In fact, the total payroll for all 228 WNBA players in 2008 was about $10.5 million, the amount that O'Neill and ten other NBA players each made in the first half of the 2007–2008 season. Overall, for every salary dollar that an NBA player makes, a WNBA player makes about 1 cent, and NBA players outnumber WNBA players about four to one.

The National Women's Basketball League (NWBL) existed from 1997 through 2007 when it ceased operations. It employed about ninety players on six teams, and the players usually made less than $10,000 for a twenty-four-game season. Although the WNBA has a labor agree-

"Ah, the glamorous life of a spoiled, overpaid professional athlete!"

Only a few professional athletes achieve fame and fortune. Thousands of others play in minor and semipro leagues in which salaries are low and working conditions poor.

ment taking it through the 2013 season, most of its players make no more than high school teachers with a few years of experience. There are opportunities for women in European basketball and soccer, but they are limited and salaries are low. Overall, the best advice for women who aspire to make a living as professional athletes is to have a backup plan and be ready to use it.

What about other careers in sports? There are jobs for women in coaching, training, officiating, sports medicine, sports information, public relations, marketing, and administration. As noted in Chapter 8, most of the jobs in women's sports continue to be held by men, and women seldom are hired for jobs in men's programs, except in support positions. In the United States, when men's and women's high school or college athletic programs are combined, men become the athletic directors in about 80 percent of the cases. Women in most post-industrial nations have challenged the legacy of traditional gender ideology, and progress has been made in various administrative positions in some sports organizations (see www.ncasports.org/press_releases.htm). However, a heavily gendered division of labor continues to exist in nearly all organizations

(McKay, 1997, 1999). In traditional and developing nations, the record of progress is negligible, and very few women hold positions of power in any sports organizations (Rintala and Bischoff, 1997; White and Henry, 2004).

OLC **ON THE *OLC*:**

See the OLC—Additional Readings for Chapter 10—for a discussion of situations in which women have encountered class-based barriers to sport participation.

Job opportunities for women have not increased as rapidly as women's programs have grown. This is partly due to the persistence of traditional ideas about gender and the fact that Title IX does not have precise enforcement procedures when it comes to equity in coaching and administration. Title IX enforcement focuses almost exclusively on athletes, and hasn't had as much impact in other aspects of sport organizations (Matson, 2004). Therefore, a pattern of gender underrepresentation exists in nearly all job categories and nearly all sport organizations. For example, in U.S. colleges and universities, the men and women who coach women's teams make less money than the men who coach men's teams—a possible Title IX violation (Brady, 2008). This is true in nearly all sports, even those that don't generate revenue. According to the most recent NCAA data (see NCAA, 2004), the 25,300 full- and part-time head coaches and assistants of women's teams in 1033 colleges and universities received combined salaries that were an estimated $245.3 million less than the combined salaries of the 30,279 coaches of men's teams.[2] This difference does *not* include

incentives and other perks received mostly by male coaches of high-profile football and basketball teams.

When the salaries of NCAA coaches are compared in each Division, the coaches of men's teams in Division I have average salaries that are 55 percent greater than coaches of women's Division I teams. In Divisions II and III the difference is 30 percent and 2 percent, respectively, although salaries for all coaches in Division III are so low that the difference is less than $100 per year per coach in those colleges. Because 56 percent of the coaches for women's teams are men, they also experience the effects of these gendered salary differences.

Opportunities for women in sports may continue to shift toward equity, but many people resist making the structural and ideological changes that would produce full equity. In the meantime, there will be gradual increases in the number of women coaches, sports broadcasters, athletic trainers, administrators, and referees. Changes will occur more rapidly in programs where salaries are low and in certain sport industries that target women as consumers and need women employees to increase their sales and profits. But the gender ideology used by influential decision makers *inside* many sports organizations will continue to privilege those perceived as tough, strong, competitive, and aggressive—and men are more likely to be perceived in such terms.

Many women who work in sport organizations continue to deal with organizational cultures that are primarily based on the values and experiences of men. This contributes to low job satisfaction and high job turnover among women (Bruening et al., 2007; Bruening and Dixon, 2008; Dixon and Bruening, 2005, 2007; Dixon and Sagas, 2007; Gregory, 2008; Sagas and Cunningham, 2005b.). Professional development programs, workshops, and coaching clinics have been developed since the late 1990s to assist women as they live in and try to change these cultures and make them more inclusive. However, full equity won't occur until more men in sport organizations change their ideas

---

[2]I used NCAA data and extrapolated them to all 327 Division I, 282 Division II, and 424 Division III schools (in 2004), even though some schools did not respond to the NCAA gender equity survey.

about gender and its connection with sports and leadership (Gregory, 2009; McKay, 1997).

Opportunities for African Americans and Other Ethnic Minorities Are Growing but Remain Limited

The visibility of black athletes in certain spectator sports often leads people to conclude that sports offer abundant career opportunities for African Americans. Anecdotal support for this conclusion comes from some successful black athletes who attribute their wealth and fame to sports. However, the extent to which job opportunities for blacks exist in sports has been greatly overstated. Very little publicity is given to the actual number and proportion of blacks who play sports for a living or make a living working in sport organizations. Also ignored is the fact that sports provide very few career opportunities for black women.

African American athletes are involved almost exclusively in five professional spectator sports: boxing, basketball, football, baseball, and track. At the same time, some of the most lucrative sports for athletes are almost exclusively white—tennis, golf, hockey, and auto racing are examples. My best guess is that fewer than 6000 African Americans, or about 1 of every 6660 African Americans, currently make significant incomes as professional athletes. Data from the U.S. Department of Labor indicates that, in 2007, there were 20,746 African American men and women classified as "athletes, coaches, umpires, and related workers." In the same year, there were 49,728 African Americans physicians and surgeons, 49,049 lawyers, and 70,616 college and university teachers (http://www.bls.gov/cps/cpsaat11.pdf). Therefore, there were twenty-eight times more African Americans working in these three prestigious professions than African American athletes in top-level professional sports; and eight times more African American doctors, lawyers, and college teachers than African Americans working in all of sports. Furthermore, physicians, lawyers, and college teachers have greater *lifetime* earnings than most athletes whose playing careers, on average, last *less* than five years and whose salaries outside top pro leagues rarely exceed $50,000 per year. Department of Labor statistics for 2007 (http://146.142.4.22/cps/cpsaat39.pdf) indicate that the median (that is, the point at which half make more and half make less) incomes of male doctors and surgeons, lawyers, and college teachers were $93,392, $92,716, and $64,428, respectively; but for athletes, coaches, umpires, and related workers, it was only $41,496. Therefore, an African American male college student today has a ten times better chance of becoming a doctor, lawyer, or college teacher than being employed in sports and will make 50 to 100 percent more per year in those non-sport professions.

These data are not presented to discourage African Americans from seeking careers in sports; however, they remind us that sports don't provide exceptional upward mobility opportunities and that there are better career opportunities outside of sports—if there are educational opportunities to take advantage of them. Of course, these statistical facts are distorted in media content that presents disproportionately more images of successful black athletes than blacks in other positive roles. If young African Americans use media images as a basis for making choices and envisioning their future, there will be less progress toward achieving racial equality in the United States (Archer, Hollingworth, and Halsall, 2007).

Employment Barriers for Black Athletes When sports were first desegregated in the United States, blacks faced *entry barriers*—that is, unless they had exceptional skills and exemplary personal characteristics they were not recruited or given professional contracts (see Kooistra, Mahoney, and Bridges, 1993). Prejudices were strong and team owners assumed that players, coaches, and spectators would not accept blacks unless they made immediate, significant contributions to a team. Black athletes with good skills were passed by. Therefore, the performance statistics for black athletes surpassed those of

Of the fifty highest paid (including endorsements) athletes in the United States in 2008, there were no women on the list. Serena Williams was last on the list in 2006 when she made less than 15 percent of what Tiger Woods made and less than one-half of what Andre Agassi made. Maria Sharapova—an attractive white, blonde from Russia—consistently makes twice as much money as Serena Williams, mostly due to her endorsement contracts. (*Source:* Amy Sancetta, AP/Wide World Photos)

whites, a fact that many whites used to reinforce their stereotypes about black physicality.

As entry barriers declined between 1960 and the late 1970s, new barriers related to retention took their place. *Retention barriers* existed when contracts for experienced black players were not renewed unless the players had significantly better performance records than white players at the same career stage (Lapchick, 1984). This pattern existed through the early 1990s (Kooistra et al., 1993), but it no longer exists (Leonard, 1995). Race-based salary discrimination existed

in most sports immediately following desegregation, but evidence suggests that it has faded in major team sports (Singh, Sack, and Dick, 2003). This is because performance can be objectively measured, tracked, and compared to the performances of other players. Statistics are now kept on nearly every conceivable dimension of an athlete's skill. Players' agents use these statistics when in salary negotiations, and they have an incentive to do so because they receive a percentage of players' salaries and don't want racial discrimination to decrease their incomes.

Employment Barriers in Coaching and Off-the-Field Jobs During the 1980s and 1990s many college and professional sport teams had plantation-like hiring practices—they employed black workers but hired only white managers (Shropshire, 1996). Since the mid-1990s, the rate at which blacks have been hired in managerial positions has varied by sport. There's been slow progress in most sport organizations, especially those associated with college and professional football.

In 2002, an expert panel assembled by ESPN discussed data on hiring practices in the NFL and concluded that the lack of minority head coaches was the most serious problem facing the league. At the same time, lawyers Johnnie Cochran, Jr., and Cyrus Mehri (2002) filed a report demanding that the NFL make systematic changes in their recruitment and hiring process so that qualified black candidates for head coach positions would be treated fairly. This pressure led the NFL to adopt the "Rooney Rule" in 2003, which required teams to interview minority candidates for open coaching positions. Although the impact of this affirmative action policy is not clear, the number of black head coaches in the NFL has increased to 6 for the 32 teams in the league (19 percent in a league where nearly 70 percent of the players are black).

Discriminatory hiring patterns have been most troubling in big-time college football. This led Floyd Keith, executive director of the Black Coaches Association (BCA) to form alliances with other civil rights organizations and demand that NCAA institutions initiate fair hiring practices. Research indicates that when chief executive officers (CEOs) recruit candidates for top management positions, they favor people with backgrounds and orientations similar to their own, and they often hire people they know or have worked with in the past (Cunningham and Sagas, 2005). Familiar people are "known quantities" and perceived to be predictable and trustworthy. Therefore, if a team owner or university athletic director is a white male, which is true in nearly all cases, he may wonder about the qualifications

Black women are seriously underrepresented in coaching at the college and professional levels. In December 2004, when Vivian Stringer, head coach of the Rutgers University women's basketball team, celebrated her 700th win, she was one of only 24 black women coaching in Division I basketball (325 teams), excluding Historically Black Colleges and Universities (Orton, 2005). (*Source:* NCAA Photos)

of ethnic minority candidates, especially if he lacks exposure to diversity (Roberts, 2007a). He may wonder if he can trust them to be supportive and fit in with his managerial style and approach. If he has doubts, conscious or unconscious, he'll choose the candidate he believes is most like himself.

These dynamics, which are seldom identified as "racial" or "ethnic," often exist in sports and other organizations. But they reaffirm an organizational culture and operating procedures that cause minority men and all women to be underrepresented in positions of power and responsibility. The NCAA reports that the number of black coaches increased 75 percent between 1996 and 2006, but it does not disclose that the percentage of teams with a black head coach went from mere 4.2 percent to an embarrassingly low 5.2 percent during a decade when many people believed that sports were color-blind. The increase was "75 percent," but real progress was insignificant.

The BCA reported in 2007 that 414 Division I head football coaching vacancies had been filled between 1982 and 2007, and only 21 of the jobs had gone to black coaches! Even more startling is that as of 2007 there had been only 22 black head coaches in the history of Division I football. Keith Harrison (2007), author of the BCA report, concluded that the head football coach position "is the most segregated position in all college sports." The 2008 season began with only 6 black head coaches for 121 teams, and the historical and current record for football teams in the other NCAA divisions is even worse. According to some people in the sociology of sport, Division I college football, a sport in which nearly half the players are black, operates much like a plantation (Hawkins, 2000; Rhoden, 2006).

Men's basketball at the professional and college levels have made significant progress in hiring black coaches, but the record for women's basketball is much less impressive. Even after seven black head coaches were hired at the start of the 2007–2008 season, black coaches were only 9 percent of head coaches for Division I teams (Lapchick, 2008). At the end of the season six more black coaches were hired, bringing the percentage up to 15—still short of the 19 percent that the BCA identifies as the goal in women's basketball where 44 percent of the players are black.

> **The boosters of inequity, the true power brokers of college football . . . take comfort in their "white-like-me" hires as a perk of owning the program with their six-figure donations. . . . [But their] contribution to higher education is not enlightenment but enwhitenment. They tailgate for ignorance.** —
> Selena Roberts, sports journalist (2007b)

Outside revenue-producing sports and a few track teams, there are so few black coaches that it makes college sports look totally white—a profile that doesn't cause many whites to ask questions, but one that causes most people of color to conclude that sports do not provide a level playing field when it comes to skin color. This factor explains why blacks perceive fewer career opportunities in coaching and have lower levels of job dissatisfaction and higher rates of turnover than their white counterparts in the coaching ranks (Cunningham, 2004, 2007a; Cunningham and Sagas, 2004, 2005, 2007; Cunningham, Bruening, and Straub, 2006; Sagas and Cunningham, 2005a).

Opportunities for Ethnic Minorities The dynamics of ethnic relations in every culture are unique (see Chapter 9). Making generalizations about ethnic relations and opportunities in sports is difficult. However, dominant sport forms in any culture tend to reproduce dominant cultural values and the social structures supported by those values. This means three things:

1. Members of the dominant social class in a society may exclude or define as unqualified job candidates with characteristics and cultural backgrounds different from their own
2. Ethnic minorities often must adopt the values and orientations of the dominant social class if they want to be hired and promoted in sport organizations
3. The values and orientations of ethnic minorities are seldom represented in the culture of sport organizations.

Latinos, Asian Pacific Americans, and Native Americans are clearly underrepresented in most sports and sport organizations in the United States (Lapchick, 2004, 2005b, 2008c). Many Euro-Americans feel uncomfortable with ethnic diversity in situations in which they must trust and work closely with co-workers. Most often, this feeling is caused by a lack of knowledge about the heritage and customs of others and little exposure to ethnic diversity involving meaningful communication. Exceptions to this are found in Major League Baseball and Major League Soccer teams that have many Latino players and a fair representation of Latinos in management. However, neither Asian Pacific Americans nor Native Americans fare very well in any U.S. sport organizations, partly because they are perceived as having little sports knowledge and experience, regardless of the reality of their lives (Lapchick, 2007, 2008a).

SPORT PARTICIPATION AND OCCUPATIONAL CAREERS AMONG FORMER ATHLETES

What happens in the occupational careers of former athletes? Are athletes' career patterns different from the patterns of others? Is sport participation a stepping-stone to future occupational success and upward social mobility? Does playing sports have economic payoffs after active participation is over?

Research suggests that, as a group, young people who played sports on high school and college teams experience no more or less occupational success than others from comparable social class and educational backgrounds. This doesn't mean that playing sports has never helped anyone in special ways; it means only that research findings don't allow us to conclude that former athletes have a systematic advantage over comparable peers in their future occupational careers.

Research on this topic becomes out-of-date when the meaning and cultural significance of sport participation changes over time; such changes are likely to influence the links between playing sports and success in later careers. However, past research suggests that, if playing sports is connected with career success, the reason may involve one or more of the following factors:

> **ON THE *OLC*:**
> See the OLC- –Additional Readings for Chapter 10—for references to past studies on playing sports and career success.

- Playing sports under certain circumstances (see the numbered list below) may teach young people *interpersonal skills* that carry over and enable them to succeed in jobs requiring those skills.
- The people who hire employees may define former athletes as good job prospects and give them opportunities to develop and demonstrate work-related abilities, which then serve as the basis for career success.
- Former high-profile athletes may have reputations that help them obtain and succeed in certain jobs.
- Playing sports under certain circumstances (see the numbered list below) may enable athletes to develop social networks consisting of social relationships that help them obtain good jobs after retiring from sports.

After reviewing much of the research on this topic, I've tentatively concluded that playing sports is positively related to future occupational success and upward mobility when it does the following things:

1. Increases opportunities to complete academic degrees, develop job-related skills, and/or extend one's knowledge about the world outside of sports.
2. Increases support from significant others for *overall* growth and development, not just sport development.
3. Provides opportunities to develop social networks that are connected with career opportunities outside of sports and sport organizations.
4. Provides material resources and the guidance needed to successfully create and manage opportunities.

5. Expands experiences, identities, and abilities *unrelated* to sports.
6. Minimizes risks of disabling injuries that restrict physical movement or require expensive and/or chronic medical treatment.

This list suggests that playing sports can either expand *or* constrict a person's overall development and future career possibilities (see Chapter 4). When expansion occurs, athletes develop abilities and forms of social and cultural capital that lead to career opportunities and success. When constriction occurs, abilities and social and cultural capital may be so limited that career opportunities are scarce and unsatisfying.

Highly Paid Athletes and Career Success After Playing Sports

Conclusions about sport participation, career success, and social mobility must be qualified in light of the following recent changes related to elite and professional sports in the United States and other wealthy societies:

- An increase in salaries that began in the mid-70s has enabled athletes to save and invest money that can be used to create future career opportunities.
- An increase in the media coverage and overall visibility of sports has created greater name recognition than past athletes enjoyed; therefore, athletes today can convert themselves into a "brand" that may lead to career opportunities and success.
- Athletes have become more aware that they must carefully manage their resources to maximize future opportunities.

> A player's career is always a blink in a stare... There is a tipping point in a player's career where he goes from chasing the dream to running from a nightmare.... It is a downhill run and it spares no one. —Doug Glanville, MLB player, 1996–2004 (2008)

Of course, many professional athletes have short careers or play at levels at which they do not make much money. When they retire, they face the same career challenges encountered by their

SIDELINES

Only a few former athletes can cash in on their athletic reputations. The rest must seek opportunities and work just like the rest of us. Those opportunities vary, depending on qualifications, experience, contacts and connections, and a bit of luck. In some cases, former athletes face hard times after their sport careers end.

age peers, and they experience patterns of success and failure similar to patterns among comparable peers who didn't play sports. This means that playing sports neither ensures nor boosts one's chances of career success, but it doesn't mean that playing sports was a waste of time.

In Chapter 4 it was explained that retirement from sports is best described as a process rather than a single event, and most athletes don't retire from sports on a moment's notice—they disengage gradually and revise their priorities as they disengage. Although many athletes handle this process smoothly, develop other interests, and move into relatively satisfying occupations, some encounter adjustment problems that interfere with occupational success and overall life satisfaction.

The two challenges that face retiring athletes are to (1) reaffirm or reconstruct identities in terms of activities, abilities, and relationships that are not directly related to sport participation and (2) nurture or renegotiate relationships with family and friends so that new identities can be established and reaffirmed. Meeting these challenges successfully may take time, and it always involves forming and nurturing relationships that support non-sport identities. For retiring athletes who have poor relationship skills, professional help may be needed.

Studies also show that adjustment problems are most likely when injuries force an athlete to retire without notice (Coakley, 1983a; Swain, 1999; Weisman, 2004). Injuries link retirement with larger issues of health and self-esteem and propel a person into life-changing transitions before they're expected. When this occurs, athletes often need career-transition counselling.

When athletes encounter problems transitioning out of sports into careers and other activities, support should be and occasionally is provided by the sport organizations that benefited from their labor (Dacyshyn, 1999). Some sport organizations, including universities and national governing bodies for Olympic sports, are beginning to do this through transition programs focusing on career self-assessments, life skills training, career planning, résumé writing, job search strategies, interviewing skills, career placement contacts, and psychological counseling. Retiring athletes often find it helpful to receive guidance in identifying the skills they learned in sports and how those skills can be transferred to subsequent careers.

Athletic Grants and Occupational Success

Discussions about sport participation and social mobility in the United States often include references to athletic scholarships. Most people believe that these grants-in-aid are valuable mobility vehicles for many young people. However, NCAA data indicate that the actual number of *full* athletic scholarships is clearly exaggerated in the popular consciousness. This occurs for the following reasons:

1. High school students who receive standard recruiting letters from university coaches often tell people they are anticipating *full*

scholarships when in fact they receive only partial aid or no aid at all, and they don't disclose this disappointing outcome.
2. College students receiving tuition waivers or other forms of partial athletic aid sometimes lead people to believe that they have full scholarships.
3. Athletic scholarships are one-year renewable contracts, but when they are not renewed, many people assume that those who had them last year also have them this year and the next.
4. Many people assume that everyone who makes a college team, especially at large universities, has a scholarship, but this is not true.

There were over 6 million undergraduate students in NCAA institutions in 2008. Table 10.4 shows that 408,364 (6.8 percent) of these students were on intercollegiate teams. Division I and II schools had 73,200 full scholarships to award and split them among 138,216 athletes so that the average scholarship was worth about $8,700. Of the 249,743 athletes in Division I and II schools, 55 percent (138,216) received some amount of athletic aid, but most received only partial scholarships. NCAA researchers estimate that about 27,600 athletes—6.8 percent of all NCAA athletes in all three divisions—received full scholarships (tuition, room, and food). Overall, 66 percent (268,148) of all athletes playing college sports receive *no* athletic scholarship money, although some may receive academic scholarships from sources outside the athletic department. Additionally, teams with few allotted scholarships may divide one $16,000 full scholarship between 8 or more athletes.

When parents and athletes discover that scholarships in baseball and track are routinely under $3000 per year, that the average baseball scholarship is $5,806, that some "scholarship athletes" receive as little as $400 per year, and that many teams award no full scholarships, they are shocked, especially when the cost of room, food, books, and tuition at most NCAA institutions is between $15,000 and $45,000 a year (Pennington, 2008a, 2008b). Parental shock may turn into disbelief when they remember that they

Table 10.4   Athletes and athletic scholarships available in NCAA Divisions I, II, and III, by gender (2008)*

Division	Men			Women		
	All athletes	Scholarships awarded to one or more athletes	Athletes with full or partial scholarships	All athletes	Scholarships awarded to one or more athletes	Athletes with full or partial scholarships
D-I & DII	141,044	41,464	78,453	108,699	31,736	59,763
D-III (N = 424)	92,786	0	0	65,835	0	0
TOTAL	**233,830**	**41,464**	**78,453**	**174,534**	**31,736**	**59,763**

Summary Analysis:

- **All NCAA athletes (2007–2008): 408,364**
- **Number of full scholarships divided among all athletes: 73,200**
- **Athletes receiving athletic aid: 138,216**
- **Percentage of all athletes w/aid 34%**
  - ○ **Division I & II men**   56%
  - ○ **Division I & II women**   55%
  - ○ **Division III men**   0%
  - ○ **Division III women**   0%
  - ○ **All men**   34%
  - ○ **All women**   34%
- **Estimated percentage of all athletes with *full* scholarships: 6.8% (27,643)**
- **Percentage of all college athletes with no athletic aid: 66% (268,148)**

Source: NCAA data (NCAA, 2008) and *The New York Times* (see Pennington, 2008a, b, c, d)
Note: "Aid" comes in many forms, but this is the "official aid" declared to the NCAA.

spent $5,000 or more a year to keep their son or daughter in a sport from age 6 to 17—a minimum "investment" of $60,000 that brings an average return of $34,800 ($8,700 times 4 years) for the families lucky enough to have a child who actually receives an average scholarship. "Luck," in this case, means a loss of at least $25,000 in cash, to say nothing of the time, energy, and long weekends spent driving to and sitting at practices, games, and tournaments—and eating fast food. Additionally, their son or daughter will generally work very hard for 35 to 40 hours per week for all or nearly all of the academic year to maintain the scholarship, and this does not include travel to games and mandatory workouts during the summer and most breaks (Pennington, 2008b).

Another way to make sense of the data in Table 10.4 is to say that among all undergraduate students in NCAA schools, less than half of one percent (0.46 percent) of them have full athletic scholarships, and only 2.3 percent of all undergraduates receive some form of athletic aid. Clearly, far fewer students receive full athletic scholarships than is commonly believed. In fact, *academic* scholarships amount to many millions of dollars more than the total amount of athletic scholarships, even though many high school students and their parents don't know this.

Class, gender, and race dynamics are strongly connected with athletic scholarships. First, young people in upper-middle-class families (with household incomes of $90,000 per year or more) have resources to develop skills in highly privatized sports such as lacrosse, soccer, volleyball, rowing, swimming, water polo, field hockey, softball, and ice hockey. As a result, they are more likely than athletes in middle- and lower-income families to receive athletic scholarships, although most could afford college without athletic aid. When Tom Farrey (2008), an Emmy-Award-winning journalist at ESPN, investigated this issue he concluded that "college athletics in general are more the province of the privileged than the poor" (p. 145). He cites a U.S. Department of Education study showing that young people from families ranked in the top quarter of the population in terms of income are ten times more likely to play on a Division I sport team than young people from families in the lowest quarter. To Farrey, this indicated that "beneath the thin layer of sport entertainment that makes its way onto television are the bulk of college athletes: Well-off and white" (p. 146).

Second, the college sports that offer high school seniors the best odds for a scholarship include rowing, golf, equestrian events, gymnastics, lacrosse, swimming, fencing, and water polo—all of which are upper-middle-class, suburban, and white (Farrey, 2008). Despite this, featured stories about college sports highlight the young people who rise from poverty to achieve fame and financial security. This recycles the myth that sports are a path to a better life at the same time that it reaffirms the American Dream, reinforces the image of the United States as a true meritocracy, and promulgates the class ideology supported by those beliefs.

Third, the only college sports that consistently generate revenues are those in which the majority of players are black men: Division I football and men's basketball. On average, these men come from households with far less wealth and income than the households from which most other Division I athletes come. This creates an interesting class- and race-based scenario: Black men from middle- and lower-income households with little wealth work to generate the revenues that provide scholarships to white athletes from households generally having greater income and wealth. White students and athletes don't think about this pattern of resource distribution, but black football and basketball players are well aware of it. The irony of this scenario is seen in situations where a black athlete is perceived by others as having it easy, and when he loses his cool in

the face of such a naïve perception, he's called a thug and people conclude that he doesn't belong on campus. In this way, college sports reproduce the very ideologies that maintain and justify social and economic inequalities. And when a few black athletes sign pro contracts, people try to (mistakenly) claim that the United States is a post-racial, color-blind society.

Overall, when athletic aid goes to financially needy young people who focus on learning and earn their degrees, college sports increase their chances for career success. But this is the exception rather than the rule. This does not mean that athletic aid is a problem, but it does mean that it contributes little to upward social mobility.

summary

DO MONEY AND POWER MATTER IN SPORTS?

Social class and class relations are integrally involved in sports. Organized sports depend on resources, and those who provide them do so in ways that support their interests by establishing economic arrangements that work to their advantage. This is why dominant sport forms in the United States and other nations with market economies promote an ideology based on the belief in meritocracy that you always get what you deserve, and you always deserve what you get.

In the United States this belief combined with belief in the American Dream constitutes a class ideology that promotes favorable conclusions about the character and qualifications of wealthy and powerful people at the same time that it disadvantages the poor and powerless. Furthermore, it leads to the conclusion that economic inequality, even when it is extreme and oppressive, is natural and beneficial to society as a whole.

Class relations also are tied to patterns of sport team ownership, event sponsorship, and media coverage of sports. As public funds build stadiums and arenas, people with wealth and power receive subsidies and income, which they use to maintain their status and privilege. At the same time, economic and political elites, including powerful transnational corporations, are perceived as those who sponsor the teams, events, and media coverage that bring people pleasure and excitement. Although fans don't always give sports the meaning that sponsors would like them to, fans seldom subject sports to critical analysis and usually don't see them as perpetuating a class ideology that justifies inequality and serves as a basis for public policies that foster it.

Sport participation patterns worldwide are connected with social class and the distribution of material resources. Organized sports are a luxury that people in many regions of the world cannot afford. Even in wealthy societies, sport participation is most common among those in the middle and upper classes, and class-based lifestyles often go hand-in-hand with staging and participating in certain sports.

Sport participation patterns also are connected with the intersection of class, gender, race, and ethnicity in people's lives. This is seen in the case of girls and women who have low participation rates when resources are scarce and among men who see sports as a means of obtaining respect when they are living on the social and economic margins of society. Boxing provides an example of a sport in which class, gender, race, and ethnicity intersect in a powerful combination. As a result, the boxing gym often becomes a safe space that offers temporary refuge for minority men who live in neighborhoods where poverty, racism, and despair spawn desperate acts of violence among their peers. The same social forces that bring ethnic minority men to boxing also fuel many variations of *hoop dreams* that captivate the attention of young ethnic minorities, especially black males. These dreams are sources of hope but they seldom come to fruition amid the reality of school and gym closings, school teams being dropped, and a lack of access to the resources required for training and the development of excellence.

Patterns of watching sports also are connected with social class and class relations. This is demonstrated by the increased segregation of fans in stadiums and arenas. Luxury suites, club seating, and patterns of season-ticket allocations separate people by a combination of wealth, power, and access to resources. In the process, inequality become increasingly normalized to the point that people are less likely to object to policies that privilege those with the money to buy a spot at the front of the line, or to establish their own line-free "premier entrance" to the luxury suites.

Opportunities for careers that hold the hope of upward social mobility exist for some people in sports. For athletes, these opportunities often are scarce and short-lived, and they reflect patterns of class, gender, and ethnic relations in society. These patterns take various forms with regard to careers in sport organizations. Although opportunities in some of these jobs have become increasingly open over the past decade, white men still hold most of the power positions in sport organizations. This will change only when the organizational cultures of sport teams and athletic departments become more inclusive and provide new ways for women and ethnic minorities to participate fully in shaping the policies and norms used to determine qualifications in sports and organize social relations at the workplace.

Research generally indicates that people who use sport participation to expand their social and cultural capital often have an advantage when seeking occupational careers apart from sports. However, when sport participation constricts social and cultural capital, it's likely to have a negative effect on later career success. The relevance of this pattern varies by sport and is affected by the resources that athletes can accumulate during their playing careers.

Ending athletic careers may create stress and personal challenges, but most people move through the retirement process without experiencing excessive trauma or difficulty. Problems are most likely when identities and relationships have been built exclusively in connection with sports. Then professional help may be needed to successfully transition into satisfying careers and relationships in which mutual support encourages growth and the development of new identities.

Otherwise, it is possible to become stuck in the "glory days" of being an athlete instead of facing the challenges presented in life after sports.

Athletic scholarships help some young people further their educations and possibly achieve career success, but athletic aid is relatively scarce compared with other scholarships and forms of financial aid. Furthermore, athletic scholarships do not always change the future career patterns of young people because many recipients would attend college without sport-related financial assistance.

In conclusion, sports are clearly tied to patterns of class, class relations, and social inequality in society. Money and economic power do matter, and they matter in ways that often reproduce existing patterns of social class and life chances.

WEBSITE RESOURCES

Note: Websites often change. The following URLs were current when this book was printed. Please check our website (www.mhhe.com/coakley10e) for updates and additions.

www.mhhe.com/coakley10e Click on Chapter 10 for information on the "Top 25" from the 1996 and 2000 rankings made by *The Sporting News*, extended discussion of the odds of playing professional sports for people in various racial and ethnic groups, and references to films.

http://bcasports.cstv.com/ Black Coaches and Administrators (BCA) advocates the growth and development of ethnic minorities at all levels of sports, both nationally and internationally; it addresses issues pertaining to the participation and employment of ethnic minorities in sport, and intercollegiate athletics in particular.

www.bls.gov/oco/ocos251.htm Published by the U.S. Department of Labor, Bureau of Labor Statistics, the 2006–2007 edition of the *Occupational Outlook Handbook* includes a section on "Athletes, Coaches,

Umpires and Related Workers" that provides descriptions of work, working conditions, training and other qualifications, job outlook, earnings, and related occupations. The search engine can be used to find descriptions of other sport-related jobs.

www.finelinefeatures.com/hoop The site for *Hoop Dreams*, a classic documentary film that provides a personalized look at social class and class relations issues in the lives of two young men living in a Chicago neighborhood.

www.ncaa.org/research/prob_of_competing/ probability_of_competing2.html#m_basketball An NCAA page that contains computations of the estimated probability of competing in athletics beyond interscholastic sports; includes good information on the odds of playing in college and the pros.

www.ncasports.org/press_releases.htm The National Consortium for Academics and Sports (NCAS) is an organization of colleges, universities, and individuals that focus on the educational attainment of athletes and on using the power and appeal of sport to bring about positive social change; site provides links to recent reports on racial and gender equity in sports.

www.teammarketing.com The Fan Cost Index link provides for each year since the early 1990s ticket prices for all teams in MLB, NBA, NFL, and NHL, and shows the average price for each league and year; also lists data for concession prices, how much it costs to take a family of four to a game, and how much ticket prices and other costs have increased since the previous season.

www.tidesport.org/aboutdirectors.html The Institute for Diversity and Ethics in Sport (TIDES) is a comprehensive resource for issues related to gender and race in amateur, collegiate and professional sports. It publishes various studies, including the internationally recognized Racial and Gender Report Cards, an assessment of hiring practices in coaching and sport management in professional and college sport. TIDES works with the National Consortium for Academics and Sports to conduct diversity management training for sports organizations.

(McGraw-Hill)

SPORTS AND THE ECONOMY

What Are the Characteristics of Commercial Sports?

> IF ANOTHER PRO does a trick and you wanna keep your job, you better do it. . . . Everything [in skateboarding] is getting bigger, more dangerous.
>
> **—Colin McKay, pro skateboarder (in Thompson, 2004)**

(OLC) Visit *Sports in Society*'s Online Learning Center (OLC) at www.mhhe.com/coakley10e for additional information and study material for this chapter, including the following:

- A complete chapter outline
- Learning objectives
- Practice quizzes
- Internet resources
- Related readings
- Essays
- Student projects

YOU'VE GOT TO GET these kids [who excel on the court] in your product. You've got to get these kids walking around being a Reebok kid. . . . They will be your messengers.

—Sonny Vaccaro, Reebok representative (in Alesia, 2004)

TEAM OWNERS ARE getting rich like never before. . . . When it comes to players, owners are becoming more tight-fisted.

—Michael K. Ozanian and Kurt Badenhausen, *Forbes*, 2008

WE ARE NOW in a sports world where human beings are glorified and then destroyed for our collective amusement.

—Dave Zirin, sports journalist (2008b)

Sports have been used as public entertainment through history. However, they've never been so thoroughly commercialized as they are today. Never before have economic factors so totally dominated decisions about sports, and never before have economic organizations and corporate interests had so much power and control over the meaning, purpose, and organization of sports.

The economic stakes for athletes and sponsors have never been higher than they are today. The bottom line has replaced the goal line. Sports are now evaluated by gate receipts, concessions and merchandise sales, licensing fees, media rights contracts, and website hits. Games and events are evaluated using media criteria such as market share, ratings points, and the cost of commercial time. Athletes are evaluated by their entertainment value as well as physical skills. Stadiums, teams, and events are named after corporations and linked to corporate logos instead of people and places that have local historical meaning.

Corporate interests influence team colors, uniform designs, event schedules, media coverage, and the comments of announcers during games and matches. Media companies sponsor and plan events, and they own a growing number of sport teams. Many sports are corporate enterprises, tied to marketing concerns and processes of global capitalist expansion. The mergers of major corporate conglomerates that began in the 1990s and now continue into the twenty-first century have connected sport teams and events with media and entertainment companies. The names of transnational corporations are now synonymous with the athletes, events, and sports that bring pleasure to the lives of millions of people.

Because economic factors are so important in sports, this chapter focuses on the following questions:

1. Under what conditions do commercial sports emerge and prosper in a society?
2. What changes occur in the meaning, purpose, and organization of sports when they become commercial activities?
3. Who owns, sponsors, and promotes sports, and what are their interests?
4. What is the legal and financial status of athletes in commercial sports?

EMERGENCE AND GROWTH OF COMMERCIAL SPORTS

Commercial sports are organized and played for profit. Their success depends on gate receipts, concessions, sponsorships, the sale of media broadcasting rights, and other revenue streams associated with sport images and personalities. Therefore, commercial sports grow and prosper best under five social and economic conditions.

First, they are most prevalent in market economies where material rewards are highly valued by athletes, team owners, event sponsors, and spectators.

Second, they usually exist in societies that have large, densely populated cities with high concentrations of potential spectators. Although some forms of commercial sports can be maintained in rural, agricultural societies, their revenues would not support full-time professional athletes or sport promoters.

Third, commercial sports are a luxury, and they prosper only when the standard of living is high enough that people have time and resources to play and watch events that have no tangible products required for survival. Transportation and communications technologies must exist for sponsors to make money. Therefore, commercial sports are common in wealthy, urban, and industrial or postindustrial societies; they seldom exist in labor-intensive, poor societies where people must use all their resources to survive.

Fourth, commercial sports require *large amounts of capital* (money or credit) to build and maintain stadiums and arenas in which events can be played and watched. Capital can be accumulated in the public or private sector, but in either case, the willingness to invest in sports depends on anticipated payoffs in the form of

Sports are played in nearly all cultures, but professional sports seldom exist in labor-intensive, poor nations. The Afghan horsemen here are playing buzkashi, a popular sport in their country, but Afghanistan lacks the general conditions needed to sustain buzkashi as a professional sport with paid athletes and paying fans. (*Source:* Efren Lukatsky, AP/Wide World Photos)

publicity, profits, or power. *Private* investment in sports occurs when investors expect financial profits; *public* investment occurs when political leaders believe that commercial sports serve their interests, the interests of "the public," or a combination of both.

AT YOUR *fingertips* For more information on politics and public investment in sports, see Chapter 13, pp. 443–449.

Fifth, commercial sports flourish in cultures where lifestyles emphasize consumption and material status symbols. This enables everything associated with sports to be marketed and sold: athletes (including their names, autographs, and images), merchandise, team names and logos. When people express their identities through clothing, other possessions, and their associations with status symbols and celebrities, they will spend money on sports that have meaning in their social world. The success of commercial sports depends on selling symbols and emotional experiences to audiences, and then selling audiences to sponsors and the media (Slack, 2005).

Class Relations and Commercial Sports

As noted in Chapter 10, the sports most likely to be commercialized are those watched, played, or used for profit by people who control economic resources in society. For example, golf is a major commercial sport in the United States, even though it does not lend itself to commercial presentation. It's inconvenient to stage a golf event for a live audience or to televise it. Camera placement and media commentary are difficult to arrange, and live spectators see only a small portion of the action. Golf does not involve vigorous action or head-to-head competition, except in rare cases of match play. Usually, if you don't play golf, you have little or no reason to watch it.

But golfers include the wealthy and powerful, and they're important people to sponsors and advertisers because they make consumption decisions for themselves, their families, their businesses, and thousands of employees who work under their supervision. They buy luxury cars and other high-end products for themselves, but more important to advertisers is that they buy thousands of company cars and computers for employees and make investment decisions related to pensions and company capital.

Golfers as a group have economic clout that goes far beyond their personal and family lives. This makes golf an attractive sport for corporations that have images and products that appeal to consumers with money and influence. This is why auto companies with high-priced cars sponsor and advertise on the PGA, LPGA, and Champions (Senior) PGA tours. This also is why major television networks cover golf tournaments: They can sell commercial time at a high rate per minute because those watching golf have money to spend—their money *and* the money of the companies they control. The converse of this is also true: Sports attracting low- and middle-income audiences often are ignored by television or covered only under special circumstances. If wealthy executives bowled, we would see more bowling on television and more bowling facilities on prime

real estate in cities; but wealthy people seldom bowl, and bowling receives little coverage.

Market economies always privilege the interests of those who have the power and resources to select sports for promotion and coverage. Unless those people want to play, sponsor, or watch a sport, it won't be commercialized on a large scale, nor will it be given cultural significance in society. A sport won't become a "national pastime" or be associated with "character," community spirit, civic unity, and political loyalty unless it's favored by people with resources. This is why football is now known as "America's game"—it celebrates and privileges the values and experiences of the men who control and benefit from corporate wealth and power in North America. This is why men pay thousands of dollars to buy expensive season tickets to college and professional football games, why male executives use corporation money to buy expensive blocks of "company tickets" to football games, and why corporation presidents write hundred-thousand-dollar checks to pay for luxury boxes and club seats for themselves, friends, and clients. They enjoy football, but most important, it reproduces an ideology that fosters their interests.

Women who want to be a part of the power structure in the United States often find that they must learn to "talk football" so they can communicate with the men who have created organizational cultures and control women's careers. If female executives don't go to the next big football game and take clients with them, they risk being excluded from the "masculinity loop" that is central to corporate culture and communication (Gregory, 2009). When they go to work every Monday during the fall, they know that their ability to "talk football" can keep them in touch with many of the men around them.

The Creation of Spectator Interest

Sport spectators are likely to be plentiful in societies where there's a general quest for excitement, an ideological emphasis on material success, childhood experiences with sports, and easy access to sports through the media.

The Quest for Excitement   When social life is highly controlled and organized, everyday routines often cause people to feel emotionally constrained. This fosters a search for activities that offer tension-excitement and emotional arousal. According to sociologists Eric Dunning and Norbert Elias, historical evidence suggests that this is common in modern societies. Sports, they contend, provide activities in which rules and norms can be shaped to foster emotional arousal and exciting actions, thereby eliminating boredom without disrupting social order in society (Dunning, 1999; Elias and Dunning, 1986).

Sports generally involve a tension between order and disruption. To manage this tension, norms and rules in sports must be loose enough to allow exciting action, but not so loose that they permit uncontrolled violence or other forms of destructive deviance. When norms and rules are too constraining, sports are boring and people lose interest; when they are too loose, sports become sites for reckless and dangerous actions that jeopardize health and social order. The challenge is to find and maintain a balance. This explanation of spectator interest raises the question, "Why do so many people give priority to sports over other activities in their quest for excitement?" Cultural theorists suggest that answers can be found by looking at the connection between ideology and cultural practices. This leads us to consider the following factors.

Class Ideology and Spectator Interest   Many people watch games live or on video, but spectator involvement is highest among those who believe in a meritocratic ideal: the idea that success is always based on skill and hard work, and skill and hard work always lead to success. This belief supports a widely held class ideology in societies with capitalist economies. Those who hold it often use sports as a model for how

the social world should operate. When sports promote the idea that success is achieved only through hard work and skill, their ideology is reaffirmed, and they become more secure in their beliefs. This is why sport media commentators emphasize that athletes and teams succeed when they work hard and have talent. This also is why corporations use the bodies of elite athletes to represent their public relations and marketing images—the finely tuned bodies of athletes are concrete examples of skill, power, and success as well as the use of science and technology (Hoberman, 1994). When high-profile athletes can deliver this message for corporations, lucrative endorsements come their way.

AT YOUR fingertips   For information on class ideology, see Chapter 10, pp. 318–320.

Youth Sport Programs and Spectator Interest   Spectator interest often is initiated during childhood sport experiences. When organized youth sport programs emphasize skills, competition, and success, participants are likely to grow up wanting to watch elite athletes. For young people who continue to play sports, watching elite athletes provides them with models for playing and improving skills; for those who discontinue active participation, watching elite athletes provides continuous connections with the images and experiences of success that they learned playing organized youth sports.

Media Coverage and Spectator Interest   Media promote the commercialization of sports by publicizing and covering events in ways that sustain spectator interest. Television increases spectator access to events and athletes worldwide and provides unique representations of sports. Camera coverage enables viewers to focus on the action and view replays in slow motion as they listen to

Football is the most widely watched sport in the United States. It offers excitement in the form of rule-governed violence, and it reaffirms the notion that success is achieved through competition and dominating opponents. Youth football teams are very popular, and more young men play high school football than any other high school sport. Football lends itself to media coverage during which replays, slow motion, and expert commentary are used to dissect plays and game plans. (*Source:* McGraw-Hill)

the "insider" comments of announcers—all of which further immerses spectators into vicarious and potentially exciting sport experiences.

On-air commentators serve the media audience as fellow spectators who embellish the action and heighten identification with athletes and teams. Commentators provide inside stories, analyze strategies, describe athletes as personalities, and magnify the importance of the entire event.

Television recruits new spectators by providing a means of learning the rules and strategies of a sport without purchasing expensive tickets. Furthermore, newcomers to a sport can learn at home with family and friends. This is a painless

way to become socialized into a spectator role, and it increases the number of people who will eventually buy tickets, watch televised games, pay for cable and satellite sports programming, and even become pay-per-view customers in the future.

Economic Factors and the Globalization of Commercial Sports

Commercial sports are now global in scope. Globalization has occurred because (1) those who control, sponsor, and promote sports seek new ways to expand markets and maximize profits, and (2) transnational corporations use sports as vehicles for introducing their products and services around the world. This makes sports a form of global cultural trade that is exported and imported in a manner similar to other products.

Sport Organizations Look for Global Markets
Commercial sport organizations are businesses, and their goal is to expand into as many markets as possible. In fact, future profits for major professional sports depend on selling media rights and consumer merchandise. Most leagues now market themselves outside their home countries and use various strategies to develop identification with their sport, teams, and players. In this way, sport organizations become exporters of culture as well as products to be consumed. The complex export–import processes that occur in connection with sports are now topics studied by scholars in the sociology of sport.

AT YOUR *fingertips*
pp. 450–466.

For more information on sport and global relations, see Chapter 13,

The desire for global expansion was the main reason why the NBA allowed its players to compose the so-called Dream Team that played in the 1992 Olympics. The global media attention received by Michael Jordan, Magic Johnson, and other players provided the NBA with publicity worth many millions of dollars. This exposure helped market NBA broadcasting rights and official NBA products worldwide. Today, the NBA finals and the NBA All-Star games are televised annually in over 200 countries and there are 76 international players from 31 countries now playing in the league. Outside the United States, China constitutes the largest NBA market and player development focus (Bradsher, 2007; Rhoden, 2007). More than 50,000 stores in China

sell NBA merchandise, and about 30 percent of all visitors to NBA.com enter through the Mandarin language portal at the site.

The desire for global expansion has led NFL, NBA, NHL, and MLB teams to play games in Mexico, Japan, England, France, Germany, and Australia and to subsidize leagues and outreach programs for marketing purposes. This spirit of globalization is neither new nor limited to North American sport organizations. The International Olympic Committee (IOC) gradually has incorporated national Olympic committees from every nation worldwide and has turned the Olympic Games into the most successful and financially lucrative media sport events in history. Furthermore, the IOC, like some other powerful sport organizations, has turned itself and the Olympics into a global brand. This branding process also has had serious implications for the Paralympic Games, as explained in Breaking Barriers on page 360.

The sport with the longest history of global expansion is soccer, which is governed by FIFA—the Fédération Internationale de Football Association (Sugden and Tomlinson, 1998, 1999). The top soccer clubs in Europe have used multiple strategies to expand their global marketing reach. The best current example is Manchester United in the English Premier league. "Man U," as it is known worldwide, is now a global brand, which has boosted the value of the club beyond $1.5 billion.

Corporations Use Sports as Vehicles for Global Expansion Because certain sports capture the attention, emotions, and allegiance of so many people worldwide, corporations are eager to sponsor them. Corporations need symbols of success and productivity that they can use as "marketing hooks" for products and as representations of their images. For example, people around the world still associate Michael Jordan with the "Air Jordan" trademark copyrighted by Nike; and many people now assume a connection between the Olympics and both McDonald's and Coca-Cola. In the

Brand Barriers
There Was Nothing We Could Do

When is a flag not a flag? Dr. Jens Bromann discovered in 1983 that this is not a trick question. As a representative of athletes with disabilities, he attended a meeting called by Juan Antonio Samaranch, the president of the International Olympic Committee (IOC). Samaranch told Bromann and others from disability sport organizations that they could no longer use Olympic images at the Paralympics or the trials leading up to them. Samaranch explained that among other things, the Olympic flag and the five interlocking rings were symbols that now represented a global brand with its own commercial interests and goals. The flag, therefore, was not so much a flag as it was a licensed logo, and it could be used only by those who paid for the right to do so. As Bromann left the meeting, he told reporters that the Olympics was now an exclusive commercial brand, and "there was nothing we could do" to maintain the interests of the Paralympics (Jennings, 1996a).

Upset, but not wanting to cut ties with the IOC, Bromann and his peers in disability sports turned their attention to the Paralympic Games that would follow the 1984 Los Angeles Olympics. But neither the Los Angeles Olympic Organizing Committee nor the United States Olympic Committee (USOC) would support them and their event. So they left Los Angeles and split their events between New York and Stoke Mandeville, England. They also formed the International Coordinating Committee of World Organizations for the Disabled (ICC) and made it the governing body for the Paralympic Games.

As president of the new ICC, Bromann focused on organizing the 1988 Paralympic Games in Seoul, Korea. With support from Korean Olympic officials, the games were a huge success, bringing together over 3000 athletes from sixty-one nations. At the opening ceremonies, Bromann, who had once competed in sports for blind athletes, received from the Korean organizers a flag that they had designed specifically for the Korean Paralympic Games. It was white and had five *tae geuks*, or traditional Korean line symbols, that

resembled teardrops in the same positions and colors as the five interlocking rings on the Olympic flag. This was meant to show that the Paralympics were related to the Olympic movement and that Paralympians train and compete as Olympians do (Sheil, 2000).

The ICC reorganized in 1989 and after the 1992 Paralympic Games in Barcelona, Spain, it became the International Paralympic Committee (IPC). In the meantime, it continued to use the tae geuks flag as its symbol, but this infuriated the IOC. The flag, claimed IOC officials, was too similar to their brand logo. In 1991 the IOC told the ICC to change its flag or face sanctions. This prompted investigative journalist Andrew Jennings to ask sarcastically, "Sanctions against the disabled? What would they do? Shoot some guide dogs? Smash up a few wheelchairs?" (1996a, p. 228). But the ICC knew the sanctions meant there would be no more funding from the IOC—an action that would destroy many disability sports.

To appease the IOC, a new symbol with three tae geuks was officially launched at the 1994 IPC World Championships. The tae geuks again appeared as teardrops, but officials explained that they now represented the Paralympic motto: "Mind, Body, and Spirit." This flag was used through the 2004 Paralympic Games in Athens. But in 2003, after years of failed attempts to gain full IOC recognition and support, the IPC separated from the IOC and adopted a new symbol and flag to represent the unique purpose and identity of the Paralympic Games. It consisted of three elements in red, blue, and green—the colors most often used in national flags. The elements are known as *Agitos* (a Latin word meaning, *I move*), and they appear to be in motion around a central point, representing a dynamic, global "Spirit in Motion"—the new motto of the Paralympics. This new representation emphasizes that the IPC goal is to sponsor sports that bring together athletes from all regions of the globe. The Spirit in Motion flag flew at the 2008 Paralympics in Beijing, and there was nothing the IOC could do to prevent it.

A.

C.

B.

International Paralympic Committee

These three flags have been used by the Paralympics in response to IOC demands that they not use any image that could be compared to the five-rings Olympic logo and flag. The five-teardrops flag (A) was used in Seoul, Korea in 1988; the three-teardrops flag (B) was used from 1994 through 2004, and the new Spirit in Motion flag (C) was used at the Beijing Paralympic Games in 2008. (*Source: Flag images courtesy of the International Paralympic Committee*)

Today, the IPC has adopted a commercial approach to disability model of sport as a survival strategy. Its flag is now a licensed logo—like the IOC flag. But this change raises the question of who will benefit from and be hurt by the commercialization of elite disability sports. Athletes who can attract spectators along with their sponsors will certainly benefit, but will this inspire sport participation among others or will it turn them into spectators? Will people be inclined to donate money to elite athletes, leaving everyone else to say, "There's nothing we could do"? Hopefully, this is not where commercialization will take disability sports.

United States, the "gold medal" achievement for a corporation is to convert the company into a brand that can be associated with various forms of status and identity. Sports serve as effective sites for doing this as sport images and products can be used to represent people's identities at the same time that they can represent other things that give them status in particular social worlds. This dynamic drives consumption and corporate profits (Walker, 2008).

Companies whose profits depend on the sales of alcohol, tobacco, fast food, soft drinks, and candy are especially eager to have their products associated with sports (Dewhirst and Sparks, 2003). This enables them to defuse negative publicity about the unhealthy aspects of their products. They want people to think that "if the sports we love are brought to us by beer, cigarettes, soft drinks, beef burgers, deep-fried foods, and candy bars, these things must have some redeeming qualities."

Scholars and journalists have identified Michael Jordan as a key figure in the process of using sports for corporate interests (Andrews, 2001; Andrews and Jackson, 2001). Jordan

> commercialized his sport and himself, turning both into brands for an emerging legion of sports marketers . . . . In his own way, Jordan . . . spread an ideology. It was that sports are not just games but tools for advertisers. It was that basketball isn't a playground thing, but a corporate thing (in Weiner, 1999, p. 77).

We now live in an era of transnational corporations (TNCs) that influence economic activity worldwide, affecting who has jobs, the kinds of work people do, salaries and working conditions, the products that people can buy, where they can buy them, and what they cost. When these corporations sponsor sports, they negotiate deals that promote their interests, increase their power, and create positive images of themselves as "global citizens and leaders." This is worth an investment of billions of dollars each year. For example, General Motors and Coca-Cola each

spent over $2 billion to sponsor Olympic sports between 1998 and 2008; and Anheuser-Busch (Budweiser) spent about $300 million for commercial time during Super Bowls between 1988 and 2008. Like other multinational corporations, these companies buy commercial time during sport events to promote the belief that pleasure and excitement in people's everyday lives depend on them. They use this belief as an ideological outpost in the minds of people worldwide, and as information is filtered through these outposts, corporate executives hope to defuse opposition to the products and operational practices of their companies (see Chapter 4). When successful, this strategy boosts their legitimacy and contributes to corporate hegemony worldwide.

AT YOUR *fingertips* For more information on ideological outposts and how they're used in processes of hegemony, see Chapter 4, pp. 115–117.

The success of this strategy led a Coca-Cola executive to tell IOC officials before the 1996 Olympic Games in Atlanta that they owed loyalty to Coke. He explained that

> Just as sponsors have the responsibility to preserve the integrity of the sport, enhance its image, help grow its prestige and its attendance, so too, do you [in sports] have responsibility and accountability to the sponsor (in Reid, 1996, p. 4BB).

IOC officials knew that drinking cola did not meet the nutritional needs of elite athletes or the health goals of the Olympic movement, but they did not resist the executive's message. Coca-Cola had worked for eight decades to colonize their minds and establish the outposts through which this message was transmitted. During the 2000 Olympic Games in Sydney, Australia, the inside cover of the official program explained the importance of sponsors with these words:

> Without sponsors, there would be no Olympic Games. Without the Olympic Games, there would be no dreams. Without dreams, there would be nothing (in Horne, 2007).

Of course, the sponsors themselves could not have written a statement better suited to their purposes. They want people to focus on dreams rather than the realities related to consumption and global corporate expansion; the Olympic Games in Beijing was awash in Coca-Cola imagery as outposts were being established in the heads of 1.3 billion potential consumers of soft drinks.

Outposts in Action: Branding Sports When ranchers want to show ownership of animals, they burn their logos into the animals' hides. The brand is their mark of ownership. And in the realm of sports, nearly all major stadiums and arenas in North America now display the brands of airlines, banks, brewers, and a gang of companies selling cars, oil, auto parts, energy, soft drinks, and communications services and products. For the venues in which NFL, NBA, and MLB teams play, these branding or naming rights sell for $3 million to $20 million per year. Deals usually are for ten to thirty years and often include signage in and around the venue, the use of luxury boxes and club seats, promotional rights for events, and exclusive concession rights (for example, the four Pepsi Centers in the United States sell only Pepsi products to fans). This benefits corporations, especially in major cities where four large billboards can cost up to $100,000 a month ($1.2 million per year). Having multiple billboard-like surfaces inside and outside a stadium is viewed as a good investment by corporate executives, especially when the name of their company is used in everyday conversations and they receive "sport perks" for themselves, customers, and friends.

The branding of sports also is apparent inside stadiums, where nearly every available surface is sold for corporate displays. Surfaces without corporate messages are now defined as wasted space, even in publicly owned facilities. This occurs at all levels of sports. For instance, many corporations desperately want to establish outposts in the minds of high school students who are in the process of forming lifelong preferences for products such as soft drinks. David Carter from the Sports Marketing Company in California knows that high school sports need revenues, so he predicts that "commercialism is coming to a school near you: the high school cheerleaders will be brought to you by Gatorade, and the football team will be presented by Outback [Steakhouse]" (in Pennington, 2004, p. 1).

As corporations brand public spaces, community identities often come to be linked with brands, thereby converting the physical embodiments of local traditions and histories into highly visible signs that promote consumption and identify corporations as providers of pleasure and excitement. In the process, the public good is replaced by the corporate good, even in spaces paid for and owned by citizen-taxpayers.

Sport events also are branded. College football fans in the United States watch everything from the Tostitos Fiesta Bowl and FedEx Orange Bowl to the Outback Bowl and Papajohns.com Bowl during December and early January. College football is clearly branded, as are the athletes who wear corporate logos on their shirts, shoes, helmets, and warm-up clothing.

NASCAR auto racing may be the most classic example of corporate branding. People watch Nextel Cup races named the Crown Royal 400, Lipton Tea 250, Pep Boys Auto 500, Subway Fresh Fit 500, Samsung 500, Kobalt Tools 500, Coca-Cola 600, Coke Zero 400, Pepsi 500, Bank of America 500, Dickies 500, Sharpie 500, Dodge Challenger 500, and UAW-Dodge 400 (the only major race or sport event with a workers' organization as a sponsor). Additionally, race cars are billboards with surface spaces purchased by companies selling products that often cannot be advertised on network television, such as hard

"This is Pepsi McDonald at Spielberg Jurassic Park where the Microsoft Raiders will battle the Wal-Mart Titans. Team captains, Nike Jones and Budweiser Williams, prepare for the Franklin Mint Coin Toss, right after this message from our sponsor, Ford trucks—giving you power on demand!"

Televised versions of commercial sports have become inseparable from the logos and products of corporate sponsors. It is not too far fetched to imagine this scene in the near future.

liquor and tobacco. This is why it was so important for NASCAR to be nationally televised—the liquor and tobacco companies wanted their brand names in front of a national audience for 250 to 600 laps during races.

PGA golfers in 2005 competed in the Mercedes-Benz Championships, BMW Championship, Merrill Lynch Shootout, Crown Plaza Invitational, Wachovia Championship, Chevron World Challenge, Shell Houston Open, LG Skins Game, Cialis Western Open, The Honda Classic, Bob Hope Chrysler Classic, Verizon Heritage, AT&T Pebble Beach National Pro-Am, Buick Invitational, and Sony Open, among many others. Men's pro tennis players competed in the Mercedes Cup, BMW Open, Pacific Life Open, Sony Ericsson Open, RCA Championships, and the Heineken Open, among others. Professional women's tennis is called the Sony Ericsson WTA Tour, and players competed in the Porsche Tennis Grand Prix, Pilot Pen Tennis, Bausch & Lomb

Championships, Family Circle Cup, Qatar Telecom German Open, Qatar Total Open, Medibank International, and Estoril Open.

Corporations also brand teams worldwide in cycling, soccer, rugby, and many other sports. Seven-time Tour de France winner Lance Armstrong and his cycling teammates rode for The Discovery Channel. Professional baseball teams in Japan are named after corporations, not cities. Players and even referees in most sports wear the corporate logos of sponsors on their uniforms. Because European soccer was televised for many years by public TV stations that had no commercials, corporations put their logos on the players themselves and around the walls of the playing fields so that spectators would see them constantly. This tradition continues. For example, in 2006, AIG (American International Group), a global investment and insurance company, paid nearly $120 million for a four-year deal that put "AIG" on the players' shirts for Manchester United, the world's most recognized sport team with over 50 million fans around the globe. The team also has sponsorship deals with Nike ($450 million for thirteen years, 2002–2015), Audi, Budweiser, Air Asia, and Tourism Malaysia, among others.

Corporate branders now give priority to sports that appeal to young males, a demographic category defined as "hard to reach." So there are the ESPN X Games, Dew Action Sport Tour, numerous events sponsored by Red Bull Energy Drink, Van's Triple Crown (surfing, skateboarding, snowboarding), McDonald's All-American High School Basketball Games, the Sprite Rising Stars Slam Dunk Contest, and the Nike Hoop Summit.

Sports agents today tell athletes that they can be brands in themselves and that their goal should be to merge with other commercial entities rather than simply endorse a company's products. Michael Jordan was the first to do this. He initially endorsed Nike products but gradually became a brand in his own right. Today he has his own line of products in addition to

"Air Jordan." Tony Hawk has done this with his own line of skateboards and other products. However, this strategy is possible only for athletes whose celebrity is great enough to be converted into a brand.

In all other cases, it is corporations who choose who and what they wish to brand. For example, some athletes as young as twelve years old may be known as Nike, Adidas, or Reebok athletes. Corporate executives now try to brand athletes as early as possible so that they can socialize the athletes to develop marketable personas that can be used to effectively promote corporate interests. This is why Nike signed Freddy Adu, currently a professional soccer player, to a $1 million endorsement contract when he was thirteen years old and gave seventeen-year-old high school senior LeBron James a $90-million contract before he was drafted by an NBA team.

The Super Bowl, far too expensive for any single corporation to brand on its own, is known as much for its ads as for the game itself. Corporate sponsors of the 2009 Super Bowl paid $3 million or more for thirty-second commercial spots during the telecast of the game—that's $100,000 per second! This generated about $160 million in revenues for NBC and General Electric. Corporate sponsors pay this rate because their ads receive exposure beyond the game itself—in terms of previews, summaries, highlights, evaluations, and rankings in other media coverage— and they will be available for years on the Internet where people can see every ad starting with the 1969 Super Bowl. Anheuser-Busch (Budweiser) spent over $25 million for commercials during the 2009 game, not including the money spent to produce the commercials. Corporations have branded the Super Bowl to such an extent that it has been described as a program where the commercials are the entertainment, and the entertainment is the commercials.

Future forms of corporate branding are difficult to predict because it's hard to say where people will draw the line and prevent corporations from colonizing their lives. Ads during television coverage are now inserted digitally on the field, court, and other surfaces of arenas and stadiums so that viewers cannot escape them even when they record events and delete commercials. Corporations spend more of their advertising money today to purchase brand-placement rights, so their names, logos, and products appear directly in the content of sports. This maximizes the branding of playing fields/spaces, uniforms, and athletes' bodies. For example, boxers have gone into the ring with henna tattoos of corporations on their backs. English soccer player Robbie Savage has an Armani logo tattooed on his arm. Action sport legend Shaun Palmer, arguably the best athlete in the world, has Cadillac tattoos. But what would happen if Cadillac used a photo of his body in one of their ads? Who owns Shaun Palmer's body and the images on its surface? Do the images belong to Palmer himself, to the artist who created the tattoos, or to Cadillac, who owns copyrights on all Cadillac images? Lawsuits in cases like this are becoming more common.

The Limits of Corporate Branding   Can corporations go too far in their branding of sports? People in New Jersey didn't resist when a local elementary school sold naming rights for its gym to ShopRite, a supermarket chain. Most high school and college sport programs have not resisted. Football fans didn't object when Burger King became the Official Fast-Food Sponsor of the NFL, and Olympic officials, who claim to be dedicated to health and fitness, accepted McDonald's as the Official Restaurant of the 2004, 2006, and 2008 Olympics However, people did object when CBS journalists wore Nike logos on their jackets as they covered the 1998 Winter Olympics in Nagano, Japan. Similarly, baseball fans were so upset in 2004 that Major League Baseball canceled a deal with Columbia Pictures that called for decorating bases, pitching mounds, and on-deck circles with spider-web patterns at fifteen home fields of teams playing games on the weekend before the release of *Spider Man 2*. But despite a few cases of resistance,

The goal of branding is to establish outposts in people's heads by connecting pleasure and excitement with corporations and their products. Golden Palace sponsored and branded this boxer because boxing fans often place bets, and the Golden Palace is an online casino that takes bets. (*Source*: Jeff Zelevansky, AP/Wide World Photos)

sports generally are for sale, and corporations are willing buyers when deals boost their power and profits and promote consumption as a lifestyle.

In less than a generation, sports have been so thoroughly branded that many people, especially those younger than thirty years old, see this situation as "normal"—as the way it is and should be. Does this mean that corporations have established ideological outposts in people's heads to the point that most people accept corporate power as inevitable and even desirable? If so, corporate hegemony is deeply entrenched, even if some people resist and argue that the control of sports should not rest in the hands of corporate entities accountable only to market forces. If so, commercial sports are a site where people with political and financial resources can package their values and ideas and present them in a form that most people see as normal.

COMMERCIALIZATION AND CHANGES IN SPORTS

What happens to sports as they shift from being activities organized for players to activities organized for paying spectators and sponsors? Do they change, and, if so, in what ways?

When a sport is converted into commercial entertainment, its success depends on spectator appeal. Although spectators watch sports for many reasons, their interest is tied to a combination of four factors:

- Attachment to those involved ("Do I know or like players and/or teams?")
- The uncertainty of an event's outcome ("Will it be a close contest?" and "Who might win?")
- The risk or financial rewards associated with participating in an event ("How much money, ego, or personal well-being is at stake in the contest?")
- The anticipated display of excellence, heroics, or dramatic expression by the athletes ("Are the players and/or teams skilled and entertaining?")

When spectators say they saw "a good game," they usually mean that it was one in which (1) they were attached personally or emotionally to people involved, (2) the outcome was in doubt until the last minutes or seconds, (3) the stakes were so high that players were totally committed to and engrossed in the action, or (4) there were skilled and dramatic performances. Events containing all four of these factors are remembered and discussed for many years.

Because attachment, uncertainty, high stakes, and performance attract spectators, successful commercial sports are organized to maximize the probability that all four factors will exist in an event. To understand how this affects sports, we will consider the impact of commercialization on the following three aspects of sports:

1. The internal structure and goals of sports
2. The orientations of athletes, coaches, and sponsors

3. The people and organizations that control sports

Internal Structure and Goals of Sports

Commercialization influences the internal structure and goals of newly developed sports, but it has less influence on long-established sports. New sports developed explicitly for commercial purposes are organized to maximize action that a target audience will find entertaining. This is not the only factor that influences the internal structure and goals of new sports, but it is the *primary* one. It is apparent in indoor soccer, indoor lacrosse, arena football, beach volleyball, roller hockey, and commercial action sports. Therefore, rules in the X Games are designed to maximize "big air," dangerous and spectacular moves, and the technical aspects of equipment, often manufactured by event sponsors.

The rules in more established sports also undergo changes to make the action more exciting and understandable for spectators, but the changes seldom alter the basic internal organization and goals of the sports. For example, rules in the NFL have been changed to protect quarterbacks, increase passing as an offensive strategy, discourage field goals, protect players from career-ending injuries, establish "television/commercial time-outs," and set game schedules to fit the interests of commercial sponsors.

Changes in commercialized spectator sports usually do one or more of these six things: (1) speed up the action, (2) increase scoring, (3) balance competition, (4) maximize drama, (5) heighten attachment to players and teams, and (6) provide "commercial time-outs." A review of rule changes in many sports shows the importance of these factors. For example, the designated hitter position in baseball's American League was added to increase scoring opportunities and heighten dramatic action. Soccer rules were changed to prevent matches from ending in ties. Tennis scoring was changed to meet the time requirements of television networks. Golf tournaments now involve total stroke counts rather than match play, so that big-name players aren't eliminated in an early round of a televised event. Free throws were minimized in basketball to speed up action. Sudden-death overtime periods and shootouts were added to National Hockey League games so that outcomes would be clearly understood by those spectators who define the meaning of sports exclusively in terms of who wins.

Although these changes are grounded in commercialization, they haven't altered the internal structure and goals of long-established sports: Teams remain the same size with similar positions, and outscoring opponents remains the primary goal. Some of these changes reflect the concerns of athletes, who have more fun when there is more action, more scoring, and a closer contest. Players may object to TV time-outs, but they and their coaches now use them in game strategies. This is new, but the structure and goal of the games hasn't changed.

Because sports are social constructions, they change as there are shifts in social conditions and power relations in society. This means that people who control sports are always influenced by social and cultural conditions at the time they make or revise rules. However, commercial issues remain the guiding focus. For example, commercial sport events are now organized as *total entertainment experiences*. There's loud music, rapidly changing video displays, light displays, cheerleaders and mascots that present entertaining performances, and announcers that heighten drama with excited and colorful descriptions of the action. This entertainment package represents a change, but it affects the context surrounding a game or match rather than the structure and goals of the sport itself.

Orientations of Athletes, Coaches, and Sponsors

Commercial sports occur within a promotional culture created to sell athletic performances to audiences and sell audiences to sponsors. These sports are promoted through marketing hype based on stories, myths, and images created around players, teams, and even stadiums or arenas. Athletes become entertainers, and the orientations of nearly everyone in sports shift toward an emphasis on heroics and away from aesthetics. As illustrated in Figure 11.1, this shift is made to attract a mass audience to buy tickets and watch televised events. Because many people in a *mass* audience lack technical knowledge about the sport they watch, they are entertained mostly by intense action, danger, the dramatic expressions of athletes and coaches, and manifestations of commitment to victory. These things are easily understood by spectators who don't know enough about the sport to be captivated by precise physical skills and subtle strategies.

When spectators lack technical knowledge about football, for example, they are entertained more by a running back's end-zone dance after a touchdown than by the lineman's block that enabled the running back to score the touchdown. Those who know little about the technical aspects of ice skating are entertained more by triple and quadruple jumps than routines that are carefully choreographed and flawlessly executed. Without dangerous jumps, naïve spectators become bored because they don't recognize subtle differences in the skills and routines of skaters. Those who lack technical knowledge about basketball are more impressed by slam dunks than a well-coordinated defensive strategy that wins a game.

Players realize what a mass audience wants and often "play to the crowd" with heroic displays and exciting or controversial personas. They may even refer to games as "showtime." In commercial terms, a player's style and persona often are as valuable as technical skills. This is why announcers and journalists focus on athletes who can make the big plays and are willing to talk in dramatic terms about their performances.

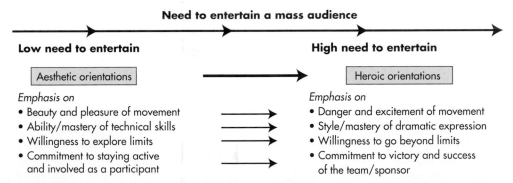

Note: The orientations associated with commercial spectator sports involve a shift from aesthetics to heroics. Spectators need technical knowledge about a sport to be entertained by aesthetic action; when spectators lack this knowledge, they seek and focus on heroic action. Therefore, athletes and others associated with the game emphasize heroic orientations in their performances. "Heroic," as used in this chapter and figure, refers to those who engage in deviant overconformity or "play to the crowd" with entertaining forms of dramatic expression. The extreme version of this practice occurs in professional wrestling where stereotypical heroes and villains engage in heroic, dramatic, spectacular, dangerous, and convincing performances in the ring. Concerns about beauty, mastery, reasoned engagement in an activity, and a commitment to well-being are not the stuff of mass entertainment sports.

FIGURE 11.1 Shifting orientations: what happens when there is a need to entertain a mass audience.

A mass audience is thrilled by long touchdown passes, home runs, and athletes who collapse as they surpass physical limits.

Overall, commercialization involves a shift in orientations so that the danger of movement becomes important *in addition to* the beauty of movement; style and dramatic expression become important *in addition to* skills; pushing beyond personal limits becomes important *in addition to* exploring limits; and commitment to victory for the team and sponsor becomes important *in addition to* commitment to participation. Aesthetic orientations don't disappear in commercial sports, but they are combined with heroic orientations to produce changes in what constitutes a memorable sport event.

Because there are dangers associated with heroic orientations, some athletes try to regulate heroic actions in their sports. This has occurred in figure skating as some athletes favor restrictions on the number of triple jumps required in skating programs. They worry that the quest for commercial success jeopardizes their bodies. Other skaters, however, adopt heroic orientations to please audiences and conform to shifts in the orientations of judges, coaches, and other skaters (Mihoces, 2005). As a result, they train to successfully land a succession of triple jumps along with quad jumps without breaking bones or destroying the continuity of their skating programs. Aesthetic orientations still exist, but heroic orientations have been woven into popular definitions of "quality" in skating performances.

As heroic orientations become more important, so do concerns about representing sponsors. This occurred in NASCAR racing when it signed a $3.2 billion, eight-year television deal with four major television companies. Veteran driver Kyle Petty notes that being a good racecar driver and being a good product representative are two different things and that racing teams today walk a fine line "between performance and promotion" (in Jenkins, 2002, p. 2A). This doesn't mean that performance is unimportant,

but it does mean that the "ability" of drivers is increasingly judged in terms of the sponsors' interests off the track. If a driver does not win races but boosts a sponsor's sales, the driver's team and car will stay on the track. If a driver consistently finishes well in races but doesn't boost the sponsor's bottom line, the driver's career may be short. According to one observer, this means that there are racers today "who can't drive a nail" but they continue to race "because they're good spokespeople for corporations" (Zengerle, 2002).

Winning, however, remains important because brand and logo visibility increase as camera coverage focuses on the leading cars during races. Winning drivers show off their logo-laden racing suits as they pop corks on champagne bottles in the winner's circle after the race. Winning drivers are interviewed and promote their sponsors as millions of people listen to what they say. At the same time, NASCAR fans have observed that announcers favor younger drivers in the television coverage of races. Darrell Waltrip, a former driver and now a television race analyst, says that older drivers often are better and faster on the track, but they want more money to race, and they don't receive attention from the younger male demographic segment of the audience that the sponsors want to attract (in Jenkins, 2002, p. 2A). Furthermore, sponsors often prefer a new face that hasn't endorsed other products in the past, so they look for young drivers with exciting personas and then train them to represent their products without sounding like walking paid commercials, even though that's what they are.

What happens to a sport when heroic orientations are pushed to extremes? Are spectators willing to have aesthetic orientations abandoned in favor of the heroic? What would events be like if this happened? One way to answer this question is to study professional wrestling—a sport turned into heroic spectacle in a quest to be entertaining. This topic is discussed in the box "Extreme Heroic Action."

Extreme Heroic Action:
Professional Wrestling as "Sportainment"

Professional wrestling is commercialization pushed to an extreme. It isolates elements of commercial sports and dramatizes them through parody and caricature (Atkinson, 2002; B. Maguire, 2005; Rinehart, 1998; Sammond, 2005; Schiesel, 2007a; Smith, 2008). In the process, it abandons aesthetic orientations and highlights the heroic.

From the late 1990s through 2001, professional wrestling captured widespread spectator interest and was a smashing commercial success. It bodyslammed its way into popular culture worldwide (Leland, 2000; McShane, 1999). Its featured events sold out stadiums nearly every night in North American cities. *Raw Is War* and *Smackdown!* were top-ranked programs on ad-supported cable television. Pay-per-view events often subscribed over half a million viewers at $30 per month and up to $50 for special events. Matches were televised in nine languages in 120 countries, wrestling videos were the best-selling "sports videos" in the world, and wrestling action figures outsold all other characters in popular culture.

Through 2001, pro wrestling was a mainstay on major cable channels with events televised four nights a week. The popular *Monday Night Nitro* cut into the audience for Monday Night Football and the finals of the NCAA men's basketball tournament. Most wrestling programs had viewer ratings consistently higher than NBA games and always higher than NHL games.

The popularity of professional wrestling was grounded in the heroic actions of performers combined with storylines and personas that engaged spectators' concerns with issues related to social class, gender, ethnicity, job security, and national identity. In most cases, storylines and personas were performed by hypermasculine, heterosexual, and homophobic strong men who were arbitrarily victimized or privileged by greedy, underhanded corporate bosses or random, unpredictable events. The men were either supported or undermined by women, represented as alluring and vulnerable sex objects or exotic and heavily muscled

sadomasochists. Overall, events were staged to represent male fantasies and fears about sex and power, and their concerns about work in a world where men felt they were losing control (B. Maguire, 2005).

During 2002 and 2003, pro wrestling lost some of its popularity, but Linda and Vince McMahon, the daughter–father executive team that runs World Wrestling Entertainment (WWE), staged a comeback in 2004 and 2005, especially among males between twelve and twenty-eight years old, who make up two-thirds of the pro wrestling audience. It also attracted fans worldwide, with The Wrestling Channel in Europe televising seventeen hours of wrestling programs every day, and with people in Mexico and the rest of Central America eager to watch Latino wrestlers.

The WWE faced a public relations and financial crisis in 2007 when Chris Benoit, a high-profile wrestler, killed his wife and son and then hanged himself. Benoit was a known steroid user and the WWE was accused of ignoring drug issues among wrestlers. But the McMahons executed successful damage control and wrestling regained popularity to the point that in April 2008, each of the presidential frontrunners for the 2008 election (Hillary Clinton, Barack Obama, and John McCain) felt compelled to appear on *Monday Night Raw* (a.k.a. *Raw Is War*) to promote themselves (Schneiderman, 2008). They even portrayed themselves through personas similar to the ones that wrestlers use and talked tough to wrestling fan/voters.

Sociologist Brendan Maguire uses structural theory to hypothesize that pro wrestling is popular because it "addresses the anxiety and angst associated with community breakdown, social disenchantment, and political correctness" (2005, p. 174). He explains that when community ties are strong and social satisfaction is high and social control is not overly constraining, people have little anxiety and little need to be entertained by dramatic parodies of heroic wrestling action. Cultural theories, on the other hand, lead to other hypotheses based on past evidence that the popularity

Professional wrestling emphasizes heroic orientations and storylines that constitute soap operas for men. These action figures of WWE (formerly WWF) president Vince McMahon and wrestlers Ken Shamrock and the Undertaker were popular toys/dolls for young boys who were wrestling fans in 1999. In 2010 these boys will be college age. Do they still watch the WWE and have their reasons for doing so changed? (*Source:* Jay Coakley)

of any cultural practice, including professional wrestling, depends on the extent to which it reaffirms the ideologies that people use to make sense of their lives and the world around them. Therefore, the goal of those who produce sport entertainment is to provide people with pleasure and excitement without fostering opposition to the power structure that sustains commercial entertainment. In this way, professional wrestling and commercial sports generally tend to reproduce the status quo and existing forms of power relations by presenting actions, storylines, and characters that constitute soap operas for men of all ages and for the women who identify with the orientations and perspectives of men (Schiesel, 2007a).

What do you think?

The People and Organizations That Control Sports

Commercialization changes the location of control in and over sports. When sports depend on the revenues they generate, control in sport organizations shifts away from the athletes and toward those with the resources to produce and promote sports. Athletes in heavily commercialized sports generally lose effective control over the conditions of their own sport participation. These conditions are controlled by a combination of general managers, team owners, corporate sponsors, advertisers, media personnel, marketing and publicity staff, professional management staff, accountants, and agents.

The organizations that control commercial sports are designed to maximize profits. Decision making promotes economic interests and deals with athletes as commodities to be managed. Therefore, athletes in commercial sports usually are cut out of decision-making processes, even when the decisions affect their health and the rewards they receive for playing. This leads them to develop strategies to represent their interests relative to the interests of team owners, agents, advertising executives, media people, and corporate sponsors. For example, athletes in ESPN's X Games constantly struggle to maintain the spirit and norms of their sport cultures as they participate under conditions controlled by ESPN and corporate sponsors.

Like many athletes before them, the athletes in action sports find it difficult to oppose the power of the media and corporate sponsors. If they want the rewards offered in commercial sports, they answer first to the sponsors. This isn't new; sponsors traditionally define the conditions of sport participation (Rinehart and Grenfell, 2002). But some people view the power shifts that come with commercialization in critical terms, assessing carefully the pros and cons of a commercial model in which corporations set the terms and conditions of playing sports. Commercialization may not significantly change the structure and goals of some sports, but it does come with major changes in the organizational contexts in which sports are played.

THE ORGANIZATION OF PROFESSIONAL SPORTS IN NORTH AMERICA

Professional sports in North America are privately owned by individuals, partnerships, or corporations. The wealth and power of owners is greatest at the top levels of professional sports and less so in minor leagues and sports with relatively small audiences. Similarly, sponsors and event promoters range from individuals to large transnational corporations, depending on the size of the events.

The Owners of Sport Teams

Most of the individuals who own minor-league teams in North America don't make much money. Many are happy to break even and avoid the losses that are commonplace at this level of sports ownership. Also, many teams, leagues, and events have been financial disasters over the past forty years. Four football leagues, a hockey league, a few soccer leagues, a volleyball league, four men's and five women's basketball leagues, a team tennis league, and a number of basketball and soccer teams have gone out of business, leaving many owners, sponsors, and promoters in debt. This list covers only the United States and doesn't include all those who have lost money on tournaments and special events.

The owners of major men's professional sport franchises in North America are very different from owners at other levels of commercial sports. Teams or franchises in the NFL, NBA, NHL, and MLB in 2008 were valued from about $100 million (Carolina Hurricanes in the NHL) to about $1.5 billion (Dallas Cowboys and Washington Redskins [sic] in the NFL, and the New York Yankees in MLB). Therefore, the owners of teams in these leagues are large corporations and one or more very wealthy individuals with assets ranging from hundreds of millions to many billions of dollars. Each of these four major men's leagues is organized as a monopoly, most teams in these leagues play in publicly subsidized facilities, owners make good to excellent returns on their investments, and support from media companies and corporate sponsors almost guarantees continued financial success at this level of ownership.

> **ON THE *OLC*:**
>
> See the OLC—Additional Readings for Chapter 11—for information on how a monopoly enables owners to increase their wealth.

Similarly, the large corporations that sponsor particular events, from major golf and tennis tournaments to NASCAR and Grand Prix races, know the costs and benefits involved. Their association with top events provides them with advertising platforms and connects them with clearly identified categories of consumers. Media companies also sponsor events so they can control their own programming, as in the case of ESPN's X Games.

Major sport sponsorships enable companies that sell tobacco, alcohol, and foods with questionable nutritional value to link their products and logos to popular activities. Executives at these companies know that people associate sports with strong, healthy bodies instead of cancer, heart disease, diabetes, obesity, tooth decay, and other forms of poor health associated with their products. Their hope is to use sports to increase their legitimacy as "corporate citizens" and defuse resistance to their policies, practices, and products.

Investments in sports and sport events are motivated by many factors. In some cases, investors are wealthy fans looking to satisfy lifelong fantasies, build their egos, or socialize with

> **Being able to share the [team] ownership experience with clients is . . . a huge competitive advantage in business.** —Raul Fernandez, 10 percent owner, Washington Capitals (in Heath, 2003)

celebrity athletes. Buying a team or sponsoring major events gives them more enjoyment and prestige than other business ventures, often making them instant celebrities in their cities. A multimillionaire part-owner of the NFL's Atlanta Falcons between 1994 and 2004 described his experience by saying that over those 10 years, he made a 500 percent return on his investment "and had a heck of a good time." Another multimillionaire explains that his investment was worthwhile because "owning a sports team is a label that differentiates one millionaire from another" (quotes in Heath, 2003, p. A1).

Those who invest in sports enjoy their status, but they don't allow fun and fantasy to interfere with business and the growth of their capital. They don't enjoy losing money or sharing power. They may look at their athletes as heroes, but they want to control them and maximize their investment returns. They may be civic boosters and supporters of public projects, but they define the "public good" in terms that emphasize capitalist expansion and their own business interests, usually to the exclusion of other definitions (Ingham and McDonald, 2003; Schimmel, Ingham, and Howell, 1993). They may not agree with fellow owners and sponsors on all issues, but they do agree that their investments must be protected and their profits maximized.

Team Owners and Sport Leagues as Cartels

The tendency to think alike has been especially strong among the owners of teams in the major North American sport leagues. Unity among owners has led to the formation of effective cartels. A **cartel** is *a centralized organizing group that coordinates the actions of a collection of people or businesses.* Therefore, even though each sport franchise in each league is usually a separate business, the team owners in each sport come together to form a cartel representing their collective interests (Downward and Dawson, 2000). The cartel is used to control inter-team competition for players, fans, media revenues, and sales of licensed merchandise. Additionally, it's used to eliminate competition from others who might form teams and leagues in the same sports. When a cartel succeeds, as it has in each of the major men's professional team sports, it becomes a **monopoly**—*the* one and only *provider of a particular product or service.*

Each league—the NBA, NFL, NHL, and MLB—is also a **monopsony,** or a single buyer of a product or service—in this case, athletic labor in a particular sport. This means that if a college football player wants to play professional football in the United States, he has one choice: the NFL. And the NFL, like other monopsony leagues, has developed a system to force new players to negotiate contracts only with the team that drafts them. This enables owners to sign new players to contracts without bidding against other teams, which might be willing to pay particular players more money.

"Winning is easy when you form a cartel and prevent others from playing."

The growth and profitability of commercial sports worldwide have little to do with athletes. Owners, sponsors, and media executives control sports today, and they make money when governments allow them to operate as cartels and keep competitors out of the game.

As a cartel, the owners prevent new leagues from being established and competing with them for players, and they also prevent new teams from entering their league without their permission. When permission is given, it involves conditions set by the cartel. For example, the new team owner is charged an entry fee to become a part of the league and must give back to the cartel some of the team's profits for a certain number of years. Since the 1960s when these fees were first assessed, they have escalated dramatically. For example, the Dallas Cowboys paid $600,000 to join the NFL in 1960, and the Houston Texans paid $700 million in 2002, and in each case, the entry payment was divided among the owners of existing NFL teams. These are just *entry* fees—they don't include other start-up expenses, player salaries, or operating costs; nor do they include "infringement payments" made to the owners of other NFL teams in the same TV markets or the mandatory forfeiture of TV revenues during the first year(s) of operation. Furthermore, a new owner can locate only in a city approved by the cartel, and no current owner can move a team to another city without cartel approval.

Acting as a cartel, the owners in each sport league collectively sell national broadcasting rights to their games and then share the revenues from national media contracts. This maintains the cartel's control over the conditions under which fans can view televised games. This is why games are not televised in the home team's region when they're not sold out, and why cable and satellite fees are so high when fans wish to purchase access to more than the primary games telecast by the major networks. Such a strategy enables team owners to make huge sums of money in their media contracts while forcing people to buy tickets to games and pay high monthly cable or satellite service bills. The U.S. Congress has approved this monopolistic method of doing business, and thereby guarantees relatively predictable revenues for team owners and gives them control over the media coverage of their games. This is why announcers sound like cheerleaders for the sports that their media companies pay to broadcast, and also why people rarely, if ever, hear or read critical analyses of sports in society. Furthermore, team owners are allowed to negotiate exclusive-use clauses in their contracts with the stadiums or arenas that they use, and this prevents new leagues and teams from using the venues they need to exist. When team owner cartels are allowed to operate this way, they can eliminate business competition, raise ticket prices, and guarantee the financial appreciation of their team's value.

Being part of a legal cartel enables most team owners to make impressive sums of money. During the mid-1960s, NFL teams were bought and sold for about $10 million; in 2008 the average franchise value was $957 million. That's an average per-team capital gain of $947 million, which amounts to an average annual return of $24 million on an original investment of $10 million. This is what a cartel does: it limits the supply of teams and drives up the value of existing teams. Of course, team owners do not include capital gains when they announce that their annual profits are low and they must raise ticket prices and have a new stadium so that they can be "competitive" with other teams. When you are part of a cartel, you can get away with this type of deception and blackmail without going to jail.

Even though the NBA, NFL, NHL, and MLB are grouped together in this section, these leagues differ in many important ways. The differences are complicated, and they change from year to year as each league encounters new economic challenges and opportunities. For example, contracts with networks and major cable television companies vary by league. The NHL is the least successful in negotiating contracts, whereas the NFL clearly has been the most successful in recent years.

Each league also has unique internal agreements regulating how teams can negotiate the sale of local broadcasting rights to their games. The NFL does not allow teams to sign independent television or radio contracts for local broadcasts of their games, but MLB does. This creates significant disparities in the incomes of baseball teams, because the New York Yankees can negotiate a local media rights deal that may be a hundred times higher than what the Kansas City Royals can negotiate, because its media market is so large.

The biggest differences between the major men's sport leagues are related to their contractual agreements with the players' association in each league. Although each league gives players as few rights and as little money as possible, athletes have struggled over the last five decades to gain control over their careers, regulate the conditions of their sport participation, and increase their salaries. This topic is discussed in the section titled "Legal Status and Incomes of Athletes in Commercial Sports."

Team Owners and Public Assistance

The belief that cities cannot have "major league status" unless they have professional sports teams and sports megaevents has enabled sports team owners and promoters to receive public money (Delaney and Eckstein, 2003; deMause and Cagan, 2008; Silk, 2004). Most common is the use of public funds to build arenas and stadiums. As noted in Chapter 10 (pp. 326–327), this "stadium socialism" enables wealthy and powerful capitalists to use public money for personal gain, but when the media discuss this transfer of funds, it is usually described as "economic development" rather than "welfare for the rich."

Team owners and their supporters justify stadium subsidies and other forms of public assistance with a five-point argument (Lavoie, 2000):

1. A stadium and pro team creates jobs; those who hold the jobs spend money and pay taxes in the city so that everyone benefits.
2. Stadium construction infuses money into the local economy; this money is spent over and over as it circulates, generating tax revenues in the process.

3. The team attracts businesses to the city, and this increases local revenues.
4. The team attracts regional and national media attention, which boosts tourism and contributes to overall economic development.
5. The team creates positive psychic and social benefits, boosting social unity and feelings of pride and well-being in the local population.

These arguments often are supported by the economic impact studies commissioned by team owners. However, impact studies done by *independent* researchers generally reach the following conclusions:[1]

1. Teams and stadiums create jobs, but apart from highly paid athletes and team executives, these jobs are low paid, part-time, and seasonal. Football stadiums, for example, are used less than twenty days per year for team games, and the ushers, parking lot attendants, ticket agents, and concessions workers don't make full-time living wages. Additionally, many athletes on the team don't live in the city or spend their money there.
2. The companies that design and build stadiums are seldom local, and construction materials and workers on major projects often come from outside the region. Therefore, much of the money spent on a stadium or arena does not circulate multiple times in the host city.
3. Stadiums attract other businesses, but most are restaurant and entertainment franchises headquartered in other cities. These franchises often have enough cash to undercut and drive out locally owned businesses.

Some out-of-town people come to the city to attend games, but most people who buy tickets live close enough to make day trips to games, and their purchases inside the stadium don't benefit businesses outside the stadium gates.

4. Stadiums and teams generate public relations for the city, but this has mixed results for tourism because some people stay away from cities on game days. Most important, *regional* economic development often is limited by a new facility because fans who spend money in and around the stadium have fewer dollars to spend in their neighborhoods. A stadium often helps nearby businesses, but it often hurts outlying businesses (Hudson, 2001). For example, when a family of four spends $10,742 for average NBA season tickets, and another $3000 for meals and parking for 41 home games, it will spend less money on dinners and entertainment close to home—if they have any money left!
5. A pro sport team can make some people feel good and may enhance general perceptions of a city, but this is difficult to measure. Additionally, the feelings of fans often vary with the success of a team, and the feelings of those who are not fans may not be improved by a men's sport team that reaffirms traditional masculinity and values related to domination and conquest (Adams, 2006; Wilson, 2006).

Independent researchers explain that positive effects are bound to occur when a city spends $500 million to a billion dollars of public money on a project. However, they also point out that the public good might be better served if tax money were spent on things other than a stadium. For example, during the mid-1990s, the city of Cleveland spent nearly a billion dollars of public money to build three sport facilities and related infrastructure. Inner-city residents during the same years pleaded with the city to install a drinking fountain in a park in a working-class neighborhood, and teachers held classes in renovated

---

[1]Studies of this issue are numerous; see Bandow (2003); Bast (1998); Brown et al., (2004); Chapin (2002); Curry, Schwirian, and Woldoff (2004), Delaney and Eckstein (2003); deMause and Cagan (2008); Eckstein and Delaney (2002); Friedman et al. (2004); Hudson (2001); Noll and Zimbalist (1997); Rosentraub (1997); Silk (2004); Smith and Ingham (2003); Spirou and Bennett (2003); Troutman (2004); and Weiner (2000).

New Soldier Field, home of the Chicago Bears, was remodeled in 2002 with private funds and $432 million of public money—a large government subsidy for a private, family-owned business. Used only 10 times a year by the Bears, it is maintained and managed year-round by the city of Chicago. This arrangement made the McCaskey family and other team owners happy because it helped to increase the franchise value of the Chicago Bears from $362 million prior to opening of the new stadium to $1.06 billion six years later. Chicago residents built the stadium and pay maintenance bills, and the team owners enjoy a $702-million increase in team value. (*Source:* Mike Smith of Aerial Views Publishing, October 5, 2003)

shower rooms in local public schools because there was no money to fund new educational facilities for inner-city students. At the same time, the owners of the three sport teams received a fifty-year exemption on taxes related to their teams and facilities, and $120 million in tax abatements on other real estate development in the area around the stadiums (Bartimole, 1999). This means that the city annually forfeited about $50 million in city and county tax revenues. In the meantime, the franchise values for the NFL, NBA, and MLB teams in Cleveland have increased dramatically, giving multimillion-dollar capital gains to each of the wealthy owners.

Sociologists Kevin Delaney and Rick Eckstein (2003) studied the Cleveland case along with eight other cities where public money was used to build stadiums for private use. They concluded that the results in Cleveland were better than in the other cities. However, they found no evidence that the three stadiums fostered a downtown rejuvenation, as stadium proponents had predicted. Neither the number of businesses nor job creation rates increased, and in the three years following the construction, the cost for each new job created was $231,000, nearly 20 times higher than it costs to develop jobs with public programs. The new sport facilities failed to lower poverty rates, improve schools, or increase the availability of safe, low-cost housing (deMause and Cagan, 2008), but they did force poor people to move to other areas of town to make room for development.

> **ON THE *OLC*:**
> See the OLC—Additional Readings for Chapter 11—Strategies to Obtain Public Money.

The people who object to stadium subsidies seldom have resources to oppose the well-financed, professionally packaged proposals developed by the consultants hired by team owners. The social activists who might lead the opposition already deal full time with problems related to unemployment, underfunded schools, homelessness, poor health, drug use, and the lack of needed social services in cities. They cannot abandon these tasks to lobby against using public money to benefit billionaire team owners and millionaire celebrity athletes. At the same time, local people are persuaded to think that team owners will abandon their city if they don't pony up public money to build a new facility with the requisite number of luxury suites and club seats.

When thinking about public subsidies to sport teams, it's helpful to consider alternative uses of public funds. For example, my former hometown of Colorado Springs used $6 million of public money in 2000 to construct a youth sport complex consisting of twelve baseball, softball, and T-ball fields of various sizes with bleacher seating; ten soccer/football fields; six volleyball courts; an in-line skating rink; a batting cage (for baseball hitting practice); and multiple basketball courts. Meanwhile, $300 million of tax money from six Denver metro counties was used to build a new stadium for Pat Bowlen, the very wealthy Canadian owner of the Denver Broncos. Instead of doing this, the counties could have used the $300 million to build 600 baseball, softball, and T-ball fields; 500 soccer/football fields; 300 volleyball courts; 50 in-line skating rinks; 50 batting cages; and 250 basketball courts around the metro area.

Which of these two alternatives would best improve the overall quality of life in the metro area? The local facilities would be open seven days a week to everyone in the community for nominal fees; the new stadium hosts 72,000 people who pay an average of $85 per ticket nine times a year, and many local people will watch the games on TV. Some people prefer the former alternative, some the latter. But those preferring the latter usually have the power and resources to obtain what they want, and they want new stadiums more than recreational facilities that most people could use year-round. This is hegemony in action.

Sources of Income for Team Owners

The owners of top pro teams in the major men's sports make money from (1) gate receipts, (2) media revenues, (3) stadium revenue, (4) licensing fees, and (5) merchandise sales. The amounts and proportions of each of these revenue sources vary from league to league.

The recent and continuing wave of new stadiums is the result of owners who demand venues that can generate new revenue streams. This is why these stadiums resemble shopping malls built around

> **I feel for the schools. I feel for welfare. But look at the positive effects of pro football on a community, the emotional investment of people at large. You can't equate that with fixing up the schools.** —Art Modell, owner, Baltimore Ravens (in Brady, 1996, p. 19C)

playing fields. Sociologist George Ritzer (2005) describes them as "cathedrals of consumption" designed so that consumption is seamlessly included in spectator experiences. Owners see this as important because it enables them to capture a greater share of the entertainment dollar in a highly competitive urban market. According to a report in *Forbes* magazine, team owners use the following formula:

> Build new facilities with fewer seats and more luxury boxes, charge higher prices, earn more revenue, hire better players and reap more wins. Then turn around and raise ticket prices (Van Riper, 2008)

The rest of the formula is to build the stadium mostly with public money so if things go wrong, the owners can split the losses with local taxpayers (Van Riper, 2008).

When a new stadium is built, the value of the team that plays there increases about 25 percent. This means that if a city builds a $700 million stadium for an NFL team that is valued at $900 million, the franchise value will increase about $225 million to $1.125 billion. This increase goes directly to the owner as part of the assets of the franchise. To prevent people from realizing how public money is used to subsidize their wealth, the owners make sure that announcers describe their team as "your" New York Giants, Cleveland Cavaliers, Detroit Red Wings, or Colorado Rockies. The owners are happy to support the illusion that their teams belong to the community, as long as they collect the revenues and capital gains while taxpayers take the risks and receive little benefit.

THE ORGANIZATION OF AMATEUR SPORTS IN NORTH AMERICA

Amateur sports don't have owners, but they do have commercial sponsors and governing bodies that control events and athletes. Generally, the sponsors are corporations interested in using

Recently built stadiums resemble shopping malls, and some fans see attendance as a shopping opportunity. They're a captive audience, and team owners want to capture as many of their entertainment dollars as possible. This fan has taken the consumption bait and is less interested in the game than buying products to prove he was there.

amateur sports for publicity and advertising purposes. The governing bodies of amateur sports operate on a nonprofit basis, although they use revenues from events to maintain their organizations and exert control over amateur sports.

Centralized sport authorities administer amateur sports in most countries. They work with the national governing bodies (NGBs) of individual sports, and together they control events, athletes, and revenues. Sport Canada and the Canadian Olympic Association are examples of such centralized authorities; they develop the policies that govern the various national sport organizations in Canada.

In the United States, the organization and control of amateur sports is much less centralized. Policies, rules, fund-raising strategies, and methods of operating all vary from one organization to the next. For example, the major governing body in intercollegiate sports is the National Collegiate Athletic Association (NCAA). For amateur sports not connected with universities, the major controlling organization is the United States Olympic Committee (USOC). However, within the USOC, each of more than fifty separate NGBs regulates and controls a particular amateur sport. NGBs raise most of their own funds through corporate and individual sponsors, and each one sets its own policies to supplement the rules and policies of the USOC and IOC. The USOC has long tried to establish continuity in American amateur sports, but the NGBs and other organizations are very protective of their own turf, and they seldom give up power; instead, they fight to maintain exclusive control over rules, revenues, and athletes. This has caused many political battles in and among organizations.

All amateur sport organizations share an interest in two things: (1) controlling the athletes in their sports and (2) controlling the money generated from sponsorships and competitive events. Sponsorship patterns in amateur sports take many forms. Universities, for example, "sell" their athletic departments, allowing corporations to brand their athletic teams and the bodies of athletes in exchange for money, scholarships, equipment, and apparel. Corporations and universities usually enter these agreements outside of any democratic processes involving votes by students, athletes, or the citizens whose taxes fund the universities.

The NGBs of U.S. amateur sports now depend on corporate sponsorships to pay for athlete training, operating expenses, and competitive events. Corporate logos appear on the clothing and equipment of amateur athletes. In some cases, athletes sign deals as individuals, but they cannot do so when the deals conflict with the interests of NGB sponsors. When this model of corporate sponsorship is used, the economics of sports are linked to the fluctuations of market economies and the profits of large corporations. Corporations sponsor only sports that foster their interests, and economic conditions influence their ability and willingness to maintain sponsorships. For example, when the Women's United Soccer Association (WUSA) and its 180 professional athletes needed $20 million in 2003 to survive another year, Nike signed a $90-million endorsement deal with seventeen-year-old LeBron James and a $21-million deal with nineteen-year-old Carmelo Anthony, both basketball players who had not yet played in an NBA game. Nike decided that this was a better business investment than supporting women's professional soccer for five years. Or Nike could have reduced the $450-million deal they made with Manchester United, a men's soccer team in England, so it could support WUSA. But corporations are about profits, and women's soccer didn't fit into their business plans.

Corporate sponsorships also vary with changing economic conditions. For example, as rap artists became more popular than athletes with many young consumers, shoe companies have reduced sponsorships of high school teams, summer leagues and camps, athletic events, and individual athletes in favor of sponsoring rap concerts and contests, rap groups in schools, and high-profile rap artists (McCarthy, 2005). Therefore, instead of signing a female athlete in 2005, Adidas signed rapper Missy Elliott to endorse "Respect Me" sneakers, bags, and jackets. And Reebok paid 50 Cent to endorse his GXT II cross-training shoe instead of signing an athlete to endorse the shoe. Similarly, NASCAR faces possible collapse if automakers decide that supplying racing teams with hundreds of expensive, gas-guzzling cars is not creating the marketing buzz they want (Jenkins, 2005). But such are the risks of depending on corporations.

LEGAL STATUS AND INCOMES OF ATHLETES IN COMMERCIAL SPORTS

When sports are commercialized, athletes are entertainers. This is obvious at the professional level, but it's also true in other commercial sports such as big-time college football and basketball.

Professional athletes are paid for their efforts, whereas amateur athletes receive rewards within limits set by the organizations that govern their lives. This raises these two questions:

1. What is the legal status of the athlete-entertainers who work in "amateur" sports?
2. How are athlete-entertainers rewarded for their work?

Many people don't think of athletes as workers, and they overlook owner–player relations in professional sports as a form of labor relations. Most people associate sports with play, and they see athletes as having fun rather than working. However, when sports are businesses, players are workers, even though they may have fun on the job. This isn't unique; many workers enjoy their jobs. But regardless of enjoyment, issues of legal status and fair rewards for work are important.

This section focuses on the United States and does not consider sports that collect gate receipts but never make enough money to pay for anything but basic expenses, if that. Therefore, we don't discuss high school sports, nonrevenue-producing college sports, or other nonprofit local sports in which teams sell tickets to events.

Professional Athletes

The legal status of athletes always has been the most controversial issue in professional team sports.

Legal Status: Team Sports Until the mid-1970s, professional athletes in the major sport leagues had little or no legal power to control their careers. They could play only for the team that drafted and owned them. They could not control when and to whom they might be traded during their careers, even when their contracts expired. Furthermore, they were obliged to sign standard contracts saying that they agreed to forfeit to their owners all rights over their careers. Basically, they were bought and sold like property and seldom consulted about their wishes. They

were at the mercy of team owners, managers, and coaches. In all sports, this form of employee restriction was called the **reserve** system because it was *a set of practices that enabled team owners to* reserve *the labor of athletes for themselves and control the movement of athletes from team to team.*

As long as the reserve system was legal, owners could maintain low salaries and near-total control over the conditions under which athletes played their sports. Parts of the reserve system continue to exist in professional sports, but players' associations in each of the major professional leagues for men have challenged the system in court and forced significant changes that increased their rights as workers.

In any other business, a reserve system of the type that has been used in sports would violate antitrust laws. Companies cannot control employee movement from firm to firm, and they certainly cannot draft employees so that no other company can hire them, nor can they trade them to another company at will. But this type of reserve system, with modifications since the 1970s, has been defined as legal in sports, and owners have used it with minimal interference from any government agency.

Team owners justify the reserve system by saying that it's needed to maintain competitive balance between teams in their leagues. They argue that, if athletes could play with any team, the wealthiest owners in the biggest cities and TV markets would buy all the good athletes and prevent teams in smaller cities and TV markets from being winners. The irony of this argument is that team owners are free-market capitalists who argue that free-market processes would destroy the business of sports! They embrace regulation and "sport socialism" because it protects their power and wealth; they form cartels to restrict athletes' rights and salaries, *but* they advocate deregulation in the economy as a whole. Their positions are ideologically inconsistent, but profitable for them.

Professional athletes always have objected to the reserve system, but it wasn't until 1976 that court rulings gave professional athletes the right to become *free agents* under certain conditions. The meaning of free agency varies, but in all leagues it allows some players whose contracts have expired to seek contracts with other teams that bid for their services. This change has had a dramatic effect on the salaries of top professional athletes from the late 1970s to the present. Table 11.1 lists average salaries in major sport leagues from 1950 to 2008, and the data show the dramatic changes that have occurred after the mid-1970s. Players' salaries increased slowly from after World War II through the mid-1970s. During those years, pro athletes made from two to four times the median family income in the United States. After free agency was allowed in the 1970s, salaries began to skyrocket. With rising revenues from gate receipts and media rights, salaries increased rapidly as teams competed for players and negotiated new Collective Bargaining Agreements (CBAs) with players' unions. In 2007 the ratio of average salaries relative to median family income was 75:1 for the NBA;

54:1 for MLB; 28:1 for the NHL; 26:1 for the NFL; 2:1 for the MLS, and 1:1 for the WNBA.

Between 1976 and about 1991, team owners in the NFL and the NHL tried to avoid the consequences of free agency by negotiating restrictions in the Collective Bargaining Agreements made with players' unions. But players' unions have consistently mounted challenges to lift restrictions; therefore, owner–athlete relations change every time a new case is resolved or a new CBA is negotiated and signed. Although team owners, league officials, and some fans dislike the players' unions, these organizations have enabled players to gain more control over their salaries and working conditions. Labor negotiations and players' strikes in professional team sports have focused primarily on issues of freedom and control over careers, rather than money, although money has certain been an issue. As a result, free agency now exists for all players after they've been under contract for a certain number of years, and owners no longer have absolute control over players' careers.

Table 11.1   Average salaries in major U.S. professional leagues, compared with median family income, 1950–2008*

Year	SPORT LEAGUE						Median U.S. Family Income†
	NFL	NBA	WNBA	NHL	MLB	MLS	
1950	15,000	5,100		5,000	13,300	NA	4,000
1960	17,100	13,000		14,100	19,000	NA	5,620
1970	23,000	40,000		25,000	29,300	NA	9,867
1980	79,000	190,000		110,000	143,000	NA	21,023
1990	395,400	824,000		247,000	598,000	NA	35,353
2000	1,116,100	3,600,000	60,000	1,050,000	1,988,034	100,000	50,732
2007/08	1,538,000	4,392,000	52,000‡	1,645,000	3,142,000	115,000	58,480

*Data on players' salaries come from many sources, but I try to be fair and accurate. Average salaries before 1971 are estimates because players' associations did not exist and teams had notoriously inconsistent payroll data. I use data from players' associations when possible.

†This is median annual income for households consisting of parents and children. Half of all families fall above the median, and half fall below it. Data are from the U.S. Census; figures for 1950 and 2007 are estimates based on trends (http://www.census.gov/hhes/www/income/histinc/f07ar.html).

‡Estimate based on the salary cap and stated salaries based on years in the league and the round in which players were drafted.

Although it's been a struggle for professional team athletes to maintain their unions, they realize that crucial labor issues must be negotiated every time they renew their CBA with the owners' cartel. At this time, the main issues negotiated in CBAs include the following:

1. The percentage of league revenues that are dedicated to "player costs" (salaries and benefits), and what is included in "league revenues"
2. The extent to which teams can share revenues with one another
3. Salary limits for rookies signing their first pro contract, salary restrictions for veteran players, and minimum salary levels for all players
4. The conditions under which players can become free agents and the rights of athletes who are free agents
5. A salary cap that sets the maximum player payroll for teams and a formula determining the fines that an owner must pay if the team's payroll exceeds the cap
6. A salary floor that sets the minimum team payroll for each team in a league
7. The conditions under which an individual player or team can request an outside arbitrator to determine the fairness of an existing or proposed contract
8. Changes in the rules of the game

To illustrate the importance of these eight factors, let's consider the contract signed in 2005 between the National Hockey League and the NHL Players Association after a 301-day lockout that canceled the entire 2004–2005 season.[2] The contract was nearly 600 pages long, but these eight issues were central negotiating points, and they were resolved in the following way:

1. Player costs cannot exceed 54 percent of hockey-related revenue collected by all the teams, and if contracted salaries are greater than 54 percent, salaries are cut proportionately to meet the limit.
2. The ten teams that earn the most money must share some of their income with the ten teams that earn the least money (this concerns players because this form of sharing revenues, gives owners less incentive to pay high salaries to good players).
3. Rookie players cannot be paid more than $850,000; a veteran player may not make over 20 percent of his team's payroll (a maximum salary of $7.8 million in 2005–2006); and the minimum salary is $450,000—an important issue because 15 to 25 percent of all players in all pro leagues receive the minimum salary during any given year.
4. A player must be thirty-one years old to become an unrestricted free agent in 2005–2006. This age decreases by one year each season until the 2008–2009 season, when a player must be twenty-seven years old *or* have a minimum of seven years of experience in the league to become a free agent.
5. The maximum payroll for teams during the 2005–2006 season was $39 million (this is a "hard cap," which means there are no exceptions for any team; a "soft cap" means that teams may exceed the maximum under certain conditions by paying a fine that goes into a pool of money that is divided among "poorer" teams).
6. The minimum payroll for teams during the 2005–2006 season was $21.5 million.
7. Players *and* teams may request salary or contract arbitration (in other leagues, only players can request arbitration).
8. Hockey rules were changed to limit violent body contact during games, which also increased the pace or speed of the games and increased scoring opportunities for teams; another change was to institute "shootouts" to reduce the number of games ending in a tie.

The hockey players were at a serious disadvantage when negotiating this contract because

---

[2]A lockout occurs when a CBA has expired and the owners decide to cease all games until an agreement is reached. A lockout is initiated by owners, whereas a strike is initiated by a players' union.

some NHL teams were losing money before they locked out the players in 2004. The players knew changes were needed, so they agreed that all salaries be cut by 24 percent in addition to the other points (Ozanian and Badenhausen, 2007).

Players in the other top men's leagues generally negotiate contracts under more favorable conditions. Therefore, they face less-restrictive salary limits and can negotiate better terms on other issues. Owners and players tend to be more agreeable when money is plentiful, but regardless of the money available, there are always questions about what proportion of revenues goes to workers and what proportion goes to management/owners (Forbes, 2007; Ozanian, 2007).

As opposed to athletes in high-revenue sports, athletes in most minor leagues and lower-revenue sports have few rights and little control over their careers. The players at this level far outnumber players in the top levels of professional sports, and they often work for low pay under uncertain conditions, and with few rights. Owners almost always have the last word in these sports, although the owners don't usually make large amounts of money.

> **OLC** **ON THE *OLC*:**
> See the OLC—Additional Readings for Chapter 11—for essays on athletes' salaries and endorsements.

Legal Status: Individual Sports   The legal status of professional athletes in individual sports varies greatly from sport to sport and even from one athlete to another. Although there are important differences between boxing, bowling, golf, tennis, auto racing, rodeo, horse racing, track and field, skiing, biking, and a number of recently professionalized alternative and action sports, a few generalizations can be made.

The legal status of athletes in individual sports largely depends on what athletes must do to train and qualify for competitions. For example,

few athletes can afford to pay for all the training needed to develop professional-level skills in a sport. Furthermore, they don't have the knowledge or connections to meet the formal requirements to become an official competitor in their sport, which may include having a recognized agent or manager (as in boxing), being formally accepted by other participants (as in most auto racing), obtaining membership in a professional organization (as in most bowling, golf, and tennis tournaments), or gaining a special invitation through an official selection group (as in pro track and field meets).

Whenever athletes need sponsors to pay for training or agents to help them meet participation requirements, their legal status is shaped by the contracts they sign with these people and then with the organizations that regulate participation. This is why the legal status of athletes in individual sports varies so widely.

Let's use boxing as an example. Because many boxers come from low-income backgrounds, they lack the resources to develop high-level boxing skills and arrange official bouts with other boxers. They must have trainers, managers, and sponsors, and the support of these people always comes with conditions that are written in formal contracts or based on informal agreements. In either case, boxers must forfeit control over much of their lives and a portion of the rewards they may earn in future bouts. This means that few boxers have much control over their careers, even when they win large amounts of prize money. They are forced to trade control over their bodies and careers for the opportunity to continue boxing. This is an example of how class relations operate in sports: when people lack resources, they are limited in the ways they can negotiate the conditions under which their sport careers occur.

The legal status of athletes in individual sports usually is defined in the bylaws of professional organizations such as the Professional Golf Association (PGA), the Ladies' Professional Golf Association (LPGA), the Association of Tennis Professionals (ATP), and the Professional

Rodeo Cowboys Association (PRCA). Because athletes control many of these organizations, their policies support athletes' rights and enable them to control some of the conditions under which they compete. Without these organizations, athletes in these sports would have few rights as workers.

Income: Team Sports   Despite publicity given to the supercontracts of some athletes in the top professional leagues, salaries vary widely across the levels and divisions of professional team sports. For example, in 2008, there were about 3500 Minor League Baseball players on 176 teams in North America, and they made from $150 a game at the lowest levels to a high of about $75,000 per year at the top minor league level. The same was true in minor league hockey, where there were at least 2000 players in 2008. The average salary in the nine-team Canadian Football League was about $100,000 but the median salary was half that amount. Major League Soccer in the United States had an average salary of $115,000 in 2008, but 30 percent of the players made less than $18,000 per year. In the Major Lacrosse League (outdoor) and National League Lacrosse (indoor), average salaries were about $13,000 and $15,400, respectively; and the *most* an NLL player could make was $27,948. The average salary in the increasingly popular Arena Football League was increased to $85,000 in 2008. WNBA players averaged about $52,000 per season, with a $34,500 minimum for rookies and $95,000 maximum for veterans. In most cases, being a professional athlete in team sports continues to be a seasonal job with few benefits and little or no career security.

To understand the range of incomes in pro sports, consider that in recent seasons the total salaries of 15 percent of MLB players were about the same as the total salaries of the other 85 percent. This is why the average—or *mean*—salary in Major League Baseball has been about $3.2 million per year, whereas the median salary is less than one-third that amount at $900,000 per

SIDELINES

©1982 M.T.F.-T.W.S.-Lakewood, CO

"Help me, Doc! I make $20 million a year, and I don't feel guilty."

Most athletes generate revenues that match their salaries or prize money. Like other entertainers, a few of them benefit from national and international media exposure. Sport events are now marketed in connection with the celebrity status and lifestyles of high-profile athlete-entertainers.

year. The big salaries for a few players drive up the average for the entire league.

The megasalaries in men's professional team sports did not exist before the 1980s. The data in Table 11.1 shows that players' average salaries have grown far beyond median family income in the United States. For example, players in 1950 had salaries not much higher than median family income at that time. In 2007–2008, the average NBA salary was over eighty times greater than the median family income!

The dramatic increase in salaries at the top level of pro sports since 1980 can be attributed to two factors: (1) changes in the legal status and rights of players, which have led to free agency and the use of a salary arbitration process, and (2) increased revenues, especially through the sale of media rights, flowing to leagues and owners (see Chapter 12). Data in Table 11.1 show that the increases in player salaries correspond closely with court decisions and labor agreements that changed the legal status of athletes and gave them bargaining power in contract negotiations with team owners.

Income: Individual Sports As with team sports, publicity is given to the highest-paid athletes in individual sports. However, the reality is that many players in these sports don't make enough money from tournament winnings to pay all their expenses and support themselves comfortably. Many golfers, tennis players, bowlers, track and field athletes, auto and motorcycle racers, rodeo riders, figure skaters, and others must carefully manage their money so that they don't spend more than they win as they travel from event to event. When tournament winnings are listed in the newspaper, nothing is said about the expenses for airfares, hotels, food, and transportation or about other expenses for coaches, agents, managers, and various support people. The top money winners don't worry about these expenses, but most athletes in individual sports are not big money winners.

Typical of many individual sports, the disparity between the top money winners and others has increased considerably on the men's and women's golf and tennis tours. In 2007 Tiger Woods made $10.6 million in prize money and $87 million in endorsements. Golfer Lorena Ochoa, who won eight tournaments in 2007, made about $14.5 million in prize money and endorsements, about 15 percent of Woods' annual earnings; but both Woods and Ochoa made far more than other golfers. Maria Sharapova, the highest-paid woman athlete in 2007, won $1.7 million but had endorsements of about $20 million. But these are unique cases. Many people are surprised to learn that the top 15 to 20 players on the Women's Tennis Association (WTA) Tour make as much prize money as the rest of the 1800 registered WTA players combined during the tour year.

The majority of men and women playing professional tennis, golf, and other individual sports do not make enough prize money to pay their competition expenses each year, although some have sponsors who pay for training and travel. Some athletes with sponsors may be under contract to share their winnings with them; the sponsors/investors cover expenses during the lean years but then take a percentage of prize money if and when the athletes win matches or tournaments.

Sponsorship agreements cause problems for professional athletes in many individual sports. Being contractually tied, for example, to an equipment manufacturer or another sponsor often puts athletes in a state of dependency. They may not have the freedom to choose when or how often they will compete, and sponsors may require them to attend social functions, at which they talk with fan-consumers, sign autographs, and promote products. For example, when Kim Clijsters (Belgium), the world's number-2–ranked tennis player, discovered that the IOC would not allow her to wear clothing bearing her sponsor's logo if she played in the 2004 Olympics, she withdrew from the games.

Overall, a few athletes in individual sports make good money, whereas most others struggle to cover expenses. Only when sport events are broadcast on television can athletes expect to compete for major prize money and earn large incomes, unless they are amateurs or have not bargained for their rights as workers.

Amateur Athletes in Commercial Sports

Amateur athletes often have a confusing and contradictory status in commercial sports. Understanding their situation requires knowledge of their legal status and the income restrictions they face in their sports.

Legal Status of Amateur Athletes The primary goal of amateur athletes is simple: to train and compete. However, achieving this goal has not always been easy because amateur athletes have little control over the conditions of their sport participation. Instead, control rests in the hands of amateur sport organizations, each setting rules that specify the conditions under which training and competition may occur. Although many rules ensure fairness in competition, others simply protect the power and interests of governing organizations and their leaders.

The powerlessness of amateur athletes in the United States led to the formation of the U.S. President's Commission on Olympic Sports in 1975. The commission's report was instrumental in the passage of the Amateur Sports Act of 1978. The Amateur Sports Act did not guarantee amateur athletes any rights, but it did create the USOC and clarified relationships among various sports organizations so that officials would be less likely to interfere with participation opportunities for athletes. Interference continues today, but it is less disruptive of training and competition than in the past.

The continued lack of power among amateur athletes is especially evident in U.S. intercollegiate sports. Even in revenue-producing college sports, athletes have few rights and no formal means of filing complaints when they've been treated unfairly or denied the right to play their sports. The athletes are not allowed to share the revenues that they may generate and have no control over how their skills, names, and images can be used by the university or the NCAA. For example, when college athletes become local or national celebrities, they have no way to benefit from the status that they've earned. They cannot endorse products or be paid when universities use their identities and images to promote events and sell merchandise.

Many amateur athletes recognize that they lack rights, but it has been difficult for them to lobby for changes. Challenging universities or the NCAA in court is expensive and would take years of a young person's life. Forming an athletes' organization would make it possible to bargain for rights, but bringing together athletes from many campuses would require resources. Additionally, some athletes have adjusted to their dependency and powerlessness and would be difficult to recruit into such an organization.

The prospect of college athletes' engaging in collective bargaining to gain rights and benefits would be a serious threat to the structure of big-time college sports. Athletes often are treated like employees by coaches and athletic departments, but if they were legally defined as employees, they would be eligible for the same considerations granted to other workers in the United States. To suggest this makes coaches, athletic directors, university presidents, and boosters very nervous.

Although athletes are now members of certain NCAA committees, these committees are not likely to increase athletes' rights. Athlete advisory committees now exist at the NCAA, conference, and campus levels, but there are no formal structures for effectively gaining more control over the conditions of training and competition. Coaches even call their athletes "kids," a word that puts them in a dependent status and keeps them there. The only way these "kids" will gain at least some control over their sport lives is for an outside group to develop a recognized athlete advocacy organization that represents athletes in their relationships with universities and the NCAA. Kids, after all, are not entitled to real power, which is why the word continues to be used by coaches and others associated with college sports.

Amateur athletes in Olympic sports have made some strides to gain control over their training and competition, but as sports become more commercialized, the centers of power move further away from athletes. Athletes are now included on advisory boards for NGBs, but NGBs take a back seat to sponsors and media in the case of commercial events. Paradoxically, as athletes gain more resources to train and compete, the control of their training and competition moves further away from them. The exceptions are a few "stars" with national visibility and the individual power to negotiate support that meets their interests.

Income of Amateur Athletes   Amateur athletes in commercial sports face another paradox: They

The NCAA strictly limits rewards received by college athletes, even those who generate millions of dollars of income for their universities and the NCAA. A ticket to this Notre Dame football game costs more than a ticket to an NFL game, but the players make a small fraction of what NFL players make. Universities profit from big-time football and men's basketball because they have access to cheap athletic labor. (*Source:* Jay Coakley)

generate money through their performances, but they cannot directly benefit financially from participating in sports. American college athletes may receive limited athletic aid while they are students in good academic standing, and elite international athletes may receive stipends for living expenses while they train, but many amateur athletes receive no compensation, even when they create revenues. This is not new, but there are times now when amateurs compete in multimillion-dollar events such as the Olympics and big-time intercollegiate football and basketball. Even when it is clear that individual athletes generate $2 to $3 million for their universities,

NCAA rules prohibit them from receiving more than one-year, renewable scholarships. Therefore, a football or basketball player from a low-income family can bring fame and fortune to a university for one to four years and not receive more than basic expenses for tuition, room, meals, books, and other necessities except in rare circumstances.

The unfairness of this situation for certain athletes promotes under-the-table forms of compensation. Although there have been many calls for the NCAA to revise its policies on compensation for athletes, developing a fair method of compensation has been beyond the NCAA's capabilities so far. Therefore, some college athletes desiring fair compensation for their abilities and work decide to leave college before graduation in hope of playing professional sports.

International amateur rules now permit athletes to be paid living expenses. However, they cannot make money beyond approved cost-of-living stipends and travel expenses related to training and competition. Therefore, if a sixteen-year-old gymnast on the U.S. national team takes money to be in an exhibition tour after the Olympics, she is not eligible to participate in NCAA college gymnastics. This also means she cannot receive athletic aid to attend college. Furthermore, if an Olympic figure skater participates in a professional skating competition, her amateur status may be revoked, even if she has accepted no money. This would make her ineligible for future Olympic competitions. These constraints make it difficult for athletes from lower-income backgrounds to maintain amateur status and continue doing their sports (Sokolove, 2004c).

Questions about the fairness of this situation have been raised by an increasing number of athletes. University of Ottawa economist Mark Lavoie (2000) notes that there may be a time "when the so-called amateur athletes will threaten to go on strike in order to get their share of the huge revenues generated by worldwide mega-events such as the Olympic Games" (p. 167).

summary

WHAT ARE THE CHARACTERISTICS OF COMMERCIAL SPORTS?

Commercial sports are visible parts of many societies today. They grow and prosper best in urban, industrial and postindustrial nations with relatively efficient transportation and communications systems, a standard of living that allows people the time and money to play and watch sports, and a culture that emphasizes consumption and material status symbols. Spectator interest in commercial sports is based on a combination of a quest for excitement, ideologies emphasizing success, the existence of youth sport programs, and media coverage that introduces people to the rules of sports and the athletes who play them.

The recent worldwide growth of commercial sports has been fueled by sport organizations seeking global markets and corporations using sports as vehicles for global capitalist expansion. This growth will continue as long as it serves the interests of multinational corporations. As it does, sports, sport facilities, sport events, and athletes are branded with corporate logos and ideological messages promoting consumption and dependence on corporations for excitement and pleasure.

Commercialization leads to changes in the internal structure and goals of certain sports, the orientations of people involved in sports, and the people and organizations that control sports. Rules are changed to make events more fan-friendly. People in sports, especially athletes, emphasize heroic orientations over aesthetic orientations and use style and dramatic expression to impress mass audiences. Overall, commercial sports are packaged as total entertainment experiences for spectators, mostly for the benefit of spectators who lack technical knowledge about the games or events they're watching.

Commercial sports are unique businesses. At the minor league level, they generate modest revenues for owners and sponsors. However, team owners at the top levels of professional sports have formed cartels to generate significant revenues. Like event sponsors and promoters, team owners are involved with commercial sports to make money while having fun and establishing good public images for themselves or their corporations and corporate products, policies, and practices. Their cartels enable them to control costs, stifle competition, and increase revenues, especially those coming from the sale of broadcasting rights to media companies. Profits also are enhanced by public support and subsidies, often associated with the construction and operation of stadiums and arenas.

It is ironic that North American professional sports often are used as models of democracy and free enterprise when, in fact, they've been built through carefully planned autocratic control and monopolistic business practices. As one NFL team owner said about himself and other owners, "We're twenty-eight Republicans who vote socialist" when it comes to their own business interests. What he meant was that NFL owners are political conservatives who have effectively eliminated free-market competition in their sport businesses and used public money and facilities to increase their wealth and power.

The administration and control of amateur commercial sports rest in the hands of numerous sport organizations. Although these organizations exist to support the training and competition of amateur athletes, their primary goal is to control both athletes and revenue. Those with the most money and influence usually win the power struggles in amateur sports, and athletes seldom have the resources to promote their interests in these struggles. Corporate sponsors are now a major force in amateur sports, and their goals strongly influence what happens in these sports.

Commercialization transforms athletes into entertainers. Because athletes generate revenues through their performances, issues related to players' rights and their fair share of revenues generated by their performances are very important. As rights and revenues have increased, so have players' incomes. Media coverage and the rights fees paid by media companies have been key in this process.

Most athletes in professional sports do not make vast sums of money. Players outside the top men's sports and golf and tennis for women have incomes that are surprisingly low. Income among amateur athletes is limited by the rules of governing bodies in particular sports. Intercollegiate athletes in the United States have what amounts to a regulated maximum wage in the form of athletic scholarships, which many

people see as unfair when some athletes generate millions of dollars of revenue for their universities. In other amateur sports, athletes may receive direct cash payments for performances and endorsements, and some receive support from the organizations to which they belong, but relatively few make large amounts of money.

The structure and dynamics of commercial sports vary from nation to nation. Commercial sports in most of the world have not generated the massive revenues associated with a few high-profile, heavily televised sports in North America, Australia, Western Europe, and parts of Latin America and eastern Asia. Profits for owners and promoters around the world depend on supportive relationships with the media, large corporations, and governments. These relationships have shaped the character of all commercial sports, professional and amateur.

The commercial model of sports is not the only one that might provide athletes and spectators with enjoyable and satisfying experiences. However, because most people are unaware of alternative models, they continue to express a desire for what they get, even though it is largely determined by the interests of people with wealth and power (Sewart, 1987). Therefore, changes will occur only when spectators and people in sports develop visions for what sports could and should look like if they were not shaped so much by the economic interests of wealthy and powerful people.

WEBSITE RESOURCES

Note: Websites often change. The following URLs were current when this book was printed. Please check our website (www.mhhe.com/coakley10e) for updates and additions.

http://asp.usatoday.com/sports/salaries/ *USA Today* maintains salary databases containing year-by-year listings of salaries for Major League Baseball, National Football League, National Basketball

Association, and National Hockey League players; data are compiled annually and include salaries for specific players, highest paid by position, plus median and total salaries for each team.

www.mhhe.com/coakley10e Click on chapter 11 for information on "outposts in action" and financial data on escalating franchise fees and franchise values, discussions of top athletes' salaries and endorsements, and explanations of rapid increases in ticket prices to top events.

www.tidesport.org/racialgenderreportcard.html Site for The Institute for Diversity and Ethics in Sports (TIDES); links to the 2008 Racial and Gender Report Cards for the NFL, WNBA, NBA, MLB, the Associated Press Sports Editors; plus an overall complete Report Card for major sports in 2007. The director of TIDES is Richard Lapchick.

www.fieldofschemes.com An information-rich companion website to the book of the same name by Joanna Cagan and Neil deMause; presents information from the book, updates on stadium issues, and links to recent articles and related sites.

www.forbes.com/lists/ Go to link for sport lists to see franchise values for all teams in MLB, NFL, NBA, NHL, and global soccer; each list of franchise values for leagues can be sorted by rank, team, current value, revenue, and operating income.

www.hockeyzoneplus.com/salair_e.htm Hockey-ZonePlus provides data on the business and economics of hockey worldwide, including salary information for teams, NHL players, and players in leagues around the world, including the professional hockey league in Russia and minor league hockey; information on the values of franchises, team ownership, attendance, coaches' salaries, and the cost of arenas.

www.nfl.com Any of the sites for professional sport leagues provide a picture of how they present themselves for commercial purposes; don't expect to find any critical information at these sites, and note the emphasis on "fantasy football" information for site visitors.

www.sportengland.org/ The Sport England site is a good example of how sports are presented in a nation where funding comes primarily from the public sector and sports have not been as commercialized as they have been in the United States.

www.sportslaw.org/ The Sports Lawyers Association publishes the Sports Lawyers Journal; this site lists articles, many of which are devoted to the legal issues associated with the special legal context in which professional sport teams operate.

http://sportsvenues.com/info.htm A business-oriented site with information on major stadiums and arenas (excluding all universities) that are the homes of major and minor league teams in North America; provides data on luxury suites, club seats, and naming rights fees.

www.teammarketing.com/ Team Marketing Report provides information on ticket prices and a fan cost index for all teams in MLB, NBA, NFL, and NHL; computes an average for each league.

www.wwe.com The World Wrestling Entertainment site provides an example of an "entertainment sport" that has remained popular among various segments of the population worldwide; as I write this, the WWE Raw! program on Monday nights is consistently the top-rated cable program of the week, beating both NHL and NBA playoff games.

(Jay Coakley)

SPORTS AND THE MEDIA

Could They Survive Without Each Other?

> IT IS CLEAR THAT the main function of sports news
> is to serve as the molehill on which mountains of
> opinion are built.
>
> —LeAnne Schreiber, ESPN Ombudsman (in
>   Hiestand, 2007, 3C).

(OLC) Visit *Sports in Society*'s Online Learning Center (OLC) at www.mhhe.com/coakley10e for additional information and study material for this chapter, including the following:

- A complete chapter outline
- Learning objectives
- Practice quizzes
- Internet resources
- Related readings
- Essays
- Student projects

ESPN HAS MADE a nation of highlight watchers out of us.

> —Barry Frank, vice president, IMG (global sport management), 2004

THE FAIRY TALE that once upon a time was sports is no more. If our televised sports don't tell us that, our sports section does.

> —Christine Brennan, sport journalist, USA Today (2008)

IT'S A BOLD NEW WORLD, and traditional sportswriters, with all their puffery and pretension, should step back from the team-sponsored buffet and open bar and get their hands dirty in the virtual sporting scrum taking place online.

> —Dave Zirin, sport journalist (2008a)

The media, including newspapers, magazines, books, films, radio, television, the Internet, mobile phones, and video games, pervade culture. Although each of us incorporates media into our lives in different ways, the things we read, hear, and see in the media are important parts of our experience. They frame and influence many of our thoughts, conversations, decisions, and experiences.

We use media images and narratives as we evaluate ourselves, give meaning to other people and events, form ideas, and envision the future. This does *not* mean that we are slaves to the media or passive dupes of those who produce and present media content to us. The media don't tell us *what* to think, but they greatly influence what we *think about* and, therefore what we discuss in everyday conversations. Additionally, our experiences are clearly informed by media content, and if the media didn't exist, our lives would be different.

Sports and the media are interconnected parts of our lives. Sports provide valuable media content, and many sports depend on the media for publicity and revenues. To better understand these interconnections, five questions are considered in this chapter:

1. What are the characteristics of the media?
2. How are sports and the media interconnected?
3. What images and messages are emphasized in the media coverage of sports in the United States?
4. What are the experiences and consequences of consuming media sports?
5. What are the characteristics of sport journalism?

CHARACTERISTICS OF THE MEDIA

Revolutionary changes are occurring in the media. Personal computers, the Internet, and wireless technology have propelled us into a transition from an era of sponsored and programmed media for mass consumption into an era of multifaceted, on-demand, interactive, and personalized media content and experiences. The pace and implications of this transition are significant, and college students today are on the cutting edge of this media revolution. Although it's important to discuss new trends and explain what may occur in the future, our discussions should be based on a general understanding of the traditional media and their connections with sports.

Media research in the past often distinguished between print and electronic media. **Print media** included *newspapers, magazines, fanzines, books, catalogues, event programs*, and even *trading cards*—words and images on paper. **Electronic media** included *radio, television, and film*. But video games, the Internet, mobile phones, and online publications have nearly eliminated the dividing line between these media forms. Today, media provide *information, interpretation, entertainment*, and *opportunities for interactivity*. On some occasions they provide all these features simultaneously. When media content is provided for commercial purposes, entertainment is emphasized more than information, interpretation, or opportunities for interactivity. In the process, media consumers become commodities sold to advertisers with the goal of promoting lifestyles based on consumption.

The media also put us in touch with information, experiences, people, images, and ideas outside the realm of our everyday, real-time lives. But most media content is edited and "re-presented" to us by others—producers, editors, program directors, programmers, camerapersons, writers, journalists, commentators, sponsors, bloggers, and website providers. These people provide information, interpretation, entertainment, and even opportunities for interactivity to achieve one or more of five goals: (1) make financial profits, (2) influence cultural values, (3) provide a public service, (4) enhance personal status and reputation, and (5) express themselves in technical, artistic, or personal ways.

In nations where most media are privately owned, the dominant goals are to make profits and to distribute content that promotes the ideas and beliefs of people in positions of power and influence. These aren't the only goals, but they are the most influential. Media expert Michael Real explains that there has been no greater force in the construction of media sport reality than "commercial television and its institutionalized value system [emphasizing] profit making, sponsorship, expanded markets, commodification, and competition" (1998, p. 17). As the Internet and wireless technology extend content and access, media sport reality is being constructed in diverse ways. This can be a contentious process as corporations and powerful individuals attempt to control online access and content. The resulting struggle is a crucial feature of contemporary social worlds.

In nations where media are controlled primarily by the state, the primary goals are to provide a public service and promote identification with the state and its officials (Lund, 2007). However, state control of the media has steadily declined as television companies and newspapers have become privatized and deregulated, and as more individuals obtain online access to information, interpretation, entertainment, and opportunities for interactivity.

Power relations in a society influence the priority given to the five goals that drive media content. Those who make content decisions act as filters as they select and create the images and messages that they present in the media. In the filtering and presentation process, these people usually emphasize images and narratives consistent with ideologies that support their interests in addition to attracting large audiences. As deregulation and private ownership have increased, the media have become hypercommercialized and media content has focused more on consumption, individualism,

competition, and class inequality as natural and necessary in society. Seldom included in the content of commercial media is an emphasis on civic values, conservation, anticommercial activities, and political action (McChesney, 1999; Walker, 2005). In fact, when groups with anticommercial messages want to buy commercial time on television, media corporations and networks have refused to sell it to them (Lasn, 2000).

There are exceptions to this pattern, but when people use media to challenge dominant ideologies, they encounter difficulties. This discourages counter-hegemonic programming and leads people to censor media content in ways that defer to the interests of the powerful. Even when there is legal protection for freedom of speech, as in the United States, those who work in the media often think carefully before presenting images and messages that challenge the interests of those who have power and influence in society, especially when those people own the media or support it by sponsoring programs.

This does not mean that those who control the media ignore what consumers think and "force" media audiences to read, hear, and see things unrelated to their interests. But it does mean that, apart from content that individuals create online, average people influence the media only through program ratings. Therefore, the public receives edited information, interpretation, entertainment, and interactive experiences that are constructed to boost profits and maintain a business and political climate in which commercial media can thrive. In the process, people who control media are concerned with what attracts readers, listeners, and viewers within the legal limits set by government agencies and the preference parameters of individuals and corporations that buy advertising time. As they make programming decisions, they

> Sport and the media must surely be the most potent combination of forces amongst the key factors in the globalization game. They have a unique synergy. —Robert Davies, chief executive, International Business Leaders Forum (2002b)

"Quick! Bring the camera—the viewers will love this crash!"

Media representations of sports are carefully selected and edited. Commentary and images highlight dramatic action, even when it's a minor part of an event.

see audiences as collections of consumers that can be sold to advertisers.

In the case of sports, those who control media not only decide which sports and events to cover but also the kinds of images and commentary that are presented in the coverage (Andrews and Jackson, 2001; Arsenault and Castells, 2008; Bernstein and Blain, 2003; Brookes, 2002; Bruce, 2007; Dempsey, 2006; Horne, 2007a; Martzke and Cherner, 2004; Rowe, 2004a, 2004b; Whannel, 2002). When they do this, they play an important role in constructing the overall frameworks that people in media audiences use to define and incorporate sports in their lives.

Most people don't think critically about media content. For example, when we watch sports on television, we don't often notice that the images and messages we see and hear have been carefully presented to heighten the dramatic content of the event and emphasize dominant ideologies in American society. The pregame analysis, the camera coverage, the camera angles, the close-ups, the slow-motion shots, the attention given

to particular athletes, the announcers' play-by-play descriptions, the color commentary, the quotes from athletes, the postgame summary and analysis, and all associated website content are presented to entertain media audiences and keep sponsors happy.

Television commentaries (narratives) and images in the United States highlight action, competition, aggression, hard work, individual heroism and achievement, playing despite pain, teamwork, and competitive outcomes. Television coverage has become so seamless in its representations of sports that we often define televised games as "real" games—more real than what is seen in person at the stadium. Longtime magazine editor Kerry Temple explains:

> It's not just games you're watching. It's soap operas, complete with story lines and plots and plot twists. And good guys and villains, heroes and underdogs. And all this gets scripted into cliff-hanger morality plays. . . . And you get all caught up in this until you begin to believe it really matters (1992, p. 29).

Temple's point is especially relevant today. The focus on profits has increased soap opera storytelling as a means of developing and maintaining audience interest in commercial media sports coverage. Sports programming is now "a never-ending series of episodes—the results of one game create implications for the next one (or next week's) to be broadcast" (Wittebols, 2004, p. 4). Sports rivalries are hyped and used to serialize stories through and across seasons; conflict and chaos are highlighted with a predictable cast of "good guys," "bad guys," and "redemption" or "comeback" stories; and the story lines are designed to reproduce ideologies favored by upper-middle-class media consumers—the ones that corporate sponsors want to reach with their ads. This was apparent in NBC's standard references to the "Redeem Team" in their coverage of the USA basketball team at the 2008 Olympics.

Even though media coverage of sports is carefully edited and represented in total entertainment packages, most of us believe that when we see a sport event on television, we are seeing it "the way it is." We don't usually think that what we see, hear, and read is a series of narratives and images selected for particular reasons and grounded in the social worlds and interests of those producing the event, controlling the images, and delivering the commentary (Crawford, 2004; McCullagh, 2002). Television coverage provides only one of many possible sets of images and narratives related to a sport event, and there are many images and messages that audiences do not receive (Knoppers and Elling, 2004). If we went to an event in person, we would see something quite different from the images that are selected and presented on television, and we would develop our own descriptions and interpretations, which would be very different from those carefully presented by media commentators.

This occurs during the Olympics, for example, as NBC strategically creates entertaining drama by presenting "plausible realities" in their broadcasts of events. To do this, they deliberately withhold information to frame events in entertaining ways, even though the real-time events were experienced differently by the athletes and others involved. They give priority to entertainment over news and factual information. Former Olympic swimmer Diana Nyad noticed this at the 1996 Olympic Games in Atlanta and pointed out during an interview on National Public Radio that "Compared to the TV audience, the people [at the events] have seen a completely different Olympics." She also noted that television and other media coverage of the Olympic Games focuses on gold medals and distorts the experiences and priorities of athletes and spectators alike.

New York Times writer Robert Lipsyte (1996c) describes televised sports as "sportainment"— the equivalent of a TV movie that purports to be based on a true story but actually provides fictionalized history. In other words, television constructs sports and viewer experiences. But the process occurs so smoothly that most television viewers believe they experience sports in a "true and natural" form. This, of course, is the goal of

the directors, editors, and on-camera announcers who select images and narratives, frame them with the stories they wish to tell, and make sure they don't alienate sponsors in the process.

To illustrate this point, think about this question: What if all prime-time television programs were sponsored by environmental groups, women's organizations, and labor unions? Would program content be different from the way it is now? Would the political biases built into the images and commentary be the same as they are now? It is unlikely that they would be the same, and we would be quick to identify all the ways that the interests and political agendas of the environmentalists, feminists, or labor leaders influenced images, narratives, and overall program content.

Now think about this: Capitalist corporations sponsor nearly 100 percent of all sports programming in commercial media, and their goals are to create consumers loyal to capitalism and generate profits for corporations and their shareholders. As media consumers realize the implications of this approach, they often turn to the Internet and seek content provided by bloggers and independent journalists. Of course, online content is presented for many reasons, and those who want to use it as an alternative to the content in commercial media must critically assess its validity and reliability. For those who remain "tuned in" to the commercial media, their experiences as spectators are heavily influenced—that is, "mediated"—by the decisions of those who control the media.

New Media and Sports

New media, including the Internet, extend and radically change media representations of sports because they provide virtual access to potentially unlimited and individually created and selected information, interpretation, and entertainment. Additionally, the interactivity of being online is like having open voice, video, and text connections with everyone in the world who also is online.

The X Games were created by ESPN. ESPN is owned by ABC. ABC is owned by the Walt Disney Company. The power behind the X Games makes it difficult for the athletes to maintain the culture of their sports on their terms. (*Source:* Becky Beal)

In the case of sports, online access can provide active involvement with sports content. We can interact with fellow fans in chat rooms, ask questions of players and coaches, identify scores and statistics, and play online games that either simulate sports or are associated with real-time sport events around the world. We can even create media content to match our interests and the interests of others worldwide. This gives us control in ways that potentially transform media experiences and mediated realities (Crawford, 2004; Halverson and Halverson, 2008).

Although people often access online sport content to complement content they consume in traditional media, many now use new media to replace traditional content. This shift in consumption patterns concerns people in media companies that broadcast live sports worldwide, because their revenues in the past have depended on controlling this content and maintaining large audiences to sell to advertisers. At the same time, sport organizations such as MLB, the NFL, and the English Premier Football (Soccer) Division are becoming more active in managing media representations of their sports so they can directly control information, analysis, and entertainment to promote themselves on their terms. For example, MLB.com (http://mlb.mlb .com/mlb/radio/index.jsp) gives paid subscribers real-time coverage of all 2,430 regular season games streamed in a widescreen format at a rate that provides clear images, even on hand-held, mobile devices. The site also provides game previews, highlights, statistics, and general commentary, among dozens of other video, audio, and text materials on baseball. Soon it will be feasible for MLB and other professional sports to provide media content *and* media coverage, giving them near-total control over the ways that their brands are represented and consumed.

As we are witnessing today, content in the new media often blurs the lines between entertainment, journalism, and marketing so that it invariably promotes lifestyles of consumption (Halverson and Halverson, 2008; Maguire et al., 2008a, 2008b; Scherer, 2007; Scherer and Jackson, 2008). This was illustrated in the United States when NBCOlympics.com provided more than 1.2 billion online pages and more than 72 million video streams of online access to 2200 hours of live events and all 3600 hours of video (and much commentary) taken at the 2008 Olympic Games (Stetler, 2008).

At the same time that corporations try to maximize control over online representations of sports, YouTube and other sites provide people with video cameras opportunities to upload their own representations of alternative and action sports. For more than three decades, young people in alternative sports have found ways to photograph, film, and distribute images of their activities. In the past, photos and VCR tapes were mailed and passed person-to-person, but distribution today occurs online with images accessible worldwide. Although these images represent what may be described as "performance sports," they're central to the media experiences of many young people who find highly structured, overtly competitive sports such as baseball or football to be constraining and uncreative.

In some cases, young people use new media to represent sports involving transgressive actions such as skating in empty private swimming pools at night or doing **parkour** ("PK"), *an activity in which young men and a few young women use their bodies to move rapidly and efficiently through existing landscapes,* especially in urban areas where walls, buildings, and other obstacles normally impede movement (http://en.wikipedia.org/wiki/Parkour; www.americanparkour.com/). Research on the new media representations of these activities is sorely needed.

The major sociological question related to the Internet and new media generally is this: Will they democratize social life by enabling people to freely share information and ideas, or will they become tools controlled by corporations to expand their capital, increase consumption, reproduce ideologies that drive market economies, and maintain the illusion that we need them to provide pleasure and excitement in our lives?

The answer to this question lies in struggles over the ways that online access is controlled, funded, and incorporated into our lives. For example, giant cable and satellite companies have effectively lobbied lawmakers to pass legislation that prevents communities in some parts of the United States from establishing wireless connectivity as a public service for all citizens. These companies want the "information highway" to forever be a toll road on which they charge and collect fees; efforts to convert the toll road to a publicly maintained "state highway" attached to local public streets would take away their profits and remove one avenue of their control in the culture-creation process.

Sociologist Brian Wilson suggests that open and accessible avenues of online communication create "an immense revolutionary potential in sport-related contexts, and [also] for sociologists [of sport] interested in contributing to activist projects" (Wilson, 2007, p. 457)—and this is the last thing that commercial providers want.

New media account for the dramatic growth of online "Fantasy Leagues." Although the first fantasy sport league, invented in 1979 by a baseball fan, didn't require online access, most fantasy sports today are played online. If we use the NFL as an example, playing fantasy football makes every participant a "team owner" who constructs a team roster by taking turns with other "owners" to draft real NFL players for positions on their fantasy teams. The weekly performance statistics of the players on an owner's team roster are converted into points so that each fantasy team owner competes against other team owners. Usually, all participants pay fees to one of many online services that compile players' statistics, compute scores, and keep track of team records.

An estimated 15 to 18 million people play fantasy sports. Players are mostly college-educated white men (93 percent) between 25 and 50 years old with higher-than-average incomes. Collectively, they spend over $2 billion annually to obtain data about players and compete in organized fantasy leagues. Individually, each owner devotes many hours to watching sports and about three hours per week managing his team, a portion of which occurs at work (Ballard, 2004; Petrecca, 2005; Wendel, 2004).

Fantasy football, baseball, NASCAR, basketball, hockey, and other sports alter sport consumption patterns (Levy, 2005; Wendel, 2004). Real games often matter little to fantasy players who focus on the performance statistics of their players, who play on many different teams in real-time games. Although they often subscribe to expensive cable and satellite television "sport packages" that enable them to watch their players, they aren't too concerned about the outcomes of those games. While they watch, they also scout other players and take note of injuries because during the season they can cut, trade, and acquire new players on their fantasy rosters.

Fantasy sports also reposition fans relative to players (Davis and Duncan, 2004; Halverson and Halverson, 2008; Kusz, 2001; Zirin, 2008b). They provide the white men who play them with a sense of power and control over players unlike them at the same time that it connects them with others who share their interests and backgrounds (Bell, 2008; Levy, 2005).

> **Know the media. Change the media. Be the media.** —Adbusters, 2004

Overall, issues related to access will cause the Internet to be contested terrain well into the future as people struggle over the rights of users to share information and ideas (Totilo, 2008). Sports leagues and teams will use the Internet more widely in the future, but they will charge fees for access to events for which they have also sold media rights to television and radio. Furthermore, sponsors of TV and radio broadcasts will oppose Internet coverage that interferes with selling products and services to their sport audiences. For example, in 2008 MLB argued that rights fees must be paid by anyone using players' names and performance statistics in a for-profit online fantasy league. But the U.S. Supreme Court ruled that the free speech rights of fantasy league organizers allowed them to use this information because players' names and statistics are part of the "public domain" (Savage, 2008).

As media technology becomes more accessible, new forms of Internet-based sports coverage will emerge. For example, grandparents in distant locations will watch their grandchild play a high school basketball game simply by logging on to the high school website. The filming, commentary, and production of the game might be done for academic credit by students in a media course. This could lead to creative, non-commercial or nonprofit forms of sport media coverage. How this will change the reality of mediated sports and our experience of them remains to be seen.

The future is difficult to predict. Will people choose 500-channel, high-definition digital television over the medium of the Internet? Will InternetTV replace television as we know it today? Will the economics of technology and the "digital divide" between technology haves and have-nots segregate spectators even further by social class? Will the culture of the Internet favor some people over others, or will it enable all spectators to create realities that fit their interests and preferences?

Answers to these questions depend on the social, political, and economic forces shaping the future of the Internet. Economic forces guarantee that the first people to enjoy new spectator experiences and realities will be those who can buy the hardware, software, and bandwidth to move around the Internet at will. Social class will influence Internet access to spectator experiences because broadband providers overlook lower-income neighborhoods where profits are scarce. But progressive public policies and programs could mandate the provision of access in these neighborhoods or provide wireless access as a public service, thereby blurring class differences in future access to the Internet. This latter possibility, however, depends on the public good being given priority over the corporate good when it comes to online access. All of us will participate in creating the future, either actively or passively, as we make our choices and influence political decisions and regulations.

Video Games and Virtual Sports

Sports also come into our lives through video games and virtual experiences. Sport video games are popular in wealthy nations, and some people have even participated in virtual sports of various types although most virtual sports are experimental and not available for general participation.

The images in digital games have become increasingly lifelike, and those who play them have uniquely active spectator experiences, even when they occur in solitude. Social science research has focused mostly on violence and gender issues, and there is little information about the actual experiences of people who play video games modeled after "real" sports.

Video games that simulate sports have become so realistic that some athletes even use them to train. The games offer high-definition graphics, intense interactivity, control of the action, and opportunities to create, train, and be your own player competing with and against representations of "real" players.

Organized, online video sports tournaments now attract thousands of players worldwide, many of whom identify themselves as cyberathletes and participate in gaming tournaments (Snider, 2007). They train regularly, have fans and agents, and if they are high-profile players, endorse products related to the games. Between 1997 and 2008 the Cyberathlete Professional League sponsored about fifty major international tournaments and awarded over $3 million in prizes to competitors. Events in Major League Gaming have attracted audiences of hundreds of thousands, and participants have come from many parts of the world (Caplan and Coates, 2007).

It is clear that sport video games provide different experiences from consuming televised sports or playing sports. For example, golf fans can match their video golf skills with the physical skills of pro golfers by going online and golfing on the same course as Tiger Woods or other high-profile players whose shots have been represented and archived through digitized images. This is a new media experience, and research has not been done to show how people integrate such experiences into their lives.

Those who play video sports are usually regular consumers of standard sport media events. Their interest and enjoyment of the video games is tied to their knowledge about a sport, sport teams, and athletes. However, the experience of digital gaming is changing as more people play one another on the Internet in organized tournaments while others watch.

Interactive video games will be continuously modified to attract new consumers. Older fans will match NFL stars of the past with those of today (Schiesel, 2007b), others will have opportunities to manage their favorite teams in virtual games (Schiesel, 2006), controlling David Beckham's body as "he" plays on a soccer team in the United States, or participating in a digital skateboarding competition with representations of Eric Koston or Lyn-Z Adams Hawkins. We don't know if interactive sport video games will eventually replace or simply extend other forms of sports media consumption (Crawford, 2004). This and related issues are discussed in the box "Win at Any Cost" on page 402.

Game players have choices, but those choices are not unlimited, nor are they ideologically neutral. The experiences of video game players are influenced by the ethos that underlies the programmed images and actions in the games. The games clearly highlight corporate brands, affirm traditional masculinity, and support other values associated with most major media sports today (Baerg, 2007; Scherer, 2007). It is important that we increase our understanding of how people integrate video game experiences into their lives.

Studies of virtual sports have not been done in the sociology of sport. But as the technology for creating virtual reality evolves, people will become immersed in physical activities in new ways. Although we don't know exactly what this means, it's possible that many people in the future will prefer virtual sports to what we define as sports today. Instead of going to a gym or fitness center, people may go to virtual sports complexes where they can put on lightweight headsets that provide visual spaces enabling them to physically engage in sport challenges that transcend time and space. This futuristic

"Win at Any Cost"
Video Games as Simulated Sports

John Madden, known to football fans over the age of forty as a former NFL coach and longtime NFL commentator (most recently on Monday Night Football), is known to the under-forty-year-old game player as a video game brand. *Madden NFL* games are among the most popular video products on the market. When Madden was asked to comment on the video game craze, he said that designers have made video games that look so much like the games on television that television producers are now using special lenses and filters to make televised NFL games appear more like video games.

Game developers work with athletes so that video game situations and players' movements are lifelike. Leagues and players cooperate because they want to be portrayed accurately in video games. Even unique mannerisms related to their dramatic on-field personas are included in the game action.

Professional team coaches now worry that video games distract players from live games. Some NFL and NBA players prefer to play video game sports over watching live games. NASCAR, Formula One, and Indy Car video games are so realistic that some racecar drivers use the games to familiarize themselves with the tracks and prepare for the split-second responses required during actual races (Bernstein, 2007).

The financial stakes associated with creating realistic and entertaining games are significant. This constantly pushes designers to refine graphics, action, and game possibilities. It also leads them to talk with potential sponsors about product placements and advertisements built into the story lines and actions in the games. As more young people play these games and watch fewer television broadcasts, corporations

The graphics in EA Sports™ *Madden NFL* are amazingly lifelike, and television producers now use filtering software to make live games appear more like images from video games. In the process, video simulations merge with televised representations of sports. (© 2005 Electronic Arts, Inc.; © 2005 NFL Players; reproduced with permission)

see video games as vehicles for developing outposts in the heads of game players and fostering their commitment to a lifestyle based on consumption (Richtel, 2005). This makes product placement in games important, and it generates revenues for game producers.

A major issue for game developers is obtaining the rights to use the names and images of athletes and sport leagues in their games. *Madden NFL 09*, for example, is produced by EA Sports with permission from the NFL and the NFL Players Association,

arcade will allow cyclists in the year 2050 to race with Lance Armstrong's granddaughter as they pedal and sweat their way along the virtual roads of the Tour de France on bikes and in environments where they experience feelings of speed, wind and rain in their faces, and the excitement of developing and carrying out strategies with

virtual teammates in the Tour de France. Other sports will merge virtual and real spaces in other ways, changing the meaning of reality when it comes to sports (Marriott, 2004). The Wii gaming console and Wii Fit represent a minor step in that direction and provide a basic introduction to new forms of gaming (Trumbo, 2008).

which receive rights fees from sales of the games. But this also means that everything in the game is subject to NFL approval. Midway Games, on the other hand, developed *Blitz: The League*, a video game modeled after pro football, without buying rights from the NFL. Therefore, they can't use references to the NFL or NFL players' names and images. But they also have the freedom to include, if they wish, images of blood and gory injuries, near-naked cheerleaders, dirty hits, in-your-face celebrations after big plays, drug use (for energy and strength), and off-field controversies (Ives, 2004) that might boost sales.

Meanwhile, a small but growing number of children are now introduced to sports through video games. For example, children who play games on Nintendo's Wii platform learn rules and game strategies as they play. They see the moves involved in a sport as they manipulate images in the games, and their initial emotional experiences in certain sports are felt in front of computer monitors or televisions rather than on playing fields.

This raises many research questions. After playing interactive went video sports, will six-year-olds want to listen to whistle-blowing coaches when they're accustomed to being in complete control of players, game strategies, and game conditions? Will these children bring new forms of game knowledge to situations in which they play informal and formally organized games? How will that knowledge influence the games they play? Will some children simply stay home in front of their monitors as they control their own games without worrying about coaches, playing time, or parental pressure? Will they learn to be critical video game consumers, discovering and critiquing the ideologies built into the games they play? And finally, to whom are game developers accountable other than market forces, and to whom should they be accountable?

Adult game players outnumber children who play, and the majority of players are males between the ages of 12 and 30. Many male college students are regular game players to the point that status in certain groups reflects prowess in video game sports. Playing games also provides regular social occasions similar to those provided by live sport events, although the players set schedules for video games and can play them when they wish.

As bandwidth and high-speed online connections have increased, video game players now compete online with opponents worldwide and form teams with rosters of players who have never met one another in person. Spectators can watch games online and even listen to the voices of the players as they compete. Will schools sponsor online teams and will bookies develop betting odds and take bets on video sport game outcomes? If so, online sports could grow exponentially.

At this point, studies of simulated sports and video games are rare. We know little about the experiences of players and the social worlds created around the games. Future research will try to answer questions such as these: Does playing video games influence how people play live sports? Are the norms in live, real-time sports influenced by players' experiences in simulated sports? If children are introduced to sports through video games, will their experiences influence their expectations and the meanings they give to experiences in live, real-time games? Will the corporations that produce video games replace the major media companies that are so powerful today? *What do you think?*

But future virtual sport possibilities will replace Wii in rapid succession and provide experiences going far beyond responding to video images.

In the meantime, it's important to understand the relationship between sports and the media in the early twenty-first century and to know how each has influenced the other.

SPORTS AND THE MEDIA: A TWO-WAY RELATIONSHIP

The media and commercialization are closely related topics in the sociology of sport. The media intensify and extend the process and consequences of commercialization. For this reason, much attention has been given to the interdependence between the media and commercialized forms of sports. Each of these spheres of life has influenced the other, and each depends on the other for part of its popularity and commercial success.

Sports Depend on the Media

People played sports long before media coverage of sport events. When sports exist just for the participants, there's no need to advertise games, report the action, publish results, and interpret what happened. The players already know these things, and they're the only ones who matter. It is only when sports become commercial entertainment that they depend on the media.

Commercial sports require media to provide a combination of coverage and news. For example, when a stage play is over, it's over—except for a review after opening night and the conversations of those who attended the play. When a sport event is over, many people wish to know about and discuss statistics; important plays, records, standings; the overall performances of the players and teams; upcoming games or matches; the importance of the outcome in terms of the season as a whole and the postseason and the next season; and so on. The media provide this knowledge and facilitate these discussions, which in turn generate interest that can be converted into revenues from the sale of tickets, luxury suites, club seats, concessions, parking, team logo merchandise, and licensing rights. After games or matches are played, the scores become news, and interpretations of the action become entertainment for fans, regardless of whether they saw an event or not. This is the case worldwide—for bullfights in Mexico, hockey games in Canada, soccer matches in Brazil, sumo wrestling in Japan, and cricket in India.

Sports promoters and team owners know the value of media coverage, and they provide free access to reporters, commentators, and photographers. For example, the Beijing Organizing Committee credentialed 4,500 written press journalists and 1,100 photographers for the 2008 Olympic Games. Credentialed media personnel often are given comfortable seats in press boxes, access to the playing field and locker rooms, and summaries of statistics and player information. In return, promoters and owners expect and usually receive supportive media coverage.

Although commercial spectator sports depend on media, some have a special dependence on television because television companies pay for the rights to broadcast games and other events. Table 12.1 and Figure 12.1 indicate that "rights fees" provide sports with predictable, significant, and increasing sources of income. Once "rights contracts" are signed, revenues are guaranteed regardless of bad weather, injuries to key players, and the other factors that interfere with ticket sales and on-site revenue streams. Without television contracts, spectator sports seldom generate profits.

Television revenues also have greater growth potential than revenues from gate receipts. The number of seats in a stadium limits ticket sales, and ticket costs are limited by demand. But television audiences can include literally billions of viewers now that satellite technology transmits signals to most locations worldwide. For example, a goal of the IOC and the sponsors of other sport megaevents is to turn the entire world into an audience that can be sold to sponsors (Billings, 2007; Horne, 2007b; Horne and Manzenreiter, 2006b; Maguire et al., 2008a, 2008b). The size of the potential TV audience and the deregulation of the television industry are the reasons that television rights fees have increased at phenomenal rates since the early 1970s. This rapid increase is illustrated in Figure 12.1 and Table 12.1. In 1986 the NFL received $400 million in television rights fees, and in 2008 it received over $3.7 billion. Similarly, the rights fees paid to televise the 1984 Olympic Games in Los Angeles amounted to $287 million—ten times *more* than were paid to televise the 1976 Olympic Games in Montreal, and nearly seven

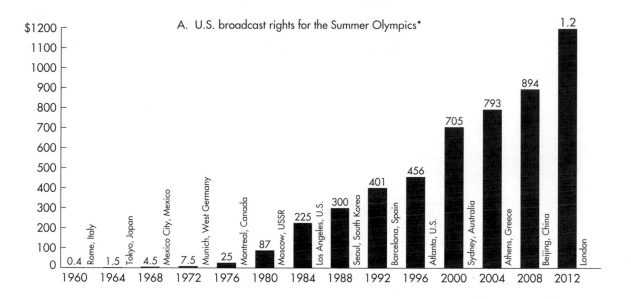

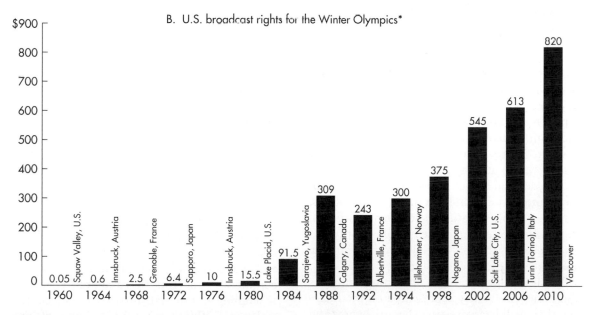

FIGURE 12.1 Escalating media rights fees paid by U.S. media companies to televise the Olympics (in millions of dollars).

*The local organizing committee for the Olympic Games also receives rights fees from other television companies around the world. Europe, Japan, and continental Asia are paying increasingly higher fees. For example, in 1984 ABC paid $225 million and other media companies worldwide paid an additional $62 million to the Los Angeles Olympic Organizing Committee; in 2012 NBC will pay a total of $1.2 billion in television rights fees and other media companies worldwide will pay about $700 million to the London Organizing Committee of the Olympic Games (LOCOG).

Table 12.1 Escalating annual media rights fees for major commercial sports in the United States (in millions of dollars)*

Sport	1986	1991	1996	2001	2008
NFL	400	900	1100	2200	3,750
MLB†	183	365	420	417	670
NBA	30	219	275	660	765
NHL‡	22	38	77	120	70
NASCAR	3	NA	NA	412	560
NCAA Men's Basketball Tournament	31	143	216	216	560§
NCAA (all women's championship)	NA	NA	NA	NA	18.5
WNBA	0	0	0	¶	¶

*These amounts have not been adjusted for inflation. Data come from multiple sources, and amounts change whenever new contracts are negotiated.

†Amounts for baseball do not include local television and radio rights fees negotiated by individual teams, national radio rights fees negotiated by the league, or Internet revenues received by the league from individual subscriptions paid to receive games on MLB.com; amount for 1996 includes national radio rights.

‡Includes U.S. rights only for 2001 and 2006; there also are Canadian rights and European rights.

§Will gradually increase through 2016, and includes rights to broadcast on television, radio, and the Internet the men's basketball tournament and other championship events, excluding football.

¶Information not available; however, the amount for 2008 is much higher than in past years, making it possible for the WNBA and teams with local media contracts to become profitable in the near future.

times *less* than the $1.9 billion that has been paid to televise the 2012 Olympic Games in London.

This growth in television rights fees makes commercial sports more profitable for promoters and team owners and increases the attractiveness of sports as sites for national and global advertising. Increased attention allows professional athletes to demand higher salaries and turns a few of them into national and international celebrities, who then use their status to endorse products sold worldwide. For example, the global celebrity and endorsement value of Tiger Woods is primarily due to the invention of satellite television.

As the quality of video streaming improves and events are widely represented on the Internet, there will be interesting changes in how and with whom media rights are negotiated. The global reach of the web creates new possibilities for large corporations wanting to "teach the world" to consume. However, it also creates challenges because new corporations will compete with traditional media companies for the video rights to sports. This is why NBC developed NBCOlympics.com in 2008, a portal enabling consumers to view events in the 2008 Olympic Games in Beijing, along with on-demand replays and highlights. Coverage was available on mobile devices and cable VOD packages, and other features were available for consumers interested in athlete profiles and gaming experiences. As this approach is used more frequently, traditional television coverage may become obsolete.

Have Commercial Sports Sold Out to the Media? Most commercial sports depend on television and online coverage for revenues and publicity. Accommodating the interests of commercial television has required changes in scheduling and rules that have made sports more "telegenic" (Hiestand, 2008). Some of these changes include the following:

- The schedules and starting times for many sport events have been altered to fit television's programming needs.
- Halftime periods in certain sports have been shortened to keep television viewers tuned to events.

The media enable some athletes to become global celebrities and benefit from windfall income related to their popularity. They know that their celebrity depends on using and maintaining close connections with the media. New England Patriots quarterback Tom Brady, like many players today, is adept at dealing with the media in ways that work to his advantage. (*Source:* Stephan Savoia; AP/Wide World)

- Prearranged schedules of time-outs have been added to games and matches to make time for as many commercials as possible.
- Teams, leagues, and tournaments have been formed or realigned to take advantage of regional media markets and build national and international fan support for sports, leagues, and teams.

In other cases, the lure of television money has encouraged changes that eventually would have occurred as sports became increasingly commercialized. For example, college football teams added an eleventh and twelfth game to their season schedules, and professional teams extended their seasons by adding games and playoffs. But these changes would have occurred without the influence of television money as people in commercial sports tried to increase gate receipts and venue revenues. The same is true for the additions of sudden death overtime periods in some sports, the tiebreaker-scoring method in tennis, the addition of medal play in golf, the 3-point shot in basketball, and the shootout in soccer and hockey. These changes are grounded in general commercial interests; television simply expands and intensifies the financial stakes associated with producing more marketable entertainment for all spectators and a more attractive commercial package for sponsors and advertisers.

Most changes associated with television coverage have been made willingly by sport organizations. The trade-offs usually are defined as attractive by players and sponsors. In fact, many sports and athletes not currently receiving coverage gladly would make changes if they could gain the attention and/or money associated with television contracts. Bowling, for example, added cheerleaders, a "VIP" bar to attract celebrities, sudden death overtime, single-ball "bowl off" to break ties, and man-versus-woman finals to make one of its events more marketable as a televised sport (Hiestand, 2008).

There are limits to what sport organizations and athletes will do to obtain television coverage, and these usually involve the issue of sharing control over the conditions of sports participation. For example, surfers have turned down television contracts because they didn't want television companies to dictate the conditions under which they would compete. The companies wanted events to occur at pre-scheduled times, even when waves were too dangerous, but most surfers have consistently decided that risking their lives was not worth the money.

Have the Media Corrupted Sports? Some people complain that dependence on the media, especially television, corrupts the "true nature" of sports. However, these people fail to take into account two factors:

1. *Sports are not shaped primarily by media.* The idea that television has somehow transformed the essential nature of sports does not hold up under careful examination. Sports are social constructions, and commercial sports are created over time through interactions among and between athletes, facility directors, sport team owners, event promoters, media representatives, sponsors, advertisers, agents, and spectators—all of whom have diverse interests. The dynamics of these interactions are grounded in power relations and shaped by the resources held by different people at different times. It is unrealistic to think that those who control the media can shape sports to fit their interests alone, but it is equally unrealistic to ignore their power.

2. *Media do not exist in a political and economic vacuum.* People who control commercial media are influenced by the social, political, and economic contexts in which they do business. Government agencies, policies, and laws regulate media in most nations.

Although media deregulation has occurred since the 1980s, the media must negotiate contracts with teams and leagues under legal constraints. Economic factors also constrain the media by setting limits on the values of sponsorships and advertising time and by influencing the climate in which pay-per-view sports and cable and satellite subscriptions might be profitable. Finally, the media are constrained by social factors, which influence people's decisions to consume sports.

Connections between media and commercial sports are grounded in complex sets of social, economic, and political relationships, which change over time and vary from society to society. These relationships limit the impact of media on sports. Media are influential, but to conclude that they corrupt sports is based on an incomplete understanding of how the social world works and how sports are connected with social relations in society.

With that said, it is also important to remember that nearly all of the most powerful people in sports around the world are CEOs or owners of major, global corporations. Nearly all of them are white men from English-speaking nations, and each wants to offer programming that people around the globe will watch and corporations will sponsor. The sports selected for national and global coverage depend on the media for their commercial success, and the salaries and endorsement income of top athletes also depend on media coverage (Delaney and Eckstein, 2008; Jeanrenaud and Kesenne, 2006; Nicholson, 2007; Raney and Bryant, 2006; Trumpbour, 2007). However, there are two sides to this process, as discussed in the following sections.

The Media Depend on Sports

Most media do not depend on sports. This is especially true for magazines, books, radio, film, and the Internet, although it is less true for newspapers and television. The Internet does not depend on sports, but certain online services make money when sports fans use the Internet to get up-to-the-minute scores, obtain insider information about particular events, participate in fantasy sports, place bets with offshore bookies, access coverage of events, and enter exclusive online chats about athletes, teams, and events.

Neither book publishing nor the film industry depends on sports. Until recently, there were very few successful books or films about sports. The urgency and uncertainty that are so compelling in live sports are difficult to capture in these media. However, since the late 1980s, both publishers and film studios have produced projects with tragic, inspiring, or outrageous stories about sports figures, including *Rocky* (1976) and its five sequels, *Hoop Dreams* (documentary, 1994), and *Million Dollar Baby* (2004) (Williams, 2006).

Many radio stations give coverage to sports only in their news segments, although local football, baseball, and men's basketball games often are broadcast live on local radio stations. Some communities have talk radio stations that feature sports talk programs that attract certain advertisers who want to reach young men with higher-than-average incomes. Most magazines devote little or no attention to sports coverage, although the number of general- and special-interest sport magazines and "fanzines" in the United States and other countries is significant. A visit to a local magazine rack shows that magazines are devoted to information about skiing, skateboarding, snowboarding, biking, motocross, car racing, and dozens of other sports.

The media most dependent on sports for commercial success are newspapers and television. This is especially true in the United States.

Newspapers Newspapers at the beginning of the twentieth century had a sports page, which consisted of a few notices about upcoming activities, a short story or two about races or college games, and possibly some scores of local games. Today, there are daily and weekly newspapers devoted exclusively to sports, and nearly all daily newspapers have sports sections often making up about 25 percent of their news content.

Major North American newspapers give more daily coverage to sports than any other single topic of interest, including business or politics. The sports section is the most widely read section of the paper. It accounts for at least one-third of the total circulation and a significant amount of the advertising revenues for big-city newspapers. It attracts advertisers who want to reach young to middle-aged males with ads for tires, automobile supplies, new cars, car leases, airline tickets for business travelers, alcoholic beverages, power tools, building supplies, sporting goods, hair-growth products, Viagra, testosterone, and hormone therapies. Additionally, there are ads for bars or clubs providing naked or near-naked female models and dancers, all-night massage parlors, and organizations offering gambling advice and opportunities (see a sample of major-city newspapers to confirm this). Ads for these products and services are unique to the (men's) sports section, and they generate needed revenues for newspapers.

As the Internet has become a primary source of information about big-time sports nationally and worldwide, many newspapers have established online sites for breaking news, regular columns, and blogs. Their print editions may contain this content, but they are beginning to focus more on local sports, including high school varsity teams, small college teams, and even youth sports. In fact, many major-city newspapers now publish weekly "prep sections" and regularly highlight local athletes.

Newspapers also are influenced by other aspects of a changing commercial environment. For example, some sport organizations, such as the NCAA, now sell "live Internet rights" to the same media companies that buy television rights to their events. At the same time, newspapers post more content online to generate income as subscriptions and ad revenues for their print version decline. This has led the NCAA in particular to redefine what it considers to be "news" and

As more people go online for coverage of national sports, city newspapers promote their coverage of local high school and college sports in an effort to maintain circulation rates and advertising income. (*Source:* Jay Coakley)

what newspapers can post online. Therefore, if newspaper journalists who possess credentials to cover NCAA events want to blog live, they must do so on the official NCAA site and *not* on their newspaper site. If journalists don't comply, the NCAA will revoke their press credentials, meaning that the newspaper will no longer have press access to live events.

Newspaper people argue that these restrictions infringe on their First Amendment rights ("freedom of the press") guaranteed by the U.S. Constitution, and the NCAA argues that it is rightfully protecting the contracted interests of its media partners—and its own financial interests

(Pickle, 2008). This disagreement raises important issues about the definition of "news" and "the press." Is blogging part of the press, and should bloggers be credentialed as "journalists" by sports organizations? Is everything written by a newspaper journalist considered to be news and therefore, protected by the U.S. Constitution? Can sport organizations define "news" to maintain their financial interests, and does this violate the notion that sports are part of the public trust because they are defined as unique public activities and often subsidized with public money? These are some of the questions raised by new media; many more will be raised in the future.

Television Some television companies in North America also depend on sports for programming content and advertising revenues. Sports are a major part of the programming schedules of national television networks and many cable/satellite companies. Television companies even create and sponsor events that they promote and televise, such as ESPN's ownership and presentation of the X Games. This approach has become increasingly common worldwide: if there are not enough mega-events to generate media profits, media companies will create them (Horne and Manzenreiter, 2006b).

Sports account for a growing proportion of income for television companies, which use sport programming to attract viewers and subscribers with demographic profiles that advertisers wish to target. For example, ESPN's multiple networks (ESPN, ESPN2, ESPNews, ESPN Classic, ESPN Deportes, ESPN HD, ESPN Today, ESPNU, and ESPN International) reach people in all but a few nations in the world. These networks provide content for ESPN.com, ESPN Radio, ESPN Deportes Radio, ESPN Broadband, ESPN Mobile, ESPNDeportes.com, ESPNRadio.com, ESPNSoccernet.com, EXPN.com, ESPN Radio, ESPN The Magazine, Bassmaster Magazine, BASS Times, ESPN Books, ESPN Interactive, ESPN On Demand, ESPN 360, ESPN HD, and ESPN2 HD. And all of these create consumer demand for products available at ESPN Zone, TeamStore@ ESPN, and Fishing Tackle Retailer. This is the current model for media organization.

Both ESPN and Fox became major television networks after they risked massive amounts of money to buy the rights to cover NFL games in 1987 and 1993, respectively. The risk paid off and both companies grew and increased their profits. Today, Fox Sports and other Fox networks televise a range of sports around the world. Additionally, there are dozens of multimedia companies that broadcast sports, including CSTV, a twenty-four-hour college sports television network that combines with CSTV.com, college sports radio, and SIRIUS College Sports Radio. Others include the Sports Network, Turner Sports Network, OLN (Outdoor Life Network), the Tennis Channel, Blackbelt TV, MLB.com, NBA TV, and The Football Network. The prime-time broadcast audience has declined in recent years, but more people view sports outside of prime time and use the websites sponsored by the same media companies that present broadcasts.

An attractive feature of sport programming for the major U.S. networks (ABC, CBS, Fox, and NBC) is that events often are scheduled on Saturdays and Sundays—the slowest days of the week for general television viewing. Sport events are the most popular weekend programs, especially among male viewers who may not watch much television at other times. For example, NFL games are the most-watched TV programs among men aged eighteen to forty-nine years old, and networks can sell advertising time at relatively high rates during what normally would be dead time for programming.

> **ON THE *OLC*:**
> See the OLC—Additional Readings for Chapter 12—for the author's essay on the marriage of mutual interest between U.S. media networks and the International Olympic Committee.

Media corporations also use sport programming to attract commercial sponsors that might invest advertising dollars elsewhere if television stations did not cover certain sports. For example, games in major men's team sports are ideal for promoting sales of beer, life insurance, trucks and cars, computers, investment services, credit cards, and air travel. Advertising executives in major corporations realize that sports attract male viewers who make business decisions related to travel and equipment purchases and often make family decisions for purchases of beer, cars, computers, investments, and life insurance.

Golf and tennis are special cases for television programming. They attract few viewers and the ratings are exceptionally low, but the audience for these sports is very attractive to certain advertisers. It comprises people from upper income groups, including many professionals and business executives. This is why television coverage of golf and tennis is sponsored by companies selling luxury cars and high-priced sports cars, business and personal computers, imported beers, investment opportunities with brokers and consultants, and trips to exclusive vacation areas. This is also why the networks continue to carry these programs despite low ratings. Advertisers will pay high fees to reach high-income consumers and corporate executives who make decisions to buy thousands of "company cars" and computers at the same time that they invest millions of dollars for employee pension plans or 401k plans. With such valued viewers, golf and tennis don't need high ratings to sell their television rights for high fees.

In the mid-1990s, television executives "discovered" women viewers and women's sports. Data indicate that women have constituted more than half the audiences for both Winter and Summer Olympic Games since 1988. This led NBC to hype and focus on women's sports, appeal to female viewers during recent telecasts of the games, and emphasize gender equity in scripted studio commentary.

Other women's sports also attract television coverage although the amount pales in comparison with coverage of men's sports. Women's events don't receive more coverage partly because female viewers of women's games have not been identified as a target demographic by advertisers who reach women through other means. Furthermore, men make up over half the viewing audience for most women's sports, but they also watch men's sports where sponsors already advertise.

Specialized cable and satellite television companies attract advertising money by covering sports that appeal to clearly identified segments of consumers. The X Games, for example, attract young males between twelve and thirty years old, which in turn attracts corporate sponsors selling soft drinks, beer, telecommunications products, and sports equipment such as helmets, shoes, skateboards, and dozens of other sport-specific products.

Over the past two decades, television companies have paid rapidly increasing amounts of money for the rights to televise certain sports, as indicated in Table 12.1. The contracts for these rights are negotiated every few years. In the case of the major men's spectator sports, contracts involve hundreds of millions of dollars for each league and the rights for the Olympics, the NFL, NASCAR, NCAA Men's College Basketball Tournament, soccer's World Cup, and premier-level soccer in England are currently around $1 billion.

Table 12.2 shows that in the United States nineteen of the top twenty-five television programs in U.S. history have been Super Bowls, that the cost of advertising on the top sport events is generally much higher than it is for other types of programs ($3.1 million for a thirty-second slot during the 2009 Super Bowl), that sports events involve minimal production costs, and that they have relatively predictable ratings. Television companies occasionally lose money on sports programming, but profits and other benefits are usually worth any risks. Furthermore, regular sports programming is a platform to promote other programs and boost ratings during the rest of the week; and it enhances the image and legitimacy of television among people who watch little other than sports.

As choices for sports television viewing have increased, audiences have fragmented and ratings for many sports have declined, especially during prime-time hours, even as the total number of people watching television sports has remained relatively steady. This means that rights fees for the very large events will remain high, but fees for other events, including "special-interest" events such as bowling, in-line skating

Table 12.2 The top twenty-five U.S. network telecasts as ranked by average household ratings

Program	Date	Average Household Rating (in millions of households)*
1. M*A*S*H* (special)	2/28/83	50.2
	1/24/82	49.1
2. Super Bowl XVI		
3. Winter Olympics	2/23/94†	45.7
4. Super Bowl XXX	1/28/96	44.2
5. Super Bowl XXXII	1/25/98	43.6
6. Super Bowl XXXIV	1/30/00	43.6
	2/3/08	43.3
7. Super Bowl XLII		
8. Super Bowl XXVIII	1/30/94	42.9
9. Super Bowl XXXVI	2/3/02	42.6
10. Cheers	1/20/93	42.4
	2/4/07	42.0
11 Super Bowl XLI		
12. Super Bowl XXXI		
	1/26/97	42.0
13. Super Bowl XXVII	1/31/93	42.0
14. Super Bowl XL	2/5/06	41.6
15. Winter Olympics	2/25/94†	41.5
16. Super Bowl XX	1/26/86	41.5
17. Dallas	11/21/80	41.5
18. Super Bowl XXXVIII	2/1/04	41.4
19. Super Bowl XXXV	1/28/01	41.3
20. Super Bowl XXXIX	2/6/05	41.1
21. Super Bowl XXXVII	1/26/03	40.7
22. Seinfeld	5/14/98	40.5
23. Super Bowl XVII	1/30/83	40.5
24. Super Bowl XXI	1/25/87	40.0
25. Super Bowl XVI	1/24/84	40.0

Source: Based on cumulative data from A. C. Nielsen as of March 1, 2008.
*Numbers refer to the average number of households tuned in to the program from the start to the end of the telecast; average telecast for a Super Bowl game is about 210 minutes (although it contains less than 15 minutes of football action).
†Telecasts on these days featured women's figure skating—specifically, the programs skated by Nancy Kerrigan and Tonya Harding.

championships, and international skiing races will be limited. When interest in special events is especially strong among particular viewers, pay-per-view (PPV) sports programming can push rights fees to high levels; this continues to occur for championship boxing, professional wrestling, and mixed martial arts. PPV can generate massive revenues, but events must be chosen selectively because most people are not willing to pay upfront for a single event on television. In the meantime, pay TV has become part of people's lives in the form of subscription fees for cable and satellite connections and special sports channels and packages. Such subscription fees in the United States increased nearly 400 percent between 1985 and 2008, partly due to rights fees paid by cable and satellite companies to leagues and sport governing bodies.

Finally, sports programming has been used as a centerpiece for the global expansion of emerging sport networks. For example, in 1994, Rupert Murdoch, owner of News Corp and Fox Television Network, successfully used the coverage of sports to leverage his acquisition of local television affiliates around the United States and thereby compete with ABC, CBS, and NBC. Murdoch also used sports coverage as part of a global expansion strategy. He has been successful, and his News Corp conglomerate is the most powerful media organization in the world.

Other corporations have used their ownership of sports rights and programming as a key component of their mergers and acquisitions in the entertainment, news, sports, television, and Internet industries. This economic strategy influences which sports programs we see and don't see, what we hear and don't hear in commentary, the existence of certain types of online sites that we are likely to visit, and the corporate messages presented in connection with athletes, teams, events, and sport places. More important, it has implications for the viability of democracy around the world because democracy depends on the free flow of information from diverse sources. When only a few corporations control the media, the flow of ideas is restricted—and cable and satellite fees increase, if they are not regulated.

Sports and the Media: A Relationship Fueled by Economics and Ideology

Commercial spectator sports depend heavily on the media, although noncommercial sports continue to exist and often thrive without media coverage. Similarly, some media companies that publish daily newspapers in the United States and produce television programs depend on sports to generate circulation and viewer ratings.

When large corporations control the media, the interdependence of sports and the media revolves around revenue streams and profits.

Sports generate identifiable audiences that can be sold to capitalists seeking consumers for products and services. In turn, the media generate revenues for sport organizations and create sport-related images, which can be sold in connection with everything from coffee mugs and credit cards to sweat suits and soccer balls.

Since the 1970s, global economic factors have intensified the interdependence between commercial sports and the media. Major transnational corporations have needed vehicles to develop global name recognition, cultural legitimacy, and product familiarity. They also want to promote ideologies that support a way of life based on consumption, competition, and individual achievement. Media sports offer global corporations a means of meeting these needs: Certain sport events attract worldwide attention; satellite technology takes television signals around the world; sport images are associated with recognizable symbols and pleasurable experiences by billions of people; sports and athletes usually can be presented in politically safe ways by linking them with local identities and then using them to market products, values, and lifestyles related to local cultures or popular forms of global culture (Maguire, J., 2005; Maguire et al., 2008b). Therefore, powerful transnational corporations now spend billions of dollars annually to sponsor the media coverage of sports. This in turn gives global media companies significant power over sports worldwide.

Finally, many male executives of large media corporations are dedicated sports fans, and they like to be associated with sports as sponsors. Masculine culture is deeply embedded in most of the corporations that they control, and they use their sponsorship money to receive VIP (very important person) treatment at sports events and reaffirm the legitimacy of the masculinized corporate cultures in the organizations they control. Furthermore, they use sport events to entertain clients, fellow executives, and friends as they pay with company credit cards. This combination of masculine ideology and government-supported

A few powerful global media companies control most of the media representations of sports worldwide. This monopoly has serious implications for what sports we see or don't see.

tax deductions for sport entertainment in the United States is a key factor in the media dependence on sports.

The long-time marriage of sports and the media is clearly held together and strengthened by vast amounts of money from corporations whose executives use sports as tools for promoting profits and ideologies consistent with their personal and corporate interests. Ideology is a key factor in the sport–media marriage. This is not a marriage based solely on money, but the goal of the sport–media partnership is to create a global family of eager consumers.

IMAGES AND NARRATIVES IN MEDIA SPORTS

To say that sports are "mediated" is to say that they consist of selected images and narratives. Much research in the sociology of sport has deconstructed these images and narratives and analyzed the ideas or themes on which they are based. The scholars who have done these studies assume that media sports are symbolic constructions, much like Hollywood action films, television soap operas, and Disney cartoons (Andrews and Jackson, 2001; Bruce, 2007; Crawford, 2004; Rowe, 2004a, 2004b; Whannel, 2002).

To say that a telecast of an American football game is a symbolic construction means that it presents the ideas that certain people have about football, values, social life, and the characteristics of the viewing audience. Although each of us interprets media images and narratives differently, many of us use mediated sports as reference points as we form, revise, and extend our ideas about sports, social life, and social relations.

Because media sports are part of everyday experience today, it's important to consider the following:

1. The media construction of sports
2. The ideological themes underlying media coverage
3. The influence of media coverage on those who consume it

The Media Construction of Sports

When media are privately owned and organized to make financial profits, sports are selected for coverage on the basis of their entertainment

breaking BARRIERS

Image and Narrative Barriers
From a Special-Interest Story to a Sports Story

Athletes with a disability receive little or no media coverage. The Paralympics, for example, have seldom been televised or covered in newspapers in the United States, even though they occur only once every four years. World Championships and other major events receive no mainstream-media coverage.

Most people who make decisions about media coverage assume that covering disability sports is a poor commercial risk. Additionally, most media people have never played or even seen disability sports, so they lack the words and experiences that would enable them to provide coverage that might build a media audience.

Research shows that when disability sports have been covered in mainstream media, athletes often are portrayed as "courageous victims" or as "heroic super-crips" who engage in inspiring athletic performances—they're always described as "inspiring." When sociologist Ian Brittain (2004) analyzed this coverage he found that media images and narratives usually fell into one of the following categories:

Patronizing—"Aren't they marvelous! They're so courageous."
Curiosity—"Let's see if she can do this!"
Tragedy—"On that fateful day, his life was changed forever."
Inspiration—"She's an inspiration—a true hero and role model."
Mystification—"I can't believe he just did that! That chair must be jet-propelled."
Pity—"He tried his best without a leg, so let's give him a hand."

Surprise—"Stay tuned and see physical feats you can't imagine!"

Images and narratives organized around these seven themes construct disability in terms of a medical model—focusing on personal impairments that must be overcome. This treatment ignores *why* particular social meanings are given to disabilities and *how* they shape the lives of many people with specific impairments (Brittain, 2004; Smith and Thomas, 2005). Consequently, media coverage often perpetuates the belief that disabilities are abnormalities and that people with disabilities have one-dimensional identities based on abnormalities.

AT YOUR *fingertips*   For more information on the medical model, see Chapter 2, *Breaking Barriers*, pp. 50–51.

Despite these misguided media representations, most athletes with a disability will accept distorted coverage rather than have no coverage at all. Like other athletes, they want to be acknowledged for their physical competence, but they also hope that by being visible in the media, they can challenge traditional stereotypes and make people aware of the need to maximize access and inclusion in all spheres of society.

Developing a media audience for disability sports begins at the local, recreational level. This point is made by Jil Gravink, founder and director of Northeast

value and revenue-generating potential. Media images and narratives are selected to represent the event so it meets the perceived interests of the audience and sponsors. Sports that are difficult to cover profitably usually are ignored by the media or covered only with selected highlights.

Sports coverage generally consists of images and narratives that exaggerate the spectacular,

such as heroic injuries or achievements; invent and highlight rivalries; and explain why events are important. Furthermore, they strive to create and maintain the celebrity status of athletes and teams. Cultural studies scholar Garry Crawford explains:

The mass media construction of celebrity often lacks depth of character, as figures are frequently painted in one-dimensional terms. . . . Much of

People in the media often treat the Paralympics as a special-interest story rather than a sports story. This is not an effective way to break down stereotypes, and it doesn't give the athletes the credit they deserve for their training and achievements. (*Source:* David Biene; photo courtesy of Ossur)

Passage, an organization that develops local programs that increase the relevance of disability sports for people with disabilities and the general population in a community. The programs provide opportunities for (dis)abled and temporarily able-bodied people to interact, play sports, and identify one another in terms of multiple characteristics and abilities.

Gravink explains that only when average people with disabilities play sports and become fully integrated into the community can disability sports "move from a special interest story to a sport story" (in Joukowsky and Rothstein, 2002a, p. 98). Only then will "courageous victims" and "heroic supercrips" be exposed for the myths they are.

the language used to describe sport stars . . . draws on the narrative of melodrama. Heroes rise and fall, villains are defeated, and women play out their roles as supporting cast members to men's central dramatic roles (2004, p. 133).

Narratives even redeem villains who demonstrate that they can be heroic warriors, with commentators often describing them as "loyal blue-collar players"—"willing to take figurative bullets for their teammates"—and "always being there when the chips are down," even if they sometimes have been nasty and broken rules in the past.

The major media also emphasize elite sport competition (Crawford, 2004; Horne and Manzenreiter, 2006b). For example, U.S.

newspapers and television networks increased their coverage of professional sports through the twentieth century and decreased coverage of amateur sports, except for big-time college football and men's basketball. This shift was accompanied by a growing emphasis on the importance of winning and heroic actions and the desire to attract corporate sponsors and a mass audience. It's important to understand this process and the ways that particular images and narratives in media coverage inform popular ideas about sports and about social relations and social life in general. This topic is discussed below and in the Breaking Barriers box on pages 416–417.

Ideological Themes in Media Images and Narratives

Sports are complex and are represented in the media through images and narratives that are selected from a vast array of possibilities (Knoppers and Elling, 2004). The traditional media resemble windows through which we view what others choose to put in our range of sight and hear what others choose to say. Therefore, the only way to avoid being duped is to become a critical media consumer or work with others to create grassroots media representations of sports.

To become a critical media consumer involves learning to identify the ideologies that guide others as they construct media representations for us. In the case of sports, the most central ideologies that influence what we see and hear are those related to success, consumption, gender, race, ethnicity, and nationality.

ON THE *OLC*:
See the OLC—Additional Readings for Chapter 12—for a discussion of additional ideological themes central in U.S. sports media coverage (nationalism, individualism, teamwork, aggression).

Success as a Theme in Media Representations of Sports   Media coverage of sports in the United States emphasizes success through individual effort, self-control, competition, teamwork, aggression, adherence to rules, and effective game plans; also important are big individual plays such as home runs, long touchdown passes, and single-handed goals. The idea that success can be based on empathy, support for others, sharing resources, autonomy, intrinsic satisfaction, personal growth, compromise, incremental changes, or the achievement of equality is seldom included in media representations of sports, even though these elements are there. This was highlighted in 2008 when a college softball player hit a home run over the fence in a crucial game, turned her ankle on first base, and was carried around the bases by her opponents because the umpire ruled (mistakenly) that her teammates could not help her around the bases without nullifying her home run—which would cause her team to lose the game. The actions of the opposing players encouraged people to acknowledge that sports are much more than what is normally represented in media coverage.

Media representations exaggerate the importance of competitive rivalries as well as winning and losing in athletes' lives. For example, ESPN has organized its coverage of the X Games around the competitive quest for medals when, in fact, many of the athletes and the spectators aren't very concerned about competition or medals (Honea, 2005). Athletes in the X Games and similar events enjoy the external rewards that come with winning, and they certainly want to demonstrate their competence, but they often emphasize self-expression and creativity more than the final scores determined by official judges. Furthermore, friendships with others in the event are more important than media-hyped rivalries and competitive outcomes. However, media narratives highlight rivalries and the desire to win because this reaffirms widely accepted cultural values and can be used to attract sponsors and consumers who may not understand the culture and skills possessed by athletes in action sports.

The success ideology regularly emphasized in U.S. media coverage is less apparent in the coverage that occurs in other nations. Narratives in the United States focus on winners, records, and final scores. Even silver and bronze Olympic medals are often viewed as consolation prizes, and games for third place are seldom played or covered by the media. The "We're number 1" conceptualization of success that is so common among Americans is seldom used as a media focus in other nations where tie scores are acceptable competitive outcomes and aren't seen as the equivalent of "kissing your sister."

Sportswriters and announcers in the United States focus on "shootouts," sudden-death play-offs, dominating others, and big plays or big hits. Rare are references to learning, enjoyment, and competing with others, even though many players see their participation in these terms. Thus, the media don't "tell it like it is" as much as they tell it to reaffirm a discourse of competitive success that closely matches the interests of sponsors and advertisers. This ideological bias does not undermine the enjoyment of sports for most people, but it ignores that there are many ways to enjoy sports, even when they are organized to promote corporate interests.

Consumption Themes in Media Representations of Sports The emphasis on consumption is clear in most media coverage of sports (Scherer, 2007; Scherer and Jackson, 2008). About 20 percent of televised sports in the United States consists of commercial time. Ads fill newspapers and magazines, and Internet sites use multiple strategies to present ads mixed with content. "TV time-outs" are now standard in football, basketball, and hockey games. And announcers remind media spectators that "This game is being brought to you by [corporate name]."

Commercials are so central in the telecast of the Super Bowl that the media audience is polled to rate them. Audiences for media sports

are encouraged to express their connections to teams and athletes by purchasing thousands of branded objects. For example, Florida State proudly sells its mascot, Chief Osceola, on stadium seat cushions, bean bag chairs, kitchen cutting boards, car floor mats, and napkins so that fans can sit on, cut on, stand on, and wipe their mouths with images of their honored chief. This is clearly consistent with consumer ideology in American society. "You are what you buy" is one of the tenets of a market economy, and Florida State fans become "Seminoles" by consuming "their chief."

Gender Themes in Media Representations of Sports Masculinity rules in media sports (Kian, Vincent, and Mondello, 2008). Men's sports receive about 90 percent of the coverage in all the media, and both images and narratives tend to reproduce traditional ideas and beliefs about gender (Messner, 2007a, section 4). For example, after buying rights to telecast National Hockey League games in 2005–2007, the vice president of programming said that OLN (Outdoor Life Network) was "very male-oriented" and emphasized competition by showing sports that involved "man versus man, man versus nature, man versus beast" (in Bechtel and Cannella, 2005, p. 17). Therefore, it wasn't surprising in 2006 when the U.S. version of the Canadian company changed its name to Versus (versus.com) and now covers World Extreme Cagefighting, World Combat League, Professional Bull Riders events, big game hunting and killing, and similar sports that idealize traditional masculinity.

Coverage of women's sports has not been a media priority, but since the mid-1990s it has been taken more seriously in connection with the Olympics, figure skating events, major tennis and golf tournaments, and some professional and college basketball games. Soccer received attention in 1999 when the U.S. Women's team won the World Cup and were described as the "(middle-class, white) girls next door" and "babe city." People even sexualized Brandi Chastain's spontaneous removal of her jersey—a common celebratory action in men's elite soccer—after scoring the winning goal in the final match against China. But coverage of women's soccer now occurs only when the World Cup is being played (2003 and 2007).

Overall, the coverage of women's sports in major newspapers remains less than 15 percent of the sports section in U.S. papers and even less in major papers in most other countries. Sports magazines have been notoriously slow to cover female athletes and women's sports, although they frequently include sexualized images of women in ads accompanying the coverage of men's sports (Bishop, 2003). This pattern of underrepresentation of women's sports in the media exists worldwide.

Coverage of women's sports has increased in some cases, but it is uneven and does not support a pattern of consistent growth. Recent research suggests that for a few major sport events that generate global interest, such as the Olympic Games and the Wimbledon Tennis Championships, women athletes are treated seriously and occasionally receive as much coverage as men receive (Crossman, Vincent, and Speed, 2007; King, 2007). But this is not true in everyday media coverage of sports. For example, a longitudinal study of sport news on the ABC, CBS, and NBC stations in Los Angeles and on ESPN's Sports Center and Fox's Southern California Sports Report indicates that between 1989 and 2004 the coverage given to women's sports peaked in 1999 at 8.7 percent and fell to 6.3 percent in 2004. Women were featured in less than 3 percent of the highlights shown on the ESPN and Fox programs in 2004, when the proportion of coverage given to women's sports was about the same as it had been in 1989, despite significant increases in women's sport participation over those 15 years (Duncan and Messner, 2005; see Chapter 2).

Tennis receives about one-third of all coverage given to women's sports on the major networks, although this varies depending on the physical appearance of high-profile players. When Maria Sharapova plays, she receives extensive coverage. Anticipating her participation in a major tournament, a Fox Sports announcer introduced a segment on his show by saying, "She's young, she's talented, and very beautiful, but can [she] stay focused tonight?"; another sport news "teaser" before a commercial said, "They slapped her on a billboard that read 'the closer you get, the hotter it gets'" (in Duncan and Messner, 2005, p. 15). But despite male announcers who talk about Sharapova differently from the way they talk about physically attractive male athletes, most television coverage of women's sports no longer trivializes female athletes as it has in the past. Sport talk shows still make women the butt of jokes, but this is accepted only among men who have trouble talking about women as athletes; apparently, they find it easier to pretend that they're still in the boys' locker room where girls are the focus of adolescent male fantasies.

Olympic media coverage in the United States highlights women gymnasts, swimmers, and divers in the Summer Games and women figure skaters and skiers in the Winter Games. But individual sports have consistently received more coverage than team sports, except for the coverage of two-person women's beach volleyball during the 2008 Olympic Games in Beijing. The men's sports most often covered in the media emphasize physical strength, speed, size, and the use of physical force and intimidation to dominate opponents—attributes consistent with traditional images of masculinity.

Men's sport events often are promoted or described as if they had special historical importance, whereas women's sports events usually are promoted in a less dramatic manner (Kian, Vincent, and Mondello, 2008). Men's events usually are unmarked by references to gender, whereas women's events almost always are referred to as women's events. For instance, there has always been "The World Cup" and "The Women's World Cup" in soccer coverage. This terminology reflects the low priority given

Football is the most popular media sport in the United States (Carroll, 2007). The coverage reproduces traditional gender ideology. (*Source:* University of Colorado Media Relations)

to women's sports in all media. For example, when *Sports Illustrated* published in 2002 a list of the best 100 sport books of all time, only three books about women's sports were on the list: one on a high school basketball team (number 65), one on figure skating (number 81), and one on figure skating and gymnastics (number 100) (McEntegart et al., 2002).

ERASING HOMOSEXUALITY Homosexuality is ignored in nearly all media coverage, whereas heterosexuality is regularly acknowledged directly and indirectly in men's and women's sports. Heterosexual female athletes are repeatedly shown with husbands, children, fiancés and boyfriends; heterosexual men are featured with their wives in the *Sports Illustrated* swimsuit edition, although their heterosexuality is so widely taken for granted that it is mentioned

only in passing. Gay athletes are assumed to be absent from sports. Lesbian images are carefully erased from coverage, even though the partners of players and coaches are known and visible to many spectators (Collins, 2004; Kian, Vincent, and Mondello, 2008). Lesbian relationships are ignored for fear of offending media audiences and "damaging" the image of sports.

Lesbian athletes in golf, tennis, and basketball aren't profiled to acknowledge partners or certain aspects of their lifestyles—those parts of their personal stories are not told. In media-constructed sport reality, lesbians and gay men in sports generally are invisible unless they publicly come "out" as gay. Even then, they are marginalized in coverage. "Homosexuality doesn't sell" beyond a coming-out announcement (Creedon, 1998, p. 96), whereas heterosexual athletes and their partners are discussed and pictured in everything from the

Sports Illustrated swimsuit edition to the television coverage of postgame victory celebrations, and nobody accuses these heterosexual athletes and coaches of pushing their values and agendas on others.

Living in a heterosexual-dominated culture is especially difficult for female coaches and players who want to acknowledge the support they receive from longtime same-sex partners. As the spouses of heterosexual athletes and coaches share the spotlight after important victories, lesbian and gay partners remain in the stands or at home wondering if their very existence could jeopardize their partners' careers. Completely unknown are the men who discreetly watch their male partners win Super Bowls, World Series titles, Stanley Cup championships, and NBA titles. To the media, they are invisible.

MEDIA ORGANIZATIONS ARE GENDERED Traditional gender patterns in media coverage have been slow to change partly because sports media organizations worldwide have cultures and structures that are deeply gendered. They've been organized and scheduled around men's sports, just like the work routines and assignments of sport reporters. Therefore, the coverage of women's events often requires changes in institutionalized patterns of sports media work. Furthermore, the vast majority of sports media personnel are men, and the highest-status assignments in sports media are those that deal with men's sports.

Female reporters and announcers today understand that their upward mobility in the sports media industry demands that they cover men's events in much the same ways that men cover them. If they insist on covering only women's events or if they are assigned only to women's events, they won't move up the corporate ladder in media organizations (Coventry, 2004). Advancement also may be limited if they insist on covering men's sports in new ways that don't reaffirm the "correctness" of the coverage patterns and styles developed by men. Although

women in the print media regularly cover men's sports, very few women have done regular commentary for men's sports in the electronic media apart from occasional "sideline reporters" who often are expected to look cute and talk to the guys as if they were at a "frat house" with no other women around (White, 2005). One of the increasing exceptions to this pattern occurred in 2008 when Doris Burke was a color commentator for NBA playoff games. Online comments, nearly all from men, were generally supportive of Burke and appreciated her competence. But a few men were upset. One stated, "I just don't want to hear a woman caller announce *my* game" (emphasis added), and another wrote, "I watched the entire 2nd half on mute because everytime i hear her talk it ruins the game for me" (www.topix.com/forum/sports/TG03GH7SCF1NSMMQ0).

Female reporters who cover men's sports are more readily accepted in the locker rooms of men's teams than they were in the past, although male athletes and coaches have been very protective of this masculinized space where men have had total control (Ricchiardi, 2005). Changes have occurred partly because men have discovered clever ways to maintain their privacy, such as wearing a robe and having designated interview times—just as female athletes have always done and continue to do when male reporters cover their events. However, it took the men nearly two decades to even think of wearing a robe because deeply rooted gender ideology impeded their ability to think creatively and responsively.

The sports coverage most often consumed by boys in the United States depicts aggression and violence as normal and exciting, portrays athletes who play in pain as heroes, uses military metaphors and terminology, and highlights conflict between individuals and teams (Messner, Hunt, and Dunbar, 1999). Women are seldom seen except when portrayed in sexual terms, or as cheerleaders, spectators, and supportive spouses and mothers on the sidelines.

reflect on SPORTS

Meet the Press:
It's Not Always Easy for Female Athletes

Johnny Miller is a former pro golfer. In July 2002, he was the NBC analyst covering the U.S. Women's Open. Julie Inkster, a forty-two-year-old veteran of the women's tour and winner of many tournaments, had just won the Open, the most prestigious event of the season. Miller met her as she was declared the winner and said excitedly, "It's big stuff when you win at 42. You're supposed to be home cooking meals at 42—you'd think, for most women." Apparently, when Miller looked at this champion golfer, he saw a mother and wife, standing in the kitchen preparing meals for her two children and husband. His vision was blurred by an ideology that distracted him as he interviewed a long-time champion golfer who had just won the most important tournament of the year.

Miller knew he'd made a mistake in allowing his gender ideology to influence his spontaneous comment. Inkster was gracious in her response, saying that she had achieved balance in her life by coordinating her career and family life. She was tactful as she dealt with Miller's gendered view of her, and she focused on her excitement about playing better golf than any woman in the world during the previous three days.

A few months before Miller interviewed Inkster, Tiffany Milbrett, the best soccer player in the United States during the 2002 professional Women's United Soccer Association season, was being photographed for a magazine story about her. During the photo shoot, the photographer asked her to remove her bra. Milbrett was shocked at the request. Without hesitating, she stated, "I'm not a model. I'm an athlete. I only want to make money doing my trade. The rest I don't really care for. I don't give a rat's ass about being sexy" (in Adelson, 2002, p. 76).

Like Milbrett, many young female athletes face a dilemma when people in the media insist on sexualizing them. They must decide if they should just play sports and hope they will be rewarded as athletes or if they should also present their bodies in sexualized terms to attract attention, sponsors, and media support. Milbrett decided against allowing her body to be sexualized, but other female athletes either conform to or exploit expectations based on traditional ideas and beliefs about what women should be.

When Anita Marks, the quarterback for the Miami Fury in the Independent Women's Football League, explained her appearance in *Playboy* magazine, she said, "Women in sport need to have two personas. What they believe is right is not going to make them money. It isn't going to make you famous" (in Adelson, 2002, p. 76). Marks let the photographers call the shots, although she chose from a limited and highly gendered set of alternatives to do what she hoped would make her famous.

Brandi Chastain took a different approach when she posed nude in *Gear* magazine. She stressed that she had "worked her ass off" to get her body in shape and was proud to have her physical strength and beauty represented in the media. Some female athletes agree with Chastain, and others do not.

Many people find it difficult to analyze these issues. In the case of Miller's interview with Inkster, should cultural definitions of gender and their consequences be irrelevant in media coverage, even though they have influenced athletes' lives? Can meaningful interviews be conducted with athletes so that ideological factors are recognized without legitimizing or perpetuating them, especially when they have disadvantaged entire categories of people in society?

In the case of Milbrett, Marks, Chastain, and other female athletes, such as Formula One racecar driver Danica Patrick and tennis player Maria Sharapova, what are the guidelines and limits for media representations of athletes' bodies? More to the point, who should determine those guidelines and limits, and what can be done to increase the chances that those determinations will be based on critically informed choices? Tiffany Milbrett, along with many other female athletes, doesn't "give a rat's ass" about being sexy, at least in front of a camera under conditions that do not match her sense of herself (Thorpe, 2008). But, if other athletes choose to be represented as sexy in the media, should they be targets of criticism and defined as "bad" for women's sports?

These questions are best answered if we consider issues of power and ideology: if female athletes had the power to control their media representations *and* they critically understood the importance of media images in our culture, it would be much easier for them to decide how they wished to meet the press. But that leaves the toughest question unanswered: How do women gain that power in sports and society? *What do you think?*

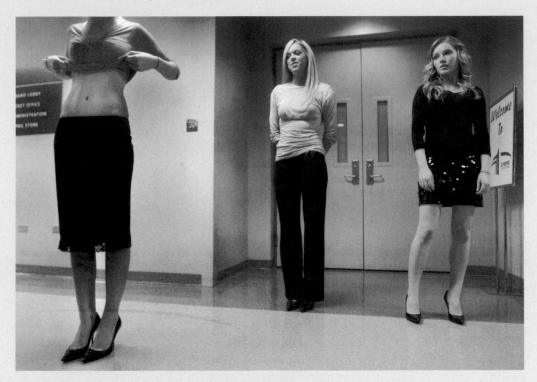

The gendered choices faced by athletes are also faced by women who apply for cheerleading and dance teams in men's professional sports. The bodies of these women are being assessed to see if they meet the criteria of the "judges" for an NBA team. If they do, they will be allowed to try out. In the process, the women view one another in objectified ways, as this photo illustrates. If these women had the power to choose how they are included and represented in sports, would they choose this? (Evan Semon; Rocky Mountain News/Polaris)

Overall, gender ideology continues to influence media representations of sports (Curry, Arriagada, and Cornwell, 2002; Thorpe, 2008). This is highlighted in the box "Meet the Press." However, it is important to note that many of us who consume media coverage of sports do not accept media representations at face value. We make sense of representations in our own terms although we are heavily influenced by the cultures in which we have been socialized. When we have special knowledge or personal connections with a sport or the athletes involved, we often give our own meanings to media representations, even if we are not critical in our assessments of them (Bruce, 2007; van Sterkenburg and Knoppers, 2004).

Race, Ethnicity, and Nationality Themes in Media Representations of Sports

Just as gender ideology influences media coverage, so does racial and ethnic ideology and the stereotypes associated with it (Bruce, 2004, 2007; Curry, Arriagada, and Cornwell, 2002; Davis and Harris, 1998; Kian, Vincent, and Mondello, 2008; van Sterkenburg and Knoppers, 2004). For example, in 1935, Grantland Rice, often identified by white journalists as the best sportswriter of the early twentieth century, described black heavyweight boxing champion Joe Louis as the "brown cobra" and wrote that Louis brought into the boxing ring "the speed of the jungle, the instinctive speed of the wild" (in Mead, 1985, p. 91). Louis was described very differently in the black press, but millions of whites read Rice's words and accepted them without question.

Of course, racial ideology and stereotypes were revised during the second half of the twentieth century, and white announcers commonly described black athletes as having natural abilities, good instincts, unique physical attributes, and tendencies to be undisciplined players; references to "jungle" and "the wild" were replaced with racialized code words such as "the ghetto," and more recently, "the streets." At the same time, white journalists described white athletes as hard-working, intelligent, highly disciplined, and driven by character rather than instincts (Bruce, 2004, 2007; Davis and Harris, 1998).

Research in the 1970s and 1980s discredited the assumed factual basis of racial and ethnic stereotypes at the same time that media studies identified the ways that ideology influenced sport stories and commentaries, particularly in reference to black athletes. This made white journalists and commentators increasingly aware that

the quality of their work depended on avoiding words and inferences based on discredited racial stereotypes (Sabo et al., 1996). As a result, most of them became more critical about what they wrote and said, and they chose their words more carefully.

But making these changes was difficult for whites who accepted dominant racial ideology and had never viewed it critically or from the perspectives of blacks, Latinos, Asians, and Native Americans. Some made careless or naïve mistakes, and a few media people were fired for them. For example, a white sport talk-radio host in San Francisco was fired in 2005 when he complained that the local Giants baseball team was losing games because its "brain-dead Caribbean hitters" lacked the discipline to avoid swinging at bad pitches, and because Felipe Alou, the team's Latino manager, had a mind that had "turned to Cream of Wheat." The white station manager felt that these comments were "good for ratings," so he played them repeatedly on the following day's programs. The other white host on the show added to the controversy by mocking Felipe Alou's response to his cohost's comments. Neither the hosts nor the program manager knew anything about the perspectives or experiences of Latino players or about the blatant and consistent racism that Felipe Alou had endured quietly as an all-star player on the Giants forty-five years earlier. Most white listeners were outraged by the firings, apparently thinking that insensitivity and a lack of knowledge about baseball players were not sufficient reasons for terminating people paid to know and comment about baseball.

Avoiding stereotypes and covering racial and ethnic relations in an informed way are two different things. Sports coverage today pretends that race and ethnicity don't exist; it assumes that sports is a racially and ethnically level playing field and that everyone in sports faces the same challenges and odds for success. But race and ethnicity are influential to such an extent that people cannot talk about them without discovering real, meaningful, and socially important racial and ethnic differences in what they think and feel. Ignoring this story about real differences allows whites in the media and media audiences to be comfortably color blind and deny the legacy and continuing relevance of skin color and cultural heritage in American society and in sports.

At the same time, blacks, Latinos, Asian Americans, and Native Americans are reminded that acceptance in the dominant culture requires them to "be like whites" in how they think, talk, and act. They understand that to be embraced by the media and white fans they should smile in accommodating ways on camera and during interviews, just like Magic Johnson and Michael Jordan did so effectively for many years (Davis and Harris, 1998). But they also admire athletes who express their racial or ethnic identities and "don't forget where they came from." This creates tension for ethnic minority athletes and unique social dynamics in sports where players are racially and ethnically mixed. This is a newsworthy story, but it would make many people, especially white sports fans, uncomfortable, and it would be difficult for most journalists to tell. But as long as it remains untold, white privilege in sports will persist without being recognized. Finally, if ethnic minority players or coaches try to tell the story, they're quickly accused of "playing the race card," being arrogant and ungrateful, or being bitter because of "imagined abuse."

IDEOLOGY AND OVERLOOKING WHITENESS Media coverage unwittingly reaffirms dominant racial ideology when whiteness is overlooked. This is best illustrated with an example unrelated to sports: When two young men killed twelve students and a teacher at Colorado's Columbine High School in 1999, people in the media overlooked the whiteness of the killers, even though the shooters in the twelve preceding mass killings in U.S. schools during the 1990s had also been white males. Whiteness was never an issue in the coverage because it is overlooked in a white-centered culture to the point that white people don't "see" it. As a result, stories and

analysis in mainstream media never contained generalizations about the problem of violence among white male teens, and nobody talked about crossing the street to avoid a white male teen on the sidewalk. However, if the two killers had been black, Latino, Asian, or Native American, the coverage and audience responses would have made race or ethnicity the central focus of stories, with other factors reduced to secondary importance or ignored. This is how racial and ethnic ideology influences coverage and stifles critical questions about the accuracy of media representations of reality.

When journalists ignore the dynamics of living in a white-dominated, white-identified, and white-centered society, they unwittingly reproduce racial and ethnic stereotypes at the same time that they claim to be color blind (Hartmann, 2007). For example, when black male athletes are portrayed as deviant, angry, physically powerful, and intimidating, some whites in society perceive them differently from the way they might perceive white male athletes who were portrayed in similar ways. Dominant racial ideology in the United States is deeply grounded in widespread (1) awe of the physical movements and "natural talent" of black male bodies and (2) fears of their imagined sexual prowess and physical power. This means that seeing a powerful and potentially violent black male athlete reaffirms, in the minds of some people, long-held ideas and beliefs about all black men. This is different from the ways in which a powerful and potentially violent white male athlete is perceived. Representations of white males are not seen in racial terms or given racial meanings, nor are they used to make generalizations about all white men.

AT YOUR *fingertips*   For more information on racial stereotypes about black male bodies, see Chapter 9, pp. 290–292.

Pretending to be color blind in a culture where a skin color–based racial ideology has existed for over three centuries ensures that white privilege is seamlessly incorporated into the media coverage of sports. It allows people in sports media to avoid asking why nearly all sports at the high school, college, and professional level are exclusively white or becoming so. It allows the editors at *Sports Illustrated* to avoid publishing an article titled "What Ever Happened to Black and Brown Athletes?" (see Price, 1997), even when they live in communities where hundreds of high school and college teams in swimming, volleyball, softball, tennis, golf, soccer, lacrosse, rowing, gymnastics, wrestling, and other sports are *all* white. It also allows journalists to avoid asking critical questions about new patterns of residential and school segregation and growing income and wealth disparity that deeply influence who plays what sports in the United States today. They can put aside questions about why there are fewer African/Asian/Native American and Latino professional golfers today than there were in 1981—fifteen years before Tiger Woods won his first PGA tournament as a professional in 1996. Most important, pretending to be color blind allows media people to ignore whiteness and all racial issues, thereby maintaining a high racial comfort level among white media consumers and advertisers (Hartmann, 2007); ignoring reality turns nice profits.

Scholars of ethnic studies explain that this self-declared colorblindness denies the real history and relevance of skin color and ethnicity in societies where previously unquestioned racism has clearly shaped the distribution of income and wealth and the everyday living conditions of nearly all people (Bonilla-Silva, 2001, 2003; Brown et al., 2005; Doane and Bonilla-Silva, 2003). When a color-blind approach governs the coverage of sports, media stories miss significant sport realities and reproduce the racial and ethnic status quo. This allows people in dominant racial and ethnic populations to see and use sports as forms of social escapism—as whitewashed worlds devoid of the complex,

messy issues that characterize real everyday life. At the same time, it constantly reminds people in racial and ethnic minority populations that their histories, heritages, and experiences are unrecognized in sports. As a result, some ethnic minority people avoid some or all sports, or they use sports as sites for seeking recognition and respect in the dominant culture. When we view media critically, it becomes increasingly clear that they don't "tell it like it is" as much as they tell it as their target demographics and advertisers want it told.

ETHNICITY AND NATIONALITY IN A GLOBAL CONTEXT Themes related to ethnicity and nationality also exist in sports media coverage worldwide. Although some sports reporters and broadcasters are careful to avoid using ethnic and national stereotypes in their representations of athletes and teams, evidence suggests that subtle stereotypes regularly influence sports coverage (Mayeda, 1999; McCarthy, Jones, and Potrac, 2003; Sabo and Jansen, 1998; Sabo et al., 1996; van Sterkenburg and Knoppers, 2004). For example, some media coverage has portrayed Asian athletes as methodical, mechanical, machinelike, mysterious, industrious, self-disciplined, and intelligent. Their achievements are more often attributed to cognitive than to physical abilities, and stereotypes about height and other physiological characteristics are sometimes used to explain success or failure in sports. Latinos, on the other hand, have been described as flamboyant, exotic, emotional, passionate, moody, and hot-blooded (Blain, Boyle, and O'Donnell, 1993).

The sports journalists most likely to avoid such stereotypes are those who have worked to learn about national and ethnic histories and those parts of the world in which teams and athletes live. This is what all good journalists do when they cover events and people. For example, when 26 percent of MLB players are Latino and more players are coming from certain Asian countries, it is reasonable to expect the journalists covering baseball to do their homework and learn about the cultures and baseball histories in those countries, and about the experiences of the athletes who have grown up there. Additionally, it would be professionally responsible for media companies to hire sports reporters and broadcasters who are bilingual and culturally informed so that they could talk meaningfully with players whose lives on and off the field are not understood by most baseball fans. These are important stories as all sports become increasingly globalized. For the media to ignore them is to ignore reality and the meanings given to sports today.

The most effective way to reduce subtle forms of racial, ethnic, and national bias in the media is to hire reporters, editors, photographers, writers, producers, directors, camerapersons, commentators, and statisticians from diverse racial, ethnic, and national backgrounds (Lapchick, 2008c; Rowe, 2004a, 2004b). Lip service is paid to this goal, and progress has been made in certain media, but members of racial and ethnic minorities are clearly underrepresented in nearly all sports newsrooms, press boxes, broadcast booths, and media executive offices. This was documented in research initiated by Richard Lapchick and The Institute for Diversity and Ethics in Sports. Data collected from 378 Associated Press websites and papers indicated that in 2008, "94 percent of the sports editors, 89 percent of the assistant sports editors, 88 percent of our columnists, 87 percent of our reporters and 89 percent of our copy editors/designers are white, and those same positions are 94, 90, 94, 91 and 84 percent male" (Lapchick, 2008c, p. 1).

This skewed pattern is unfortunate because ethnic diversity among media people would enrich stories and provide multiple perspectives for understanding sports and the people who play and coach them. Of course, neither skin color nor gender precludes knowledge about sports or the people involved in them, but knowledge is based on a combination of experience and the richness of the perspectives one uses to make sense of the ethnically and racially diverse social worlds that constitute sports today.

ON THE *OLC*:

See the OLC—Additional Readings for Chapter 12—for the author's essay on the consequences of watching violence in sports.

EXPERIENCES AND CONSEQUENCES OF CONSUMING MEDIA SPORTS

Media sports provide topics of conversation, occasions for social interaction, a sense of belonging and identity, opportunities to express emotions, and an exciting distraction for those who are passing time alone. However, few studies have investigated audience experiences to see how people give meaning to media sports coverage and integrate it into their lives. Similarly, we know that media images and narratives influence what people feel, think, and do, but few studies have investigated the consequences of media sport consumption at the individual or collective level.

Audience Experiences

Studies of audience experiences suggest that people interpret media content and integrate media sport consumption into their lives in diverse ways (Bruce, 2007; Wenner and Gantz, 1998). More men than women are strongly committed to consuming media sports, and strongly committed consumers constitute a relatively small segment of the overall population in most societies, including the United States and Canada (Adams, 2006). However, these studies don't tell us much about the ways that people give meaning to and include the consumption of media sports in their lives.

One exception is a creative study of twenty white men and a few women who had grown up in various towns in western Pennsylvania but had moved to Fort Worth, Texas (Kraszewski, 2008).

By various means each person joined with others who had started a tradition of meeting in a sports bar where they watched Pittsburgh Steelers games from August through December. As they met each week their interaction focused on rekindling and nurturing their sense of western Pennsylvania as "home" and their identities associated with their geographical origins. In the process they created a place-image of western Pennsylvania that matched the blue-collar, white European-American, steelworker image of the Steelers. They wore Steelers jerseys, drank Iron City (Pittsburgh) beer in aluminum bottles, and were identified as Steelers fans by the

Dallas Cowboys fans in the rest of the bar. They avoided talking about social class, race, and jobs and focused on "where they were from"—talking about roads, towns, and other features of the landscape of western Pennsylvania. For them, watching the Steelers on television was a social occasion for interacting with others who reaffirmed their sense of home and their regional identities, despite living over 1200 miles away from where they grew up.

About 12,000 miles from Texas and Pittsburgh, a study of the Grog Squad in South Australia identified the ways that fans use the medium of the Internet to "construct and

As large, outdoor screens are used to televise major sport events, such as the Rugby World Cup in Paris (2007), there are new social dynamics associated with media consumption. This crowd was predominantly French, but there were groups of fans from at least ten other nations. Access to this plaza was open, and spectators were orderly despite a packed crowd and no reserved seats. No sociological research has been done on this phenomenon. (*Source:* Jay Coakley)

communicate their allegiance to their team and to each other" (Palmer and Thompson, 2007). Grog Squads are collections of hard-drinking male fans of various Australian Rules Football teams in South Australia. They use multiple websites (for example, see www.rocketrooster.com and http://aftergrogblog.blogs.com/) to nurture social connections that serve many purposes at the same time that they enact a very aggressive, sexist, and sometimes racist and destructive form of hegemonic masculinity. The Internet enables these men to stay in touch and share stories that secure and enhance their status among fellow Grog Squaders.

A U.S. study of people who watch televised sports in the context of marriage indicated that male-female married couples often watch televised sports together and that this usually is a positive activity in their relationships (Wenner and Gantz, 1998). The men watched sports more than the women did and were more likely to be committed fans, but when women were committed fans, their patterns of watching and responding to sports on television were similar to men's patterns. Some couples experienced conflicts related to viewing sports, but most resolved them successfully. Partners usually learned to adjust to each other's viewing habits over time, and when they didn't, it usually meant that the couple had general relationship problems unrelated to watching sports.

Future studies will tell us more about the ways that media sport experiences are integrated into people's lives and when media sports become important sites at which social relationships occur. It will be important to include the use of the Internet and video games in these studies.

Consequences of Consuming Media Sports

Research on the consequences of consuming media sports has focused on a wide variety of issues. Here we'll focus on three: active participation in sports, attendance at sport events, and betting on sport events.

Active Participation in Sports Does consuming media sports lead people to be more active sport participants or turn them into couch potatoes? This is an important issue, given the health problems associated with physical inactivity in many societies today.

When children watch sports on television, some copy what they see *if* they have or can make opportunities to do so. Children are great imitators with active imaginations, so when they see and identify with athletes, they may create informal activities or seek to join youth sport programs to pursue television-inspired dreams. Participation grounded in these dreams usually fades quickly, especially after children discover that it takes years of tedious, repetitive, and boring practice to compete successfully and reach the victory podium. Of course, it's possible that initial participation can stimulate other motives that sustain a commitment to playing sports, but research suggests that this is not a regular occurrence (Lines, 2007). In light of this evidence it appears that a positive link between watching and doing sports may exist only when parents, teachers, or physical educators strategically connect media representations with everyday sport participation. Research is needed to explore this possibility.

Many adults don't play the sports they consume in the media, but some do and use media sports as entertainment and a source of inspiration for their own participation. In the absence of research on this topic, we can say only that consuming sports through the media may be connected with activity or inactivity in different situations and with different people.

Attendance at Sport Events Game attendance is related to many factors, including the consumption of media sports. On the one hand, the owners of many professional teams enforce a television blackout rule based on the belief that television coverage reduces game attendance and ticket sales. In support of this belief, many people say that they would rather watch certain sport events on television than attend them in person. On the other hand, the media publicize sports, promote interest, and provide information that helps people to identify with athletes and teams and become potential ticket purchasers for events (Wann et al., 2001b; Weiss, 1996; Zhang, Pease, and Smith, 1998).

At this point in time, it appears that people who consume media sports also attend games in person (Zhang and Smith, 1997). However, as ticket prices increase and the number of elite, "live" games increase across various sports, people may limit attendance when they can watch the same game on television. Additionally, as media focus attention on elite sports, such as NBA basketball, people may ignore less elite events such as local high school games, but we don't know if or when this occurs. Overall, it is reasonable to conclude that consumption of media sports is positively related to attendance at the top levels of competition but may interfere with attendance at lower levels of competition (Zhang, Pease, and Jambor, 1997).

Betting on Sport Events Consuming media sports is clearly connected with betting on sport events, but there is no evidence that it causes gambling. Nearly 70 percent of all sport bets are made informally with family members, friends, and co-workers in so-called office pools (Jones, 2008). Formal gambling on sports dates back centuries (Cashmore, 2007) and continues today at horse and dog tracks and in Las Vegas "sports books" where people may bet legally on nearly every possible outcome in many sport events—such as number of points, who scores first, points in first half or second half, who beats the point spread, and so on.

Online gambling accounts for about $20 billion out of a total of $150 billion bet illegally on sports in the United States (Drape, 2008). Sport gambling is most popular among younger men

> IF [teams and ticket prices] are chasing people out of the arena and onto their couches, it doesn't matter as long as those people are watching sports on television. Television is where corporate America makes its money. —David Carter, sports marketing consultant (2002)

who have above-average income and at least some college education (Jones, 2008). Male college students have higher rates of gambling than other categories of people, mostly because they think they know more about sports than everyone else (Brown, 2000; Crist, 1998; Jenkins, 2000; Layden, 1995a, 1995b, 1995c).

Sport gambling debts can have destructive consequences, but betting on sports is not generally seen as an important moral or legal issue. In fact, a Gallup poll in 2008 shows that gambling on sports has declined between 1992 and 2008, even though online gambling opportunities are accessible to more people today than ever before (Jones, 2008). In 2008, 7 percent of people in a national poll said they had bet on a professional sport event during the previous year, whereas 12 percent admitted having done so in 1992. Similarly, in 2008, 14 percent said they had participated in an office pool during the previous year, whereas 22 percent admitted having done so in 1992.

Many people today are accustomed to buying state lottery tickets and going to casinos, and they don't favor new restrictions that would limit or ban betting on sports, nor are they seduced by online betting opportunities. However, gambling constitutes a threat to sports because it elevates the stakes associated with competitive outcomes and may lead people to seek an edge by convincing one or more athletes to control the scores of games and matches so that bets can be won when point spreads are not covered by favored teams or athletes. Even a rumor of game fixing or point shaving seriously threatens the integrity of competitive outcomes and destroys the foundation for much sport spectatorship. In this sense, consuming media sports does not influence gambling as much as gambling could influence media sport consumption.

THE PROFESSION OF SPORT JOURNALISM

Some people trivialize sport journalism by saying that it provides information about people and events that is entertaining but unrelated to important issues in everyday life. However, sports do matter—not because they produce a tangible product or make essential contributions to our survival, but because they represent ideas about how the world works and what is important in life. Sports are not merely reflections of social worlds; they also are constitutive of those worlds—that is, they're sites at which social worlds are produced, reproduced, and changed. Sport journalists are key players in these constitutive processes, because their representations of sports can influence the ideas and beliefs that people use to define and give meaning to themselves, their experiences, and the organization of social worlds.

Sport Journalists Are Not All the Same

Entertainment is a focus for nearly everyone working in commercial media. Sportswriters generally provide specific information and in-depth analysis, whereas the announcers and commentators for visual electronic media usually focus on providing images and narratives that create anticipation and a sense of urgency among their audience. Exceptions sometimes occur in sport talk radio when analysis and "call-in" interactivity are structured into program format. Additionally, television also includes some sport programming that provides in-depth analysis, but this is relatively rare in the overall programming format of television.

At the present time, people representing sports online emphasize information and analysis, much like people in print media, but they also provide their audiences with opportunities to respond or comment on their representations. This interactivity alters the relationship between journalists and their audiences and influences the overall content of online sports coverage.

"I used to work at FIXR Sports, so I know the rule at FIXR: if it bleeds, it leads."

The media coverage of sports news is much like other news in that it presents so much violence and drama that it misrepresents what generally happens in sports and the rest of the community.

As athletes, agents, team publicity directors, bloggers, and others contribute online content, traditional sport journalism is changing (Aleindor, 2008). Research is needed on the production and consumption of this new media and its impact on the definition and role of journalism in sports and society (Ballard, 2006).

Sport Journalists on the Job: Relationships with Athletes

As access to information about sports has increased, sportswriters have had to create stories that go beyond the action and scores in sports. This leads them to seek increasingly intimate information about the personal lives of athletes, and this creates tension in athlete–journalist relationships. Athletes today realize that they cannot trust journalists to hold information in confidence, even if the disclosure took place in the privacy of the locker room. Furthermore, the stakes associated with "bad press" are so great for athletes and teams that everyone in sport organizations limits what they say when talking with journalists. As a result, sport stories tend to contain similar statements and quotes from athletes game after game, week after week, and season after season (Doaks, 2004).

Differences in the salaries and personal backgrounds of players and sport journalists increase tensions in their relationships. Wealthy black and Latino athletes without college degrees have little in common with middle-class, college-educated, white, Euro-American journalists. As a result, some journalists don't refrain from using compromising information about athletes to enhance stories, and athletes define journalists as "outsiders" looking for a good story regardless of whose reputation they may damage.

Team owners and university athletic departments are so conscious of tensions between athletes and media personnel that they now provide players with training on how to handle interviews without saying things that might sound bad or be misinterpreted. However, tensions sometimes reach a point at which players threaten people from the media, and sportswriters, in particular, quit their jobs to find less stressful occupations.

Tensions also call attention to ethical issues in sport journalism. Many, but not all journalists are aware that they should not jeopardize athletes' reputations simply for the sake of entertainment, and they should not hurt them unintentionally or without good reason. Dan Le Batard, a regular columnist for *ESPN—The Magazine*, explains that he tries to be "nonjudgmental"

ON THE *OLC*:
See the OLC—Additional Readings for Chapter 12—for links to articles in which Dave Zirin, an award-winning sport journalist, discusses problems in sport journalism today.

when he covers athletes because all people have flaws and exposing the flaws of an athlete who disappoints you with their actions smacks of self-righteousness and raises the ethical issue of invasion of privacy (2005, p. 14). However, journalists constantly face gray areas in which ethical guidelines are not clear, and the need to present attractive stories often encourages them to push ethical limits. As a result, tensions are likely to remain in athlete-journalist relationships.

summary

COULD SPORTS AND THE MEDIA SURVIVE WITHOUT EACH OTHER?

Media and media experiences have become ever-present in the lives of people living in many parts of the world today. This is why we study the relationship between sports and the media.

Media sports, like other aspects of culture, are social constructions. They're created, organized, and controlled by human beings whose motives and ideas are grounded in their social worlds, experiences, and ideologies. The media represent sports to us through selected images and narratives that usually reaffirm dominant ideologies and promote the interests of wealthy and powerful people who own media companies. A hopeful exception to this is the Internet, a medium that offers revolutionary potential for people to create and control images and narratives in ways that foster grassroots interests.

Video games and virtual sports are important components of the new media. At this time, they complement existing media, but they're beginning to provide unique sport-related experiences unlike those occasioned by traditional media. As technology enables people to immerse themselves in virtual realities and participate in physical challenges with real and virtual others, the meaning, purpose, and organization of sports will change.

Sports and the media have become increasingly interdependent as both have become more important parts of social worlds. They could survive without each other, but they would be different from the way they are now. Commercial sports have grown and prospered because of media coverage and the rights fees paid by media companies. Without the publicity and money provided by media, commercial sports would be reduced to local business operations with much less scope than they have today, and less emphasis would be placed on elite, competitive sports in people's lives.

Media could survive without sports, but newspapers and television would be different from their current format if they did not have sports content and programming to attract young male audiences and the sponsors who wish to buy access to those audiences. Without sports, newspaper circulation would decrease, and television programming on weekends and holidays would be different and less profitable for television broadcasters.

The symbiotic relationship between sports and the media in most societies today exists because certain sports can be used to attract audiences that sponsors want to convert into consumers of their products and services. The dynamics of this relationship are also influenced by the interaction that occurs between athletes, agents, coaches, administrators, sport team owners, sponsors, advertisers, media representatives, and a diverse collection of spectators. Power relations are a crucial feature of this interaction process, and it is important to understand them when studying the sports-media relationship.

Research indicates that media coverage of sports in the United States emphasizes images and narratives reproducing dominant ideologies related to success, consumption, gender, race, ethnicity, and nationality. As a result, current patterns of power and privilege are portrayed as normal and natural and remain unquestioned. Future research utilizing cultural, interactionist, and structural theories combined with a critical approach will tell us more about the various ways that people make sense of the media representations they consume. This is especially important in connection with the Internet and video games. Patterns of media sport consumption are changing rapidly, and it is important to study them in ways that promote critical media literacy rather than the uncritical celebration of media technology and the promotional culture of most sports coverage (Kellner, 2003a, 2003b, 2004).

Few studies have investigated the experiences and consequences of consuming media sports. We know that people make sense of sports media images and narratives on their own terms and that this interpretive process of sense-making is influenced by the social, cultural, and historical conditions under which it occurs. People also integrate media sport experiences into their lives in diverse ways, but we know little about the patterns and consequences of this integration process. For example, research is needed to help us identify the conditions under which the consumption of media sports influences active participation in sports, attendance at live sport events, and gambling on sports.

To understand sports and the media, it helps to become familiar with basic features of sports journalism today. Journalists are key players in the overall process of representing sports to large audiences. In the process they influence ideas and beliefs about sports and social worlds. The interactivity made possible by new media has made journalists more accessible to their audiences while bringing members of the audience into the process of creating media content. Additionally, the need to create stories that capture the attention of media consumers has led journalists to seek stories that disclose private and personal information about athletes. This creates tensions between journalists and athletes, which then influence media representations of sports and the people who play them today.

Sports and the media need each other, especially when making profits is a primary goal for each. The sports-media relationship changes as it is negotiated by athletes, facility directors, sport team owners, event promoters, media representatives, sponsors, advertisers, agents, and spectators. Studying the dynamics of this relationship helps us understand sports in society more fully.

WEBSITE RESOURCES

Note: Websites often change. The following URLs were current when this book was printed. Please check our website (www.mhhe.com/coakley10e) for updates and additions.

www.mhhe.com/coakley10e Click on Chapter 12 for information on topics related to material in this chapter.

www.americanparkour.com/ This site provides an example of how alternative/action sports use the Internet; see links to videos, photo gallery, and pics of the week.

www.edgeofsports.com/ Site maintained by Dave Zirin, an independent sports journalist; Zirin presents information and analysis that is critically informed and free of most of the commercial influences that shape the work of other sport journalists.

http://espn.go.com/ ESPN provides a combination of traditional and new media coverage of sports.

www.esportstv.com/buylan2007/ eSports TV provides videos of gaming competitions; an example of new media sports.

http://fantasygames.sportingnews.com/ Fantasy games and in-depth fantasy analysis is available on this site; another example of how the traditional media have expanded to seek an audience that can be sold to sponsors.

http://games-ak.espn.go.com/s/ff101/ff101.htm?campaign=ff07&source=in_tools_101 Fantasy 101 tutorial provided by ESPN in an effort to recruit fantasy football participants.

www.la84foundation.org/11pub/over_frmst.htm The Amateur Athletic Foundation has links to a series of studies focused on sports and media.

www.real-sports.com An online sporting magazine that clearly illustrates the emphasis on consumption in sports media.

http://mlb.mlb.com/mlb/mediacenter/programs.jsp This is the home page of Major League Baseball's multimedia website; fans can spend hours here watching videos and listening to interviews about baseball worldwide (and learning little).

www.nfl.com The NFL home page is designed to provide fans with "everything they need to know"—so they won't have to go to any other media source.

www.since1865.com/sections/sports Includes links to every sport-related article published in *The Nation*, the longest-running weekly news magazine in the United States; it does not depend on corporate advertising, so its writers and editors view sports through a less filtered lens than writers and editors in commercial media.

www.sportingnews.com/ A good example of how the traditional print media have developed online content as a complement to their regular sports coverage.

www.wnba.com/ The WNBA site provides a combination of entertainment, information, analysis, and interactivity for fans.

(Elizabeth Pike)

SPORTS AND POLITICS

How Do Governments and Global Political Processes Influence Sports?

NO PERSON SHALL play ball or any game of sport
with a ball or football in, over, across, along or
upon any street or sidewalk or in any public park,
except on those portions of said park set apart for
such purposes.

—Los Angeles Municipal Code (2008a)

OLC Visit *Sports in Society*'s Online Learning
Center (OLC) at www.mhhe.com/coakley10e
for additional information and study material
for this chapter, including the following:

- A complete chapter outline
- Learning objectives
- Practice quizzes
- Internet resources
- Related readings
- Essays
- Student projects

WE CONSIDER SPORTS participation an indicator of
civilization, and the wellness and happiness of a
country.

    —**Filippo Fossati, Italian Union of Sport for All
    (2008)**

WE HAVE WAGED a lengthy and tireless battle to
create a [revolutionary] sports culture. . . . This
is what has allowed our country to reach a place
of honour in sports . . . recognized by the entire
world.

    —**Fidel Castro, president of Cuba, 2001**

INTERNATIONAL COMPETITIONS, such as the
Olympic Games, encourage all of our nations to
set aside their differences in the spirit of fair play.
They provide everyone with a venue for cultural
exchange and an opportunity to share national
traditions and customs.

    —**Stuart C. Gilman, U.S. Office of Government
    Ethics (in UN, 2003)**

437

Organized competitive sports have long been connected with politics, governments, and global political processes. When people say that politics has no place in sports, they usually mean that there is no place in sports for politics that differ from their own.

Politics refers to the *processes of organizing social power and making decisions that affect the lives of people in a social world.* Politics occur at all levels of social life, from the politics of friendship and family relationships to national, international, and global affairs (Volpi, 2006). People in the sociology of sport study political processes in communities, local and national sport organizations, societies, and large nongovernment organizations (NGOs) such as the International Olympic Committee (IOC) or Fédération Internationale de Football Association (FIFA), the international federation that governs world soccer.

Governments are *formal organizations with the power to make and enforce rules in a particular territory or collection of people.* Because governments make decisions affecting people's lives, they are political organizations by definition. Governments operate on various levels from local parks and recreation departments to nation-states, and they influence sports whether they occur in a public park or a privately owned stadium that hosts international competitions. People in the sociology of sport often refer to **"the state"** because this concept *includes the formal institution of a national government plus those parts of civil society—such as education, family, media, and churches—that teach values and ideologies that extend the influence and control of the political agencies that make and enforce laws and govern a society.*

Politics often involve the actions and interactions of governments, but rule-making in sports today goes beyond the political boundaries of the state and occurs in connection with global processes. For example, soccer is a global sport because British workers, students, and teachers brought the game to South America and British soldiers and missionaries brought it to Africa, Asia, the West Indies, and other colonized areas

of the nineteenth-century British Empire. Soccer grew around the world through the global processes of migration, capitalist expansion, British imperialism, and colonization—all of which involve politics. Governments usually are involved in political processes, but today's world includes such rapid global movements of people, products, ideas, technologies, and money that these processes transcend particular states and involve transnational corporations and nongovernmental organizations such as Greenpeace, the Red Cross, and sport organizations such as the IOC and FIFA.

This chapter focuses on the relationships between sports and politics. The goal is to explain the ways in which sports are connected with governments, the state, and global political processes. Chapter content focuses on four major questions:

1. Why do governments often sponsor and control sports?
2. How are sports connected with global politics that involve nation-states, transnational corporations, and nongovernmental organizations?
3. What is the role of the Olympic Games in global politics and processes?
4. What are the ways that political processes occur in sports and sport organizations?

When you are reading this chapter, remember that power and authority are the key concepts used when studying politics and political processes. **Power** refers to *an ability to influence people and achieve goals, even in the face of opposition from others* (Weber, 1922). And **authority** is *a form of power that comes with a recognized and legitimate status or office in a government, an organization, or an established set of relationships.* For example, a large corporation, such as Nike or McDonald's, has power if it can influence how people think about and play sports and if it can use sports to achieve its goals. Sport organizations such as the IOC, FIFA, the NCAA, and a local parks and recreation department have the *authority* to administer particular sports as long as the people associated with those sports accept the organizations as legitimate governing bodies. This highlights the fact that *politics* refers to the power to make decisions that affect sports and sport participation.

THE SPORTS–GOVERNMENT CONNECTION

As sports grow in popularity, government involvement usually increases. Many sports require sponsorship, organization, and facilities—all of which depend on resources that few individuals possess on their own. Sport facilities may be so expensive that regional and national governments are the only entities with the power and resources to build and maintain them. Government involvement also occurs when there is a need for a third party to regulate and control sports and sport organizations in ways that promote the overall good of people in a community or society.

The nature and extent of government involvement in sports varies by society, but it generally serves one or more of the following purposes (Houlihan, 2000):

1. Safeguard the public order
2. Ensure fairness and protect human rights
3. Maintain health and fitness among citizens
4. Promote the prestige and power of a group, community, or nation
5. Promote a sense of identity, belonging, and unity among citizens
6. Reproduce values consistent with dominant ideology in a community or society
7. Increase support for political leaders and government
8. Facilitate economic and social development in a community or society

Safeguard the Public Order

Governments are responsible for maintaining order in public areas, including parks, sidewalks, and streets, among other places. Here are two sections from the Los Angeles Municipal Code, enforced by the city in an effort to safeguard citizens and the public order:

> No person shall ride, operate or use a bicycle, unicycle, skateboard, cart, wagon, wheelchair, roller skates, or any other device moved exclusively by human power, on a sidewalk, bikeway or boardwalk in a willful or wanton disregard for the safety of persons or property. (Los Angeles Municipal Code, 2008b)

> Within the limit of any park or portion thereof designated by the Board as a skateboard facility, whether the facility is supervised or unsupervised,

> 1. No person shall ride a skateboard unless that person is wearing a helmet, elbow pads and knee pads.
> 2. No person shall ride a bicycle or scooter in the skating area
> 3. . . . skate parks shall also be closed during periods of wet weather or when conditions, such as wet weather, make it unsafe to skate (Los Angeles Municipal Code, 2008c)

Laws similar to these, full of bureaucratic language, exist in nearly all cities and towns. They set boundaries for where, when, and under what circumstances sports may be played.

Ideally, these laws promote safety and reduce conflict between multiple users of public spaces. For example, state and local governments in the United States (and other countries) ban barefisted boxing, bungee jumping off public bridges, and basketball playing on public streets. In the case of commercial sports, governments may regulate the rights and responsibilities of team owners, sponsors, promoters, and athletes.

Local governments may regulate sport participation by requiring people to obtain permits to use public facilities and playing fields. Likewise, local officials may close streets or parks to the general public so that sport events can be held under controlled and safe conditions. For example, annual marathons in New York City and London require the involvement of the government and government agencies such as the city police.

Local governments often regulate where and when certain sports can occur. This is true in Philadelphia's "Love Park," although "street skaters" do break the rules on weekends, holidays, and late at night. (*Source:* Jay Coakley)

Safeguarding the public order also involves policing sport events where safety may be threatened by crowds or unruly individuals. During the Olympics, for example, the host city and nation provide thousands of military and law enforcement officials to safeguard the public order. In the face of possible protests and terrorist actions, it is estimated that the Chinese government spent up to $6.5 billion to police and monitor the Beijing area in connection with the 2008 Olympic Games—more than the $1.5 billion spent by Athens and Greece to secure the 2004 Olympic Games (Latimer, 2008; Waterford, 2004). The government also employed over 43,000 soldiers, 47 helicopters, 74 airplanes, 33 naval ships, 6,000 security guards on 18,000 buses, 30,000 guards at bus stops and terminals, and tens of thousands of surveillance cameras in Beijing and other cities, along with the personnel to monitor them.

Governments sponsor sports that are used during military and police training so that soldiers and police will be more effective protectors of the public order (Mangan, 2003). Military academies in the United States sponsor sports for cadets, and the World Police and Fire Games are held every two years because people believe that sport participation keeps law enforcement officials and firefighters prepared to safeguard the public order.

Finally, some governments sponsor sport events and programs for people defined as potential threats to the public order. When public officials believe that sports will keep young people—especially those labeled "at risk"—off the streets and thereby reduce crime rates, vandalism, loneliness, and alienation, they may provide funding and facilities for sport programs. Midnight basketball was an example of this (Hartmann, 2001, 2003b; Hartmann and Depro, 2006; Hartmann and Wheelock, 2002). These programs are seldom effective unless they are tied to other efforts to reduce the deprivation, racism, poverty, dislocation, unemployment, community disintegration, and political powerlessness that often create "at-risk youth" and social problems in communities and societies (Coakley, 2002).

A study by Doug Hartmann and Brooks Depro (2006) suggests that programs like midnight basketball might be effective in reducing crime rates when they are sponsored in connection with other public efforts that make people in a particular neighborhood aware that the city government and law enforcement is taking them seriously and can be trusted to maintain public order. However, Wheelock and Hartmann (2007) also found that when members of the U.S. Congress debated anti-crime program funding in the 1990s, references to midnight basketball increased their fears of crime by "at-risk" populations (especially black men) and shifted their focus from funding similar preventive programs to funding traditional social control approaches emphasizing policing and incarceration.

Overall, when safeguarding the public order is the reason for government involvement in sports, the focus of that involvement can influence sports in many ways—sometimes restricting certain forms of sport participation at the same time that other forms are supported.

Ensure Fairness and Protect Human Rights

Governments may intervene in sports by passing laws, establishing policies, or ruling in court cases that protect the rights of citizens to participate in public sport programs. A classic example of this is Title IX in the United States and similar laws in other countries that were passed to promote gender equity in sports (Mitchell and Ennis, 2007).

Today, many national governments are considering or have already enacted laws mandating the provision of sport participation opportunities for people with disabilities. For example, the United States Supreme Court made a ruling in 2001 that ensured fair treatment for Tracy Martin, Tiger Woods's former roommate and golf teammate at

Stanford University. Martin's case is presented in Breaking Barriers, p. 442. Additionally, a federal court in 2008 ruled in favor of the Michigan Paralyzed Veterans of America and forced the University of Michigan to increase its accessible seats for football fans from 88 (in 2007) to 329 in 2010 (out of 107,501 total seats) and to make restrooms accessible even though they were built in previous years not covered by existing ADA law (Lapointe, 2008; Pear, 2008). A similar ruling forced Madison Square Garden in New York City to expand to 40 its accessible seats for fans with disabilities.[1]

In other examples of government actions to guarantee fairness and human rights, the U.S. Congress passed the Amateur Sports Act in 1978 and created the USOC, now the official NGO responsible for coordinating amateur sports in the United States. A major reason for doing this was to protect athletes from being exploited by multiple, unconnected, and self-interested sport-governing bodies that controlled amateur sports through much of the twentieth century. In 1998 the act was revised to require the USOC to support and fund Paralympic athletes because people with disabilities were systematically denied opportunities to play elite amateur sports. Unfortunately, people have differing opinions on how the act should be interpreted and this has led athletes with disabilities to file lawsuits to receive the support and funding that they and many others consider to be fair.

Disputes about fairness and human rights in sports are not always settled by legislative or judicial actions, but as the stakes associated with sports and sport participation increase,

---

[1]As I wrote this chapter during the summer of 2008, the Bush Administration was about to propose an extension of ADA law that would make facilities such as miniature golf courses, swimming pools, and playgrounds more accessible (Pear, 2008). The administration was responding to a new generation of young people with disabilities created by the Iraq war, and to data showing that about 30 million Americans (1 in 10 Americans) have serious disabilities and that this number will increase as the average age of the population increases.

breaking BARRIERS

Political Barriers
I Think . . . This Opens Some Doors for People

When we talk about sports and people with disabilities, we must talk politics. Consider the legal case of PGA golfer Casey Martin. In 1994 as a junior at Stanford, he was voted captain of the golf team and led it to the collegiate championship. Tiger Woods joined the team in 1995, and Martin was his roommate when Stanford played tournaments away from Palo Alto. Martin won the U.S. Intercollegiate Golf Championship that year and led Stanford to the NCAA finals.

But all was not well with Martin. A congenital defect in his right leg prevented normal blood circulation and was gradually eroding his bone and causing him increasingly severe, chronic pain. There were times when he could barely walk, so his coach convinced him to use a golf cart that was permissible under NCAA rules, given his medical condition. After graduating, Martin played professional golf and by 1997 found that there were times when he couldn't walk and needed a motorized cart to complete eighteen holes. But the PGA ruled that Martin had to walk or quit the tour. Martin sued and won an injunction allowing him to use a cart. The PGA appealed and the case went to the U.S. Supreme Court. In a split decision, the court ruled in 2001 that under the Americans with Disabilities Act of 1990, Martin must be allowed to use a cart because doing so would not force the PGA to make "an unreasonable accommodation" in his case.

Martin spent over $100,000 of his money to play politics with the PGA for four years. His pain and fatigue continued to increase and he played only nine tournaments between 2001 and late 2005. Today at 36 years old (in 2008), he is the men's golf coach at the University of Oregon. He knows that a leg amputation is needed, but he puts it off because, as he puts it, "I'm attached to it" (Yocom, 2008).

In the meantime, Nike has established the Casey Martin Nike Award, which honors an individual with a disability who has taken a public stand and engaged in political battles to inspire or expand sport participation rights for people with disabilities. Representatives from Nike explain that "If you have a body, you are an athlete."

The Casey Martin story is not unique. People with disabilities have always fought political battles to avoid being invisible in the world of sport (DePauw, 1997). For example, in 2005 as representatives of London, Madrid, Moscow, New York, and Paris gave detailed presentations in the hope of being chosen by the IOC to host the 2012 Olympics and Paralympics, only Madrid mentioned the Paralympics in their overall plan. The invisibility of disability was in plain sight.

After the Supreme Court decision in 2001, Casey Martin said, "I'm thrilled . . . I think in the future this opens some doors for people." However, in the real world of sport where eligibility rules are frequently exclusive, people with disabilities know that if they don't play politics, they may not play at all.

government officials are more likely to pass laws and accept sport-related legal cases for judicial rulings.

Maintain Health and Fitness

Governments often become involved in sports to promote health and fitness among citizens. In nations with state-funded, universal health care programs, governments often sponsor sports and physical activity programs to improve health and reduce expenditures for medical care. Nations without universal health care may also sponsor or promote sports for health reasons, but they have a lower stake in preventive approaches and less incentive to fund them.

Although people generally believe that sport participation improves health and reduces medical costs, there's a growing awareness that the relationship between sports participation and health must be qualified because of the following research findings (Waddington, 2000a, 2007):

- Many illnesses that increase health-care costs are caused by environmental factors and living conditions that cannot be changed through sport or fitness programs.
- Some forms of sport participation do not produce overall health benefits.
- The win-at-all-cost orientation in certain competitive sports often contributes to injuries and increased health-care costs; for example, over 40,000 high school and college athletes in the United States have serious knee injuries each year, and 136,000 high school athletes suffer concussions (Gessel et al., 2007).
- The demand for health care often increases among competitive athletes because they seek specialized medical care to treat and rehabilitate any injury or physical condition that might impede their performance.

Therefore, some government officials are now cautious and selective when they sponsor sports for health purposes, and they are more likely to support noncompetitive physical activities with clear aerobic benefits than sports with high injury rates.

> When we Uruguayans suffer a humiliating defeat, we confirm that we are no more than a fiction in history, a mistake on the map, a bad joke of God or Devil. —Eduardo Galeano, journalist and author (in Agovino, 2007)

AT YOUR *fingertips* For more information on the health benefits and risks of sport participation, see Chapter 4, pp. 107–109 and Chapter 6, pp. 164–166.

Between 2005 and 2008, the U.S. Congress convened a committee, commissioned a $20-million investigation of performance-enhancing drugs and human growth hormones in baseball, and involved the U.S. Justice Department, the Federal Bureau of Investigation (FBI) and the Internal Revenue Service (IRS) largely because the legislators were concerned about the health of young people who might take drugs used by professional athletes they admire. This also is why the U.S. government provides about 60 percent of the funding for the United States Anti-Doping Agency (USADA), the organization responsible for most testing in U.S. sports.

Promote the Prestige and Power of a Community or Nation

Government involvement in sports frequently is motivated by a quest for recognition and prestige (Allison, 2004; Bairner, 2005). This occurs on local, national, and even global levels. For example, the 1996 Olympic Games were used by Atlanta to present itself as a world-class city symbolizing the "new South," now open to all people regardless of race or national background. Sydney, host of the 2000 Summer Games, presented itself as a city with clean air in a country with a pleasant climate and vital business connections with emerging nations in Asia. Salt Lake City used the 2002 Winter Olympics to present itself as an economically progressive area and an attractive tourist destination. Athens used the 2004 Summer Games to show the world that Greece was part of the new Europe and that it was a nation that had more than monuments of a past era. China, according to some estimates, spent nearly $65 billion on the 2008 Olympic Games in an effort to present itself as a powerful and dynamic nation that was attractive for business investments and tourism (Brownell, 2008; Close, Askew, and Xu, 2006).

This quest for recognition and prestige also underlies government subsidies for national teams across a wide range of sports, usually those designated as Olympic sports. Government officials use international sports to establish their nation's legitimacy in the international sphere, and they often believe that winning medals enhances their image around the world. This is why many governments provide cash rewards to their athletes who win medals. At the 2008 Olympic Games in Beijing, Greek athletes were promised $300,000 for gold, $200,000 for silver, and about $107,000 for bronze medals plus civil service jobs and advertising contracts worth up to a half-million dollars. Russia paid $50,000, $30,000, and $20,000 for medals, but medal winners also received bonuses amounting to about $500,000. The U.S. Olympic Committee paid $25,000, $15,000, and $10,000 to gold, silver, and bronze medal winners, although the largest financial rewards were given to gold medal winners by corporations seeking celebrity endorsements. In China the rewards for medals came from the national, provincial, and city governments, and from a foundation that traditionally awards medal winners with $80,000 and a kilo of gold. Many other nations had instituted and continued to maintain similar reward systems for medal winners (Grohmann, 2008).

Attempts to gain recognition and prestige also underlie local governments' involvement in sports. Cities fund sport clubs and teams and then use them to promote themselves as good places to live, work, locate a business, or vacation. Many people in North America feel that if their city does not have one or more major professional sport team franchises, it cannot claim world-class status (Delaney and Eckstein, 2003, 2008; deMause and Cagan, 2008; Silk, 2004; Silk and Andrews, 2008). Even small towns use road signs to announce the success of local high school teams to everyone driving into the town: "You are now entering the home of the state champions" in this or that sport. State governments in the United States subsidize sport programs at colleges and universities for similar reasons: Competitive success is believed to bring prestige to the entire state as well as the school represented by winning athletes and teams; prestige, it is believed, attracts students, students pay tuition, and tuition pays for educational programs.

When governments fund sports and sport facilities to boost the profile of a city or nation, they often become caught in a cycle where increased funding is regularly required to compete with other cities and nations doing the same thing with bigger budgets or newer facilities (Bourdieu, 1998; Coakley, 2008b; Hall, 2006). This continuously pushes up the funds and other resources that must be allocated to sports, and it decreases resources for programs having more direct and concrete positive impact on citizens. Government officials often find that using this strategy to boost prestige for a city or nation is costly relative to the public benefits created, especially when most of the benefits go to a relatively small and predominantly wealthy segment of their constituency.

Promote Identity and Unity

When people identify strongly with a sport, government officials often use public money to support athletes and teams as a representation of a city or nation. The emotional unity created by a sport or team can be used to establish or reaffirm an identity that further connects people with the city or nation (Sorek, 2007). For example, when the Brazilian men's soccer team plays in the World Cup, the people of Brazil experience a form of emotional unity and a related sense of attachment to the nation. This attachment may mean different things to different people, but the expectation is that it will reaffirm national loyalty and highlight everything from the nation's history and traditions to its geography and its place in the world economic or political order.

Research on national identity indicates that it is a much more dynamic social construct than many people have imagined.[2] Its intensity, meaning, and the forms through which it is expressed vary widely between and even within nations.

---

[2]Beginning in the mid-1990s, the topic of national identity and sport has received much attention in the sociology of sport. The research done over the last decade has been extensive. The following references are a good starting point for people interested in this topic: Allison (2000, 2004); Bairner (2001, 2005); Bartoluci and Perasović (2008); Brownell (2008); Burdsey (2006); Crolley and Hand (2006); Falk (2005); Hall (2006); Hallinan and Judd (2007); Hogan (2003); Hong

Quantifying and measuring the long-term social impact of sports is difficult. Will this girl's identity and her sense of Australia's place in the world be different when she seeks a job in 2021 because Sydney hosted the 2000 Olympics? Sports provide immediate and temporary emotional experiences, but it takes careful planning to make those experiences the basis for real changes in a city or nation. (*Source:* McGraw-Hill)

Additionally, it changes over time with shifts in national experiences such as those that occur between times of peace and times of war, in the face of positive or negative economic conditions, or when immigration patterns alter a nation's demographic profile. Consider a recent Olympic qualifying tournament for men's team handball held in Zadar, Croatia. A city of 71,000 people on the coast of the Adriatic Sea, Zadar was repeatedly attacked during the early and mid-1990s by Yugoslav and Serbian forces as Croatia fought

(2006); Horne and Manzenreiter (2006); Jutel (2002); Lechner (2007); Lee, Jackson, and Lee (2007); Magdalinski (1999); J. Maguire (1999, 2005); Maguire and Burrows (2005); Maguire and Nakayama (2006); Maguire and Possamai (2005); Maguire and Stead (2005); Maguire and Tuck (2005); Manzenreiter (2006); McCarthy (2007); Millward (2006); Nalapat and Parker (2005); Newman (2007a); Poulton (2004); Sam (2003); Sato (2005); Tomlinson and Young (2006); Xu (2006).

a war to break away from the Soviet-aligned Yugoslavia and become an independent nation. Croatia succeeded in gaining its independence, but the people in the Zadar region have only recently felt that the war and its aftermath are behind them. Therefore, when they hosted the handball tournament, the tickets sold out immediately and people from the city and surrounding area used the team and its matches as opportunities to express deep personal feelings of nationhood shaped by war, economic hardship, recent peace, and hope for future prosperity.

The expressions of national identity in Zadar can be viewed as a sign of resilience and unity with the rest of Croatia, but their intensity, and the ways that they reaffirm a strong sense of separation from people in neighboring Serbia and Bosnia-Herzegovena, cause some people to be wary (Bartoluci and Perasović, 2008). This suggests a point that has been clearly highlighted in recent history: sport-related expressions of national unity, pride, and identity can be dangerous under conditions that turn them into chauvinism and militaristic forms of nationalism (Silk and Falcous, 2005).

When government involvement in sport is intended to promote identity and unity, it usually benefits some people more than others. Although emotional unity seldom lasts long, it often serves the interests of people with power and influence because they have the resources to connect it with the images, traditions, and memories that constitute their ideas of nationhood and the importance of loyalty to the status quo. For example, when men's sports are sponsored and women's sports are ignored, the sense of national identity and unity among men may be strong, but women may feel alienated (Adams, 2006). When sports involve participants from only one ethnic group or a particular social class, there are similar divisions in the "imagined community" and the "invented traditions" constructed around sports (Kusz, 2001, 2007; Newman, 2007a, 2007b).

National and local identities are political in that they can be constructed around many different ideas about who or what the nation or community is. Of course, these ideas can vary widely between particular categories of people. Furthermore, neither the identity nor the emotional unity created by sports changes the social, political, and economic realities of life. When games end, people go their separate ways. Old social distinctions become relevant again, and the people who were disadvantaged prior to the game or tournament remain disadvantaged after it (Smith and Ingham, 2003). But this raises an interesting set of questions: Do privileged people feel more justified in their privilege, and do people who are systematically disadvantaged in a city or nation feel less justified in making their disadvantage a political issue because everyone, even

> **Sport is an important tool for "imagining" nationhood. It is a perfect forum for constructing identity.** —Annemarie Jutel, physical educator (2002)

the rich and powerful, is part of the big "we" that is reaffirmed at sport events? The identity and unity created by sports clearly feels good to many people, and it can inspire a sense of possibility and hope, but it may obscure the need for social transformations that would make social worlds more fair and just.

The recent growth of global labor migration has intensified interest in the relationship between sport and national identity. As globalization has blurred national boundaries and made them less relevant for many people, government officials have used sports and national teams to rekindle the idea of nationhood at the same time that they have used sports and multinational teams to inspire identification with newly created political and economic entities (Houlihan, 1994; J. Maguire, 1999, 2005). For example, as European nations sponsor national sports to reinvigorate old feelings of national identity at a time when immigrant workers bring diverse identities to various nations, representatives of the 27-nation European Union use golf's Ryder Cup pitting Team Europe against Team USA to promote the formation of a European identity. Satellite and cable companies (Eurosport and Sky Sports) that serve most European nations have fostered both forms of identification with their sports programming, depending on which one will increase ratings.

These developments complicate national identity and make it more difficult to study and understand its connection with sports. Governments continue to use sports to promote identity and unity, but the long-term effectiveness of this strategy is difficult to assess. Many government officials *believe* that sports create more than temporary good feelings of national "we-ness," but nearly all these officials are men, and the sports they support usually have long histories of privileging men. Multiple layers of politics are associated with sports.

Reproduce Values Consistent with Dominant Political Ideology

Governments also become involved in sports to promote specific political values and ideas among their citizens. This is especially true when there is a need to reaffirm the idea that success is based on discipline, loyalty, determination, and hard work, even in the face of hardship and bad times. Sports are useful platforms to promote these values and foster a particular ideology that contains taken-for-granted assumptions about the way social life is organized and how it does and should operate.

It's difficult to determine the extent to which people are influenced by sports that are represented in specific ideological terms, but we do know that in capitalist societies, such as the United States, sports provide people with a vocabulary and real-life examples that are consistent with dominant ideology. The images, narratives, and the often-repeated stories that accompany sports in market economies emphasize that competition is clearly the best and most natural way to achieve personal success and allocate rewards to people, whereas alternative approaches to success and allocating rewards—democratic socialism, socialism, communism, and the like—are ineffective, unnatural, and even immoral.

A classic example of a government's use of sport to promote its own political ideology occurred in Nazi Germany in 1936 (Walters, 2006). Most countries hosting the Olympic Games use the occasion to present themselves favorably to their own citizens and the rest of the world. However, Adolf Hitler was especially interested in using the games to promote the Nazi ideology of "Nordic (white, northern European) supremacy" through the "Berlin Games," which preceded World War II. The Nazi government devoted considerable resources to training German athletes, who won eighty-nine medals in Berlin—twenty-three more than U.S. athletes won and over four times as many as any other country won during the games. This is why the outstanding performance of Jesse Owens, an African American, was so important to countries aligned against Germany at that point in history. Owens's four gold medals and world records challenged Hitler's ideology of Nordic supremacy, although it did not deter Nazi commitment to a destructive political and cultural ideology that set the stage for World War II.

The Cold War era following World War II was also a time when nations, especially the United States, the former Soviet Union (USSR—the Union of Soviet Socialist Republics), and East Germany (GDR—the German Democratic Republic), used the Olympics and other international sport competitions to make claims about the superiority of their political and economic ideologies. The Cold War is over and powerful corporations now use sports to promote free-market ideology, but governments have not stopped using sports to promote values consistent with ideologies that support their interests. In fact, since the late 1950s the U.S. military has provided "color guard" units to present the American flag at sporting events and has sponsored demonstration "fly-overs" by fighter jet teams to connect the status and place of the military with certain sports, especially football, in the minds of Americans.

> **Boxing is well suited to the Cuban character: we are brave, resolute, selfless. We have strong convictions and clear definition. We are pugnacious and we like to fight.** —Alcides Sagarra, former Olympic boxing coach in Cuba (in Reuters, 2004).

Increase Support for Political Leaders and Government

Government authority rests ultimately in legitimacy. If people do not perceive political leaders and the government as legitimate, it is difficult to maintain social order. In the quest to maintain

President George W. Bush was frequently photographed with championship teams and successful athletes. Here he displays swim trunks received from the Auburn University Women's Swimming and Diving Team as Crystal Langhorne, captain of the University of Maryland basketball team, looks on. This White House event honored NCAA champions from 2005 to 2006. As former partial owner of the Texas Rangers MLB team, Bush learned that being associated with elite sports is good for public relations. (*Source:* Charles Dharapak, AP/Wide World Photos)

their legitimacy, political officials may use athletes, teams, and particular sports to boost their acceptance in the minds of citizens. They assume, as Antonio Gramsci predicted they would, that if they support the things that people value and enjoy, they can maintain their legitimacy as leaders. This is why so many political leaders present themselves as friends of sport, even as faithful fans. They attend highly publicized sport events and associate themselves with high-profile athletes and teams that win major competitions. U.S. presidents traditionally have associated themselves with successful athletes and teams and have invited champions to the White House for photo opportunities.

Some male former athletes and coaches in the United States have used their celebrity status from sports to gain popular support for their political candidacy. A highly publicized example

AT YOUR *fingertips*   For more information on Gramsci and his discussion of power and hegemony, see Chapter 4, pp. 115–117.

is Jesse Ventura, a former professional wrestler, who was elected governor of Minnesota in 1998 and flirted with the idea of running for president in 2000. Other former athletes and coaches have been elected to state legislatures and to the U.S. Congress and Senate by using their status from sports and their sport personas to increase their legitimacy as "tough," "hard-working," and "loyal" candidates who are "decisive under pressure" and "dedicated to being winners." Arnold Schwarzenegger used his tough-terminator, masculinized image combined with his compassionate conservative image (from *Kindergarten Cop*) to become the celebrity governor of California (Messner, 2007b), although some would argue that he was never an athlete.

Facilitate Economic and Social Development

Since the early 1980s, government involvement in sports often has occurred to facilitate a particular form of urban economic development (Delaney and Eckstein, 2003; Gold and Gold, 2007; Hall, 2006; Horne and Manzenreiter, 2006b; Lenskyj, 2000, 2008; Schimmel, 2000, 2002, 2006; Silk and Andrews, 2008). National and city governments spend millions of tax dollars on their bids to host the Olympic Games, World Cup tournaments, world or national championships, Super Bowls, College Bowl games, All-Star Games, high-profile auto races, golf tournaments, and track and field meets. In many cases, these expenditures of public money are connected with private entrepreneurial projects designed to increase private capital and "renew" blighted or declining areas. By using a sport team, a new stadium, or a major sport event to justify spending public money, business-oriented public officials can partner with developers to gentrify "downtown" by bringing in upscale businesses, shoppers, and residents, and moving out low-income residents and homeless people.

Using sports is an effective way to create public support for this type of development project, but many of the projects are risky and controversial as public investments. Most fail to meet the optimistic economic impact projections provided by developers, and benefits are enjoyed by relatively few people, (Shaffer, Green, and Mauboules, 2003).

> Winter Olympiads are largely a way to put a ski village on the map; the Summer Games can be an image-changing urban-renewal tool.
>
> —Nick Summers, *Newsweek* journalist, 2007.

and were put in touch with valuable resources in the realm of sports. At the same time, however, their involvement in other spheres was limited and non-sport social networks declined in scope (Harvey, Levesque, and Donnelly, 2007). Another study done in Canada found that people who had played youth sports were more likely to be involved in community activities through adulthood (Perks, 2007). Taken together, these studies indicate that sports may be associated with social development under certain conditions and that the social effects of this association may not be immediately observable in people's lives. This doesn't confirm the beliefs of public officials who use sports to promote social development as much as it provides information about how and when government can effectively facilitate social development and what can realistically be expected in terms of social effects.

AT YOUR *fingertips* For more information on the economic aspects of sports, see Chapter 10, pp. 317–322, and Chapter 11, pp. 358–366 and 372–380.

Government involvement in sports may also be based on the presumed social effects of sports in a community or society. Many public officials believe that sports, in almost any form, bring people together and create social bonds that carry into other spheres of life and increase the social vitality of a city or society. Research generally contradicts this belief, often finding that relationships formed in connection with sports seldom carry over to other spheres, and that some relationships between individuals and groups are characterized by conflicts that can interfere with social development.

Two recent studies have raised additional questions about this issue. Researchers doing an exploratory (or "pilot") study in Canada found that people who worked as volunteers with non-profit sport organizations for longer than one year expanded their network of relationships

Additional Examples of Government Involvement in Sports

The previous eight sections did not identify all types of government involvement in sports. Examples of other types of involvement include the following:

- Making laws that ban animal sports such as bullfighting or dog and cock fighting and protect the well-being of animals in horse and dog racing, fox hunting, and rodeo
- Making laws that ban, restrict, or regulate gambling on sports, thereby protecting the credibility of competitive sport outcomes and reining in athletes who might be coerced to shave points or fix competitions
- Adjusting the tax code (in the United States) so that the cost of tickets and luxury suites at sport events are partially tax-deductible business expenses

- Interpreting tax laws so that profit-making college sports are officially defined as non-profit educational programs
- Interpreting anti-trust and labor law in ways that benefit professional sport team owners
- Making public funding decisions that influence where public sport facilities are located and what sports they serve

Even though many people say that politics have no place in sports, governments play a key role in sponsoring and regulating sports. People generally take issue with government involvement only when it does not bring the results they want; otherwise, they seldom notice it.

Critical Issues and Government Involvement in Sports

Advocates of government involvement in sports justify it as serving the "public good." It would be ideal if governments promoted equally the interests of all citizens, but differences between individuals and groups make this impossible. Therefore, public investments in sports often benefit some people more than others. Those who benefit most are the persons or groups who are capable of directly influencing policy makers. This doesn't mean that government policies reflect only the interests of wealthy and powerful people, but it does mean that policy making is often contentious and creates power struggles among various segments of the population in a city or society.

Governments worldwide make decisions about allocating funds between elite sports and sports for all. Elite sports are highly organized, have strong backing from other organized groups, and base their requests for support on visible accomplishments achieved in the name of the entire country or city. Recreational sports serving large numbers of people are less organized, less likely to have powerful supporters, and less able to give precise statements of their goals and the political significance of their programs. This does not mean that government decision makers ignore

mass participation, but it does mean that "sport for all" usually has lower priority for funding and support (Green, 2004, 2006; Green and Houlihan, 2004; Sam, 2003).

Those who believe the myth that there is no connection between sports and government are most likely to be ignored by public officials, whereas those who are aware of government involvement are most likely to benefit when it does occur. Sports are connected with power relations in society as a whole; therefore, sports and politics cannot be separated.

SPORTS AND GLOBAL POLITICAL PROCESSES

Most people have lofty expectations about the impact of sports on global relations. It has long been hoped that sports would serve diplomatic functions by contributing to cultural understanding and world peace. Unfortunately, the realities of sports seldom match ideals. Nation-states and transnational corporations (TNCs) regularly use sports to promote their ideologies, and sports have become much more global today as athletes, teams, events, equipment, and capital investments and profits cross national borders as if they no longer exist. Issues related to these global processes often are linked with politics, so it is useful to understand them when studying sports in society.

International Sports: Ideals Versus Realities

Achieving peace and friendship among nations was emphasized by Baron Pierre de Coubertin when he founded the modern Olympic Games in 1896. For over a century, his goals have been embraced by many people who assumed or hoped that sports would do the following things:

- Create open communication lines between people and leaders from different nations.
- Highlight shared interests among people from different cultures and nations.

- Demonstrate that friendly international relationships are possible.
- Foster cultural understanding and eliminate the use of national stereotypes.
- Create a global model for cultural, economic, and political relationships.
- Establish processes that develop effective leaders in emerging nations and close the resource gap between wealthy and poor nations.

Recent history shows that sports can be useful in the realm of **public diplomacy,** which consists of *public expressions of togetherness in the form of cultural exchanges and general communication among officials from various nations.* However, sports have no impact in the realm of **serious diplomacy,** which consists of *discussions and decisions about political issues of vital national interest.* In other words, international sports provide opportunities for political leaders to meet and talk, but they don't influence the content of their discussions or their policy decisions.

Likewise, sports bring together athletes who may learn from and about one another, but athletes have seldom tried to make or influence political decisions, and their relationships with one another have no serious political significance. These points were illustrated clearly in 1999, when the Cuban National Baseball Team played the Baltimore Orioles in Cuba and then again in Baltimore. Media coverage and public conversations were affected temporarily, but the games had no impact on the adversarial political relations between the United States and Cuba (Pettavino and Brenner, 1999).

Recent history shows that most nations use sports and sport events, especially the Olympic Games, to pursue their own interests rather than to achieve international understanding, friendship, and peace (Jennings, 2006). Nationalist themes going beyond respectful expressions of patriotism have been clearly evident in many events, and most nations regularly use sport events to promote their own military, economic, political, and cultural agendas and ideologies. This was particularly apparent during the Cold War era following World War II and extending into the early 1990s. During these years, the Olympics were extensions of "superpower politics" between the United States and its allies and the former Soviet Union and its allies.

The inherent links between international sports and politics were so clear in the early 1980s that Peter Ueberroth, president of the committee that organized the 1984 Olympic Games in Los Angeles, said that "we now have to face the reality that the Olympics constitute not only an athletic event but a political event" (U.S. News & World Report, 1983). Ueberroth was not being prophetic; he was simply summarizing his observations of events leading up to the 1984 games. He saw that nations were more interested in benefiting themselves than in pursuing global friendship and peace. The demonstration of national superiority through sports was a major focus of world powers, and many nations that lacked political and economic power used sports to gain international recognition and legitimacy. For smaller nations, the Olympics, World Cups, and international championships have long been stages for showing that their athletes and teams can stand up to and sometimes defeat athletes and teams from wealthy and powerful nations. For example, when the cricket teams from the West Indies or India play teams from England, Indian and West Indian athletes and fans view the matches as opportunities to show the world that they are now equal to the nation that once colonized their land and controlled their people. When their teams win, it is cause for political affirmation and great celebration.

National and city leaders know that hosting the Olympics is a special opportunity to generate international recognition, display national power and resources to a global audience, and invite investments into their economies. This is why the bid committees from prospective host cities and nations have regularly used gifts, bribes, and financial incentives to encourage

The sports of wealthy and powerful nations in the Western Hemisphere form the foundation of the Olympic Games. This photo of the 1936 Olympic Games in Berlin shows the U.S. team saluting, in contrast to the straight-arm Nazi gesture of the Germans. The Nazi flag (far right) is prominently displayed by the host nation, and Adolf Hitler used the Olympics to promote Nazi ideology. (*Source:* USOC Archives)

IOC members to vote for them in the bid selection process. Illegal and illicit strategies reached their peak during the bidding for the 2002 Winter Olympics, when officials from Salt Lake City offered to IOC members and their families money, jobs, scholarships, lavish gifts, vacations, and the sexual services of "escorts" as they successfully secured the votes needed to host the games (Jennings, 1996a, 1996b; Jennings and Sambrook, 2000).

The link between sports and politics has been clearly exposed by protests and boycotts directed at the Olympics and other international sport events. For example, when Mexican college students used the 1968 Olympic Games hosted by Mexico City as an occasion for protesting police violence and the oppressive political regime that the violence supported, the police and military massacred hundreds of students and others in a public plaza in the Tlatelolco neighborhood of Mexico City (Poniatowska, 1975). Representatives of governments and National Olympic Committees said little or nothing about the murders because they wanted a "secure" Olympic Games.

In 1980, the United States and sixty-two of its political allies boycotted the Olympic Games in Moscow, which was then the capital of the Soviet Union (USSR), to protest the Soviet Union's decision to unilaterally invade Afghanistan to eliminate Islamic rebels, including Osama bin Laden, because the rebels were subverting Soviet control of the region. The United States supported the autonomy of Afghanistan, armed the rebels, and helped to create the terrorist infrastructure that later became Al-Qaeda. In retaliation, the Soviet Union and at least fourteen of its allies boycotted the 1984 Olympic Games in Los Angeles to protest the commercialization of the games and avoid terrorist actions they expected from jingoistic Americans. Each of these Olympic Games was held despite the boycotts, and each host nation unashamedly displayed its power and resources to the world and touted the fact that they topped the medal count for the respective games. Neither the boycotts nor hosting the games had any major effects on American or Soviet political policies, although they did intensify Cold War feelings and fears.

Global media coverage of sport mega-events has added new dimensions to the link between sports and politics. Television companies, especially the American networks, have used political controversies to hype the games and increase audience ratings, and they edit programming to highlight the American flag and melodramatic stories about athletes who overcame disadvantage to achieve success and participate in the American Dream (Greider, 2006). Networks claim that Americans won't watch an Olympics unless the dominant ideologies and global power of the United States are woven into the coverage. Of course, the U.S. media aren't the only ones to do this, but their impact far surpasses the impact of nationalist and ethnocentric coverage in other nations, because the military and economic power and policies of the United States affect the world much more than do the power and policies of other nation-states.

Nationalistic themes in media coverage of international sports are now accompanied and sometimes obscured by images and narratives promoting capitalist expansion and the products and services of transnational corporations. These issues are discussed in the box titled "Olympism and the Olympic Games."

> **ON THE *OLC*:**
> See the OLC—Additional Readings for Chapter 13—for a summary of recent Olympic Games at which there have been significant protests and boycotts related to political issues.

Nation-States, Sports, and Ideological Hegemony

Global politics often revolve around issues of ideological hegemony—that is, whose ideas and beliefs are most widely accepted worldwide and used to guide everything from world trade to who starts wars with whom. In this process, sports usually serve the interests of wealthy and powerful nations. For example, when nations with few resources want to participate in major international sports, they must look to wealthy nations for assistance in the form of coaching, equipment, and training support. As this occurs, people in poorer nations often de-emphasize their traditional folk games and focus on the global sports developed around the values and experiences of nations powerful enough to export their games around the globe and make them the centerpieces of international competitions. If they want to play, those are the sports that will put them on the program. To the extent that this makes them dependent, sports become vehicles for economically powerful nations to extend their control over important forms of popular culture worldwide—and to claim that it is part of the "foreign aid" that they give to assist poor people and struggling nations (Miller et al., 2001, 2003).

If people in traditional cultures want to preserve their native games, they must resist a dependency status, but this is difficult in international sports when the rules and other structural characteristics of the sports reflect and privilege the ideologies of powerful nations (Ben-Porat and Ben-Porat, 2004; Gems, 2006; Klein, 2008a; Mills and Dimeo, 2003). For example,

reflect on **SPORTS**

Olympism and the Olympic Games:
Are They Special?

According to the Olympic Charter, the Olympic Games are based on a special philosophy described in these words:

> Olympism is a philosophy of life, exalting and combining in a balanced whole the qualities of body, will and mind. Blending sport with culture and education, Olympism seeks to create a way of life based on the joy found in effort, the educational value of good example and respect for universal fundamental ethical principles.

The fundamental principles of the Olympic Charter are simple and straightforward. They emphasize that the Olympics should provide opportunities for people worldwide to learn about and connect with one another—a commendable goal given that our future and the future of the earth itself depends on global cooperation.

The spirit of Olympism emphasizes learning to understand and appreciate human diversity and working to sustain healthy and safe lifestyles worldwide. If the Olympic Games inspire this spirit, they are indeed special. But nationalism and commercialism exert so much influence on today's Olympic Games that the goals of global understanding and health promotion receive only token attention (Carrington, 2004; Lenskyj, 2008).

One of the factors undermining Olympism is the current method of selling media broadcasting rights for the Olympic Games (Andrews, 2007; Real, 1996). Television companies buy the rights to take the video images they want from the Olympics and combine them with their own narratives to attract audiences in their countries. So instead of bringing the world together around a single unifying experience, the coverage consists of many heavily nationalized and commercialized versions of the Olympic Games. Of course, media consumers give their own meanings to this coverage, but they have images and narratives from only their nation as starting points for making sense of and talking about the Olympics.

Media consumers who want to use the Olympics to visualize a global community constructed around cultural differences and mutual understanding can do so, but current media coverage provides little assistance in this quest. Most coverage highlights the association between human achievement, selected cultural values, and corporate sponsors. In the process, many people come to believe that corporations really do make the Olympics possible. As they watch television coverage in the United States, about 20 percent of the programming consists of commercial messages from corporations, many of which claim to "bring you the Olympics."

People don't accept media images and narratives in literal terms, but corporate sponsors now bet nearly a billion dollars every two years on the possibility that associating their products and logos with the Olympics will discourage criticism of their products, encourage people to consume those products regularly, and normalize a lifestyle organized around ceaseless consumption.

The overt commercialism that now pervades the Olympics has led some people to question the meaning of the games themselves. "The Olympics is not about sports any more," says a multiple-medal-winning Olympian. "It's about who can win the most money. It's like going to Disneyland" (in Reid, 1996, p. 4BB). A similar observation was expressed by a high-ranking Olympic official who said,

> I'm on the verge of joining those who think it's time for the Olympics, in their present context, to die. And they need to die for the same reason the ancient Olympic Games died—greed and corruption (in Reid, 1996, p. 4BB).

Charles Barkley, a member of the U.S. men's basketball "Dream Team" in 1992, noted that Olympic ideals had little to do with his experience at the games. He said that the U.S. team came to the Olympics "to spread basketball internationally and make more money for somebody" and when it's over, "poor people will still be poor and racism and sexism will still exist" (in DuPree, 1992, p. 7E). Barkley's conclusion is supported by Kevin Walmsley, director of the International Center for Olympic Studies, who describes the Olympic Ideal as "an empty vessel filled up by the ideas of the day" (in Price, 2004).

These statements indicate that the Olympic Games must be changed. The IOC issues regular press releases full of rhetoric about friendship and peace, but it does little to fund, foster, and institutionalize programs and processes focused explicitly on cultural understanding and social responsibility. Bruce Kidd (1996a), a former Olympian and a physical and health educator at the University of Toronto, argues that if the Olympic Games are to be special, they must use sports to make people aware of global injustice and promote social responsibility worldwide.

Kidd says that in the spirit of Olympism, athletes should be selected for participation in the games on the basis of their actions as global citizens as well as their athletic accomplishments. There also should be a curriculum enabling athletes to learn about fellow competitors and their cultures. The games should involve formal, televised opportunities for intercultural exchanges, and athletes should be ready to discuss their ideas about world peace and social responsibility during media interviews.

The IOC should sponsor projects enabling citizen-athletes to build on their Olympic experiences through service to others around the world. A proportion of the windfall profits coming from rapidly escalating TV rights fees should fund such projects, thereby giving IOC members opportunities to talk about real examples of social responsibility that they support. The "up close and personal" stories presented in the media could then highlight the socially responsible actions of athletes, rather than creating soap-opera–like stories of personal tragedies and triumphs. Media consumers are increasingly aware that they don't live in isolation from the rest of the world and may find such coverage more entertaining and hopeful than tabloid-like stories of trouble and trauma.

Additionally, the IOC could control nationalism and commercialism more carefully as it organizes the games and sells broadcasting rights. There is no single best way to do this, but I would suggest that some of the following nine changes be made:

1. *Eliminate national uniforms for athletes.* Let athletes choose from uniforms created by designers selected to express cultural themes from various regions of the world. This change would reduce nationalism, highlight creativity and cultural learning, and incorporate art into the Olympics—effects that the ancient Greeks would

Coca-Cola spent well over half a billion dollars to present corporate images and messages in connection with the 2008 Olympic Games in Beijing. Here, as part of their "Red Around the World" campaign (nearly everything is red in this photo), the company dressed NBA star Yao Ming and world-record-holding hurdler Liu Xiang to represent a Coke bottle and can, respectively. Associating China and its two most popular athletes with their brand and logo is a key political strategy in a nation where government permission is needed to do business as Coca-Cola wants to do. (Imaginechina/AP Wide World Photos)

endorse. The specially designed uniforms could be trademarked and sold by an "Olympic Artists Foundation," with incoming revenue used to support artists in developing regions of the world and to empower the workers who make sport equipment and apparel for less than a living wage under oppressive conditions.

reflect on SPORTS

Olympism and the Olympic Games (Continued)

2. *Revise the opening ceremonies so that athletes enter the arena by event instead of by nation.* This would emphasize global unity rather than the nation-states into which athletes were born by chance. Artists from around the world would be commissioned to design flags for various sports, and the flags of nation-states would be displayed in the middle of the field to emphasize that unity can exist with difference.

3. *Eliminate national anthems and flags during award ceremonies.* Medals would be presented at the end of each day of competition in an area designed to present the athletes first as representatives of all humanity, and second as representatives of their nations. This would highlight global unity rather than the superiority of some nations over others.

4. *Promote a fair method of calculating medal counts.* National medal counts are contrary to the spirit and official principles of Olympism. They foster chauvinism, present the achievements of athletes in divisive rather than unifying ways, and privilege large, wealthy nations with the resources to create excellence in sports. To defuse the meaning that people give to traditional medal counts, members of the Olympic Academy (scholars who study Olympism) should publish an "official medal count" in which the size and/or wealth of nations is statistically controlled. Table 13.1 provides an example of how rankings would change if only national population size were controlled. Column A ranks nations in traditional terms—by the total number of medals won in all the Olympic Games from 1896 through 2004. But Column B ranks nations in terms of the medals won per capita (for every ten million people, in this case). Therefore, if a nation with ten million people has an athlete who wins one medal, it would have the same significance as a nation with 100 million people having athletes who win 10 medals.

5. *Eliminate or revise team sports.* Organizing team sports by nation encourages players and spectators to perceive games in we-versus-they terms. Therefore, eliminate all team sports or develop methods of choosing teams so that athletes from different countries play on the same teams and athletes from a particular nation play on different teams. Then "dream teams" would emphasize international unity rather than specific national and commercial interests. And athletes might make more friends worldwide and learn about other cultures.

6. *Add to each games "demonstration sports" native to the cultural regions where the games are held.* The IOC should specify that all media companies purchasing broadcasting rights and receiving press credentials must devote 5 percent of their coverage to these native games. Because the media influence the ways that people imagine, create, and play sports around the world, this would provide expanded images of physical activities and facilitate creative approaches to sport participation worldwide. At present, many Olympic sports are simply a legacy of former colonial powers that exported their games as they conquered around the world (Bale and Christensen, 2004).

7. *Use multiple sites for each Olympic Games.* The cost of hosting the summer Olympic Games was $14.6 billion for Athens in 2004 and well over $40 billion for Beijing in 2008; and as I write this, London has already spent nearly $10 billion, about 300 percent over their original budget projections. Such costs privilege wealthy nations and prevent less wealthy nations from hosting the games and highlighting their cultures. If Olympic events were split into three successive "event packages," it would be possible for some developing nations to host one of the event packages and enjoy the benefits of staging the events at the same time that media spectators would see a wider range of cultural settings as they viewed events over the eighteen days of coverage. When one nation hosts the entire games, it is required to build massive, highly specialized facilities that may never be regularly used or filled to capacity in the future. This is economically and ecologically irresponsible and often leaves citizens in cities or smaller nations with a legacy of massive debts and underused facilities.

Table 13.1   Olympic medal count by total medals and medals per capita, 2007

Total medals rank		Medals per 10 million people*	
Nation	**Medals**	**Nation**	**Medals**
1. United States	2309	1. Liechtenstein	2669
2. France	670	2. Norway	864
3. United Kingdom	664	3. Finland	839
4. Sweden	577	4. Sweden	641
5. Italy	568	5. Hungary	448
6. Germany	560	6. Switzerland	382
7. Hungary	449	7. Austria	303
8. Finland	438	8. Denmark	298
9. Norway	398	9. Bulgaria	269
10. Australia	354	10. St. Kitts & Nevis	257
11. Canada	326	11. Estonia	217
12. Japan	296	12. Bahamas	199
13. Switzerland	286	13. New Zealand	185
14. Netherlands	282	14. Australia	176
15. Romania	266	15. Netherlands	172
16. Austria	248	16. Bermuda	153
17. Poland	247	17. Belgium	140
18. China	245	18. Jamaica	135
19. Russia	214	19. Cuba	120
20. Bulgaria	200	20. Romania	119
21. Korea, South	174	21. Greece	118
22. Denmark	162	22. France	111
23. Belgium	145	23. United Kingdom	109
24. Cuba	137	24. Luxembourg	106
25. Greece	126	25. Trinidad & Tobago	102
		(31. United States	79)

(*Source:* Adapted from four data sets provided by NationMaster: http://www.nationmaster.com/graph/spo_sum_oly_med_all_tim-summer-olympic-medals-all-time (retrieved June 10, 2008). The data cover all medals won from 1896 to 2004. This is problematic because many countries today did not exist prior to the end of World War I and World War II when the victors split or combined existing nations to meet their interests and concerns.

* In the per capita list, the United States ranks #31 (79 medals per 10 million people), behind Iceland (#26), Canada (#27), Italy (#28), Virgin Islands (#29), and Tonga (#30). If per capita income were also taken into account, the list would shift and the United States would drop much lower than #31 (see http://www.symworld.com/medals/index.php?sort=totalnormal and http://www.billmitchell.org/sport/medal_tally_2008).

8. *Emphasize global responsibility in media coverage.* Television contracts should mandate an emphasis on global social responsibility in the media coverage of the games. Athlete committees, working with scholars from the Olympic Academy, could identify individuals, organizations, and corporations that have engaged in noteworthy forms of social responsibility and assist media companies in producing coverage of these cases. Additionally, a mandated amount of media time should

be dedicated to public service announcements from nonprofit human rights groups that work with athletes and sport organizations to promote social justice and sustainable forms of development. This would guarantee that media consumers would have access to messages that are not created or censored by corporations and market forces.

9. *Integrate the Olympics and Paralympics.* Just as the Olympic Movement supports gender equality and opposes racial apartheid in sports, it should include people with disabilities in the Olympic Movement (Wolff, 2005). This could be done by having common opening and closing ceremonies, awarding the same Olympic medals to athletes in both events, and referring to both as "Olympics." This would send a powerful message to the world

saying that the full inclusion of people with disabilities is an achievable goal in all spheres of life.

People will say that these suggestions are idealistic or that the IOC, the global media, and corporate sponsors constitute a power base that cannot be challenged successfully. However, the Olympic movement was founded on idealism and intended to inspire visions of what our world could and should be; additionally, it emphasizes that progress comes only through effort and participation. If the Olympic Games of today are little more than global-marketing opportunities for transnational corporations and a stage for global power displays by wealthy nations with medal-winning athletes, now is a good time to take action. A good starting point would be to replace "Citius, Altius, Fortius" ("Faster, Higher, Stronger") with "Excellence, Unity, and Peace" as the new Olympic motto. *What do you think?*

when an American sport such as football is introduced to another country, it comes with an emphasis on ideas about individual achievement, competition, winning, hierarchical authority structures, physical power and domination, the body, and the use of technology to shape bodies into efficient machines. These ideas may not be completely accepted by everyone who plays or watches football, but they reaffirm orientations that privilege U.S. interests and obscure the cooperative values that are common and even necessary for the collective survival of most traditional cultures. As an editor at *Newsweek* noted, "Sports may be America's most successful export to the world. . . . Our most visible symbol has evolved from the Stars and Stripes to Coke and the Nike Swoosh" (Starr, 1999, p. 44).

> **Sport is beautifully trivial. In the World Cup, it's the trivial magnified to global mega-drama. One of the democratic tasks of critically engaged sports fans is to rescue that triviality from the exploitative forces that pump it up with dubious meanings.** —Mark Perryman, author, *Ingerland: Travels with a Football Nation*

Ideally, sports facilitate cultural exchanges through which people from different nations share information and develop mutual cultural understanding. But true 50–50 sharing and mutual understanding are rare when nations have unequal power and resources. Therefore, sports often become cultural exports from wealthy nations incorporated into the everyday lives of people worldwide. Local people are free to reject, revise, or redefine these sports (Ben-Porat and Ben-Porat, 2004; Denham, 2004; Falcous and Maguire, 2006; Falcous and Silk, 2006; J. Maguire, 2005), but when "cultural trade routes" are opened through sports, nations that import sports often become increasingly open to importing and consuming additional goods, services, and ideas from the nations that export sports (Jackson and Andrews, 2004). To avoid this outcome, the less

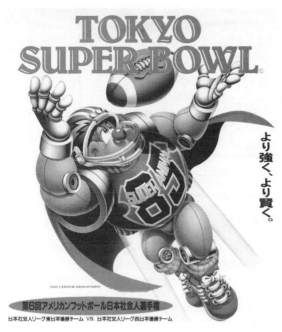

より強く、より賢く。

第6回アメリカンフットボール日本社会人選手権

日本社会人リーグ東日本優勝チーム VS. 日本社会人リーグ西日本優勝チーム

Efforts by the NFL to export football to other nations have failed, largely because it requires expensive equipment and facilities and is tied to meanings and ideologies unique to history and culture in the United States. This advertising poster shows how the NFL was represented by and for Japanese people as they hosted an NFL preseason game played in Tokyo in 1992. The caricature shows a "superanimal" with bionic joints, protective equipment, and a cape. (*Source:* Jay Coakley)

powerful nations must increase their political power and economic resources; if the imbalance is not corrected it becomes more difficult to resist the ideological hegemony of wealthy and powerful nations.

New Political Realities in an Era of Transnational Corporations

Global politics have changed dramatically since the 1970s. Massive corporations are now among the largest economies in the world today, and they share the global political stage with nation-states. This change occurred as nation-states embraced a policy of deregulation, lifted trade restrictions, lowered tariffs, and made it easier for capital, labor, and goods to flow freely around the globe. Although nation-states remain central in global relations, the differences between national and corporate interests and identities have nearly disappeared in connection with sports. This was implied by Phil Knight, CEO of U.S.-based Nike, when he discussed shifts in fan loyalties in the Men's World Cup in soccer:

> We see a natural evolution . . . dividing the world into their athletes and ours. And we glory ours. When the U.S. played Brazil in the World Cup, I rooted for Brazil because it was a Nike team. America was Adidas (in Lipsyte, 1996a, p. 9).

For Knight, teams and athletes now represent corporations as much or more than nations; and corporate logos have become more visible than national flags at international events. When Nike paid to sponsor Brazil's national team and used its players to market Nike products worldwide, Knight was pushing consumption and brand loyalty over patriotism and public service as the most important global values. For him, sports were outposts in the heads of sport fans worldwide and could be used as receptors and transmitters for the messages coming from Nike and other corporate sponsors seeking further global capitalist expansion. Like executives from other transnational corporations (TNCs), he believes that sports contribute to the growth of global well-being when they are used to promote a lifestyle of consumption and the ideologies that support it.

Corporate sponsors now exert significant influence over sport events, at least to the point of directing sport images and narratives toward spectator-consumers rather than spectator-citizens. Sports that can't be covered this way—such as those that aren't organized to attract spectators with high purchasing power, or those that don't emphasize competitive outcomes and setting performance/production records—are not sponsored. When spectators and potential media audiences are not valued consumers, and when sports don't represent an ideology of competition

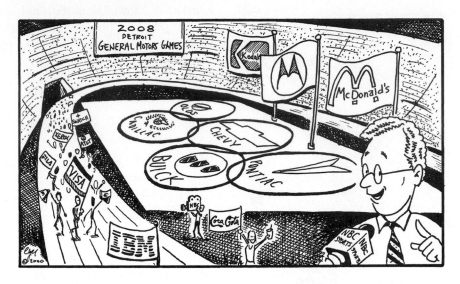

"NBC Sports has eliminated nationalism in our Olympic coverage and replaced it with global consumer capitalism. Now our commentary will be full of references to individualism, competition, and success by conquest. Enjoy the games—and the commercials!"

Global politics today involve the interaction of nation-states and transnational corporations. As a result the media coverage of global mega-events is organized around images and messages that link transnational corporations with flags, anthems, and athletes representing nation-states. Patriotic feelings and consumer desires are seamlessly woven together.

and success, corporations don't become sponsors and commercial media have no reason to cover them.

The global power of transnational corporations is neither unlimited nor uncontested. Individuals and local populations have used their own cultural perspectives to make sense of the images and narratives that come with global sports and give them meanings that fit with their lives (Foer, 2004; J. Maguire, 1999, 2005). However, research that combines cultural theory and a critical approach shows that global media sports and the commercial messages that accompany them often cleverly fuse the global and the local through thoughtfully and carefully edited images that combine local traditions, sport action, and consumer products in seamless and technically brilliant media representations (Andrews and Silk, 1999; Carrington and Sugden, 1999; Jackson and Andrews, 2004; Jackson

and Hokowhitu, 2002; Jackson and Scherer, 2002; Miller et al., 2001, 2003; Silk, 1999; Tomlinson, 2005). These researchers argue that such fused images tend to "detraditionalize" local cultures by representing local symbols and lifestyles in connection with consumer products that, by themselves, have nothing to do with traditional local culture.

The process of destabilizing local cultures and creating a culture of consumption is based on the corporate application of research findings in anthropology, sociology, and psychology (Goodman, 2001; Klein, 2002)—and it occurs in a broader context than traditional cultures in developing regions of the world. For example, a company that produces shoes and apparel suited for physical activity may hire qualitative researchers to observe young people and identify new, popular activities that they've invented and incorporated into their lives. When an activity is identified, it is described in fine detail, and the "homemade" apparel of participants is carefully studied. Then the company "produces" a version of the shoes and apparel that represents the culture created around the activity and gives "samples" to the most popular participants and asks them to try them out. People from the company hope that after they have taken the creations of the young people and used them to produce consumer items, they can sell the items back to the young people for a profit. Additionally, they patent, trademark, and copyright the items so that what was originally created by the participants in the local activity is now owned and controlled by the company and used for its purpose.

On a slightly less subversive level, Coca-Cola claims that it sponsors the Olympics because it wants the whole world "to sing," to "live Olympic," to experience "unity on the Coke side of life," to be "red around the world," to "go red for China," or to be "friends forever," but when Coke executives envision "one world one dream," they see 6.7 billion people drinking Coke after Coke for life. McDonald's uses a similar approach as the Official Restaurant of the Olympic Games from 1996 through 2012.

Corporations that sponsor global sports and use them as advertising platforms know that sooner or later the images and narratives associated with sources of pleasure and entertainment in people's lives will in some form enter the imaginations and conversations of those who see and hear them. Commercial images and messages do not dictate what people think, but they certainly influence what people think about, and in this way, they become a part of the overall discourse that occurs in cultures around the globe.

This description of new global political realities does not mean that sports have fallen victim to a worldwide conspiracy hatched by transnational corporations. It means only that transnational corporations have joined nation-states in the global political context in which sports are defined, organized, promoted, played, presented, and given meaning around the world (Jackson and Scherer, 2002; Silk, 1999).

Other Global Political Issues

As sports become increasingly commercialized and national boundaries become less relevant, more athletes become global migrant workers. As they increasingly go where they can develop their skills and earn rewards, the global migration of athletes has raised new political issues for sports. Similarly, as the demand for sports equipment and clothing has increased in wealthy nations, transnational corporations have opted to cut costs for those products by manufacturing them in poor countries where wages are extremely low and workers are plentiful. A result of these two developments is a clear split between the world's haves and have-nots when it comes to sports. Those born into privilege in wealthy nations manage and host sports and consume sport products, and those born into disadvantaged circumstances struggle to make a living on the field or in the factory. This gap between rich and poor is not new, but it reminds us that sports are integrally linked with global political processes in many ways.

Athletes as Global Migrant Workers When Team USA competed in Beijing during the 2008 Olympic Games, some of the potential medal winners included table tennis players from China, a kayaker from Poland, a record-setting distance runner from Kenya (with a Chinese coach), a former gold medalist equestrian from Australia, and a triathlete from New Zealand (Wilson and Lehren, 2008). Each was a new U.S. citizen, and each competed in a sport that attracts few elite American athletes.

Like other forms of labor migration, the global recruitment and migration of athletes blurs national borders. But in sports, it also blurs the meaning of success in both national and international events (Bale and Maguire, 1994; Maguire, 2004; Maguire and Stead, 2005). For example, what does it mean to people in China and the United States when a Chinese-born and -trained table tennis player wins a medal as a member of the U.S. team? In another case, Yamilé Aldama is one of the best triple jumpers in the world. She was born in Cuba, currently lives in

London, is a naturalized citizen of Sudan, and has applied for British citizenship; at this point, she is basically "stateless." On whose national team should she compete? To make things more interesting without being unrealistic, let's imagine that she married a Jamaican and gave birth to a child in the United States and still wants to compete in the Olympics.

These examples highlight the fluidity of citizenship in a global sport world where boundaries have been blurred and erased by a growing number of athletes and fans. When athletes move from one nation to another, it may be due to personal choice, a need to obtain political asylum, or being recruited by a talent scout, a coach, or an organization that represents elite athletes. Regardless of the reason, the move raises issues related to (1) personal adjustments by migrating athletes, (2) the rights of athletes as workers, (3) the impact of talent migration on the nations from and to which athletes migrate, and (4) the impact of athlete migration on the identities of athletes and fans.

Some migration patterns are seasonal, involving temporary moves as athletes travel from one climate area to another to play their sports. Patterns may follow annual tour schedules as athletes travel from tournament to tournament around a region or the world, or they may involve longterm or permanent moves from one region or nation to another. For example, baseball players and snow skiers may travel alternately to the northern and southern hemispheres to play ball or ski year-round.

The range of personal experiences among migrating athletes is great. They vary from major forms of culture shock and chronic loneliness to minor homesickness and lifestyle adjustments. Some athletes are exploited by teams or clubs, whereas others make great amounts of money and receive a hero's welcome when they return home in the off-season. Some encounter prejudice against foreigners or various forms of racial and ethnic bigotry, whereas others are socially accepted and form close friendships. Some cling to their national identities and socialize with fellow athletes from their homelands, whereas others develop more global identities unrelated to one national or cultural background. In some cases, teams and clubs expect foreign athletes to adjust on their own, whereas others provide support for those who need to learn a new language or become familiar with new cultural settings (Burgos, 2007; Klein, 1991, 2006; J. Maguire, 2004, 2005).

Athletic talent migration also has an impact on the nations involved. For example, when the top baseball players in Latin America, Japan, and Korea are recruited by North American Major League Baseball (MLB) teams, it depletes talent from professional teams and leagues in those nations and forces their local fans to watch MLB games to see the best players from their nations. As they watch MLB games, attendance and television ratings for games in their home countries decline, teams and leagues experience financial problems, and soon the training infrastructure and resources to develop top players erodes; in the process, young people lose the support and inspiration needed to develop elite skills in those sports.

This process has already created serious concerns in European soccer. For example, when Premier League clubs in England recruit players worldwide, they invest less money in the development of local talent. As fewer young people are inspired to play a game in which the majority of top players are from other nations, local talent fades and the local fan base declines. This is not an immediate issue for teams with a global fan base, but who will those teams play when other clubs fail financially? Will a global league be practical, and will it support the talent creation that makes a sport attractive to fans? These are unanswered questions, but current trends suggest that answers are needed.

The global migration of athletes also may influence how people think about and identify themselves in connection with nation-states, but this topic has not been studied. Many people appreciate athletic talent regardless of the athlete's nationality (Cyphers, 2003), but they may also feel special affection for athletes born and raised in their own nation. Does this make people more open-minded and knowledgeable about other cultures, or does it make them more defensive and ethnocentric? This question is important because many teams and leagues now recruit players from a wide range of national and cultural backgrounds. For example, during the 2007–2008 season, less than 20 percent of NHL players were U.S.-born; about half were from Canada, and about 30 percent were from European nations. Over one-fourth of the players on MLB teams and over 40 percent of the players at all levels of professional baseball in North America were born outside the United States. Among the 450 players in the NBA during the 2007–2008 season, there were eighty-one international players from thirty-five countries; over 25 percent of the 2007 NBA All-Star selections were players born outside the United States.

These trends worry some people and have led to quotas on the number of foreign-born or foreign-nationality players that teams may sign to contracts. For example, in the early 1990s, Japan banned U.S. female basketball players from its professional league. At the same time, professional leagues in Italy, Spain, and France allowed their teams to have up to two foreign players, many of whom were from the United States. In 1996 England lifted all quotas for both men's and women's pro basketball teams; during the same year, the new Major League Soccer (MLS) organization in the United States limited the number of non–U.S. players to four per team. Currently, some people in the United States want limits on the number of foreign athletes who can play on intercollegiate teams, but college coaches continue to recruit more athletes from outside the United States.

Another dimension of this issue is related to global team ownership patterns. As new multibillionaires around the world recruit top athletes for teams in their countries, it's possible that an entire professional league could lose its best players to a new league that could buy the talent needed to create the most elite league in the world. For example, wealthy and powerful people in Russia want hockey to be centered in their country, and they're now luring players to the Russian professional Superliga (Schwirtz, 2008).

As commercial sport organizations expand their franchise locations across national borders and compete for athletes worldwide, the global migration of athletes will continue to increase. Researchers in the sociology of sport have studied some of the implications of this migration, but much remains to be learned (Elliott and Maguire, 2008; Takahashi and Horne, 2006; Taylor, 2007).

Global Politics and the Production of Sports Equipment and Apparel Free-trade agreements allowing money and goods to flow across national borders without the constraints of taxes and tariffs have created a new global economic environment. This change makes it even more cost-effective for large corporations selling products to people in wealthy nations to locate production facilities in labor-intensive, poor nations. Workers in these nations are desperate for jobs and will work for low wages under conditions that would be considered oppressive by everyone who buys the products.

Through the first few years of this century, many athletic shoes costing well over $100 a pair in the United States were cut and sewn by Chinese, Indonesian, and Thai workers, some of them children, making less than $2 per day (Sage, 1999). Children in Pakistan, India, and Bangladesh, where working conditions and pay often are reprehensible, stitched soccer balls. Outrage among people who became aware of these situations in the late 1990s led to widespread social activism, much of which was fueled by Internet communication. After years of confronting and struggling with companies such as Nike, Reebok, Adidas, and others, human rights activists forced some of these corporations to create anti–child labor policies and to allow their factories to be monitored so that acceptable working conditions could be established and maintained. But child labor and sweatshop conditions continue to exist, and a wide range of sporting goods and apparel consumed in

When activists such as the Maquila Solidarity Network, the Global March Against Child Labour, and other social justice groups sparked global pressure to stop companies from using children to sew soccer balls in India and Pakistan, some sewing operations moved to Africa, where people are desperate for jobs and not yet organized to demand fair wages. Instead of setting up factories, companies contract with individuals who work in their homes or small local facilities like this one outside of Nairobi, Kenya. (Photo compliments of Kevin Young)

wealthy nations is made by people living below local poverty levels and working under conditions that make individual and family survival a daily challenge (Play Fair, 2008; Oxfam International, 2008; WRC, 2007).

A report in 2004 showed that MLB used balls stitched in Costa Rica by people who worked eleven hours a day, six days a week, for about $2750 per year. This compares poorly with the $2.5-million average salary for MLB players. Starting at 6 a.m. and quitting at 5 p.m., unless forced to work overtime, the people in Costa Rican factories earn about 30 cents for sewing 108 perfect stitches on the seams of a ball. The work is hard, says a thirty-seven-year-old man who sews baseballs in a factory where the temperature often is above 90 degrees. "Sometimes," he explains, "it messes up your hands, warps your fingers and hurts your shoulders" (Weiner, 2004). This man's 30 cents of labor produces a ball that Rawlings Sporting Goods sells for

$15 (as of June 2008; http://www.rawlingsgear .com/Baseball/Balls).

Research shows that it's possible to improve working conditions among people who produce sporting goods and other products if enough people in wealthy nations participate in actions that make corporations accountable and also provide exploited workers with the resources they need to demand higher wages and better working conditions. For example, when the Nike Transnational Advocacy Network, a worldwide Internet-based activist organization, exposed the exploitive practices used in Nike factories in the late 1990s, they forced significant changes in the conditions under which workers produced Nike products in certain nations (Sage, 1999). However, Jim Keady, co-director of Educating for Justice and an expert on working conditions in Nike factories in Southeast Asia, reported in mid-2008 that wages and collective bargaining have not changed and the "spending power for

Nike's production workers is actually worse than it was in 2000, even though Nike profits in 2007 hit a record $1.5 billion." As Keady notes, "This is truly a case of the rich getting richer and the poor getting poorer" (EFJ, 2008).

In Indonesia, where Keady has done extensive research on living conditions, workers are trying to bargain for cost-of-living wage increases. In response, Nike is threatening to leave town and take 7300 jobs elsewhere. This relocation would devastate this already poverty-stricken area and threaten thousands of lives. But stockholders always want Nike to hit quarterly revenue projections, and Nike can do this only by continuing to exploit current workers or by moving their production to a part of the world where workers are just as desperate but not yet organized. Of course, Nike is not the only source of this injustice; many other companies use the same exploitive practices despite the work of activists between 1995 and the 2004 Olympic Games in Athens, Greece. Two different research reports issued in 2008 provide evidence that serious violations of workers' rights continue to be the norm in the production of sports brands (Oxfam International, 2008; Play Fair, 2008).

Politics is relevant to this sport-related labor issue because neither the local (Indonesian, Thai, Chinese, Sri Lankan, Cambodian, and others) nor U.S. governments see fit to intervene for the sake of the workers, and people in the United States and other wealthy nations are not yet concerned enough about these issues to politicize their consumption of sport equipment, shoes, and apparel by boycotting all products not certified by worker advocacy organizations. Unless consumer-citizens in wealthy nations become concerned enough about the people who make their products to take action, social justice activists will not by themselves be able to make significant changes in an under-regulated global marketplace where transnational corporations can pursue profits with little or no oversight or accountability.

Students at a number of universities in the United States have organized to demand that the apparel and equipment sold in their campus stores and used in the athletic departments are made in conformity with an antisweatshop code. This is a useful step in reducing worker exploitation in poor nations where governments don't regulate corporations to protect workers. In the case of Nike, Champion, Adidas, Reebok, Puma, and others, this strategy can be effective because these companies have contracts with many universities and athletic departments. Human rights and social justice groups have fought these battles for many years, and organizational structures are in place that enable students to help them without ever leaving campus.

Making Sense of Political Realities

It's not easy to explain the relationships between sports and global political processes. Are sports today merely tools of capitalist expansion and new forms of cultural imperialism? Are they being used by wealthy nations to make poor, developing nations dependent on them, or do they enable emerging nations to achieve cultural and economic independence? As globalization occurs, are traditional sports and folk games being replaced by the organized, competitive sports favored by wealthy and powerful nations?

Finding answers to these questions requires research at local *and* global levels. Existing studies suggest that sports that are favored by wealthy nations are not simply imposed on people worldwide. Even when people play sports that come from powerful nations, they give them meanings that are grounded in local cultures and the experiences of the people who play them. Global trends are important, but so are the local expressions of and responses to those trends (Bale and Christensen, 2004; Bale and Cronin, 2003; Ben-Porat and Ben-Porat, 2004; Denham, 2004; Donnelly, 1996a; Foer, 2004; Hastings, Cable, and Zahran, 2005; J. Maguire, 1999, 2004, 2005; Okubu, 2004). Power is a process, and it is always exercised through relationships and current forms of social organization. Therefore, research on sports worldwide must examine the processes through which powerful nations exert control over sports in other nations as well as the processes through which people worldwide integrate sports and sport experiences into their lives on their own terms.

POLITICS IN SPORTS

The term *politics* usually is associated with formal government entities in the public sphere. However, politics include all processes of governing people and administering policies, at all levels of organization, both public and private. Therefore, politics are an integral part of sports, and many local, national, and international sport organizations are referred to as "governing bodies."

Most sport organizations provide and regulate sport participation opportunities, establish and enforce policies, control and standardize competitions, and acknowledge the accomplishments of athletes. This sounds like a straightforward set of tasks, but they seldom are accomplished without opposition, debate, and compromise. Members of sport organizations agree on many things, but conflicts often arise as decisions are made in connection with the following seven questions:

OLC ON THE *OLC*:
See the OLC—Additional Readings for Chapter 13—for a full discussion of the ways that politics are an inherent part of all organized sports, from "T-ball" to the Olympic Games.

1. What qualifies as a sport? There is no universal definition of sport, so each nation, community, and international event, such as the Olympic Games, must develop a definition that makes sense within its circumstances. As a result, official as well as unofficial definitions of "sport" vary widely.
2. What are the rules of a sport? The rules in all sports are arbitrary and changeable. The governing bodies of sports often change

Outside Southeast Asia, Sepak Takraw might be called kick volleyball with no hands or arms allowed; only feet, head, knees, and chest may contact the ball. Based on cuju, an ancient Chinese game, Sepak Takraw has been played by people in Vietnam, Malaysia, Indonesia, Laos, Thailand, and Myanmar for five centuries. If these nations had conquered and colonized other parts of the world and used this game to socialize colonial subjects into their cultures, as did Europeans with their sports, it would exist in enough countries to qualify as an Olympic sport. This is how politics has influenced even the definition of sports. Note: to watch women from Myanmar and Vietnam play a gold medal point in the 2006 Doha Asian Games Doha 2006, see www.youtube.com/watch?v=0pL-9ozKn1Y. (*Source:* Ng Han Guan; AP/Wide World Photos)

them to fit their interests or the circumstances in which the sports are played.
3. Who makes and enforces the rules in sports? The official rules of every sport are determined by the sport's governing body, but confusion often results when various organizations representing the interests of different

people all claim to be the primary governing body of a sport.

4. Who organizes and controls sport events? Until recently, members of the governing body of a sport organized and controlled competitions, but events today may be organized and partially controlled by third parties such as sponsors, media companies, or management groups that specialize in event organization.

5. Where do sport events take place? When athletes decide where to play a sport, they choose a place that is convenient for them or for the spectators they wish to attract. When events are staged for commercial purposes, they take place wherever they will generate the most revenue. In the case of international events such as the Olympic Games, various cities make bids to be the host and the members of the IOC select the bidding city that provides the most attractive venue for the games and the commercial interests associated with them.

6. Who is eligible to participate in a sport? Eligibility decisions take into account factors that are defined as relevant by members of a governing body or people managing an event. Age, skill level, academic performance, gender, race/ethnicity, nationality, citizenship, place of residence, and other factors have been used to limit eligibility depending on the concerns and ideologies of the people making eligibility decisions.

7. How are rewards distributed to athletes and others associated with sports? When rewards are associated with participating in or staging an event, the question of "Who gets what?" is crucial to everyone involved. Rewards may include affirmations of status, such as a Most Valuable Player award, or monetary compensation as in the case of revenue-producing sports. The distribution of money often creates friction between the players and the people who organize and manage the team or event.

These questions are inherently political because answers are determined in contexts where there are differences of interest that must be resolved through political processes and the use of both power and authority. Most people understand this, but they complain about politics in sports when resolutions and answers are not the ones they want to hear.

summary

HOW DO GOVERNMENTS AND GLOBAL POLITICAL PROCESSES INFLUENCE SPORTS?

Sports and politics are inseparable. Government involvement in sports is generally related to the need for sponsorship, organization, and facilities. The fact that sports are important in people's lives and can be sites for social conflict often leads to government involvement. The forms of involvement vary by society, but their purposes are generally to (1) safeguard the public order; (2) ensure fairness and protect human rights; (3) maintain health and fitness among citizens; (4) promote the prestige and power of a group, community, or nation; (5) promote a sense of identity, belonging, and unity among citizens; (6) reproduce values consistent with dominant ideology; (7) increase support for political leaders and governmental structures; and (8) facilitate economic development.

The rules, policies, and funding priorities set by government officials and agencies reflect political differences and struggles among groups within a society. This doesn't mean that the same people always benefit when government involvement occurs, but involvement seldom results in equal benefits for everyone. For example, when funds are dedicated to the development and training of elite athletes, fewer funds are available to support general participation programs. Funding priorities could favor mass participation instead of elite sports, but the priorities themselves are subject to debate and negotiation. This political process is an inevitable part of organized sports.

History shows government intervention in sports usually favors groups with the greatest quantity of resources and the highest degree of organization, and with goals that support the ideological orientations of public officials. The groups least likely to be favored are those that fail to understand the connection between sports and politics or lack resources to effectively influence political decisions. When people believe the myth that sports and politics are unrelated, they're likely to be disappointed when officials develop policies and allocate funds.

The connection between sports and global political processes is complex. Ideally, sports bring nations together in contexts supportive of peace and friendship. Although this can and does occur, most nations use sports to satisfy their own interests. Displays of nationalism have been and continue to be common at international events. The Olympic Games are a good case in point. People who work with, promote, or follow the Olympics often focus on national medal counts and use them to support their claims for national status.

If mega-events such as the Olympics are indeed special events with positive potential, efforts should be made to maximize that potential. Limiting nationalism and commercialism and emphasizing the interdependence of nations and people would be helpful and could be done by any number of strategies.

Powerful transnational corporations have joined nation-states as major participants in global political processes. As a result, sports are used increasingly for economic as well as political purposes. Nationalism and the promotion of national interests remain part of global sports, but consumerism and the promotion of capitalist expansion have become more important since 1991 and the end of the cold war.

Within the context of global relations, athletes and teams now are associated with corporate logos as well as nation-states. Global sport events have political and economic implications. They are sites for presenting numerous images and narratives associated with the interests of nation-states *and* corporate sponsors. The dominant discourses associated with sports in the United States are clearly consistent with the interests of corporate sponsors, and they promote an ideology infused with the capitalist values of individualism, competition, achievement, and consumption.

Global political processes also are associated with other aspects of sports, such as the migration patterns of elite athletes and the production of sporting goods. Political issues are raised when athletes cross national borders to play their sports and when transnational corporations produce sports equipment and clothing in labor-intensive, poor nations and then sell these products in wealthy nations.

These and other issues associated with global political processes are best understood when they are studied on both global and local levels. Data in these studies help determine when sports involve reciprocal cultural exchanges leading to mutual understanding among people and when they involve processes through which powerful nations and corporations exercise subtle influence over the social life and political events in less powerful nations.

Politics also are part of the very structure and organization of sports. Political processes exist because people in sport organizations must answer questions about what qualifies as a sport, the rules of a sport, procedures for enforcing rules, organization and control of sport events, locations of sport events, eligibility criteria for participants, and distribution of rewards. These political issues are central to sports, and they illustrate why the organizations that make decisions about sports are often described as governing bodies. This is another example highlighting that sports are inseparable from politics and political processes.

WEBSITE RESOURCES

Note: Websites often change. The following URLs were current when this book was printed. Please check our website (www.mhhe.com/coakley10e) for updates and additions.

www.mhhe.com/coakley10e Click on Chapter 13 for information on sports and international relations, gift-giving and Olympic scandals, and politics and the Paralympic movement.

www.aafla.com The Amateur Athletic Foundation in Los Angeles is now called LA84 Foundation. Established with the profits from the 1984 Olympic Games in Los Angeles, the foundation maintains an outstanding library and digital archive containing historical and political material on sports, along with many useful publications and resources, some of which I have used as references in writing this book.

www.educatingforjustice.org/ Educating for Justice is an activist organization formed by a former college soccer coach and a friend who began a grassroots campaign to investigate the factories in Indonesia that produced Nike shoes (see www.sweatthefilm.org); today the organization works to bring social justice to sweatshops producing athletic apparel and other products frequently sold in college bookstores.

http://ec.europa.eu/sport/index_en.htm The Sport section of the European Commission covers issues related to the development of sport through the European Union, providing information about programs, government influence on sports, and the politics of coordinating national sport governing bodies with this international governing body.

www.gamesmonitor.org.uk Games Monitor is a network of people debunking Olympic myths, deconstructing the hype created by Olympic boosterism, and raising awareness of problems associated with hosting the 2012 Games in London.

www.globalmarch.org/campaigns/worldcupcampaign/Index.php The Global March Against Child Labour is an international movement based in India and focused on eliminating exploitive working conditions that condemn millions of children to lives of servitude and suffering; it continues to focus on the children in India and Pakistan who in 2008 were still stitching soccer balls without any worker rights.

www.iwg-gti.org The International Working Group on Women and Sport provides information on programs, policy issues, and problems faced by girls and women in nearly 100 countries; information reveals different patterns of government involvement as well as the cultural issues that influence programs, policies, and problems; provides key links to other international sport organizations.

www.olympic.org Official site of the International Olympic Committee; presents information favorable to the IOC, the Olympic Games, and anything to do with either.

http://olympicstudies.uab.es/eng/index.asp The Olympic Studies Center at the Universitat Autònoma de Barcelona provides many links to official information about the Olympics.

www.playfair2008.org/index.php?option=com_frontpage&Itemid=65 Play Fair 2008 is an international campaign that originated prior to the 2008 Olympic Games to push for respect for workers' rights in the global sporting goods industry; go to "Reports" to download the Play Fair 2008 study on working conditions.

www.policyalternatives.ca/reports_studies/index.cfm The Canadian Centre for Policy Alternatives has very useful research on sports generally and the Olympics in particular; a "Quick Search" for "Olympics" will provide a list of useful studies and reports, including a full cost–benefit analysis of the Vancouver 2010 Winter Olympic and Paralympic Games.

http://purl.access.gpo.gov/GPO/LPS31547 Does the U.S. Olympic Committee's organizational structure impede its mission? This report was produced by the U.S. Congressional Subcommittee on Commerce, Trade and Consumer Protection; it provides an extensive critique of the USOC.

www.ucalgary.ca/library/ssportsite/ Scroll down to "International Sport Federations" and to "National Sport Structures and Organizations" to find links to nearly every established sport organization in the world.

www.un.org/sport2005/ Information on sports and development; links to reports and projects such as www.un.org/Depts/dhl/resguide/r58.htm—a UN resolution on "Building a Peaceful and Better World Through Sport and the Olympic Ideal" (http://www.olympicspirit.org/press_071031_truce.php)

www.usoc.org Official site of the United States Olympic Committee; provides links to forty-five national governing bodies for Olympic and Pan American sports, twenty-four Paralympic sports, and "feel good" stories about athletes, teams, and events.

(Rich Clarkson/NCAA Photos)

SPORTS IN HIGH SCHOOL AND COLLEGE

Do Competitive Sports Contribute to Education?

WHEN I PLAYED, you had to make the team. . . .
Now we can't let anyone get injured. We don't
have enough guys out there as it is. Almost all the
players have jobs to support their families. And
many don't have health insurance.

—**High school football coach (in Sherry, 2007)**

Visit *Sports in Society*'s Online Learning Center (OLC) at www.mhhe.com/coakley10e for additional information and study material for this chapter, including the following:

- A complete chapter outline
- Learning objectives
- Practice quizes
- Internet resources
- Related readings
- Essays
- Student projects

WE LET STUDENTS KNOW: If you participate [in sports], we will control your study life. For kids who really want to play, they've been playing their whole lives and they'll do almost anything to play.

—Jay Sailes, high school principal (in Riede, 2006)

IN FACT, COLLEGE ATHLETICS in general are more the province of the privileged than the poor. . . . [B]eneath the thin layer of sport entertainment that makes its way onto television are the bulk of college athletes: Well-off and white.

—Tom Farrey, ESPN, in *Game On* (2008)

The NCAA basketball tournament has everything I like: corporate sponsorship, unpaid labor and blind partisan allegiance.

—Stephen Colbert, *I Am America (And So Can You!)* (2007)

The emergence of today's organized sports is closely linked with schools in England and North America. However, the United States is the only nation in the world where it is taken for granted that high schools and colleges sponsor and fund interschool or varsity sport programs. In most countries, organized sports for school-aged young people are sponsored by community-based athletic clubs that are funded by members or by a combination of public and private sources (Hyland, 2008). Only Canada and Japan have some schools that sponsor competitive teams, but they usually are no more important than other co-curricular activities. Interscholastic sports are an accepted and important part of U.S. high schools and colleges, but when they dominate the cultures and public profiles of schools, many people become concerned about their role in education.

This chapter is organized around four major questions related to interscholastic sport programs:

1. What claims do people make when they argue for and against the programs?
2. How are sport programs related to education and the experiences of students?
3. What effects do sports programs have on the organization of schools and the achievement of educational goals?
4. What are the major problems associated with sport programs and how might they be solved?

ARGUMENTS FOR AND AGAINST INTERSCHOLASTIC SPORTS

Most people in the United States don't question the existence of interscholastic sports in high schools and colleges. However, budget cutbacks and highly publicized problems in some programs raise questions about the relationship between these sports, the development of young people, and the achievement of educational goals. Responses to these questions vary and almost always are based on strong emotions. Program supporters claim that interscholastic sports support the educational mission of schools and the development of young people, whereas critics claim that they interfere with that mission and distract students from learning to be responsible citizens. The main points made on both sides of this debate are summarized in Table 14.1.

Table 14.1   Claims that are made in arguments for and against interscholastic sports

Claims For	Claims Against
1. They involve students in school activities and increase interest in academic activities.	1. They distract students from academic activities and distort values in school culture.
2. They build self-esteem, responsibility, achievement orientation, and teamwork skills required for occupational success today.	2. They perpetuate dependence, conformity, and a power and performance orientation that is no longer useful in society.
3. They foster fitness and stimulate interest in physical activities among students.	3. They turn most students into passive spectators and cause too many serious injuries to athletes.
4. They generate spirit and unity and maintain the school as a viable organization.	4. They create a superficial, transitory spirit that is unrelated to educational goals.
5. They promote parental, alumni, and community support for school programs.	5. They deprive educational programs of resources, facilities, staff, and community support.
6. They give students opportunities to develop and display skills in activities valued in society and to be recognized for their competence.	6. They create pressure on athletes and support a hierarchical status system in which athletes are unfairly privileged over other students.

When people enter this debate, they often exaggerate the benefits and problems associated with interscholastic sports. Supporters emphasize glowing success stories, and critics emphasize shocking cases of excess and abuse, but the most accurate descriptions lie somewhere in between. Nonetheless, supporters and critics call our attention to the relationship between sports and education. This chapter focuses on that relationship.

INTERSCHOLASTIC SPORTS AND THE EXPERIENCES OF HIGH SCHOOL STUDENTS

Do interscholastic sport programs affect the educational and developmental experiences of high school students? This question is difficult to answer. Education and development occur in connection with many activities and relationships. Even though interscholastic sports are important in most schools and the lives of many students, they constitute only one of many potentially influential experiences. Quantitative research on this issue has seldom been guided by social theories, and it generally consists of comparing the characteristics of athletes and other students. Qualitative research, often based on a critical approach and guided by combinations of cultural, interactionist, and structural theories, has focused on the connections between interscholastic sports, the culture and organization of high schools, and the everyday lives of students.

High School Athletes[1]

Studies in the United States consistently show that high school athletes as a group generally have higher grade point averages, more positive attitudes toward school, lower rates of absenteeism, more interest in attending college, more years of college completed, greater career success, and better health than students who don't play school-sponsored sports.[2] These differences usually are modest, and it's difficult for researchers to separate the effects of sport participation from the effects of social class, family background, support from friends, identity issues, and other factors related to educational attitudes and achievement.

Membership on a school team is a valued status in many U.S. schools, and for some students it seems to go hand in hand with positive educational experiences, reduced dropout rates, and increased identification with the school (Hartmann, 2008; Lipscomb, 2006; Marsh and Kleitman, 2003; McNeal, 1995; Miller et al., 2005). However, research doesn't explain much about why sport participation affects students, and why it affects some differently from others (Hartmann and Massoglia, 2007).

Why Are Athletes Different?   The most logical explanation for differences between athletes on school teams and other students is that school-sponsored sports, like other sponsored activities, attract students who have good grades and are socially popular in school. Most researchers don't have information about the pre-participation characteristics of athletes because they collect data at one point in time and simply compare students who play on sport teams with students who don't. These studies are limited because they don't prove that playing school sports changes young people

---

[1]The term "student-athlete" is not used because *all* members of school teams are students, just like band members and debaters. The NCAA promotes the use of this term as a political strategy to deflect the criticism that big-time college athletic programs are overcommercialized, overprofessionalized, and generally unrelated to the academic mission of universities. This NCAA agenda is not supported by the author.

[2]There are hundreds of these studies; the most recent and methodologically respectable of these include the following: Barber et al. (2001); Broh (2002); Carlson et al. (2005); Child Trends (2008); Curtis et al. (2003); Eitle (2005); Eitle and Eitle (2002); Fullinwider (2006); Guest and Schneider (2003); Harrison and Narayan (2003); Hartmann (2008); Hill (2007); Hoffman (2006); Hunt (2005); Leeds, Miller, and Stull (2007); Marsh and Kleitman (2002); Miller et al. (2000, 2005); Miracle and Rees (1994); Rees and Miracle (2000); Troutman and Dufur (2007); Videon (2002); Whitley (1999).

in ways that would not have occurred otherwise. Fourteen- to eighteen-year-olds grow and develop in many ways whether they play school sports or do other things. This is an important point, because young people who play on varsity sport teams are more likely to come from economically privileged backgrounds and have above-average cognitive abilities, self-esteem, and past academic performance records, including grades and test scores (Child Trends, 2008; Carlson et al., 2005; Eitle, 2005; Hunt, 2005; Rees and Miracle, 2000). Therefore, students who try out for, make, and stay on school teams are different from other students before they play high school sports.

This *selection-in process* is common; students who participate in official, school-sponsored activities tend to be different from other students. This difference is greatest in activities in which student self-selection is combined with eligibility requirements and formal tryouts when teachers or coaches select students for participation. Additionally, this combination of self-selection, coach selection, and eligibility is an extension of a long-term process that begins in youth sports. Over time, students with lower grades and poor disciplinary records decide they don't want to be involved in sports, or they aren't academically eligible to participate, or coaches see them as troublemakers and cut them during tryouts.

Research also shows that students who play varsity sports for three years during high school are different from those who are cut from or quit teams. Those who are cut or quit are more likely to come from less advantaged economic backgrounds and have lower cognitive abilities, lower self-esteem, and lower grade point averages than those who remain on teams (Child Trends, 2008; Crosnoe, 2002; Spreitzer, 1995; White and Gager, 2007). Furthermore, athletes who receive failing grades are declared ineligible and become "nonathletes" and have low grades when

> **Because of soccer, we've been able to bring our Hispanic students and our white students together in a way we never thought was possible. When they put on that jersey, they feel like they're part of this school.** —High school athletic director in rural Colorado (in Sanchez, 2006)

researchers collect data and compare their grades with the grades of eligible athletes!

Another factor that has not been studied is the control that parents, teachers, and coaches have over the lives of athletes on school teams, especially when the athletes are "in season" and their daily activities, especially academic activities, are closely monitored by coaches and parents (Riede, 2006). Homework checks, study halls, grade checks, and class attendance are standard procedures in the lives of athletes when their season is ongoing. Although this probably adds structure to daily schedules, its impact on learning and academic growth is not known.

Overall, school sports have selection-in, filtering-out, and in-season control processes, each of which contributes to differences between athletes and other students. To control for these processes and determine if and when playing sports produces unique, positive educational or developmental outcomes, researchers must collect data at regular intervals from an entire sample of students so they can measure and track changes that are due to sports participation rather than other things.

Studying Athletes in Context Research published between the 1950s and today presents mixed and confusing findings about the effects of playing school sports. This is because most researchers assume that playing on a school team has the same meaning in all contexts for all athletes in all sports and therefore must have the same consequences. But this is not true. Meanings vary widely depending on three factors:

1. The status given to athletes and sports in various contexts
2. The identities young people develop as they play sports

Self-selection, combined with academic eligibility and coach selection, ensures that athletes often have different characteristics from other students before they ever play on school teams. Athletes may learn positive and/or negative things in sports, but it's difficult to separate those things from other forms of learning and development that occur during adolescence. (*Source:* Marc Piscotty, *Rocky Mountain News*)

3. The ways that young people integrate sports and an athlete identity into their lives

For example, playing on a junior varsity team or being a mediocre player on the varsity fencing team often involves different implications for the status and identity of a young man in comparison with being an all-state football or basketball player on a state-championship team—even if the young man is on a fencing team at a private school that has produced many college and Olympic champions. Similarly, being a young woman ranked the number-one high school tennis player in the state would involve different status and identity implications from being

a young woman who is a record-setting heavyweight powerlifter or a substitute on the junior varsity softball team.

When researchers at the University of Chicago used data collected over four years from two large samples of high school students, they found that interscholastic athletes at schools located in low-income areas were more likely to be identified as good students than were athletes playing at schools located in upper-middle-income and wealthy areas (Guest and Schneider, 2003). Additionally, having an athlete identity was positively associated with grades in schools located in lower-income areas but negatively associated with grades in wealthier areas where taking sports too seriously was seen as interfering with preparing for college and careers. Therefore, the academic implications of being an interscholastic athlete depended on the different meanings given to playing sports and having an athlete identity in different social class contexts during the 1990s in American society.

Research also indicates that the meanings given to playing interscholastic sports also vary by gender and have changed since the late 1960s (Hoffman, 2006; Miller et al., 1998, 1999, 2000, 2005; Troutman and Dufur, 2007). For example, young women on school teams have had lower rates of sexual activity (fewer sex partners, lower frequency of intercourse, and later initiation of sexual activity) than their female peers who didn't play sports, whereas young men on school teams had higher rates of sexual activity than other young men in the schools (Miller et al., 1998, 1999). This difference may exist because playing on school teams enhances the social status of young people and gives them more power to regulate sexual activity on their own terms. During the 1990s, it appears that many young women used this power to resist sexual relationships that they defined as inappropriate or exploitive, whereas young men used their power to gain sexual favors from young women (Risman and Schwartz, 2002). But these patterns could change in the future as the meanings given to being on school sport teams change and as there are shifts in students' ideas about sex.

Research also suggests that identifying oneself as a "jock" in some U.S. high schools connects a student with peers who are socially gregarious and more likely than other students to engage in risky actions such as heavy and binge drinking (Miller et al., 2005). This issue needs more study, but it seems that playing on certain school teams provides students with more choices for aligning themselves with various cliques or social groups that have different priorities for what they like to do. The choices made by athletes probably influence how others identify them and where they fit into the overall culture of the school. In some cases, this "positions" them in the overall social structure of the school so that they value academic work, whereas in other cases, it positions them so that they focus on social activities with other jocks who like to party even if it detracts from academic achievement.

Identifying the influence of playing high school sports in a person's adult life is much more difficult than identifying the effects that occur during late adolescence. The meanings people give to sport participation change over time and vary with a wide range of social and cultural factors related to gender, race and ethnicity, and social class. For example, when we hear that many CEOs of large corporations played sports in high school, it tells us nothing about the role of sport participation in the long, complex process of becoming a CEO. The occupational experiences of top CEOs, most of whom are white men, are strongly related to their family backgrounds and social networks, and cannot be separated from the gender, ethnic, and class relations that have characterized American and other societies during the past sixty years. This does not mean that these men haven't worked hard or that sport participation is irrelevant to who they are and what they do, but the importance of playing varsity sports cannot be understood apart from many other factors that are clearly related to occupational success.

> **Athletes and jocks are not the same. . . . Together they represent the two faces of sport: one ascetic and disciplined, the other gregarious and risk-oriented.** —Kathleen Miller et al., educational researchers (2005)

Overall, research in the sociology of sport indicates that the effects of playing school sports depend on the contexts in which sports are played, the organization of sport programs and teams, and the social characteristics of athletes (Crissey and Honea, 2006; Hartmann, 2008; Hartmann and Massoglia, 2007). Therefore, when young, white women from upper-middle-class families play lacrosse in a small, private, elite prep school where grades are all-important, the effects of participation are likely to be different from the effects that occur when young ethnic minority men from working-class families play football in a large public school where "jock culture" norms emphasize physical toughness, male camaraderie, and high-risk activities more than academic excellence.

Student Culture in High Schools

Sports are usually among the most important activities sponsored by high schools, and being on a school team can bring students prestige among peers, formal rewards in the school, and recognition from teachers, administrators, and people in the local community. Athletes, especially boys in high-profile sports, often are accorded recognition that enhances their popularity in student culture. Pep rallies, homecomings, and other sports events are major social occasions on school calendars. Students often enjoy these events because they provide opportunities for social interaction outside the classroom. Parents favor them because they're associated with the school and crowds are controlled by school authorities; therefore, they will allow their children to attend games and matches even when they forbid them from going to other places.

The popularity of school sports has led sociologists to ask questions about their impact on student culture in high schools. It seems that sports and sport events have the potential to influence

reflect on SPORTS

Status and Privilege in Student Culture
Do Athletes Rule U.S. High Schools?

After fourteen students and a teacher-coach were killed in a shooting at Columbine High School in Littleton, Colorado (1999), some people raised questions about interscholastic sports and the dynamics of status and privilege in student culture. "Anti-jock" statements were made by the killers, who had previously been involved in a confrontation with members of a school team. As people tried to explain this horrific event, some wondered if high school athletes are given forms of privilege that other students perceive to be unfair and that make some athletes feel that they have the right to demean others whom they identify as "deviant" within the normative structure of the school.

Shortly after the Columbine killings, a number of "anti-jock" webzines and websites emerged. Current and former students used them to express their resentment of high school cultures in which certain athletes were privileged and students in some other groups were marginalized (Wilson, 2002). Most of these sites no longer exist, but discussions with anti-jock themes continue.

Most high schools have complex status systems and multiple popularity criteria. Students identify and differentiate one another in many ways, depending on what they define as important in their social lives. These definitions vary from one school to another and across different groups in the same school, but a process of identification and differentiation occurs in all high schools. However, when differences are used to rank students as superior and inferior and identify particular students as targets for harassment or intimidation, there is cause for concern. When students, teachers, and administrators ignore systematic and chronic harassment and intimidation, problems can become serious and volatile.

School sports are commonly associated with status hierarchies in U.S. high schools, but this is not an issue that has attracted much research—mostly because school administrators don't want to open their doors to researchers who might find problems

that could jeopardize their jobs. An ESPN survey done a month after the Columbine shootings indicated that one-third of the high school students interviewed said that tension existed between athletes and nonathletes in their schools (ESPN, 1999). About half of the students knew of athletes who had physically mistreated nonathletes, and about 70 percent knew of athletes who had verbally mistreated nonathletes. Seventy percent identified football players as the athletes who most often mistreated nonathletes, 10 percent identified male basketball players, 2 percent identified wrestlers, and 1 percent identified female basketball players. Nearly 80 percent said that athletes sometimes or often received special treatment from teachers or administrators. These data are sketchy, but they indicate a need for research on the ways that athletes, especially young men who play high-profile sports in a school, use their status as they engage and interact with others.

At this point, it appears that chronic harassment and bullying is most likely in schools where there is little social, ethnic, and social-class diversity and where acceptance requires conformity with norms governing clothes, hairstyles, music preferences, and general presentation of self. In these schools some students in high-status groups equate "difference" with "deviance" and feel that they should enforce these norms.

Students who assume the role of "policing student culture" are not always athletes or identified as "jocks." Furthermore, being on a school team and being labeled a "jock" in student cultures often are *not* one and the same thing. However, male athletes on certain teams are perceived to "police" and intimidate other students often enough for those of us concerned with student culture to critically examine (1) the impact of school sports on students' lives, (2) the forms of status and privilege enjoyed by athletes on different sport teams, and (3) the ways that athletes from various teams use their status and privilege in their relationships with others. *What do you think?*

students' values, attitudes, actions, and experiences. This topic is discussed in the box titled "Status and Privilege in Student Culture" on page 477.

High School Sports and Popularity   For many years, student culture was studied simply in terms of the factors that high school students used to determine popularity. Research usually found that male students wished they could be remembered as "athletic stars" in high school, whereas female students wished to be remembered as "brilliant students" or "the most popular." Although these priorities have changed over the last two generations, the link between popularity and being an athlete has remained relatively strong for male students. At the same time, the link between popularity and being an athlete has become stronger for female students, although other characteristics, such as physical appearance and social skills, are also important—more important than they are for young men.

Most high school students today are concerned with academic achievement and attending college; furthermore, their parents regularly emphasize these priorities. But students also are concerned with four other things: (1) social acceptance, (2) personal autonomy, (3) sexual identity, and (4) becoming an adult. They want to fit in with peers and have friends they can depend on, to control their lives, to feel comfortable with their sexual identity, and to be taken seriously as young adults. Because males and females in North America are still treated and evaluated differently, adolescents use different strategies for seeking acceptance, autonomy, sexual identity, and recognition as young adults. For young men, sports provide opportunities to demonstrate the physical and emotional toughness that is associated with masculinity today, and successfully claiming a masculine identity is assumed to bring acceptance, autonomy, and recognition as an adult. For young women, sports are not used so much to claim a feminine identity that brings acceptance, autonomy, and recognition as an adult, but they are used

to achieve and express the personal power that enables women to achieve these things. My hypothesis is that young women in high school at this point in time are less likely than their male peers to view sports as an identificational focal point in their lives and more likely to view them as part of a larger project of achievement that involves academic, social, and other personal accomplishments. If this is the case, the visibility and status gained by high school athletes have different implications for young men than for young women in high school student culture and beyond (Carlson et al., 2005).

High School Sports and Ideology   Interscholastic sport programs do more than simply affect the status structures of high schools. When Pulitzer Prize–winning author H. G. Bissinger wrote the book *Friday Night Lights* about a high school football team in Odessa, Texas, he observed that

Sport participation often gives young women opportunities to establish personal and social identities based on skills respected by peers and people in the general community. However, playing sports usually does not bring as much status and popularity to girls as it does to boys in U.S. high schools. (*Source:* Tini Campbell)

football "stood at the very core of what the town was about. . . . It had nothing to do with entertainment and everything to do with how people felt about themselves" (1990: 237).

Bissinger noted that football in Odessa and across the United States was important because it celebrated a male cult of toughness and sacrifice and a female cult of nurturance and servitude. Team losses were blamed on coaches who weren't tough enough and players who weren't disciplined and aggressive. Women stayed on the sidelines and faithfully tried to support and please the men who battled on behalf of the school and town. Attending football games enabled students and townspeople to reaffirm their ideas about "natural differences" between men and women. Young men who did not hit hard, physically intimidate opponents, or play with pain were described as "ladies," and a player's willingness to sacrifice his body for the team was taken as a sign of commitment, character, and manhood.

Bissinger also noted that high school sports were closely linked with a long history of racism in Odessa, and that football was organized and played in ways that reaffirmed traditional racial ideology among whites and produced racial resentment among African Americans. Ideas about race and certain aspects of racial dynamics have changed since 1988 when many whites in the Odessa area still referred to blacks as "niggers" and blamed blacks and Mexicans for most of the town's social and economic problems. White people are not as likely today to say that blacks succeed on the football field because of their "natural physical abilities," whereas whites succeed due to character, discipline, and intelligence.

Bissinger's book fails to deal with many aspects of high school sports, but a study by anthropologist Doug Foley (1990b, 1999a) provides a more complete description and analysis of the place of sports in a high school and the town in which it exists. Foley studied an entire small Texas town but paid special attention to the ways that people incorporated the local high school football team and its games into the overall social life of the

school and the community. He also studied the social and academic activities of a wide range of students, including those who ignored or avoided sports.

Foley's findings revealed that student culture in the high school "was varied, changing, and inherently full of contradictions" (1990b, p. 100). Football and other sports provided important social occasions and defused the anxiety associated with tests and overcontrolling teachers, but sports were only one part of the lives of the students. Athletes used their status as a basis for "identity performances" with other students and certain adults, but for most students, identity was grounded more deeply in gender, class, and ethnicity than in sport participation.

Foley concluded that sports were socially important because they presented students with a vocabulary they could use to identify values and interpret their everyday experiences. For example, most sports came with a vocabulary that extolled individualism, competition, and "natural" differences related to sex, skin color, ethnicity, and social class. As students learned and used this vocabulary, they perpetuated the culture and social organization of their school and town. In the process, traditional ideologies related to gender, race, and class continued to influence social relations in the town's culture, even though some people questioned and revised those ideologies and redefined their importance in their lives.

The point of Foley's study and other research on socialization as a community process is that the most important social consequences of high school sports are not their impact on grades and

AT YOUR *fingertips* For more information on socialization as a community process, see Chapter 4, pp. 114–120.

popularity but their impact on young people's ideas about social life and social relations.

High School Sports as Learning Experiences

Early in the twentieth century, educators included physical education and sports in U.S. schools because they believed that learning should encompass body and mind (Hyland, 2008). Physical activities and sports, they thought, could be organized to teach important things. But the widespread belief that "sports build character" led to the assumption that playing sports automatically transformed young people in positive ways, no matter how the sports were organized. There was no need for research to identify what participants learned or how to teach things beyond tactics and techniques. Individual testimonials about "sport making me what I am today" fueled the mythology that sport was like an automatic car wash: anyone who enters will be cleansed, dried, and sent off with a shiny new look.

As a result, there are no "learning evaluations" at the end of a season, coaches aren't held accountable as teachers, and there is an amazing lack of systematically collected evidence documenting the dynamics of teaching and learning in various sports played by over seven million high school students every year. The downside of this lack of knowledge is that we can't prove what young people learn in sports or when and why they learn certain things, both positive and negative. Nor can we rate the effectiveness of various coaching strategies for teaching what we want young people to learn in sports. And what is it that we want young people to learn? If we knew these things, we could present evidence to school boards when they make funding decisions. Too many sports and sport programs are being cut today, or "outsourced" to club programs because they're considered "extra"-curricular rather than co-curricular activities and there is no evidence to show otherwise.

INTERCOLLEGIATE SPORTS AND THE EXPERIENCES OF COLLEGE STUDENTS

Does varsity sport participation affect the educational and developmental experiences of college athletes?[3] This question cannot be answered unless we understand that college sport programs are very diverse. If we assume that all programs are like the ones we see or read about in the media, we are bound to have distorted views of athletes, coaches, and intercollegiate sports.

> **OLC ON THE *OLC*:**
> See the OLC—Additional Readings for Chapter 14—for the author's paper on why research faculty have not been eager to study intercollegiate sports.

Intercollegiate Sports Are *Not* All the Same

The amount of money spent every year on intercollegiate sports varies from less than $250,000 at some small colleges to over $100 million at Ohio State University and the University of Texas. Large universities usually sponsor ten to eighteen varsity sports for men and a similar number for women, whereas small colleges may have only a few varsity sports and many club teams (Pennington, 2008). In small colleges, coaches may be responsible for two or more teams and teach courses as well. Larger universities may have ten or more coaches for football alone and multiple coaches for most sports. Few of these coaches teach courses, and most have no

---

[3]This chapter focuses primarily on four-year institutions in the United States. Although junior colleges and two-year community colleges comprise 22 percent of all higher education insitutions with intercollegiate sport programs and have 10 percent of all intercollegiate athletes, there is little research on them.

formal connection with academic programs at universities.

Schools with intercollegiate sports are generally affiliated with one of two national associations: the National Collegiate Athletic Association (NCAA) or the National Association of Intercollegiate Athletics (NAIA). The NCAA is the largest and most powerful association, with 1200 member institutions, about 403,000 athletes, and a budget of over $500 million per year. Member institutions are divided into five major categories, reflecting program size, level of competition, and the rules that govern sport programs. Division I includes (in 2008–2009) 330 schools with "big-time" programs. This division contains three subdivisions:

(1) Football Bowl Subdivision (FBS) consists of 121 universities that have big-time football teams; each institution is allotted 85 full scholarships for football players.
(2) Football Championship Subdivision (FCS) consists of 221 universities that have football programs and are allotted only 63 scholarships that can be awarded to (or split between) no more than 85 students.
(3) Non-Football (NF) subdivision consists of 90 universities that do not have football teams but have big-time basketball and/or other big-time sports.

NCAA Divisions II and III contain 293 and 444 schools, respectively. These schools have smaller programs and compete at less than a big-time level, although competition often is intense. Division II schools may award limited scholarships but rarely give a full scholarship to an athlete. Division III schools do not award athletic scholarships.

Some colleges and universities choose to affiliate with the NAIA rather than the NCAA. The NAIA has about 290 members, 45,000 athletes, and a $4-million budget—less than 1 percent of the NCAA budget. NAIA schools have teams in up to twelve sports for men and eleven for women. Athletic scholarships may or may not be given, and most programs and teams are not considered big-time. The NAIA struggles to maintain members in the face of NCAA power and influence, although the organizations are discussing the possibility of member institutions scheduling games and matches with schools from the other organization—a move that would save many millions of dollars in travel money every year. However, this would not break the monopoly control the NCAA has over intercollegiate sports.

Christian colleges and Bible schools also have sport programs. Ninety-nine of these are affiliated with the National Christian College Athletic Association (NCCAA), although many have dual membership in the NCCAA and either the NAIA or NCAA Division III. The National Junior College Athletic Association consists of over 500 junior and community colleges; some of its 50,000 athletes receive scholarships, nearly all of which cover only partial expenses.

Even though the vast majority of intercollegiate sport teams are not big-time, people use what they see and read in the media to make conclusions about all college sports. But this is a mistake because most sports at most schools do not resemble the sports covered by the mainstream media. Tables 14.2 and 14.3 clarify this complex college sport bureaucracy by showing the percentage of schools in each category and the percentage of athletes that play in each category. For example, Table 14.2 shows that FBS universities comprise only 3 percent of all institutions of higher education with intercollegiate sports; and Table 14.3 shows that only 8 percent of all intercollegiate athletes play on teams in FBS universities—that is, the ones that have big-time football teams eligible to play in major bowl games. NCAA Division III has the highest proportion of athletes—28 percent—in 444 schools that award no scholarships.

Although it's important to study all these categories, most research focuses on the Division I

Table 14.2 Percentage Distribution of All Colleges and Universities with Sport Programs by Athletic Organization and Division, 2005

Organization	Division	Percent of All Institutions
NCAA	FBS (I)	3
NCAA	FCS (I)	10
NCAA	NF (I)	4
NCAA	Div. II	14
NCAA	Div. III	21
NAIA		13
NJCAA*		22
All Others§		13

Table 14.3 Percentage Distribution of All College Athletes by Athletic Organization and Division, 2005

Organization	Division	Percent of All Institutions
NCAA	FBS (I)	8
NCAA	FCS (I)	16
NCAA	NF (I)	6
NCAA	Div. II	15
NCAA	Div. III	28
NAIA		10
NJCAA*		10
All Others§		7

Source: Adapted from Cheslock (2007).

* National Junior College Athletic Association
§ Includes all colleges and universities having sport programs but not maintaining membership in any of the above organizations.

Sports in Divisions II and III receive little attention. Little coverage was given the 2008 D III national basketball championship games in which Washington University defeated Amherst College. The everyday experiences of athletes in these programs differ from the experiences of athletes in big-time programs, but research documenting and analyzing the differences and their educational implications is lacking. (*Source:* Andres Alonso/NCAA Photos)

universities (see Coakley, 2008a, 2008c). Therefore, this chapter, based on the literature in the sociology of sport and other disciplines, provides a limited view of intercollegiate sports. This is important to remember when we discuss issues and problems because they vary widely from one division to the next.

Athletes in Big-Time Programs

Being an athlete in a big-time intercollegiate program is not always compatible with being a student. A recent survey of 21,000 NCAA athletes showed that most of them spend close to 40 hours per week doing their sports; football players reported spending 45 hours a week on their sport (Wolverton, 2008), and most athletes said they spent more time on their sport than on their academic work (Wieberg, 2008a).

Research by sociologists Patricia and Peter Adler (1991, 1999) helps to put these data in context. After five years of observing, interviewing, traveling with, and hanging out with athletes and coaches for a big-time college basketball team, the Adlers concluded that playing on such a team and being seriously involved in academic courses seldom go hand in hand. The young men on the team began their first year of coursework with optimism and idealism because they expected their academic experiences to contribute to their future occupational success. However, after one or two semesters, the demands of playing basketball, the social isolation that goes along with being an athlete, and the powerful influence of the team culture drew them away from academic life.

The men discovered that selecting easier courses and majors was necessary if they were to meet coaches' expectations for team members. Fatigue, the pressures of games, and over 40 hours a week devoted to basketball kept them from focusing seriously on academic tasks. Furthermore, nobody ever asked them about their academic lives; attention always was focused on basketball, and few people expected these young men to identify themselves as students or give priority to coursework. Racial ideology and stereotypes accentuated this social dynamic as many people assumed that young black men playing basketball had no interests or abilities other than their sport.

When these young men received positive feedback, it was for athletic, not academic, achievement. Difficulties in their courses often led them to view academic life with pragmatic detachment—that is, they didn't become emotionally invested in coursework and they chose classes and arranged course schedules that enabled them to meet the demands of their sport. They knew what they had to do to stay eligible, and coaches would make sure their course schedules kept them eligible. Gradually, most of the players detached themselves from academic life on the campus.

Academic detachment was supported in the team culture. These young men were with one another constantly—in the dorms, at meals, during practices, on trips to away games, in the weight room, and on nights when there were no games. During these times, they seldom talked about academic or intellectual topics, unless it was in negative terms. They encouraged cutting classes, and they joked about bad tests and failing papers. They provided each other with support for their identities as athletes, not students.

Academic detachment did not occur for all team members. Those who managed to balance their athletic and academic lives were the ones who entered college with realistic ideas about academic demands, had parents and peers who actively supported academic achievement, and entered the university with solid high school preparation and the ability to develop relationships with faculty and other students. These relationships were important because they emphasized academic achievement and provided day-to-day support for academic identities.

The Adlers also found that the structure of big-time intercollegiate sports worked against maintaining a balance between athletics and academics. For example, as high-profile people on campus, these young men had many social opportunities, and it was difficult for them to focus on coursework instead of their social lives. Road trips to away games and tournaments took them away from classes for extended periods. They missed lectures, study groups, and tests. Their tight connections with fellow athletes isolated them from the academic life of the university.

Unlike other students, these young men generated revenue and publicity for the university, the athletic program, and coaches. Academic detachment was not a problem for the school as long as the young men did not get caught doing something illegal or resist the control of their coach. It became a problem only when it caused them to be ineligible. But from the university's perspective, there was always another collection of eager young men who could be recruited to attract fans and generate revenues with their exceptional basketball skills.

The Diversity of Athlete Experiences

Many entertainment-oriented intercollegiate sport teams are characterized by chronic problems, low graduation rates, and hypocrisy when it comes to education. However, teams in nonrevenue-producing sports are more likely to be organized so that athletes can combine sport participation with academic and social development. This combination is most likely when athletes enter college with positive attitudes about school and the value of a college education

and then receive support for academic involvement and the formation of academic identities (Neinas, 2003; Shulman and Bowen, 2001).

Athletes on teams in which there is strong support for academic success may train hard and define athletic success as important, but most of them take their education seriously and try to maintain a balance between their academic and athletic commitments. The athletes who do this most effectively are those who have the following: (1) past experiences that consistently reaffirm the importance of education, (2) social networks that support academic identities, (3) perceived access to career opportunities following graduation, and (4) social relationships and experiences that expand confidence and skills apart from sports.

Athletes in big-time college sports face difficult choices when allocating time and energy to academic work, sport participation, and social activities. When academic work is given a low priority, the educational relevance of intercollegiate sports fades. Studying for tests is difficult when the stakes associated with your games often involve millions of dollars for your school and when your coach wants you to be totally committed to "being all you can be" on the field. Also, playing in front of 80,000 people in a stadium with millions watching on television may distract some 18- to 22-year-olds, even when the media don't critique their every move on the field. (*Source:* Jamie Schwaberow/NCAA Photos)

Coaches in programs that actively support academic success may schedule practices and games that do not interfere with coursework. Athletes may miss games and meets because they must study for or take tests, write papers, or give presentations. Team members may discuss academic issues and support one another when it comes to academic performance. In other words, there are sport programs and teams that do not subvert the academic mission of higher education (Simon, 2008). Usually they're found in the NCAA Division III and some NAIA programs, but they also exist in some low-profile, nonrevenue-producing Division I and II sports and in many women's sports. However, as sports cultures are organized more strongly around dedication, sacrifice, paying the price, and giving it up for the game and the team, and as coaches must develop winning teams to keep their jobs, it becomes difficult to balance athletics and academics even in Division III sports (Hyland, 2008).

Grades and Graduation Rates: Athletes in Big-Time College Sports

Unlike athletes in low-profile intercollegiate programs, athletes in big-time, revenue-producing sports often have different backgrounds from other students on campus. They're more likely to be African American, come from lower socioeconomic backgrounds, and be a first generation college student in their families (Bray, 2001). This makes it difficult to compare their academic achievements with the achievements of other students. Comparisons are also difficult because grade point averages (GPAs) have different meanings from one university to another and from department to department within a single university. Even graduation rates are poor indicators of academic outcomes because academic standards and requirements vary from one university to another and between programs in universities.

> The growing gap between college athletics and educational values is a major, unavoidable issue. —James Shulman and William Bowen (2001)

Some studies report that athletes earn higher grades than other students, and some report the exact opposite. Some studies show athletes attending graduate school more often than nonathletes, and others show athletes taking an abundance of courses requiring little or no intellectual effort. Therefore, making sense of grades must take into account these two possibilities:

1. Athletes in certain sports are overrepresented in specific courses and majors. This phenomenon is known as *clustering*. It occurs most often among athletes facing rigid and demanding expectations on their teams, making it difficult to compare the academic experiences of athletes across different teams at different universities.

2. Athletes in football and men's basketball often enter college with lower average high school GPAs and lower ACT and SAT scores than other students, including most other athletes, at their universities (Alesia, 2008). Their academic goals may differ from the goals of other students, and this influences their academic choices and performance (Bracklin, 2008).

Data on graduation rates also are confusing because they're computed in many ways. The NCAA now publishes standardized "six-year graduation rates" for all member institutions and for each major division, which has made is possible to do basic comparisons of universities and sports. These rates for Division I universities during 2006–2007 provide the following information about athletes who receive full or partial athletic scholarships (NCAA, 2007):

- Sixty-three percent of the athletes who entered Division I universities in 2000 graduated within six years, whereas 62 percent of the general student body graduated in six years. Therefore, athletes as a group have a graduation rate similar to other college students—even though athletes have a higher proportion of men and African Americans and a lower proportion of Asian Pacific Americans than there are in the general student body.

- The graduation rate for female athletes is 71 percent, whereas women in the general student population had a 64 percent graduation rate; the rate for male student athletes was 55 percent compared with 59 percent among men in the general student population. These statistics suggest that women's sport teams have cultures that are much more supportive of academic achievement than is the case for men's teams.

- Graduation rates are lowest in revenue-producing sports, especially men's basketball (46 percent) and football (55 percent); these rates are below the rates for all athletes (63 percent) and the general student body (62 percent).

- The graduation rate for African American male athletes (48 percent) is significantly higher than the rate for African American men in the general student population (39 percent). The rate for black female athletes (63 percent) is higher than the rate for black women generally (50 percent). Graduation rates for black male athletes have increased since 1986 when minimum academic standards for scholarship athletes were established for Division I universities. However, the data on graduation rates among blacks continue to indicate that too many "predominantly white campuses are not welcoming places for students of color, whether or not they are athletes" (Lapchick, 2005b).

What do these patterns mean? With whom should we compare athletes when we assess the

Graduation rates for female athletes are higher than for men who play college sports. However, as women's teams have become entertainment oriented, graduation rates have declined slightly. Research shows that women tend to allocate more time to academic work as they make choices between school, sport, and social life (*Source:* Jamie Schwaberow/NCAA Photos)

academic integrity of big-time sports—with regular full-time students who work full time, who have equivalent scholarships, who enter college with similar grades and test scores, or who come from similar socioeconomic backgrounds? There is no single ideal comparison. Furthermore, even though graduation is an important educational goal, it should not be the only criterion used to judge academic success. College degrees are important, but they don't mean much unless sufficient learning has occurred. It's difficult to measure learning in a survey of athletes, but it is possible to hold athletic departments academically accountable.

The Challenge of Achieving Academic Goals

Since 1983 when the NCAA first set minimum standards for first-year students to be eligible to play on Division I college teams, there have been repeated attempts to make intercollegiate programs educationally responsible. Graduation rates among athletes have increased as eligibility rules have become stricter. The most recent new rules for eligibility went into effect in 2003; today athletes must complete 40 percent of their graduation requirements with a GPA of at least 1.8 by the end of their second year; 60 percent of requirements must be completed with a GPA of 2.0 by the end of their third year, and 80 percent must be completed with a GPA of 2.0 by the end of their fourth year. Eligibility among first-year athletes now requires completion of fourteen English, math, science, and other core high school courses.

> **OLC** **ON THE *OLC*:**
>   See the OLC—Additional Readings for Chapter 14—for a brief history of recent NCAA reforms, including information about the new Academic Progress Rate (APR) formula and how it is being used.

First-year athletes also must meet minimum requirements on a sliding scale that combines high school GPAs and ACT/SAT scores. The scale is designed so that higher GPAs offset lower standardized test scores. This approach was adopted because research shows that (a) standardized tests disadvantage students who aren't from middle-class, Euro-American backgrounds, and (b) scores on such tests are poor predictors of academic success for individual students, especially those from academically weak high schools.

Changes in NCAA eligibility rules are now designed to do three things: (1) send messages to high schools and high school athletes that a commitment to academic achievement is required to play college sports, (2) set new guidelines for universities that haven't taken seriously the academic lives of athletes, and (3) encourage universities to provide athletes with the support they need to succeed academically.

Boosting eligibility standards has been somewhat successful, but many intercollegiate programs still fall short of meeting reasonable academic goals (Benford, 2007; Bowen and Levine, 2003; Knight Commission, 2001; Lapchick, 2008b, Shulman and Bowen, 2001; Sperber, 2000). Reforming big-time college sports is difficult because they are tied to many interests that have nothing to do with education. Some young people in those sports are in college only to obtain the coaching and experiences needed to stay competitive in amateur Olympic sports or to enter professional sports as soon as an opportunity presents itself. Coaches view their sports as businesses, and they are hired and fired on the basis of win–loss records and the amount of revenue that they create for the athletic program. Academic administrators, including college presidents, generally use high-profile sports as public relations and fund-raising tools instead of focusing on them as educational programs. The corporations that sponsor teams and buy advertising on telecasts of college sports don't care about athletes' education as long as their teams attract positive attention to the company's products. Similarly, local businesses that make money when the home team attracts fans are not concerned about graduation rates as long as sports fill the town with spectators for every home game.

Because of persisting problems, the NCAA passed new academic rules in 2005. These rules shift more responsibility for academic reform to athletic departments in Division I universities. The rules, which now apply to over 6,200 Division I teams, establish a minimum academic progress rate (APR) *and* a minimum graduation success rate (GSR). The APR is calculated at the beginning of each semester by awarding a team 1 point for each of its players who is academically eligible and 1 point for each player who has returned to school for that semester. A formula is used to adjust the calculations for teams of different sizes, but the perfect score for all teams is 1000 points. A team that does not have a score of at least 925 points—which would imply a graduation rate of about 60 percent—is subject to losing in the following year one or more of its allotted scholarships, depending on the difference between the team's score and the minimum 925 points. The APR is based on rolling data from the previous four academic years so that one bad year doesn't affect a team unfairly.

The GSR also is calculated by using four years of rolling data. Therefore, the rate to 2010 is based on the proportion of athletes who entered the university in 2000 through 2003 and graduated within six years after they first registered for courses. The GSR is not reduced when athletes in good academic standing transfer to other universities or enter professional sports (Wieberg, 2005a).

In May 2008, the NCAA announced that over 200 college teams did not meet the APR standards and would lose athletic scholarships they could have awarded for the 2008–2009 academic year. Twenty-six teams, mostly in football, men's basketball, and baseball, were designated "chronic

> **We don't have a football team and we're a research-heavy school, so we give chess scholarships to attract smart students.** —Dr. Alan T. Sherman, Chess Program Director, University of Maryland in Baltimore (in Bick, 2006).

underperformers" and given more severe penalties, including mandatory reductions in team practice time. If these teams did not show improvement over the next year, they faced bans from postseason tournaments. Overall, one-third of all Division I universities had at least one team penalized for APR scores under the 925 minimum.

When these penalties were announced, Myles Brand, president of the NCAA, stated that "Academic reform is here to stay . . . [and] coaches, ADs, presidents and student-athletes . . . should understand that's the order of the day" (Wieberg, 2008b, p. 1C). He also told university presidents and athletic directors that with these new rules, it "makes more sense to put the money into academic support for student-athletes than it does in the development of new [luxury stadium] suites" (Wieberg, 2008c, p. 10C).

If the NCAA continues to enforce these rules, it means that the financial stakes associated with academic integrity in big-time intercollegiate sports may be high enough to make them take academic issues more seriously.

"I like your new recruit, coach; he's an excellent example of higher education!"

In big-time intercollegiate sports, coaches and university presidents have frequently distorted the meaning of higher education.

Academic Support Programs   Athletic departments with big-time sport programs now maintain their own academic support programs. Although the stated role of people working in these programs is to help athletes succeed in their academic work, the fact that they are administered by and located in athletic departments raises questions about their real goals. These questions are asked every time it is reported that paid staff wrote papers and did other assignments for athletes (Carter, 2008; Potuto, 2007).

Although these programs have existed at least since the early 1980s, they've attracted little research. A study in the mid-1990s suggested that academic support programs for athletes were useful but that they didn't necessarily boost graduation rates (Sellers and Keiper, 1998). The first published evaluation of an academic support program was done at the University of Minnesota in 2007 (Kane, Leo, and Holleran, 2008). The evaluation resulted in the development of a model and recommendations for how to improve academic support for athletes and how to measure improvements through regular program evaluations. This model was well received by others concerned about academic integrity in college sports (Callahan, 2008; Chelladurai, 2008), but it remains to be seen how the University of Minnesota or other universities might use it. In the meantime, there is very little basis for assessing the usefulness of academic support programs for athletes.

Future Reforms   At the same time that the NCAA reports improved graduation rates among athletes, other research suggests that there is a growing separation between the culture of intercollegiate sports and the general university culture (Bowen and Levine, 2003; Bowen et al., 2005; Lawrence, Hendricks, and Ott, 2007; Shulman and Bowen, 2001). This separation is fueled by powerful historical, commercial, and political factors that currently shape the culture of college sports. These factors are so powerful that college professors concerned with defending academic integrity in the face of sport programs striving to meet financial goals formed The Drake Group (TDG, www.thedrakegroup.org/) to develop and lobby for proposals to reform intercollegiate sports. TDG lobbied the U.S. Congress, asking it to investigate the nonprofit status of college sport teams organized to make profits. When the Congress formed an investigative committee, the NCAA acted quickly to highlight academic success stories in college sports. However, TDG states that until intercollegiate sports are monitored by an independent agency that is not connected with the NCAA, the educational mission of universities will continue to be compromised.

The failed long-term history of reform efforts, the powerful commercial forces affecting big-time college sports, and the lack of faculty knowledge of and control over intercollegiate sports creates skepticism about the real impact of current reform efforts (Coakley, 2008b; Morgan, 2008; Thelin, 2008). But others are hopeful that meaningful changes will occur now that the NCAA has made a commitment to enforcing academic standards by using penalties that have serious financial and reputational consequences (Chelladurai, 2008; Simon, 2008).

> I'm a UCLA Prostitute. I sell my body to them. They pay me to perform for them. When my teammates and I perform well, the school makes lots of money . . . Regardless of how much money the school makes, we get the same, just our scholarship. —College football player (in Anderson, 2004)

DO SCHOOLS BENEFIT FROM VARSITY SPORTS?

High school and college sports affect more than just athletes. In this section, we look at the influence of these programs on high schools and colleges as organizations. In particular, we examine school spirit and budgets.

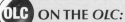

ON THE *OLC*:
See the OLC—Additional Readings for Chapter 14—for a discussion of school-community relations.

School Spirit

Anyone who has attended a well-staged student pep rally or watched the student cheering section at a well-attended high school or college game or meet realizes that sports can generate impressive displays of energy and spirit. This doesn't happen with all sport teams, nor does it happen in all schools. Teams in low-profile sports usually play games with few, if any, student spectators. Teams with long histories of losing records seldom create a spirited response among more than

a few students. Many students don't care about school teams and resent the attention given to some teams and athletes. But there are regular occasions when sports are sites at which students and others associated with a school express their spirited feelings about teams and the school as a whole.

Proponents of varsity sports say that displays of school spirit at sport events strengthen student identification with schools and create solidarity organized around the school. In making this case, a high school principal in Texas says, "Look, we don't get 10,000 people showing up to watch a math teacher solve X" (McCallum, 2003, p. 42). Critics say that the spirit created by sports is temporary, superficial, and unrelated to educational goals.

Being a part of any group or organization is more enjoyable when people have collective

Is this a display of school spirit? If it is, what does it mean? Will these students study harder, graduate at a higher rate, or donate more money to the school than other students? Is this an expression of identification with the school, and what does that mean? Unless we can answer these questions, how do we know if school sports should be supported because they foster school spirit and identification? (*Source:* Jamie Schwaberow/NCAA Photos)

opportunities to express their feelings of togetherness. However, there is nothing magical about sports in producing this outcome. Schools in other countries don't have interscholastic sports, but they have other ways to bring students together and provide enjoyable, educational experiences revolving around recreation, student-controlled clubs, and community service. In fact, most educators worldwide see little value in sports played by a few young people while their classmates are spectators when resources could be used to fund other integrative activities that would connect students more meaningfully with their communities. Instead of trying to "keep kids off the streets," they say that co-curricular programs should enable young people to make "the streets" safer and more vibrant public spaces.

The spirit associated with high-profile intercollegiate sports is exciting for some students, but only a small proportion of the student body attends even highly publicized games. Either the students aren't interested or the athletic department limits student tickets so they can sell seats at a higher price to other fans. The games of big-time sport teams often are major social occasions that inspire displays of spirit on many university campuses, but there's no research that enables us to say when this spirit supports the educational mission of the university and when it simply creates social dynamics that support binge drinking and generally ignoring norms that exist on and around campuses during the rest of the week (Higgins, Tewksbury, and Mustaine, 2007).

School Budgets

High schools and colleges with big-time sport programs have different budget issues because the financial stakes associated with big-time intercollegiate sports can be exceptionally high. For example, when a nineteen-year-old sophomore at a major university eligible for a bowl game with a big payout is sent onto the field to kick a field goal during the final minute of the last game of the season, his kick may mean the difference between his university receiving $18.5 million for an invitation to the 2010 Fed Ex Orange Bowl or $2.5 million for an invitation to another bowl game. With $16 million and uncounted other benefits riding on the kick, the stakes are high for him, his coach, team, and school—and this does not include the estimated $30 million that will be won or lost by gamblers who have bet on the game. This is not the case in high school sports. Therefore, high school and college budget issues are discussed separately.

High Schools Most interscholastic sport programs are funded through school district appropriations that come from property taxes. In most cases, expenditures for these programs account for less than 1 percent of school budgets. When certain sports have large budgets, money also comes from gate receipts and booster clubs (Brady and Sylwester, 2004).

Interscholastic sports usually don't cut into resources for basic educational programs, but neither do they add to those resources. When educational funding is tight and classroom teachers try to do their jobs without adequate resources, they and others may call for cuts in athletic funding. In the face of recent budget shortfalls, this is a common occurrence in schools around the United States. As a result schools have used various fund-raising strategies: (1) collecting sport participation fees from the families of students who play on school teams, (2) fostering booster clubs, and (3) seeking corporate sponsorships. But each of these alternatives creates problems.

Participation fees privilege students from well-to-do families, discourage students from low-income families, and create socioeconomic divisions in the student body (Carlson et al., 2005). But they are widely used and range from a low of $25 to a high of over $1000 for some sports that require big budgets to pay for equipment and facilities. Some families pay thousands of dollars for their children to play school sports (Brady and Glier, 2004), which creates serious problems for coaches when parents who have just written a check for $500 make it known that they don't want their child sitting on the bench (Glier, 2004).

Relying on booster club support also creates problems because most community boosters want to fund boys' football or basketball teams rather than the athletic program as a whole, and many parent booster clubs focus only on the sports that their children play (Fry, 2006). This practice intensifies existing gender inequities and has led to Title IX lawsuits, none of which have been decided in favor of boosters who ignore girls' teams (Sanchez, 2003). Additionally, some boosters feel that they have the right to give advice to coaches and players, intervene in team decision-making, and influence the process of hiring coaches. Community boosters may focus on win–loss records so they can tout their influence when they interact with friends and business associates; for them, educational issues may take a back seat to building a team that will win a state championship.

Corporate sponsorships connect the future of interscholastic sports to the advertising budgets and revenue streams of businesses. This means that schools can be left empty-handed when advertising budgets are cut or sponsorships are not paying off enough to satisfy company owners, stockholders, and top executives. Other problems occur when the interests of corporate sponsors don't match the educational goals of high schools. For example, promoting candy, soft drinks, and fast-food consumption with ads and logos on gym walls, scoreboards, and team buses contradicts health and nutrition principles taught in high school courses. This subverts education and makes students cynical about the meaningfulness of their curriculum. But certain corporations want to "brand" students as young as possible and may make strong arguments when they mark a school as a place they want their name to be.

> Decades after marketers began selling products by capitalizing on consumer interest in professional teams, then college teams, they are becoming big boosters of high school sports. —Stuart Elliott, journalist, *The New York Times* (2007)

Colleges and Universities The relationship between sports and school budgets at the college level is complex. Intercollegiate sports at small colleges are usually low-budget activities funded through student fees and money from the general fund and the college president's office. The budgets at NCAA FBS universities range from about $30 million to $110 million. However, athletic departments use many different accounting methods, making it difficult to compare them. For example, some departments may "hide" profits to maintain their nonprofit status for tax purposes, and others may "hide" losses to avoid criticisms that sport teams are too costly and take money away from academic programs.

There are about 1900 intercollegiate sport programs in the United States. Less than 25 of them consistently make more money than they spend (Fulks, 2008), and these programs have football teams that play in major bowl games each year and receive payouts of $18.5 (in 2009). Overall, about $230 million of bowl money is distributed to 68 football teams, but over 75 percent of all bowl money ($180 million) goes to only 10 teams, leaving the rest ($50 million) to be split by 58 teams. Table 14.4 shows the amount of debt incurred in 2006 by universities with the biggest and "most successful" sport programs. Among the 119 FBS universities—the ones with top-rated football and basketball programs—losses averaged about $7.3 million per university. Among the 118 FCS universities, average losses were $7.1 million per university, and among the 94 universities in the No Football Subdivision, average losses were $6.6 million (Berkowitz, 2008; Fulks, 2008).

When these figures were published in 2008, they shocked people who thought that athletic departments with winning football teams made handsome profits each year (Kelderman, 2008a, 2008b). What these people didn't know is that

Table 14.4   Median Revenues and Expenditures by Division I Subdivisions, 2006

	Median Total Revenues	Median Generated Revenues	Median Total Expenses	Median Net Revenue (or Deficit)
Football Bowl Subdivision (N = 119)	$35,400,000	$26,342,000	$35,756,000	−$7,265,000
Football Championship Subdivision (N = 118)	$9,642,000	$2,345,000	$9,485,000	−$7,121,000
Division I—No Football (N = 94)	$8,771,000	$1,828,000	$8,918,000	−$6,607,000

Source: Fulks, 2008; Lederman, 2008

profits reported in past years counted as *income* millions of dollars from student fees, boosters' donations, the university foundation, and the university president's office. When these dollars were subtracted from "income" on athletic department accounting statements, it became clear that sport programs operate with large annual losses and exist only because they are subsidized by student fees and general fund money. This information, in turn, shocked many students and faculty members who were eager to discuss alternative uses of these funds.

Another surprise in the data was that in financial terms sport programs for women in most universities are more cost effective than sport programs for men—that is, they lose less money, are less costly, and spend far less per athlete than men's programs. Of course, football teams are the biggest money makers *and* money losers in the top NCAA subdivisions. When a big-time football or men's basketball team has a financial surplus, the money usually pays for other sports along with rapidly escalating coach salaries, perks for athletic directors and "friends" of the athletic department, and academic support programs to assist athletes with coursework. However, when an athletic department loses money, the losses are covered by increased student fees, higher ticket prices for games, special fund-raising directed at boosters and corporate sponsors, and the general funds that come from tuition, state tax money,

and/or endowments. In 2006, about 20 percent of the money for athletic departments in the top Division I level—the BFS—came from student fees and other university funds; at FCS and NF universities making up the rest of Division I, about 75 percent of athletic department costs are paid from student fees and institutional support!

Overall, about $1 billion in public money, including $507 million coming from student fees, was used by athletic departments in major state universities in 2006 (Alesia, 2006a). This does not take into account the indirect subsidies paid by taxpayers when the people who buy luxury suites and high-priced tickets to football and men's basketball games deduct up to 100 percent of their costs as either "business expenses" or "charitable contributions," thereby cutting about 40 percent of total costs off their taxes—money that could be used to fund public programs; additionally, tax-free bonds, often held by wealthy individuals and institutions, are used to build new university sport stadiums with luxury suites for wealthy fans and their friends (Alesia, 2006a).

This information is important because it clearly contradicts the widely held belief that revenues from men's teams pay for women's teams. In reality, this is true in 50 universities out of nearly 350 with big-time programs. Additionally, female students outnumber male students (about 53 percent to 47 percent) on most

In most NCAA schools, women's sport programs have smaller financial deficits than men's sports. This means that men's sports have a higher net cost than women's sports in most schools. The budget for this 2008 Division I championship bowling team at the University of Maryland Eastern Shore is small compared to the cost of most men's sports. (*Source:* Alyssa Schukar/NCAA Photos)

Recent NCAA data also clear up other fallacies about Division I intercollegiate sports. Here is a summary of these findings (Orszag and Orszag, 2005):

- Between 2001 and 2003, spending on intercollegiate athletics increased 20 percent, whereas spending in the rest of the university increased by less than 5 percent.
- The amount of money spent on big-time sports has no effect on academic quality or the academic qualifications of incoming students.
- Increasing the budget for sports does not increase alumni donations to the university.
- Increasing the budget for football and men's basketball does not produce more profits by those sport teams in a university, nor does it improve their win–loss records.
- Between 1993 and 2003, the "wealth gap" widened between financially successful Division I football and men's basketball teams and the teams that struggle financially.
- Increases in the budgets of athletic departments sometimes occur due to a desire to match athletic budgets at other institutions— a strategy that will never change the fact that every Division I game always ends with one winning team and one losing team.

Other research shows that when universities decrease athletic spending they do not experience declines in alumni giving or the number and quality of student applicants (Frank, 2004). It's true that when universities have winning sport teams their athletic departments receive more donations, but when this occurs, less money is donated to the universities' general funds (Stinson and Howard, 2004). In other words, many of the widely held beliefs about the benefits of big-time sports are myths perpetuated by people who ignore facts or simply repeat individual success stories to support what they wish to believe.

campuses, meaning that student fees from women contribute more to athletic teams than men contribute. This could be a violation of Title IX law, but many people associated with men's sports ignore these data and continue to insist that they are victims of gender equity.

In a number of our major institutions with large athletic departments, expectations have become unsustainable.
—Myles Brand, president, NCAA (in Roberts, 2005)

Even though research shows that sports do not have the positive effects that many people think they have, most large universities could not drop intercollegiate sports without encountering problems. Campus cultures and the public images of universities are tied to sport teams, and it would be a challenge to tie them to other things. However, many universities with top academic reputations don't have highly visible sport programs, nor do they use sports to obtain research grants and major donations. Their public profiles stand on academic and research quality rather than number of bowl games and final four appearances, and they attract the best students and maintain interesting campus cultures. This raises the following question: Sports are fun, entertaining, and great topics of conversation, but is their educational value worth what is spent on them? At this point, research suggests that elite intercollegiate programs are not worth what they cost, but more research remains to be done.

OLC ON THE *OLC*:

See the OLC—Additional Readings for Chapter 14—for a multidisciplinary bibliography of research on college sports and other issues related to the costs and benefits of intercollegiate sports.

Hidden Costs of Intercollegiate Sports   Discussions about intercollegiate sports became especially heated after James Shulman and William Bowen (2001), respected experts on higher education, identified hidden costs associated with college sports. After analyzing data from 1951 through the 1990s for thirty colleges and universities that have highly selective admissions policies, they reported the following findings:

- Students recruited as athletes are regularly given greater advantage in college admissions decisions than the relatives of alumni or underrepresented minorities.

- The difference between the ACT/SAT scores of recruited athletes and other students has grown consistently since the late 1980s, with athletes scoring significantly lower on these tests than other students admitted to the same schools.

- Since the late 1980s, the academic performance of athletes has been consistently lower than expected on the basis of test scores and other factors considered in the admissions process; and underperformance is most likely to occur when athletes are exclusively immersed in a sport culture in which athletic excellence is the central focus of their lives.

- The lives of athletes on college campuses have become increasingly separate from the lives of other students, due mostly to their immersion in a sport culture in which year-round training and continuous togetherness with teammates is expected.

- As the emphasis and per-student funding dedicated to intercollegiate sport teams have increased, the popularity, status, and per-student funding of other extracurricular activities have decreased, even though other activities are controlled more directly by students, have more clearly documented positive and complementary educational outcomes, and cost far less than sport teams.

Shulman and Bowen's study focused on highly rated academic institutions, so their findings can't be generalized to all colleges and universities. However, when their findings are combined with more recent evidence presented in follow-up studies, it appears that, even on campuses that don't have big-time sports programs, there is increasing tension between core educational values and decisions that favor intercollegiate sports in admissions and resource allocation in campus budgets (Bowen and Levine, 2003; Bowen et al., 2005). This tension has been building since the 1980s, and some faculty members now believe that academic quality suffers when so many campus resources are dedicated to recruiting

*"Our daughter goes to a truly great university!
Her basketball team just beat Stanford!"*

Some people equate athletic success with academic quality, but research shows no relationship between these two factors. Spending money on sports does not enhance academic programs or learning in the classroom; and winning teams do not bring more money to academic programs.

athletes, financially supporting teams that have ever-growing training and travel expenses, and building facilities for sports that are not organized or treated as educational.

This research on "hidden costs" has evoked widespread controversy. Bowen and his colleagues point out that they are not antisport when they question the organization, funding, and campus impact of intercollegiate programs. They ask if it is sensible to provide coaches with money to recruit students with highly specialized sport skills when the head of the sociology department or the faculty advisor for the school newspaper does not have a similar recruiting budget. Sports, they say, can exist without recruiting because many students want to play on school teams for reasons other than athletic scholarships and media coverage.

As this debate continues, it is important to gather systematic evidence about intercollegiate sports. Current research indicates that sports and sport experiences have a wide range of

consequences depending on the meanings that people give to them and the ways they are integrated into people's lives in particular social and cultural contexts. Interestingly, we've only begun to study those meanings, contexts, and consequences in education, even though U.S. schools have sponsored competitive sport teams for well over a century.

VARSITY HIGH SCHOOL SPORTS: PROBLEMS AND RECOMMENDATIONS

High school sport programs are widely supported, and many influential people want to keep them as they are. Some programs provide opportunities for students to develop and display physical skills in ways that have educational relevance. Others have lost their connection with education and distracted some students from learning in their classrooms. Problems vary by schools, sports, and teams, but the most serious include (1) an overemphasis on "sports development," (2) limited participation access, and (3) school cultures in which certain athletes are privileged over other students.

Overemphasis on "Sports Development"

The Problem   Some high school administrators, athletic directors, and coaches think that high school sports should emulate big-time intercollegiate sports. This leads to excessive concerns with winning records and building high-profile programs that become the focus of attention in the school and community. These programs often center on football or boys' basketball, but other teams may be highlighted in certain regions and schools. Creating and maintaining high-profile programs often leads to administrative decisions that overlook the educational needs of all students in the school. Instead, decisions focus on maximizing wins, minimizing losses, and being "ranked" in the state (Moore, 2007; Saslow, 2006a, 2006b, 2006c).

People who focus on sports development often give lip service to keeping sports in proper perspective as they fail to see that emphasizing sports in the school often marginalizes many students with no interest in sports (Saslow, 2007). Additionally, the students who play sports often are encouraged to specialize in a single sport for twelve months each year, even though this may restrict overall social and educational development (Farrey, 2008; Prisbell, 2006; Wolff, 2002). This turns off students who want to play sports but don't want to make them the center of their lives. Other students become so dedicated to sports that they overconform to the sport ethic to the point that they jeopardize other important activities and relationships in their lives.

AT YOUR *fingertips* For more information on overconformity to the norms of the sport ethic, see Chapter 6, pp. 162–169.

Adherence to a sports development model often is driven by boosters and booster organizations that raise funds and provide other types of support to one or more sport teams in a school. A high school football player describes this support:

> [Boosters] bring in uncountable money and nonstop help, whether it is buying uniforms or providing good meals after every game (Fry, 2006, A2).

However, individual boosters and booster organizations are seldom regulated by schools or school districts and they exist primarily in wealthier areas, often giving unfair advantage to a single team in a school or to an entire athletic program relative to programs in poor areas where resources are scarce and teams struggle to

exist. When boosters provide resources, sometimes out of their own pockets, they often feel they have a right to intervene in the process of evaluating and hiring coaches, and they generally focus on coaches' win–loss records rather than teaching abilities, because they often assume that winning is educational.

The ultimate example of a sports development approach is high schools that are organized around sports. Students in these high schools, many of which have been opened by IMG Academies in Florida, train in a particular sport and schedule classes around training (King, 2002, 2005; Latimer, 2005; Sokolove, 2004b). Tuition ranges from about $25,000 for "day students" to over $80,000 for boarding students who buy private lessons in their sport (soccer, baseball, softball, basketball, tennis, golf, swimming, mountain sports, and fishing). And it costs even more to attend the high-tech "education centers" for specialized physical or mental training. Students play their sports year-round in an atmosphere that, it is claimed, will "breathe life into their dreams" (http://www.imgacademies.com/HQ/default.sps?itype=7939).

Those dreams focus on obtaining an athletic scholarship to college, becoming a professional athlete, or graduating with highly developed and specialized skills. It's not known if the students learn in their courses that fifteen to twenty times more college scholarship dollars are awarded for academic achievements than for athletic skills.

> **High school sports will continue to fester into shameful overemphasis in too many places, will continue to emulate the college sports model that is America's educational shame.** —H. G. "Buzz" Bissinger (2004), author, *Friday Night Lights*

Recommendations for Change

Keeping high school sports in perspective requires regular evaluations and opportunities for program reorganization, coach-teacher education programs, and parent/booster education. State education departments should conduct research on the educational value of state and national rankings and post season tournaments. Furthermore, if sport participation produces important educational outcomes, it is important that all schools have adequate resources to provide teams for students wishing to play.

Limited Participation Access

The Problem   Organizing interscholastic sports so that all students in the United States play the same sports ignores educational theory and the diversity of sport interests among high school students. Furthermore, when high schools emphasize power and performance sports, they discourage participation by some boys and many girls who prefer sports emphasizing pleasure and participation. This is one reason why schools don't meet gender equity goals, despite persistent attempts to provide "opportunities" for girls. Not surprisingly, many girls prefer sports that are not organized around particular ideas about masculinity. "Proving who the better man is" through sports does not resonate with many high school girls.

And where are disability sports in high schools? The "adapted sports" of basketball, bowling, floor hockey, soccer, softball, and track are sanctioned by the National Federation of State High School Associations, but fewer than 70 out of nearly 18,000 U.S. high schools have teams in any of these sports (0.4 percent), and these are located in only 3 of 50 states. Over 7.43 million students play on "standard" high school sport teams, and less than 3700 students play on adapted sport teams (NFHS, 2008). Some athletes with disabilities play on standard teams, but apart from them, there is only 1 varsity athlete in adapted sports for every 5000 athletes on able-bodied varsity teams! Students with disabilities are "invisible" in high school sports. Consequently, able-bodied students miss opportunities to see their peers with disabilities compete and to share sport experiences with them. This represents a missed educational opportunity for able-bodied students and students with disabilities.

Recommendations for Change   Many students are not interested in playing interscholastic

ON THE *OLC*:
See the OLC—Additional Readings for Chapter 14—for a discussion of ethnicity and increased sport participation among girls.

sports, especially sports based on a power and performance model. Those who do not measure up to their bigger, faster, taller, and stronger classmates require alternatives to traditional power and performance sports or adaptations of those sports. For example, there could be three varsity boys' basketball teams organized by skill level and scheduled to play similarly skill-ranked teams from other schools.

Although sports like football and basketball receive much attention and many resources, there is a need for teams in Ultimate Frisbee, disc golf, racquetball, flag football, softball, in-line skating, skateboarding, and other sports for which there is enough local interest to field teams. With guidance, the students themselves could administer and coach these teams and coordinate exhibitions or meets and games with teams from other schools.

Girls' sports still lack the support that boys' sports enjoy. This problem has a history that goes far beyond high school, but the result, as illustrated in Figure 14.1, is that many more boys than girls play high school sports—about 1.3 million more in 2008.

One strategy for achieving gender equity is to have more gender-mixed (co-ed) sports such as long-distance running, doubles tennis and badminton, bowling, golf, cycling and tandem cycling, soccer, hacky sack, climbing, archery and shooting, volleyball, swimming, racquetball, and billiards. Gender-mixed sports would facilitate social development, promote interest in lifetime sports, and improve overall fitness. Why is football the centerpiece of many programs when few men and no women play football after they leave high school?

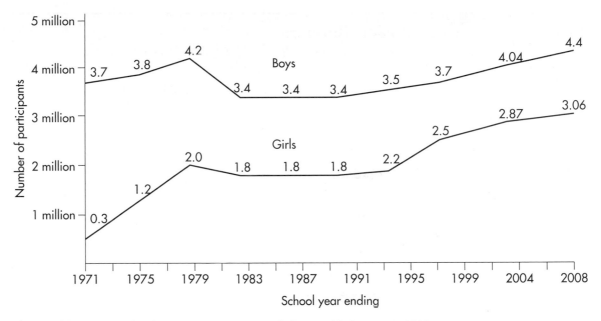

FIGURE 14.1 Boys and girls participating in interscholastic athletics, 1971–2008. (*Source.* NFHS, 2008)

When participation fees exist, they should be automatically waived for all students who qualify for subsidized federal lunch programs. Other strategies are needed as well so that "equality of educational opportunity" is more than a meaningless national slogan. When financial status becomes a criterion for sport participation in public schools, it is time to raise public money (taxes) or drop interscholastic sports.

Competitive sport participation by students with disabilities should occur through a combination of creatively designed programs. There are sports in which athletes with disabilities can be included in standard games, meets, and matches, but when this isn't possible there should be school teams in one or more adapted sports, or teams from districts or combinations of schools when there's a shortage of athletes. Furthermore, when students play on community-based teams sponsored by disability organizations, their participation should be publicized, supported, and

formally rewarded as is done with other athletes in the schools. There are many ways to support athletes with disabilities. Strategies will vary from one school to another, but they can be developed if people are creatively inclusive in how they organize sports. This issue is discussed in the Breaking Barriers box, page 500.

Athletes Are Privileged Over Other Students

The Problem   This issue was raised in Reflect on Sports box on page 477. It's included here because the growing emphasis on sports in U.S. culture carries over into high school culture. In many schools this creates or perpetuates status structures in which athletes are privileged over other students. This favoritism generates tension and feelings of animosity among other students and leads some athletes to believe that they have the power to do as they wish.

breaking BARRIERS

Inclusion Barriers
How Can I Wear Shoes if I Don't Have Feet?

Seventeen-year-old Bobby Martin says, "I stand 3 foot 1 inch but I've got the soul of a 6-foot-4 person" (Grossfeld, 2005). Martin played backup noseguard and on special teams for Dayton's (Ohio) Colonel White High School football team in 2005. He was born without legs, but he wrestled, bowled, danced, and moved around school hallways and classrooms on a custom skateboard.

On the football field, Martin moved with his hands and hips. "I love the reaction people have when I make a tackle. People don't believe I can play, and I love to prove them wrong." But he was stopped from playing when a referee told his coach that the Ohio high school rules required all players to wear shoes, knee pads, and thigh pads. Martin had all the necessary permissions to play, but the referees were not aware of them. As Martin pleaded his case on the field, he asked, "How can I wear shoes if I don't have feet?" (in Reilly, 2005, p. 90). For the rest of the season, Martin's coach presented referees with a letter in which the Dayton Public Schools declared his eligibility.

Bobby Martin's experiences received nationwide media coverage (Coffey, 2005; Grossfeld, 2005; Reilly, 2005), but none of the coverage mentioned that no U.S. high school in 2005 had a varsity team for students with disabilities. Nor was it noted that only a handful of universities field even one "paravarsity team," or that the NCAA does not recognize any championships in sports for athletes with disabilities. The few universities with wheelchair basketball teams fund the teams through disability services rather than the athletic department, and paid coaches and scholarships are very rare. All of this perpetuates the

"invisibility" of (dis)ability and the resultant lack of opportunities in U.S. schools.

Bob Szyman is a teacher-coach at the Chicago High School of Agricultural Sciences. He left his position as secretary general of the International Wheelchair Basketball Federation (IWBF) to teach special education and physical education. His goal is to establish a wheelchair basketball league in Chicago public schools, but his biggest challenge has been finding people who are excited about such a league. He explains that "there is no wheelchair sport culture" in the schools, so students with disabilities have no expectations and make no demands, especially in lower-income and ethnic minority communities; nor do administrators, teachers, and coaches ask why there are no "paravarsity teams." When Szyman organizes wheelchair sports camps and competitions, the participants go out of their way to thank him, but they don't ask why their schools have no sports programs for them. They're accustomed to being ignored when it comes to sports.

The Americans with Disabilities Act (ADA) calls for access and equity, but it contains no mandate to establish paravarsity sports or make teachers, administrators, and coaches think creatively about developing them. Few students can do what Bobby Martin did. Certain (dis)abilities require games, rules, and equipment adapted to physical characteristics. Therefore, if Bobby Martin were speaking to educators about this issue, he might ask, "How can students with a disability play sports if we have no teams?" This question begs for an answer.

Leon Botstein, long-time president of Bard College, has noted that today's high schools must be reformed because they "trap [adolescents] in a world of jock values and anti-intellectualism, like trying to cram a large person into a small, childish uniform" (1997; and in Applebome, 1999). These are harsh words, but they highlight the

need for critical assessments of school cultures in which the most revered students are those who can "kick ass" on a football field or hit 20-foot jumpers at the buzzer.

Recommendations for Change   Administrators, teachers, and coaches are responsible for knowing

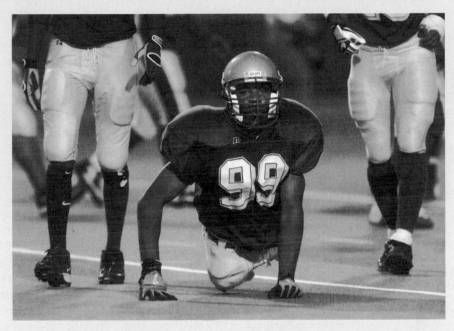

Public schools are traditionally places where temporarily able-bodied young people develop and display their sports skills, but the myth that people with disabilities aren't interested in sports subverts opportunities for them. Bobby Martin is an assertive and determined young man with an undeniable desire to play football. But mainstreaming young people with disabilities in existing school sports is not always practical. Does that mean it is fair to deny young people the learning experiences that can occur in high school and college sports? (*Source: Dayton Daily News*, Jim Witmer/AP Wide World Photos)

about the ways that systems of privilege operate in schools. This is not easy because most adults are unaware of the subtle manifestations of privilege that occur between students in classrooms, hallways, cafeterias, parking lots, and other common spaces in and around the schools. The challenge is to become aware and develop methods to control them without using high-tech surveillance devices that invade students' privacy and turn the schools into mini–police states.

An effective strategy is to bring diverse students together in policy-assessing and policy-making groups so that they can learn about one another and develop reasons for interacting in civil and respectful ways. Friendship groups are crucial factors in the development of adolescents, so it's important to accept the selective interaction patterns that young people prefer, while ensuring that friendship groups are not pitted against each other in school-based status dynamics.

> **ON THE *OLC*:**
> See the OLC—Additional Readings for Chapter 14—for a discussion of whether high schools sports emphasize conformity or leadership.

Another effective strategy to equalize treatment is to give equal attention and recognition to students' accomplishments in activities other than sports—and to encourage local media to do the same. When high school athletes are exclusively privileged in the culture of their schools and communities, some of them will exploit that privilege. If this goes unchecked, it can distort school cultures and undermine the educational and social development of many students, including athletes (Weiner, 2000).

INTERCOLLEGIATE SPORTS: PROBLEMS AND RECOMMENDATIONS

Problems are not new to intercollegiate sports. Even in the late 1800s, college teams were accused of being too commercial and professional. In the mid-1920s, a Carnegie Corporation study found intercollegiate programs were so commercialized and professionalized that they undermined education (Savage, 1929). But these problems continued to grow along with the size, popularity, and scope of intercollegiate sports, and they were identified again in a 1973 study by the American Council on Education (Hanford, 1974, 1979). Between 1991 and 2001, the Knight Foundation Commission on Intercollegiate Athletics issued four reports calling

for reforms and the elimination of the excessive commercialization of college sports (Knight Commission, 1991, 1992, 1993, 2001). These reports, combined with other research, identify at least four major problems confronting college sports today: (1) commercialization, (2) a lack of athletes' rights, (3) gender inequities, and (4) distorted racial and ethnic priorities.

Commercialization

The Problem   Big-time college sports have been turned into part of the entertainment industry, with commercial goals and operating methods that are unrelated to or in conflict with the educational mission of U.S. universities. Evidence shows that financial issues have become so important that they interfere with the academic progress of many college athletes. Media companies and corporate sponsors are unconcerned with educational issues because their profits don't require academic accomplishments among athletes—as long as the most entertaining athletes retain their eligibility. Nor are those corporations concerned with sports and teams that don't attract large media audiences.

As a result, many big-time college sport programs are riddled with inconsistencies related to amateurism and education. For example, basketball players on big-time teams are classified as amateurs as they devote most of their college lives to their sport for scholarships of $4000 to $25,000 per year (Wieberg, 2008a). At the same time, their coaches have salary packages averaging over $1 million a year and uncounted perks and endorsement money, their universities profit from media and ticket revenues and the sales of jerseys with their numbers on the back, and others, including athletic directors and NCAA officials, become wealthy because of their labor as amateurs. This hypocrisy intensifies the expectation of privilege among many athletes—which regularly gets them in trouble—and makes a mockery of college basketball as a nonprofit, educational activity (Sack, 2008).

Commercialization and organizing sports around an entertainment model undermines most efforts to sponsor sports for athletes with disabilities. This isn't the only factor that accounts for the invisibility of students with disabilities in the 150-year history of intercollegiate sports, but the existence of an entertainment model that emphasizes revenue-generating sports makes it more difficult to establish teams for athletes with disabilities.

Recommendations for Change   As they are currently organized, intercollegiate sports require significant funding, and the NCAA tends to see commercialism as a solution rather than a problem. This is one of the factors that has led The

Drake Group to say that the only way to bring about real change is for the U.S. Congress to intervene and force universities to follow certain rules or lose their status as tax-exempt, nonprofit educational organizations—an outcome that would have serious financial consequences for the NCAA, universities, and the boosters who support big-time programs. The following recommendations for reform proposed by The Drake Group are designed to organize college sports around educational rather than commercial goals:

1. Disclose the courses taken by athletes, the average grades for all students in those courses, and the names of instructors who teach those courses.

Powerful vested interests are linked with major revenue-producing college sports, such as the men's final four basketball tournament. For example, about 90 percent of the NCAA's operational funds come from the sale of media rights to this tournament. Various business interests in the cities that host the regional and final games also make money from the tournament. In the face of such strong financial interests, changes in these sports are unlikely. (*Source:* NCAA Photos)

2. Restore the rule that makes first-year students ineligible to play on varsity teams and apply the rule to transfer students.[4]

3. Restore multiyear athletic scholarships by giving athletes five-year, need-based, grants-in-aid that can't be revoked because of injury or poor performance.[5]

4. Redefine athletic eligibility so that students on sport teams must maintain a 2.0 GPA, quarter-by-quarter or semester-by-semester, in accredited, degree-track courses.

5. Require all athletic departments to use the same system of financial accounting so that all income and expenses are clearly stated and open to public financial audits.

6. Reorganize academic counseling and support services so that they are the same for all athletes and outside the control of athletic departments.

7. Reduce the number of athletic events and change game schedules so that students are not forced to miss classes or give higher priority to athletic participation than to class attendance.

These proposals are not radical; all are consistent with standard norms and processes in public universities. However, they are controversial because they would reduce the control that the NCAA and athletic departments have over athletes' lives and

> Exploitation, hypocrisy, duplicity are harsh words yet precisely describe the workings of the NCAA and its member schools in their treatment of college revenue athletes, the young men and women upon whose backs this multi-billion-dollar college revenue sports empire rests. It is America's modern plantation.
>
> —David Meggyesy, NFL Players Association, Western Regional Director, retired (in Sack, 2008)

subject teams to normal standards of academic and financial accountability.

Corporate support should also be regulated so that intercollegiate sport programs are not dependent on the advertising and profit needs of private companies. Requiring athletes to wear particular corporate logos is inconsistent with freedom of speech for athletes and the accepted idea that critical thinking should be encouraged among all students. Classroom teachers and academic departments are not allowed to sell their students to corporations, and this policy should also apply to coaches and athletic departments. If corporate sponsorships occur, they should be negotiated openly so that students may evaluate them in critical terms. For example, students may decide that no sweatshop labor will be used to produce the apparel worn by athletes and the equipment used in school sports.

If these recommendations cannot be implemented, student-controlled club and intramural sports should replace intercollegiate sports. This is an extreme suggestion, but the chronic problems and hypocrisy in commercial-entertainment sports necessitate extreme actions.

Lack of Athletes' Rights

The Problem The lives of many intercollegiate athletes are controlled by coaches whose careers depend on making sure that athletes are completely dedicated to their sports. If they have athletic scholarships, they are at the mercy of coaches who determine whether their scholarships will be renewed each year (Wolverton, 2008). If athletes have a grievance with the coach or athletic department, they risk loss of team membership and their scholarships if they speak out. There's no union or arbitration board to which they can go, and they are seldom

---

[4]Until 1973 first-year students weren't eligible to play on intercollegiate teams. It was believed that students needed one year to become acclimated to the academic demands of college before playing big-time sports. Through the 1960s, many athletic scholarships were four-year grants-in-aid, and they were guaranteed even if the recipient did not play sports. Today, all athletic scholarships are one-year grants that are renewed each July at the discretion of the head coach for each team.

[5]See footnote 4.

represented on committees that make decisions about the conditions of their sport participation. In short, they have no institutionalized mechanism or process for challenging the system that controls them (Moye and Harrison, 2002).

In the face of this system in which they had no rights, four athletes filed a federal antitrust lawsuit claiming that the NCAA engaged in unlawful restraint of trade when it restricted their scholarships only to the cost of tuition, books, housing, and meals. The students won the suit and forced the NCAA to do four things: (1) make $10 million available for the football and men's basketball players who were on major conference teams between 2002–2003 and 2007–2008 and had "bona fide educational expenses" of $500 to $2500 per year over what their scholarships paid; (2) allocate $218 million to Division I universities so that athletes from 2008 to 2013 with demonstrated financial or academic need for funds can receive assistance; (3) permit Division I schools to provide year-round health insurance for athletes so they can be taken off the insurance policies of their parents; and (4) pay up to $8.6 million of the legal fees for the four students and provide $100,000 to cover the expense of notifying all students eligible for the settlement (Carey and Gardiner, 2008a, 2008b, 2008c).

This lawsuit rectifies one of the injustices built into NCAA sports. Others remain, and there will be additional lawsuits unless the NCAA makes reforms in other areas. An obvious one is that a few athletes generate millions of dollars for their universities and have no way of benefiting from their athletic labor beyond their scholarships and basic educational expenses that they can demonstrate (Alesia, 2006b). These athletes must make four-year commitments to schools, but schools make only year-to-year scholarship commitments to them. In the meantime, universities and even a corporate sponsor who has a signed agreement with a university can use the likenesses of athletes in their game promotions and commercials without compensating the players, but the athletes cannot sell their own likenesses (Smith, 2007).

Intercollegiate sports are described as educational, but athletes are in a position where they are basically owned by their coach to the point that their opportunities to learn are constrained. If this can be demonstrated, there will be another lawsuit.

> **ON THE *OLC*:**
>   See the OLC—Additional Readings for Chapter 14—for a discussion of pay for college athletes

Recommendations for Change   Athlete representatives should be voting members on certain NCAA and all university athletic committees; they should have a formal means to register complaints and have them investigated without jeopardizing their status on teams; they should have regular opportunities, like students in courses, to evaluate coaches and team programs on their educational merits; and they should be in charge of athlete advisory/disciplinary committees that handle team issues. Furthermore, every university should provide an independent ombudsperson— an appointed official who investigates issues raised by "employees"—to whom athletes can go when they think their rights have been compromised.

Unless sport participation is part of an open and democratic educational experience, big-time sports should be treated as businesses, with employees who have a right to be paid and receive other workers' benefits. As they now exist, big-time college sports are a major form of show business in which the entertainers earn less than minimum wage. As revenues have increased in college sports, some of them are beginning to look much like gilded plantations where workers are fed and housed but have no opportunity to share in the fruits of their labor (Hawkins, 2000). Therefore, there should be guidelines for allowing athletes to earn money and form economic relationships outside the university. This would eliminate the myth of amateurism and some of the hypocrisy in intercollegiate sports (Sack, 2008; Sack and Staurowsky, 1998).

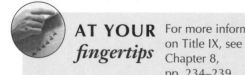

AT YOUR *fingertips*   For more information on Title IX, see Chapter 8, pp. 234–239.

Gender Inequities

The Problem   For many years female students paid fees that subsidized intercollegiate sports that basically excluded them. Men became accustomed to this sexist arrangement, and when Title IX became law in 1972, many of them resisted the mandate to share resources: They said sharing would hurt them because they had organized athletic programs for the previous eighty years around their interests and the assumption that they controlled all the resources. The notion of gender equity took them by surprise and some men

have continued to resist it for the last 37 years. As a result, there are no intercollegiate programs that have achieved full gender equity.

Figure 14.2 shows that women made up 53 percent of the student body but only 43 percent of the athletes in 325 Division I universities in 2006. Additionally, they received 45 percent of the scholarship dollars, 32 percent of recruiting dollars, 34 percent of the total athletic department operating budget, and 35 percent of all salaries for head coaches.

As of 2008, 43 percent of the athletes at *all* NCAA Division levels were women (174,534), and 57 percent were men (233,830). At the same time, nearly 57 percent of all undergraduate students at those schools were women, and 43 percent were men. Although proportionality may not be the best way to measure equity, current patterns of opportunities and financial support show that inequities continue to exist. For example, in 2008 there were about 59,300 more men than women playing intercollegiate sports,

After having all the "athletic toys" in high schools and colleges, rules mandating that boys share half of the "toys" with the girls were strongly resisted by boys. Many men who have administered school athletic programs over the past thirty years grew up when boys and men had all the athletic toys and learned that this was the right way to organize sports.

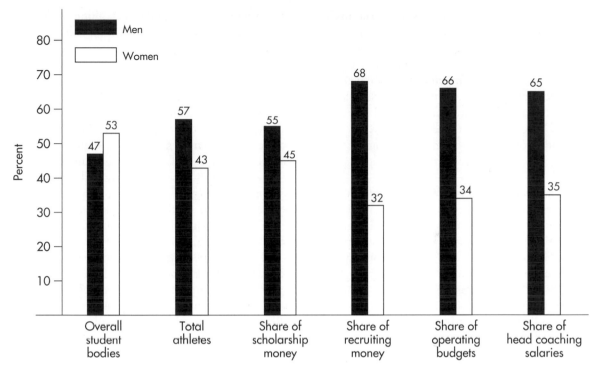

FIGURE 14.2 Gender equity in NCAA Division I universities, 2005–2006. (*Source:* Correspondence with research staff at the National Collegiate Athletic Association, 2008)

and between 2002 and 2008, the number of men and women playing sports in all NCAA schools increased by 23,940 and 20,933, respectively. These differences are due primarily to the size of football teams and the number of universities adding or expanding their football programs.[6]

---

[6]Research is needed on the ironic possibility that Title IX has provided a major boost to college football teams and players. When the number of scholarships for football teams was cut from 105 to 85 to meet gender equity goals, the 30 top teams could no longer hoard "extra" players to prevent their opponents from recruiting them. This meant that about 600 players who would have accepted scholarships from those universities could be recruited by other teams that were able to become contenders for conference championships and big-money bowl games. As television and sponsorship money also increased, other schools decided to expand their football programs. Therefore, many football players owe their scholarships and their playing time to Title IX!

In 73 universities in the top six intercollegiate conferences (the Atlantic Coast, Big East, Big Ten, Big 12, Pacific-10, and Southeastern), football and men's basketball often make enough money, due to massive increases in television rights fees, to boost the overall budgets for women's sports. However, at the same time, the expenses for football and men's basketball have increased dramatically. Therefore, women's programs at these universities have grown although they still operate on half the dollars spent on men's programs. The schools with the largest gender inequities are those with football programs that don't share the recent windfall television revenues enjoyed by universities in the major conferences.

In terms of gender equity, the supporters of intercollegiate football face a glaring contradiction. On the one hand, they say that football is an educational activity and is not responsible for paying taxes or treating players as employees. On the other hand, when gender equity in education is discussed, they claim that college football is a business affected by objective market forces out of their control and it should not be treated as an educational activity. This is why Title IX remains controversial—it exposes the contradictions of big-time sport programs and turns football supporters into flip-floppers.

Recommendations for Change The current organization and operation of intercollegiate football is the primary cause of persistent gender inequity in college sports. If football was played so that it did not require 85+ players on big-time teams and if there were "expense ceilings" for all FBS and FCS teams, gender equity would be achievable and all teams would be able to compete on fairer basis. If all football teams in each NCAA division or subdivision had the same budget limits as the teams they played, football rankings would reflect good coaching and team organization rather than who has the biggest budget.

Many people forget that it took nearly a century to build intercollegiate football and men's basketball into sports that attract popular attention. Women should be given the same amount of time to build their programs and make one or two of their sports into popular attractions. This means that women's programs have until 2072—one hundred years after Title IX was passed—to build their programs with the full support of universities, including the use of student fees from male students. In the meantime, there's no educational justification for paying women any less for coaching teams similar to those coached by men, and there's no educational justification for paying the coaches of women's teams less than the coaches of similar men's teams. To argue that market forces alone determine coaches' salaries and team budgets is

> **Football is the S.U.V. of the college campus: aggressively big, resource-guzzling, lots and lots of fun and potentially destructive of everything around it.**
> —Michael Sokolove, journalist (2002)

like saying that market forces alone determine the annual profits of large oil companies.

Distorted Racial and Ethnic Priorities

The Problem NCAA data in 2007 indicated that blacks constituted about 10 percent of the student body at Division I universities, but they comprised 21 percent of the athletes, 46 percent of the football players, and 60 percent of the men's and 47 percent of the women's basketball players with scholarships. Nearly 70 percent of all black male athletes played football or basketball—the only sports that produced revenues and the sports with the lowest graduation rates.

This also means that, in some big-time sport programs, black male athletes have consistently generated revenues that funded other sport teams on which all or nearly all of the players were white. Black athletes have long been keenly aware of their contributions to white athletes and become frustrated when they're perceived by whites to be privileged on campus.

Overall, one of every 6 black men on Division I campuses is an athlete; this is the case for 1 of every 29 white men, 1 of every 25 black women, and 1 of every 33 white women. This gives many people the impression that black males are superathletes who attend college because of their physical skills. At the same time, it leads people to overlook the fact that over 99.5 percent of all black American men between the ages of eighteen and twenty-three do not have athletic scholarships (Alesia, 2005).

Figure 14.3 highlights data on race, ethnicity, and big-time intercollegiate sports. The data suggest that if African Americans excel in revenue-producing sports, universities will actively identify and recruit them, but the same universities do a terrible job of recruiting African American students who don't excel at scoring touchdowns or making jump shots. There is no denying that a few African Americans benefit from athletic scholarships. But the problem is that universities have capitalized on the racist myth that blacks can use sports to improve their lives, while ignoring their responsibility to recruit black students and to change the social climate on the campus so that black students feel welcome, supported, and respected, even if they don't score touchdowns or score 20 points a game.

A related problem is that many black athletes feel isolated on campuses where there are few black students, faculty, and administrators (Harrison and Lawrence, 2004; Lawrence, 2005). This isolation is intensified by many

factors (Dempsey, 2004; Fudzie and Hayes, 1995; Hawkins, 2000), including these:

1. Racial and athletic stereotypes make it difficult for black athletes to feel welcome on campus and develop relationships that support academic success.
2. Athletes must devote so much time to their sports that it is difficult to become involved in other spheres of campus life.
3. Campus activities often fail to represent the interests and experiences of black students, which makes them feel unwelcome.

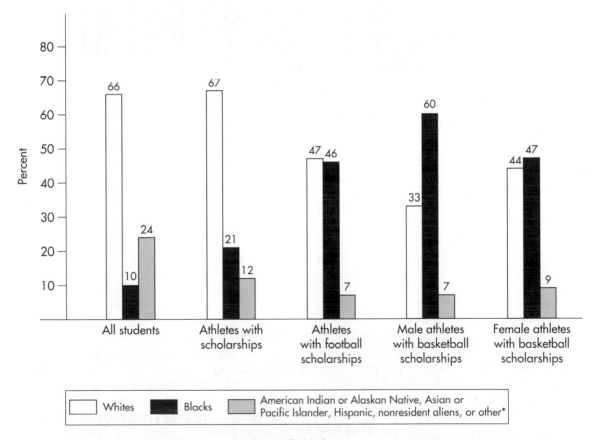

*Racial and ethnic classifications are based on self-identifications.

FIGURE 14.3 Percentages of students and athletes in NCAA Division I universities by skin color and ethnicity, 2007. (*Source:* 1999–2000—2006–2007 NCAA Student-Athlete Race and Ethnicity Report; http://www.ncaapublications.com/Uploads/PDF/Race-Ethnicity_2008bc054067-3afd-4d76-b1cc-c1e9422eca18.pdf)

4. When campus life is unrelated to their experiences, black athletes may withdraw from activities that could connect them with other students.

5. When white students lack experience in racially diverse groups, they may feel uncomfortable interacting with black students from backgrounds unlike their own.

6. When white students conclude that black athletes have things easy and are unfairly privileged, it creates tension that undermines meaningful interaction.

Feelings of social isolation are especially intense when black athletes come from working-class or low-income backgrounds and white students come from upper-middle-income backgrounds. This combination of ethnic and socioeconomic differences can create problems unless the administration, faculty, and professional staff provide regular opportunities for students to interact in ways that increase their knowledge of others from different backgrounds. Putting athletes in their own dorm wings, creating special academic support programs for them, and giving them athlete centers where they can hang out with other athletes may make general campus isolation more endurable, but it does not foster learning and development (Hawkins, 2000).

Most research in the sociology of sport has focused on black men, so we don't know much about the experiences of black women who play sports in predominantly white institutions. Additionally, black women face the dual challenge of coping with complex racial and gender dynamics on campus and in the athletic department (Bruening, 2004, 2005; Bruening et al., 2005; Corbett and Johnson, 2000; Daniels, 2000; Smith, 1999; Stratta, 1995, 1998; Suggs, 2001; Winlock, 2000). They see few women of color in positions of power and authority in their schools and athletic departments, so may not feel fully included in either sphere.

A key issue for some black women is that Title IX law has benefited white women more

than black women. For example, 74 percent of all black women with scholarships in Division I NCAA schools in 2007 were playing on basketball or track teams, and black women received only 4.6 percent of the scholarships in the other 16 women's sports. This means that nearly 25 percent of all black women with scholarships play on teams where they may be the only black athlete, and it's likely that their experiences are different from the experiences of black women on basketball and track teams.

Title IX has fueled the growth of soccer, crew (rowing), golf, rifle, and lacrosse, but these sports are played primarily by white girls and young women in upper-middle-class families. When black women do play them, they seldom have black teammates and their experiences can be socially isolating (Bruening et al., 2005). For this reason, Tina Sloan Green of the Black Women in Sport Foundation claims that "Title IX was for white women" and that the experiences of black girls and women have been overlooked in the expansion of college sports for women (Suggs, 2001). This is an issue that most whites ignore because they assume that race and ethnicity are irrelevant when crew, a nearly all-white activity, is designated as a college sport, whereas double dutch, played almost exclusively by black girls, is never even considered as a sport in high schools or colleges (see the cover of this book for an image representing double dutch). In other words, Title IX does not recognize that the activities of some people are more likely to be considered sports than the activities of other people.

Recommendations for Change Universities must be more aggressive and creative in recruiting and supporting ethnic minority students who aren't athletes and in doing the same for ethnic minority coaches and faculty. It's not fair to recruit black or other ethnic minority athletes to campuses where they have little social support and feel that students and faculty don't know much about their history, heritage, and experiences (Perlmutter, 2003). If universities effectively included racial and cultural diversity within all spheres of campus life, recruiting black athletes would not indicate a distorted set of campus priorities. When universities present to the world images of physically talented black athletes and intellectually talented white scientists, racism is perpetuated, whether intentionally or not.

DO COMPETITIVE SPORTS CONTRIBUTE TO EDUCATION?

The United States is the only nation in the world where it is taken for granted that high schools and colleges will sponsor and fund interschool sport programs. There are arguments for and against this practice, but most of the claims made on both sides are not based on good research.

Generalizing about high school and college sport programs is difficult because programs and the conditions under which participation occurs are so diverse. However, it's important to study school sports to determine if and when they contribute to positive educational outcomes for athletes, the overall organization of the school, and students in general. At a minimum, if the programs provide no educational benefits for the athletes, they cannot be justified as school-sponsored activities.

Research shows that young people who play on high school teams have better overall academic records than those who don't. But much of this difference is explained by the processes through which students are selected-in and filtered-out of school teams. Young people with characteristics consistent with academic achievement are favored in these processes, so it is not surprising that athletes, on average, have different characteristics from other students.

The most effective way to determine what occurs in connection with school sport participation is to study athletes and teams in context over time. This enables a researcher to identify the factors that influence sport experiences, the meanings that young people give to those experiences, and how young people integrate them into their identities and everyday lives.

Sport experiences vary widely and are given different meanings that tend to be influenced by gender, race and ethnicity, social class, (dis)ability, and the social and cultural context of the family, school, and local community. Although there is reasonably consistent evidence indicating that the social dynamics on certain high school sport teams increase the likelihood of binge drinking among all athletes and higher rates of sexual activity and bullying among certain male athletes, most studies suggest that sport participation has positive outcomes for most young people.

Research also indicates that some schools, coaches, parents, and athletes lose sight of educational goals in their pursuit of competitive success in sports. Sports can be seductive, and people connected with high school teams usually require guidance to keep their programs in balance with the academic curriculum. Unless sport teams are explicitly organized to achieve positive educational outcomes, the chances of achieving them decrease. When people assume that sport participation automatically builds personal character and enhances learning, it undermines the planning and evaluation that must be a part of any school activity, especially those that are as costly as many school sports.

The possibility that sport participation interferes with the education of athletes is greatest in big-time intercollegiate programs. The status and identity that often comes with membership on highly visible and publicized sport teams makes it difficult for many young people to focus on and give priority to academic work. This is especially the case among young men who see their destinies being shaped by sport achievements, not academic achievements. With this said, data indicate that athletes as a category have higher graduation rates than the general student population. However, graduation rates among athletes vary widely by gender, race, and sport.

High school and college sports usually create spirited feelings among some students, faculty, and staff in schools. But little is known about the characteristics of this spirit or if and when it contributes to the achievement of educational goals—or disrupts the achievement of those goals. Although many different activities can be used to unite students and link them with community and society, sports often are used to do this in the United States. Sports often are popular activities, but there is much to be learned about the conditions under which they are most and least likely to produce particular educational and developmental outcomes.

Most high school sport programs don't seriously cut into funds for academic programs. The money they require is well spent if they provide students with opportunities to learn about their physicality, develop physical and interpersonal skills, and display their skills in ways that lead them to be recognized and rewarded by others. However, when budgets are strained, many sport programs depend on participation fees, boosters, and/or corporate sponsors to survive. When this occurs, school in lower-income areas are at a serious competitive disadvantage. Over time, these strategies to fund school sports lead to and intensify social class and racial/ethnic divisions in schools and school districts.

Funding issues are complex and often confusing in intercollegiate sports. However, it's clear that very few programs are self-supporting and nearly all of them depend on subsidies from student fees, donations, and general campus funds. As intercollegiate programs boost their focus on achieving commercial goals, the likelihood of achieving educational goals usually declines. The allocation of general funds and student fees to intercollegiate sports becomes an increasingly contentious issue when athletic departments and sport teams have become so separate from the rest of campus culture that faculty and students see no reason to support them.

The major problems facing high school sport programs are (1) an excessive emphasis on sports development, (2) limited participation access among certain segments of the student body, and (3) a school status system and organizational culture that is perceived to unfairly privilege certain athletes. Similarly, intercollegiate programs face problems related to (1) an overcommercialization of certain sports, (2) lack of institutionalized mechanisms to secure and protect athletes' rights, (3) a nearly universal failure to achieve full gender equity, and (4) distorted priorities for recruiting athletes and students from various racial and ethnic backgrounds.

Dealing with these problems is necessary if school sports in high schools and colleges are to produce outcomes making them viable educational activities supported by institutional resources. School sport programs will always face challenges, making it necessary to assess them critically on a regular basis—as occurs with all parts of the curriculum.

WEBSITE RESOURCES

Note: Websites often change. The following URLs were current when this book was printed. Please check our website (www.mhhe.com/coakley10e) for updates and additions.

www.mhhe.com/coakley10e Click on Chater 14 for a bibliography of research on college sports and discussions of NCAA reforms, pay for college athletes, school-community relations, and ethnicity in girls' high school sports.

www.aahperd.org/nagws/template.cfm The National Association for Girls and Women in Sport is a member organization of AAHPERD; this site provides good information on Title IX issues.

www.bus.ucf.edu/sport/cgi-bin/site/sitew.cgi?page= /ides/media.htx The Institute for Diversity and Ethics in Sport provides independent studies of graduation rates for university teams in postseason tournament and bowl games as well as other diversity patterns in intercollegiate sports.

www.childtrendsdatabank.org/pdf/37%5FPDF.pdf Provides data on participation in school athletics and data comparing participation in 1991 and 2006; encompasses variables not covered by data from the National High Schools Activity Association. The data are collected by Child Trends Data Bank, Washington, DC (2003).

www.cstv.com The home page of College Sports TV; provides schedules of television and online programming; highlights of games; scores and standings; and fan interaction platforms.

www.disability.uiuc.edu/athletics/ Site of the University of Illinois Adapted Varsity Athletics Program; offers complete information on the university's support of leadership and excellence in wheelchair sports.

www.ed.gov/about/offices/list/ocr/docs/title9guidanceadditional.html The site of the U.S. Department of Education and the Office of Civil Rights provides a full explanation of new (2005) enforcement guidelines related to Title IX.

www.insidehighered.com/views/why_the_u_s_should_intervene_in_college_sports Explanation of why the U.S. government should intervene in intercollegiate sports; presented by Frank Splitt (2/16/05); it focuses on the tax-exempt status of revenue-producing sports.

www.knightcommission.org The Knight Commission on Intercollegiate Athletics provides all of its policy statements and research reports based on the studies it commissions.

www.naia.org Site of the National Association of Intercollegiate Athletics provides information about this organization and its nearly 300-member organizations.

www.ncaa.org The National Collegiate Athletic Association provides information about intercollegiate sports and links to NCAA sport sciences programs and NCAA-sponsored studies, including graduation rate data at http://www.ncaa.org/wps/ncaa?ContentID=10.

www.nfhs.org The National Federation of State High School Associations has information about varsity high school sports in the United States and historical and recent data on participation totals by sport and gender, rules, and other topics.

www.njcaa.org The National Junior College Athletic Association presents information related to intercollegiate sports at over 500 community/junior colleges in the United States.

www.thedrakegroup.org/ The Drake Group assists faculty and staff maintain academic integrity as they deal with pressures from commercialized intercollegiate sports; provides a network of college faculty that lobbies for academic standards, and offers general information about college sports and academic issues.

www.thenccaa.org Site of the National Christian College Athletic Association provides general information and news for its ninety-nine member colleges.

(Jay Coakley)

SPORTS AND RELIGIONS

Is It a Promising Combination?

I AM A MEMBER OF TEAM JESUS CHRIST

—Sign posted in the locker room by Fisher
DeBerry, head football coach, U.S. Air Force
Academy, 2005

chapter outline

How Do Sociologists Define and Study Religion?

Similarities and Differences Between Sports and Religions
    Sports as Religion
    Sport and Religion Are Essentially Different
    Religions and Sports as Cultural Practices
    Studying Sports and Religions: An Assessment

Modern Sports and Religious Beliefs and Organizations
    The Protestant Ethic and the Spirit of Sports
    Sports and World Religions
    REFLECT ON SPORTS: Allah's Will: Dilemmas for Islamic Women in Sports?
    How Have Christians and Christian Organizations Used Sports?
    How Have Athletes, Coaches, and Teams Used Religion?
    REFLECT ON SPORTS: Public Prayers at Sport Events: What's Legal and What's Not?

The Challenges of Combining Sports and Religious Beliefs
    Challenges for Christian Athletes
    Challenges for Christian Sport Organizations
    Adapting Religious Beliefs to Fit Sports
    BREAKING BARRIERS: Belief Barriers: I Was "One of God's Favorites"

Summary: Is It a Promising Combination?

Visit *Sports in Society*'s Online Learning Center (OLC) at www.mhhe.com/coakley10e for additional information and study material for this chapter, including the following:

- A complete chapter outline
- Learning objectives
- Practice quizzes
- Internet resources
- Related readings
- Essays
- Student projects

YOU LOOK AT some of the games we're winning. Those aren't just a coincidence. God has definitely had a hand in this.

—**Dan O'Dowd, general manager, Colorado Rockies (in Nightengale,2006)**

I HOPE I DON'T have to spend my time telling my players I'm a Christian. I hope they see it in my everyday life.

—**Lovie Smith, Head Coach, Chicago Bears (in Moring, 2007)**

WE SHOULD KEEP our daughters away from competitive sports and spend our time training them how to be Biblically feminine women, wives and mothers.

—**Scott Jonas, BeautifulWomanhood.org, 2005**

515

The relationship between sports and religions varies by time and place. As noted in Chapter 3, physical activities and sports in many traditional cultures are included in rituals that are linked to the supernatural. For example, the histories of many Native America cultures show that games and running races often had spiritual significance. The histories of Jews and Christians in Europe and North America indicate that there have been times and places in which religious authorities approved of physical activities, games, and sports; and in other cases, authorities condemned them as indulgent and sinful. There have been religious approaches to the body—sometimes linking it with weakness and sin, and other times linking it with strength and godliness.

During the last half of the twentieth century, most religious organizations in North America and Europe approved of sports and, at times, even sponsored them. Furthermore, individuals today combine sport participation with their religious beliefs and publicly proclaim the personal importance of this combination. This is especially common among Christian athletes in the United States.

The purpose of this chapter is to examine the connections between religions and sports. This relationship is complex because similar religious beliefs are combined with sports in diverse ways, depending on the experiences, relationships, and interests of individuals and groups.

The major questions we'll discuss in this chapter are these:

1. How is *religion* defined, and why do sociologists study it?
2. What are the similarities and differences between sports and religions?
3. Why have people combined sports and religious beliefs, and why are Christians more vocal about this combination than are Jews, Muslims, Hindus, Buddhists, Sikhs, and other people whose religious beliefs are not based on Christianity?
4. What are the issues and controversies associated with combining religious beliefs and sport participation?

When discussing the last question, special attention is given to the prospect of using religion as a platform for eliminating racism, sexism, deviance, violence, and other problems in sports and sport organizations.

HOW DO SOCIOLOGISTS DEFINE AND STUDY RELIGION?

A sociological discussion of religion may create controversy because people often use their own religious beliefs and practices as their only point of reference. Tensions are inevitable whenever people are asked to think critically and analytically about the beliefs and meanings that they use to make sense of their experiences and the world around them.

In sociological terms, **religions** are *integrated and socially shared beliefs and rituals that people accept on faith and use as a source of meaning, guidance, and transcendence* (Cipriani, 2007). Religious beliefs and rituals link people's lives with a supernatural realm or a divinity, including God or gods.[1] This link is grounded in faith—the foundation of all religions.

Religions are powerful because people use them as sense-making perspectives and guides for action. In this sense, they share certain characteristics with ideologies. For example, both are components of culture organized around beliefs accepted on faith or taken for granted, and both are used to explain the meaning of objects, events, and experiences and to guide choices and actions. However, ideologies focus mostly on secular, here-and-now, material world issues, and they're neither automatically nor inevitably linked with the supernatural or a divinity. Religions, on the other hand, always bring a divinity or the supernatural into the sense-making process and connect meaning and

---

[1]The word *God* refers to the Supreme Being or the Creator in monotheistic religions. The words *god(s)* and *godliness* refer to deities across all religions, including polytheistic religions, in which people believe in multiple deities, or gods.

understanding to a sacred realm that transcends the here-and-now material world.

Although ideologies are linked with the secular world and religions are linked with a supernatural realm, they often overlap, making it difficult to clearly differentiate them. For example, if people have a religious belief that God created male and female as two distinct human forms, they could use it to develop and support a gender ideology organized around male-female sex differences and the assumption that it is neither moral nor natural to blur or make light of those differences. When this occurs, secular ideologies take on moral significance and ideologically-based actions become morally righteous actions. This is why jihadist ideology is a powerful force in the world today—it establishes a connection between (selected) Islamist beliefs and a here-and-now quest for political control; as a result, the actions of jihadists are given moral urgency and legitimacy.

Because religion informs widespread views of the world and influences social relationships and the organization of social life, it also informs ideas and beliefs about the body, movement, physical activities, and even sports. However, as we examine the relationship between religions and sports, it's useful to know that religions are linked with the supernatural and sacred—that is, with things that inspire awe, mystery, and reverence. For example, many Christians define churches as sacred places by connecting them with their God. Therefore, the meaning of a church to Christians can be understood only in terms of its perceived link with the supernatural. On the other hand, sport stadiums and arenas are secular places and have no connection with the sacred or supernatural as defined by Christians. They may be important to people, but they are understandable in terms of secular meanings and experiences.

The importance of distinguishing between the sacred and secular is illustrated by answers to the following pair of questions. First, do you think that people in your town would object to a sport stadium having Pepsi, Budweiser, and McDonald's logos on the scorer's table and on scoreboards placed around the venue? Second, do you think

the same people would object to the same logos placed on the pulpit and incorporated into its stained-glass windows in their church, temple, or mosque? My guess is that having logos in the stadium is a non-issue, but that putting logos in a place of religious worship is certain to cause controversy, with people saying that the logos degrade the sacred meaning given to their (God's) house of worship and the sacred objects in it.

The diversity of religions and religious beliefs around the world is extensive (Cipriani, 2007). Human beings have dealt with inescapable problems of human existence and ultimate questions about life and death in many ways. In the process, they've developed thousands of rich and widely varied religions. When sociologists study religions, they examine the ways that believers use religion as they give meaning to themselves, their experiences, and the world in which they live. They also focus on the ways that religious beliefs inform people's feelings, thoughts, and actions. When religious beliefs set some people apart from others and connect power, authority, and wisdom in the secular world with a divinity or supernatural forces, religion has significant and powerful social consequences.

The social consequences of religion and religious beliefs vary widely, but they can include the following:

- Powerful forms of group unity and social integration, *and* devastating forms of group conflict and violent warfare
- A spirit of love and acceptance *and* forms of moral rejection and condemnation
- Humble conformity with prevailing social norms *and* a righteous rejection of prevailing norms
- A commitment to social equity *and* commitment to policies and practices that produce inequalities between men and women, racial and ethnic groups, social classes, homosexuals and heterosexuals, and able-bodied and disabled people

Of course, none of these consequences is inevitable. Each occurs only in connection with the

In societies where Christianity is dominant, there usually are reasonably clear distinctions between the secular and sacred. However, in societies where Islam and Hinduism are dominant, it is very difficult to make this distinction because the secular and sacred are almost seamlessly merged in daily life. (*Source:* Marco Di Lauro, AP/Wide World Photos)

ways that people interpret religious beliefs and incorporate them into their lives.

SIMILARITIES AND DIFFERENCES BETWEEN SPORTS AND RELIGIONS

Discussions about sports and religions often are confusing. Some people view sport as a form of religion, or at least "religion-like," whereas others assume that the "true nature" of religion is essentially different from the "true nature" of sport. Still others view sports and religions as two distinct sets of cultural practices, which may be similar or different depending on how people create, define, and use them. The purpose of this section is to explain and clarify each of these three positions.

Sports as Religion

Attending an NFL game or a World Cup soccer match and being a part of 75,000 or more people yelling, chanting, and moving in unison reminds some people of a religious experience. Some people go so far as to say that sports *are* religion because they involve passions, dedication, identities, and ritualistic actions and they are played with bodies made in the image of God (Prebish, 1993; Thoennes, 2008). Others stop short of this position and say that sports are simply religion-like because both share some characteristics and can produce similar consequences (Baker, 2007; Hubbard, 1998; Mathisen, 1992; Novak, 1976). In both cases, the following similarities between sports and religious have been noted:

- Both have places or buildings for communal gatherings and special events—sports have stadiums and arenas where fans attend games or contests, and religions have churches and temples where believers attend services.
- Both emerge out of a disciplined quest for perfection in body, mind, and spirit—sports emphasize perfection in a disciplined physical performance, and religions emphasize perfection in a disciplined moral purity.
- Both are controlled through structured organizations and hierarchical systems of authority—sports have commissioners, athletic directors, and coaches; and religions have bishops, pastors, and priests/ministers/rabbis.
- Both have events that celebrate widely shared values—sports involve contests that celebrate competition, hard work, and achievement; and religions involve ceremonies and rituals that celebrate commitment, community, and redemption.
- Both have rituals before, during, and after major events—sports have initiations, national anthems, halftime pep talks, hand slapping, and band parades; and religions have baptisms, opening hymns, regular sermons, the joining of hands, and ceremonial processions.
- Both have heroes and legends about heroic accomplishments—sports heroes are elected to "halls of fame," and their stories are told repeatedly by journalists, coaches, and

fans; and religious heroes are elevated to sainthood, and their stories are told repeatedly by religious writers, ministers, and believers.
- Both evoke intense emotions and give meaning to people's lives—sports inspire players and fans to contemplate human potential, and religions inspire theologians and believers to contemplate the meaning of existence.
- Both can be used to distract attention from important social, political, and economic issues and thereby become "opiates" of the masses—sports focus attention on athlete-celebrities, scores, and championships; and religions focus attention on everlasting life and a personal relationship with the supernatural, rather than here-and-now issues and the material conditions of people's lives.

This list helps us understand why some people describe sport as religion or religion-like.

Sport and Religion Are Essentially Different

Some people argue that religion and sport each have a unique, separate truth, or "essence." The essence of religion, they believe, is grounded in divine inspiration, whereas the essence of sport is grounded in human nature.[2] They argue that religion and sport reveal basic truths that transcend time and space, and people "live out" these truths every day, *but* the truths offered by religion are clearly different from the truths offered by sport.

People who think this way are called **essentialists** because *they assume that the universe is governed by unchanging laws and that meaning and truth are inherent in nature.* When they study religion and sport, they argue that the fundamental character of religion is essentially different from

---

[2]These people use the singular rather than the plural form when they refer to *sport* and *religion*. This is because they assume that all forms of sport contain and express the same essence, as do all forms of religion. I explain the problems associated with this "essentialist" approach in chapter 1, page 12.

Although this statue is created by a Christian business, it suggests that Christianity, like sports, is a collection of socially constructed cultural practices, which change in connection with larger social forces and contexts. Few other religions would create a statue representing their prophet/"Savior" playing a heavy-contact sport that involves brutal body contact and borderline violence. (*Source:* Jay Coakley)

the fundamental character of sport, and they identify the following differences:

- Religious beliefs, meanings, rituals, and events are fundamentally mystical and sacred, whereas sport beliefs, meanings, rituals, and events are fundamentally clear-cut and secular.
- The purpose of religion is to transcend the circumstances and conditions of the material world in the pursuit of eternal life, whereas the purpose of sport is to embrace material reality and seek victories through physical performance.
- Religion involves faith in one's beliefs, whereas sport involves competition to establish superiority.
- Religion emphasizes humility and love, whereas sport emphasizes personal achievement and conquest.

- Religious services highlight a collective process of acknowledging the sacred and supernatural, whereas sport events highlight a collective commitment to a here-and-now outcome with transitory and secular significance.

Essentialists argue that there are fundamental differences between Super Bowl Sunday and Easter Sunday, even though both are important days in the lives of many people. Similarly, they see fundamental differences between a hockey team's initiation ceremony and a baptism, a seventh-inning stretch and a scheduled prayer, a cathedral and a stadium.

Some essentialists are religious people who believe that religion and sport are fundamentally different because religion is divinely inspired and sport is not. They often claim that the essentially sacred character of religion is corrupted when combined with the essentially secular character of sport (Hoffman, 1992b, 1992c, 1992d, 1999; Ramsey, 2005; White, 2008). Nonreligious essentialists don't believe in divine inspiration, but they also argue that the cultural meanings and social consequences of religion and sport are fundamentally different.

Religions and Sports as Cultural Practices

Most sociologists study religions and sports as cultural practices that are created by people over time as they live with each other and give meaning to their experiences and the world around them. This is a *social constructionist approach*, and it is based on evidence showing that religions and sports have diverse forms and meanings that are understandable only in connection with the social and cultural conditions under which people create and maintain them. Furthermore, these forms and meanings change over time as social and cultural conditions change.

Social constructionists generally use cultural and interactionist theories to guide their work. They focus on social relations and issues of power and study the meanings given to the body by people who have different religious beliefs.

They also examine the ways that religious beliefs influence movement, physical activity, sport participation, and even the organization of sports. They ask why sports and religions are male-dominated spheres of life and then they study gender ideology in relation to religion, the body, and sports. They also investigate the ways that people combine religious beliefs with sport participation and the social consequences of those combinations in particular social worlds.

Social constructionists realize that the meanings and practices that constitute sports and religions vary by time and place. Religious beliefs and rituals change with new revelations and visions, new prophets and prophecies, new interpretations of sacred writings, and new teachers and teachings. These changes often reproduce the cultural contexts in which they occur, but there are times when they inspire transformations in social relations and social life. Sports are viewed in similar terms—as socially constructed and varying cultural practices that usually reproduce existing meanings and social organization but have the potential to challenge and transform them.

Studying Sports and Religions: An Assessment

The question of whether sports and religions are essentially the same or different does not inspire critical sociological analysis. More important to sociologists are the ways that people participate in the formation and transformation of social and cultural life and how sports and religions are involved in those processes. A constructionist approach guided by cultural, interactionist, and structural theories leads directly to questions about people's experiences and relationships. It also focuses on the different meanings that religions and sports hold for different people and how those meanings are influenced by the social and cultural contexts in which they are formed and changed.

Unfortunately, research on sports and religions is scarce. Scholars who study religions are seldom interested in studying sports, and scholars who study sports are seldom interested in studying religions. The studies that do exist focus primarily on Christian belief systems, particularly those in North America. Therefore, we know little about sports and other world religions, even though there is a need to know about the ways that different religious beliefs are related to conceptions of the body, expressions of human movement, the integration of physical activity into everyday life, and participation in sports. Such knowledge could be used to establish programs that improve health and reduce the cost of medical care.

There have been a few studies of the influence of Islamic beliefs on the sport participation of Muslim women (Hargreaves, 2000; Nakamura, 2002; Pfister, 2001). For those who study sports and gender, it is helpful to understand that religious beliefs often define, in moral terms, expectations related to femininity and masculinity. This makes religion an important topic to include in their analyses because these expectations regulate bodies and influence sport participation patterns in different cultures (Chandler, 2002; Randels and Beal, 2002). Islam has received more attention than other religions in this regard, because it has very specific beliefs about the clothing that must be worn by women when they might be seen by men.

Despite the scarcity of information about sports and religions other than Christianity and Judaism, issues related to this topic are discussed in the section, "Sports and World Religions on page 524." But first, we focus on why certain forms of Christianity have become closely associated with organized competitive sports.

MODERN SPORTS AND RELIGIOUS BELIEFS AND ORGANIZATIONS

Despite important differences between the organization and stated goals of sports and religions, people have combined these two spheres of life in mutually supportive ways (Baker, 2007; Deardorff and White, 2008; Ladd and Mathisen, 1999; Putney, 2003). In some cases, people with certain religious beliefs have used sports for religious purposes, and in other cases, people in sports have used religion in the pursuit of performance goals.

The frequency with which people combine Christian beliefs and sports raises interesting questions. Why have Christian organizations and beliefs, in particular, been combined directly and explicitly with sports? Why haven't other religions been combined with sports and sport participation to the same extent? How have Christian organizations used sports, and how have athletes and sport organizations used Christianity and Christian beliefs? What are the dynamics and social significance of these combinations? These are the major issues discussed in the rest of the chapter.

The Protestant Ethic and the Spirit of Sports

Historical evidence helps explain links between modern sports and contemporary Christian beliefs. In the late nineteenth century, German sociologist-economist Max Weber did a classic study titled *The Protestant Ethic and the Spirit of Capitalism* (1904/1958). His research focused on the connection between the ideas embodied in the Protestant Reformation and the values underlying the growth of capitalist economic systems. He concluded that Protestant religious beliefs, especially those promoted by the reformer John Calvin, helped create a social and cultural environment in which capitalism could develop and grow. For example, Weber explained that Protestantism promoted a "code of ethics" and a general value system that created in people deep moral suspicions about erotic pleasure, physical desire, and all forms of idleness. "Idle hands are the devil's workshop" was a popular Protestant slogan.

> The union between religion and sport began as a quest for physical and moral health.
> —William J. Baker, historian (2007)

Weber also used historical data to show that this "Protestant ethic," as he referred to it, emphasized a rationally controlled lifestyle in which emotions and feelings were suppressed in a quest for worldly success and eternal salvation. This orientation, developed further in Calvin's notion of predestination, led people to define their occupation as a "calling" from God and to view work as an activity through which one's spiritual worth could be proven and displayed for others to see. This was socially significant because it linked material success with moral worth: Being rich was a sign of "being saved"—as long as you didn't spend the money on yourself.

The Protestant work ethic has been integrated into different cultures in different ways since the nineteenth century. However, it has always emphasized values that are consistent with the spirit that underlies organized competitive sports as they've been developed in Europe and North America. Sociologist Steven Overman explains this in his book, *The Influence of the Protestant Ethic on Sport and Recreation* (1997). Overman shows that the Protestant ethic has emphasized a combination of the following seven key *virtues*:

1. *Worldly asceticism*—the ideas that suffering and the endurance of pain has a spiritual purpose, that goodness is linked with self-denial and a disdain for self-indulgence, and that spiritual redemption is achieved only through self-control and self-discipline.
2. *Rationalization*—the idea that truth can be discovered through human reason, and that virtue is expressed through efficiency and measurable achievements.
3. *Goal directedness*—the idea that spiritual salvation and the spiritual worth of human action depend on achievement and success.
4. *Individualism*—the ideas that salvation is a matter of individual responsibility, initiative,

and choice, and that people control their spititual destiny by accepting a personal relationship with God/Christ.

5. *Achieved status*—the idea that worldly success is associated with goodness and salvation, whereas failure is associated with sin and damnation.

6. *The work ethic*—the ideas that work is a calling from God and that people honor God by working hard and developing their "God-given potential" through work.

7. *The time ethic*—the ideas that time has a moral quality and that wasting time is sinful and a sign of weak moral character.

Overman theorizes that these seven virtues are closely matched with the orientation and spirit that informs the meaning, purpose, and organization of modern sports, especially power and performance sports in the United States. This theory is only partially supported by evidence because these virtues have been integrated into people's lives in many different ways, depending on historical and cultural factors. Furthermore, some of these virtues are not exclusive to Protestantism—they also exist in certain forms of Catholicism and other religions, although no religion other than mainstream Protestantism is organized around a set of virtues exactly the same as these seven.

Overman's theory requires revision, but his seven virtues help to explain some of the ways that people in Europe and North America view the body and sports. Traditional Catholic beliefs, for example, emphasize that the body is a divine vessel—a "temple of the Holy Spirit"

Organized competitive sports emphasize work and achievement. These values are compatible with values underlying Protestant religious beliefs. Therefore, playing football on a church-sponsored team is believed to be consistent with secular and Protestant-Christian values. (*Source:* Kristie Ebert)

(I Corinthians 6:19). As a result, Catholics living in the nineteenth and early twentieth century were taught to keep the body pure, but purity was achieved through sexual abstinence and restraint, not through having fun playing sports. Most Protestant believers, on the other hand, emphasized that the body was a divine tool to be used in establishing mastery over the physical world (Genesis 1:28; I Corinthians 9:24–27; Philippians 4:13). The perfect body, therefore, was a mark of a righteous soul (Hutchinson, 2008; Overman, 1997).

Protestant beliefs have also supported the idea that individual competitive success is a means of demonstrating individual achievement and moral worth. Overall, organized competitive sports, because they're oriented around work and achievement, are logical sites for the application of Protestant beliefs. Unlike free and expressive play, these sports are work-like and demand sacrifice and the endurance of pain. Therefore, Protestant/Christian athletes can define sport participation as their calling (from God) and make the claim that God wants them to be the best they can be in sports, even if sports sometimes require the physical domination of others. Furthermore, Christian athletes can define sport participation as a valuable form of religious witness and link success in sports to moral worth and personal salvation.

Evidence supports this aspect of Overman's theory in that athletes from Protestant nations disproportionately outnumber athletes from nations where people are primarily Muslim, Hindu, or Buddhist (Lüschen, 1967; Overman, 1997, pp. 150–157). Even the international success of athletes from non-Protestant nations is often traceable to the influence of cultures where Protestant beliefs are dominant. However, the recent and rapid global diffusion of work-related achievement values has muted the influence of religious beliefs on athletic success. As a result, many athletes from non-Protestant nations excel in sports and win international competitions today.

Sports and World Religions

Most of what we in North America know about sports and religions focuses on various forms of Christianity, especially evangelical fundamentalism. Little is written about sports and Buddhism, Confucianism, Hinduism, Islam, Judaism, Sikhism, Shinto, Taoism, or the hundreds of variations of these and other religions. The beliefs and meanings associated with each of these religions influence how people perceive their bodies, define and give meaning to physical activities, and relate to each other through human movement. However, few people other than evangelical fundamentalist Christians use sports to publicly proclaim their religions beliefs, or use their religious beliefs to give spiritual meaning to sport participation.

It appears that no religion has an equivalent of the self-proclaimed "Christian athlete," which is an increasingly visible character in competitive sports in North America, Australia, New Zealand, and parts of Western Europe. This may be due in part to the Christian notion of individual salvation and how certain believers have applied it to everyday life. Additionally, some world religions focus on the transcendence of self—meaning that believers seek to merge the self with spiritual forces rather than distinguishing the self through a quest for personal growth and spiritual salvation through sport participation. In fact, the idea of using physical competition against others to publicly distinguish the self violates the core beliefs of many religions.

Unfortunately, our knowledge of these issues is limited. We know more about the ways that some North American athletes and coaches convert Zen Buddhist beliefs into strategies for improving golf scores, marathon times, and basketball teamwork than we do about the ways that Buddhism is related to sports and sport participation among 400 million Buddhists around the world. This is because much of our knowledge is grounded in Eurocentric science and limited personal experiences.

"Well, fans, this is the race we've waited for. The winner of this one will lead us to Ultimate Truth!"

Scholars who study religions and sports are not concerned with the truth or falsity of religious beliefs as much as they are concerned with the ways that religions influence the meaning, purpose, and organization of sports in society.

Buddhism and Hinduism: Transcending Self Buddhism and philosophical Hinduism emphasize physical and spiritual discipline, but they do not inspire believers to strive for Olympic medals or physically outperform or dominate other human beings in organized competitive sports. Instead, most of the current expressions of Buddhism and Hinduism focus on transcending the self and the material world. Beliefs emphasize that reality is transient and the human condition is inherently fragile—neither of which is consistent with training to be an elite athlete, signing endorsement contracts, or being inducted into a sport hall of fame. Overall, the central beliefs of Hindus and Buddhists don't lead to seeking competitive success in physical activities.

It is primarily elite athletes from Christian, capitalist countries that use the meditation practices and rituals from these religions to improve

sport performances and give spiritual meaning to competitive sports. However, a segment of a growing Hindu nationalist movement in India uses exercises, games, and sports combined with yoga and prayers to develop loyalty and affection for Hindu culture and Hindu nationhood (McDonald, 1999). This is consistent with historical evidence showing that sports have long been used as sites for training minds and bodies for military service and "defending culture." However, when this training is tied to religion and religious practices, it takes on new meaning because the secular and the sacred are combined for political purposes. When this occurs, sports become irrelevant because the focus often turns to identifying secular enemies and morally justifying wars against them.

People revise religious beliefs as changes occur in their cultures and as beliefs travel from one culture to another. This is true for Buddhism and Hinduism as well as other world religions. For example, traditional Hindu practices in India call for women to be secluded and veiled—that is, confined to private, family-based spaces and covered with robes and scarves. These practices were originally linked with a caste system in which religion was used to justify and maintain social inequalities. The caste system consisted of complex norms and beliefs that regulated activities and relationships throughout Indian society. Individuals were born into a particular caste, and their caste position marked their social status in society as a whole. Officially, the caste system is illegal today, but its cultural legacy continues to exist. This explains why women with a heritage traced back to middle and upper castes have considerable freedom, but women and many men from lower-caste heritage live with persistent poverty, unemployment, and illiteracy. Current patterns of sport participation are influenced by these factors, even though people may embrace "modernized" Hindu beliefs that accommodate increasing secularization in Indian society. Although the caste system was never grounded exclusively in Hindu religious beliefs, Hinduism was organized so that it reproduced the social importance of castes and caste membership. This topic has yet to be studied in terms of its connection with sports and other physical activities. Additionally, there is a need for research on how contemporary Hindus in India and other areas combine religious beliefs with their passion for cricket.

Islam: Submission to Allah's Will   Studying Islam and sports is a challenge because Muslims, like many Buddhists and Hindus, make few distinctions between the secular and the sacred. Every action is done to please Allah (God) and is therefore a form of worship. Religious beliefs and cultural norms are merged into a single theology/ideology, with an emphasis on peace through submission to Allah's will.

Muslims have long participated in physical activities and sports, but participation is regulated by their beliefs about what pleases Allah. The connection between sports and the Islamic mandate to submit to Allah's will has not been studied. However, historical research has referred to a form of "muscular Islam" that existed in a region of South Africa during the apartheid era (Nauright, 1997; Nauright and Magdalinski, 2002). For example, Muslim rugby players between 1930 and 1970 used a highly aggressive style of play to symbolize their struggle against racial apartheid. But we don't know if the players, or the women and families who supported them, connected rugby or their use of intimidation and violence on the field to Allah's will.

There are noteworthy examples in the United States of African American Muslims who have excelled at sports. Boxer Cassius Clay's conversion to Islam in the 1960s created global publicity. When he changed his name to Muhammad Ali and articulated his Muslim beliefs, most Americans did not understand Islam or why some African Americans embraced it. Since then, other black male athletes who have grown up as Muslims or converted to Islam have played elite sports. However, the traditions of sport

participation and the quest for excellence in sports are not as strong in Muslim countries as they are in secularized, Christian-Protestant countries, partly because low per capita income makes full-time training nearly impossible for many Muslims in rural and less developed regions of the world.

Although Muslim nations in many parts of Central and Southeast Asia have no religious restrictions on girls and women playing sports, Islamic beliefs in other parts of the world legitimize patriarchal structures and maintain definitions of male and female bodies that discourage girls and women from playing sports and restrict their everyday access to sport participation opportunities (Fatwa Bank, 2004; Good, 2002; Moore, 2004; Taheri, 2004; Walseth and Fasting, 2003).[3] For example, physical activities in many Muslim nations are sex segregated. Men are not allowed to look at women in public settings, and women must cover their bodies with robes and head scarves, even when they exercise. These norms are especially strong among fundamentalist Muslims. This is why national Olympic teams from some Muslim nations have few or no women athletes. For example, in 1992 thirty-five nations, half of them Muslim, sent no women to the Olympic Games in Barcelona. In 2004 only four Muslim nations had no women on their teams, but the total number of women from Muslim nations was the lowest since the 1960 Olympics (Taheri, 2004). The nations with the tightest restrictions include Iran, Afghanistan, Oman, Kuwait, Pakistan, Qatar, Saudi Arabia, the United Arab Emirates, and Sudan. However, an increasing number of women from Islamic countries participated in the Asian Games, held in 2006 and 2008 in Doha, Qatar. Iran regularly holds events exclusively for women, the latest being the Fourth Women Islamic Games in

---

[3]Patriarchy is a form of gender relations in which men are officially privileged relative to women, especially in regard to legal status and access to political power and economic resources.

reflect on SPORTS

Allah's Will
Dilemmas for Islamic Women in Sports?

Imagine winning an Olympic gold medal, receiving death threats from people in your country who brand you as an immoral and corrupt woman, and then being forced to live in exile. At the same time, imagine that you are a heroine to many young women, who see you as inspirational in their quest for equal rights and opportunities to play sports.

This was the situation faced by Hassiba Boulmerka, the gold medalist in the 1500 meters at the 1992 Olympic Games in Barcelona, Spain. As an Algerian Muslim woman, she believed that being an international athlete did not require her to abandon her faith or her commitment to Islam. But those who condemned Boulmerka said that although it is permissible for women to participate in sports, it was not permissible to do so in shorts or T-shirts, or while men are watching, or when men and women train together, or

when facilities do not permit total privacy, or, if you are married, unless your husband gives his permission (Beiruty, 2002).

To complicate matters, some Islamic feminists accused Boulmerka of allowing herself to be used by a sport system based on men's values and sponsored by corporations that promote a soulless, worldwide consumer culture. To participate in such a system, they said, was to endorse global forces that oppress humankind.

More recently, 18-year-old tennis phenomenon Sania Mirza from India was given heavy police security at a tournament in Calcutta, India, after receiving alleged threats from Muslim men saying that she violated Sharia Law stating that any woman in public must cover her entire body except for her hands and face. Mirza's shorts and sleeveless shirts were called

The participation of Muslim women in sports, regardless of their clothing, initiate heated debates about religion and gender. Even though record-setting sprinter Ruqaya Al Ghasara runs in clothes that conform to Muslim expectations, she tests the meaning of the hijab and veil. She explains that the relationship between the hijab and her sense of purpose gives her strength on the track and support from like-minded believers. (*Source:* Junji Kurokawa, AP/Wide World Photos)

"indecent" and "corrupting," and in 2008, the disputes over her tennis clothes led her to consider quitting her tennis career. Instead, she decided to boycott tournaments in her home country. At the same time, Indian corporations seek the now 21-year-old Mirza to endorse their products, knowing that many young Indian women look up to her.

The issues facing Mirza are avoided by 25-year-old Bahrain-born sprinter Ruqaya Al Ghasara. Since 2004 she has been winning medals and setting records while wearing her trademark white headscarf and red bodysuit. When Al Ghasara won the 100-meters at the West Asian Games in 2007, she told reporters, "I have no problems with the hijab. I have a great desire to show that there are no problems with wearing these clothes. Wearing a veil proves that Muslim women face no obstacles and encourages them to compete in sport" (Algazeera, 2006). When pressed further, she said, "It's not just a matter of wearing a piece of cloth. There is something very special about wearing the hijab. It gives me strength. I feel lots of support from society because I am wearing the Islamic hijab. There is a relationship between the hijab and the heart" (IAAF, 2007).

These three scenarios illustrate clearly that the bodies of Muslim women are "contested terrain." They're at the centre of deep political, cultural, and religious struggles about what is important, what is right and wrong, and how social life should be organized. Muslim women in sports embody and personify these struggles. On the one hand, these women are active subjects asserting new ideas about what it means to be a Muslim woman. On the other hand, they're passive objects used in debates about morality and social change in the world today.

Struggles over issues of religion and gender will continue for Muslim women participating publicly in sports. At the same time, Muslim women living in predominantly Christian countries sometimes use sports played in private as a refuge and an opportunity to spend time with women who share their beliefs. This is the case in Norway (Walseth, 2006) and England (Kay, 2006), but when a small gym at Harvard University was reserved for Muslim women to use for 6 hours a week, it caused nationwide debate for months (in the United States) (Pollitt, 2008). Overall, understanding and coming to terms with "Allah's will" is not easy. *What do you think?*

· ·

September 2005. But these games are not televised because the women are allowed to dress as they wish, and there is a fear that men may watch them. No men are allowed in or near the event, and armed women guards guarantee that men keep their distance. The connection between gender, sport, and Islam is discussed further in the box "Allah's Will on page 527."

The popularity of sports among men in Islamic countries is often tied to expressions of political and cultural nationalism rather than to religious beliefs (Stokes, 1996). Similarly, when Muslims migrate from Islamic countries to Europe or North America, they sometimes play sports, but their participation is tied more to learning about life and gaining acceptance in their new cultures than expressing Muslim beliefs through

sports. Muslim girls and women in non-Islamic countries have very low sport participation rates (Kay, 2006; Nakamura, 2002; Verma and Darby, 1994), and Muslim organizations are unlikely to sponsor sports for their members. However, some people, including scholars in the sociology of sport, have organized programs that enable Muslim women to train and play sports under conditions consistent with their modesty norms. So far, these programs have been successful in attracting and providing participation opportunities for girls and young women (Kay, 2006; Weaver, 2005).

Judaism: Sports and Struggle The link between Judaism and sports is weak, but the link between Jews and sport participation is strong.

This apparent contradiction is understandable when we remember that Jews constitute an ethnic population as well as a religion, and that Jews have faced discrimination in nearly every society in which they've lived, except Israel. The following two statements help us understand sport participation among Jews:

> Jews are not sportsmen. Whether this is due to their physical lethargy, their dislike of unnecessary physical action or their serious cast of mind—it is nevertheless a fact . . .
>
> Sport valorized Gentile masculine values like aggression, strength, speed, and combativeness. . . . I loved it. Nothing my father could do or say stopped me from embracing baseball, basketball, or football over religion.

The first statement was made in 1921 by Henry Ford, possibly the most influential man in the United States at that time. The second statement was made by Alan Klein (2008), a Jew born in Germany just after the gas chambers had been shut down following World War II. Ford invented the assembly line and founded the Ford Motor Company; Klein came to the United States, played sports, earned a Ph.D., and became an anthropologist noted for his excellent research on sports.

Like many Jews, Klein was attracted to sports as a reaction to anti-Semitism (Brenner and Reuveni, 2006). He played typical American sports to assimilate, to fit in at a time when being like everyone else kept him from feeling different in his school and community. Excelling in sports disrupted the stereotype that Jews were "thinkers instead of doers"—smart people with frail bodies. Similar dynamics led Jews to dominate professional basketball from 1920 through the late 1940s, and boxing from 1910 to 1940 (Klein, 2008a).

AT YOUR *fingertips*   For more information on ethnicity and sport participation, see Chapter 9, pages 292–305.

Today Jews sponsor the quadrennial Maccabiah Games in the year following the Olympics. These games are cultural rather than religious in origin and purpose; they were founded to foster Jewish identity and traditions and to showcase highly skilled Jewish athletes. The International Jewish Sports Hall of Fame serves a similar purpose, as does J-Grit: The Internet Index of Tough Jews (www.j-grit.com/index.html), a website designed to discount "ugly stereotypes about Jews."

Shinto: Sumo in Japan   Sumo, or traditional Japanese wrestling, has strong historical ties to Shinto, a traditional Japanese religion (Light and Kinnaird, 2002). Shinto means "the way of the gods," and it consists of a system of rituals and ceremonies designed to worship nature rather than reaffirm an established theology. Modern sumo is a nonreligious activity, although it remains steeped in Shinto ritual and ceremony. The dohyo (rings) in which the bouts take place are defined as sacred sites. Religious symbols are integrated into their design and construction, and the rings are consecrated through purification ceremonies, during which referees, dressed as priests, ask the gods to bless the scheduled bouts. Only the wrestlers and recognized sumo officials are allowed in the dohyo. Shoes must not be worn, and women are never allowed to stand on or near the ring.

The wrestlers take great care to preserve the purity of the dohyo. Prior to their bouts, they ritualistically throw salt into the ring to symbolize their respect for its sacredness and purity; they even wipe sweat off their bodies and rinse their mouths with water presented to them by fellow wrestlers. If a wrestler sheds blood during a bout, the stains are cleaned and purified before the bouts continue. Shinto motifs are included in the architecture and decorations on and around the dohyo. However, wrestlers do not personally express their commitment to Shinto, nor do Shinto organizations sponsor or promote sumo or other sports.

Sumo wrestling in Japan is steeped in centuries-old Shinto rituals of purification. However, sumo wrestlers never refer to their own religious beliefs in connection with their sport. (*Source:* Katsumi Kasullara, AP/Wide World Photos)

Religion and Life Philosophies in China   Anthropologist Susan Brownell (1995, 2008) has studied physical culture and forms of Taoist, Confucian, and Buddhist ideas and practices in her comprehensive studies of the body and sport in China. She notes that each of these life philosophies is actually a general theory of the nature and principles of the universe. As with Islam, this makes it difficult to separate "religious beliefs" from cultural ideology as a whole. Each of these life philosophies emphasizes the notion that all human beings should strive to live in accord with the energy and forces of nature. The body and physical exercise are seen as important parts of nature, but the goal of movement is to seek

harmony with nature rather than to overcome or dominate nature or other human beings.

Tai chi is a form of exercise based on this cultural approach to life and living. Some versions of the martial arts are practiced in this spirit, but others, including practices outside China, are grounded in secular traditions of self-defense and military training. China's success in recent international competitions, including the 2008 Olympic Games in Beijing, raises other questions about the possible connections between religious beliefs and sport participation. Therefore, it is possible that future research will examine the implications of Taoism, Confucianism, and Buddhism as they have been integrated into the lives of various segments of the vast and diverse Chinese population.

Native Americans: Merging the Spiritual and Physical Historically, Native Americans have often included physical games and running races in religious rituals (Nabokov, 1981). However, the purpose of doing this is to reaffirm social connections within specific native cultural groups and gain skills needed for group survival. Outside these rituals, sport participation has had no specific religious meaning.

Making general statements about religious beliefs and sport participation among Native Americans is difficult because beliefs vary from one native culture to another. However, many native cultures maintain animistic religious beliefs emphasizing the spiritual integration of material elements, such as the earth, wind, sun, moon, plants, and animals. Many native games contain features that imply this integration, and, when Native Americans play sports constructed by people from European or other backgrounds, they often use their religious beliefs to give their participation a meaning that reaffirms their ways of viewing the world and their connection with the sacred.

Anthropologist Peter Nabokov has studied running among Native Americans and notes that prior to their contact with Europeans they ran for practical purposes such as hunting, communicating, and fighting; but they also ran to reenact myths and legends and to reaffirm their connection with the forces of nature and the universe. More recently, Native American athletes whose identities are grounded in native cultures often define sport participation in terms of their cultural traditions and beliefs. However, little is known about how they incorporate specific religious beliefs and traditions, which vary across native cultures, into sport participation that occurs outside of their native cultures or how young Native Americans who play sports connect their participation to religious beliefs.

Sports and World Religions: Waiting for Research We need more information about the connections between various world religions, ideas about the body, and participation in physical activities and sports. This information would help us understand the lives of billions of people who participate in various forms of physical activities and sports but do not connect them directly with religious organizations or use them as sites for religious witness. This is different from the tendency of some Christians to attach their religion to institutionalized, competitive sports that already exist for nonreligious purposes.

How Have Christians and Christian Organizations Used Sports?

Unlike other religions, Christianity has inspired believers to use sports for many purposes. These include (a) promoting spiritual growth, (b) recruiting new members and promoting religious beliefs and organizations, and (c) promoting fundamentalist beliefs and evangelical orientations.

> **OLC** **ON THE *OLC:***
> See the OLC—Additional Readings for Chapter 15—for a list of Christian sport organizations.

To Promote Spiritual Growth During the mid-1800s, influential Christian men, described as "muscular Christians" in England and New England, promoted the idea that the physical condition of a man's body had religious significance. They believed that the male body was an instrument of good works and that meeting the physical demands of godly behavior required good health and physical conditioning. Although most religious people at the time didn't agree with this approach, the idea that there might be a connection between the physical and spiritual dimensions of human beings grew increasingly popular (Baker, 2007; Guttmann, 1978, 1988).

The idea that the body had moral significance and that moral character could be strengthened with physical conditioning encouraged many religious organizations to use sports in their efforts to recruit boys and men. For example, the YMCA grew rapidly between 1880 and 1920 as the organization built athletic facilities in many communities and sponsored sport teams. Canadian James Naismith invented basketball in 1891 while he was a student at the Springfield, Massachusetts, YMCA. William Morgan, the physical activities director at a YMCA in Holyoke, Massachusetts, invented volleyball in 1895.

Religious beliefs about developing and strengthening the body were not applied to girls or women during the nineteenth and early twentieth centuries. For most people, "a female muscular Christian was a contradiction in terms [and] . . . Muscular Christianity represented a reaction against the 'femininization' of American middle-class culture" (Baker, 2007, pp. 44–45). In fact, when activist women opened the first YWCA in Boston in 1866 their focus was on "prayer, Bible study, and Christian witness" devoted to helping women find decent housing and obtain job training so they could work and support themselves; playing sports was not part of the program (Baker, 2007, p. 62).

Although mainline Protestants endorsed sports for boys and men through the end of the nineteenth century, some of them came to wonder about the religious relevance of the highly competitive sports that emerged during the first half of the twentieth century. Scandals, violence, and other problems in sports caused evangelicals, in particular, to question their value. Protestant leaders were also wary of women playing sports because it contradicted their belief that God created men and women to be different and that female athletes would subvert God's plan

> I promise . . . to be faithful and true to my obligations as a Christian, a man, and a citizen . . . I bind myself to promote, by word and example, clean, wholesome, and manly sport. — from the "Pledge of Sportsmanship" recited by participants in the Catholic Youth Organization (CYO) boxing teams (Baker, 2007, p. 179)

that sex differences must be preserved by keeping women out of sports (Jonas, 2005).

It wasn't until the late 1940s that evangelical Christians again made a direct connection between sports and their religious beliefs (Ladd and Mathisen, 1999). And they were not alone in embracing sports in the years following World War II. Protestant churches and congregations, Catholic dioceses and parishes, Mormon wards, the B'nai B'rith, and some Jewish synagogues also embraced sports as worthwhile activities, especially for young men. These organizations sponsored sports and sport programs because their members and leaders believed that sport participation developed moral character and prepared young men for the military.

For example, as World War II was ending in 1945, Pope Pius XII gave a worldwide address in which he talked about the moral value of sports from a Catholic perspective:

> Those who accuse the Church of not caring for the body and physical culture . . . are far from the truth. . . . In the final analysis, what is sport if not a form of education for the body? This education is closely related to morality. . . . Sport is an effective antidote to softness and easy living (in Feeney, 1995, pp. 27–29).

Other religious leaders delivered similar messages about sports. In 1971 evangelist Billy Graham, a long-time outspoken promoter of sports as a builder of moral character, summarized the spirit in which many religious organizations have viewed sports over the last century:

> The Bible says leisure and lying around are morally dangerous for us. Sports keep us busy; athletes, you notice, don't take drugs. There are probably more committed Christians in sports, both collegiate and professional, than in any other occupation in America (in *Newsweek*, 1971, p. 51).

Part of Graham's statement sounds naïve today, but he accurately noted that many Christians use sports as activities that symbolize and promote moral development—especially among boys and young men. This commitment remains strong in North America.

To Recruit New Members and Promote Religious Beliefs and Organizations Using sports to promote particular religious beliefs was a key strategy of Christian missionaries who accompanied European and North Americans who colonized traditional cultures (Brownell, 1995; Hong, 2006). Since the mid-1800s this strategy was used to attract and recruit boys and men to churches and religious organizations, especially in England and the United States (Putney, 2003). This practice became so common in the United States after World War II that sociologist Charles Page referred to it as "the basketballization of American religion" (in Demerath and Hammond, 1969, p. 182).

In the early 1990s, for example, Bill McCartney, the former football coach at the University of Colorado, used sport images as he founded his religious organization, The Promise Keepers, and recruited men to join. McCartney and others in the evangelical men's organization preached that a "manly man is a Godly man." Similarly, other Christian fundamentalist organizations have used images of tough athletes to represent ideal "Christian men." This strategy of presenting a "masculinized Christianity" is designed to attract men into churches so that they can "rescue the Bible from women and overly refined preachers" (Flake, 1992, p. 165).

Church-affiliated colleges and universities in the United States have also used sports as recruiting and public relations tools. Administrators from these schools know that seventeen-year-olds today are more likely to listen to recruiting advertisements that uses terminology, images, and spokespeople from sports. For example, when the famous preacher Oral Roberts founded his university in Tulsa, Oklahoma,

in 1965, he highlighted the importance of its sport programs in this way:

> Athletics is part of our Christian witness. . . . Nearly every man in America reads the sports pages, and a Christian school cannot ignore these people. . . . Sports are becoming the No. 1 interest of people in America. For us to be relevant, we had to gain the attention of millions of people in a way that they could understand. (in Boyle, 1970, p. 64)

Jerry Falwell, noted television evangelist, introduced intercollegiate athletics at his Liberty University in the 1970s with a similar explanation:

> To me, athletics are a way of making a statement. And I believe you have a better Christian witness to the youth of the world when you competitively, head-to-head, prove yourself their equal on the playing field. (in Capouya, 1986, p. 75)

Then, in his opening prayer, Falwell declared, "Father, we don't want to be mediocre, we don't want to fail. We want to honor You by winning" (in Capouya, 1986, p. 72).

Other church-affiliated colleges and universities have used sports in similar but less overt ways to attract students. Catholic schools—including the University of Notre Dame, Gonzaga, Georgetown, and Boston College—have used football and/or basketball programs to build their prestige as church-affiliated institutions. Brigham Young University, affiliated with the Church of Latter Day Saints (Mormons), also has done this. Smaller Christian colleges around the United States formed the National Christian Collegiate Athletic Association (NCCAA) in the mid-1960s to sponsor championships and recruit Christian student-athletes to their schools (Ladd and Mathisen, 1999).

Some religious organizations are developed around sports to attract people to Christian beliefs and provide support for athletes who hold Christian beliefs. Examples include Sports Ambassadors, the Fellowship of Christian Athletes (FCA), Athletes in Action (AIA), Pro Athletes Outreach (PAO), Sports Outreach America (SOA),

The public profiles of some universities are linked to both sports and religion. This is the football stadium at the University of Notre Dame, with the library in the background. The outside wall of the library presents a mural image of Christ, now known as "Touchdown Jesus" among Notre Dame fans. (*Source:* Jay Coakley)

and dozens of smaller groups associated with particular sports. These organizations often have a strong evangelical emphasis, and members are usually eager to share their beliefs in the hope that others will embrace Christianity as they do. For example, an athlete departing for Guatemala on a trip sponsored by the AIA said, "I am really looking forward to sharing God's word and introducing a personal relationship with Jesus Christ to others" (Lynch, 2005).

Many Christian organizations and groups also use sports as sites for evangelizing. Thousands of organized volunteers at recent Olympic Games have distributed Bibles, books, videos, audiotapes, CDs, magazines, pamphlets, pins, sport ministry kits, and sport-planning and clinic

guides.[4] Most of these feature athletes giving witness to the importance of Bible-based religious beliefs in their lives. Such efforts to evangelize are not new, but today they are highly organized and coordinated in connection with major events, such as the Super Bowl.

---

[4]The exception to this was the 2008 Olympic Games in Beijing. The Chinese government banned cause-related public displays and this discouraged organized evangelizing; additionally, the government also identified missionaries as potential threats to social order and did not allow them in the country during the games. However, the Evangelical Press released a book on Eric Liddell (Keddie, 2008), one of the athletes featured in the film, *Chariots of Fire*, and used it to highlight Liddell's many years of missionary work in China between the mid-1920s and the early 1940s.

Apart from major events, RBC Ministries and the FCA, both fundamentalist Christian organizations, publish *SportsSpectrum* and *Sharing the Victory (STV)*, widely circulated magazines that use a biblically informed perspective to report on sports and athletes. Articles highlight Christian athletes and their religious testimony. Most athlete profiles emphasize that life "without a commitment to Christ" is superficial and meaningless, even if one wins in sports. This method of using athletes to evangelize is now a key strategy. As one FCA official asked, "If athletes can sell razor blades and soft drinks, why can't they sell the Gospel?"

In 2004 Pope John Paul II established a new Vatican office dedicated to "Church and Sport" (Glatz, 2004; Pontifical Council for the Laity, 2006). Although its primary stated goal is to reform the culture of sport, it is also concerned with making Catholicism relevant in the lives of people, especially men, who are no longer involved in their parishes or using Catholic beliefs to guide their lives. The office now sponsors a talk radio sport program to attract Italian men who no longer see the Catholic Church as relevant to them; soccer is a central focus of the program on Vatican radio (Gladstone, 2005).

To Promote Fundamentalist Beliefs and Evangelical Orientations

Most of the religious groups and organizations previously mentioned promote a specific form of Christianity—one based on a loosely articulated conservative ideology and a fundamentalist orientation toward life.

Religious fundamentalism is based on the belief that the secular foundation of modern societies is inherently corrupt and can be redeemed only if people reorganize their personal lives and the entire social order to manifest the absolute and unchanging Truth contained in a sacred text (Hadden, 2000; Marty and Appleby, 1995;

> **Our youth basketball team is back in action Wednesday at 8 PM in the school recreation hall. Come out and watch us kill Christ the King.**
> — Poster announcing an elementary school basketball game (2002)

Pace, 2007). Religious fundamentalists emphasize that this reorganization requires people to be personally committed to the supernatural source of truth (God, Allah, Christ, Mohammed, "the universe," the spirit world), which provides clear answers to all problems. These answers are revealed through sacred writings, the verbal teachings of divinely inspired leaders and prophets, and personal revelations.

Fundamentalist movements arise when people perceive moral threats to a way of life that was ideal in the past when, according to their beliefs, it was based on religious principles. Therefore, fundamentalists emphasize the "moral decline of society" and the need to return to a time when religious truth was the foundation for culture and social organization. This belief may be so deeply held that it divides fundamentalists from other people in a society.

Ladd and Mathisen (1999) explain that fundamentalist Christians in the United States have used sports, in part, to reduce their separation from society and increase their legitimacy in it. The tendencies of Christian fundamentalist movements in other English-speaking, predominantly Protestant societies to use sports to promote their beliefs support this explanation, although there certainly are important variations between countries.

How Have Athletes, Coaches, and Teams Used Religion?

Athletes, coaches, and teams use religion, religious beliefs, prayers, and rituals in many ways. Research on this topic is scarce, but there is much anecdotal information suggesting that athletes and coaches use religion for one or more of the following purposes:

1. To cope with uncertainty
2. To stay out of trouble
3. To give meaning to sport participation

4. To put sport participation into a balanced perspective
5. To establish team solidarity and unity
6. To reaffirm expectations, rules, and social control on teams
7. To assert autonomy in the face of power
8. To achieve personal and competitive success
9. To market games and sell tickets

To Cope with Uncertainty   Through history, people have used prayers and rituals based on religion, magic, and/or superstition to cope with uncertainties in their lives (Ciborowski, 1997; Womack, 1992). Because sport competition involves uncertainty, it is not surprising that many athletes use rituals, some based in religion, to help them feel as if they have some control over what happens to them on the playing field.

Wrestler Kurt Angle, a gold medalist in the 1996 Olympic Games, explained that when he had a serious neck injury before his qualifying matches, he prayed to God for guidance. His doctor advised him not to wrestle because he would risk paralysis if he injured his neck again. However, in answer to his prayers, "God said to do it." Thus, before each match, his doctor shot novocaine into his neck so that he could endure the pain. After he won the gold medal, he said,

> I knew my neck was hurt . . . I knew when I was wrestling in the Olympic Games that He was watching over me. I knew when I won the gold medal that He intended me to win. He wanted someone like me to spread the Word and be a role model for kids (in Hubbard, 1998, p. 147).

The use of prayers and rituals is not limited to Christian athletes. Former NBA player Hakeem Olajuwon engaged in a regular Islamic prayer ritual as he faced challenges in his life as a professional athlete. He explained that "my religion gives me direction, inner strength. I feel more comfortable. You can take life head on" (*USA Today*, 1994, p. 6C).

Not all religious athletes use prayer and religious rituals in this manner, but many call on their religion to help them face challenges and uncertainty. Therefore, many athletes who pray before or during games seldom pray before or during practices when uncertainty isn't an issue. For example, Catholic athletes who make the sign of the cross when they come up to bat or shoot a free throw during a game don't do the same thing when they bat or shoot free throws at practices. It is the actual competition that produces the level of uncertainty that evokes the prayer or religious ritual.

Sometimes it's difficult to separate the use of religion from the use of magic and superstition among athletes (Baker, 2007). **Magic** consists of *recipe-like rituals designed to produce immediate and practical results in the material world.* **Superstitions** consist of *regularized, ritualistic actions performed to give a person or group a sense of control and predictability in the face of challenges.* Thus, when athletes pray, it may be a form of religion or magic and superstition, but in many cases, its primary goal is to control or deal with the uncertainty that exists in competitive sports.

To Stay Out of Trouble   The late Reggie White was an ordained minister and a retired defensive lineman in the NFL; he was called the "minister of defense". When he was asked about his religious beliefs during his years in the NFL, he said that "studying God's Word helped keep my life on track, even though there were bad influences like drugs and crime all around me" (IBS, 1996b, Section A). Other athletes say similar things about religion helping them to avoid the risky lifestyles that often exist in the social worlds that develop around certain sports. NFL player Sean Gilbert has said, "Before I found the Lord, I drank! I whoremongered! I cussed! I cheated! I manipulated! I deceived!" (in Corsello, 1999, p. 435).

The fact that religious beliefs may separate athletes from risky off-the-field lifestyles and keep them focused on training in their sports has not been lost on coaches (Plotz, 2000). Journalist Andrew Corsello explains that "regardless of their own beliefs, coaches are attracted to the self-control that Christian convictions instill in a man" (1999, p. 435). Furthermore, team owners may see "born-again athletes" as better long-term investments because they believe that religious athletes "are less likely to get arrested" (Nightengale, 2006; Smith, 1997). Finally, religious beliefs also may keep athletes out of trouble by encouraging them to become involved in church-related and community-based service programs. This involvement also separates them from risky off-the-field lifestyles.

To Give Meaning to Sport Participation Sport participation emphasizes personal achievement and self-promotion, and it involves playing games that produce no essential goods or services, even though people create important social occasions around sport events. This makes sport participation a self-centered, self-indulgent activity. Although training often involves personal sacrifices and pain, it focuses on the development and use of personal physical skills, often to the exclusion of other activities and relationships. Realizing this can create a crisis of meaning for athletes who have dedicated their lives to personal achievements in sports.

One way to deal with this crisis of meaning is to define sport participation as an act of worship, a platform for giving witness, or a manifestation of God's plan for their lives (Hoffman, 1992a, 1992b, 1992c, 1999). Many Christian athletes and coaches like to quote Colossians 3:23 in the Bible: "Whatever you do, work at it with all your heart, working for the Lord, not for men." This enables them to define their sport as a sacred rather than a secular activity. As a result, their doubts about the worthiness of what they do are eliminated because playing sports is sanctified as a calling from God.

To Put Sport Participation into a Balanced Perspective It's easy to lose perspective in sports, to let it define you and foreclose other parts of your life. In the face of this threat, some athletes feel that religious beliefs enable them to transcend sports and bring balance back to their lives. For example, former Olympic runner Elana Meyer explains that "running is a way God can use me for His glory. Athletics is not my life" (IBS, 1996b, Section G). Domonique Foxworth, a defensive back on the Atlanta Falcons, explains that "there is no better way to calm an eager rookie before a big game than to put the game in perspective by reminding him of his spiritual beliefs" (Foxworth, 2005, 2D). This makes playing sports part of God's plan, and it becomes easier for athletes to face challenges and deal with the inevitable disappointments experienced in sports. In the process, they keep sports in perspective.

To Establish Team Solidarity and Unity Religious beliefs and rituals can be powerful tools in creating bonds between people. When they're combined with sport participation, they can link athletes together as spiritual teammates, building team solidarity and unity in the process. Many coaches know this, and some have used Christian beliefs as rallying points for their teams. For example, Fisher DeBerry, a committed Christian and former head football coach at the U.S. Air Force Academy, used religion to establish an esprit de corps on his team by hanging a sign in the locker room saying "I AM A MEMBER OF TEAM JESUS CHRIST"—a statement that is in the Competitor's Creed for the Fellowship of Christian Athletes.

This use of religion can backfire when athletes object to expectations to pray or profess agreement with religious statements. This occurred recently at New Mexico State University when four Muslim football players filed a lawsuit accusing their coach of religious discrimination because he labeled them "troublemakers" after they objected to reciting the Lord's Prayer in a team huddle after each practice and before each game. The university settled the case out of court, suggesting that they agreed that a football coach doesn't have the right to turn his team into a religious brotherhood (Fleming, 2007).

"She says this prayer is 'voluntary.' Who's she trying to fool?!?"

When coaches use religious beliefs and rituals on sport teams, they may create solidarity or dissent. Coaches say that team prayers are voluntary, but players may feel pressure to pray or not play, regardless of their religious beliefs.

Objections to pregame prayers in public schools have led some U.S. students and their parents to file lawsuits to ban religious expression in connection with sport events. However, coaches and athletes continue to insist that prayers bring team members together in positive ways and serve a spiritual purpose in players' lives. This controversial issue is discussed in the box "Public Prayers at Sport Events."

To Reaffirm Expectations, Rules, and Social Control on Teams Religion also can sanctify norms and rules by connecting them with divinities. Therefore, it can be used to connect the moral worth of athletes with the quality of their play and their conformity to team rules and the commands of coaches. This combination of religion and sport is very powerful, and coaches have been known to use it as a means of controlling athletes. Coaches see obedience to their rules as necessary for team success, and religious

beliefs promote obedience by converting it into a divine mandate.

> **ON THE *OLC*:**
> See the OLC—Additional Readings for Chapter 15—for a description of what some Christian athletes call a "Total Release Performance."

To Assert Autonomy in the Face of Power After interviewing NFL players about religion, journalist Andrew Corsello (1999) noted that "it should come as no surprise that the assertion of individuality through religious testimony in the NFL comes at a time when the game has never been more corporatized, more dehumanized" (p. 439). Corsello's point is that religion enables a player to establish an identity outside of the rigid, hierarchical structure of organized sports and therefore resist the power of coaches and team owners who control their lives. Corsello thinks that this is especially important for black athletes, who may have more reason to seek ways to assert their individuality and identity and feel personally empowered in the face of the white-dominated governance structures in sports, especially in college and professional football in the United States. This possibility has never been studied, but it is worth investigating.

To Achieve or Explain Competitive Success People often debate whether it is appropriate to pray for victories or other forms of athletic success. Some argue that using prayer this way trivializes religion by turning it into a training strategy. However, Howard Griffith, a former NFL running back, says, "It's not that we're trivializing anything. The question was posed to [the Christians on our team], 'Does He [God] control wins and losses?' Yes, He does. . . . It is not anti-Christian to pray for wins" (in Nack, 1998, p. 47).

Some Christian athletes believe that God intervenes in sports. Isaac Bruce, a wide receiver

reflect on SPORTS

Public Prayers at Sport Events
What's Legal and What's Not?

Prayers before sport events are common in the United States. They're said silently by individuals, aloud by small groups of players or entire teams in pregame huddles, and over public address systems by students or local residents.

Public prayers are allowed at private events, and all people in the United States have the right to say silent, private prayers for any purpose at any time. As long as an event is sponsored by private organizations or as long as people pray privately and silently, prayers are legal in connection with sports.

According to a 1962 U.S. Supreme Court decision, which banned organized prayers in public schools, prayers may not be legal when they are said publicly and collectively at sport events sponsored by state organizations, such as public schools. This ruling caused controversy in Texas in 1992, when two families near Houston filed a lawsuit requesting a ban on prayers in public schools. They appealed to the First Amendment of the U.S. Constitution, which says, "Congress shall make no law respecting an establishment of religion." The federal district judge in the case ruled that public prayers are permitted as long as they are nonsectarian and general in content, initiated by students, and not said in connection with attempts to convert anyone to a particular religion. But this decision was qualified during an appeal when the appellate judges ruled that sport events are not serious enough occasions to require the solemnity of public prayer; therefore, the prayers are inappropriate.

Despite this decision and two similar decisions in 1995 and 1999, people in many U.S. towns continue to say public prayers before public school sport events. Students often include references to "Jesus," "Lord," and "Heavenly Father" when they say prayers over the public address system, and athletes do the same when they pray with their teams. These prayers often are "local traditions," and people object when federal government judges tell them that they are unconstitutional. They argue that it violates their constitutional right to "freedom of speech."

Those who have filed lawsuits argue that the prayers are grounded in Christian beliefs and create informal pressures to give priority to those beliefs over others. They also say that those who don't join in and pray are subject to ridicule, social rejection, or efforts to convert them to Christianity. The people who support public prayers say they don't pressure anyone and that Christianity is the dominant religion in their towns and in the United States. However, they also assume that the public prayers will not be Jewish, Islamic, Hindu, Buddhist, Baha'i, or Sikh prayers and that they will not contradict their Christian beliefs.

When judges rule on these cases they usually consider what would occur if prayers at public school sports events represented beliefs that contradicted Christian beliefs. Would Christians object if public prayers praised Allah, the Goddess, or multiple deities? What would happen if Muslim students said their daily prayers over the public address system in conjunction with a basketball game, if teams were asked to pray to Allah or the Prophet Muhammad, or if all football games were rescheduled to accommodate Muslim customs during their three- to four-week observance of Ramadan in October? These are important questions because over 4 billion people in the world do not hold Christian beliefs and nearly 1 in 4 Americans have beliefs that are not Christian.

These are the reasons that judges have regularly ruled that public prayers are not allowed at sport events sponsored by state organizations such as public schools. The U.S. Supreme Court made the latest decision in July 2000, reaffirming that officially sanctioned public prayers at sport events sponsored by public schools are illegal.

What do you think?

in the NFL, said that prayers "work" for him: "Like when we played Minnesota last year. I had a pretty good first half, but God really manifested in the third quarter—I had eighty-nine yards!" (in Corsello, 1999, p. 435).

Colorado Rockies chairman and CEO Charlie Monfort assembled a team that in 2006 had many Christians in management, coaching, and on the roster. When the team experienced success, Monfort said, "I think character-wise we're stronger than anyone in baseball. Christians . . . are some of the strongest people in baseball. I believe God sends signs, and we're seeing those." Dan O'Dowd, the team's general manager concurred with his boss, saying, "You look at some of the games we're winning. Those aren't just a coincidence. God has definitely had a hand in this."

To Market Games and Sell Tickets   After the Nashville Sounds, a minor league baseball team, joined forces with a local entertainment and sports marketing company in 2001 to sponsor a Faith Night™ promotion, the idea has become increasingly popular. As a promotion it includes performances by Christian rock groups, a Bible giveaway, and a raffle for bobble-head dolls of Moses, Jonah, and other biblical characters. Now Faith Night™ is a registered trademark of the team, and baseball teams throughout the South use it regularly to boost game attendance.

As a marketing tool, Faith Night has been successful, targeting churches where fans can be recruited. The CEO of the Nashville Sounds says that "Faith Nights are the biggest thing we do here. It is big, big business for us." And a marketing director for another minor league team puts it simply: "Baseball, faith and Americana, it's a perfect fit" (Cherner, 2005).

The success of Faith Night has attracted the attention of marketing people for NFL and NBA teams, and it is likley to be used when there's a need to sell more tickets (Chass, 2008). The Nashville Sounds general manager explains that it fits with their overall marketing profile, saying, "We do 'Thirsty Thursday' on Thursday nights. It's beer today, God tomorrow—it's managing the expectations of your fan base" (NPR, 2006).

THE CHALLENGES OF COMBINING SPORTS AND RELIGIOUS BELIEFS

Organized competitive sports and religion are cultural practices with different histories, traditions, and goals. Each has been socially constructed in different ways, around different issues, and through different types of relationships. This means that combining religious beliefs with sport participation may require adjustments—either in a person's religious beliefs or in the way a person plays sports. Although a growing number of athletes around the world combine Islamic beliefs with their sport lives, this section focuses specifically on the challenges faced by Christian athletes.

Challenges for Christian Athletes

Physical educator Shirl Hoffman (1992b, 1992d, 1999) has made the case that there are built-in conflicts between some Christian religious beliefs and the actions required in many elite power and performance sports. Christianity, he explains, is based on an ethic that emphasizes the importance of means over ends, process over product, quality over quantity, and caring for others over caring for self. But power and performance sports emphasize winning, final scores, season records, personal performance statistics, and self-display.

Do these differences present challenges to Christian athletes? If so, how do athletes deal with them? For example, do Christian athletes wonder if their actions in sports are proper acts of worship? Do Christian boxers wonder if pummeling another human being into senseless submission and risking the infliction of a fatal injury, is an appropriate spiritual offering? Do Christian football players see problems associated with using intimidation and "taking out" opponents with potentially injurious hits and then saying that such behaviors are "acts of worship"? Do athletes really believe that they can use harmful actions as expressions of religious commitment simply by saying that they are motivated by Christian love? Does this heal the concussions and broken bones of those injured by their "loving hits"?

What about Christian pitchers who throw fastballs high and inside to batters as part of their pitching strategy? Does a strategy that

"I just want to thank my Lord and Savior, who made this knockout possible."

Statements like this are common in postgame interviews. They assume that the "Lord and Savior" is somehow glorified by what occurs in sports. Data suggest that most Christian athletes don't question the logic of this assumption.

deliberately risks hitting a batter's head with a ball thrown at 80 miles per hour qualify as an act of worship? Is it part of God's plan for a Christian base runner to slide into second base with spikes aimed at the opposing player's leg in an attempt to break up a double play? Do Christian athletes ask such questions, and if so, how do they answer them?

Research suggests that Christian athletes combine their religious beliefs with sport participation in diverse ways (Baker, 2007). A study by Betty Kelley and her colleagues (1990) found that, at small liberal arts colleges, Christian varsity athletes who valued religion as a tool for achieving secular goals emphasized the importance of winning in sports, but those who valued religion for its own sake emphasized personal goals and the enjoyment of competition. Overall, the Christian athletes didn't question the

"fit" between their religious beliefs and actions in sports. However, these were athletes in small colleges where a power and performance orientation was not heavily emphasized.

A Canadian study (Dunn and Stevenson, 1998) reported that members of a local church-sponsored hockey league were successful when they collectively decided to play hockey in a manner that reflected Christian values. Fair play was a stated goal in the league; prohibited were body contact, fights, swearing on the ice, and drinking beer in the locker rooms. There was a public prayer before each game, and official league standings were not kept although game scores were kept. Interviews with twenty players indicated that most of them met the spirit of the rules although some had difficulty applying Christian principles in all game situations, especially when they were emotionally caught up in the action. A few others seemed to be only nominally committed Christians, and they were more interested in being "good hockey players" than "Christian hockey players." The authors concluded that, in a recreational league, it is possible to have a reasonably good fit between Christian values and playing a sport. Similar outcomes have been reported in basketball leagues sponsored by The Church of Jesus Christ of Latter-day Saints (Mormons). In an effort to restore order to games that had gotten out of hand, the league authorities, all Mormons, developed a "sportsmanship scoring system" that reduced technical fouls and conflicts on the court (Saxton, 2008).

Stevenson's (1991a, 1991b, 1997) research on elite athletes associated with Athletes in Action (AIA) indicated slightly different patterns. Some of the elite athletes avoided conflicts by clearly separating their religious beliefs from sport participation. They ignored the possibility that their actions in sports were not compatible with Christian values. They asked no questions and played as everyone else did. However, most of the elite Christian athletes in Stevenson's sample were troubled by conflicts between their religious beliefs and what they did as athletes. In most cases, they resolved conflicts by emphasizing that it was their Christian duty to perfect their skills because to do so would increase their effectiveness as evangelizers.

OLC **ON THE *OLC*:**
See the OLC—Additional Readings for Chapter 15—for the author's discussion of issues to consider when combining religion and sport participation.

Stevenson's research focused on young men in the AIA, but there have been no studies of Christian athletes who are not members of similar organizations. Anecdotal evidence suggests that elite athletes who identify themselves as Christians don't play sports differently from others. Some even say that their religious beliefs make them more intense and aggressive on the playing field. Mike Barrows, an NFL linebacker and a devout Christian, proudly declared that his violent hits on the field were attempts to "knock the sin out of somebody" (Saunders, 2001).

Statements from some Christian athletes, and stories about their lives (as described in Christian publications), suggest that they merge their religious beliefs and sport participation by emphasizing the ascetic aspects of sport. **Asceticism** refers to *discipline, self-denial, and avoiding bodily pleasures*, and embracing this philosophy helps athletes give moral meaning to their actions in sports. For Christian athletes who view sports in this way, "Jesus the teacher" becomes "Christ the competitor," and, "if Jesus were alive today, he would play sports like everyone else, only better." For example, the Competitor's Creed of the FCA highlights the importance of asceticism in these words:

> My sweat is an offering to my Master. My soreness is a sacrifice to my Savior. I give my all—all of the time. I do not give up. I do not give in. I do not give out. I am the Lord's warrior—a competitor by conviction and a disciple of determination (www .fca.org/TEAMFCA/CompetitorsCreed.lsp).

Most Christian athletes don't express any doubts about the moral suitability of what they do in sports, but when they do, research suggests that they do one of three things to reduce their doubts:

1. They focus on the ascetic aspects of sports and see themselves as enduring pain for God's sake.
2. They strive to be the best they can be as athletes so they can more effectively use sport as a platform for evangelizing or for doing good works off the field.
3. They drop out of power and performance sports, and seek other sports and activities that fit with their beliefs.

A model that identifies the origin of doubts experienced by athletes and the strategies used to reduce doubts is depicted in Figure 15.1

Challenges for Christian Sport Organizations

The record of Christian organizations shows that they give primary emphasis to building faith one person at a time. Consequently, they haven't tried to eliminate problems in sports other than to condemn overcommercialization and drug use by athletes (Ladd and Mathisen, 1999). When journalist Frank Deford did a feature story on sports and Christianity in a 1976 issue of *Sports Illustrated*, he observed,

> No one in the movement—much less in any organization—speaks out against dirty play, no one attacks the evils of recruiting, racism or any of the many other well-known excesses and abuses. Sport owns Sunday now, and religion is content to lease a few minutes before the big games. (p. 100)

Noted sports historian William Baker points out that despite all their emphasis on athletics, "evangelicals have yet to produce anything approximating a theology of sport" (2007, p. 217). They assume that reform occurs only when

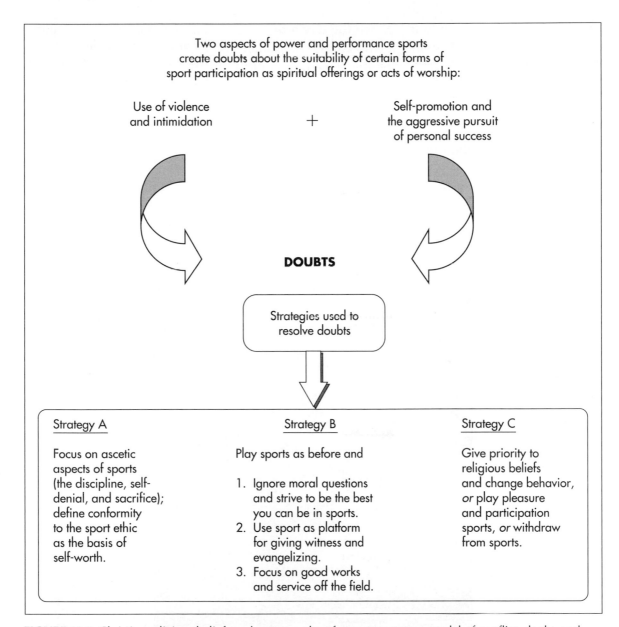

FIGURE 15.1 Christian religious beliefs and power and performance sports: a model of conflict, doubt, and resolution.

individual athletes accept Christ into their lives, so their emphasis is on evangelizing over action.

This approach is based on the "primacy of faith"—the idea that faith rather than good works alone is the basis for spiritual salvation. Critics of this approach argue that faith without

good works is meaningless, and that people who do good works as ends in themselves can be saved even if they haven't given their lives to Christ.

This debate has interesting implications for people with disabilities and their sport participation. Do religions influence ideas about disabilities and do they foster good works in the form of providing opportunities for people with disabilities to play sports? These questions are examined in *Breaking Barriers* on page 545.

Adapting Religious Beliefs to Fit Sports

Religions and sports change as people's values and interests change and as power shifts in society, but it appears that sports change little, if at all, when combined with religion. Instead, it seems that religious beliefs and rituals are

Since the dawn of civilization, we human beings have persistently created God in our own image. —William J. Baker (2000, p. 6).

called into the service of sports, or modified to fit the ways that dominant sports are defined, organized, and played in society.

Robert Higgs makes this point in his book *God in the Stadium: Sports and Religion in America* (1995). He explains that the combination of sports and Christian beliefs has led religion to become "muscularized" so that it emphasizes a gospel of discipline, duty, and self-righteousness rather than a gospel of stewardship, social responsibility, and humility. Muscularized religion gives priority to the image of the knight with a sword over the image

"Not by might nor by power, but by my spirit." History shows that people construct images of deities to fit their values and ideals (Baker, 2000, 2007). This is shown by an image of a pumped-up Christ on a T-shirt sold in a Christian shop. Among Christians who value muscles, their image of Christ often is a muscular one. (*Source:* Jay Coakley)

breaking BARRIERS | Belief Barriers
I Was "One of God's Favorites"

Religious beliefs have long informed popular ideas and beliefs about bodies and embodied experiences, including experiences of disability. For instance, as a child, Margaret Orlinski contracted a virus that partially paralyzed her legs. She could walk, but everyone saw that it was a struggle. Margaret's family lived in a Catholic neighborhood and attended mass every week at their local parish church. Margaret explains that everyone she knew used Catholic beliefs to explain her paralysis:

> I was called a saint. "God loves her so much to have given her this cross to bear." I heard that so many times. I felt an enormous amount of pressure to be perfect because I was "one of God's favorites." (in Phillips, 1988, p. 206)

The pressure felt by Margaret has origins that are traceable to Paul's letter to the Hebrews (12:6–10) in which he explains that hardship is a gift from God and provides a unique opportunity to submit to God's will and share in His holiness.

Do religious beliefs influence cultural definitions of disability, and do those definitions influence opportunities and inclinations to play sports? Existing research doesn't answer these questions, but sacred writings serve as a starting point for thinking critically about possible answers.

Other than the Bible, most sacred texts make only passing references to disabilities, if they mention them at all (see the Koran, 24.61 and 48.17). But the Bible speaks occasionally about disability (Hutchinson, 2008). For instance, the Lord in the Old Testament told Moses to tell Aaron that people with disabilities were unworthy of bringing gifts to his altar. The words in Leviticus are ominous:

> No man who . . . is blind or lame, disfigured or deformed . . . with a crippled foot or hand, or who is a hunchback or a dwarf . . . is to come near to present the food offerings to the LORD . . . or approach the altar, and so desecrate my sanctuary. (Leviticus 21:16–23)

This has led some people to say that Christians often equated deformity and disability with sin and uncleanliness, thereby casting people with disabilities as "others" to be avoided (Mellor and Shilling, 1997). However, in the New Testament, Jesus embraced people with disabilities, treated disabilities as defects to be healed, and taught that people should care for and be charitable to people with disabilities (for example, see Matthew 11:4–6; 15:29–31; 21:12–14).

Despite apparent contradictions in Christian approaches to disability, the provision of care and services to people with disabilities has often been sponsored by Christian organizations. But neither Christian nor other religious organizations have given priority to the provision of sport opportunities to people with disabilities. This could change in the future if religious people read their sacred texts more closely, as each of the world's religions emphasizes the importance of following a norm of reciprocity. For example, writing in 500 BC, Confucius highlighted this norm with a story:

> Tsze-kung asked . . . "Is there one word which may serve as a rule of practice for all of one's life?" The Master said, "Is not RECIPROCITY such a word? What you do not want done to yourself, do not do unto others" (The Confucian Analects, Chapter 15).

Although research on religious beliefs about the body is scarce, sociologists have frequently studied the "norm of reciprocity" in human interaction. Whether we connect this norm with religion or humanism, it states that if able-bodied people don't wish to be denied opportunities to play sports, they should not deny people with disabilities those opportunities. And Margaret Orlinski would add that opportunities should be organized so that people with disabilities won't ever feel that their moral worth depends on being perfect.

- -

of the shepherd with a staff (Higgs, 1995). This approach, emphasizing a Christian's role as "the Lord's warrior," fits nicely with the power and performance sports that are popular today.

Similarly, Higgs points out that Christian religious beliefs have been used more often to transform winning, obedience to coaches, and a commitment to excellence in sports into moral virtues than to identify and seek solutions to problems in sports. Therefore, Christian beliefs generally reproduce sports as they currently exist. At this point, the only exception to this appears to be recreational sports where athletes have agreed upfront to use Christian beliefs to guide their actions during play.

summary

IS IT A PROMISING COMBINATION?

Religion focuses on a connection with the sacred and supernatural, and religious beliefs influence the feelings, thoughts, and actions of believers. This makes religion significant in sociological terms.

Discussions about sports and religions often focus on how these two spheres of cultural life are similar or different. Certainly, they are socially similar because both create strong collective emotions and celebrate collective values through rituals and public events. Furthermore, both have heroes, legends, special buildings for communal gatherings, and institutionalized organizational structures.

On the other hand, those who assume that sport and religion each have unique fundamental essences that are fixed in nature argue that the inherent differences between these spheres of life are more important than any similarities. Some have even argued that sports corrupt religious beliefs.

Most scholars in the sociology of sport conceptualize religions and sports as socially constructed cultural practices and meanings that may overlap or differ, depending on the social circumstances. This constructionist approach is based on evidence that sports and religions are subject to change as people struggle over what is important in their lives and how to organize their collective lives.

Little is known about the relationships between sports and major world religions other than particular forms of Christianity. It seems that certain dimensions of Christian beliefs and meanings have been constructed in ways that fit well with the beliefs and meanings underlying participation and success in organized competitive sports. Organized competitive sports seem to offer a combination of experiences and meanings that are uniquely compatible with the major characteristics of the Protestant ethic.

Sports and certain expressions of Christianity have been combined for a number of reasons. Some Christians promote sports because they believe that sport participation fosters spiritual growth and the development of strong character. Christian groups and organizations have used sports to promote their belief systems and attract new members, especially young males who wish to see themselves as having "manly virtues." They also have used popular athletes as spokespersons for their messages about fundamentalist beliefs.

Athletes and coaches have used religious beliefs and rituals for many reasons: to cope with the uncertainty of competition; to stay out of trouble; to give meaning to sport participation; to put sport participation into a balanced perspective; to establish team solidarity and unity; to reaffirm expectations, rules, and social control on teams; to assert autonomy in the face of power; to achieve and explain competitive success; and to sell tickets to sport events.

Although the differences between the dominant ethos of Christianity and the dominant ethos of competitive sports would seem to create problems for Christian athletes and sport organizations, research suggests that this rarely occurs. With the exception of sports played at the recreational level and sponsored by Christian organizations, data indicate that many athletes define their religious beliefs in ways that generally reaffirm and intensify the orientations that lead to success in competitive sports.

Neither Christian athletes nor Christian organizations have paid much attention to what might be identified as moral and ethical problems in sports. Instead, they've focused their resources on spreading religious beliefs in connection with sport events and sport involvement. Their emphasis has been on playing sports for the glory of God, using athletic performances as a platform for giving Christian witness, and working in off-the-field church and community programs.

In conclusion, the combination of sports and religious beliefs offers little promise for changing dominant forms of sport, especially in the United States. Of course, individual athletes may alter their sport-related behaviors when they combine sports and religion in their own lives, but at this time such changes have had no observable effect on what occurs in elite, competitive sports.

WEBSITE RESOURCES

Note: Websites often change. The following URLs were current when this book was printed. Please check our website (www.mhhe.com/coakley10e) for updates and additions.

www.mhhe.com/coakley10e Click on Chapter 15 for a list of Christian sport organizations; discussion of "Total Release Performance," a concept developed by a Christian sport organization; discussion of the uses of rituals and magic in sports.

www.athletesinaction.org Athletes in Action is a Christian evangelical organization that has a global mission; site provides information about its mission, organization, and programs.

www.fca.org Fellowship of Christian Athletes is the most popular Christian evangelical organization in the United States; site provides information about its mission, organization, and programs.

www.hinduonnet.com/ Online edition of India's national newspaper; the sports section provides an overview of the range of sports popular in India.

www.infinitysports.com Site of an organization that mobilizes churches, sports ministries, campus ministries, and other Christian groups to use sports to evangelize around the world; the organization is committed to Christianizing every person in the world.

www.sportsspectrum.com/ *Sports Spectrum* is an established national publication that highlights Christian athletes in ways designed to motivate others to embrace their faith; provides links to dozens of Christian sport ministries and organizations such as Christian Bowhunters, Christian Rodders and Racers, Christian Surfers, and others.

www.themodernreligion.com/women/w_sport.htm This site presents an article by Hikmat Beiruty who outlines fundamentalist Islamic moral guidelines for girls and women in sports; this article is reprinted on dozens of sites, including http://www.zawaj.com/articles/women_sports.html

www.thenccaa.org This is the site of the 98-member National Christian College Athletic Association; provides general information and news.

www.traditioninaction.org/Cultural/B003cpWomenSports.htm Author Marian T. Horvat, Ph.D., outlines fundamentalist Catholic moral guidelines for girls and women in sports; although ignored by nearly all Catholics today, these guidelines are based on statements from popes prior to the 1960s, but they've influenced sport participation patterns among millions of girls and women worldwide.

(Royalty-Free/CORBIS)

SPORTS IN THE FUTURE

Are We Agents of Change?

FORECASTING THE FUTURE is futile. Predictions are
a reflection of a single perspective: the present's.
    —Luke Cyphers, journalist, ESPN
      The Magazine (2008)

(OLC) Visit *Sports in Society*'s Online Learning Center (OLC) at www.mhhe.com/coakley10e for additional information and study material for this chapter, including the following:

• A complete chapter outline
• Learning objectives
• Practice quizzes
• Internet resources
• Related readings
• Essays
• Student projects

THE PRIMARY GOAL of futurists is not to predict the future but to uncover images of possible, probable, and preferable futures that enable people to make informed decisions about their lives.

—Wendell Bell, futurist (1997)

WHEN I DREAM, I see myself running so fast that I can bring us up from our living standards and buy all the girls of Ethiopia sneakers.

—Meseret Defar, 2004 Olympic gold medalist,
5000 meters (in Wax, 2005)

AS GLOBAL WARMING CHANGES the planet, it . . . is changing the way we play and the sports we watch.

—Alexander Wolff, journalist, Sports
Illustrated (2007)

Discussions of the future often involve exaggerations. Predicting dramatic changes always is more exciting than declaring that tomorrow will be a variation of today. Therefore, people often describe the future in science-fiction terms that arouse extreme hopes or fears. This sparks our interest, but such images of the future are rarely helpful because the future seldom unfolds as rapidly or dramatically as some forecasters would have us believe.

Social change is driven primarily by the efforts of people who work to create a future that fits their visions of what life should be like. Some people have more power and resources to turn their visions into reality, but they seldom want revolutionary changes because their privileged positions depend on stability and controlled change. This often impedes progressive changes in favor of increasing the efficiency and profitability of existing ways of life. In the case of capitalist societies, this involves fostering growth in the production and distribution of consumer goods.

Although power relations cannot be ignored, many aspects of sports are contested as people integrate them into their lives. Accordingly, the goal of this chapter is to respond to the following questions:

1. What models of sports might we use to envision possibilities for the future?
2. What current trends must be acknowledged as we consider the future of sports?
3. What major factors underlie existing trends, and how will they influence the future of sports?
4. How can we become effective agents in creating the future of sports?

ENVISIONING POSSIBILITIES FOR THE FUTURE

Sports are social constructions. This means that dominant sports at any particular place and time are likely to be consistent with the values, ideas,

interests, and experiences of those who have power in a social world. However, dominant sports are not accepted by everyone, and people often modify them or develop alternatives in the process of resisting or challenging them.

Dominant sports in most societies have been and continue to be grounded in the values and experiences of men who value military conquest, political control, and economic expansion. As noted in previous chapters and explained in Chapter 4, these sports are organized around a **power and performance model.** However, people may reject all or part of dominant sport forms as they seek experiences grounded in alternative values and interests. Many of these people create sports organized around one of more elements of a **pleasure and participation model.**

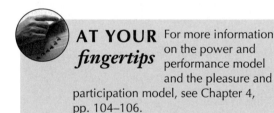

AT YOUR *fingertips* For more information on the power and performance model and the pleasure and participation model, see Chapter 4, pp. 104–106.

These two models do not encompass all possibilities for envisioning sports in the future. But they represent two popular conceptions of sports in contemporary societies, and they are practical starting points for thinking about what we'd like sports to be in the future.

Power and Performance Sports

Power and performance sports will continue to be highly visible and publicized sport forms in the near future. They're based on key aspects of dominant ideologies in most postindustrial societies, as demonstrated by their emphasis on strength, power, speed, competition, and competitive outcomes.

Although power and performance sports take many forms, they're all built upon the idea that excellence is proved through competitive success and achieved through dedication, hard work, and a willingness to take risks. They stress setting records, pushing human limits, using the body as a machine, and employing science and technology. According to many athletes in power and performance sports, the body is to be disciplined and monitored so as to meet the demands of sports.

Power and performance sports are exclusive in that participants are selected for their physical skills and abilities to achieve competitive success. Those who lack these "qualities" are cut or relegated to lower-status programs. Organizations and teams have hierarchical authority structures in which athletes are subordinate to coaches and coaches are subordinate to owners and administrators. It is widely accepted that coaches can exceed standard normative limits when motivating and training athletes to outperform others.

Club sports and intramurals may include elements from both power and performance sports and pleasure and participation sports. Ultimate Frisbee is a good example. (*Source:* Bob Byrne, Ultimate Players Association)

Athletes are expected to obey coaches and show that they are willing to make sacrifices in their quest for competitive success.

The sponsors of power and performance sports stress the value of winning; being endorsed by winning athletes and teams is important when selling products and promoting the sponsor's brand. Sponsors assume that their association with winning athletes and teams enhances their status and makes them special in the eyes of people they wish to impress and influence. As long as current sponsors desire this connection, power and performance sports will remain dominant for the foreseeable future in most societies.

Pleasure and Participation Sports

Although power and performance sports are highly visible, many people realize that there are other ways to organize and play sports that more closely match their values and interests. This realization has led to the creation of numerous sport forms organized around *pleasure and participation* and emphasizing freedom, authenticity, self-expression, enjoyment, holistic health, support for others, and respect for the environment. They focus on personal empowerment and the notion that the body is to be nurtured and enjoyed in a quest to experience challenges rather than trained and subordinated in a quest to achieve competitive success.

Pleasure and participation sports tend to be inclusive, and skill differences among participants often are accommodated by using "handicaps" that allow everyone to experience exciting challenges associated with organized physical activities. Sport organizations and teams based on this model have democratic decision-making structures characterized by cooperation, power sharing, and give-and-take relationships between coaches and athletes. Humiliation, shame, and derogation are inconsistent with the spirit underlying these sports.

Pleasure and participation sports are characteristically sponsored by public and nonprofit organizations and by corporations seeking exposure to a defined collection of consumers. Additionally, some corporations may sponsor these sports as part of an overall emphasis on social responsibility and a commitment to health promotion, among other commendable goals.

CURRENT TRENDS RELATED TO SPORTS IN SOCIETY

Becoming aware of current trends and the factors that influence them is the starting point for being effective agents in creating the futures we want to see. The complexity of social worlds complicates the identification of trends, so it's useful to think of the factors that support the growth of power and performance sports on the one hand, and pleasure and participation sports on the other. Making this distinction helps us clarify our goals and use social theories more effectively as we participate in the process of influencing the culture and organization of sports.

Factors Supporting the Growth of Power and Performance Sports

There are strong vested interests in power and performance sports among those who have power and influence in wealthy postindustrial societies. For example, when the goal is to use strength, power, and speed to outperform others, sports reaffirm gender differences and a form of gender ideology that privileges men. As long as men control corporate resources there will be an emphasis on sponsoring power and performance sports. Currently, this helps to explain why American football, the classic embodiment of these sports, has become the most popular spectator sport in the United States and continues to attract billions of dollars in television rights fees and other revenues. Athletes in the NFL and other power and performance sports are portrayed in the media as heroic figures, as warriors who embody a corporate emphasis on productivity, efficiency, and dedication to performance in the face of all barriers. Spectators are encouraged to identify with these athletes and express their identification through the consumption of licensed merchandise and other products.

Because power and performance sports often involve pushing human and normative limits, they are relatively easy to market and sell when combined with storylines that resonate with the experience of consumers. This is why the media now emphasize the personal lives of athletes and their families. Dedicated, long-time fans may be satisfied with coverage focused on games, scores, and statistics, but new and less knowledgeable fans often are attracted to more dramatic and tabloid-style information about players' lives. For instance, in 2005 the Tour de France set a new precedent by allowing Lance Armstrong to bring his three children to the victory podium after winning his seventh consecutive Tour. The television cameras focused on his six-year-old son and three-year-old twin daughters and turned to Armstrong's then-girlfriend, rock star Sheryl Crow, who traveled with him, the children, and their nanny during the three-week, 2250-mile race. Viewers asked, where was his ex-wife, the mother of his children? Does she get along with Sheryl Crow? Do Armstrong and Crow want children of their own? If so, did Armstrong freeze enough sperm cells before the testicular cancer treatment made him sterile? And what would happen to Crow's career if she had a child with Armstrong? Such were the questions of viewers who knew relatively little about cycling but were attracted to Armstrong as a celebrity and cancer survivor as well as an athlete. This type of media coverage is common in many power and performance sports, because it provides the storylines that maintain interest in these sports even when people know little about the tactics and techniques involved in doing the sport from an athlete's perspective.

Factors Supporting the Growth of Pleasure and Participation Sports

Sports have always been social occasions in people's lives, and people incorporate into them the things that give them pleasure or reaffirm their values. Pleasure and participation sports today are popular to the extent that people define them as attractive alternatives to the more culturally dominant power and performance sports. Factors that motivate this search for alternatives today are (1) concerns about health and fitness, (2) participation preferences among older people, (3) values and experiences brought to sports by women, and (4) groups seeking alternatives to highly structured, competitive sports that constrain their experiences.

Concerns About Health and Fitness As health-care policies and programs emphasize prevention rather than expensive cures, people generally become more sensitive to health and fitness issues. In North America, health-care and insurance companies now encourage strategies for staying well as they seek to cut costs and maximize profits. This encourages people to pursue activities with health benefits, and many pleasure and participation sports meet this need (Waddington, 2000b, 2007).

In the United States, where physical education classes have been eliminated in many schools, growing concerns about health, fitness, and obesity are creating interests in new forms of physical education that focus on lifetime activities, noncompetitive challenges, inclusive participation philosophies, respect and support for other participants, and responsible attitudes toward the environment—all of which are characteristics of pleasure and participation sports. If these concerns continue to grow, they will influence the sport preferences of people through the life course. If this happens, people may decide that their tax money should be used to build local recreation complexes rather than stadiums for professional teams and that spending a

Concerns about health and fitness frequently lead people to engage in pleasure and participation sports such as in-line skating. In Piran, Slovenia, this man in his 60s stays fit by skating and teaching young people how to negotiate town streets and sidewalks on their skates. (*Source:* Jay Coakley)

day playing recreational sports with family and friends is more important than spending significant amounts of money to attend professional games and buy satellite/cable packages so they can sit and watch sports day after day.

When people realize that healthy exercise can be incorporated into challenging pleasure and participation sports that connect them with others and their environment and create enjoyment and a sense of community, they are likely to give higher priority to them—but this depends on how people choose to create the future for themselves and their families, within their schools and communities (O'Connor and Brown, 2007).

Participation Preferences Among Older People As the median age of the population increases in many societies and older people represent an increasingly larger proportion of the world's population, there will be more interest in sports that do not involve intimidation, physical force, the domination of opponents, and the risk of serious injuries.

As people age, they're less likely to risk physical well-being to establish a reputation in sports. Older people are more likely to see sports as social activities and make them inclusive rather than exclusive. They also realize that they have but one body, and it can be enjoyed only if they cultivate it as though it were a garden rather than using it like a machine.

People in the baby-boomer generation in the United States are now in their mid-40s to mid-60s. They grew up playing and watching competitive sports and are not likely to abandon them as they age, but most of them will avoid participation in power and performance sports that have high injury rates. Instead, they'll redefine what it means to be an athlete and they will play modified versions of competitive activities in which rules emphasize the pleasure of movement, connections between people, and controlled challenges (Dionigi and O'Flynn, 2007; Tulle, 2007). Additionally, pleasure and participation sports will also be sites where older

people challenge the notion that aging always involves increasing dependency and incapacity. "Seniors" and "masters" sport programs will increase as people demand them. As a result, images of older people who are fit, healthy, and accomplished athletes will become more visible and serve as models for others seeking pleasure and participation.

Values and Experiences Brought to Sports by Women As women gain more power and resources, many will revise or reject traditional power and performance sports. In the process, they'll create new sport forms that emphasize one or more dimensions of pleasure and participation sports. For instance, when women play sports such as rugby, soccer, and hockey, they often emphasize inclusiveness and support for teammates and opponents in explicit ways that are less common in men's versions of these sports. The "in-your-face" power and performance orientation exhibited by some men is replaced by a more cooperative orientation that highlights connections between participants.

Women often face difficulties when recruiting corporate sponsors for pleasure and participation sports, although this is beginning to change as people in corporations see that these sports can make employees healthier and create new realms of consumption for which products and services can be sold.

Groups Seeking Alternative Sports People who reject certain aspects of power and performance sports have a history of creating alternative sports and unique sport cultures organized around them (Borden, 2001; Rinehart and Syndor, 2003). Studies of skateboarders, snowboarders, surfers, BMX riders, in-line skaters, and others show that some people in these sports resist turning them into commercialized, competitive forms (Beal, 1995; Honea, 2005, 2007). Even in official, formally sponsored contests, skaters have deliberately subverted the power and performance dimensions of events.

Unregistered skaters have crashed the events. Registered skaters have pinned their competition numbers upside down on their shirts, boycotted award ceremonies, and focused on expressing themselves and supporting "opponents." Mass demonstrations have been staged at a few events where nonconforming athletes were disqualified for their actions. Of course, none of this is shown on television broadcasts that are edited to attract young viewers, but they are indicative of resistance to events organized around a power and performance model (Crissey, 1999).

Some people also resist attempts to change the pleasure and participation emphasis in their activities. They don't want competition and the domination of opponents to replace the expression and support for fellow participants. For example, when a twelve-year-old snowboarder was asked about adding his sport to the Olympics, he said, "Don't kill the ride, dude. Let us be free." Even at age twelve, he knew that the ideology of power and performance would subvert desired elements of pleasure and participation in his sport. After snowboarding was added to the Olympics in 1996, Terje Haakonsen, reputedly the best boarder in the world, refused to compete in Nagano, Japan. He said, "Snowboarding is about fresh tracks and carving powder and being yourself and not being judged by others; it's not about nationalism and politics and money" (in Perman, 1998, p. 61).

After skateboarding had been turned into a traditional competitive sport by the X Games, legendary skater Tony Hawk declared that "it's about time the riders took the competitions into their own hands" because others were destroying many of the expressive and pleasurable elements of boarding (in Higgins, 2005). Hawk organized his Boom Boom HuckJam tour to preserve the spirit of action and lifestyle sports in a format that could generate revenues to support elite athletes as well as media coverage to grow the sports. Similarly, Terje Haakonsen and other snowboarders created "Ticket To Ride" (www.ttrworldtour.com/) in 2002—a series of rider-controlled events designed to preserve the ethos of their sports through "a movement connected to the core of snowboarding's identity [and an emphasis on a] sense of fun and friendship, the appreciation of nature, the travel and the unique experiences, the freedom and creativity . . ." The challenge for these sports today is to resist pressure to align with corporate sponsors and incorporate into their activities more power and performance elements that will attract mass audiences (Wheaton, 2004).

People with physical or intellectual disabilities have also developed alternative sports or adapted dominant sports to fit their interests and needs. Although some of these sports emphasize elements of power and performance, most emphasize pleasure and participation. Concern and support for teammates and opponents, as well as inclusiveness related to physical abilities, characterize these sports.

When people with a disability participate with able-bodied people in sports organized around a power and performance model, it presents an opportunity for all athletes, regardless of age or ability, to deal with the reality that human relationships always involve accommodating difference and uniqueness. Dealing with this reality requires making a choice: maintain power and performance sports as they are and marginalize those with a disability, or organize them around the pleasure and performance model to be inclusive. It's difficult to predict how people in different situations and at different points in their lives will handle this choice, but it's certain that their decisions will create the future of sports (Nixon, 2007).

The Gay Games, the World Outgames, and the EuroGames provide additional examples of alternative sport forms emphasizing participation, support, inclusiveness, and the enjoyment of physical movement. The seventh quadrennial Gay Games in Chicago and the 1st World Outgames in Montreal each drew over 10,000 athletes in 2006, and the EuroGames draws nearly 3000 athletes to its annual event. Participants

Disc golf, invented in the 1960s, initially used lampposts and fire hydrants as "holes." Since then it has become less "alternative," but it continues to attract people seeking a sport without coaches, schedules, referees, and other constraints that limit freedom and creativity. (*Source:* Jay Coakley)

include gay men, lesbians, bisexuals, and trans-sexuals (GLBTs) in sports emphasizing inclusion and other aspects of the pleasure and participation model. GLBTs also organize sports at the community level to provide experiences free of the homophobia that can destroy enjoyment in other sports (Ravel and Rail, 2007).

The range of sports that incorporate elements of the pleasure and participation model grows as more people realize that sports are social constructions that can be created to fit even temporary interests and passing situations. This has been illustrated recently by people forming local adult kickball leagues and freerunning groups, and joining with others to surf on sand, play bike polo, go streetsurfing, and create uncounted other sports.

Although it often is a challenge to find corporate sponsors, various pleasure and participation sports usually survive because people are creative enough to find resources to maintain them. Furthermore, corporate or media sponsors are needed only when a sport hires administrators,

stages national and international tournaments, and involves expensive equipment and travel expenses. When a sport exists simply for pleasure and participation, the primary resource needed is people wishing to play it.

> **OLC ON THE *OLC*:**
>
> See the OLC—Additional Readings for Chapter 16—for the author's essay on the challenges and conflicts that will emerge when increasing numbers of people participate in sports and seek outdoor areas that fit their interests.

Trends in Sport Spheres

Predicting the future is less important than knowing about current trends and using that knowledge to participate in creating the future. For instance, some people study trends so that they can more effectively plan strategies to create sports that are humane, accessible, inclusive, and democratically organized. Others have different goals, but in any case, our knowledge of current trends in various sport spheres is useful. If the result is *multiple futures and greater sport participation choices and opportunities*, that's ideal.

Professional Sports   Current trends in professional sports involve the following:

- Profit-driven national and global expansion
- Staging mega-events connected with national and urban "redevelopment" projects
- Using public funds to build facilities and expand private consumer attractions
- Athletes and owner/promoters seeking "collective bargaining agreements" (CBAs) that fairly reward athlete labor and owner/promoter investments
- Growing resistance from people who disapprove of using public money to subsidize private investments in professional sports

Although people think that they have no control over these trends, most professional sports exist in democratic societies where citizens often vote on use of public funds to build sport stadiums and arenas. They also elect political representatives who determine the legal environment in which businesses, including professional sports, operate. More people now realize that they can organize to resist the construction of publicly funded stadiums that are used only by professional teams, and they can pressure local legislators to regulate the use of public facilities so that corporations with deep pockets for entertainment expenses cannot drive up the price of all tickets to games. As people view themselves more as citizens and less as consumers, they'll create futures more in line with their values, interests, and resources. In the meantime, the allocation of financial rewards will remain an issue in all professional sports where revenues are split between athletes and owner/promoters.

Intercollegiate Sports   Current trends in intercollegiate sports in the United States involve the following elements:

- Escalating expenses for big-time spectator sports
- Struggles over gender equity
- Athletes in revenue-producing sports seeking rights to profit from their skills
- Students seeking more opportunities to play school-sponsored sports
- Faculty resisting the use of university resources to subsidize big-time sports

Knowing about and understanding these trends is important for students, administrators, and legislators making decisions about the use of student fees and campus sport facilities (see Wolverton, 2007b). As athletic department budgets increase much faster than academic budgets, faculty are becoming more concerned about these decisions and how they affect higher education, and students increasingly want opportunities to participate in organized sports that enable them to have fun and develop and display physical skills. At the same time, athletes on existing teams are more assertive about their rights, and those on revenue-producing teams are increasingly concerned about receiving fair rewards for their labor. Concerns about and struggles over gender equity influence each of these trends.

The possibilities for students to create futures in connection with these trends are many. Students on large campuses are like community citizens who can influence the use of local resources to support their sport interests, and more of them want campus decisions to be made democratically rather than by administrators, athletic directors, coaches, and boosters.

High School Sports   Current trends in high school sports involve the following elements:

- Increasing financial and public relations stakes associated with sports
- Parents and athletes viewing high school sports as a way to obtain college scholarships and admission into the college of their choice
- Struggles over gender equity
- Increasing elitism favoring skilled and highly specialized athletes
- Emphasis on playoffs, championships, state titles, and national rankings
- "Outsourcing" certain sport teams to private clubs

As the stakes become greater with an emphasis on playoffs, championships, college scholarships for athletes, and school reputations, debates about the meaning, purpose, and organization of high school sports become more contentious. Historically, "boosters" who covet state titles and want high school sports to resemble big-time college sports have dominated these debates, but many students, parents, teachers, and local citizens have different visions of what school sports should be in the future. At the same time, many of the best athletes in certain sports now play on community-based club teams rather than school teams, making it more feasible to restructure interscholastic sports if people wish to do so.

Overall, the future of high school sports depends on who argues their case most convincingly to school boards and district athletic directors. Because school sports are funded with tax money and their stated goal is education, these people will seek research on sports, sport participation, and education to support their arguments.

Youth Sports Current trends in organized youth sports involve the following elements:

- Declining public programs due to budget constraints
- Increased privatization benefiting people who can pay club and facility fees
- Increasing de facto segregation of sports by socioeconomic status, race, and ethnicity
- Decreasing availability of opportunities for children in low-income families and communities
- More children seeking alternatives to adult-controlled organized sports

These trends mimic general trends in society. As ideology emphasizes individualism and a form of "family values" that expects every family to provide for itself, people with resources will create playgrounds on their own property and buy access to private sport programs and facilities for themselves and their children. They don't need public parks or publicly funded programs and seldom vote to support them. As a result, public sport programs and facilities are disappearing and youth sports are becoming less accessible to people in middle-class, working-class, and low-income families. Resistance to these trends is currently weak, but there is a possibility that people will demand more accessible youth sports in the coming years.

Sports for People with a Disability Current trends in sports for people with a disability involve the following elements:

Athletes with disabilities are participating in sports in greater numbers. Creatively designed equipment permits new forms of sports involvement for people of all ability levels, as shown by these trail riders. (*Source:* Rob Schoenbaum)

- More people disabled by war, land mines, lack of medical care, and poverty
- Increasing recognition that people with disabilities want to play sports and have a right to do so
- Continuing use of sport participation as therapy for people with disabilities
- More sports programs for elite athletes with disabilities
- New technologies that facilitate sport participation

There is a growing popular awareness that disability is multifaceted and more common than previously recognized. As a result, emerging ideas, vocabularies, and orientations are supportive of opportunities for people with disabilities to play sports. The use of the medical model that encouraged people to seek technical or medical "fixes" or "cures" for disabilities is slowly giving way to a social model recognizing that impairments are a normal part of the human condition

breaking BARRIERS

Vision Barriers
I Have to Believe

In 1997 a youth baseball coach in Conyers, Georgia, noticed that one of his five-year-old players came to every practice and game with his seven-year-old brother. The seven-year-old loved baseball, but there were no teams for children in wheelchairs. So the coach invited him to play.

This coach's action precipitated a series of events. The following season, local adults organized the Conyers "Miracle League" for children with disabilities. It was the first baseball league of its kind, and the rules were adapted to fit the players. For example, every player on a team would bat each inning, all base runners were safe, and every player scored a run. Able-bodied young people and volunteers served as buddies, assisting players when the need arose.

During the first year there were thirty-five players on four teams. Watching them play inspired Dean Alford, a former Georgia state representative and president of the local Rotary Club. He saw that a conventional ball field with grass, dirt, and elevated bases created barriers for players who were blind or using wheelchairs, walkers, and crutches. Alford worked with local Rotary Clubs to raise money to design and construct a rubberized turf playing field plus accessible restrooms, concession stand, and picnic area. Three other grass fields were designed so they could be converted to synthetic surfaces as the Miracle League grew.

The field, 25 miles east of Atlanta, opened in 2000. It attracted national media attention and interest among the families of more than 75,000 children with disabilities in the Atlanta area. In 2008 there were about 200 Miracle League organizations in the United States, Puerto Rico, and Canada.

When people hear of the Miracle League, visit websites, and watch games, their idealism often pushes them to think further outside the box of traditional parks and playing fields. Some communities have built universally accessible playgrounds adjacent to the smooth-surface baseball fields. Playground designers today are more likely to create environments that attract children with varying physical (dis)abilities. This type of design enables families and friends to play safely as they encounter physical challenges and have fun regardless of abilities.

When people see a Miracle League game played on a barrier-free field adjoining a barrier-free play area, they usually say: "This makes so much sense," and then they ask, "Why doesn't my community have one of these?" This response along with the development of more sport programs like the Miracle League is heartening for the 6 million U.S. children with (dis)abilities who may find that it is difficult or impossible to play sports in traditional programs that assume high ability among participants.

The more recent development of Miracle Leagues for adults is heartening to the thousands of veterans returning from Iraq and Afghanistan with amputated limbs, sight and hearing impairments, and injuries that impede walking. Making sports accessible to them is a no-brainer, even among those who lack idealism. As veterans return to communities, universities, gyms, parks, trails, and workplaces, idealism is essential if barriers are to be broken.

Jayne Craike, who competes on the New Zealand Equestrian Federation national dressage circuit and also represents her country in the Paralympics, encourages people to be idealistic as they envision and work to create the future. She says, "*I have to believe* that there is still more to come in a world that is continually changing, and that we can make a difference" (Joukowsky and Rothstein, 2002b, p. 55, emphasis added). Craike knows that sports are more than therapy for people with (dis)abilities. When sports are highly valued, participation is a normalizing activity enabling people with (dis)abilities to establish positive identities, meet others, and force everyone who watches them to acknowledge that (dis)abilities are a normal part of the human condition. It may be idealistic to envision and work for universal accessibility, but who wants to settle for the alternative?

and that there is a need for changes that increase access to sport participation across all ability levels (Howe, 2008; Nixon, 2007). This change of thinking is leading more people to view ability in terms of a continuum rather than simply reducing it to the two mutually exclusive categories of able-bodied and disabled. As more people think this way, many futures become possible, as illustrated in Breaking Barriers, p. 559.

Spectators and Spectator Sports Current trends related to spectators and spectator sports involve the following elements:

- Consuming live and media sports as a central leisure activity
- Using new media that provide exciting spectator experiences
- Treating spectators as consumers receptive to advertising messages

Spectator sports are deeply embedded in many cultures. However, people decide how much they will pay in terms of money, time, and effort to be spectators; what meanings they'll give to experiences; and how they'll integrate experiences into their lives. Some also seek futures that deviate from those envisioned by corporate sponsors and media executives. For example, if people voted to bring free or low-cost wireless (Wi-Fi) Internet access to their communities, the future would involve incredibly diverse spectator experiences. But if people allow giant cable and telecom corporations to control the conditions of broadband access, their futures as spectators will be limited and expensive. Imagine futures in which broadband access is publicly provided like other essential services, such as roads and schools, and is available to people worldwide. This future is much more feasible than building roads worldwide, and as more people share this vision, spectator sports will change dramatically.

FACTORS INFLUENCING TRENDS TODAY

When we're creating futures it's useful to know about factors that influence current trends. This enables us to anticipate possibilities, prevent or overcome resistance, and make more informed decisions as we participate in social worlds.

Many factors influence trends in sports, but the discussion here is limited to five: technology, telecommunications and electronic media, a widespread commitment to organization and rationalization, a cultural emphasis on commercialism and consumption, and the changing demographic composition of communities and societies.

Technology

Technology is the *application of scientific or other organized knowledge to solve problems, expand experiences, or alter the conditions of reality*. It is used to make sports safer, detect and treat injuries more effectively, assess physical limits and potential, expand the experiences available in sports, train bodies to perform more efficiently, provide athletes with more control of their bodies, increase the speeds at which bodies move, decrease the risks involved in sports, enhance the size and strength of bodies, alter bodies to match the demands of particular sports, identify rule infractions and enforce rules more accurately, measure and compare performances with precision, and improve the durability and functionality of equipment (Assael, 2007c; Atkinson, 2007a; Dimeo, 2007; Pennington, 2007; Yessis, 2006).

The major issue related to technology is when and how to use and regulate it. The governing bodies of sports try to regulate the technologies used by coaches, officials, trainers, and athletes, but the rapid expansion of new technologies makes this difficult. Assessing the full

AT YOUR *fingertips* For more information on technologies altering the athletic body, see Chapter 6, pp. 184–186. Also see the OLC—Additional Readings for Chapter 16—for a discussion of the unknown consequences of new technologies in sports.

implications of particular technologies is not easy (Crouse, 2008; Magdalinski, 2008). Consistent and sensible decisions about them are made only when we know what we want sports to be in the future. Consider genetic-enhancement technologies. They can be used to improve human performance, heal injured bodies, and eliminate some physical impairments. If we want to create a future in which sports are organized around the power and performance model, the framework and criteria for assessing genetic enhancement would be different from the way they would be if we want sports organized around a pleasure and participation model. This is why it is important to have a clear sense of what we want the meaning, purpose, and organizations of sports to be in the future.

> **The use of drugs, and, perhaps more startling, the engineering of genes to enhance performance, raises questions about the notion of what an athlete is.** —Richard Sandomir, journalist (2002)

the sports that dominate popular discourse and influence what we envision for the future. If we realize this, we can seek images and narratives about sports that are not represented exclusively through commercial media. This expands our experience and enables us to think more creatively about the present and future. The more versions of sports we see and talk about, the more we can create futures to match our interests and circumstances.

Organization and Rationalization

All sports contain the element of play (Tomc, 2008). But sports today focus so much on planning and productivity that play has been pushed

Telecommunications and Electronic Media

Television, computers, the Internet, wireless phones, and other handheld devices are technologies with implications for sports. Television and the Internet, for instance, provide visual images and narratives that many people use to imagine future possibilities for sports; the same is true for video games. Some people even use electronic images to inform their choices about participation and formulate standards for assessing sport experiences. Therefore, media producers worldwide have considerable power to create the future. The events, athletes, and stories represented in the media influence popular discourse about sports, and it is out of that discourse that people form their ideas about what sports could and should be in the future.

To understand this process, imagine that football is the only sport you've ever seen on television. You would have a seriously limited sense of what sports are and what they could be. A version of this occurs as media companies select for coverage only those sports that generate profits on commercial television. As a result, those are

"Oh, Mom! I'm not going outside to play when I can play on my virtual World Cup Team right here."

The future of sports is difficult to predict. Will children prefer video games and virtual sports over the dominant sport forms of today? Will playing virtual sports serve as a "gateway" into real-time sports by teaching children the rules and challenges that characterize real-time sports?

to the sidelines. "Fun" in organized, purpose-driven sports is associated with achieving goals rather than physical expression and joy. Process is now secondary to product, and the journey is secondary to the destination.

People in postindustrial societies live with the legacy of industrialization. They emphasize organization according to rational principles based, whenever possible, on systematic research. Being organized and making plans to accomplish goals is so important that spontaneity, expression, creativity, and joy—the elements of play—are given low priority or may even be considered frivolous by event planners, coaches, and spectators. This is why legendary snowboarder Terje Haakonsen decided against participating in the Olympics; he didn't want to endorse a form of sport in which organization and rationalization had subverted play. His thoughts are summarized in this description of snowboarding:

> That was a fun time . . . I was always learning new tricks, figuring out ways to get better. When I'm having fun snowboarding, it's like meditation. I'm not thinking about anything but what I'm doing right now. No past, no future. . . . [But today, too many] people get stuck and all they do the whole year is pipe, and that's too bad for them. They do the same routine over and over, get the moves down. It becomes like this really precise, synchronized movement, like they're little ballerinas or something. It's no longer this spontaneous sport, like when you're a kid screwing around (in Greenfeld, 1999).

Haakonsen felt that fun and effort merge together in sports when they are done on terms set by participants; this merger breaks down when sports are done for judges using criteria that ignore the subjective experience of participation.

When we are creating sports, these are important things to keep in mind because there is a tendency in postindustrial cultures to organize all physical activities for the purposes of rationally assessing skills and performances. Working to improve physical skills so we can expand

possibilities for new experiences is one thing, but spending years perfecting a specialized skill to conform to someone else's idea of technical perfection is another. Once we "feel" this distinction in our own sport participation, we become more creative when thinking about the future.

Commercialism and Consumption

Many people today are so deeply embedded in commercial culture that they think of themselves as customers instead of citizens. This changes the basis for evaluating self, others, and experiences (Buscombe et al., 2006). When commercial ideology pervades sports, play becomes secondary to playoffs and payoffs; games, athletes, and sport participation itself become commodities—things bought and sold for bottom-line purposes. Participation then revolves around the consumption of equipment, lessons, clothing, nutritional supplements, gym and club memberships, and other material things. Status is based on where you do sports, the equipment that you use, and the clothing that you wear—not the joy of playing.

Many people are turned off by this approach, but unless they've experienced alternatives, it may be difficult to envision sports devoid of commercialism and consumption. This is why it's important to have public spaces where people can play sports that don't require fees, permits, or memberships (Bale and Vertinsky, 2004). Creativity thrives in such spaces. In this sense, public policies at all levels of government can create or subvert possibilities for noncommercial sport futures.

Changing Demographic Composition of Communities and Societies

Sports are social constructions, and some of the richest sport environments are those in which people have diverse cultural backgrounds and sport experiences. Even when people play the same sport, strategies and styles often vary with their cultural backgrounds. For example,

Trying to improve skills on your own terms is different from doing a routine over and over to meet someone else's idea of technical perfection. Once we "feel" this distinction in our own sport participation, we become much more creative as we think of how to do sports and incorporate them into our lives. (*Source:* PhotoLink/ Getty Images)

Canadians created a secular and rationalized version of lacrosse that was different from the traditional, sacred game invented and played by Native Peoples in North America (King, 2007b). People in the United States took the sport of rugby as played in England and adapted it to fit their preferences; the result was American football, a game that is relatively unique in the world (Riesman and Denny, 1951). In 2004 the New York Mets hired a Latino general manager, signed notable Latino players, and developed a style of play that was fast, assertive, and spirited. This style is now part of a larger cultural shift in Major League Baseball, a shift that celebrates diversity by incorporating it into everything from on-the-field strategy to marketing the game to Latinos in the United States and Latin America (Mahler, 2005).

Although demographic diversity presents challenges, it also presents possibilities for creating new forms and versions of sports. As geographical mobility, labor migration, and political turmoil push and pull people across national borders, there will be opportunities to borrow and blend different sports, styles of play, and game strategies. If people take advantage of those opportunities without systematically privileging games from one culture and marginalizing games from other cultures, it will be possible to envision and create sports that fit a wide range of interests and abilities.

At the same time that global blending occurs, there will be increased divisions between people from different social classes and certain racial and ethnic groups within societies where inequalities are great. As a result, people from certain ethnic minorities will play only a few sports, whereas those in the dominant population will have diverse opportunities to play sports and develop skills.

BECOMING AGENTS OF CHANGE AND CREATING THE FUTURE

Robert Davies, chief executive of the International Business Leaders Forum, an organization dedicated to promoting global social responsibility, tells corporate leaders worldwide that the visibility and popularity of sports at the local and global levels provides opportunities to improve health, develop communities, boost education and literacy, and empower girls and women. He says that "the power and influence of sport is only just being understood" by people concerned with social responsibility (Davies, 2002b). He also told an international assembly of journalists and media representatives that "high-profile global sporting events are seen as a frontier for raising issues of injustice and social responsibility" and that the media have a responsibility to explore that frontier (Davies, 2002a).

> **OLC** **ON THE *OLC*:**
> See the OLC—Additional Readings for Chapter 16—for a list of groups and organizations using sports to bring about progressive changes.

As Davies thinks about the future from the perspective of corporate social responsibility, he sees possibilities for changing sports and using them to facilitate changes beyond playing fields and locker rooms. Other perspectives alert us to even more possibilities. To assess them and work to convert selected possibilities into realities, there is a need to understand connections between sports and the rest of the world. Therefore the process of creating the future involves identifying goals, using theories to plan strategies, and choosing a vantage point for making changes.

Identifying Goals

Change means different things to different people because their goals for the future are different. For most people in sports, the primary goal is *growth*—strengthening and expanding what exists today. For others, the primary goal is *improvement*—eliminating problems and promoting justice and fairness in sports. And for a few people, the primary goal is *social transformation*—reorganizing social relationships and creating new sport forms that are healthy, inclusive, humane, and widely accessible.

Growth is a **conservative goal** based on the belief that sports are inherently positive activities that should be strengthened and expanded in their current forms. Accomplishing this goal requires using management and marketing techniques to expand and make sport organizations more efficient while maintaining the culture and structure of sports as they are. The belief is that increased efficiency will create resources that inevitably fuel expansion. Most people in organized sports are dedicated to this goal for both ideological and personal reasons: they believe that the growth of sports as they are currently organized will improve society and create opportunities for people working in sport organizations, including themselves.

Improvement is a **reformist goal** based on beliefs that sport participation produces positive consequences, that the ethical foundations of sports must be restored and maintained, and that participation opportunities must be increased. Accomplishing this goal requires changes that promote fair competition, character-building experiences, and appropriate opportunities for everyone to participate. Cheating, deviance, and drug use must be controlled, discrimination must be eliminated from policies and programs, and participation must be made more accessible in schools and communities. Improvement is a widely accepted goal, although people may differ on the priorities for specific reforms.

Professional sport teams sometimes fund community programs and services for children. The teams encourage players, even those with reformist and radical goals, to be engaged in them. The (NBA's Indiana) Pacers Academy in central Indianapolis provides a "Read to Achieve" program and a middle and high school curriculum for about 100 at-risk students. This is helpful, but it focuses on changing a few individuals rather than changing the social conditions that put thousands of children at risk. Other teams take a similar approach by supporting youth sports, providing disaster relief, and working with health-related charities. (*Source:* Jay Coakley)

Transformation is a **radical goal** based on the belief that dominant forms of sports are systemically flawed and must be reorganized or replaced to create new meaning and purpose. Accomplishing this goal requires a critical assessment of dominant sports and the ability to create reorganized or new sports in which previously disenfranchised segments of the population share power with others in determining policies, controlling sport resources and facilities, and developing opportunities that meet their needs and concerns. Few people associated with sports support transformation as a goal, and those in positions of control usually are quick to use their resources to impede or undermine anyone espousing radical transformation.

My experience indicates that most people who read this book give priority to *growth*, with *reform* being an important but secondary goal.

In the context of many sport organizations, reformists often are labeled as "anti-sport" and marginalized. For example, because a few of my colleagues and I have regularly called for reforms of the IOC and the USOC, some of us are no longer welcome at the Olympic Training Center (OTC) in Colorado Springs.

Radicals are especially unwelcome in or around sport organizations, although most radicals don't see this as a problem because their work focuses primarily on issues of poverty, homelessness, universal health care, quality education for children, accessible public transportation, full employment, and guaranteed minimum standards of living. A few radicals have used sports as sites for challenging dominant definitions of masculinity and femininity, raising questions about the meaning of race, exposing the poverty and inequalities that prevent meaningful participation in society, destroying stereotypes about (dis)abilities, and critiquing the antidemocratic, exclusive, and hierarchical structures that characterize most organized sports today. In the process, they often inspire creative visions of what sports could be in the future and, in doing so, encourage others to critically assess sports and sport organizations and to become involved in progressive programs in which political awareness and community activism is combined with playing sports (Zirin, 2005b; 2008a).

Using Theories

Throughout this book it is noted that sociologists study and explain social worlds in terms of culture, interaction, and social structure. Theories related to each of these dimensions of social worlds are useful when thinking about the future of sports and developing strategies to create particular futures. In fact, without theories, it's impossible to predict or accurately anticipate the consequences of change-oriented strategies, regardless of the goals a person wants to achieve.

Cultural Theories   People who wish to be agents of change in sports use cultural theories because these theories explain the processes through which social worlds are produced, reproduced, and transformed. Cultural theories explain that to change sports, we must change the symbols, values, norms, vocabularies, beliefs, and ideologies that people use to make sense of and give meaning to sports and sport experiences. For example, the process of creating gender equity in sports has involved, among many things, changing the vocabulary used by media announcers covering women's sports. In the past, female athletes were identified by their first names, which gave the impression that their sports were not as serious as those played by men. As this vocabulary issue was identified, often by researchers in the sociology of sport, announcers changed how they talked about women athletes. This was a relatively minor change, but it altered narratives in ways that presented women's sports more seriously.

Overall, cultural theories focus attention on issues of ideology, representation, and power dynamics in society. They explain how people use power to maintain cultural practices and social structures that represent their interests, and they identify how people resist or oppose those practices and structures. This information is required to use a critical approach to develop strategies for changing sports.

Research using cultural theories helps us envision sports that are: (a) free of exploitation and oppression; (b) organized to be inclusive in terms of age, gender, race, ethnicity, religion, and (dis)ability; and (c) used to empower people to participate actively in the social worlds in which they live. Goals based on cultural theories usually are reformist, seldom conservative, and occasionally radical. For this reason, cultural theories may be seen as threatening by many people who want only to grow sports as they are currently defined and organized.

Interactionist Theories   When people use interactionist theories, they focus on processes

AT YOUR *fingertips*   For more information on using theories in the sociology of sport, see Chapter 2, pp. 36–38. See the OLC—Additional Readings for Chapter 16—for explanations of how specific theories, such as structural-functionalism, conflict theory, feminist theory, and figurational theory, are used to identity strategies for bringing about social change.

of social learning and development and the relationships through which people come to know and give meaning to the world. Interactionist theories explain that changing sports involves changing socialization processes, self-concepts and identities, and the priorities given to particular role models and significant others. For example, people often resist reformist and radical changes because their self-concepts and identities are grounded in and supported by the current culture and organization of sports. This is useful to know because it helps us anticipate that people will often be personally defensive in the face of recommended changes in sports. Changes may threaten their identities and provoke resistance. Therefore, strategies must be presented tactfully, based on clear research evidence, and implemented to include as allies those currently working in sports. Creating the future in this way requires patience, persistence, and a keen awareness of how others perceive and identify themselves with and through sports.

Interactionist theories can be used to support conservative, reformist, or radical goals, but they generally emphasize the need to include multiple voices and perspectives in the change process. The assumption underlying these theories is that when voices are represented in social worlds, the organization of those worlds will eventually represent their interests and concerns. However, those using a critical approach usually combine interactionist theory with cultural theory and focus on power as well as representation. This often takes them in the direction of reform and transformation (Becker and McCall, 1993; Denzin, 2007).

Structural Theories When people use structural theories, they focus on relationships between social organization and access to power, authority, material resources, and economic opportunities. Structural theories explain that changing sports involves changing the organization of relationships and the larger context in which relationships exist. Functionalism is a form of structural theory based on the assumption that all social worlds are organized around shared values and need only to be preserved or tweaked here and there to improve efficiency and social integration. This approach appeals to people with vested interests in the status quo because it supports growth and minor reforms. As a result it is consistent with conservative and slightly reformist goals.

Conflict theory, based on the ideas of Karl Marx, is another form of structural theory. It identifies the economic factors that create social class divisions in society and determine life chances and lifestyles among people in all social classes. Conflict theory is most consistent with reformist or radical goals such as redistributing power and economic resources so that relationships are more egalitarian and social policies are more responsive to people who have the greatest needs in a society. When strategies for creating the future of sports are based on conflict theory, they identify the racism, sexism, nationalism, and militarism that distort the meaning, purpose, and organization of sports and recognize that eliminating the profit motive would allow sports to be organized around the needs of those who play them rather than those who own them.

Social theories can be used to achieve conservative, reformist, or radical goals. But people interested in the sociology of sport are more likely than others, especially those working in

sport organizations, to use a critical approach that focuses on reform and transformation (McDonald, 2002). They focus on what can be done to make sports more democratic, accessible, and humane so that physical activities represent the needs of all people rather than the needs of powerful people who are interested in preserving things as they are. Sociologist Ian McDonald (2007) explains that sports are so complex and paradoxical that many of us in this field denounce sports at the same time that we seek to perpetuate them. And this often is a tricky task.

Assessing Vantage Points

There are at least four different vantage points or strategic positions for initiating changes in and through sports (Hall et al., 1991). We can work inside sport organizations, join opposition groups to resist the growth of certain sport forms, create new and alternative sports, or work outside of sports to create structures and ideologies that support desired sport forms. Being aware of our personal vantage point is important because each comes with its own constraints and opportunities for creating the future of sports.

1. *Working inside sport organizations.*
An "insider" vantage point is constraining because promotions and job security depend on a certain degree of conformity to the values and culture of the organization where you work. This means that even though you may favor certain reforms or transformations, your commitment to change may decrease as you move up the organization into positions of power. Once people reach positions of power, they often set conservative goals and focus on the growth and efficiency of their organization. This isn't inevitable, but it's customary.

On the other hand, an insider vantage point provides information about the structure and culture of sport organizations and enables a person to directly intervene in the processes that affect the meaning, purpose, and organization of

Athletes as Change Agents
Activism Is a High-Risk Activity

Athletes are visible and popular. Some have the highest name and face recognition of any human beings in history. This puts them in good positions to serve as effective change agents in society—or does it?

The visibility and popularity of athletes depends heavily on media coverage and overall public image. Leagues, teams, and corporations use athletes' images to promote events and products, but this does not mean that athletes can readily convert their celebrity status into power related to serious social, political, or economic issues.

The social context of sport celebrity limits the extent to which athletes can be effective agents of change. If the words and actions of athletes don't match the interests of those who control their images, they risk losing the coverage and support that sustains their celebrity. Team owners and corporate sponsors usually avoid relationships with athletes who speak out on social issues; neither owners nor corporations want to alienate fans and consumers.

Adonal Foyle, a social and political activist who has played in the NBA since 1997, notes that few athletes speak out, even though many have strong thoughts and feelings on certain issues. He says that they're "cautious because they don't want to stand out of the crowd and be controversial in that way" (in Zirin, 2004a).

When Tiger Woods was selected by *Time* magazine as one of "the 25 most influential Americans" in 1997, he was widely condemned for saying that "Golf has shied away from [racism] for too long, [and] I hope . . . [to] change that" (*Time*, 1997). But his status, he discovered, did not by itself make him an effective agent of change in a context where country clubs are run by powerful white men. Since 1997 Woods has teamed up with major corporations to fund his Tiger Woods Foundation, which helps young people by developing their character, awarding scholarships, and maintaining a "learning center." This conservative approach focuses on changing individuals rather than structures, and it allows Woods to avoid taking on the powerful people who now provide him with endorsement income of $75 to $90 million per year.

South-African-born, Canadian NBA player Steve Nash faced criticism in 2003 when he came to all-star media day interviews wearing a T-shirt that said, "No War. Shoot for Peace." The NBA All-Star game was in Atlanta, and Nash simply wanted to express his strongly held belief that violence does not effectively resolve conflicts. By the end of the day he had discovered that being anti-war in the United States could jeopardize his credibility and influence as a spokesperson on any issue (Candaele and Dreier, 2004). After his experience, the Steve Nash Foundation focused solely on helping children by funding needed services and promoting healthy individual development.

It's not surprising that socially concerned athletes use conservative strategies often dedicated to helping individual children. Building playgrounds, visiting children in hospitals, promoting literacy, and delivering antidrug messages in high schools is noncontroversial because it reaffirms dominant societal values and strengthens the status quo. Even when retired athletes enter politics, they generally represent conservative political positions aligned with preserving the status quo. If athletes in the United States promoted radical or disruptive reformist changes that involved transforming the culture or structure of sport organizations or society, they would subject themselves to powerful criticisms that could threaten their careers.

Individual athletes have resisted the sports establishment and fostered progressive changes, but they have usually endured many negative consequences when doing so (Snyder, 2006; Zirin, 2005a, 2005b). Evidence suggests that athletes can lessen the risks of promoting reformist and radical goals by working in or through established organizations that can provide them with cover, support, and resources that connect them with larger efforts to promote change. For example, Sport in Society, a center at Northeastern University, and the National Consortium for Academics and Sports, each founded by scholar-activist Richard Lapchick, are reformist organizations that sponsor programs in which current and former athletes team up with others to make progressive changes in sports, communities, the media, and society. Among other things, these programs train high school students to think critically about social issues, form local Human

Tommy Smith and John Carlos took off their shoes and raised gloved fists to protest poverty and racism as they stood on the victory podium during the 1968 Olympic Games in Mexico City (*Source:* AP/Wide World Photos). This action caused them to be expelled from the U.S. team and sent back to the United States, where they were widely criticized and demeaned for more than twenty years. Nearly four decades later—in 2005—they received honorary doctorates from San Jose State University, where a 23-foot-high statue (right) commemorates their commitment to the then-radical goals of racial justice and the elimination of poverty. (*Source:* Jay Johnson)

Rights Squads, and become involved in community projects designed to reduce prejudice, violence, and other problems. Since 1990 these programs have enabled athletes to be agents of change by working in established organizations that have resources and favorable public profiles.

NBA player Adonal Foyle realized the importance of having this form of institutional legitimacy and support when he established his foundation,

Democracy Matters (www.democracymatters.org). Through the organization he speaks out on selected issues, but he also uses it to recruit college students to become involved in political efforts to reduce government corruption and increase democratic participation. Foyle also has been a team representative in the NBA players' association because he believes that a "player's rights should not be violated by powerful owners." Foyle is unique in that he grew up in

reflect on SPORTS   Athletes as Change Agents *(Continued)*

poverty in the West Indies and came to the United States at the invitation of a sociologist and an economist (Joan and Jay Mangle at Colgate University) who endorsed reformist and radical goals. He completed high school and college as a dedicated student who knew that bringing about real cultural and structural changes involved more than just helping individuals and doing charity.

Recent history shows that even suggesting the need for social and cultural transformation can create problems for athletes. When Cassius Clay (Muhammad Ali) spoke against racism during the 1960s and, as a Muslim,

refused induction into the military during the Vietnam War, he was stripped of his boxing title and sentenced to five years in prison. When 400-meter champions Tommy Smith and John Carlos stood on the victory podium during the 1968 Olympics in Mexico City and used symbolic gestures to protest poverty and racism in the United States, they faced contempt and rejection for the next twenty years (see the photo of Smith and Carlos; F. Murphy, 2006; Smith and Steele, 2007). Is this why athletes today use their names and fame to promote corporate brands instead of social and cultural change? *What do you think?*

sports. If a person reaches a position of power in a sport organization, the opportunities to make and influence changes increase.

To use insider information, access, and power effectively, it helps to be aware of contraints. This is highlighted in the box titled "Athletes as Change Agents."

2. *Joining "opposition" groups.*

History shows that the future often is influenced by groups that oppose the status quo and promote policies and programs that alter the direction of change. For example, opposition groups in recent years have effectively lobbied against using public funds to build costly stadiums that primarily serve the interests of privileged people (Delaney and Eckstein, 2003, 2007). Opposition groups have been less effective in opposing plans to host mega-events, such as the Olympics, but these groups will be more effective in the future as research continues to document the debts and other problems that come with hosting such events.

Local groups opposing specific policies and programs have often been effective, whether it be to promote gender equity, build a new skatepark or disc golf course, or reserve public spaces for pleasure and participation sports. As these groups

alter the sport landscape they help create more a more diverse and representative future for sports.

3. *Creating new or alternative sports.*

Altering the future of sports also occurs when people reject dominant power and performance sports and develop new sports grounded in alternative ideas about what sports should be. This is not easy to do because resources are seldom available to entrepreneurs who are not in the mainstream of sports programs and organizations. However, working from this outsider vantage point can be effective when it influences others to consider and participate in alternatives to existing sport forms. Former Olympian and current health and physical educator Bruce Kidd says that creating "alternatives to the commercial sport culture [is] .. an uphill fight," but he also notes that efforts to create these alternatives "have a long, rich, and proud history" (1997, p. 270).

When new or alternative sports are successfully created, they become targets of commercial interests that want to convert them into commodified forms of power and performance sports. Resisting this co-optation is difficult and not always successful, but the process of creating new and alternative sports is needed to inspire creative visions of the future of sports.

4. *Working outside sports*

Creating the future of sports from outside vantage points requires foresight and a good grasp of how social change occurs. For example, when feminists created the women's movement during the 1960s it provided an opportunity for activists, educators, and progressive politicians to draft Title IX as part of the Education Amendments to the Civil Rights Restoration Act. When this act became law in 1972 it changed the legal context in which sports were organized, sponsored, and played and eventually altered the future of sports in dramatic ways.

Similarly, people working in military veterans' organizations today may effectively change how "disabilities" are defined in U.S. culture and, in the process, encourage others to draft laws and create programs that provide equal opportunities for people with disabilities to play sports as others do. In this sense, anyone who works to eliminate social injustice and create opportunities for new voices to be expressed and taken seriously in social worlds also lays the groundwork for creating more humane and accessible sports in the future.

Regardless of one's vantage point, being an effective agent of change always requires the following qualities:

1. Visions of what sports and social life *could* and *should* be like
2. Willingness to work hard on the strategies needed to turn visions into realities
3. Political abilities to rally the resources that make strategies effective

Bringing these qualities together requires individual and collective efforts. But if we don't make these efforts, the meaning, purpose, and organization of sports will be created for us by others, and the future is unlikely to match our visions of what sports could and should be.

> I started Democracy Matters to help students fight for progressive change by standing up to big money interests corrupting our democracy. I hope you will join me. —Adonal Foyle, NBA player, www.democracymatters.org, 2005

summary

ARE WE AGENTS OF CHANGE?

Sports are social constructions. This means that we play a role in making them what they are today and what they will be in the future. We can play this role actively by envisioning what we'd like sports to be and then working to make them so, or we can play it passively by doing nothing and allowing others to create sports as they'd like them to be.

This chapter emphasized that the meaning, purpose, and organization of sports will become increasingly diverse in the future, and that power and performance sports will remain dominant because they continue to attract wealthy and powerful sponsors. Pleasure and participation sports will grow in connection with demographic trends and ideological changes, but they will not attract as much sponsorship as is enjoyed by sports organized around the power and performance model.

Sports at all levels of participation will be sites for struggles over who should play and how sports should be organized. Current trends suggest that pleasure and participation sports are supported by concerns about health and fitness, the participation preferences of older people whose influence will increase in the future, the values and experiences brought to sports by women, and groups seeking alternative sports.

In all sport spheres, trends are influenced by many factors, including technology, telecommunications and electronic media, values supportive of organization and rationalization, a cultural emphasis on commercialism and consumption, and the changing demographic composition of communities and societies.

Creating the sports of the future is a process that involves identifying goals, using theories to plan strategies, and assessing what can be done from the vantage point that one occupies relative to sports in society. Goals can be growth, reform, or transformation. Most people, especially those who are advantaged by the status quo, focus on the conservative goal of growth because they want to expand and strengthen sports as they are currently played and organized. Some people focus on the goal of reform because they want more people to enjoy the benefits that sports have to offer. And a few people focus on the radical goal of transformation because they think that sports should be "reconstructed" with new meaning and purpose.

Strategies for creating futures can utilize cultural, interactionist, and structural theories, regardless of goals. Cultural theories emphasize that the future of sports is linked with the symbols, values, norms, vocabularies, beliefs, and ideologies that people use as they make sense of and give meaning to sports and sport experiences. Interactionist theories emphasize that the future of sports is linked with socialization processes, self-concepts, identities, and the influence of peers and significant others. Structural theories emphasize that the future of sports is linked with the organization of the larger context in which sports exist.

Social theories can support conservative, reformist, or radical goals. Scholars in the sociology of sport tend to be reformist and occasionally radical rather than conservative, and they often focus on making sports more democratic, accessible, inclusive, and humane.

The effectiveness of people who want to be agents of change requires a clear understanding of the vantage point they occupy in the relationship between sports and society. The four major vantage points are in (a) sport organizations, (b) opposition groups, (c) groups that create new and alternative sport forms, and (d) groups working to transform the larger society in ways that will change sports.

Regardless of one's vantage point, effectively creating the future depends on having a clear vision of what sports could and should be in the future, a willingness to work hard to turn visions into realities, and the political abilities to initiate and maintain strategies that produce results. Unless we work to create the sports we want in the future, sports will represent the interests of those who want us to play on their terms and for their purposes.

This leaves us with an interesting choice: we can be consumers who accept sports as they are, or we can be citizens who actively engage in the process of making the world and sports humane and sustainable. The goal of this book is to provide a foundation for informed and active citizenship.

WEBSITE RESOURCES

Note: Websites often change. The following URLs were current when this book was printed. Please check our website (www.mhhe.com/coakley10e) for updates and additions.

www.mhhe.com/coakley10e Click on Chapter 16 to read predictions about what happens to the control and organization of sports when more people play them; also provides information on the impact of technology on sports and athletes.

www.AforBW.org The site of Athletes for a Better World, an organization with a mission of changing the culture of sport by strengthening the character of athletes and providing them with a Code for Living that will enhance the integrity of sports activities; teamwork and civic responsibility are primary values in the code.

www.ast.com/ Site of the Dew Tour, now called the Action Sports Tour; it now has the same "corporate feel" as mlb.com and nfl.com.

www.boomboomhuckjam.com/ Site for Tony Hawk's (and Mat Hoffman's) tour that ideally provides skaters and BMX bikers the opportunities to display skills in a format of their own choosing rather than a competitive format established by media companies or outside organizations; but corporate sponsors now have a major stake in the Boom Boom HuckJam tour.

www.bmxweb.com/ Links to hundreds of sites used by BMX and freestyle riders; illustrates how athletes in alternative/action sports form networks worldwide.

www.educatingforjustice.org This site was originally the home of the Olympic Living Wage Project, part of an international effort to make athletes in the 2000 Olympic Games in Sydney aware of labor abuses related to the production of their equipment and uniforms; today it is a nonprofit organization that presents justice-oriented programming and content for educational purposes and to raise awareness that sparks social change.

www.gaygames.com The site of the Federation of Gay Games; provides links to coverage of each games since 1982, including the most recent Gay Games VII in Chicago (2006) and what's in store for 2010 in Cologne, Germany.

www.hotrails.com/ Site for aggressive in-line skaters; provides a "feel" for the sport, who participates, and the norms underlying participation; note gender, racial/ethnic, and social-class patterns among participants because they provide information about the social dynamics of certain alternative sports as they develop.

www.ncasports.org/home.htm The National Consortium for Academics and Sports (NCAS) is an organization of colleges, universities, and individuals dedicated to creating a better society by focusing on educational attainment and using the power and appeal of sport to bring about positive social change; the program provides tuition to former athletes without degrees in exchange for their involvement in service.

www.paralympic.org The official website of the International Paralympic Committee.

www.pdga.com/ and http://www.discgolfassoc.com/ Disc golf "official" sites illustrating how quickly an alternative sport can be institutionalized and inserted into a power and performance format. However, most participants emphasize the elements of pleasure and participation when they play.

http://scienceofsport.blogspot.com/ An informative blog maintained by two South African exercise physiologists who discuss current issues in sports and sport performance from a physical science and technology perspective; they often provide useful information for social scientists concerned with performance issues and the future of sports.

www.space.com/missionlaunches/ 080425-space-station-sports.html The Future of Space Sports describes the games that astronauts are developing as they exercise in zero gravity.

www.sportinsociety.org Sport in Society, a center at Northeastern University (Boston), uses sports as a basis for civic actions designed to promote change and social justice; provides links to the center's programs—Athletes in Service to America, Disability in Sport, Mentors in Violence Prevention (MVP) Program, Project TEAMWORK, Urban Youth Sports—all focused on making progressive changes in communities and society, while involving sports and athletes in the process.

www.sportsphilanthropyproject.com/ This is the site of the Sports Philanthropy Project; provides services to professional sports teams to set up foundations in their communities to enhance social development and community programs.

www.un.org/Depts/dhl/resguide/r58.htm This site has links to two UN Resolutions: 'Building a Peaceful and Better World Through Sport and the Olympic Ideal" (A/RES/58/6) and "Sport as a Means to Promote Education, Health, Development and Peace" (A/RES/58/5).

www.un.org/sport2005/ The site of the UN International Year for Sport and Physical Education 2005; also provides a link to a Sport for Development and Peace report entitled "Sport as a Tool for Development and Peace: Towards Achieving the United Nations Millennium Development Goals" (33 pages).

REFERENCES

AAA. 1998. Statement on "Race." Washington, DC: American Anthropological Association. Online: www.aaanet.org/stmts/racepp.htm (retrieved June 2005).

Abernathy, Liz, and Chris Bleakley. 2007. Strategies to prevent injuries in adolescent sport: A systematic review. *British Journal of Sport Medicine* 41: 627–638.

Acosta, R. Vivian. 1999. Hispanic women in sport. *Journal of Physical Education, Recreation and Dance* 70, 4: 44–46.

Acosta, R. Vivian, and Linda Jean Carpenter. 2004. Women in intercollegiate sport: A longitudinal, national study twenty-seven year update, 1977–2004. Online: http://webpages.charter.net/womeninsport/.

Adams, Mary Louise. 2006. The game of whose lives? Gender, race and entitlement in Canada's 'national' game. In David Whitson and Richard Gruneau, eds., *Artificial ice: Hockey, culture, and commerce* (pp. 71–84). Peterborough, Ontario: Broadview Press.

Adbusters. 2004. #3: The battle for media carta. *Adbusters: Journal of the Mental Environment* 51 (Jan/Feb): (no page numbers)

Adelson, Eric. 2002. Hot to trot. *ESPN The Magazine* (June 24): 74–76.

Adelson, Eric. 2003. Driven. *ESPN The Magazine* (December 22): 70–71.

Adelson, Eric. 2006. Michelle Wie can change the world. *ESPN The Magazine* 9.03 (February 13): 65–66.

Adler, Patricia A., and Peter Adler. 1991. *Backboards and blackboards: College athletes and role engulfment.* New York: Columbia University Press.

Adler, Patricia A., and Peter Adler. 1998. *Peer power: Preadolescent culture and identity.* New Brunswick, NJ: Rutgers University Press.

Adler, Patricia A., and Peter Adler. 1999. College athletes in high-profile media sports: The consequences of glory. In Jay Coakley and Peter Donnelly, eds., *Inside Sports* (pp. 162–170). London: Routledge.

Adler, Patricia A., and Peter Adler. 2003. The promise and pitfalls of going into the field. *Contexts* 2, 2: 41–47.

Agovino, Michael J. 2007. Losses, and the losing losers who hate them. *The New York Times* (June 18). Online: http://select.nytimes.com/mem/tnt.html?emc=tnt&tntget=2006/06/18/weekinreview/18agovino.html.

Albert, Edward. 2004. Normalizing risk in the sport of cycling. In Kevin Young, ed., *Sporting bodies, damaged selves: Sociological studies of sports-related injury* (pp. 181–194). Amsterdam: Elsevier.

Alcindor, Habiba. 2008. Did you know that *The Nation* has a sportswriter? *The Nation Associate* 28, 1: 5–9.

Alesia, Mark. 2004. Lawmaker to the NCAA: Get tougher or be taxed. *Indianapolis Star* (May 19). Online: www.indystar.com/articles/0/147733-6820-036.html.

Alesia, Mark. 2005. Off court, schools lacking color: Most players are black, but few male students are. *Indianapolis Star* (March 17): 1A

Alesia, Mark. 2006a. Colleges play, public pays $1 billion: That's how much university general funds and students contributed to athletic departments last year. *Indianapolis Star* (March 30). Online: www.indystar.com/apps/pbcs.dll/article?AID=/20060330/SPORTS/603300460.

Alesia, Mark. 2006b. Tourney money fuels pay-to-play debate: Fewer than 1% of athletes help make more than 90% of the NCAA's money. *Indianapolis Star* (April 1). Online: www.indystar.com/apps/pbcs.dll/article?AID=/20060401/SPORTS/604010509.

Alesia, Mark, 2008. 'Special' treatment for athletes—little accountability: Only schools know how far they bend admission requirements and how many such students graduate. *Indianapolis Star* (September 7): http://www.indystar.com/ apps/pbcs.dll/article?AID=/20080907/ SPORTS/809070375

Algazeera. 2006. Glory for Al Ghasara. *Algazeera.net* (December 11). Online: http://english.aljazeera .net/NR/exeres/A3E2CB0F-A9CA-4327- A07B-4675C98E13C7.htm.

Allison, Lincoln. 2000. Sport and nationalism. In Jay Coakley and Eric Dunning, eds., *Handbook of sports studies* (pp. 344–355). London: Sage.

Allison, Lincoln. 2004. *The global politics of sport: The role of global institutions in sport.* London/New York: Routledge.

AMA (J. Stephenson). 1996. Female Olympians' sex tests outmoded. *Journal of the American Medical Association* 276, 3 (July 17): 177–178.

American Academy of Pediatrics. 2000. Intensive training and sports specialization in young athletes. (RE9906). *Pediatrics* 106, 01: 154–157. Online: http://www.aap.org/policy/RE9906.html.

Anderson, Eric. 2000. *Trailblazing: America's first openly gay track coach.* Hollywood, CA: Alyson.

Anderson, Eric. 2002. Gays in sport: Contesting hegemonic masculinity in a homophobic environment. *Gender and Society* 16, 6: 860–877.

Anderson, Eric. 2004. Exploitation of the scholarship athlete. Unpublished manuscript.

Anderson, Eric. 2005. *In the game: Gay athletes and the cult of masculinity.* Albany: State University of New York Press.

Anderson, Jason. 2005. Most dangerous game. Online: www.eye.net/eye/issue/issue_04.21.05/ film/murderball.html (retrieved November 2005).

Anderson, Kristen L. 1999. Snowboarding: The construction of gender in an emerging sport. *Journal of Sport and Social Issues* 23, 1: 55–79.

Andrews, David L., ed. 1996a. Deconstructing Michael Jordan: Reconstructing postindustrial America. *Sociology of Sport Journal* 13, 4. Special issue.

Andrews, David L. 1996b. The fact(s) of Michael Jordan's blackness: Excavating a floating racial signifier. *Sociology of Sport Journal* 13, 2: 125–158.

Andrews, David L., ed. 2001a. *Michael Jordan, Inc.: Corporate sport, media culture, and late modern America.* Albany, NY: State University of New York Press.

Andrews, David L. 2001b. Sport. In R. Maxwell, ed., *Culture works: The political economy of culture*

(pp. 131–162). Minneapolis: University of Minnesota Press.

Andrews, David L. 2007. Sport as spectacle. In George Ritzer, ed., *Encyclopedia of sociology* (pp. 4702–4704). London/New York: Blackwell.

Andrews, David L., and Steven J. Jackson. 2001. *Sport stars: The cultural politics of sporting celebrity.* London/New York: Routledge.

Andrews, David L., and Michael Silk. 1999. Football consumption communities, trans-national advertising, and spatial transformation. Paper presented at the annual conference of the North American Society for the Sociology of Sport, Cleveland, OH (November).

Angelini, James R. 2008. How did sport make you feel? Looking at the three dimensions of emotion through a gender lens. *Sex Roles: A Journal of Research* 58, 1–2: 127–135.

Anonymous. 1999. Confessions of a cheater. *ESPN The Magazine* (November 1): 80–82.

AP (Associated Press). 2000. Fox relishes his role as Lakers' enforcer. *Denver Post* (June 20): C10.

Applebome, Peter. 1999. Alma maters: Two words behind the massacre. Online: www.lieye.com/ articles/littletonli/nytimes.shtml.

Archer, Louise, Sumi Hollingworth, and Anna Halsall. 2007. 'University's not for me — I'm a Nike person': Urban, working-class young people's negotiations of 'style,' identity and educational engagement. *Sociology* 41, 2: 219–237.

Armstrong, Gary. 1998. *Football hooligans: Knowing the score.* Oxford: Berg.

Armstrong, Gary. 2007. Football hooliganism. In George Ritzer, ed., *Encyclopedia of sociology* (pp. 1767–1769). London/New York: Blackwell.

Armstrong, Ken, and Nick Perry. 2008a. Convicted of assault and accused of rape, star player received raft of second chances. *Seattle Times* (January 31). Online: http://seattletimes.nwsource.com/html/ localnews/2004147460_rbstevens270.html.

Armstrong, Ken, and Nick Perry. 2008b. Key UW linebacker played entire season after his bloody print was tied to shooting. *Seattle Times* (January 30). Online: http://seattletimes.nwsource.com/ html/localnews/2004148820_rbpharms280.html.

Armstrong, Ken, and Nick Perry. 2008c. To Huskies fans a tragic hero, to the courts a wanted felon. *Seattle Times* (January 30). Online: http://seattletimes.nwsource.com/html/ localnews/2004150796_rbwilliams281.html.

Arsenault, Amelia, and Manuel Castells. 2008. Switching power: Rupert Murdoch and the global business of media politics: A sociological analysis. *International Sociology* 23, 4: 488–513.

Ashe, Arthur. 1993. *A hard road to glory*. 3 vols. New York: Amistad.

Assael, Shaun. 2003. Cut and run. *ESPN The Magazine* (July 70): 40–49.

Assael, Shaun. 2005. Shape shifter. *ESPN The Magazine* (May 90): 88–96.

Assael, Shaun. 2007a. Business as usual. *ESPN The Magazine* 10.06 (March 26): 99–100.

Assael, Shaun. 2007b. Made in China. *ESPN The Magazine* 10.20 (October 18): 90–95.

Assael, Shaun. 2007c. *Steroid nation: Juiced home run totals, anti-aging miracles, and a Hercules in every high school: The secret history of America's true drug addiction*. New York: ESPN Books.

Associated Press, 2007. Payne brings old set of ideals as new Augusta chairman. Online: http://www.pga.com/masters/2007/news/masters_t2021606.html (retrieved April 1, 2008).

Atencio, Matthew, and Jan Wright. 2008. "We be killin' them": Hierarchies of black masculinity in urban basketball spaces. *Sociology of Sport Journal* 25, 2: 263–280.

Atkinson, Michael. 2002. Fifty million viewers can't be wrong: Professional wrestling, sports-entertainment, and mimesis. *Sociology of Sport Journal* 19, 1: 47–66.

Atkinson, Michael. 2007a. Playing with fire: Masculinity, health, and sports supplements. *Sociology of Sport Journal* 24, 2: 165–186.

Atkinson, Michael. 2007b. Virtual sports. In George Ritzer, ed., *The Blackwell Encyclopedia of Sociology* (pp. 5208–5211). London: Blackwell Publishing/Blackwell Reference.

Atkinson, Michael, and Kevin Young. 2008. *Deviance and social control in sport*. Champaign, IL: Human Kinetics.

Atlanta Journal/Constitution. 1996. America's Olympic teams are increasingly marked by less diversity, more elitism (October 1): H7. Special report.

Avery, Derek, R., Scott Tonidandel, and McKensy G. Phillips. 2008. Similarity on sports sidelines: How mentor-protégé sex similarity affects mentoring. *Sex Roles: A Journal of Research* 58, 1–2: 72–80

Axthelm, Pete. 1970. *The city game*. New York: Harper and Row.

Azzarito, L., and M. Solmon. 2006a. A feminist poststructuralist view on student bodies in physical education: Sites of compliance, resistance, and transformation. *Journal of Teaching in Physical Education* 25 (April): 200–225.

Azzarito, L., and M. Solmon. 2006b. A poststructural analysis of high school students' gender and racialized bodily meanings. *Journal of Teaching in Physical Education* 25 (January): 75–98.

Azzarito, L., M. Solmon, and L. Harrison. 2006c. "If I had a choice I would." A feminist poststructuralist perspective on girls in physical education. *Research Quarterly for Exercise and Sport* 77 (June): 222–239.

Bacon, Victoria L., and Pamela J. Russell. 2004. Addiction and the college athlete: The Multiple Addictive Behaviors Questionnaire (MABQ) with college athletes. *The Sport Journal* 7, 2. Online: www.thesportjournal.org/2004Journal/Vol7-No2/.

Baerg, Andrew. 2007. Fight Night Round 2: Mediating the body and digital boxing. *Sociology of Sport Journal* 24, 3: 325–345.

Bailey, Richard, I. Wellard, and H. Dismore. 2004. *Girls' participation in physical activities and sports: Benefits, patterns, influences and ways forward*. United Kingdom: Canterbury Christ Church University College Centre for Physical Education and Sport Research. Online: www.icsspe.org/portal/download/Girls.pdf?PHPSESSID=002ba9b543c789519ae82d8eaf0862b8.

Bairner, Alan. 2001. *Sport, nationalism, and globalization: European and North American perspectives*. Albany: State University of New York Press.

Bairner, Alan, ed. 2005. *Sport and the Irish: Histories, identities, issues*. Dublin: University College Dublin Press.

Bairner, Alan. 2007. Back to basics: Class, social theory, and sport. *Sociology of Sport Journal* 24, 1: 20–36.

Baker, Joseph, and Jean Côté. 2006. Shifting training requirements during athlete development: The relationship among deliberate practice, deliberate play and other sport involvement in the acquisition of sport expertise. In D. Hackfort and G. Tenenbaum, eds., *Essential processes for attaining peak performance* (pp. 93–110). Germany: Meyer and Meyer.

Baker, William J. 1988. *Sports in the Western world.* Urbana: University of Illinois Press.

Baker, William J. 2000. *If Christ came to the Olympics.* Sydney, Australia: University of New South Wales Press, Ltd.

Baker, William J. 2007. *Playing with God: Religion and modern sport.* Cambridge, MA: Harvard University Press.

Bale, John, and Mette Christensen, eds. 2004. *Post-Olympism: Questioning sport in the twenty-first century.* Oxford/New York: Berg.

Bale, John, and Mike Cronin, eds. 2003. *Sport and postcolonialism.* Oxford/New York: Berg.

Bale, John, and Joseph Maguire, eds. 1994. *The global sports arena: Athletic talent migration in an interdependent world.* London: Frank Cass.

Bale, John, and Patricia Vertinsky, eds. 2004. *Sites of sport: Space, place and experience.* New York/London: Routledge.

Ballard, Chris. 2004. Fantasy world. *Sports Illustrated* (June 21): 80–89.

Ballard, Chris. 2006. Writing up a storm. *Sports Illustrated* 104, 13 (March 27): 58–65.

Ballard, Steve. 1996. Broken back doesn't stall Indy winner. *USA Today* (May 28): A1.

Bandow, Doug. 2003. *Surprise: Stadiums don't pay after all!* Cato Institute Report (October 19). Washington, DC: Cato Institute.

Banet-Weiser, Sarah. 1999. Hoop dreams: Professional basketball and the politics of race and gender. *Journal of Sport and Social Issues* 23, 4: 403–420.

Barber, Bonnie L., Jacquelynne S. Eccles, and M. R. Stone. 2001. Whatever happened to the jock, the brain, and the princess? Young adult pathways linked to adolescent activity involvement and social identity. *Journal of Adolescent Research* 16, 5: 429–455.

Barkley, Charles. 2006. *Who's afraid of a large black man? Race, power, fame, identity, and why everyone should read my book.* New York: Riverhead Freestyle.

Barnes, Simon. 2006. Football destined to remain the last bastion of homophobia—that's the straight, naked truth. *London Times* (October 6). Online: www.timesonline.co.uk/article/0,,8303-2391153,00.html.

Barry, Patrick. 2008. Finding the golden genes. *Science News* 174, 3 (August 2). Online: http://www.sciencenews.org/view/feature/id/34225/title/Finding_the_Golden_Genes.

Bartimole, Roldo. 1999. The city and the stadia (panel). Presentation at the annual conference of the North American Society for the Sociology of Sport, Cleveland, OH (November).

Bartoluci, Sunćica, and Benjamin Perasović. 2008. National identity and sport—the example of Croatia. Paper presented at the 5th Conference of the European Association for Sociology of Sport (Bled, Slovenia, May 23).

Bast, Joseph L. 1998. *Sports stadium madness: Why it started, how to stop it.* Heartland Policy Study, No. 85. Chicago: Heartland Institute.

BBC Sport Academy. 2005. Rugby League—Disability. Online: http://news.bbc.co.uk/sportacademy/hi/sa/rugby_league/disability/newsid_4019000/4019549.stm (retrieved November 2005).

Beal, Becky. 1995. Disqualifying the official: An exploration of social resistance through the subculture of skateboarding. *Sociology of Sport Journal* 12, 3: 252–267.

Beal, Becky, and Lisa Weidman. 2003. Authenticity in the skateboarding world. In Robert E. Rinehart and Synthia Sydnor, eds., *To the extreme: Alternative sports, inside and out* (pp. 337–352). Albany: State University of New York Press.

Beals, Katherine A. 2000. Subclinical eating disorders in female athletes. *Journal of Physical Education, Recreation and Dance* 71, 7: 3–29.

Beals, Katherine A., and Amanda K. Hill. 2006. The prevalence of disordered eating, menstrual dysfunction, and low bone mineral density among US collegiate athletes. *International Journal of Sport Nutrition and Exercise Metabolism* 16, 1: 1–23.

Bechtel, Mark, and Stephen Cannella. 2005. Scorecard: Cable ready. *Sports Illustrated* (August 29): 16–17.

Becker, Debbie, 1996. Nothstein: "I enjoy the pain." *USA Today* (July 24): 14E, 17E.

Becker, Debbie. 1999. Leaping past the pain. *USA Today* (April 1): 1E, 4E.

Becker, Howard S., and Michael M. McCall. 1993. *Symbolic interaction and cultural studies.* Chicago: University of Chicago Press.

Beiruty, Hikmat. 2002. Muslim women in sport. *Nida'ul Islam Magazine.* Online: www.islamzine .com/women/women-sports.html (retrieved October 15, 2005).

Bell, Christopher. 2008. *Bigger, stronger, faster: The side effects of being American.* Magnolia Pictures and BSF Films. Online: http:// biggerstrongerfastermovie.com/.

Bell, Jack. 2008. Making it to the major league of fantasy sports. *The New York Times* (April 5). Online: www.nytimes.com/2008/04/05/ technology/05interview-web.html.

Bell, Wendell. 1997. *Foundations of futures studies.* 2 vols. New Brunswick, NJ: Transaction.

Bell, Wendell, and James Mau. 1971. Images of the future: Theory and research. In W. Bell and J. Mau, eds., *The sociology of the future* (pp. 6–44). New York: Russell Sage Foundation.

Belson, Matthew. 2002. Assistive technology and sports. In Artemis A. W. Joukowsky III and Larry Rothstein, eds., *Raising the bar* (pp. 124–129). New York: Umbrage Editions.

Benedict, Jeff. 1997. *Public heroes, private felons: Athletes and crimes against women.* Boston: Northeastern University Press.

Benedict, Jeff. 1998. *Athletes and acquaintance rape.* Thousand Oaks, CA: Sage.

Benedict, Jeff. 2004. *Out of bounds: Inside the NBA's culture of rape, violence, and crime.* New York: HarperCollins.

Benedict, Jeff, and Don Yaeger. 1998. *Pros and cons: The criminals who play in the NFL.* New York: Warner Books.

Benford, Robert D. 2007. The college sports reform movement: Reframing the "edutainment" industry. *The Sociological Quarterly* 48, 1: 1–28.

Ben-Porat, Guy, and Amir Ben-Porat. 2004. (Un)bounded soccer: Globalization and localization of the game in Israel. *International Review for the Sociology of Sport* 39, 4: 421–436.

Berger, Jody. 2002. Pain game. *Rocky Mountain News* (February 23): 6S.

Berger, Jody. 2004. Straight shooter. *Denver Post* (January 24): 1B.

Berkowitz, Steve. 2008. Few athletics programs in black; most need aid. *USA Today* (May 16): 12C. Online: http://www.usatoday.com/printedition/ sports/20080516/c12schools16.art.htm

Berlage, Gai Ingham. 1994. *Women in baseball: The forgotten history.* Westport, CT: Praeger Publishers.

Bernstein, Alina, and Neil Blain, eds. 2003. *Sport, media, culture: Global and local dimensions.* London: Frank Cass.

Bernstein, Viv. 2007. Simulated racing gives a real advantage to drivers. *The New York Times* (March 4): Sports 3; online, www.nytimes .com/2007/03/04/sports/othersports/ 04nascar.html.

Berra, Lindsey. 2005. This is how they roll. *ESPN The Magazine* (December 5): 104–111.

Berry, Donald A. 2008. The science of doping. *Nature* 454 (August 7): 692–693.

Bhana, Deevia. 2008. 'Six packs and big muscles, and stuff like that': Primary school-aged South African boys, black and white, on sport. *British Journal of Sociology of Education* 29, 1: 3–14.

Bick, Julie. 2006. Low-cost workouts for young minds. *The New York Times* (April 2). Online: http://select.nytimes.com/mem/tnt.html?_r=1 &emc=tnt&tntget=2006/04/02/business/ yourmoney/02mate.html.

Bick, Julie. 2007. Looking for an edge? Private coaching, by the hour. *The New York Times* (February 25). Online: www.nytimes.com/2007/ 02/25/business/yourmoney/25coach.html.

Bilger, Burkhard. 2004. The height gap. *New Yorker* (April 5): 38–45.

Billings, Andrew C. 2007. *Olympic media: Inside the biggest show on television.* New York: Routledge.

Bishop, Ronald. 2003. Missing in action: Feature coverage of women's sports in *Sports Illustrated. Journal of Sport and Social Issues* 27, 2: 184–194.

Bissinger, H. G. 1990. *Friday night lights.* Reading, MA: Addison-Wesley.

Bissinger, H. G. "Buzz." 2004. Innocents Afield. *The New York Times* (December 16): www.nytimes. com/2004/12/16/opinion/16bissinger_.html.

Bjerklie, David, and Alice Park. 2004. How doctors help the dopers. *Time* (August 16): 58–62.

Blackshaw, Tony, and Tim Crabbe. 2004. *New perspectives on sport and 'deviance': Consumption, performativity and social control.* London/New York: Routledge.

Blades, Nicole. 2005. Lucia Rijker. *ESPN The Magazine* (June 6): 96–97.

Blain, Neil, Raymond Boyle, and Hugh O'Donnell. 1993. *Sport and national identity in the European media*. Leicester, England: Leicester University Press.

Blake, Andrew. 1996. *The body language: The meaning of modern sport*. London: Lawrence and Wisehart.

Blauvelt, Harry. 2003. Stephenson says Asian players hurt LPGA tour. *USA Today* (October 10): 13C.

Blinde, Elaine M., Diane E. Taub, and Lingling Han. 1994. Sport as a site for women's group and societal empowerment: Perspectives from the college athlete. *Sociology of Sport Journal* 11, 1: 51–59.

Block, Martin E. 1995. Americans with Disability Act: Its impact on youth sports. *Journal of Health, Physical Education, Recreation and Dance* 66, 1: 28–32.

Bloom, Benjamin S. 1985. *Developing Talent in Young People*. New York: Ballantine Books.

Bloom, John. 2000. *To show what an Indian can do: Sports at Native American boarding schools*. Minneapolis: University of Minnesota Press.

Bloom, Marc. 1998. Slower times at American high schools. *The New York Times* (January 29): C27.

Blue, Laura. 2008. Do clean athletes have a chance? *Time* (August 20). Online: http://www.time.com/time/health/article/0,8599,1834144,00.htmlLoland.

Blumenthal, Karen. 2005. *Let me play: The story of Title IX: The law that changed the future of girls in America*. New York: Atheneum.

Blumenthal, Ralph. 2004. Texas tough, in lipstick, fishnet and skates. *The New York Times*, section 1 (August 1): 14.

Blumstein, Alfred, and Jeff Benedict. 1999. Criminal violence of NFL players compared to the general population. *Chance* 12, 3: 12–15.

Boland, Robert. 2008. Athletes behaving badly: A problem solved by degrees? School of Continuing and Professional Studies. NYU Preston Robert Tisch Center for Hospitality, Tourism, and Sports Management. Online: http://www.scps.nyu.edu/about-scps/scps-faculty/robert-boland.html (retrieved 9/12/08).

Bonde, H. 2006. *Gymnastics and politics. Niels Bukh and male aesthetics*. Copenhagen: Museum Tusculanum Press

Bonilla-Silva, Eduardo. 2001. White supremacy and racism in the post-civil rights era. Boulder, CO: Lynne Rienner.

Bonilla-Silva, Eduardo. 2003. *Racism without racists: Color-blind racism and the persistence of racial inequality in the United States*. Lanham, MD: Rowman & Littlefield.

Booth, Douglas, and John Loy. 1999. Sport, status and style. *Sport History Review* 30: 1–26.

Borden, Iain. 2001. *Skateboarding, space and the city: Architecture and the body*. Oxford, UK: Berg.

Botstein, Leon. 1997. *Jefferson's children: Education and the promise of American culture*. New York: Doubleday.

Bourdieu, Pierre. 1986a. *Distinction: A social critique of the judgment of taste*. London: Routledge.

Bourdieu, Pierre. 1986b. The forms of capital. In J. G. Richards, ed., *Handbook of Theory and Research for the Sociology of Education* (pp. 242–258). New York: Greenwood Press.

Bourdieu, Pierre. 1998. The essence of neoliberalism (trans. by Jeremy J. Shapiro). *Le Monde diplomatique* (December). Online: http://mondediplo.com/1998/12/08bourdieu.

Bowden, Mark. 2008. Sacks, lies and videotape. *The New York Times* (May 18). Online: http://www.nytimes.com/2008/05/18/opinion/18bowden.html.

Bowen, William G., and Martin A. Kurzweil, Eugene M. Tobin, and Suzanne C. Pichler. 2005. *Equity and excellence in American higher education*. Charlottesville, VA: University Press of Virginia.

Bowen, William G., and Sarah Levine. 2003. *Reclaiming the game: College sports and educational values*. Princeton, NJ: Princeton University Press.

Boylan, Jennifer Finney. 2008. The XY games. *The New York Times* (August 3). Online: http://www.nytimes.com/2008/08/03/opinion/03boylan.html.

Boyle, Robert H. 1970. Oral Roberts: Small but OH MY. *Sports Illustrated* (November 30): 64–66.

Brackenridge, Celia. 2001. *Spoilsports: Understanding and preventing sexual exploitation in sport*. London: Routledge.

Brackenridge, Celia, and Kari Fasting, eds. 2003 *Sexual harassment and abuse in sport: International research and policy perspectives*. London: Whiting and Birch. (See also *Journal of Sexual Aggression* 8, 2 [2002].)

Brackin, Dennis. 2008. U freshmen post lowest reported ACTs in conference. *Minneapolis Star Tribune* (August 26): http://www.startribune.com/sports/gophers/27512199.html

Braddock, Jomills Henry, et al. 1991. Bouncing back: Sports and academic resilience among African-American males. *Education and Urban Society* 24, 1: 113–131.

Braddock, Jomills Henry, Jan Sokol-Katz, Anthony Greene, and Lorrine Basinger-Fleischman. 2005. Uneven playing fields: State variations in boys' and girls' access to and participation in high school interscholastic sports. *Sociological Spectrum* 25, 2: 231–250.

Bradsher, Keith. 2007. New push into China by N.B.A. *The New York Times* (September 19). Online: http://www.nytimes.com/2007/09/19/business/worldbusiness/19hoops.html.

Brady, Erik. 1996. Some legislators say Baltimore's money misspent. *USA Today* (September 6): 19C.

Brady, Erik. 2008. Pay gap could mean schools are in violation. *USA Today* (May 23): 10C.

Brady, Erik, and Ray Glier, 2004. No free ride: Many students pay to play sports. *USA Today* (July 30): 14C.

Brady, Erik, and D. Howlett. 1996. Ballpark construction booming. *USA Today* (September 6): 13C–21C.

Brady, Erik, and MaryJo Sylwester. 2004. Kentucky school maintains edge with fundraising booster groups. *USA Today* (June 17): A4.

Bray, Corey. 2001. *NCAA Research Report 99-05: Academic Characteristics by Income Group of Division I Recruits in the 1997 and 1998 NCAA Initial-Eligibility Clearinghouse.* Indianapolis, IN: National Collegiate Athletic Association. Online: http://www.ncaa.org/library/research/05Series/report_99-05.pdf.

Bredemeier, Brenda Jo Light, Ellen Brooke Carlton, Laura Ann Hills, and Carole Ann Oglesby. 1999. Changers and the changed: Moral aspects of coming out in physical education. *Quest* 51, 4: 418–431.

Brennan, Christine. 1996. *Inside edge: A revealing journey into the secret world of figure skating.* New York. Scribner.

Brennan, Christine. 2002. Augusta sticks with boyish act. *USA Today* (July 11): 3C.

Brennan, Christine. 2008. Sports world spills onto news pages. *USA Today* (May 8): 3C.

Online: http://www.usatoday.com/printedition/sports/20080508/c3chris08.art.htm.

Brenner, Michael, and Gideon Reuveni, eds. 2006. *Emancipation through muscles: Jews and sports in Europe.* Lincoln: University of Nebraska Press.

Bretón, Marcos. 2000. Field of broken dreams: Latinos and baseball. *ColorLines* 3, 1: 13–17.

Bretón, Marcos, and José Luis Villegas. 1999. *Away games: The life and times of a Latin baseball player.* Albuquerque: University of New Mexico Press.

Briggs, Bill. 2002. A heavy burden: Way of life leads to early death for many NFL linemen. *Denver Post* (October 20): 1J, 8J.

Briggs, Bill. 2004. Crowds gone wild. *Denver Post* (November 28): 1B.

Brittain, Ian. 2004. Perceptions of disability and their impact upon involvement in sport for people with disabilities at all levels. *Journal of Sport and Social Issues* 28, 4: 429–452.

Broh, Beckett A. 2002. Linking extracurricular programming to academic achievement: Who benefits and why? *Sociology of Education* 75, 1: 69–95.

Brookes, Rod. 2002. *Representing sport.* New York: Oxford University Press.

Brooks, Dana, and Ronald Althouse. 2000. African American head coaches and administrators: Progress but . . .? In D. D. Brooks and R. C. Althouse, eds., *Racism in college athletics: The African-American athlete's experience* (pp. 85–118). Morgantown, WV: Fitness Information Technology.

Brown, Adam, ed. 1998. *Fanatics! Power, identity and fandom in football.* London/New York: Routledge.

Brown, Bruce Eamon. 2003. *Teaching character through sport: Developing a positive coaching legacy.* Monterey, CA: Coaches Choice. Online: www.coacheschoice.com/.

Brown, Gary T. 2000. Beating the odds. *NCAA News*, extra section (December 18): A1, A4.

Brown, Jeffrey A. 2004. Gender, sexuality, and toughness: The bad girls of action film and comic books. In S. Inness, ed., *Action chicks* (pp. 47–74). New York: Palgrave Macmillan.

Brown, Matthew, Mark Nagell, Chad McEvoy, and Daniel Rascher. 2004. Revenue and wealth maximization in the National Football League: The impact of stadia. *Sport Marketing Quarterly* 13, 4: 227–236.

Brown, Michael F. 2003. *Who owns native culture?* Cambridge, MA: Harvard University Press.

Brown, Michael K., et al., eds. 2005. *Whitewashing race: The myth of a color-blind society.* Berkeley: University of California Press.

Brown, Tony N., James S. Jackson, Kendrick T. Brown, Robert M. Sellers, Shelley Keiper, and Warde J. Manuel. 2003. "There's no race on the playing field": Perceptions of racial discrimination among white and black athletes. *Journal of Sport and Social Issues* 27, 2: 162–183.

Brownell, Susan. 1995. *Training the body for China: Sports in the moral order of the People's Republic.* Chicago: University of Chicago Press.

Brownell, Susan. 2008. *Beijing's games: What the Olympics mean to China.* Lanham, MD: Rowman & Littlefield.

Bruce, Toni. 2004. Marking the boundaries of the 'normal' in televised sports: the play-by-play of race. *Media, Culture and Society* 26, 6: 861–879.

Bruce, Toni. 2007. Media and sport. In George Ritzer, ed., *The Blackwell Encyclopedia of Sociology* (pp. 2916–2921). London: Blackwell Publishing and Blackwell Reference Online.

Bruening, Jennifer E. 2004. Coaching difference: A case study of four African American female student-athletes. *Journal of Strength and Conditioning Research* 18, 2: 242–251.

Bruening, Jennifer E. 2005. Gender and racial analysis in sport: Are all the women white and all the blacks men? *Quest* 57, 3: 330–349.

Bruening, Jennifer E., et al. 2007. Work-family conflict in coaching ll: Managing role conflict. *Journal of Sport Management* 21, 4: 471–496.

Bruening, Jennifer E., Ketra. L. Armstrong, and Donna L. Pastore. 2005. Listening to the voices: The experiences of African American female student-athletes. *Research Quarterly for Exercise and Sport* 76, 1: 82–100.

Bruening, Jennifer E., and Marlene A. Dixon. 2008. Situating work-family negotiations within a life course perspective: Insights on the gendered experiences of NCAA Division I head coaching mothers. *Sex Roles: A Journal of Research* 58, 1–2: 10–23.

Buffington, Daniel. 2005. Contesting race on Sundays: Making meaning out of the rise in the number of black quarterbacks. *Sociology of Sport Journal* 22, 1: 19–37.

Bull, Chris. 2004. The healer. *ESPN The Magazine* (February 16): 90–95.

Burawoy, Michael. 2004. Public sociologies: Contradictions, dilemmas and possibilities. *Social Forces* 82, 4: 1603–1618.

Burdsey, Daniel. 2006. 'If I ever play football, dad, can i play for England or India?': British Asians, Sport and Diasporic National Identities. *Sociology* 40: 11–28

Burgos, Adrian. 2007. *Playing America's game: Baseball, Latinos, and the color line.* Berkeley: University of California Press.

Burstyn, Varda. 1999. *The rites of men: Manhood, politics, and the culture of sport.* Toronto, Ontario: University of Toronto Press.

Busch, Angela. 2007. Cross country women keep running health risks. *Women's eNews* (January 25). Online: www.womensnews.org/article.cfm/dyn/aid/3044/context/archive (retrieved March 1, 2008).

Buscombe, Richard, Iain Greenlees, Tim Holder, Richard Thelwell, and Matt Rimmer. 2006. Expectancy effects in tennis: The impact of opponents' pre-match non-verbal behaviour on male tennis players. *Journal of Sports Sciences* 24, 12: 1265–1272.

Butler, Judith. 2004. *Undoing gender.* New York: Routledge.

Buysse, Jo Ann M., and Melissa Sheridan Embser-Herbert. 2004. Constructions of gender in sport: An analysis of intercollegiate media guide cover photographs. *Gender and Society* 18, 1: 66–81.

Cagan, Joanna, and Neil deMause. 1998. *Field of schemes: How the great stadium swindle turns public money into private profit.* Monroe, ME: Common Courage Press.

Callahan, Carolyn M. 2008. Response to "Issues of academic support and performance of Division I student-athlete: A case study at the University of Minnesota." *Journal of Intercollegiate Sport* 1, 1: 139–146.

Callahan, L. F. et al. 2002. Osteoarthritis in retired national football league (NFL) players: The role of injuries and playing position. *Arthritis & Rheumatism* 46: S415.

Campbell, Alan. 2008. For their own good: Recruiting children for research. *Childhood* 15, 1: 30–49.

Canavan, Tom. 2003. Mourning risked heart attack if he continued playing. *The Coloradoan* (November 26): C3.

Candaele, Kelly, and Peter Dreier. 2004. Where are the jocks for justice? *The Nation* 278, 25 (June 28). Online: www.thenation.com/doc.mhtml?i=20040 628&s=candaele.

Cannella, Stephen. 2006. Scorecard. *Sports Illustrated* 105, 9 (September 4): 42.

Caplan, Jeremy, and Ta-Nehisi Paul Coates. 2007. Tiger. Jordan. Hawk. Wendel? *Time* (February 01). Online: www.time.com/time/magazine/article/0,9171,1584772,00.html.

Capouya, John. 1986. Jerry Falwell's team. *Sport* 77, 9: 72–81.

Carey, Jack, and Andy Gardiner. 2008a. NCAA settles antitrust lawsuit. *USA Today* (January 30): 1C; online, www.usatoday.com/printedition/sports/20080130/c1story30.art.htm.

Carey, Jack, and Andy Gardiner. 2008b. Settlement gives aid to athletes. *USA Today* (January 30): 1C. Online: www.usatoday.com/printedition/sports/20080130/ncaa30.art.htm.

Carey, Jack, and Andy Gardiner. 2008c. Settlement terms. *USA Today* (January 30): 6C. Online: www.usatoday.com/printedition/sports/20080130/ncaabreak30.art.htm.

Carlson, Deven, Leslie Scott, Michael Planty, and Jennifer Thompson. 2005. *Statistics in brief: What is the status of high school athletes 8 years after their senior year?* Washington, DC: U.S. Department of Education, Institute of Education Sciences, National Center for Educational Statistics (NCES 2005-303; http://nces.ed.gov/pubs2005/2005303.pdf).

Carpenter, Linda Jean, and R. Vivian Acosta. 2005. *Title IX.* Champaign, IL: Human Kinetics.

Carpenter, Linda Jean, and R. Vivian Acosta. 2008. Women in intercollegiate sport, 1977–2008. Online: http://webpages.charter.net/womeninsport/.

Carrington, Ben. 2004. Cosmopolitan Olympism, humanism and the spectacle of race. In John Bale and Mette Christensen, eds., *Post-Olympism: Questioning sport in the twenty-first century* (pp. 81–98). Oxford/New York: Berg.

Carrington, Ben. 2007. Sport and race. In George Ritzer, ed., *The Blackwell encyclopedia of sociology* (pp. 4686–4690). London: Blackwell Publishing

Carrington, Ben, and Ian McDonald, eds. 2001. *"Race," sport, and British society.* New York/London: Routledge.

Carrington, Ben, and John Sugden. 1999. Transnational capitalism and the incorporation of world football. Paper presented at the annual conference of the North American Society for the Sociology of Sport, Cleveland, OH (November).

Carroll, Joseph. 2007. Football reaches historic popularity levels in Gallup poll. *Gallup News Service* (January 19). Online: http://www.galluppoll.com/content/?ci=26188.

Carter, Andrew. 2008. FSU investigation: Academic fraud. *OrlandoSentinel.com* (September 13). Online: http://www.orlandosentinel.com/sports/orl-fsuncaa1308sep13,0,4566802.story

Cashmore, Ellis, 2007. Gambling and sports. In George Ritzer, ed., *Encyclopedia of sociology* (pp. 1818–1821). London/New York: Blackwell.

Caudwell, Jayne, ed. 2006. *Queer theory and sport: Challenges and controversies.* London: Routledge.

Cavallo, Dominick. 1981. *Muscles and morals.* Philadelphia: University of Pennsylvania Press.

Cavanagh, Sheila and Heather Sykes. 2006. Transsexual bodies at the Olympics: The International Olympic Committee's policy on Transsexual Athletes at the 2004 Summer Games. *Body and Society* 12, 3: 75–102. Online: http://dx.doi.org/10.1177/1357034X06067157.

CBC Sports. 2007. Minor hockey association investigates weekend brawl. Canadian Broadcasting Company Online (November 27). Online: www.cbc.ca/canada/toronto/story/2007/11/27/hockey-brawl.html (retrieved November 28, 2007).

CBC—The Conference Board of Canada. 2005. *Strengthening Canada: The socio-economic benefits of sport participation in Canada.* Gatineau, Quebec: Sport Canada. Online: www.pch.gc.ca/progs/sc/pubs/socio-eco/index_e.cfm.

Chafetz, Janet S., and Joseph A. Kotarba. 1995. Son worshippers: The role of Little League mothers in recreating gender. *Studies in Symbolic Interaction* 18: 219–243.

Chafetz, Janet, and Joseph Kotarba, 1999. Little League mothers and the reproduction of gender. In Jay Coakley and Peter Donnelly, eds., *Inside Sports* (pp. 46–54). London: Routledge.

Chandler, Timothy J. L. 2002. Manly Catholicism: Making men in Catholic public schools, 1945–80. In Tara Magdalinski and Timothy J. L. Chandler, eds., *With God on their side: Sport in the service of religion* (pp. 99–119). London/New York: Routledge.

Chapin, Tim. 2002. *Identifying the real costs and benefits of sports facilities.* Cambridge, MA: Lincoln Institute of Land Policy. Online: www.lincolninst .edu/pubs/dl/671_chapin-web.pdf.

Chappell, Robert. 2007. *Sport in developing countries.* Ewell, UK: International Sports Publications.

Charlesworth, Hannah, and Kevin Young. 2004. Why English female university athletes play with pain: Motivations and rationalizations. In Kevin Young, ed., *Sporting bodies, damaged selves: Sociological studies of sports-related injury* (pp. 163–180). Amsterdam: Elsevier.

Chass, Murray. 2008. Is a night devoted to faith really about the money? *The New York Times* (March 14). Online: http://query.nytimes.com/ gst/fullpage.html?res=9A05E2DD1238F937A25 750C0A96E9C8B63&partner=rssnyt&emc=rss (retrieved May 5, 2008).

Chastain, Brandi. 2004. *It's not about the bra.* New York: Harper Resource.

Chelladurai, Packianathan. 2008. Athletics IS education: A response to Kan, Leo, and Holleran's case study of University of Minnesota student-athletes. *Journal of Intercollegiate Sport* 1, 1: 130–138.

Cherner, Reid. 2005. If you billed it around faith, they will certainly come. *USA Today* (July 21). Online: http://www.usatoday.com/sports/baseball/ minors/2005-07-21-faith-night_x.htm (retrieved May 5, 2008).

Cheshire, Jane, and Marguerite Valentine. 2007. Special issue on femininity. *British Journal of Psychotherapy* 23, 4:

Cheslock, John. 2007. *Who's playing college sports? Trends in participation.* East Meadow, NY: Women's Sports Foundation. Online: http:// www.womenssportsfoundation.org/~/media/Files/ Research%20Reports/Whos%20Playing% 20College%20Sports/fullreport.pdf.

Child Trends, 2008. *Participation in school athletics.* Child Trends Data Bank. Online: http:// www.childtrendsdatabank.org/indicators/ 37SchoolAthletics.cfm (retrieved June 20, 2008).

Christenson, Marcus, and Paul Kelso. 2004. Soccer chief's plan to boost women's game? Hotpants. *The Guardian*—United Kingdom (January 16).

Online: http://football.guardian.co.uk/ News_Story/0,,1124460,00.html (retrieved December 1, 2005).

Chudacoff, Howard. 2007. *Children at play: An American history.* New York: New York University Press.

Ciborowski, Tom. 1997. "Superstition" in the collegiate baseball player. *Sport Psychologist* 11, 3: 305–317.

Cipriani, Roberto. 2007. Religion. In George Ritzer, ed., *The Blackwell Encyclopedia of Sociology* (pp. 3853–3864). London: Blackwell Publishing and Blackwell Reference Online.

Cisneros-Puebla, César A. 2007. Qualitative computing. In George Ritzer, ed., *Encyclopedia of sociology* (pp. 3725–3726). London/New York: Blackwell.

Clancy, F. 1999. Warriors. *USA Weekend* (February 12–14): 4–6.

Claringbould, Inge, and Annelies Knoppers. 2008. Doing and undoing gender in sport governance. *Sex Roles: A Journal of Research* 58, 1–2: 81–92.

Clark, John. 1978. Football and working class fans: Tradition and change. In R. Ingham, ed., *Football hooliganism: The wider context.* London: Inter-Action Imprint.

Clark, Sheryl, and Carrie Paechter. 2007. 'Why can't girls play football?' Gender dynamics and the playground. *Sport, Education and Society* 12, 3: 261–276.

Clayton, Ben, and Barbara Humberstone. 2006. Men's talk: A (pro)feminist analysis of male university football players' discourse. *International Review for the Sociology of Sport* 41, 3–4: 295–316.

Close, Paul, David Askew, and Xin Xu. 2006. *The Beijing Olympiad: The political economy of a sporting mega-event.* Abingdon, UK/New York: Routledge.

Coakley, Jay. 1983a. Leaving competitive sport: Retirement or rebirth? *Quest* 35, 1: 1–11.

Coakley, Jay. 1983b. Play, games and sports: Developmental implications for young people. In Janet C. Harris and Roberta J. Park, eds., *Play, games and sports in cultural contexts* (pp. 431–450). Champaign, IL: Human Kinetics.

Coakley, Jay. 1988–1989. Media coverage of sports and violent behavior: An elusive connection. *Current Psychology: Research and Reviews* 7, 4: 322–330.

Coakley, Jay. 1992. Burnout among adolescent athletes: A personal failure or social problem? *Sociology of Sport Journal* 9, 3: 271–285.

Coakley, Jay. 1993. Sport and socialization. *Exercise and Sport Science Reviews* 21: 169–200.

Coakley, Jay. 1994. Ethics in coaching: Child development or child abuse? *Coaching Volleyball* (December–January): 18–23.

Coakley, Jay. 1998. *Sport in society: Issues and controversies* (6th ed.). New York: McGraw-Hill.

Coakley, Jay. 2002. Using sports to control deviance and violence among youths: Let's be critical and cautious. In M. Gatz, M. A. Messner, and S. J. Ball-Rokeach, eds., *Paradoxes of Youth and Sport* (pp. 13–30). Albany: State University of New York Press.

Coakley, Jay. 2006. The good father: Parental expectations and youth sports. *Leisure Studies* 25, 2: forthcoming.

Coakley, Jay. 2007. Socialization and sports. In George Ritzer, ed., *Encyclopedia of sociology* (pp. 4576–4580). London/New York: Blackwell.

Coakley, Jay, ed. 2008a. Research on intercollegiate sports: A working bibliography. *Journal of Intercollegiate Sport* 1, 1: 147–169.

Coakley, Jay. 2008b. Sports don't just happen: Physical activity and cultural production in neoliberal societies. Keynote address at the Fifth Conference of the European Association for Sociology of Sport (Bled, Slovenia, May 23).

Coakley, Jay. 2008c. Studying intercollegiate sport: High stakes, low rewards. *Journal of Intercollegiate Sport* 1, 1: 14–28.

Coakley, Jay. (forthcoming). Sport specialization: Does it create excellence or "one-trick ponies"? In Sandra Spickard Prettyman and Brian Lampman, eds., *Learning culture through sports* (2nd ed.). Lanham, MD: Rowman & Littlefield.

Coakley, Jay, and Peter Donnelly. 2004. *Sports in society: Issues and controversies* (1st Canadian edition). Toronto: McGraw-Hill Ryerson.

Coakley, Jay, and Anita White. 1999. Making decisions: How young people become involved and stay involved in sports. In Jay Coakley and Peter Donnelly, eds., *Inside Sports* (pp. 77–85). London: Routledge.

Cochran, Johnnie L., and Cyrus Mehri. 2002. *Black coaches in the National Football League: Superior performance, inferior opportunities.* Report presented to the National Football League (October).

Coffey, Wayne. 2005. Player without legs shows the heart of a champion. *New York Daily News KRT* (October 12). Online: www.isubengal.com/media/paper275/news/2005/10/12/Sports/Player.Without.Legs.Shows.The.Heart.Of.A.Champion-1017369.shtml.

Cohen, Greta L. 1994. Media portrayal of the female athlete. In Greta L. Cohen, ed. *Women in sport: Issues and controversies* (pp. 171–184). Newbury Park, CA: Sage.

Colbert, Stephen. 2007. *I am America (and so can you!).* New York: Grand Central Publishing.

Cole, Cheryl L. 2000a. Body studies in the sociology of sport. In Jay Coakley and Eric Dunning, eds. *Handbook of sport studies* (pp. 439–460). London: Sage.

Cole, C. L. 2000b. The year that girls ruled. *Journal of Sport and Social Issues* 24, 1: 3–7.

Cole, C. L. 2006. Nicole Franklin's double dutch. *Journal of Sport and Social Issues* 30, 2: 119–121.

Collins, Chuck, and Felice Yeskel. 2005. *Economic apartheid in America.* New York: New Press.

Collins, Michael F., and James R. Buller. 2003. Social exclusion from high-performance sport: Are all talented young sports people being given an equal opportunity of reaching the Olympic podium? *Journal of Sport and Social Issues* 27, 4: 420–442.

Collins, Patricia Hill. 2004. *Black sexual politics: African Americans, gender, and the new racism.* New York/London: Routledge.

Connell, R. W. 1995. *Masculinities.* Berkeley, CA: University of California Press.

Conroy, Pat. 1986. *The prince of tides.* Boston: Houghton Mifflin.

Cooky, Cheryl. 2004. Raising the bar?: Urban girls' negotiations of structural barriers in recreational sports. Paper presented at the annual meeting of the American Sociological Association, San Francisco, CA, Aug 14.

Cooky, Cheryl. 2006. Strong enough to be a man, but made a woman: Discourses on sport and femininity in *Sports Illustrated for Women.* In Linda K. Fuller, ed., *Sport, rhetoric, and gender* (pp. 97–106). New York: Palgrave Macmillan.

Cooky, Cheryl, and Mary G. McDonald. 2005. 'If you let me play': Young girls' inside-other narratives of sport. *Sociology of Sport Journal* 22, 2: 158–177.

Corbett, Doris, and William Johnson. 2000. The African American female in collegiate sport: Sexism and racism. In D. Brooks and R. Althouse, eds., *Racism in college athletics: The African American athlete's experience* (pp. 199–226). Morgantown, WV: Fitness Information Technology.

Corsello, Andrew. 1999. Hallowed be thy game. *Gentlemen's Quarterly* (September): 432–440.

Côté, Jean, Joseph Baker, and Bruce Abernethy. 2008. Practice and play in the development of sport expertise. In R. Eklund and G. Tenenbaum (eds.), *Handbook of sport psychology* (3rd ed.). Hoboken, NJ: Wiley.

Côté, Jean, and Jessica L. Fraser-Thomas. 2007. Youth involvement in sport. In P. R. E. Crocker (ed.), *Introduction to sport psychology: A Canadian perspective* (pp. 266–294). Toronto: Pearson Prentice Hall.

Côté, Jean, and John Hay. 2002 Children's involvement in sport: A developmental perspective. In J. M. Silva and D. E. Stevens, eds., *Psychological foundations of sport* (pp. 484–502). Boston: Allyn & Bacon.

Cotton, Anthony. 2005. Pain in the grass. *Denver Post* (October 16): 1J.

Couser, G. Thomas. 2000. The empire of the "normal": A forum on disability and self-representation—introduction. *American Quarterly* 52, 2: 305–310.

Coventry, Barbara. 2004. On the sidelines: Sex and racial segregation in television sports broadcasting. *Sociology of Sport Journal* 21, 3: 322–341.

Craig, Maxine Leeds, and Rita Liberti. 2007. 'Cause that's what girls do': The making of a feminized gym. *Gender and Society* 21, 5: 676–699.

Crawford, Garry. 2004. *Consuming sport: Fans, sport, and culture.* London/New York: Routledge.

Crawley, Sara L., Lara J. Foley, and Constance L. Shehan. 2007. *Gendering bodies.* Lanham, MD: Rowman & Littlefield.

Creedon, Pamela J. 1998. Women, sport, and media institutions: Issues in sports journalism and marketing. In Lawrence A. Wenner, ed., *MediaSport* (pp. 88–99). London/New York: Routledge.

Cresswell, Scott, and Robert C. Eklund. 2006. The nature of player burnout in rugby: Key characteristics and attributions. *Journal of Applied Sport Psychology* 18, 3 (September): 219–239.

Cresswell, Scott L., and Robert C. Eklund. 2007. Athlete burnout: A longitudinal qualitative study. *Sport Psychologist* 21, 1: 1–20.

Crissey, Joy. 1999. *Corporate cooptation of sport: The case of snowboarding.* Master's thesis, Sociology Department, Colorado State University, Ft. Collins, CO.

Crissey, Sarah R., and Joy Crissey Honea. 2006. The relationship between athletic participation and perceptions of body size and weight control in adolescent girls: The role of sports. *Sociology of Sport Journal* 23, 3: 248–272.

Crist, Steven. 1998. All bets are off. *Sports Illustrated* (January 26): 82–92.

Critcher, Charles. 1979. Football since the war. In J. Clark, ed., *Working class culture* (pp. 161–184). London: Hutchinson.

Crolley, Liz, and Hand, David. 2006. *Football and European identity: Historical narratives through the press.* London/New York: Routledge.

Cronin, Don. 1998. Violent athletes targeted. *USA Today* (March 6): 1C.

Crosnoe, Robert. 2002. Academic and health-related trajectories in adolescence: The intersection of gender and athletics. *Journal of Health and Social Behavior* 43, 3: 317–335.

Crosset, Todd. 1995. *Outsiders in the clubhouse: The world of women's professional golf.* Albany: State University of New York Press.

Crosset, Todd. 1999. Male athletes' violence against women: A critical assessment of the athletic affiliation, violence against women debate. *Quest* 52, 3: 244–257.

Crossman, Jane, John Vincent, and Harriet Speed. 2007. 'The times they are a-changin': Gender comparisons in three national newspapers of the 2004 Wimbledon Championships. *International Review for the Sociology of Sport* 42, 1: 27–42.

Crouse, Karen. 2007. Torres is getting older, but swimming faster. *The New York Times* (November 18). Online: www.nytimes.com/2007/11/18/sports/othersports/18torres.html.

Crouse, Karen. 2008. Scrutiny of suit rises as world records fall. *The New York Times* (April 11). Online: www.nytimes.com/2008/04/11/sports/othersports/11swim.html.

Crowther, Nigel B. 2007. *Sport in ancient times.* Westport, CT: Praeger Publishers.

Cunningham, George B. 2004. Already aware of the glass ceiling: Race-related effects of perceived opportunity on the career choices of college athletes. *Journal of African American Studies* 7, 1: 57–71.

Cunningham, George B. 2007a. *Diversity in sport organizations.* Scottsdale, AZ: Holcomb Hathaway Publishers.

Cunningham, George B. 2007b. Opening the black box: The influence of perceived diversity and a common in-group identity in diverse groups. *Journal of Sport Management* 21: 58–78.

Cunningham, George B. 2008. Creating and sustaining gender diversity in sport organizations. *Sex Roles: A Journal of Research* 58, 1–2: 136–145.

Cunningham, George B., Jennifer E. Bruening, and Thomas Straub. 2006. Examining the under-representation of African Americans in NCAA Division I head-coaching positions. *Journal of Sport Management* 20: 387–417.

Cunningham, George B., and Michael Sagas. 2004. Racial differences in occupational turnover intent among NCAA Division IA assistant football coaches. *Sociology of Sport Journal* 21, 1: 84–92.

Cunningham, George B., and Michael Sagas. 2005. Access discrimination in intercollegiate athletics. *Journal of Sport and Social Issues* 29, 2: 148–163.

Cunningham, George B., and Michael Sagas. 2007. Perceived treatment discrimination among coaches: The influence of race and sport coached. *International Journal of Sport Management* 8: 1–20.

Cunningham, George B., and Michael Sagas. 2008. Gender and sex diversity in sport organizations: Introduction to the special issue. *Sex Roles: A Journal of Research* 58, 1–2: 3–9.

Curry, Timothy. 1991. Fraternal bonding in the locker room: A profeminist analysis of talk about competition and women. *Sociology of Sport Journal* 8, 2: 119–135.

Curry, Timothy. 1993. A little pain never hurt anyone: Athletic career socialization and the normalization of sports injury. *Symbolic Interaction* 16, 3: 273–290.

Curry, Timothy. 1996. Beyond the locker room: Sexual assault and the college athlete. Presidential Address, North American Society for the Sociology of Sport Conference (Birmingham, AL).

Curry, Timothy. 1998. Beyond the locker room: Campus bars and college athletes. *Sociology of Sport Journal* 15, 3: 205–215.

Curry, Timothy J., Paula A. Arriagada, and Benjamin Cornwell. 2002. Images of sport in popular nonsport magazines: Power and performance versus pleasure and participation. *Sociological Perspectives* 45, 4: 397–413.

Curry, Timothy J., Kent P. Schwirian, and Rachael Woldoff. 2004. *High stakes: Big time sports and downtown redevelopment.* Columbus: Ohio State University Press.

Curry, Timothy, and R. H. Strauss. 1994. A little pain never hurt anybody: A photo-essay on the normalization of sport injuries. *Sociology of Sport Journal* 11, 2: 195–208.

Curtis, James, William McTeer, and Philip White. 2003. Do high school athletes earn more pay? Youth sport participation and earnings as an adult. *Sociology of Sport Journal* 20, 1: 60–76.

Cyphers, Luke. 2003. Next. *ESPN The Magazine* (December 22): 58–66.

Cyphers, Luke. 2008. Project X. *ESPN The Magazine* 11.06 (March 24): 47–51.

Dacyshyn, Anna. 1999. When the balance is gone: The sport and retirement experiences of elite female gymnasts. In Jay Coakley and Peter Donnelly, eds., *Inside sports* (pp. 214–222). London: Routledge.

Daily Show, The. 2003. Episode Number 736 (April 7): Online: http://www.tv.com/the-daily-show/martha-burk/episode/498113/summary.html"www.tv.com/the-daily-show/martha-burk/episode/498113/summary.html.

Daniels, Donna. 2000. Gazing at the new black woman athlete. *ColorLines* 3, 1: 25–26.

Dannheisser, Ralph. 2008. Baseball, once just an American game, extends reach worldwide. America.gov (March 31). Online, www.america.gov/st/sports-english/2008/March/20080331164120zjsredna0.6307947.html.

Dater, Adrian. 2005. Female boxer, 34, dies after Golden Gloves bout. *Denver Post* (April 5): 1D.

Davids, K., et al. 2007. Genes, environment and sport performance: Why the nature-nurture dualism is no longer relevant. *Sports Medicine* 37, 11: 961–980.

Davies, Robert. 2002a. Media power and responsibility in sport and globalisation.

Presentation made to the Third International Conference for Media Professionals in a Globalised Sport World, Copenhagen (November). (See www.iblf.org.)

Davies, Robert. 2002b. Sports, citizenship and development: Challenges and opportunities for sport sponsors. Presentation at the World Sports Forum Lausanne (September). (See www.iblf.org.)

Davis, Caroline. 1999. Eating disorders, physical activity, and sport: Biological, psychological, and sociological factors. In Philip White and Kevin Young, eds., *Sport and gender in Canada* (pp. 85–106). Don Mills, Ontario: Oxford University Press.

Davis, F. James. 2001. *Who is black: One nation's definition.* University Park, PA: Penn State University Press.

Davis, Laurel, and Othello Harris. 1998. Race and ethnicity in U.S. sports media. In L. A. Wenner, ed., *Media Sport* (pp. 154–169). London/New York: Routledge.

Davis, Nickolas W., and Margaret Carlisle Duncan. 2006. Sports knowledge is power: Reinforcing masculine privilege through fantasy sport league participation. *Journal of Sport and Social Issues* 30, 3: 244–264.

Davis-Delano, Laurel R. 2007. Eliminating Native American mascots. *Journal of Sport and Social Issues* 31, 4: 340–373.

Deardorff, Donald Lee, and John White, eds. 2008. *The image of God in the human body: Essays on Christianity and sports.* Lewiston, NY: Edwin Mellen Press.

Deford, Frank. 1976. Religion in sport. *Sports Illustrated* 44, 16: 88–100.

DeHass, Denise. 2008. *1999-00–2006-07 NCAA student-athlete race and ethnicity report.* Indianapolis: National Collegiate Athletic Association.

Delaney, Kevin J., and Rick Eckstein. 2003. The devil is in the details: Neutralizing critical studies of publicly subsidized stadiums. *Critical Sociology* 29, 2: 189–210.

Delaney, Kevin J., and Rick Eckstein. 2007. *Public dollars, private stadiums: The battle over building sports stadiums.* Piscataway, NJ: Rutgers University Press.

Delaney, Kevin, and Rick Eckstein. 2008. Local media coverage of sports stadium initiatives. *Journal of Sport and Social Issues* 32, 1: 72–93.

deMause, Neil, and Joanna Cagan. 2008. *Field of schemes: How the great stadium swindle turns public money into private profit* (revised/expanded edition). Lincoln: University of Nebraska Press.

Demerath, Nicholas J., and Philip Hammond. 1969. *Religion in social context: Tradition and transition.* New York: Random House.

Dempsey, Chris. 2004. Many blacks feel isolation at CU. *Denver Post* (June 27): 1A, 19A.

Dempsey, John Mark, ed. 2006. *Sports-talk radio in America: its context and culture.* Binghamton, NY: Haworth Half-Court Press.

Denham, Bryan E. 2004. Hero or hypocrite?: United States and international media portrayals of Carl Lewis amid revelations of a positive drug test. *International Review for the Sociology of Sport* 39, 2: 167–185.

Denham, Bryan. 2006a. The Anabolic Steroid Control Act of 2004: A study in the political economy of drug policy. *Journal of Health & Social Policy* 22, 2: 51–78.

Denham, Bryan. 2006b. Effects of mass communication on attitudes toward anabolic steroids: An analysis of high school seniors. *Journal of Drug Issues* 36, 4: 809–830.

Denham, Bryan. 2007a. Calling out the heavy hitters: What performance-enhancing drug use in professional baseball reveals about the politics and mass communication of sport. *International Journal of Sport Communication* 1, 1: 3–16.

Denham, Bryan. 2007b. Government and the pursuit of rigorous drug testing in Major League Baseball: A study in political negotiation and reciprocity. *International Journal of Sport Management and Marketing* 2, 4: 379–395.

Denver Post. 2004. Toughen up. *Denver Post* (August 1): 2B.

Denzin, Norman. 2001. Representing Michael. In David L. Andrews, ed., *Michael Jordan, Inc.: Corporate sport, media culture, and late modern America* (pp. 3–14). Albany, NY: State University of New York Press.

Denzin, Norman K. 2007. *Symbolic interactionism and cultural studies: The politics of interpretation.* Oxford, UK: Wiley-Blackwell.

Denzin, Norman K., and Yvonna S. Lincoln. 2000. Introduction: The discipline and practice of qualitative research. In Norman K. Denzin and

Y. S. Lincoln, eds., *Handbook of qualitative research* (2ⁿᵈ ed., pp. 1–29). Thousand Oaks, CA: Sage.

DePauw, Karen. 1997. The (in)visibility of disability: Cultural contexts and "sporting bodies." *Quest* 49, 4: 416–430.

Dewhirst, Timothy, and Robert Sparks. 2003. Intertextuality, tobacco sponsorship of sports, and adolescent male smoking culture: A selective review of tobacco industry documents. *Journal of Sport and Social Issues* 27, 4: 372–398.

Dick, Randall, Margot Putukian, Julie Agel, Todd A. Evans, and Stephen W. Marshall. 2007. Descriptive epidemiology of collegiate women's soccer injuries: National Collegiate Athletic Association Injury Surveillance System, 1988–1989 through 2002–2003. *Journal of Athletic Training* 42, 2: 278–285.

Dimeo, Paul. 2007. *A history of drug use in sport, 1876–1976.* London/New York: Routledge.

Dionigi, Rylee, and Gabrielle O'Flynn. 2007. Performance discourses and old age: What does it mean to be an older athlete? *Sociology of Sport Journal* 24, 4: 359–377.

DiPasquale, Mauro G. 1992. Editorial: Why athletes use drugs. *Drugs in Sports* 1, 1: 2–3.

Director. 2008. A great day at the Oscar(s). The National Center on Physical Activity and Disability—*NCPAD NEWS* 7, 6 (June). Online: www.ncpad.org/director/fact_sheet.php?sheet=622.

Dixon, Marlene A., and Jennifer E. Bruening. 2005. Perspectives on work–family conflict: A review and integrative approach. *Sport Management Review* 8: 227–254.

Dixon, Marlene A., and Jennifer E. Bruening. 2007. Work–family conflict in coaching I: A Top-down perspective. *Journal of Sport Management* 21: 377–406.

Dixon, Marlene A., and Michael Sagas. 2007. The relationship between organizational support, work–family conflict, and the job-life satisfaction of university coaches. *Research Quarterly for Exercise and Sport* 78: 236–247.

Doaks, Clinton. 2004. We can handle the truth. *Mile High Sport Magazine* (November): 10.

Doane, Ashley W., and Eduardo Bonilla-Silva. 2003. *White out: The continuing significance of racism.* New York/London: Routledge.

Dobie, Michael. 1987. Facing a brave new world. *Newsday* (November 8): 13.

Dodd, Mike. 2002. Tiger: Membership up to Muirfield. *USA Today* (July 17): 1C.

Domi, Tie. 1992. Tough tradition of hockey fights should be preserved. *USA Today* (October 27): C3.

Donnelly, Michele. 2006. Studying extreme sports: Beyond the core participants. *Journal of Sport and Social Issues* 30, 2: 219–224.

Donnelly, Peter. 1993. Problems associated with youth involvement in high-performance sports. In B. R. Cahill and A. J. Pearl, eds., *Intensive participation in children's sports* (pp. 95–126). Champaign, IL: Human Kinetics.

Donnelly, Peter. 1996a. The local and the global: Globalization in the sociology of sport. *Journal of Sport and Social Issues* 20, 3: 239–257.

Donnelly, Peter. 1996b. Prolympism: Sport monoculture as crisis and opportunity. *Quest* 48, 1: 25–42.

Donnelly, Peter. 1997. Child labour, sport labour: Applying child labor laws to sport. *International Review for the Sociology of Sport* 32, 4: 389–406.

Donnelly, Peter. 1999. Who's fair game? Sport, sexual harassment, and abuse. In P. White and K. Young, eds., *Sport and gender in Canada* (pp. 107–128). Don Mills, Ontario: Oxford University Press.

Donnelly, Peter. 2000. Interpretive approaches to the study of sports. In Jay Coakley and Eric Dunning, eds., *Handbook of sport and society* (pp. 77–91). London: Sage.

Donnelly, Peter, and Jay Coakley. 2003. *The role of recreation in promoting social inclusion.* Monograph in the Working Paper Series on Social Inclusion published by the Laidlaw Foundation, Toronto, Ontario.

Donnelly, Peter (with Simon Darnell, Sandy Wells, and Jay Coakley). 2007. The use of sport to foster child and youth development and education. In Sport for Development and Peace, International Working Group (SDP/IWG), *Literature Reviews on Sport for Development and Peace* (pp. 7–47). Toronto, Ontario: University of Toronto, Faculty of Physical Education and health. Online: http://iwg.sportanddev.org/data/htmleditor/file/Lit.%20Reviews/literature%20review%20SDP.pdf (retrieved September 10, 2008).

Donnelly, Peter, and Jean Harvey. 1999. Class and gender: Intersections in sport and physical activity. In Phillip White and Kevin Young, eds., *Sport and gender in Canada* (pp. 40–64). Don Mills, Ontario: Oxford University Press.

Donnelly, Peter, and Jean Harvey, 2007. Social class and gender: Intersections in sport and physical activity. In Kevin Young and Philip White, eds., *Sport and gender in Canada* (2nd edition, pp. 95–119). Don Mills, Ontario: Oxford University Press.

Donnelly, Peter, and LeAnne Petherick. 2004. Workers' playtime?: Child labour at the extremes of the sporting spectrum. *Sport in Society* 7, 3: 301–321.

Donnelly, Peter, and Kevin Young. 1999. Rock climbers and rugby players: Identity construction and confirmation. In Jay Coakley and Peter Donnelly, eds., *Inside Sports* (pp. 67–76). London: Routledge.

Downward, Paul, and Alistair Dawson, 2000. *The economics of professional team sports*. London/New York: Routledge.

Drahota, Jo Ann T., and D. Stanley Eitzen. 1998. The role exit of professional athletes. *Sociology of Sport Journal* 15, 3: 263–278.

Drape, Joe. 2008. Web Site Puts Focus on the Fix in Sports Bets. *The New York Times* (May 25). Online: http://www.nytimes.com/2008/05/25/sports/othersports/25betfair.html.

Draper, Electa. 2005. Trying to turn the game into more than a dead end. *Denver Post* (May 17): 1A, 10A

DuBois, William Edward Burghardt. 1935. *Black reconstruction in America*. New York: Harcourt, Brace.

Dukes, Richard L., and Jay Coakley. 2002. Parental commitment to competitive swimming. *Free Inquiry in Creative Sociology* 30, 2: 185–197.

Duncan, Margaret Carlisle. 2008. The personal is political. *Sociology of Sport Journal* 25, 1: 1–6.

Duncan, Margaret Carlisle, and Michael A. Messner. 2000. *Gender in televised sports: 1989, 1993, and 1999.* Los Angeles: Amateur Athletic Foundation.

Duncan, Margaret Carlisle, and Michael A. Messner. 2005. *Gender in televised sports: News and highlights shows, 1989–2004.* Los Angeles: Amateur Athletic Foundation. Online: www.aafla.org/9arr/ResearchReports/tv2004.pdf.

Dunn, Katherine. 1994. Just as fierce. *Mother Jones* (November–December): 35–39.

Dunn, Robert, and Christopher Stevenson. 1998. The paradox of the Church Hockey League. *International Review for the Sociology of Sport* 33, 2: 131–141.

Dunning, Eric. 1986. Social bonding and violence in sport. In Norbert Elias and Eric Dunning, eds., *Quest for excitement: Sport and leisure in the civilizing process* (pp. 224–244). Oxford, UK/Cambridge, MA: Blackwell.

Dunning, Eric. 1999. *Sport matters: Sociological studies of sport, violence and civilization*. London: Routledge.

Dunning, Eric, Patrick Murphy, Ivan Waddington, and Antonios E. Astrinakis, eds. 2002. *Fighting fans: Football hooliganism as a world phenomenon.* Dublin: University College Dublin Press.

Dunning, Eric, Patrick Murphy, and John Williams. 1988. *The foots of football hooliganism: An historical and sociological study*. London: Routledge and Kegan Paul.

Dunning, Eric, and Kenneth Sheard. 1979. *Barbarians, gentlemen and players: A sociological study of the development of rugby football*. New York: University Press.

DuPree, David. 1992. Controversy wears down Dream Team. *USA Today* (August 5): 7E.

Duquin, Mary. 2000. Sport and emotions. In Jay Coakley and Eric Dunning, eds., *Handbook of sports studies* (pp. 477–489). London: Sage.

Dworkin, Shari L. 2001. "Holding back": Negotiating a glass ceiling on women's muscular strength. *Sociological Perspectives* 44, 3: 333–351.

Dworkin, Shari L. 2003. A woman's place is in the . . . cardiovascular room? Gender relations, the body, and the gym. In Anne Bolin and Jane Granskog, eds., *Athletic Intruders: Ethnographic research on women, culture, and exercise* (pp. 131–158). Albany: State University of New York Press.

Early, Gerald. 1998. Performance and reality: Race, sports and the modern world. *The Nation* 267, 5: 11–20.

Eccles, Jacquelynne S., and Bonnie L. Barber. 1999. Student council, volunteering, basketball, or marching band: What kind of extracurricular involvement matters? *Journal of Adolescent Research* 14, 1: 10–43.

Eckstein, Rick, and Kevin Delaney. 2002. New sports stadiums, community self-esteem, and community collective conscience. *Journal of Sport and Social Issues* 26, 3: 236–248.

Edwards, Harry. 1973. *Sociology of sport.* Homewood, IL: Dorsey Press.

Edwards, Harry. 2000. The decline of the black athlete (as interviewed by D. Leonard). *ColorLines* 3, 1: 24–29.

EFJ, 2008. Keady reports on current conditions for Nike's Indonesian workers. *Educating for Justice Newsletter.* Online: http://www.educatingforjustice .org/ (retrieved September 3, 2008).

Eichberg, Henning. 2008. Pyramid or democracy in sports? Alternative ways in European sports policies. *Nordic Sport Science Forum* (February 6). Online: http://idrottsforum.org/articles/eichberg/ eichberg080206.html (retrieved July 20, 2008).

Eitle, Tamela McNulty. 2005. Do gender and race matter? Explaining the relationship between sports participation and achievement. *Sociological Spectrum* 25, 2: 177–195.

Eitle, Tamela McNulty, and David J. Eitle. 2002. Just don't do it: High school sports participation and young female adult sexual behavior. *Sociology of Sport Journal* 19, 4: 403–418.

El Qarany, Hosna. 2006. Saudi women take up martial arts. *Asharq Alawsat* (Arabic International Daily-English Edition; August 8). Online: http://aawsat.com/english/news .asp?section=7&id=6092.

Elias, Norbert. 1986. An essay on sport and violence. In Norbert Elias and Eric Dunning, eds., *Quest for excitement* (pp. 150–174). New York: Basil Blackwell.

Elias, Norbert, and Eric Dunning. 1986. *Quest for excitement.* New York: Basil Blackwell.

Eliasoph, Nina. 1999. "Everyday racism" in a culture of political avoidance: Civil society, speech, and taboo. *Social Problems* 46, 4: 479–502.

Elkind, David. 2007. *The hurried child.* Cambridge, MA: Da Capo Lifelong Books.

Elkind, David. 2008. *The power of play: Learning what comes naturally.* Cambridge, MA: Da Capo Lifelong Books.

Elkington, John. 2004. Praying for rain. *SustainAbility Radar* (sports issue, August–September): 4–5.

Ellin, Abby. 2008. The high price of raising an Olympian. MSN.com. Online: http://articles .moneycentral.msn.com/Investing/StockInvesting Trading/TheHighPriceOfRaisingAnOlympian .aspx (retrieved August 20, 2008).

Elling, Agnes, Paul de Knop, and Annelies Knoppers. 2003. Gay/lesbian sport clubs and events: Places of homo-social bonding and cultural resistance? *International Review for the Sociology of Sport* 38, 4: 441–456.

Elliott, Richard, and Joseph Maguire. 2008. "Getting caught in the net": Examining the recruitment of Canadian players in British professional ice hockey. *Journal of Sport and Social Issues* 32, 2: 158–176.

Elliott, Stuart. 2007. Marketers are joining the varsity. *The New York Times* (June 11). Online: http://select .nytimes.com/mem/tnt.html?emc=tnt&tntget= 2007/06/11/business/media/11adcol.html.

Elliott, Stuart. 2008. Anheuser-Busch pushes the big beers for the Super Bowl. *The New York Times* (January 22). Online: http://select.nytimes.com/ mem/tnt.html?emc=tnt&tntget=2008/01/22/ business/media/22adco.html.

Ellis, Carolyn, and Arthur Bouchner. 2000. Autoethnography, personal narrative, reflexivity: Researcher as subject. In Norman K. Denzin and Yvonna S. Lincoln, eds., *Handbook of qualitative research* (2nd ed., pp. 733–768). Thousand Oaks, CA: Sage.

Elman, Jeremy T. 2006. Can trademark law help minority groups eliminate negative stereotypes? *Law.com* (October 12). Online: www.law.com/jsp/ law/LawArticleFriendly.jsp?id=1160557519218 (accessed September 8, 2008).

Engh, Fred. 1999. *Why Johnny hates sports.* Garden City Park, NY: Avery.

ESPN. 1999. High school athletes: Do jocks rule the school? In T. Farrey, ed., *Outside the Lines* (June 20–June 24). Online: www.espn.com/gen/ features/jocks.

ESPN The Magazine. 2005. Special report: Turning a blind eye to steroids—The inside story of baseball's open secret. *ESPN The Magazine* (November 21): 69–84.

Etkin, Jack. 2008. Intentional walk for Gossage. *Rocky Mountain News* (May 13): Sports 4–5. Online: http://www.rockymountainnews.com/news/2008/ may/13/intentional-walk-for-gossage/.

Ewald, Keith, and Robert M. Jiobu. 1985. Explaining positive deviance: Becker's model and the case of runners and bodybuilders. *Sociology of Sport Journal* 2, 2: 144–156.

Falcous, Mark, and Joseph Maguire. 2006. Imagining 'America': The NBA and local-global mediascapes. *International Review for the Sociology of Sport* 41, 1: 59–78.

Falcous, Mark, and Michael Silk. 2006. Global regimes, local agendas: Sport, resistance and the mediation of dissent. *International Review for the Sociology of Sport* 41, 3–4: 317–338.

Falk, Gerhard. 2005. *Football and American identity.* New York: Haworth Press.

Falk, William B. 1995. Bringing home the violence. *Newsday* (January 8): 12–13.

Farber, Michael. 2002. Clubhouse confidential. *Sports Illustrated* (January 14): 52–57.

Farber, Michael. 2004. Code red. *Sports Illustrated* (March 22): 56–60.

Farhood, Steve. 2000. Typical girls. *Boxing Monthly* 12, 1. Online: www.boxing-monthly.co.uk/content/0005/thrcc.htm.

Farrey, Tom. 2005. Baby you're the greatest: Genetic testing for athletic traits. *ESPN The Magazine* 8.03 (February 14): 80–87. Online: http://sports.espn.go.com/espn/news/story?id=2022781.

Farrey, Tom. 2006a. The guru of growth. *ESPN The Magazine* 9.18 (September 11): 158–164.

Farrey, Tom. 2006b. The MAN. *ESPN The Magazine* 9.15 (July 31): 88–93.

Farrey, Tom. 2007. The case for HGH. *ESPN The Magazine* 10.02 (January 29): 48–52.

Farrey, Tom. 2008. *Game on: The all-American race to make champions of our children.* New York: ESPN Books.

Fasting, Kari. 1996. 40,000 female runners: The Grete Waitz Run—Sport, culture, and counterculture. Paper presented at International Pre-Olympic Scientific Congress, Dallas (July).

Fasting, Kari, Celia Brackenridge, and Jorunn Sundgot-Borgen. 2004. Prevalence of sexual harassment among Norwegian female elite athletes in relation to sport type. *International Review for the Sociology of Sport* 39, 4: 373–386.

Fatwa Bank. 2004. Islam's stance on women's practicing sport. Online: www.islamonline.net/fatwa/english/FatwaDisplay.asp?hFatwaID=48375 (retrieved July 5, 2005).

Fausto-Sterling, Anne. 2000. *Sexing the body: Gender politics and the construction of sexuality.* New York: Basic Books.

Feeney, Robert. 1995. *A Catholic perspective: Physical exercise and sports.* Allentown, PA: Aquinas Press.

Feldman, Bruce. 2007. A recruiting pitch of another kind. *ESPN The Magazine* (May 28). Online: http://espn.go.com/gen/s/2002/0527/1387550.html.

Fenstermaker, Sarah, and Candace West, eds. 2002. *Doing gender, doing difference: Inequality, power, and institutional change.* New York: Routledge.

Ferber, Abby L. 2007. The construction of black masculinity: White supremacy now and then. *Journal of Sport and Social Issues* 31, 1: 11–24.

Ference, Ruth, and K. Denise Muth. 2004. Helping middle school females form a sense of self through team sports and exercise. *Women in Sport and Physical Activity* 13, 1: 28–35.

Fielding-Lloyd, Beth, and Lindsey J. Meân. 2008. Standards and separatism: The discursive construction of gender in English soccer coach education. *Sex Roles: A Journal of Research* 58, 1–2: 24–39.

Fields, Barbara J. 1982. Ideology and race in American history. In J. Morgan Kousser and James M. McPherson, eds., *Region, race, and reconstruction: Essays in honor of C. Vann Woodward* (pp. 143–177). New York: Oxford University Press.

Fine, Gary Alan. 1987. *With the boys: Little League baseball and preadolescent culture.* Chicago: University of Chicago Press.

Finger, Dave. 2004. Before they were next. *ESPN The Magazine* 7.12 (June 7): 83–86.

Fink, Janet S. 2008. Gender and sex diversity in sport organizations: Concluding comments. *Sex Roles: A Journal of Research* 58, 1–2: 146–147.

Fink, Janet S., and George B. Cunningham. 2005. The effects of racial and gender dyad diversity on work experiences of university athletics personnel. *International Journal of Sport Management* 6: 199–213.

Flake, Carol. 1992. The spirit of winning: Sports and the total man. In S. Hoffman, ed., *Sport and religion* (pp. 161–176). Champaign, IL: Human Kinetics.

Fleming, David. 2005. Stunt men. *ESPN The Magazine* (December 5): 64–70.

Fleming, David. 2007. Does God want John Kitna to win? *ESPN—The Magazine* 10.20 (October 8): 48–54.

Fleming, Scott, and Alan Tomlinson. 2007. Racism and xenophobia in English football. In Alan Tomlinson, ed., *The sport studies reader* (pp. 304–315). London/New York: Routledge.

Foer, Franklin. 2004. *How soccer explains the world: An unlikely theory of globalization.* New York: HarperCollins.

Foley, Douglas E. 1990a. *Learning capitalist culture.* Philadelphia: University of Pennsylvania Press.

Foley, Douglas E. 1990b. The great American football ritual: Reproducing race, class, and gender inequality. *Sociology of Sport Journal* 7, 2: 111–135.

Foley, Douglas E. 1999a. High school football: Deep in the heart of south Tejas. In Jay Coakley and Peter Donnelly, eds., *Inside Sports* (pp. 133–138). London: Routledge.

Foley, Douglas E. 1999b. Jay White Hawk: Mesquaki athlete, AIM hellraiser, and anthropological informant. In Jay Coakley and Peter Donnelly, eds., *Inside Sports* (pp. 156–161). London: Routledge.

Forbes. 2007. The business of basketball. *Forbes* (December 6). Online: www.forbes .com/2007/12/06/nba-team-valuations-biz-07nba -cz_kb_mo_cs_1206nba_land.html.

Foucault, Michel. 1961/1967. *Madness and civilization.* London: Travistock.

Foxworth, Domonique. 2005. Ties that bind team begin with prayer. *Denver Post* (October 19): 2D.

Frank, Robert H. 2004. *Challenging the myth: A review of the links among college athletic success, student quality, and donations.* Miami: Knight Foundation Commission on Intercollegiate Athletics. Online: www.knightfdn.org/.

Franseen, L., and S. McCann. 1996. Causes of eating disorders in elite female athletes. *Olympic Coach* 6, 3 (Summer): 15–17.

Fredrickson, Barbara L., and Kristen Harrison. 2005. Throwing like a girl: Self-objectification predicts adolescent girls' motor performance. *Journal of Sport and Social Issues* 29, 1: 79–101.

Fredrickson, George M. 2003. *Racism: A Short History.* Princeton, NJ: Princeton University Press.

Freedman, Jonah. 2008a. A crash-course in foreign-exchange rates. *SI.com.* Online: http:// sportsillustrated.cnn.com/more/specials/ fortunate50/2008/index.20.html.

Freedman, Jonah. 2008b. Ranking the 50 highest-earning athletes in the U.S. *SI.com.* Online: http://sportsillustrated.cnn.com/more/specials/ fortunate50/2008/.

Freeman, Mike. 1998. A cycle of violence, on the field and off. *The New York Times*, section 8 (September 6): 1.

Frias, Carlos, and William M. Hartnett. 2006. Heavy pressure: NFL players struggle with weight game. *Palm Beach Post* (October 29). Online: www.palmbeachpost.com/sports/content/sports/ epaper/2006/10/29/a1b_nflweight_1029.html.

Friedman, Michael T., David L. Andrews, and Michael L. Silk. 2004. Sport and the façade of redevelopment in the postindustrial city. *Sociology of Sport Journal* 21, 2: 119–139.

Friedman, Vicki A., Linda G. Martin, and Robert F. Schoeni. 2004. An overview of disability in America. *Population Bulletin* 59, 3 (special issue, "Disability in America").

Fry, Hap. 2006. Boosters take different roads to same goal. *The Coloradoan* (January 27): A1, A2.

Fudzie, Vince, and Andre Hayes. 1995. *The sport of learning: A comprehensive survival guide for African-American student-athletes.* North Hollywood, CA: Doubleplay.

Fulks, Daniel L. 2008. *Revenues and Expenses of NCAA Division I Intercollegiate Athletics Programs.* Indianapolis, IN: National Collegiate Athletic Association. Online: http://www.ncaapublications .com/Uploads/PDF/Revenue_Expenses_ 200860cc123e-54d9-45e7-acbd-a1f195b345e6.pdf.

Fuller, Linda K., ed. 2006. *Sport, rhetoric, and gender: Historical perspectives and media representations.* Basingstoke: Palgrave Macmillan.

Fullinwider, Robert K. 2006. *Sports, youth and character: A critical survey.* Circle Working Paper 44, The Center for Information and Research on Civic Learning and Engagement. College Park, MD: University of Maryland.

GAO. 2006. *Olympic security: Better planning can enhance U.S. support to future Olympic Games.* Report to the Committee on International Relations, House of Representatives. Washington, DC: United States Government Accountability Office. Online: www.gao.gov/new.items/d06753.pdf.

Garbarino, James. 2006. *See Jane hit: Why girls are growing more violent and what we can do about it.* New York: Penguin.

Garber, Greg. 2007a. The Dominican Republic of the NFL *ESPN The Magazine* (May 28). Online: http://espn.go.com/gen/s/2002/0527/1387626.html.

Garber, Greg. 2007b. They might be giants. *ESPN The Magazine* (May 28). Online: http://espn.go.com/gen/s/2002/0527/1387627.html.

Garrett, Robyne. 2004. Negotiating a physical identity: Girls, bodies and physical education. *Sport, Education and Society* 9, 2: 223–237.

Gaunt, Kyra D. 2006. *The games black girls play.* New York: New York University Press.

Gavora, Jessica. 2002. *Tilting the playing field: Schools, sports, sex and Title IX.* San Francisco: Encounter Books.

Geffner, David. 2002. Just one of z-boys. *AmericaWest Magazine,* May: 41–43.

Gems, Gerald R. 2006. *The athletic crusade: Sport and American cultural imperialism.* Lincoln: University of Nebraska Press.

Genel, Myron. 2000. Gender verification no more? *Medscape Women's Health* 5, 3. Online: http://ai.eecs.umich.edu/people/conway/TS/OlympicGenderTesting.html (retrieved August 20, 2008).

George, John. 1994. The virtual disappearance of the white male sprinter in the United States: A speculative essay. *Sociology of Sport Journal* 11, 1: 70–78.

Gessel, Luke M., Sarah K. Fields, Christy L. Collins, Randall W. Dick, and R. Dawn Comstock. 2007. Concussions among high school and college athletes. *Journal of Athletic Training* 42, 4: 495–503. Online: http://www.pubmedcentral.nih.gov/articlerender.fcgi?artid=2140075.

Gibbons, Tim, Alicia McConnell, Tammie Forster, Suzie Tuffey Riewald, and Kirsten Peterson. 2003. *Reflections on success: U.S. Olympians describe the success factors and obstacles that most influenced their Olympic development.* Colorado Springs, CO: United States Olympic Committee. Online: www.usolympicteam.com/ReflectionsonSucces.pdf.

Gibbs, Nancy. 2008. Cool running. *Time* 171, 4 (January 28): 116. Online: www.time.com/time/magazine/article/0,9171,1704675,00.html.

Giles, Audrey. 2004. Kevlar®, Crisco®, and menstruation: "Tradition" and Dene games. *Sociology of Sport Journal* 21, 1: 18–35

Ginsburg, Kenneth R. 2007. The importance of play in promoting healthy child development and maintaining strong parent-child bonds. *Pediatrics* 119, 1. Online: www.aap.org/pressroom/playFINAL.pdf.

Giordano, Rita, and Kristen A Graham, 2004. An early leg up. *Philadelphia Inquirer* (February 24): D1, D3.

Giulianotti, Richard, and Gary Armstrong. 2002. Avenues of contestation: Football hooligans, running and ruling urban spaces. *Social Anthropology* 10, 2: 211–238.

Gladstone, Brooke. 2005. The passion of the pitch. PBS, WNYC Radio. Online: www.onthemedia.org/transcripts/transcripts_052705_pitch.html (retrieved July 10, 2005).

Glanville, Doug. 2008a. In baseball, fear bats at the top of the order. *The New York Times* (January 16). Online, www.nytimes.com/2008/01/16/opinion/16glanville.html.

Glanville, Doug. 2008b. Lovers, not fighters. *The New York Times* (May 25). Online: http://www.nytimes.com/2008/05/25/opinion/25glanville.html.

Glatz, Carol. 2004. New Vatican office to promote culture of sport. *BC Catholic* (Vancouver diocesan paper): Online: http://bcc.rcav.org/04-08-16/ (retrieved July 10, 2005).

Glier, Ray. 2004. Reserve finds $425 a high price to sit. *USA Today* (July 30): 14C.

Glock, Allison. 2005. The look of love. *ESPN The Magazine* (June 20): 66–74.

Godley, Amanda. 1999. The creation of the student/athlete dichotomy in urban high school culture. Paper presented at the annual conference of the North American Society for the Sociology of Sport, Cleveland (November).

Goffman, Erving. 1963. *Stigma: Notes on the management of spoiled identities.* Englewood Cliffs, NJ: Prentice-Hall.

Gold, John Robert, and Margaret M. Gold. 2007. *Olympic cities: City agendas, planning, and the world's games, 1896–2012.* New York: Routledge.

Golden, Mark. 1998. *Sport and society in ancient Greece.* Cambridge, UK: Cambridge University Press.

Good, Regan. 2002. Women's share at Olympic competitions drops. Online: www.womensenews.org/article.cfm/dyn/aid/824 (retrieved July 5, 2005).

Goode, Erich. 1991. Positive deviance: A viable concept? *Deviant Behavior* 12: 289–309.

Goodger, Kate, Trish Gorely, David Lavalee, and Chris Harwood. 2007. Burnout in sport: A systematic review. *Sport Psychologist* 21, 2: 127–151.

Goodman, Barak. 2001. *The merchants of cool: A report on the creators and marketers of popular culture for teenagers.* PBS Frontline. Online: http://www.pbs .org/wgbh/pages/frontline/shows/cool/.

Goodman, Cary. 1979. *Choosing sides: Playground and street life on the lower east side.* New York: Schocken Books.

Gordon, Ian. 2007. Caught looking. *ESPN The Magazine* 10.11 (June 4): 100–104.

Gorman, Christine. 2005. Why more kids are getting hurt. *Time* (June 6): 58.

Gramsci, Antonio. 1971. *Selections from the prison notebook* (Q. Hoare and G. N. Smith, trans). New York: International Publishers (original work published in 1947).

Gramsci, Antonio. 1988. Selected writings: 1918–1935 (D. Forgacs, ed.). New York: Shocken.

Grant, Alan. 2002a. Body shop. *ESPN The Magazine* 5.03 (February 4): 50–54.

Grant, Alan. 2002b. A painful reality. ESPNMag .com (January 30). Online: http://espn.go.com/ magazine/grant_20020130.html (retrieved June 2005).

Grant, Alan. 2008. Rogue spear. *ESPN The Magazine* 11.05 (March 10): 68–72.

Grasmuck, Sherri. 2005. *Protecting home: Class, race, and masculinity in boys' baseball.* New Brunswick, NJ: Rutgers University Press.

Graves, Joseph L. Jr. 2002. *The emperor's new clothes: Biological theories of race at the millennium.* New Brunswick, NJ: Rutgers University Press.

Graves, Joseph L., Jr. 2004. *The race myth: Why we pretend race exists in America.* New York: Penguin Books.

Green, Mick. 2004. Power, policy, and political priorities: Elite sport development in Canada and the United Kingdom. *Sociology of Sport Journal* 21, 4: 376–396.

Green, Mick. 2006. From "sport for all' to not about "sport" at all?: Interrogating sport policy interventions in the United Kingdom. *European Sport Management Quarterly* 6, 3: 217–238.

Green, Mick, and Barrie Houlihan. 2004. Advocacy coalitions and elite sport policy change in Canada and the United Kingdom. *International Review for the Sociology of Sport* 39, 4: 387–403.

Green, Tina Sloan. 2000. The future of African American female athletes. In D. Brooks and R. Althouse, eds., *Racism in college athletics: The African American athlete's experience* (pp. 227–243). Morgantown, WV: Fitness Information Technology.

Greenfeld, Karl Taro. 1999. Adjustment in mid-flight. *Outside* (February). Online: http://outside .away.com/magazine/0299/9902terje_2.html.

Gregory, Michele. 2009. Inside the locker room: Homosociability in the advertising industry. *Gender, Work and Organization* (forthcoming).

Gregory, Sean. 2006. Olympic-size controversy. *Time* 167, 3 (January 16): 21.

Greider, William. 2006. Olympic swagger. *The Nation* (February 28). Online: www.thenation .com/doc/20060313/greider2.

Grenfell, Christopher C., and Robert E. Rinehart. 2003. Skating on thin ice: Human rights in youth figure skating. *International Review for the Sociology of Sport* 38, 1: 79–97.

Grey, Mark. 1999. Playing sports and social acceptance: The experiences of immigrant and refugee students in Garden City, Kansas. In Jay Coakley and Peter Donnelly, eds., *Inside Sports* (pp. 28–36). London: Routledge.

Griffin, Pat. 1998. *Strong women, deep closets: Lesbians and homophobia in sport.* Champaign, IL: Human Kinetics.

Grohmann, Karolos. 2008. Teams put a price on Beijing Games medals. *International Herald Tribune* (March 5). Online: http://www.iht.com/ articles/reuters/2008/03/05/sports/OUKSP-UK-OLYMPICS-MEDALS.php.

Grossfeld, Stan. 2005. New spin on rugby: Quadriplegic athletes take sport to the extreme with wheelchair version. *Boston Globe* (May 31): D1.

Gruneau, Richard. 1988. Modernization or hegemony: Two views of sports and social development. In Jean Harvey and Hart Cantelon, eds., *Not just a game* (pp. 9–32). Ottawa, Ontario: University of Ottawa Press.

Gruneau, Richard. 1999. *Class, sports, and social development.* Champaign, IL: Human Kinetics.

Guérandel, Carine, and Christine Mennesson. 2007. Gender construction in judo interactions.

International Review for the Sociology of Sport 42, 2: 167–186.

Guest, Andrew, and Barbara Schneider. 2003. Adolescents' extracurricular participation in context: The mediating effects of schools, communities, and identity. *Sociology of Education* 76, 2: 89–109.

Guilbert, Sèbastien. 2004. Sport and violence: A typological analysis. *International Review for the Sociology of Sport* 39, 1: 45–55.

Gulick, Luther. 1906. Team games and civic loyalty. *School Review* 14: 676–679.

Guskiewicz, Kevin M. et al. 2007. Recurrent concussion and risk of depression in retired professional football players. *Medicine and Science in Sports and Exercise.* 39, 6: 903–909.

Guskiewicz, Kevin M., et al. 2003. Recurrent sport-related concussion linked to clinical depression. ACSM Annual Meeting, Free Communications, San Francisco, CA. *Medicine and Science in Sports & Exercise* 35, 5: S50.

Guskiewicz, Kevin M., et al. 2005. Association between recurrent concussion, mild cognitive impairment, and Alzheimer's disease in retired professional football players. *Neurosurgery* 57, 4: 719–724.

Gustafsson, Henrik, Göran Kenttä, Peter Hassman, and Carolina Lundqvist. 2007. Prevalence of burnout in competitive adolescent athletes. *Sport Psychologist* 21, 1: 21–37.

Guttmann, Allen. 1978. *From ritual to record: The nature of modern sports.* New York: Columbia University Press.

Guttmann, Allen. 1986. *Sport spectators.* New York: Columbia University Press.

Guttmann, Allen. 1988. *A whole new ball game: An interpretation of American sports.* Chapel Hill: University of North Carolina Press.

Guttmann, Allen. 1998. The appeal of violent sports. In J. Goldstein, ed., *Why we watch: The attractions of violent entertainment* (pp. 7–26). New York: Oxford University Press.

Guttmann, Allen. 2004. *Sports: The first five millennia.* Amherst: University of Massachusetts Press.

Hadden, Jeffrey. K. 2000. Religious movements. In E. F. Borgotta, and R. J. V. Montgomery, eds., *Encyclopedia of sociology* (pp. 2364–2376). New York: Macmillan Reference.

Hall, C. Michael. 2006. Urban entrepreneurship, corporate interests and sports mega-events: The thin policies of competitiveness within the hard outcomes of neoliberalism. *The Sociological Review* 54, Supplement 2: 59–70.

Hall, M. Ann. 2002. *The girl and the game: A history of women's sport in Canada.* Peterborough, Ontario: Broadview Press.

Hall, M. Ann, Trevor Slack, Gerry Smith, and David Whitson. 1991. *Sport in Canadian society.* Toronto: McClelland and Stewart.

Hallinan, Chris, and Barry Judd. 2007. "Blackfellas" basketball: Aboriginal identity and Anglo-Australian race relations in regional basketball. *Sociology of Sport Journal* 24, 4: 421–436.

Halverson, Erica Rosenfeld, and Richard Halverson. 2008. Fantasy baseball: The case for competitive fandom. *Games and Culture* 3, 3–4: 286–308.

Hammersley, Martyn. 2007. Ethnography. In George Ritzer, ed., *Encyclopedia of sociology* (pp. 1479–1483). London/New York: Blackwell.

Haney, C. Allen, and Demetrius W. Pearson. 1999. Rodeo injuries: An examination of risk factors. *Journal of Sport Behavior* 22, 4: 443–467.

Hanford, George. 1974. *An inquiry into the need for and the feasibility of a national study of intercollegiate athletics.* Washington, DC: American Council on Education.

Hanford, George. 1979. Controversies in college sports. *Annals of the American Academy of Political Science* 445: 66–79.

Hargreaves, Jennifer, 1994. *Sporting females: Critical issues in the history and sociology of women's sport.* London: Routledge.

Hargreaves, Jennifer. 2000. *Heroines of sport: The politics of difference and identity.* London: Routledge.

Hargreaves, Jennifer, and Patricia Anne Vertinsky, eds. 2006. *Physical culture, power and the body.* Abingdon/New York: Routledge.

Harp, Joyce B., and Lindsay Hecht. 2005. Obesity in the National Football League. *Journal of the American Medical Association* 293, 9: 1061–1062.

Harrison, C. Keith. 1998. Themes that thread through society: Racism and athletic manifestation in the African-American community. *Race, Ethnicity and Education* 1, 1: 63–74.

Harrison, C. Keith (with Sharon Yee). 2007. *The big game in sport management and higher education.*

The hiring practices of Division IA and IAA Head Football Coaches. Indianapolis: Black Coaches and Administrators.

Harrison, C. Keith, and Suzanne Malia Lawrence. 2004. College students' perceptions, myths, and stereotypes about African American athletes: A qualitative investigation. *Sport, Education and Society* 9, 1: 33–52.

Harrison, Louis, Jr., Laura Azzarito, and Joe Burden, Jr. 2004. Perceptions of athletic superiority: A view from the other side. *Race Ethnicity and Education* 7, 2: 149–166.

Harrison, Louis, Jr., Amelia M Lee, and Don Belcher. 1999. Race and gender differences in sport participation as a function of self-schema. *Journal of Sport and Social Issues* 23, 3: 287–307.

Harrison, Patricia A., and Gopalakrishnan Narayan. 2003. Differences in behavior, psychological factors, and environmental factors associated with participation in school sports and other activities in adolescence. *Journal of School Health*, 73, 3: 113–121.

Hart, M. Marie. 1981. On being female in sport. In M. M. Hart and S. Birrell, eds., *Sport in the socio-cultural process* (pp. 291–301). Dubuque, IA: Brown.

Hartmann, Douglas. 2001. Notes on midnight basketball and the cultural politics of recreation, race, and at-risk urban youth. *Journal of Sport and Social Issues* 25, 4: 339–371.

Hartmann, Douglas. 2003a. The sanctity of Sunday afternoon football: Why men love sports. *Contexts* 2, 4: 13–21.

Hartmann, Douglas. 2003b. Theorizing sport as social intervention: A view from the grassroots. *Quest* 55, 2: 118–140.

Hartmann, Douglas. 2004. *Race, culture, and the revolt of the black athlete: The 1968 Olympic protests and their aftermath*. Chicago: University of Chicago Press.

Hartmann, Douglas. 2007. Rush Limbaugh, Donovan McNabb, and "a little social concern": Reflections on the problems of whiteness in contemporary American sport. *Journal of Sport and Social Issues* 31, 1: 45–60.

Hartmann, Douglas. 2008. High school sports participation and educational attainment: Recognizing, assessing, and utilizing the relationship. Report to the LA84 Foundation. Online: http://www.la84foundation.org/3ce/HighSchoolSportsParticipation.pdf.

Hartmann, Douglas, and Brooks Depro. 2006. Rethinking sports-based community crime prevention: A preliminary analysis of the relationship between midnight basketball and urban crime rates. *Journal of Sport and Social Issues* 30, 2: 180–196.

Hartmann, Douglas, and Michael Massoglia. 2007. Re-assessing high school sports participation and deviance in early adulthood: Evidence of enduring, bifurcated effects. *The Sociological Quarterly*, 48: 485–505.

Hartmann, Douglas, and D. Wheelock. 2002. Sport as prevention? Minneapolis's experiment with late-night basketball. *CURA Reporter* 32, 3: 13–17.

Harvey, Jean, Alan Law, and Michael Cantelon. 2001. North American professional team sport franchises ownership patterns and global entertainment conglomerates. *Sociology of Sport Journal* 18, 4: 435–457.

Harvey, Jean, Maurice Levesque, and Peter Donnelly. 2007. Sport volunteerism and social capital. *Sociology of Sport Journal* 24, 2: 206–223.

Hastings, Donald W., Sherry Cable, and Sammy Zahran. 2005. The globalization of a minor sport: The diffusion and commodification of masters swimming. *Sociological Spectrum* 25, 2: 133–154.

Hawes, Kay. 2001. Mirror, mirror. *NCAA News*, special report (September 24): A1–4.

Hawkins, Billy. 2000. *The new plantation: The internal colonialization of black student athletes*. Winterville, GA: Sadiki.

Heath, Thomas. 2003. For the investor who has everything. *Washington Post* (October 14): A1. Online: www.washingtonpost.com/ac2/wp-dyn/A21700-2003Oct13 (retrieved July 20, 2005).

Heckert, Alex, and Druann Heckert. 2002. A new typology of deviance: Integrating normative and reactivist definitions of deviance. *Deviant Behavior* 23: 449–479.

Heckert, Druann Maria, and Daniel Alex Heckert. 2007. Positive deviance. In George Ritzer, ed., *Encyclopedia of sociology* (pp. 3542–3544). London/New York: Blackwell.

Henderson, John. 2004. Cycling's other race. *The Denver Post* (July 4): 13B.

Henricks, Thomas S. 2006. *Play reconsidered: Sociological perspectives on human expression*. Urbana: University of Illinois Press.

Heywood, Leslie, and Shari Dworkin. 2003. *Built to win: The female athlete as cultural icon.* Minneapolis: University of Minnesota Press.

Hiestand, Michael. 2007. Sports on TV: Facts or opinions? *USA Today* (October 12): 3C.

Hiestand, Michael. 2008. Sports on TV: Event puts a new spin on bowling. *USA Today* (May 7): 3C. Online: http://www.usatoday.com/printedition/sports/20080507/c3mike07.art.htm.

Higgins, George E., Richard Tewksbury, and Elizabeth Ehrhardt Mustaine. 2007. Sports fan binge drinking: An examination using low self-control and peer association. *Sociological Spectrum* 27, 4: 389–404.

Higgins, Matt. 2005. A sport so popular, they added a second boom. *The New York Times* (July 25). Online: http://query.nytimes.com/mem/tnt.html?emc=tnt&tntget=2005/07/25/sports/othersports/25boom.html.

Higgins, Matt. 2007. It's a kids' world on the halfpipe. *The New York Times* (July 15). Online: www.nytimes.com/2007/07/15/sports/othersports/15skate.html.

Higgins, Paul C. 1992. *Making disability: Exploring the transformation of human variation.* Springfield, IL: Thomas.

Higgs, Robert J. 1995. *God in the stadium: Sports and religion in America.* Lexington: University of Kentucky Press.

Hill, Michael. 2007. Achievement and athletics: Issues and concerns for state boards of education. *State Education Standard* 8, 1: 22–31.

Hills, Laura. 2007. Friendship, physicality, and physical education: An exploration of the social and embodied dynamics of girls' physical education experiences. *Sport, Education and Society* 12, 3: 317–336.

Hilvoorde, Ivo M. 2008. Elite sport and national pride. Paper presented at the Fifth Conference of the European Association for Sociology of Sport (Bled, Slovenia, May 23).

Hnida, Katie. 2006. *Still kicking: My journey as the first woman to play Division I college football.* New York: Scribner.

Hoberman, John M. 1992. *Mortal engines: The science of performance and the dehumanization of sport.* New York: Free Press.

Hoberman, John M. 1994. The sportive-dynamic body as a symbol of productivity. In T. Siebers, ed., *Heterotopia: Postmodern utopia and the body politic* (pp. 199–228). Ann Arbor: University of Michigan Press.

Hoberman, John M. 2004. *Testosterone dreams: Rejuvenation, aphrodisia, doping.* Berkeley: University of California Press.

Hodge, Ken, Chris Lonsdale, and Johan Y. Y. Ng. 2008. Burnout in elite rugby: Relationships with basic psychological needs fulfilment. *Journal of Sport Sciences* 26, 8: 835–844.

Hoeber, Larena. 2007. Exploring the gaps between meanings and practices of gender equity in a sport organization. *Gender, Work and Organization* 14, 3: 259–280.

Hoeber, Larena. 2008. Gender equity for athletes: Multiple understandings of an organizational value. *Sex Roles: A Journal of Research* 58, 1–2: 58–71.

Hoffman, John P. 2006. Extracurricular activities, athletic participation, and adolescent alcohol use: Gender-differentiated and school-contextual effects. *Journal of Health and Social Behavior* 47, 3: 275–290.

Hoffman, Mathew (with Alyssa Roenigk). 2005. Fall guy. *ESPN The Magazine* (August 1): 62–70.

Hoffman, Shirl. 1992a. Evangelicalism and the revitalization of religious ritual in sport. In S. Hoffman, ed., *Sport and religion* (pp. 111–125). Champaign, IL: Human Kinetics.

Hoffman, Shirl. 1992b. Nimrod, nephilim, and the athletae dei. In S. Hoffman, ed., *Sport and religion* (pp. 275–286). Champaign, IL: Human Kinetics.

Hoffman, Shirl. 1992c. Recovering a sense of the sacred in sport. In S. Hoffman, ed., *Sport and religion* (pp. 153–160). Champaign, IL: Human Kinetics.

Hoffman, Shirl. 1992d. *Sport and religion.* Champaign, IL: Human Kinetics.

Hoffman, Shirl. 1999. The decline of civility and the rise of religion in American sport. *Quest* 51, 1: 69–84.

Hogan, Jackie. 2003. Staging the nation: Gendered and ethnicized discourses of national identity in Olympic opening ceremonies. *Journal of Sport and Social Issues* 27, 2: 100–123.

Hogshead-Makar, Nancy, and Andrew S. Zimbalist, eds. 2007. *Equal play: Title IX and social change.* Philadelphia: Temple University Press.

Holt, Nicholas, L., ed. 2007. *Positive youth development through sport.* Milton Park/New York: Routledge.

Honea, Joy. 2005. *Youth cultures and consumerism: Sport subcultures and possibilities for resistance.* Ph.D. dissertation, Sociology Department, Colorado State University; Fort Collins, CO.

Honea, Joy Crissey. 2007. Sport, alternative. In George Ritzer, ed., *Encyclopedia of sociology* (pp. 4653–4656). London/New York: Blackwell.

Hong, Fan, ed. 2006. *Sport, nationalism and orientalism: The Asian Games.* London/New York: Routledge.

hooks, bell. 2000. *Where we stand: Class matters.* New York/London: Routledge.

Horne, John D. 2007a. Controlling the spin: The political discourses of Boosters and Sceptics before, during and after major sports events (MSEs). Paper presented at the annual conference of the International Sociology of Sport Association, Copenhagen, Denmark.

Horne, John D. 2007b. The four 'knowns' of sports mega-events. *Leisure Studies* 26, 1: 81–96.

Horne, John, and Wolfram Manzenreiter, 2006a. An introduction to the sociology of sports mega-events. In John Horne and Wolfram Manzenreiter, eds., *Sports mega-events: Social scientific analyses of a global phenomenon* (pp. 1–24). Oxford: Blackwell.

Horne, John, and Wolfram Manzenreiter, 2006b. *Sports mega-events: Social scientific analyses of a global phenomenon.* Oxford: Blackwell (also published in 2006 as *The Sociological Review* 54, Supplement 2).

Houlihan, Barrie. 1994. *Sport and international politics.* Hemel Hempstead, England: Harvester-Wheatsheaf.

Houlihan, Barrie. 2000. Politics and sport. In Jay Coakley and Eric Dunning, eds., *Handbook of sport studies* (pp. 213–227). London: Sage.

Houlihan, Barrie, and Mick Green, eds. 2007. *Comparative elite sport development: systems, structures and public policy.* Amsterdam/Boston: Elsevier/Butterworth-Heinemann.

Hovden, J. 2000. Gender and leadership selection processes in Norwegian sporting organizations. *International Review for the Sociology of Sport* 35, 1: 75–82.

Howard, Theresa. 2007. Nike serves up new ads supporting women. *USA Today* (August 27): 5B. Online: www.usatoday.com/printedition/money/20070827/adtracklead27.art.htm.

Howe, David. 2008. *The cultural politics of the Paralympic movement.* London: Routledge.

Howe, P. David. 2003. Kicking stereotypes into touch: An ethnographic account of women's rugby. In Anne Bolin and Jane Granskog, eds., *Athletic intruders: Ethnographic research on women, culture, and exercise* (pp. 227–246). Albany: State University of New York Press.

Howe, P. David. 2004. *Sport, professionalism and pain: Ethnographies of injury and risk.* London/New York: Routledge.

Huang, Chin-Ju, and Ian Brittain. 2006. Negotiating identities through disability sport. *Sociology of Sport Journal* 23, 4: 352–375.

Hubbard, Steve. 1998. *Faith in sports: Athletes and their religion on and off the field.* New York: Doubleday.

Hudson, Ian. 2001. The use and misuse of economic impact analysis: The case of professional sports. *Journal of Sport and Social Issues* 25, 1: 20–39.

Hughes, Glyn. 2004. Managing black guys: Representation, corporate culture, and the NBA. *Sociology of Sport Journal* 21, 2: 163–184.

Hughes, Robert, and Jay Coakley. 1991. Positive deviance among athletes: The implications of overconformity to the sport ethic. *Sociology of Sport Journal* 8, 4: 307–325.

Hughson, John. 2000. The boys are back in town: Soccer support and the social reproduction of masculinity. *Journal of Sport and Social Issues* 24, 1: 8–23.

Hunt, H. David. 2005. The effect of extracurricular activities in the educational process: Influence on academic outcomes? *Sociological Spectrum* 25, 4: 417–445.

Hutchinson, Nichola. 2008. Disabling beliefs? Impaired embodiment in the religious tradition of the West. *Body & Society* 12, 4: 1–23.

Hyland, Drew A. 2008. Paidia and paideia: The educational power of athletics. *Journal of Intercollegiate Sport* 1, 1: 66–71.

IAAF. 2007. A first for Bahrain. *IAAF Magazine* (Issue 1, June 1). Online: http://www.iaaf.org/news/magazine/newsid=38867.html (retrieved, May 6, 2008).

Iber, Jorge, and Regalado, Samuel O., eds. 2007. *Mexican Americans and sports: A reader on athletics and barrio life.* College Station: Texas A&M University Press.

IBS (International Bible Society). 1996a. *More than gold.* Colorado Springs: IBS.

IBS (International Bible Society). 1996b. *Path to victory: A sports New Testament with the testimonies of athletes who are winning in life* (no. 1144). Colorado Springs: IBS.

Ingham, Alan G., B. J. Blissmer, and K. W. Davidson. 1999. The expendable prolympic self: Going beyond the boundaries of the sociology and psychology of sport. *Sociology of Sport Journal* 16, 3: 236–268.

Ingham, Alan G., Melissa A. Chase, and Joanne Butt. 2002. From the performance principle to the developmental principle: Every kid a winner? *Quest* 4, 4: 308–332.

Ingham, Alan, and Alison Dewar. 1999. Through the eyes of youth: "Deep play" in peewee ice hockey. In Jay Coakley and Peter Donnelly, eds. *Inside Sports* (pp. 7–16). London: Routledge.

Ingham, Alan, and Mary McDonald. 2003. Sport and community/communitas. In R. Wilcox, D. L. Andrews, R. L. Irwin, and R. Pitter, eds., *Sporting dystopias: The making and meaning of urban sport cultures* (pp. 17–34). Albany: State University of New York Press.

Inness, Sherrie A. 2004. 'Boxing gloves and bustiers': New images of tough women. In Sherrie A. Inness, ed., *Action chicks* (pp. 1–17). New York: Palgrave Macmillan.

Interlandi, Jeneen. 2008. Myth meets science. *Newsweek* 151, 8 (February 25): 48.

IPC, 2008. IPC Position Statement on IAAF's Commissioned Research on Oscar Pistorius. International Paralympic Committee. Online: www.paralympic.org/release/Main_Sections _Menu/News/Press_Releases/2008_01_14_a.html.

Ives, Nat. 2004. Coming for gamers: Football unfettered. *The New York Times* (December 20): C8.

Jackson, Steven J., and David L. Andrews, eds. 2004. *Sport, culture and advertising: Identities, commodities and the politics of representation.* London/ New York: Routledge.

Jackson, Steven J., and Brendan Hokowhitu. 2002. Sport, tribes, and technology: The New Zealand All Blacks Haka and the politics of identity. *Journal of Sport and Social Issues* 26, 2: 125–139.

Jackson, Steven J., and Jay Scherer. 2002. Screening the nation's past: Adidas, advertising and corporate nationalism in New Zealand. Paper presented at the annual meetings of the North American Society for the Sociology of Sport, Indianapolis (November).

Jaffe, Eric. 2007. Overuse injuries cutting short pitching careers before they even begin. *The Columbia Journalist*, May 1. Online: http:// columbiajournalist.org/sports_reporting_ padwe/2005/article.asp?subj=sports&course= sports_reporting_padwe&id=1031.

James, C. L. R. 1984. *Beyond a boundary* (American edition). New York: Pantheon Books.

Jamieson, Katherine. 1998. Navigating the system: The case of Latina student-athletes in women's collegiate sports. Paper presented at the annual conference of the American Alliance for Health, Physical Education, Recreation and Dance, Reno, NV (April).

Jamieson, Katherine. 2005. "All my hopes and dreams": Families, schools, and subjectivities in collegiate softball. *Journal of Sport and Social Issues* 29, 2: 133–147.

Jamieson, Katherine M. 2007. Advance at your own risk: Latinas, families, and collegiate softball. In Jorge Iber and Samuel O. Regalado, eds. *Mexican Americans and sports: A reader on athletics and barrio life* (pp. 213–232). College Station: Texas A&M University Press.

Jayson, Sharon. 2004. On or off the field, it's a "civility" war out there. *USA Today* (November 30): 9D.

Jeanrenaud, Claude, and Kesenne, Stefan, eds. 2006. *The economics of sport and the media.* Northampton, MA: Edward Elgar.

Jenkins, Chris. 2000. Caught in gambling's web. *USA Today* (March 13): 1C–2C.

Jenkins, Chris. 2002. The new face of NASCAR. *USA Today* (May 24): 1A–2A.

Jenkins, Chris. 2005. Steroid policy hits Latin Americans. *USA Today* (May 6): 7C.

Jennings, Andrew. 1996a. *The new lords of the rings.* London: Pocket Books.

Jennings, Andrew. 1996b. Power, corruption, and lies. *Esquire* (May): 99–104.

Jennings, Andrew. 2006. *Foul! The secret world of FIFA—bribes, vote rigging, and ticket scandals.* New York: HarperSport.

Jennings, Andrew, and Clare Sambrook. 2000. *The great Olympic swindle: When the world wanted its games back.* New York: Simon and Schuster.

Johns, David. 1992. Starving for gold: A case study in overconformity in high performance sport. Paper presented at the annual conference of the North American Society for the Sociology of Sport, Toledo (November).

Johns, David. 1996. Positive deviance and the sport ethic: Examining weight loss strategies in rhythmic gymnastics. *Hong Kong Journal of Sports Medicine and Sport Science* 2 (May): 49–56.

Johns, David. 1997. Fasting and feasting: Paradoxes in the sport ethic. *Sociology of Sport Journal* 15, 1: 41–63.

Johns, David. 2004. Weight management as sport injury: Deconstructing disciplinary power in the sport ethic. In Kevin Young, ed., *Sporting bodies, damaged selves: Sociological studies of sports-related injury* (pp. 117–133). Amsterdam: Elsevier.

Johns, David P., and Jennifer S. Johns. 2000. Surveillance, subjectivism and technologies of power. *International Review for the Sociology of Sport* 35, 2: 219–234.

Johnson, Allan G. 2006. *Privilege, power, and difference* (2nd ed.). New York: McGraw-Hill.

Joiner, Lottie L. 2007. Superkids might be missing out on childhood fun. *Coloradoan* (August 19): B7.

Jonas, Scott. 2005. Should women play sports? Online: www.jesus-is-savior.com/Womens%20Page/christian_women_and_sports.htm (retrieved July 8, 2005).

Jones, Jeffrey M. 2008. One in six Americans gamble on sports. *Gallup News Service* (February 1). Online: http://www.gallup.com/poll/104086/One-Six-Americans-Gamble-Sports.aspx.

Joukowsky, Artemis A. W., III, and Larry Rothstein. 2002a. New horizons in disability sport. In Artemis A. W. Joukowsky, III, and Larry Rothstein, eds., *Raising the bar* (pp. 8–17). New York: Umbrage Editions.

Joukowsky, Artemis A. W., III, and Larry Rothstein, eds. 2002b. *Raising the bar*. New York: Umbrage Editions.

Jutel, Annemarie. 2002. Olympic road cycling and national identity: Where is Germany? *Journal of Sport and Social Issues* 26, 2: 195–208.

Kane, Mary Jo. 2002. Playing unfair: The media image of the female athlete (video). Media Education Foundation. Online: http://www.mediaed.org/videos/MediaGenderAndDiversity/PlayingUnfair.

Kane, Mary Jo, and Jo Ann Buysse. 2005. Intercollegiate media guides as contested terrain: A longitudinal analysis. *Sociology of Sport Journal* 22, 2: 214–238.

Kane, Mary Jo, Perry Leo, and Lynn K. Holleran. 2008. Issues related to academic support and performance of Division I student-athlete: A case study at the University of Minnesota. *Journal of Intercollegiate Sport* 1, 1: 98–129.

Kassandra Project, 2007. *Kassandra Report* (December 27). Online: http://kassandraproject.files.wordpress.com/2008/02/kassandra_report.pdf.

Katz, Jackson. 2003. When you're asked about the Kobe Bryant case. Online: www.jacksonkatz.com/bryant.html.

Kay, Joanne, and Suzanne Laberge. 2003. Oh say can you ski? In Robert E. Rinehart and Synthia Sydnor, eds., *To the extreme: Alternative sports, inside and out* (pp. 381–398). Albany: State University of New York Press.

Kay, Tess. 2006. Daughters of Islam: Family influences on Muslim young women's participation in sport. *International Review for the Sociology of Sport* 41, 3–4: 357–374.

Kayser, Bengt, Alexandre Mauron, and Andy Miah. 2005. Viewpoint: Legalisation of performance-enhancing drugs. *The Lancet* 366 (December): S21. Online: http://www.thelancet.com/journals/lancet/article/PIIS0140673605678312/fulltext.

Kayser, Bengt, and Aaron C. T. Smith. 2008. Globalisation of anti-doping: The reverse side of the medal. *British Medical Journal* 337 (July 4): a584.

Keating, Peter. 2004a. The biz. *ESPN The Magazine* (December 6): 14.

Keating, Peter. 2004b. Insurance run. *ESPN The Magazine* 7.14 (July 5): 70–73.

Keating, Peter. 2005. Baseball has solved its steroid problem—at least that's what they want you to believe. *ESPN The Magazine* (December 5): 16.

Keddie, John. 2008. *Running the race: Eric Liddell, Olympic champion and missionary*. Faverdale North, Darlington, UK: Evangelical Press.

Keith, Susan. 1999. Native American women in sport. *Journal of Physical Education, Recreation and Dance* 70, 4: 47–49.

Kelderman, Eric. 2008a. Athletic directors cry foul over NCAA's data. *The Chronicle of Higher*

Education 54, 38 (May 30): A4. Online: http://chronicle.com/weekly/v54/i38/38a00401.htm.

Kelderman, Eric. 2008b. New data show many colleges footing large share of athletics expenses. *The Chronicle of Higher Education* 54, 37 (May 23): A15. Online: http://chronicle.com/weekly/v54/i37/37a01502.htm.

Keller, Josh. 2007. As football players get bigger, more of them risk a dangerous sleep disorder. *Chronicle of Higher Education* 53, 27 (March 9): 43.

Kelley, Betty C., Shirl J. Hoffman, and Diane. L. Gill. 1990. The relationship between competitive orientation and religious orientation. *Journal of Sport Behavior* 13, 3: 145–156.

Kellner, Douglas. 2003a. *Media spectacle*. London/New York: Routledge.

Kellner, Douglas. 2003b. Toward a critical theory of education. *Democracy and Nature* 9, 1: 51–64. Online: www.gseis.ucla.edu/faculty/kelllner/.

Kellner, Douglas. 2004. The sports spectacle, Michael Jordan, and Nike. In Patrick B. Miller and David K. Wiggins, eds., *Sport and the color line* (pp. 305–326). New York/London: Routledge.

Kensler, Tom. 2005. Wie playing PGA Tour event seems out of bounds to some. *Denver Post* (July 3): 1B, 10B.

Keown, Tim. 2004. World of hurt. *ESPN The Magazine* (August 2): 57–77.

Kian, Edward (Ted) M., John Vincent, and Michael Mondello. 2008. Masculine hegemonic hoops: An analysis of media coverage of March madness. *Sociology of Sport Journal* 25, 2: 223–242.

Kidd, Bruce. 1984. The myth of the ancient games. In A. Tomlinson and G. Whannel, eds., *Five-ring circus* (pp. 71–83). London: Pluto Press.

Kidd, Bruce. 1987. Sports and masculinity. In M. Kaufman, ed., *Beyond patriarchy: Essays by men on pleasure, power, and change* (pp. 250–265). New York: Oxford University Press.

Kidd, Bruce. 1995. Inequality in sport, the corporation, and the state: An agenda for social scientists. *Journal of Sport and Social Issues* 19, 3: 232–248.

Kidd, Bruce. 1996a. Taking the rhetoric seriously: Proposals for Olympic education. *Quest* 48, 1: 82–92.

Kidd, Bruce. 1996b. Worker sport in the New World: The Canadian story. In A. Kruger and J. Riordan, eds., *The story of worker sport* (pp. 143–156). Champaign, IL: Human Kinetics.

Kidd, Bruce. 1997. *The struggle for Canadian sport*. Toronto: University of Toronto Press.

Kidd, Bruce (with Maggie MacDonnell). 2007. Peace, sport and development. In Sport for Development and Peace, International Working Group (SDP/IWG), *Literature Reviews on Sport for Development and Peace* (pp. 158–194). Toronto, Ontario: University of Toronto, Faculty of Physical Education and health. Online: http://iwg.sportanddev.org/data/htmleditor/file/Lit.%20Reviews/literature%20review%20SDP.pdf (retrieved January 24, 2008).

Kihl, L. 2007. Moral codes, moral tensions and hiding behind the rules: A snapshot of athletic administrators' practical morality. *Sport Management Review* 10, 3: 279–305.

Kilbourne, Jean. 2007. The naked truth: Advertising's image of women. Address given at the annual White Privilege Conference, April 20, Colorado Springs, CO.

King, C. Richard, and Charles Fruehling Springwood. 2001a. *Beyond the cheers: Race as a spectacle in college sport*. Albany: State University of New York Press.

King, C. Richard, and Charles Fruehling Springwood, eds. 2001b. *Team spirits: The Native American mascots controversy*. Lincoln: Bison Books and University of Nebraska Press.

King, C. Richard, ed. 2004a. *Native Americans in sports*. Armonk, NY: Sharpe Reference.

King, C. Richard. 2004b. Re/claiming Indianness: Critical perspectives on Native American mascots. *Journal of Sport and Social Issues* 28, 1 (special issue).

King, C. Richard. 2007a. Postcolonialism and sports. In George Ritzer, ed., *Encyclopedia of sociology* (pp. 3547–3548). London/New York: Blackwell.

King, C. Richard. 2007b. Sport and ethnicity. In George Ritzer, ed., *Encyclopedia of sociology* (pp. 4681–4684). London/New York: Blackwell.

King, C. Richard. 2007c. Staging the White Olympics. *Journal of Sport and Social Issues* 31, 1: 89–94.

King, Kelley. 2002. The ultimate jock school. *Sports Illustrated* (November 25): 48–54.

King, Kelley. 2005. Little shred schoolhouse. *Sports Illustrated* (March 21): (in Scorecard section).

King, Peter. 2004. Painful reality. *Sports Illustrated* (October 11): 6063.

Kiszla, Mark. 2001. Denver "D" short for "dark side." *Denver Post* (March 20): 1D, 3D.

Kiszla, Mark. 2007. Injury shakes up tough guys. *Denver Post* (September 11). Online: http://www.denverpost.com/broncos/ci_6856716.

Kix, Paul. 2007. Muscling up. *ESPN The Magazine* 10.10 (May 21): 44.

Klein, Alan. 1991. *Sugarball: The American game, the Dominican dream.* New Haven, CT: Yale University Press.

Klein, Alan. 1993. *Little big men: Bodybuilding subculture and gender construction.* Albany: State University of New York Press.

Klein, Alan. 2006. *Growing the game: The globalization of major league baseball.* New Haven: Yale University Press.

Klein, Alan. 2008a. Anti-semitism and anti-somatism: Seeking the elusive sporting Jew. In Alan Klein, ed., *American sports: An anthropological approach* (pp. 1120–1137). New York/London: Routledge (also published in *Sociology of Sport Journal* 17, 3: 213–228).

Klein, Alan. 2008b. Progressive ethnocentrism: Ideology and understanding in Dominican baseball. *Journal of Sport and Social Issues* 32, 2: 121–138.

Klein, Naomi. 2002. *No logo.* New York: Picador USA.

Klis, Mike. 2008. Pain takes back seat for Big Game. *The Denver Post* (February 1): 1D, 7D. Online: http://www.denverpost.com/sports/ci_8134531.

Knight Commission. 1991. *Keeping faith with the student-athlete.* Report of the Knight Foundation Commission on Intercollegiate Athletics. Miami, FL: Knight Foundation.

Knight Commission. 1992. *A solid start: A report on reform of intercollegiate athletics.* Report of the Knight Foundation Commission on Intercollegiate Athletics. Miami: Knight Foundation.

Knight Commission. 1993. *A new beginning for a new century: Intercollegiate athletics in the United States.* Report of the Knight Foundation Commission on Intercollegiate Athletics. Miami: Knight Foundation.

Knight Commission. 2001. *A call to action: Reconnecting college sports and higher education.* Report of the Knight Foundation Commission on Intercollegiate Athletics. Miami. Online: Knight Foundation http://www.knightfdn.org/.

Knoppers, Annelies, and Anton Anthonissen. 2008. Gendered managerial discourses in sport organizations: Multiplicity and complexity. *Sex Roles: A Journal of Research* 58, 1–2: 93–103.

Knoppers, Annelies, and Agnes Elling. 2004. "We do not engage in promotional journalism": Discursive strategies used by sport journalists to describe the selection process. *International Review for the Sociology of Sport* 39, 1: 57–73.

Knudson, Mark. 2005. The Mark: The whole IX yards. *Mile High Sports Magazine* (May): 21–23.

Kohn, Alfie. 1986. *No contest: The case against competition.* Boston: Houghton Mifflin.

Komlos, John, and Benjamin E. Lauderdale. 2007. Underperformance in affluence: The remarkable relative decline in U.S. heights in the second half of the 20th century. *Social Science Quarterly* 88, 2: 283–305.

Kooistra, Paul. 2005. Bend it like Bourdieu: Class, gender and race in American youth soccer. Paper presented at the annual meeting of the American Sociological Association, Philadelphia, PA (August 12).

Kooistra, Paul, John S. Mahoney, and Lisha Bridges. 1993. The unequal opportunity for equal ability hypothesis: Racism in the National Football League. *Sociology of Sport Journal* 10, 3: 241–255.

Koukouris, Konstantinos. 1994. Constructed case studies: Athletes' perspectives of disengaging from organized competitive sport. *Sociology of Sport Journal* 11, 2: 114–139.

Kozol, Jonathan. 1991. *Savage inequalities.* New York: Crown.

Kozol, Jonathan. 2002. Malign neglect. *The Nation* 274, 22: 20–23.

Kozol, Jonathan. 2005. *The shame of the nation: The restoration of apartheid schooling in America.* New York: Crown Publishers.

Krane, Vikki. 2001. We can be athletic and feminine, but do we want to? Challenging hegemonic femininity in women's sport. *Quest* 53, 1: 115–133.

Krane, Vikki, Precilla Y. L. Choi, Shannon M. Baird, Christine M. Aimar, and Kerrie J. Kauer. 2004. Living the paradox: Female athletes negotiate femininity and muscularity. *Sex Roles* 50, 5/6: 315–329.

Krane, Vikki, Jennifer Waldron, Jennifer Michalenok, and Julie Stiles-Shipley. 2001. Body image concerns in female exercisers and athletes: A feminist cultural studies perspective. *Women in Sport and Physical Activity Journal* 10, 1: 17–54.

Kraszewski, Jon. 2008. Pittsburgh in Fort Worth: Football bars, sports television, sports fandom, and the management of home. *Journal of Sport and Social Issues* 32, 2: 139–157.

Kreager, Derek A. 2007. Unnecessary roughness? School sports, peer networks, and male adolescent violence. *American Sociological Review* 72, 5: 705–724.

Kristal, Nicole. 2005. "Tutoring" rich kids cost me my dreams. *Newsweek* (April 11): 19.

Kruger, J., S., H. Carlson, and H. Kohl. 2006. Trends in strength training—United States, 1998–2004. *CDC Morbidity and Mortality Weekly Report* 55, 28 (July 21): 769–772. Online: http://www.cdc.gov/mmwr/preview/mmwrhtml/mm5528a1.htm.

Kusz, Kyle. 2001. "I want to be the minority." The politics of youthful white masculinities in sport and popular culture in 1990s America. *Journal of Sport and Social Issues* 25, 4: 390–416.

Kusz, Kyle W. 2007. From NASCAR nation to Pat Tillman: Notes on sport and the politics of white cultural nationalism in post-9/11 America. *Journal of Sport & Social Issues*, 30, 1: 77–88.

Laberge, Suzanne, and Mathieu Albert. 1999. Conceptions of masculinity and of gender transgressions in sport among adolescent boys: Hegemony, contestation, and social class dynamic. *Men and Masculinities* 1, 3: 243–267.

Laberge, Suzanne, and David Sankoff. 1988. Physical activities, body *habitus*, and lifestyles. In J. Harvey and H. Cantelon, eds., *Not just a game* (pp. 267–286). Ottawa: University of Ottawa Press.

Ladd, Tony, and James A. Mathisen. 1999. *Muscular Christianity: Evangelical Protestants and the development of American sport.* Grand Rapids, MI: Baker Books.

Lafferty, Yvonne, and Jim McKay. 2004. "Suffragettes in satin shorts"? Gender and competitive boxing. *Qualitative Sociology* 27, 3: 249–276.

Lamb, Julie. 2007. In George Ritzer, ed., *Encyclopedia of sociology* (pp. 3726–3728). London/New York: Blackwell.

Lamb, L. 2000. Can women save sports? An interview with Mary Jo Kane. *Utne Reader* 97: 56–57.

Lance, Larry. M. 2005. Violence in sport: A theoretical note. *Sociological Spectrum* 25, 2: 213–214.

Lapchick, Richard. 1984. *Broken promises: Racism in American sports.* New York: St. Martin's Press/Marek.

Lapchick, Richard. 2004. *Racial and gender report card, 2003.* Orlando: Institute for Diversity and Ethics in Sports, University of Central Florida.

Lapchick, Richard. 2005a. *Keeping score when it counts: Graduation rates for 2005 NCAA men's and women's Division I basketball tournament teams.* Orlando: Institute for Diversity and Ethics in Sport at the DeVos Sport Business Management Graduate Program, University of Central Florida.

Lapchick, Richard. 2005b. *2004 racial and gender report card.* Orlando: Institute for Diversity and Ethics in Sports, University of Central Florida.

Lapchick, Richard E. 2007. Asian American athletes: past, present and future. *ESPN The Magazine* (May 1). Online: http://espn.go.com/gen/s/2002/0430/1376346.html.

Lapchick, Richard. 2008a. Games could have lasting impact for Asian-Americans. *Sports Business Journal* 11, 17 (August 25–31): 29.

Lapchick, Richard. 2008b. *NCAA graduation rates* (21 online reports, 2003-2008). Orlando, FL: The Institute for Diversity and Ethics in Sports (University of Central Florida). Online: http://www.tidesport.org/ncaagraduationrates.html.

Lapchick, Richard. 2008c. *"Scoring the hire": A hiring report for NCAA Division I women's basketball head coaching positions.* Indianapolis: Black Coaches and Administrators. Online: http://bcasports.cstv.com/auto_pdf/p_hotos/s_chools/bca/genrel/auto_pdf/0406-report-card.

Lapointe, Joe. 2008. Michigan stadium will expand seating for disabled fans. *The New York Times* (March 11). Online: http://www.nytimes.com/2008/03/11/sports/ncaafootball/11michigan.html.

Laqueur, Thomas. 1990. *Making sex.* Cambridge, MA: Harvard University Press.

Lardner, James, and David A. Smith, eds. 2005. *Inequality matters: The growing economic divide in America and its poisonous consequences.* New York: The New Press.

Large, David Clay. 2007. *Nazi Games: The Olympics of 1936.* New York: Norton.

Lasn, Kalle. 2000. *Culture jam.* New York: Quill.

Latimer, Clay. 2005. More than child's play: Studies in determination. *Rocky Mountain News* (December 20): 1C, 11C–14C.

Latimer, Clay. 2008. "Before, I ran from danger and death. Now, I run for sport." *Rocky Mountain News* (August 8): Olympics8.

Laumann, Silken. 2006a. Athlete quotes. Right To Play (website), www.righttoplay.com/site/PageServer?pagename=athletequotes (retrieved January 15, 2008).

Laumann, Silken. 2006b. *Child's play: Rediscovering the joy of play in our families and our communities.* Toronto: Random House Canada.

Laurendeau, Jason. 2004. The "crack choir" and the "cock chorus": The intersection of gender and sexuality in skydiving texts. *Sociology of Sport Journal* 21, 4: 397–417.

Laurendeau, Jason. 2008. "Gendered risk regimes": A theoretical consideration of edgework and gender. *Sociology of Sport Journal* 25, 3: 293–309.

Laurendeau, Jason, and Nancy Sharara. 2008. "Women could be every bit as good as guys": Reproductive and resistant agency in two "action" sports. *Journal of Sport and Social Issues* 32, 1: 24–47.

Laurson, Kelly R., and Joey C. Eisenmann. 2007. Prevalence of overweight among high school football linemen. *Journal of the American Medical Association* 297, 4 (January 24/31). Online: http://jama.ama-assn.org/cgi/content/full/297/4/363.

Lavoie, Marc. 2000. Economics and sport. In J. Coakley and E. Dunning, eds., *Handbook of sports studies* (pp. 157–170). London: Sage.

Lawler, Jennifer. 2002. *Punch: Why women participate in violent sports.* Terre Haute, IN: Wish Publishing.

Lawrence, Janet H., Lori A. Hendricks, and Molly C. Ott. 2007. *Faculty perceptions of intercollegiate athletics: A national study of faculty at NCAA Division I Football Bowl Subdivision institutions.* A report prepared for the Knight Commission on Intercollegiate Athletics. Ann Arbor, MI: University of Michigan, Center for the Study of Higher and Postsecondary Education.

Lawrence, Suzanne Malia. 2005. African American athletes' experiences of race in sport. *International Review for the Sociology of Sport* 40, 1: 99–110.

Layden, Tim. 1995a. Better education. *Sports Illustrated* (April 3): 68–90.

Layden, Tim. 1995b. Book smart. *Sports Illustrated* (April 10): 68–79.

Layden, Tim. 1995c. You bet your life. *Sports Illustrated* (April 17): 46–55.

Layden, Tim. 2001. Does anyone remember the Titans? *Sports Illustrated* (October 15): 72–83.

Layden, Tim. 2002. The loneliest losers. *Sports Illustrated* (November 18): 69–72.

Layden, Tim. 2007. The big hit. *Sports Illustrated* 107, 4 (July 30): 53–62.

Le Batard, Dan. 2005a. Open look: The fight that tore the NBA apart? *ESPN The Magazine* (May 9): 14.

Le Batard, Dan. 2005b. Open look: Is it cheating if you don't understand the rules? *Es posible. ESPN The Magazine* (May 23): 14.

Leahy, Michael. 2008. The Pain Game. *Washington Post* (February 3): W08. Online: www.washingtonpost.com/wp-dyn/content/article/2008/01/29/AR2008012904015.html.

Lechner, Frank J. 2007. Imagined communities in the global game: Soccer and the development of Dutch national identity. In Richard Giulianotti and Roland Robertson, eds., *Globalization and sport* (pp. 107–121). Oxford, UK: Blackwell.

Lederman, Doug. 2008. A (money) losing proposition. *Inside Higher Ed* (May 16). Online: http://www.insidehighered.com/news/2008/05/16/ncaa.

Lee, Nammi, Steven J. Jackson, and Keunmo Lee. 2007. South Korea's "glocal" hero: The Hiddink syndrome and the rearticulation of national citizenship and identity. *Sociology of Sport Journal* 24, 3: 283–301.

Leeds, Michael A., Cristen Miller, and Judith Stull. 2007. Interscholastic athletics and investment in human capital. *Social Science Quarterly* 88, 3: 729–744.

Lefkowitz, Bernard. 1997. *Our guys: The Glen Ridge rape and the secret life of the perfect suburb.* Berkeley: University of California Press.

Le Gall, Franck, Christopher Carling, and Thomas Reilly. 2008. Injuries in Young Elite Female Soccer Players: An 8-Season Prospective Study. *The American Journal of Sports Medicine* 36: 276–284.

Lehrman, Sally. 1997. Forget *Men are from Mars, women are from Venus.* Stanford Today.

Online: www.stanford.edu/dept/news/ stanfordtoday/ed/9705/9705fea401.shtml (retrieved December 1, 2005).

Leland, J. 2000. Why America's hooked on wrestling. *Newsweek* (February 7): 46–55.

Lemert, Charles. 2002. *Social things*. Lanham, MD: Rowman & Littlefield.

Lenskyj, Helen J. 1986. *Out of bounds: Women, sport and sexuality*. Toronto: Women's Press.

Lenskyj, Helen J. 1999. Women, sport, and sexualities: Breaking the silences. In Phillip White and Kevin Young, eds., *Sport and gender in Canada* (pp. 170–181). Don Mills, ON: Oxford University Press.

Lenskyj, Helen J. 2000. *Inside the Olympics industry: Power, politics, and activism*. Albany: State University of New York Press.

Lenskyj, Helen. 2003. *Out in the field: Gender, sport and sexualities*. Toronto: Women's Press. Online: http://www.womenspress.ca/.

Lenskyj, Helen Jefferson. 2008. *Olympic industry resistance: Challenging Olympic power and propaganda*. Albany, NY: State University of New York Press.

Leonard, Wilbert Marcellus II. 1995. Economic discrimination in major league baseball: Marginal revenue products of majority and minority group members. *Journal of Sport and Social Issues* 19, 2: 180–190.

Levy, Don. 2005. Fantasy sports and fanship habitus: Understanding the process of sport consumption. Paper presented at the annual conference of the American Sociological Society, Philadelphia (August).

Lewin, Tamar. 2002. Ruling fuels drug-test debate in schools. *Denver Post* (September 29): 12A.

Lewis, Jerry. 2007. *Sports fan violence in North America*. New York: Rowman & Littlefield.

Liang, Ursula. 2007. The emphasis is not on 'Asian' but 'American.' *ESPN The Magazine* (May 1). Online: http://espn.go.com/gen/ s/2002/0429/1375733.html.

Liddle, Eric. 2003. Black is best. Online: www .spectator.co.uk (retrieved June 2005).

Lieber, Jill. 2003. Playing dirty, playing mean. *USA Today* (January 3): 1C–2C.

Light, Richard, and Louise Kinnaird. 2002. Appeasing the Gods: Shinto, sumo and "true" Japanese spirit. In T. Magdalinski and T. J. L.

Chandler, eds., *With God on their side: Sport in the service of religion* (pp. 139–159). London/New York: Routledge.

Ligutom-Kimura, Donna Ann. 1995. The invisible women. *Journal of Physical Education, Recreation and Dance* 66, 7: 34–41.

Lines, Gill. 2007. The impact of media sport events on the active participation of young people and some implications for PE pedagogy. *Sport, Education and Society* 12, 4: 349–366.

Lippi, Giuseppe, Giuseppe Banfi, Massimo Franchini, and Gian Cesare Guidi. 2008. New strategies for doping control. *Journal of Sports Sciences* 26, 5: 441–445.

Lipscomb, Stephen. 2006. Secondary school extracurricular involvement and academic achievement: A fixed effects approach. *Economics of Education Review* 26, 4: 463–472.

Lipsyte, Robert, 1996a. Farewell to sport, welcome to sportainment. *The New York Times* (August 4). Online: http://www.nytimes.com/specials/ olympics/0804/oly-lipyte-column.html.

Lipsyte, Robert. 1996b. Little girls in a staged spectacle for big bucks? That's sportainment! *The New York Times* (August 4): 28.

Lipsyte, Robert.1996c. One fell swoosh: Can a logo conquer all? *The New York Times*, section B (February 7): 9.

Lipsyte, Robert. 1998. A step in the healing process. *The New York Times* (March 5): C22.

Lipsyte, Robert. 1999. The jock culture: Time to debate questions. *The New York Times*, section 8 (May 9): 11.

Lipsyte, R. 2001. In purest form, basketball is a playground game. *The New York Times* (October 28): S13.

Liston, Katie. 2007. Revisiting the feminist-figurational sociology exchange. *Sport in Society* 10, 4: 623–645.

Liston, Katie, Dean Reacher, Andy Smith, and Ivan Waddington. 2006. Managing pain and injury in non-elite rugby union and rugby league: A case study of players at a British university. *Sport in Society* 9, 3: 388–402.

Loland, Sigmund. 2003. Three Ideal-typical views and their implications. *Nordic Sport Science Forum* (October 9). Online: http:// idrottsforum.org/articles/loland/loland _2.html.

Long, Jonathan, Ben Carrington, and Karl Spracklin. 2007. 'Asians cannot wear turbans in the scrum': Explorations of racist discourse within professional rugby league. In Alan Tomlinson, ed., *The sport studies reader* (pp. 283–288). London/New York: Routledge.

Long, Jonathan A., and Mike J. McNamee. 2004. On the moral economy of racism and racist rationalizations in sport. *International Review for the Sociology of Sport* 39, 4: 405–420.

Longman, Jeré. 1996. Slow down, speed up. *The New York Times* (May 1): B11.

Longman, Jeré. 2001. Getting the athletic edge may mean altering genes. *The New York Times* May 11). Online: http://www.nytimes .com/2001/05/11/sports/11GENE.html.

Longman, Jeré. 2007a. An amputee sprinter: Is he disabled or too-abled? *The New York Times* (May 15). Online: www.nytimes.com/2007/05/15/ sports/othersports/15runner.html.

Longman, Jeré. 2007b. Putting on weight for football glory. *The New York Times* (November 30). Online: www.nytimes.com/2007/11/30/sports/ 30obesity.html.

Los Angeles Municipal Code. 2008a. Chapter V, Public Safety and Protection; Article 6—Public Hazards; Section 56.15—Bicycle Riding—Sidewalks, #1. Online: www.amlegal .com/nxt/gateway.dll?f=templates&fn=default .htm&vid=amlegal:lamc_ca.

Los Angeles Municipal Code. 2008b. Chapter V, Public Safety and Protection; Article 6—Public Hazards; Section 56.16—Streets—Sidewalks— Playing ball or games of sport. Online: www .amlegal.com/nxt/gateway.dll?f=templates&fn= default.htm&vid=amlegal:lamc_ca.

Los Angeles Municipal Code. 2008c. Chapter VI— Public Works and Property; Article 3—Public Parks, Playgrounds, Beaches and Other Property; Section 63.44—Regulations Affecting Park and Recreation Areas. New Subsection N. Online: www.amlegal.com/nxt/gateway.dll?f=templates& fn=default.htm&vid=amlegal:lamc_ca (retrieved June 15, 2008).

Loveless, Tom. 2002. *The 2002 Brown Center report on American education: How well are American students learning?* Washington, DC: Brookings Institution.

Lowe, Maria R. 1998. *Women of steel: Female bodybuilders and the struggle for self-definition.* New York: New York University Press.

Lüschen, Günther. 1967. The interdependence of sport and culture. *International Review of Sport Sociology* 2, 127–141.

Lund, Anker Brink. 2007. The political economy of mass mediated sports. Keynote address at the ISHPES and ISSA Joint World Congress, Copenhagen (August 3).

Lupton, Deborah. 2000. The social construction of medicine and the body. In G. Albrecht, R. Fitzpatrick, and S. Scrimshaw, eds., *The handbook of social studies in health and medicine* (pp. 50–63). London: Sage.

Lynch, Andy. 2005. Three track teammates head to Guatemala. Online: www.athletesinaction.org/ news.aspx?newsitem=41 (retrieved July 8, 2005).

Lyons, B. 2002. Fallen legends were beset by life's frailties. *Denver Post* (September 29): 4C.

MacArthur, Linda. 2008. *The drive to strive: Exploring the experiences of elite-level adolescent artistic performers.* PhD dissertation, Department of Curriculum, Teaching, and Learning, Ontario Institute for Studies in Education of the University of Toronto.

MacLeod, Calum. 2008. Paralympics aim to change Chinese prejudices. *USA Today* (September 5): 12A; Online: http://www.usatoday.com/ printedition/news/20080905/a_china05.art.htm.

MacNeill, Margaret. 1999. Social marketing, gender, and the science of fitness: A case-study of ParticiPACTION campaigns. In P. White and K. Young, eds., *Sport and gender in Canada* (pp. 215– 231). Don Mills, ON: Oxford University Press.

Madison, James K., and Sarita L. Ruma. 2003. Exercise and athletic involvement as moderators of severity in adolescents with eating disorders. *Journal of Applied Sport Psychology* 15, 3: 213–222.

Magdalinski, Tara. 1999. Sports history and East German national identity. *Peace Review* 11, 4: 539–545.

Magdalinski, Tara. 2008. *Sport, technology and the body: The nature of performance.* London/New York: Routledge.

Maguire, Brendan. 2005. American professional wrestling: Evolution, content, and popular appeal. *Sociological Spectrum* 25, 2: 155–176.

Maguire, Jennifer Smith. 2006. Exercising control: Empowerment and the fitness discourse. In Linda K. Fuller, ed., *Sport, rhetoric, and gender* (pp. 119–130). New York: Palgrave Macmillan.

Maguire, Jennifer Smith. 2008. *Fit for consumption: Sociology and the business of fitness.* London/New York: Routledge.

Maguire, Joseph. 1988. Race and position assignment in English soccer: A preliminary analysis of ethnicity and sport in Britain. *Sociology of Sport Journal* 5, 3: 257–269.

Maguire, Joseph. 1999. *Global sport: Identities, societies, civilizations.* Cambridge, England: Polity Press.

Maguire, Joseph. 2004. Sport labor migration research revisited. *Journal of Sport and Social Issues* 28, 4: 477–482.

Maguire, Joseph. 2005, ed. *Power and global sport: Zones of prestige, emulation and resistance.* London/New York: Routledge.

Maguire, Joseph A., Sarah Barnard, Katie Butler, and Peter Golding. 2008a. Celebrate Humanity or consumers?: Building markets, constructing brands and glocalising identities. *Social Identities, 14*, 1: 63–77.

Maguire, Joseph A., Katie Butler, Sarah Barnard, and Peter Golding. 2008b. Olympism and consumption: An analysis of advertising in the British media coverage of the 2004 Athens Olympic Games. *Sociology of Sport Journal* 25, 2: 167–186.

Maguire, Joseph, and Mike Burrows. 2005. 'Not the Germans again': Soccer, identity politics and the media. In Joseph Maguire, ed., *Power and global sport: Zones of prestige, emulation and resistance* (pp. 130–142). London/New York: Routledge.

Maguire, Joseph A., and Masayoshi Nakayama, eds. 2006. *Japan, sport and society: Tradition and change in a globalizing world.* London/New York: Routledge.

Maguire, Joseph, and Catherine Possamai. 2005. 'In league together': Global rugby league and local identities. In Joseph Maguire, ed., *Power and global sport: Zones of \prestige, emulation and resistance* (pp. 87–106). London/New York: Routledge.

Maguire, Joseph, and David Stead. 2005. "Cricketers of the Empire": Cash crops, mercenaries and symbols of sporting emancipation? In Joseph Maguire, ed., *Power and global sport: Zones of*

prestige, emulation and resistance (pp. 63–86). London/New York: Routledge.

Maguire, Joseph, and Jason Tuck. 2005. 'A world in union': Rugby, globalization, and Irish identity. In Joseph Maguire, ed., *Power and global sport: Zones of prestige, emulation and resistance* (pp. 109–129). London/New York: Routledge.

Mahany, Barbara. 1999. Parents drive free time from lives of kids. *Chicago Tribune* (May 27): LIFE1.

Mahler, Jonathan. 2005. Building the béisbol brand. *The New York Times*, section 6. Online: www.nytimes.com/2005/07/31/magazine/31METS.html?oref=login.

Majors, Richard. 1986. Cool pose: The proud signature of black survival. *Changing Men: Issues in Gender, Sex and Politics* 17 (Winter): 184–185.

Majors, Richard. 1998. Cool pose: Black masculinity and sports. In G. Sailes, ed., *African Americans in sport* (pp. 15–22). New Brunswick, NJ: Transaction.

Malcolmson, Robert W. 1984. Sports in society: A historical perspective. *British Journal of Sport History* 1, 1: 60–72.

Malloy, D. C., and Dwight H. Zakus. 2002. Ethics of drug testing in sport—an invasion of privacy justified? *Sport, Education and Society* 2: 203–218.

Mangan, J. A., ed. 2003. *Militarism, sport, Europe: War without weapons.* London/New York: Routledge.

Manzenreiter, Wolfram. 2006. Sport spectacles, uniformities and the search for identity in late modern Japan. *The Sociological Review* 54, 2: 144–159.

Markula, Pirkku. 1995. Firm but shapely, fit but sexy, strong but thin: The postmodern aerobicizing female bodies. *Sociology of Sport Journal* 12, 4: 424–453.

Marriott, Michel. 2004. Your shot, he said, distantly. *The New York Times*, circuits (August 26): 1.

Marriott, Michel. 2005. Cyberbodies: Robo-legs. *The New York Times* (June 20): F1.

Marsh, Herbert W. 1993. The effect of participation in sport during the last two years of high school. *Sociology of Sport Journal* 10, 1: 18–43.

Marsh, Herbert W., and Sabina Kleitman. 2002. Extracurricular school activities: The good, the bad, and the nonlinear. *Harvard Educational Review* 72, 4: 464–511.

Marsh, Herbert W., and Sabina Kleitman. 2003. School athletic participation: Mostly gain with little pain. *Journal of Sport and Exercise Psychology* 25, 2: 205–228.

Marsh, Peter. 1982. Social order on the British soccer terraces. *International Social Science Journal* 34, 2: 247–256.

Marsh, Peter, and A. Campbell, eds. 1982. *Aggression and violence.* Oxford, UK: Basil Blackwell.

Martin, Randy, and Toby Miller, eds. 1999. *SportCult.* Minneapolis: University of Minnesota Press.

Marty, Martin E., and R. S. Appleby, eds. 1995. *Fundamentalisms comprehended* (vol. 5 of *The fundamentalism project*). Chicago: University of Chicago Press.

Martzke, Rudy, and Reid Cherner, 2004. Channeling how to view sports. *USA Today* (August 17): 1C–2C.

Marx, Jeffrey. 2004. He turns boys into men. *Parade* (August 29): 4–6.

Maslach, Christina, and Michael P. Leiter. 1997. *The truth about burnout: How organizations cause personal stress and what to do about it.* San Francisco: Jossey-Bass.

Mathisen, James. 1992. From civil religion to folk religion: The case of American sport. In S. Hoffman, ed., *Sport and religion* (pp. 17–34). Champaign, IL: Human Kinetics.

Matson, Barbara. 2004. A growth sport is stunting female coaches. *Boston Globe* (Dec. 5): www.boston.com/sports/articles/2004/12/05/a_growth_sport_is_stunting_female_coaches/.

May, Reuben A. Buford. 2008. *Living through the hoop: High school basketball, race, and the American dream.* New York: New York University Press.

Mayeda, David Tokiharu. 1999. From model minority to economic threat: Media portrayals of major league baseball pitchers Hideo Nomo and Hideki Irabu. *Journal of Sport and Social Issues* 23, 2: 203–217.

McCallum, Jack. 2002. Citizen Barkley. *Sports Illustrated* (March 11): 38.

McCallum, Jack. 2003. Thank God it's Friday. *Sports Illustrated* (September 29): 40–42.

McCarthy, Cameron. 2007. To interpose a little ease: Making sense of sport and intellectual labor in C.L.R. James's *Beyond a Boundary* and his other works. Paper presented at the annual conference of the North American Society for the Sociology of Sport, Pittsburgh, November 2.

McCarthy, D., R. L. Jones, and P. Potrac. 2003. Constructing images and interpreting realities: The case of the black soccer player on television. *International Review for the Sociology of Sport* 38, 2: 217–238.

McCarthy, Michael. 2005. Athletes on the outs in ads: Hip-hop artists outscore jocks in endorsements. *USA Today* (July 5): 1C–2C.

McChesney, Robert W. 1999. The new global media: It's a small world of big conglomerates. *The Nation* 269, 18: 11–15.

McClung, Lisa R., and Elaine M. Blinde. 1998. Negotiation of the gendered ideology of sport: Experiences of women intercollegiate athletes. Paper presented at the annual conference of the North American Society for the Sociology of Sport, Las Vegas (November).

McCormack, Jane B., and Laurence Chalip. 1988. Sport as socialization: A critique of methodological premises. *Social Science Journal* 25, 1: 83–92.

McCullagh, Ciaran. 2002. *Media power.* New York: Palgrave.

McDonagh, Eileen, and Laura Pappana. 2007. *Playing with the boys: Why separate is not equal in sports.* New York: Oxford University Press.

McDonald, Ian. 1999. "Physiological patriots"?: The politics of physical culture and Hindu nationalism in India. *International Review for the Sociology of Sport* 34, 4: 343–358.

McDonald, Ian. 2002. Critical social research and political intervention. In John Sugden and Alan Tomlinson, eds., *Power games: A critical sociology of sport* (pp. 100–116). London/New York: Routledge.

McDonald, Ian. 2007. One-dimensional sport. *Nordic Sport Science Forum* (December 12). Online: http://idrottsforum.org/articles/mcdonald/mcdonald071212.html.

McDonald, Mary G., and David L. Andrews, 2001. Michael Jordan: Corporate sport and postmodern celebryhood. In David L. Andrews and Steven J. Jackson, eds., *Sport stars: The cultural politics of sporting celebrity* (pp. 20–35). London/New York: Routledge.

McElwain, David (Max). 2004. *The only dance in Iowa: A history of six-player girls' basketball.* Winnipeg, Manitoba: Bison Books.

McEntegart, Pete, et al. 2002. The top 100 sports books of all time. *Sports Illustrated* (December 16): 128–148.

McHale, James P., Penelope G. Vindon, Loren Bush, Derek Richer, David Shaw, and Brienne Smith. 2005. Patterns of personal and social adjustment among sport-involved and noninvolved urban middle-school children. *Sociology of Sport Journal* 22, 2: 119–136.

McHugh, Josh. 2007. Blade runner. *Wired* 15.03 (March). Online: www.wired.com/wired/archive/15.03/blade.html.

McKay, James, and Helen Johnson. 2008. Pornographic eroticism and sexual grotesquerie in representations of African American sportswomen. *Social Identities: Journal for the Study of Race, Nation and Culture* 14, 4: 491–504.

McKay, Jim. 1997. *Managing gender: Affirmative action and organizational power in Australian, Canadian, and New Zealand sport.* Albany: State University of New York Press.

McKay, Jim. 1999. Gender and organizational power in Canadian sport. In Phillip White and Kevin Young, eds., *Sport and gender in Canada* (pp. 197–215). Don Mills, ON: Oxford University Press.

McKay, Jim. 2005. Americans with Disabilities Act: A job not done (yet). *Pittsburgh Post-Gazette* (July 15). Online: www.post-gazette.com/pg/05196/538181.stm (retrieved July 21, 2005).

McMahon, Regan. 2007a. *Revolution in the bleachers: How parents can take back family life in a world gone crazy over youth sports.* New York: Gotham Books.

McMahon, Regan. 2007b. Unhealthy competition: Young kids are training like professionals, and have the injuries to prove it. *San Francisco Chronicle* (April 15): CM-9. Online: http://sfgate.com/cgi-bin/article.cgi?f=/c/a/2007/04/15/CMG7OOP5OB1.DTL.

McNeal, Ralf B., Jr. 1995. Extracurricular activities and high school dropouts. *Sociology of Education* 64, 1: 62–81.

McShane, Larry. 1999. Winner take all (Associated Press). *Colorado Springs Gazette* (July 4): LIFE4.

Mead, C. 1985. *Champion Joe Louis: Black hero in white America.* New York: Scribner.

Meadows, James A. 2006. 'X' marks the spot to party. *Rocky Mountain News* (January 27): 6A.

Mellor, P. A., and C. Shilling (1997) *Re-forming the body: Religion, community and modernity.* London: Sage.

Mendelsohn, Daniel. 2004. What Olympic ideal? *The New York Times Magazine* (August 8). Online: www.nytimes.com/2004/08/08/magazine/WLN130551.html.

Mendoza, Alexander. 2007. Beating the odds: Mexican American distance runners in Texas, 1950–1995. In Jorge Iber and Samuel O. Regalado, eds., *Mexican Americans and sports: A reader on athletics and barrio life* (pp. 188–191). College Station: Texas A&M University Press.

Merron, Jeff. 1999. Running on empty. *SportsJones* 3 (June). Online: www.sportsjones.com/running.htm.

Messner, Michael A. 1992. *Power at play.* Boston: Beacon Press.

Messner, Michael A. 1996. Studying up on sex. *Sociology of Sport Journal* 13, 3: 221–237.

Messner, Michael A. 2000. Barbie girls versus sea monsters: Children constructing gender *Gender and Society* 14, 6: 765–784.

Messner, Michael A. 2002. *Taking the field: Women, men, and sports.* Minneapolis: University of Minnesota Press.

Messner, Michael A. 2007a. The masculinity of the governator: Muscle and compassion in American politics. *Gender and Society* 21, 4: 461–480.

Messner, Michael A. 2007b. *Out of play: Critical essay on gender and sport.* Albany, NY: State University of New York Press.

Messner, Michael A., Michele Dunbar, and Darnell Hunt. 2000. The televised sports manhood formula. *Journal of Sport and Social Issues* 24, 4: 380–394.

Messner, Michael A., Margaret Carlisle Duncan, and Cheryl Cooky. 2003. Silence, sports bras, and wrestling porn: Women in televised sports news and highlights shows. *Journal of Sport and Social Issues* 27, 1: 38–51.

Messner, Michael A., Darnell Hunt, and Michele Dunbar. 1999. *Boys to men: Sports media messages about masculinity.* Oakland, CA: Children Now.

Messner, Michael A., and Donald F. Sabo, eds. 1994. *Sex, violence and power in sports.* Freedom, CA: The Crossing Press.

Messner, Michael A., and Mark A. Stevens. 2002. Scoring without consent: Confronting male athletes' violence against women. In M. Gatz, M. A. Messner, and S. J. Ball-Rokeach, eds., *Paradoxes of youth and sport* (pp. 225–240). Albany: State University of New York Press.

Meyer, Jeremy. 2002. Ward's fire within. *Denver Post* (July 14): 1C, 12C.

Miah, Andy. 2004. *Genetically modified athletes: Biomedical ethics, gene doping and sport.* London: Routledge.

Middleton, Richard T. 2008. Institutions, inculcation, and black racial identity: pigmentocracy vs. the rule of hypodescent. *Social Identities* 14, 5: 567–585.

Midol, Nancy, and Gerard Broyer. 1995. Toward an anthropological analysis of new sport cultures: The case of whiz sports in France. *Sociology of Sport Journal* 12, 2: 204–212.

Midol, Nancy, and Gerard Broyer. 1995. Toward an anthropological analysis of new sport cultures: The case of whiz sports in France. *Sociology of Sport Journal* 12, 2: 204–212.

Migliaccio, Todd A., and Ellen C. Berg. 2008. Women's participation in tackle football: An exploration of benefits and constraints. *International Review for the Sociology of Sport* 43, 2: 271–288.

Mihoces, Gary. 2005. Injured skaters struggle in world championships. *USA Today* (March 15): 7C. Online: www.usatoday.com/sports/olympics/winter/2005-03-14-skating-worlds_x.htm.

Mihoces, Gary. 2007a. Concussions command NFL's attention. *USA Today* (June 19): 1C-2C.

Mihoces, Gary. 2007b. Sport's risks lurk in each ride. *USA Today* (January 4): 9C. Online: http://www.usatoday.com/printedition/sports/20080104/pbrtwo.art.htm.

Miller, Kathleen E., Grace M. Barnes, Donald F. Sabo, Merrill J. Melnick, and Michael P. Farrell. 2002. Anabolic-androgenic steroid use and other adolescent problem behaviors: Rethinking the male athlete assumption. *Sociological Perspectives* 45, 4: 467–490.

Miller, Kathleen E., Merrill J. Melnick, Grace M. Barnes, Michael P. Farrell, and Don Sabo. 2005. Untangling the links among athletic involvement, gender, race, and adolescent academic outcomes. *Sociology of Sport Journal* 22, 2: 178–193.

Miller, Kathleen E., Don F. Sabo, Michael P. Farrell, Grace M. Barnes, and Merrill J. Melnick. 1998.

Athletic participation and sexual behavior in adolescents: The different world of boys and girls. *Journal of Health and Social Behavior* 39, 108–123.

Miller, Kathleen E., Don F. Sabo, Michael P. Farrell, Grace M. Barnes, and Merrill J. Melnick. 1999. Sports, sexual behavior, contraceptive use, and pregnancy among female and male high school students: Testing cultural resource theory. *Sociology of Sport Journal* 16, 4: 366–387.

Miller, Kathleen E., Don F. Sabo, Merrill J. Melnick, Michael P. Farrell, and Grace M. Barnes. 2000. *The Women's Sports Foundation report: Health risks and the teen athlete.* East Meadow, NY: Women's Sports Foundation.

Miller, Patricia S., and Gretchen Kerr. 2003. The role experimentation of intercollegiate student athletes. *The Sport Psychologist* 17, 2: 196–219.

Miller, Patrick B., and David K. Wiggins, eds. 2003. *Sport and the color line: Black athletes and race relations in twentieth-century America.* London/New York: Routledge.

Miller, Phillip. 2007. Private financing and sports franchise values: The case of Major League Baseball. *Journal of Sports Economics* 8, 5: 449–467.

Miller, Ted. 2007. American football, Samoan style. *ESPN The Magazine* (May 28). Online: http://espn.go.com/gen/s/2002/0527/1387562.html.

Miller, Toby, Geoffrey Lawrence, Jim McKay, and David Rowe. 2001. *Globalization and sport: Playing the world.* London: Sage.

Miller, Toby, David Rowe, Jim McKay, and Geoffrey Lawrence. 2003. The over-production of U.S. sports and the new international division of cultural labor. *International Review for the Sociology of Sport* 38, 4: 427–440.

Mills, C. Wright. 1956. *The power elite.* New York: Oxford University Press.

Mills, C. Wright. 1959. *The sociological imagination.* New York: Oxford University Press.

Mills, James, and Paul Dimeo. 2003. "When gold is fired it shines": Sport, the imagination and the body in colonial and postcolonial India. In John Bale and Mike Cronin, eds., *Sport and postcolonialism* (pp. 107–122). Oxford, UK/New York: Berg.

Millward, Peter. 2006. 'We've all got the bug for Euro-aways': What fans say about European football club competition. *International Review for the Sociology of Sport* 41, 3: 375–393.

Mindegaard, Peter. 2007. Towards new forms of popular football? *Nordic Sport Science Forum* (June 6). Online: http://idrottsforum.org/articles/mindegaard/mindegaard070606.html (retrieved July 20, 2008).

Mintz, Steven. 2006. *Huck's raft: A history of American childhood.* Belknap Press.

Miracle, Andrew W., and C. Roger Rees. 1994. *Lessons of the locker room: The myth of school sports.* Amherst, NY: Prometheus Books.

Mitchell, Nicole, and Lisa A. Ennis. 2007. *Encyclopedia of Title IX and sports.* Westport, CT: Greenwood Press.

Montville, Leigh. 1999. Shall we dance? *Sports Illustrated* (December 6): 98–109.

Mooney, Chris. 2003. Teen herbicide. *Mother Jones* (May–June): 18–22.

Moore, David Leon. 2002. Parents pay dearly to coach kids for stardom. *USA Today* (July 26): 1A–2A. Online: www.usatoday.com/educate/college/firstyear/casestudies/20040106-coaching.pdf.

Moore, David Leon. 2007. Do prep basketball teams go too far? *USA Today* (February 9): 1C–2C. Online: www.usatoday.com/printedition/sports/20070209/c1scov09.art.htm.

Moore, Kathleen. 2004. Olympics 2004: Muslim women athletes move ahead, but don't leave faith behind. Online: www.payvand.com/news/04/aug/1056.html (retrieved July 5, 2005).

Morgan, Robert. 1993. The 'Great Emancipator' and the issue of race. *The Journal for Historical Review* 13, 5: 4. Online: www.ihr.org/jhr/v13/v13n5p-4_Morgan.html.

Morgan, William J. 2008. Markets and intercollegiate sports: An unholy alliance? *Journal of Intercollegiate Sport* 1, 1: 59–65.

Moring, Mark. 2007. Fumbling religion? *Christianity Today* (September): 32–36.

Morris, Jenny. 1996. Introduction. In J. Morris, ed., *Encounters with strangers: Feminism and disability* (pp. 1–12). London: Women's Free Press.

Moye, Jim, and C. Keith Harrison. 2002. Don't believe the hype: Do the automatic suspensions of student-athletes for alleged misconduct withstand constitutional scrutiny? *Texas Entertainment and Sports Law Journal* 11, 1: 5–15.

Mrozek, Donald J. 1983. *Sport and American mentality, 1880–1920.* Knoxville: University of Tennessee Press.

Mueller, Frederick O., and Robert C. Cantu. 2008. *National Center for Catastrophic Sport Injury Research: Twenty-Fifth Annual Report, Fall 1982–Spring 2007.* Online: http://www.unc.edu/depts/nccsi/AllSport.htm (retrieved August 8, 2008).

Murderball. 2004. A documentary film by Think Film Company, New York. Online: www.thinkfilmcompany.com/.

Murphy, Austin. 2006. Buffalo soldier. *Sports Illustrated* 104, 17 (April 17): 62–66.

Murphy, Frank. 2006. *The last protest: Lee Evans in Mexico City.* Kansas City: Windsprint Press.

Murphy, Geraldine M., Al J. Petipas, and Britton W. Brewer. 1996. Identity foreclosure, athletic identity, and career maturity in intercollegiate athletics. *Sport Psychologist* 10, 3: 239–246.

Murphy, Patrick, and Ivan Waddington. 2007. Are elite athletes exploited? *Sport in Society* 10, 2: 239–255.

Murphy, Patrick, John Williams, and Eric Dunning. 1990. *Football on trial: Spectator violence and development in the world of football.* London: Routledge.

Myers, J. 2000. *Afraid of the dark: What whites and blacks need to know about each other.* Chicago: Lawrence Hill Books.

Nabokov, Peter. 1981. *Indian running: Native American history and tradition.* Santa Fe, NM: Ancient City Press.

Nack, William. 1998. Does God care who wins the Super Bowl? *Sports Illustrated* 88, 3 (January 26): 47–48.

Nack, William, and Lester Munson. 1995. Sports' dirty secret. *Sports Illustrated* (July 31): 62–75.

Nack, William, and Lester Munson. 2000. Out of control. *Sports Illustrated* (July 24): 86–95.

Nack, William, and Don Yaeger. 1999. Every parent's nightmare. *Sports Illustrated* 91, 10 (September 13): 40–53.

Nakamura, Yuka. 2002. Beyond the hijab: Female Muslims and physical activity. *Women's Sport and Physical Activity Journal* 11, 2: 21–48.

Nalapat, Abilash, and Andrew Parker. 2005. Sport, celebrity and popular culture: Sachin Tendulkar, cricket and Indian nationalisms. *International Review for the Sociology of Sport* 40, 4: 433–446.

Nash, Bruce, and Allan Zullo. 1989. *The baseball hall of shame(2).* New York: Pocket Books.

Naughton, Jim. 1996. Alcohol abuse by athletes poses big problems for colleges. *Chronicle of Higher Education* 43, 4: A47–A48.

Nauright, John. 1997. Masculinity, muscular Islam and popular culture: "Colored" rugby's cultural symbolism in working class Cape Town c. 1930–70. *International Journal of the History of Sport* 14, 1: 184–190.

Nauright, John, and Tara Magdalinski. 2002. Religion, race and rugby in "coloured" Cape Town. In T. Magdalinski and T. J. L. Chandler, eds., *With God on their side: Sport in the service of religion* (pp. 120–138). London/New York: Routledge.

NBC/USA Network. 2005. Homosexuality and sports. Full-survey results online at http://sportsillustrated.cnn.com/2005/magazine/04/12/survey.expanded/; discussion and partial results in Wertheim (2005) and Smith (2005a).

NCAA. 2007. Research related to graduation rates of Division I student-athletes1984-2000. NCAA Research Staff. Indianapolis: National Collegiate Athletic Association. Online: http://www2.ncaa.org/portal/academics_and_athletes/education_and_research/academic_reform/grad_rate/2007/d1_summary.pdf.

NCAA, 2008. *1981-82 – 2006-07 NCAA Sports Sponsorship and Participation Rates Report* (prepared by Denise M. DeHass, Research Consultant). Indianapolis: The National Collegiate Athletic Association.

Neinas, Chuck. 2003. *2003 AFCA player survey.* American Football Coaches Association. Online: www.afca.com/lev1.cfm/88) (retrieved September 10, 2005).

Nelson, Mariah Burton. 1994. *The stronger women get, the more men love football: Sexism and the American culture of sports.* New York: Harcourt Brace.

Nelson, Mariah Burton. 1998. *Embracing victory: Life lessons in competition and compassion.* New York: Morrow.

Newman, Joshua I. 2007a. Army of whiteness? Colonel Reb and the sporting South's cultural and corporate symbolic. *Journal of Sport and Social Issues,* 31, 4: 315–339.

Newman, Joshua I. 2007b. Old times there are not forgotten: Sport, identity, and the Confederate flag in the Dixie South. *Sociology of Sport Journal,* 24, 3: 261–282.

Newsweek. 1971. Are sports good for the soul? (January 11): 51–52.

Newsweek. 2004. Perspectives: Entertainment. *Newsweek* (December29–January 5): 122.

NFHS. 2008. *2007-08 high school athletics participation survey.* Indianapolis: National Federation of State High School Associations. Online: http://www.nfhs.org/core/contentmanager/uploads/2007-08%20Participation%20Survey.pdf.

NHANES—National Health and Nutrition Examination Survey. 2002. *Prevalence of overweight and obesity among adults: United States, 1999–2000.* Hyattsville, MD: National Center for Health Statistics.

Nichol, Jon P., Patricia Coleman, and B. T. Williams. 1993. *Injuries in sport and exercise: Main report.* London: Sports Council.

Nicholson, Mathew. 2007. *Sport and the media: Managing the nexus.* London: Elsevier.

Nightengale, Bob. 2006. Team's rebuilding effort focuses on Christianity, character. *USA Today* (May 31): 1A–2A.

Niiya, Brian, ed. 2000. *More than a game: Sport in the Japanese American community.* Los Angeles: Japanese American National Museum.

Nixon, Howard L., II. 1993a. Accepting the risks and pain of injury in sport: Mediated cultural influences on playing hurt. *Sociology of Sport Journal* 10, 2: 183–196.

Nixon, Howard L., II. 1993b. A social network analysis of influences on athletes to play with pain and injuries. *Journal of Sport and Social Issues* 16, 2: 127–135.

Nixon, Howard L., II. 1994a. Coaches' views of risk, pain, and injury in sport, with special reference to gender differences. *Sociology of Sport Journal* 11, 1: 79–87.

Nixon, Howard L., II. 1994b. Social pressure, social support, and help seeking for pain and injuries in college sports networks. *Journal of Sport and Social Issues* 18, 4: 340–355.

Nixon, Howard. L., II. 1996a. Explaining pain and injury attitudes and experiences in sport in terms of gender, race, and sports status factors. *Journal of Sport and Social Issues* 20, 1: 33–44.

Nixon, Howard L., II. 1996b. The relationship of friendship networks, sports experiences, and gender to expressed pain thresholds. *Sociology of Sport Journal* 13, 1: 78–86.

Nixon, Howard L., II. 2000. Sport and disability. In J. Coakley and E. Dunning, eds., *Handbook of sport studies* (pp. 422–438). London: Sage.

Nixon, Howard L., II. 2007. Constructing diverse sports opportunities for people with disabilities. *Journal of Sport and Social Issues* 31, 4: 417–433.

Nobles, Melissa. 2000. *Shades of citizenship: Race and the census in modern politics*. Stanford, CA: Stanford University Press.

Noll, R., and A. Zimbalist, eds. 1997. *Sports, jobs, and taxes*. Washington, DC: Brookings Institution.

Novak, Michael. 1976. *The joy of sports*. New York: Basic Books.

Nowinski, Christopher. 2007. *Head games: Football's concussion crisis from the NFL to youth leagues*. East Bridgewater, MA: Drummond Publishing Group.

NPR (National Public Radio). 2006. All things considered (May 26). Online: http://www.npr .org/templates/story/story.php?storyId=5434639 (retrieved, May 5, 2008).

O'Connor, Justen P., and Trent D. Brown. 2007. Real cyclists don't race. *International Review for the Sociology of Sport* 42, 1: 83–97.

Oglesby, Carole A. (with the International Working Group on Women and Sport, WomenSport International, the International Association of Physical Education for Women and Girls, and the International Council of Sport Science and Physical Education). 2006. *Positive embodiment: Contributions of sport, exercise and physical recreation to the life-long development of girls and women*. Report for the United Nations Division for the Advancement of Women.

Oglesby, Carole A. (with the International Working Group on Women and Sport and WomenSport International). 2008. *Women 2000 and Beyond*. New York: Division for the Advancement of Women of the United Nations Secretariat.

Okubu, Hideaki. 2004. *Local identity and sport: Historical study of integration and differentiation*. Sankt Augustin, Germany: Academica Verlag.

Oliver, Michael. 1996. *Understanding disability: From theory to practice*. New York: St. Martin's Press.

Olney, Buster. 2006. Why pitchers use. *ESPN The Magazine* 9.13 (July 3): 46–47.

Omi, Michael, and Howard Winant. 1994. *Racial formation in the United States*. New York/London: Routledge.

Opdyke, Jeff. 2007. Love and money: When a kid's game becomes your life. *Wall Street Journal*

Online, May 6. Online: http://online.wsj.com/ article/SB117840716307293503.html (retrieved January 24, 2008).

Orenstein, Peggy. 2008. The way we live now: Girls will be girls. *The New York Times Magazine* (February 10). Online: www.nytimes .com/2008/02/10/magazine/10wwln-lede-t.html.

Orszag, Jonathan M., and Peter R. Orszag. 2005. *The empirical effects of collegiate athletics: An update*. Indianapolis: National Collegiate Athletic Association.

Orton, Kathy. 2005. Black female coaches few and far between. *Washington Post* (March 16): D09. Online: http://www.washingtonpost.com/wp-dyn/ content/article/2005/03/26/AR2005032600511_ 2.html.

Ossur, 2008. Oscar Pistorius—Special feature. Ossur. Online: www.ossur.com/?PageID=6738 (retrieved July 15, 2008).

Otto, Allison Ann. 2003. Scoring with Latinos. *Denver Post* (May 13): 1A.

Overman, Steven J. 1997. *The influence of the Protestant ethic on sport and recreation*. Brookfield, VT: Ashgate.

Oxendine, Joseph B. 1988. *American Indian sports heritage*. Champaign, IL: Human Kinetics.

Oxfam International. 2008. *Offside! Labour rights and sportswear production in Asia*. Melbourne, Australia: Oxfam International. Online: http:// www.oxfam.org/en/policy/briefingnotes/offside_ labor_report.

Ozanian, Michael K. 2007. How 'bout them Cowboys? *Forbes* (September 13). Online: www .forbes.com/2007/09/13/dallas-cowboys-stadium -biz-07nfl_cx_mo_0913nflintro.html.

Ozanian, Michael K., and Kurt Badenhausen. 2007. The business of hockey. *Forbes* (November 8). Online: www.forbes.com/2007/11/08/nhl-team -values-biz-07nhl_cx_mo_kb_1108nhl_land.html.

Ozanian, Michael K., and Kurt Badenhausen. 2008. The business of baseball. *Forbes* (April 16). Online: http://www.forbes.com/2008/04/16/baseball -team-values-biz-sports-baseball08-cx_mo_kb_ 0416baseballintro.html.

Pace, Enzo. 2007. Fundamentalism. In George Ritzer, ed., *Encyclopedia of sociology* (pp. 1813– 1816). London/New York: Blackwell.

Palmer, Catherine, and Kirrilly Thompson. 2007. The paradoxes of football spectatorship: On-field and online expressions of social capital among the "Grog Squad." *Sociology of Sport Journal* 24, 2: 187–205.

Pappas, Nick, Patrick McKenry, and Beth Catlett. 2004. Athlete aggression on the rink and off the ice. *Men and Masculinities* 6: 291–312.

Paraschak, Victoria. 1995. The native sport and recreation program, 1972–1981: Patterns of resistance, patterns of reproduction. *Canadian Journal of History of Sport* (December): 1–18.

Paraschak, Victoria. 1999. Doing race, doing gender: First Nations, "sport," and gender relations. In Phillip White and Kevin Young, eds., *Sport and gender in Canada* (pp. 153–169). Don Mills, ON: Oxford University Press.

Parker, Heidi M., and Janet S. Fink. 2008. The effect of sport commentator framing on consumer attitudes. *Sex Roles: A Journal of Research* 58, 1–2: 116–126.

Parkhouse, Bonnie L., and Jean M. Williams 1986. Differential effects of sex and status on elevation of coaching ability. *Research Quarterly for Exercise and Sport* 57, 1: 53–59.

Parrish, Paula. 2002. The height of gaining an edge. *Rocky Mountain News* (September 21): 1B, 12B–13B.

Patrick, Dick. 2002. U.S. Anti-Doping Agency willing to administer testing for baseball. *USA Today* (June 14): 6C.

Patrick, Dick. 2005. USOC lobbies for anti-doping agency funds. *USA Today* (May 25): 7C.

Patrick, Dick. 2006. Luck, not better lab tests, helped catch athletes. *USA Today* (August 25): 10C. Online: www.usatoday.com/printedition/sports/20060825/c10olynotes25.art.htm.

PBS. 2006. *Race—The power of an illusion* (transcripts of Episodes I, II, III). Online: www.newsreel.org/nav/title.asp?tc=CN0149.

Pear, Robert. 2008. Plan seeks more access for disabled. *The New York Times* (June 16). Online: http://www.nytimes.com/2008/06/16/washington/16disabled.html.

Pelak, Cynthia Fabrizio . 2002. Women's collective identity formation in sports: A case study from women's ice hockey. *Gender and Society* 16, 1: 93–114.

Pelak, Cynthia Fabrizio. 2005. Athletes as agents of change: An examination of shifting race relations within women's netball in post-apartheid South Africa. *Sociology of Sport Journal* 22, 1: 59–77.

Pennington, Bill. 2004. Reading, writing and corporate sponsorships. *The New York Times*, section A (October 18): 1.

Pennington, Bill. 2005. Doctors see a big rise in injuries for young athletes. *The New York Times*, section A (February 22): 1.

Pennington, Bill. 2007. For athletes, the next fountain of youth? *The New York Times* (March 29). Online: www.nytimes.com/2007/03/29/sports/29stem.html.

Pennington, Bill. 2008a. The scholarship divide: Expectations lose to reality of sports scholarships. *The New York Times* (March 10). Online: www.nytimes.com/2008/03/10/sports/10scholarships.html.

Pennington, Bill. 2008b. The scholarship divide: It's not an adventure, it's a job. *The New York Times* (March 12). Online: http://www.nytimes.com/2008/03/12/sports/12lifestyles.html.

Pennington, Bill. 2008c. The scholarship divide: New rules threaten sport's tryout process. *The New York Times* (March 11). Online: http://www.nytimes.com/2008/03/11/sports/11baseball.html.

Pennington, Bill. 2008d. The scholarship divide: Recruits clamor for more from coaches with less. *The New York Times* (March 11). Online: http://www.nytimes.com/2008/03/11/sports/11coaches.html.

Peretti-Watel, Patrick, Valérie Guagliardo, Pierre Verger, Patrick Mignon, Jacques Pruvost, and Yolande Obadia. 2004a. Attitudes toward doping and recreational drug use among French elite student-athletes. *Sociology of Sport Journal* 21, 1: 1–17.

Peretti-Watel, Patrick, Valérie Guagliardo, Pierre Verger, Jacques Pruvost, Patrick Mignon, and Yolande Obadia. 2004b. Risky behaviours among young elite-student-athletes: Results from a pilot survey in South-Eastern France. *International Review for the Sociology of Sport* 39, 2: 233–244.

Perks, Thomas. 2007. Does sport foster social capital? The contribution of sport to lifestyle of community participation. *Sociology of Sport Journal* 24, 4: 378–401.

Perlmutter, David D. 2003. Black athletes and white professors: A twilight zone of uncertainty.

Chronicle of Higher Education 50, 7. Online: http://chronicle.com/weekly/v50/i07/07b00701.htm.

Perman, Stacy. 1998. The master blasts the board. *Time* (January 19): 61.

Perrottet, Tone. 2004. *The naked Olympics: The true story of the ancient games*. New York: Random House.

Perrucci, Robert, and Earl Wysong. 2003. *The new class society*. Lanham, MD: Rowman & Littlefield.

Petersen, Alan. 2007. *The body in question: A socio-cultural approach*. London/New York: Routledge.

Peterson, Tomas, 2008. The professionalization of sport in the Scandinavian countries. *Nordic Sport Science Forum* (February 20). Online: http://idrottsforum.org/articles/peterson/peterson080220.html (retrieved July 20, 2008).

Petrecca, Laura. 2005. Marketers tackle participants in fantasy football. *USA Today* (August 25): 3B.

Pettavino, P., and P. Brenner. 1999. More than just a game. *Peace Review* 11, 4: 523–530.

Pfister, G. 2001. Doing sport in a headscarf? German sport and Turkish females. *Journal of Sport History* 27: 401–428.

Phillips, M. J. 1988. Disability and ethnicity in conflict: A study in transformation. In M. Fine and A. Asch, eds., *Women with disabilities: Essays in psychology, culture, and politics*. Philadelphia: Temple University Press.

Pickle, David. 2008. New media, new issues. *NCAA Champion* (Spring): 63.

Pike, Elizabeth C. J. 2004. Risk, pain, and injury: "A natural thing in rowing"? In Kevin Young, ed., *Sporting bodies, damaged selves: Sociological studies of sports-related injury* (pp. 151–162). Amsterdam: Elsevier.

Pike, Elizabeth C. J. 2005. "Doctors just say 'Rest and take ibuprofen, ": A critical examination of the role of "non-orthodox" health care in women's sport. *International Review for the Sociology of Sport* 40, 2: 201–220.

Pike, Elizabeth C. J., and Joseph A. Maguire. 2003. Injury in women's sport: Classifying key elements of "risk encounters." *Sociology of Sport Journal* 20, 3: 232–251.

Pilz, Gunther A. 1996. Social factors influencing sport and violence: On the "problem" of football hooliganism in Germany. *International Review for Sociology of Sport* 31, 1: 49–68.

Platt, Larry. 2002. *New jack jocks: Rebels, race, and the American athlete*. Philadelphia: Temple University Press.

Play Fair 2008. *Clearing the hurdles: Steps to improving wages and working conditions in the global sportswear industry*. Written by the Maquila Solidarity Network on behalf of the Play Fair 2008 Campaign. Online: http://www.playfair2008.org/docs/Clearing_the_Hurdles.pdf.

Plotz, David. 2000. Does God care who wins the Super Bowl? *Denver Post* (February 13): 6G.

Pollitt, Katha. 2008. Sweatin' to the Koran? Subject to debate. *The Nation* 286, 16 (April 28): 14. Online: http://www.thenation.com/doc/20080428/pollitt (retrieved May 6, 2008).

Poniatowska, Elena. 1975. *Massacre in Mexico* (original title *La noche de Tlatelolco*; translated by Helen R. Lane). New York: Viking Books.

Pontifical Council for the Laity. 2006. *The world of sport today: A field of Christian mission*. Città del Vaticana: Libreria Editrice Vaticana.

Poppen, Julie. 2004. Pro performance. *Rocky Mountain News* (March 31): 6B.

Porterfield, Kitty. 1999. Late to the line: Starting sport competition as an adult. In Jay Coakley and Peter Donnelly, eds., *Inside Sports* (pp. 37–45). London: Routledge.

Portes, Alejandro. 1998. Social capital: Its origins and applications in modern sociology. *Annual Review of Sociology* 24: 1–24.

Potuto, Josephine R. 2007. Academic misconduct, athletics academic support services, and the NCAA. *Kentucky Law Journal* 95, 2: 447–480.

Poulton, Emma. 2004. Mediated patriot games: The construction and representation of national identities in the British television production of Euro '96. *International Review for the Sociology of Sport* 39, 4: 437–455.

Poulton, E. 2005. English media representation of football-related disorder: 'Brutal, short-hand and simplifying'? *Sport in Society* 8, 1: 27–47.

Powers-Beck, Jeffrey P. 2004. *The American Indian integration of baseball*. Lincoln: University of Nebraska Press.

Prebish, C. S. 1993. *Religion and sport: The meeting of sacred and profane*. Westport, CT: Greenwood.

President's Council on Physical Fitness and Sports. 1997. *Physical activity and sport in the lives of girls*.

Minneapolis: Center for Research on Girls and Women in Sport, University of Minnesota.

Preves, Sharon E. 2005. *Intersex and identity: The contested self.* New Brunswick, NJ: Rutgers University Press.

Price, Monroe E., and Daniel Dayan, eds. 2008. *Owning the Olympics: Narratives of the new China.* Ann Arbor, MI: University of Michigan Press.

Price. S. L. 1997. What ever happened to the white athlete? *Sports Illustrated* (December 8): 31–55.

Price, S. L. 2004. Flag jumper. *Sports Illustrated* (August 30.): 54–56.

Prisbell, Eric. 2006. An endless summer league. *Washington Post* (July 6): E01. Online: www .washingtonpost.com/wp-dyn/content/ article/2006/07/05/AR2006070501676.html.

Pronger, Brian. 1999. Fear and trembling: Homophobia in men's sport. In Phillip White and Kevin Young, eds., *Sport and gender in Canada* (pp. 182–197). Don Mills, ON: Oxford University Press.

Pronger, Brian. 2002. *Body fascism: Salvation in the technology of physical fitness.* Toronto/Buffalo, NY: University of Toronto Press.

Putney, Clifford. 2003. *Muscular Christianity: Manhood and sports in Protestant America, 1880–1920.* Cambridge, MA: Harvard University Press.

Q and A. 2003. Alana Beard. *Sports Illustrated* (December 1): 28.

Quart, Alissa. 2008. When girls will be boys. *The New York Times* (March 16). Online: www .nytimes.com/2008/03/16/magazine/ 16students-t.html.

Raisborough, Jayne. 2006. Getting onboard: Women, access and serious leisure. *The Sociological Review* 54, 2: 242–262.

Ramsey, David. 2005. Why? *Colorado Springs Gazette* (December 11). Online: www.gazette.com/display .php?id=1312798&secid=3.

Randels Jr., George D., and Becky Beal. 2002. What makes a man?: Religion, sport, and negotiating masculine identity in the Promise Keepers. In Tara Magdalinski and T. J. L. Chandler, eds., *With God on their side: Sport in the service of religion* (pp. 160–176). London/New York: Routledge.

Raney, Arthur A., and Jennings Bryant , eds. 2006. *Handbook of sports and media.* Mahwah, NJ: L. Erlbaum Associates.

Ravel, Barbara, and Geneviève Rail. 2006. The lightness of being 'gaie': Discursive constructions of gender and sexuality in Quebec women's sport. *International Review for the Sociology of Sport* 41, 3–4: 395–412.

Ravel, Barbara, and Geneviéve Rail. 2007. On the limits of "gaie" spaces: Discursive constructions of women's sport in Quebec. *Sociology of Sport Journal* 24, 4: 402–420.

Real, Michael. R. 1996. The postmodern Olympics: Technology and the commodification of the Olympic movement. *Quest* 48, 1: 9–24.

Real, Michael. R. 1998. MediaSport: Technology and the commodification of postmodern sport. In L. A. Wenner, ed., *MediaSport* (pp. 14–26). London/New York: Routledge.

Rees, C. Roger, and Andrew W. Miracle. 2000. Sport and education. In J. Coakley and E. Dunning, eds., *Handbook of sports studies* (pp. 291–308). London: Sage.

Regalado, Samuel O. 2006. Baseball underneath America: The Nisei game in Northern California. Paper presented at the Race and Sport Symposium, University of Iowa (October). Online: http://www.uiowa.edu/~global/index.htm.

Regalado, Samuel O. 2008. *Viva Baseball! Latin Major Leaguers and Their Special Hunger.* Urbana: University of Illinois Press.

Reid, E. 1997. My body, my weapon, my shame. *Gentlemen's Quarterly* (September), 361–367.

Reid, S. M. 1996. The selling of the Games. *Denver Post* (July 21): 4BB.

Reilly, Rick. 2004a. Another victim at Colorado. *Sports Illustrated* (February 16). Online: http:// sportsillustrated.cnn.com/2004/writers/rick_ reilly/02/16/hnida/index.html.

Reilly, Rick. 2004b. The silent treatment. *Sports Illustrated* 101, 20 (November 22): 144.

Reilly, Rick. 2005. Half the size, twice the man. *Sports Illustrated* 103, 13 (October 3): 90.

Reuters. 2004. Cuban boxing team mixes punches with ideology. *The New York Times* (June 20). Online: http://query.nytimes.com/mem/tnt .html?tntget=2004/06/20/sports/othersports/ 20BOXI.html.

Reynolds, Gretchen. 2007a. Give us this day our daily supplements. *Play: The New York Times Sports Magazine* (March 4). Online: www.nytimes

.com/2007/03/04/sports/playmagazine/
04playsupplement.html.

Reynolds, Gretchen. 2007b. Outlaw DNA. *Play: The New York Times Sports Magazine* (June 3): 18–20.

Rhoden, William C. 2006. *Forty million dollar slaves: The rise, fall, and redemption of the Black athlete.* New York: Crown Publishers.

Rhoden, William C. 2007. Basketball sees potential in China, and vice versa. *The New York Times* (May 13). Online: http://select.nytimes.com/mem/tnt.html?emc=tnt&tntget=2007/05/13/sports/basketball/13rhoden.html.

Ricchiardi, Sherry. 2005. Offensive Interference. *American Journalism Review* (December/January). Online: www.ajr.org/Article.asp?id=3788.

Rice, Ron (with David Fleming). 2005. Moment of impact. *ESPN The Magazine* (June 6): 82–83.

Richtel, Matt. 2005. A new reality in video games: Advertisements. *The New York Times* (April 11): C1.

Riede, Paul. 2006. Athletic eligibility: Struggling to raise the bar. *The School Administrator* (June). Online: http://www.aasa.org/publications/saarticledetail.cfm?ItemNumber=6314.

Riesman, David, and Reuel Denny. 1951. Football in America: A study of cultural diffusion. *American Quarterly* (Winter): 302–325.

Rigauer, Bero. 2000. Marxist theories. In Jay Coakley and Eric Dunning, eds., *Handbook of sports studies* (pp. 28–47). London: Sage.

Rinehart, Robert E. 1998. *Players all: Performances in contemporary sport.* Bloomington: Indiana University Press.

Rinehart, Robert E. 2000. Arriving sport: Alternatives to formal sports. In Jay Coakley and Eric Dunning, eds., *Handbook of Sports Studies* (pp. 504–519). London: Sage.

Rinehart, Robert. 2005. "Babes" and boards. *Journal of Sport and Social Issues* 29, 3: 232–255.

Rinehart, Robert, and Chris Grenfell, 1999. Icy relations: Parental involvement in youth figure skating. Paper presented at the annual conference of the North American Society for the Sociology of Sport, Cleveland (November).

Rinehart, Robert, and Chris Grenfell. 2002. BMX spaces: Children's "grass roots" courses and corporate-sponsored tracks. *Sociology of Sport Journal* 19, 3: 302–314.

Rinehart, Robert E., and Synthia Syndor, eds. 2003. *To the extreme: Alternative sports inside and out.* Albany: State University of New York Press.

Rintala, Jan, and Judith Bischoff. 1997. Persistent resistance: Leadership positions for women in Olympic sport governing bodies. *OLYMPIKA: The International Journal of Olympic Studies* 6, 1–24.

Riordan, James. 1996. Introduction. In Arnd Krüger and James Riordan, eds., *The story of worker sport* (pp. vii–x). Champaign, IL: Human Kinetics.

Risman, Barbara, and Pepper Schwartz. 2002. After the sexual revolution: Gender politics in teen dating. *Contexts* 1, 1: 16–24.

Ritzer, G. 2003. *Contemporary sociological theory and its classical roots: The basics.* New York: McGraw-Hill.

Ritzer, George. 2005. *Enchanting a disenchanted world: Revolutionizing the means of consumption.* Thousand Oaks, CA: Pine Forge Press.

Rivers, Caryl. 2007. Spirited play is good for boys and (yes!) girls. *WeNews* (August 8). Online: http://www.womensenews.org/article.cfm/dyn/aid/3270/context/archive.

Roberts, Selena. 2005. Big boosters calling the shots on campus. *The New York Times*, section 8 (January 2): 1

Roberts, Selena. 2006. Thin line between fabulous and flabulous. *The New York Times* (September 1). Online: http://select.nytimes.com/2006/09/01/sports/tennis/01roberts.html.

Roberts, Selena. 2007a. College booster bias is delaying minority hiring. *The New York Times* (January 28). Online: http://select.nytimes.com/2007/01/28/sports/ncaafootball/28roberts.html.

Roberts, Selena. 2007b. Entertainers in sports are grappling with reality. *The New York Times* (July 8). Online: http://select.nytimes.com/2007/07/08/sports/other sports/08roberts.html.

Robinson, Laura. 1998. *Crossing the line: Violence and sexual assault in Canada's national sport.* Toronto: McClelland and Stewart.

Robinson, Joshua, and Alan Schwarz. 2008. Olympic dream stays alive, on synthetic legs. *The New York Times* (May 17). Online: http://www.nytimes.com/2008/05/17/sports/olympics/17runner.html.

Roche, Kathleen M. 1999. *Neighborhood characteristics and social capital: Influences on the association between parenting and fighting and delinquency among adolescent males.* PhD dissertation, Department of Sociology, Johns Hopkins University, Baltimore, MD.

Rock, Steve. 2008. Removal of woman referee by religious school has some crying foul. *The Kansas City Star* (February 12). Online: www.kansascity.com/105/story/487355.html.

Roderick, Martin. 2004. English professional soccer players and the uncertainties of risk. In Kevin Young, ed., *Sporting bodies, damaged selves: Sociological studies of sports-related injury* (pp. 137–150). Amsterdam: Elsevier.

Roenigk, Alyssa. 2006. Action sports insider. *ESPN The Magazine* 9.10 (May 22): 104.

Roenigk, Alyssa. 2008. The Gretchen Bleiler show. *ESPN-The Magazine* 11.02 (January 28): 62–66.

Rose, Stephen J. 2007. *Social stratification in the United States.* New York: The New Press.

Rosenau, Pauline Vaillancourt. 2003. *The competition paradigm: America's romance with conflict, contest, and commerce.* Lanham, MA: Rowman & Littlefield.

Rosenfeld, Alvin, and Nicole Wise, 2001. *The over-scheduled child.* New York: St. Martin's Griffin Edition.

Rosentraub, M. 1997. *Major League losers: The real cost of sports and who's paying for them.* New York: Basic Books.

Ross, Sally R., and Kimberly J. Shinew. 2008. Perspectives of women college athletes on sport and gender. *Sex Roles: A Journal of Research* 58, 1–2: 40–57.

Roth, Amanda, and Susan A. Basow. 2004. Femininity, sports, and feminism: Developing a theory of physical liberation. *Journal of Sport and Social Issues* 28, 3: 245–265.

Roversi, Antonio. 1994. The birth of the "ultras": The rise of football hooliganism in Italy. In R. Giulianotti and J. Williams, eds., *Game without frontiers: Football, identity and modernity* (pp. 359–381). Aldershot, England: Arena, Ashgate.

Rowe, David, ed. 2004a. *Sport, culture and the media: Critical readings.* Maidenhead, Berkshire: Open University Press.

Rowe, David. 2004b. *Sport, culture and the media: The unruly trinity* (2nd ed.). Maidenhead, Berkshire: Open University Press.

Rowland, Thomas W. 2006. Telling boys from girls: What your mother didn't tell you. *Pediatric Exercise Science* 18, 3 (August): 277–281.

Ruck, Rob. 1987. *Sandlot seasons: Sport in black Pittsburgh.* Urbana: University of Illinois Press.

Runciman, David. 2006. They can play, but they can never win. *New Statesman* (May 29). Online: http://www.newstatesman.com/200605290007.

Ryan, Joan. 1995. *Little girls in pretty boxes: The making and breaking of elite gymnasts and figure skaters.* New York: Doubleday.

Sabo, Donald, and Sue Curry Jansen. 1998. Prometheus unbound: Constructions of masculinity in sports media. In Lawrence A. Wenner, ed., *MediaSport* (pp. 202–220). London: Routledge.

Sabo, Don., Sue Curry Jansen, Danny Tate, Margaret Carlisle Duncan, and Susan Leggett. 1996. Televising international sport: Race, ethnicity, and nationalistic bias. *Journal of Sport and Social Issues* 20, 1: 7–21.

Sabo, Don, Kathleen Miller, Michael Farrell, Grace Barnes, and Merrill Melnick. 1998. *The Women's Sports Foundation report: Sport and teen pregnancy.* East Meadows, NY: Women's Sport Foundation.

Sabo, Don, Kathleen E. Miller, Merrill J. Melnick, Michael P. Farrell, and Grace M. Barnes. 2005. High school athletic participation and adolescent suicide: A nationwide study. *International Review for the Sociology of Sport* 40, 1: 5–23.

Sabo, Don, Kathleen E. Miller, Merrill J. Melnick, and Leslie Heywood. 2004. *Her life depends on it: Sport, physical activity, and the health and well-being of American girls.* East Meadow, NY: Women's Sport Foundation.

Sachs, Carolyn J., and Lawrence D. Chu. 2000. The association between professional football games and domestic violence in Los Angeles County. *Journal of Interpersonal Violence* 15: 1192–1201.

Sack, Allen L. 2008. *Counterfeit amateurs: An athlete's journey through the sixties to the age of academic capitalism.* University Park, PA: Penn State University Press.

Sack, Allen L., and Ellen J. Staurowsky. 1998. *College athletes for hire: The evolution and legacy of the NCAA's amateur myth.* Westport, CT: Praeger.

Sadowski, Rick. 2005. Moore strikes back. *Rocky Mountain News* (February 18): 1C, 7C.

Safai, Parissa. 2003. Healing the body in the "culture of risk": Examining the negotiation of treatment between sport medicine clinicians and injured athletes in Canadian intercollegiate sport. *Sociology of Sport Journal* 20, 2: 127–146.

Sagas, Michael, and George B. Cunningham. 2005a. Racial differences in the career success of assistant football coaches: The role of discrimination, human capital, and social capital. *Journal of Applied Social Psychology* 35: 773–797.

Sagas, Michael, and George B. Cunningham. 2005b. Work and family conflict among college assistant coaches. *International Journal of Sport Management* 6: 183–197.

Sage, George H. 1996. Patriotic images and capitalist profit: Contradictions of professional team sports licensed merchandise. *Sociology of Sport Journal* 13, 1: 1–11.

Sage, George H. 1998. *Power and ideology in American sport: A critical perspective.* Champaign, IL: Human Kinetics.

Sage, George H. 1999. Justice do it! The Nike transnational advocacy network: Organization, collective actions, and outcomes. *Sociology of Sport Journal* 16, 3: 206–235.

Sage, George H. 2000. Political economy and sport. In J. Coakley and E. Dunning, eds., *Handbook of sports studies* (pp. 260–276). London: Sage.

Sam, Michael P. 2003. What's the big idea? Reading the rhetoric of a national sport policy process. *Sociology of Sport Journal* 20, 3: 189–213.

SAMHSA (Substance Abuse and Mental Health Services Administration). 2002. *The 2000 national household survey on drug abuse: Team sports participation and substance use among youths.* Rockville, MD: SAMHSA.online: http://www.DrugAbuseStatistics.samhsa.gov.

Sammond, Nicholas, ed. 2005. *Steel chair to the head: The pleasure and pain of professional wrestling.* Durham, NC: Duke University Press.

Sanchez, Robert. 2003. Holding back boosters. *Rocky Mountain News* (November 10): 20A–21A.

Sanchez, Robert. 2006. Soccer giving schools, students kick-start: Latino-led teams achieving goals on field, in classroom. *The Denver Post* (September 24): 1A, 23A. Online: www.denverpost.com/ci_4388623.

Sandomir, Richard. 2002. Athletes may next seek genetic enhancement. *The New York Times* (March 21). Online: http://nytimes.com/2002/03/21/sports/othersports/21DRUG.html.

Sandomir, Richard. 2007a. From the edge of madness to fighting's mainstream. *The New York Times* (May 25). Online: www.nytimes.com/2007/05/25/sports/othersports/25ufc.html.

Sandomir, Richard. 2007b. W.W.E.'s testing is examined after Benoit murder-suicide. *The New York Times* (July 17). Online: www.nytimes.com/2007/07/17/sports/othersports/17wrestling.html.

Sandomir, Richard. 2008a. Giants seat licenses priced from 1,000 *to* 20,000. *The New York Times* (July 18). Online: http://www.nytimes.com/2008/07/18/sports/football/18seats.html.

Sandomir, Richard. 2008b. New stadiums: Prices, and outrage, escalate. *The New York Times* (August 26). Online: http://www.nytimes.com/2008/08/26/sports/26tickets.html.

Sapolsky, Robert M. 2000. It's not all in the genes. *Newsweek* (April 10): 68.

Saporito, Bill. 2004. Why fans and players are playing so rough. *Time* (December 6): 30–34.

Saraceno, Jon. 2005. Native Americans aren't fair game for nicknames. *USA Today* (June 1): 10C.

Saslow, Eli. 2006a. Opportunity realized a world away. *Washington Post* (January 30): E01. Online: http://www.washingtonpost.com/wp-dyn/content/article/2006/01/29/AR2006012901149.html.

Saslow, Eli. 2006b. Trading Diamonds for Blue Chips. *Washington Post* (January 31): E01. Online: http://www.washingtonpost.com/wp-dyn/content/article/2006/01/30/AR2006013001305.html.

Saslow, Eli. 2006c. Turning promise into a commodity. *Washington Post* (January 29): A01. Online: http://www.washingtonpost.com/wp-dyn/content/article/2006/01/28/AR2006012801231.html.

Saslow, Eli. 2007. In Maryland, a fight to the finish line. *Washington Post* (April 12): A01.

Sato, Daisuke, 2005. Sport and identity in Tunisia. *International Journal of Sport and Health Science* 3: 27–34. Online: www.shobix.co.jp/ijshs/tempfiles/journal/3/20040072.pdf.

Saunders, Patrick. 2001. Nasty boys. *Denver Post* (January 28): 11–21.

Saunders, Patrick. 2005. NFL policy on drugs questioned. *The Denver Post* (April 12): 5D.

Savage, David G. 2008. Fantasy baseball leagues allowed to use real players' names. *Los Angeles Times* (June 2). Online: www.latimes.com/sports/la-na-scotus3-2008jun03,0,4517238.story.

Savage, Howard J., ed. 1929. *American college athletics.* Bulletin no. 23. New York: Carnegie Foundation.

Saxton, Bryon. 2008. "Church ball" is about sportsmanship. *The Denver Post* (April 13): 3C.

Schaller, Bob. 2005. Toni Davis. Online: www .blackathletesportsnetwork.net/artman/publish/ article_0510.shtml (retrieved December 3, 2005).

Scheerder, Jeroen, Bart Vanreusel, Marijke Taks, and Roland. Renson. 2002. Social sports stratification in Flanders, 1969–1999: Intergenerational reproduction of social inequalities? *International Review for the Sociology of Sport* 37, 2: 219–246.

Scheerder, Jeroen, et al., 2006. Sports participation among females from adolescence to adulthood: A longitudinal study. *International Review for the Sociology of Sport* 41, 3–4.

Schefter, Adam. 2003. Working through the pain. *Denver Post* (December 7): 1J, 6J.

Scheinin, Richard. 1994. *Field of screams: The dark underside of America's national pastime.* New York: Norton.

Scherer, Jay. 2007. Globalization, promotional culture and the production/consumption of online games: Engaging Adidas's 'Beat Rugby' Campaign. *New Media & Society* 9, 3: 475–496.

Scherer, Jay, and Steven Jackson. 2008. Producing Allblacks.com: Cultural intermediaries and the policing of electronic spaces of sporting consumption. *Sociology of Sport Journal* 25, 2: 187–205.

Schiesel, Seth. 2006. Making virtual football more like the real thing. *The New York Times* (July 6). Online: http://select.nytimes.com/mem/tnt .html?emc=tnt&tntget=2006/07/06/sports/ football/06game.html.

Schiesel, Seth. 2007a. Flashy wrestling shows grab the world by the neck and flex. *The New York Times* (April 4). Online: www.nytimes .com/2007/04/04/arts/television/04mania.html.

Schiesel, Seth. 2007b. With famed players, game takes on Madden's turf. *The New York Times* (September 17). Online: www.nytimes .com/2007/09/17/technology/17game.html.

Schilling, Mary Lou. 1997. Socialization, retirement, and sports. Online essay and links: http://edweb6 .educ.msu.edu/kin866/resschilling1.htm (retrieved June 2005).

Schimmel, Kimberly S. 2000. Take me out to the ball game: The transformation of production-consumption relations in professional team sport. In C. L. Harrington and D. D. Bielby,

eds., *Cultural production and consumption: Readings in popular culture* (pp. 36–52). Oxford, UK: Blackwell.

Schimmel, Kimberly. S. 2002. The political economy of place: Urban and sport studies perspectives. In Joseph Maguire and Kevin Young, eds., *Theory, sport and society* (pp. 335–353). Oxford, UK: JAI (Elsevier Science).

Schimmel, Kimberly S. 2006. Deep play: Sports mega-events and urban social conditions in the USA. *The Sociological Review* 54, 2: 160–174.

Schimmel, Kimberly, Alan G. Ingham, and Jeremy W. Howell. 1993. Professional team sport and the American city: Urban politics and franchise relocations. In A. G. Ingham and J. W. Loy, eds., *Sport in social development* (pp. 211–244). Champaign, IL: Human Kinetics.

Schmidt, Michael S. 2008. Baseball is challenged on rise in stimulant use. *The New York Times* (January 16). Online: www.nytimes.com/2008/01/16/ sports/baseball/16stimulant.html.

Schneider, Angela, and Theodore Friedmann, eds. 2006. *Gene doping in sports: The science and ethics of genetically modified athletes.* Boston: Elsevier Academic Press.

Schneider, Angela, and Fan Hong, eds.2007. *Doping in sport: Global ethical issues.* London: Routledge.

Schneiderman, R. M. 2008. Better days, and even the candidates, are coming to W.W.E. *The New York Times* (April 28). Online: http://www.nytimes .com/2008/04/28/business/media/28wwe.html.

Schroeder, Janice Jones. 1995. Developing self-esteem and leadership skills in Native American women: The role sports and games play. *Journal of Physical Education, Recreation and Dance* 66, 7: 48–51.

Schultz, B. 1999. The disappearance of child-directed activities. *Journal of Physical Education, Recreation and Dance* 70, 5: 9–10.

Schuman, Howard. 2002. Sense and nonsense about surveys. *Contexts* 1, 2 (Summer): 40–47.

Schwarz, Alan. 2007a. Concussions put college players in murky world. *The New York Times* (November 29). Online: www.nytimes .com/2007/11/29/sports/ncaafootball/ 29concussions.html.

Schwarz, Alan. 2007b. For Jets, silence on concussions signals unease. *The New York Times* (December 22). Online: www.nytimes

.com/2007/12/22/sports/football/22concussions
.html.

Schwarz, Alan. 2007c. Girls are often neglected victims of concussions. *The New York Times* (October 2). Online: www.nytimes .com/2007/10/02/sports/othersports/ 02concussions.html.

Schwarz, Alan. 2007d. In high school football, an injury no one sees. *The New York Times* (September 15). Online: www.nytimes.com/2007/09/15/sports/ football/15concussions.html.

Schwirtz, Michael. 2008. Russia is luring back N.H.L. stars. *The New York Times* (February 29). Online: www.nytimes.com/2008/02/29/sports/ hockey/29hockey.html.

SDP/IWG Secretariat. 2007. Introduction. In Sport for Development and Peace, International Working Group (SDP/IWG), *Literature Reviews on Sport for Development and Peace* (pp. 3–6). Toronto, Ontario: University of Toronto, Faculty of Physical Education and Health. Online: http://iwg.sportanddev.org/data/htmleditor/file/ Lit.%20Reviews/literature%20review%20SDP .pdf (retrieved January 24, 2008).

Seale, Clive, ed. 2004. *Researching society and culture.* London, Sage.

Seattle Times. 2003. *Coaches who prey: The abuse of girls and the system that allows it* (multiarticle series). Online: http://seattletimes.nwsource.com/news/ local/coaches/ (retrieved June 2005).

Seeley, Morgan, and Genevieve Rail. 2004. Youth with disabilities: Rethinking discourses of the "healthy" body. Paper presented at the annual meeting of the North American Society for the Sociology of Sport, Tucson, Arizona (November).

Sellers, Robert, and S. Keiper. 1998. Opportunity given or lost? Academic support services for NCAA Division I student-athletes. Paper presented at the annual conference of the North American Society for the Sociology of Sport, Las Vegas (November).

Selman, Robert L. 1971. Taking another's perspective: Role-taking development in early childhood. *Child Development* 42: 1721–1734.

Selman, Robert L. 1976. Social-cognitive understanding: A guide to educational and clinical practice. In T. Lickona, ed., *Moral development and behavior* (pp. 299–317). New York: Holt, Rinehart & Winston.

Sernau, Scott. 2005. *Worlds apart: Social inequalities in a global economy.* Thousand Oaks, CA: Pine Forge Press.

Sewart, James. 1987. The commodification of sport. *International Review for the Sociology of Sport* 22, 3: 171–192.

Shaffer, Marvin, Alan Greer, and Celine Mauboules. 2003. Olympic costs and benefits: A cost-benefit analysis of the proposed Vancouver 2010 Winter Olympic and Paralympic Games. Vancouver: Canadian Centre for Policy Alternatives. Online: www.policyalternatives.ca/bc/olympics/olympics_ summary.html.

Shakib, Sohaila. 2003. Female basketball participation: Negotiating the conflation of peer status and gender status from childhood through puberty. *American Behavioral Scientist* 46, 10: 1404–1422.

Shakib, Sohaila, and Michele D. Dunbar. 2002. The social construction of female and male high school basketball participation: Reproducing the gender order through a two-tiered sporting institution. *Sociological Perspectives* 45, 4: 353–378.

Shapin, Steven. 2005. Cleanup hitters: The steroid wars and the nature of what's natural. *New Yorker* (April 18): 191–194.

Shapiro, Thomas M. 2004. *The hidden cost of being African American: How wealth perpetuates inequality.* New York: Oxford University Press.

Shaw, Mark. 2002. Board with sports. Paper written in Introductory Sociology, University of Colorado, Colorado Springs, spring semester.

Sheil, Pat. 2000. Shed a tear or two . . . or else! Online: www.abc.net.au/paralympics/features/s201108.htm.

Sherry, Allison. 2007. School woes sacking DPS football teams. *Denver Post* (November 11): 1C, 5C. Online: http://www.denverpost.com/ci_7429469.

Shields, David L. L., and Brenda J. L. Bredemeier. 1995. *Character development and physical activity.* Champaign, IL: Human Kinetics.

Shields, David L. L., Brenda J. L. Bredemeier, D. E. Gardner, and A. Bostrom. 1995. Leadership, cohesion, and team norms regarding cheating and aggression. *Sociology of Sport Journal* 12, 3: 324–336.

Shilling, Chris. 1993. *The body and social theory.* London: Sage Publications.

Shilling, Chris. 2007. *Embodying sociology: Retrospect, progress and prospects.* Malden, MA: Blackwell Publishing.

Shogan, Debra, and Maureen Ford. 2000. A new sport ethics. *International Review for the Sociology of Sport* 35, 1: 49–58.

Shropshire, Kenneth L. 1996. *In black and white: Race and sports in America.* New York: New York University Press.

Shulman, James L., and William G. Bowen. 2001. *The game of life: College sports and educational values.* Princeton, NJ: Princeton University Press.

Silk, Michael L. 1999. Local/global flows and altered production practices. *International Review for the Sociology of Sport* 34, 2: 113–123.

Silk, Michael L. 2004. A tale of two cities: The social production of sterile sporting space. *Journal of Sport and Social Issues* 28, 4: 349–378.

Silk, Michael L., and David L. Andrews. 2008. Managing Memphis: Governance and regulation in sterile spaces of play. *Social Identities: Journal for the Study of Race, Nation and Culture* 14, 3: 395-414.

Silk, Michael L., and Mark Falcous. 2005. One day in September/A week in February: Mobilizing American (sporting) nationalisms. *Sociology of Sport Journal* 22, 4: 447–471.

Simon, Robert L. 2008. Does athletics undermine academics? Examining some issues. *Journal of Intercollegiate Sport 1, 1: 40–58.*

Simons, Herbert D. 2003. Race and penalized sports behaviors. *International Review for the Sociology of Sport* 38, 1: 5–22.

Simpson, Kevin, 1996. Sporting dreams die on the "rez." In D. S. Eitzen, ed., *Sport in contemporary society* (pp. 287–294). New York: St. Martin's Press.

Singh, Parbudyal, Allen Sack, and Ronald Dick. 2003. Free agency and pay discrimination in Major League Baseball. *Sociology of Sport Journal* 20, 3: 275–286.

Slack, Trevor, ed. 2005. *The commercialisation of sport.* New York/London: Routledge.

Smedley, Audrey. 1997. Origin of the idea of race. *Anthropology Newsletter* (November). Online: www .pbs.org/race/000_About/002_04-background-02 -09.htm (retrieved October 15, 2005).

Smedley, Audrey. 1999. Review of Theodore Allen, *The Invention of the White Race, vol. 2. Journal of World History* 10, 1: 234–237.

Smedley, Audrey. 2003. PBS interview for the series, *Race—the power of an illusion.* Online: www.pbs .org/race/000_About/002_04-background-02 -06.htm (retrieved June 2005).

Smith, Amanda. 1999. Back-page bylines: Newspapers, women, and sport. In Randy Martin and Toby Miller, eds., *SportCult* (pp. 253–261). Minneapolis: University of Minnesota Press.

Smith, Andrew, and Nigel Thomas. 2005. The inclusion of elite athletes with disabilities in the 2002 Manchester Commonwealth Games: An exploratory analysis of British newspaper coverage. *Sports, Education and Society* 10, 1: 49–67.

Smith, Brett, and Andrew Sparkes. 2002. Men, sport spinal cord injury and the construction of coherence: Narrative practice in action. *Qualitative Research* 2, 2: 143–171.

Smith, C. 1997. God is an .800 hitter. *The New York Times Magazine* (July 27): 26–29.

Smith, Gary. 2005a. The shadow boxer. *Sports Illustrated* (April 18): 58–68. Online: http:// sportsillustrated.cnn.com/2005/magazine/04/12/ griffith0418/ (retrieved July 2005).

Smith, Gary. 2005b. What do we do now? *Sports Illustrated* (March 28): 40–50.

Smith, Jason M., and Alan G. Ingham. 2003. On the waterfront: Retrospectives on the relationship between sport and communities. *Sociology of Sport Journal* 20, 3: 252–274.

Smith, Lauren. 2007. NCAA proposal would let colleges cash in on player images. *The Chronicle of Higher Education* 54, 6 (October 5): A1. Online: http://chronicle.com/weekly/v54/i06/ 06a00102.htm.

Smith, Michael. 1983. *Violence and sport.* Toronto: Butterworths.

Smith, R. Tyson. 2008. Passion work: The joint production of emotional labor in professional wrestling. *Social Psychology Quarterly* 71, 2: 157–176.

Smith, Ronald. E. 1986. Toward a cognitive-affective model of athletic burnout. *Journal of Sport Psychology* 8, 1: 36–50.

Smith, Tommie, and Steele, David. 2007. *Silent gesture: Autobiography of Tommie Smith.* Philadelphia: Temple University Press.

Smith, Yvonne. 2000. Sociohistorical influences on African American elite sportswomen. In D. Brooks and R. Althouse, eds., *Racism in college athletics: The African American athlete's experience* (pp. 173–198). Morgantown, WV: Fitness Information Technology.

Snider, Mike. 2007. Gamers who mean business. *USA Today* (August 14): 3D.

Snyder, Brad. 2006. *A well-paid slave: Curt Flood's fight for free agency in professional sports.* New York: Viking.

Snyder, Eldon. E. 1994. Interpretations and explanations of deviance among college athletes: A case study. *Sociology of Sport Journal* 11, 3: 231–248.

Soek, Janwillem. 2006. *The strict liability principle and the human rights of the athlete in doping cases.* The Hague: TMC Asser Press.

Sokolove, Michael. 2002. Football is a sucker's game. *The New York Times Magazine*, section 6 (December 22): 36–41, 64, 68–70.

Sokolove, Michael. 2004a. Built to swim. *The New York Times Magazine*, section 6 (August 8): 20–25.

Sokolove, Michael. 2004b. In pursuit of doped excellence. *The New York Times Magazine*, section 6 (January 18): 28–33, 48, 54, 58.

Sokolove, Michael. 2004c. The thoroughly designed American childhood: Constructing a teen phenom. *The New York Times*, section 6 (November 28): 80.

Sokolove, Michael. 2006. From pastime to nap time. *The New York Times* (February 5). Online: www.nytimes.com/2006/02/05/magazine/05controversy_24_25_.html.

Solomon, Alisa. 2000. Our bodies, ourselves: The mainstream embraces the athlete Amazon. *The Village Voice* (April 19–25). Online: www.villagevoice.com/issues/0016/solomon2.shtml (retrieved October 15, 2005).

Sorek, Tamir. 2007. *Arab soccer in a Jewish state: The integrative enclave.* Cambridge: Cambridge University Press.

Spaaij, Ramón. 2006. *Understanding football hooliganism: A comparison of six western European football clubs.* Amsterdam: Amsterdam University Press.

Sparkes, Andrew C. 2002. *Telling tales in sport and physical activity: A qualitative journey.* Champaign, IL: Human Kinetics Press.

Sparkes, Andrew, and Brett Smith. 2002. Sport, spinal cord injury, embodied masculinities, and the dilemmas of narrative identity. *Men and Masculinities* 4, 3: 258–285.

Sperber, Murray. 2000. *Beer and circus: How big-time college sports is crippling undergraduate education.* New York: Holt.

Spiegel, Alix. 2008. Old-fashioned play builds serious skills. PBS, *Morning Edition* (February 21). Online: http://www.npr.org/templates/story/story.php?storyId=19212514.

Spirou, Costas, and Larry Bennett. 2003. *It's hardly sporting: Stadiums, neighborhoods, and the new Chicago.* DeKalb: Northern Illinois University Press.

Spreitzer, Elmer A. 1995. Does participation in interscholastic athletics affect adult development?: A longitudinal analysis of an 18–24 age cohort. *Youth and Society* 25, 3: 368–387.

St. Louis, Brett. 2003. Sport, genetics and the 'natural athlete': The resurgence of racial science. *Body and Society* 9, 2: 75–95.

St. Louis, Catherine. 2007. Train like a pro, even if you're 12. *The New York Times* (July 19). Online: www.nytimes.com/2007/07/19/fashion/19Fitness.html.

Starr, Mark. 1999. Voices of the century: Blood, sweat, and cheers. *Newsweek* (October 25): 44–73.

Starr, Mark, and Allison Samuels. 2000. A season of shame. *Newsweek* (May 29): 56–60. Online: http://www.newsweek.com/id/84233 (retrieved July 16, 2008).

Staurowsky, Ellen J. 2007. "You know, we are all Indian": Exploring white power and privilege in reactions to the NCAA Native American Mascot Policy. *Journal of Sport and Social Issues* 31, 1: 61–76.

Sternheimer, Karen. 2006. *Kids these days: Facts and fictions about today's youth.* Lanham, MD: Rowman & Littlefield.

Stetler, Brian. 2008. Web audience for games soars for NBC and Yahoo. *The New York Times* (August 25). Online: http://www.nytimes.com/2008/08/25/sports/olympics/25online.html (retrieved August 25, 2008).

Stevenson, Christopher L. 2002. Seeking identities: Towards an understanding of the athletic careers of masters swimmers. *International Review for the Sociology of Sport* 37, 2: 131–146.

Stevenson, Christopher. 1991a. The Christian-athlete: An interactionist-developmental analysis. *Sociology of Sport Journal* 8, 4: 362–379.

Stevenson, Christopher. 1991b. Christianity as a hegemonic and counter-hegemonic device in elite sport. Paper presented at Conference of the North American Society for the Sociology of Sport, Milwaukee (November).

Stevenson, Christopher. 1997. Christian-athletes and the culture of elite sport: Dilemmas and solutions. *Sociology of Sport Journal* 14, 3: 241–262.

Stevenson, Christopher. 1999. Becoming an elite international athlete: Making decisions about identity. In J. Coakley and P. Donnelly, eds., *Inside Sports* (pp. 86–95). London: Routledge.

Stinson, Jeffrey L., and Dennis R. Howard. 2004. Scoreboards and mortarboards: Major donor behavior and intercollegiate athletics. *Sport Marketing Quarterly* 13, 3: 129–140.

Stoelting, Suzanne Marie. 2004. She's in control, she's free, she's an athlete: A qualitative analysis of sport empowerment and the lives of female athletes. Paper presented at the annual conference of the American Sociological Society, San Francisco (August).

Stokes, M. 1996. "Strong as a Turk": Power, performance and representation in Turkish wrestling. In J. MacClancy, ed., *Sport, identity and ethnicity* (pp. 21–42). Oxford, UK: Berg.

Stoll, Sharon K., and Jennifer M. Beller. 1998. Can character be measured? *Journal of Physical Education, Recreation, and Dance* 69, 1: 18–24.

Stoll, Sharon K., and Jennifer M. Beller. 2000. Do sports build character? In J. R. Gerdy, ed., *Sports in school: The future of an institution* (pp. 18–30). New York: Teachers College Press (Columbia University).

Stone, Gregory P. 1973. American sports: Play and display. In John T. Talamini and Charles H. Page, eds., *Sport and society* (pp. 65–84). Boston: Little, Brown.

Stone, Jeff, Christian I. Lynch, Mike Sjomeling, and John M. Darley. 1999. Stereotype threat effects on black and white athletic performance. *Journal of Personality and Social Psychology* 77, 6: 1213–1227.

Stone, Jeff, Zachary W. Perry, and John M. Darley. 1997. "White men can't jump": Evidence for the perceptual confirmation of racial stereotypes following a basketball game. *Basic and Applied Social Psychology* 19, 3: 291–306.

Stratta, Theresa. 1995. Cultural inclusiveness in sport—Recommendations from African-American women college athletes. *Journal of Physical Education, Recreation and Dance* 66, 7: 52–56.

Stratta, Theresa. 1998. Barriers facing African-American women in college sports: A case study approach. *Melpomene*, 17, 1: 19–26.

Sugden, John, and Alan Tomlinson. 1998. *FIFA and the contest for world football: Who rules the peoples' game?* Cambridge, UK: Polity Press.

Sugden, John, and Alan Tomlinson. 1999. *Great balls of fire: How big money is highjacking world football.* Edinburgh, Scotland: Mainstream.

Sugden, John, and Alan Tomlinson. 2000. Theorizing sport, social class and status. In Jay Coakley and Eric Dunning, eds., *Handbook of sport studies* (pp. 309–321). London: Sage.

Suggs, Welch. 2001. Left behind. *Chronicle of Higher Education* 48, 14: A35–A37.

Suggs, Welch. 2005. *A place on the team: The triumph and tragedy of Title IX.* Princeton, NJ: Princeton University Press.

Sundgot-Borgen, J. 2001. Eating disorders. In K. Christensen, A. Guttmann, and G. Pfister, eds., *International encyclopedia of women and sports* (pp. 352–358). New York: Macmillan Reference.

Swain, Derek. 1999. Moving on: Leaving pro sports. In Jay Coakley and Peter Donnelly, eds., *Inside sports* (pp. 223–231). London: Routledge.

Swartz, Jon. 2004. High death rate lingers behind fun facade of pro wrestling. *USA Today.* Online: www.usatoday.com/sports/2004-03-12-pro-wrestling_x.htm (retrieved January 24, 2008).

Swartz, Jon. 2007. WWE drug suspensions raise hopes. *USA Today* (September 5): 7C.

Sweeney, Emily. 2005. Cost of prosthetics stirs debate. *Boston Globe* (July 5): 2. Online: www.boston.com/business/globe/articles/2005/07/05/cost_of_prosthetics_stirs_debate/?page=2 (retrieved July 21, 2005).

Sweeney, H. Lee. 2004. Gene doping. *Scientific American* 291, 1: 69.

Swift, E. M., and D. Yaeger. 2001. Unnatural selection. *Sports Illustrated* (May 14): 87–93.

Swoopes, Sheryl. 2005. Outside the arc (as told to L. Z. Granderson). *ESPN The Magazine* (November 7): 120–125.

Sykes, Heather. 2006. Transsexual and transgender policies in sport. *Women in Sport and Physical Activity Journal* 15, 1: 3–13.

Sykes, Heather. 2007. Anxious identification in 'The Sopranos' and sport: Psychoanalytic and queer theories of embodiment. *Sport, Education and Society* 12, 2: 127–139.

Sylwester, MaryJo. 2005a. Girls following in Ochoa's, Fernandez's sports cleats. *USA Today* (March 29): 4C.

Sylwester, MaryJo. 2005b. Hispanic girls in sports held back by tradition. *USA Today* (March 29): 1A–2A.

Sylwester, MaryJo. 2005c. Sky's the limit for Hispanic teen. *USA Today* (March 29): 4C.

Taheri, Amir. 2004. Muslim women play only an incidental part in the Olympics. Online: www.benadorassociates.com/article/6651 (retrieved July 5, 2005).

Takahashi, Yoshio, and John Horne. 2006. Moving with the bat and the ball: Preliminary reflections on the migration of Japanese baseball labour. *International Review for the Sociology of Sport* 41, 1: 79–88.

Tamburrini, Claudio M. 2003. *Educational or genetic blueprints: What's the difference?* Nordic Sport Science Forum (June 6). Online: http://idrottsforum.org/articles/tamburrini/tamburrini.html.

Taub, Diane E., and Kimberly R. Greer. 2000. Physical activity as a normalizing experience for school-age children with physical disabilities: Implications for legitimating of social identity and enhancement of social ties. *Journal of Sport and Social Issues* 24, 4: 395–414.

Taylor, Ian. 1982a. Class, violence and sport: The case of soccer hooliganism in Britain. In Hart Cantelon and Richard Gruneau, eds., *Sport, culture and the modern state* (pp. 39–97). Toronto: University of Toronto Press.

Taylor, Ian. 1982b. On the sports violence question: Soccer hooliganism revisited. In Jennifer Hargreaves, ed., *Sport, culture and ideology* (pp. 152–196). London: Routledge and Kegan Paul.

Taylor, Ian. 1987. Putting the boot into a working-class sport: British soccer after Bradford and Brussels. *Sociology of Sport Journal* 4, 2: 171–191.

Taylor, Matthew. 2007. Football, migration and globalization: The perspective of history. *Idrottsforum*. Online: http://idrottsforum.org/articles/taylor/taylor070314.html.

Temple, Kerry. 1992. Brought to you by . . . *Notre Dame Magazine* 21, 2: 29.

Theberge, Nancy. 1999. Being physical: Sources of pleasure and satisfaction in women's ice hockey. In J. Coakley and P. Donnelly, eds., *Inside Sports* (pp. 146–155). London: Routledge.

Theberge, Nancy. 2000a. Gender and sport. In J. Coakley and E. Dunning, eds., *Handbook of sport studies* (pp. 322–333). London: Sage.

Theberge, Nancy. 2000b. *Higher goals: Women's ice hockey and the politics of gender*. Albany: State University of New York Press.

Theberge, Nancy. 2008. "Just a normal bad part of what I do": Elite athletes' accounts of the relationship between health and sport. *Sociology of Sport Journal* 25, 2: 206–222.

Thelin, John R. 2008. Academics and athletics: A part and apart in the American campus. *Journal of Intercollegiate Sport* 1, 1: 72–81.

Thiel, Art. 2008. Big-time college sports' misdeeds have many enablers. *Seattle Post Intelligencer-seattlepi.com* (January 31). Online: http://seattlepi.nwsource.com/thiel/349656_thiel01.html.

Thing, Lone, F. 2004. Scars on the body: The risk management and self-care of injured female handball players in Denmark. In Kevin Young, ed. *Sporting bodies, damaged selves: Sociological studies of sports-related injury* (pp. 195–210). Amsterdam: Elsevier.

Thoennes, K. Erik. 2008. Created to play: Thoughts on play, sport, and the Christian life. In Donald Lee Deardorff and John White, eds., *The Image of God in the human body: Essays on Christianity and Sports*. Lewiston, NY: Edwin Mellen Press.

Thomas, Carol. 1999. Narrative identity and the disabled self. In M. Corker and S. French, eds., *Disability discourse* (pp. 47–56). Milton Keynes, England: Open University Press.

Thomas, Katie. 2008a. Big game is no place for the average fan. *The New York Times* (February 3). Online: http://select.nytimes.com/mem/tnt.html?emc=tnt&tntget=2008/02/03/sports/football/03corporate.html.

Thomas, Katie. 2008b. A lab is set to test the gender of some female athletes. *The New York Times* (July 30). Online: http://www.nytimes.com/2008/07/30/sports/olympics/30gender.html?th&emc=th.

Thompson, Carmen Renee. 2004. The hook-up: McKay and Shinoda. *ESPN The Magazine* (December 20): 40.

Thompson, R., and R. T. Sherman. 1999. Athletes, athletic performance, and eating disorders: Healthier alternatives. *Journal of Social Issues* 55, 2: 317–337.

Thompson, Shona. 1999a. The game begins at home: Women's labor in the service of sport. In J. Coakley and P. Donnelly, eds., *Inside Sports* (pp. 111–120). London: Routledge.

Thompson, Shona. 1999b. *Mother's taxi: Sport and women's labor.* Albany: State University of New York Press.

Thomsen, Steven R., Danny W. Bower, and Michael D. Barnes. 2004. Photographic images in women's health, fitness, and sports magazines and the physical self-concept of a group of adolescent female volleyball players. *Journal of Sport and Social Issues* 28, 3: 266–283.

Thomson, Rosemarie Garland. 2000. Staring back: Self-representations of disabled performance artists. *American Quarterly* 52, 2: 334–338.

Thomson, Rosemarie Garland. 2002. Integrating disability, transforming feminist theory. *National Women's Studies Association Journal* 14, 3: 1–32.

Thorpe, Holly. 2008. Foucault, technologies of the self, and the media. *Journal of Sport and Social Issues* 32, 2: 199–229.

Tierney, John. 2008. Let the games be doped. *The New York Times* (August 12). Online: http://www.nytimes.com/2008/08/12/science/12tier.html.

Time. 1997. *Time*'s 25 most influential Americans. *Time* 149, 16: 40–62.

Todd, Terry. 1987. Anabolic steroids: The gremlins of sport. *Journal of Sport History* 14, 1: 87–107.

Tomc, Gregor. 2008. The nature of sport. Keynote address at the Fifth Conference of the European Association for Sociology of Sport (Bled, Slovenia, May 23).

Tomlinson, Alan. 2005. The commercialization of the Olympics: Cities, corporations, and the Olympic commodity. In Kevin Young and Kevin Wamsley, eds., *Global Olympics: Historical and sociological studies of the modern Games* (pp. 179–200). Oxford, UK: Elsevier.

Tomlinson, Alan. 2007. Sport and social class. In George Ritzer, ed., *Encyclopedia of sociology* (pp. 4695–4699). London/New York: Blackwell.

Tomlinson, Alan, and Christopher Young, eds. 2006. *National identity and global sports: Culture, politics, and spectacle in the Olympics and the Football World Cup.* Albany, NY: State University of New York Press.

Totilo, Stephen. 2008. Playing games. *The Nation* 286, 21 (June 2): 25–30.

Tracey, Jill, and T. Elcombe. 2004. A lifetime of healthy meaningful movement: Have we forgotten the athletes? *Quest* 56, 2: 241–260.

Tracy, Allison J., and Sumru Erkut. 2002. Gender and race patterns in the pathways from sports participation to self-esteem. *Sociological Perspectives* 45, 4: 445–467.

Tramontano, Gerald. 2008. Head games. *The New York Times* (September 13). Online: http://www.nytimes.com/2008/09/13/opinion/13tramontano.html

Travers, Ann. 2006. Queering sport: Lesbian softball leagues and the transgender challenge. *International Review for the Sociology of Sport* 41, 3–4: 431–446.

Trivett, Steve. 1999. Rampart goes back to smash-mouth in win over Mitchell. *Rocky Mountain News* (October 31): 30C.

Troutman, Kelly, P., and Mikaela J. Dufur. 2007. From high school jocks to college grads assessing the long-term effects of high school sport participation on females' educational attainment. *Youth & Society* 38, 4: 443–462.

Troutman, Parke. 2004. A growth machine's plan B: Legitimating development when the value-free growth ideology is under fire. *Journal of Urban Affairs* 26, 5: 611–622.

Trulson, Michael E. 1986. Martial arts training: A novel "cure" for juvenile delinquency. *Human Relations* 39, 12: 1131–1140.

Trumbo, Catherine. 2008. Going for the gold: Senior citizens shine at Wiilympics. *The Coloradoan* (August 24): A4. Online: http://www.coloradoan.com/apps/pbcs.dll/article?AID=/20080824/LOVELAND04/80824003/1192/LOVELAND (retrieved 8/26/08).

Trumpbour, Robert C. 2007. *The new cathedrals: Politics and media in the history of stadium construction.* Syracuse: Syracuse University Press.

Tuaolo, Esera. 2002. Free and clear. *ESPN The Magazine* (November 11): 72–77.

Tucker, Ross, and Jonathan Dugus, 2007a. Oscar Pistorius banned—IAAF result. *The Science of Sport*

(December 19). Online: http://scienceofsport .blogspot.com/2007/12/oscar-pistorius-banned -iaaf-result.html.

Tucker, Ross, and Jonathan Dugus, 2007b. Oscar Pistorius debut: The scientific facts and implications. *The Science of Sport* (July 17). Online: http://scienceofsport.blogspot.com/2007/07/ oscar-pistorius-debut-scientific-facts_17.html.

Tucker, Ross, and Jonathan Dugus, 2007c. Oscar Pistorius reaction: Challenge the ban. *The Science of Sport* (January 14). Online: http:// scienceofsport.blogspot.com/2008/01/oscar -pistorius-reaction-challenge-ban.html.

Tucker, Ross, and Jonathan Dugus, 2007d. Oscar Pistorius—Science and engineering vs. training. An evaluation of ALL the evidence. *The Science of Sport* (July 11). Online: http://scienceofsport .blogspot.com/2007/07/oscar-pistorius-science -and-engineering.html.

Tucker, Ross, and Jonathan Dugus. 2008. Oscar Pistorius: A case where the science does not matter. *The Science of Sport* (February 21). Online: http://scienceofsport.blogspot .com/2008/02/oscar-pistorius-case-where -science-does.html.

Tucker, Lori, and Janet B. Parks. 2001. Effects of gender and sport type on intercollegiate athletes' perceptions of the legitimacy of aggressive behaviors in sport. *Sociology of Sport Journal* 18, 4: 403–413.

Tulle, Emmanuelle. 2007. Running to run: Embodiment, structure and agency amongst veteran elite runners. *Sociology* 41, 2: 329–346.

Turner, Bryan S. 1997. *The body and society.* London: Sage.

United Nations. 2003. *Sport for peace and development.* United Nations General Assembly, Fifty-eighth session, 52nd plenary meeting (November 3). Document A/58/PV.52. Online: http:// daccessdds.un.org/doc/UNDOC/GEN/ N03/592/54/PDF/N0359254.pdf?OpenElement (retrieved 6-15-08).

Upton, Jodi. 2005. Violence at games means trouble for all. *USA Today* (November 23): 11C.

U.S. Department of Labor. 2005. *Statistics about people with disabilities and employment.* Washington, DC: Office of Disability Employment Policy. Online: www.dol.gov/odep/pubs/ek01/stats.htm (retrieved July 21, 2005).

U.S. News and World Report. 1983. A sport fan's guide to the 1984 Olympics. *U.S. News and World Report* (May 9): 124.

U.S. Surgeon General. 1999a. Fact sheet: *Physical activity and women.* National Center for Chronic Disease Prevention and Health Promotion. Atlanta, GA. Online: www.cdc.gov/nccdphp/sgr/ women.htm.

U.S. Surgeon General. 1999b. *Physical activity and health.* National Center for Chronic Disease Prevention and Health Promotion. Atlanta, GA. Online: www.cdc.gov/nccdphp/sgr/sgr.htm.

USA Today. 1994. Daily prayers are ritual for Olajuwon. *USA Today* (10 June): 6C.

USDHHS (U.S. Department of Health and Human Services). 1996. *Physical activity and health: A report of the surgeon general.* Washington, DC: USDHHS.

Van Riper, Tom. 2008. Here come the super-stadiums. *Forbes* (March 31). Online: www.forbes .com/2008/03/31/sports-stadiums-yankees-biz -sports_cx_tvr_0331stadiums.html.

van Sterkenburg, Jacco, and Annelies Knoppers. 2004. Dominant discourses about race/ethnicity and gender in sport practice and performance. *International Review for the Sociology of Sport* 39, 3: 301–321.

Vavrus, M. D. 2000. From women of the year to "soccer moms": The case of the incredible shrinking women. *Political Communication* 17, 2: 193–213.

Veblen, Thorsten. 1899. *The theory of the leisure class.* New York: Macmillan. (See also 1994 edition, New York: Penguin Classics.)

Verducci, Tom. 2002. Totally juiced. *Sports Illustrated* (June 3): 34–48.

Veri, Maria J. 1999. Homophobic discourse surrounding the female athlete. *Quest* 51, 4: 355–368.

Verma, Gajendra K., and Douglas S. Darby. 1994. *Winners and losers: Ethnic minorities in sport and recreation.* London: Falmer Press.

Vertinsky, Patricia A. 1990. *The eternally wounded woman: Women, exercise and doctors.* Manchester, UK: Manchester University Press.

Vertinsky, Patricia A. 1994. Women, sport, and exercise in the 19th century. In D. M. Costa and S. R. Guthrie, eds., *Women and sport: Interdisciplinary perspectives* (pp. 63–82). Champaign, IL: Human Kinetics.

Videon, Tami M. 2002. Who plays and who benefits: Gender, interscholastic athletics, and academic outcomes. *Sociological Perspectives* 45, 4: 415–435.

Vincent, John. 2004. Game, sex, and match: The construction of gender in British newspaper coverage of the 2000 Wimbledon Championships. *Sociology of Sport Journal* 21, 4: 435–456.

Vitello, Paul. 2006. The trouble when Jane becomes Jack. *The New York Times* (August 20). Online: http://www.nytimes.com/2006/08/20/fashion/20gender.html.

Volpi, Frederic. 2006. Politics. In Bryan S. Turner, ed., *The Cambridge dictionary of sociology* (pp. 445-447). Cambridge, UK: Cambridge University Press.

Wacquant, Loïc J. D. 1992. The social logic of boxing in black Chicago: Toward a sociology of pugilism. *Sociology of Sport Journal* 9, 3: 221–254.

Wacquant, Loïc J. D. 1995a. The pugilistic point of view: How boxers think and feel about their trade. *Theory and Society* 24: 489–535.

Wacquant, Loïc J. D. 1995b. Why men desire muscles. *Body and Society* 1, 1: 163–179.

Wacquant, Loïc. 2004. *Body and soul: Notebooks of an apprentice boxer.* Oxford, UK/New York: Oxford University Press.

Waddington, Ivan. 2000a. Sport and health: A sociological perspective. In Jay Coakley and Eric Dunning, eds., *Handbook of sports studies* (pp. 408–421). London: Sage.

Waddington, Ivan. 2000b. *Sport, health and drugs: A critical sociological perspective.* London: Routledge.

Waddington, Ivan. 2007. Health and sport. In George Ritzer, ed., *Encyclopedia of sociology* (pp. 2091–2095). London: Blackwell.

Wahl, Grant. 2003. Big bend. *Sports Illustrated* 98, 25 (June 23): 60–68.

Wahl, Grant. 2004. On safari for 7-footers. *Sports Illustrated* (June 28): 68–78.

Waldron, Jennifer, and Vikki Krane. 2005. Whatever it takes: Health compromising behaviors in female athletes. *Quest* 57, 3: 315–329.

Walker, Rob. 2005. Extreme makeover: Home edition—entertainment poverty. *The New York Times*, section 6 (December 4). Online: www.nytimes.com/2005/12/04/magazine/04wwin_consumed.html.

Walker, Rob. 2008. *Buying in: The secret dialogue between what we buy and who we are.* New York: Random House.

Walseth, Kristin. 2006. Sport and belonging. *International Review for the Sociology of Sport* 41, 3–4: 447–464.

Walseth, Kristin, and Kari Fasting. 2003. Islam's view on physical activity and sport: Egyptian women interpreting Islam. *International Review for the Sociology of Sport* 38, 1: 45–60.

Walsh, David. 2007. From Lance to Landis. *ESPN The Magazine* 10.13 (July 2): 98–107.

Walters, Guy. 2006. *Berlin games: How the Nazis stole the Olympic dream.* New York: William Morrow.

Wann, Daniel L., Gaye Haynes, B. McLean, and P. Pullen. 2003. Sport team identification and willingness to consider anonymous acts of hostile aggression. *Aggressive Behavior* 29: 406–413.

Wann, Daniel L., Jamie L. Hunter, Jacob A. Ryan, and Leigh Ann Wright. 2001a. The relationship between team identification and willingness of sport fans to consider illegally assisting their team. *Social Behavior and Personality: An International Journal* 29, 6: 531–537.

Wann, Daniel L., Merrill J. Melnick, Gordon W. Russell, and Dale G. Pease. 2001b. *Sport fans: The psychology and social impact of spectators.* New York: Routledge.

Wann, Daniel L., Robin R. Peterson, Cindy Cothran, and Michael Dykes. 1999. Sport fan aggression and anonymity: The importance of team identification. *Social Behavior and Personality: An International Journal* 27, 6: 597–602.

Wann, Daniel L., Joel L. Royalty, and A. R. Rochelle. 2002. Using motivation and team identification to predict sport fans' emotional responses to team performance. *Journal of Sport Behavior* 25, 2: 207–216.

Wann, Daniel, Paula J. Waddill, and Mardis D. Dunham. 2004. Using sex and gender role orientation to predict level of sport fandom. *Journal of Sport Behavior* 27, 4: 367–377.

Warren, Patricia Nell. 2003. The rise and fall of gender testing: How the Cold War and two "masculine" Soviet sisters led to a propaganda campaign. *Outsports.com.* Online: www.outsports.com/history/gendertesting.htm.

Waterford, Robin. 2004. Athens suffers old stereotypes. *USA Today* (August 5): 15A.

Wax, Emily. 2005. Facing servitude, Ethiopian girls run for a better life. *Washington Post* (December 29): A01. Online: http://girlsgottarun.aeomaia.com/.

Wearden, Stanley T., and Pamela J. Creedon. 2002. "We got next": Images of women in television commercials during the inaugural WNBA season. *Sport in Society* 5, 3: 189–210.

Weaver, Paul. 2005. Alma mater of Coe and Radcliffe brings sport to Muslim women. Online: www.buzzle.com/editorials/2-23-2005-66148.asp (retrieved July 8, 2005).

Weber, Max. 1904/1958. *The Protestant ethic and the spirit of capitalism* (trans. T. Parsons). New York: Scribner.

Weber, Max. 1968/1922. *Economy and society: An outline of interpretive sociology* (trans. G. Roth and G. Wittich). New York: Bedminster Press.

Wechsler, Henry, and Bernice Wuethrich. 2002. *Dying to drink: Confronting binge drinking on college campuses.* New York: Rodale and St. Martin's Press.

Wechsler, Henry, et al. 1997. Binge drinking, tobacco, and illicit drug use and involvement in college athletics. *Journal of American College Health* 45: 195–200.

Wedgewood, Nikki. 2004. Kicking like a boy: Schoolgirl Australian rules football and bi-gendered female embodiment. *Sociology of Sport Journal* 21, 2: 140–162.

Weed, Mike. 2001. Ing-ger-land at Euro 2000: How "Handbags at 20 paces" was portrayed as a full-scale riot. *International Review for the Sociology of Sport* 36, 4: 407–424.

Weil, Elizabeth. 2006. What if it's (sort of) a boy and (sort of) a girl? *The New York Times* (September 24). Online: www.nytimes.com/2006/09/24/magazine/24intersexkids.html.

Weiner, Jay. 1999. What do we want from our sports heroes? *BusinessWeek* (February 5): 77

Weiner, Jay. 2000. *Stadium games: Fifty years of big league greed and bush league boondoggles.* Minneapolis: University of Minnesota Press.

Weiner, Tim. 2004. Low-wage Costa Ricans make baseballs for millionaires. *The New York Times* (International Sunday) (January 25): 3.

Weinstein, Marc D., Michael D. Smith, and David L. Wiesenthal. 1995. Masculinity and hockey violence. *Sex Roles* 33, 11/12: 831–847.

Weir, Tom. 2000. Americans fall farther behind. *USA Today* (May 3): 3C.

Weir, Tom. 2006. Rookie always in a hurry. *USA Today* (June 30): C1–2.

Weisman, Larry. 2004. Propelled to think past NFL. *USA Today* (June 16): 1C.

Weiss, Otmar. 1996. Media sports as a social substitution pseudosocial relations with sports figures. *International Review for the Sociology of Sport* 31, 1: 109–118.

Welch, W. M. 1996. Federal taxpayers shut out of stadium payoff. *USA Today* (May 31): A1.

Wellard, Ian, ed. 2007. *Rethinking gender and youth sport.* New York: Routledge.

Wells, Steven. 2008. Bend it like Janiah. *Philadelphia Weekly* (January 23–29). Online: http://www.philadelphiaweekly.com/view.php?id=14977.

Wen, Dennis Y. 2007. Risk factors for overuse injuries in runners. *Current Sports Medicine Reports* 6: 307–313.

Wendel, Tim. 2004. How fantasy games have changed fans. *USA Today* (September 20): 23A.

Wenner, Lawrence A., and Walter Gantz. 1998. Watching sports on television: Audience experience, gender, fanship, and marriage. In L. A. Wenner, ed., *MediaSport* (pp. 233–251). London: Routledge.

Wertheim, Jon. 2005. Gays in sports: A poll. *Sports Illustrated* (April 18): 64–65. Online: http://sportsillustrated.cnn.com/2005/magazine/04/12/griffith_poll0418/ (retrieved July 2005).

West, Brad. 2003. Synergies in deviance: Revisiting the positive deviance debate. *Electronic Journal of Sociology* (November). Online: http://www.sociology.org/archive.html.

Whannel, Garry. 2002. *Media sport stars: Masculinities and moralities.* London/New York: Routledge.

Wheaton, Belinda, ed., 2004. *Understanding lifestyle sports: Consumption, identity and difference.* London: Routledge.

Wheaton, Belinda, and Becky Beal. 2003. "Keeping it real": Subcultural media and the discourses of authenticity in alternative sport. *International Review for the Sociology of Sport* 38, 2: 155–176.

Wheeler, Garry David, et al. 1996. Retirement from disability sport: A pilot study. *Adapted Physical Activity Quarterly* 13, 4: 382–399.

Wheeler, Garry David, et al. 1999. Personal investment in disability sport careers: An international study. *Adapted Physical Activity Quarterly* 16, 3: 219–237.

Wheelock, Darren, and Douglas Hartmann. 2007. Midnight basketball and the 1994 crime bill debates: The operation of a racial code. *The Sociological Quarterly* 48, 2: 315–342.

White, Amanda M., and Constance T. Gager. 2007. Idle hands and empty pockets? Youth involvement in extracurricular activities, social capital, and economic status. *Youth and Society* 39, 1, 75–111.

White, Anita, and Jay Coakley. 1986. *Making decisions: The response of young people in the Medway Towns to the "Ever Thought of Sport?" campaign.* London: Sports Council (now Sport England) and Greater London and South East Region.

White, Anita, and Ian Henry. 2004. *Women, leadership and the Olympic movement.* Loughborough, England: Institute of Sport and Policy Research, Loughborough University. Online: http://multimedia.olympic.org/pdf/en_report_885.pdf.

White, John. 2008. Idols in the stadium: Sport as an 'idol factory.' In Donald Lee Deardorff and John White, eds., *The image of God in the human body: Essays on Christianity and sports.* Lewiston, NY: Edwin Mellen Press.

White, Kelly. 2004. Discriminating airwaves. Online: www.womenssportsfoundation.org/cgi-bin/iowa/issues/article.html?record=999 (retrieved August 25, 2005).

White. Kerry. 2005. Breaking news, breaking boundaries. Online: www.womenssportsfoundation.org/cgi-bin/iowa/career/article.html?record=35 (retrieved August 25, 2005).

White, Michelle, and Joyce Kay. 2006. Who rules sport now?: White and Brackenridge revisited. *International Review for the Sociology of Sport* 41, 3–4: 465–473.

White, Philip. 2004. The cost of injury from sport, exercise and physical activity: A review of the evidence. In Kevin Young, ed., *Sporting bodies, damaged selves: Sociological studies of sports-related injury* (pp. 309–332). Amsterdam: Elsevier.

White, Philip, and Kevin Young. 1997. Masculinity, sport, and the injury process: A review of Canadian and international evidence. *Avante* 3, 2: 1–30.

White, Philip, and Kevin Young. 2007. Gender, sport and the injury process. In Kevin Young and Philip White, eds., *Sport and gender in Canada* (259–278). New York: Oxford University Press.

Whitley, Roger L. 1999. Those 'dumb jocks' are at it again: A comparison of the educational performances of athletes and nonathletes in North Carolina high schools from 1993 through 1996. *High School Journal* 82, 4: 223–233.

Whoriskey, Peter. 2002. Games played in the street out of bounds in Fairfax City. *Washington Post* (February 18): B01. Online: www.streetplay.com/stories/essays/washpostfeb17.shtml.

Wieberg, Steve. 1994. Conley nears end of six-year career. *USA Today* (November 17): 8C.

Wieberg, Steve. 2004. Boosters can provide quite a lift. *USA Today* (October 6): 10C.

Wieberg, Steve. 2005. Grad rates carry warning. *USA Today* (December 20): 12C.

Wieberg, Steve. 2008a. Study: College athletes are full-time workers. *USA Today* (January 13): 1C.

Wieberg, Steve. 2008b. 218 teams whistled for academic trouble. *USA Today* (May 7): 1C.

Wieberg, Steve. 2008c. Underachievers face sanctions. *USA Today* (May 7): 10C.

Wiggins, David K. 1994. The notion of double-consciousness and the involvement of Black athletes in American sport. In G. Eisen and D. K. Wiggins, eds., *Ethnicity and sport in North American history and culture* (pp. 133–156). Westport, CT: Greenwood Press.

Wiggins, David K., ed. 2003. *African Americans in sports.* Armonk, NY: Sharpe Reference.

Wikipedia, 2008. Oscar Pistorius. Online: http://en.wikipedia.org/wiki/Oscar_Pistorius

Williams, Dana. 2007. Where's the honor? Attitudes toward the "Fighting Sioux" nickname and logo. *Sociology of Sport Journal* 24, 4: 437–456.

Williams, Patricia J. 2005. Genetically speaking. *The Nation* 280, 24: 10.

Williams, Randy. 2006. *Sports cinema: 100 movies, the best of Hollywood's athletic heroes, losers, myths and misfits.* New York: Limelight Editions.

Williams, Timothy, and Cassi Feldman. 2007. Stickball, anyone? In a PlayStation world, maybe not. *The New York Times* (July 1): 21 (New York Report). Online: www.nytimes.com/2007/07/01/nyregion/01street.html?_r=1&scp=1&sq=Timothy+Williams%2C+stickball+&st=nyt&oref=slogin (retrieved February 1, 2008).

Willmsen, Christine, and Maureen O'Hagan. 2003. Coaches continue working for schools and private teams after being caught for sexual misconduct. *Seattle Times* (December 14). Online: http://seattletimes.nwsource.com/news/local/coaches (retrieved June 2005).

Wilmore, Jack H. 1996. Eating disorders in the young athlete. In O. bar-Or, ed., *The child and adolescent athlete* (pp. 287–303). Vol. 6 of the *Encyclopaedia of sports medicine* (IOC Medical Commission). London: Blackwell Science.

Wilson, Brian. 1999. "Cool pose" incorporated: The marketing of black masculinity in Canadian NBA coverage. In Phillip White and Kevin Young, eds., *Sport and gender in Canada* (pp. 232–253). Don Mills, ON: Oxford University Press.

Wilson, Brian. 2002. The "anti-jock" movement: Reconsidering youth resistance, masculinity, and sport culture in the age of the Internet. *Sociology of Sport Journal* 19, 2: 206–233.

Wilson, Brian. 2006. Selective memory in a global culture: Reconsidering links between youth, hockey and Canadian identity. In David Whitson and Richard Gruneau, eds., 2006. *Artificial ice: Hockey, culture, and commerce* (pp. 53–70). Peterborough, Ontario: Broadview Press.

Wilson, Brian. 2007. New media, social movements, and global sport studies: A revolutionary moment and the sociology of sport. *Sociology of Sport Journal* 24, 4: 457–477.

Wilson, Duff. 2008a. Clemens autograph seekers may have broken federal law. *The New York Times* (February 13). Online: www.nytimes .com/2008/02/13/sports/baseball/13autographs.html.

Wilson, Duff. 2008b. Friendlier tone, but plenty of tough talk. *The New York Times* (January 16). Online: www.nytimes.com/2008/01/16/sports/baseball/16baseball.html.

Wilson, Duff, and Andrew W. Lehren. 2008. Swapping passports in pursuit of Olympic medals. *The New York Times* (June 15). Online: www .nytimes.com/2008/06/15/sports/olympics/ 15citizen.html (retrieved June 15, 2008).

Wilson, Thomas C. 2002. The paradox of social class and sports involvement: The roles of cultural and economic capital. *International Review for the Sociology of Sport* 37, 1: 5–16.

Winant, Howard. 2001. *The world is a ghetto: Race and democracy since World War II*. New York: Basic Books.

Winant, Howard. 2004. *The new politics of race: Globalism, difference, justice*. Minneapolis: University of Minnesota Press.

Winant, Howard. 2006. Race and racism: Towards a global future. *Ethnic and Racial Studies* 29, 5: 986–1003.

Winlock, Colette. 2000. Running the invisible race. *ColorLines* 3, 1: 27.

Wittebols, James H. 2004. *The soap opera paradigm: Television programming and corporate priorities*. Lanham, MD: Rowman & Littlefield.

Wolfe, Tom. 1979. *The right stuff*. New York: Farrar, Straus, and Giroux.

Wolff, Alexander. 2000. Crying foul. *Sports Illustrated* (December 11): 42–47.

Wolff, Alexander. 2002. The vanishing three-sport star. *Sports Illustrated* (November 18): 80–92.

Wolff, Alexander. 2003. The American athlete: Age 10. *Sports Illustrated* 99, 13 (October 6): 59–67.

Wolff, Alexander. 2007. Going, going green. *Sports Illustrated* 106, 11 (March 12): 36–45.

Wolff, Eli A. 2005. The 2004 Athens Games and Olympians with disabilities: Triumphs, challenges, and future opportunities. Presentation at the 45th International Session for Young Participants International Olympic Academy. Athens, Greece.

Wolverton, Brad. 2007a. The athletics department of the future. *The Chronicle of Higher Education* 53, 46 (July 20): A28; Online, http://chronicle.com/ weekly/v53/i46/46a02801.htm.

Wolverton, Brad. 2007b. Minority hiring still lags; new standards may help. *The Chronicle of Higher Education* 54, 10 (November 2): A34. Online: http://chronicle.com/weekly/v54/i10/ 10a03401.htm.

Wolverton, Brad. 2008. Athletes' hours renew debate over college sports. *The Chronicle of Higher Education* 54, 20 (January 25): A1. Online: http:// chronicle.com/weekly/v54/i20/20a00101.htm.

Womack, Mari. 1992. Why athletes need ritual: A study of magic among professional athletes. In S. Hoffman, ed., *Sport and religion* (pp. 191–202). Champaign, IL: Human Kinetics.

Wong, Joyce. 1999. Asian women in sport. *Journal of Physical Education, Recreation and Dance* 70, 4: 42–43.

Wood, Skip. 2004. Leftwich's job skills include pain tolerance. *USA Today* (October 22): 15C.

Woodward. J. R. 2004. Professional football scouts: An investigation of racial stacking. *Sociology of Sport Journal* 21, 4: 356–375.

Woog, Dan. 1998. *Jocks: True stories of America's gay male athletes*. Los Angeles: Alyson Books.

World Health Organization. 2007. *Women and physical activity*. Geneva, Switzerland.

Online: www.who.int/moveforhealth/advocacy/information_sheets/woman/en/index.html.

WRC. 2007. WRC factory investigation: Jerzees Choloma and Jerzees de Honduras. *Worker Rights Consortium.* Online: http://www.workersrights.org/freports/JerzeesCholoma.asp.

Wright, Darlene, and Kevin Fitzpatrick. 2006. Social capital and adolescent violent behavior correlates of fighting and weapon use among secondary school students. *Social Forces* 4: 1435–1453.

Wulf, Steve. 2004. Basketbrawl. *ESPN The Magazine* 7.26 (December 20): 82.

Xu, Xin. 2006. Modernizing China in the Olympic spotlight: China's national identity and the 2008 Beijing Olympiad. *Sociological Review* 54, 2: 90–107.

Yessis, Michael. 2006. *Build a better athlete: What's wrong with American sports and how to fix it.* Terre Haute, IN: Equilibrium Books.

Ying, Wang. 2007. Kids forced to work too hard: Survey. *China Daily* 27, 8460 (June 5): 3

Yocom, Guy. 2008. My shot: Casey Martin. *Golf Digest* (March). Online: www.golfdigest.com/magazine/2008/03/myshot_martin (retrieved June 15, 2008).

Young, Iris Marion. 1990. *Throwing like a girl and other essays in philosophy and social theory.* Bloomington and Indianapolis: Indiana University Press.

Young, Iris Marion. 1998. Situated bodies: Throwing like a girl. In D. Welton, ed., *Body and flesh: A philosophical reader* (pp. 259–273). Oxford, UK: Blackwell.

Young, Kevin. 1993. Violence, risk, and liability in male sports culture. *Sociology of Sport Journal* 10, 4: 373–396.

Young, Kevin. 2000. Sport and violence. In J. Coakley and E. Dunning, eds., *Handbook of sport studies* (pp. 382–407). London: Sage.

Young, Kevin. 2002a. From "sports violence" to "sports crime": Aspects of violence, law, and gender in the sports process. In M. Gatz, M. A. Messner, and J. Ball-Rokeach, eds., *Paradoxes of youth and sport* (pp. 207–224). Albany: State University of New York Press.

Young, Kevin. 2002b. Standard deviations: An update on North American crowd disorder. *Sociology of Sport Journal* 19, 3: 237–275.

Young, Kevin. 2004a. The role of the courts in sports injury. In Kevin Young, ed., *Sporting bodies, damaged selves: Sociological studies of sports-related injury* (pp. 333–353). Amsterdam: Elsevier.

Young, Kevin, ed. 2004b. *Sporting bodies, damaged selves: Sociological studies of sports-related injury.* Amsterdam: Elsevier.

Young, Kevin. 2007a. Violence among athletes. In George Ritzer, ed., *Encyclopedia of sociology* (pp. 5199–5202). London/New York: Blackwell.

Young, Kevin. 2007b. Violence among fans. In George Ritzer, ed., *Encyclopedia of sociology* (pp. 5202–5206). London/New York: Blackwell.

Young, Kevin, and H. Charlesworth. 2005. *Injured female athletes: Experiential accounts from England and Canada.* London: Routledge.

Young, Kevin, and Philip White. 1995. Sport, physical danger, and injury: The experiences of elite women athletes. *Journal of Sport and Social Issues* 19, 1: 45–61.

Young, Kevin, and Phillip White, eds. 2007. *Sport and gender in Canada.* Don Mills, ON: Oxford University Press (Second Edition).

Young, Kevin, Philip White, and William McTeer. 1994. Body talk: Male athletes reflect on sport, injury, and pain. *Sociology of Sport Journal* 11, 2: 175–195.

Zakus, David, Donald Njelesani, and Simon Darnell. 2007. *The use of sport and physical activity to achieve health objectives.* In Sport for Development and Peace, International Working Group (SDP/IWG), *Literature Reviews on Sport for Development and Peace* (pp. 48–88). Toronto, Ontario: University of Toronto, Faculty of Physical Education and health. Online: http://iwg.sportanddev.org/data/htmleditor/file/Lit.%20Reviews/literature%20review%20SDP.pdf (retrieved January 24, 2008).

Zeigler, Cyd, and Jim Buzinksi. 2007. The outsports revolution: Truth and myth in the world of gay sports. Los Angeles: Alyson Publications.

Zengerle, Jason. 2002. Driving the company car. *The New York Times Magazine* (February 10): 40–43.

Zhang, James J., Dale G. Pease, and E. A. Jambor. 1997. Negative influence of market competitors on the attendance of professional sport games: The case of a minor league hockey team. *Sport Marketing Quarterly* 6, 3: 31, 34–40.

Zhang, James J., Dale G. Pease, and Dennis W. Smith. 1998. Relationship between broadcasting media and minor league hockey game attendance. *Sport Management Quarterly* 12, 2: 103–122.

Zhang, James J., and Dennis W. Smith. 1997. Impact of broadcasting on the attendance of professional basketball games. *Sport Marketing Quarterly* 6, 1: 23–29.

Zimbalist, A. 1999. *Unpaid professionals: Commercialism and conflict in big-time college sports.* Princeton, NJ: Princeton University Press.

Zirin, Dave. 2004a. An interview with Adonal Foyle: Rebounder for reforms, master of the lefty lay-up. *CounterPunch* (July 16). Online: http://www.counterpunch.org/zirin07162004.html (retrieved June 5, 2008).

Zirin, Dave. 2004b. Selective outrage in Detroit. Online: www.counterpunch.com/zirin11222004.html (retrieved June 2005).

Zirin, Dave. 2005a. What's my name, fool? *The Nation Online* (August2): www.thenation.com/doc/20050815/zirin.

Zirin, Dave. 2005b. *What's My Name, Fool? Sports and resistance in the United States.* Chicago, IL: Haymarket Books.

Zirin, Dave. 2007. *Welcome to the Terrordome: The pain, politics, and promise of sports.* Chicago: Haymarket Books.

Zirin, Dave. 2008a. *A people's history of sports in the United States.* New York/London: The New Press.

Zirin, Dave. 2008b. Blogged down: The seduction of Buzz Bissinger. *Edge of Sports* (May 8). Online: http://edgeofsports.com/2008-05-07-341/index.html (retrieved May 8, 2008).

Zirin, Dave. 2008c. Butts on parade: Clemens meets Wallace. *The Edge of Sports* (January 7). Online: http://www.edgeofsports.com/2008-01-07-308/index.html

Zirin, Dave. 2008d. Olympics wrap-up: Marco Polo would be proud. *The Nation* (August 24). Online: http://www.thenation.com/blogs/notion/348214 (retrieved 8/25/08).

Zirin, Dave. 2008e. The Super Bowl: Who stole the soul? *The Edge of Sports* (February 1). Online: http://edgeofsports.com/2008-02-01-314/index.html.

Zirin, Dave. 2008f. Washington DC's sporting shock doctrine. *The Edge of Sports* (March 30). Online: http://edgeofsports.com/2008-03-30-333/index.html.

Zorpette, Glenn. 2000. The chemical games. *Scientific American* 11, 3: 16–23.

NAME INDEX

Note: n indicates notes; f indicates figures; t indicates tables

A

Aaron (Old Testament), 545
Abernathy, Bruce, 135n3
Abernathy, Liz, 107
Acosta, R. Vivian, 239, 242, 252, 253t, 299
Adams, Mary Louise, 376, 428, 446
Adelson, Eric, 275, 304, 423
Adler, Patricia A., 47, 112, 139, 288, 483
Adler, Peter, 47, 112, 139, 288, 483
Adu, Freddy, 365
Agassi, Andre, 342f
Agel, Julie, 107
Agovino, Michael J., 443
Aikman, Troy, 164
Aimar, Christine M., 239, 245
Al Ghasara, Ruqaya, 527f, 528
Albert, Edward, 45, 167
Aldama, Yamile, 461–462
Alesia, Mark, 353, 493, 505, 508
Alford, Dean, 559
Ali, David, 324
Ali, Laila, 201
Ali, Muhammad (Cassius Clay), 82t, 201, 268, 526, 568
Allison, Lincoln, 443, 444n2
Almada, Anthony, 181
Alonso, Andres, 482f
Alou, Felipe, 425
Althouse, Ronald, 292
Anderson, Eric, 47, 112, 257, 266, 267, 268, 489
Anderson, Jason, 205f
Anderson, Kristen L., 250
Andrews, David L., 117, 118, 119, 326, 362, 376n1, 396, 415, 444, 448, 454, 458, 460
Angle, Kurt, 536
Anthonissen, Anton, 255

Anthony, Carmelo, 142–143, 380
Applebome, Peter, 500
Appleby, R. S., 535
Arase, Lauren, 230
Archer, Louise, 341
Armstead, Jessie, 210
Armstrong, Gary, 221
Armstrong, Ken, 170, 177, 213
Armstrong, Ketra L., 290, 294, 510
Armstrong, Lance, 364, 402, 552
Arriagada, Paula A., 424, 425
Arsenault, Amelia, 396
Ashe, Arthur, 71, 82t
Assael, Shaun, 179, 181–182, 183, 186, 188, 560
Astrinakis, Antonios E., 221
Atencio, Matthew, 47
Atkinson, Michael, 12, 154, 173, 370, 560
Axthelm, Pete, 79
Azzarito, Laura, 286

B

Bacon, Victoria L., 176
Badenhausen, Kurt, 353
Baerg, Andrew, 401
Bailey, Richard, 238
Baird, Shannon M., 239, 245
Bairner, Alan, 317, 443, 444n2
Baker, Joseph, 135, 135n3
Baker, William J., 62, 64, 66, 519, 522, 531, 532, 536, 541, 542, 544, 544f
Bale, John, 456, 461, 465, 562
Ballard, Chris, 399, 432
Ballard, Steve, 165
Bandow, Doug, 376n1
Banet-Weiser, Sarah, 292
Banfi, Giuseppe, 179
Barber, Bonnie L., 176, 473n2

Barkley, Charles, 275, 286, 454
Barnard, Sarah, 398, 404, 414
Barnes, Grace M., 93, 173, 473, 473n2, 475, 476
Barnes, Michael D., 240
Barnes, Simon, 262, 267, 268
Barrows, Mike, 542
Barry, Patrick, 186, 188
Bartel, Cameron, 131
Bartimole, Roldo, 377
Bartoluci, Suncica, 444n2, 445
Basinger-Fleischman, Lorrine, 241
Basow, Susan A., 256
Bast, Joseph L., 376n1
Beal, Becky, 133, 147, 250, 398f, 521, 554
Beals, Katherine A., 163n1, 243
Beard, Alana, 103
Bechtel, Mark, 419
Becker, Debbie, 164, 206
Becker, Howard S., 567
Beckham, David, 267, 401
Beiruty, Hikmat, 527
Belcher, Don, 289
Bell, Christopher, 181, 182
Bell, Jack, 400
Bell, Wendell, 549
Beller, Jennifer M., 102, 173
Belson, Matthew, 332
Ben-Porat, Amir, 453, 458, 465
Ben-Porat, Guy, 453, 458, 465
Benedict, Jeff, 170, 176–177, 213
Benford, Robert D., 487
Bennett, Larry, 376n1
Benoit, Chris, 370
Berger, Jody, 164, 315
Berlage, Gai Ingham, 78
Bernstein, Alina, 396
Bernstein, Viv, 402
Berra, Lindsey, 205

SUBJECT INDEX